The Motet in the Late Middle Ages

The Motet in the Late Middle Ages

The Motet in the Late Middle Ages

MARGARET BENT

OXFORD
UNIVERSITY PRESS

Oxford University Press is a department of the University of Oxford. It furthers the University's objective of excellence in research, scholarship, and education by publishing worldwide. Oxford is a registered trade mark of Oxford University Press in the UK and certain other countries.

Published in the United States of America by Oxford University Press
198 Madison Avenue, New York, NY 10016, United States of America.

© Oxford University Press 2023

All rights reserved. No part of this publication may be reproduced, stored in a retrieval system, or transmitted, in any form or by any means, without the prior permission in writing of Oxford University Press, or as expressly permitted by law, by license, or under terms agreed with the appropriate reproduction rights organization. Inquiries concerning reproduction outside the scope of the above should be sent to the Rights Department, Oxford University Press, at the address above.

You must not circulate this work in any other form
and you must impose this same condition on any acquirer.

Library of Congress Cataloging-in-Publication Data
Names: Bent, Margaret, author.
Title: The motet in the late middle ages / Margaret Bent.
Description: [1.] | New York : Oxford University Press, 2023. | Includes index. |
Identifiers: LCCN 2022044679 (print) | LCCN 2022044680 (ebook) |
ISBN 9780190063771 (hardback) | ISBN 9780190063801 (epub) |
ISBN 9780190063788
Subjects: LCSH: Motets—500-1400—History and criticism. |
Motets—14th century—History and criticism.
Classification: LCC ML190 .B45 2023 (print) | LCC ML190 (ebook) |
DDC 782.209/02—dc23
LC record available at https://lccn.loc.gov/2022044679
LC ebook record available at https://lccn.loc.gov/2022044680

DOI: 10.1093/oso/9780190063771.001.0001

Printed by Integrated Books International, United States of America

The publisher gratefully acknowledges support from the Kenneth Levy Fund of the American Musicological Society, supported in part by the National Endowment for the Humanities and the Andrew W. Mellon Foundation.

Amicis optimis

Bonnie, Leofranc, and David

Contents

Preface and Acknowledgements	xi
About the Companion Website	xv
List of Illustrations	xvii
List of Tables	xix
List of Music Examples	xxi
List of Sound Clips	xxv
List of Manuscripts	xxvii
Other Abbreviations	xxxv
Introduction	1

PART I. COMPOSITIONAL TECHNIQUES 15

1. Theoretical and Terminological Issues	17
2. What is Isorhythm?	39

PART II. THE MARIGNY MOTETS, BEYOND *FAUVEL*, AND VITRY 65

3. Fauvel and Marigny: Which Came First?	67
4. *Tribum que non abhorruit/Quoniam secta latronum/Merito hec patimur* and its 'Quotations', and *Garrit gallus/In nova*	83
Appendix: Commentary to *Tribum/Quoniam*; Commentary to *Garrit/In nova*	108
5. *Aman novi/Heu Fortuna/Heu me*	111
6. *Floret/Florens*: Intended for *Fauvel*?	131
7. Related Manuscripts, Related Motets; Vitry	139
8. *Vos quid admiramini/Gratissima virginis species/Gaude gloriosa*	151

PART III. MACHAUT 169

9. Words and Music in Machaut's Motet 9	171
10. Deception, Exegesis and Sounding Number in Machaut's Motet 15	197
11. The 'Harmony' of the Machaut Mass	209

viii CONTENTS

12. Machaut's Motet 10 and its Interconnections — 231

13. Motet 18: *Bone pastor Guillerme/Bone pastor, qui pastores/Bone pastor* — 245

14. Text–Music Relationships in Motets 4 and 8 — 263

PART IV. *MUSICORUM COLLEGIUM*: THE MUSICIAN MOTETS 281

15. *Apollinis eclipsatur*, its Progeny and their Sources — 283

16. *Apollinis eclipsatur/Zodiacum signis/In omnem terram* and Later Versions with Added Parts — 301

Appendix: Commentaries to Web Transcriptions for the Pieces with Multiple Sources — 321

17. *Musicalis sciencia/Sciencie laudabili* and the Musicians Named in *Apollinis* and *Musicalis* — 325

18. *Musicorum collegio/In templo Dei/Avete* — 343

19. *Alma polis religio/Axe poli cum artica/[Et] in ore eorum* and its Named Musicians — 353

Appendix: Commentary Notes to Example 19.1, *Alma polis religio/Axe poli cum artica/[Et] in ore eorum* — 367

20. *Sub arturo plebs/Fons citharizancium/In omnem terram* and its Musicians — 369

Appendix: Variants in *Sub Arturo plebs/Fons citharizancium/In omnem terram* — 388

21. Fragmentary Motets and Other Possibly Linked Compositions — 389

PART V. ENGLISH MOTETS C. 1400–1420 399

22. The Yoxford Manuscript and the Motet *O amicus/Precursoris* — 401

Appendix: Musical Transcription of *O amicus/Precursoris* (Ex. 22.1), with Musical and Textual Commentary — 423

23. The Yoxford Credo — 431

Appendix: Notes to Credo Transcription (Ex. 23.1) — 443

24. Mayshuet and the *Deo gratias* Motets in the Old Hall Manuscript — 445

25. Old Hall, the Agincourt Motets, and Dunstaple — 465

CONTENTS ix

PART VI. ITALIAN MOTETS 495

26. The Fourteenth-Century Italian Motet — 497

27. The Motet Collection of San Lorenzo 2211 (**SL2211**) and the Composer Hubertus de Salinis — 531

28. The Motets of Johannes Ciconia — 551

29. Ciconia, Prosdocimus, and the Workings of Musical Grammar as Exemplified in *O felix templum* and *O Padua* — 575

PART VII. MUSIC FOR POPES AND THE COURTS OF BURGUNDY AND CYPRUS 603

30. Early Papal Motets — 605

    Appendix: Music for Popes John XXII(?) to Eugene IV — 638

31. Trémoïlle Revisited — 641

    Appendix: Transcription of Incipits as Listed in the **Trém** Index, with Identifications and Sources — 653

32. Some Aspects of the Cyprus Manuscript and its Motets — 661

    Appendix: The Cyprus Motets — 682

Bibliography — 687
Index of Compositions — 715
Index of Manuscripts — 723
General Index — 727

Preface and Acknowledgements

Like *Fauvel*, this book is a hybrid in more than one sense. It is part print and part digital; many music examples essential to the text but too large in format to be printed legibly in the book are displayed only as downloadable files on the companion website; see p. xv. The book is also a hybrid in that it was neither conceived *ab initio*, nor is it a simple collection of previously published writings. Had it started from a blank slate, the coverage would have been more even, more comprehensive. It was originally planned and commissioned as a compilation of the many articles I have published on various aspects of late medieval motets over several decades, together with a significant proportion of previously unpublished material that had arisen from teaching and from work on individual motets presented at seminars and conferences. Almost half the chapters are completely new, most substantially those of Part IV (Chs. 15–21) on the musician motets, but also most of Chapters 1, 6–8, 13, 14, 25 and 28. But as I came to work on the updating commentaries planned to introduce or frame each chapter, I felt the need to rewrite or extensively revise most of the previously published work (about half of the book), both to take account of revisions necessitated by discovery of new sources and of more recent work by myself and others. It made sense to group related chapters into the seven Parts of this book, with new material worked in. Suzanne Ryan, then commissioning editor for OUP, readily agreed that this would make a better book.

I also eliminated some duplication and intermediate stages towards my current views, which include, I hope, a clearer understanding of the appropriate use of terms such as isorhythm, and of distinctions between, for example, diminution and proportion. I have tried to indicate where and how my stance has significantly changed over the years, and my views are often differently nuanced; but for the record, most of the older articles (written before the internet) are available on the web, some on my academia.edu page.

The chapters vary considerably with respect to technical and notational description, and hence of the level of readership addressed. Chapter 9, for example (on Machaut's Motet 9, with sound examples), was designed for pedagogical use as an introduction suitable for students, while chapters with more detailed analysis and technical details of notation and commentary are directed at specialists or advanced graduate students. In many cases, readers will be able to skip the more technical discussions if their interests lie more in verbal texts and contextual considerations. The Introduction gives an overview of the contents which may guide readers to the chapters most relevant to their interests.

The original form of some of this work dates back over many decades. Some has never been published, some only in occasional or obscure publications that are not currently accessible online. Despite attempts to do justice to work by others more recent than my original articles, coverage and acknowledgements are inevitably incomplete, especially with respect to older oral contributions by colleagues and students.

xii PREFACE AND ACKNOWLEDGEMENTS

Many colleagues have given me valuable feedback over the years. Foremost among them are the three long-standing friends to whom this book is dedicated: Bonnie Blackburn, Leofranc Holford-Strevens and David Howlett. It was a huge privilege that Bonnie was willing not only to undertake copy-editing prior to submission but also to prepare the index. Her thorough vigilance has saved me from many errors, omissions and inconsistencies, though it is inevitable in a book of this size that many will remain, and for these I am responsible. In Leofranc and David I have benefited from two of the most resourceful Latinists anywhere: Leofranc has been ready to answer queries and translate difficult Latin, and the stimulus of collaborating with David in the late 1980s opened my eyes to a range of textual subtleties.

Much of the work presented here has been enriched by those and other interdisciplinary contacts that I have been fortunate enough to enjoy over the years. Kevin Brownlee had major input on the French texts of Machaut motets in Chapters 10, 12 and 14 on which we worked together and presented in seminars. I observed that he had read every word Machaut wrote except the motets, and that someone as deeply concerned as he with intertextuality should find a rich harvest in motets with simultaneous texts in which each syllable had a precise placement in time and in relation to the other text. He rose magnificently to the challenge. Chapter 5 presents my contribution to our published collaboration on the Fauvel motet *Aman novi*. Colleagues who joined Andrew Wathey and me in the seminars and conferences that resulted in *Fauvel Studies* have provided stimulus, often ongoing: especially Elizabeth A. R. Brown, Ardis Butterfield, Emma Dillon, Christopher Page, Nancy Freeman Regalado, Alison Stones and Jane Taylor.

I had not intended to inflict the entire text of the book on any one colleague for prepublication reading, but Lawrence Earp, after giving sharply focused and critical feedback on several chapters at an early stage, has now gone through the entire manuscript; I am most grateful to him and to Michael Scott Cuthbert for saving me from numerous errors and omissions. Exchanges with Jacques Boogaart about Machaut motets and with Elena Abramov-van Rijk on Italian matters have been particularly helpful, as were conversations about thirteenth-century precedents with Catherine A. Bradley and Sean Curran.

It would be impossible to list all my scholarly debts over a lifetime. I beg forgiveness of any I have neglected to list below among the many other friends, colleagues and students who, in addition to those named above, have contributed observations and helpful criticism over the years in seminars, conversations and correspondence. I am grateful to Cristina Alís Raurich, Jon Michael Allsen, Alexander Blachly, Calvin Bower, Roger Bowers, Anna Maria Busse Berger, John Caldwell, Antonio Calvia, David Catalunya, Alice Clark, Suzannah Clark, Lisa Colton, Karen Cook, Julie Cumming, Karen Desmond, Brianne Dolce, Richard Dudas, Ross Duffin, Theodor Dumitrescu, David Fallows, Manuel Pedro Ferreira, Sarah Fuller, Paweł Gancarczyk, Julian Gardner, Maria Carmen Gómez, Barbara Haggh-Huglo, Anne Hallmark, Elina Hamilton, George Harne, Jared Hartt, Jan Herlinger, Andrew Hicks, Martin Horyna, Anthony Hunt, Andreas Janke, Jonathan Katz, Andrew Kirkman, Paul Kolb, Karl Kügle, Elizabeth Eva Leach, Daniel Leech-Wilkinson, Peter Lefferts, Christian Thomas Leitmeir, Manon Louviot, Grantley McDonald, Pedro Memelsdorff, John Milsom, John Nádas, Virginia Newest†, Robert Nosow, Alejandro Enrique Planchart†, Yolanda Plumley, Harold

PREFACE AND ACKNOWLEDGEMENTS xiii

Powers†, Susan Rankin, Zoltán Rihmer, Anne Robertson, Edward Roesner†, Kévin Roger, Uri Smilansky, Jason Stoessel, Anne Stone, Reinhard Strohm, Johanna-Pauline Thöne, Philippe Vendrix, Andrew Wathey, Rob Wegman, Elżbieta Witkowska-Zaremba, Mary Wolinski, Peter Wright†, Anna Zayaruznaya, Emily Zazulia and Francesco Zimei.

This list includes some with whom brief exchanges or conversations have proved stimulating on individual points or chapters, and some with whom I have had more wide-ranging exchanges. Specific debts are acknowledged in place, and I am grateful to them all. In particular, I have almost certainly failed to incorporate some contributions of more recent scholarship, for which I apologise. Errors and inconsistencies inevitably remain. All shortcomings are mine alone.

Transcriptions are provided in scored diplomatic copies in an adapted form of the original notation, or in modern notation, for most but not all of the motets discussed in detail, either in the book or on the companion website (see p. xv). Manuscript images for most of the compositions are available on https://gallica.bnf.fr/, https://www.diamm. ac.uk/, or the websites of individual libraries. A few music examples have been taken over from previous publications, notably those set for Chapter 29 by Vincent Besson. Most of the transcriptions of whole motets are on the companion website, and are mine unless otherwise stated. Most of those, and music examples throughout the book, have been newly set by Timothy Symons, who was able to transform my handwritten copies into things of beauty before his untimely death. I was enormously relieved when he also agreed to organise the illustrative material (figures, music examples and tables) both for the book and for web display. Ronald Woodley has graciously allowed me to use his Bentivoglio and Accidentals fonts for the in-text music symbols.

My debt of gratitude to All Souls College for generous support over three decades is incalculable. I am indebted for cooperation and many kindnesses to the staff of the numerous libraries in which I have worked, to Julia Craig-McFeely of DIAMM, and to Ugo Giani of LIM (Libreria Musicale Italiana). Suzanne Ryan, formerly of OUP, encouraged and handled the original proposal for this book; I am grateful to her and to her successor Norman Hirschy, and to Rachel Ruisard of OUP. Together with the production team at Newgen, led by Stuart Allison, they have worked together to transform this long and complex manuscript into printed and digital form, and I thank them for their skill and patience.

About the Companion Website

www.oup.com/us/TheMotetintheLateMiddleAges

Oxford has created a companion website to accompany *The Motet in the Late Middle Ages*. Material that cannot be made available in full form in the book, namely larger-format music examples and tables, is provided here, and can be downloaded. Examples and figures are each numbered consecutively in each chapter, whether they are in the book or on the website. The reader will need to consult this essential resource in conjunction with the chapters. Examples available online are indicated in the text with Oxford's symbol ⊙.

Chapters 9 and 13 also have audio clips, numbered as ⊙ mp3 files and linked to the numbered music examples. To download the audio clips individually, right-click (on a Mac: Control-click) on the audio player and save the file to your computer. You may need to select 'Allow Download' if your browser asks permission to download the file. There is also the option to bulk-download a zip file that contains all audio clips for Chapters 9 and 13, found under the 'Resources' tab.

List of Illustrations

3.1	A much-simplified diagram of part of the *Fauvel* narrative, left to right, and historical narrative, right to left	80
4.1	Schematic diagram of *Tribum/Quoniam/Merito*	93
4.2	Palindromic rhythm of the (first) tenor *talea* of *Garrit gallus* in **Paris146**, f. 44ᵛ	102
4.3	*Garrit gallus* in **Pic**, f. 67ʳ	103
4.4	Periodic structure of *Garrit gallus*	105
5.1	Triplum incipit of *Aman/Heu* in **Paris146**, f. 30	114
5.2	Notated sharp in **Paris146**, f. 30, tenor, bottom staff	123
8.1	The tenor and contratenor *taleae* of the two *colores* of *Vos/Gratissima*	158
8.2	The chiasm of triplum *Vos–Ista* alternations	162
8.3	Some instances of prevalent rhythmic motives (*Vos* and *Gratissima*)	164
8.4	**Ivrea**, f. 9ʳ, staff 4: 'eye music' in *Vos/Gratissima*	164
8.5	The hockets of *Vos/Gratissima*	165
9.1	Motetus rhyme-words in Machaut, Motet 9	188
9.2	Some verbal correspondences between triplum and motetus in Machaut, Motet 9	189
13.1	Texts with hockets in Machaut, Motet 18, bar 97–end	249
13.2	**Paris146**, Lescurel, f. 58ʳ: rests in *Belle com loiaus*	257
13.3	Proposed original notation of the tenor of Machaut, Motet 2	261
16.1	Staggered periods in *Apollinis*	306
17.1	*Musicalis sciencia* in **Pic**, f. 67ᵛ	327
17.2	Opening rhythms of *Musicalis sciencia* and *Musicorum*	330
19.1	Tenor and contratenor of *Alma polis* in **Chantilly**, f. 68	361
20.1	Opening triplum rhythms of *Apollinis* and *Sub Arturo*	381
▶ 21.1	*Non eclipsis atra ferrugine* in **Leiden2515** f. 1ᵛ	
▶ 23.1	Structural diagram of the Yoxford Credo	
23.2	Responsory *Omni tempore*, AS, pl. 317	433
23.3	Tenor *talea* of Yoxford Credo as notated, with ligatures resolved, followed by the reducing derivations. Breves altered in perfect mensurations are so marked	435
25.1	Tenor of Byttering, *En Katerine*, tenor *Sponsus amat sponsum* [*sic*] in **OH**, f. 111	467

xviii   LIST OF ILLUSTRATIONS

25.2   Text of *Carbunculus ignitus lilie*, with aligned isorhythm, showing that rests never divide words   470

25.3   Tenor of Sturgeon, *Salve mater/Salve templum* in **OH**, f. 92   479

27.1   The structure of Gathering XIX of **SL2211**   532

28.1   The three stages of *O felix templum* in **Q15**; also at ⏵ Fig. 28.1   557

28.2   Tenor of *Doctorum principem* in **Q15**, f. A299ᵛ   562

List of Tables

▶ 5.1 Comparative editions of the triplum text of *Aman novi/Heu Fortuna/Heu me, tristis est anima mea*

6.1 Textual correspondences between the prose *Carnalitas* and the motet triplum *Floret*   134

7.1 Contents of **Br19606**   141

8.1 Texts and translations of *Vos/Gratissima* by David Howlett   152

9.1 Cadencing opportunities in Machaut, Motet 9   182

9.2 Machaut motets with one or both texts in Latin (out of a total of 23)   184

9.3 Distribution of text in Machaut, Motet 9   186

9.4 Rhythmic vocabulary of upper parts in Machaut, Motet 9   191

9.5 Calendrical dimensions in Machaut, Motet 9   191

10.1 Texts of Machaut's, Motet 15   204

12.1 Verses lined up with *taleae* in Machaut, Motet 10   233

13.1 Texts and translations of Machaut, Motet 18; translations by Leofranc Holford-Strevens   246

13.2 The hocket passage laid out by stanzas in Machaut, Motet 18   250

14.1 Texts and translation of Machaut, Motet 4   264

14.2 Texts and translation of Machaut, Motet 8   273

22.1 Texts and translation of *O amicus/Precursoris*   407

▶ 25.1 Inventory of the Royal Choirbook (RC)

25.2 Distribution of the sequence texts in Dunstaple's motets nos. 32 and 33   489

25.3 The Dunstaple motets classed by Bukofzer as isorhythmic   490

26.1 Italian motets *c.* 1310–1410   504

27.1 Motets in **SL2211**   534

27.2 Mass music and motets by Hubertus de Salinis   540

27.3 Songs by or possibly by Salinis   546

28.1 Ciconia's motets (numbered as in PMFC 24)   554

32.1 The 'O' Antiphons   677

List of Music Examples

'Modern notation' is specified for complete transcriptions or substantial excerpts. Unspecified complete transcriptions (mostly on the website) are in a scored form of the original notation. Shorter examples are notated as convenient for that example.

1.1	Standard 10/6–12/8 cadence, and non-coincidental final cadences in three Machaut motets (M4, M10, M15)	22
1.2	The end of M17 from Machaut, *The Motets*, ed. Boogaart (modern notation)	24
1.3	Endings of *O Maria/O Maria*: (a) **Pad1106**; (b) **Q15**; (c) **MuEm**	27
▶ 4.1	Transcription of *Tribum que non abhorruit/Quoniam secta latronum/ Merito hec patimur*	
4.2	Tenor and chant of *Merito hec patimur*	92
4.3	Three notes of the chant as used in the motetus of each block of *Tribum*	95
4.4	Triplum of *Tribum* showing chant paraphrase of tenor *Merito*	96
▶ 4.5	Transcription of *Garrit gallus/In nova*	
4.6	Musical relations between *Garrit Gallus/In nova fert* and *Tribum/Quoniam*	106
4.7	Musical relations between *Garrit Gallus* and *Tribum* at the word *leo*	108
5.1	Edition of music of *Aman novi/Heu Fortuna/Heu me, tristis est anima mea*	119
7.1	Tenor of *Orbis orbatus/Vos pastores*: three *taleae*, three statements	148
8.1	The tenor of *Vos/Gratissima*	154
▶ 8.2	Transcription of *Vos/Gratissima* by Richard Dudas, based mainly on **Durham20**	
8.3	The main structural junction of *Vos/Gratissima*, demonstrating several instantiations of *simili*	166
▶ 9.1	Transcription of Machaut, Motet 9, *Fons tocius superbie/O livoris feritas/Fera pessima*	
9.2	Structure of the tenor of Motet 9	176
9.3	The tenor *color* of Motet 4, and its articulation by *talea* repetition	178
9.4	Opening of tenor of Motet 16	179
9.5	Chant tenor of the *Fauvel* motet *Tribum/Quoniam/Merito hec patimur*	179
9.6	Standard cadences in Motet 9	182
9.7	Partial cadences in Motet 9	183
9.8	Displaced cadence in Motet 9, B47–B49	183
9.9	Displaced cadences in Motet 9 in B112–B115	184
9.10	Motet 9: inversion (upper brackets) and retrograde (lower brackets) patterns in the tenor *color*	193

xxii LIST OF MUSIC EXAMPLES

9.11 Similarities between openings of Motet 9 and Motet 15   194

10.1 Machaut, Motet 15, *Amours qui a le pouoir/Faus Samblant m'a deceü/Vidi dominum* (modern notation)   198

11.1 Gloria of Machaut's mass, excluding Amen (modern notation)   216

▶ 12.1 Transcription of Machaut, Motet 10, *Hareu! hareu! le feu/Helas! ou sera pris confors/Obediens usque ad mortem*

12.2 The tenor of Motet 10   235

12.3 Prominent motives in Motet 10   236

12.4 Openings of Motets 15 and 10 and the 'Amours' motive   243

▶ 13.1 Machaut, Motet 18, from Machaut, *The Motets*, ed. Boogaart (modern notation)

▶ 14.1 Transcription of Machaut, Motet 4, *De Bon Espoir/Puis que la douce/Speravi*

14.2 The tenor *color* of Motet 4, showing its overlap with Motet 9 and its articulation by *talea* repetition   266

▶ 14.3 Transcription of Machaut, Motet 8, *Qui es promesses/Ha! Fortune/Et non est qui adjuvat*

14.4 Tenor of Motet 8, showing leaps of 4ths and 5ths, the x and y motives and their retrogrades and inversions, and the derivation of four-note minim formulas of the top parts from the chant   276

14.5 Similar phrases leading to death in Motet 10 and Motet 8   278

▶ 16.1 Transcription of *Apollinis eclipsatur/Zodiacum signis/In omnem terram*

▶ 16.2 Transcription of *Apollinis* with textless triplum from **Barc853**

▶ 16.3 Transcription of *Apollinis* with added triplum *Pantheon abluitur* and textless quadruplum from **LoTNA** and **SL2211**

▶ 16.4 Transcription of *Apollinis* with added triplum *Psallentes zinzugia* and contratenor from **LoTNA**

▶ 17.1 Transcription of *Musicalis sciencia/Sciencie laudabili*

▶ 18.1 Transcription of *Musicorum collegio/In templo Dei*

18.2 Chant melisma on *Avete* (GS 120) and the tenor of *Musicorum*   349

▶ 19.1 Transcription of *Alma polis religio/Axe poli cum artica/[Et] in ore eorum*

19.2 Comparison of the tenor of *Alma polis* with chant melody from **Fribourg2**   358

19.3 The first *talea* pair of each *color* of *Alma polis* in simplified modern notation   361

▶ 20.1 Transcription of *Sub Arturo plebs/Fons citharizancium*

20.2 Tenors of *Apollinis* and *Sub Arturo*   376

▶ 21.1 Transcription of *Arta/Musicus est ille* (modern notation)

21.2 *Arta/Musicus est ille*: contratenor with three isorhythmic *taleae*   390

21.3 Opening rhythm in motetus of *Sub Arturo/Fons citharizancium* and triplum of *Fons origo musicorum*   395

22.1 Musical Transcription of *O amicus/Precursoris* (Ex. 22.1), with Musical and Textual Commentary (modern notation)   423

22.2 Comparison of tenor of *O amicus* with proposed chant   403

LIST OF MUSIC EXAMPLES   xxiii

22.3 Solus tenor, tenor and contratenor of *O amicus* — 413

22.4 Tenor and contratenor of *O amicus* — 413

▶ 23.1 Transcription of the Yoxford Credo (modern notation)

23.2 Tenor of Yoxford Credo, with relevant portions of chant — 434

24.1 Transcription of *Post missarum sollennia/Post misse modulamina* (modern notation) — 451

24.2 Reconstructed tenor of *Post missarum* — 458

24.3 Tenor of *Are post libamina* — 459

24.4 Tenor of *Herodis in pretorio/Herodis in atrio/Hey, hure lure* from **Durham20** — 459

▶ 25.1 Transcription of Dunstaple, *Descendi in ortum meum* (modern notation)

▶ 25.2 Transcription of Dunstaple (?), *Gaude flore virginali* (modern notation)

▶ 25.3 Transcription of Dunstaple, Gloria in canon (modern notation)

26.1 Excerpt from fragmentary motet on S. Cristina in **Ox16** (modern notation) — 518

26.2 *Florentia mundi/Marce pater*, transcribed from **Egidi** and **SL2211** (modern notation) — 521

▶ 26.3 Transcription of *O Antoni expulsor demonum* (modern notation)

27.1 Salinis, *Jhesu salvator*, first textless interlude with strict rhythmic canon — 549

27.2 Salinis, *Jhesu salvator*, second textless interlude, with two strict rhythmic canons — 549

27.3 Salinis, *Psallat chorus*, first textless rhythmic sequential passage — 550

28.1 Final systems of *O virum omnimoda* (modern notation) — 559

29.1 Johannes Boen, *Musica*, example from *Se grace/Cum venerint*, Mass of Tournai — 580

29.2 Prosdocimus, *Contrapunctus*, example of *musica ficta* — 584

29.3 Ciconia, *Venecie mundi splendor*, bb. 85–end (modern notation) — 587

29.4 Ciconia, *O felix templum jubila*, bb. 1–27 (modern notation) — 591

29.5 Ciconia, *O felix templum jubila*, contrapuntal reduction of bb. 1–27 (modern notation) — 592

29.6 Ciconia, *O felix templum jubila*, bb. 47–62 (modern notation) — 595

29.7 Ciconia, *O Padua* (modern notation) — 596

29.8 Ciconia, *O Padua*, bb. 9–10, showing the contrapuntal reduction of each upper voice with the tenor (modern notation) — 599

▶ 31.1 *Plausu querulo*, transcribed by Richard Dudas

31.2 Tenor of *Plausu querulo* — 651

List of Sound Clips

These can be downloaded individually or in bulk; see p. xv for instructions.

- 9.1.mp3 — Machaut Motet 9 (Ex. 9.1)
- 9.2.mp3 — Chant segment (Ex. 9.2a)
- 9.3.mp3 — Structure of the *color* (Ex. 9.2b)
- 9.4.mp3 — Rhythmicised tenor (Ex. 9.2d and 9.2e)
- 9.5.mp3 — *Color* and *talea* (Ex. 9.2f)
- 9.6.mp3 — Tenor of Motet 4, marking *color* and *talea* (Ex. 9.3)
- 9.7.mp3 — Tenor of Motet 16, beginning (Ex. 9.4)
- 9.8.mp3 — Chant tenor of *Tribum/Quoniam* (Ex. 9.5)
- 9.9.mp3 — Motet 9 (Ex. 9.1, tr B18–B19, B33–B34; mo B16–B20, B31–B35)
- 9.10.mp3 — Motet 9 (Ex. 9.1, tr B63–B65, B77–B79; mo B65–B67, B84–B86; tr B51–B54, B92–B95)
- 9.11.mp3 — Motet 9 (Ex. 9.1, mo B17–B21, B137–B140)
- 9.12.mp3 — Motet 9 (Ex. 9.1, tr B25–B32.1)
- 9.13.mp3 — Motet 9 (Ex. 9.1, tr and mo, B25–B32.1)
- 9.14.mp3 — Motet 9 (Ex. 9.1, tr, mo, tenor, B25–B32.1)
- 9.15.mp3 — 6/3–8/5 cadences (Ex. 9.6a and 9.6b)
- 9.16.mp3 — 10/6–12/8 cadences (Ex. 9.6c)
- 9.17.mp3 — Partial cadences, B24–B25, B123–B124 (Ex. 9.7)
- 9.18.mp3 — Simple cadence form (Ex. 9.8a)
- 9.19.mp3 — Displaced cadence, B47–B49 simplified (Ex. 9.8b)
- 9.20.mp3 — Displaced cadences, B112–B115 (Ex. 9.9a–9.9d)
- 9.21.mp3 — Motet 9 (Ex. 9.1, B46–B83)
- 9.22.mp3 — Motet 9 (Ex. 9.1, mo alone, B91–B115)
- 9.23.mp3 — Motet 9 (Ex. 9.1, motetus progressions: B100–B102, B111–B114.1)
- 9.24.mp3 — Motet 9 (Ex. 9.1, a3, B91–B115)
- 9.25.mp3 — Motet 9 (Ex. 9.1, tr B6–B9)
- 9.26.mp3 — Motet 9 (Ex. 9.1, mo B109–B111)
- 9.27.mp3 — Openings of Motets 9 and 15 (Ex. 9.11)
- 13.1.mp3 — Machaut Motet 18, hocket section, b. 97–end, triplum
- 13.2.mp3 — Machaut Motet 18, hocket section, b. 97–end, motetus
- 13.3.mp3 — Machaut Motet 18, hocket section, b. 97–end, all three parts

List of Manuscripts

Items not in bold are either manuscripts cited without a siglum or names for groups of fragments or parts of a manuscript. Most archival documents are footnoted but not listed here.

Aachen	Aachen, Stadtbibliothek Aachen, MS Beis E14
Ao	Aosta, Seminario Maggiore, MS 15 (*olim* A 1° D 19)
Apt	Apt, Basilique Sainte-Anne, Trésor, MS 16bis
Arras983	Arras, Bibliothèque municipale, MS 983 (766), flyleaf
Autun152	Autun, Bibliothèque municipale, MS 152
Bamberg	Bamberg, Staatsbibliothek, MS Lit. 115
Barc853	Barcelona, Biblioteca Nacional de Catalunya (*olim* Central), MS 853c/d (BarcA, BarcE)
Barc971	Barcelona, Biblioteca Nacional de Catalunya, MS 971 (BarcC)
Basel71	Basel, Öffentliche Bibliothek der Universität, MS F.IX.71 (formerly Musikfragment I)
Basel72	Basel, Öffentliche Bibliothek der Universität, MS N.I.6 Nr 72 (formerly Musikfragment II)
Belfast	Belfast, Queen's University Library, MS 1-21-1
Ber49	Berlin, Staatsbibliothek, Stiftung Preußischer Kulturbesitz, MS lat 2° 49
Ber190	Berlin, Staatsbibliothek, Stiftung Preußischer Kulturbesitz, MS germ. 8° 280
Bergamo589	Bergamo, Civica Biblioteca 'Angelo Mai', MS MA 589 (Delta VIII.26)
Berlin, Staatsbibliothek, MS Mus. theor. 1325	
Bern	Bern, Burgerbibliothek, MS A 471 (flyleaves of A 421)[1]
Bologna	See also **Q1, Q15**
Boverio	Turin, Biblioteca Nazionale Universitaria, MS T.III.2
BOZ1	Warsaw, Biblioteka Narodowa, BOZ 61, treatise 1
BOZ2	Warsaw, Biblioteka Narodowa, BOZ 61, treatise 2
BOZ3	Warsaw, Biblioteka Narodowa, BOZ 61, treatise 3
Brescia5	Brescia, Biblioteca Queriniana, MS C.VI.5
Brive, Bibliothèque municipale, MS 1	
Brno	Brno, Archiv města Brna (City of Brno Archive), Fond V 2, Svatojakubská knihovna, 94/106, rear pastedown
Brussels758	Brussels, Archives du Royaume, Archives Ecclésiastiques, MS 758
Brussels5170	Brussels, Algemeen Rijksarchief, Fonds Sint-Goedele, MS 5170 (*olim* 758)
Br19606	Brussels, KBR, MS 19606
Bu2216	Bologna, Biblioteca Universitaria, MS 2216
Bud298	Budapest, Egyetemi Könyvtár, MS U.Fr.l.m. 298

---

[1] Also known as MS A 421. The ambiguity arose from an original cataloguing error, but it is now standard to refer to the host MS as A 421, the music fragments in its binding as A 471, following Steiger, *Das Berner Chansonnier-Fragment.*

xxviii LIST OF MANUSCRIPTS

Cambridge	See also **Pepys**
Cambridge, MA	See **Houghton**
Canberra	Canberra, National Library of Australia, Nan Kivell Calligraphy Collection, MS 4052/2/1 (part of RC)
Ca29	Cambrai, Le Labo (*olim* Médiathèque d'agglomération, Médiathèque municipale, Bibliothèque municipale), MS 29
Ca165	Cambrai, Le Labo (*olim* Médiathèque d'agglomération, Médiathèque municipale, Bibliothèque municipale), Inc. B 165
Ca1328	Cambrai, Le Labo (*olim* Médiathèque d'agglomération, Médiathèque municipale, Bibliothèque municipale) MS B 1328
Cant128/6	Canterbury, Cathedral Archives, CCA-DCc/AddMS/128/6 (*olim* CANT 3)
Ce70	Cambridge, Emmanuel College, MS 70
Ce300	Cambridge, Emmanuel College, MS 300
Chantilly (or **Ch**)	Chantilly, Bibliothèque du Château de Chantilly, MS 564 (*olim* 1047)
Chicago	See **Newberry**
Civ57	Cividale del Friuli, Museo Archeologico Nazionale, Cod. LVII
Civ98	Cividale del Friuli, Museo Archeologico Nazionale, Cod. XCVIII
Columbia	New York, Columbia University, Rare Book and Manuscript Library, Goff T172 (previously noted as Butler Library, and on Digital Scriptorium as Incunable T-172) (part of RC)
Cop17a	Copenhagen, Det Kongelige Bibliotek, Fragm. 17a, inv. 2400–2409
Cortona1	Cortona, Archivio storico del Comune, Frammento Musicali Medioevale (uno foglio) 'Cortona 1'
Cortona2	Cortona, Archivio storico del Comune, Frammento Musicali Medioevale (due foglia) 'Cortona 2'
Cu710	Cambridge, University Library, Add. MS 710 (the Dublin Troper)
Cu4435	Cambridge, University Library, Add. MS 4435 (16) (part of RC)
Cu5963	Cambridge, University Library, Add. MS 5963 (8) (part of RC)
Cyprus	Turin, Biblioteca nazionale universitaria, MS J.II.9 (TuB)
Darmstadt521	Darmstadt, Hessische Landes- und Hochschulbibliothek, MS MS 521
Darmstadt3471	Darmstadt, Hessische Landes- und Hochschulbibliothek, MS MS 3471
Darmstadt, Hessische Landes- und Hochschulbibliothek MS 705	
Dor	Dorchester, Dorset History Centre (D.H.C.), D-FSI, acc.10959
Douai74	Douai, Bibliothèque Marceline Desbordes-Valmore, MS 1105/3 fragment 74.4/1
Durham20	Durham, Chapter Library, MS C I 20
Egerton	London, British Library, Egerton MS 3307
Egidi	Montefiore dell'Aso, Biblioteca-Archivio di Francesco Egidi (lost)
Esc10	Escorial, Real Monasterio de San Lorenzo del Escorial, Biblioteca y Archivo de Música, MS O.II.10
Fauvel	This refers to the interpolated version of the *Roman de Fauvel* in Paris, Bibliothèque nationale de France, fonds fr. 146. **Paris146** includes other contents of the volume
Faenza	Faenza, Biblioteca comunale, MS 117
Ferrell(Vg)	Private Collection of James E. and Elizabeth J. Ferrell, Kansas City, United States, MS 1 (Machaut manuscript, formerly Vogüé, Wildenstein)
Fleischer	Rochester, New York, Sibley Music Library, Fleischer Fragment 44
Florence	See also **Redi71, SL2211**
Florence29	Florence, Biblioteca Medicea Laurenziana, MS Pluteus 29.1
Fountains	London, British Library, Add. MS 40011B

LIST OF MANUSCRIPTS   xxix

Fp 26	Florence, Biblioteca nazionale centrale, MS Panciatichiano 26
Franus	Hradec Králové, Muzeum východních Čech (Regional Museum, Library), MS II A 6 (Franus Cantional)
Fribourg2	Fribourg, Bibliothèque des Cordeliers, MS 2
Fribourg260	Fribourg, Bibliothèque cantonale et universitaire, MS Z 260
Gdańsk2315	Danzig, Stadtbibliothek, MS 2315, lost since Second World War
Ghent3360	Ghent, Rijksarchief, MS 3360
GR219	Grottaferrata, Biblioteca del Monumento Nazionale (*olim* Biblioteca dell'Abbazia di S. Nilo (Badia Greca)), Kript.Lat. 219 (*olim* 374 or E.β.XVI)
GR224	Grottaferrata, Biblioteca del Monumento Nazionale, Kript. Lat. 224, *olim* Collocazione provvisoria 197 [belongs with Dartmouth College, MS 002387 (*olim* Santa Barbara, collection of Denis Stevens)]
GRss	Grottaferrata, Biblioteca del Monumento Nazionale, Grottaferrata fragment s.s.
Houghton122	Cambridge, MA, Harvard University, Houghton Library, fMS Typ 122
Innsbruck	See **WolkB**
Ipswich	See **Yox**
Ivrea	Ivrea, Biblioteca capitolare, MS 115
Jena105	Jena, Thüringer Universitäts- und Landesbibliothek, MS Buder 4° 105
Karlsruhe82	Karlsruhe, Badische Landesbibliothek, Codex Lichtenthal 82, flyleaf
Kassel1	Kassel, Universitätsbibliothek Kassel; Landesbibliothek und Murhardsche Bibliothek der Stadt Kassel, 4° Ms. med. 1
Koblenz701	Koblenz, Landeshauptarchiv, Best. 701 Nr. 243
Kras	See **Warsaw8054**
Kremsmünster149	Kremsmünster, Stiftsbibliothek, MS 149
Lausanne8076	Lausanne, Bibliothèque et Archives de la Ville, fonds C 09 (service de la culture), carton 8076
Leiden342A	Leiden, Bibliotheek der Rijksuniversiteit, Fragment L.T.K. 342A
Leiden2515	Leiden, Bibliotheek der Rijksuniversiteit, Fragment B.P.L. 2515
Leiden2720	Leiden, Bibliotheek der Rijksuniversiteit, Fragment B.P.L. 2720
Leipzig223	Leipzig, Universitätsbibliothek der Karl-Marx Universität, Fragm lat. 223a (taken from D-LEu MS 1440)
Leipzig431	Leipzig, Universitätsbibliothek der Karl-Marx Universität, Fragm lat. 431
Lo4	London, British Library, Cotton MS Julius E. IV
Lo6	London, British Library, Royal MS 12 C VI
Lo12	London, British Library, Cotton MS Vitellius D. XII
Lo13	London, British Library, Cotton MS Vespasian D. XIII
Lo24	London, British Library, Cotton MS Titus D. XXIV
Lo36	London, British Library, Cotton MS Titus A. XXXVI
Lo53	London, British Library, Harley MS 53
Lo565	London, British Library, Harley MS 565
Lo763	London, British Library, Lansdowne MS 763
Lo861	London, British Library, Harley MS 861
Lo978	London, British Library, Harley MS 978
Lo1776	London, British Library, Sloane MS 1776
Lo4909	London, British Library, Add. MS 4909
Lo24198	London, British Library, Add. MS 24198
Lo29987	London, British Library, Add. MS 29987
Lo36579	London, British Library, Add. MS 36579
Lo40725	London, British Library, Add. MS 40725

XXX   LIST OF MANUSCRIPTS

Lo41667	London, British Library, Add. MS 41667
Lo54324	London, British Library, Add. MS 54324
Lo62132A	London, British Library, Add. MS 62132A
London	see also **Egerton, Fountains, McV, OH, Robertsbridge, V&A**
LoTNA	London, The National Archives, E.163/22/1/24
Lwa12185	London, Westminster Abbey, MS 12185
Lwa33327	London, Westminster Abbey, MS 33327
Lucca184	Lucca, Archivio di Stato, MS 184 (including 2 folios discovered in 1988 and 4 folios discovered in 1998) (also known, with **Perugia3065,** as the Mancini codex)
MachautA	Paris, Bibliothèque nationale de France, f. fr. 1584
MachautB	Paris, Bibliothèque nationale de France, f. fr. 1585
MachautC	Paris, Bibliothèque nationale de France, f. fr. 1586
MachautE	Paris, Bibliothèque nationale de France, f. fr. 9221
MachautG	Paris, Bibliothèque nationale de France, f. fr. 22546
Maidstone	Maidstone, Centre for Kentish Studies, PRC 50/5 (*olim* PRC 49/20)
Mainz, Stadtbibliothek, MS II 375	
Mancini Codex	See **Lucca184** and **Perugia3065**
McV	London, British Library, Add. MS 41667 (the McVeagh fragment)
Melk391	Melk, Benediktinerstift, Stiftsbibliothek MS 391
Melk950	Melk, Benediktinerstift, Stiftsbibliothek MS 950
Michaelbeuren10	Michaelbeuren, Stiftsbibliothek, Man. Cart. 10
Mo	Montpellier, Bibliothèque interuniversitaire, Section médecine, H 196
ModA	Modena, Biblioteca Estense e Universitaria, MS α.M.5.24 (formerly lat. 568)
ModB	Modena, Biblioteca Estense e Universitaria, MS α.X.I.11 (formerly lat. 471)
Montefiore	See **Egidi**
Montefortino	Archivio di Stato Ascoli Piceno, Notarile di Montefortino, vol. 142
Morgan396	New York, Morgan Library, MS M.396
Morgan978	New York, Morgan Library, MS M.978
Mu716	Munich, Bayerische Staatsbibliothek, Cgm 716
Mu3223	Munich, Bayerische Staatsbibliothek, Mus. MS 3223
Mu3224	Munich, Bayerische Staatsbibliothek, Mus. MS 3224
Munich 3232a	See **MuEm**
Mu15611	Munich, Bayerische Staatsbibliothek, Clm 15611
Mu29775	Munich, Bayerische Staatsbibliothek, Clm 29775/10 (formerly Clm 5362 Kasten D IV and [31])
MuEm	Munich, Bayerische Staatsbibliothek, MS clm 14274 (formerly mus. MS 3232a) (Codex St Emmeram)
New York	See **Columbia, Morgan396, Morgan978**
Newberry	Chicago, Newberry Library, MS 54.1
Norwich6	Norwich, Cathedral Library, T6
Nuremberg9, 9a	Nuremberg, Stadtbibliothek, Fragments lat. 9 and lat. 9a (originally from binding Cent. V 61, and Nuremberg 25)
OH	London, British Library, Add. MS 57950 (Old Hall)
Ox7	Oxford, Bodleian Library, MS e Mus. 7
Ox16	Oxford, Bodleian Library, MS Canon. ital. 16
Ox27	Oxford, Bodleian Library, MS Fairfax 27
Ox31	Oxford, Bodleian Library, MS Don. b. 3l (part of RC)
Ox32	Oxford, Bodleian Library, MS Don. b. 32 (part of RC)
Ox42	Oxford, Bodleian Library, MS Lat. liturg. e. 42 (Missale Bugallense, Codex Lowe)

LIST OF MANUSCRIPTS   xxxi

Ox81	Oxford, Bodleian Library, MS Hatton 81
Ox112	Oxford, Bodleian Library, MS Canon. Class. lat. 112
Ox213	Oxford, Bodleian Library, MS Canon. misc. 213
Ox229	Oxford, Bodleian Library, MS Canon. Pat. Lat. 229 (PadA)
Ox271*	Oxford, Bodleian Library, MS Bodley 271*
Ox308	Oxford, Bodleian Library, MS Douce 308
OxAS56	Oxford, All Souls College, MS 56
OxC118	Oxford, Corpus Christi College, MS 118
OxM267	Oxford, Magdalen College, MS 267
OxNC362	Oxford, New College, MS 362
OxS26	Oxford, Bodleian Library, MS Arch. Selden B26
OxU192	Oxford, Bodleian Library, University College MS 192
Pad14	Padua, Archivio di Stato, S. Giustina, catastico VII, busta 14
Pad658	Padua, Biblioteca Universitaria, MS 658 (PadC)
Pad675	Padua, Biblioteca Universitaria, MS 675 (PadD)
Pad684	Padua, Biblioteca Universitaria, MS 684 (PadA)
Pad1106	Padua, Biblioteca Universitaria, MS 1106 (PadD)
Pad1115	Padua, Biblioteca Universitaria, MS 1115 (PadB)
Pad1225	Padua, Biblioteca Universitaria, MS 1225 (PadD)
Pad1283	Padua, Biblioteca Universitaria, MS 1283 (PadD)
Pad1475	Padua, Biblioteca Universitaria, MS 1475(PadA)
PadA	= **Ox229, Pad684, Pad1475**
PadB	= **Pad1115**
PadC	= **Pad658**
PadD	= **Pad675, Pad1106, Pad1225, Pad1283**
Paris146	Paris, Bibliothèque nationale de France, fr. 146; see also *Fauvel*
Paris196	Paris, Bibliothèque de l'Arsenal, MS 196
Paris279	Paris, Bibliothèque de l'Arsenal, MS 279
Paris568	Paris, Bibliothèque nationale de France, f. it. 568 (Pit)
Paris571	Paris, Bibliothèque nationale de France, f. fr. 571
Paris837	Paris, Bibliothèque nationale de France, f. fr. 837
Paris844	Paris, Bibliothèque nationale de France, f. fr. 844 (trouvère MS M; *chansonnier du roi*, from Artois)
Paris934	Paris, Bibliothèque nationale de France, nouv. acq. fr. 934
Paris2195	Paris, Bibliothèque nationale de France, f. fr. 2195
Paris2444	Paris, Bibliothèque nationale de France, nouv. acq. lat. 2444
Paris3343	Paris, Bibliothèque nationale de France, f. lat. 3343
Paris4917	Paris, Bibliothèque nationale de France, nouv. acq. fr. 4917
Paris11411	Paris, Bibliothèque nationale de France, f. lat. 11411
Paris12044	Paris, Bibliothèque nationale de France, f. lat. 12044
Paris14741	Paris, Bibliothèque nationale de France, f. lat. 14741
Paris22069	Paris, Bibliothèque nationale de France, nouv. acq. fr. 22069
Paris	See also *Fauvel*, **Machaut, Pic, Reina, Trém**
Pepys1594	Cambridge, Magdalene College, Pepysian Library, MS 1594
Perugia2	Perugia, Biblioteca Sala del Dottorato dell'Università degli Studi, Inc. 2 (*olim* Cas. 3, Incunabolo inv. 15755 N.F.), 'Cialini fragment'. ('Cas. 3' was the old location of the Incunabolo, even if Brumana-Ciliberti in their book used the inventory number (15755 N.F.). The fragments are now held together with the incunabulum—though detached—with the new shelfmark "Inc. 2")
Perugia3065	Perugia, Biblioteca comunale "Augusta", MS 3065 (with **Lucca184** forms of the Mancini Codex, ManP)

xxxii LIST OF MANUSCRIPTS

Philadelphia15	Philadelphia, University of Pennsylvania Libraries, MS 15
Philadelphia614	Philadelphia, University of Pennsylvania Libraries, MS 614
Philadelphia658	Philadelphia, Free Library, MS Lewis T658 (*olim* T 489b)
Pic	Paris, Bibliothèque nationale de France, Collection de Picardie 67, f. 67, in black and white on Gallica at https://gallica.bnf.fr/ark:/12148/btv1b10033904t/f211.item and https://gallica.bnf.fr/ark:/12148/btv1b10033904t/f212.item
Pra9	Prague, Státni knihovna CSSR-Universitní knihovna, XI E 9
Pra103	Prague, Archiv Pražského Hradu, Knihovna Metropolitní Kapituly, MS M.CIII
Princeton103	Princeton, University Library, MS 103
Q1	Bologna, Museo Internazionale e Biblioteca della Musica di Bologna, MS Q.1 (*olim* Cod. 12)
Q15	Bologna, Museo Internazionale e Biblioteca della Musica di Bologna, MS Q.15 (*olim* Civico Museo Bibliografico Musicale, MS Q.15; *olim* Liceo Musicale 37)
RC	Eighteen fragments from a dismantled royal choirbook. See EECM 62 for description, inventory and facsimiles; an abbreviated inventory is in ⊙ Table 25.1. The manuscripts involved are: **Canberra**; **Columbia**; **Cu4435**; **Cu5963**; **Ox31**; **Ox32**; **OxM267**; **OxU192**; **Tallinn**; **V&A**
Redi71	Florence, Biblioteca Medicea Laurenziana, MS Redi 71
Reina	Paris, Bibliothèque nationale de France, nouv. acq. fr. 6771 (codex Reina)
Robertsbridge	London, British Library, Add. MS 28550
Rochester	See **Fleischer**
Rostock	Rostock, Universitätsbibliothek, MS. Phil.100/2 (Rostock Liederhandschrift, compiled by Rostock students between 1465 and 1487), http://rosdok.uni-rostock.de/resolve/id/rosdok_document_0000000269
San Marino	See **SM19914**
SanGiorgio	Venice, Abbazia di San Giorgio Maggiore, frammento musicale (currently lost)
Seville25	Seville, Biblioteca Capitular y Colombina, MS 5-2-25
Siena30	Siena, Biblioteca Comunale, MS L.V.30
Siena36	Siena, Biblioteca Comunale, MS L.V.36
SienaRavi3	Siena, Archivio di Stato, Fondo Vicariati, Vicariato di Gavoranno, registro Ravi 3 (1568–69)
SL2211	Florence, Archivio del Capitolo di San Lorenzo, MS 2211
SM19914	San Marino, CA, Huntington Library, HM 19914
Solsona109	Solsona, Arxiu Diocesi, MS 109
Speciálník	Hradec Králové, Muzeum východních Čech (Regional Museum, Library), MS Hr-7 (II A 7) (Codex Speciálník)
Sq	Florence, Biblioteca Medicea Laurenziana, Cod. Mediceo Palatino 87
St Petersburg	See **Warsaw378**
Stockholm, Kungliga Biblioteket, MS V.u.22	
Stras	Strasbourg, Bibliothèque municipale (*olim* Bibliothèque de la Ville), MS 222 C.22 (destroyed 1871); see Coussemaker, *Le Manuscrit musical M 222 C 22* for partial transcription
Tallinn	Tallinn, Estonian Theatre and Music Museum (Tallinn, Eesti Teatri- ja Muusikamuuseum) ETMM M8: 2/1–1 (part of RC)
Tarragona1	Tarragona, Archivo Histórico Archidiocesano, Fragment 1
Tarragona2	Tarragona, Archivo Histórico Archidiocesano, Fragment 2

LIST OF MANUSCRIPTS xxxiii

Todi	Todi, Biblioteca comunale Lorenzo Leoni, Fondo Congregazione di Carità Istituto dei Sartori
Toul94	Toulouse, Bibliothèque d'Études et du Patrimoine (*olim* Bibliothèque municipale), MS 94
Tourn27	Tournai, Chapitre de la Cathédrale, MS A 27 (*olim* 476)
Trém	Paris, Bibliothèque nationale de France, nouv. acq. fr. MS 23190 (*olim* Serrant, Duchesse de la Trémoïlle)
Trent	Trent codices
TR	Refers to the first part of **Tr87** and the second part of **Tr92**
Tr87	Trent, Castello del Buonconsiglio, Monumenti e Collezioni Provinciali (*olim* Museo Provinciale d'Arte), MS 1374 (*olim* 87)
Tr90	Trent, Castello del Buonconsiglio, Monumenti e Collezioni Provinciali (*olim* Museo Provinciale d'Arte), MS 1377 (*olim* 90)
Tr92	Trent, Castello del Buonconsiglio, Monumenti e Collezioni Provinciali (*olim* Museo Provinciale d'Arte), MS 1379 (*olim* 92)
Tr93	Biblioteca Capitolare/Museo Diocesano di Trento, MS BL ['Trent 93']
Troyes1397	Troyes, Bibliothèque municipale, MS 1397
Troyes1949	Troyes, Bibliothèque municipale, MS 1949
Turin10	Turin, Archivio di Stato, J.b.IX.10
Turin	See also **Cyprus**
Utrecht37	Utrecht, Bibliotheek der Rijksuniversiteit, MS 6 E 37 (Cat. 1846), part I
V&A	London, Victoria and Albert Museum, Prints and Drawings Study Room, Level E, Case I, shelf 197, box 5, Circ. 526–1923 (part of RC)
Vat307	Vatican City, Biblioteca Apostolica Vaticana, Barb. lat. 307
Vat1260	Vatican City, Biblioteca Apostolica Vaticana, Pal. Lat. 1260
Vat5321	Vatican City, Biblioteca Apostolica Vaticana, Vat. Lat. 5321
Venice24	Venice, Biblioteca nazionale Marciana, MS lat. app. cl. VIII/24 (coll. 3434)
Venice97	Venice, Biblioteca nazionale Marciana, Lat. CI. XII.97 [4125])
Venice145	Venice, Biblioteca nazionale Marciana, MS ital. IX,145 (coll. 7554)
Venice	See also **SanGiorgio**
Vg	See **Ferrell(Vg)**
Vienna123a	Vienna, Österreichische Nationalbibliothek, Fragm 123a
Vienna661	Vienna, Österreichische Nationalbibliothek, Fragm. 661
Vienna922	Vienna, Österreichische Nationalbibliothek, Fragm. 922
Vienna2856	Vienna, Osterreichische Nationalbibliothek, MS 2856
Vienna3244	Vienna, Österreichische Nationalbibliothek, MS 3244
Vienna4195	Vienna, Österreichische Nationalbibliothek, MS 4195
Vienna5094	Vienna, Österreichische Nationalbibliothek, MS 5094
Vienna	See also **WolkA**
W1	Wolfenbüttel, Herzog-August Bibliothek, Cod. Guelf. 628 Helmst.
Warsaw378	Warsaw, Biblioteka Narodowa, MS Lat. F. I. 378 (*olim* St Petersburg, Imperatorskaia Publichnaia biblioteka (Imperial Public Library), Lat. F. I. 378). Manuscript lost; known through photographs in Poznań
Warsaw8054	Warsaw, Biblioteka Narodowa, MS III. 8054 (*olim* Biblioteka Świdzińskich, then Biblioteka Krasiński 52)
Warsaw	See also **BOZ**
Washington1400	Washington, Library of Congress, MS M2.1 C6 1400 Case
WashingtonJ6	Washington, Library of Congress, MS ML171.J6 Case
WolkA	Vienna, Osterreichische Nationalbibliothek, Cod. 2777 (WolkensteinA)
WolkB	Innsbruck, Universitätsbibliothek, MS without shelfmark (WolkensteinB)

xxxiv LIST OF MANUSCRIPTS

Worcester160   Worcester Cathedral, MS F.160 (*olim* 1247)
Wrocław16   Wrocław, Biblioteka Uniwersytecka, MS IV Q 16
Wrocław411   Wrocław, Biblioteka Uniwersytecka, MS I Q 411, *olim* Ak1955/KN 195
Würz   Würzburg, Franziskanerkloster, MS I 10
YorkN3   York Minster, MS xvi.N.3
Yox   Ipswich, Suffolk Record Office, HA30: 50/22/13.15

Other Abbreviations

AfMw	*Archiv für Musikwissenschaft*
AH	Analecta Hymnica
alt.	alteration
AM	*Acta musicologica*
AMS	American Musicological Society
AAV	Archivio Apostolico Vaticano (formerly Archivio Segreto Vaticano, ASV)
AS	*Antiphonale Sarisburiense*, ed. Walter H. Frere, Plainsong and Mediaeval Music Society (London, 1901–25)
B	breve
b	bar
BJHM	*Basler Jahrbuch für Historische Musikpraxis*
BnF	Bibliothèque nationale de France
C	Cantus, *color* or clef, depending on context: (CI = Cantus I; C1 = *color* or clef)
CAO	*Corpus Antiphonalium Officii*, ed. René-Jean Hesbert and René Prévost (Rome, 1963–79)
CCR	Calendar of Close Rolls
CEKM	Corpus of Early Keyboard Music (The American Institute of Musicology)
CM	*Current Musicology*
CMM	Corpus Mensurabilis Musicae (The American Institute of Musicology)

1/2 Guillaume Dufay, *Motetti* [*isorithmici dicti*], ed. Guillaume De Van, *Opera Omnia*, 2, CMM 1 (Rome, 1948) re-edited with current numbering as:

1/1 Guillaume Dufay, *Motetti*, ed. Heinrich Besseler, *Opera Omnia*, CMM 1 (Rome, 1966)

1/6 Guillaume Dufay, *Cantiones*, revised ed. David Fallows, *Opera Omnia*, 6, CMM 1 (n.p., 1995) (commentary volume is Fallows, *The Songs of Guillaume Dufay*)

8/3 *The Collected Works of Laurentius Masii de Florentia, Donatus de Florentia, Rosso da Collegrano, and Nine Anonymous Pieces*, ed. Nino Pirrotta, CMM 8/3 (n.p., 1962)

11/1–7 *Early Fifteenth-Century Music*, ed. Gilbert Reaney, 8 vols., CMM 11 (n.p. and Neuhausen, 1955–83). Vol. 1 (1955), Vol. 2 (1959), Vol. 3 (1966), Vol. 7 (1983)

21 *The Cypriot-French Repertory of the Manuscript Torino, Biblioteca Nazionale, J.II.9*, ed. Richard H. Hoppin, 4 vols., CMM 21 (Rome, 1960–3)

29 *Fourteenth-Century Mass Music in France*, ed. Hanna Stäblein-Harder, CMM 29 (Rome, 1962)

35/1–2 Johannes Brassart, *Opera Omnia*, ed. Keith E. Mixter, 2 vols., CMM 35 (n.p., 1965).

39 *The Motets of the Manuscripts Chantilly, Musée Condé, 564 (olim 1047) and Modena, Biblioteca Estense, α.M.5.24 (olim lat. 568)*, ed. Ursula Günther, CMM 39 (n.p., 1965)

46/1–3 *The Old Hall Manuscript*, ed. Andrew Hughes and Margaret Bent, 3 vols., CMM 46 (n.p., 1969)

xxxvi OTHER ABBREVIATIONS

	50/1 Leonel Power, *Complete Works*, ed. Charles Hamm, CMM 50 (n.p., 1969)
	53/1–3 *French Secular Compositions of the Fourteenth Century*, ed. Willi Apel, 3 vols., CMM 53 (n.p., 1970–72)
col.	coloration
CPR	Calendar of Patent Rolls
CS	*Scriptorum de musica medii aevi nova series*, ed. Edmond de Coussemaker, 4 vols. (Paris, 1864–76; repr. Hildesheim, 1963)
CSM	Corpus Scriptorum de Musica (The American Institute of Musicology)
	5 Anon., *Notitia del valore delle note del canto misurato*, ed. Armen Carapetyan, CSM 5 (n.p., 1957)
	8 Philippe de Vitry, *Ars nova*, ed. Gilbert Reaney, André Gilles and Jean Maillard, CSM 8 (n.p., 1964)
	13 Anonymous, *De musica mensurabili* (ca. 1380), ed. Cecily Sweeney 1971. Anonymous, *De semibrevibus caudatis* (ca. 1400), ed. André Gilles and Cecily Sweeney, CSM 13 (n.p., 1971)
Ct	Contratenor
Curtis–Wathey	Gareth Curtis and Andrew Wathey, 'Fifteenth-Century English Liturgical Music: A List of the Surviving Repertory', *Royal Musical Association Research Chronicle*, 27 (1994), 1–69. Revised version by James Cook and Peter Wright (2017) available at http://www.eecm.ac.uk/media/sites/researchwebsites/eecm/Revised%20Curtis-Wathey%20handlist%20(2017).pdf)
DIAMM	Digital Image Archive of Medieval Music; https://www.diamm.ac.uk/
DSB	*Dictionary of Scientific Biography*, ed. C. G. Gillespie, 16 vols. (New York, 1970–81)
EECM	Early English Church Music
	22 *Fifteenth-Century Liturgical Music*, II: *Four Anonymous Masses*, ed. Margaret Bent, EECM 22 (London, 1979)
	42 *Fifteenth-Century Liturgical Music*, IV: *Early Masses and Mass Pairs*, ed. Gareth Curtis, EECM 42 (London, 2001)
	55 *Fifteenth-Century Liturgical Music*, VIII: *Settings of the Gloria and Credo*, ed. Peter Wright, EECM 55 (London, 2013)
	62 *English Fifteenth-Century Polyphonic Fragments: A Facsimile Edition*, ed. Margaret Bent and Andrew Wathey, EECM 62 (London, 2022)
EM	*Early Music*
EMH	*Early Music History*
GR	*Graduale Sacrosanctae Romanae Ecclesiae de tempore et de sanctis* (*Graduale Romanum*) (Tournai, 1974)
GS	*Graduale Sarisburiense*, ed. Walter Howard Frere (London, 1894; repr. Farnborough, 1966)
GS	*Scriptores Ecclesiastici de Musica Sacra Potissimum*, ed. Martin Gerbert, 3 vols. (Sankt Blasien, 1784; repr. Hildesheim, 1963)
HMT	*Handwörterbuch der musikalischen Terminologie* (Wiesbaden, 1971–2006).
JAF	*Journal of the Alamire Foundation*
JAMS	*Journal of the American Musicological Society*
JM	*Journal of Musicology*
JMT	*Journal of Music Theory*
lig.	ligature
L	long
LML	*Lexikon Musicum Latinum Medii Aevi = Wörterbuch der lateinischen Musikterminologie des Mittelalters bis zum Ausgang des 15.*

OTHER ABBREVIATIONS   xxxvii

	Jahrhunderts = *Dictionary of Medieval Latin Musical Terminology to the End of the 15th Century*, ed. Michael Bernhard, Bernhold Schmid, and Calvin M. Bower (Munich, 1992–2016)
LU	*Liber usualis* (Tournai, 1959)
M	minim
Mo	motetus
M&L	*Music & Letters*
MB	Musica Britannica
	8 John Dunstable, *Complete Works*, ed. Manfred Bukofzer, MB 8 (London, 1953)
	8rev John Dunstable, *Complete Works*, ed. Manfred Bukofzer, rev. edn. by Margaret Bent, Ian Bent, and Brian Trowell, MB 8rev (London, 1970)
MD	*Musica disciplina*
MGG1	*Die Musik in Geschichte und Gegenwart*, ed. Friedrich Blume (Kassel, 1949–86)
MGG2	*Die Musik in Geschichte und Gegenwart*, 2nd edn., ed. Laurenz Lütteken (Kassel, 1994–2008)
MMMA	Monumenta monodica medii aevi (Kassel, 1956–)
mo	Motetus
MQ	*The Musical Quarterly*
MR	*Music Review*
MT	*The Musical Times*
Mx	maxima
NDB	*Neue Deutsche Biographie*, 4 (Berlin, 1957)
NG1	*The New Grove Dictionary of Music and Musicians*, ed. Stanley Sadie (London, 1980)
NG2	*The New Grove Dictionary of Music and Musicians*, 2nd edn., ed. Stanley Sadie and John Tyrrell (London, 2001)
PM	*Processionale monasticum*
PMFC	Polyphonic Music of the Fourteenth Century
	1 *The Roman de Fauvel; the Works of Philippe de Vitry; French Cycles of the Ordinarium Missae*, ed. Leo Schrade, PMFC 1 (Monaco, 1956)
	2–3 *The Works of Guillaume de Machaut*, ed. Leo Schrade, PMFC 2–3 (Monaco, 1974)
	5 *Motets of French Provenance*, ed. Frank Ll. Harrison, PMFC 5 (Monaco, 1965)
	12 *Italian Sacred Music*, ed. Kurt von Fischer and F. Alberto Gallo, PMFC 12 (Monaco, 1976)
	13 *Italian Sacred and Ceremonial Music*, ed. Kurt von Fischer and F. Alberto Gallo, PMFC 13 (Monaco, 1987)
	15 *Motets of English Provenance*, ed. Frank Ll. Harrison; texts ed. and trans. Peter Lefferts, PMFC 15 (Paris and Monaco, 1980)
	16–17 *English Music for Mass and Offices*, ed. Ernest H. Sanders, Frank Ll. Harrison, and Peter M. Lefferts, 2 vols., PMFC 16–17 (Paris and Monaco, 1983–86)
	23A, 23B *French Sacred Music*, ed. Giulio Cattin and Francesco Facchin, 2 vols., PMFC 23A, 23B (Monaco, 1991)
	24 *The Works of Johannes Ciconia*, ed. Margaret Bent and Anne Hallmark, PMFC 24 (Paris and Monaco, 1984–85)
PMM	*Plainsong and Medieval Music*
p.mus.	pieces in *Fauvel* as numbered in Dahnk, *L'Hérésie de Fauvel*

xxxviii OTHER ABBREVIATIONS

PRMA	*Proceedings of the Royal Musical Association*
Qu	Quadruplum
RBM	*Revue belge de musicologie*
RC	Royal Choirbook
RIM	*Rivista italiana di musicologia*
RISM	Repertoire international des sources musicales
RM	*Revista de musicología*
RMA	Royal Musical Association
S	semibreve
SaM	*Il saggiatore musicale*
SBM	*Schweizer Beiträge zur Musikwissenschaft*
SIMG	*Sammelbände der Internationalen Musikgesellschaft*
SMed	*Studi medievali*
SMus	*Studi musicali*
ST	Solus tenor
TKVNM	*Tijdschrift van de Koninklijke Vereniging voor Nederlandse Muziekgeschiedenis*
T	Tenor (or *talea*, depending on context)
TML	Thesaurus Musicarum Latinarum; http://www.chmtl.indiana.edu/tml/
tr	triplum
TVNM	*Tijdschrift van de Vereniging voor Nederlandse Muziekgeschiedenis*
WA	*Antiphonaire monastique, XIIIe siècle: Codex F. 160 de la bibliothèque de la Cathédrale de Worcester*, Paléographie musicale, 12 (Tournai, 1922)

Introduction

The Preface acknowledges at least some of the many collegial debts I have incurred over several decades. It also sets out the genesis and mechanical aspects of this book, whose relationship to the companion website is explained on p. xv. The examples on the website are mostly too large to be printed in the book, but form an essential part of the chapters under which they are located on the website. Here I give an overview of the contents of the book, and of what I see as some of its contributions. But first a few words on the origins and definitions of the motet.

What was a Motet?

Just as generic terms such as symphony, concerto, fantasy and sonata have changed their meanings over the centuries, so also 'motet'. From the eighteenth century onwards the term was understood mostly to denote a sacred choral work of a very different sort from the genre that had its origins in the early thirteenth century. Jared C. Hartt's *A Critical Companion to Medieval Motets* covers many aspects of early motet composition; his Introduction stresses their plural characters. Building on work by previous generations of scholars, more than half of the contributions to that book focus on the thirteenth century, some drawing attention to exceptional cases that do not fit well with our broader narratives of the genre.[1] I will not attempt to synthesise those narratives here. The present book is mostly about motets in the fourteenth century, extending in some chapters into the early fifteenth. It starts with some of the more advanced motets in the *Roman de Fauvel* (**Paris146**). Rather than tracing continuities and disjunctions from earlier repertories, the focus is largely on individual compositions, teasing out something of the range of strategies employed to serve their uniqueness and interrelationships.

Definitions of the motet from this period point to a multi-voice composition to which verbal texts are fundamental, as the name suggests ('mot' = word). The famous definition by Johannes de Grocheio (*c.* 1300) is explicitly polyphonic and polytextual ('Motetus vero est cantus ex pluribus compositus, habens plura dictamina': a motet is a song put together from several, having several texts), with a tenor which may or may not be texted ('quia quilibet debet habere dictamen et in aliquibus non, tenore excepto').[2] Even such a minimal definition as this is challenged by the existence of monophonic motets without tenors (albeit a minority) in the thirteenth and fourteenth centuries. They are perhaps implied in the 'Capitulum de vocibus applicatis verbis', now dated after

---

[1] For some of these exceptional cases see Bradley, 'Origins and Interactions'.

[2] Besseler's dating *c.* 1300 was upheld by Page, 'Johannes de Grocheio', 17, which I find more plausible than the reversion to Ernst Rohloff's dating as *c.* 1275, in *Johannes de Grocheio, Ars Musice*, ed. Mews et al., 10–12, q.v. for bibliographical references to datings by earlier scholars. The definition quoted is on pp. 84–85. Grocheio here distinguishes the tenor from the 'cantus' parts; it is not always clear if the tenor is counted as one of those plural texts.

The Motet in the Late Middle Ages. Margaret Bent, Oxford University Press. © Oxford University Press 2023.
DOI: 10.1093/so/9780190063771.003.0001

2 INTRODUCTION

1332: 'Motteti sunt cantus applicati verbis . . . Fiunt etiam ad unum et ad plures cantus' (motets are melodies applied to words. . . . They are made with one or more melodies).[3] 'Cantus' could of course apply to melodies added to a tenor, but no mention is made of a tenor. The modern editors of this treatise understand it to mean monophonic motets, but comment that none are transmitted, though they were acknowledged by Ludwig, and more recently investigated by Judith Peraino, Elizabeth Eva Leach and Gaël Saint-Cricq.[4] So what remains of the traditional definition of a motet? Given the plurality already apparent thirty years ago, I ventured that ' "A piece of music in several parts with words" is as precise a definition of the motet as will serve from the thirteenth to the late sixteenth century and beyond'.[5] But given recent revisions and exceptions, all that remains is 'music with words'.

By contrast, a much higher bar for motet definition was set by Frank Ll. Harrison for his editions in PMFC 5, thirty-three complete fourteenth-century motets of French provenance from **Paris146** and **Ivrea** and, a bit later, **Chantilly**.[6] Fragmentary sources considerably augment this number, and discoveries continue. In addition, of course, there are the twenty-three motets by Machaut, which form a very significant proportion of the surviving French motets. Harrison required two differently texted upper parts, a cantus firmus and, usually, isorhythm.[7] Because fourteenth-century French motets were the first to be discovered, codified and edited, some of their normative criteria were misfittingly applied to English and Italian motets, which survive in much more fragmentary form, and whose distinctiveness was recognised only decades later. In PMFC 15 (36 motets of English provenance), Harrison implicitly acknowledged that the strict criteria he had set for French motets had to be applied more flexibly for England. He nevertheless admitted *Salve cleri speculum* (PMFC 15, no. 11) to honourable status as a motet, qualified by having chant paraphrase in the tenor, although only from section 2 onwards. But he excluded its generic companions, *A solis* and *Hostis Herodes*, likewise voice-exchange motets from the same manuscript, **Ox81** (the Hatton MS), both with chant paraphrase, not in the tenor, but at the beginning of the upper parts. These were relegated to less prestigious categories in PMFC 16 (nos. 94–95 and 96), thus applying an artificial criterion to separate identically structured compositions.[8]

For motet definition we can also turn to instances of contemporary labelling and classification. Fourteenth-century manuscripts, indexes or lists which describe pieces as motets cast the net wider than Harrison's restrictive definition. The **Paris146** index

---

[3] See Ch. 26 and n. 44 for this passage and Elena Abramov-van Rijk's recent dating. Originally made known in Debenedetti, 'Un trattatello', and more recently in an edition and translation by Burkard and Huck, 'Voces applicatae verbis'. This definition appears to invert the motet definition: 'Ballade sunt verba applicata sonis'. Burkard and Huck (p. 21) caution against treating this as a chronological claim for the order of words and music in either case.

[4] 'Weder überliefert noch anderswo besprochen'; ibid., 12; but see Ludwig, *Repertorium*, i/1, 305–15. Peraino, 'Monophonic Motets', explains how monophonic refrains and grafted monophonic melodies were associated with the term 'motet' in the 13th c., and observes that scholars have not 'stepped outside a principal concern with polyphonic genres or questions of compositional procedure' (pp. 644, 646). Among other recent accounts of monophonic motets see Leach, 'The Genre(s) of Medieval Motets', and Saint-Cricq, 'Motets in Chansonniers'.

[5] Bent, 'The Late-medieval Motet', 114.

[6] **Paris146** dates from the late 1310s, **Ivrea** has been dated between *c.* 1360 and 1390, **Chantilly** to the early 15th c. The Chantilly motets were also edited by Günther in CMM 39.

[7] See Ch. 2 for a historiographical unpicking of this over-widely used modern term.

[8] For more on voice-exchange motets, see Bent, Hartt and Lefferts, *The Dorset Rotulus*.

INTRODUCTION 3

classifies motets as 'motez a trebles et a tenures', for three-part motets, and 'motez a tenures sanz trebles' for two-part motets.[9] With very few exceptions, thirteenth- and fourteenth-century motets are named and indexed by their motetus parts, at the end of the fourteenth century and in the fifteenth by tripla.[10] The **Trém** index is classified in two columns as 'motez' and 'balades et rondeaus' respectively. Motets are indeed listed by motetus parts, but that column also includes *chaces* and mass movements; I suggest in Chapter 31 that the division may be practical rather than generic, separating long pieces from shorter songs that could serve as page-fillers. Motets are also labelled thus in the table of contents of **MachautA**, and their sections so headed in the other Machaut manuscripts.

We also have the authority of theorists who attach the term to titles of known motets. After Franco, these include fourteenth-century treatises attributed to Philippe de Vitry, Johannes de Muris, Robertus de Handlo, John of Tewkesbury, Johannes Boen, Philippus de Caserta, Theodoricus de Campo, Heinrich Eger von Kalkar, and many anonymous authors. As in the preceding century, it is sometimes clear that a whole motet or a specified voice-part is being referred to, and sometimes the reference is just to the eponymous motetus voice.[11]

Moving into the fifteenth century, the thirteen motets in **Chantilly** are grouped together at the end and headed 'Motes' in the table of contents. **OH** also groups its motets together, but they are not so labelled and there is no index. **ModB** is unique in having a table of contents with musical incipits. The section headed 'Hic incipiunt motteti' includes the newer 'song' or cantilena motets (with a texted top part and accompanying tenor and—usually inessential—contratenor, both usually untexted), as well as periodically structured compositions with isorhythm.[12] **Q15** was originally planned with sections devoted to mass movements (mostly paired) and to motets, though not so labelled.[13] Cantilena motets are again grouped with periodic motets; the motet section also includes Du Fay's setting of Petrarch's *Vergene bella*, classified by Heinrich Besseler

[9] A similar classification occurs in the slightly earlier **Lo978** (the Harley index): 'Moteti cum una littera et duplici nota', 'Moteti cum duplici littera', 'Moteti cum duplici nota'.

[10] A few motets are already cited by triplum in treatises in the 14th c., including *Orbis orbatus*. The index of **MachautE** of the 1390s lists the motets by triplum, that of the earlier **MachautA** mostly by motetus, except that Motets 1 and 18 are exceptionally cited by triplum. Both indexes are analysed in Earp, 'Scribal Practice', 52–82. The often-cited *Rex Karole* (late 1370s) is never named other than by its triplum. The thirteen motets of **Chantilly** are all listed by triplum except for *Ida capillorum*, the motetus, which is presented there and in **Ivrea** as the triplum; see Ch. 31.

[11] *Motetus* can refer to the whole composition: 'In moteti tenore qui vocatur . . .' (as in the tenor of the motet called . . .) and similar formulations occur repeatedly in Vitry, *Ars nova*, Boen, *Ars*, and elsewhere. Or it can refer just to the motetus voice: Jacobus Leodiensis, *Speculum musicae*, VII ch. 3: 'Cum autem quis facit discantum qui triplum vocatur, debet aspicere non solum ad voces tenoris, sed etiam moteti, ut concordet et cum tenore similiter et cum moteto' (Whoever who makes a discant called triplum should look not only at the tenor notes, but also those of the motetus, in order that it may concord with both tenor and motetus). The *Lexikon Musicum Latinum* (*LML*) accordingly defines *motetus* as (1) Genre of mensural music based on a tenor and with different texts in individual voices; (2) Term that designates the voice of a motet immediately adjacent to the tenor, giving supporting citations. For more on the term, see Hofmann, 'Zur Entstehungs- und Frühgeschichte des Terminus Motette'.

[12] For the distinction between classified indexes and lists of contents in Machaut, see Earp, 'Scribal Practice', 52–82. The index of **MachautA** is a prescriptive table of contents from which the manuscript made some departures. The index of **MachautE** is a *post facto* table of contents. For a more general discussion, see Bent, 'Indexes' and, more specifically, for **Chantilly** see Bent, 'The Absent First Gathering', also 'The Trent 92 and Aosta Indexes'. For an Italian list of mostly non-extant pieces, see Zimei, 'Un Elenco veneto' and Ch. 26.

[13] See Bent, *Q15*. There appears originally to have been a section (subsequently removed) devoted to songs, but songs were also added as page-fillers late in the first stage of compilation.

4   INTRODUCTION

(CMM 1/VI) as a song. By the time of **Q15** and **ModB**, such groupings imply a broader understanding of motets to embrace newer styles.

Gradually in the fifteenth century, these new song-like kinds of motet came to the fore.[14] Simpler styles have been broadly related to humanist impulses, placing more emphasis on rhetorical communication and new approaches to the expression of semantic meaning, though mostly now using existing and often liturgical texts, which sets them apart from the predominance in the fourteenth century of texts newly composed in close conjunction with their music. It may have been these new trends that partly informed Tinctoris's famous statement in the 1470s that only music of the last forty years was worth hearing, though his writings address complex notational issues.[15] The general move towards simpler textures might be compared to the eighteenth-century shift to the *style galant*, insofar as that was a reaction against perceived contrapuntal complexity. Major composers in the fifteenth century, however (including Du Fay and Dunstaple), continued to cultivate both types of motet. The delight in puzzles, notational subtleties and ingenious constructions continued alongside newer forms throughout the century and beyond; the fascination with intellectual challenges was never lost.

Overview of This Book's Contents

Most of the motets discussed here date from the fourteenth century. Some are from the first two decades of the fifteenth century, notably English motets in Part V, some Italian motets in Part VI, the Cyprus motets in Chapter 32, and the later papal motets in Chapter 31. The book thus, by chance rather than design, somewhat complements the thirteenth-century concentration of Hartt's *Critical Companion*.[16] Datings of motets are a continuing challenge. Recent scholarship has refined the dating of some of the manuscripts containing (or treatises naming) them, thus changing *termini ante quem* for their contents. Occasions for composition or performance have been proposed or removed; suggested dedicatees have been revised, and competing narratives of stylistic and notational development continue to play out. Several new datings of individual works are proposed. Chronology is hampered by the fact that most compositions are anonymous, and that few known composers, apart from Machaut and Vitry, have known careers and death dates. A cluster of dates in the 1370s helps orientation: Machaut died in 1377, which obviously provides a terminus for any late works not included in manuscripts prepared earlier in his lifetime. The enormous repertory indexed in the largely lost manuscript **Trém** must date mostly from before a 1376 inscription, though later additions may extend a few years beyond that (Ch. 31). Not in **Trém** was the motet *Rex Karole/Leticie pacis*, dated *c.* 1375 by Günther, 1378 by Carolann Buff (see Ch. 27

---

[14] The standard survey and classification of 15th-c. motets is Cumming, *The Motet in the Age of Du Fay*, who notes their amorphous character.

[15] Tinctoris, *Liber de arte contrapuncti* (1477), Prologue: 'Et si visa auditaque referre liceat nonnulla vetusta carmina ignotae auctoritatis quae apocrypha dicuntur in manibus aliquando habui, adeo inepte, adeo insulse composita ut multo potius aures offendebant quam delectabant' (I have had in my hands certain old anonymous songs, called apocrypha, so stupidly and absurdly composed that they rather offended than pleased the ear).

[16] And an entire recent book has been devoted to the eighth fascicle of **Mo**: Bradley and Desmond, *The Montpellier Codex*.

n. 8), which must in any case antedate the 1380 death of its dedicatee Charles V. It was adjacent (in **Basel72**) to what appears to be a contrafact (*Novum sidus*) of the little-known *Gaudeat et exultet* (in **Basel72**), a motet which celebrates a French antipope and must date from soon after 1378 (Chs. 30 and 26). The newest and most exciting addition to this cluster is a unique motet in **Douai74**, *Ferre solet/Anatheos*, deciphered by Manon Louviot. It is internally signed through an acrostic by the composer, Johannes Vavassoris, and dated 1373.[17] However, proposed datings for individual pieces can vary by at least twenty years where such help is lacking.

The two chapters of Part I address various aspects of compositional technique that underpin fourteenth-century motets. Chapter 1 considers the often-cited prescriptions for motet composition traditionally attributed to 'Egidius' and proposes restoring the treatise to anonymity. Also addressed are the phenomenon of middle-voice tenors with a lower motetus, the definition and terminology for *introitus* and *cadentia*, the problem of non-coincident or dissonant endings, and the status of lower parts. I have dealt in other publications with questions of musical grammar, counterpoint, and the roles of solus tenor and contratenor parts.[18] The principles set out in those studies will be alluded to but not repeated in detail here, though they underlie my compositional assumptions.

Chapter 2 is an only slightly adapted version of a previously published paper on the history and limitations of the modern term isorhythm. A preamble to the chapter notes recent work by Lawrence Earp and Anna Zayaruznaya. I suggest that the term has been misapplied in ways that distort the historiography of the motet and imply more uniformity than is justified by the rich variety of techniques and strategies encountered. Many chapters in this book (some originally published decades ago but to varying degrees rewritten) draw attention to some of these strategies, constructional, notational, and particularly the role of text and music together in shaping each motet as an individual conception, some of these in ways little noticed previously.

The early chapters in Part II (the Marigny motets, beyond *Fauvel*, and Vitry) are adapted from previously published articles, reordered and now amplified with unpublished material: Chapter 3, 'Fauvel and Marigny' (1998); Chapter 4, '*Tribum*' (1997), here with added material on *Garrit gallus/In nova*; and Chapter 5, *Aman/Heu*, my contribution to the joint article with Kevin Brownlee, 'Icarus, Phaeton, Haman' (2019). Chapter 6 on *Floret/Florens* has been added, partly moved from 'Fauvel and Marigny'; also new are Chapter 7, with observations on related manuscripts, and on motets by or perhaps by Vitry, and Chapter 8 on the intimate relationship of words and music in his *Vos/Gratissima*.

The chapters of Part III deal with individual motets by Machaut and address various aspects and audiences. Chapter 9, on Motet 9 (*Fons tocius superbie/O livoris feritas/Fera pessima*), was written in 2003 with pedagogical intent and is accompanied by sound clips accessible on the companion website. It suggests a number of hitherto

---

[17] Presented in a seminar at All Souls College on 20 Nov. 2020. See Louviot, 'Uncovering the Douai Fragment'.

[18] Bent, *Counterpoint, Composition, and Musica Ficta* (2002) includes previously published articles. See ch. 8 on the Solus tenor, and especially the Introduction with updating commentaries. Subsequent relevant publications include 'The Grammar of Early Music' (1989); 'Naming of Parts: Notes on the Contratenor' (2008); and 'Reading, Memory, Listening, Improvisation' (2014).

6 INTRODUCTION

unremarked or little-remarked directions and opportunities for motet analysis, some of which have since been extended by others. Chapter 10 on M15 (*Amours qui a le pouoir/ Faus Samblant m'a deceü/ Vidi dominum*) is a revised version of a 1991 paper twinned with one by Kevin Brownlee ('Machaut's Motet 15'), part of our otherwise largely un-published collaboration (in seminars) on some of Machaut's French-texted motets. This collaboration also included Motet 10 (*Hareu! hareu! le feu/Helas! ou sera pris confors/Obediens usque ad mortem*), on which his contribution on the texts appeared as Brownlee, 'Fire, Desire, Duration, Death', mine not until 2018 as 'Machaut's Motet 10', and here Chapter 12. Chapter 13 addresses issues of notation and dating in Motet 18 (*Bone pastor Guillerme/Bone pastor qui pastores/Bone pastor*, extracted and ex-panded from Bent, 'Words and Music in Machaut's Motet 9'), with a new postscript on the tenor of Motet 2 (*Tous corps qui de bien amer/ De souspirant cuer dolent me pleing/ Suspiro*). Chapter 14, on Motets 4 (*De Bon Espoir/ Puis que la douce/ Speravi*) and 8 (*Qui es promesses de Fortune/ Ha! Fortune, trop suis mis/Et non est qui adjuvet*), is previously unpublished but was delivered as lectures together with Brownlee's comments on the texts, which were summarised in his 'Textual Polyphony in Machaut's Motets 8 and 4'. These discussions were also directed towards an interdisciplinary audience and should be considered together with, and in some cases updated by, more recent work by others on these motets. Chapter 11 is not about a motet but a mass movement, the Gloria of Machaut's Mass, raising questions of compositional and contrapuntal priority that are also relevant to motet composition.

The chapters of Part IV (*Musicorum collegium*: the Musician Motets) are hith-erto unpublished, though much of the material has been presented in lectures and seminars from the 1980s onwards, most recently in a draft circulated to participants in the International Symposium on Late Medieval and Early Renaissance Music, Novacella 2017. As elsewhere, these chapters are designed to be read in conjunction with the musical transcriptions on the companion website, in addition to examples in the printed book. Early work on this repertory received stimulus from dialogue and joint presentations with David Howlett, and I am grateful for his insights on the verbal texts. Plans for joint publication stalled when our views diverged on the extent to which his ingenious letter countings, anagrams and golden sections should domi-nate the discussion. I hope he will publish his work on these texts separately. Readers of my earlier articles may notice that in some revisions in Parts II and III I now place less emphasis on irrational proportions such as the golden section, except where the counted components are objectively (structurally) separated, as for example, in Part IV, between the two texts of *Musicorum* discussed in Chapter 18, or the musical division between the *color* statements of *Arta/Musicus* in Chapter 21. That chapter considers incomplete compositions that may be connected to the family of musician motets, and also lists other compositions, not so connected, that deal with music or musicians. Chapter 20 addresses the unique and brilliant English motet with named musicians, *Sub Arturo plebs*, an English contribution to this originally French subgenre, and its disputed dating. It thus forms a bridge from the mainly French motets considered so far to English compositions around and after 1400 in Part V, and then to Italian motets be-fore and after 1400 in Part VI.

A word of explanation is needed as to why Part V (English motets *c.* 1400–1420) includes nothing relating to my interests in the rich tradition of English motets dating from most of the fourteenth century. A much-revised version of my reconstruction of a major English motet from before 1326, *Rota versatilis*, is now published in Bent, Hartt and Lefferts, *The Dorset Rotulus*, which includes a new survey of English fourteenth-century motet composition superseding anything else I might have included here. The first quarter of the fifteenth century was a remarkably productive time for English music, though not necessarily more so than the fourteenth, which is marked by a great variety of inventive compositional strategies surviving in numerous but mostly fragmentary forms, a tragic shadow of what must have been.[19] Although some French motets are found in English sources from the mid-fourteenth century (**Durham20** and **Ox7**), there is no evidence of travel in the opposite direction. None of the identified motets listed in **Trém** in the late 1370s (Ch. 31) has English sources or can be confidently claimed as English on stylistic grounds, though questions have been raised about its inclusion of at least two motets on St Thomas Becket, who was, however, also widely venerated on the Continent. The new century is better documented in the toweringly important Old Hall manuscript (**OH**), the first English music book to survive in anything approaching complete form since the Winchester Troper 400 years earlier.[20] This Part addresses, first, two unique and complex compositions in the Yoxford fragment (**Yox**), *O amicus/Precursoris* and the Credo *Omni tempore*, and then motets in the Old Hall manuscript and by Dunstaple. Chapters 22–25 bring together revised forms of previously published and unpublished work on these English compositions from the years around 1400, some of them conceptually and notationally quite complex.

Part VI (Italian motets) begins with a paper first presented at Certaldo in 1984, here revised as Chapter 26, in which I sought to define the distinctive genre of the Italian motet, despite its absence from the large retrospective anthologies of the early fifteenth century dominated by the madrigal, ballata and caccia. Much that I said then has now been absorbed into mainstream scholarship, its arguments taken further by others. Most of those motets are fragmentary; a few were included in PMFC 12–13.[21] Most or all of Ciconia's motets date from the first decade of the fifteenth century (PMFC 24) and spawned a flow of similarly formed compositions in the ensuing generation. Many features distinguish them from French motets. Some are isorhythmic in the truest sense, two sections of which the second rhythmically replicates the first; such cases were discounted as too simplistically constructed to qualify as isorhythmic by older inflated definitions. The upper parts usually have different texts, but increasingly often a single text; those parts are usually of equal or nearly equal range and activity. Most have freely composed tenors; exceptions are Marchetto's only surviving motet and those by Du Fay a century later. It still remains for the motet output of Du Fay to be fully evaluated in the light of his absorption of Italian precedents.

---

[19] Complete compositions are published in PMFC 15–17. Some idea of the further range and extent of English motet composition furnished by fragments can be gained from the path-breaking dissertation of Peter Lefferts, 'Motet in England' (1983), and especially from his musical appendix (available on DIAMM resources).

[20] The possible exception to this generalisation would be **W1**: a book of Parisian polyphony that was at St Andrews early in its life, and was almost certainly produced in Scotland—which is not England. None of this changes the fundamental problem that there is a dearth of near-complete insular sources.

[21] Those volumes were published in 1976 and 1987, the latter including reconstructions based on material signalled by me.

8 INTRODUCTION

Chapter 27 is an almost unchanged version of my assessment of the motets in the palimpsest manuscript **SL2211** and the composer Hubertus de Salinis.[22] Chapter 28 is a previously unpublished overview of the motets of Johannes Ciconia. Chapter 29 is an almost unchanged version of my attempt to bring the theories of Prosdocimus de Beldemandis to bear on the analysis of compositions by his Paduan contemporary Johannes Ciconia.[23] There is no documentary evidence that they knew each other, and their respective theoretical writings have little in common, either in content or purpose. Nevertheless, I found it instructive to bring Prosdocimus's counterpoint teaching into dialogue with the background counterpoint of Ciconia's motets, to show how the bare counterpoint is elaborated, and how dyadic principles are mapped onto a three-part texture.

Part VII (Music for Popes and the Courts of Burgundy and Cyprus) brings together three unrelated essays, all considerably revised from their original published forms. Chapter 30, 'Early Papal Motets', has been reworked to take account of subsequent writings and discoveries, including a discussion of the incomplete motet *Per grama protho paret*. Chapter 31 updates my earlier essay on the Trémoïlle 'index' (**Trém**), including some new identifications. Although for convenience I refer to it as an index, it lies in status between a classified index and a table of contents in that it separates motets and other long compositions from ballades and shorter works (rondeaux, a virelai and a hymn) which evidently served as page-fillers in this large-format manuscript; but otherwise it lists compositions in order as in a table of contents, and later additions were indexed as they were copied. Some of the songs are numerically out of order, presumably listed in order of copying where space had been found for them on an earlier opening.

Chapter 32, on the motets of the manuscript Turin, Biblioteca Nazionale Universitaria J.II.9 (**Cyprus**), is here enlarged with a survey of the probable origins of the repertory and the manuscript, taking account of more recent work. Most important is Karl Kügle's identification of Jean Hanelle as a musician from Cambrai who, together with the composer Gilet Velut, accompanied Charlotte of Bourbon to Cyprus in 1411 when she became the queen of King Janus. It was already known that Hanelle was still nominally in musical service to the new King John of Cyprus, the son of Janus and Charlotte, when he (Hanelle) accompanied their daughter Anne to Savoy for her marriage to Duke Louis in 1434; the continuity from Hanelle's earlier arrival in Cyprus suggests a role for him in the compilation and possibly the creation of this isolated repertory. A Postscript to this chapter considers a 2012 hypothesis (Kügle, 'Glorious Sounds for a Holy Warrior'), finding it ingenious but unconvincing. However, at a conference in Turin, 30 September–1 October 2021, Kügle drew back from that hypothesis for some of the same reasons that I found it problematic, and replaced it with a new theory that he has yet to publish and submit to peer evaluation. I have therefore curtailed my original draft of this critique. The many questions raised about the manuscript's origins must be considered work in progress, which may be taken further in the proceedings of that conference.

---

[22] Bent, 'The Motet Collection of San Lorenzo 2211'.
[23] Bent, 'Ciconia, Prosdocimus'.

New Ways to Explore Motets

It is not easy to draw together what contributions these essays may have made, over several decades, either in their original forms or in the current revisions. But what follows is an attempt to set out some of the directions that were new at the time, or are new for previously unpublished chapters.

A unique property of measured music is the capacity to give fixed places to words within a relative time frame. In most fourteenth-century motets, not just one but two different simultaneous texts thus arranged are precisely placed in relation to each other, with full control at the level of syllables, in a detailed design that can be as purposeful as that of the different but coordinated musical strands attached to them. Coordinated words and music exponentially increase the layers of integrated polyphonic complexity. Motets of French provenance usually have two secular or semi-secular texts, both or either in French or Latin, and a chant tenor whose source words mirror theirs (sometimes provocatively) and implies its own biblical and liturgical context, symbolically and semantically. Counted and coordinated lines, words, syllables are cunningly woven together on the more familiar ground of counted musical elements. This book explores opportunities available from such a precise and literal kind of intertextuality. Words and music planned together can enhance and add to verbal sense; music alone can create semantic and symbolic sense by depiction or motivic association. Beyond the purely semantic, many more dimensions (three musical strands, three textual strands) are available for a complex interplay of symbolism, ingenuity and sonic adventure, including the application of musical techniques such as recapitulation and motives associated (almost leitmotivically) to the verbal structures, in turn conditioning the ways the texts were composed, often in demonstrable conjunction with the musical concept. Connections and allusions between motets abound, particularly in the musician motets of Part IV.

Unlike most other musico-poetic genres, few motet texts (with one exception, not even those by Machaut) were transmitted without their music; most were evidently not reckoned to stand alone as poetry. Modern studies of lyric and narrative verbal texts have largely ignored the polyphonic motet, even including the twenty-three by Machaut. Most of those texts that were copied later without music have at some time or other been attributed to Vitry, perhaps signalling a special regard for his often distinctive learned and polemical style. There are almost no instances from this period of pre-existent motet texts subsequently 'set to music'. Many motets have almost a syllable-per-note relationship. In general, the relationship between words and music is deliberate and unique; they are sometimes demonstrably conceived and planned together. Irregularities or changes of verse metre or structure may confirm this, notably in the Marigny motets, or when the verse pattern changes for a hocket section, as in Machaut's Motet 18 (Ch. 13). Accordingly, contrafaction is rare; fourteenth-century examples involving adaptations for England are discussed in Chapter 24, and a papal motet, *Gaudeat et exultet*, possibly also in a contrafacted version, in Chapters 26 and 30.

Whereas most thirteenth-century motets had only minimal rhythmic contrast between the tenor and texted parts, the great augmentation of rhythmic vocabulary that took place in the second and third decades of the fourteenth century allowed a higher degree of contrast between long sustained notes in the tenor and smaller note-values in the texted upper parts, giving greatly increased opportunities for rhythmic variety.

10   INTRODUCTION

That variety was sometimes exploited by limiting the rhythmic vocabulary in any one motet, the better to mark significant moments with deviations from the background (for example, in *Vos/Gratissima*, Ch. 8). At the same time, much longer compositions became possible, their overall structure controlled by the slower-moving tenors. Five levels of note-values (minim, semibreve, breve, long, maxima, variously named, already set out in the gradus system of Muris's *Notitia* in 1319) were eventually further extended by devices including augmentation, diminution, proportions and coloration. The composers of the fourteenth and early fifteenth centuries whose works are explored here gleefully exploited these new resources to the full.

Several chapters draw attention to new ways of understanding and analysing motets. Some common ground in compositional resources notwithstanding, most fourteenth-century motets are highly individual constructions of words and music, governed more by the chosen material (the *materia* of the newly anonymised treatise discussed in Ch. 1), subject, words and music, than by any external or received template. Liberated from generalisations arising from umbrella (and sometimes inaccurate) definitions of isorhythm (Ch. 2) and an assumption that composers were following templates, their differences as original creations are often more interesting than what they have in common. Verbal texts have usually been examined for their semantic content and any hints they may give about the use, date and purpose of the motet. A valuable instance is Anne Walters Robertson's thorough and revealing study of the texts of the Machaut motets.[24] Such studies have sometimes operated at arm's length from musical detail, the precise fit of note and syllable, the sonic properties of the words themselves, the placing of vowels and consonants, including alliteration and assonance, vowel rhyme and onomatopoeia. I consider how the mutual placement of syllables in the texted parts may be symbolically significant, as well as their relationships to their notes; self-imposed disciplines that may have governed them (such as the choice to make word-breaks and hocket rests coincide, as exemplified in Chs. 9, 13 and 25); how puns, symbolic constructs or citations, or the desire to place these at structurally significant musical points, may enhance semantic sense, or even deform or obscure it where ambitious double meanings are attempted. The embedding of a secondary or double meaning in the text may produce an opaque result, as in the double, contrary chronology of the Marigny motets of Part II, and in the motetus of *O amicus/Precursoris* (Ch. 22), which encodes the musical structure in the motetus text. The motetus of *Sub Arturo* (Ch. 20) describes the tenor structure, but more directly: 'twice by hemiola'; and the text of *Are post libamina* (Ch. 24) embodies a declaration that it is a contrafact. Recapitulations of text and music, separately or together, are significant in *Tribum/Quoniam*, in *Vos/Gratissima*, in Machaut's motets 10 and 15, and elsewhere. Several motet texts have proved difficult or impossible to translate and incurred the low opinion of classicists, perhaps even because semantic sense was not their makers' only or primary consideration (notably *Apta caro/Flos virginum*, not examined here). Musical techniques of repetition and recapitulation are applied to significant words (or their synonyms) for verbal recapitulation. Sometimes musical motives are associated with particular words (for example, love, fire and death in Machaut's Motet 10, Ch. 12); repeated rhythmic or melodic motives often underscore verbal recapitulations.

[24] Robertson, *Guillaume de Machaut and Reims*.

INTRODUCTION   11

Many motets have what I call a main density area, often at a musically or textually significant point, and involving musical or verbal recapitulation. Conspicuous examples
include *Vos/Gratissima* (Ch. 8) and Machaut's Motets 4 and 8 (Ch. 14). In Machaut's
Motet 10 this area occurs at B79–83 (see ⊙ Ex. 12.1), the three-quarters mark, at the
start of the minim hockets, where the words *Amours* (love) and *ardoir* (burning) coincide on the highest tenor note. *Doublement* marks the only place in the motet where a
three-minim figure is heard twice ('doubly') in immediate succession, also initiating a
direct verbal and musical cross-citation shared with Motet 15 (of the words *Amours, qui
est mes chiés*). Citation and allusion between texts of different motets, sometimes with
the same music, occur here, between the Marigny motets (Part II), and among the musician motets (Part IV).

Word-painting is ubiquitous. Reversals and voice-crossings reflect the reversal, inversion and usurpation themes of *Fauvel* in Part II; see Chapter 3. Text-driven crossing
of differently texted parts occurs in *Aman novi*, where Fauvel's aspirations, Icarus's fall
and Fortune's putting down of Haman all occasion crossings of triplum and motetus
(Ch. 5). In Machaut's Motet 9 (Ch. 9) extremes of range convey height and depth;
Lucifer flies high before his descent, and the triplum crosses below the motetus for
abysses and caverns. Depiction goes far beyond madrigalisms such as simple ascent and
descent, and even ascent and descent here are not simple when two different texts are
involved. The crucifixial sharps in *Aman novi* are both visible and audible (Fig. 5.2). In
Vos/Gratissima, 'occulum occulo' (eye to eye) is made visible and audible by an exact
repeat ('eye music') which sets itself purposefully apart by momentarily departing from
the expected isorhythm (Fig. 8.4).

Local puns abound. In Machaut's Motet 9, the rhyme scheme is reversed following
the words *retro pungit* (stings from behind), and *pungit* is represented by puncturing
hockets. Solmisation puns may be direct (*mi-fa* in *Musicorum*, Ch. 18), or by vowel
rhyme. Alliteration or vowel rhyme between the texted parts can unite them sonically.
The same word from the two different texts may be given emphasis by being made to coincide, as when both voices sing *amours* together in Machaut's Motet 4. Sometimes there
is semantic play when the two texts interact, as in the second section of *Vos/Gratissima*,
where the audible insertion of triplum words while the motetus rests changes (even if
not grammatically) the sense of the motetus text. Onomatopoeia is effectively used in
Motet 9, with abundant 'ss' for the hissing serpent.

Structural puns are also a major resource. In *Musicorum collegio* (Ch. 18) the junc-
ture of the two *color* statements falls between *acuto* and *gladio* (*cum bis acuto | gladio*);
it is cut 'with a twice-sharp sword', recalling an earlier structural join on a cutting
word: *nemo . . . posset incide-| re* (no one will be able to cut). *Talea* means a cutting,
what tailors do; words of division or proportion often mark such structural points. In
Tribum (Ch. 4), the words *trans metam ascenderit* ('should ascend across the limit') take
us across the midpoint of the sixty-two triplum words, and cross the boundary to the
second *color*. In *Vos/Gratissima* (Ch. 8) the structural join is marked and laid bare by a
wound-word (*vulnere*), the recapitulations nudged by *simili*. In Machaut's Motets 10
and 4, the word *souvenir* (memory) underlines a structural or a verbal and musical recapitulation. In Machaut's Motet 4 (Ch. 14), an unsignalled shift to perfect modus is
punningly marked by *blesse* (wound) in TI, *Je ne puis avoir duree* ('I'm unable to last',
referring to use of a longer measure) in TII, and *desmesuree* (beyond measure) in TIII,

12   INTRODUCTION

again attesting the close planning of words and music together. Particularly striking in *O amicus/Precursoris* is the realisation in a tenor mensuration canon of the Baptist as precursor of Christ (Ch. 22).

In Bent, 'Polyphony of Texts and Music', on *Tribum* (now incorporated into Ch. 4), I argued that its pre-existing material—the classical couplets that end each verbal text, and the chant tenor—were fundamental constructional pillars for both text and music, and that neither preceded the other. In other motets that show a tight syllabic connection (such as Machaut's Motet 18, Ch. 13), the composer and poet were either one and the same, or worked in very close collaboration, neither preceding the other. Linkage and cross-reference between the three Marigny motets in *Fauvel* (Chs. 3–6) also suggest a single hand, that of Vitry, as does their carefully crafted double narrative conveying opposite chronological directions (Ch. 3), reinforced by calendrical play. Other groups of motets, notably the musician motets of Part IV, are rich in citation and mutual reference, but obviously by different composers over time—some are internally signed. The similar placing of linking factors between some of these motets (composer signatures, or the naming of Boethius at the textual midpoint) confirms deliberate modelling.

It is a commonplace that most tenors were chosen for their verbal relevance to the theme of the texted parts, even if this involved, for example, a bold if not blasphemous juxtaposition of earthly and heavenly love. Symbolic or numerical musical play with the tenor's words is found in the double cantus firmus derivation of the tenor of *Aman novi* (Ch. 5), in the cosmic message of the musician motets (*In omnem terram*, Chs. 16, 20), in the precise words of the chant fragment selected for the tenor of *O amicus/Precursoris* (Ch. 22), and in the six mensurally varied statements of the Credo *Omni tempore*, whose tenor punningly so labelled has only a loose relationship to the only identifiable chant with those words (Ch. 23).

But it seems that chant excerpts were often selected for their purely musical properties as well, as a note-row might be chosen: for suitably placed stepwise progressions that would suit cadences; for the number and divisibility of its notes into—sometimes overlapping—*colores* and *taleae*, and for how it facilitated disposition of those *taleae* around structural joins and cadencing points; for its properties of range, interval, number, symmetry or palindrome. It may have been selected for its depictive qualities: for the restraint of using a limited pitch range; for its intervallic tenor leaps as in Machaut's Motet 8; or the serpentine slithering quality of the entirely conjunct tenor of Machaut's Motet 9 (Ch. 9). Sometimes a chant is musically related to another, different chant (the short tenor melody of Machaut's Motet 9 is wholly contained in that of Motet 4). A tenor may have textual identity with another, different chant: two different *In omnem terram* chants are used for two of the musician motets, a form of reference which is unmistakable but not literal. Allusion or citation with difference is ubiquitous in the musician motets and may be deliberately varied; often just one or two out of the three elements of text, rhythm, melody suffice to mark a quotation, not all three.

Calendrical allusions and their expression in number are fundamental to the managed chronology of the Marigny motets (Ch. 3) and to the interrelated musician motets of Part IV. The tenor of *Musicalis* is a Christmas Alleluia, that of *Musicorum* an Easter Alleluia. *Musicorum* cites the Apocalypse, *Sub Arturo* Genesis, the last and first books of the Bible, reflecting the global reach (*In omnem terram*) of the A–Z of *Apollinis/Zodiacum*. The number of musicians celebrated in each is reflected in the ways both music and text are counted: the zodiacal twelve musicians named in *Apollinis/Zodiacum* (Ch. 16) are embedded in the 12^2 (144) breves of the motet's length, disposed in three *color* statements, each of two 24-breve *taleae* and in the number and multiples of lines and syllables, totalling 240 + 120 = 360 (see ⊙ Ex. 16.1), as David Howlett observed. They are counted as *bis sex*, twice six, counting the months of the year as well as the signs of the zodiac. *Musicorum* goes one better than six with its seven musicians (Ch. 18 and ⊙ Ex. 18.1) embodied not only in the Apocalyptic seven candlesticks and the seven churches of Asia, but in a descending scale of seven notes borrowed from *Apollinis*, and in seven statements of a quoted motive (rhythm and text), also from the parent motet. Calendrical aspects are woven into both the text and music of *Musicorum collegio/In templo Dei*, with sevens (for days of the week), fours (weeks in a month), twelves (months of the year); and the total number of poetic lines is fifty-two (weeks of the year). *Sub Arturo/Fons* (Ch. 20) nods at both these predecessors with its fourteen musicians, twice seven. The two other motets in this group, *Musicalis sciencia/Sciencie laudabili* and *Alma polis/Axe poli*, both name twenty musicians (twice ten, ten being the number of Boethius referred to in *Apollinis/Zodiacum*).

Melodic material from the chant is often incorporated in the upper parts. In *Tribum/Quoniam* (Ch. 3), the tenor's one disjunct progression (*e g d*) comes prominently three times in the motetus, transposed as *a c g*. Machaut's Motet 9 (Ch. 9) uses motives derived from its conjunct and serpentine tenor in the upper parts. By contrast, for the vagaries of *Fortune* in Motet 8, Machaut chose a tenor with intervallic leaps, where similar leaps in the upper parts, together with syncopated rocking motion, underline the instability of Fortuna (Ch. 14). Besides melodic affinities, I have noted in Motet 10 (Ch. 12) an upper-voice rhythm derived inversely by diminution from that assigned to the tenor.

Chapter 9 surveys some of these resources in Machaut's Motet 9, including the relationship between *color* and *talea*, criteria for tenor selection, part ranges and cadence choices, the marking of *talea* ends, devices such as alliteration or vowel rhyme, and exploitation of the purely sonic qualities of a specially composed text. A restricted rhythmic vocabulary is sometimes chosen, the better to make purposeful deviations stand out against it (instances are noted in Chs. 8 and 9).

Interesting variety is achieved by different rates of distribution of verbal texts in relation to music and to each other. In Machaut's Motet 9, the entire second half of the motetus text is confined to the final third of the piece, and is thus declaimed twice as fast as the first half, creating a climactic acceleration towards the end, in a similar way to that provided musically when there is tenor diminution or upper-part hocketing. In *Sub Arturo plebs* (Ch. 20), each of the nine triplum stanzas is set to a new *talea*, three per *color*. Because the *colores* successively reduce, the text is also delivered much faster towards the end, the excitement further increased by complex cross-rhythms.

Audience

Who *were* motets for? Who *are* they for? The simultaneous dimensions of the motet have not had a smooth modern reception; bitextuality hardly meets criteria of clear and audible presentation. Besseler went so far as to declare that early motets were not intended for aesthetic enjoyment by listeners, but rather as supports to the devout for prayer and

14   INTRODUCTION

reflection—even though many of them are by no standards sacred.[25] For many unprepared listeners, the sound of a modern performance can give pleasure, though Grocheio thought otherwise: not only did the common laity not understand motets, they did not enjoy hearing them. He famously wrote that only the *litterati* could appreciate motets, and that was even before the cultivation of some of the subtler strategies documented here.[26] But for those who might aspire to count among present-day musical *litterati*, there is so much more. We have garnered plentiful evidence that the construction and placement of those texts is not casually chaotic, as has sometimes been implied, but deliberate and artful. The many subtleties could never have been grasped at a single or first hearing by an unprepared listener, but this was not how the primary audience—the performers—first encountered a motet. Singers, at first, saw just their own part, text and music inseparable. Only when putting it together in sound with the other strands could the full polyphonic texture of words and music happen, when singers were enabled to explore and savour the interactions, the interplay, the puns, the quotations, the ingenuity, against the background of their shared culture (which included the Bible, the liturgy, Boethius, and much more).

Some readers may find the enterprise of identifying these strategies cerebral. This book is not for them. It was just such a debate that fuelled my exchanges with Christopher Page in the early 1990s.[27] My own appreciation of these extraordinary multifaceted compositions has been enhanced by teasing out at least some of the craft and erudition that composer-poets had lovingly woven into them. The intricate patterning based on number, structure, word sounds as well as sense, uncovering at least some aspects of their ingenuity, playfulness, juxtapositions, boundless invention, and even at times subversion: all these give a precious window into the thought processes of our medieval colleagues and enrich the overall experience of what are often stunningly beautiful compositions, eloquent, dramatic and expressive.

In most cases, such observations arise in studies of individual motets or between related motets; the genesis of the present compilation means that these aspects have not been treated systematically over larger repertories. There is much more to discover; many footnotes here are invitations to follow up on little-explored manuscripts and pieces, and sharp observers will find much to correct and loose ends to resolve. I offer this book to readers who are curious to pursue these and other paths, in the hope that younger scholars in the future may find some of these directions fruitful for further exploration of this inexhaustibly fascinating genre. To engage deeply with individual motets allows the imaginative exercise of craft and resourceful creativity to sing to us from many centuries ago.

---

[25]   Besseler, 'Studien II', 144.

[26]   'Cantus autem iste non debet coram vulgaribus propinari, eo quod eius subtilitatem non animadvertunt nec in eius auditu delectantur, sed coram litteratis et illis, qui subtilitates artium sunt quaerentes. Et solet in eorum festis decantari ad eorum decorationem, quemadmodum cantilena, quae dicitur rotundellus, in festis vulgarium laicorum.' *Johannes de Grocheio, Ars Musice*, ed. Mews et al., 84. 'This kind of music should not be presented to the common people (Page, 'Johannes de Grocheio': lay public) because they neither observe its subtlety nor take pleasure in hearing it; but to the educated (Page: clergy) and those who seek out subtleties in the arts. It is customarily sung to adorn their feasts, just as the songs called *rotundelli* (are sung) at feasts of the common laity.'

[27]   Page, *Discarding Images*; Bent, 'Reflections on Christopher Page's *Reflections*'; Page, 'A Reply to Margaret Bent'.

PART I
COMPOSITIONAL TECHNIQUES

16 COMPOSITIONAL TECHNIQUES

I have dealt in other publications with questions of musical grammar, counterpoint, and the roles of solus tenor and contratenor parts.[1] The views set out in those studies will be alluded to but not repeated in detail here, though they underlie the compositional assumptions in this book. These first two chapters address a few other recurrent issues of compositional technique: in Chapter 1, the prescriptions for motet composition traditionally (but unreliably) attributed to Egidius and the phenomenon of middle-voice tenors; the definition and terminology for *introitus* and *cadentia*; the problem of non-coincident or dissonant endings; lower parts; and, in Chapter 2, a slightly adapted version of my previously published paper on isorhythm.

---

[1] Bent, *Counterpoint, Composition, and Musica Ficta* (2002), which includes previously published articles. See there ch. 8 on the solus tenor, and especially the Introduction. Subsequent relevant publications include 'The Grammar of Early Music' (1989); 'Naming of Parts: Notes on the Contratenor' (2008); and 'Reading, Memory, Listening, Improvisation' (2014).

1

Theoretical and Terminological Issues

Instructions for Motet Composition: 'Egidius'

'Primo accipe tenorem' ('first take a tenor'). Thus begins the only and often-cited fourteenth-century treatise which purports to enlighten us about motet composition, *De modo componendi tenores motettorum*. 'First take a tenor' was also the starting point of Alice Clark's invaluable compendium of tenor chant sources. Her title, *Concordare cum materia*, gives the crucial further precept of the treatise, namely that the choice of tenor is preceded by that of the *materia* of the motet; but the textual and musical nature, relationship and priority of that *materia*, beyond its influence on the choice of tenor, has fuelled continuing discussion. Modern scholars have unquestioningly assigned this little treatise to Egidius de Morino or Murino. Its five manuscript sources were set out by Daniel Leech-Wilkinson, who presents most of the text, with translation and commentary; a fuller version of the text is given more recently by Anna Zayaruznaya, whose paragraph numbers will be used here.[1] All five sources of the motet treatise also contain a more widely distributed treatise on note-shapes, the *Tractatus figurarum*, ascribed in **Faenza** to 'Philippi de Caserta', in **Newberry** to 'Magistri Phillipoti Andree'. The authorship of this companion treatise was excellently assessed by Wulf Arlt, and more recently edited by Philip Schreur, now with access to fourteen sources.[2] The *Tractatus figurarum* has been thought to date from the end of the century, though the manuscripts containing similar note-shapes are now dated after *c.* 1400; but the authorship of Philipoctus is in doubt, as the note-shapes described do not correspond to his compositions as transmitted.[3] It is ascribed to Egidius in four sources (in **Lo4909** to 'Egidium de Muris vel de Morino', where it is followed anonymously by *De modo componendi tenores motettorum*). Although the confusion of Muris and Morino may be telling, the numerical weight of the attribution for the *Tractatus figurarum* is

---

[1] The treatise is entitled *De modo componendi tenores motettorum* in **WashingtonJ6**, but the incipits of two sources do not specify tenors: **Seville25** has *Incipit ars qualiter et quomodo debent fieri mottetti*, **Siena30** *Ordo ad componendum motettum cum tribus vel quatuor*. Extracts from the text of *CS* iii. 124–28 (in full on TML: https://chmtl.indiana.edu/tml/14th/AEGTRA, consulted 23.3.2022) are presented in improved form with glossed translation and variants in Leech-Wilkinson, *Compositional Techniques*, i. 18–24 and Appendix I, 223; and now a fuller text with adaptation of Leech-Wilkinson's translation is in Zayaruznaya, *Upper-Voice Structures*, Appendix, 110–16, with the promise of the full text in a new edition and translation by Zayaruznaya and Andrew Hicks. Petrus Picardus's *Ars motettorum* is a short treatise on mensural notation which gives no motet-specific instructions. A treatise entitled *Modus componendi rotam versatilem* is tantalisingly missing from **Lo6** which, according to its listed contents, once contained it. This apparently refers to one of the most fascinating compositions of the early 14th c., a large-scale English voice-exchange motet. See Bent, '*Rota versatilis*', and its revision in Bent, Hartt and Lefferts, *The Dorset Rotulus*, ch. 5.

[2] Arlt, 'Der *Tractatus figurarum*'. *Tractatus figurarum*, ed. Schreur, gives source descriptions; the report on **Lo4909** is inaccurate with respect to these treatises and needs correction from *Robertus de Handlo*, ed. Lefferts, 71–72.

[3] See Ch. 26 n. 5. Schreur, in *Tractatus figurarum*, sets out the case for and (largely) against the authorship of Philipoctus.

The Motet in the Late Middle Ages. Margaret Bent, Oxford University Press. © Oxford University Press 2023.
DOI: 10.1093/so/9780190063771.003.0002

18   COMPOSITIONAL TECHNIQUES

diminished, as this version derives from a single witness, and Egidius is not regarded as a candidate for its authorship. The sources are mostly of Italian provenance; it is unlikely that such an Italianate treatise would be by a Frenchman from Thérouanne (Morino).

De modo componendi tenores motettorum is adjacent to the *Tractatus figurarum* in four of its five sources (all except **Seville25**). It is anonymous in three sources (**Seville25**, **Lo4909**, **Siena30**), but in the other two it is conflated with the *Tractatus figurarum*, and ascribed at the end of both treatises: to 'magistri Egidii' in **WashingtonJ6** and to 'Magistrum Egidium de Murino' in **Vat5321**. **WashingtonJ6** also ascribes the *Tractatus figurarum* at the beginning to 'Egidium monachum'. (Coussemaker, using **Vat5321**, recognised that they were separate treatises.) Since these two sources conflate the treatises, and bear the only attributions to Egidius (now discredited for the *Tractatus figurarum*), their authority for his authorship of the motet treatise too comes into question. It is not clear whether they can be treated as separate attributions applying to the motet treatise, but in any case, they appear not to have independent stemmatic authority. The attribution may have gained modern traction from eagerness to attach a name to the treatise, however tenuous the authority, and from a short-circuited temptation to identify the author with the Egidius de Morino named as a musician in *Apollinis* and *Musicalis*, which we shall show to be unlikely. The content is hard to date; a general consensus places the treatise in the third quarter of the fourteenth century (as assumed by Zayaruznaya), but I now think it could date from closer to 1400. In either case, this probably excludes authorship by the earlier Egidius de Morino named in those motets datable *c.* 1330, who may be identifiable with one Egidius de Flagiaco (Chs. 16 and 17).[4] I propose that *De modo componendi tenores motettorum* should revert to anonymous status.

The motet treatise promises much but delivers disappointingly little. Indeed, the text is specifically directed to the teaching of children ('ad doctrinam parvulorum', §23);[5] and although it speaks vaguely of further subtleties (for which the reader is referred to the grace of the Almighty, §24), it does not even begin to venture into most of the territory of the advanced motets covered in this book, while at the same time introducing other complexities, prematurely for beginners. Its many puzzling aspects will only briefly be touched on here. Four-part composition is introduced almost at the beginning, §4, prescribing an (optional) contratenor *above* the tenor (i.e., one that is not contrapuntally essential). These two parts are then treated as the foundation with which the triplum and then the motetus should be concordant (§5, §8). For the tenor and contratenor to be treated as a supporting pair in this way usually applies where the contratenor goes below the tenor (as in *Vos/Gratissima*, Ch. 8) and is contrapuntally essential.[6] Priority is given to the triplum; it is not until the very late fourteenth

---

[4] Clark, '*Concordare cum materia*', 5, suggests that if the motet treatise could be dated decades earlier than the *Tractatus figurarum*, it could be by the Egidius de Flagiaco who is a candidate for identity with the Egidius de Morino of *Apollinis* and *Musicalis* (see Ch. 17). In support of this is that he was *magister puerorum* of the royal chapel in Paris (Hoppin and Clercx, 'Notes biographiques', 85), and the treatise is addressed to children. But the gap between the documentation of Flagiaco and the probable date of the treatise seems to me too wide. Egidius de Aurolia (Orleans) can be excluded as being from the wrong city, though he must be closer in date to the treatise; he is named in the text of the very complex *Alma polis* as its composer (Ch. 19). *Alma polis* is the only one of the musician motets composed with an original contratenor, in that case essential.

[5] The paragraph numbers used here for reference are those of Zayaruznaya, *Upper-Voice Structures*, Appendix.

[6] The only kind of composition where the contratenor must be the next thing to compose would be those instances where it would share the contrapuntal foundation with the tenor in such a way as to invite or

century that a shift is apparent in indexes and treatises whereby motets are more often cited by triplum than by motetus. The motetus is described as being lower ('at the fifth', 'ad quintam'), which would not apply to the many motetus parts that are closer in range to their tripla, even if they supply the fifth at triplum-tenor octave cadences. It is at this stage in the treatise that there seems to be a prescription for upper-part isorhythm ('figurata sicut prima pars'; 'the same note-shapes as the first section', §6). Upper-part isorhythm was usually only partial in the early decades of the fourteenth century (as in *Vos/Gratissima*, Ch. 8, and Machaut's Motet 9, Ch. 9). The author appears to propose four equal musical sections, not allowing for diminution. The corresponding division of the text into four equal portions (§9) likewise excludes the possibility that less text would be required for an accelerated section.[7] The detailed text distribution is left somewhat vague (to be 'distributed over the music as well as possible', §§9–10).[8] Only then come more detailed instructions to rhythmicise the tenor and contratenor (here, *colorare*, §11), to manage and specify repetitions (§13), and a spelling-out of perfect and imperfect modus (§§14–20). This section should probably have preceded the addition of the upper parts; advance notice is given that it is prerequisite to them ('quod inferius patebit', §2). These anomalies discourage treating its statements about priority as strongly applicable to motet composition. Indications of a date for the treatise possibly as late as *c.* 1400 are the precedence accorded to the triplum over the motetus (as noted previously, from §5); the reference to imperfect notes as void rather than red (§§15–16); and the advocacy of arabic numerals over the roman ones of the 'antiquos magistros' ('old masters', §13), arabic numerals not being common much before the fifteenth century.

Most surprising for a self-proclaimed elementary treatise is a final section which follows an apparent peroration (§§21–24) and is absent from one of the five sources (**Lo4909**), so it could be treated as a supplement and might therefore be a later addition. But, given the previously noted pointers to a date close to 1400 for the body of the treatise, it cannot be much later. While linked to what precedes it, this final section lurches into 'another way' of composing motets by placing the tenor as the middle voice. As noted in the next section of this chapter, only about five motets in the French repertory have middle-voice tenors, some of them then quite old. Why would a child attempt this unusual type of motet when so much else goes unexplained? The description, set out in the present Chapter 16, fits the three-part *Apollinis/Zodiacum* better than any other known motet. §31 allows for four-part writing with a contratenor. Finally, §32 allows

necessitate the composition of a solus tenor, which I have argued is found only in motets with contrapuntally essential contratenors. The solus tenor, a *basso seguente* conflation of those parts, would then serve as a foundation on which the upper parts could be more easily constructed. Examples here are in *Vos* (Ch. 8) and *O amicus* (Ch. 22). See also Bent, 'Pycard's Double Canon: Evidence of Revision?', where revisions of the lower canon surviving in the solus tenor demonstrably show the role of that voice in the compositional process as providing a basis onto which the upper-voice canon could be projected.

[7] See Ch. 26 n. 17 for a corresponding instance in *Argi vices Polyphemus/Tum Philemon rebus*. The motet is in four sections without diminution, and with equal distribution of text.

[8] 'Egidius' instructions on texting have been widely quoted, but find almost no support among surviving compositions': Leech-Wilkinson, *Compositional Techniques*, 22. They are very far from the detailed and purposeful text–music relationships demonstrable in many of the motets discussed in this book. There are indeed some motets where the relationship seems to be more casual, but in many cases it is so precisely calculated that the words must have been designed for or with the music.

20   COMPOSITIONAL TECHNIQUES

for five-part motets, the fifth voice being a quadruplum (§35), but there are no such motets from the fourteenth century; the only five-part motets are the later-added extra parts to *Apollinis*.[9] In Chapter 16 I argue that this striking passage applies precisely to the only five-part motets from the period, namely the later-added parts to *Apollinis* (one of which is labelled quadruplum, as in the treatise), which must date from around or after 1400, as must at least this final section of the treatise. Taken together with other indications of late dating, this further eliminates the musician named in motets of seventy years earlier as the author of the treatise.

Middle-Voice Tenors

The known motets with a central tenor, triplum above it and contrapuntally essential motetus below, are usefully assembled in Virginia Newes, 'Early Fourteenth-Century Motets with Middle-Voice Tenors'. Besides *Apollinis/Zodiacum*, French motets with middle-voice tenors include *Tribum/Quoniam*, *Amer amours/Durement* (first *color*; the tenor of the second is transposed down), *Se grace/Cum venerint*, and *D'ardant desir/Se fus d'amer*. To these can now be added the Marian motet *Flos vernalis/Fiat intencio*, of uncertain national origin, previously known only from its intabulation in **Robertsbridge** and fragments in **OxAS56**; further fragments of the original motet have now been discovered by Cristina Alís Raurich in **Karlsruhe82** and an almost complete version by Karl Kügle in **Koblenz701** (see Alís Raurich, 'The *Flores* of *Flos vernalis*'). It is also in the index to **Trém** (see Ch. 31). Italian motets with middle-voice tenors are *Ave regina/Mater innocencie* (Marchetto), *Ave corpus sanctum/Protomartiris* (**SanGiorgio**), and *Gratiosus fervidus/Magnanimus opere*.

Of the twenty-four English motets in PMFC 15, six have a middle-voice tenor, and more incomplete motets also had or may have had a *medius cantus*.[10] Given that duet motets with central cantus firmus were favoured in England, it is interesting that of the few motets of French provenance with middle-part tenors, four also occur in English sources, *Apollinis* (with added voices) in **LoTNA,** arrangements of *Tribum* and *Flos vernalis* in **Robertsbridge**, and *Amer/Amours* in **Durham**. In addition, the widespread *Degentis vita/Cum vix artidici* (also in the English source **Yox**) has the tenor and motetus frequently crossing so that the tenor is partly in the middle. Did those motets appeal to the English because of this scoring, comparable to the stylistic reasons I suggest in Chapter 27 for the choice of Italian motets in **SL2211**, or did these examples influence the English habit? *O dira nacio/Mens in nequicia* (uniquely preserved in **Trém**) has the tenor partly in the middle, and is published as an English work in PMFC 17. The jury is out on the national origin of this motet on St Thomas Becket, as also of two other motets with a central tenor: *Plausu querulo* (also on St Thomas of Canterbury) and *Flos vernalis* (mentioned previously). Apart from the keyboard arrangement of *Flos vernalis* in **Robertsbridge**, none of the vocal versions is in an English source. All three motets were in **Trém** (see Ch. 31).

---

[9] The only other case is a fifth part added to the **OH** motet *Are post libamina* (Ch. 24).

[10] For English motets see Lefferts, 'Motet in England' and *Motet in England*; Hartt, 'The Duet Motet in England' and 'A Missing Middle-Voice Melody'.

Non-coincident Endings

Inconsistent notation of final durations is ubiquitous, with casual interchangeability of breves, longs, maximas or conventional decorative longs. These are invariably and uncontroversially regularised—usually silently—in editions and performances. Sometimes they are caused by the literal iteration of an isorhythmic *talea*, in diminution or not, written out or not, whose last note would need to be elongated in performance to end together with the upper parts.[11] In *Apollinis* (see Ch. 16, ▶ Ex. 16.1) the tenor's isorhythm determines the last note as a breve plus rest, whereas the outer parts have a long; the breve needs to be extended to end with the upper parts. In *Alma polis* (▶ Ex. 19.1) the homographic tenor in diminished form ends with a semibreve plus rest and the contratenor with a breve, both of which need to be lengthened in order to finish together with the longs of the upper parts.[12] Here, unusually, the triplum maintains its isorhythmic pattern after the cadential arrival, but without dissonance. Such elongations invite the simplest kind of initiative and can generally be taken for granted. Initiatives are often required when performers have to determine empirically, in the absence of an instruction, whether a repeated tenor *color* is to be diminished, how to resolve an unsignalled canon, the entry point for a *fuga* or where the *comes* should end, or to infer from what point in a ballade repeat to jump to a notated *clos* ending.[13]

Quite a high proportion of even the limited number of motets considered in this book have non-coincident endings, so notated that not only does the duration of the final cadence not coincide in all parts, but also the arrival on it, usually on account of the completion of an isorhythmic tenor *talea* which might have to be cut short if the cadential arrival is to coincide. (Similar initiatives are needed for the *comes* of a canon whose termination is unsigned.) Some instances do not incur dissonance (as in *Sub Arturo*, ▶ Ex. 20.1, for a motetus *talea* completion) and some do. Many of these cases are disguised in modern editions by being silently editorially 'corrected', which masks the fact that they are not uncommon. The question is: given that initiatives are expected of performers in the simpler cases just mentioned, should such endings be allowed to stand as notated, or was it assumed that they would be adjusted to simultaneity?

Five Machaut motets have anomalous final cadences: M4, M9, M10, M15, M17. These include the only three of Machaut's motets that end with 10/6–12/8 cadences on *f* (Ex. 1.1a): M4 (Ex. 1.1b), M10 (Ex. 1.1c) and M15 (Ex. 1.1d).[14] There are many

---

[11] This agrees with Leech-Wilkinson, *Compositional Techniques*, i. 140 n. 76, who lists a number of motets where a literal repetition of the *talea* results in such irregularity at the end, 'disregarding the need for all voices to conclude upon a final of theoretically equal length', but makes no mention of the dissonant endings.

[12] For the term 'homographic', see Ch. 2.

[13] Ends of mass movements in **OH** show considerable notational variance, despite editorial initiatives by the main scribe, for example, in shortening the finals of section endings in score settings from longs to breves. Although there are no dissonant endings inviting emendation, some final decorative longs are separated from their approach notes by single or double barlines, sometimes where they stand outside an isorhythmic structure. The last note of a diminished tenor iteration often needs to be conventionally prolonged. Instances of untidy endings that would surely have been adjusted by performers are **OH**, no. 23, f. 19, and no. 24, f. 20, given as alternatives in CMM 46.

[14] For full transcriptions see Ch. 14, ▶ Ex. 14.1, Ch. 12, ▶ Ex. 12.1, Ch. 10, Ex. 10.1. Verbal networks between these three motets include the following: *malgré* near the end of the triplum of M4 and M10; *morir* at the end of the motetus of M4 and near the end of the triplum of M10; *-ture* as the final triplum rhyme of M10 and M15; *-oir* as the final motetus rhyme of M10 and M15 and near the end of the motetus of M4.

22 COMPOSITIONAL TECHNIQUES

Ex. 1.1 Non-coincidental final cadences in three Machaut motets: (a) standard 10/6–12/8 cadence; (b) final cadence of M4; (c) final cadence of M10; (d) final cadence of M15

points of verbal and musical interrelationship between these three motets, and indeed between each of them and other motets. In M4 and M10, taken literally, the tenor does not arrive with the upper parts; in M15, it is the triplum that cadences later, with what we would call a dissonant appoggiatura (see Ch. 10 and Ex. 10.1). M15 is also the only instance of these three where the dissonance does not appear to result from a literal, perhaps over-literal, continuation of an isorhythmic pattern: M15 has no tenor diminution. The last two triplum notes are ◼ ◖, whereas the isorhythmically corresponding places have ♦ ♦ ⊥ ◼. The endings of M4 and M10 have been adjusted in the editions of Friedrich Ludwig and Leo Schrade, I think rightly, by shortening the penultimate notated tenor value so that the parts cadence together. M15, however, is transcribed (by Ludwig, followed as usual by Schrade) with its concluding triplum appoggiatura—perhaps because a delayed upper-voice resolution (Ex. 1.1d) sounds less offensive to our ears (acclimatised by progressions such as the appoggiatura that concludes the Bach *St Matthew Passion*) than does a dissonant tenor delay. I have suggested (in Ex. 10.1) a possible emendation for the end of M15, although the appoggiatura in the top part could stand. The problem of these endings remains unresolved, and has hitherto been largely swept under the carpet. In M15, the last words of triplum and motetus are *desconfiture* and *nonchaloir*, which arguably justify the dissonance by affective word-painting. But Machaut does not consistently take such text-suggested opportunities. If he was inclined to respond to unstable words with dissonant destabilising endings, he did not do so in M8, whose last word is also *desconfiture*, nor in M1, which ends with 'bitter' (*amer*), nor in M2 ('keeping too long silent' could have prompted a delayed cadence), nor in M7, which ends 'exceeding moderation and good sense' (*trespasser mesure et scens outrer*), nor in M18, whose triplum ends 'grant a stable dominion instead of this unstable one' (*pro labili*), all of which could have invited a punning depictive delay or dissonance.[15]

Cases involving late or early arrival of the tenor because of the literal application of a *color* and/or *talea* repeat are harder to accept where the delay is in the lowest part. In M10, it is the tenor that arrives late; are we to take the ending literally? To allow the tenor its full notated span would require extension of the upper parts from 107 to 108 breves, making their final long perfect (possible, and yielding a nice total number), not otherwise signalled; but more seriously, a dissonant delay in the tenor's arrival on the cadence to join the upper parts (Ex. 1.1c, and ▶ Ex. 12.1).[16] I think singers, on balance, would probably have decided to arrive together, by delaying the upper parts' cadence by a semibreve, or by shortening the penultimate tenor breve, and cheating the tenor of its final semibreve and semibreve rest. Ludwig simply stated that the final *talea* should be truncated, and he may have been right.[17] In favour of a dissonant delayed final cadence for M10 we could invoke the textual encouragement of *desnature* (tr B97), 'Ne puet longue durée avoir' (mo B101–6) and 'malgré Nature' (tr B104–6). ▶ Example 12.1 gives the dissonant version, which follows the manuscripts and the isorhythm, with the safer option of a simultaneous ending on a small staff beneath.

---

[15] For speculations on Machaut's working methods that may have resulted in such irregularities see Leech-Wilkinson, *Compositional Techniques*, vol. 1, 140 n. 76.

[16] Boogaart, 'Encompassing Past and Present', 54–55, and Hartt, 'Tonal and Structural Implications', 67–70, also address the non-coincident final cadence of M10.

[17] Ludwig, *Guillaume de Machaut*, iii. 40 (144).

There is disagreement between the manuscripts at a similar crux at the end of M4 (Ex. 1.1b and ▶ Ex. 14.1), where there is no comparable verbal prompt, except possibly the final motetus words 'jusqu'au morir'. For the penultimate note two sources (**Ferrell(Vg)**, **MachautG**) follow the diminution strictly with a long, so that the tenor cadences after the upper parts, while in two others (**MachautA**, **MachautE**) the long has been shortened to a breve, perhaps in a failed attempt to normalise the cadence, which only succeeds in making the tenor cadence ahead of the upper parts. Neither version produces simultaneity, but this contemporary editorial attempt to do so may again encourage the safer option of simultaneous arrival, as in M10. Taken in isolation, any of these would seem to be a self-evident case for adjustment, to avoid serious musical anomaly. An alternative ending is indicated in ▶ Example 14.1.

All Machaut's tenors are homographic, including those with diminution (i.e., the diminution could have been derived from the first statement without renotation), but all have the diminution written out in all the Machaut manuscripts, as was normal in motets of the time. The single exception is his Motet 2, which I argue (in a Postscript to Ch. 13) was originally homographic despite an irregularity in the currently notated form. Singers applying what may originally have been an unnotated diminution may have been expected to normalise the final cadences of M4 and M10. A mechanical writing-out of the diminution seems to prescribe the anomaly more strongly than may have been intended had it been left to the performers to adjust the second statement. I am inclined to reject the delayed dissonant final cadences for M4 and M10, on the grounds that the scribe/editor may have failed to make a self-evident editorial adjustment in that mechanical copying of the repeat.

The other two of the five affected Machaut motets have 6/3–8/5 final cadences. Both M9 and M17 have undiminished tenor repeats, marked for repetition but not written out. In M9, if the isorhythm is followed literally, the tenor resolution on *g* is delayed by a semibreve rest, leaving an unsupported fourth between the upper parts until the final note sounds, but no other dissonance. Here there is no verbal encouragement for a delay, unless it be a final sting of the serpent; the *materia* of the ending is resolved, turning as it does from multiple evils to the Virgin and Christ. A normalised arrival for the tenor is given as an alternative in ▶ Example 9.1, although the delayed ending remains possible.

Not so, however, in M17, which has a more problematic 6/3–8/5 cadence (see Ex. 1.2). As in M9, there is no diminution, and no verbal encouragement. The tenor's final

Ex. 1.2 The end of Motet 17 from Guillaume de Machaut, *The Complete Poetry and Music*, ix: *The Motets*, ed. Jacques Boogaart, trans. R. Barton Palmer, TEAMS Middle English Texts Series (Kalamazoo, 2018). Reproduced by kind permission of Jacques Boogaart and Medieval Institute Publications

THEORETICAL AND TERMINOLOGICAL ISSUES   25

descent on $d\,c$ (breve–long) falls a breve later than the parallel fourths of the cadence of the upper parts, making what is surely an unacceptable dissonance. The tenor's long rest before that final cadential progression has to be shortened (unsignalled) to a breve rest in order to make the tenor $d\,c$ descent coincide with the upper parts $b\,c$ and $f\sharp\,g$.

In a series of studies, Jacques Boogaart has eloquently defended Machaut's dissonant endings on the basis of textual clues, adopting them in his recent edition.[18] He offers some reasons why obvious opportunities might not always have been taken, or suggests that the words are indeed depicted but in other, subtler ways. Although he allows for alternatives, his stance provocatively propels the issue into wider notice. He believes that such final dissonances are intentional, in Machaut and elsewhere; I maintain that at least in some cases it was self-evident to performers that they should be adjusted to produce consonance. Boogaart's edition presents the dissonant ending for M17 (Ex. 1.2), but holds the problem at arm's length by allowing 'Performers who prefer not to end on a dissonance' to avoid it, as surely must be done, and as in Ludwig's and Schrade's editions, by shortening the preceding long rest to a breve rest, to make the 6/3–8/5 cadence coincide in all three parts. In an earlier article, 'Playing with the Performer', Boogaart analysed the text and music of this motet with great sensitivity, but still left a decision about the ending to the performers. He highlighted the concluding triplum words 'Car qui .ij. fois vuet denree, Le marcheant conchie' ('he who wants goods a second time cheats the merchant'), offering 'disharmony' as a synonym for *conchie*, referring to the final dissonance that results if the second tenor statement is sung the same way as the first.[19] The *color* is notated only once and marked for (unreduced) repetition. I believe the need to shorten the rest would have been self-evident to performers without the need to read the text prescriptively, though they may have enjoyed the enigma by hindsight. Boogaart, in Machaut, *The Motets*, transcribes—and defends—all the non-coincident endings literally, including in M17.

It is cases like M17 that raise the question more generally: were performers expected to make the arrival on the final cadence coincide, as well as its termination? On the basis of the more difficult instances, I have come to the conclusion that such initiatives were indeed expected, no doubt involving trial and error, that it was not only the most challenging cases that invite adjustment, and that the need to adjust in M17 may encourage similar adjustments in at least M4 and M10 to make the parts cadence together.

Let us now turn to some motets by other composers considered in this volume. In Vitry's *Vos/Gratissima* the tenor had to be fully written out, because the second *color* is differently rhythmicised and could never have been homographic. The penultimate tenor note is notated as a long which, preceding another long, should be perfect, arriving after the other parts and creating a severe dissonance, with f and g sounding simultaneously. ⏵ Example 8.2 reduces the penultimate long to an altered breve, while showing the notated (perfect) long as an alternative.[20] This adjustment, like those in M4 and M10, invites a small departure from strict isorhythm to produce an acceptable ending.

---

[18] See Machaut, *The Motets*, ed. Boogaart, 15 for his defence; see here Ch. 12. Lavacek, 'Hidden Colouration', discusses some of these endings, especially in Motet 4; this article came to my attention too late to be considered here.

[19] The Ferrara Ensemble (on Arcana A 305) perform the dissonant ending of M17 at Boogaart's instigation, but align the ending of M4 in consonance by adjusting the upper parts.

[20] This transcription, adjusted in discussion, was kindly provided by Richard Dudas. See also his 'Another Look at *Vos/Gratissima*'.

26   COMPOSITIONAL TECHNIQUES

In **Ivrea**, however, the penultimate note was originally a breve, but the shortening stem on the ligature has been erased. Chapter 8 and Figure 8.1 demonstrate other places in this tenor where that scribe struggled, which at the same time may give clues about his exemplar; there are many erasures. The final *talea* is curtailed, as happens in other motets, including *Garrit gallus/In nova*, ⊙ Example 4.5. It could be asked why, if fully written out, was the opportunity not taken to change the tenor ending of *Vos/Gratissima*. But the twinned contratenor (unsyncopated in the second *color*) *was* suitably adjusted (compare B139 with B157 of ⊙ Ex. 8.2, omitting the breve rest that in other *taleae* precedes the second long), giving further encouragement that the tenor should do likewise. The problem is avoided in the solus tenor (in **Ivrea**), which has three breves (*e f g*) for the penultimate long (B154–56), again confirming the arrival of the *tenorizans* cadence on B157.

All the instances cited here involve tenor repetition. In some cases with no diminution (M9 and M17), it might be argued that marking the tenor for repetition but not notating it in full leaves the performer responsible for making any necessary adjustment at the end of a second iteration. As noted previously, in all Machaut's motets with a reduced second *color*, the tenors are homographic and so conceived.[21] But, as usual at the time, the reductions are written out, redundantly. This has the effect of making them appear more prescriptive than they would have been, had the realisation of the reduction been left to performers, as just proposed for M17. Such adjustment is always (and uncontroversially) necessary when the final cadence stands outside the isorhythmic structure, or when it falls on the beginning of the last modus grouping, thus cutting short any subsequent patterning set up in previous *taleae*. This foreshortening is more conspicuous when the modus is perfect: *Musicorum*, ⊙ Example 18.1; *Tribum*, ⊙ Example 4.1; Machaut M8, ⊙ Example 14.3; M10, ⊙ Example 12.1; M15, Example 10.1, but it also occurs in imperfect modus, as in M18, ⊙ Example 13.1.

M15, as noted, is an instance of a delayed ending in a part other than the tenor. The motetus of *Sub Arturo plebs* has a similar delay in **Yox**, which follows the isorhythm literally and brings in the fifth of the final chord after the octave has sounded, also making that final note a breve. **Chantilly** does likewise, but elongates the final note to a maxima. This involves no dissonance, no unsupported fourths, and is shown thus in ⊙ Example 20.1. **Q15**, however, omits the rest, making the last two notes void (coloured) longs, so that they arrive together; this adaptation by the **Q15** scribe is noted for ⊙ Example 20.1, and may reflect what he as a performer would expect to do.

A more dramatic case of indecision which seems to confirm that an initiative was expected and attempted is provided by the chaotically notated ending of *O amicus* in its only source, Example 22.1. The final sonority stands outside the isorhythmic structure. It is omitted in cantus I and the tenor, both of which stop abruptly after the penultimate. Cantus I departs from the isorhythm of the preceding *taleae* for the last two notes of bar 69, as if to make a strong cadence, but omits the final long, *f*, which clearly must be supplied (though a *b c* ending in cantus I would have avoided the parallel unisons with cantus II). The tenor mechanically reproduces the isorhythmic *talea* and the pitch of the undiminished first *color*, whose penultimate note fails to fit with or provide the needed resolution, ending with a dissonant red semibreve *f*, preceded by an S-rest (⌐ ♦) instead of the editorially supplied *a g* in Example 22.1; here, both pitch and rhythm require

---

[21] But see Ch. 13 for a proposal that the tenor notation of M2 was originally homographic.

adjustment. The contratenor is derived from the tenor and needs to adapt its final cadence; the whole voice is bracketed in Example 22.1. Derived canonic parts, indeed, require common-sense initiatives from performers comparable to what I am suggesting for final cadences. For *O amicus*, the manuscript provides cadential resolutions only in cantus II and the solus tenor. Cantus II provides a suitable cadential arrival outside the isorhythmic structure. The end of the solus tenor corresponds to the preceding *taleae*, without making an adjustment to support the final progression but, unlike the tenor, it does correctly supply the final cadential note outside that structure, together with cantus II. There was clearly here an attempt, albeit only partially successful (i.e., not in all voice-parts), to take appropriate initiatives at the ending.

Another extreme example of variant readings at the end of a motet is in *O Maria virgo davitica/O Maria maris stella* (PMFC 12, no. 41), where uncertainty at the final cadence affects the uppermost part; its three sources make three different attempts to adapt the ending. Example 1.3a, **Pad1106**, comes close to a cadence in bar 82 by varying the isorhythm in bars 81–82 and placing the 'unnecessary' two minims on the first beat of bar 82. In Example 1.3b, in **Q15**, cantus I faithfully reproduces the isorhythm in bars

Ex. 1.3 Endings of *O Maria/O Maria*: (a) **Pad1106**; (b) **Q15**; (c) **MuEm**

28 COMPOSITIONAL TECHNIQUES

79–83 instead of resolving with a long on bar 82. Example 1.3c in **MuEm** maintains the triplum isorhythm in bars 79–82, but might have done better, like Example 1.3a, to squeeze the *a b* into the previous bar to achieve a simultaneous arrival.

The existence in the manuscripts of two versions of the end of M4, together with the three different notations of the ending of the *Sub Arturo* motetus, and of the *O Maria* triplum, attest different editorial attempts by contemporaries to regularise endings. *O amicus*, with its partially failed adaptation of the various parts of a single piece in a single source, similarly attests an attempted adjustment. Scribes sometimes did take initiatives at this point, apparently attempting what performers would have been expected to do.[22] Such examples of unsuccessful or conflicting initiatives support the claim that anomalous endings were in most cases not intentional and would have been normalised. Successfully adjusted endings may have left no such trace.

This stance goes against the judgement of several respected colleagues, and I expect it to be controversial. But the dissonant endings, if accepted, have no precedents in the contrapuntal vocabulary of the time, and they would raise profound questions about how we understand the musical grammar.[23] The decisions are finely balanced. How far can normal musical procedures be transgressed in the interests of expressing the *materia*? I wavered in the past about M15, and still do;[24] but now find at least the more extreme dissonant endings in other motets unacceptable. With some of the other cases we enter a grey area. A systematic study of the notation, in their various manuscript sources, of endings that have been silently normalised in modern editions, could well cast more light on this under-explored issue.

Introitus

Many motets have introductions (sometimes melismatic) for the texted parts before the lower parts enter. These may be within but are more often outside the periodic structure of those lower parts. They may be texted or untexted, self-contained or not. Any such introduction is usually referred to in the scholarly literature as an *introitus*, and will usually be so called here. Only a minority are thus labelled in the manuscripts. The term seems to have been applied more or less strictly by different scribes or composers. **Q15** uses the term quite restrictively, to refer only to self-contained textless introductions.[25] Machaut's motets 21–23 have introductions that are generally referred to as *introitus*. Indeed, in **MachautA** all parts of M21 (*Christe, qui lux es et dies/Veni creator spiritus*) are so labelled, and in this motet alone the *introitus* is indeed untexted and self-contained.

---

[22] I long ago entitled a contribution to a Round Table 'Manuscripts as Répertoires, Scribal Performance and the Performing Scribe', giving examples of scribal modifications which achieved initiatives that performers would have been expected to take.

[23] No less a scholar than Lawrence Earp ('Isorhythm', 98 n. 66) accepts this dissonance in *Vos/Gratissima*, as he does in the Machaut motets. He argues that the *Vos* triplum's final injunction to 'hurry' could reflect its earlier arrival at the cadence; but on the model of the textual clue in M17, it could equally well mean that the tenor must hasten to its final note.

[24] As pointed out by Boogaart, 'Thought-provoking Dissonances', 286 n. 36.

[25] See Bent, *Q15* i. 151.

THEORETICAL AND TERMINOLOGICAL ISSUES   29

The lower parts enter for its last three maximas to support the cadence of the upper parts. The complex and divergent transmission of this section in the various Machaut manuscripts is fully expounded in Zayaruznaya, '[In]troitus: Untexted Beginnings', and commented on more briefly in Machaut, *Motets*, ed. Boogaart. The (unlabelled) *Introitus* to M9 (*Fons tocius superbie/O livoris feritas*) is discussed in Chapter 9, and the presence or absence of such introductions noted in Table 9.2. In M23 (*Felix virgo, mater Christi/Inviolata genitrix*) the introduction is self-contained but texted. The lower parts again enter towards its end and are labelled *introitus*. But none of the sources labels the introduction to M22 (*Tu qui gregem/Plange, regni respublica*), which is short, texted, and not self-contained.

Of the motets in PMFC 5, nos. 1 (*O Philippe/O bone dux*), 4 (*Apta caro/Flos virginum*), 8 (*Almifonis/Rosa*), 19, 24 and 26 (*Rex Karole/Leticie pacis*) have introductions. That for *O Philippe/Bone dux* is very long, textless and self-contained, and accompanied by a solus tenor. It meets the stricter criteria for an *introitus*, though not so labelled.[26] Several motets usually attributed to Vitry have unlabelled introductions, including *Tuba sacre/In arboris* and *Virtutibus/Impudenter*. His *Petre clemens/Lugentium* was until recently known only from **Ivrea**, where it has an accompanied introduction. The **Aachen** version now shows that 'tenor' to have been a solus tenor, and also gives the hitherto unknown contratenor and tenor, which do not enter until breves 9 and 13 respectively, leaving the imitative opening for triplum and motetus unaccompanied.[27] The incomplete motet *O vos omnes/Locus iste* (**Durham20**, f. 337ᵛ), lacking a triplum, has a long, self-contained, textless introduction, of which the tenor enters towards the end and is labelled *introitus tenoris*. This motet could possibly be English but, partly on grounds of its vituperative text, it has also been proposed with more confidence that it might be added to the Vitry canon.[28]

Cadentia

Throughout this book, I use the terms *cadentia* or cadence for the two-part progression of an imperfect to a perfect interval (3–5, 6–8, 3–1), whether the progression is closural or ongoing, and also where the two-part progression occurs within a texture of more than two parts, whether or not superimposed with another cadential progression. Dyadic counterpoint theory deals almost entirely in local successions, not long-term goals. It does not in principle distinguish internal or ongoing progressions from closural ones, and in most cases I do not find it useful to do so. The same term can serve identical progressions, for example in Ciconia's *Venecie mundi splendor* (Ex. 29.3) at bars

---

[26] This *introitus* is partly illegible and was not transcribed in Johnson, 'The Motets', nor, following her without acknowledgement, by Harrison in PMFC 5. A general study of these introductions in Zayaruznaya, '[In]troitus: Untexted Beginnings', includes analysis of an obscure mention of *introitus* by Ugolino of Orvieto; it lists works with labelled *introitus* on p. 4, and presents an ingenious discussion and transcription of what she deduces to be multiple versions of an *introitus* for *O Philippe*, pp. 23–30 and Appendix Aii. Lawrence Earp has drawn my attention to a partial transcription in Raitzig, *Codex Ivrea*, with some alternative readings in what that author treats as a single *introitus*.

[27] Commented and transcribed in Zayaruznaya, 'New Voices for Vitry'.

[28] Lefferts, 'The Motet in England', 38, 157–62, 339, 569–75; Hamilton, 'Philippe de Vitry in England', 40–44.

30 COMPOSITIONAL TECHNIQUES

89–90 (ongoing) and the conclusion of the motet, in both cases superimposed pairs of dyads, 6–8 and 10–12.[29] Treating the two locations as different has resulted in a number of recorded performances that fail to connect the ongoing progression at bars 89–90 as such, separating the antecedent from the resolution onto the beginning of the Amen, but connecting the identical progression of the final cadence. Unlike *clausula*, the term *cadentia* (or cadence) has no inherent meaning of closure. It literally means 'falling', thus suiting the stepwise *tenorizans* descent of most such progressions. Sarah Fuller ('Tendencies and Resolutions') proposed the now widely used term 'directed progression', presumably to avoid the connotations of closure acquired by the word 'cadence' in modern usage, connotations which the ubiquitous local processes of tendency and resolution did not have in the late Middle Ages. While 'directed progression' is approximately synonymous with *cadentia*, that term too has taken on broader connotations, just as 'cadence' has acquired connotations of closure. Fuller herself extends it from two-part counterpoint to 'three-voice *contrapunctus*'.[30] I do not recognise any theory of three-voice counterpoint before the late fifteenth century, but confine 'cadence' here to dyadically based progressions. These include separable consideration of superimposed dyads between different pairs of parts within a three-voice texture that may or may not cadence together (as shown in Ch. 29), sometimes with changing roles of those voices within a piece. Dyadic principles also underlie contrapuntally based composition in four or five parts, just as dominant thirteenths can be explained in terms of triadically based harmony. The relatively recent closural connotations of 'cadence' may be considered problematic when using the term non-closurally, but so may 'directed progression' be for the broader and non-dyadic connotations it has acquired. Either term is acceptable, provided its associative disadvantages are recognised. Exercising a general preference for an available medieval term, albeit one thinly documented, I will use *cadentia* with strictly dyadic application, and without inherent distinction between closural or nonclosural context.

Cadentia is not the only term to have just a single contemporary documentation; others include *res facta* (Tinctoris in the 1470s) and *opus perfectum et absolutum* (Listenius, *Musica*, 1537), terms which have entered common usage despite solitary and often anachronistic attestations. Conversely, a number of terms introduced by modern writers have taken hold with apparent authority because they have been presented in Latin (these include *minor color*, *extensio modi*, *tempus perfectum diminutum*), but with no contemporary theoretical support that I have been able to find for the meanings assigned to them.[31] In addition, terms such as *tactus* and *integer valor* have been applied anachronistically, and with different nuance, to much earlier music than that which their first users had in mind.

---

[29] As this discussion of *cadentia* has general application, it has been moved here and extended from the earlier version of Ch. 29. See also Ch. 9 n. 22.

[30] Fuller, 'Guillaume de Machaut: *De toutes flours*', 55; see also Fuller, 'On Sonority'.

[31] For *tempus perfectum diminutum* see Bent, 'The Myth'. I have elsewhere pointed out that there was no single term for what we call either 'pitch' or 'rhythm', but rather a rich range of terms in each case, many of which lack precise modern equivalents: 'Diatonic *ficta*', 1–2. See also Bain, 'Theorizing the Cadence', 325–26. On the other hand, modern writers have felt the need for a single term (like isorhythm, or chromaticism, both in various ways inappropriate) for a phenomenon which in the late Middle Ages involved circumlocutions (*color* and *talea*, 'the signs of musica ficta'). On *minor color* see Woodley, 'Minor Coloration Revisited'.

THEORETICAL AND TERMINOLOGICAL ISSUES   31

Several scholars have invoked the relevant passages in Jacobus's *Speculum musice*.[32] The longer account in *Speculum* book IV is more informative than the shorter mention in the better-known book VII, and corresponds more fully to an understanding of *cadentia* as the progression of an imperfect to a perfect interval. Some of the intervals named (fourth, seventh, ninth) rarely or never occur as cadential antecedents in fourteenth-century counterpoint and were presumably included for completeness. Jacobus is absolutely clear, however, about the contraction of a minor third to a unison, the outward resolution of a major third to a fifth, a major sixth to an octave, and a major tenth to a twelfth. He describes an imperfect concord striving to reach a neighbouring perfect concord to which it is joined above and below, and resolves or 'falls' into that concord:[33]

Antequam concordantes, quantum ad cadentiam, comparentur, quid sit cadentia videatur.	Before concords are compared with respect to *cadentia*, let it be seen what a *cadentia* is.
Cadentia, quantum ad praesens spectat propositum, videtur dicere quendam ordinem vel naturalem inclinationem imperfectioris concordiae ad perfectiorem. Imperfectum enim ad perfectionem naturaliter videtur inclinari, sicut ad melius esse, et quod est debile per rem fortiorem et stabilem cupit sustentari. Cadentia igitur in consonantiis dicitur, cum imperfecta concordia perfectiorem concordiam sibi propinquam attingere nititur ut cadat in illam et illi iungatur secundum sub et supra, descendendo videlicet vel ascendendo.	A *cadentia*, insofar as it pertains to the present purpose, seems to mean a certain ordering or natural inclination of an imperfect concord to a more perfect one. For an imperfect thing seems to incline by nature towards perfection, as towards [a] better [state of] being, and what is weak aspires to be sustained through something stronger and stable. Therefore, [the term] *cadentia* is used in [the context of] consonances, when an imperfect concord strives to reach a neighbouring perfect concord, so that it resolves (falls) into that [perfect concord] and is accordingly joined to it above and below, by descending or ascending.
Quantum igitur ad cadentiam, una secunda sive tonus sub vel supra petit unisonum. Et similiter una tertia in semiditono. Sed una tertia in ditono petit quintum. Et similiter una quarta in diatessaron, aut petit unisonum, aut quintam. Quinta, scilicet diapente, propter bonitatem suam, tenet locum suum. Perficitur tamen in unisono aut in diapason. Sexta, scilicet tonus cum diapente, petit duplum vel quintam.	Therefore, with respect to *cadentia*, a second or a tone below or above seeks a unison. Likewise, a [minor] third, the semiditone, [seeks a unison]. But a [major] third, the ditone, seeks a fifth. And similarly, a fourth, the diatessaron, seeks either a unison or a fifth. A fifth, a diapente, on account of its own goodness, holds its place. Nevertheless, it is perfected in the unison or in the diapason. The [major] sixth, namely the tone with diapente, seeks the duple [i.e., octave] or fifth.

---

[32] Including Fuller, 'Tendencies and Resolutions' (1992); Bain, 'Theorizing the Cadence' (2003); Bent, 'Ciconia, Prosdocimus' (2003); and Hartt, 'Rehearing Machaut's Motets' (2010). In a learned and interesting article, David Maw ('Redemption and Retrospection') offers a different interpretation, reading Jacobus's use of the term as 'a process whereby imperfect concords were redeemed for perfection'.

[33] Jacobus, *Speculum* book 4, ch. 50, ed. Bragard, iv. 122–23. Translation by George Harne, adapted.

32 COMPOSITIONAL TECHNIQUES

Septima in semiditono cum diapente petit diapente vel diapason, ut praecedens. Octava, scilicet diapason, stat in se ipsa, non perfectibilis per aliam, nisi per unisonum. Nona, idest tonus cum diapason vel bis diapente, petit diapason vel in diapente revertitur. Decima in semiditono cum diapason petit diapason. Decima in ditono cum diapason petit duodecimam, scilicet diapason cum diapente, vel revertitur in diapason. Et consimiliter est de undecima, scilicet de diatessaron cum diapason. Duodecima autem, scilicet diapente cum diapason, quiescit in se ipsa, aut, ascendendo, petit quintam decimam, idest bis diapason, apud eum qui altam habet vocem, vel, descendendo, revertitur in diapason.

The [minor] seventh, the semiditone with diapente, seeks the diapente or diapason, as the preceding [does]. The octave, the diapason, stands firm, not perfectible through another, unless through a unison. The ninth, that is the tone with a diapason (or the double diapente), seeks the diapason or returns to the fifth. The tenth, the semiditone with diapason, seeks the diapason. The [major] tenth, the ditone with diapason, seeks the twelfth, namely the diapason with diapente, or reverts to the diapason. And similarly concerning the eleventh, namely concerning the diatessaron with diapason. And the twelfth, the diapente with diapason, rests in itself, or ascending, seeks a fifteenth, i.e., the double diapason, on the part of the one [i.e., the singer] who has the upper voice, or, descending, returns to the diapason.

He returns to the topic in book VII, ch. 8:

Quodsi concordia imperfecta ante perfectam perficiatur propter cadentiam in ipsam, rationabile videtur ut concordia aliqua, puta diatessaron, augeatur ex perfectiore si communicet cum illa.

But if an imperfect concord prior to a perfect [concord] is perfected on account of a 'cadential' [movement] into it, it seems reasonable that some concord, for example, a diatessaron, may be increased [in perfection] by the more perfect [concord] if it communes with it.

Insofar as *cadentia* means a falling (a downward step of one part) it did not necessarily have closural connotations. The absence of any mention of closure leaves open the possibility that such *cadentie* (or directed progressions) can at least function as anchors and staging posts, minor punctuation, not necessarily for closure. They are described in purely intervallic terms corresponding to the tension and resolution implied by 'directed progression'.[34] Jared Hartt makes a good distinction, using '*cadentia* to denote a two-voice progression (usually an imperfect interval moving to its nearest perfect), but . . . "directed progression" in a more general sense, that which encompasses the possibility for various paths of resolution involving three-voice sonorities. . . . Like

---

[34] Fuller's 'more generalized formulation separates the type of progression from the act of cadence' ('Tendencies and Resolutions', 231); her reluctance to adopt 'cadence' is clear from her report that Jacobus 'goes so far as to introduce the term *cadentia* for certain types of intervallic progression' (p. 230). Indeed he does; that is how I propose to use it here.

the directed progression, a *cadentia* does not necessarily feature the closure that is associated with *cadence*.'[35]

Some *cadentie* do of course coincide with closure, whether at ends of pieces or sections, such as phrase endings in most songs, where musical and poetic units correspond. Two-part pieces are straightforward, but a contratenor can artfully redefine, weaken or subvert an otherwise clear discant-tenor *cadentia* (see Ch. 29). In motets and similarly complex constructions, internal joins are often deliberately overlapped or elided, and text and music units do not necessarily coincide. A *cadentia* may form a bridge onto the beginning of a new section, as often happens in structured motets (or as indeed into the recapitulation in a sonata movement). The duration of the perfect interval thus approached may bear upon whether it is perceived as closural or ongoing. But even after a brief arrival point, the counterpoint can take off in a new direction.

The duration of the approaching imperfect interval can be deceptive. In Ciconia's motets, long held notes are often not points of arrival or repose (perfect intervals), but carry the tension and expectancy of imperfect intervals awaiting resolution. The same is argued in Chapter 11 for some of the long held notes in the Gloria of the Machaut Mass. They may heighten expectation of closure by prolonging the approach and delaying closure, as often happens with lengthy cadential preparation in later music. Theorists including Prosdocimus often use terminology suggesting that an imperfect interval aspires to resolution in perfection. Any sonority containing a third would be defined both by Prosdocimus and by Ciconia's own practice as an approach sonority, a penultimate. That third should be connected to its destination by a semitone in one part, a major third if rising or expanding, a minor third if descending or contracting. Any perfect interval or superimposed combination of perfect intervals approached from such an imperfect interval can be treated as a strong arrival point, whether or not it immediately takes off on a new beginning. A *cadentia* is defined more by its context and approach than by the length of the perfect interval on which it arrives.

The stepwise descending tenor function in a cadence (*tenorizans*) can be taken by a voice other than the tenor, for example when two upper parts form a self-contained duet before the tenor entry, where they are inverted, or where an essential contratenor works together on equal terms with the tenor (as in *Vos/Gratissima*: see Ex. 8.1). The choice of a portion of chant ending with a stepwise descent is nearly universal in motet tenors. A notable exception is Dunstaple's four-part *Veni sancte spiritus* (MB 8, no. 32), whose tenor excerpt ends with a descending fifth. In Machaut's motets M22 and M23 the tenor ascends at the end but, in those cases, the essential contratenor is the lowest voice and descends by step to form the final cadence. In *Vos/Gratissima* and Machaut's motet 21, the tenor descends by step but is not the lowest voice; it is equally twinned with the contratenor. The only other four-part motet by Machaut is the probably early Motet 5 (*Aucune gent/Qui plus aimme*), which presents huge problems, though tenor and contratenor work together and are both essential. The four-part Gloria of the Mass, however, has a problematic and grammatically inessential contratenor (see Ch. 3).

---

[35] Hartt, 'Rehearing Machaut's Motets', 194–95.

COMPOSITIONAL TECHNIQUES

Lower Parts

Solus tenors

All known solus tenor parts provide a conflation of the lowest notes of tenor and contratenor, with varying degrees of exact correspondence. They survive only for compositions where a contrapuntally essential contratenor complements the tenor to support the upper parts, especially where the composer chose not to require a chant-carrying tenor to serve also as the contrapuntal tenor. Tenor and contratenor may work together in a fully equal partnership, as in *Vos/Gratissima*: Example 8.1 shows the complete reciprocity of their 'strict' counterpoint, and Chapter 8 sets out their rhythmic reciprocity, switching syncopating roles in the two sections of the motet. In some cases, the members of this lower-voice pair are referred to interchangeably as tenor and contratenor, or in the plural as *tenores*.

Since the visual control of score format was not available to musicians back then, I have argued that the solus tenor could have been an aid in the compositional process, providing a *basso seguente* foundation on which the upper parts could be erected, especially in complex pieces involving canon, or a twinned tenor and contratenor.[36] Even if they do represent preparatory work, solus tenor parts were often retained in manuscripts, as they could provide help in rehearsal, or even substitute for the pair of lower parts. In some cases only the solus tenor was copied: for *Petre clemens/Lugentium* and *O Philippe/O bone dux* in **Ivrea**, for *O Maria* in **Q15** and **MuEm**. Zayaruznaya has uncovered the true tenor and contratenor of *Petre clemens* in **Aachen**;[37] other cases of unidentified tenors may similarly turn out to be solus tenors. *O Maria* survives with all five parts in **Pad1106**, including tenor and contratenor, but its tenor is unidentified (see Chs. 26, 28); **Q15** and **MuEm** give only the solus tenor. Rarely, there is an additional solus tenor part of unknown function; *Vos/Gratissima* also has a second solus tenor in **Ivrea**, marked for deletion ('vacat iste'). A later, textless and unlabelled addition to **Br19606** gives a different version of the solus tenor for Vitry's *Impudenter/Virtutibus*.[38] In at least one case, an extra part was composed against a solus tenor: in **Basel72** the second part of *Novum sidus orientis, De scintilla*, has a *Contratenor cum solo tenore*.[39] In that second section alone, a contratenor is essential, the qualifying condition for a solus tenor, but the complex career of this motet and its contrafaction needs further work. Such parts may have been provided by musicians who had access only to a solus tenor but not to the original tenor and contratenor.

---

[36] Bent, *Counterpoint, Composition and Musica Ficta*, ch. 8, and its Introduction, pp. 38–46. Score notation at this period was confined to homophonic textures, and complex notation requiring linear contextual reading was in any case unsuited to vertical presentation in score.

[37] Zayaruznaya, 'New Voices for Vitry'. Unlike the solus tenor, the newly found tenor is the verse 'Non est inventus similis illi qui conservavit legem excelsi' from the Gradual *Ecce sacerdos magnus*. This of course corresponds much more closely than the solus tenor to known versions of the chant specified as *Non est inventus similis illi* in **Vienna4195**, a text-only source. See Wathey, 'The Motets of Philippe de Vitry', 126.

[38] See Kügle, 'Two Abbots and a Rotulus', 146, and Table 27.1 for sources of *Impudenter/Virtutibus*. For another contratenor to *Impudenter/Virtutibus*, composed against the solus tenor (in **Bern**), see Steiger, 'Das Berner Chansonnier-Fragment', 57–60.

[39] This motet appears to be a contrafact of *Gaudeat et exultet* in **Basel71**, with the second part *Papam querentes*. See Chs. 26 and 30.

Any deviations by the solus tenor from a strict lower-voice conflation may betray its origin at an earlier compositional stage, as I have proposed for Pycard's virtuosic **OH** Gloria no. 27 with double canon, where its deviations from the definitive tenor and contratenor parts at the lower-voice canon's five-breve interval may attest an earlier version of the canon.[40] In some cases, conflation would eradicate a clever compositional conceit, as in that canon and that of *O amicus*; see Chapter 22.

The lower parts of *Rex Karole/Leticie pacis* (CMM 39, no. 5; PMFC 5, no. 26), are confused in **Chantilly**, where the only support is provided by the solus tenor. A unique contratenor is so labelled in a different, informal script, and does not underpin the tenor, which is absent. **Stras** preserves the **Chantilly** solus tenor, labelled 'tenor', and the missing tenor, labelled 'contratenor'. What is lacking is the original contratenor from which the tenor–contratenor conflation of the solus tenor was made. Terminology for such parts, and for substitute or added parts, was quite often inconsistent.

Many motets which qualify by contratenor function are not transmitted with solus tenors, perhaps because their preparatory role was no longer needed. This applies to Dunstaple's motets, most notably to the well-known four-part *Veni sancte spiritus* (MB 8, no. 32) whose chosen chant segment, as noted, does not even end with a stepwise descent. The jagged texted contratenor leaps above and below the tenor and could have been conflated to form a supporting solus tenor. A part so labelled for that motet in **Mu3224** is in fact not a solus tenor but a tenor *ad longum*.

Tenors *ad longum*

A small repertory of eight motets dating from about 1400 to 1430 survives with tenor parts marked *ad longum*—substitute parts for notationally difficult tenors: works by Dunstaple, Binchois, Ciconia, Brassart, Velut, Carmen and Antonius de Civitate. Ciconia's *Petrum Marcello* also has a *contratenor ad longum*.[41] As J. Michael Allsen pointed out, at least three of the *ad longum* parts in these manuscripts seem to have been later additions by the scribe who initially copied the motet. The tenor *ad longum* accompanying Brassart's *Magne Deus potencie* in **Q15** was written on a formerly blank staff at the bottom of the page (f. R253ᵛ). Likewise, both of the *ad longum* parts in **Ox213**—for *Clarus ortu* and *Benedicta viscera*—were added at the bottom of an opening, in a different ink colour from the rest of the motet. The tenor *ad longum* of Dunstaple's three-part *Veni sancte spiritus* (MB 8, no. 33) appears only in the **Tr92** copy, and would have been necessary here to overcome the omission of rests at the end of the tenor, which disables this already difficult part.

Perhaps the earliest instance of a tenor *ad longum* is for the motet *Inter densas* in **Chantilly**, although there labelled 'solus tenor'. Among the few motet tenors with mensural reinterpretation of a homographic tenor, which include *Sub Arturo* and *Portio nature/Ida capillorum*, *Inter densas/Imbribus irriguis* is the most extreme instance, without

---

[40] 'Pycard's Double Canon: Evidence of Revision?', and Bent, *Counterpoint, Composition and Musica Ficta*, ch. 9.

[41] They have been admirably investigated by Allsen, '*Tenores ad longum*', which discusses reasons for the inclusion of such parts or of other rhythmic cues.

36 COMPOSITIONAL TECHNIQUES

precedent or consequence.[42] It is an essay in difference, virtuosically exploiting the potential of its full series of note values: the tenor *color* consists of just six notes: ♩♩ ♦ ◼ ◗ ◗. Eight statements of strikingly different overall length exploit most available permutations of imperfection and alteration, modus, tempus, and prolation, although there are no consistent modus-level groupings. Despite the equivalence of the unaltered minim in all statements, the overall lengths of its tenor statements are contrived to be as diversely proportioned as 27:12, 12:8, 18:8, 18:8, a series framed by the cubes of 3 and of 2 but in no discernible order.

Tenor relationships of *Inter densas*:

statement	prolation	tempus	Modus	maximodus	semibreves of C in upper parts
1	3	3	3	3	54
2	3	2	3	2	24
3	2	3	2	3	24
4	2	2	2	2	16
5	2	3	3	3	36
6	2	2	3	2	16
7	3	3	2	3	36
8	3	3	2	2	12 +Mx(8) = 20

The relationships are spelt out in a verbal canon. Without that help, and even with it, a correct solution to the tenor of *Inter densas* is quite challenging, more so had it not been resolved in the provision of a part labelled 'solus tenor' (as noted, in fact a tenor *ad longum*). It incorporates (sometimes only approximately) the contratenor's short interludes only in the rests between the long tenor statements. The contratenor provides essential support in those interludes but the only otherwise unsupported fourth it underpins is the very first note of the motet. The tenor *ad longum* accommodates the actual tenor to the major prolation of the other parts, with awkward results when the tenor statements are in minor prolation. A solus tenor would have taken the lowest notes of an essential tenor–contratenor pair, which this does not do. A tenor *ad longum* is a simplified spelling out of a complex or riddle tenor, relieving the singer of the need to solve a mensural rereading. Later this would more commonly be called a 'resolutio'. This could be done *post facto* as an aid to singers or, like a solus tenor, may well have served as a basis for the composition of the upper parts of this particularly complex piece. Perhaps significantly, the gnomic six-note tenor is notated after the tenor *ad longum*, on the same staff; perhaps this was how the composer worked out its permutations in relation to the upper parts.

Since Ursula Günther (CMM 39) the text has been treated as referring to Gaston Fébus, Count of Foix. If indeed it refers to him it must probably be dated in the 1380s,

---

[42] Its tenor *Admirabile* is misprinted as *Admirabilem* in some scholarly writings, including, alas, one of mine. This motet is also discussed in Bent, 'The Measurement' (1998) and Zazulia, 'A Motet Ahead of its Time?', 349. Most recently, Kévin Roger has identified precisely this rhythmic sequence in the *Libellus* attributed to Jean de Muris, as his ninth example of alteration. Roger, 'La composition du tenor', 193–96.

or at least before his death in 1391, which is very early for its advanced and unique features. But Karl Kügle has recently argued (in an unpublished paper, June 2017) that the associations described in the text apply only weakly to the Count of Foix, and that a stronger candidate for the milieu described is the entourage of Giangaleazzo Visconti (d. 1402), or even that of his advisor Pietro Filargo, later Pope Alexander V. This striking conclusion has the merit of offering a more plausible dating closer to 1400. But Anne Stone, also in an unpublished paper (December 2017), believes that it can only refer to Gaston Fébus, and certainly the imagery suggests this. In subsequent correspondence (25 November 2020) she notes that the triplum text 'is cast as a dream-vision, so that the subject described appears in a dream rather than in reality'. Rather than the poet encountering the dedicatee and his men in the forest (Günther), 'the text actually says that the poet is in the forest, falls asleep, and then sees the red-haired, jewel-encrusted figure. Could the dedicatee be someone who is no longer living?' That would open the possibility of a later dating. Certainly the motet tenor's extreme mensural conceit is unique, whether before or after 1400, and seems technically precocious for an earlier date.

Tenors and contratenors

I have discussed these roles elsewhere, notably in 'Naming of Parts'. Here I will simply reiterate the crucial distinction in four-part motets between contratenors that are contrapuntally inessential and those that are essential. The inessential kind may not always be above the tenor; it can be omitted without damage to the texture and is indeed often demonstrably a later addition, as in the case of Ciconia's motets and of later versions of *Apollinis*, or it is at least unstable in transmission. Essential contratenors on the other hand were usually designed and composed together with tenors, often providing contrapuntal support (to otherwise unsupported fourths), especially where the chant-carrying function of the tenor does not allow it to be the contrapuntal basis as well. It is presumably this kind of contratenor that the author of *De modo componendi tenores motettorum* prescribed to be written immediately after the organisation of the tenor. *Vos/Gratissima* (Ch. 8) and Dunstaple's four-part *Veni sancte spiritus* (MB 8, no. 32) provide clear examples of essential contratenors.

Four-part Compositional Types

Under half of the PMFC 5 motets (13/30) are *a*4, and of those, only two, *Rex Karole/ Leticie pacis* and *Post missarum/Post misse*, have essential contratenors; both have solus tenors. Of motets attributed to Vitry, on the other hand, four, *Petre clemens/Lugentium, Vos/Gratissima, Impudenter/Virtutibus* and *O canenda/Rex* have essential contratenors, and all but the last are transmitted with a solus tenor.[43] Criteria for an inessential

---

[43] Although there are no obvious reasons to attribute *Post missarum* to Vitry, it may be worth noting that it has an essential contratenor and a solus tenor, and that the other three motets preserved with it in **Aachen** all have a strong claim on his authorship.

COMPOSITIONAL TECHNIQUES

contratenor are that it does not provide essential support when the tenor is resting, and that, when below the tenor, it does not support otherwise unsupported fourths. All Ciconia's contratenors are inessential, some demonstrably added later. Inessential contratenors are often unstably transmitted, sometimes in alternative versions. These criteria underlie the two main distinct types of four-part motets and mass compositions. Most involve the addition of a grammatically expendable contratenor to a self-contained three-part structure. No solus tenor parts survive for such motets. Some of these contratenor parts can not only be omitted without damage to the contrapuntal core, but they seem to operate outside the grammar of contrapuntally based composition, their conventions little understood. The other type of four-part motet is a small class where the tenor carries a cantus firmus that prevents it from also supporting the counterpoint. Here, exceptionally, the contratenor takes over or shares the tenor's contrapuntal role, providing some essential notes, especially by supporting structural fourths from below the tenor, such as *Vos/Gratissima* (Ch. 8). This is the defining characteristic of all pieces that have, or any that could have had, a solus tenor part.

Conclusion

This first chapter has addressed a number of technical issues about how motets were made, a recurrent theme of this book. Many of the following chapters raise more questions than they answer, especially about the order in which the interrelationships of text and music were worked out, often demonstrably together, and how they were constrained by pre-existent material, verbal or musical, and by self-imposed structural disciplines. The answers are different for each of the motets examined in detail, which, together with the hegemony of isorhythm interrogated in Chapter 2, invites a view of these works as unique and individual conceptions, far removed from *a priori* templates or prescriptions, such as those given in *De modo componendi tenores motettorum*, which opened this chapter. Apparent instances of word-painting sometimes challenge decisions about whether musical anomalies are intentional or erroneous, as in the non-coincident endings treated above. All this is fertile territory for further work, for which I hope this book may provide an incentive and an invitation.

2

What is Isorhythm?

Preamble

My 2008 essay was an attempt to articulate and sharpen a growing discomfort with a disjunction between the modern term isorhythm and the way it had come to be used and understood.[1] Ernest Sanders, Daniel Leech-Wilkinson and others had drawn back from the term, or used it with some care. My own position evolved through several writings, notably NG2 (Isorhythm), 'The Measurement', and 'Yoxford Credo' (here Ch. 23). In most cases, my earlier statements as this view evolved have been superseded, and in other chapters in this volume have been removed from their original locations.

I had expected that this would be one of the chapters of this book least in need of updating, but two significant recent contributions to the subject demand notice: one is Anna Zayaruznaya, *Upper-Voice Structures*, the other Lawrence Earp, 'Isorhythm', both published in 2018. Instead of attempting to work them into a revision of my essay, I will preface a lightly edited version with these brief comments.

I appreciate the thoughtful critique of Lawrence Earp, rooted in his deep knowledge both of the musical antecedents and in detail of the writings of Friedrich Ludwig and Heinrich Besseler. Those have led him to offer refinements to my historiographical report, while broadly accepting my premise, by arguing that although Ludwig said 'equal' he often intended periodic recurrence, not in the sense of literal rhythmic repetition—what we might call isoperiodic rather than isorhythmic in the strict sense.[2] He cites Besseler's recognition that much of what Ludwig called isorhythmic was in fact isoperiodic, and states 'the problem with "isorhythm" has been that the term is too easily interpreted in the wrong sense'; this indeed was the recognition that had prompted my article.[3] It is the wrong term. Had Besseler stuck to his preferred term, the 'isoperiodic motet', much misunderstanding would have been avoided. 'Isoperiodic' works well for motets without a reduced second (or third) section, like Machaut's Motet 9 (Ch. 9), with its rhythmically identical tenor *taleae*, but its partial isorhythmic correspondence in the upper parts is insufficient to earn their overall designation as 'isorhythmic' or their periods as *taleae*. It also serves where upper-part periods embrace multiple tenor *taleae*, as in Machaut's Motet 15 (Ch. 10), or in rarer cases, fewer. And it could

---

[1] This paper under the same title, 'What is Isorhythm?', was originally published in David Butler Cannata, with Gabriela Ilnitchi Currie, Rena Charnin Mueller, and John Nádas (eds.), *Quomodo Cantabimus Canticum? Studies in Honor of Edward H. Roesner* (Middleton, WI, 2008), 121–43. The present adaptation is published with permission from the American Institute of Musicology. The late Edward Roesner has been a career-long inspiration and a cherished friend. In dedicating the revision of this essay to his memory, I am grateful for stimulus in all aspects of 14th-c. music as well as for sharing his unsurpassed knowledge of Wagner performance. Other colleagues previously thanked are now listed in the Preface and Acknowledgements.

[2] Though I stand by my translation of 'rhythmisch exakt gleich' as implying rhythmical identity and not merely periodic correspondence.

[3] Earp, 'Isorhythm', 87 n. 30 and 88.

The Motet in the Late Middle Ages. Margaret Bent, Oxford University Press. © Oxford University Press 2023.
DOI: 10.1093/so/9780190063771.003.0003

40   COMPOSITIONAL TECHNIQUES

serve for cases where regular upper-voice periods bounded by rests can be defined as bridging and overlapping with tenor *taleae*, as for example by application of Sanders's modular numbers in *Garrit gallus* (see Fig. 4.3) or the wraparound isorhythmic ends and beginnings of *taleae* in Machaut's Motet 9 (⏵ Ex. 9.1). But for tenor iterations that accelerate, whether by diminution, mensural change or proportion, 'isoperiodic' will serve no better than 'isorhythmic'.

There is much agreement and some overlap in our respective accounts. Earp's is more concerned with the roots of repetition strategies in the thirteenth century and their transition into the fourteenth, mine more with how the isorhythmic yoke historiographically imposed on fourteenth-century works has skewed the way both they and fifteenth-century developments are viewed. One key area of agreement is that rhythmic replication is not in itself the goal or indeed the most interesting feature of a motet, but rather underpins how an individual motet's unique design serves a complex web of verbal and musical meanings. Earp cites instances which might qualify as programme music.[4] Precisely. The many ways in which individual motets bear meaning is a central premiss of this book, and I have here and previously demonstrated instances of the wide range of ways in which this is achieved, at structural, symbolic, numerical, verbal, programmatic and depictive levels. It will be clear from many chapters that I believe that at least the most original motets are unique creations, in no way following templates.

Zayaruznaya, *Upper-Voice Structures*, also published in 2018, seeks to modify the common understanding that tenors are the primary shaping force, prior in conception to the upper voices. Her interesting counter-hypothesis is that in some cases the musical design of the upper voices could have been in place before the tenor was planned or chosen. It is certainly possible that the prior *materia* of a motet before the choice of tenor, as specified in *De modo componendi tenores motettorum*, could include musical as well as textual material. My study of *Tribum* (now absorbed into Ch. 4) set out to show that pre-existent textual material was a building block of equal importance to the music *and* text of the pre-existent tenor in that motet. But where it can be demonstrated (again in *Tribum* and elsewhere) that melodic and rhythmic material from the tenor is worked into the upper parts, it is harder to maintain that they preceded the tenor. In what may have been an extreme case, Zayaruznaya argues that the composer of *Colla/ Bona* had already written the texts and worked out the periodic structure of the upper parts before choosing the tenor and giving it a repetition pattern that is at odds with its upper voices.[5] Could it not equally well be that the upper parts are given a pattern that is at odds with the tenor? At least for Vitry and Machaut, and for other internally signed texts, it seems that motet composers usually wrote their own texts (except in rare cases of specified collaboration). Internal evidence suggests a complex relationship between borrowed and newly composed material, both text and music, often closely planned and adjusted together, and with different priorities in different motets, such as to defy

---

[4] Earp, 'Isorhythm', citing Zayaruznaya, *The Monstrous New Art*, 46–52.

[5] Zayaruznaya, *Upper-Voice Structures*, ch. 6, and '*Materia* Matters'. I find it hard to agree with her conclusion; and Earp, '"The spirit moves me"', 290–95 gives a convincing counter-argument. Zayaruznaya, *The Monstrous New Art*, 4–5, draws attention to anticipations of parts of my argument in several contributions to *Les Colloques de Wégimont. II, 1955, L'ars nova: Recueil d'études sur la musique du XIVᵉ siècle* (Paris, 1959).

generalisations about the order of the compositional process in these most individual works. Zayaruznaya's valuable contributions on the terminology of *color* and *talea* are reported below.

What is Isorhythm?

The isorhythmic motet is assuredly one of the most splendid creations of the musical thought of mankind. The rigid laws governing its composition brought about a rationalisation of that most irrational of psychic activities—artistic inspiration; and by means of numbers, of which it is a sonorous expression, they succeeded in subjugating the movements of musical fantasy to the solid framework of a preconceived idea, product of the rational mind. What could be further removed from our present conception of music than this art, whose smallest details were foreordained, and to which any sort of lyric sentiment was as foreign as to the numbers that determined the form and dimension of the work. It is indeed hardly proper to call by the same word 'music' that product of scholastic rationalism, and the creations of today, whose fundamental laws were edicted in order to make of music the vehicle of sentiments born in the heart of man. . . . The isorhythmic motet is the purest expression of a hermetic art, whose subtleness can only be grasped by the innermost regions of the mind, by those faculties which seem to lie midway between the *mens* and the *anima*. Such music was not written to please the ear, and those who seek therein a message for the heart must needs be disappointed.

Isorhythmy [*sic*] was the finest expression of the XIVth century musical ideal, the *arcanum* which only the few could penetrate, and which constituted the supreme test of the composer's ability. However, excessive rationalisation brought about its decadence, inasmuch as the rigidity of its character determined a *nec plus ultra* against which a reaction was inevitable. The embryo of this salutary escape from the sterility of the *ratio* was hidden in the music of the Italian schools, animated by the golden dawn of Humanism.[6]

In these elevated terms, Guillaume De Van introduced his edition of Du Fay's motets in 1948, less than half a century after the modern term isorhythm had first been appropriated for musicology. The language may be unusually extravagant, but the status of the isorhythmic motet which it presents has long been taken for granted. It is regularly referred to in terms such as 'the grandiose manifestation of the speculative medieval view', 'that great monument of medieval rationalism', and chapter headings such as 'Die Spätblüte der isorhythmischen Motette' or 'The Pride of the Isorhythmic Motet' are not uncommon.[7]

---

[6] CMM 1/2, ed. De Van, pp. i–ii. The volumes produced by De Van were later re-edited, and the edition completed, by Heinrich Besseler.

[7] Respectively: Dammann, 'Spätformen der isorhythmischen Motette'; Cumming, *The Motet in the Age of Du Fay*, 82; Finscher and Laubenthal, '"Cantiones quae vulgo motectae vocantur"'; Strohm, *The Rise*, 39. See also the important study by Lütteken, *Guillaume Dufay und die isorhythmische Motette*, which in ch. 2 ('Umrisse eines Gattungstypologischen Entwurfs') reviews the history and definitions of the term as it has

42   COMPOSITIONAL TECHNIQUES

It is one of three substantial genres that feature in any survey of the early centuries of Western polyphony: *organum*, the isorhythmic motet, and the cyclic mass. It was on the basis of such instances of sustained compositional planning that composers of seven hundred years ago could be hailed, seventy years ago, as intellectually sophisticated, worthy forebears of their more recent successors in the Western tradition. Now that the study of music has opened up to non-Western and non-literate musics, criteria that find guarantees of artistic quality in large-scale form, musical unity and mathematical underpinnings sound dated as a basis for value judgement.

The isorhythmic motet was compared by Heinrich Besseler to sonata form at a time when that term carried unchallenged generic force. Charles Rosen described his book on sonata forms as

> an attempt to see what can be salvaged of the traditional view of sonata form. Its insufficiencies, its absurdities, even, have become steadily more glaring. The more enlightened musicologists today apply the term to works of the eighteenth century only prudently, sceptically, half-heartedly, and with many reservations, spoken and unspoken. Yet I think we still need the term for an understanding of that period as well as for those which came after.[8]

'Isorhythm' has not yet undergone the unpicking that Rosen and others have applied to 'sonata form', now more prudently used (as he did) in the plural; it is time that it did. 'Isorhythmic' as an adjective invites more limited and critical use while, as a genre label, '*the* isorhythmic motet' presents serious problems, terminologically and historiographically. This essay calls for a more critical application of the term 'isorhythm' (Gr. ἴσος, equal, and ῥυθμός, rhythm). It has been stretched well beyond the original meaning for which it was first used, quite properly, in 1904, and applied to kinds of repetition which it no longer accurately describes, namely things which are either not equal or do not refer to rhythm or only to rhythm.

Even the word 'rhythm' is never used in the Middle Ages to mean what we now understand by musical rhythm, which from at least the early fourteenth century was expressed in terms of measure, *mensura*, mensuration.[9] But since the intended meaning of the 'rhythm' part of isorhythm is well established in modern usage I will merely signal the problem here and use 'rhythm' in its commonly understood sense, hard though modern dictionaries find that to define beyond 'patterns of duration', aspects of musical movement as ordered in time. However, many instances of equality purported to be 'isorhythm' turn out not to require isolation of the rhythmic dimension, either because:

(1) Both melody and rhythm are repeated, whether as (a) simple repetition, with melody and rhythm coinciding, not requiring rhythm to be isolated; or

---

been used; his concern is to situate the genre historically and philosophically, rather than to challenge the appropriateness of the term and its boundaries. For the main purposes of his book, he retains the received distinction between Du Fay's 'isorhythmic' and 'non-isorhythmic' motets, discussing only the former.

[8] Rosen, *Sonata Forms*, Preface.

[9] See Crocker, 'Musica Rhythmica', and Bent, 'Diatonic *Ficta*', pp. 1–3, for the absence of single medieval terms for what we understand by pitch and rhythm, and Wilhelm Seidel's thirty-six-page article 'Rhythmus/numerus' (1980) in *HMT*.

(b) overlapping repetitions of melody and rhythm requiring separate specification not just of rhythm, but of both melody and rhythm; or

(2) the melody rather than the rhythm is repeated. This category includes cases both (a) where the internal relationships between repetitions are by no standards rhythmically equal, to the extent that they require separate notation for successive statements; and (b) where the same notation may yield different results, whether or not the subsequent statements are separately written out or respelt.

Derivation from the same notation will here be called homographic.[10]

In both cases, exaggerated or misplaced emphasis on rhythm (at the expense of melody or counterpoint) as a structuring technique has not only deformed teaching and analysis of the motet repertory, but has also placed a central distorting construction on late-medieval music history.

'Iso', 'equal', is the main focus of this essay. Beyond the cases where rhythm is wrongly emphasised at the expense of the melodic component, the claim of rhythmic equality will be challenged on further levels (developed from 2(b), above): cases where the internal relationships, even where derived from the same notation, are described as 'the same rhythm but faster'. Thus, many cases of tenor repetitions in so-called 'isorhythmic' motets are subjected to various kinds of (usually) accelerating transformation, some of which result in slight rhythmic differences that again undermine the designation 'iso'. Where there are slight internal differences of rhythm, the result could be described as similar (homoeorhythmic) but not 'equal' (iso). Where there is no difference of internal relationships, the result might well be described as 'the same (homorhythmic), but faster', where to say 'equal (isorhythmic), but faster' would make no sense. While both 'homoeorhythmic' and 'homorhythmic' may prove useful in describing the results of different readings of a single notated (homographic) tenor, they may obscure, and fail to align with, the different processes by which those results are derived. It is processes that lie at the heart of this challenge to the concept; isorhythm describes a resulting structure, not usually the process by which it was attained. While it is true to say that 'equal' is not always the same as 'same', it is nonsense to say that 'same' is *equal* to 'equal'. In an isosceles triangle, two sides are *equal* to each other but not the *same* as each other. If one of those sides is reduced to half its previous length, the triangle is no longer isosceles.

Color and *talea*

Medieval music theorists neither had nor needed a single term for what we call isorhythm. They used the terms *color* and *talea* for the articulation and segmentation of the tenor *cantus firmus*. It has long been known that contemporary theorists gave inconsistent definitions of these terms, using them synonymously or even with apparently reversed meanings, but the full extent of that inconsistency has only recently been

---

[10] Leofranc Holford-Strevens proposed the elegant Greek-derived word 'isosemantic' to replace my mongrel 'isonotational', offering 'isosemasy' (Gr. ἰσοσημασία) for the abstract noun, noting that σημασία (semasia) is actually found in Greek for musical notation. However, discussion with a number of colleagues has shown a slight preference for 'homography' and 'homographic' as serviceable English words, and preferable to 'equinotational'.

44 COMPOSITIONAL TECHNIQUES

set out by Zayaruznaya in a challenge to current usage.[11] Her useful and comprehensive demonstration very effectively makes the point that the terms were at least as often used with meanings other than those in current usage. Her welcome edition and translation of the treatise discussed at the beginning of Chapter 1, *De modo componendi tenores motettorum*, hitherto attributed to Egidius, is presented in the context of documenting the varying definitions. Although the theoretical testimony favours *color* as a general term for repetition of pitch or rhythm, with a bias to rhythm rather than melody, when *talea* is separately defined, it does always seem to refer to the same note-shapes, i.e. rhythm. Unequivocal support for the modern usage comes only from the *Ars cantus mensurabilis mensurata per modos iuris*. While fully acknowledging this confusion, for reasons of clarity I retain the settled modern usage of *color* for repeated pitch content, *talea* for rhythm, pending further suggestions. Where upper-voice periodicity subsumes multiple short tenor *taleae* into larger units (as in *Tribum/Quoniam*, *Cum statua/Hugo*, *Vos/Gratissima*, several Machaut motets including M15), Georg Reichert called such larger periods *Großtalea*, Jacques Boogaart *supertalea*, and Zayaruznaya blocks. The term 'double *talea*' can apply where a pair of identical tenor *taleae* serves a single upper-voice *talea*, or 'period' where those larger units have deviations, as when the upper-part structures are, as often, not fully isorhythmic. I try to reserve the term *talea* for iterations that are either exact or homographic.[12] Despite these problems, *color* and *talea* offer a starting point for developing a more responsive analytical vocabulary to balance the components of motet construction. In modern usage, the single term isorhythm came to be applied—often misleadingly—to a wide range of late-medieval motet and mass compositional strategies. The twin structuring role of melody is marginalised by a term which sets priority on rhythm and has been wrongly used both for simple repetitions and for melodic repeats with changed or overlapping rhythm (categories 1 and 2 above).

Origins and History

Let us review the origins and history of the term. The German word *Isorhythmie* was coined for music by Friedrich Ludwig in 1904 to describe the local application of equal, non-diminishing, rhythmic repetitions to different melodic units in the motetus part of the thirteenth-century motet *On parole/A Paris/Frese nouvele*:[13]

> Both [upper] voices have completely freed themselves from the old [rhythmic] modes, as has the tenor. Instead, the motetus, at least for the first five bars of each period, and despite the completely different verse metres which occur within those periods, realises a structure rhythmically exactly identical (isorhythmic), which, as I have indicated before, is the rule for motets of the fourteenth century. The triplum, in a few noteworthy instances, also participates in the isorhythmic treatment of the individual periods. It is not yet consistently carried through for the entire motet, however, not even in the motetus. . . . While up

---

[11] The appendix of Zayaruznaya, *Upper-Voice Structures*, conveniently assembles the relevant theoretical writings. See also the Preamble to the present chapter.

[12] These statements are documented in Ch. 12 n. 18. See also Ch. 10 n. 4.

[13] *On parole/A Paris/Frese nouvele* is in **Mo**, ff. 368ᵛ–369ᵛ, no. 302 in RISM, 319 (in the editions of Rokseth and Tischler).

WHAT IS ISORHYTHM? 45

to this point it was the norm, especially for the motetus, to maintain the verse metre in its melodic declamation, and at most to abandon it for special reasons in a few places, in this motet [on the contrary], a purely rhythmic principle prevails over verse metre and word accent, which soon establishes itself just as despotically as at the beginning of the history of the motet when, conversely, text metre completely governed the musical rhythm. The latter principle is indeed valid as an internal structural device, even if its exclusive application can lead to monotony, short-changing melody in the interests of rhythm. The new principle [on the contrary] even extends the application of isorhythm to the upper voices (since the tenor is constructed in this manner, and the complexity of its rhythm, which repeats several times, requires in compensation a rhythmically unified layout of the upper voices as well). This necessarily leads to acts of violence, which are even present in this first composition (in a lighter genre), which takes this as its point of departure.[14]

As usual in these motets, the tenor part has a straightforward repetition of both rhythm and melody, so there is no need to isolate the rhythmic element. 'Isorhythmic' does, however, accurately denote the rhythmic identity applied to changing melody in the motetus. Had Ludwig and his followers simply retained that local, descriptive sense, this essay would not be necessary. However, even here, the references to *despotisch* and *Gewalttätigkeiten* ('despotic', and 'violent acts') already suggest the iron grip of an a priori scheme whose ideal was to achieve a complete conformity, measured against which other tactics were found wanting.

Ludwig next applied the term in 1905, in a long review of Johannes Wolf's *Geschichte der Mensural-Notation von 1250–1460* (Leipzig, 1904). Wolf had pointed out the shortening of tenor note-values in the second part of many Machaut motets, which Ludwig glosses as 'Diminution, wie er es nennt', perhaps distancing himself from this use of the term. Ludwig comments on his transcription of Machaut's Motet 3, *Fine Amour/ He! Mors/Quare non sum mortuus*, where the tenor *color* of twenty-five notes, first presented as longs and maximas, then as breves and longs, is divided into three and a half *völlig gleichgebaute Abschnitte* (completely equally constructed sections). Wolf's transcription of the first section in imperfect modus is approved, but criticised for continuing this modus into the second *rhythmisch veränderten Teil* (rhythmically altered

---

[14] 'Beide Stimmen haben sich vom alten Modus völlig gelöst, ebenso wie der Tenor; statt dessen führt der Motetus wenigstens für die fünf ersten Takte der Perioden trotz der ganz verschiedenen Metren, die in sie fallen, einen rhythmisch exakt gleichen (isorhythmischen) Bau durch, der, wie ich schon einmal andeutete, in den Motetten des 14. Jahrhunderts die Regel ist. Auch das Triplum beteiligt sich an der isorhythmischen Behandlung der einzelnen Perioden mit einigen beachtenswerten Ansätzen; eine konsequente Durchführung für die ganze Motette liegt aber auch im Motetus hier noch nicht vor. . . . Galt es bisher besonders für den Motetus immer noch als Regel, das Versmetrum auch in der melodischen Deklamation zu bewahren und höchstens aus speziellen Gründen es an einzelnen Stellen aufzugeben, so hat in dieser Motette ein rein rhythmisches Prinzip über Versmetrum und Wortbetonung den Sieg davongetragen, und bald setzt es sich ebenso despotisch durch, wie am Anfang der Geschichte der Motette umgekehrt das Textmetrum den musikalischen Rhythmus völlig beherrschte. Ist das letztere Prinzip etwas innerlich durchaus Berechtigtes, wenn auch seine ausschließliche Durchführung zur Eintönigkeit führen kann und die Melodie auf Kosten des Rhythmus verkürzt, so führt das neue, die Durchführung der Isorhythmik auch in den Oberstimmen, nur weil der Tenor so baut und die Kompliziertheit des sich mehrere Male wiederholenden Tenorrhythmus bald die rhythmische einheitliche Anordnung auch der Oberstimmen als Gegengewicht verlangt, notwendig zu Gewalttätigkeiten, die auch in dieser ersten Komposition leichteren Genres, die diesen Standpunkt aufzeigt, nicht fehlen.' Ludwig, 'Studien', 223–24. The English term isorhythm first appears in late 19th-c. classical studies to describe lines with the same number of poetic feet, or for two poems in the same metre (*Oxford English Dictionary*), but I have yet to find a classicist colleague familiar with the term.

46 COMPOSITIONAL TECHNIQUES

part), where 'it here completely destroys the phrase structure; not only in the tenor do the analogous notes fall in rhythmically different places, but also in the upper voices, since these also mark out the isorhythm of the individual tenor sections very clearly'.[15] Ludwig is careful to limit isorhythm (here as a noun) to the identical *taleae* within each *color*, to refer to the second reduced section as 'rhythmically altered' (its note values as analogous, not equal), and to be cautious in applying the term 'diminution'.

The next mention is in 1910, again for thirteenth-century motets, but recognising its extension into the fourteenth century and beyond:

> Musically, on superficial examination, the motet at first gives a more antiquated impression, since the motetus is entirely in the old second rhythmic mode. . . . But on thorough analysis, a completely new way of disposing the periodic structure of the upper voices becomes apparent for the first time. This new disposition, which attained absolute dominance in the fourteenth-century motet and which would continue to play this role into the fifteenth century, is that of—as I would like to call this structure—isorhythm of the upper-voice periods in the individual tenor statements.[16]

Ludwig here applied this to the motet *Amor vincens omnia/Marie preconio/Aptatur*, which has some successive phrases of equal length, but with similar rather than the same rhythm.[17] The fourteenth-century use of this phenomenon, already a departure from the original sense, was later called by Besseler 'isoperiodic', a term subsequently explained by Ursula Günther as meaning that 'the upper voices only follow the plan of the lower voices in a general way, or have merely a few bars rhythmically identical in each Tenor period'.[18]

Ludwig contributed the major medieval section to Adler's *Handbuch* (1924), entitled: 'Die geistliche, nichtliturgische, weltliche einstimmige und die mehrstimmige Musik des Mittelalters'. The heading of sub-chapter IV reads: 'Die französischen Balladen, Virelais und Rondeaux des 14. Jahrhunderts; die isorhythmische Motette des 14. und beginnenden 15. Jahrhunderts; die italienischen Madrigale, Balladen und Cacce; die mehrstimmige Messe des 14. Jahrhunderts. Etwa 1300–1430.'[19] Here for the first time we find recognition of 'the isorhythmic motet' as a genre label for the fourteenth

---

[15] 'zerstört er hier die Periodenbildung völlig: nicht nur im Tenor kommen jedesmal die analogen Töne der einzelnen Abschnitte auf rhythmisch verschiedene Stellen, sondern auch in den Oberstimmen, da diese die Isorhythmie der einzelnen Tenorabschnitte ebenfalls ganz scharf ausprägen'. Review of Wolf by Friedrich Ludwig, in *SIMG* 6/4 (July 1905), 597–641. I owe this reference to Busse Berger, *Art of Memory*, 13.

[16] 'Musikalisch macht die Motette bei oberflächlicher Betrachtung zunächst einen älteren Eindruck, da der Mot. ganz im alten 2. Modus . . . Bei eingehender Untersuchung aber zeigt sich hier zum 1. Mal eine ganz neue Art der Disposition der Periodenbildung der Oberstimmen, die dann im 14. Jahrhundert zur Alleinherrschaft in der Motette gelangen und diese Rolle weiter bis in das 15. Jahrhundert hinein spielen sollte: die, wie ich diesen Bau nennen möchte, Isorhythmie der Oberstimmenperioden in den einzelnen T.-Durchführungen.' Ludwig, *Repertorium*, 444 ff.

[17] **Mo**, ff. 321ᵛ–322ᵛ, no. 266 in RISM, no. 283 in the editions of Rokseth and Tischler.

[18] Günther, 'The 14th-century Motet', 29. Besseler, 'Studien II', 201 n. 1, noun, *Isoperiodik*. The term was also taken up by Handschin, *Musikgeschichte im Überblick*, 201. The observation is consonant with Ernest Sanders's discovery of what he calls modular numbers, isoperiodic (but not isorhythmic) upper-voice phrases separated by rests, sometimes strikingly juxtaposed over a different underlying number structure in the lower parts. See Sanders, 'The Medieval Motet'. Sanders is careful not to overwork the term: 'It does not seem particularly helpful to apply the term "isorhythm" to motets with upper voices whose phrases, while showing an ordered arrangement, exhibit no isorhythmic parallelisms whatsoever' (561 n. 268).

[19] Adler, *Handbuch* (1924), i. 228.

WHAT IS ISORHYTHM? 47

and indeed the fifteenth centuries. This was followed by the *Habilitationsschrift* of Ludwig's sometime student Heinrich Besseler, published in two instalments ('Studien' I and II, 1925 and 1926), which demonstrated a further significant escalation of the status of isorhythm:

> From now on [*c.* 1316, and **Paris146**], all fourteenth-century French motets are, with a few insignificant exceptions, isorhythmic. This constructional principle, which for over a century, i.e. until the age of Dunstable and Dufay, held 'canonical status', is to be named on an equal footing with the two great forms of Baroque and classical music, the *da capo* aria and sonata form. It must, accordingly, have been consciously presented for the first time shortly before 1316, between two such closely related works as *Adesto* and *Quoniam*, maintained and seized upon as the ideal new motet form . . . that Vitry is to be regarded as the creator of the isorhythmic *ars nova* motet.[20]

It must have been his exchanges with Besseler that prompted the normally judicious Ludwig to endorse this leap, first in 1924 and, more strongly after the publication of Besseler's work, in the revision of his chapter in the *Handbuch*, attested by the shared language of their newly formulated descriptions. In Ludwig's revision of his essay for the 1930 edition of Adler's *Handbuch*, the isorhythmic motet (note the paradigmatic singular) has moved up to take pride of place: 'Die isorhythmische Motette des 14. und beginnenden 15. Jahrhunderts; die französischen Chaces, Balladen, Virelais und Rondeaux des 14. Jahrhunderts; die italienischen Madrigale, Balladen und Cacce; die mehrstimmige Messe des 14. Jahrhunderts. Etwa 1300–1430.'[21]

Ludwig now endorses Besseler's 1926 coronation of Vitry as the *Schöpfer* (creator) of 'the isorhythmic motet', exalted by both men to an epochal plane of *kanonische Geltung* (canonical status), which remained 'fixed, unchanged into the first decades of the fifteenth century':

> As H. Besseler has plausibly suggested, they probably include several early works of Philippe de Vitry, in which the young master, then about 25 years old, inaugurates the epoch of the 'isorhythmic motet'. The high pathos that once permeated the *conductus* now lays hold of the motet, whose outward dimensions increase and whose texts throughout the entire century often serve politics or personal participation in contemporary events. . . .
>
> Machaut's motets [. . . stand] stylistically on the foundation of a completely new motet style, of which the first traces are to be observed in the repertory of the seventh and eighth fascicles of the Montpellier MS. This style had already received a new instantiation in some works of Machaut's somewhat older contemporary Philippe

---

[20] 'Von jetzt an sind alle Motetten des französischen 14. Jahrhunderts mit wenigen belanglosen Ausnahmen isorhythmisch. Dieses Aufbauprinzip, das über ein Jahrhundert lang, bis in die Zeit Dunstables und Dufays in "kanonischer Geltung" geblieben und ebenbürtig neben den beiden größten Formprägungen des Barock und des Klassizismus, der Dacapo-Arie und Sonate zu nennen ist, muß demnach kurz vor 1316, zwischen zwei so nahe verwandten Werken wie *Adesto* und *Quoniam* zum erstenmal bewußt hingestellt und als vorbildliche neue Motettenform beibehalten und aufgegriffen worden sein . . . daß Philippe von Vitry als Schöpfer der isorhythmischen Ars nova-Motette anzusehen ist.' Besseler, 'Studien II', 194–95. On Besseler, see most recently Schipperges, *Die Akte Heinrich Besseler*. Pages 30–34 give a brief report on Besseler's *Habilitationsschrift*.
[21] Adler, *Handbuch* (1930), i. 265.

48   COMPOSITIONAL TECHNIQUES

de Vitry, but it prevails universally and almost without exception in Machaut's entire motet corpus, and has attained such perfection that it could be said to be endowed with canonical status, unchanged into the first decades of the fifteenth century, providing the formal scaffold for motet structure, which in other details as well was becoming more and more overcharged, namely the 'isorhythmic' construction of the new motet, wherein each tenor statement falls into two or more periods, which not only in the tenor (and when present, the contratenor), but (disregarding the text structure of the motetus and triplum) also in the upper voices are rhythmically completely analogous or even completely identical rhythmically, sometimes corresponding down to the smallest rhythmic detail, often of considerable length and frequently in more complicated combinations of bars of different length—Machaut, for example, wrote motets in which the first tenor statement had 11, 17 or 19 longs, and the second [statement] the same number of breves.[22]

Both men extended isorhythm to fourteenth-century repertory, on the basis of work on the motets of Machaut, Vitry and the Ivrea manuscript (first inventoried by Besseler).[23] Ludwig's Machaut edition, which aligns the *taleae* to show correspondences, was published in 1929.[24] But instead of serving as an appropriate adjective to describe rhythm-only repetition, it now appears as an over-arching prescriptive title for an epoch-making, canonical genre, crowning the French *ars nova* motet repertory between the 1310s and the 1440s. It was from this point that 'the isorhythmic motet' attained a hegemonic status that dominated the standard narrative of music history for the fourteenth and fifteenth centuries, and underwent further escalation in the next decades.

Motet Classification

Besseler divided isorhythmic motets into *einfach* (without diminution) and *zweiteilig* (bipartite, with some kind of diminution):

---

[22] 'unter ihnen, wie H. Besseler wahrscheinlich machte, mehrere Jugendwerke von Philipp de Vitry, in denen der damals etwa 25 jährige junge Meister die Epoche der 'isorhythmischen Motette' (vgl. unten S. 273) inauguriert. Das hohe Pathos, das einst namentlich die Conductus durchzog, ergreift jetzt die Motette, die auch in ihrer äußeren Ausdehnung wächst und deren Texte durch das ganze Jahrhundert oft der Politik oder persönlicher Anteilnahme am Zeitgeschehen dienen'. Ibid., 267.
'Machauts Motetten [stehen . . .] stilistisch auf dem Boden eines völlig neuen Motettenstils, zu dem erste Ansätze zwar wohl schon im Repertoire des siebenten und des achten Faszikels von Montpellier zu beobachten sind, der dann bereits in einigen Werken von Machauts etwas älterem Zeitgenossen Philipp von Vitry seine neue Ausprägung erfahren hatte (vgl. oben S. 267), der in Machauts Motettenschaffen nun aber in weitestem Umfang, fast ausnahmslos, herrscht und jetzt so fertig dasteht, daß er, man möchte sagen: mit kanonischer Geltung, unverändert bis in die ersten Jahrzehnte des 15. Jahrhunderts das Formgerüst für den ebenfalls im einzelnen immer überladener werdenden Motettenbau abgeben konnte: das ist der "isorhythmische" Aufbau der neuen Motette, bei dem jede Tenordurchführung in zwei oder mehr Perioden zerfällt, die nicht nur im Tenor und gegebenenfalls im Kontratenor, sondern (ohne Rücksicht auf die Textgliederung des Motetus und Triplum) auch in den Oberstimmen rhythmisch völlig analog gegliedert oder sogar völlig rhythmisch gleich, gelegentlich bis in die kleinste rhythmische Einzelheit sich entsprechend, gebaut werden, oft von beträchtlicher Ausdehnung sind und vielfach in komplizierteren Kombinationen von Takten verschiedener Ausdehnung verlaufen (Machaut schrieb z.B. Motetten, in denen die erste Tenordurchführung 11, 17 oder 19 *longe* und die zweite die gleiche Zahl von *breves* mißt).' Ibid., 272–73.
[23] Besseler, 'Studien I', at 249–52.
[24] Machaut, *Musikalische Werke*, ed. Ludwig, 4/2 (Leipzig, 1929).

WHAT IS ISORHYTHM? 49

As far as the isorhythmic structure is concerned, two main types emerge which are already found in the works of Vitry. Either a segment is repeated unchanged several times isorhythmically . . . or the initial principal periods are followed by a second part, exactly corresponding but shortened, in which normally each tenor note is diminished by half or by a third.[25]

Günther translated *einfach* as unipartite and *zweiteilig* as bipartite. This translation is misleading, because motets without diminution, such as Ciconia's, are by any standards bipartite when the second half rhythmically replicates the first half. Those two halves are fully isorhythmic in the strict sense. Günther's 'simple' category (perhaps a more suitable rendering of *einfach*) has no diminution. In other cases, where both rhythm and melody of the tenor are repeated entire, there is no need to distinguish the rhythmic repetition from the melodic (category 1(a) above). Besseler and Günther treat simple repetition as a less advanced, less prestigious kind of isorhythm than where diminution of some kind is present. But equal proportion, 1:1, far from having lower status, was deemed the foremost of the proportions, and was so recognised by Boethius in *De arithmetica*. Any other proportion is not equal, and therefore not 'iso'. So even in describing proportional relationships, 'iso' cannot properly mean 'the same internal relationships but faster', even if the transformation is derived from the same notated form. To resume the previous analogy with triangles: two triangles with the same internal angles, of which one has sides twice as long as the other, are not *equal* to each other (congruent), but similar. Where there is an unequal proportional relationship between two homographic tenor statements, the result might be described as 'the same (homorhythmic), but faster', if the internal relationships are preserved; or 'similar (homoeorhythmic), but faster', if there are internal differences usually due to a mensural reinterpretation; but in neither case 'equal'. A term unequivocally meaning 'equal' is problematic when the dimension for which equality is claimed (in this case, rhythm) is subject to any kind of transformation. When the term 'isorhythm' was stretched from its original, localised, analytical meaning into one which expressed a generic judgement about the large-scale form of the motet, there was an attendant irony: in order to fit the category, there could be very little that was 'iso' about a particular motet, for its status as an 'isorhythmic motet' came to depend on whether the composer had manipulated or altered its tenor from one statement to the next, so as to create a varied (therefore unequal) but cohesive high-level structure. According to the rigorous standards devised for it by its twentieth-century creators, the 'isorhythmic motet' was a contradiction in terms.

The hurdles for the genre were raised by Günther to limit it to what Willi Apel called panisorhythm: 'If the upper voices also follow this scheme, the composition is an isorhythmic motet.'[26] An evolutionary progression emerged: first, motets with isorhythm in the tenor only,[27] then tenors with diminution, then motets with partial isorhythm

---

[25] 'Nach dem isorhythmischen Bauplan ergeben sich zunächst zwei Haupttypen, die beide schon bei Vitry vorkommen. Entweder wird ein Abschnitt unverändert mehrmals isorhythmisch wiederholt . . . oder es schließt sich an die ersten Hauptperioden ein genau entsprechender, verkürzter zweiter Teil an, bei dem in der Regel jede Tenornote auf die Hälfte bzw. ein Drittel diminuiert.' Besseler, 'Studien II', 219–21.

[26] Günther, 'The 14th-century Motet', 29, and Apel, 'Remarks'.

[27] That is, no longer following Ludwig's restriction to non-tenor parts; unlike some later commentators, Ludwig, at least at first, recognised when the tenor statements were full repetitions.

50 COMPOSITIONAL TECHNIQUES

in upper parts culminating in panisorhythm, motets with two or (later) three succes-sively reducing tenor *color* statements, each usually containing two or three rhythmi-cally identical—isorhythmic—*taleae* in which every note in the corresponding upper parts was accounted for in at least one equal, 'isorhythmic' section over another *talea* of the same *color*.[28] This last type is very common for a relatively short period (Dunstaple's motets are representative) and is often chosen as the paradigmatic isorhythmic motet, a template reused even more frequently than was previously recognised. Jon Michael Allsen has catalogued more than a hundred examples from the early fifteenth cen-tury: 'The fifteenth-century isorhythmic motet was not, as often suggested, an archaic form practiced by few composers—rather, it was a vital genre that continued to evolve in the hands of the most skilled and musically ambitious late medieval composers.'[29]

In other words, works were arranged and even dated not by observing how they culti-vated variety (as they did spectacularly in the fourteenth century), but rather according to how closely they approached an ideal of identity (in the early fifteenth). This is just the period when composers, according to the standard narrative, were supposed to be waking up to humanism and becoming impatient with rigid forms. There is, of course, some justification for the perception of predictable uniformity in relation to such a tight construction, and it is dissonant with that narrative. But even here, the relationship be-tween the *color* statements was either proportional, diminishing, or mensural, or some combination of these (category 2(b) above), which precludes true isorhythm. Other strategies may simply incur the negative label 'not isorhythmic'. These include motets on song-form tenors, motets without pre-existing tenor, tenor derivations by retrograde or inversion, and more extreme cases of mensural manipulation. Interestingly, such va-riety was celebrated in Ludwig's magisterial 1902 survey of fourteenth-century music before isorhythm established its iron grip on historiography.[30]

Misplaced emphasis on identity has fostered a view of the isorhythmic motet as a clever but restrictive rule-bound monolith, a view which masks both the ingenuity and continuing cultivation of a wide range of compositional strategies that are either covered by or excluded from it. In stressing its intellectual rigour and difficulty, both Ludwig and Besseler embraced a cerebral image of the isorhythmic motet which has plagued it ever since, including its extension to Du Fay by De Van with which this essay opened; this image plays a large role in the structuralist, monumentalist cathedralism deplored by Christopher Page.[31] Late twentieth-century scholarship inherited an en-trenched and largely unquestioned tool that was in some cases downright wrong, in others too blunt and rigid for most of the manifestations to which it has been applied.

Rhythmic equality between tenor *color* statements can occur throughout a motet, as opposed to within *colores*, only when there is no tenor diminution or other trans-formation of the *color* (and then they are usually straightforward repeats). Over non-diminishing tenor *taleae*, there can (but may not) be full or partial upper-part isorhythm throughout. Full isorhythm in such a case is relatively rare, but occurs, for example, in the anonymous motet *Musicalis scientia/Scientie laudabilis*, in which all voices are rhythmically identical in seven *taleae* disposed over a single *color* (see Ch. 17). In a

---

[28] Apel, 'Remarks', 139 ff.; Sanders called this strophic identity ('Isorhythm', *NG1*, x. 351–54).
[29] Allsen, 'Style and Intertextuality', p. ii.
[30] Ludwig, 'Die mehrstimmige Musik'.
[31] Page, *Discarding Images*.

motet with tenor reduction, true isorhythm can occur only between the *taleae* within each *color* statement, not between those statements. Any upper-part correspondences, likewise, can only be rhythmically 'the same' between the *taleae* within each *color*, not between reducing *colores*, because the tenor segments become shorter; this occurs, for example, in all the so-called panisorhythmic motets by Dunstaple. Unless panisorhythm is defined to mean that every note in a motet is accounted for by a rhythmic repetition, at least within if not between sections, these can at least be called 'motets with isorhythm', if not, overall, 'isorhythmic motets'. 'Periodic motets' might be a more accurate and serviceable term, just because it is less precise and may therefore cover a wider range of procedures. If the tenor melody *and* rhythm repeat completely and exactly, without diminution, such repetition has no reason to be called iso*rhythmic*, nor is the overall form of the motet determined by isorhythm; it is just a straightforward repetition, requiring neither melody nor rhythm to be singled out (category 1(a) above). An example is B. de Cluni's motet *Apollinis eclipsatur/Zodiacum signis/In omnem terram* (Ch. 16), which has three identical tenor *color* statements, each divided into two isorhythmic *taleae*. The only isorhythm in this motet is confined to the tenor *taleae* within each *color*; the three tenor *color* statements are identical in rhythm and melody, and there is no upper-part isorhythm.

Color and *talea* often overlap, with non-coincident repetitions of both (category 1(b) above). In the tenor of Machaut's Motet 9, *Fons tocius superbie/O livoris feritas/Fera pessima*, for example, each pair of *color* statements spans three *taleae* (Ch. 9). The terms *color* and *talea* (in their current understanding) serve well to describe the separate constituents, especially where the overlapping is less regular. If isorhythm denotes the application of the same rhythm to a different melody, then the corresponding term for a repeated melody differently rhythmicised is isomely (isomelic). 'Isorhythm' is here redundant or misleading without reference also to isomelism (or isomely), though the upper-part repetitions around the hockets linking the *taleae* in this case can usefully be described as isorhythmic. In other motets by Machaut and others, significant rhythmic and melodic repetitions have often been overlooked because they are not aligned with the tenor *talea*. It is often the case that only regular repetition is signalled, to the end of charting a qualitative crescendo towards tidy and mechanical rhythmic identity. The result is that subtler kinds of variation are neglected.

Vitry

One can understand Besseler's satisfaction in 1926 at being able to list, over three pages, the then known isorhythmic motets, mostly from the Fauvel, Machaut and Ivrea manuscripts.[32] To his credit, he took the important first steps in identifying the motet output of Philippe de Vitry. However, three out of the very small corpus of 'isorhythmic' motets attributable to Vitry have second *color* statements which are not diminutions or even rhythmic transformations of the first, but are newly rhythmicised and require renotation (category 2(a) above). These motets are *Firmissime fidem teneamus/*

---

[32] Besseler, 'Studien II', 222–24. The list also includes motets with simple tenor repetition (for example, *Apollinis eclipsatur*).

52   COMPOSITIONAL TECHNIQUES

Adesto, sancta trinitas/Alleluya; *Douce playsence/Garison selon nature/Neuma quinti toni*; and *Vos quid admiramini/Gratissima virginis species/Gaude gloriosa* (Ch. 8); the latter two are among the most securely attributed. Each tenor *color* statement is internally divided into short isorhythmic *taleae*, with some sporadic isorhythmic repetition in the upper parts of these motets, but the entire rhythmic scheme for the second tenor *color* in each case is quite independent of the first. At most, it is within but not between sections of such motets that isorhythm occurs, as tenor *talea* repetitions within a *color*, and as portions of isorhythm appear in the upper parts (notably in hockets). These three Vitry motets, central to Besseler's genre-defining group, cannot therefore be considered to be structured isorhythmically overall; the second *color* statement is neither homoeorhythmic (similar in rhythm) nor homographic (notated the same).[33]

The one thing that is repeated exactly over the entire span of a tenor motet with new or transformed rhythm, including diminution, is not the rhythm but the melody; that is, it is not isorhythmic but isomelic (equal melody). This rarely used term, first used by Besseler, has often been confined to relatively minor or approximate similarities in corresponding places in the upper parts.[34] Its lowly status is still evident in *NG2*:

> Isomelism was once regarded as highly significant, but its importance has since been disputed. Scholars at first interpreted it as a product of conscious compositional procedure: either as a means of 'symbolizing' isorhythmic structures . . . or simply as a device which could be inserted to mark off isorhythmic sections. At the other extreme, Sanders regarded it as a mere byproduct of motet composition.[35]

This presentation of isomelism reveals the extent to which isorhythm has been allowed to dominate. But isomelism deserves to be redefined and restored alongside isorhythm as an equal and useful descriptive partner. Where *color* and *talea* repetitions overlap, there is no reason to choose a single overall term that privileges the rhythmic repetition to the exclusion of the melodic.

Homographic Tenors and 'Unequal' Results

I now turn to cases—the majority—where mensurally transformed versions are derived from the same notated tenor. In contrast to the new rhythmicisations used by Vitry, which require renotation, this covers all cases that can be derived by mensural transformation or diminution from a single notated (homographic) form. This does not preclude the rewriting or respelling of such derivations, which is often the case if they are complex, or if in a two-opening copy they lie across a page turn. The fourteenth-century theorists Muris and Boen (already cited with respect to *color* and *talea*) both use a

---

[33] Other motets attributable to Vitry have a single *color* divided into isorhythmic *taleae*. These include *Garrit gallus/In nova fert*.

[34] It appears only as a footnote in Reese, *Music in the Renaissance*, 92. Of Le Rouge's mass on Frye's balade, *So ys emprentid*, Reese writes: 'The isorhythmic technique is here provided with a counterpart; whereas in the former the rhythmic pattern remains the same but the melodic content may vary, in the latter the melodic material remains the same but the rhythmic pattern varies. This technique has been called isomelic.' For another application, see S. E. Brown, 'New Evidence'.

[35] Laurenz Lütteken, 'Isomelism', *NG2* xii. 617–18.

WHAT IS ISORHYTHM?   53

common notational touchstone of rhythmic comparability, *figure* or *corpora*, and not the criterion of similarity in realised results that underlie most diagnoses of 'isorhythm'. The same applies to motet tenors that are to be realised in canon, by retrograde or inversion; they are strictly derived from the same notational basis (homographic), but the spelt-out results may look or sound very different, and could by no means be called 'the same'.

Confusion has long existed between diminution, proportion, and mensural transformation. Old definitions of coloration, as removing a third of the value of a note, are largely to blame for failure to make important distinctions of principle. Problems arise where the point of reference is the modern transcription, where only a reader with a good grasp of the original notation can discern deceptively similar results arising from different notational procedures, or different results deriving from the same original notation. I have long proposed distinguishing between different uses of coloration, most notably whether for mensural or for proportional change. On the one hand, its use for imperfection corresponds to a mensural shift, usually from perfect to imperfect time, fixing coloured notes at their imperfect and unaltered values. This is not proportional. Sesquialtera coloration, on the other hand, *is* proportional; it reduces everything by a third, or, rather, occasions a precise acceleration of tempo in which three minims take the time of two, but where imperfection and alteration still apply as required by the governing mensuration.[36] In special cases colours, signs or numerals can be used to code proportions other than 3:2 (for example, Ɔ for 4:3). Such usages are truly proportional. The same distinctions between proportional and mensural manipulation apply beyond coloration, as in tenor derivations required by the phrases *per medium*, *per semi*, *ad tertiam*, and *dupla proportione* when the relevant mensurations permit proportional division by two or three. Instances of mensural reinterpretation of the same tenor include *Inter densas* (Ch. 1), *Alma polis regia* (Ch. 19) and *Sub Arturo plebs* (Ch. 20).

Another clear case of mensural transformation without diminution is Machaut's Motet 6, *S'il estoit/S'amours/Et gaudebit* (see Ch. 13 and Machaut, *Motets*, ed. Boogaart). The first tenor statement is in perfect modus, with alteration of the first breve; the second, neither renotated, nor rewritten, nor specified, is still in perfect modus, but displaced by a long rest so that a different breve is altered. Even the modern reader unschooled in *ars nova* notation would see difference, but have no way of knowing that this tenor was homographic, while those of the three Vitry motets cited above are not.

I have been using the word 'diminution' in its commonly understood sense of some kind of acceleration or reduction of values, usually expressed as a proportion (1:2, 2:3). A thorough investigation of fourteenth-century understandings of diminution is beyond the scope of this essay.[37] A few cases do indeed specify diminution proportionally.[38] But this is not how diminution is explained by theorists, for whom it is a shift of notes to the next level down: a notated long is read as a breve, a breve as a semibreve. In most cases, lacking telltale note-values, the results will not be distinguishable from

---

[36] See, for example, 'Notation, III, 3 (vii)', *NG*1 and *NG*2, and EECM 22, p. xiii.

[37] For 14th-c. definitions of diminution see Bent, 'The Myth'.

[38] For example, in the motet *Alma polis/Axe poli* (music and text respectively attributed within the text to Egidius de Aurolia and J. de Porta), **Chantilly**, ff. 67ᵛ–68ʳ, where the newly identified tenor is labelled *cum diminucione eiusdem per semi*. See Ch. 19 and Ex. 19.1. Edited in Harrison (PMFC 5, no. 28) and Günther (CMM 39, no. 10).

54   COMPOSITIONAL TECHNIQUES

proportional reduction, but if the shift of note-levels also involves an asymmetrical shift of modus, tempus and prolation relationships, different duple and triple combinations at any of those levels may result, rather than proportioned internal relationships that could be described as 'the same but faster'. Similarity of results may simply be due to a limited range of original note-values that did not exploit the range of permutations of twos and threes required by the various levels of mensuration, and thus did not expose difference, as in *Sub Arturo plebs*. The great majority of reducing tenors appears to be proportional and can be so expressed, that is, the internal relationships are the same in successive statements in shorter values; but their derivation may nevertheless be, and sometimes is demonstrably, by shift of note values.

The tenor of Dunstaple's St John the Baptist motet, *Dies dignus decorari/Demon dolens/Iste confessor*, is notated not in the values of the first statement, but of its third and final statement, in imperfect modus and perfect tempus with altered semibreves (see also Ch. 25).[39] Instead of the second and third statements being diminutions of the first, the first two are derived by augmentation of the third in relation to the upper parts, up a note level from the written values, as is the case in all those Dunstaple motets which result in sections proportioned 6:4:3. The semibreve pairs in the third statement (the single notated statement) require alteration; but when read up a note-level as breve pairs in the first and second statements, the modus is in both cases imperfect, so there is no alteration. Those breves (written semibreves) are counted out with reference to the upper parts by perfect tempus in the first *color* and imperfect modus in the second. Strict isorhythm, again, occurs in all parts, but only within each *color*, not between *colores*. This is a case of mensural reinterpretation, though with much slighter consequences than in *Inter densas* and *Sub Arturo plebs*.

Mensural transformation and diminution may be combined, as in the Credo *Omni tempore* (Ch. 23), where six different forms are derived from one notated statement. Each tenor *color* is read first in perfect and then in imperfect modus (mensural transformation, with and without alteration of the breve); each successive pair of statements is then read in diminution, at the next note level down. Only within each *color* are there rhythmically identical *taleae* (in this case three).[40]

The various fault lines concerning definitions of identity were to bedevil not merely the definition of isorhythmic motets, but also motet definitions and hierarchies throughout the fourteenth and fifteenth centuries, privileging the 'isorhythmic' kind and widening the gulf that separated it from other, implicitly inferior motet forms. The question of motet definitions and classifications, and how editorial policies have shaped the way motets are studied, demands separate investigation. Students and performers who browse the slim volumes containing those flagship pieces which were able to jump all the hurdles will be circularly misled into thinking that most motets worthy of the name were isorhythmic. Misfits lurk in other volumes, pieces which counted as motets for their composers and contemporaries. 'Isorhythmicmotet' soon became coterminous with a restrictive definition of the high-status, late-medieval motet, an inseparable term like 'functionalharmony'.

---

[39]   MB 8, no. 26; and Bent, 'The Measurement', ex. 2.
[40]   See Ch. 23 on the Yoxford Credo, and Bent, 'The Measurement', ex. 3.

Truly Isorhythmic Motets?

Having questioned the appropriateness of an isorhythmic classification for many of the motets commonly so designated, are there any truly isorhythmic motets? The only pieces whose entire form could be said to be governed by isorhythm are those relatively rare motets with a single tenor *color* divided into rhythmically identical *taleae* (like Vitry's *Petre Clemens/Lugentium siccentur*); such motets may—or may not—have complete or partial isorhythm in the upper parts. Complete isorhythm is found in motets where the entire second half rhythmically replicates the first, but with different pitches, notably the three truly isorhythmic motets of Ciconia (which have no pre-existent tenors).[41] I repent the presentation of *Doctorum principem* among the isorhythmic motets in the Ciconia edition; it is now abundantly clear that it should not have been included under that heading. It is a motet based on three different mensural readings of a homographic tenor; these lie midway on a spectrum whose extremes are marked by *Inter densas* and Dunstaple's *Dies dignus*. The other three Ciconia motets presented there, *Albane misse celitus/Albane doctor maxime*, *Ut te per omnes/Ingens alumnus Padue* and *Petrum Marcello/O Petre antistes* (in addition to two fragmentary *opera dubia*: see Ch. 28) belong to the very small category of motets that can be called wholly isorhythmic. In each case, the second half exactly replicates the rhythm of the first. In addition, *Petrum Marcello venetum/O Petre antistes inclite* has rhythmic diminution of the *color* within each of these halves. Isorhythm applies between the two sections but not within them. Similar patterns are found in other post-Ciconian motets from the 1420s, including the Du Fay motets *Vasilissa ergo gaude/Concupivit* and *Rite maiorem/Artibus summis/Ora pro nobis*, although these have pre-existent tenors and a single tenor *color*. However, the Ciconia motets are not always considered fully-fledged, high-status isorhythmic motets, for which not only a pre-existent tenor but, paradoxically, non-identical diminishing repetition came to be an ideal if not indeed a qualifying feature.[42]

Besseler's list included (implicitly as 'isorhythmic', but wrongly so):

- motets with repeating *colores* that are differently rhythmicised and need separate notation;
- motets whose tenor repetitions are not rhythmically identical, although derived from the same notated form (homographic);
- motets whose tenor repetitions had to be renotated because the rhythmic and melodic patterns are overlapped and staggered; and

---

[41] The claim that *Petrum Marcello venetum/O Petre antistes inclite* may use a cantus prius factus (S. E. Brown, 'A Possible Cantus Firmus') is not generally accepted.

[42] Finscher and Laubenthal, '"Cantiones quae vulgo motectae vocantur"', reiterate an escalating view. While they do not refer to PMFC 24 they nonetheless report its new datings and the tally of four isorhythmic motets. However, contrary to my view expressed here, that one of those is not isorhythmic, but the other three are, in the most literal sense, they dismiss Ciconia's isorhythm in the following terms: 'ist vom ganzen isorhythmischen System nur die rhythmische Identität der beiden Teile (in allen vier Stimmen) geblieben' (p. 295). Having subscribed to a crescendo of complexity, setting the hurdles increasingly high, they find 'only' rhythmic replication remaining in Ciconia's 'simplified' system—but this is the one feature that I now argue merits the term isorhythm.

56 COMPOSITIONAL TECHNIQUES

- motets with simple tenor repetition of rhythm *and* melody, not requiring terminological separation of the rhythmic repetition.

None of the above can properly be called isorhythmic. Conversely, Besseler also designated as 'nicht isorhythmisch' some motets with irregular tenor repetition patterns,
including at least one motet that contains true isorhythm, Machaut's Motet 20, *Trop
plus est bele/Biaute paree/Je ne sui mie*, which did not fit his mould because the tenor
repetitions are determined by the tenor's rondeau form. But within its total duration
of forty-eight perfect breves plus final long, this motet, in fact, has three irregularly
placed blocks of complete isorhythm in the upper parts, over differing tenor pitches,
at bars 8–11, 42–45, and 25–27 (with differing tenor rhythm, and a slight motetus variant in bar 28) in Machaut, *The Motets*, ed. Boogaart. Thus, it makes more use of true
isorhythm than some motets that have been unquestioningly so described, and it links
with the thirteenth-century repertory which first gave rise to the term.[43] Isorhythm
remains a useful descriptive term for such blocks of upper-part repetition, whether
or not coordinated with tenor repetitions, as it does also for tenor *taleae* within a *color*
statement.

Fifteenth-Century Decline

Many historians have subscribed to the outworn, cerebral, bloodless image that the isorhythmic motet had accumulated by the second half of the twentieth century, voicing
its need to give way to the currents of humanism, and to the human feeling and ex-
pressiveness that seems to characterise music from the late fifteenth century on. David
Fallows wrote:

> By the middle of the century the isorhythmic motet had fallen from favour. It is as though
> musicians and their patrons now realized that it was an empty form based on aesthetic
> criteria of an age long gone, principles scarcely relevant to the age of humanism, of sen-
> suality in the arts, of the individual. The two main features of the motet were entirely
> contrary to those modern beliefs. Normally the motet had at least two different texts
> sounding simultaneously; and while the texts were usually related in some way, perhaps
> even sharing rhyme-words, their simultaneous singing inevitably resulted in a richness
> born partly of aural confusion which may have pleased the Gothic mind but must have
> seemed hopelessly unrealistic in fifteenth-century Italy. And the isorhythmic structure—a
> form based on the idea that at least one voice should contain a rhythmic pattern which
> was repeated with different pitches—was a neat and ingenious scheme that appealed to
> the thirteenth-century desire for numerical system and entelechy but had relatively little
> to say to the contemporaries of Donatello and Brunelleschi who felt that their art should
> actually be perceived as perfect. [. . . Dufay] was continually adapting the form to his own
> purposes, finding ways of reconciling the motet with fifteenth-century cultural values.
> Dufay's motets contain an unsurpassed range of techniques, expanding some features of

---

[43] Sanders, 'Isorhythm', gives as ex. 2 the extensive parallel isorhythmic passages in *Se je chante/Bien doi
amer/Et sperabit*, **Mo**, ff. 357ᵛ–359ᵛ, no. 294 in RISM, no. 311 in Rokseth, Tischler.

the old style, rejecting others, experimenting and re-experimenting with various musical figures, constantly reconsidering the form. . . . works of classical purity combined with personal vision. For composers of the early fifteenth century the position of the motet was in many ways similar to that of the fugue for nineteenth-century composers. It was a style based on aesthetic criteria that had obtained nearly two hundred years earlier but had little to do with the ideas that were now current; and it was increasingly a style associated with seriousness of tone and scholasticism, a style used to suggest formality, to be used for auspicious occasions. Yet another feature shared by the motet and the fugue in the later stages of their history was that while their difficulties and formality often drove a lesser composer to produce his most pompous and turgid efforts, they equally spurred a certain kind of resourceful mind to sublime heights of musical invention. The evidence suggests that Dufay's was such a mind.[44]

Life after isorhythm was also articulated by Sanders who, despite being fastidious about use of the word, subscribed to the general view of its demise:

In the end, there appeared mensuration motets without isorhythm. Three compositions by Dufay represent this final structural type of the medieval motet, which is related to the Burgundian cantus-firmus mass. . . . As in the case of the symphony of the early 20th century, the huge proportions to which the isorhythmic motet of English, Burgundian and Franco-Flemish composers of the early 15th century had grown were indications of its imminent demise as a species.[45]

Compared by Besseler to the *da capo* aria and sonata form, by Sanders to the late-romantic symphony, and by Fallows to fugue, we are presented with the image of a massive construction that, dinosaur-like, had risen, overreached itself, and needed to fall. Yet these 'overblown' motets take about two to a maximum of five minutes to perform. They are supposed to have given way in their last gasp to the—paradoxically—much longer constructions of the unified mass cycle, where each related movement may take five minutes, resulting in a half-hour work, maintaining unity over an even longer time-span when performed in a liturgical context. These parallels variously imply extended duration (the Romantic symphony), taut construction (fugue), or offer status in the musical mainstream (aria and sonata). In all cases, the comparison seeks to legitimate strange and distant music, bringing it closer to home.

Examples of recognisably similar techniques from the later fifteenth century are seen as vestigial throwbacks after a break with the tradition:

The legacy of the isorhythmic motet can be heard in fainter and fainter echoes throughout the second half of the fifteenth century. As the genre waned near the end of the first half of the century, it was succeeded by motets and masses employing a cantus firmus in the tenor but, with a few significant exceptions, eschewing most techniques explicitly associated with isorhythm. . . . The use of strict diminution of a cantus firmus, laying out the temporal plan of a piece according to strict numerical ratios, the use of perfect modus, and

---

[44] Fallows, *Dufay*, 103–4, 123.
[45] Sanders, 'Medieval Motet', 567–68, and similarly in his 'Isorhythm'.

58   COMPOSITIONAL TECHNIQUES

a compositional technique that will be referred to as modus disposition all can be understood as vestiges of the isorhythmic tradition.[46]

However, to unpick some of the unfounded assumptions about isorhythm and its accumulated mythology would permit these to be seen, rather, as processes of natural growth and continuation. I fell into the trap myself, and would no longer write 'It is perhaps paradoxical that the waning principle of isorhythm, seen at its most classical and polished in Dunstaple's isorhythmic motets, should for a short period have acted as a vital catalyst in begetting the unity of the cyclic Mass, the area of activity which was clearly a crucible of new creative vigour during at least the 1420s.'[47]

Many have noted the affinity and indeed the historical connection between the isorhythmic motet and the tenor mass, while subscribing to the demise of the former. The continuity is in fact greater than often recognised, but has been masked by misdescription of motets. The underlying and unifying processes of these cycles are not new, but were already in place from the early fourteenth century, most notably:

(1)   Identical tenors between movements that do not require separate consideration of rhythm and melody, such as the *Caput* masses; and

(2)   isomelic tenors differently rhythmicised in each movement of a mass, or for each tenor statement within a motet or mass movement where there is a double *cursus* (again, as in the *Caput* masses). This is what happens in the re-rhythmicised second *colores* of some Vitry motets (now disqualified from isorhythm).

These, of course, correspond to the types 1 and 2 set out at the beginning of this essay. Impostors in the isorhythmic canon require reconsideration both of what the tenor mass does, and what the isorhythmic motet does not do. The confining shackles of the chilly medieval motet, from which warm-blooded Renaissance composers were eager to escape, have been positively reformulated for the 'new' tenor mass. A historiographical agenda which sought to sharpen the medieval–Renaissance contrast was not well served by emphasising unbroken continuity, and hence that continuity has been underplayed. This is understandable, given that some of the relevant characteristics have lurked unrecognised under the umbrella of isorhythm.

Manfred Bukofzer famously linked the 'end' of the isorhythmic motet tradition to mass cycles such as *Caput*: 'The idea of writing a Mass setting on a tenor not borrowed from plainsongs of the Ordinary was prompted by a medieval form, the isorhythmic motet. The fountainhead of the development is the transfer of the isorhythmic technique to the Mass.'[48] Techniques were indeed transferred, but not quite in the way he describes. He called several mass cycles 'isorhythmic', foremost among them the anonymous English *Caput* cycle formerly thought to be by Du Fay, which presents two melodic statements of the tenor in each movement (a 'double *cursus*'), differently rhythmicised

---

[46] Brothers, 'Vestiges of the Isorhythmic Tradition'; see also Dammann, 'Spätformen der isorhythmischen Motette'.

[47] Bent, *Dunstaple*, 78.

[48] Bukofzer, *Studies*, 221–23.

WHAT IS ISORHYTHM? 59

in triple and duple time, requiring separate notation.[49] The second part of each movement is therefore an isomelic, not an isorhythmic variant in imperfect time of the first perfect-time statement. But this entire double-cursus tenor appears identically, melody *and* rhythm—therefore not isor*hythmic*—in all movements of the mass. What is more, the two later *Caput* masses by Ockeghem and Obrecht use exactly the same tenor, in the same rhythmicisation. So much for the claim that late fifteenth-century composers turned their backs on such constructions. Large-scale motets of around the year 1500 share many features with their antecedents. Obrecht's *Sub tuum praesidium* mass is another example of the continuing tradition of structural and mensural transformation between movements of a mass cycle, as are many of the *L'homme armé* masses.

Caput, therefore, is not an isorhythmic mass. Dunstaple's *Da gaudiorum premia* and Power's *Alma redemptoris* masses likewise have complete tenor identity between, but not within, movements, with a single *color* in each movement which changes from perfect to imperfect time; *pace* Bukofzer, they too are not isorhythmic. Dunstaple's mass movements on *Jesu Christe Fili Dei* are likewise related not by isor*hythm*, but by tenor *identity*. But within each movement, the tenor is stated twice (a double *cursus*). Its (potentially single) notated form is in the values not of the first, but of the last statement,[50] the first being derived from it by augmentation, to be read up a note value. Each of the statements is notated entirely in breves, including a change from (unnotated) perfect to notated imperfect tempus (C), allowing no scope for perceptible mensural change within the different signatures. Where the tenor statements are identical between movements, melodically and rhythmically, as in *Caput* and other English masses, it is inappropriate to single out rhythmic identity (isorhythm), as also for the identical statements in *Apollinis eclipsatur* and several other fourteenth-century motets.

The *Rex seculorum* mass by Dunstaple or Power presents a differently rhythmicised version of the same chant in each movement, freely varied and therefore not strictly isomelic, but it retains the same chant divisions between perfect and imperfect time sections. Re-rhythmicisation requiring renotation within each movement (as in the two isomelic *colores* of each *Caput* movement), or between movements (as in *Rex seculorum*), is what happens between the *color* statements of the re-rhythmicised Vitry motet tenors a century earlier.[51]

These mass techniques constitute neither a rejection nor a throwback, but rather a continuing development of precisely the same resources for motet composition that had been in place since the early fourteenth century. To have defined the original control

[49] Ibid., 256–71, and the example on p. 260, which sets out the *Caput* tenor; pitches and rhythms are the same in each movement of all three masses. Each movement presents the tenor melody first in triple, then in duple time, renotated, therefore isomelically.

[50] In fact, it is written out twice in the only source because the movements occupy more than one opening. For Bukofzer's isorhythmic mass classifications see MB 8.

[51] Sanders, 'Isorhythm', rightly observes that there is no isorhythm in the English masses mentioned here, because the *color* is not divided into *taleae*, and 'identity arises not from their rhythms, but from the pitch content of the tenor'. However, he does not invoke the criterion of simple identity. He states that in *Rex seculorum* 'even this [rhythmic] connection with the isorhythmic tradition is severed'. In other words, despite these important cautions and qualifications, he does not challenge the credentials of the isorhythmic motet as commonly understood, or the suitability of the term. *Rex seculorum* differs from the Vitry motets in that the restatements are not completely isomelic. A great variety of patterns is found in the English mass compositions of **OH**. See, for example, the Gloria *Ad Thome*, no. 24 (anonymous, but perhaps by Power), where the irregularly overlapping *color* and *talea* result in the second *color* (with slight melodic variants) being differently rhythmicised from the first.

60 COMPOSITIONAL TECHNIQUES

group of Vitry motets as 'isorhythmic', without recognising that the second *colores* are newly rhythmicised, has led to a misconstruction of exactly the same technique in the 'freely rhythmicised' (and sometimes isomelic) tenors of fifteenth-century mass cycles. Far from breaking free of the shackles of isorhythm, they are simply mapping out the century-old technique of newly rhythmicised forms of tenor melodies onto a larger canvas for the melodic unification of tenor masses. This distinction has gone largely unremarked. If it was legitimate (but wrong) to extend the term isorhythm to such new rhythmicisation in the early fourteenth century, it becomes illogical to disqualify later tenor mass cycles and other large-scale structures which do likewise. Conversely, if isorhythm is not the right term for the late fifteenth century, as generally agreed, then neither is it right for much of the earlier repertory to which it is now unquestioningly applied. What disqualifies the tenor mass as isorhythmic also disqualifies Vitry as the creator of isorhythm. Isorhythm was redefined by Ludwig and Besseler to reflect musical developments between the thirteenth and fourteenth centuries, even if the term had become unsuitable, but it was not similarly stretched or adapted for the transition from the fourteenth to the fifteenth. The term ossified but the musical development moved on. A gradual but insidious historiographical shift crept in that affected not just the changing definition of isorhythm, but even the criteria for accepting a work as a motet. All along, there were motet constructions that were not by any definition isorhythmic. The later they are, the more likely are such compositions to be disqualified from a narrowed definition of the most uniform and prestigious kind of motets, especially following an arbitrary mid-fifteenth-century cut-off point in the stretching of the term isorhythm.

Alternative Terms?

We have seen mathematical rigidity caricatured to an absurd extreme, a preposterous monster doomed to die, in order to give way to new humane, humanistic musical standards (De Van, Fallows). The historiographical shift is clear through the twentieth century, during the first half of which we saw the term coined and stretched to the point where it no longer accurately described the processes. It then became encumbered with the negative discourse of cerebral, medieval, number-bound sterility which the second half of the twentieth century sought to shed on behalf of Renaissance humanists, men of feeling. Restraint in use of the umbrella term 'isorhythmic motet' removes one of the key planks of this historiography.

The question always asked at this stage is 'what can we call it instead?' But to ask this raises the question 'what is IT?' I have tried here to draw attention to the variety rather than the sameness of strategies of motet composition in the fourteenth and fifteenth centuries, showing that they can even less be accommodated within a single model than can sonata forms. 'It' (isorhythm) has been loosely applied to a congeries of techniques, including:

- simple isorhythmic replication either over a whole motet or within sections (intra-*color*);

WHAT IS ISORHYTHM? 61

- diminution or augmentation of successive tenor statements, not in the common current sense of proportional reduction, but reading them at the next note-level down or up, perhaps resulting in different mensural combinations;
- proportional reduction of successive tenor statements, for example, 2:1;
- mensural rereading of successive homographic tenor statements, resulting in great or slight differences (*Inter densas*, *Doctorum principem*, *Sub Arturo plebs*, Dunstaple's 6:4:3 motets);
- exact tenor repetition of both rhythm and melody, not requiring 'rhythm' to be singled out, as in the *Caput* masses;
- repetition of melody to a different rhythm (isomelic, but not isorhythmic), as in the tenors of *Vos/Gratissima* and other Vitry motets; and, finally,
- other forms of structuring such as canon, retrograde, etc.

Most motets are in some way 'structured'; but then so, if to a lesser extent, are pieces that use no tenor manipulation. Most but not all are 'tenor' motets, a term used for some late fifteenth-century forms that could well be applied much earlier, and which serves to signal a real continuity with the tenor mass.[52] But not all tenor motets are isorhythmic and not all motets with isorhythm have pre-existent tenors. 'Periodic motet', or 'structured motet' may be the only terms that meet all cases. I look forward to a period of experimental terminology, more open to recognising a variety of compositional techniques, and to clearing the way for an appreciation of the wide range of motet structuring that anticipates and nourishes the growth of the cyclic mass and late fifteenth-century motet.[53] Far from repudiating motet techniques, or artificially reviving them, later forms adapt and extend them in an unbroken evolution.

I have rejected 'isorhythm' for overall description of many of the pieces to which it has been applied, and applied it, locally, to some pieces from which it has been withheld. The term remains useful and valid, however, to describe occurrences of true isorhythm, even in motets that have previously been excluded from isorhythmic definition, such as the song-tenor motets of Machaut, or down-played, as with some motets of Ciconia. But I do suggest that we draw back from grandiose and normative use as an overall genre label, and confine it to procedures for which it provides an accurate description, not necessarily to whole motets, very few of which are wholly isorhythmic, and take care to put other strategies on a level playing field with the particular kinds of motets that have been disproportionately privileged (even if misnamed) as isorhythmic. I hope that a wider palette of descriptive terms—more use of *color–talea* permutations, and distinctions between diminutional, proportional and mensural transformations—will increase awareness of the great variety of motet strategies. But by all means we can talk about motets 'with isorhythm'.

---

[52] Finscher and Laubenthal, '"Cantiones quae vulgo motectae vocantur"', 306.

[53] A good start on such classifications has been made in Cumming, *The Motet in the Age of Du Fay*. She writes (p. 82): '"Isorhythm" is a modern term with a variety of possible meanings; different scholars use it in different ways. Excessive emphasis on the distinction between "isorhythmic" and "non-isorhythmic" limits our understanding of different kinds of rhythmic structures, and the relationships among "isorhythmic" and other works.'

62 COMPOSITIONAL TECHNIQUES

Summary and Conclusions

1. Since Ludwig coined the term isorhythm, its application has escalated from an accurate description of local procedures to a prescriptive definition of a genre. Isorhythm remains a useful description of *talea* repetitions within each tenor *color*, or for upper-part isorhythm, whether periodic or partial (even in motets described by Besseler as 'not isorhythmic'), but is problematic as a determinant of the motet genre.

2. The second statement of a tenor *color* is not 'iso' if differently rhythmicised (requiring different notation), whether within a Vitry motet, for the second half of a fifteenth-century tenor mass (for example, *Caput*), or between movements of a mass cycle on the same tenor melody where it is melody, not rhythm that remains constant.

3. The same notation may yield different results: a tenor is homographic rather than isorhythmic if restatements apply mensural change or diminution, whether or not those changes result in large, small or no differences of relative internal rhythms (process versus results).

4. Rhythm has been overstressed. 'Isorhythm' is inappropriate when there is total repetition of melody *and* rhythm (because falsely isolating rhythm), or just melodic repetition; in both cases, rhythmic and melodic permutations, including overlapping *color* and *talea*, can be classified using those terms. It is the tenor melody, and not its rhythm, that retains identity between diminishing or transformed sections.

5. Modern use of the term 'isorhythm' refers to results; apparent similarity in current notation may conceal differences of process. Products of mensural transformation of a homographic basis may thus have been classified according to whether they yield 'isorhythmic' results, either with the same internal relationships (Alanus's *Sub Arturo*, Ch. 20) or similar relationships (Dunstaple's *Dies dignus* and Ciconia's *Doctorem principem*, with and without alteration), or strikingly different as in a 'mensuration' motet (*Inter densas*). These differences may arise from accidents of note-value selection or mensural combination.

6. Only equal proportion (1:1) truly qualifies as 'iso'; the term 'isorhythm' is not a good choice for diminution or mensural transformation, which are by no standards 'equal'. These can be called 'the same rhythm' only by a modern understanding of 'rhythm' (which has no medieval equivalent), and then only by denying identity ('the same but faster'). Besseler's classification of motets without diminution as *einfach* and with diminution as *zweiteilig* does not address this problem, but privileges motets with some kind of diminution, even if that diminution disqualifies a strictly isorhythmic classification.

7. Only motets with single-*color* or non-diminishing tenors, or those (not necessarily tenor-based) with a second half (as in Ciconia) or subsequent *taleae* (as in *Musicalis scientia*) rhythmically replicating the first in all voices can be judged wholly (rather than intra-sectionally) isorhythmic.

8. Careless naming has led to historiographical distortion for both the fourteenth and the fifteenth centuries. The promotion of rhythmic identity and predetermined

conformity as primary generic features of more than a century of motet development has:

(a) impeded recognition of the great variety of strategies in motet composition
     from the early *ars nova* throughout the fourteenth century;
(b) narrowed the definition of motet to exclude some interestingly varied
     works;
(c) short-changed simple repetition, melodic repetition, and complex repetition
     patterns (including song tenors and non-coincident *talea–color* patterns);
(d) imposed ill-fitting French criteria on English and Italian motet traditions;
(e) historiographically distorted an evolving fourteenth-century genre, demo-
     nising artificially restrictive criteria as cerebral 'gothic' shackles;
(f) historiographically distorted the fifteenth-century evolution of the same
     underlying processes in the cyclic mass and structured motets by—
     wrongly—stressing their rejection of earlier processes, which now come to
     be redefined positively in terms of new humanistic expression.

Afterword

Some have responded coyly to my plea for a more thoughtful use of the term isorhythm,
using it as before, but apologetically or in scare quotes. It should be clear from the
foregoing that I do not outlaw 'isorhythm', but advocate restricting it to appropriate
applications. 'Isorhythmic' serves perfectly well for exact rhythmic iterations, where
rhythm but not pitch is repeated. If there is diminution, call it diminution; if there is
mensural redefinition or some other kind of reduction, call it that; if the same tenor notation is manipulated mensurally, call it homographic—a term that several colleagues
have found useful. And if there is repetition of rhythm *and* pitch, call it repetition,
without isolating rhythm. Reduced sections, however achieved, can be called reduced
or accelerated; they do not always correspond to a stricter definition of diminution.
Diminution is not a general term for acceleration in fourteenth-century theory; in
classic definitions by Johannes de Muris, it specifically required the notation to be
reinterpreted at the next lower level of note values.[54] If the relevant adjacent note-levels
correspond, with respect to duple or triple quality, the result may be the same as halving,
or duple proportion, a descriptive short-cut often taken then as now. But diminution is
not appropriate if the process is mensural, as in *Sub Arturo* or *Doctorum principem*; and
indeed in the extreme case of *Inter densas* the mensural manipulations do not achieve
successive reductions. If the tenor is notated at the level not of the first but of the final
statement (as in the Dunstaple motets mentioned above), its first statement may be in
augmentation, which problematises the term *integer valor*. Motets 'with isorhythm'
may serve where 'isorhythmic motet' claims too much. For a minority of motets before 1400 with reducing sections, and a majority in the early fifteenth century, complete isorhythm in all parts may be observed between the statements within each *color*
but not between *colores*. 'Pan-isorhythm' may be a suitable term for motets in which

---

[54] Bent, 'The Myth'.

64 COMPOSITIONAL TECHNIQUES

every note is rhythmically accounted for in one or more exact repetitions, as long as it is understood that the identity applies within and not between each successive reducing section.[55] 'Isoperiodic' will serve where sections of equal length are not isorhythmic, but it will not do for reduced or mensurally changed periods, where the periods are of different lengths. 'Proportioned' may serve to describe the consequences of diminution or mensural manipulation, but so to describe just the overall result may obscure the process by which that result was reached (as has been the case with the two different processes used by Dunstaple; see Ch. 25). By seeking greater refinement of classification and terminology to meet the challenge of this variety, we can hope to release motets without rhythmic reduction from the stigma of being more primitive, when they may explore *varietas* in other ways. To forgo the monolithic generic concept of 'the isorhythmic motet' may fruitfully complicate the writing of synthetic music history; but to interrogate and refine use of the term may open up the wide varieties of text–music constructions that characterise the surviving corpus of fourteenth-century motets in all their individuality.

---

[55] Earp calls Machaut's Motet 4 'highly "panisorhythmic"'; although there is a notable amount of rhythmic alignment between *taleae*, there is also sufficient deviation from exact replication to discourage the use of the term here.

PART II
THE MARIGNY MOTETS, BEYOND *FAUVEL*, AND VITRY

66 FAUVEL AND VITRY

Part II reflects a long-term interest in the interpolated version of the early fourteenth-century *Roman de Fauvel* in **Paris146**, whose components (music, poetic texts, narrative, history and art) had often been studied separately without reference to the others. A series of interdisciplinary seminars in Oxford and a conference in Paris culminated in the publication of Bent and Wathey (eds.), *Fauvel Studies* (1998). Chapter 3 is lightly revised from my contribution to that volume, a new view of the three motets on the historical figure of Enguerrand de Marigny and their double function in the Fauvel narrative. Chapters 4 and 5 deal at length with those motets; Chapter 6 deals with a motet that may have originally been intended for inclusion but was partially cannibalised for the Fauvellian agenda. Chapter 7 addresses related motets and manuscripts and their relation to Philippe de Vitry, whose motet *Vos/Gratissima* is the subject of Chapter 8.

3

Fauvel and Marigny: Which Came First?

The extended version of the *Roman de Fauvel* in Paris, BnF fr. 146 (**Paris146**) is famous for its many interpolations of music, text and images.[1] Three motets have been much discussed on account of their coded references to political events associated with the reign of Philip IV (the Fair) and the rise and fall of his opportunistic and treacherous counsellor Enguerrand de Marigny, allegorised in the incongruous rise of the bestial hybrid Fauvel and his deserved downfall. The three motets are all preserved anonymously and occur in this order in the *Fauvel* narrative:[2]

Aman novi/Heu Fortuna/Heu me, tristis est anima mea (f. 30ʳ, F 25, p.mus. 71): Ex. 5.1

Tribum/Quoniam/Merito hec patimur (ff. 41ᵛ–42ʳ, F 27, p.mus. 120): ▶ Ex. 4.1

Garrit gallus/In nova fert/Neuma (f. 44ᵛ, F 30, p.mus. 129): ▶ Ex. 4.5[3]

The texts are multivalent; obfuscation and veiled references do not always make it easy to distinguish primary from secondary meanings. Here the distinction matters, not least because of the arguments that have been offered with respect to the purpose, dating and authorship of these motets. Several other motets relate to historical events

---

[1] This chapter is revised from the version published as 'Fauvel and Marigny: Which Came First?' in Bent and Andrew Wathey (eds.), *Fauvel Studies: Allegory, Chronicle, Music and Image in Paris, Bibliothèque nationale de France, MS français 146* (Oxford, 1998), 35–52. It meets OUP's conditions for reuse without obtaining formal permission.

'Fauvel' in this chapter has two meanings: *Fauvel* is the interpolated *Roman de Fauvel* in **Paris146** (Paris, BnF fr. 146) and Fauvel is the character therein. Verse numbers are given in the editions of Långfors, *Le Roman de Fauvel* (L), whose text is used; S gives references in a more recent edition: Strubel, *Le Roman de Fauvel*; 'p.mus.' numbers refer to the texts of musical pieces as numbered in Dahnk, *L'Hérésie de Fauvel*, taken over by Strubel, and given in parentheses in Leo Schrade's edition after Schrade's sequential numbering of motets in PMFC 1 ('F'). L is also used for Long; context makes clear which is meant.

Paris146 can be viewed on Gallica at https://gallica.bnf.fr/ark:/12148/btv1b8454675g/f1.image.r= roman%20de%20fauvel (accessed 9.7.2020). The verbal text of the *roman* is edited in Långfors, *Le Roman de Fauvel*, that of the musical additions in Dahnk, *L'Hérésie de Fauvel*. The complete text of the expanded *roman* in **Paris146**, together with the texts of the musical interpolations, is published with a modern French translation by Strubel, *Le Roman de Fauvel*. The numerations of these three editions are cited here as Långfors, Dahnk, and Strubel. For full accounts of the short and long versions of *Fauvel* and of the other contents of **Paris146**, see the introduction to the facsimile of the complete manuscript in *Le Roman de Fauvel*, ed. Roesner et al., and also Bent and Wathey (eds.), *Fauvel Studies*. More recent studies of *Fauvel* include Dillon, *Medieval Music-Making*, and Marinescu, 'The Politics of Deception', q.v. for other recent bibliography.

[2] The coded political meanings were first identified by Becker, 'Fauvel', 36–42, and were brought to the attention of musicologists in Schrade, 'Philippe de Vitry'. Modern editions of the music of the motets are published in PMFC 1, and here as noted above. The motets (except *Garrit gallus*) were recorded by the Orlando Consort on 'Philippe de Vitry and the Ars Nova', CD-SAR 49, with accompanying translations by David Howlett. A rhythmically flexible performance of *Aman novi* was recorded by Sequentia on Deutsche Harmonia Mundi/BMG Classics (RD 77095).

[3] Transcriptions of *Garrit gallus* and *Tribum* are on the website (▶Exx. 4.1 and ▶4.5), of *Aman* in the book as Ex. 5.1, all designed to be used in conjunction with the commentaries in the relevant chapters. *Aman* and *Tribum* are numbered in longs, *Garrit gallus* in breves.

The Motet in the Late Middle Ages. Margaret Bent, Oxford University Press. © Oxford University Press 2023.
DOI: 10.1093/so/9780190063771.003.0004

68 FAUVEL AND VITRY

of the 1310s: the Templar crisis, the death of the emperor Henry VII in 1313, and the reigns of the French kings Louis X (1314–16) and Philip V (1316–22), sons of Philip the Fair (d. 1314):

Scariotis geniture/Jure quod/Superne matris, f. 2ʳ (F 5, p.mus. 5)

On the death of Emperor Henry VII, 24 August 1313

Nulla pestis est gravior/Plange, nostra regia/Vergente, f. 3ʳ (F 8, p.mus. 9)

Sense of crisis towards the end of the reign of Philip IV (d. 1314)

Detractor est nequissima/Qui secuntur castra/Verbum iniquum, f. 4ʳ (F 9, p.mus. 12)[4]

This has been conjectured to be in support of the Templars following their arrest on 14 September 1307. In his harsh review of Dahnk in *Neuphilologische Mitteilungen*, 37 (1936), 58–65, Långfors proposed an identification of Picquigny with the vidames of Amiens. Roesner et al., in *Le Roman de Fauvel*, 21 suggest that it might rather refer to the period after the death of Philip and to Messire Ferri de Piquegny who, according to the *Chronique métrique* in **Paris146**, led the purge of Marigny: see below

Desolata mater/Que nutritos/Filios enutrivi, f. 8ᵛ (F 13, p.mus. 27)

Against the Templars, referring to the campaign of 1312–14 and the Bulls of April and May 1312

Se cuers ioans/Rex beatus/Ave, f. 10ᵛ (F 15, p.mus. 32)

For Louis X, crowned 3 August 1315

Servant regem/O Philippe/Rex regum, ff. 10ᵛ–11ʳ (F 16, p.mus. 33)

For Philip V, and therefore not before mid-November 1316, following the death of Jehan, short-lived posthumous baby son of Louis X. Philip's coronation was in January 1317.[5]

An impetus to the publication of *Fauvel Studies* was that the many elements of **Paris146** had been edited and studied on separate tracks with little regard for their context.[6] Musicologists had tended to consider the motets as self-contained compositions, treating **Paris146** as just one of several sources transmitting them, and not seeing the project of the enlarged and interpolated *roman* as the primary reason for

---

[4] *Detractor est nequissima vulpis/Qui secuntur castra*: Dahnk identified the allusion to Lucan in the first line of the motetus. These words are also echoed in the last line of the triplum text of *Colla iugo/Bona condit*: 'Nulla fides pietasque viris qui castra secuntur' (There is no faith or piety in men who follow camps). The texts of *Colla/Bona* are preserved separately in a number of literary manuscripts, including the text of a non-extant contratenor: Wathey, 'The Motets of Vitry', 123 and 138. The vituperative nature of these texts, and the cross-references between them, suggest Vitry's authorship.

[5] The version of **Paris571** replacing Philip with 'Ludowice' is a later adaptation for St Louis, not for Louis X, and is therefore not the original version: 'Wathey, 'The Marriage of Edward III', 17–19.

[6] Bent and Wathey (eds.), *Fauvel Studies*, Introduction, especially 19, 22. Mühlethaler, *Fauvel au pouvoir*, 279. An excellent account of many aspects of the manuscript is given in *Le Roman de Fauvel*, ed. Roesner et al.

their existence.[7] It had usually been assumed that their real-life documentary function came first, that they were imported into or adapted for that manuscript, having been written outside it, and hence that their compositional order must be that of the historical narrative to which they refer. Concentration on their 'documentary' content has led to neglect of the fact that the three 'Marigny' motets also chart the forwards narrative of Fauvel, left to right through the manuscript of the *roman*, most explicitly in *Heu Fortuna*, the motetus which is placed in Fauvel's mouth following Fortuna's rejection of his marriage suit. But they also chart the backwards narrative of biting contemporary historical satire, which runs back to front, right to left, from the end of the *roman*.[8]

The motet texts point up the satirical allegory of current events and emphasise the unnatural reversals that are a constant theme of *Fauvel*.[9] The major source for the detail of these events is the *Chronique métrique* attributed to Geffroy de Paris, which ends **Paris146** (ff. 63ʳ–88ʳ). It provides much of the specific historical information relating to Marigny which underlies and complements the narrative in *Fauvel*.[10] Insofar as the other contents can be seen as part of the same project, the *Chronique* may not be an entirely impartial witness. The right order for that historical narrative is the wrong order for the topsy-turvy progress of Fauvel the hybrid horse–man; a fusion between these apparently colliding worlds is produced when the motets are seen in context. The text of the *roman* itself strongly invites this reading: Fauvel *fait tout par bestourne* (Långfors 1119, Strubel 1125), *Meine tout per antifrasin | C'est a dire par le contraire* (L 1184–85, S 1190–91). The wheel of Fortuna turns incessantly, changing high to low, far to near, back to front, signalling chronological paradoxes at many levels; it reverses Fauvel's fortunes. A striking example is the black baptism of the famous Fountain of Youth illustration that accompanies the motet *Tribum/Quoniam*, by both counts the central motet of the three (ff. 41ᵛ–42); by bathing (being baptised) in ordure, old men (Fauvel's vainglorious progeny) are rejuvenated, another trick of reversed chronology. A further subtlety is that they move (old to young) from right to left, a reversal within the order of the left-to-right *Fauvel* narrative. These reversals correspond to the description in *Fauvel* of Fortuna's wheels which move in contrary motion (see below), thus signalling the bi-directional narrative that is underscored by many markers in the texts as well as by musical and visual symbolism.[11] Fortuna also controls the elements: fire, earth, air (wind) and water are all present in the triplum of *Aman novi*.

---

[7] Some of the more modern *Fauvel* motets with *ars nova* characteristics (duple time, with up to five semibreves to the breve) are also found in later sources with updated notation. None of these copies pre-dates *Fauvel*; nor are any of the surviving manuscripts of the uninterpolated *Fauvel* earlier than **Paris146**.

[8] Roesner (*Le Roman de Fauvel*, 20) downplays the historical import and the relevance of Marigny: in *Aman/Heu* 'Haman, Phaeton, and Icarus are often used as *exempla* of pride ready to suffer a fall'. And despite a clear unfolding of the historical events, the authors say that 'the main point of their inclusion was to illustrate the moral fable of Fauvel, who was to be understood as himself, not merely a stand-in for Marigny'.

[9] Many aspects of reversal in *Fauvel* have been pointed out, for example in the analysis of *Je voi/Fauvel nous a fait/Autant* in Zayaruznaya, *The Monstrous New Art*, 46–52. Lawrence Earp alerted me to a remarkable publication by Riemann, 'Noch zwei verkannte Kanons', in which he interprets the text of p.mus.29, *Fauvel nous a fait present* (Fauvel: *autant m'est si poise arriere comme avant* and *car tout ce fait par contraire*) as an instruction to perform the piece in retrograde. Without cadences, the result is not very satisfactory.

[10] The chronicle is edited by Diverrès, *La Chronique métrique*. See also Dunbabin, 'The Metrical Chronicle', and especially Regalado, 'The *Chronique métrique*'.

[11] Illustrated by textual citations in Bent, 'Marigny', 40–43; the wheel, surprisingly, is not illustrated in **Paris146**. An excellent essay on this central character, Hunt, 'The Christianization of Fortune', was not ready in time to be included in Bent and Wathey (eds.), *Fauvel Studies*.

70 FAUVEL AND VITRY

The motets self-consciously emphasise this historical order with verb tenses suggesting not only self-evident *termini post quos* for their composition, but also *termini ante quos*. In *Garrit gallus/In nova*, Philip IV, the 'blind lion', is still alive (*monarchisat*, present tense), and the motet, it has been argued, must therefore have been composed before his death on 29 November 1314.[12] In *Tribum/Quoniam* the past tense (*regnaverat*) indicates that Philip is no longer reigning and that the motet must date from after his death (true) but, goes the argument, before Marigny's execution on 30 April 1315. In *Aman novi/Heu Fortuna* the body of Marigny has been washed by the rain on the gallows of Montfaucon; therefore it may date from up to two years after his execution, the period during which his body was left there as an example before it was finally released for burial in 1317.[13] Indeed the motet must be at least that late. But that is not the same as asserting that it must have been the last of the three motets to be composed, a claim that may not stand up to scrutiny.

The role and position of these topical motets in the interpolated *Fauvel* itself had hardly been addressed. Even the valuable study by Ernest Sanders considered only the external historical events and not any relevance they might have to the *Fauvel* narrative, neglecting to observe that the motetus *Heu Fortuna* is primarily Fauvel's first-person lament on his rejection by Fortuna.[14] *Heu Fortuna* also invokes Haman's execution: '*velud Aman morior*', says Fauvel in his love-death response to that rejection. The simultaneous triplum *Aman novi* further emphasises in its first word the image of Haman applied *post mortem* to Marigny, recapitulated and brought home in the same text as *noster Aman* (line 18, first person plural). 'In monte falconis' indicates Montfaucon, the gallows of Paris, on which Marigny had already been hanged. The Haman–Marigny link in the triplum makes sense of *velut Aman morior* in the motetus and connects Marigny, Haman and Fauvel, as will be recounted in Chapter 5. Marigny's death, like Haman's, is a real one on the gallows, but real death is not yet part of Fauvel's narrative. Downfall is predicted but withheld. Fauvel's words do double duty as Marigny's *ante mortem* lament, invoking Haman, at his execution, spoken by, or as if by, one not yet dead. The tenor is fashioned, exceptionally, from two chants: one from the Office of the Dead (*Heu me*) and the other from the Maundy Thursday chant *Tristis est anima mea*, expressing Christ's agony in Gethsemane.[15] Both, again, affirm the first person singular.

Liturgically the latter chant indicates the eve of Christ's crucifixion. In historical time the motetus signals the eve of Ascension, when Marigny was hanged (that is, Wednesday, 30 April 1315), with much play in the motet texts and the *Chronique métrique* on height, ascent, and fall. The triplum refers to that hanging after the fact. In

---

[12] Thus Sanders, 'The Early Motets of Philippe de Vitry', 36: 'probably October–November 1314, certainly no later, since it reflects the state of affairs before Philippe's death'; Schrade, 'Philippe de Vitry', 338; and Leech-Wilkinson, 'The Emergence of Ars nova', 307: 'before 29.xi.14'. Roesner et al., in *Le Roman de Fauvel* (24b) are prepared to stretch this to 'cannot be later than the beginning of 1315'.

[13] *Le Roman de Fauvel*, ed. Roesner et al., 52. See Chs. 4 and 5.

[14] Sanders, 'The Early Motets of Philippe de Vitry'. Besseler and Schrade had also made the same assumption.

[15] *Aman* is a clearer case than in others that have been suggested; see Rankin, 'The Divine Truth of Scripture'. One such, in a motet securely attributed to Vitry by internal signature and in the *Quatuor principalia*, is *Cum statua/Hugo*, ingeniously argued in Zayaruznaya, *The Monstrous New Art*, 113–18, where she engages with Clark, 'New Tenor Sources', 121–24. And it has been suggested that Machaut's Motet 5, *Aucune gent/Qui plus aimme/Fiat voluntas tua* is either a conflation of two chants or an extensively manipulated chant. See Boogaart, *Guillaume de Machaut ... Motets*, 198–99.

Fauvel's time, his lament is on the eve of Pentecost; the following day will mark his marriage to Vaine Gloire. Similar counterpoints and conflicts between liturgical time and the narrative time of *Fauvel* are worked out on a large scale.[16]

The three Marigny motets are presented in **Paris146** in reverse chronological order from that in which the historical events to which they refer took place and which their verb tenses underscore. This fact is known, but has usually been mentioned without comment, or even been taken to imply support for the view that the motets were imperfectly adapted to their new context, having originally been intended for a different one. It is my goal here to show that this order might have been purposeful, and hence to propose that they were designed from the beginning for *Fauvel*. In the *Fauvel* narrative, *Aman novi/Heu Fortuna* precedes *Tribum/Quoniam*, which precedes *Garrit gallus/In nova*. Fauvel's lament in the motetus *Heu Fortuna*, at least, is in the correct order in relation to *Fauvel*. The other two motets have more oblique and generalised references to Fauvel, which has led to their function in *Fauvel* being considered secondary, as has the apparently wrong order of their reference to historical events. But many planning details of **Paris146** show increasingly that nothing about its contents or order was casual. If the motets are made to act their parts in the narrative, as are the masked characters of the charivari, they may not be literally documentary. The tenses of their ostensible order tell us not about their order of composition, as has been assumed, but rather about the fiction of their reversal and double use. *Garrit gallus/In nova* presents events that are current and about to happen; if, as I suggest, it is merely feigning the present tense, its actual composition is no more confined to the time while Philip IV was still alive than the *post factum* prophecies in the Divine Comedy are bound to the time before those events occurred.[17] Not only were all these motets of current interest; they were planned as *exempla* for this grand *admonitio* to the royal house, and are its *raison d'être*. The *Roman de Fauvel* is not, after all, a newspaper to be discarded when topical interest is lost. It has already made recent or even current events into art of timeless and lasting value. As Ezra Pound put it, 'Literature is news that stays news'.

The chronology that has resulted from a documentary reading of the political texts apart from their context in *Fauvel* has led to arguments about the stylistic development of their composer(s). Schrade had dated the Marigny motets by historical event and proposed that all three were by Philippe de Vitry. Sanders used those datings in conjunction with his analyses to argue a chronological progression from less to more tightly ordered pieces, applying that hypothesis, in turn, to cast doubt upon Philippe de Vitry's authorship of the less 'tidy' pieces.[18] Like Schrade before him, he was concerned to refine the Vitry canon. Schrade had built it up; Sanders added and subtracted pieces, partly on grounds of style, on a rather rigid formal criterion of 'modular numbers', and of association with other compositions. Edward Roesner further trimmed Vitry's oeuvre—and indeed his role in the creation of *Fauvel*—to a cautious minimum, arguing that only five

---

[16] See Dillon, 'The Profile of Philip V'.

[17] Dante's *Purgatorio* dates from about 1310, but refers prophetically to 1300 and 1306, the kidnap of Boniface VIII, and the transfer of the papacy to Avignon.

[18] Schrade, 'Philippe de Vitry'; Sanders, 'The Early Motets of Philippe de Vitry', 36: 'Apart from the fact, however, that these two works would be the only motets by Vitry to be preserved as *unica* in f.fr. 146, their attribution to him would force us to postulate a curious inconsistency in the composer's development: both motets, written after as advanced a piece as *Garrit gallus*, lack a coherent phrase structure and generally exhibit a conservative facture.'

72 FAUVEL AND VITRY

or at most seven motets (all or most outside *Fauvel*) are likely to be his, one of which (the late *Phi millies ad te/O creator*) survived only as text without music. Most of the triplum has since been recovered.[19]

First, it may be responded that more criteria for compositional ingenuity can be proposed than the particular one demonstrated by Sanders. Neither isorhythm nor upper-part periodicity is the only criterion of craft. *Aman novi/Heu Fortuna* is a superbly well-made piece, if not conventionally so with respect to isorhythm and upper-voice periodicity. Broader criteria should restrain the judgement as to whether a piece is by the same or a different composer until a wider range of techniques has been established and until there is a clearer consensus about features that are likely or not to be imitable. The quest for a single line of development along which compositions can be neatly arranged chronologically fails to allow for outliers, the cultivation of deliberate effects, innovative originality or deliberate archaising, all of which are arguably present in *Fauvel*. It also fails to recognise that many early *ars nova* motets are unique essays that neither conform to nor create a template. To rescue *Aman novi/Heu Fortuna* and *Orbis orbatus/Vos pastores* from charges of untidiness may undo Sanders's reasons for taking them away from Vitry, but that does not yet prove that they or any other motets are *by* Vitry.[20]

Sanders accepts Vitry's authorship for *Garrit gallus/In nova* on grounds of its shared cantus firmus with the ascribed (non-*Fauvel*) motet *Douce plaisance/Garison* and supports Vitry's authorship of *Floret/Florens* on the same grounds (discussed in Ch. 6). Sanders argues that the same cantus firmus makes it likely that those pieces are by the same composer, without consideration of the ease with which this could be a copied feature or a homage, and without observing that shared tenors occur in motets by different composers (Machaut and Vitry, Damett and Sturgeon, and many more).[21] He removes *Aman novi/Heu Fortuna*, even though it is on Marigny, as being too untidy to have been written after the 'tidier' *Garrit gallus/In nova*. As will be shown below, this is inconsistent with his bid to add the 'untidy' *Floret/Florens* to the Vitry canon, but to remove it from the *Fauvel* project on grounds that it was already obsolete.[22] This argument cannot be invoked without raising the question why this consideration did not prevent the inclusion in *Fauvel* of the other motets that deal with the same series of events and would be similarly obsolete.

Second, even if style chronology could be demonstrated, we still need not assume that the piece referring to the latest events was composed last. And even if the composer is the same, a few months is probably too narrow a time frame for such a finely tuned range of stylistic nuance to be established as the basis for a compositional chronology.

---

[19] *Le Roman de Fauvel*, ed. Roesner et al., 39–42. For the triplum see Lüdtke, 'Kleinüberlieferung'; Zayaruznaya, 'New Voices'; Zayaruznaya, *The Monstrous New Art*.

[20] *Orbis/Vos* can now be added to the list of motets surviving outside *Fauvel* (in **Koblenz701**). See Kügle, 'The Aesthetics of Fragments'. Most of the *Fauvel* motets also found in later copies have at some point been tentatively attributed to Vitry. Whether his authorship played any part in their continued transmission, or should play any part in our attributions, remains to be investigated.

[21] See Leech-Wilkinson, 'Related Motets', for relationships between motets by, for example, Vitry and Machaut. In **OH** nos. 112, 113, Damett and Sturgeon divide a chant between them as the cantus firmus of those two motets; Machaut's Motet 17 uses part of the same tenor as Vitry, *Vos quid admiramini: Gaude virgo gloriosa, super omnes speciosa* (see Ch. 8); Motet 13 has the unidentified tenor *Ruina*, also used in *Super/Presidentes* in **Paris146**.

[22] Sanders, 'The Early Motets of Philippe de Vitry', 35–36, and Clark, 'The Flowering', 178 n. 12.

A complex Ovidian textual-musical quotation, to be explored below, seemed to suggest that *Garrit gallus/In nova* and *Tribum/Quoniam* were indeed composed in the order implied by their ostensible historical narrative sequence. I would now argue that the motets could equally well have been worked out concurrently so that the material seems to refer to itself, without necessarily confining the compositional dates to the apparent historical sequence. With respect to chronological assumptions, one might ask, further: why should the master of the *Fauvel* miniatures have painted more conventionally in his later work, after painting with such originality, verve, and imagination in **Paris146**?[23]

Third, we cannot assume that Vitry, simply because, apart from Machaut, he is the only known composer of the time by whom we knowingly have any motets, must be the author of all competent motets or only of the most competent ones. The issue of personal stylistic development becomes moot, even if Vitry's authorship of these pieces can be argued on other grounds. Roesner has objected that the three motets are unlikely to be by the same composer because this would show an undue obsession with Marigny.[24] But there is no shortage of obsession in *Fauvel*, whether it be manifested in the historical events in which Marigny was the villain, in the collective obsession of the compilers, or in the fauvelisation of pre-existent pieces. Daniel Leech-Wilkinson narrowed the composition dates and the compositional progression of the *Fauvel* motets.[25] He distinguished two composers for the advanced motets. One may be Vitry; the other he called 'the Master of the Royal Motets'. He assumed the evident *termini post quos* that refer to events that have happened—the king has died, Marigny has been hanged. This is obviously true. But like Sanders and Roesner, he went on to impose *termini ante quos*, assuming that a piece would not have been written after a later event that overtakes it. All these writers have assumed or implied that the compiler assembled his material, both old material for refurbishing and modern pieces, from older and current repertory external to the *Fauvel* project itself. This is very probably true of the imported older material, some of which was purposefully customised for *Fauvel*. But the issue here is rather: were the most modern motets, up-to-date in style and topical content, written for some other purpose independent of the *Fauvel* project, or were they purpose-made for it?[26]

As Roesner pointed out in private correspondence, a consequence of assuming that all three motets were written for *Fauvel* is to place them at the very centre of the early *ars nova* and at the apex of the transmission of this repertory. There is clearly a problem with this assumption with respect to their transmission, for the copies in **Paris146** have errors of text and music that disqualify them from being the source for other surviving or ideally correct copies. But is it not possible that the problem here lies in the **Paris146** copies themselves? The material collected for the compilation must have existed in some more temporary form before being copied into the manuscript, and those working materials could themselves have formed the stemmatic apex of the often inaccurate copies. Other interpolated *Fauvel* manuscripts with music are known to have

---

[23] Listed by Avril in *Le Roman de Fauvel*, ed. Roesner et al., 46.
[24] Ibid. 42b.
[25] Leech-Wilkinson, 'The Emergence of *Ars nova*'.
[26] The consensus seems to have moved since the first publication of this chapter towards recognising that the newest *Fauvel* motets were indeed newly composed for the **Paris146** compilation.

74 FAUVEL AND VITRY

existed. Some of the material included in or rejected from this compilation may have been used in those other versions. **Paris146** may not have been the only or even the best repository of compositions designed for a larger *Fauvel* enterprise.

But if these motets were from the start conceived as admonitory exempla, serving the dual purposes of *Fauvel* narrative and of historical narrative, their actual order of composition remains undetermined and perhaps irrelevant, undermining attempts to establish composer chronology based on the historical dates. They take their place in *Fauvel* as reflective 'arias' glossing the main text and, in the pivotal case of the motetus *Heu Fortuna*, as direct speech by Fauvel after Fortuna's rejection. Book II has more direct speech by the protagonists, in line with greatly increased interpolation. Fortuna, in the guise of a woman, has two aspects, a counterpart to the hybrid presentation of Fauvel. The *Fauvel* story itself is her deceptively pleasant side, while the dark and melancholic underside is that of the historical exemplum. To each of Fortuna's two wheels is fixed another smaller wheel within the larger that turns in the opposite direction. It is through these that Fortuna controls time, and it is their motions that constantly cause the world's affairs to change. Fortuna's wheels, her control of time, and her contrary nature may be illustrated as follows:

Fortuna's two wheels and their contrary subwheels

La seignorie temporel,
Que deust estre basse Iune,
Est par la roe de Fortune
Souveraine de sainte Eglise.

Sainte Yglise est au dessous mise
Si qu'el donne poi de lumiere;
Ainsi va ce devant derriere:
Les membres sont dessus le chief.
  (L 472–9; S 470–77)

Deux roez ot devant Fortune
Qui tous jours tournient, mes l'une
Va tost et l'autre lentement,
Et en chascune vraiement
A une mendre roe mise
Tout par dedens et a, tel guise
Que mouvement contraire tient
Contre la roe ou el se tient
Ices roez sans séjourner
Font l'estat du monde tourner.
  (L 1931–40; S 1966–75)

Aussi dois des roes entendre
Dont chascune en a une mendre,
Et ont contraires mouvemens

Fortuna's doubleness and control of time

Mes diversement mi transporte,
Et ma maniere si est double
As uns sui belle, as autres trouble.
Je sui fille du roy des rois.
  (L 2179–83; S 2215–19)

Le pouoir m'est commis en temps
Par quoy tout mouvement terminent;
Par moi commencent et definent,
Et temps n'est fors que la mesure
De tous mouvemens de nature.
. . . .

Le temps ay, par quoy je mesure
Du monde tout l'ambleure.
Onques si tost n'amble ne point
Que du temps n'y mete le point,
Par le quel je tantost compasse,
Le present ainsi com il passe,
Tout soit le present si menuz
Qu'il ne puisse estre retenuz.
Mez ma dite commission

Faudra quant faudra motion,
Car le monde adonc finera
Tantost que mouvoir cessera.

Et par divers entendemens.
(L 2689–92; S 2721–24)

Ainsi cil qui est haut montez,
Soit plain de mal ou de bontez,
Mainte chose le contrarie
Par verite ou par envie

Ou par grant tristece ou par cure,
Par maladie ou aventure.
Et ce dit la roe petite
Qui contre la grant tous jours lite;
Car il n'est nul, sachiez sans doute,
A qui Fortune se doint toute.
(L 2711–20; S 2743–52)

(L2218–22, 2229–40; S 2254–58,
2265–76)

Fortune si n'est autre chose
Que la providence divine,
Qui dispose, mesure et termine
Par compas de droite reson.
(L 2254–57; S 2290–93)

Fortune's two wheels illustrate contrary motion, back-to-front and up-and-down reversals. The large wheel finds a parallel in the daily east–west motion of the *primum mobile*—the heaven of the fixed stars—and the contrary small wheel in the proper, periodic movements of the seven planetary heavens, which move south-west to north-east on an inclined plane. It is surprising that Fortuna's all-important wheels are not illustrated in **Paris146**, and that depictions of her and her attributes are here less interesting and varied than those of the hybrid Fauvel himself. By contrast, another copy of the uninterpolated *roman* is prefaced by a striking image of Fortuna.[27] The most conspicuous wheels in **Paris146** are the four on the chariot of Hellequin. Was the manuscript perhaps at one stage intended to have four Marigny motets, or four royal motets? There is some evidence for both suggestions.

The emphasis on Fortuna's wheels in the text suggests why *Fauvel* presents us with different chronological tracks. The *roman* is unfolded in a main wheel, while the little wheel, the contemporary political narrative, goes against it in the opposite direction. This notion is echoed in musical and verbal palindromes, in superimposed motet texts, in strong hints of reversal in all three Marigny motet texts, and in the arrangement of the *roman* itself. The last line of the triplum *Aman novi* is 'Non eodem cursu respondent ultima primis'—not by the same revolution do the last respond to the first. 'Sic nec est reversus' (line 10) likewise suggests the cursus of Fortuna's wheels within wheels described in the motetus text *Heu Fortuna*. Soon after Fortuna has described her wheels the effect is manifested: Fauvel feels the reversal of his own fortunes. The motets are placed in the 'correct' historical order until the effect of Fortuna's wheels is felt at *Aman novi/Heu Fortuna*, a turning point of the *Fauvel* narrative. The motetus *Heu Fortuna* is central to the *Fauvel* narrative as well as being historically the most explicit of the three

[27] **Paris2195**, f. 156ᵛ. See https://gallica.bnf.fr/ark:/12148/btv1b60003385/f320.item (last accessed 18.7.2020); reproduced in black and white in Bent and Wathey (eds.), *Fauvel Studies*, 42. See also **MachautC**, f. 30, reproduced in Zayaruznaya, 'She has a Wheel', 197 and in Earp and Hartt (eds.), *Poetry, Art, and Music*, Fig. 4.18.

motets. It must have been written for *Fauvel*, but at the same time with very precise historical resonances, and is announced in the lines preceding the motetus as *Fauvel's* lament in his own voice, as will be set out in Chapter 5.

These motets are not pre-existent compositions or hasty adaptations; they must have been written expressly for *Fauvel* with deliberately double meaning, their political message tailored to their place in *Fauvel*. If we turn the focus to their primary role in **Paris146**, a view largely absent from discussions of the motets, factors other than external historical narrative must determine that role, their dating, and their order in the manuscript. The habit of making texts do double duty was embedded in the motet tradition from the start, when sacred and profane love were boldly pitted against each other in the juxtaposition of liturgical and secular texts and tunes. The opportunity to exercise and develop new notational possibilities in the early fourteenth century must also have been stimulated by the *Fauvel* project, another sense in which *Fauvel* may have prompted the compositions rather than being prompted by them.

Among many hybrid aspects of **Paris146** are the fauvelised musical compositions in which older chants or motets are changed or patched up with *Fauvel* material, or placed in contexts wildly different from their original ones, with purposeful perversity. But some of the newer compositions are unlikely to have had a previous existence and are more likely to have been composed for *Fauvel*. Some of the texts mix French and Latin, biblical and classical quotations, rhythmic and metrical lines. Juxtapositions in the same motet, as will be shown for *Aman novi/Heu Fortuna*, may perhaps be considered a further enhancement of the hybrid theme.[28] The Renard tradition unnaturally substitutes animals for humans, as also happens in *Tribum/Quoniam* and *Garrit gallus/In nova*. Roesner et al. write (*Le Roman de Fauvel*, 20b): 'The fox who rules in place of the blind lion, who gorges on chickens, and who sucks the blood of the sheep while the cock crows weeping is meant to be understood as Fauvel himself, and not merely as a stand-in for Marigny'. Surely it can be both. The blind lion is Philip IV, so identified (there as *debonair*) at the end of Book I, as well as in the *dits* in **Paris146**. *Fauvel* is the primary narrative, but Fortuna's reverse wheel carries the Marigny story, backwards, as counter-plot, and in that counter-plot Marigny is primary.

The climax of the transformational symbolism comes in the final two Marigny motets that are linked to each other and to *Fauvel* by building on different lines from Ovid—final in their present manuscript order, *Tribum* and *Garrit gallus*. The final column of the body of *Fauvel* is headed by the first line of the *Metamorphoses*, 'In nova fert animus mutatas dicere formas', that most famous of first lines, and most famous signal of animal transformation. Fauvel does everything in reverse, by its opposite; how better to depict that than to start from the end with a famous beginning, signalling the reverse counter-narrative. *Garrit gallus/In nova* presents the lamenting Frenchman in the voice of the lamenting author (maybe Vitry), for Ovidian purposes a cock, lamenting the fox. The fox is not only Marigny but also the antecedent of Fauvel and the Renard of earlier *romans*, in which the lion-king Noble is deceived

---

[28] Assuming only the historical meaning, Sanders ('The Early Motets of Philippe de Vitry', 32) states that Haman is Marigny, here and in *Floret/Florens*. But Fauvel is also Haman and Fauvel is also Marigny.

FAUVEL AND MARIGNY   77

by Renard the wily fox, a clear model for King Philip as the blind lion and Marigny as the fox.[29] This reading of the motets is supported from the text: Fauvel's palace was painted with the story of Renard (L 1357–58, S 1393–94), implying that the fox of earlier *romans* is metamorphosed here into the horse Fauvel, or at least is his role model. The Ovidian motets gloss the bestial transformations of *Fauvel*, to show how humans become animals, or by currying Fauvel (as in 'currying favour') reduce themselves to the status of animals.[30] The extra twist here is that Fauvel the horse, led by Fortuna upstairs from the stable on the first folio as the first stage of *his* hybrid metamorphosis, becomes Fauvel the half-human hybrid who flouts nature. Marigny the human, through his Renard-like fox identity, the *vulpis* of *Garrit gallus/In nova*, becomes Fauvel the hybrid. Marigny's transformation is 'first' recounted, as reverse narrative, in *Garrit gallus* at the end of *Fauvel*, 'starting' at the end, at the top of the last column, with *In nova* [*sic*] *fert* at its 'beginning', and balancing Fauvel's fully equine appearance at the beginning of the manuscript.

Apart from a short *envoi* on f. 45 (the final drinking song), starting from the end, *Garrit gallus* ends the body of the *roman*, whose final folio (f. 44^v, the 'backside' of the last full folio, and its right-hand column, which is the beginning of the backwards sequence) records the grim consequences of this transformation with a famous introductory line that not only serves both narratives, but also puts the beginning at the end, underscored throughout by musical and textual puns on ideas of metamorphosis and reversal. Indeed, it almost amounts to a palindrome for the bi-directional narrative, also reflected in the musically palindromic tenor of *Garrit gallus*, to be discussed below.

Ovid's famous opening line not only signals a beginning, starting from the end, but also parallels the first recto folio of the 'forwards' narrative of *Fauvel*, with its striking illustrations, generically hybrid musical transformations, and ostentatiously innovative musical notation: there are three oblique minim upstems at the end of staff 3 of *Quare fremuerunt* on f. 1^r, probably the earliest instance of stemmed minims. Fauvel started there as fully horse, but by the end of the narrative, in the Fountain of Youth scene, his progeny (begotten with his human hind quarters on Vain Glory, as shown in the nuptial miniature on f. 34) appear fully human. Already old men, they are transformed (backwards) into youths, albeit by black baptism in ordure and sins, making the solemn Christian ritual of rebirth into a mere trick with time. They move from right to left, in the direction of the 'backwards' narrative. This scene is accompanied by the second-from-the-end, second in narrative order Marigny motet, *Tribum/Quoniam*, a piece strongly marked with respect to reversal.

---

[29] The fox is also the subject of the motetus of another Fauvel motet, *Detractor est nequissimus vulpis/Qui secuntur castra*, which is also in **Paris571**. Both upper voices in both sources have a pair of little strokes at the beginning, as does the motetus of *Servant/Ludowice*, implying some level of duple mensuration. In both motets the modus is perfect and tempus imperfect; major prolation would be expected from the Fauvel notation, but **Paris571** is more ambiguous and inconsistent. While some groups clearly specify major prolation by stemming, up and down, there are some groups of four, all with minim stems, that might suggest minor prolation. (The triplum of both motets is not in the left- but in the right-hand column.)

[30] L 335–37, S 333–35: *Mes or est du tout berstorne | Ce que Diex avoit atourne | Que hommes sont devenus bestes*. And L 416–18, S 414–16: *Mes Fauvel, qui trestout desvoie, | A tant fait que cest luminare | Est tout berstornei* [**Paris146**: *bestourne*] *au contraire*'. With respect to the substitution of a horse for a fox, Jean-Claude Mühlethaler (*Fauvel au pouvoir*, pt. I, ch. 2) has pointed out that the horse has associations with *luxuria* (a particular vice of the *Fauvel* programme) and the Apocalypse, also strongly evoked here.

78   FAUVEL AND VITRY

That motet could have been planned to start at the top of f. 42^r but in fact begins two lines earlier at the end of f. 41^v. The layout is so contrived that the words *Fortuna cito vertere*, set to a melodic palindrome, appear at the top of the page, another strong hint of reversal. The tenor is redundantly notated twice to fill the space gained by starting the triplum early. In this context we are surely to understand the 'tribe' as referring to Fauvel's progeny too. As the central of the three Marigny motets, *Tribum/Quoniam* is the pivot for their reverse historical order. Marigny is most clearly Fauvel when the two voices of Marigny and Fauvel are united in *Aman novi/Heu Fortuna*, the third of the Marigny motets (Ch. 5) and the third from the end of *Fauvel* (other motets and musical items intervene—the sequence of Marigny motets is not uninterrupted). Here, too, there is a contrary direction, animal to hybrid, hybrid to man, and man to hybrid in the lament that serves them both.[31] In addition, the use of animals to represent human forces at the most pointed part of the *admonitio* is an essential part of the apocalyptic strand of the *roman*.

All three Marigny motets, and several other *Fauvel* motets as well, are saturated with themes and structures of reversal and inversion in music and text.[32] The wrong order for the historical narrative is the correct order for the topsy-turvy world of *Fauvel*, and it is that world we deal with when the motets are seen in context. Fauvel operates in reverse, as shown above. Fortuna has raised up Fauvel against reason, *contraire a raison* (L, S 23); and *fortune va sans reson | et si regne en toute seson* (L 297–98; S 295–96). She is unstable; her wheel turns incessantly, changing high to low and far to near, back to front: *Que Fortune qui n'est pas ferme, | Et qui de torneir ne se terme, | Le plus avant retornera, | De haut bas, de loing pres fera* (L, S 79–82). Above all, Fortuna controls time, the beginning and end of time (L 2218–36; S 2254–72), and this is contrived in the art of time, measured music. We need hardly look further than Fortuna's bidirectional wheels to corroborate the bold execution of chronological paradoxes at so many levels in *Fauvel*, a narrative that is already *contre raison*, a grand double negative, a vivid manifestation of Fortuna.

Let us return briefly to the junction of Books I and II, ff. 10–11.[33] Fortuna's control of time by means of liturgical reference starts precisely here, immediately before the three royal references that are placed between the date of book I, 1310, on f. 10 (c) and its *explicit* on f. 11. The first of these royal references is one of the few insertions of new verse lines into book I of the *roman*; most of those insertions are on this page, and the remainder are in book II. Philip IV, the young debonair lion, grandson of St Louis, reigned *jadis* and is now dead. The addition recording his death—in 1314, a striking juxtaposition of dates after the just-advertised 1310—also offers a deliberate emphasis on verb tenses:[34]

> Regnaut li lyons debonaires
> De qui fu plus douz li afaires

---

[31] The Trinity motet *Firmissime/Adesto* stands between the two Ovidian motets, its accompanying miniatures displaying the figure of Christ crucified that alludes to the tenor of *Aman novi/Heu Fortuna*. But Fauvel as a transformed Renard is equally present in *Tribum/Quoniam* and *Garrit gallus/In nova*.

[32] See *Le Roman de Fauvel*, ed. Roesner et al., 41b for discussion of change and reversal.

[33] Discussed also in Brown, 'Rex ioians' and Dillon, 'The Profile of Philip V'.

[34] Philip the Fair died on 29 November 1314. This is not the first mention of Philip IV (who succeeded his father in 1285); the 'neveu St Louis' is mentioned as having dealt with the Templars (L 1005, S 1011). The date 6 December 1314 given in some manuscripts (but not this one) for the completion of Book II is exactly one week after the death of Philip IV. Both days were Fridays, respectively preceding and following the first Sunday of Advent, which may tie them to the liturgical calendar played out in *Fauvel* and provide the occasion for some of its portrayals of a double narrative.

Que il n'eust besoing este;

Ce li fist la grant honeste

Qui en li tout ades regna.

Certes ie croi qu'il le regne a

Du roiaume de paradis.

Cilz fu Phelippes, fius iadis

Du tres bon roi hardi Phelippes

Qui en Arragon lessa les pippes;

Ci si fu filz de saint Loys.

Du tout ci mons dit assoys

[f. 10^v] Recitant de lui un motet.

Ha, sire diex! comme il flotet

Par mer du cueur et marchoit terre

Pour le saint sepucre conquerre!

Se li autre a li garde preissent,

D'amer Fauvel ne s'entremeissent:

Car loiaute et verite

Retornassent, Fauvel gite.

(f. 10^{r-v}; Dahnk, vv. 15–34, Strubel 1241–60)

We are led at this moment to expect a motet for Philip IV, but instead there follows one for his son and successor, Louis X (*Se cuers ioians/Rex beatus/Ave*: F 15, p.mus. 32), and then the motet for his younger son Philip V *qui regne ores* (*Servant regem/O Philippe/Rex regum*, ff. 10^v–11^r (F 16, p.mus. 33).[35] The added verses emphasising Philip IV's descent from St Louis, and the motets for the two brother kings, are placed in historically correct order at the very end of Book I (ff. 10^v–11^r), unlike the historical Marigny motets distributed in deliberately reverse order towards the end of book II. Were there once intended to be three motets here, for the three adult kings who have come blasphemously to curry Fauvel, anticipating the Antichrist of book II?[36] Fauvel is depicted on the facing page (f. 11), mocking them in royal majesty while usurping (sitting on) their throne.

And the current pair of royal motets is preceded by the first wholly French-texted motet in the collection, *Je voi douleur/Fauvel nous a fait/Autant* (F 14, p.mus. 29), a motet that emphasises Fauvel both in the motetus and in the tenor, which is put into Fauvel's mouth in the first person and signals reversal: *autant m'est si poise arriere comme avant*.[37] French was previously used in a *Fauvel* motet only for alternating lines in the 'hybrid' triplum of *Detractor est/Qui secuntur/Verbum iniquum* (F 9,

---

[35] Capital F here denotes Fauvel numbers, not folios.

[36] The author tells of a dream of four kings. The fourth king, the infant John (known as the bean king), is also mentioned in *Un songe*, cited in Morin, 'Jehannot de Lescurel'. See also Brown, 'Rex ioians' and Dillon, 'The Profile of Philip V'. The three kings could also be a blasphemous allusion to the three kings who came to worship the infant Christ.

[37] The triplum is framed (palindromically) by the couplet *Je voi doulour avenir | car tout ce fait par contraire* reflecting the tenor's 'weighing the same at the beginning and the end', another instance of reversal. Zayaruznaya, *The Monstrous New Art*, 46 presents this motet as 'the superimposition of a body on a piece of music', also discussed in Earp, 'Isorhythm', 90–91. The upper-part texts reinforce and augment the lessons of the tenor, as they do in *Aman*.

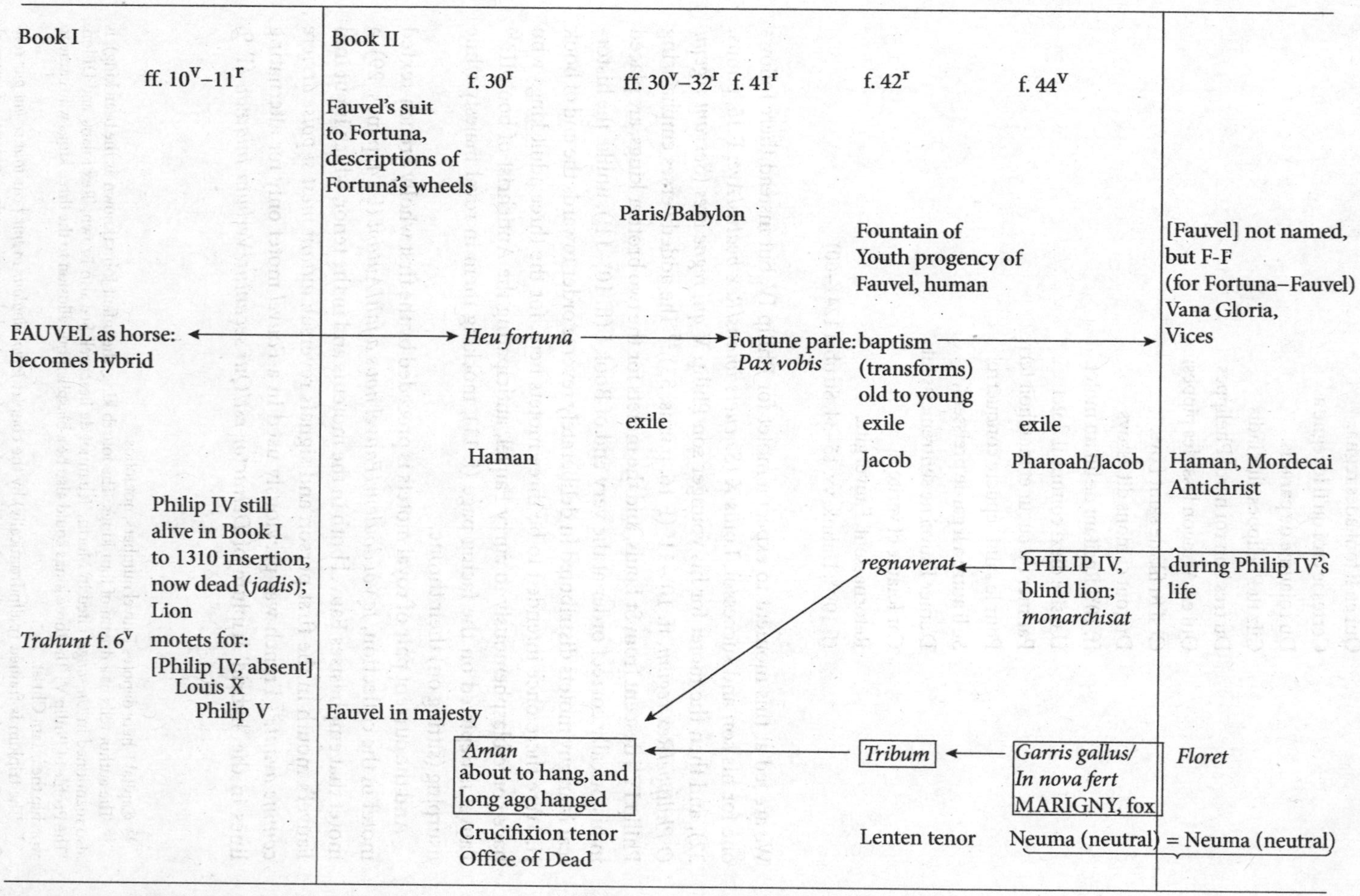

Book I | **Book II**

ff. 10ᵛ–11ʳ

- FAUVEL as horse: becomes hybrid
- Philip IV still alive in Book I to 1310 insertion, now dead (*jadis*); Lion
- motets for: [Philip IV, absent] Louis X, Lion, Philip V
- *Trahunt* f. 6ᵛ
- Fauvel in majesty

f. 30ʳ

- Fauvel's suit to Fortuna, descriptions of Fortuna's wheels
- *Heu fortuna*
- Haman
- *Aman* about to hang, and long ago hanged
- Crucifixion tenor Office of Dead

ff. 30ᵛ–32ʳ

- Paris/Babylon
- exile

f. 41ʳ

- Fortune parle: *Pax vobis* — baptism (transforms) old to young
- exile

f. 42ʳ

- Fountain of Youth progeny of Fauvel, human
- Jacob
- exile
- *regnaverat*
- *Tribum*
- Lenten tenor

f. 44ᵛ

- [Fauvel] not named, but F-F (for Fortuna–Fauvel) Vana Gloria, Vices
- Haman, Mordecai Antichrist
- Pharoah/Jacob
- exile
- PHILIP IV, blind lion; *monarchisat* — during Philip IV's life
- *Garris gallus/In nova fert* MARIGNY, fox
- *Floret*
- Neuma (neutral) = Neuma (neutral)
- Lenten tenor

Fig. 3.1 A much-simplified diagram of part of the *Fauvel* narrative, left to right, and historical narrative, right to left

p.mus. 12) in book I, which perhaps has a vaguer reference to Marigny dating from the time of Philip the Fair, but it is not discussed here as a Marigny motet. The use of French in a motet is thus set up in immediate anticipation of the very next motet, for Louis X, *Se cuers ioians/Rex beatus/Ave*, whose French triplum creates an irreverent hybrid with the royal Latin motetus: the French-speaking Fauvel has inserted himself most unsuitably into a royal context, just before the invocation of the Holy Spirit at the anointing (into which in turn is inserted with calculated incongruence the rondeau *Porchier miex*, p.mus. 30): 'I'd rather be a swineherd than curry Fauvel', as he will in the miniature following the royal motets defile the royal throne of France.[38]

The trio of kings at the junction of books I and II points forward to the trio of motets at the end of the *Fauvel* narrative, where the contrary motion of the motet sequence begins.[39] The young debonair lion at the end of book I, Philip the Fair, is the blind lion of the two Marigny motets placed at the end of book II. Are we also meant to read *Garrit gallus/In nova*, where Philip is alive, as balancing a missing motet for him at the end of book I which marks his death, with a similar emphasis on tenses in both places? The three royal statements are in correct, or 'forward', chronological order, which already suggests that the project may have been fashioned retrospectively after the death of at least one of them. Some of these forwards and backwards directions are shown in simplified form in Fig. 3.1. If the double function of these motets in *Fauvel* is primary, their actual order of composition becomes moot. Relationships between the motets do not prevent them from being written at roughly the same time, after all the events to which they refer had happened. This places them after 1317, probably by *c.* 1320, but in any case before the death of Philip V in 1322. In any case, they are too close together in time to encourage any secure stylistic separation. The Marigny motets, at least, must have been planned together, whether or not they are the work of the same composer, and whatever was the precise order of their composition, both words and music. Such planning may be partially extended to other motets, some of them less clearly or not at all topical, by means of cross-references, reversals, palindromes and other structural features. These considerations blur questions of individual authorship and also increase the likelihood that some of the non-topical motets, too, were purpose-made for *Fauvel*. Not only do they offer a caution against over-literal dating according to the topical references, but beyond that they mark a rich new strand of contrivance in this remarkable *Gesamtkunstwerk*.

---

[38] The accompanying miniature shows the Holy Spirit descending as a dove to a clerk in prayer. The text greets this as *He unccion espirital*, which I read as the 'unction' of a royal anointing; Strubel (line 1211) renders it as *He, unicorn espirital*.

[39] *Fauvel* is rich in trios. The three modern Marigny motets at the end also mirror the three old but adapted pieces on f. 1. Trios of words are also conspicuous; see the discussion of 'three words' and puns on three in *Tribum*, Ch. 4.

4

Tribum que non abhorruit/Quoniam secta latronum/Merito hec patimur and its 'Quotations', and *Garrit gallus/In nova*

In the preceding chapter I argued for the conceptual unity of the three Marigny motets as a group and their double function in the forwards narrative of *Fauvel* and the backwards narrative relating to Marigny and recent political events. It anticipates some of what will be expanded here about the motets and their relationship to each other.[1] These two motets, *Tribum* and *Garrit*, together with the Trinity motet on f. 43ʳ, *Firmissime/Adesto*, are frequently cited as the most advanced motets in *Fauvel* and as candidates for the authorship of Philippe de Vitry. Much has been written about them, embodying as they do major musical and notational innovations of the early *ars nova*, including duple (imperfect) tempus; a wide range of note values within one piece, from maximodus to what would later be called prolation, with minims, laying the foundations for much longer compositions than motets of the thirteenth century; changes of modus and tempus (in the case of *Garrit gallus*, coded by the earliest known use of red notation for this purpose); and mostly unstemmed semibreve groups divided by dots to be evaluated according to default rhythms set out in a group of contemporary treatises in which *Garrit* and *Firmissime* are also cited.[2]

However, they are very far from being the only compositions in *Fauvel* to display some of these features. *Aman/Heu* has usually been left out of this 'advanced' group, presumably because it lacks the element of tenor repetition and regular periodicity present in *Garrit* and *Tribum*. In Chapter 5 it will be shown to have considerable ingenuity of a different kind while being closely tied to those motets. Leo Schrade treated the three Marigny motets as inseparable; I hope to show that the nature of their interconnections and coordination makes it highly probable that the three motets, different and unique as they are, indeed stem from a single mind. At least a dozen of the other *Fauvel* motets use imperfect tempus and major prolation *avant la lettre*. Some of the monophonic pieces, too, lend themselves to the same rhythmic interpretation of semibreve groups as the motets, even though such a reading is not corroborated by being locked into a contrapuntal structure. Christopher Page's rhythmic rendition of the monophonic ballade *Ay*

---

[1] This chapter includes and extends material revised from the chapter published as 'Polyphony of Texts and Music in the Fourteenth-Century Motet: *Tribum que non abhorruit/Quoniam secta latronum/Merito hec patimur* and its "Quotations"', in Pesce (ed.), *Hearing the Motet*, 82–103. It meets OUP's conditions for reuse without obtaining formal permission.

[2] Besseler gave remarkably prescient analyses of these motets. However, I think he was wrong to call this notation Petronian: none of these motets uses more than four S to the B (five only in *Quare fremuerunt*), and they are all in duple tempus, which was unknown to Petrus and abhorrent to Jacobus. Besseler, 'Studien II'. See Bent, *Jacobus*, ch. 2, on this terminology. Leech-Wilkinson considers *Tribum* and *Firmissime* more closely related to each other than to *Garrit gallus*.

The Motet in the Late Middle Ages. Margaret Bent, Oxford University Press. © Oxford University Press 2023.
DOI: 10.1093/so/9780190063771.003.0005

amours (ff. 16ᵛ–17) is brilliantly vindicated by its use as a motet tenor with those explicitly notated rhythms in **Paris934**.[3] And as noted, *Quare fremuerunt* on the opening 'display' page of **Paris146** boasts three minim upstems, angled to the right as in the slightly later **Paris571**. I will start in the middle, with the pivotal motet of the three, *Tribum*, pivotal because of its central role in both the forward (*Fauvel*) and backward (historical) narrative.

Tribum/Quoniam (▶ Ex. 4.1) survives in three main sources, the interpolated *Fauvel* in **Paris146**, **Stras** and the rotulus **Br19606**, six of whose nine motets are in **Paris146** or in some way related to its repertory.[4] Three later adaptations will not be considered here, though they attest to a long reception history.[5] As with *Garrit gallus* (▶ Ex. 4.5, and see below), the transcription conflates the largely unstemmed semibreves of **Paris146** with the clarifying minim stems of later sources. The few downstems (indicating a long note on the first of a group of three) are only in **Paris146**. In *Fauvel* it shares a page (f. 42ʳ) with the famous Fountain of Youth miniature, around whose triangulated top music and text are arranged. The remaining text and music on the page are closely coordinated with the image, which presents a black baptism in which the progeny of Fauvel, shown as old men, are rejuvenated in filth and vice, moving from right to left (i.e. backwards); the motet can be read as a further gloss on the same theme.

Chapter 3 demonstrated the relationship of the texts of *Tribum* to a given political situation involving the fall from power of a corrupt minister in early fourteenth-century France and his subsequent execution. Each of the texts for the upper voices ends with a 'quotation' (actually a foundational element) in the form of a couplet of quantitative verse commenting proverbially on the 'tragic fall'. The tenor is drawn from the opening of a chant melody for a passage in Genesis relating to the story of Joseph, which makes a not-too-oblique comment on the contemporary political situation. I will show (1) that the freely composed remaining texts for the upper voices in the motet (in rhymed syllabic verse) are built up from certain key words and sound patterns in their final metrical 'quotations'; (2) that the two apparently independent texts are ingeniously related by the fact that three of the same words or their roots are placed in a chained pattern that connects the triplum, motetus and tenor; (3) that the melodies of the upper voices both use elements of the tenor chant melody (the tenor being limited, significantly, to the first three words of that chant); and (4) that they are so composed that the motetus and triplum reflect and enhance the patterns found in the texts considered independently

---

[3] Page, 'Tradition and Innovation', 355; Dudas and Earp, *Four Early Ars nova Motets*.

[4] The motet was previously edited in PMFC 1, 54–56 and is in **Paris146**, ff. 41ᵛ–42. A musical omission in the motetus in **Paris146** renders it unperformable without emendation from the other sources. The Appendix to this chapter gives the manuscript variants. My transcription differs from Schrade's in several places. The identities are better seen if the plicas are left unrealised in the transcriptions, as they are in the later sources. Bent, '*Tribum*' neglected to take the **Stras** source into account, here rectified.

[5] One of these is an ornamented keyboard adaptation of (mainly) triplum and motetus in **Robertsbridge**, strikingly transposed up a tone (ed. Apel, *Keyboard Music*, 6–8). Images of **Robertsbridge** are on DIAMM, and a facsimile is in Wooldridge, *Early English Harmony*, plates 42–45. These motet intabulations, especially that of *Flos vernalis* (ed. Apel, *Keyboard Music*, 9) of which the original vocal model has now been identified, are the subject of Alís Raurich, 'The *Flores* of *Flos vernalis*'. Second is a small single leaf in **Mu29775**, preserving a curiously notated and textually corrupt version of the triplum alone, transposed down a seventh (to the *g* an octave below the keyboard version), and with a page turn. Upstemmed, flagged, and downstemmed minims are used, with no obvious relationship to the rhythms of the motet. Staehelin, 'Münchner Fragmente', 176–77 and pl. 5 (facsimile) dates it early 15th c., but the downstemmed minims might suggest an even later date, despite their appearance in some early German organ tablatures, which this is not. Third, **Rostock** has what can only be described as an approximation of the motetus of *Tribum/Quoniam* on f. 43 with a triplum texted *Dixit, dixit iracundus homo* which breaks the tenor into repeated notes to accommodate text. Both German sources appear to be attempting minor prolation, which may indicate that they were copying from unstemmed semibreves.

and contrive 'consonances' between related words and sounds in the texts. After identifying some significant features of its musical construction and the status of its pre-existent material, I will demonstrate textual-musical references between the motets *Tribum/Quoniam/Merito* and *Garrit gallus/In nova fert*, and offer further discussion of *Garrit gallus*.

It has long been recognised that *Tribum* is one of a group of motets alluding to events and people prominent in the crises that afflicted the French royal house and the series of accessions to the monarchy in the second decade of the fourteenth century. Philip IV (the Fair) died on 29 November 1314, and his discredited counsellor Enguerrand de Marigny was hanged on 30 March 1315. Philip was succeeded in turn by his sons Louis X and Philip V, both of whose coronations are celebrated in motets at the junction of books I and II (as noted above), but the three Marigny motets at the end of book II (*Garrit gallus/In nova fert*, *Tribum/Quoniam*, *Aman novi/Heu Fortuna*) refer only to Philip IV, as a blind lion whose reign is first present, in *Garrit gallus*, then past, in *Tribum*, and to Marigny's fall and execution in *Aman*.[6]

The last two lines of the motetus of *Tribum/Quoniam* 'quote' an elegiac couplet from one of the letters Ovid wrote in exile, *Epistulae ex Ponto* IV. 3, lines 35–36, a work that arises out of Ovid's own fall and banishment. The tenor is the beginning (on the first three words) of the Matins responsory for the third Sunday in Lent, *Merito hec patimur quia peccavimus in fratrem nostrum*, ℣ *Dixit Ruben fratribus suis* (Justly we suffer these things because we sinned against our brother. Reuben said to his brothers . . .). Its biblical source is Genesis 42:21, which concerns Joseph's incognito meeting with his brothers in Egypt. Both Ovid and Genesis deal with exile; both provide significant context for the newly written motet texts, underscoring the immediate and contemporary message and the calamitous events to which they refer. Ovid's letter was written from exile to an unnamed (and unidentified) faithless friend. The subject and unstated context of the tenor text from Genesis is the remorse of Joseph's brothers after deceiving their father Jacob about their abuse of Joseph, which led to his exile in Egypt. The Ovid couplet is introduced by the words *que dolum acuunt*. The author 'sharpens the deceit' (or evil) by counterpointing Ovid's exile to the exile of the Israelites in Egypt reported in Genesis as well as drawing both into service to lament the woes of France in a motet written for this amplified and politically pointed version of *Fauvel*.[7]

We have seen the central role played by Fortuna and her turning wheel in the interpolated version of *Fauvel* for which the motet was written, and in whose triplum Fortuna is likewise central. She also figures importantly in Ovid's letter. Lines 7 and 29 of

---

[6] Wathey, 'Myth and Mythography', 84 and 95–97, reported that the final hexameter couplet of the triplum *Tribum que non abhorruit* is not an independent proverb but derives from Joseph of Exeter's *De bello troiano*, VI. 804–5, in the context of the reversal of King Priam's fortunes and his murder, a significant referent in the historical context of *Fauvel*. In turn, the sentiment, but not the wording, derives from Lucretius, *De rerum natura*. Even more strikingly, Vitry used this same couplet to annotate a passage in his own copy of the *Chronicon of Guillaume de Nangis*, which recounts Parthian defeat (38 BC) and subsequent tragedies, in moral and historical conditions parallel to those of the motet, where, too, it was better to have nothing than to suffer a calamitous loss. This discovery offers further support for Vitry's authorship of the motet, as well as for his direct involvement in the *Fauvel* project. For a quotation from *De bello trojano* in *Garrit gallus*, see below n. 35.

[7] Exile and eclipse are central themes of **Paris146**, particularly in the *dits* of Geffroy de Paris. One of his French poems uses an eclipse of the sun and the moon to stand for the vacant papacy in 1314–16 and also for the uncertainties of the French royal succession and the eclipse of its dignity at the same period (*De la Comète et de l'Eclipse de la Lune et du Soulail*); another deals with the exile of the papacy from Rome to Avignon (*La Desputoison de l'Eglise de Romme et de l'Eglise de France pour le Siège du Pape*). See *Six Historical Poems*. The Latin poem *Natus ego* also treats of this topic, but applies the theme of Babylonian captivity more generally (and traditionally) to the sins and sufferings of the Church. See Holford-Strevens, 'The Latin *Dits*'.

86   FAUVEL AND VITRY

the letter name Fortuna, who is described in the lines preceding those used in the motet (italics mine):

> 7   nunc, quia contraxit vultum *Fortuna* recedis
>
>   ...
>
>   quid facis, a! demens? Cur, si *Fortuna* recedat
>
> 30   naufragio lacrimas eripis ipse tuo?
>
>   Haec dea non stabili, quam sit levis, orbe fatetur,
>
>   quae summum dubio sub pede semper habet.
>
>   quolibet est folio, quavis incertior aura:
>
>   par illi levitas, improbe, sola tua est.
>
> 35   *Omnia sunt hominum tenui pendentia filo*
>
>   *et subito casu quae valuere, ruunt.*

Now that Fortune has frowned, you draw back ... Ah, what are you doing, madman? Why, if Fortune draws back, do you yourself thus refuse your shipwreck its tears? This goddess declares by her unsteady wheel that she is fickle; she always has its top under her faltering foot. She is more uncertain than any leaf, than any breeze; the only thing that matches her inconstancy, reprobate, is yours. All human affairs hang by a slender thread, and things that were strong collapse in a sudden fall.[8]

Here are the texts, lightly adapted from the versions as edited and translated by David Howlett:

Triplum	Disyllabic rhymes: octosyllables
Tribum que non abhorruit	a
indecenter ascendere	b
furibunda non metuit	a
Fortuna cito vertere,	b
5 dum duci prefate **tribus**	c
in sempiternum speculum	c
parare palam omnibus	c
non pepercit patibulum.	d
Populus ergo venturus	e
10 si trans metam | ascenderit,	f
quidam forsitan **casurus**,	e
cum tanta **tribus ruerit**,	f

---

[8] This passage is a vivid choice to evoke the theme of Marigny, whose hanging is more literally presented in *Aman novi/Heu Fortuna*. The text is here quoted and the translation adapted from Ovid, *Ex ponto*, IV. 3. 35. This reference to the fragility of life also recalls *Disticha Catonis*, I. 19 (*Cum dubia et fragilis sit nobis vita tributa*), providing a link to the direct quotation of the immediately preceding *Disticha* I. 18 in *Aman novi* (Ch. 5).

sciat eciam quis fructus	g
delabi sit in profundum.	h
15 *Post zephyros plus ledit hyems, post gaudia luctus;*	g (hexameter couplet)
unde nichil melius, quam nil habuisse secundum.	h

Motetus	**Disyllabic rhymes: octosyllables, lines 1–9**
Quoniam secta latronum	a
spelunca vispilionum	a
vulpes que Gallos roderat	b
tempore quo regnaverat	b
5 leo cecatus **subito**	c
suo **ruere merito**	c
in mortem privatam bonis:	d
concinat Gallus Nasonis	d
dicta que dolum acuunt:	e
10 *omnia sunt hominum tenui pendencia filo*	elegiac couplet, lines 10–11
et **subito casu** *que valuere* **ruunt.**	e

Tenor: *Merito hec patimur*

Triplum: Furious Fortune has not feared to bring down swiftly the tribe which did not shrink from ascending indecently, while for the leader of the foresaid tribe she has not refrained from preparing the gallows as an eternal mirror in the sight of everyone. Therefore if the people to come should ascend across the limit, let a certain man who might, perhaps, fall, since such a tribe has collapsed, know also what an outcome it would be to fall into the depth. Winter harms more after gentle west winds, grief after joys; and so nothing is better than to have had no good fortune [i.e., 'there is nothing better than not to have enjoyed any good fortune', because to have enjoyed good fortune makes the less good fortune (that follows it) feel so much the worse].[9]

Motetus: Since the gang of thieves from a cave of reprobates (and) the fox which had gnawed the cocks in the time in which the blinded lion had ruled have fallen suddenly by their own deserts into a death deprived of good things, let the cock shout Ovid's

---

[9] See n. 6 above for the derivation from Joseph of Exeter. David Howlett translated the last couplet as 'Winter harms more after gentle west winds, griefs [harm more] after joys; whence nothing is better than to have had nothing for the second time [*that is,* better to have nothing at all than to have enjoyed good fortune in the past]). Zoltán Rihmer, on the other hand, offered for the last phrase: [*that is,* better to have nothing at all than not to have enjoyed good fortune in the past]. I am indebted to Jonathan Katz for the version offered here: 'unde nichil melius <est> quam nil habuisse secundum', this last word also meaning 'successful' or 'fortunate'. He also treats *luctus* (grief) as singular, understood to govern the same verb as 'hyems'.

words which intensify the deceit: 'All human affairs are hanging by a slender thread, and with a sudden fall things which were strong crash.'

Tenor: Justly we suffer these things.

Tribum/Quoniam: Texts

A network of verbal repetitions (distinguished in boldface above) underpins and gives structure to the two texts. In accusative (*tribum*) or nominative form (*tribus*), the word 'tribe' occurs three times in the triplum, thus punning on *tribus* (three) to reinforce a central feature of the motet. The third *tribus* directly precedes *ruerit*, which (as *ruunt*) is the last word of the motetus and hence of the Ovid couplet. This verb (as *ruunt* and *ruere*) occurs twice in the motetus, with *ruere* directly preceding *merito*, which in turn is the first of the three tenor words. The first word of the triplum and the last word of the motetus are thus linked in a pattern that is structurally fundamental to the motet and exists independently of verbal sense, although it is used to reinforce that sense. The lattice is further reinforced by—though by no means dependent upon—the proportioned positions of the words within their own texts.[10] The motetus *casu* in the final Ovid line is picked up in the triplum's *casurus*. Note how many of these words are adjacent to each other or in rhyme positions; that *subito*, *casu* and *ruunt* in the pre-existent Ovid couplet link the motetus to the triplum, and that the tenor's pre-existent *Merito* links it to the motetus.

The triplum's fourteen octosyllabic lines are followed by a hexameter couplet, a self-contained proverb without literary context.[11] The couplet, despite its own innocence of rhyme and its longer lines, is integrated into the overall rhyme scheme, abab cdcd efef ghgh. Thus, of the triplum's eight disyllabic rhymes, the last two are made to rhyme with these pre-existent hexameters. The motetus has nine octosyllabic lines rhymed in pairs, followed by an elegiac couplet. The last (odd, uncoupled) line of its syllabic verse (*dicta que dolum acuunt*) is made to rhyme (*-uunt*) with the pre-existent pentameter; it also shares *-u -u* assonance (vowel rhyme) with the triplum *fructus*, tying together the eight double *-u -u* vowel rhymes of the triplum with the rhymed pair in the motetus, *acuunt* introducing the Ovid couplet and *ruunt* ending it. This insistence on the same vowel is all the more striking because both the final rhymes are disyllabic (paroxytone: *fructus*, *luctus*; *profundum*, *secundum*), that is, showing identity from the stressed syllable to the end; the musical setting, however, suggests French end-stressing. (The first six pairs would be considered 'imperfect' in vernacular verse of this period, because the identity is limited to the two unstressed syllables.) There is confirmation that this insistence on the one vowel is deliberate: the final two vowels of the last word in the last line of the motetus, *ruunt*, which rhymes with *acuunt* in the antepenultimate (and last rhythmic) line, also have the repeated *u u* vowels, something that can take on an audible dimension in musical performance. On the assumption that both texts are constructed

---

[10] David Howlett points out that *Tribus/m* recurs at words 16 and 38, that is, at or immediately adjacent to the major and minor parts of the golden section (extreme and mean ratio—a + b is to a as a is to b) of its text by word count (62), and that *Ruunt* to *ruere* span the major part of the same ratio, counting words from the end of the motetus: *ruere merito* are the 25th and 24th words from the end of a total of 41 words.

[11] Walther, *Proverbia sententiaeque*, no. 22073 (*Carminum proverbialium, loci communes . . .*).

backwards from the Ovidian quotation at the end of the motetus, this insistence on *u-u* may be a way of reinforcing the idea of 'collapse' or 'downfall' in the verb *ruunt*. The intentions of this densely crafted writing are confirmed and underscored by their musical setting. *Fructus* closes a line (triplum 13) in which triplum and motetus coincide musically in identical rhythm, at (longs) L51–L55; this immediately follows the triplum's crucial *tribus ruerit*, suitably set to a striking descending scale in semibreves in L50–L51.[12] The Ovid couplet is integrated into both texts. The single-rhymed triplum words *profundum* and motetus *hominum* arrive together on L61 (see ⓟ Ex. 4.1): the internal *-um* of the motetus hexameter is thus brought into rhyming and musical alignment with the triplum word that is in turn arranged to rhyme with the last word of *its* pre-existent hexameter couplet. Although not used as rhyme words or line ends in their respective couplets, triplum *gaudia* and motetus *pendencia* arrive together on L67, and thus similarly connect the separate texts by 'imperfect' rhyme. The vowels and two of the consonants of the first motetus word *Quoniam* are those of the first word of the Ovid couplet, *omnia* (and the vowels *o-i-a* are reversed at the end of the same line, *-a filo*). In addition the motet concludes with musically aligned vowel rhyme between the ends of both borrowed couplets:

> Tr   *meli -us quam nil ha-buis-se se-cun-dum*
> Mo   *ca- su que   va -lu- e-re ru- unt* (u q a u e e u u).

Such vowel rhyme was contrived to be a conspicuous feature of these texts. The treatment of individual syllables, and their adjacent and simultaneous combination, mark them as words carefully calculated for musical treatment. Many are easily audible from outside, though some would remain privy to participating performers. To someone already familiar with the motet, the triplum's *abhorruit* can then be heard (in a solo opening, uncomplicated by other voices) as relating to *ruit*, further underscored by the palindrome of the opening vowels *i–u, u–i*: tr*i*b*u*m–horr*u*it. The 62 words of the triplum divide in half between *metam* and *ascenderit* (31 + 31). The words *trans metam ascende-|rit* take us 'over the boundary' to the second *color*, set to a melodic palindrome that hinges around the structural centre of the motet (ⓟ Ex. 4.1, third system, *a g f e f e f g a*). The two *-tam* syllables in triplum and motetus coincide: *trans metam* and *mortem privatam* (the middle word of the motetus, 21st of 41), hooking the parts firmly together at the *color* join, to words that mean 'across the limit'. Puns with words of measure are quite common in fourteenth-century motets at such positions of structural or proportional importance in text or music (other instances are noted in Chapters 8 and 18).

Words denoting 'fall' abound in both texts (*vertere, delabi, profundum, casurus*), ending with the fundamental *ruunt*. Ovid alludes in the letter to the fall of his exile: 'insultare iacenti te mihi' (you insult me in my fall), lines 27–28. *Casu* and *ruunt* in the pentameter of the Ovid motetus couplet are echoed by *casurus–ruerit* in the triplum. Both *color* statements are introduced with the rising word *ascendere* or *ascenderit* at verse line ends, and with the same notes *a g f e f*. Their descending reversals, *vertere*,

---

[12] Musical references are given by longs (L) as numbered in ⓟ Ex. 4.1, or the values referred to as breves (B), semibreves (S). The golden section of the structured music (that is, discounting the introductory 6L) falls halfway through L51 on *ru|- erit* (triplum) and *dicta* (motetus).

profundum, patibulum, also occur at line ends, as do the three recapitulated words, two of which mean 'fall': *subito, casurus, ruunt. Patibulum* and *patimur* also create a pun as well as a vowel rhyme.

Ovid wrote 'sum tamen haec passus' (I however have suffered this [line 55 of the letter]; first person singular). The motet tenor's three words, *Merito hec patimur*, use the same deponent verb in the first person plural. Only the three words *Merito hec patimur* are provided, and only their music from the chant is used. This leads us to another very significant connection (in lines 25–26 of the letter):

si mihi rebus opem nullam factisque ferebas, venisset verbis charta notata tribus

(Even if you brought me no aid in facts, in deeds, you might have sent me three words on a sheet of paper.)

Puns on three are central to the motet, starting with the triplum's *tribum/tribus. Tribum* of course means tribe, not three, but as the opening word of the triplum, it is unquestionably used with punning intent; the word *tribum* or *tribus* occurs three times in the *triplum* text. We have seen that three words from Ovid's pentameter line, *subito, casu, ruunt*, are all worked into the new motet texts, emphasised by repetition, and given significant positions, both as proportioned, and by adjacent words. *Subito* in the motetus follows *leo cecatus* and ends the line immediately preceding *ruere merito. Casurus* ends the triplum line immediately preceding *tribus ruerit. Ruere/ruunt* have already been singled out as fundamental and specially placed. But even more telling is the choice of tenor, just the three words, *Merito hec patimur*, linked in various ways to the texts of the motet and determining its musical form and substance. The portion of chant selected corresponds to those three words and no more.

Cumulatively, the evidence which has just been presented makes it certain that the newly written rhythmical parts of the two texts were composed very carefully, on the foundations of the quotations, in conjunction with each other, and in conjunction with the intended musical setting and the chosen tenor words.[13] Verbal recapitulations, and the distance between them, are calculated in the same way that musical elements are recapitulated, spaced and proportioned. The Ovid couplet has yielded the sense and the verbal units that govern the composition of both texts; it is as fundamental to the verbal composition as is the choice of plainsong for the musical construction, a choice strongly governed in turn by the words. Indeed, these words underpin the verbal structure in the same way that the notes of a derived tenor underpin the musical structure. It appears that the chant tenor was chosen to fit Ovid rather than Ovid to fit the tenor. A common assumption has been that the notes of the chant tenor were the first compositional constraint to be adopted once the general subject of the texts (the *materia*) had been decided. I think it can here be proposed instead that the texts had been planned precisely and in detail; that the Ovid couplet

---

[13] Patrick Boyde alerted me to an interesting case of strategic quotation (probably before 1340) in the Petrarch *canzone, Lasso me, ch'i' non so in qual parte pieghi* (no. 70 in the *Canzoniere*). It has five stanzas of ten lines each. The last line of each stanza is the first line of an existing *canzone* by a noted poet, respectively by Arnaut Daniel (so Petrarch believed), Cavalcanti, Dante, Cino, and finally Petrarch's own *Nel dolce tempo de la prima etade* (no. 23, his first *canzone*, on the theme of metamorphosis). In each case the penultimate line of the stanza forms a rhyming couplet with the final imported line.

was primary to those texts, and must have been chosen at least as early as, or before, the Genesis source of the motet tenor. These twin pillars of text and music are intimately linked and provide a striking marriage of pagan and Christian elements.[14] The status of 'pre-compositional' material must therefore be accorded in equal measure to the Ovid couplet and to the choice of tenor. The one is no more a quotation than the other; both are starting points and building material for the texts and music. The treatise *De modo componendi tenores motettorum* (usually attributed to Egidius, but see Chapters 1 and 16) already implied that the words might exist before a tenor was chosen to go with them: first choose your *materia*.[15] The close interdependence of text and music in this and some other motets suggests that this *materia* was more precisely worked out than simply a general indication of the intended subject matter. Here we have internal evidence that they must have done so, but in conjunction with the music; this gives a twin central role in the creation of this motet to the composition and disposition of the words as well as the music.

Tribum/*Quoniam*: Music

We turn now to an analysis of the music (see ⊙ Ex. 4.1), having already noted some features of the texts that were so planned in relation to the music that they would be heard simultaneously.

The particular preoccupation with the word(s) *Tribus/m* seems to have affected all the main proportions of the motet, textual and musical. The motet is 78 imperfect longs in duration, arranged in perfect maximodus (with longs grouped in threes). The triplum enters alone, for three longs, followed by the motetus, for three longs, then the tenor. Each of the two equal *color* statements occupies 12 × 3 longs:

$$3 + 3 + (color\,1)\,12 \times 3 + (color\,2)\,12 \times 3 = 78L$$

Without the 6L (12B) introduction, the motet is 72L (= 144 breves) in length; several fourteenth-century motets work with this number, 12^2, notably in the musician motets group (see Part IV). For purposes of these calculations, the final long is considered to extend to its official full length of three longs (a perfect maxima), corresponding to the rests that complete *color* 1.

As already noted, the tenor is the beginning of the Matins responsory for the third Sunday in Lent, *Merito hec patimur quia peccavimus in fratrem nostrum*. The chant is transposed up a fifth from *f* to *c*. AS 174 had presented the hitherto closest available version of the melody, differing in only one note from the motet tenor, but Anne Walters Robertson has now found a perfect match in a Parisian source from St-Maur,

---

[14] It is tempting to see in this some support for Vitry's authorship. It would not be surprising that Vitry, a friend and respected associate of Petrarch, should pioneer such boldly clerical-humanistic juxtapositions. This is entirely in line with the further pointers to Vitry's humanist identity that result from Andrew Wathey's discovery of some of his motet texts in humanist poetry manuscripts. See Wathey, 'The Motets of Vitry' and 'The Motet Texts of Philippe de Vitry'.

[15] For this treatise see Leech-Wilkinson, *Compositional Techniques*, i. 18–24; and now the appendix of Zayaruznaya, *Upper-Voice Structures*, offers text and translation of this, together with other theoretical texts relating to *color* and *talea*.

Paris12044, f. 80.[16] This removes any need to assume that the chant was even slightly manipulated by the composer in order to achieve a tidy structure of 6 × 3 short *talea* groups which then yield three identical three-note groups (*a g g* transposed, for the motet, to *e d d*) within each of the two *colores*.[17] The composer contrived that the recurring pattern *e*-rest-*d* (♩ 𝄽♩) from this group should provide six equidistant and identical bases on which two alternating sets of three blocks of music, identical in all parts, are erected (A B A B A B): see Ex. 4.2. In ▶ Ex. 4.1 the A blocks are shaded light, the B blocks darker. The commentary to this transcription is in the Appendix to this chapter. To ensure this equidistancing required the tenor to be rhythmicised before the blocks were superimposed on it, contrary to suggestions that the blocks could have been planned before the rhythmicisation of the tenor.[18] Ex. 4.2 brackets the palindromic elements of the tenor: the first three notes, *c d e*, are inverted at the end. They are used in the motetus in each of the A blocks at the chant pitch, *f g a*. The three disjunct notes *e g d* (notes 12–14, interrupting the palindrome) are transposed to the chant pitch, *a c g*, in the motetus in each of the B blocks. The rest of the motetus is saturated with melodic cells derived from the chant: *f g a*, *f g a b♭*, *a g*, *b♭ a g a*, *a g a b♭*, *g a g f* and more, including transpositions. Some of them are, appropriately, retrogrades or inversions of each other (cf. Machaut M8, Ch. 14, for a comparable instance of tight motivic relationship between the tenor and the texted parts).

Ex. 4.2 Tenor and chant of *Merito hec patimur*

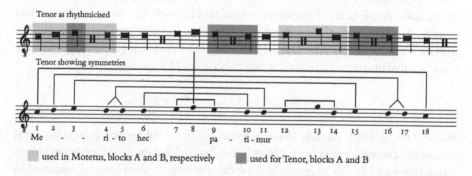

Figure 4.1 shows the musical plan schematically. While the tenor has the same rhythmic pattern in both *color* statements, the patterns of sound and silence in the upper parts differ slightly, corresponding to the alternating cadential patterns (x and y) that link the blocks to 'non-block' music and give a special place to the phrase marked at 'z', whose significance will become clear later.

---

[16] Robertson, 'Local Chant Readings', 518–19.
[17] There is an extra minim in the triplum at the end of L12. The other corrections in the present edition that bring out this identity are based on alternative manuscript readings and supported by musical sense (parallel readings, and avoidance of unsupported simultaneous fourths).
[18] I claim that both musical and textual pre-existing material (*materia*) together formed twin pillars for this motet's construction, but not that the rhythmic structuring of the upper parts preceded that of the tenor, as implied in Zayaruznaya, *The Monstrous New Art*, p. 8, and see below, n. 19.

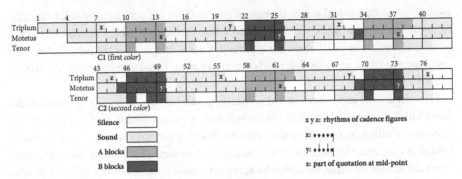

Fig. 4.1 Schematic diagram of *Tribum/Quoniam/Merito*

Each trio of 4L blocks (three of A, three of B) is identical not only in pitch but also in rhythm in all parts. With thrice two blocks of music arranged over twice three identical places in the tenor, the composition becomes a grand hemiola of threefold form arranged over a twice-stated tenor *color*. An analysis committed to isorhythmic primacy, and particularly to demonstrating the primacy of the lower parts, will give only subsidiary attention to the amazing interlocked tripartite structure, with its own internal identities, that is counterpointed against the two identical tenor *color* statements, and to the ternary pattern set up by the three pairs of A + B that cut across those two statements. While the tenor can at the most basic level be described as isorhythmic, with six short *taleae* or *ordines* in each *color*, the upper parts might be said to superimpose an overlapping, tight, but counter-isorhythmic structure upon it.[19]

A few previous analysts have noted the outlines of this structure, though their significance and extent has largely been passed over.[20] It has not previously been proposed that Schrade's transcription be emended to match these observations; the blocks can easily be made fully identical, as in ⏵ Ex. 4.1, on the authority of the other two sources. Our understanding of musical language at this period is still so fragile that we timidly fail to recognise as nonsense some manuscript readings that demand to be corrected in

---

[19] I loosened the received notion of tenor priority by claiming in this case that it was shared with pre-existent textual material. Zayaruznaya, *Upper-Voice Structures*, further eroded tenor priority by placing upper-voice musical structures ahead of tenor structuring, which is for me a step too far. She kindly acknowledges the new proposals of my 1997 analysis, but objects (n. 10) that 'even there, the presence of three longer periods in the upper voices is described as a "counter-isorhythmic structure" superimposed on the "isorhythmic" tenor, and framed as an exceptional aspect of *Tribum/Quoniam* closely tied to its meaning, rather than a compositional tool in use in the broader repertory'. My diagram and the layout of my edition are said to privilege the two tenor *colores* over the three periods of the upper parts, though I think it is clear that I see these as twin structural components. But the tenor in this case had to be planned and rhythmicised before the upper parts, in order to ensure that the three instances of *e d* in each *color* fall equidistantly to accommodate the alternating A and B blocks (Ex. 4.2 above). Zayaruznaya would rather see the tenor as fitting into those blocks. One can line up the tenor *colores*, as I did, or the identical blocks as in Earp, 'Isorhythm', 95. Both layouts are valid. My analysis was indeed focused on this one motet as an individual and original composition of text and music, laden with specific meaning, and without attempting to generalise. If such patterning did become a general tool, *Tribum* was one of the earliest motets to implement it, and thus a pioneering work.

[20] They seem to have been published only in Fuller, *European Musical Heritage*, 99–103, albeit noted in less detail. The translation is improved by Howlett's reading, Schrade's musical transcription (reproduced by Fuller) by the present version. Sanders partly makes this observation ('The Early Motets of Philippe de Vitry', 27) when he says that the *taleae* could be treated as 3 × 4 instead of 2 × 6, reflecting isomelic correspondences, and notes with approval the periodicity of the upper parts.

accordance with musical sense, though of course there are also equally valid variants. Analysis can provide a text-critical tool to refine the edition where deviations from a pattern of identity or parallelism are apparently casual. In this case, the new readings are corroborated by an analysis that treats the motet as an equal and interrelated partnership of text and music.

Is isorhythm or any other kind of recurrent pattern a conscious background model from which purposeful deviation is intended to be recognised as such, or is it simply a means of filling in neutral space between primary formal events? Can it be both? I think it can, and the balance differs in different pieces. Textual and musical events often cut across or dislocate hitherto accepted measurements of the tidiness or maturity of a motet. When analysis upholds the purposefulness of such 'deviations' they cannot be dismissed as manifestations of untidiness or early date. Such analysis may demonstrate that more than one formal pattern is at work in the music, just as there may be deliberate ambiguity in the text when a biblical and a secular sense, or two different narratives, are superimposed.

A common weakness of judgements about orderliness of structure, or of analytical bases for determining chronology, occurs when only a single criterion, or criteria that are too limited, are taken into account. Sanders demonstrated the extent and importance of regular periodicity of phrases between rests in the upper parts of motets, even where there is no regular isorhythm between those phrases.[21] Ursula Günther's study of the fourteenth-century motet invoked the amount and extent of isorhythm as a measure of chronology.[22] Neither of them takes closely into account either the text–music relationship of individual parts or networks of relationships between texts and musical lines, within and between pieces, which are just one aspect of the compositional possibilities.[23] In short, each motet is different, unique, and can only in the most limited and approximate senses be measured by conventional standards of periodicity. Several of the motets on Heinrich Besseler's list of isorhythmic motets are not in a strict or primary sense isorhythmic. *Vos quid/Gratissima*, *Firmissime/Adesto* and *Douce/Garison* are among motets (all deemed early) that use a newly rhythmicised second *color* rather than diminution or mensural derivation from a homographic notation; others may balance a variety of constructional resources much more complex than simple tenor replication, as in the Marigny group.[24] Any isorhythm in these motets is between *taleae* within each *color*, not between *colores*.

The portion of melody used (and transposed) for the *Tribum* tenor has several palindromic features (see Ex. 4.2 above): the beginning and end, *cded–dedc* (*ut re mi re–re mi re ut*), resemble the *Neuma quinti toni* of *Garrit gallus*, which starts and ends with *fga–agf* (*ut re mi–mi re ut*). A conjunct palindrome from notes 5 to 11 of the tenor, *d d e f e d d*, abuts the only melodically disjunct group *e g d* (notes 12–14), and at the same time contributes to a melodic sequence with the opening four notes. Discounting repeated

---

[21] Sanders, 'The Medieval Motet'.
[22] Günther, 'The 14th-Century Motet'.
[23] Examined by scholars including Reichert, 'Das Verhältnis'.
[24] Besseler, 'Studien II', 222–24. See Ch. 2 above. Sanders rightly rejects diminution as the appropriate term for the new rhythmicisations of the tenors of *Douce/Garison* and *Firmissime/Adesto*; 'The Early Motets of Philippe de Vitry', 28.

notes, the whole melody can be seen as a conjunct palindrome into which the disjunct group is inserted; this is the way the composer must have treated it in fashioning the upper parts (see Ex. 4.4 below).

Each of the six blocks (ABABAB in Fig. 4.1, ▶ Ex. 4.1) starts on an octave *a* in triplum and motetus flanking the tenor *e*, and each is always preceded by triplum rests and followed by motetus rests. Each block begins a new triplum text line and contains only that line (lines 3, 6, 8, 11, 14, 16); the longer last hexameter line, 16, extends beyond the block to the final cadence. The identity is sometimes extended into adjacent groups. The middle A block and the second and third B blocks are introduced by motetus semibreves *b♭ d c b♭*, and the central A and B blocks followed by triplum semibreves *d d c b♭*. Each block presents three prominent notes of the chant in its motetus (see Ex. 4.3). Block A has *c d e*, the opening of the chant. In the central A block indeed these notes coincide with the motetus word *merito*, underscoring, both in its musical placing and in its notes, the significance of the first word of the tenor (*Merito*) in the verbal lattice of the upper parts.[25] The only disjunct group of notes in the tenor, *e g d*, makes a prominent appearance at its original chant pitch, *a c g*, in the motetus of each of the B blocks, for the words—all significant— reg*na*verat, *Na*sonis, sub*ito casu*. Example 4.4 shows how the first triplum phrase of *Tribum* freely paraphrases the entire chant segment on *f*, except for the three-note disjunct cell *a c g*. The omission of these three notes at this stage leaves a perfectly palindromic phrase; the final four notes of the chant are repeated in parentheses. The triplum then proceeds to paraphrase the disjunct cell *a c g* in its next phrase. In ▶ Ex. 4.1 this is at L10, avoiding any further *f* cadences until the new *color* at L43 and the final cadence. This paraphrase of the disjunct cell forms the triplum of the A block and combines with the motetus presentation of the first three notes of the chant (at tenor pitch, *c d e*).

Ex. 4.3 Three notes of the chant as used in the motetus of each block of *Tribum*, respectively *c d e* and *a c g* (transposed from *f g a* and *e g d*)

Block A, motetus:
long 10   vispi - li -   o   num
      34   subito suo rue - re   me   ri   to
      58   ho - mi   num

Block B, motetus:
long 22   reg - na   ve   rat
      46   concinat Gallus Na - so   nis
      70   subi - to   ca   su

---

[25] The other two occurrences of this musical phrase fall on *vispilionum* and *hominum*, thus drawing attention to the first 'rhyme' of the motetus (*latronum–vispilionum*) with the caesural *hominum* of the Ovid hexameter.

Ex. 4.4 Triplum of *Tribum* showing chant paraphrase of tenor *Merito*

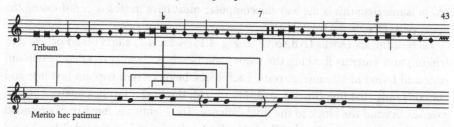

The triplum presents three text lines, nine words, 3 × 3, before the critical word *Fortuna*, which in **Paris146** is made to stand at the top of the recto page; the thrice three words preceding it are at the foot of the preceding verso.[26] Fortuna is central to Ovid's letter, to *Fauvel* and to the observations on the career of Marigny, developed covertly here but more overtly in *Aman novi/Heu Fortuna*. The three voices of the motet enter in succession, at intervals of three longs, triplum, motetus, tenor, that is, first one, then two, then all three parts sound. The verbal repetition pattern involves three triplum words, two motetus words and one tenor word. As noted, the beginning and end of the tenor melody are on scale degrees 1, 2 and 3; 3, 2, 1 (*ut re mi ... mi re ut*). There are twice three blocks of identical material in all three parts. The tenor has two *color* statements, each of six three-note *ordines* separated by rests. The maximodus is perfect, three longs to the maxima. The total number of lines (27) is 3 cubed.[27]

This motet is one of a significant minority in which the tenor is not the lowest in range but the middle voice of the texture.[28] It mostly sounds fifths between the triplum–motetus octaves. The motetus is the contrapuntal foundation, and is always a fifth below the tenor on downbeats of the large modus groups, except at L67, where exceptionally an octave is used, for an exceptional position (accommodating a triplum–motetus imitation that links the two borrowed texts). The motetus here twice makes its own insistence on the distinctive disjunct *a c g* motive, at L64–L67, and then in the final B block from L70, independently of its adhesion to the tenor. The motetus deceptively usurps the tenor's role as the true foundation of the piece—perhaps a further mirror of a series of deceptions in the Genesis story (recalled by the tenor), since Jacob had previously cheated his brother Esau out of his birthright before himself being deceived by his own sons about the fate of Joseph. Deception and usurpation are central themes of *Fauvel*.

Whether or not they thought it was by Vitry, *Tribum* has been accepted as an 'advanced' composition by most scholars including Sanders, Edward Roesner and Lawrence Earp.[29] Karen Desmond, on the other hand, argues that it is a conservative

---

[26] It was not necessary to space the piece in this way. It could have been accommodated on the recto, starting at the top of the page, without displacing any other material, by the simple expedient of writing a single statement of the tenor. The tenor is notated once only in **Br19606**, twice (redundantly) in **Paris146**.

[27] There are 27 words in the motetus of the neighbouring *Adesto/Firmissime*, a strongly trinitarian piece studied in Robertson, 'Local Chant Readings'.

[28] It may be one of the earliest in which this is consistently true, though a few motets in **Mo** have the tenor in the middle for some of the time. Here the placing of the tenor as the middle voice emphasises its role as the palindromic middle of the trio of motets. See Ch. 1 for middle-voice tenors, including *Apollinis*, and now the early *Flos vernalis*: Alís Raurich, 'The *Flores* of *Flos vernalis*'.

[29] Leech-Wilkinson 'The Emergence of *Ars nova*', 298–99 stresses the close similarity of the musical language of *Tribum/Quoniam* and *Firmissime/Adesto* and assigns them to the same composer. Earp indeed noted ('Isorhythm', 97–98) 'that the parallel perfect intervals in *Tribum/Quoniam* help to convey a message, and must not be considered as evidence of inept composition'.

piece, seen by a later writer as relatively crude in comparison with the 'subtler' *Apta caro*. This hangs on her misapplying the theorist's *grosso modo* as a judgement of *Tribum* as 'simple, plain or even crude and unrefined'.[30] This is perhaps to understate the status of *Tribum* in its own time and the many subtleties that have been pointed out since. Its wide dissemination, well into the fifteenth century, would certainly suggest that it was valued long after its original composition.[31] *Tribum* is set up in such a way as to encourage parallel part-writing, especially if viewed in the long term rather than in a contrapuntally local way. Parallel octaves and fifths occur between triplum and motetus, parallels with the tenor only at L20, L44, and L55. Considering the extent of tenor paraphrase in the triplum, it is surprising that there is not even more parallelism. Rather than regarding such parallels as archaic, or even crude, they could well be part of the self-conscious playing with time that is a constant feature of the *Fauvel* project, stylistic (and notational) evolutionary time, both archaising and ultramodern, forwards and backwards. Innovation and novelty are relative. *Tribum* was highly original in many such ways, including for its departure from the *ars antiqua* in using perfect (rather than imperfect) maximodus, imperfect (rather than perfect) modus and tempus, and what would later become trochaic major prolation, as well as for its role in the Marigny trio.

Garrit gallus/In nova: Texts

Before setting out further links between *Tribum* and *Garrit gallus*, we will consider *Garrit gallus/In nova*, which is preserved in two sources, **Paris146**, f. 44^v and **Pic**, 67^r, and transcribed as ▶ Ex. 4.5.[32]

Texts and translations by David Howlett, lightly adapted:

Triplum	Disyllabic rhymes
Garrit Gallus flendo dolorose,	a
luget quippe **Gallorum** concio,	b
que satrape traditur dolose,	a
excubitus sedens officio,	b

---

[30] Schreur, *Tractatus Figurarum*, 66–69, who unconvincingly translates *grosso modo* as 'grand'. Desmond, *Music and the moderni*, 2: 'But perhaps the intended meaning here is closer to "simple" or "plain", or even as a synonym for "crassus"—that is, crude and unrefined'. Grantley McDonald and Leofranc Holford-Strevens confirmed (personal communications) that *grosso modo* is a generalised comment rather than a judgement of the piece, certainly not implying that it was crude. The correct sense was already recognised in Stone, 'Che cosa c'è', and see now Bent, '*Artes novae*'. Desmond transcribes the opening (L1–L36) on p. 54, and the parallel fifths and octaves at L50–L62 on p. 63, offering her own analysis, building partly on that in Bent, '*Tribum*', but missing the demonstration of text–music relationships that could have qualified it for a higher subtlety rating. The parallel fifths and octaves create a deliberate effect of rawness, perhaps self-consciously atavistic. Earp, 'Isorhythm', 94–96, offers an insightful tonal analysis of this motet; he sees the archaising parallel intervals as a deliberately desolate gesture and the placing of the tenor in the middle as an expression of the 'slender thread' of the text. On Hartt, 'The Problem of the Vitry Motet Corpus', see Ch. 7 and n. 38.

[31] One late manuscript of the treatise, **Faenza**, incomprehensibly groups *Rex Karole* (dated in the late 1370s) together with the 'unsubtle' *Tribum* of the late 1310s, whereas the 'subtler' *Apta caro* is probably from the 1350s or earlier. *Rex Karole* therefore must be considered a late addition to the **Faenza** text. It is also a late addition to Boen, *Ars (Musicae)*, as Boen died in 1367. See Ch. 15 n. 15.

[32] Ch. 17 discusses the notation of *Musicalis* on the **Pic** rotulus, which, exceptionally, spatially aligns isorhythmic periods within each of the two upper parts, inapplicable to *Garrit gallus*. For the **Pic** version of *Garrit gallus* see Fig. 4.3.

FAUVEL AND VITRY

5	atque **vulpes**, tamquam vispilio	b
	in Belial vigens astucia,	c
	de **leonis** consensu proprio	b
	monarchisat, artat angaria.	c
	Rursus, ecce, Jacob familia	c
10	Pharaone altero fugatur;	d
	non ut olim Jude vestigia	c
	subintrare potens, lacrimatur;	d
	in deserto fame flagellatur,	d
	adiutoris carens armatura.	e
15	Quamquam clamat, tamen spoliatur,	d
	continuo forsan moritura;	e
	miserorum exulum vox dura!	e
	O **Gallorum garritus** doloris,	f
	cum **leonis cecitas** obscura	e
20	fraudi paret **vulpis** proditoris.	f
	Eius fastus sustinens erroris	f
	insurgito: alias labitur	g
	et labetur quod habes honoris,	f
	*quod **mox** in facinus tardis ultoribus itur.*	g

The cock gabbles, weeping grievously; indeed the whole flock of cocks performing the duty of the watch mourns; it is betrayed deceitfully to the satrap. And the fox, as the lowest sort of reprobate, flourishing with the cunning of Belial, behaves like a monarch with the lion's own consent; he imposes compulsory duties. Again, behold, the family of Jacob is put to flight by another pharaoh; not, as formerly, able to follow the tracks of Judah, it wails; it is scourged by famine in the desert, lacking the armament of a helper. Although it cries out, nonetheless it is robbed, perhaps about to die on the spot. The harsh voice of wretched exiles. O the gabble of the grief of the cocks, since the dark blindness of the lion lies subject to the fraud of the traitor fox. Bearing the arrogance of his error, rise up! Otherwise what you have of honour falls, and it will fall, because when avengers are slow people soon turn to crime.

Motetus	Disyllabic rhymes	
*In nova fert animus **mutatas** dicere formas.*		
Draco nequam quem olim penitus	b	
mirabili crucis potencia	c	
debellavit Michaël inclitus,	b	
5 **mox** Absalon munitus gracia,	c	
mox Ulixis gaudens facundia,	c	
mox lupinis dentibus armatus,	d	
sub Tersitis miles milicia	c	
rursus vivit in **vulpem mutatus**;	d	

10	fraudi cuius lumine privatus	d
	leo, vulpe imperante, paret.	e
	Oves suggit **pullis** saciatus.	d
	Heu! Suggere non cessat et aret;	e
	ad nupcias carnibus non caret.	e
15	Ve **pullis**! Mox ve **ceco leoni**!	f
	Coram Christo tandem ve **draconi**!	f

Tenor: Neuma

My mind brings [me] to speak of forms changed into new [bodies]. The evil dragon which long ago the renowned Michael utterly vanquished by the wondrous power of the Cross, now fortified with the good looks of Absalom, now rejoicing in the eloquence of Ulysses, now a soldier in the army of Thersites, armed with wolfish teeth, lives again changed into a fox. With the fox commanding, the lion, deprived of sight, lies subject to his fraud. Sated with chicks he sucks the sheep. Alas! he does not cease to suck, and he is (still) thirsty. He does not lack meats for the wedding feast. Woe to the chicks! Soon, woe to the blind lion! At the last, before Christ, woe to the dragon!

The motetus opens with one of the most famous of classical opening lines (Ovid, *Metamorphoses* I.1) about animal transformations, the hexameter 'In nova fert animus mutatas dicere formas [corpora]'; (My mind brings [me] to speak of forms changed into new bodies—the quotation stops short of Ovid's *corpora*). This is the literary work, widely known and quoted then as now, which above all others deals with and stands for metamorphoses between gods, humans, and animals. The protagonist of *Fauvel* is a horse unnaturally transformed to human estate and kingly status. *In nova fert* on the last full folio of the *roman* (f. 44^v) thus comes full circle from the first folio in which Fortuna raised (transformed) Fauvel from stable to palace. Both motet texts are beast fables, the triplum about a flock of cocks, a blind lion, and a fox, the motetus about a dragon, which, changed into an insatiable fox, at a wedding feast first consumes the chicks, then sucks the blood of sheep, and yet remains thirsty. We have already noted how its status as a famous opening marks the beginning of the backwards historical narrative.

Gallus is the opening gambit of *Garrit gallus*, perhaps authorial, surely multivalent. *Gallus* is both a cockerel (rooster) who gives a warning cry and a Frenchman (and in the plural form *gallorum*, Frenchmen). Gallus was Petrarch's sobriquet for Vitry, whose identity as the Gallus of the fourth eclogue of Petrarch's *Bucolicum carmen* has been cautiously reaffirmed.[33] Gallus was the name of an earlier Latin poet regarded as one of Ovid's important models and predecessors, but of whose work almost nothing

---

[33] Mann, 'In margine'. Vitry remains one of several candidates for identification as the 'Gallus' of Petrarch's fourth eclogue. Despite a number of early testimonies, he is rejected in Petrarch, *Bucolicum carmen*, ed. François and Bachmann, and cautiously left in play by Mann. However, none of these authors adduces these earlier and

100 FAUVEL AND VITRY

survives. 'Gallus' may gain further significance from the 'cock' king, as Philip V is represented, particularly in *Un songe*, one of the French *dits* in **Paris146**.[34]

The last line of the triplum of *Garrit gallus* is a hexameter from a medieval Latin epic about the ruin of a nation: Joseph of Exeter, *De bello trojano* (I. 386), the same work that provided the last couplet of the triplum of *Tribum*, another link between the two motets.[35] Here, likewise, it is worked into the chained scheme of disyllabic rhymes, with only the Ovidian first motetus line standing outside the rhyme scheme. The 24 triplum lines relate 3:2 to the 16 lines of the motetus; all the lines are decasyllabic except for the two hexameters.

The techniques of verbal construction are similar to those of *Tribum*: *mutatas* and *mox* from the hexameter lines are worked foundationally into the new rhythmic text. The fox, cockerel and chickens (as *vulpes*, *gallus* and *pullis*), and the blind lion are among the verbal links between the two texts. Significant words are sometimes adjacent, and Howlett has found many to be significantly spaced by word count. The biblical allusions are strong. In the triplum, the cocks (Frenchmen) are compared with the Israelites, the family of Jacob pursued by an unnamed pharaoh into the desert and starved; in the motetus they are eaten. Old Testament figures Jacob and Judah are named in the triplum, as is the 'bad' character Belial, forming a trio (threes are also a conspicuous theme of *Tribum*). Absalom is named in the motetus together with the New Testament figures, the Apocalyptic archangel Michael and Christ, forming another trio. The motetus presents Absalom in another, overlapping trio together with two classical characters in the triple anaphora of lines beginning with *mox*: a traitor with deceptive good looks like Absalom (2 Kings 14: 25),[36] a liar of eloquent cunning like Ulysses (*Aeneid* II. 164, IX. 602), and a forceful brute like Thersites (*Iliad* II), is the fox Enguerrand de Marigny, financial counsellor to the blind lion Philippe IV.

Garrit gallus: Music and Notation

Tribum (▶ Ex. 4.1 above) and *Aman* (Ex. 5.1 below) are barred and numbered in longs, *Garrit* (▶ Ex. 4.5) in breves, the better to mark the alternation between perfect

---

apparently Vitriacan self-presentations as a *gallus*, which could add weight to his candidacy. On the other hand, Zoltán Rihmer (email correspondence of Nov. 2015) is of the opinion that the content would be so insulting to Vitry as to make his candidacy highly unlikely. Wathey, 'The Motets of Vitry', 120, adds (with sources) other testimonies, including that of Francesco Piendibeni da Montepulciano, chancellor of Perugia, who, in a commentary on the *Bucolicum carmen* completed in 1394, makes clear not only that Vitry's reputation had survived into the first generation of Petrarch scholarship but also that it was rapidly established in the exegesis of the poet's works. Identifying Vitry with the 'Gallus' of the Fourth Eclogue—'Gallus hic fuit Phylippus de Victriaco, clarissimus musicus et philosophus et Petrarce summe notus'—Piendibeni comments that 'Gallus erat unus famulus francigena musicus qui Petrarcham infestabat assidue ut poesym et rhetoricam edoceret' ('this Gallus was Philippe de Vitry, most famous musician and philosopher, and well known to Petrarch', and 'Gallus was a servant, born in France, a musician who pestered Petrarch to teach him poesy and rhetoric').

[34] *Six Historical Poems*, ed. Storer and Rochedieu.
[35] First pointed out by David Howlett in a seminar in Oxford in Feb. 1992. This is reported, together with many valuable insights on classical allusions in *Fauvel* motets, in Holford-Strevens, 'Fauvel Goes to School', 64. See n. 6 above for the citation in *Tribum*.
[36] Or could the good-looking Absalom represent Philip the Fair?

and imperfect modus.[37] The commentary to this transcription is in the Appendix to this chapter.

The novelty and strangeness of the events portrayed are signalled not only by Ovid's words but also by the earliest surviving use of red notation in the tenor of *Garrit gallus* to signify mensural, indeed temporal, metamorphosis of perfect to imperfect modus, possibly punning on Marigny's red hair as well as on mutation (black and red to change modus, standing for human and animal metamorphoses).[38] This motet is cited along with others in the early *ars nova* treatises for a range of different usages of red notes to change modus or tempus or both, in either direction. For *Garrit gallus* this is defined negatively: red notes can be placed to prevent a long before a long having three breves, and to prevent alteration of the second of two breves preceding a long.[39] But the forms of the black tenor notes are transformed into new red bodies, which literally embody many of the themes of the motet. The mutation of colour causes temporal change. At B79, *mutatus* is marked by a strong dissonant appoggiatura in the motetus. **Paris146** marks a $b\flat$ against $f\sharp$, perhaps punning on mutation in a hexachordal sense; **Pic** delays the $\sharp$ until B80. This comes just after the fox T̲h̲e̲r̲sites is punningly given a t̲e̲r̲nary long.

The tenor has two *color* statements, each consisting of three *taleae*. The black notes of the tenor are in perfect modus, the red in imperfect (in Fig. 4.2 grey, with coloration brackets). It is rhythmically a 'nominal' palindrome, formed by the status of the notes (as longs or breves) rather than of their counted values, which include altered and unaltered breves: see Fig. 4.2.[40] The third note, the second black ■, followed by a dot, is altered before the following red ■, and the penultimate note (■) is altered before the final ◄. By later standards, alteration can take place only before a note of the next higher value, a dot alone being insufficient, though several early theorists, all in similar language, know a *punctum alterationis*, of which this may be an example.[41] Not only each

---

[37] Desmond, *Music and the moderni*, discusses this motet with respect to 'destabilisation of modus', 215–19, drawing attention to the triplum dot at B137 (near the end), which cuts across the imperfect modus of the other parts. She rightly observes that, despite the upper-part rests that articulate the tenor's modal changes, the upper parts do not follow them in lockstep, but have their directed arrivals on perfect sonorities which do not always coincide with the tenor's modal changes.

[38] Red notation is also used in the tenor of *Thalamus/Quomodo*, **Paris146**, f. 32, but apparently with no mensural function. Sanders suggests it might correspond to a distinction between plainsong and non-chant, one of the meanings possibly implied in the *ars nova* treatises. More significantly, and less well known, is that red notation is used in an English source that cannot be much later, **Lwa12185**, probably from the 1320s, as it includes (other, non-red) notations described in Handlo's treatise of 1326. In *Beatus vir*, red notation turns the long and breve from perfect to imperfect, while in *Nos orphanos*, red coloration turns the long from perfect to imperfect but does not change the character of the breve. These fragmentary motets are transcribed in Lefferts, 'Motet in England', 713, 719. This raises intriguing questions of influence and direction, as the mensural use of red notation is unlikely to have been devised independently. Red notation is not mentioned by any English theorist at this period, notably Handlo, whose knowledge of French motets may not have extended beyond Petrus de Cruce, for whose authorship of motets he and Jacobus's *Speculum musice* VII are the major and earliest authorities. Additions by a later scribe to **Lo62132A** use red notation for middle chant-bearing parts in score; see Bent, *The Fountains Fragments*. See now Bradley, 'Fragments from a Medieval Motet Book' for the only known use of the theoretically prescribed use of coloration for octave transposition.

[39] 'Aliquociens uero ponuntur ut longa ante longam non ualeat tria tempora uel ut secunda duarum breuium inter longas positarum non alteretur ut in tenore In noua fert animus.' Anonymous version of the *Compendium* in **Paris14741** (TML), fuller than that in CSM.

[40] 'Nominal': term suggested by Leofranc Holford-Strevens.

[41] Wolf, 'Ein anonymer Musiktraktat'; *De musica mensurabili* (Pseudo-Theodonus) and *De semibrevibus caudatis*, both in CSM 13. *Quatuor Principalia* IV, ch. 26 (*CS* iv. 266, now in Aluas, *Quatuor principalia*) rejects the use of a dot for alteration as absurd: 'licet quidam posuerunt punctum duabus aliis de causis, et male, videlicet causa imperfectionis et alterationis, quod absurdum est dicere', so by 1351 this usage seems to have fallen from favour.

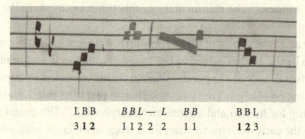

LBB	BBL—	L	BB		BBL
3 1 2	1 1 2 2	2	1 1		1 2 3

Fig. 4.2 Palindromic rhythm of the (first) tenor *talea* of *Garrit gallus* in Paris, Bibliothèque nationale de France, fr. 146, f. 44ᵛ. © BnF. Red notes are labelled in italics, with note values numerically below. Bold numbers signal where the nominal palindrome is not also numerical

talea, but the entire tenor is a nominal rhythmic palindrome, with no rest at the beginning or end.

The upper parts are in imperfect time throughout, its semibreves in what would later be called major prolation, as confirmed by later sources with minim stems. The tenor's red notation has no effect on them at the prolation level, which remains major; later in the century, red notation usually fixed notes at their imperfect values at all levels. Whether the upper parts are in perfect or imperfect modus is moot: two successive longs at motetus B45 and B47 seem to confirm imperfect modus (if in perfect modus, the first would have to be perfect), as does the fact that all longs in the upper parts in both sources that need to be perfect have dots, except in **Paris146** at B101. The final tenor is perfect, so if the final notes are equal, the upper parts may also be deemed perfect. But the twenty-five breves of each of the six *taleae* divide neither by two nor three, so some irregularity (or mutation) is inevitable. As a convenient compromise, the upper parts are here barred following the perfections and imperfections of the tenor, but some independence and ambiguity are possible.

For demonstration purposes, the accompanying transcription (▶ Ex. 4.5) is a hybrid between the two sources. The downstems are present only in **Paris146**, and are sometimes so small or tentative as to be almost absent, but they are not, as Apel thought, later additions. *Garrit* has no upstemmed minims in **Paris146**; those in the transcription are from **Pic**, Fig. 4.3. That **Pic** was copying from an unstemmed exemplar is apparent from its redundant retention of most dots between groups of S whose values are now made explicit by minim stems, including one passage (over *o miserum*) where the scribe was confused and allowed dots to stand after each of a succession of five semibreves. The few plicas are present only in **Paris146**. Works attributed to Vitry (including late and recently reconstructed works like *Phi millies* and *Beatius/Cum humanum*) never imperfect the breve in ℂ by a minim, except by using a plica.[42] This usage could be a negative authorial marker for Vitry, or at least a reason for doubting his authorship of

---

[42] The triplum of *Phi millies* is transcribed and reconstructed in Zayaruznaya, *The Monstrous New Art*, appendix 3, who proposes a dating of 1356–57 in 'Evidence of Reworkings', 174 n. 41. She suggests *Beatius* may be by Vitry in Zayaruznaya, 'Quotation, Perfection', and in 'Evidence of Reworkings', 165–66, she argues that the central hocket section might have been added later. In *The Monstrous New Art*, 206–15 she reveals a passage of triplum text and music quoted directly from *Firmissime/Adesto*.

TRIBUM/QUONIAM AND GARRIT GALLUS/IN NOVA   103

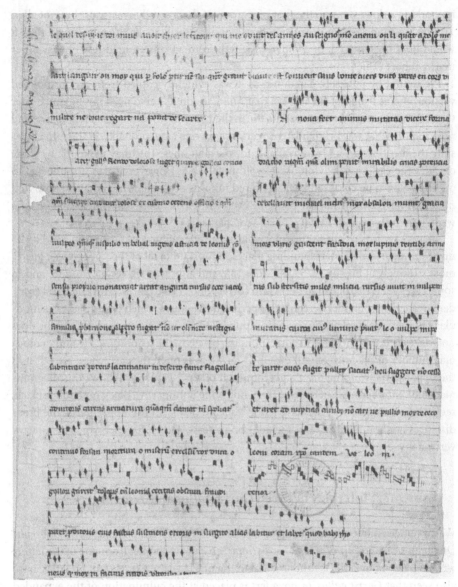

Fig. 4.3 *Garrit gallus* in Paris, Bibliothèque nationale de France, Collection de Picardie 67, f. 67[r]. © BnF

motets with breves imperfected by minims. The plicas in *Fauvel* are never spelt out as minims in the later more precisely notated sources of the unstemmed motets. **Paris146** also places some semibreves almost adjacent to unison breves, never with a new syllable, suggesting tied notes, here shown with dotted ties, at tr B18, B20, B34, B45, B59, B88, mo B27, B43, B59, B77, B102.[43] In **Paris146**, *Garrit* and *Aman* are fairly consistent

---

[43] Semibreves actually touching each other, or 'one-note ligatures', are more decisively notated in Italian sources. In pure Italian notation, the breve is not imperfected. Successive unisons judged here to be of this type are shown by dotted ties.

104 *FAUVEL* AND VITRY

in marking a downstem on the first of a group of three semibreves; most but not all in *Tribum* are so marked. A downstem does not necessarily make the note longer than it would be if unstemmed, or a different length from an unstemmed note, but it never marks a short value.[44]

Pic cannot be precisely dated, but as it was evidently copied from an unstemmed version, and as I suggest (in Ch. 17) that *Musicalis* on its verso need not be much later than 1330, I see no reason not to date **Pic** in the 1330s. Both these motet tenors use void notation for what was originally red (certainly in one case, probably in the other), despite the fact that red ink was available for the staff lines. This may make **Pic** by some decades the earliest surviving use of void notation.[45] However, it was not unusual to outline notes to be coloured later when red ink was available, which may be how void notation started. Informal use could be even earlier, as in the tenor of *Vos*/*Gratissima* written in the margin of **Esc10** *c.* 1330; see Chapter 8.

There is no isorhythm in the upper parts, but the aligned transcription (ⓑ Ex. 4.5 invites comparison of corresponding places in most if not all of the upper-voice *taleae*, most strikingly at breves 32, 57, 82, 107, 132; and at breves 15, 40, 65, 90, 115, and in some cases a few surrounding notes also correspond. These places, with B + B rest (∎ ⌐), demarcate Ernest Sanders's regular isoperiodic structures which he expresses as modular numbers, defined as the periodic number of breves between rests, though he does not make clear that these fall at corresponding places in the tenor *talea*. He finds a modular number of the *talea* length of 25B (17 + 8); as is often the case, these are offset in the upper parts from the *talea* and from each other.[46] Figure 4.4 shows this diagrammatically. Numbering is in breves. The tenor is the bottom row. Black notation is black, red notation is grey, and the long tenor rests are blank. In the upper parts, the breve distances are bounded by (and include) breve rests, shown for each voice by a heavy vertical line.

Interplay between *Garrit gallus* and *Tribum*

We have seen how the last couplet of the motetus of *Tribum que non abhorruit*/ *Quoniam secta latronum*/*Merito hec patimur*, an elegiac couplet from one of the letters written by Ovid in exile, is fundamental to the newly written texts built on it. We have also seen that *Garrit gallus*/*In nova fert* is placed at the culmination of the expanded and interpolated version of *Fauvel*. It is a grand *admonitio* which is also a motet about

---

[44] In four of the Lescurel songs in **Paris146**, there is often a downstem on the first of a group of four or three S; groups of S separated by dots are mostly melismatic, but some are syllabic, for example on ff. 59ᵛ–60, 61, 62, when perfect time seems to prevail.

[45] Musical commentary in Appendix to this chapter. A clear case is in the motet *Ferre solet* in **Douai74**, where the red notes were filled in from void outlines. The canon specifies them as red, but the word *vacue* is added above. They must have been first outlined in void, the canon copied from a source with red notation specifying red, the canon here corrected to correspond to the void notation, and then red notation supplied. The motet is discussed in Louviot, 'Uncovering the Douai Fragment'.

[46] This happens also in *Musicorum*, *Apollinis*, and elsewhere. Sanders's numbers for *Garrit gallus* (total 147B) are shown diagrammatically in Fig. 4.4 above.

  tr 16B + (17 + 8 + 17 + 8 + 17 + 8 + 17 + 8 + 17B) + 14B
  mo 15B + (17 + 8 + 17 + 8 + 17 + 8 + 17 + 8 + 17B) + 15B
  Tenor 6B + (*10* + 15 + *10* + 15 + *10* + 15 + *10* + 15 + *10*B) + 6B (coloration italicised).

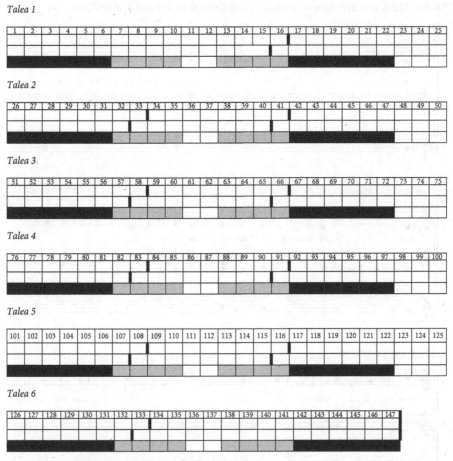

Fig. 4.4 Periodic structure of *Garrit gallus*

bestial transformation, Fauvel as a horse metamorphosed into a horse-human hybrid, embodying a range of animals that stand in for human subjects. It is therefore particularly appropriate that the first line of its motetus 'quotes', or rather, presents, the first line of Ovid's *Metamorphoses*. As in the case of *Tribum*, it can likewise be argued for *Garrit gallus* that its Ovidian line is not so much a quotation as a foundational building block.

The middle system of Ex. 4.6 shows the beginning of *Garrit gallus*. Above it on the first system is the free musical recapitulation at *talea* V to coincide with the verbal recapitulation of the opening words as *Gallorum garritus*. *Gallus* opens the triplum and then comes twice more as *Gallorum*, the second with this musical recapitulation, but both times in distress from the fox. Below it on the lowest system of Ex. 4.6 is the beginning of the second half of *Tribum/Quoniam*, at the second *color* statement, which starts with a clearly audible musical quotation of the beginning of *Garrit gallus*. It is a quotation that involves all three parts, changing their roles (mutating, again) and applying light camouflage. The motetus (as noted) is the lowest voice, and the triplum outlines the *Tribum* tenor *Merito* (Ex. 4.4 above). The Ovidian motetus *In nova fert* lies above the triplum at the beginning of *Garrit gallus* for the duration of the quoted line and

Ex. 4.6 Musical relations between *Garrit Gallus/In nova fert* and *Tribum/Quoniam*

beyond; it is echoed again at the midpoint of *Tribum* at *ascenderit*. *Tribum*'s motetus also picks up the strongly derogatory *vispilio* (*vispilionum*, motetus line 2) from *Garrit gallus* (triplum line 5).

All this suggests that the composition of *Garrit gallus* preceded *Tribum*, as do its tenses; it would be harder to explain the quotation if the order was reversed, though they must surely have been planned together. Indeed, recognition of the full resonances of the quotation depends on considering the text and music combinations together. In *Tribum*, the quotation directly follows the central words of the triplum, *trans metam* (across the boundary)—a kind of 'meta'morphosis, possibly a further Ovidian pun— and is followed by the words *concinat Gallus Nasonis*. *Concinat* is the verb used by Philippe de Vitry to signal his authorship in the motet *Cum statua/Hugo, Hugo* as 'hec concino Philippus publice'. Then comes the word *gallus* which, as we saw above, has multiple meanings in this context. *Gallus* comes twice in the motetus of *Tribum*; the *gallos* are gnawed by the fox, and the *Gallus* ventriloquises Ovid. Philip IV, still alive (present tense) in *Garrit gallus*, is now dead in *Tribum/Quoniam*, motetus line 4, past tense: 'tempore quo <u>regnaverat</u> leo cecatus'. Ovid named himself (Naso) in line 10 of the letter: 'quisquis sit, audito nomine, Naso, rogas'. Naso is named in line 8 of the *Tribum* motetus as the author of the couplet from the letter. Naso is Ovid's signature name: the author aligns himself with Ovid by announcing the couplet from *Epistulae ex Ponto* from both authorial mouths, Ovid's and his own ('concinat gallus nasonis dicta'). At the same time, *Tribum* alludes to the opening of *Garrit gallus/In nova fert* which presents the declaiming *Gallus* simultaneously with *In nova fert*, the first line of Ovid's *Metamorphoses*.

The multiple quotation cements the authorial link between the Gallus 'singing out' (*concinat*) in *Tribum*, 'prating' (*garrit*) in *Garrit gallus*, and the Ovid whose words are present in and fundamental to both motets. [*Con-*]-*cinat Gallus* is set to a prominent four-note motive (*b d c b*) that precedes three of the *Tribum* blocks, and it recurs in conjunction with words whose special significance we have already observed. It introduces the second (central) A block at L33 (*ruere* before *merito*), the central B block at L45 (*Gallus Nasonis*) and the final B block with the Ovid couplet at L69 (*subito/casu*). This placing of motetus *casu* (fall) reflects the triplum *casurus* in the middle B block.

The Ovidian *In nova fert* is located as prominently as it could be at the beginning of *Garrit gallus*. The middle of the central B block in *Tribum/Quoniam* falls on *Nasonis*. Thus the same words and music are emphasised by repetition and quotation and by positions that are proportioned in relation to each other as well as internally. We now see that the central interruption to the pattern of musical rhyme (*z* in Fig. 4.1 above) is made precisely to enable the centrally placed quotation from *Garrit gallus*. There are significant coincidences at the junction with *color* 2: the middle words of both parts, which occur in those lines; a palindrome in triplum and motetus melodies; and a repetition of *ascendere/-it* that introduces *color* 2 with a coincidence of music and words.

Tribum/Quoniam and *Garrit gallus/In nova fert* share the same beasts: *gallus, vulpes, pullis* and *leo* (cockerel, foxes, chicks and lion). *Garrit gallus* twice has in the tenor (at B92 and B129) the notes *b♭ a* at the motetus's *leo* (see Ex. 4.7). The two triplum lions fall at the midpoint of each *color* (B36 and B111 in ⓟ Ex. 4.5). The *Garrit gallus* tenor notes *b♭ a* at *leo* become the long and deliberate *b♭ a* for *leo* in the motetus of *Tribum/Quoniam* at L27–L28 in ⓟ Ex. 4.1. These notes sound, as they do in the tenor of *Garrit gallus*, as the lowest notes of the texture (despite the tenor being the middle voice in *Tribum*), and are written at the same pitch in both motets. They are preceded, in the first B block, by the emphatic past-tense verb *regnaverat*, also set to long notes, as if to emphasise the past tense, and to suggest that he (Philip IV) reigned too long. The particular prominence given here to the lion (albeit the blind lion, Philip IV) recalls Vitry's personal seals, both surviving instances of which date from the late 1340s and appropriate classical imagery in portraying the figures of Hercules and the lion. The second seal shows Hercules and David conquering the lion, precisely as the text of *Tribum* does in what, above, I called a 'striking marriage of pagan and Christian elements'. The lion in the seal is overpowered, and the regal lion in *Garrit gallus* is blind, so it would hardly

Ex. 4.7 Musical relations between *Garrit Gallus* and *Tribum* at the word *leo*

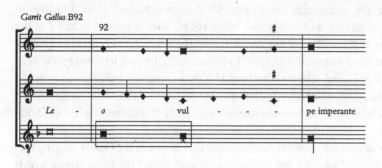

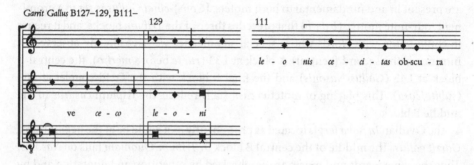

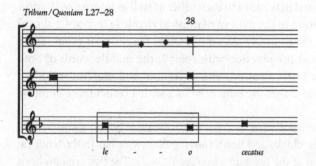

qualify as an honourable Vitry signature alongside the likelier *Gallus*, prominent in both motets.[47]

Appendix
Commentary to Tribum/Quoniam (musical edition, ▶ Ex. 4.1)

Sources: **Paris146**, ff. 41ᵛ–42; **Br19606**, recto, no. 3; **Stras**, f. 71ᵛ, no. 115, in Coussemaker, *Le Manuscrit de Strasbourg*, 110–11, which I neglected to use in Bent, 'Tribum'. Plicas and the few downstems are in **Paris146** only; in **Br19606** and **Stras** the

---

[47] Wathey, 'The Motets of Vitry', 145–46. I thank Julian Gardner for his observation of this correspondence between seal and text.

rhythms are confirmed by minim stems. None of the **Paris146** plicas are realised as additional notes in those sources. But for the motetus *b♭*s, triplum *f♯* would be suggested.

Triplum: **Paris146** 36.4, 60.4 *e* ♦; rhythm matched to 12 (♦ ♦) on authority of **Br19606** and **Stras**, equalising the A blocks; **Br19606** and **Stras** 27.2–29.2 one lig; **Br19606** tr 35.2–4 *b a b g* ♦ ♦ ♦ ♦; 54 no ♭; **Stras** 3, ⌐ before 3.3; 4 *ab* dotted ▪; 11. 2–4, 35. 2–4, 59.2–4 *c b a g* ♦ ♦ ♦♦; 27.2–3 *g* ▪; 51 *a g f e* ▪ ♦ ♦ ♦; 54.4 ♦ ♦ ♦♦.

Motetus: **Paris146** ♭ signature appears only at the beginnings of staves 2, 5, 6 (preceding the clef), 8, but ♭ precedes the first *b* on the other staves except staff 4 where it precedes the second *b* (33), not the first (31). **Br19606** ♭ sig every staff except the last; *c* and *f* clefs on first two staves; **Stras** ♭ sig on every staff; **Paris146** 34 long plica followed by ♦ ♦ *a g*; 35–39 om (thus for 33–40 it has: *b d c b a–a g f*); 60.3–4 no lig, **Paris146** over erasure; **Br19606** and **Stras** 54 no ♭; **Br19606** 56.2–4 *a g a b* ♦ ♦ ♦♦; 57.2–3 lig; 66.2–67 *e d c b a*; **Stras** mo 1–3 3rd rest ⌐ instead of ⌐; 12.3–13, 33.3–4, 57.2–3 lig; 67 ▪ 68.3 ▪; **Paris146** 47, 71 *d*: correctly *c* in **Br19606**.

My transcription of the motetus differs from Schrade's in several places: at 34 (as **Br19606**: **Paris146** omits 35–39, giving just two semibreves *a g*), 47 (*c* as **Br19606**), 66 (as **Paris146**, rescuing the imitation by descent from *d*), 71 (*c* as **Br19606**; this and 47, 66 are confirmed both by **Stras** and by the intabulation in **Lo28550**). L74 is a possible further candidate for emendation, but without support from the manuscripts. There are no plicas in the later sources, which between them confirm details of the identical passages.

Commentary to *Garrit/In nova* (musical edition, ⓟ Ex. 4.5)

Paris146 has been followed unless **Pic** is clearly preferable. **Pic**'s variants are mostly equally good.

The tenor repetition is marked in **Pic** by two little strokes, in **Paris146** by an inscription that appears to have four minims followed by 'etc'. In the same paler ink, the tenor is preceded by 'n', probably for 'Neuma'.

Pic no ♭ at tr 12, 79, 129, 142, mo 12, 26, 41, 54, 98, 139; **Pic** no ♯ at tr 8, 59, 125, mo 6, 18, 136; 78, ♯ before 80 not 79; mo 104 ♭ **Pic** (placed before 101), not in **Paris146**.

Pic tr 8.1 *g*; 61.2 *d*; 101 dotted ▪; 106.2 *c*; 111.2 ♦ ♦ *g f*; 114 lig; 135.3 *d*; 144.1 *d*; mo 28.2–3 ♦ *g*; 44 ♦♦ ♦ *g f e*; 45 downstem ▪; 85.2 ♦ ♦ *g a*; 119 ♦♦ ♦ *e d c*; 123–4 ♦♦ ♦ ♦ ♦ *c c c e f*; 128.2–3 ♦ *f*; 142–4 *fe ed cb*; 144 lig.

Paris146 tr 27.1–2 *a g* (at line change); 41 rest om **Paris146**; 95 ▪; tr 101 no dot, therefore implying perfect modus (dot in **Pic**), but 137 is dotted; dot after mo 119, 124, 128.

5

Aman novi/Heu Fortuna/Heu me

As we have seen in the preceding chapters, the three motets fit the *Fauvel* narrative in manuscript order: *Aman—Tribum—Garrit gallus*, and the historical narrative in reverse order. *Aman novi* comes just beyond where the short version of *Fauvel* ended,[1] at the most serious crux in that narrative (f. 30), immediately after Fortuna has rejected Fauvel's presumptuous marriage suit. The other two motets (*Tribum*, *Garrit gallus*) go on, in that order and in *Fauvel* time, to increasingly bitter reflections on the bad times and reversals of nature brought about by Fauvel and his progeny. On the manuscript opening containing *Aman novi/Heu Fortuna* (ff. 29ᵛ–30), both central characters, Fortuna and Fauvel, reach climactic crisis.[2] In *Aman novi*, Fauvel sings the motetus, *Heu Fortuna*, the (mostly) lower of the two differently texted upper voices. He usually sings in 'vulgar' (vernacular) French, but here, as noted, he laments in the higher register of Latin, signalling aspiration above his station.[3] His first-person sung lament is addressed to Fortuna, who has rejected his suit after raising his expectations, only then with her wheel to sink him in the lake of tears. She has promised him much, but now deceived him. If he will die like Haman (i.e. be hanged), this is no more than Fortuna predicted in the final stanza of her lai (f. 19ʳ⁻ᵛ), that he and his tribe will be hanged ('Puis soit Fauvel a seür | que j'entendré | a li honnir | et destruire | et de sa gent mainz pandré': Strubel vv. 61–65, preceding Långfors 2115). The motetus is introduced with the following words in French, which describe his face as being wet with tears, and place the motetus specifically in his mouth ('Ha fait le motet qui s'ensuit'):[4]

> Fauvel oi et entendu
> Ce que la dame li a rendu,
> Esperduz est, ne set que face

Older versions of this chapter, as 'Icarus, Phaeton, Haman: Fauvel and Dante?', were presented jointly by Bent and Kevin Brownlee to the Oxford Medieval Society on 23.5.1996, at the Vitry conference at Yale in 2015, and now published as Bent and Kevin Brownlee, 'Icarus, Phaeton, Haman: Did Vitry Know Dante?', *Romania*, 137 (2019), 85–129. I thank the editors of *Romania* for permission to reuse my part of that article here.

[1] On the short and expanded versions of *Fauvel*, see Ch. 3 n. 1. *Aman novi/Heu Fortuna/Heu me* is in **Paris 146**, f. 30.

[2] The opening is so arranged that the names of Fauvel and Fortuna alternate in the top lines of four of the six columns, one pair on each page. There are many examples of similarly contrived choreographies of layout; on ff. 41ᵛ–42, as noted in Ch. 4, the triplum of *Tribum* starts at the end of f. 41ᵛ so that the first word on f. 42 will be 'Fortuna'. The third column of f. 30 deals with the wise and foolish virgins. In part, they are prophetic of Fauvel's wedding with Fortuna's daughter Vaine Gloire, for which unhallowed nuptials he is attended by (female) virtues and vices. For 'F–F' see also Fig. 3.1.

[3] This motet is the final musical item in the courtship episode, of which Ruxandra Marinescu gives an excellent account, including its use and reversals of French and Latin between Fauvel and Fortuna ('The Politics of Deception', 51–78). Shortly afterwards, Fauvel sings for the last time, once more in Latin, in a fragment of pseudochant based on Ps. 80: 4, to give *gravitas* to his wedding invitation: *Buccinate in neomenia* (p.mus. 76, f. 31ᵛ).

[4] In addition it is a piece of the utmost sophistication. The argument in Sanders, 'The Early Motets of Philippe de Vitry', that it is untidy and unworthy, fades under an expanded range of criteria for the evaluation of quality and competence, as does his claim that it cannot have been written by Vitry later than 'tidier' but 'earlier' pieces. *Le Roman de Fauvel*, ed. Roesner et al., 20–21a, 24b, refer mainly to the topical references in this group: 'none of these pieces includes explicit reference to the figure of Fauvel', and it is further implied that none of the newly composed motets in modern style began life with a text specific to Fauvel. But at other

---

The Motet in the Late Middle Ages. Margaret Bent, Oxford University Press. © Oxford University Press 2023.
DOI: 10.1093/so/9780190063771.003.0006

112 FAUVEL AND VITRY

En plourant mouilliee la face

Non sachant quel chemin tenir

Doie, n'a quel fin doit venir,

Ha fait le motet qui s'ensuit:

Mes il n'i prent point deduit.

(Compare the last line of the motetus: 'hoc me docuisti'.)

(L 1032–39; S 4094–4101; cf. Dahnk 1032–1039.[5] Strubel 4094–4101 follows Långfors 3145–52.)

Fauvel heard and understood what the lady said. He is lost and doesn't know what to do. Weeping, his face wet, he doesn't know what route he should take, nor to what end he should come. [He] made the motetus which follows, but took scarcely any pleasure in it.

Triplum (ed. Rihmer)	Syllable count and rhymes
Aman novi probatur exitu,	10a
quantum prosit inflari spiritu	10a
superbie, quid plus appetere	10b
quam deceat, et que suscipere	10b
5 non liceat, tantumque scandere	10b
quod tedeat, ut alter Ycarus,	10c
qui tanquam **ignarus**	6c
in mari **est mersus**,	6d
aquis iam submersus.	6d
10 Sic nec est reversus	6d
Pheton usurpato	6e
Solis regimine,	6f
ed ipso cremato	6e
victo conamine	6f
15 est exterminatus.	6g
Sic nimis elatus,	6g
Ycari volatus	6g
affectans transcendere	7b
noster Aman, vincere	7b
20 rapinam Phetontis,	6h
in **Falconis** montis	6h
loco collocatus,	6g
evectus a pulvere	7b
ymbre sepe lavatur,	7i

points in the introductory essay it is shown that the motetus of *Aman novi/Heu fortuna* is indeed introduced as the words of Fauvel (18b), and that the Fauvel and Marigny ingredients are linked (51b–52a).

[5] Dahnk (Da) refers to the separately numbered verses of the Långfors edition (as 'texte') and the 1808 verses of the 'addicions' printed in its appendix ('La'), and introduces a new numeration in parentheses for the further 1069 verses published together with the texts of the musical interpolations, which are now additionally in Strubel.

25	aura flante siccatur	7i
	suis delictis in ymis:	8k
	Non eodem cursu respondent ultima primis.	hex k

The end of a new Haman proves what good it brings to swell with the spirit of pride, what [it means] to grasp after more than is appropriate and what one is not allowed to receive, and to rise so much that it offends, like another Icarus, who unaware, as it were, sank into the sea, now drowned in the waters. So [too] Phaeton did not return, having usurped the command of the Sun['s chariot], but, himself burned, [his] effort defeated, was exterminated. So [too] our Haman, excessively elevated, affecting to transcend the flight of Icarus, to surpass the theft of Phaeton, set up in the place of Montfaucon, lifted up from the dust, is repeatedly washed by the rain, dried by the blowing wind, [and yet is] in the depths because of his crimes: Not by the same course do the last things accord with the first.

The triplum text is corrupt and has undergone emendations, which are compared in ⏵ Table 5.1. These include Zoltan Rihmer's version, used here and in Ex. 5.1.

Then follows the motetus, *Heu Fortuna*, Fauvel's sung Latin lament on his rejection by Fortuna.[6]

Motetus text: Fauvel's words, first person[7]	Disyllabic rhymes
Heu Fortuna subdola,	7a
que semper diastola	7a
usque nunc fuisti,	6b
promittendo frivola	7a
5 tanquam vera sistola	7a
nunc apparuisti.	6b
Heu, quociens prospera,	7c
longe ponens aspera	7c
mihi promisisti,	6b

---

[6] Another instance of a motetus text being introduced in the surrounding verse, in this case by the author or narrator: 'Pour Phelippes qui regne ores/Ci metreiz ce motet onquores: O Philippe prelustris francorum' (Da vv. 35–36, p.mus. 33). See also (above and below) on the absence of a motet for Philip IV, apparently announced with 'Recitant de lui un motet. Ha, sire diex'. Another instance is the first fully French motet, *Je voi douleur/Fauvel nous a fait/Autant* (F 14, p.mus. 29), whose tenor is put into Fauvel's mouth in the first person.

[7] Commentary on motetus text by ZR:

1 *Fortuna* capitalised as a personified concept, like a number of similar notions in Vitry's motets (for example, *Fides, Ratio*), and, ultimately, Fauvel himself.

2, 5 *Diastola* (from the Greek word *diastole*) and *sistola* (from Greek *systole*) are the categories of ancient rhetoric (and medieval grammar), the former meaning the lengthening of a short vowel, the latter the shortening of a long one. Strubel (p. 529) points out that diastola and sistola are medical metaphors for cardiac expansion and contraction.

11 *ad* deleted, restoring the regular pattern of the syllable count.

12–13 As Becker pointed out, this stanza lacks its expected first half—or perhaps its second. The composer, even if he wrote this verse, could not have accommodated a further twenty syllables in the setting as it stands. It was either a deliberate irregularity by the poet, there being no obvious lacuna in the sense, or its omission was a musical compositional decision.

10	me ditans innumera	7c
	gaza usque ethera	7c
	nomen extulisti.	6b
	Nunc tua volubili	7d
	rota lacu flebili	7d
15	nudum demersisti.	6b
	Velud Aman morior;	7e
	de te sic experior	7e
	quod me decepisti;	6b
	quanto gradus alcior,	7e
20	*tanto casus gravior:*	7e
	hoc me docuisti.	6b

Tenor: Heu me, tristis est anima mea

Motetus: Alas, deceitful Fortune, you who have until now always been a means of expansion, by promising worthless things you have now appeared as a true means of contraction. Alas, how many times have you promised me prosperity, putting troubles far off; enriching me with countless treasures, you have exalted [my] name to the heavens. Now with your revolving wheel you have sunk me naked in the lake of tears. I die like Haman; thus do I find out about you by experience that you have deceived me. The higher the step, the graver the fall: this you have taught me.

Tenor: Alas for me, my soul is sad [even unto death].

While *Tribum* and *Garrit* are also preserved in later sources with explicit notation of minims, *Aman novi* is uniquely preserved in **Paris146**, f. 30[r]. The triplum begins not with not an ornamental 'A' but with 'Q': see Fig. 5.1. The obvious explanation is that the flourisher saw three minims (*ma*) with macron over the *a*, following the space for the initial and, in the absence of a guide letter, read it as *niam*, supplying the 'Q' for *Quoniam*. The three minims were likewise construed by Dahnk as *ni*, the macron over

Fig. 5.1 Triplum incipit of *Aman/Heu* in Paris, Bibliothèque nationale de France, fr. 146, f. 30[r]. © BnF

the *a* as representing *m*, reading the word as *Quoniam*, irregularly abbreviated. This would create an eleven-syllable line. In a long critical review, Becker, 'Fauvel', recognised this as an error for what would at first sight seem the apparently less likely word *Aman*, as confirmed later within both texts, and that the initial letter should have been 'A'.[8] So in the absence of a visible guide letter, the 'Q' was assumed to be a crass error, the scribe perhaps short-circuiting to the *Quoniam secta latronum* motetus of *Tribum que non abhorruit*. Although the correct reading *Aman* is beyond doubt, it is possible that the Q might not after all be an error. I was alerted to the phenomenon of *fausses lettres* by Elizabeth Cullinane ('Les *Dits entés*', 49–50), who gives an instance of 'Q' being substituted for 'A' in a vertical acrostic in the final *dit enté* of the Lescurel songs, *Gracieus temps est quant rosier*, which reads J E Q N (n) E (Jeanne), the additional 'n's in the 'N' line being provided alliteratively. In the 'ABC' of the thirteenth-century self-styled 'Huon, le roi de Cambrai', 'Q' has negative connotations as a reversal of 'P'.[9] P stands for *Père* and *Paradis*; Q is *bestourné*: 'Q étant un P tourné à l'envers, est une vilaine lettre, comme son nom.' Thus associated with retrogression and negativity, it may just possibly have been in this case a deliberate substitution for 'A', all the more telling for suggesting yet another link between *Fauvel* and the songs of Lescurel.

Fauvel's lament in the motetus (*Heu Fortuna subdola*) would sit equally well in the voice of Marigny, likewise raised by Fortuna and then dashed down. Fauvel speaks in the first person singular and in the present tense (both also used for the tenor) and aligns himself with Haman ('like Haman I die'), but he is still alive to say so. There are clear parallels between Haman's career and Marigny's, and obviously also with Fauvel's. Marigny was raised from relatively modest estate to disproportionate advancement, basked in royal favour and honour, and was finally hoist on his own petard. Haman rose to favour and then presumed to usurp royal status and its insignia (in his case, garments, crown, and indeed a horse), and was hanged for his treachery on the gallows he had prepared for Mordecai, as recounted in the Book of Esther.[10] The hanging of Haman's ten sons also mirrors the *roman*'s emphasis on the foul offspring of Fauvel. In dying 'like Haman', Fauvel's progeny are implicitly included in his fate. From this point on, in Fauvel's progress, his nuptial celebrations are very firmly located in Paris. Indeed, Montfaucon (the gallows of Paris) is named here in the triplum of *Aman novi*, as it is in the *Chronique*;[11] the manuscript's famous and recognisable depiction of fourteenth-century Paris is on the verso of the same leaf (f. 30), just one example of the subtle and subversive choreography of *Fauvel*'s physical layout.

---

[8] Becker, 'Fauvel', 40; reported in Schrade, 'Philippe de Vitry', 336.

[9] *Huon, le roi de Cambrai: Oeuvres*, ed. Artur Långfors (Paris, 1913). Cullinane cites **Paris837**, f. 127ʳ, in a context which emphasises reversal ('Si com li q va bestournant').

[10] In the English MS **Morgan978**, the text of *Singularis laudis digna* invokes Esther and Ahasuerus in the course of beseeching the Virgin for English victory: Bowers, 'Fixed Points', 315–17, dates it to 1369, rejecting the interpretation of Sanders, 'English Polyphony', 172–73. The motetus of *Rex Karole/Leticie pacis* (datable in the late 1370s) names Esther, Ahasuserus, Haman and Mordecai in a prayer to the Virgin to grant victory to France.

[11] The gallows of Montfaucon were constructed in the late 13th c. and remained in use until the time of Louis XIII. Strubel says (p. 527) that they were constructed on the orders of Enguerrand de Marigny (born *c.* 1260), but does not document this statement. Strubel further notes (p. 529) that the image of hanged men being washed by the rain and dried in the sun is found elsewhere, notably in *Roman de la Rose*, ed. Strubel, v. 6485.

116 *FAUVEL* AND VITRY

Verb tenses are a significant aid to managing and signposting the fictive chronology of the double narrative, and especially to reinforcing the secondary historical strand. The triplum *Aman novi* sounds simultaneously with this motetus. It stands (physically as well as in import) as the final culminating text of the backwards historical sequence. It is a past-tense narrative, not in Fauvel's voice, but in the third person, except for the first person plural of 'noster Aman', our Haman, the historical Marigny. Fauvel's narrative is in the present tense, the historical narrative in the past. 'Our' Haman is now dead, like the long-past hanging of Marigny (the 'new Haman') on Montfaucon, in the last of the three motets in historical, 'backwards' order. As we learn from the *Chronique métrique*, the body of Marigny, washed by rain on the gallows, fell or was cut down. It was found naked on the ground, and on the vigil of St John the Baptist (23 July 1315), dressed, like a *cloche*, and re-hanged (see below). It remained there as an example for two years after his execution, before finally being released for burial in 1317, when Marigny's reputation enjoyed some rehabilitation by Philip V. The triplum text confirms that the exposed body of this 'new Haman' was left hanging in the rain and wind, therefore dating the motet no earlier. All sources unanimously attest the terribly wet weather of the summer of 1315, which gives added point to the inclusion in the motet texts of the watery ends of Icarus and Phaeton, Fortuna sinking Fauvel (with his tear-wet face) 'naked in the lake of tears', and Marigny's rain-washed corpse. In the myth, Phaeton fell burning into the river and his sisters swelled the waters with their tears.[12] Indeed, in the triplum, Icarus is paralleled directly by Phaeton and then by 'our' Haman, the unnamed Marigny. Both Phaeton and Marigny committed crimes while still on high, and both paid for them with a fatal fall. In Marigny's case, ironically, his fall incurred the punishment of being raised on high in a different, negative and terminal sense, on a mount which in turn parallels the mount of crucifixion, a gallows from which he, in turn, fell. Fauvel's metaphorical death from a love-rejection in the motetus is literally aligned (by simultaneous presentation of the two texts) with the account in the triplum of a death (Marigny's) which, like Haman's, was a real one on the gallows; but real death is not yet part of Fauvel's narrative. Downfall is predicted but withheld. Fauvel's words become Marigny's *ante mortem* lament, invoking Haman, at his execution, spoken by, or as if by, one not yet dead.

The Tenor

It is highly unusual for a motet tenor to combine two chants. The tenor of *Aman novi* is just such a hybrid, combining a chant for the Office of the Dead, *Heu me* (Alas for me), with one for Maundy Thursday, *Tristis est anima mea* (My soul is sad), implying its continuation, *usque ad mortem*.[13] Both texts are the first-person words of Christ. The first seven tenor notes (the entirety of the *Heu me* chant excerpt), rhythmicised in short note-values, form the opening of the triplum, *Aman novi*. After the second

---

[12] Wathey, 'Myth and Mythography', 87.
[13] For sources see Rankin, 'The Divine Truth of Scripture', 241–42, ex. 10.

chant, the tenor ends with three iterations of the opening four notes (to *Heu me*), another trio to add to those already pointed out in *Tribum* and *Garrit gallus*; the placing between those two of the Trinity motet *Firmissime/Adesto* may not be accidental. Christ's agonised first-person words on the eve of His crucifixion in the tenor sound simultaneously with the account of Marigny's hanging in the triplum and Fauvel's first-person lament in the motetus. If Fauvel is indeed Marigny, another first-person dimension is added to the lament put into his mouth, combining (besides Haman) Fauvel, Marigny and Christ in a deliberately incongruous trinity of voices. Both tenor texts affirm the first person singular, but the second chant's words are those of Christ, not of Fauvel's first-person motetus. The striking, indeed blasphemous juxtaposition rolls the trinity of villains—Haman (biblical), Fauvel (fable), and Marigny (historical)—together with His words. Haman's hanging, or crucifixion, was often seen as an antitype of Christ's. While in liturgical time the chant tenor signifies the eve of Christ's crucifixion, in historical time the triplum text refers (after the fact) to the hanging of Marigny, which took place on the eve of Ascension (Wednesday, 30 April 1315), with much play in the texts on height, ascent and fall. Here is a small sample from the *Chronique métrique*:[14]

vv. 7274–88

Reprouchié li sera tozjors
Monfaucon; la fu mis en cage,
Mat en angle, au plus haut estage
Tele sepulture esleü
N'avoit pas, s'en fu deceü.
Je ne sai se saint ert trouvé
Car bien haut a esté levé;
et puis tel[le] cortoisie ot,
Desouz ses piez un Paviot.
En la fin d'avril lors fina,
Por ce que d'embler ne fina,
La veille de l'Ascention
En cest an d'incarnation
Couvert sis vints et onze quines;
C'est en cest an, or le devines.
. . .

vv. 7313–18:

Et du remanant du lignage
Engerran, qui t'a fet damage
Et qui vis encore demeurent,
Oste les, si que plus ne queurent:
Tout ont escorchié et plumé.
Chascun en crie: 'Heu me!' (initiating a fourteen-line citation).

---

[14] Diverrès, *La Chronique métrique*. Between the lines cited here are vv. 7301–5, which tantalisingly include three obliterated lines rendered wholly illegible by earlier chemical attempts to recover them: 'Puis Engerran de Marregni/Que . . ./D . . ./F . . ./Et de Michiel de Bordenaï'.

118 *FAUVEL* AND VITRY

...

vv. 7333–46:
En cele annee voirement,
Ne say par quel consentement,
Ont aucuns si bien entendu
Qu'il ont Engerran despendu;
Et despoillé fu trestout nu,
Tout ainsi l'en fu avenu.
Por ce commandé ra esté
Que pendu fust et remonté;
Et si fu il en une cloche,
Ainsi sa besoingne li cloche.
Autrement eust esté crevé
Charles, s'il ne fust relevé.
Ce fu la veille Saint Jehan
Que rependu fu en cel an.

Heu me in v. 7318 is, as noted above, the tenor incipit of the motet, one of many close links between *Fauvel* and the chronicle. In Fauvel's chronology, his lament in the motetus text precedes the next major Christian festival following the Ascension, Pentecost, the day following which will mark his marriage to Fortuna's handmaid Vaine Gloire. So he did not die, but in a sense heightened the blasphemy by rising again (resurrecting), marrying, on Pentecost. Similar counterpoints and collisions between liturgical time and narrative chronology are worked out on a large scale in *Fauvel*, here with maximum play on the eves of the crucial dates, whether historical (Marigny's execution, specified precisely in the chronicle), fictional (Fauvel) or biblical (Christ's crucifixion). Liturgically, these refer to the eves of Good Friday (the Crucifixion), Ascension (Marigny's execution), Pentecost (Fauvel's marriage) and John the Baptist (Marigny's re-hanging, specified in the chronicle).

The Music of *Aman novi*

For a diplomatic transcription of *Aman* from its only source (**Paris146**) see Ex. 5.1. As in *Tribum* and *Garrit gallus* the semibreves are separated into breve groups by dots, and either unstemmed, or with downstems on some first beats. These downstems are much more copious in *Aman*. They indicate that a note is long but, when there are just two semibreves in the space of a breve, not necessarily longer than the second one; they are equal. Although this is not corroborated for *Aman* by a later source with minim stems, the intention is clear from the later notations of other motets. Views of the musical quality of *Aman* have varied widely. Ernest Sanders rejected Vitry's authorship partly on grounds that, although referring to a later event, it was less tidy than the 'earlier' *Garrit gallus*. He neglected to observe that the tenor chant of *Aman* is structured in segments, measured in longs, of 12 + 1, 13 + 1, 12 + 1, 13 + 1, 3 + 1, 3, where each '1' is a long rest, and the final two short segments are the repetitions of *Heu me* at the end.

Ex. 5.1 Edition of music of *Aman novi/Heu Fortuna/Heu me, tristis est anima mea*, with text as emended by Zoltán Rihmer: see ▶ Table 5.1

Ex. 5.1 Continued

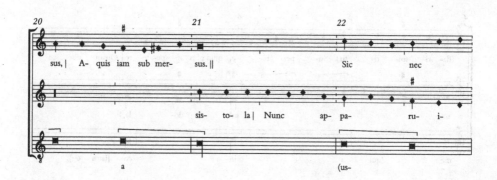

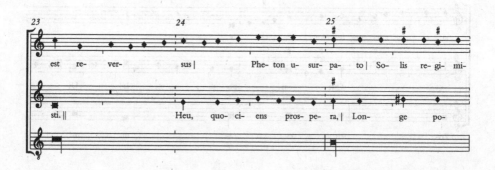

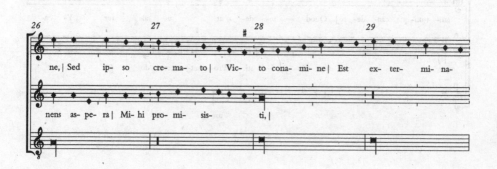

Ex. 5.1 Continued

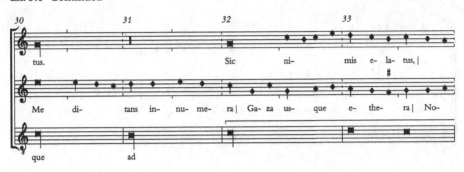

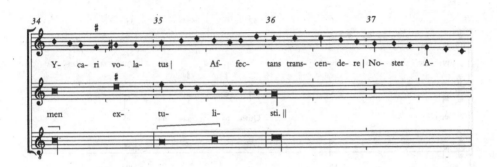

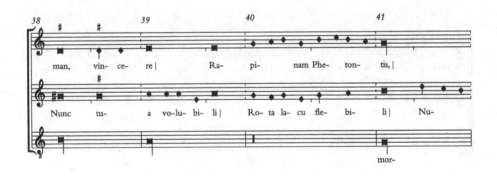

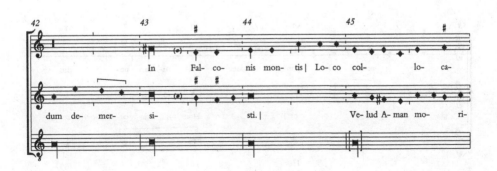

Ex. 5.1 Continued

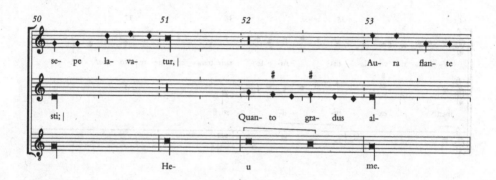

This is precisely the kind of patterning that qualified his more favourable rating of the other Marigny motets. The upper parts are indeed more irregular, but the composer avoids simultaneous rests between any two parts. By contrast, Alexander Blachly championed Vitry's authorship of *Aman novi* for its 'melodically superior . . . excitement, surprise, and imaginative juxtaposition of fast and slow rhythms'.[15] He is one of very few writers to have found this a composition of superior quality. He discerns a numerical structure which is deployed with skill, avoiding simultaneous rests, although requiring special pleading by the tidier numerical criteria used by his teacher Ernest Sanders. He commented on the 'thrilling' and 'novel' effects of the notated and implied sharps, but without linking them to the text, as I do here. Sanders noted incipient imitation within and between voices, comparing (in Ex. 5.1) triplum L1, L12–L13 and L36 and motetus L21–L22; triplum L26 is echoed at motetus L30 and L35. The melodic writing is predominantly stepwise, with a fourth or fifth only at L44, L50, L53. In three instances, the rhythm ♦ ♦ ♩ occurs two or more times consecutively (Ex. 5.1, motetus L32–L33, triplum L36–L37 and L56–L57). Blachly relates the framing principle of the threefold repetition of the tenor notes *c c b a* at the end to the tenor of Vitry's motet *Tuba sacre/In arboris/Virgo sum*, whose opening two-note motive *a g* is repeated three times at the end, and similarly the repetitions of the opening *a g f* at the end of *Colla jugo/Bona condit/Libera me*. The case for Vitry's authorship will be further considered in Chapter 7 in relation to *Orbis orbatus/Vos pastores*.

Musically, the many visually and audibly conspicuous sharps in *Aman novi* (notated on *f* and *g* by cross-like signs, and necessitating unnotated *d♯*s, unusual and extreme in this repertory) may suggest crucifixion (in later music a commonplace of word-painting). The one notated *g♯* in the tenor (Ex. 5.1 at L46) is on the chant melisma of <u>mortem</u> and coincides with Fauvel's 'velud Aman mori<u>or</u>' in the motetus, aligning the cross sign of Christ's crucifixion in the tenor with Haman's in the motetus, and further suggesting the gibbet of Montfaucon ('Falconis montis'). (See Fig. 5.2.)

In addition, the audible harmonic twist (with *d♯*s) at 'noster Aman' (Marigny) in this motet (L38) might indicate that the composer was aware of Jewish Purim traditions of noise-making to drown out the name of Haman. Those festivities could have been perceived by Christians as a parody of the crucifixion. The striking harmonies of this motet might also relate to the *Fauvel* charivari, where instruments such as *cliquetes* and

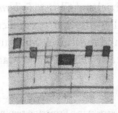

Fig. 5.2 Notated sharp in Paris, Bibliothèque nationale de France, fr. 146, f. 30ʳ, tenor, bottom staff. © BnF

---

[15] Blachly, 'The Motets of Philippe de Vitry', 56–77 at 56.

124 *FAUVEL AND VITRY*

macequotes (making *hauz brais* and *hautes notes*; see Långfors, vv. 717–18) recall the rattles traditionally used in Purim ceremonies.[16]

Recent work has drawn attention to the creative use of voice-crossing in motets, sometimes in ways that suggest metaphorical word-painting.[17] We have noted a striking instance at the beginning of *Garrit gallus*, where the Ovidian first line in the motetus rises prominently above the triplum. In *Aman* at L37–L39 this sharp-laden introduction of 'noster Aman' in the triplum is surmounted (metaphorically 'put down') by Fortuna, who is addressed in the motetus, which at this point symbolically crosses the triplum to sing above it. The progression at L24–L25 following 'Pheton usurpato' also allows the motetus to usurp the triplum range, rising above it; at L34–L35 Fauvel's reference to his elevation in the motetus rises above 'Ycarus' in the triplum. At L18–L21 the motetus rises above the 'watery' triplum at the point where Icarus is submerged. This happens again at L29–L30, where Phaeton too is 'exterminated', and at L42–L44, where Montfaucon in the triplum dips below the motetus. This is followed by Fauvel's 'velut Aman morior', where the motetus still rises above the triplum, which in turn overtakes the motetus to reach the top of its range as the dead Marigny is raised from the dust to be displayed ghoulishly on high; at L57–L59 the 'fall' in the motetus perversely rises over the triplum. The extent of this metaphorical play on rise and fall, height and depth, is particularly suited to the concept of this motet, and is one of many instances that go beyond a general perception that word-painting in early repertories barely exists.

Here we are dealing not only with classical citations and allusions, but with biblical ones too. Fauvel and Christ are alive at the time of their first-person soliloquies, though anticipating different kinds of death. We are clearly meant to read Fauvel's motetus in the light of the 'hangings' of Haman and Marigny, a trio of crucifixions sounding simultaneously with Christ's in the tenor. (Christ's crucifixion was itself a trio in which he was flanked by the two malefactors.) The gallows of Montfaucon in the triplum becomes the Parisian mount of crucifixion. Fauvel, however, does not die but lives on to marry Vaine Gloire and beget his wretched progeny, who are rejuvenated in the heresy and filth of the Fountain of Youth. Christ rose again; Marigny's body was re-erected as an example, another blasphemous parallel. These resurrections or rebirths anticipate the rise of Antichrist, which is made quite specific in the apocalyptic *Fauvel*, both referred to by Fortuna, embodied in Haman, and implicitly also in Marigny. The motets that form this trio are further connected by trios of names, as noted above, and packed with allusions that carry unstated context with them. We have noted that *Garrit gallus* names the trio of Absalom (a traitor), Ulysses (a liar), both deceptively attractive, and Thersites (a churl), but also Absalom, Michael and Christ. *Tribum* (another pun on three, *tribus*) names its protagonists allegorically—the lion, fox and cockerel. *Aman* has a double trio all of whose components also stand for Fauvel: Marigny, Haman and (blasphemously) Christ, all hanged or crucified; Icarus, Phaeton and Marigny, who aspired too high and

---

[16] First pointed out by Manuel Pedro Ferreira in a Princeton seminar paper in 1989, published as Ferreira, 'Vitry', where he also calls attention to a notated diminished fifth in *Floret* on the word 'Aman'; Sanders, 'The Early Motets of Philippe de Vitry', also invoked Purim in connection with *Floret*. Jews were expelled from France and readmitted at several dates during this period. The great Jewish exile of 1306 was followed by their return in 1315.

[17] Bent, 'Words and Music in Machaut's Motet 9' (2003, here Ch. 9), and Zayaruznaya, 'She Has a Wheel' (2009).

fell. The names of Icarus, Phaeton and Haman each occur twice in the triplum text; the repetitions of key words (here, names) will by now be a familiar technique from the other two Marigny motets, like the well-placed musical recapitulations in these motets. There could also be here a trinitarian link to the *Fauvel* motet *Firmissime/Adesto sancta Trinitas* (f. 43^{r-v}), the most advanced of five motets placed between *Tribum* and *Garrit gallus*; just one motet stands between *Aman* and *Tribum*.[18]

The 'other Pharaoh' of *Garrit gallus* parallels the 'new Haman' of *Aman novi*. Both Pharaoh and Haman are Old Testament oppressors of the chosen people, here the French, who should be properly ruled over by heirs of the recently canonised Saint Louis. 'Noster Aman' in the triplum of *Aman*, the word recapitulated in the first person plural, speaks for 'us', the contemporary Frenchmen who have been oppressed by Marigny. The beast fable themes played out in *Fauvel* and augmented from *Renard* are present in *Garrit gallus* as the *galli* (cockerels/roosters and Frenchmen), the blind lion (King Philip IV) and the traitorous fox (red-headed Marigny). The Archangel Michael conquers the dragon, Satan, whose fall from grace allegedly punished the sin of pride, his bid to be equal to and independent of God. Satan and Haman in their different ways bid too high, and fell, as did Marigny 'the satrap', Fauvel his beastly literary embodiment, as well as Icarus and Phaeton. A series of bestial metamorphoses and reversals unfolds in both narratives. In 'backwards' historical order, the beast allegories of *Garrit gallus* become increasingly human throughout the three motets, culminating in *Aman novi*, which by naming Montfaucon alludes as specifically to Marigny as it can do without naming him. The motet tenors also become increasingly personalised, from the neutral melisma (*Neuma*) of *Garrit gallus*, through the first person plural of *Tribum*'s tenor *Merito hec patimur*, to the double first person singular of the hybrid tenor of *Aman*, with its additional blasphemous dimension of the words of Christ.

Aman is if anything even more densely packed than *Tribum* and *Garrit* with quotations and allusions. Ovid is present as the source for the stories of Icarus and Phaeton, though not quoted or named directly. Dahnk identified a citation from Lucan, one of several in the *Fauvel* motets.[19] Leofranc Holford-Strevens locates this to the report of a 'deceitful dream' of Pompey before a disastrous defeat, and reports that this 'would be a very apt parallel, if the position in the text, the presence of *innumera(m)*, and the raising of the name above the earth can establish it'; it could so be argued, since the elements of pride before a fall and deception are clearly present.[20] The last line of the triplum is from the distichs of Cato, a hexameter couplet:

cum fueris felix, quae sunt aduersa caueto:
non eodem cursu respondent ultima primis.[21]

(When you prosper, beware of adversity: the end does not match the beginning.[22])

---

[18] For *Firmissime/Adesto* see Robertson, 'Which Vitry?'
[19] Dahnk, *L'Hérésie de Fauvel*, p.mus. 71, 173, points out that the phrase *ad ethera . . . nomen* in motetus lines 10–12 'est fréquent dans le latin classique de même qu'au moyen âge, mais le voisinage du mot *innumera* fait croire qu'il s'agit ici d'un souvenir de Lucain VII.10: *innumeram effigiem Romanae cernere plebis/attolique suum laetis ad sidera nomen/vocibus et plausu cuneos certare sonantes*'.
[20] In *Bellum civile* 7.10–12. Holford-Strevens, 'Fauvel Goes to School', at 61–62.
[21] *Disticha Catonis*, I. 18.
[22] Translated by Leofranc Holford-Strevens.

126 FAUVEL AND VITRY

In addition to the moral message, there is yet more play on symmetries and on inversions of beginnings and ends. The final line sums up the preceding content of the triplum: Marigny's being raised on high corresponds to his previous elevation (*respondent*). This is also reflected in the voice crossing at L57–L59 noted above, which suggests the great difference (*non eodem cursu*) between hanging on the gallows (*ultima*) and enjoying his previous royal favour (*primis*), words spanning time between situations, both of which were of notable duration, and apply also to Fauvel's identification with Haman (*velud Aman morior*). The hexameter not only seals the unity of the three motets and confirms the bi-directional narrative, but it is also reflected in the music: whereas both *Garrit gallus* and *Tribum* begin and end on *f* (*f–c–f*), *Aman* starts on *c* (*c–g–c*) and ends in a different place, on *a* (*a–e–a*): the end does not match the beginning. Andrew Wathey points out that the use of *sistola* and *diastola* (motetus, lines 2 and 5) to criticise Fortuna alludes to the critical tradition around the Cato commentaries, and that the (syllabic) couplet at the end of the motetus, 'Quanto gradus altior/tanto casus gravior' (as the ascent is higher, so the fall is graver) is also elaborated in a thirteenth-century commentary to *Esopus*, fable 35 (in the widely circulated distichs of Gualterus Anglicus); the allusion to a beast fable is clearly particularly appropriate in this context.[23] Thus all three Marigny motets introduce the voices of older authors in a rich textual polyphony, by beginning, including or ending with citations or allusions. In several cases these are highlighted by standing outside metrical structures that are already extremely irregular with respect to line length and rhyme structure, mixing classical metres with goliardic or medieval rhythmic verse.[24] The triplum text of *Aman* as transmitted is notably irregular, while the motetus falls neatly into tercets of seven, seven and six syllables.[25] These are texts crafted for music, not texts that happen to have received a musical setting; their purposeful irregularities are easily undervalued if treated as self-standing verse.

Despite their presentation in a 'wrong' historical order, we have seen in Chapter 3 that the topical content of the motets has been taken literally by most scholars, as if they were newspaper reports, to provide *termini post* and *ante quem* for dating the motets.[26] It has been assumed that their real-life documentary function came first, that they were imported or adapted for *Fauvel*, and therefore that their compositional order must be

---

[23] Wathey, 'Auctoritas', 72. In fact, many classical authors are cited for this sentiment in *Thesaurus Proverbiorum*, iii, s.v. 'Fall', 143–45.

[24] *Garrit gallus*: Ovid (*Metamorphoses*, 'In nova fert'), and Joseph of Exeter, *De bello troiano*, I. 386 (Howlett). *Tribum*: Ovid (*Ex Ponto*), and Joseph of Exeter. *De bello troiano*, VI. 804–5. See Ch. 4 nn. 9 and 35. Vitry used this couplet to annotate a passage in his own copy of the *Chronicon* of Guillaume de Nangis. See Wathey, 'Myth and Mythography'. In *Aman novi*: Ovid (*Metamorphoses*, Phaeton and Icarus); Lucan; Cato's commentary to Gualterus Anglicus, *Esopus*, fable 35; Bible (Book of Esther; the name of Haman is marked in the Nangis chronicle owned by Vitry); Christ's words in the tenor. In all these cases, animals standing in for human agency goes back to Aesop. Kügle, *The Manuscript Ivrea*, 107 n. 60 locates in the University of Paris the prevalence of quotations from the Bible, Ovid, Lucan, and Horace, and notes that some of the motets cite the same quotations: Matt. 7: 15 appears in *Scariotis/Jure*, *Super/Presidentes* and *Cum statua/Hugo*; Lucan, *De bello civili* 10. 407 is quoted in both *Colla/Bona* and *Detractor/Qui secuntur*. Holford-Strevens, 'Fauvel Goes to School', 60. *Secuntur* is the last word of *Colla/Bona*.

[25] See ▶ Table 5.1 for an emended version by Zoltán Rihmer, used here in the musical edition Ex. 5.1. His revision makes better sense of the syllable count and rhyme scheme, and it stays much closer to the manuscript text than Becker's drastic (and undefended) revision used in Schrade's musical edition. Rihmer's version also fits the music better than either Becker's or Strubel's emendations with respect to text underlay.

[26] Schrade, 'Philippe de Vitry', 338; Sanders, 'The Early Motets of Philippe de Vitry'.

that of the historical narrative to which they refer, as set out above. Working from the end of the book, in *Garrit gallus*, the 'blind lion' (Philip IV) is still reigning (present tense, *monarchisat*), so, it is argued, it must antedate his death on 29 November 1314; in *Tribum* his reign is already past (past tense, *regnaverat*), but it antedates Marigny's execution on 30 April 1315; the gallows has been prepared, but his imminent execution is still in the future: '[Fortuna] has not refrained from preparing the gallows ... [for] a certain man who might, perhaps, fall'. *Aman novi*, the third motet of the historical narrative, reports the situation two years after the execution, in 1317.

Thus, the unity of the three *Fauvel* motets as a group is even tighter than previously recognised. The careful planning of their double narrative function means that all were composed retrospectively no earlier than 1317, later than the events to which they refer, later than datings which assumed their simple documentary chronicle function. Even if the conception and compilation of *Fauvel* started before 1317, these motets at least must be later; the project must have been completed at the latest by the death of Philip V in 1322. The masterly programme of the trio of motets makes their common authorship virtually certain: if *Garrit* and *Tribum* are by Vitry, so too is *Aman*.

From Ovid to Dante: The Pairing of Icarus and Phaeton

Ovid, as noted, is present in all three Marigny motets. In *Fauvel* order, the Ovidian references increase in explicitness through the three texts. Ovid's myths (Icarus and Phaeton) are present but not attributed in *Aman*, he is cited as Naso in *Tribum*, and the motetus of *Garrit* opens with the first line of the *Metamorphoses*. *Garrit gallus/In nova fert* is the last piece before the *envoi*. In 'Marigny' order it is the beginning, so advertised by using that famous first line, and the Ovidian text leads the story through the three motets from nature's first beginnings, through exile (*Tribum*) to modern catastrophes (*Aman*). The central doom-laden motet, *Tribum*, builds its texts from an elegiac couplet from the letters Ovid wrote in exile, the *Ex Ponto*, reproaching a faithless friend for failing to contact him. Thus, in Marigny order, starting from the end, the three motets start with a very clear Ovidian reference in *Garrit gallus/In nova fert* (the first line of the *Metamorphoses*), a less familiar but attributed one in *Tribum*, and an unsignalled pair of references in *Aman*, now to be discussed.

The Ovidian link concerns two key over-ambitious high flyers, Icarus and Phaeton, to whom the 'new Haman' is likened. The high flyer Fauvel was raised by Fortuna from the stable to the palace. The naming twice each of the trio Haman, Phaeton and Icarus in the triplum of *Aman novi* gives unmistakable emphasis (lines 1, 6, 11, 17, 19, 20). And although this motet (the first in *Fauvel* order and the third in Marigny order) neither names nor quotes Ovid, the *Metamorphoses* are its source for the stories—there quite separate—of Icarus and Phaeton. At the end of *Metamorphoses* 1 and the opening of *Metamorphoses* 2, Apollo promised his son Phaeton whatever he wished, and he tried in vain to dissuade him from his request to drive the sun's chariot. He described the route and its dangers, advising a middle course, and how to discipline the horses. The young Phaeton was unable to control them and plunged to his watery death, after causing great and unnatural damage on earth. (Fauvel is also an out-of-control horse.)

128 FAUVEL AND VITRY

In *Metamorphoses* 8, Daedalus encouraged his son Icarus to take the feathered wings he had made for them both for their flight out of their imprisonment in Crete, likewise advising a middle course. The son ignored this advice and flew too close to the sun; the wax on his wings melted and he crashed down into the sea.

The two stories obviously have much in common. In one case a son is encouraged by his father to fly, in the other reluctantly permitted to do so; both sons are advised to moderate their course; both fail disastrously and fall from on high to a catastrophic and watery end. Fauvel's horrid progeny are rejuvenated by a black baptism in the Fountain of Youth. Fauvel's wet face links him (via an albeit dry Haman) to Marigny's rain-washed body post-execution; but it also links him directly and explicitly to Phaeton and Icarus, who are named in the triplum, and whose deaths involve plunging into the sea. To link Icarus and Phaeton is an obvious strategy, but precedents for this linkage are extremely rare.[27]

By far the most striking classical-medieval presentation that explicitly combines the fall of Phaeton with that of Icarus is in Dante's *Inferno* 17, where the author-protagonist compares his fear to theirs.[28] Dante uses both Phaeton and Icarus programmatically in the rest of the *Commedia*, where their flight serves as a key negative model for the protagonist's ascent. *Purgatorio* 17, the central canto not only of the second *cantica* but of the *Commedia* as a whole, is important—for present purposes—both for its reading of the Dantean Phaeton and because it contains the *Commedia*'s only reference to Haman. He is not explicitly named in the canto, but he is there as clearly as Marigny (also unnamed) is in the motet text. In *Purgatorio* 17 Haman is referred to as 'one crucified' ('un crucifisso', line 26), preceding the naming of the trio of Ahasuerus, Esther and Mordecai (ll. 28–9). He also 'rains down' (*piovve*, l. 25) in a striking formulation, which adds a watery dimension to his alignment both by Dante and, in this motet, with Icarus and Phaeton, as well as the rain-washed corpse of Marigny.

Given these striking juxtapositions, and knowing Kevin Brownlee's articles on Dante, Phaeton and Icarus, led me to ask him: did anyone before Dante link Phaeton, Icarus and Haman in this same way? How early were the *Inferno* and the *Purgatorio* known in Paris? Lacking other evidence of such an early French circulation of the *Commedia*, is this connection merely coincidental, or is it strong enough to provide a link with the *Roman de Fauvel* in **Paris146**? The discussion that followed resulted in a few joint oral presentations from the 1990s onwards, eventually published as Bent and Brownlee, 'Icarus, Phaeton, Haman'. The reader is referred to the second half of that article for Brownlee's extensive and brilliant exploration of the Dante connection. Our conclusion was:

It does not seem to be mere coincidence that two innovative Romance authors around 1307–17, Dante and Vitry, should not only have linked the Icarus and Phaeton stories, but

---

[27] This double reference occurs in the pseudo-Seneca's *Hercules Oetaeus*, a late play, which many critics do not attribute to Seneca himself but to an educated imitator. In the passage involving lines 675–90, the *puer* of 678 is Phaeton, and Icarus is explicitly cited in 687, a key citation kindly communicated by Pedro Memelsdorff. For further details, see Bent and Brownlee, 'Icarus, Phaeton, Haman', 104 n. 54.

[28] It was two articles by Brownlee, 'Phaeton's Fall' and 'Dante's Transfigured Models', that first suggested the Dante–Fauvel parallel to me. The *Metamorphoses* is the Ovidian work that Dante cites by far the most frequently and elaborately. While he also references Ovid's erotic poetry (*Amores*, *Ars amatoria*, *Remedia amoris*), Dante never cites the Ovidian exilic works. The only Ovidian *loci* containing the combined reference to Phaeton and Icarus are thus only found in a work that is systematically and purposefully ignored by Dante: *Tristia* I. 1. 79–90 and III. 4. 21–30. I thank Pedro Memelsdorff for this reference.

also linked them to the story of Haman in the book of Esther and to Christ's crucifixion. While they might have arrived independently at these connections (with in Vitry's case an application to contemporary events), we would prefer to infer from this commonality that some knowledge of the first two *cantiche* of the *Commedia* was available in Paris at an earlier date than hitherto documented.[29]

[29] Bent and Brownlee, 'Icarus, Phaeton, Haman', 121.

6

Floret/Florens: Intended for *Fauvel*?

Ernest Sanders has convincingly connected a fourth motet to the three Marigny motets in *Fauvel*.[1] This is *Floret cum Vana Gloria/Florens vigor/Neuma*, based on the same tenor (*Neuma quinti toni*) as *Garrit gallus* (which is in *Fauvel*) and *Douce playsance/Garison* (which is not, but is accepted as a work by Vitry). *Floret* is preserved not in **Paris146** but in two other sources: **Ca1328**, which, although much damaged, identifies the tenor as *Neuma*, hence the 'N' by the *Garrit* tenor in **Paris146** (as noted by Schrade, 'Philippe de Vitry', 339), and in the rotulus **Br19606**, no fewer than six of whose ten pieces, including this, have a version in *Fauvel*. Schrade, Sanders, Edward Roesner and others have assumed that the topical motets were adapted from obsolete historical motets and interpolated in **Paris146**. They, and Daniel Leech-Wilkinson, took the historical datings as compositional dates, which strongly influenced the style chronology and composer assignations they proposed (see Ch. 3 above), and indirectly allowed the now-rejected datings of *Per grama* and *Flos/Celsa* in the mid- to late 1310s (see Ch. 30 below). By contrast, I have proposed that especially the three Marigny motets, and perhaps also *Floret*, were custom made for **Paris146** specifically with a double function in the two narratives. If this is right, then arguments about stylistic development within a short period, or what is and is not possible from the same composer in a particular order, fall away.

Triplum and motetus texts and translation, based on translations by Sanders and David Howlett:

Triplum	Translation
Floret cum vana gloria	Together with Vain Glory there flourishes
novitatum presumpcio	the presumptuousness of novelties,
ypocrisis iactancia	as do hypocrisy, boastfulness,
discordia contencio	discord, contentiousness,
5 ac inobediencia	and disobedience,
pertinencie captio	seizure of property;
procedit ex invidia	from envy proceeds
in prosperis afflictio	affliction in prosperity,
detractio et odia	slander, hatreds and
10 nocensque susurratio	harmful whispering,
de proximi iniuria	gleeful exultation at misfortune
iocunda exultacio	befalling neighbours;
ex ira contumelia	from anger arise
exit et indignacio	insult and indignation,

[1] Sanders, 'The Early Motets of Philippe de Vitry', with a transcription of the motet on pp. 37–42. Whether he has equally convincingly attributed *Floret* to Vitry must remain open. He argues (p. 31): 'Like *Tribum/Quoniam/Merito* [*Floret/Florens*] must be attributed to [Vitry] for the two reasons that it seems characteristic of his early style and that it is one of the most advanced motets to be utilised by Chaillou in fr. 146. Moreover, the other motets based on the same or closely related cantus firmus are both by Vitry.' See also Ch. 7 n. 26.

The Motet in the Late Middle Ages. Margaret Bent, Oxford University Press. © Oxford University Press 2023.
DOI: 10.1093/so/9780190063771.003.0007

15	clamor rixe blasphemia	the clamor of strife, blasphemy;
	mentis viget inflacio	conceit flourishes and
	profluit et accidia	disgust is spreading,
	foras mentis vagacio	as are mental derangement,
	malicia pigricia	malice, sloth,
20	rancor et desperacio	rancour, and despair;
	manat ex avaricia	from avarice flow
	fallacia prodicio	intrigue, treachery,
	iniquitas periuria	iniquity, perjury,
	fraus cordis obduracio	fraud, hardheartedness;
25	ex gula inmundicia	from gluttony come uncleanness
	sensus hebes in genio	and dulled sensation in spirit;
	scurrilitas leticia	scurrility, vain pleasure
	vana cum multiloquio	and garrulousness,
	sequitur ex luxuria	From self-indulgence follows
30	huius mundi affectio	the love of this world,
	cecitas inconstancia	blindness, inconstancy,
	ac inconsideratio	and inconsiderateness;
	horror futura gloria	future glory will become horror,
	gravis precipitacio	grave headlong descent;
35	in deum perit odia	odious love of our flesh
	nostre carnis dilectio.	begets hatred of God.

	Motetus	Translation
	Florens vigor ulciscendo	Flourishing power, in your avenging
	iuste vincens omnia	justly winning all
	ad tibi fides loquendo	to you, Faith, speaking
	fastus ad supplicia	for punishment for arrogance
5	qui Aman genu flectendo	those who by bending the knee to Haman
	impediunt obsequia	impede proper observances,
	causatori adherendo	by adhering to the plaintiff seek
	fugiunt causaria	to avoid adversity;
	sicque falsum sustinendo	and thus by sustaining falseness,
10	succumbit iusticia	justice succumbs;
	Mardocheo detrahendo	by humiliating Mordecai
	preparant exidia	they prepare ruin,
	que in ipsos convertendo	which as it turns on themselves
	sencient duplicia	will suffer doubly,
15	cum iudex discuciendo	when the deliberating Judge
	iusta dabit premia.	will give just rewards.

FLORET/FLORENS: INTENDED FOR FAUVEL? 133

Dahnk recognised that a monophonic 'prose' (so designated) in *Fauvel, Carnalitas, luxuria* (f. 12^{r–v}), was an adapted version of the triplum of *Floret*, and not vice versa; Schrade (later) thought the motet was an elaboration of the prose.[2] The motetus text is not used in the prose adaptation. *Carnalitas* retains the long rests of the motet triplum, which would be unlikely in an original monophonic composition; and it is the only monophonic composition in *Fauvel* to use syllabic semibreves, though there are some among the Lescurel songs. Nowhere does Sanders hint that *Floret* had anything to do with *Fauvel* before it was fauvelised by Chaillou.

Almost every line of the motet triplum *Floret* has a direct correspondence in *Carnalitas*, with lines 7–28 almost identical to lines 7–28 of *Carnalitas*. The triplum text has been topped and tailed, and the correspondences reordered at the beginning and end, as shown in Table 6.1. The first six lines of the *Carnalitas* text replace the motet's opening six lines, name Fauvel, and associate with him the predominant vices of carnality and *luxuria*. The next twenty-two lines in *Carnalitas* have preposition changes which enhance the presentness of Fauvel's courtier vices there listed.[3] The motet triplum's last eight lines are replaced by eight new lines referring to the future marriage of Fauvel (named) and Vain Glory, and warning Fortune of trouble ahead. Then follow lines 3–6 moved from the opening of the triplum, and then by three more new lines.[4] The purpose of the prose adaptation was to fauvelise the text, to associate the vices specifically with the court of Fauvel, and to make it appropriate to its planned location in the *roman* by placing his marital flourishing still in the future. The text of the prose carefully takes account of the fact that the marriage is in the future ('harbinger'), whereas in the motet Fauvel is already flourishing with Vain Glory: *Floret cum Vana Gloria*.

All four Marigny motets are laments or complaints about the events they report, and all forecast a disastrous fall, in this case a 'gravis precipitacio'. This motet does not actually name Fauvel, though it is clearly he; and it incidentally plays into the letter emphasis of 'F', as for Fauvel and Fortuna. Sanders treated *Floret/Florens* as primarily a political text dating from when Philip IV was still alive (as he, the blind lion, is in *Garrit gallus*), thus no later than 1314. He elucidated the motetus text as a thinly veiled attack on the unnamed Marigny in the guise of Haman, who was hanged on the gallows prepared for Mordecai, identified by Sanders as standing for Charles de Valois.[5] But this is still in the future in the historical dimension of the *Floret/Florens* text. Its references to Haman and Mordecai (from the Book of Esther) anticipate the explicit Fauvel–Haman alignment in

---

[2] Dahnk, *L'Hérésie de Fauvel*, 74–77. Schrade, 'Philippe de Vitry', 350–51, but he added the identification of the **Ca1328** source of the motet and the tenor label *Neuma*.

[3] Texts and translations are printed in Sanders, 'The Early Motets of Philippe de Vitry': the motetus on p. 32, triplum pp. 42–43, musical editions of the motet pp. 37–42, and the end of *Carnalitas* on p. 45 from breve 118, from which point it differs from the motet. Comparative texts and Howlett's translations of the triplum *Floret* and the prose *Carnalitas* are given in Clark, 'The Flowering', at 183–86.

[4] This expansion of seven lines adds about 40 breves of music. *Floret* is 153 breves long, *Carnalitas* 191 breves; the music differs from B118 to the end. There is an interesting copying miscalculation: exactly the right number of staves was provided, but there is a blank staff at the foot of f. 12, which necessitated the insertion of an extra staff at the foot of f. 12^{v}, perhaps because the text scribe turned the page too soon.

[5] Nicolaus de Lyra (*c.* 1270–1349) had become professor of theology at the University of Paris in 1308. For him Haman and Mordecai were the prototypes of the evil and the just courtier. Sanders, 'The Early Motets of Philippe de Vitry', 33–34.

134 FAUVEL, AND VITRY

Table 6.1 Textual correspondences between the prose *Carnalitas* and the motet triplum *Floret*

Beginning and end of the prose (translation David Howlett)	Prose, *Fauvel*, f. 12^r−v		Motet triplum, with corresponding line numbers in the prose
Carnality, lechery rule in Fauvel's palace, and inconstancy; with them, worldly deceit, blindness, horror. Idleness, drunkenness, passion; (see *Floret* triplum translation for lines 7–28)	Carnalitas, Luxuria in Favelli palacio presunt et Inconstancia cum hiis mundana Fictio, Cecitas, Horror, Octia, Ebriositas, Passio.	5	Floret cum vana gloria. = 29 novitatum presumpcio = 41 ypocrisis iactancia. = 37, 40 discordia contencio. = 40, 37 ac inobediencia = 38 pertinencie captio = 39
	post procedit Invidia in prosperis, Afflictio, Detractio et Odia nocensque Susurracio, de proximi Iniuria iocunda Exultacio. Ira hinc, Contumelia exit et Indignacio, Clamor, Rixe, Blasphemia, mentis urget Inflacio. Non longe sunt Accidia, falax mentis Vagacio, Malicia, Pigricia, Rancor et Desperacio. Assistit Avaricia, Fallacio, Prodicio, Inequitas, Pariuria, Fraus, cordis Oduracio. Post gula Immundicia, Sensus habet in gremio. Scurrilitas, Leticia vana cum Multiloquio.	7 10 15 20 25 28	procedit ex invidia in prosperis afflictio detractio et odia nocensque susurratio de proximi iniuria iocunda exultacio ex ira contumelia exit et indignacio clamor rixe blasphemia mentis viget inflacio profluit et accidia foras mentis vagacio malicia pigricia rancor et desperacio manat ex avaricia fallacia prodicio iniquitas periuria fraus cordis obduracio ex gula inmundicia sensus hebes in genio scurrilitas leticia vana cum multiloquio
Finally, Vain Glory by a harbinger vision of Fortune is joined in matrimony with Fauvel, to whom let his name be a warning. A commission is given on the depravity of the coming of Antichrist. Woe to the messenger. Hypocrisy, daughter of Vain Glory, contention and disobedience, the seizing of property, boastfulness, discord, the enjoyment of vanities lead the bride through devious ways. May they fall from a great height.	in fine Vana Gloria visu Fortune previo. iungitur matrimonio cum Fauvello cui quod nuncia vox sit, datur commissio de adventus nequicia Antichristi. Ve nuncio! Vane Glorie filia Ypocrisis; Contencio, hac Inobediencia, Pertinacie Capcio, Iactancia, Discordia, Vanitatum Presumpcio Sponsam ducunt per devia. cadant in precipicio!	30 (34) 35 40	sequitur ex luxuria. = 1 huius mundi affectio = 4 cecitas inconstancia = 5, 3 ac inconsideratio horror futura gloria = 5 gravis precipitacio = 43 in deum perit odia =?9, ?5 nostre carnis dilectio. =?1

FLORET/FLORENS: INTENDED FOR FAUVEL? 135

Aman novi/Heu Fortuna, where Haman's hanging is far in the past, Fauvel–Marigny's imminent, on the gallows whose preparation is announced in the triplum text of *Tribum* (line 8).[6] Sanders noted the Haman connection with *Aman*, but in missing the double meanings did not yet realise that not only the explicitly fauvelised adaptation *Carnalitas* in **Paris146**, but also the motet, relate as closely to *Fauvel* as they do to external historical events. Fauvel is not named in the triplum (*Floret*), but he is present in the first two lines by already 'flourishing with' (marrying) Vain Glory and all the vices. Recognition of the dual function of all four Marigny motet texts raises the question whether *Floret/Florens* was originally intended to have a place in the double narrative of the interpolated *Fauvel*: it is so closely related to both narratives that it was surely originally planned to carry this double function in *Fauvel*. The motet differs from the prose (where the marriage is in the future) in that it follows the marriage and would have been appropriately placed at the very end of the *Fauvel* narrative, near where *Garrit gallus* is now, after the 'flourishing' with Vain Glory with which the triplum begins has produced the 'Fauveaux nouveaux' (a *lieto fine*, however sardonically reported), and at the beginning of the backwards Marigny sub-narrative that will culminate in the hanging of Haman in *Aman novi/Heu Fortuna*, together with all the other threads that are drawn together in that motet.

If *Floret/Florens* was indeed planned for this position, why was it not included? It has been pointed out (*Le Roman de Fauvel*, ed. Roesner et al., 6b) that the blank verso after the *envoi*, f. 45[v], is ruled in two columns as if for another motet comparable to *Garrit gallus/In nova*. Folio 45[r] was likewise originally ruled with a central margin that would have accommodated a two-column motet, as well as having superimposed the prevalent three-column ruling that was used for the *envoi*. Could *Floret/Florens* have been intended for one of these places? Could it have followed *Garrit gallus*, i.e. preceded it in the backwards cycle of historical motets? There is already an alliterating alphabetical backwards sequence starting with the present explicit on f. 45, '*Ferrant fina . . .*', *Garrit gallus/In nova/Neuma* (on the pitch *f*: the initial letters of Fauvel and Fortuna), and [H]*Aman novi/Heu Fortuna/Heu me*, perhaps intended to reinforce the order of the historical narrative (F G H). Such a placing of *Floret/Florens* (on the same neuma) would have contributed to that sequence. (*Tribum/Quoniam* and *In nova fert* lie outside this alphabetical pattern.) Alphabetical order up to the letter G is given particular prominence in **Paris146**. It is the ordering principle for the songs of Jehannot de Lescurel, which finish at G, rounded off by two final pieces that are different generically from their predecessors (*dits entés* rather than rondeaux or ballades), perhaps indicating that the cut-off at G was not accidental. Another 'F/F' motet of similar date (late 1310s or early 1320s) has recently been reconstructed by Cristina Alís Raurich: *Flos vernalis/Fiat intencio*. The subject is Marian, and there is no reason to connect it to *Fauvel*, though the floral beginning in both cases (*Floret/Florens*), and the 'F' alliteration are suggestive.[7]

---

[6] Sanders, 'The Early Motets of Philippe de Vitry', 32 expands this idea; see also Bent, 'Marigny' (Ch. 3 above).

[7] Alís Raurich, 'The *Flores* of *Flos vernalis*' (forthcoming); first presented at a seminar in All Souls College, 4.3.2021. *Flos vernalis/Fiat intencio* has been reconstructed from three fragmentary sources, is listed in **Trém**, and has long been known only from its intabulation in **Robertsbridge** in company with two *Fauvel* motets, *Firmissime/Adesto* and *Tribum/Quoniam*.

136 FAUVEL AND VITRY

Chronologically, for both forwards and backwards narratives, *Floret* would have had to come either before or after *Garrit gallus/In nova*, probably after, given that f. 45ʳ may have been ruled to accommodate another motet; to have placed it after *Garrit gallus*, however, would have diluted the strong beginning-at-the-end now provided by *In nova fert*. But there is another possibility: could *Floret/Florens* originally have been intended to be placed where *Garrit gallus/In nova* now is? In *Garrit gallus/In nova* the political allegory is more developed, and the *Fauvel* narrative recedes behind the fox of antecedent beast-fable *romans* as well as yielding place to a sharper apocalyptic message. The two motets are on the same tenor, surely not a coincidence, a neuma that is liturgically neutral, both in perfect modus, imperfect tempus.[8] There is also a link with *Tribum*: the *Floret* tenor likewise has two *color* statements without reduction, each bipartite with a different ending; the first three units of its *talea* ◼ ╻ ◼ ╪ share their rhythm with *Tribum's* short *talea* ╻ ╻ ╻ ╪╪. *Garrit gallus/In nova* is the stronger piece with respect to both text and music, infinitely rich and closely interconnected with *Tribum/Quoniam* and *Aman/Heu*. *Floret* offers an upbeat end to Fauvel's story, celebrating his union with Vaine Gloire; was it decided to replace that happy ending with the darker and cleverer *Garrit gallus/In nova* that more strongly initiates the reverse motion of the Marigny story and the overriding apocalyptic foreboding? Once it had been decided to exclude the motet, its triplum could then be cannibalised for the prose on the vices, *Carnalitas, luxuria*, and the motet itself discarded, at least for purposes of this manuscript. If this is what happened, it has considerable implications for the planning of the interpolated *Fauvel*. *Floret* would have been not only earlier than *Garrit gallus*, but earlier than all three of the Marigny motets; even so, I cannot believe it is by the same composer.[9] It is musically and textually much less tightly linked to them than they to each other. It is a vigorous piece, dominated by repeated notes for text declamation and melodic leaps of fourths, but I must confess to finding it less interesting and less sophisticated, lacking similar musical and textual citational play.[10] It lacks the Ovidian ingredient and classical quotations which, after their roles in the double narratives of *Fauvel* and current events, are among the strong factors binding the trio of motets as presented, and its simple catalogue of vices falls short of the tone and learnedness of the other Fauvel–Marigny motets.[11] We may therefore have here a precious relic from the cutting-room floor in the process of compiling *Fauvel*. Even if Sanders's chronology of the Marigny motets no longer applies, and if the more palpably structured *Garrit gallus* was indeed

---

[8] The three tenors are set out comparatively by Sanders, 'The Early Motets of Philippe de Vitry'.

[9] Daniel Leech-Wilkinson finds 'its counterpoint . . . far more crude with ugly upper-voice clashes, monotonous decorations of lengthy sonorities (often by leaping up and down over a fourth, the last resort of a composer lacking voice-leading skills) and inconsequential progressions'. Leech-Wilkinson, 'The Emergence of *Ars nova*', 302.

[10] Immediately after an illuminating explanation of the counterpoint at the beginning of *Se grace/Cum venerint* (see Ch. 29 below), *Johannes Boens Musica*, 68, cites this motet for the much less challenging seconds with the tenor, which can be explained as passing notes: 'Sic et secunda admittitur in motheto Florens vigor super verbo Mardocheo et secunda et quarta in tenore motheti Rex quem metrorum' ('Likewise explained is the second admitted in the motet *Florens vigor* on the word "Mardocheo" [bb. 94–100], and the second and fourth in the tenor of the motet *Rex quem metrorum*'). The motet is transcribed in Sanders, 'The Early Motets of Philippe de Vitry'.

[11] Bent, 'Tribum', and Bent, 'Marigny', incorporated above. Sanders observes that 'If "Haman" is Marigny, "Mordecai" can only be Charles de Valois' ('The Early Motets of Philippe de Vitry', 32). He also gives the context for *Floret* from the book of Esther.

(as I now suggest) a late and better replacement for *Floret/Florens*, it could still be the case that *Garrit gallus* was composed after *Aman*. Their musical and textual interrelatedness notwithstanding, the three (or four) Marigny motets are different from each other, with deliberately cultivated distinctiveness that cannot be plotted on a chronology of style evolution.

7

Related Manuscripts, Related Motets; Vitry

The challenge to the setting of terminal composition dates for 'historical' motets also has implications for the completion of the interpolated *Fauvel* itself, and for the wheels within wheels of its own assembly. Consequent upon the removal of firm terminal dates for the Marigny motets, the whole compilation may not be bound by a *terminus ante quem* as early as *c.* 1317, as had been proposed; there may have been more time for the careful planning, adaptation of pieces, editing, and replacement to which the possible substitution of *Garrit gallus/In nova* for *Floret/Florens* might attest, as suggested in Chapter 6, and with it the intimately linked trio of Marigny motets now in **Paris146** and the double narrative to which they contribute.

Evidence of adaptations and fauvelisations in **Paris146** from earlier motets and conducti is well documented. More scattered, and inviting further interpretation, is the evidence from later sources of discards and adaptations. Since Ernest Sanders, 'The Early Motets of Philippe de Vitry', the preparation of two early manuscripts that contain concordances to *Fauvel* motets, **Paris571** and **Br19606**, both originally thought to be earlier than or contemporary with **Paris146**, have been moved later by a decade or more, **Paris571** to 1326 and **Br19606** to 1335, though in both cases their repertories are demonstrably older. The contents of **Paris571** include Raoul le Petit's beautifully illustrated *Dit de Fauvain*, a she-ass counterpart of Fauvel.[1] Just preceding *Fauvain* in **Paris571** are two *Fauvel* motets once thought to have preceded their inclusion in **Paris146**: *Servant regem/O Philippe (Ludowice)/Rex regum* (F 16, p.mus. 33) also listed in **Trém**; *Detractor/Qui secuntur/Verbum iniquum* (F 9, p.mus. 12).

The motetus of *Servant regem/O Philippe* is presented in the left-hand column in **Paris571**, as if it were the triplum, with a text beginning not *O Philippe* but *Ludowice*.[2] This was assumed to refer to Louis X (1314–16), and therefore an earlier version of a motet that was recycled for his younger brother, Philip V. Sanders hence dated **Paris571** 1315–16,[3] to accommodate the presumed earlier form of the motet, just before its adaptation for **Paris146**. In other words, it was claimed that both royal motets in *Fauvel* were originally written for Louis X.

But Andrew Wathey has shown that **Paris571** was written and illuminated in 1326, at least partly in England, as a presentation book celebrating the marriage contract of Prince Edward of England (later Edward III) and Philippa of Hainaut, organised by Edward's mother, Queen Isabella, daughter of Philip IV, as the arms on the opening miniature on f. 6 establish. Besides *Fauvain*, the volume includes Brunetto Latini's *Livre*

---

[1] Taylor, 'Le Roman de Fauvain'.

[2] **Paris571**, f. 144. A three-staff indentation was left for initial 'L'; this was not provided, but 'ludovice' is written (small) in the margin. *Servant regem/O Philippe* was attributed to Vitry by Schrade, 'Philippe de Vitry', and more recently affirmed by Robertson, 'A Musical Lesson', 259.

[3] Citing RISM B IV 2, 173.

The Motet in the Late Middle Ages. Margaret Bent, Oxford University Press. © Oxford University Press 2023.
DOI: 10.1093/so/9780190063771.003.0008

140 FAUVEL AND VITRY

du Trésor, a rule for princes, a coronation rite and other moralising works on kingship in the 'Mirror of Princes' tradition. Isabella spent much of 1325 in Paris on diplomatic missions, including arranging the marriage. Wathey argues that, in view of this dating, *O Philippe* has been adapted for Louis IX, St Louis, the common ancestor of Edward and Philippa, and a saintly model for them, invoked more than once as the forebear of the recent kings. Wathey has removed any grounds for regarding *O Philippe* as a hastily updated contrafact of a motet for Louis X. The companion royal motet that precedes it in **Paris146** and in historical time, though not necessarily in order of composition, was indeed written for Louis X (*Se cuers ioans/Rex beatus/Ave*, F 15, p.mus. 32). *O Philippe* was written for Philip V and no one else, no earlier than mid-November 1316 or early 1317, the latest such *terminus* in *Fauvel*. Indeed, the triplum *Servant regem* is a stern reminder of kingly duty, and the tenor *Rex regum* is also appropriate to the purpose of the book. The other *Fauvel* motet in **Paris571**, *Detractor/Qui secuntur* (f. 4, F 9, p.mus 12) also elaborates the theme of wise kingship, and the triplum and motetus parts are similarly reversed on the page. Prince Edward performed a homage in September 1325, attested by royal notaries of whom the most senior was none other than Gervais du Bus, one of the authors of *Fauvel*. Philippe de Vitry was also in the royal chancery at this time; this suggests the opportunity for a direct line of transmission to England for these two French motets from **Paris146** that nicely complemented the aims of the presentation book.[4]

Fully six of the ten pieces in **Br19606** (see Table 7.1) are in **Paris146** in some form, two heavily adapted. All of them have the notation updated with minim stems, confirming (along with other later sources) the default readings of the stemless or downstemmed semibreves in **Paris146**. They form the core repertory of the rotulus, and five of them are also known from other sources, as shown in Table 7.1. Three are copied consecutively on the recto (face) and three on the verso (dorse). The other four pieces are the (conventional and old-fashioned) opening conductus *Deus in adiutorium*, the notational and stylistic outlier *Mater formosa/Gaude virgo* at the bottom of the recto,[5] and the two pieces at the bottom of the verso, the incomplete *O/Nostris lumen tenebris* and the later partial addition of Vitry's *Impudenter circumivi/Virtutibus*. Sanders dated **Br19606** *c.* 1320 with repertory going back to 1300. Even if that now seems too early, Karl Kügle's dating to *c.* 1335 on the strength of its coat of arms is surprisingly late, and surely reflects either a very conservative patron or a late copy of earlier material. Without Kügle's evidence, I would have placed its repertory and notational stage in the 1320s. I will now consider **Br19606**'s status as a repository for versions of the *Fauvel* material.

The other motet in **Br19606** besides *Floret/Florens* that was subjected to even more radical adaptation, and immediately follows it, is *Trahunt in precipitia/An diex/*

---

[4] Wathey, 'The Marriage', especially 14–18. Brown, 'Rex ioians', 62, still accepted that the motet was written for Louis X and adapted for Philip. Dillon, 'The Profile of Philip V', 219, acknowledged Wathey's new dating, but hesitated to accept its implications. Robertson, 'A Musical Lesson', also leaves the question open. See Taylor, '*Le Roman de Fauvain*' for further historical speculation. See below for two further English sources of Fauvel motets, **Robertsbridge** and **YorkN3**.

[5] See Kügle, 'Two Abbots and a Rotulus', and **Koblenz701**. Discussed by Desmond, ' "One is the loneliest" ', as an example of a piece that was updated from *Fauvel* notation. **Koblenz701** had descending and ascending stems and dots, some of which were erased, strongly suggesting that we are witnessing a hesitant process of conversion.

RELATED MANUSCRIPTS, RELATED MOTETS; VITRY   141

Table 7.1 Contents of **Br19606**

Compositions in **Paris146** are in boldface (*Floret* in adapted form).

Composition	Other sources of Paris146 pieces
RECTO	
Deus in adiutorium	
Super cathedram/Presidentes in thronis/Ruina	**Ca165, Troyes1949, Ox271***
Tribum que non abhorruit/Quoniam secta latronum/Merito [hec patimur]	**Stras, Robertsbridge** (and two other later adaptations)
Firmissime fidem teneamus/Adesto sancta Trinitas/Alleluia	**Koblenz701 and Robertsbridge**
Mater formosa, tu nobilis/Gaude virgo mater Christi/[Tenor]	
VERSO	
Floret cum vana gloria/Florens vigor ulciscendo/[Neuma quinti toni]	**Ca1328**
Trahunt in precipitia/An diex/[Displicebat ei]	
Se cuers joians/Rex beatus, confessor domini/[Ave]	**McV, Trém**
O/Nostris lumen tenebris dat [motetus only]	
Impudenter circumivi solum/Virtutibus laudabilis/Alma redemptoris mater [solus tenor II and contratenor only]	

Displicebat, presumably its original form. It appears as a motet quite early in **Paris146** with a new added quadruplum, *Quasi non ministerium*, and with the French-texted motetus replaced by the Latin *Ve qui gregi* (the motet occupies the whole of f. 6ᵛ, F 11, p.mus. 21).[6] The monophonic composition on f. 26ᵛ intersperses the music and text of the dismembered French motetus *Han Diex! ou pourai je trouver* with further text (without music) starting *Han Diex! de tout le monde sire*. Ardis Butterfield has outlined the complex network of this formally anomalous piece that leaves its mark all over *Fauvel*.[7] She describes a central complex including 'two pieces of seemingly inscrutable generic complexity', to which she applies the term 'semi-lyric'. They frame a central ballade (*Se j'onques a mon vivant*, p.mus. 57, f. 26). The first, *Amour dont tele est la puissance*, is placed in Fauvel's mouth as he presents it to Fortune. It is described in the classified table of contents as a *dit*; Butterfield calls it a *dit à refrains*. The refrains have musical notation but the intervening 'narrative' sections do not. The second semi-lyric piece is quite different. It consists of the text and music of the fourteen-line French motetus of *Trahunt in precipicia/An diex* dismembered into

---

   6 The tenor, *Displicebat*, has been identified as the verse of a responsory for St Augustine beginning *Volebat enim* (Clark, 'The Flowering', 175 n. 2 and Clark, 'New Tenor Sources', 108–16). There may be some play on letters here: *Quasi* and *Trahunt* alliterate with what would be their part-names quadruplum and triplum, as well as with *Quoniam* and *Tribum*. The words 'gravis precipitacio', *Floret*, line 34, also occur in the triplum *Trahunt in precipicia*.

   7 Butterfield, 'The Refrain', 132, 146–48 reports 'a pre-existent 14-line motetus part, *An diex on* [*ou?*] *pora ge trover* found without music on the guard leaf of BN lat.7682'. See also Brown, 'Rex ioians', 63.

142 *FAUVEL AND VITRY*

consecutive fragments (with just the music of the second line omitted), each of which is used as a 'refrain' heading a six-line strophe that amplifies, purely textually, each so-called refrain. The Latin version of the melody in **Paris146** is more ornamented than the original French-texted one in **Br19606**, but it is this more ornamented version whose original French text is restored for its generic conversion, signalling a complex relationship both with **Br19606** and the **Paris146** adaptation. Six of the lines, which come to be treated as refrains, are identical with part of the fourth strophe of the *Dit d'Amour* by Nevelon d'Amiens.[8] There is further remarkable recycling within **Paris146**: one of these newly created refrain lines is in turn quoted in Jehannot de Lescurel's *dit enté Gracieus temps est* (on this alphabetical series ending at G, see Ch. 6), just as the first line of this piece and the **Br19606** motetus, *Han Diex! ou pourai je trouver*, is the first line (words and music) in the *enté* structure of a *sotte chanson* later in the *Fauvel* manuscript on f. 34[v]. This creates a network of verbal and musical recapitulation at three positions within *Fauvel*, and beyond it in the Lescurel section of **Paris146**. In that context, it may not be too far-fetched to connect the interpolated *Han Diex! de tout le monde sire* with *Ha, sire Dieux!* (Strubel v. 1254), the exclamation that seems to announce an absent motet for Philip IV on f. 10[v], preceding the two 'royal' motets for his sons Louis X and Philip V. The Latin substitution of this motetus suits the purposes of a royal *admonitio* rather well. Was it perhaps to a version of this motet that the rubric refers? In **Br19606** it immediately precedes the Louis X motet *Se cuers ioans/Rex beatus/Ave*, which it would likewise have preceded at this point in the interpolated *Fauvel* had it been part of an *admonitio* intended for Philip IV while he was still alive.[9] The tenses at the end of Book I are managed with deliberation: Philip IV, the debonair lion, reigned *jadis*; then Philip V is referred to as reigning now (*ores*). The tenses are self-consciously mirrored by their reversal at the end of Book II: Philip IV, the lion, now blind, reigns (*monarchisat*) in *Garrit gallus/In nova*; he reigned (*regnaverat*) in *Tribum/Quoniam*. The regal blind lion at the end of Book II, no longer debonair, mirrors the blind goddess Fortuna, portrayed with blindfold only at the beginning of Book I. The fact that Fortuna holds a mirror in some images (ff. 12, 12[v]) is a further hint of reversal.

Other later copies of *Fauvel* or *Fauvel*-related motets:

Servant/O Philippe	**Paris571** (Ludowice), **Trém**
Detractor/Qui secuntur/Verbum iniquum	**Paris571**
Tribum/Quoniam	**Br19606**, **Robertsbridge**, **Stras** and two later adaptations, **Rostock** and **Mu29775**[10]

[8] Butterfield, 'The Refrain'; see also Plumley, *Grafted Song*, 112.

[9] It could have been placed on f. 6[v] for reasons of space (it would have taken up too much space in the tight composition of ff. 10–11); this is also a good place for it, because it follows a complaint about the king's false counsellors, and we know that king to be Philip IV (the Fair). The upper-voice texts draw heavily on the conductus repertory. See Dahnk, *L'Hérésie de Fauvel*, pp. li–lxvi. Together with a series of musical interpolations, the motet follows line L 668, S 666 (close to or at the number of the beast, 666). Fauvel allots the alms. The king is complicit in taxing the church, which is riven with simony (in the text following the motet) and other vices.

[10] The text only was preserved in Lübeck, Stadtbibliothek, MS 152 (destroyed in 1945). See Wathey, 'The Motets of Philippe de Vitry', 123.

RELATED MANUSCRIPTS, RELATED MOTETS; VITRY   143

Super cathedram/Presidentes	**Br19606, Ca165, Ox271*, Troyes1949**
Firmissime/Adesto	**Br19606, Robertsbridge, Koblenz701, Darmstadt521** (tr text)
Floret/Florens (in *Fauvel* only as the prose *Carnalitas*)	**Br19606, Ca165**
Trahunt in precipitia/An diex/ Displicebat	**Br19606**
Se cuers/Rex beatus	**Br19606, McV, Trém**
Garrit gallus/In nova fert	**Pic**
Orbis orbatus/Vos pastores	**Koblenz701**
Scariotis/Jure	**Trém**
Inter amenitatis/O livor/Revertenti	**Trém, YorkN3, Tr87**

Super cathedram/Presidentes/Ruina with five witnesses is one of the most widely circulated of the *Fauvel* motets; exceptionally, all its later sources retain unstemmed semibreves with dots. Only *Tribum* has more sources (six, including later arrangements).[11]

The two leaves of the considerably later **Ca165** clearly belong together, and are consistent with each other and with **Ca1328**. F. 1, however, has unstemmed semibreves on both sides, the only leaf in the related Cambrai complex without stems; f. 2 has stemmed minims. Surprisingly, at the evidently later date, it presents the whole motet with semibreves separated by dots, presumably following an exemplar without updating the notation.[12] The triplum text of *Super/Presidentes* mentions Hercules. Both of Vitry's seals, dating from the late 1340s, show the figures of Hercules and the lion.[13] Together with its wide circulation and vitriolic texts, the presence of Hercules in *Super/Presidentes* may further support Vitry's authorship of this motet. I increasingly favour the view that many of the motets in *Fauvel* generally judged 'less advanced', but which already deploy imperfect tempus, and especially those with vituperative texts, are likely to be early works of Vitry, as he found his way to the 'more advanced' motets generally accepted as his. *Fauvel* in any case documents a transition from the **Mo** repertory to what we know as the *ars nova*. *Ars nova* innovations, foremost of which is imperfect time, are well established in *Fauvel* long before a further wave of innovation made it necessary to notate their rhythms with stems. Recent controversies about the term fall away if we can accept that there were multiple waves of newness; and that some writers are using the term *ars nova* to indicate the musical concepts and rhythms, as I continue to do, while others define it as a stage of notational evolution, increased precision, and systematisation

[11] **Ox271*** contains fragments of *Super cathedram*, notated in grouped semibreves with dots and with no stems, no plicas. Folios numbered 6ᵛ–1 have the beginning of the motetus (with a gap in between); f. 3ᵛ sits below f. 6ᵛ with the end of the motetus ('-uli caret basis'), tenor, and the end of the triplum ('delictum atr' . . .' and 'sanius'), presumably overflowing onto this original recto from the preceding verso.

[12] The motet is discussed by Desmond, 'Notations', 112–19, who mentions the motetus fragment in **Ox271*** (on ff. 6ᵛ–1), but misses the continuation and the triplum fragment on f. 3ᵛ.

[13] See above, Ch. 4 n. 47, and Wathey, 'The Motets of Vitry', 145. Also *leo in vulpem* occurs in *Presum preces* (p.mus. 18), perhaps anticipating these beasts in *Tribum* and *Garrit*. Hercules is also mentioned in stanza 2 of *Mundus a mundicia*, the polemical conductus by Philip the Chancellor of which stanza 1 was adapted for *Fauvel* (p.mus.2). See Welker, 'Polyphonic Reworkings'.

144 FAUVEL AND VITRY

that lagged behind the musical phenomena.[14] **Troyes1949** has only the tenor, *Ruina*, and the final line of the triplum text written across the full page width. Presumably the upper parts started in two columns, and the triplum reverted to full width after the end of the shorter motetus. Only unstemmed semibreves are used throughout this fragment, so we can assume that the missing upper parts of *Super/Presidentes* were likewise unstemmed.[15]

Given the wide range of mostly fragmentary sources preserving versions of *Fauvel* motets, it is surprising that none is in **Ivrea**. However, three more *Fauvel* motets besides *Servant regem/O Philippe/Rex regum* (Philippe V)[16] were cited by their motetus parts in the index to **Trém**: *Scariotis/Jure* (F 5, p.mus 5), and, as a later addition, *Se cuers ioans/Rex beatus/Ave* (for Louis X). **Trém** thus contained both the 'royal' motets. **Trém** also lists *O livor*, the motetus of *Inter amenitatis/O livor/Reverenti*, a three-part motet preserved in the much later Battre fascicle of **Tr87**, probably from the 1430s (ff. 231ᵛ–232), as reported by Emilie Dahnk. **Paris146** gives only the two outer parts without that motetus (f. 21ᵛ, F 22, p.mus. 50), reduced from what must have been the three-part original. It is very surprising to find this motet more than a century later, in a version very close to **Paris146**, but of course by then and long since with explicit minims. Thus the motetus does not survive until more than a century after Fauvel, but is documented in **Trém**. The triplum alone appears on a musically isolated page in **YorkN3** (f. 10ᵛ), in an early fourteenth-century English hand and notation with groups of up to four stemless semibreves separated by breves or dots; the possibility of English origin for the motet has been suggested.[17] The early date of this copy, together with the English associations of **Paris571**, for which contact with Vitry could have been a conduit for those motets, points at least to an early circulation in England of some of the *Fauvel* material, as do the two later keyboard arrangements in **Robertsbridge**.[18]

Marigny, *Floret*, 'Quotations', and Possible Attributions to Vitry

All preserved anonymously, three tightly linked motets have floated in and out of the unstable canon of works by Philippe de Vitry (1291–1361), with *Aman* considered the most doubtful. Vitry was a considerable, even towering, intellectual, poet and composer, protégé of Louis of Bourbon, French royal secretary, papal familiar of Clement VI, close friend of Petrarch, and bishop of Meaux.[19] Of the *Fauvel* motets, Heinrich

---

[14] See especially Desmond, *Music and the moderni*, and Bent, '*Artes Novae*'.

[15] **Troyes1949** was discovered by Dominique Gatté. See Catalunya, 'Nuns, Polyphony', which gives photomontages of the still pasted-down sides, revealing capital letters and a few notes. I wondered if the 'D' tenor in the photomontage of fragment b could be the *Displicebat* tenor of (Quasi) *Trahunt/Ve/Displicebat*. What can be discerned of the tenor has some similarities of shape and range. It is to be hoped that the paste-down can be lifted.

[16] As **Trém** cites motets by motetus, this motet is a likelier identification than the *O Philippe* triplum which opens **Ivrea**.

[17] Bent, Hart and Lefferts, *The Dorset Rotulus*, 32 n. 27. See also Colton, 'Making Sense of *Omnis/Habenti*', 224 n. 15.

[18] It is striking that the **Robertsbridge** arrangements of *Tribum/Quoniam* and *Firmissime/Adesto* are copied on successive folios in **Paris146** and are directly adjacent in **Br19606**. For the similarly early motet *Flos/Fiat*, also intabulated in **Robertsbridge**, see Ch. 6 n. 7.

[19] For Philippe de Vitry, see NG2 (and Grove online), s.v. Vitry, by Bent and Wathey. Errors in the print edition of the NG2 worklist have now been corrected online and include the following: *Cum statua/Hugo* and

RELATED MANUSCRIPTS, RELATED MOTETS; VITRY   145

Besseler attributed *Tribum/Quoniam*, *Firmissime/Adesto* and *Garrit gallus/In nova* (but not *Aman*) to Vitry, and as the most obviously advanced motets in *Fauvel*, these attributions have won wide if not universal acceptance. Ph. Aug. Becker stated that *Garrit* and *Tribum* 'are said to be by Philippe de Vitry, and [*Aman*] might also be'.[20] Leo Schrade correctly affirmed the three motets as inseparably linked by their historical order, though wrongly equating that with their dates of composition. He thought they must be by the same composer, and endorsed Vitry's authorship of *Aman*.[21] If *Tribum* and *Garrit* are by Vitry, so must *Aman* be; I agree. Others including Daniel Leech-Wilkinson have rejected *Aman*, which seemed to lack the indirect testimony that attributes *Garrit gallus* and *Tribum* to him with more confidence; Edward Roesner even rejected *Garrit gallus*.[22]

Many of the arguments put forward by Sanders against Vitry's authorship of *Aman* are challenged by the case made here with respect to the chronology, function and conceptual unity of the three motets in *Fauvel* as well as their historical coding, and by new arguments in favour of the musical and textual quality of *Aman*. As set out in Chapter 3, Schrade, Sanders, Roesner and Leech-Wilkinson all assumed the historical dates to be dates of composition, and this conditioned their inferences about composer identity and stylistic chronology. All except Schrade leave *Aman* aside. Sanders adopted and extended Schrade's motet datings based on a literal reading of the historical events, leading him to reject *Aman* on grounds that, as a historically 'later' composition than *Garrit* and *Tribum*, it was less advanced, arguing that Vitry would not have composed a less coherent or more conservative piece (as he judged it by the rather narrow criteria he sets out) after 'as advanced a piece as *Garrit gallus*'.[23]

Sanders then linked *Floret/Florens* to the Marigny group, though because he only recognised their historical associations but not their central role in the *Fauvel* programme, he drew different conclusions from those put forward above. In favour of Vitry's authorship, he invoked the neutral *Neuma quinti toni* tenor that underpins three motets: Vitry's *Douce playsance/Garison* (not in *Fauvel*), *Garrit gallus/In nova* (widely accepted as a work by Vitry), and *Floret/Florens*.[24] Use of a version of the same tenor is arguably an imitable feature, given the number of cantus firmi common to different composers; Sanders admits this is insufficient in itself. The choice of the same tenor for *Floret* and *Garrit* may be significant for a composition designed for *Fauvel*, for the

---

Vos/Gratissima are *not* named in the *ars nova* tradition; *Douce/Garison* and *Firmissime/Adesto* are listed in *Ars nova*.

[20] Besseler, 'Studien II', 203; Becker, 'Fauvel', 36–37.

[21] 'But if we assume Philippe to be the composer of one of the works in the group, the inseparable association of the three motets as well as their close stylistic affinity make the same authorship for all three mandatory', and 'safely establishes the dates' (Schrade, 'Philippe de Vitry', 335–39).

[22] *Le Roman de Fauvel*, ed. Roesner et al., 39–42.

[23] Sanders, 'The Early Motets of Philippe de Vitry', 36. Sanders continues: 'their attribution to [Vitry] would force us to postulate a curious inconsistency in the composer's development: . . . written after as advanced a piece as *Garrit gallus*, lack a coherent phrase structure and generally exhibit a conservative facture in some ways reminiscent of the time of Petrus de Cruce'. This argument has many problems. Apart from the fallacious assumption of a developmental crescendo, Sanders's criteria for structural coherence are too narrow for a repertory where ingenuity takes many varied forms. They have largely to do with regular periodicity ('modular numbers') and are set out in Sanders, 'The Early Motets of Philippe de Vitry', and in Sanders, 'The Medieval Motet'.

[24] Sanders, 'The Early Motets of Philippe de Vitry', 35.

146 FAUVEL AND VITRY

reasons given in Chapter 6, but is not a reliable indicator of authorship. He also pointed out that *Floret* has the same clefs and opening sonority as *Garrit gallus* (likewise hardly a confirmation of authorship), and claims (more convincingly) that the text's original character and tone are clear Vitriacan hallmarks, going on to argue that the melodic, rhythmic and contrapuntal vocabulary falls within the style range of the larger group of motets that have been attributed to Vitry.

Still following chronological criteria, Sanders says *Floret* would have been out of date by the time Chaillou de Pesstain was making his edition in 1316, hence the recycling to the purposes of *Fauvel* of a motet triplum, from an obsolete external political context, as the prose *Carnalitas, luxuria*.[25] While admitting that *Floret* is 'less advanced in technique' and 'somewhat untidy', because he evaluated it as an early work, he did not hold it to the same criteria of numerical tidiness which led him to deny Vitry's authorship to the different artfulness of *Aman/Heu*, which he assumed to be a couple of years later. This chronological case for Vitry's authorship of *Floret* but not of *Aman* is weakened if the compositions, as suggested here, could all be later than the events. At this innovative period in the early *ars nova* when nearly every motet explores a different challenge, and there is no such thing as a standard template, the application of a single criterion can be limiting.[26]

Although noting the Haman link with *Floret*, Sanders regarded *Aman* rather as the creation of a lesser, anonymous musician, who 'was apparently reminded by Marigny's hanging of the biblical imagery so originally used in Vitry's early motet' [*Floret*], 'even though, admittedly, [*Aman*'s] melodic lines are somewhat reminiscent of the élan of Vitry's style'.[27] Perhaps Sanders realised that, in his enthusiasm to claim *Floret* for Vitry, with his belief in the documentary datings, and with his criteria of numerical tidiness, he was underestimating the originality of *Aman novi*; he certainly underestimated the textual richness and its interrelatedness with the other two motets brought out above. Indeed, *Floret* and the more complex *Aman* share many musical features, including rhythmic vocabulary, similar amounts of repeated-note sub-breve declamation and striking use of sharps (especially pronounced in *Aman*), not to mention textual bite. In the absence of attributed comparands, there is no compelling stylistic reason why both *Floret* and *Aman* could not be by Vitry.[28] Leaving

---

[25] 'The motetus poem can certainly, though not inevitably, be understood as reflecting the situation that prevailed between Sept. and Nov. of 1314. In 1316, however, when Chaillou was making his edition of the *Roman de Fauvel*, this text was no longer topical; nor is it in any way pertinent to the passage of the roman to which he added the triplum. The latter, being an impassioned diatribe against an impressively comprehensive catalogue of flourishing evils, suited the context well, and so, altering it somewhat, he incorporated it.' Sanders, 'The Early Motets of Philippe de Vitry', 33. Neither Sanders nor Schrade, 'Philippe de Vitry', gives any indication that they thought the political motets (the Marigny motets, and those listed in Ch. 3) had any connection to the *Fauvel* story.

[26] Sanders on modular numbers ('The Early Motets of Philippe de Vitry', 29): 'The phrase structure of *Floret*, utilizing the first nine multiples of the number 3, is still somewhat untidy, not unlike that of *Firmissime/ Adesto/Alleluya*.' His number analysis of *Floret* is as follows (but changing his count in longs to breves, for a total of 153):

> [Triplum] (30B + 27B) + (18B + 21B) + (15B + 21B) + 9B + 12B
> [Motetus] 24B+ (18B + 21B + 18B) + 12B + (21B + 21B +18B)
> [Tenor] [2(6B + 6B + 27B)] + [(6B + 6B + 27B) + (6B + 6B + 24B)].

[27] Ibid., 36.

[28] Schrade, 'Philippe de Vitry', 350. In the case of *Aman*, as Sanders, 'The Early Motets of Philippe de Vitry' put it, 'throwing Becker's caution to the winds', 36. See also PMFC 1, Commentary.

Sanders's chronological argument aside, and adding the Fauvellian programme to the historical one, if *Floret* is by Vitry, as he claims, so could *Aman* be; and if *Aman* is, as I claim, so could *Floret* be. However, as stated above, I find *Floret* musically and textually less interesting than the three established Marigny motets, and certainly less conceptually entwined with them; other *Fauvel* motets may have a stronger claim on Vitry's authorship than *Floret*.

Orbis orbatus/Vos pastores

Hitherto unique to **Paris146**, this motet was recently uncovered in **Koblenz701** by Karl Kügle, headed *de prelatorum avaricia*. It is complete, though the end of the tenor is damaged. Some dots are curiously placed over the tenor, apparently to show alteration. Others between some groups of semibreves, and the occasional downstem, betray its transcription from a source with mainly stemless semibreves; the provision of minim stems is inconsistent and unreliable, showing this to be a bungled attempt by an inexperienced notator to resolve the intended rhythms.[29]

Besides the three *Fauvel* motets named above, *Firmissime/Adesto*, *Tribum/Quoniam* and *Garrit/In nova*, Besseler first also counted *Orbis/Vos* as a work of Vitry, the earliest and most doubtful, but not *Aman*; he then backed off from this attribution and affirmed the other three.[30] Schrade claimed a close affinity of textual and musical style ('stylistic identity') between *Aman* and *Orbis/Vos*, which he thought was also by Vitry, particularly noting the characteristically vituperative texts, rhythmic vocabulary and declamation. If *Aman* is by Vitry, so might *Orbis* be. But both attributions have been brushed aside, rejected by Sanders, Leech-Wilkinson and Roesner. Schrade further pointed out that the tripla of *Aman* and *Orbis/Vos* share their opening rhythm and pitches (with the differences that the *g* in *Orbis* is sharp, and *Orbis* is in perfect modus) and also the first six tenor notes, transposed.[31] What he did not point out is that since *Aman*'s tenor is chant-based, and that of *Orbis/Vos* is unidentified, *Aman* may have come first, which brings Besseler's stylistic ordering into question. Moreover, as noted above, the triplum of *Aman* (and hence of *Orbis*) is a diminished version of that chant opening, another reason for placing *Aman* first. The text of *Orbis/Vos* is vitriolic in the way we have come to associate with Vitry. Moreover, there are clear links with the texts of other Marigny motets, which further helps an attribution to Vitry. In addition to other shared bestial imagery, line 7 of *In nova fert* is 'mox lupinis dentibus armatus'; the final couplet of *Orbis* is 'Nec ut lupos armamini | horum armati dentibus'—armed with wolves' teeth, again. The *Orbis/Vos* tenor carries the biblical quotation 'Fur non venit nisi ut furetur, et mactet, et perdat' (John 10: 10), but no melody for this non-liturgical text is known or likely. Each *color* contains three nearly identical periods. This serpentine conjunct tenor within a narrow range is strongly reminiscent of the *Fera pessima* tenor *color* of Machaut 9 (*a bb a g/a bb a g/f g a g*) (Ex. 9.10 below) and other tenors there cited. (See Ex. 7.1.)

---

[29] Kügle, 'The Aesthetics of Fragments'.
[30] Besseler, 'Studien II', 192.
[31] Schrade, 'Philippe de Vitry', 335–39.

Ex. 7.1 Tenor of *Orbis orbatus/Vos pastores*: three *taleae*, three *color* statements

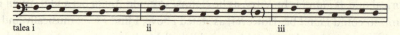

We saw above that the choice of chant for *Tribum* related to *Garrit gallus*, and that the opening of the triplum of *Tribum* was likewise a diminished version of the same chant. Use of this strategy in both pairs of motets may further help to support a claim of common authorship. The incorporation of chant tenor material into upper parts has received little notice in this repertory, where it is in fact quite widespread. There are famous fifteenth-century examples, such as Dunstaple's four-part *Veni sancte spiritus/Veni creator*, which paraphrases the opening of the chant in the upper parts before the tenor takes over at the point where the triplum leaves off, and earlier instances in the early fourteenth-century English voice-exchange motets in **Ox81**.[32] These earlier instances are perhaps less obvious but still quite striking; they augment the arsenal of craft which can be built up alongside narrower criteria.

Sanders rejected both *Aman* and *Orbis*. He objected that, if by Vitry, *Orbis* and *Aman* would be the only such works preserved as *unica* in **Paris146**. This criterion is made dangerous by the regular discovery of new sources; although it remains true of *Aman*, it is no longer applies to *Orbis*, whose recent appearance in **Koblenz701** would by Sanders's criteria elevate its eligibility.[33] A high proportion of *Fauvel* motets that are also preserved in later sources have at some point been tentatively attributed to Vitry; their later circulation could possibly indicate the regard in which these works and their author were held, though it would be rash to confirm their status on this basis. Most attributable motets whose verbal texts are separately preserved in later manuscripts are by Vitry. *Orbis* is also the only *Fauvel* motet cited in any of the *ars nova* treatises (here, **Vat307**) besides the Vitriacan candidates *Garrit* and *Firmissime*. It also appears to be the only motet to be cited in that complex of treatises by its triplum, *Orbis*, rather than the presumed motetus, *Vos*, which, however, has a higher overall range and lies predominantly above *Orbis*. The layout in both surviving manuscripts assigns triplum status to *Orbis*, and it is clear that the parts have not been reversed. *Orbis*, laden with biblical references, is much more active, and gallops largely syllabically through three seven-line octosyllabic stanzas against the single similar stanza in the slower-moving *Vos*, with its strong invective against sinful priests. The status of these voices may have been ambiguous then, as now. The motetus voices of *Garrit gallus* and *Floret* also spend significant time above the triplum, and in terms of voice order, *Tribum* innovates with a central tenor above the motetus. Some of these reversals and voice-crossings may accord with the reversal and inversion themes of *Fauvel*.[34]

On the strength of his study of motet texts, Leofranc Holford-Strevens believes Vitry to have been the author of all three Marigny texts in **Paris146**. Their often-biting tone

---

[32] *A solis* and *Hostis Herodes* quote in the first seven longs of their upper parts the openings, respectively, of well-known Christmas and Epiphany hymns (PMFC 16). Harrison in PMFC 15 sequesters their stylistic sibling *Salve clere speculum* into a different (motet) classification on the strength of chant paraphrase (but only from section 2) in its tenor. On the Hatton pieces, see now Bent, Hartt and Lefferts, *The Dorset Rotulus*.

[33] Sanders, 'The Early Motets of Philippe de Vitry', 36 and 31.

[34] Voice-crossing is also a major strategy in several Machaut motets, as shown in Ch. 9 for Motet 9 and elsewhere, and has since been fruitfully pursued in Zayaruznaya, 'She has a Wheel', and Shaffer, 'Finding Fortune'.

RELATED MANUSCRIPTS, RELATED MOTETS; VITRY   149

and learned frame of reference is entirely consistent with the texts of later motets more certainly attributed to him. Because of the intimate relationship of text and music, I cannot believe that text and music are not by the same author, and therefore give my vote to Vitry as the composer. If they reinforce the climax of *Fauvel*, it is not to be excluded that other *Fauvel* motets that have from time to time been attributed to Vitry, without general acceptance, but which already exploit the then-novel imperfect tempus, may be earlier works by him. The elaborate process of adaptation, both of earlier repertory, and of pieces such as the two heavily reworked motets in **Br19606**, open his authorship as a possibility. Born in 1291, he was already in his mid- to late twenties when **Paris146** was compiled, so experiments with the imperfect tempus that is new to the *ars nova* and copiously present in **Paris146**, but in no earlier source, could well have started a few years earlier and included his earliest work, not yet considered as such by modern scholars. If he was centrally involved in devising the musical programme for *Fauvel*, could he have learned his craft partly by making those arrangements of older repertory? What was he writing before he began his more radical innovations? I would place a strong bet on his authorship of some of the other *Fauvel* motets which also innovate in imperfect time, if not yet with modus changes and coloration. Some of the earlier motet texts in *Fauvel* are learned and vituperative, in a style later confirmed in Vitry's texts, and for which the *Fauvel* project was a natural outlet. Schrade also noted similarities between the triplum texts of *Orbis* and *Garrit* (p. 339). They share a level of invective rhetoric that is characteristic of more securely attributed Vitry works.

Internal punning 'signatures' (including the Frenchmen/cockerels, the *galli* of *Garrit gallus*), and a pattern of musico-textual cross-references and allusions, link especially *Garrit* and *Tribum*, but all three motets were carefully planned as a unit, with often irregular verbal texts written 'for' music and conceived together with it, and *Aman* is replete with allusions.[35] All three motets incorporate one or more classical lines, and each motet ends with a classical 'quotation' (which, as argued for *Tribum*, may be a building block rather than a quotation). Possible authorial signatures include the *gallus* who speaks in *Garrit gallus*; in *Tribum* Ovid's words are voiced or ventriloquised by this same *gallus* who *concinat Gallus Nasonis dicta* (sings the words of Ovid). Vitry's authorship receives further support from the discovery that the hexameter couplet from Joseph of Exeter's *De bello troiano* that ends *Tribum* (see above) was later written into his own copy of the chronicle of Guillaume de Nangis, as a marginal autograph annotation to a historical passage parallel to the contemporary events criticised in *Fauvel*: 'Nota: Post zephiros plus ledit hiems, post gaudia luctus, etc.'[36]

There has been widespread but not universal acceptance of Vitry's authorship of *Garrit* and *Firmissime*, and probably also of *Tribum*, all named in *ars nova* treatises.

---

[35] Wathey, 'The Motet Texts', 195, also advances the view that the words and music were conceived together.

[36] The *Chronicon* of Guillaume de Nangis (a monk of Saint-Denis, and the main historiographer of the French royal house at the end of the 13th c.) exists in two states. Vitry owned one of two surviving copies of the first redaction, Vat. Reg. lat. 544, as reported by Wathey, 'Auctoritas'. See also Wathey, 'Philippe de Vitry's Books', where Vitry's annotations are further discussed, and Wathey, 'Words and Music'. *De bello troiano* VI. 784–87 and 818–52 give Hecuba's lament, which has some similarity with the language of *Aman*; Wathey, 'Myth and Mythography', 96 n. 39. He notes Hecuba's *Heu meus* at VI. 814–15 (cf. *Aman*'s tenor *Heu me*) and the references by both Hecuba (VI. 838) and the motet triplum to the fires that consumed Phaeton and their 'common emphasis on the cruelty of fate'. Following earlier studies that underestimate the *Fauvel* component, he calls the motetus *Heu Fortuna* the lament of Marigny. It may be that too, but it is explicitly placed in the mouth of Fauvel.

150 *FAUVEL* AND VITRY

Both have innovations beyond the primary one of duple time; *Garrit* by using tenor coloration to change modus, *Firmissime* by newly rhythmicising the first *color* in longs in perfect maximodus to become the second *color* in breves in imperfect modus, all fully and necessarily written out (but over a page turn, **Paris146**, f. 43[r-v]). It has proved less straightforward to claim advanced technical and musical innovation for *Tribum* than for *Garrit gallus*, though all three (and only those of the *Fauvel* motets) have been accepted as Vitry's by Besseler, Sanders, Leech-Wilkinson and others. Sanders excluded *Aman* on style-chronological grounds we have judged to be weak, and excluded *Orbis/ Vos* despite the shared material pointed out by Schrade.[37] He depended, too heavily I believe, on criteria which he found lacking in *Aman*. Hartt's computation of sonority in some Vitry motets also, in my view, depends too heavily on a single criterion as a tool for attribution, and takes too little account of layered dissonance, resolved appoggiaturas, and text–music relationships.[38] Above all, neither of these authors, and some others, seem ready to concede that a composer may deliberately cultivate different styles and strategies in different compositions, as I believe to be the case with the Marigny motets.

All three Marigny motets are masterly and strikingly original constructions of text and music, musically very different from each other, despite their coordinated substance and musical cross-referencing. I hope by augmenting the tight links between them, and broadening the criteria for evaluating craft, to have revived the case for Vitry's authorship of *Aman* and *Orbis*, and with them perhaps that of other imperfect-tempus *Fauvel* motets.

---

[37] A shared tenor was sufficient to persuade Sanders that the same composer was responsible for *Floret* and *Garrit*, but he included *Floret* despite it lacking the regular periodicity on which basis he excluded *Aman*. A shared tenor is no guarantee of composer identity. Many instances of sharing by different composers include *Ruina*, in *Super/Presidentes* and Machaut M13; *Gaude virgo gloriosa . . . Super omnes speciosa* in *Vos/ Gratissima* and Machaut M17. See Ch. 8. The striking vocative of *Vos pastores* may be reflected in that of Vitry's *Vos quid admiramini*. Shared opening words sometimes link motets.

[38] Hartt, 'The Problem of the Vitry Motet Corpus'. In view of the close text–music relationships demonstrated for these and other motets, I cannot agree with his suggestion that Vitry could in some cases have provided words for others to set.

8

Vos quid admiramini/Gratissima virginis species/Gaude gloriosa

Sources

Two motets considered to be among the most certain works by Vitry are attributed to him by John of Tewkesbury, the author of the *Quatuor principalia*, whose earliest source is dated 1351. One, *Cum statua/Hugo*, is also authorially signed in the triplum: 'hec concino Philippus publice'; the other is *Vos/Gratissima*.[1] Both are anyway probably considerably earlier than this by criteria of their upper-voice rhythms, which go only minimally beyond the *Fauvel* defaults for stemless semibreves, but they are among the earliest indications that French repertory was circulating in England by this date.[2] Leo Schrade knew *Vos/Gratissima* only from **Ivrea** and the partly illegible copy in **Ca1328**, and its listing in **Trém**. Since then, it was identified in **Brussels5170** (announced by Gilbert Reaney in 1965; triplum and beginning of motetus only), the English source **Durham20** (announced by Frank Ll. Harrison in 1967), and **Aachen** (announced by Joachim Lüdtke in 2001; motetus and lower parts only).[3]

Esc10 is a collection of mostly standard astronomical writings heavily annotated by Johannes de Muris, together with many miscellaneous personal notes, calculations and observations (for example, of eclipses), financial transactions and book loans. It is thus a hugely important source for his biography; datable entries range from 1321 to 1344. An incomplete version of the tenor of *Vos/Gratissima* was copied sideways in void notation in the margin on f. 223ᵛ, in a section of the manuscript thought to

---

This chapter is based on the oral presentations on *Vos/Gratissima* that I gave in the late 1980s in Princeton and then in Oxford and elsewhere (some jointly with David Howlett); since then, much has been discovered and written about this motet. The present observations, not previously published, are here partly (and imperfectly) updated to take account of sources that have since come to light and to note work by others. Among many discussions of this motet are Leech-Wilkinson, *Compositional Techniques*, 50–67; Hamilton, 'Philippe de Vitry in England'; Desmond, *Music and the moderni*, 198–202, 222–28; Clark, 'Super omnes speciosa'; Dudas, 'Another Look at *Vos/Gratissima*'.

[1] Aluas, *Quatuor principalia*. This treatise also refers to Vitry having used red coloration in 'several motets' ('pluribus motetis') to change modus, tempus or prolation. For *Cum statua/Hugo* see Zayaruznaya, *The Monstrous New Art*, ch. 4 and appendix 2. A more recently discovered source is in **Leipzig431**. See Maschke, 'Entfernte Einbandfragmente'.

[2] Tabulated in Earp, 'Tradition and Innovation'; he accepts paired minim rests in hockets ⌐ ♦ as equivalent to ♦ ♦; see Ch. 13 below. Zayaruznaya, 'Reworkings', 156, shows how the **Ivrea** semibreve hockets of *Cum statua/Hugo* were revised with minims for **Ca1328**; but those too do not involve single minim rests.

[3] Reaney, 'New Sources'; Harrison, 'Ars Nova in England'; Lüdtke, 'Kleinüberlieferung'; and Zayaruznaya, *The Monstrous New Art*. It is published in PMFC 1, Vitry no. 7, p. 76. The essential contratenor and the twinned nature of the two supporting lower parts qualify this as a piece for which a solus tenor could be expected. **Ivrea** preserves two versions of a solus tenor. The first, with many dissonant departures from a

152 FAUVEL AND VITRY

date around 1330 or soon after.[4] On the same page, Muris records the loan to Vitry of his Boethius (with commentary) and the *Didascalicon* of Hugh of St-Victor: 'Magister Philippus de Vitriaco habet musicam Boecii cum (commento) et didascalicon Hugonis'; and in a longer list of book loans on f. 225[v]: 'Magister Philippus de Vitriaco habet meum commentum super musicam' and 'Dominus D. Legrant habet tabulas Tholetanas et speram, compotum, astrolabium, theoriam planetarum etc.'. Both Vitry and Denis le Grant were composers who later became bishops, and were evidently in social and intellectual contact with Muris.[5] It seems plausible that the likely presence together of two or all three musicians may have occasioned a discussion of this tenor and its annotation in **Esc10**. Both on notational grounds and on the evidence of **Esc10**, *Vos/Gratissima* has been dated before or around 1330.[6] On stylistic and notational grounds, I am inclined to accept a date around the middle or second half of the 1320s.

Texts

Some of the most remarkable features of this motet arise from the structuring of the texts and from the text–music relationships. The texts are given here in Table 8.1, showing textual alignment between triplum and motetus, but discussion of them and those relationships will follow the resolution of some musical and notational issues.

Table 8.1 Texts and translations of *Vos quid admiramini/Gratissima virginis species*

		Triplum		Motetus
C1T I	1	**Vos**, quid admiramini,	1	**Gratissima** virginis species
	2	virgines, si virgini		
	3	pre ceteris eligende		
T II	4	dignati fuerimus	2	quam decorat carnis mundicies
	5	nubere, dum nupsimus		
	6	tanquam valde diligende.	3	usque centrum plagasti intima
T III	7	**Ista** pulcra specie,		
	8	humilis manerie		
	9	ac opere virtuosa;		

lower-voice conflation, is marked *vacat iste* and is followed by a 'normal' solus tenor, also partially preserved in **Aachen**.

---

[4] **Esc10** was announced by Gushee, 'New Sources' (1969), noting its connections with Muris, Vitry and Denis le Grant; but the unlabelled tenor on f. 223[v] was not identified as that of Vitry's motet until 1991: Kügle, 'Frankreich und sein direkter Einflußbereich', 354. The tenor is reproduced and parsed in Hamilton, 'Philippe de Vitry in England'.

[5] See Ch. 31 for a new attribution to Denis le Grant in the **Trém** index.

[6] Some dating criteria are summarised in Desmond, *Music and the moderni*, 198.

Table 8.1 Continued

		Triplum		Motetus
T IV	10	turpis vestrum altera,	4	mei cordis plaga dulcissima,
	11	ausu nimis aspera		
	12	necnon virtutes exosa.	5	intra stillans amoris spiritum
T V	13	**Ista** lux, **vos** nubila,		
	14	**ista** velox aquila,		
	15	**vos** colubres gradientes;		
	16	**ista** super ethera	6	nescientem pectoris exitum.
T VI	17	regnat, **vos** in misera		
	18	valle languetis egentes.	7	**Gratissime** simili vulnere
	19	**Ista** virgo **regia**		
C2T i	20	dulcis est amasia		
	21	mea sponsaque pia.	8	peperisti mundum *me ledere.*
T ii	22	*Rex ego sum, hec regina.*		
	23	Quid tanta referimus?	9	*O regina,* tuum amplectere
T iii	24	Nos qui cuncta novimus		
	25	dignam preelegimus	10	astringendo pectus *cum ubere.*
T iv	26	*et ut rosam hanc pre spina.*		
	27	Surgite **vos** igitur,	11	*O rex regum,* oculum oculo
T v	28	quia tempus labitur		
	29	et mors **vos** persequitur.	12	et os ori junge *pro osculo*
T vi	30	*Huic servite, hanc vocate,*		
	31	quod si neclexeritis,	13	*ac inspira* verbum in labia,
T vii	32	illam non videbitis		
	33	gloriam quam cupitis.	14	quo recepto fiat caro dia.
(T viii)	34	**Vos eÿa** properate!		

Tenor: Gaude virgo gloriosa, super omnes speciosa

Source: David Howlett in the Orlando Consort recording, 'Philippe de Vitry and the Ars Nova', CD-SAR 49.

Notes: Hockets are marked in italics, *Vos* and *Ista* in bold. Unless noted, **Brussels5170**, **Ca1328** and **Aachen** agree with the given text where present and legible.

Variants: tr 23 **Durham20** *Quis*; 27 **Ivrea** *Urgete*; mo 3 **Ivrea** *placasti*; **Aachen** 8 *delere*, 9 *ampectore*, 14 *receptum*.

Triplum: You virgins, why are you astonished if in preference to the others we have deigned to wed the chosen virgin, since we have wed, so specially to be loved. She beautiful in appearance, humble in manner, and virtuous in work; the other of you filthy, too harsh in daring, and also hating virtues. She light, you cloudy; she a swift eagle, you slithering snakes; she reigns above the heavens, you languish needy in the miserable vale. She a royal virgin, is a sweet mistress and my holy spouse. I am the king, she the queen. Why do we say such things? We who know all things have forechosen her as worthy, and as this rose in preference to the thorn. Arise, therefore, because time is passing and death pursues you. Serve her, call upon her, because if you neglect her you will not see the glory which you desire. Oh hurry!

Motetus: Most gracious figure of a virgin, whom beauty of flesh adorns, you have wounded to the centre the inmost parts of my heart with a very sweet wound, pouring within a spirit of love that knows no exit from my breast. Most graciously you have brought forth a pure one to injure me with a similar wound. O queen, embrace your own one, binding bosom with breast. O king of kings, join eye to eye and mouth to mouth for a kiss, and breathe the word on my lips, which, once received, may make the flesh divine.

Tenor: Rejoice, glorious one.

The Tenor: Relationship to Other Motets

The tenor is shown in Ex. 8.1a. It has long been known that Vitry's tenor *Gaude gloriosa, super omnes speciosa* is from the middle of the Marian antiphon *Ave regina celorum*, and that the tenor of Machaut's Motet 17 uses the last part of this segment, from *Super omnes speciosa* to the end. Machaut's tenor *color* coincides with the last eighteen notes of Vitry's tenor (notes 13–30 in Ex. 8.1b); in the second *color* statement of *Vos/Gratissima* this is the passage from *talea* iv to the end.[7] The shared section is melodically identical in the two motets, though at different pitch levels (*Vos/Gratissima* on *f*, M17 on *c*) and differently rhythmicised. The fact that the version used by both differs from known chant sources led Alice Clark to infer that Machaut borrowed from Vitry, not directly from a chant.[8] She also noted that Machaut's *talea* appears to be modelled on Vitry's, rather than the other way round. Such a causal relationship would then require M17 (generally thought on grounds of notational usage to be one of Machaut's earlier motets, and dated by Lawrence Earp to the 1320s) to follow *Vos/Gratissima*, which would then need to be placed considerably earlier than its usual dating towards 1330.

The dependence of Machaut on Vitry has been called into question by the more recent discovery of **Paris934** by Richard Dudas. An anonymous motet on f. 79[r], labelled and based on *Super omnes speciosa*, uses exactly the same segment at the same pitch

Ex. 8.1 The tenor of *Vos/Gratissima*: (a) The *taleae* of *color* 1 are marked (with |) above the staff, of *color* 2, below it. Brackets show repeated cells and chiasms. (b) The background contrapuntal relationship of tenor (black noteheads) and contratenor (void)

---

[7] Clark, 'Concordare cum materia', V7 and M17, 204 and 251.

[8] Clark, 'Machaut Reading Machaut', 95. Clark, '*Super omnes speciosa*', 248, cites three instances where Machaut borrows a tenor from another motet. In Ex. 8.1a the chant text is not underlaid in detail, because the chant differs from known sources.

as Machaut M17, and is judged by Earp to date from around or even before 1320, too early to postdate Vitry's motet.[9] The tenor *color* in M17 is simply repeated without change, whereas the new motet is much more complex, with two written-out and differently rhythmicised *colores*, each of which is marked for repetition; there is no contratenor in either motet. The second reading of the second *color* statement of the **Paris934** motet, as Earp observes, reinterprets its single notated form with differently placed and evaluated alteration and imperfection in two different context-dependent rhythmicisations, pointing the way to Machaut's similar treatment of a homographic tenor in his M6. These different levels of complexity raise questions about the relative chronology and actual dating of the three motets on this shared tenor, but complicate the case for claiming direct dependence between them. Like the two main (notated) *color* statements in the **Paris934** motet, *Vos/Gratissima* provides a new rhythmicisation of the second *color*, as in two other early motets attributed to Vitry: *Firmissime/Adesto* and *Douce/Garison*. In none of these cases could the new rhythmicisation have been notated homographically; it could not have been derived from the first statement by diminution or mensural change. Machaut's M17 and **Paris934** each have a six-note *talea*, three *taleae* per *color*; the *color* in both cases contains eighteen notes and is at the same pitch (c). The relationship is thus closer between them than either is to Vitry's, suggesting that Machaut's source may have been the **Paris934** motet, whose texts, insofar as they survive, are to my eye Vitry-like in tone, and include the words *Rex regum* and *filia*, also evocative of *Vos/Gratissima*, as is the use of the first person and the learned Latinate style. Leofranc Holford-Strevens observed that the triplum text is modelled on Ovid's *Ex ponto* (I. 6.51–53), from which Vitry cites IV. 3.35–36 in *Tribum*. Another motet in **Paris934**, on f. 79ᵛ, has an essential contratenor which functions as a pair with the tenor in a manner contrapuntally similar to *Vos/Gratissima*, but with tightly interlocked mensural coloration.[10]

Yet another motet using the same tenor segment was identified by Michael Cuthbert. It is *Pura placens/Parfundement*, in **Ox7**, a mid-fourteenth-century English manuscript of similar date to **Durham20**, which includes *Vos/Gratissima* which, as noted, is attributed to Vitry in the English treatise by John of Tewkesbury, the *Quatuor principalia* dated 1351.[11] This tenor is pitched on *f* like Vitry's version (Machaut and **Paris934** being on *c*). It has one small variant, likewise not in known chant sources: in the other three tenors, notes 8–12 are *d f g f f* (in the version of Vitry; transposed to *c* in the other two) and in *Pura placens/Parfundement* they are *d f f g f*. Until a matching version of either form of this melody is found in a chant source, some relationship between the four compositions must be assumed. The probable chronological order was **Paris934**, Machaut, Vitry, *Pura placens/Parfundement*, thus reducing the reasons for

---

[9] Dudas and Earp, *Four Early* Ars nova *Motets*. It appears that the motet was originally notated without minim stems, which were added later.

[10] Dudas and Earp, 'Paris 934'; first presented at a seminar in All Souls, Oxford, 22.10.2020.

[11] Cuthbert, 'Hidden in our Publications'. The motet is in PMFC 15, no. 24, where the tenor is listed as unidentified. With two mid-century attestations to Vitry's motet being known in England, *Pura placens/Parfundement* might have borrowed its tenor. The style and alliteration suggest English origin. On the other hand, it shares an opening in **Ob7** with a motet also in **Ivrea**, so it might be a French motet in England, as suggested by its possible identity as the opening motet ('*Profondement*') of a lost French source reported (from Barrois, from the 1487 inventory of the Burgundian ducal library) in Besseler, *Studien I*, 184 and 222 n.1, and more recently in Kirkman, *The Cultural Life of the Early Polyphonic Mass*, 245.

156 FAUVEL AND VITRY

placing Vitry's motet before Machaut's, though both their motets could be of similar date in the mid-1320s.

The Tenor–Contratenor Relationship

The contratenor of *Vos/Gratissima* is grammatically essential, and works as a pair together with the chant tenor. It is shown in void notes in Ex. 8.1b. The tenor has a range of a full octave: roughly the first third explores the range a fifth above *f*, the middle third the fourth below, and the final third the fourth above. The descending fourth *bb a g f* occurs near the beginning and at the end, and the two low *c*s form the centre of a chiasm, bracketed in Ex. 8.1a. The contratenor provides a fifth below higher notes of the chant tenor at places which would otherwise have unsupported fourths, and it is above the tenor when the tenor descends to its lower range. The tenor and contratenor *colores* of *Vos/Gratissima* each have thirty notes. The first *color* is divided into six *taleae* of five notes, marked at the top of the staff in Ex. 8.1a, the second into seven *taleae* of four notes, marked at the bottom of the staff, leaving the final two cadential chant notes and their preceding rest to start an unfinished new *talea*. Each *talea* of the first *color* extends over five longs, the contratenor syncopated by an initial imperfect long rest, and each *talea* of the second extends over three longs, the tenor syncopated by an initial breve rest.

Ex. 8.1b shows the background contrapuntal relationship of tenor and contratenor. The parallel fifths at notes 10–11 are mitigated in the composed form by rests at B28–B31, but not at B113–B115, where they coincide with two bars of parallel unisons between the upper parts on *astringendo*, perhaps to emphasise, or even depict, the 'close binding of breast to breast' (motetus line 10; see Table 8.1). Such a striking effect was surely deliberate, and can be added to a growing list of instances of affective word-painting, where the music departs from an implicit norm.

My analytical comments in what follows were originally based on a transcription from **Ivrea**. Richard Dudas has graciously allowed me to use his transcription from **Durham20** (see ⏵ Ex. 8.2), which for present purposes has been adjusted at my request in a few places where I felt the readings of **Ivrea** or of other sources to be preferable.[12] The result is therefore an interpretation; readers may have different opinions on individual decisions. The relatively few variants are noted above the staff, and listed with sources in the note.[13] In this case, the lower-case roman numerals for the *taleae* of the

---

[12] Richard Dudas has offered substantial analytical insights in email correspondence in 2021, now included in Dudas, 'Another Look at *Vos/Gratissima*'.

[13] Commentary notes to ⏵ Ex. 8.2): **Ivrea, Ca1328, Brussels5170, Durham20, Aachen** (further abbreviated here to **Iv, Ca, Br, D, A**). Durham's plicas are not present in the other sources, apart from a few in **Ca** and **Br**. Where legible, breve plicas are in **Br** at mo 17, tr 52, 86, 122, 124, 135, 149, and **Ca** mo 45. If the ending is to be aligned (as here), the penultimate tenor note is, wrongly in all legible sources, an imperfect L before a L. The ligature in **Iv** had a stem (correctly) for a B (alt), but it was erased, here restored.
D: tr 40.4, 41.4, 42.4, large minims on the last of a group of four, presumably for syllabification. Elsewhere the last minim is separated, as at tr 97, 114–15, 123. These distinctions are not made where the group is melismatic. Ex. 8.2 follows **D** except as noted (changes on authority of other sources or of subjective critical judgement). **Ca** and **Br** variants are noted where legible. Music variants from Ex. 8.2: tr 44 **Iv** and **Br** ♦♦ ♦♦ preferred to **D, Ca** ♦ ♦♦♦; tr 87 **Iv** *fede* ♦♦ ♦♦ preferred to **Ca, D, Br** ♦ ♦♦ *ede*; tr 94.2 **Ca, Iv** *g* preferred to **A, D** *f*; tr 143 **Iv** *aag* ♦ ♦♦; mo 6 **Iv** *c* ■ preferred to **D, Br, A** *cbca* ♦♦ ♦♦; mo 7–9 **Iv A Br** two ligs (**D** one lig); mo 9.1 *b* **Iv, A, Br** preferred to **D** *d*; mo 30 **Iv** *gfg* ♦ ♦♦; mo 45 **Iv** *fe* ♦ ♦; mo 58.1 **Iv** *d* preferred to **Ca A D** *e*.

second *color* do not mean that they are diminished forms of the upper-case ones in the first *color*; they are newly rhythmicised.

There are surprisingly few progressions of third to fifth between the tenor–contratenor pair (Ex. 8.1b), so that normal cadences are largely avoided. At two places where one part descends by step, it is undercut by the other, making a third to unison (tenor notes 8–9, 29–30, Ct 14–15, 24–25). Progressions of third to fifth occur only at notes 3–4 on *g–f* (with Ct below), 17–18 on *d–c* and 22–23 on *g–f* (both with tenor below). The first of these falls (in ⊙ Ex. 8.2) at breves 9–10 and 97–98, the second at breves 51–52 and 127–30, and the third at breves 66–67 and 141–42. Of these, breves 9–10 and 141–42 make a normal 6/3–8/5 cadence; breves 66–67 and 97–98 make a weak cadence in the upper parts; B127–B130 avoid the cadence with rests. B51–B52 make a strong 3–5 cadence with parallel octaves *f♯–g*, requiring *f♯* in triplum and contratenor on the triplum word *aspera* (harsh)—the only occasion for any sharp in the whole motet, and arguably another instance of word-painting, taking the musical language outside an implicit norm that has been set up for the motet, such as *astringendo* (above) and *oculi oculo* (below).

Variant Notational Readings and the Reciprocal Syncopation of the Lower Parts

The annotation in **Esc10** is not the only indication that the tenor notation gave rise to debate then, as now. The *Quatuor principalia* cites both *Cum statua/Hugo* and *Vos/Gratissima* for the use of a dot to perfect the long. In the case of *Vos/Gratissima*:

> Posset tamen prima longa imperfici a parte ante per brevem precedentem vel per valorem nisi punctus immediate eam sequatur, ut patet in tenore de Gratissima.

> The first longa can be imperfected at the beginning part by a preceding brevis or its value, unless the punctus immediately follows it, as is apparent in the tenor of *Gratissima*.

This description does not apply to the first tenor *color*, but seems to describe the beginning of the second, where the first long is preceded by a breve rest, as shown in Fig. 8.1. The dot on the final long of the first *color* ensures that the newly rhythmicised second *color* starts with that breve rest. If it were not for the dot after the long, the breve rest would imperfect it. The first long of *color* 2, after the breve rest, has a dot in **Durham20**; but that long precedes another long and would be perfect by *similis ante similem*, so its dot is helpful but not essential.

Ivrea has many erasures in the second half of the tenor. The scribe (or reviser) misunderstood the syncopated *taleae* of *color* 2, failing to recognise that each group is offset by the rest, and the syncopation made up at the end of each short *talea*. He erased the (originally correct) long stem from the first long of each *talea*, making it a breve to be altered, which without the syncopation would be notationally but not musically correct. He then (wrongly) added a dot to the second long. Despite this garbled version in **Ivrea**, on which he was then dependent, Schrade was able to correct the faulty reading empirically; there is no doubt on grounds of musical sense about the intended tenor

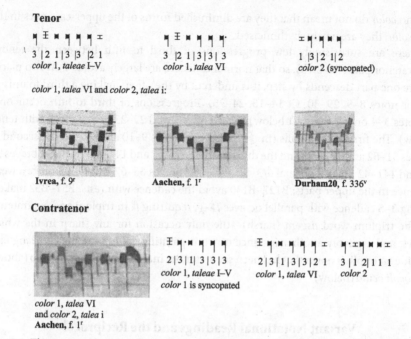

Fig. 8.1 The tenor and contratenor *taleae* of the two *colores* of *Vos/Gratissima*. The excerpts are reproduced with permission from the Biblioteca Capitolare, Ivrea for MS 115; from Stadtbibliothek Aachen, for MS Beis E14; from Durham Cathedral Library, for MS C I 20

values. These are now corroborated by **Durham20** and **Aachen**, which were not available to him. Fig. 8.1 shows the faulty **Ivrea** reading as just described, **Aachen** lacking an (accidental) dot after the long following the breve rest, and **Durham20** with dots (albeit faint) after both longs before and after the *color* join.[14]

The scribe of **Ivrea** was not the only one to be confused. The notation of **Esc10** is somewhat casual with respect to the notation of breves and longs, but the note forms are often overruled by small arabic numerals giving values as 1, 2 or 3 breve units. The indications are too imprecise to support Karen Desmond's claim that the rest 'transgressively' extends the first *color*. **Esc10** wrongly gives dots and rests to some of the breves at the ends of *taleae* in the first *color*; ironically, its final *talea* 'needs' a dot but does not have one, though it does get the numeral 3. Nor does the second *color* in **Esc10** correspond to Vitry's motet. Even where some notes appear to be breves they are assigned 'wrong' values with small numerals. It is as if one of these men (Muris, Vitry, le Grant) was puzzled by the tenor rhythm and wrote it down in Muris's notebook in the course of a discussion, quite possibly in the presence of the composer. The breve unit values given there for the tenor *talea* of the second *color*, 3 3 2 2, are wrong: they should

---

[14] **Ca1328** is illegible at this point. **Durham20** has plicas which suggest it may have been copied from an early source; *Fauvel* plicas are usually resolved or ignored even in slightly later copies. Plicas, however, were sometimes retained in England longer than elsewhere. **Durham20** also observes an English distinction between major S rests, crossing the staff line, and imperfect rests, suspended from it (⊤); that rest in major prolation in French notation came consistently to designate a major semibreve. Short rests were often irregularly or unstably notated in the early *ars nova*; see Ch. 13 and n. 9, and Earp, 'Tradition and Innovation'. **Ivrea**, **Ca1328**, **Aachen** and **Brussels5170** use pairs of M rests (⊔) for these hockets.

be, as in Fig. 8.1 (**Aachen** and **Durham20**), 1 (rest) |3 |2 1| 2, the final imperfect long of each *talea* making up a perfection with the initial breve rest that sets off the syncopation.

Much of what has recently been written about this motet hinges around that dot of perfection at the end of the first tenor *color* (*talea* VI), showing similar modern indecision.[15] The first five *taleae* of that first *color* end with a long imperfected by a breve rest, as shown in Fig. 8.1. In the sixth *talea* the long is followed instead by a dot, preventing its imperfection by the ensuing breve rest. So this final *talea* of *color* 1 appears irregular. But all becomes clear when we take the essential and complementary contratenor into account. The bottom line of Fig. 8.1 shows the contratenor for the same passage at the junction of the *colores*. The contratenor is syncopated in *color* 1, the tenor in *color* 2. The syncopation only seems more extreme in *color* 2 because it occupies a relatively greater part of the shorter *talea*. For the last note of *color* 1, the parts simply change rhythmic places, on a unison *f*.[16] The contratenor has L + rest, (▮ɪ) the tenor a perfect L dotted, ▮·, instead of the other way round, preparing both parts for their swapped functions in *color* 2 and clarifying the join: the contratenor now starts on the beat, and it is the tenor that is displaced by a rest. But in her ex. 6.2, Desmond counts the tenor breve rest as part of *color* 1 (▮· ɪ ▮), and starts *color* 2 with the long on the second beat of the modus group.[17] If the start of tenor *color* 2 were to be thus delayed, one would expect a dot after as well as before the breve rest to confirm the displacement, in order to place the first long of *color* 2 on a downbeat (▮ ɪ ·ɪ · ▮) and avoid syncopating the second *color*. This proposal fails to take account of the above-noted complementarity with the essential contratenor; the tenor breve rest at the beginning of *color* 2 is the syncopating agent, and similarly in all its short *taleae*, as the contratenor rest was in *color* 1.[18] In a notation without cumbersome barlines and ties, and where tenor and contratenor are offset against each other, complex relationships between the parts are often set up.

Desmond gives a fine detailed analysis of sonorities, attacks and directed progressions (her ex. 6.9), which brings out the wide range of interplay between different ways of achieving emphasis. It is true that the heard directed progressions in *color* 2 fall on the second beats of the modus groups, and that this creates a playful ambiguity, but complex music of all periods invites listeners to hear and enjoy surprises and playful tensions between surface and underlying metrical organisation. Beethoven and Brahms often keep one guessing where the barlines fall. Vitry is doing something similar here, brilliantly.

---

[15] The motet, and the dot, were discussed at length in Elina Hamilton's paper delivered at the Medieval and Renaissance Music Conference, Brussels, 2015, now published as Hamilton, 'Philippe de Vitry in England'. This was followed, with different conclusions, by Desmond, *Music and the moderni*, 222–28. Hamilton does take account of the contratenor, and makes a case that it, and not the tenor, is what the *Quatuor principalia* is referring to, but I think the second *color* of the tenor is a better fit; the long is preceded by a breve and followed by a dot. Desmond acknowledges the contratenor displacement in *color* 1, 224 n. 52, but considers it less pronounced.

[16] Clark, '*Super omnes speciosa*', 261, makes a similar point.

[17] Desmond, *Music and the moderni*, 201: 'This dot forces the tenor in the second *color* to transgress the mensural organisation set up in the first *color*, where its *talea* patterns now begin on the second breve of the modus unit'. I see the dot as clarifying and enabling, rather than transgressive, and the reversal of syncopating functions between tenor and contratenor in the second *color* as a balancing complement.

[18] Such offsetting and longer-term syncopation is found in other motet tenors. Desmond cites Machaut's M10, which was the subject of my paper in Hartt, *Machaut Motets*, here Ch. 12 and ⏵ Ex. 12.1. The case in M10 is clear; the syncopation starts at the beginning of the tenor, is made up at the end of each *talea* and wraps around to the next one. A more spectacular syncopated offsetting involving tenor and contratenor is in *Alma polis*, Ch. 19 and Ex. 19.1 below.

160 *FAUVEL AND VITRY*

The recurrent rhythmic motives (see below and Fig. 8.3) do not always fall at the same point in the modus group (compare B3, B6, B11 with B19, B97), and that creates a teasing instability, hinting at unrealised isorhythm in the first *color*. By contrast, in the second *color*, the strict isorhythm of the upper parts (including the hockets), for the first four and last nine breves of each double *talea* (or period) of the lower parts, establishes a clear affirmation of their perfect-modus boundaries, with one purposeful exception to be noted below. That the upper parts are not displaced by any decision about the lower-part *colores* is shown by emphatic rhythmic recurrence, and by the notation of rests, which observe the modus boundaries. The triplum rest at the beginning of each pair of tenor *taleae* in *color* 2 is an imperfect long rest in all sources including **Ca1328** and **Brussels5170**. Conversely, the motetus has two purposefully separated breve rests in each *talea* of *color* 2 in all sources, including **Ca1328** and **Aachen**; they straddle the modus division.[19] The difference in rest notation between triplum and motetus shows the notator's sensitivity to maintaining a regular perfect modus division in the upper parts. The upper parts are construed in perfect modus while the syncopated tenor sings against them, rather than, as Desmond suggests, that they 'sing against the implied mensuration of the tenor' (p. 224).[20]

The ending is problematic. The last two notes of the tenor of *Vos/Gratissima* appear to begin a new *talea*. As two successive longs, the first (B155) should be perfect (syncopated, as in the other *taleae*). To continue the syncopation here would, however, dissonantly delay the tenor's arrival on the final cadence. In order for the parts to cadence together the penultimate *g* should be an altered breve, as shown on the main staff in ⊙ Ex. 8.2, though this is no longer the notation of any source. Among **Ivrea**'s many tenor erasures, this note originally had a stem, correctly specifying a breve, but the stem was erased. Thus, at some point, perhaps in **Ivrea**'s exemplar, the end was correctly adjusted. Earp accepts the non-coincident cadence as intentional, **Ivrea**'s originally normalised notation notwithstanding.[21] The contratenor is adjusted here to achieve a coincident ending; the breve rest of the other *taleae* is omitted, placing the final long together with the upper parts, as must surely have been intended also in the tenor, whose two final longs as notated appear visually to coincide, but without allowing for the syncopation. It may not be too fanciful to see both the truncated final *talea* and the curtailed penultimate notes (the actual omission of the contratenor rest and the needed shortening of the tenor long) as reflections of the final line of the triplum text: 'O hurry!'

Texts and Text–Music Relationships

The opening words of the triplum recall the Introit antiphon for the Feast of the Ascension, *Viri Galilei,* **quid admiramini** *aspicientes in celum* (Ye men of Galilee, why

[19] Two separate breve rests are notated at mo breves 93–94, 111–12, 129–30, 147–48.

[20] Her statement that 'One might even go so far as to say that the compositional conceit of this entire motet is this dot' seems to me somewhat exaggerated. Desmond, *Music and the moderni*, 228, 201.

[21] Earp, 'Isorhythm', 98 n. 66. For possibly non-coincident endings in Machaut's motets 9, 15, 4 and 10 see Chs. 9, 10, 12 and Exx. 12.2–12.4 below, and especially, for an overview, Ch. 1 above.

stand you looking up to heaven?). Even closer to Vitry is the second text and refrain of an English motet *Ascendenti sonet geminacio/Viri Galilei, quid vos admiramini?*[22]

The texts (Table 8.1 above) are carefully structured for music. In *color* 1 the triplum has three six-line stanzas of 778, 778 (aabccb), 18 lines. The *color* 2 triplum has two longer (eight-line) stanzas each of 7778, 7778 (aaabcccb), 16 lines. The motetus has 14 decasyllabic lines, rhymed in couplets, seven lines in each *color*. The first two triplum stanzas are tidily distributed over the music, one half stanza for each of the first four *taleae*; but the text setting and general density are accelerated in the central stanza 3, where an extra line is squeezed into *color* 1 (line 19, the first line of stanza 4), and the accelerating alternation of the key words *Vos* and *Ista* is at its most dense. The last *Ista*, in line 19, is the 55th word of 109, the middle word of the triplum. This line (**Ista** *virgo regia*) is the first of the '*color* 2' stanzas 4 and 5, but it is placed at the end of *color* 1, anticipating the new *color* and binding the *colores* together. These new stanzas actually bridge the main structural join (at B90–B91), of which more below.

First person singular and plural forms seem to be used somewhat interchangeably (singular, tr 21, 22, mo 4, 8; plural, tr 4, 5, 23, 24, 25), though the singular (*mei*) is linked to the 'intimate wound' in motetus line 4. The first person plural occurs first in tr lines 4–5: 'We have wed . . . the chosen virgin', next in the rhetorical question in line 23, 'Why do we say such things?', followed immediately in lines 24–25 with a reprise of the declaration of choice: 'We . . . have forechosen her.' The use of the plural form with such deliberation by the solo protagonist of a marriage which appears to be both mystical and physical can perhaps be explained as the royal or 'majestic' plural, used interchangeably with the singular ('I am the king'). But a clear distinction is maintained between the use of the second persons plural and singular. The plural forms are all in the triplum (1, 10, 13, 15, 17, 18, 27, 29, 30, 31, 32, 33, 34), all for 'you' (bad). The second person singular forms (all good), are all in the motetus (3, 8, 9), addressed to the virgin, holy bride, queen (the *ista* of the triplum, here *gratissima*), linked to the intimacies of embrace, eyes, breasts, kissing mouths, lips.

Fig. 8.2 shows the grand chiasm of these triplum *Vos–Ista* alternations, contrasting 'you' (plural), bad, with 'her', good. Those words are absent from the motetus. The alternation, as noted, is most dense in the central stanza 3, where *Vos* occurs three times, three times in stanza 5, seven times altogether in the triplum; *Ista* five times. The last *Ista* is the first line of stanza 4; the placing of this final *Ista* of the chiasm before the join confines this key word to *color* 1. The main part of the chiasm concludes at the climactic end of the first *color*, with triplum line 19, *Ista virgo regia*, whose pivotal placement was discussed above. We are kept waiting for the last *Vos* until the very end, the final triplum line, framing the chiasm: *Vos* begins the first and last triplum lines. Fig. 8.2 also shows a secondary chiasm in *color* 2, framed by *regia* (line 19 again), the last triplum word of the first *color*, and *eÿa* in the final line, with which it forms vowel rhyme. In between are the symmetrical *rex – regina – regina – rex* of the hockets, also with e-i-a vowel rhyme on *regina*. The beginnings and ends of these chiasms thus bridge the two *colores* and stitch them together.

---

[22] The ultimate source of these words is Acts 1: 10–11, 'viri Galilei quid statis aspicientes in caelum', but without the word *admiramini*. The motet is in **Dor** and **Lwa12185**. See Bent, Hartt and Lefferts, *The Dorset Rotulus*, ch. 3.

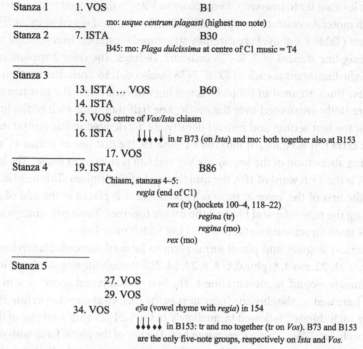

Fig. 8.2 The chiasm of triplum *Vos–Ista* alternations

Parallels with the erotic language of the Song of Songs have been noted, as have textual similarities with *Impudenter/Virtutibus*, which is specifically Marian.[23] Like Desmond, I associate *vulnere* with the striking moment at the beginning of *color* 2 (B91), when this word is heard alone while the triplum has an imperfect long rest (= two breves), laid bare with an imperfect sonority on *vulnere* at B91.[24] She stresses the association of the wound both with the crucifixion and the birth of Christ and with its importance in fourteenth-century devotion, as well as its demarcation of the junction between the *colores*. But I have also taken this striking image in directions more literally associated with the verbal and musical material of this motet. The wound is inserted (inflicted?) by the motetus into the exposed interrupted (wounded) triplum phrase: 'She a royal virgin' (motetus, 'by a wound') 'is a sweet mistress and my holy spouse'. The same opportunity to interpose a suggestive motetus three-syllable word during the triplum rests also occurs at each periodic recurrence in the upper parts, coinciding with the beginning of each odd-numbered tenor *talea* in *color* 2. At B109 'Why do we say such things?' (motetus, 'embrace') 'We (or us, *nos*) who know all things'; and perhaps more tellingly at B145 'if you neglect her' (motetus, 'lips') 'you will not see the glory'. The words that conspicuously interrupt the triplum lines at those places are 'wound', 'embrace', 'lips', giving new erotic as well as christological meaning to the way the combined texted parts are knitted together (as they were for *Ista/plagasti*)—powerfully suggesting those

---

[23] Leech-Wilkinson, *Compositional Techniques*, 50.
[24] Desmond, *Music and the moderni*, 222–33. She calls this a 'tear', 'a hole—of one breve—in the fabric of the previously harmonically audible perfect *modus* of the musical surface'.

VITRY: *VOS/GRATISSIMA*   163

connections, though it would be asking too much that they also made perfect grammatical sense between the two parts.

This is one of a growing number of motets that signal a musical structural join with words of cutting, division or proportion, in this case, a wound. The phenomenon has been noted in *Tribum*, Chapter 4 above; 'trans metam ascende-|rit' takes us 'over the boundary'. In *Musicorum*, Chapter 18, the verbal phrase 'cum bis acuto | gladio' is cut with the twice-sharp sword at the juncture of the *colores*, and the word *incidere* literally cuts an earlier *talea* division: 'incide- | re cum silice'. In Machaut's M4 (Ch. 14), *desmesuree* (beyond measure) coincides with the unsignalled switch to perfect modus. These instances can be multiplied. David Howlett's prescient suggested emendation of **Ivrea**'s *placasti* to *plagasti* is now confirmed by both **Aachen** and **Durham20**: 'you have wounded to the centre (*usque centrum*) the innermost parts of my heart with a very sweet wound'. Both *Ista* and the wound-words are proportionally placed. The first *color* is ninety breves. The motetus's noun 'plaga dulcissima' ('most sweet wound') falls at its exact centre, B45, as prepared by *usque centrum*, and is flanked at proportioned distances by the 'wounding' verbs *plagasti* (B30) and *vulnere* (following B90). The first *Ista* (stanza 2) is also at B30 in the triplum, one-third of the way through the first 90B *color*. At that point, *Ista* (tr) and *plagasti* (mo) coincide on a unison *g*, the highest note of the motetus, which occurs only this once, as if to signal that it is she who inflicts the 'sweet wound', to which height the lower-range first-person motetus aspires. The second *Ista* (stanza 3) is at B60, two-thirds of the way through the first *color*; we have already located the noun *plaga* at B45, the *centrum*.[25]

As well as pointing to the centre of *color* 1, 'usque centrum' may also point forward to the third wound-word (*vulnere*, following *plaga* and *plagasti*) at the main structural join of the motet. Although that is not the actual centre by breve count, it is certainly 'central', the centre of gravity, a striking but by no means isolated instance of ways in which words of measure can mark the passage of musical time through a motet. The 'plaga dulcissima' is echoed immediately after the join by the succession *vulnere* (motetus) and *dulcis* (triplum), once again linking those two texts. A final 'hurting' phrase, *me ledere*, punctuated with rests, initiates the hocket at B102.

Rhythmic Vocabulary

The upper parts have some detectable periodicity in the first *color*, mostly involving the rhythms of Fig. 8.3, for example at tr breves 6–9, 36–38, 65–67; 19–21, 49–51, 79–81. There is much more correspondence in the second *color*, especially for the isorhythmic hockets. I still prefer to call them periods, confining the word *talea* to rhythmic iterations, usually in the lower parts. Here, a partially isorhythmic upper-part period in *color* 2 spans two tenor *taleae*, starting at Ti, iii, v, vii. Each period reproduces isorhythmically in both upper parts the opening four breves of *color* 2 that were so strikingly shared between the triplum and motetus, as described above, which in turn is the opening *Vos* rhythm. The one deviation is the rhythmic variant at *talea* v, which can be

---

[25] **Durham20** has a descending breve plica which places *plaga* on the first beat, whereas **Ivrea**'s underlay places *pla-* on the second S of 45.

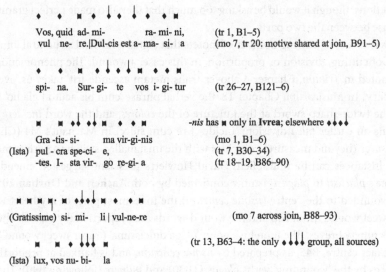

Fig. 8.3 Some instances of prevalent rhythmic motives (*Vos* and *Gratissima*)

explained by an unusual piece of literal word-painting—in this case the 'eye music' of a purposeful musical repeat for *oculum oculo*, 'eye to eye' (Fig. 8.4). This may be paralleled by the unisons on *astringere*, binding breast to breast, noted above, in that instance departing from an established contrapuntal norm, in the case of the final triplum line, 'O hurry!', by the structural curtailment of the final *talea*, and here by departing from an established isorhythmic pattern.

Fig. 8.4 Ivrea, Biblioteca capitolare, MS 115, f. 9^r, staff 4: 'eye music' in *Vos/Gratissima*. This excerpt is reproduced with permission from the Biblioteca Capitolare, Ivrea

The hockets are strictly isorhythmic, and occupy the second half of each period, corresponding to the even-numbered tenor *taleae*. Text for the hockets was precisely calculated so that the texts would coincide at those points, and so as to place monosyllables where the isolated notes would be; no words are broken by rests. Of several places where triplum and motetus have musical and textual interplay, the hockets bring them together most strikingly. The triplum hocket on 'hec regina' is interlocked with motetus *O regina*, which at words 28 and 29 are also the central motetus words of a total of fifty-eight: the queens are brought together at B102–B104, two-thirds of the way through the music. The interlocking of the hockets, shown in Fig. 8.5,

Fig. 8.5 The hockets of *Vos/Gratissima*

rhythmically equal in both parts, suggests the paired sensuous intimacies of this section of the motetus.[26]

As in some other motets, the strategy was often to establish a neutral or restricted rhythmic vocabulary for a particular motet, in order to allow purposeful deviations from it to stand out audibly (a similar phenomenon is noted in Ch. 9, on Machaut, M9). The five-note figure ♦♦♦ ♦♦ occurs just twice in the motet, both times strikingly in both triplum and motetus simultaneously, in both cases emphasising key words. The first occurrence is at B72 on the triplum word *Ista* (line 16), the second at B153, on the triplum word *Vos* (starting the final line 34), the ingredients of the chiasm shown in Fig. 8.2 above. Just as the verbal recurrences in the texts are carefully placed, so here a rhythmic figure is used sparingly to highlight these key words. In *Vos*, there is just one departure from the *Fauvel* defaults for unstemmed semibreves: *nubila* (B63) has ♦♦♦♦ in all sources, instead of the default for a four-note group ♦♦♦♦. (**Durham20** also has ♦♦♦♦ at B45 on *turpis*, but the ♦♦♦♦ of **Ivrea** and **Brussels5170** has been preferred here, in view of the way this rhythm has elsewhere been reserved for a very particular purpose.)

The Rhythmic Motives

Two distinct rhythmic motives, slightly differing in length, but composed of the same units differently ordered, stand respectively for *Vos* (♦ ♦ ■ ♦♦♦♦ ♦ ♦ ■) in the triplum and *Gratissima* (■ ■ ♦♦♦♦ ■ ♦ ♦ ■) in the motetus. (That last breve in **Ivrea** is ♦♦♦♦ *cbca* in other sources, but the ■ has been retained here, on grounds of its use as a recurring motive.) Fig. 8.3 shows some instances of these motives.

She who is the *Gratissima* of the motetus equates with the triplum's *Ista*. Fig. 8.3 shows the alignment of the opening *Gratissima* motive with the first two rhythmicisations of *Ista*. The motives associated with the words *Vos* and *Gratissima* (see also Ex. 8.3a) are almost constantly present throughout the motet, in various combinations, mingling and mutating. ♦♦♦♦ ♦ ♦ ■, for example, occurs at least fifteen times, mostly in the triplum,

---

[26] The first hocket is at B100 ('Rex ego sum'), the golden section of the 162 breves of the motet. This *Rex* is also at the golden section of triplum lines, 'hec regina' at the golden section by word count, all crucial words. For other motets that observe this discipline, see Ch. 13 below. Some of these conjunctions are noted by Daniel Leech-Wilkinson in his notes to the Orlando Recording on CD-SAR 49, p. 7.

often at different points in the modus groupings, thus loosening any sense of predictable regular recurrence.

Both motives are deployed with particular ingenuity and density around the structural join. The motetus recapitulates the opening word *Gratissima* as *Gratissime* at line 7, the last line of the first half of the text, with its three significant and significantly placed words 'Gratissime simili | vulnere' across the musical structural join. (See Ex. 8.3a–b.) Instead of initiating *color* 2, these words anticipate the new section at the end of *color* 1, just as the triplum's first line of stanza 4 does ('Ista virgo regia'). But it is also a musical recapitulation: the full *Gratissima* motive at the beginning of the motetus (■ ■ ♦♦♦♦ ■ ♦ ♦ ■) recurs for *Gratissime*, B87–B92. Moreover, in the version of **Ivrea**, used in ▶ Ex. 8.2, the triplum ('-tes, Ista virgo regia') is in exact rhythmic canon on that same motive (■ ■ ♦♦♦♦ ■ ♦ ♦ ■) with the motetus (B85–B90), as shown in Ex. 8.3b–c. (**Durham20**, **Ca1328** and **Brussels5170** have ♦♦♦ instead of ♦♦♦♦ at B87, making the rhythmic canon slightly less strict but still perceptible.)

The placing of *simili* and *vulnere* on either side of the *color* join in the motetus marks the musical form both by announcing the 'similar' second *color* and the 'wound' of the structural join. *Simili* does multiple duty. It flags the verbal recapitulation (*Gratissime*) and the new (similar) *color*; it draws attention to the (similar) verbal repetition of the wound, and to its echoing role in the (near or exact) rhythmic canon. This is the triplum's only use of that motive, seeming further to cement the identity ('similar') of the motetus's *Gratissime* with the triplum's *Ista virgo*, she who is *Gratissima*.

Ex. 8.3 The main structural junction of *Vos/Gratissima*, demonstrating several instantiations of *simili*: (a) *Vos* and *Gratissima* motives together at the motet opening B1–B6; (b) B85–B90 up to the join; (c) B91–B95, from the join, continuing the rhythmic canon, and showing the 'wounding' rests

In addition, the end of that motive and of the canonic imitation have melodic inversion across the join (*regia*, *a g f*, *vulnere*, *d e f*, to the same rhythm ♦ ♦ ■); and at the very beginning of the new *color* (*simili*), motetus and triplum combine to share the *Vos* motive (♦ ♦ ■ | ♦♦♦♦ ♦ ♦ ■) for 'vulnere | Dulcis est amasia' (B91–B95, *vulnere dulcis* recalling *plaga dulcissima*), made audibly prominent by rests in the 'other' part (Ex. 8.3a and c). It is also laid bare at the beginning of the second *color* where the lower parts have a unison *f*. In *color* 1, the upper parts provided more sonorities over that *f*; here, *vulnere* sounds a bare octave with those lower parts.

The prominent *d e f* of *vulnere*, mentioned above, recurs at the very end of the motet in the last three pitches of the triplum, for the final line 'Vos eÿa properate', whose significance in completing the verbal chiasm (*Vos*), with both pitch and vowel rhyme connection (*eÿa*, e-i-a), has been signalled above. Thus to end the motet emphatically with the three pitches of *vulnere* could identify the truncated eighth *talea* as a final musical allusion to the wound.

I hope to have demonstrated just a few of the features that contribute to this motet's inexhaustibly subtle creation of many layers of meaning within and between the texts in combination with each other and with the music. Meaning is achieved in both text and music, separately and together, by recapitulations, contrasts, chiasms, imitations, leitmotivic use of rhythmic associations, successive and simultaneous juxtapositions, different means of emphasis, by proportioned or symbolic placements, and striking instances of word-painting. Much has been written about this wonderfully rich composition, saturated as it is with musical and verbal meaning; others will surely find even more artfulness than what has been pointed out here.

PART III
MACHAUT

170 MACHAUT

The chapters of Part III deal analytically with text–music relationships in individual motets by Machaut. Chapter 9 (on Motet 9) was written with pedagogical intent, and is accompanied by sound clips and many notated examples; it explores several under-explored dimensions of those relationships that may be fruitfully employed in other analyses. Chapter 13 deals with aspects of Motet 18 (dating and text–music relationships) and Motet 2 (notation); Chapter 11 deals not with a motet but with a counterpoint-based reading of the Gloria of Machaut's Mass. Three chapters on the French-texted motets (M15 in Chapter 10, M10 in Chapter 12, M4 and M8 in Chapter 14) were stimulated by collaborations with Kevin Brownlee. Together we explored a rich seam of intertextuality, new to literary scholars, which gives precise musical placement to simultaneous texts. The earlier version of Chapter 10 (on Motet 15) was published in 1991 alongside a companion article by Brownlee, and his study of the text of Motet 10 is also published elsewhere.

9

Words and Music in Machaut's Motet 9

The article lightly revised as the present chapter on M9 (*Fons tocius superbie/O livoris feritas/Fera pessima*) was designed to serve as an introduction to a Machaut motet at an accessible level, while at the same time pointing out some features previously little noted.[1] These include text–music relationships; purposeful voice-crossing and uneven text distribution across the musical structure; and whether a self-imposed discipline of not breaking words with hocket rests is honoured. Some elementary explanations have been allowed to remain in order that this section can still serve an introductory purpose. Throughout Part III, Machaut's motets are often numbered as 'M', here M9.

Accompanying sound clips were recorded in 2003 by members of Musick's Feast, a professional ensemble based in Iowa City: Elizabeth Aubrey, director, Barbara Evans O'Donnell and Marvin Bergman, and can be accessed on the companion website for this book, for which Professor Aubrey has given permission. The style of Machaut's music can be foreign, even to those quite at home with sixteenth-century music. In the present case, newcomers may find it helpful to immerse themselves in this one piece by repeated listenings, perhaps attending to different features on different hearings.

The original article was included in an issue of *Early Music* (2003) honouring the then recently deceased John Stevens and Philip Brett, both of whom devoted much of their scholarly attention to a musicianly concern not just with issues of general mutual appropriateness of a particular set of words to its music, but also with details of tailoring and nuance at the most minute level. Music is necessarily counted, as John Stevens so eloquently argued in his book on medieval song; it is less widely recognised that verbal texts for music are counted too. Philip Brett once exhorted musicologists to 'face the music'.[2] I have chosen Machaut's Motet 9 to demonstrate an artful combining of words, music and the relationship between them that I hope both would have enjoyed, and which I believe responds to the particular relationships they both valued so highly in different repertories.

The way we listen to music today is often conditioned by changing technologies and concert habits. How often, for example, do we approach medieval music by listening or half-listening to a dozen motets in succession on a CD or playlist, or to a similar succession in a concert? The aural experience of music, like the perception of other developed arts, can lie anywhere on a spectrum from casual hearing to informed engagement. It

---

[1] Some but not all of these features had been addressed in Reichert, 'Das Verhältnis'. The present adaptation of Bent, 'Words and Music in Machaut's Motet 9', *Early Music* 31 (2003), 363–88, has been licensed by Rightslink.

[2] Stevens, *Words and Music*; Brett, 'Facing the Music'.

The Motet in the Late Middle Ages. Margaret Bent, Oxford University Press. © Oxford University Press 2023.
DOI: 10.1093/so/9780190063771.003.0010

172   MACHAUT

is my purpose here to suggest some ways of arriving at the latter position, using a single motet by Machaut as an example.

Measured music gives syllables precise values and positions within a single text, or as sense units or sonic units in relation to other texts. In the fourteenth century the notation of rhythm took a large step forward, permitting larger-scale composition and local detail, along with the precise recovery of these rhythms. Polyphonic settings from this period can position apparently disparate or incongruous texts in a precise simultaneous relationship that was unquestionably intended by the composer. A motet can also make or receive complex textual, musical and intertextual allusions to or from other motets.

Techniques of verbal disposition and recapitulation in motet texts may set them apart from other literary genres, and make them truly words for music in a way that can only be fully perceived in relation to their music. Thus understood, some texts that seemed artless can be seen to be just differently art*ful*. Conversely, the music becomes more purposefully directed, even sometimes depictive, when read in conjunction with the texts.

Motet 9, *Fons tocius superbie/O livoris feritas/Fera pessima*, is one of the most widely discussed but least performed of Machaut's motets. Its theology and its music have been extensively analysed by Hans Heinrich Eggebrecht, its verse structure by Georg Reichert, its compositional technique by Sarah Fuller, its historical dating by Kurt Markstrom, its biblical anchorage by Jacques Boogaart, and its context within Machaut's oeuvre and its interpretation by Anne Walters Robertson.[3] The complete motet is given as ⓑ Example 9.1, in a layout intended to complement this analysis, and in an adaptation of the original notation that both permits compact graphic presentation and reflects the fewer note symbols used to achieve the rhythms.[4] Each system of the score corresponds to a *talea* (a term to be explained below); to locate particular passages, I shall use these *talea* numbers (roman I–IX) as well as the bar numbers (arabic numerals with 'B' for breve) that appear above the score. The complete motet can be heard on sound clip ⓑ 9.1.

Readers are now invited to view images of Motet 9 in two of the manuscripts in which Machaut's complete works were collected.[5] In the Machaut manuscripts, the whole piece is contained, as is normal, on a single opening, so that it can be read by three singers without page turns. The beginning of each voice-part is signalled by a large decorated capital, each voice-part provided with its own different text. The lengthy triplum occupies more space than the medium-length motetus. The gnomically compact tenor occupies the least space. In performance, however, all three parts have the same duration, since the

---

[3] Eggebrecht, 'Machauts Motette Nr 9'; Reichert, 'Das Verhältnis'; Fuller, 'Modal Tenors'; Markstrom, 'Machaut and the Wild Beast'; Boogaart, 'Encompassing Past and Present'; Robertson, *Guillaume de Machaut*. Published editions of Motet 9: Ludwig, *Guillaume de Machaut*, iii. 33–36; PMFC 2, 137–40; Machaut, *The Motets*, ed. Boogaart, which see for an excellent modern-notation edition and details of manuscript variants.

[4] Emendations made to the version preserved in the manuscripts: triplum, B89, 2nd note *f* is emended to *g*. (Thus the leap *d–f* for *Dolus* becomes *d–g*, possibly rhyming with *sol-ut*. Nowhere else is this leap dissonant with the tenor, and in all other cases the spondee uses either repeated notes or a leap of a fourth.) In triplum, B136, note 2 *e* is emended to *d*.

[5] Instead of the black and white facsimiles which accompanied the original article, I have given references to online colour images, here for **MachautA** and **Ferrell(Vg)**; most other Machaut manuscripts are available on Gallica. For Motet 9, **MachautA**, ff. 422ᵛ–423 can be viewed at https://gallica.bnf.fr/ark:/12148/btv1b84490444/f866.item, and **Ferrell(Vg)**, ff. 268ᵛ–269 on https://www.diamm.ac.uk/sources/3774/#/images (images 540–541). Earp, *Guillaume de Machaut: A Guide*, gives a comprehensive guide to the Machaut manuscripts and their contents. Manuscript variants for all the motets are given in the recent modern edition: Machaut, *The Motets*, ed. Boogaart.

MACHAUT'S MOTET 9   173

tenor notes are slower and are stated three times. The three parts are presented separately, not aligned in score, so they cannot be read simultaneously by a single musician.

In **MachautA**, the topmost voice (the triplum) begins in column 1 of the verso (left-hand page), continues into column 1 of the recto (right-hand page), and is completed in the staves stretching the full width of the recto. The second upper part (motetus) begins in column 2 of the verso (the columns are parallel and equal), and is completed in the first staff of column 2 of the recto, where the longer triplum enjoys a customised ruling to accommodate its extra words and notes. The tenor occupies the second and third staves of column 2 of the recto. Each part is marked with a large decorative initial. In **Ferrell(Vg)**, there are no columns: the triplum is on the left-hand page (f. 268ᵛ), the motetus and tenor on the right (f. 269).

The motet survives in all seven of the main complete-works Machaut manuscripts, including the earliest, **MachautC**, copied by 1350.[6] In addition it was one of relatively few of Machaut's works that circulated outside those manuscripts, as we know from the index of the lost Trémoïlle manuscript (**Trém**); see Chapter 31.[7]

The Verbal Texts

As is usual in fourteenth-century motets, the two upper parts have different texts; this difference extends to length, organisation, metre and rhyme scheme. These texts are presented simultaneously. The words are locked by the musical rhythmic organisation into specific positions or durations within each text individually; they are also given precise placements in relation to the other text. In addition to relating in general terms what the motet is 'about', it appears that individual words were selected for special placement or what we might call *musical* treatment, perhaps as formal markers, by means of repetition, rhyme and contrast. Special treatment of words explores sonic qualities of alliteration and rhyme, illustrative tactics which exploit the contrasts of high and low words in relation to extremes of musical range.

	Triplum		Translation
Introitus	Fons tocius superbie,		Lucifer, source of all pride and
	Lucifer, et nequicie		all evil, who, having been
	Qui, mirabili specie		adorned with marvellous beauty
	Decoratus,		
talea I	Eras in summis locatus,	5	and set in the heights [of heaven],
	Super thronos sublimatus,		raised above the Thrones—
	Draco ferus antiquatus		you who are called the old fierce
	Qui dicere,		dragon—

---

[6] For the dating and details of all manuscripts, recordings, bibliography, see the indispensable Earp, *Guillaume de Machaut: A Guide*, and for the most recent assessment see Earp, 'Introduction' (in Earp and Hartt), 27.

[7] His motets seem to have had a more limited circulation than the songs. All the Machaut motets known to have circulated outside the Machaut manuscripts are listed in the **Trém** index (motets 8, 9, 10, 14, 15, 16, 19, 20, 23). Of those nine, only motets 8, 15 and 19 are otherwise known outside the Machaut manuscripts.

II	Ausus es sedem ponere 9	ventured to set up your seat
	Aquilone et gerere	in the North and
	Te similem in opere	to model your actions on
	Altissimo.	those of the Most High;
III	Tuo sed est in proximo 13	but your most arrogant pride
	Fastui ferocissimo	was soon thwarted
	A judice justissimo	by the Most Just Judge,
	Obviatum.	
IV	Tuum nam auffert primatum; 17	for he deprived you of your primacy;
	Ad abyssos cito stratum	you saw yourself swiftly hurled down
	Te vidisti per peccatum	for your sin to the abyss
	De supernis.	from the heights.
V	Ymis nunc regnas infernis; 21	Now you reign over the depths below;
	In speluncis et cavernis	in caves and pits you lie,
	Penis jaces et eternis	in torments and everlasting
	Agonibus.	agonies.
VI	Dolus et fraus in actibus 25	Deceit and treachery are in your deeds,
	Tuis et bonis omnibus	and with your arrows you
	Obviare missilibus	strive to thwart all good.
	Tu niteris;	
VII	Auges quod nephas sceleris 29	You increase that wicked crime
	Adam penis in asperis	that kept Adam in the harsh torments
	Tenuit Stigos carceris.	of his Stygian prison.
	Sed Maria	But I pray that the Virgin Mary,
VIII	Virgo, que, plena gratia, 33	who, full of grace,
	Sua per puerperia	freed him by her childbearing
	Illum ab hac miseria	from this misery,
	Liberavit,	
IX	Precor et anguis tedia 37	may both increase the [serpent's]
	Augeat et supplicia	sufferings and punishments,
	Et nos ducat ad gaudia	and lead us, whom she has created,
	Quos creavit.	to [heavenly] joys.

	Motetus	Translation
talea I	O livoris feritas,	O savage envy,
II	Que superna rogitas	who seek the heights
III	Et jaces inferius!	but lie in the depths,
IV	Cur inter nos habitas?	why do you dwell amongst us?
V	Tua cum garrulitas 5	While your chattering
VI	Nos affatur dulcius,	speaks to us very sweetly,
VII	Retro pungit sevius,	it stings very savagely from behind,

VIII	Ut veneno scorpius:		as the scorpion does with its poison;
	Scariothis falsitas		the treachery of Iscariot
	Latitat interius.	10	is concealed within.
IX	Det mercedes Filius		May the Son of God
	Dei tibi debitas!		give you your due rewards.

Tenor: Fera pessima (Most evil beast)

English translation by Leofranc Holford-Strevens

Tenor Melody, Borrowed Chant: *Color*

The musical foundation, the tenor, is taken, again as usual, from liturgical chant, which provides its pitches (*color*), but no rhythms. Such excerpts carry with them the verbal text which was the music's biblical and liturgical underpinning as well as its musical scaffolding. Whether or not a tenor's text appears in a motet manuscript, it can usually be located in the first instance as scriptural and in the second as having a liturgical placement. The tenor therefore brings to the motet both an implicit biblical-exegetical narrative context and a liturgical-calendrical context.

In Motet 9 the tenor text consists of just two words: *Fera pessima* ('most evil beast'). These come from the middle of a Matins responsory, *Videns Jacob vestimenta Joseph*, for the third Sunday of Lent; indeed, *Fera pessima* opens Jacob's direct speech in responding to the blood-stained coat of many colours by which he is deceived into thinking that Joseph is dead.[8] Internal portions of chant are often harder to identify than beginnings; here we are even *told* (by the motetus text, line 10) that the most evil beast hides within: *latitat interius*. Although versions of this melody vary, exact matches exist in contemporary antiphoners, so it is not necessary to posit any authorial modifications.[9]

The primary factor that led a composer to choose a tenor for a motet was to suit the symbolic, ritual or topical significance of its attached words to the subject of the texts of the upper parts (whether or not these had already been composed). However, musical features of the melodic segment should not be underestimated as additional factors in the choice. Tenor segments nearly always end with a stepwise melodic descent to facilitate the tenor's role in cadencing with the other parts.[10]

The twelve pitches of Machaut's chant segment—one of the shortest of his motet tenors (M14 has ten notes)—are given in Example 9.2a (sound clip ▶ 9.2). Those

[8] The same words and chant open the tenor of a motet by Loyset Compère (*c.* 1445–1518), *Sola caret*, whose political significance is discussed in Dean, 'The Occasion'. Compère's tenor starts at the same music and words, but uses a longer segment of the chant. Two of the five voices of Compère's motet present in canon the entire chant of which Machaut uses the first twelve notes. *Fera pessima* occurs no fewer than five times in the text of the three free voices. The second half of the text invokes the Virgin, as does Machaut's motet, and makes explicit the deception of Jacob by Joseph's brothers. Dean unravels the obscure historical allusions in the first half of the text.

[9] The tenors and their sources are listed in Clark, '*Concordare cum materia*'.

[10] Except in Motet 23, whose last two notes rise a step as if anticipating the provision of the lower (essential) contratenor. The repeated final tenor note in M10 does not affect the cadential descent. A striking example of a final irregular tenor progression is Dunstaple's four-voice motet *Veni sancte spiritus* (MB 8, no. 32), whose tenor breaks off with a descending fifth, *d–g*, not a cadential progression at this time.

176 MACHAUT

Ex. 9.2 Structure of the tenor of Motet 9:
(a) the chant segment from which the *color* is derived, with ▶ sound clip 9.2;
(b) tetrad structure of the *color*, with ▶ sound clip 9.3;
(c) symmetries in the *color*;
(d) the rhythmicised tenor in original notation;
(e) the preceding, aligned in (speeded-up) modern notation, with ▶ sound clip 9.4;
(f) reconfiguration of the *color* tetrads by the *talea*, with ▶ sound clip 9.5

twelve *color* pitches are disposed in three groups of four: two identical and one different, producing the overall form x x y, as shown in Example 9.2b (sound clip ▶ 9.3). It even seems shorter than it is, with its internal repetitions and near-repetitions, serpentine coiling and the narrow range of a fourth. Any apparent illustration of verbal sense may already be present in the pre-existent chant, though many similar melodies have no obvious verbal explanation. This tenor divides as readily into 2 × 6 as it does into 3 × 4, and has many internal symmetries and capabilities for retrograde (back-to-front) presentation. Example 9.2c shows just some of these.

- Notes 1–7 form a palindrome centred on note 4.
- Notes 2–6, 7–11 form a sequence.
- The first half of the tenor (notes 1–6) is stated a step lower in retrograde (notes 7–12).
- Notes 5–8, 9–12 form a transposed retrograde.
- There are also inbuilt inversions (upside-down segments): notes 1–3, 3–5 and notes 5–8, 8–11.

Since the tenor melody is stated continually, six times during the course of the motet, these patterns wrap around the *talea* joins and extend into the repetitions (for example, notes 4–8 = 12–4).

Rhythmic Disposition by the Composer: *Talea*

Although the tenor has a borrowed melody (*color*), its rhythmic pattern (*talea*) was applied by Machaut. In Motet 9, three identical eight-note *taleae* are superimposed on two statements of the twelve-note *color* to form a complete cycle. Thus, in ▶ Example 9.1 each twelve-note *color* occupies a system and a half of the score.

Example 9.2d shows this cycle in the original notation. Only one of these cycles is notated—two *colores* on three *taleae*. The three little rest-like lines at the end of the tenor part are repeat signs, indicating that the *color* cycle is to be stated three times. The three cycles can be seen spaced out in the lowest voice-part of the score in ▶ Example 9.1, starting at *taleae* I, IV, VII. Example 9.2e, aligned with 9.2d, is a version of the same rhythms in modern notation and speeded-up note values, applied to the two successive, rhythmically different, statements of the melody; these are heard on sound clip ▶ 9.4 (where drum = *talea*, triangle = *color*). Example 9.2f (sound clip ▶ 9.5) gives the same notes, without rhythms, grouped into fours, showing the superimposition of two *colores* and three *taleae*, and the resulting x–y combinations. The way Machaut divided up these notes discourages the actual singing of the words 'fera pessima' (most evil beast), which remain an unheard but nevertheless participating presence.

The eight-note *talea* rhythm is repeated exactly; that is to say, it is strictly isorhythmic. 'Isorhythm' ('equal rhythm') is a word of twentieth-century coinage, unpicked in Chapter 2, that has given its name to a genre: the isorhythmic motet. But the absence of a medieval word is something we might take more seriously. Rhythmic identity as the defining feature of a genre has been emphasised at the expense of the many other strategies that are ingeniously combined in motets. Some of those features cut across or prevent rhythmic identity, and are much more individual than it. As we shall see here, a disciplined background (not necessarily 'isorhythmic' as the term is strictly defined and generally understood) may be used to set off and mark out individual or highlighted moments of musical and textual significance. It is true that many motets of the early fifteenth century are rhythmically uniform and appear to follow a template, but to suggest that this is the crowning achievement of a chronological progression to uniformity easily undervalues the varied techniques that discipline and enliven musical materials in other ways; fourteenth-century motets show a great variety of compositional strategies. The term is also often used in connection with motets in which the same rhythm is repeated faster (i.e. in diminished values, so that they are no longer 'equal'), but that does not apply here, and in any case, a restatement in reduced values is not identical.

Example 9.1 sets out the nine rhythmically identical tenor statements—*taleae*—in the nine roman-numbered systems; they are preceded by a solo introduction, or introitus.[11] Each of these *taleae* comprises one tenor rhythmic unit of eight notes spanning fifteen breves. (In ▶ Example 9.1 each breve is given the value of one bar.) Machaut plays on

---

[11] On the term 'introitus' see Ch. 1; Bent, *Q15*, i. 151; and Zayaruznaya, '[In]troitus'. I shall use it here for upper-part introductions before the tenor entry, although its early use may have been more restricted. The editions of Ludwig and Schrade begin this unit at the full perfect long (three-bar group) within which the tenor enters, causing subsequent isorhythmic periods to start as upbeats. As in other cases (for example, Motet 10) Machaut sets up a long-term syncopation of the tenor structure in relation to the top parts. It starts on the final upbeat-bar of the introduction if arranged by perfect *modus*.

both sets of numbers—notes and durations—which are not necessarily related; just as in verbal texts, word-count and metrical scheme may both be counted but are not mutually dependent.

There are nine *taleae* each of eight notes, a total of 72; and six *colores* each of twelve notes, also totalling 72. In addition, this total subdivides into three identical 24-note cycles starting at systems I, IV, VII, in each of which two *colores* span three *taleae*. A total of 3 × 3 = 9 rhythmic statements therefore carry 2 × 3 = 6 melodic statements.

Measured in breves (B), equalling bars, each cycle (of three *taleae*, two *colores*) occupies 3 × 15 = 45 breves, and there are three such cycles, 3 × 45 = 135 breves. With the monophonic introduction of 14 breves, which stands outside this structure, the total length of the motet is 149 breves.

The tenor falls readily into long bars, each equal to a perfect long, containing three of the shorter top-voice bars, each equal to a breve. There are thus five perfect longs to each *talea* (5 × 3 = 15 breves). The tenor's prevailing iambic (second-mode) rhythm (short–long) is also prevalent in the motetus, while at the level of the shorter note-values, trochaic rhythms (long–short) predominate. The one-bar upbeat beginning each *talea* completes the two-bar *talea*-ends and coordinates them with subsequent *color* statements.

Melodic Affinities with Other Motet Tenors

Machaut seems to have relished the compositional challenges and symmetries of this austerely conjunct tenor melody. In Motet 4, *De bon espoir/Puis que/Speravi*, he used a longer but almost identical tenor.[12] That tenor, *Speravi*, 'I hoped', comes from Psalm 12, used as a Pentecost Introit; see Example 9.3 and sound clip ▶ 9.6 (where drum = *talea*, triangle = *color*); it embodies (as notes 3–14) the entire melody used in Motet 9 (bracketed and labelled *Fera pessima*), flanked by a few extra notes.[13] He also structured and proportioned it in the same way, this time with two eighteen-note *colores* in the time of three twelve-note *taleae*.

Ex. 9.3 The tenor *color* of Motet 4, and its articulation by *talea* repetition, with ▶ sound clip 9.6

---

[12] For Motet 4 see Ch. 14 and Ex. 14.1.

[13] The tenors of these two motets are independently derived from different chants, in both cases on words appropriate to the motet. The overlap of melodic content surely cannot be coincidental, and it may reflect Machaut's fascination with exploiting this particular sequence of notes. But other cases raise interesting questions as to when motet tenors may have been derived not directly from chant but from another motet. The family of motets on the obscure *Aptatur* tenor is one clear instance of such derivation (for an addition to this group, see now Bent, Hartt and Lefferts, *The Dorset Rotulus*); another is the unidentified *Ruina*, common to *Super/Presidentes* in *Fauvel* and Machaut's Motet 13. This has been remarked on by Clark: '*Super omnes speciosa*', in connection with the shared tenors of Vitry's *Vos/Gratissima* and Machaut's Motet 17 (see Ch. 8).

Machaut's chant-based motets with isorhythm have often been segregated from his song-tenor motets.[14] Song-forms are characterised by musical repetition in less regular orderings, but a similar effect is achieved when the music is governed by a straightforwardly repeating tenor, whether the repetitions are due to the song form or are present within a chant, or whether they are produced by repetition of a chant fragment. One such is Motet 16, *Lasse/Se j'aim mon loyal ami/Pourquoy me bat*, whose repetitive, conjunct and serpentine song tenor is not unlike that of Motet 9; the first portion is shown in Example 9.4 (sound clip ▶ 9.7).[15]

Ex. 9.4 Opening of tenor of Motet 16, with ▶ sound clip 9.7

Motet 9 also has a strong affinity with a motet in the earlier *Roman de Fauvel*: *Tribum/ Quoniam/Merito hec patimur* (Ch. 4).[16] Its mostly conjunct tenor is from another Matins responsory for the very same day as *Fera pessima*, the third Sunday of Lent.[17] 'Justly we have suffered these things' is from the same Genesis story about the envy, deceit and unfraternal behaviour of Joseph's brothers (see Ex. 9.5; sound clip ▶ 9.8). All the vices, and especially envy, deceit and overweening pride before a fall, are prominent in upper-voice texts of the *Fauvel* motets, as they are here.[18]

Ex. 9.5 Chant tenor of the *Fauvel* motet *Tribum/Quoniam/Merito hec patimur*, with ▶ sound clip 9.8

Upper Parts: Triplum and Motetus

The solo introduction to Machaut Motet 9, *Fons tocius superbie/O livoris/Fera pessima* (▶ Example 9.1) perfectly respects a three-bar grouping, but does not clearly

---

[14] These are the subject of Clark, 'Machaut's Motets on Secular Songs' and Hartt, 'The Three Tenors'.
[15] This A section ends with an *ouvert* (first-time) ending, its restatement (not shown) with a *clos* (second-time ending); that is followed by a different B section, then two more statements of A. Compare also the serpentine tenor of *Orbis orbatus/Vos pastores*, Ex. 7.1 above.
[16] See Ch. 4 and Exx. 4.2–4.4.
[17] Ch. 4. That chapter demonstrates how the musical structure in that case depends on a pre-existent tenor, the verbal structure on a pre-existent textual citation. See also Ch. 3.
[18] One *Fauvel* motet refers to the treachery of Judas, and several have similar beastly and vituperative diction. Shared words between motets from the *Fauvel* circle and Machaut's Motet 9 are shown below in bold. The motetus of *Garrit gallus* takes off from the first line of Ovid's *Metamorphoses*: 'In nova fert animus mutatas dicere formas/**Draco** nequam quem olim penitus'. Another motet from this group begins 'Floret cum vana gloria/de adventus **nequicia** ['evil']/antichristi'. *Aman novi* deals with **superbia** (pride) and reversal of fortune, a downfall from high to low. The motetus of *Orbis orbatus* (*Vos pastores adulteri*) refers to the followers of Lucifer, 'successores **Luciferi**'. The motetus of *Tribum que* starts 'Quoniam secta latronum/**spelunca** vispilionum'.

180   MACHAUT

establish it; the tenor enters in B15, an upbeat whether reckoned by triplum or by *talea*.[19] Fourteenth-century motets show varying degrees of isorhythmic correspondence in the upper parts (triplum and motetus), ranging from none to total identity. In this case, the correspondence is calculatedly partial, and is confined to hocket sections (that is, passages where the notes are 'hiccupped', or punctured, with rests, a pointillist passing of notes between all three voice-parts).

▶ Example 9.1 is shaded to show the strictly isorhythmic portions in the upper voices, beginning and ending two bars earlier in the triplum than in the motetus. Their phases are thus staggered from each other, and in turn from the tenor; but triplum and motetus still each have seven identical breves wrapped around the join to the next *talea*, leaving eight breves' worth in the middle (unshaded) that are not fully identical.[20] Anne Walters Robertson has drawn attention to other ways in which this motet plays on aspects of the ambiguous number of vices (seven or eight); here the fifteen breves of each *talea* are divided into segments that, although non-coincident in triplum and motetus, give each voice seven breves' worth that are isorhythmic, and eight that are not. ▶ Example 9.1 is also marked to show the ends of poetic lines (|), the conclusions of stanzas (separated by ||), and the starting points of *colores* as well as the roman-numeral *taleae* corresponding to systems of the score. B7–B8 of each tenor *talea*, rhythmically free in the texted parts, are often singled out for special music or words.

In fact, there are many more correspondences than those shaded in ▶ Example 9.1, but they are not consistently carried through in all *taleae*. Some correspondences outside the isorhythmic areas occur in the same position in relation to the repeating rhythm of each *talea*, and are therefore shown in vertical alignment in ▶ Example 9.1, as at triplum breves 18–19 and 33–34; motetus breves 16–20 and 31–35 (sound clip ▶ 9.9), while others appear displaced obliquely in relation to that alignment (for example, triplum breves 63–65 and 77–79; motetus breves 65–67 and 84–86; triplum breves 51–54 and 92–95; sound clip ▶ 9.10), or are repeated at a different pitch (motetus breves 17–21 and 137–40; sound clip ▶ 9.11). These displacements by pitch or rhythmic alignment from one *talea* to another stand out; some expectation of periodic repetition has been set up and then avoided by an artful displacement. They also serve to highlight, support and sometimes link significant words.

Hocket Punctuation

The obsessively conjunct tenor is strikingly punctuated (or 'punctured': see *pungit*, motetus line 7, 'stings from behind') by hockets in the upper parts, which not only fracture the melodic line but deliberately scatter their notes with exposed skips of fourths, pitch-leaps which contrast with the serpentine stepwise movement of the tenor. These leaps clearly herald each new *talea*. The nine hocket passages bridging the *taleae* are shaded on the score, ▶ Example 9.1. Sound clip ▶ 9.12 gives B25–B32.1, the triplum only; sound clip ▶ 9.13 brings together the triplum and motetus at the same place;

---

[19] Roman numerals indicate the nine *talea* periods from where the chant tenor begins, starting after the introitus.

[20] The motetus is not given separately here, but is reproduced in Boogaart, 'Encompassing Past and Present'.

finally, sound clip ⏵ 9.14 adds the tenor, illustrating three corresponding passages in the motet, bridging *taleae* I–II, II–III, III–IV (breves 25–32, 40–47, 55–62). The notes are different but the rhythm in each case is the same (isorhythm, again), and these rhythms are replicated at all other *talea* joins, making the identities audible.

Musical Range and Cadence Choices

The tenor range is limited to a fourth, *f–bb*. The triplum ranges within the octave above middle *c* (*c–c′*), with a high *c′* for 'Lucifer' (B6, touched again at III, B52, for *judice justissimo*); there are several occurrences of the lowest notes (middle *c, c♯*) for triplum words like *speluncis* in V (B78) and *Stigos* in VII (B112; caves, pits, and Stygian prisons), and sometimes to allow the motetus to keep these triplum words down by soaring above the triplum (as in IX, B135–B143). The motetus range is mostly a third lower (*a–a′*), but is extended at both ends to the large compass of a twelfth. It matches the top note, *c′*, of the triplum (at VI, B97), again rises above the triplum to *bb* at VIII, B121–B122, and descends below the tenor to *f♯* in VI–VII at B92 and B112. (Sound clip ⏵ 9.22 gives the motetus for this passage.)[21] The extraordinary compass of this part is masked when the three-part texture is heard as a unit.

A cadencing opportunity arises wherever the tenor descends by step without an intervening rest. 'Cadences' here are defined by particular progressions; the arrival points are not necessarily moments of closure.[22] Cadences are largely avoided among the rests of the hocket sections, but the final cadence of the motet is regular, notwithstanding the interruption of a tenor rest. In practice, singers might have adjusted this to make the cadence coincide on B148.[23] Despite the non-coincidence of *color* and *talea*, pitches 3–4 of each *talea* are always *a–g* (B3–B5 of each *talea*), providing a cadencing opportunity on *g* at tenor pitch 4 (B5). This opportunity is usually taken (with a normal 6/3–8/5 cadence—see next paragraph), but in a few cases where the preceding notes 2–3 are *bb–a*, the alternative opportunity to cadence on *a* is taken instead (in *taleae* IV, VI, VII). This is shown in Table 9.1, columns 2 and 3. Note 7 of each *talea* is always *a* (B11). Because of the different permutations of *x* and *y* (as in Ex. 9.2f above), notes 6–7 are *bb–a* in *taleae* I, II, IV, V, VII, VIII.

Most cadences place the tenor at the bottom of a standard progression in which a major third proceeding to a fifth is superimposed upon a major sixth proceeding to an octave (6/3–8/5).[24] These main forms, onto *g* and *a*, are given as Examples 9.6a and 9.6b (sound clip ⏵ 9.15). Exceptional cases are noted in Table 9.1. One such, not uncommon

---

[21] Introitus, *Lucifer*, high *c″* B6; and corresponding positions in the following *taleae*, I, B21–B22, *draco ferus*; III, B50–B53, *ferocissimo a judice justissimo*, highest triplum note *c″* with lowest tenor note *f*; V, *penis jaces*; VI, *obviare missilibus/affatur*, highest motetus note *c″* with lowest triplum note *c* and lowest tenor note *f*; VII, unison rhythms on *penis in asperis*, irregular progression on *stigos* at B112, with the lowest motetus note *f* ♮ on *pungit*, below the tenor, preceding *Sed Maria*; VIII, *scorpius Scariothis*; IX, *Filius*.

[22] I use the term cadence (*cadentia*) here on the authority of the 14th-c. theorist Jacobus to mean the dyadic (two-part) progression of an imperfect to a perfect interval, usually a third to a fifth or a sixth to an octave, and with a stepwise descent in one of the parts, usually the lower. For the supporting text and further comment, see Ch. 1. It is equivalent to the modern term 'directed progression', with the caveat that Sarah Fuller, who introduced the term, also applies it to three-part progressions (Fuller, 'Directed Progression').

[23] See Ch. 12, 'Endings', for non-coincident cadences, and Ch. 1.

[24] These figures indicate intervals from the lowest note, with no modern connotations of triadic inversion.

Table 9.1 Cadencing opportunities in Machaut, Motet 9

Bar (breve) and note numbers apply within each *talea*; regular cadences are in bold. Places where the tenor does not descend to provide a cadence opportunity are shaded. An asterisk (*) indicates a cadence opportunity that is not taken. Regular cadence progressions are in boldface

talea	B2–B3 in each *talea* (tenor notes 2–3 = b♭–a in I, III, IV, VI, VII, IX; = g–a in II, V, VIII)	B4–B5 in each *talea* (tenor notes 3–4 = a–g in I–IX)	B10–B11 in each *talea* (tenor notes 6–7 = b♭–a in I, II, IV, V, VII, VIII; = g–a in III, VI, IX)
I	*	6/3–8/5	tenor–motetus 3–5 (triplum c♯)
II		6/3–8/5	tenor–motetus 6–8 (triplum *e*, irregular approach)
III	*	tenor–motetus 6–8; triplum irregular (B48–9)	
IV	6/3–8/5	*	6/3–8/5
V		6/3–8/5	6/3–8/5
VI	tenor–triplum 6–8 motetus irregular (below tenor)	irregular	**motetus 10–8**
VII	6/3–8/5	*	triplum 3–5, motetus 3–1 (below tenor), irregular
VIII	**tenor–motetus 10–8**	tenor–triplum 6–8	6/3–8/5
IX	*	6/3–8/5 (triplum below motetus)	**irregular; final cadence regular, but with a rest; tenor a–g, 6/3–8/5**

elsewhere but unique in this motet, superimposes a tenth to a twelfth on a sixth to an octave (10/6–12/8: see Ex. 9.6c; sound clip ▶ 9.16). This occurs in *talea* III, B50–B52, where a climactic cadence touching the motet's extremes of range overlaps a rest between the tenor's *g* and *f* at the midpoint of the *talea*.

Ex. 9.6 Standard cadences in Motet 9:
(a) 6/3–8/5 on *g*;
(b) 6/3–8/5 on *a*, with ▶ sound clip 9.15;
(c) 10/6–12/8 on *f*, with ▶ sound clip 9.16

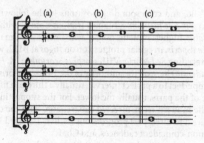

Although the contrapuntal grammar operates in two parts, cadences between pairs of parts are often superimposed in music in three or more parts. Sometimes only two of the three voices cadence together (see also Ch. 29). For example, tenor–motetus at I, B25 (Ex. 9.7a) and at II, B39 (Ex. 9.7b) both have an irregular triplum; at VIII, B124 (Ex. 9.7c), there is a triplum–tenor cadence, with irregular motetus. Sound clip ⏵ 9.17 illustrates all three moments, giving first the regular two-voice cadence, then Machaut's three-voice version.

Ex. 9.7 Partial cadences in Motet 9:
(a) B24–B25, motetus-tenor, triplum prevents closure;
(b) B39–B40 motetus-tenor, triplum approaches 5th irregularly;
(c) B123–B24, triplum-tenor, motetus approaches 5th irregularly, with ⏵ sound clip 9.17

Example 9.8 shows how the basic 6/3–8/5 progression that underlies B47–B49 (Ex. 9.8a; sound clip ⏵ 9.18) is resolved in the motetus, but that in Example 9.8b (a simplified version of the progression in the motet; sound clip ⏵ 9.19) the triplum anticipates the resolution to d, preventing closure, and moving on to cadence on f (as in Ex. 9.6c above).

Ex. 9.8 Displaced cadence in Motet 9, B47–B49:
(a) basic progression, with ⏵ sound clip 9.18;
(b) Machaut's music simplified, with ⏵ sound clip 9.19

Example 9.9 shows an even more complex cadential displacement for B112–B115. Example 9.9a shows what a normal resolution would produce for just the motetus and tenor; Example 9.9b gives the same two-voice progression with Machaut's displacement, this time delaying the progression of the motetus from $f\sharp$ to g; Example 9.9c gives the normalised three-voice version of Example 9.9a, still strange because of the angular parallel progression; and Example 9.9d gives Machaut's displacement, which sounds stranger still, but can be logically construed by the stages just illustrated.

Ex. 9.9 Displaced cadences in Motet 9 in B112–B15:
(a) motetus and tenor only, expected resolution;
(b) motetus and tenor only, with Machaut's displacement;
(c) all three parts, expected resolution;
(d) all three parts, with Machaut's displacement, with ▶ sound clip 20

Examples 9.9a–9.9d can be heard on sound clip ▶ 9.20. Other odd-sounding moments, notably the one at B68, can be similarly explained as displacements.

Verbal Texts and the Introduction

With both upper-voice texts in Latin, Motet 9 is in a minority among Machaut's 23 motets; see Table 9.2. This table also notes the presence or absence of an introitus before

Table 9.2 Machaut motets with one or both texts in Latin (out of a total of 23)

Motet no.	Triplum	Motetus	Introduction (=Introitus?)	No. of voices
9	Fons tocius	O livoris	yes—solo	3
12	Helas! pour quoy (French)	Corde mesto	no	3
17	Quant vraie amour (French)	O serie	no	3
18	Bone pastor Guillerme	Bone pastor qui	no	3
19	Martyrum gemma	Diligenter inquiramus	yes—solo	3
21	Christe qui lux	Veni creator spiritus	yes—solo and duet	4
22	Tu qui gregem	Plange regni	yes—solo and duet	4
23	Felix virgo	Inviolata genitrix	yes—solo and duet	4

MACHAUT'S MOTET 9   185

the tenor entry. All other motets are French-texted and none has an introduction outside the structure. All three four-voice Latin motets (Motets 21–23) have a duet introduction which starts as an extended solo. Motets 9 and 19 are the only three-voice Latin motets to have such an introduction, both solo only. Motet 18 is the only three-voice Latin motet not to have one. In all other cases the tenor starts with the texted voices at the beginning, albeit in Motets 13, 15 and 18 with a rest which is integral to the isorhythmic structure.

Distribution of Texts in Relation to Music

The text distribution of the triplum is simple. There are ten stanzas. One is used for the solo introduction, and the other nine receive a *talea* each, starting with the hocket just ahead of each *talea* join (see Table 9.3). Machaut has here set himself the additional discipline of not breaking any word with rests, even in the hockets.[25] This is successfully carried out in the hockets, fully in the triplum's regularly placed monosyllables and disyllables (2 + 1 + 2), and with two exceptions in the motetus to the isolated monosyllable at the beginning of each line. This must mean that the text was composed with the extra discipline of placing monosyllables and disyllables at specific points where the hockets were intended.[26] These are words tailored for music, and music for words, in a highly specific way that in this case is entirely non-affective. Motet 9 is not the only one in which Machaut contrives to avoid breaking words with musical rests: other instances are given in Chapter 13.

The distribution of the much shorter motetus text is less straightforward. Lines 1–7 receive one whole *talea* each. Then *talea* VIII gets three lines and IX gets two, so that the last five text-lines are squeezed into just two *taleae*. The higher proportion of notes to syllables in most *taleae* conspires with a seemingly more arbitrary underlay in the manuscripts to make it appear less purposeful than the triplum. In each *talea* the first motetus note is a semibreve flanked by rests (hocket), and the text has monosyllables at the beginning of most but not all lines. The manuscript underlay is inconsistent between rhythmically identical *taleae* and avoids splitting any of these words. Example 9.1 places a syllable on each of the isolated notes that opens each *talea*, in turn providing a springboard for the two hocketed triplum monosyllables. Five polysyllables at line beginnings break this pattern in the verse composition. Three of these are precisely for the lines (9, 10, 12) that do not begin a *talea* and are therefore not subject to the prevailing monosyllable discipline, and include the polysyllables *Scariothis* and *latitat*. Applying this pattern, the two remaining disyllables at line beginnings are split with hocketing rests; this has some logic, as they occur in the long sentence about twofold attack and double treachery that occupies fully half the motetus, the six lines 5–10. The words *tu-a* and *re-tro pungit* (lines 5 and 7) are, in principle, split. In the latter case, the verb *pungit* ('punctures') in motetus line 7 has already been linked with hockets.

[25] On 'monosyllable discipline' see Chs. 13, 17, 22, 25.
[26] One possible exception to this is the doubtful reading *Elanguis* at the beginning of stanza 10. The text, which did not make sense here, has been mended by Leofranc Holford-Strevens to *Et anguis*—independently of knowing the syllable/hocket constraint, which is now perfectly observed. Two other text readings were already corrected by Ludwig, *Guillaume de Machaut*; all manuscripts have *auges que* for *auges quod* (triplum line 29) and *te fuit* for *tenuit* (triplum, line 31).

186 MACHAUT

Table 9.3 Distribution of text in Machaut, Motet 9

‖ marks where musical rests do, could or should occur in relation to words, with monosyllables and disyllables placed so as to leave words intact, except where noted.

Stanza	Line	*Talea*	Triplum text	Rhyme
1	1	Introitus	Fons tocius superbie,	a
	2		Lucifer, et nequicie	a
	3		Qui, mirabili specie	b
	4		Decoratus,	a
2	5	I	Eras ‖ in ‖ summis ‖ locatus,	b
	6		Super thronos sublimatus,	b
	7		Draco ferus antiquatus	b
	8		Qui dicere, ‖	c
3	9	II	Ausus ‖ es ‖ sedem ‖ ponere	c
	10		Aquilone et gerere	c
	11		Te similem in opere	c
	12		Altissimo. ‖	d
4	13	III	Tuo ‖ sed ‖ est in ‖ proximo	d
	14		Fastui ferocissimo	d
	15		A judice justissimo	d
	16		Obviatum. ‖	e
5	17	IV	Tuum ‖ nam ‖ auffert ‖ primatum;	e
	18		Ad abyssos cito stratum	e
	19		Te vidisti per peccatum	e
	20		De supernis. ‖	f
6	21	V	Ymis ‖ nunc ‖ regnas ‖ infernis;	f
	22		In speluncis et cavernis	f
	23		Penis jaces et eternis	f
	24		Agonibus. ‖	g
7	25	VI	Dolus ‖ et ‖ fraus in ‖ actibus	g
	26		Tuis et bonis omnibus	g
	27		Obviare missilibus	h
	28		Tu niteris; ‖	g
8	29	VII	Auges ‖ quod ‖ nephas ‖ sceleris	h
	30		Adam penis in asperis	h
	31		Tenuit Stigos carceris.	h
	32		Sed Maria ‖	i
9	33	VIII	Virgo, ‖ que, ‖ plena ‖ gratia,	i
	34		Sua per puerperia	i
	35		Illum ab hac miseria	i
	36		Liberavit, ‖	k
10	37	IX	Precor ‖ et ‖ anguis ‖ tedia	i
	38		Augeat et supplicia	i
	39		Et nos ducat ad gaudia	i
	40		Quos creavit.	k

Table 9.3 Continued

			Motetus	
1	1	I	O ‖ livoris feritas,	x
	2	II	Que ‖ superna rogitas	x
	3	III	Et ‖ jaces inferius!	y
2	4	IV	Cur ‖ inter nos habitas?	x
	5	V	Tu - ‖ - a cum garrulitas	x
	6	VI	Nos ‖ affatur dulcius,	y
3	7	VII	Re - ‖ - tro pungit sevius,	y
	8	VIII	Ut ‖ veneno scorpius:	y
	9		Scariothis falsitas	x
4	10		Latitat interius.	y
	11	IX	Det ‖ mercedes Filius	y
	12		Dei tibi debitas!	x

Tenor: Fera pessima

The triplum offers the clearest possible evidence that not only the substance of the text but also the details of its word-breaks were planned together with the musical design; this purpose is less clearly transmitted for the motetus. Friedrich Ludwig's edition follows the manuscripts in distributing these monosyllables rather casually, observing the apparently intended word–rest constraints in the triplum but not in the motetus. Leo Schrade's isolates most monosyllables with rests in the motetus but not in the triplum. The accompanying examples and sound clips thus correspond to Ludwig's solution for the triplum and Schrade's for the motetus; Machaut, *The Motets*, ed. Boogaart, likewise observes both. This is a case where the internal evidence of the compositional design of words and music leads to a solution that is not literally supported by the manuscripts. As with many other editorial or performative decisions, it is less a question of establishing a composer's intent than of being alert to the internal logic and process that the composition retains as an autonomous work, however much contextual richness may be added by referential comparisons.

Rhyme-words at *Talea*-ends

In Motet 9, all triplum stanzas have chain rhyme, i.e. the last, short line of each stanza provides the rhyme for the first three lines of the next one. No rhymes are repeated except for the last two. This means that the *talea* end-words are all different until the final section, which detaches *Sed Maria* from stanza 8 and links it to the final rhyming couplet -*avit*:

188   MACHAUT

Line	
4	decoratus
8	dicere
12	altissimo
16	obviatum
20	de supernis
24	agonibus
28	tu niteris
	===
32	Sed Maria
36	liberavit
40	quos creavit

In the motetus, all six line-ends in the first half of the text (lines 1–6) also end *taleae*; in the second half, only lines 7, 10 and 12 end *taleae* in this highly uneven text distribution, which applies to the verbal declamation an acceleration commonly (though not here) found in the music of tenor repetitions. Note that the rhymes of stanzas 1 and 2 (*-itas*, *-itas*, *-ius*) are reversed in stanzas 3 and 4 (*-ius*, *-ius*, *-itas*), and that this pattern is preserved in the lines selected for *talea* rhymes. The resulting *talea* rhyme scheme x x y reflects the musical form of the three-segment tenor melody (see Ex. 9.2b above). All stanza ends have one of the two rhymes used in the motetus, a pattern very different from the triplum (see Fig. 9.1).

Alliteration

In Motet 9 Machaut has arranged many sonic verbal correspondences, some of which are marked in Fig. 9.2. *Fera pessima* links alliteratively with *fons*, the first triplum word, *feritas* in motetus line 1, *ferus* in triplum 7, *inferius* in motetus 3 (also to *interius*, motetus 10), *infernis* in triplum 21 (also to *supernis*, triplum 20). *Ferocissimo* (triplum 14) also sonically conflates *fera* with its own superlative *pessima*, and at this point (B50–B53) is bunched with another superlative, *justissimo*, at the only place in

Line	
1	feritas
2	rogitas
3	inferius
4	habitas
5	garrulitas
6	dulcius
7	sevius
10	interius
12	debitas

Fig. 9.1 Motetus rhyme-words in Machaut, Motet 9

MACHAUT'S MOTET 9   189

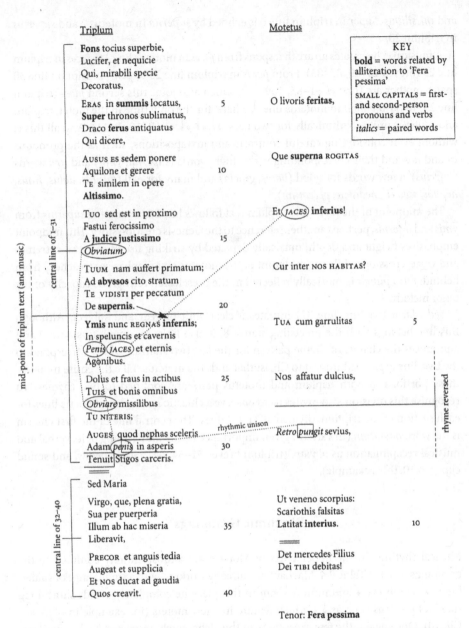

Fig. 9.2 Some verbal correspondences between triplum and motetus in Machaut, Motet 9

the piece to have the musical rhythm ♪♪ ♪♪♪, and the only time when two tribrachs come in immediate succession in the symmetrical group ♪♪ ♪♪♪ ♪♪♪ ♪♪, touching *c′*, the highest note in the piece, and linking it to other climaxes where this note is heard, all the more snakily hissy with soft French 's' sounds. Superlatives are picked up onomato-poeically from *fera pessima* not only to *fastui ferocissimo* but also the adjacent and musically underlined *judice justissimo*. These sounds are further echoed in *abyssos*

190 MACHAUT

and *missilibus*. *Super* in triplum line 6 is echoed by *superna* in motetus 2 and *supernis* in triplum 20.

A musical echo creates an arc that spans from *jaces* in motetus line 3 to *jaces* in triplum line 23 (breves 48–49, 82–83). From *penis* in triplum line 23 to *penis* in triplum line 30 spans another arc (breves 81–85, 109–15), which also joins this second *jaces* (triplum line 23) to *retro pungit* in motetus line 7, where, for the only time in the motet, triplum and motetus unite rhythmically for two bars: ♦♦ ♦♦ ♦♦ ♦♦ (B110–B111). And all this is without even considering careful contrasts and juxtapositions, such as the pronouns *tu* and *nos* and their corresponding verbs, high words (*superna, ymis*) and low words (*inferius*), a few words for good (*bonis, gracia*) and many for evil (*falsitas, dolus, fraus, nephas, sceleris, nequicie, peccatum*).

The midpoint of the forty-line triplum text follows line 20, separating *supernis* from *ymis* and *infernis*, perhaps another reference to the Genesis creation story. This midpoint emphasises height and depth, musically depicted by striking use of registral extremes and voice-crossing, while the midpoint of the motetus text emphasises treachery from behind: *retro pungit* is musically reflected in the preselected retrograde capacity of the tenor melody.

Sed Maria (triplum line 32) initiates a clear shift of gear and subject. Although this line belongs with the preceding stanza 8, it also links by rhyme to stanza 9 and announces the change of rhyme pattern for the last two stanzas, which correspond to the two-line *explicit* addressed to Christ that ends the motetus. Like the entire motetus, these portions in both triplum and motetus parts are confined to two rhymes. To recognise this division also invites us to observe a chiastic symmetry of poetic lines for each section of the triplum, divided at 31 + 9 lines. The central line of the first chiasm is the word *obviatum* (thwarted), given importance by the underlining of its verbal and musical recapitulation as *obviare* (triplum breves 51–54, 92–95; see below, and sound clip ⊙ 9.10, third example).

Rhythmic Groupings

Musical rhythms in the upper parts of Motet 9 are almost entirely confined to the groupings listed in Table 9.4. Machaut was already working with a small range of values, breve ▪, semibreve ♦ and minim ♦, but in this piece he completely avoids short–long (iambic) patterns such as ♦ ♦ which feature in a few motets (for example in M15; see Ch. 10). Once again, the few exceptions to this deliberately restricted background vo-cabulary are made to stand out as conspicuous. Verbal economy and purposeful reca-pitulation of chosen words work together with musical means to highlight particular moments. Composers often limited themselves further within the available options, for reasons that will be suggested below.

Table 9.4 Rhythmic vocabulary of upper parts in Machaut, Motet 9

Breve units	Triplum	Motetus	Total	Comments
▪	27	23	50	The rhythmic vocabulary is mostly restricted to these few patterns, against which variants stand out and are reserved for special effect.
♦♦	28	8	36	
♦♦♦	10	10	20	
♦♦♦♦	29	14	43	
♦♦♦♦♦	4	2	6	The last of these is on the pivotal words *Sed Maria*; the first is combined with one of the *unica*.
♦ ♦♦♦	1 only			Triplum B2, echoing Motet 15.
♦ ♦♦♦♦	1 only			Two rare usages are combined in triplum B51–B52, to the words *ferocissimo a judice justissimo*: ♦♦ ♦♦♦♦ ♦♦
꜔♦꜔♦ ♦꜔♦꜔	9			Hockets at *talea* beginnings occur only here.

Numbers

In addition to the musical numbers already considered, the verbal text also displays some interesting patterns, as shown in Table 9.5. In the triplum, 31 lines occur before the division: there are 28 words from *Sed Maria* to the end; both are lengths of months counted in days. Lent, for which the tenor is prescribed, has 40 days. The numbers 7, 12, 52 and 364 may suggest a calendrical plan, perhaps worth exploring in the light of other speculations about the origins of this motet.

Table 9.5 Calendrical dimensions in Machaut, Motet 9

	Triplum	Motetus	Total
Lines	**40 = 31 + 9**	**12** = 6 + 6 text = 7 + 5 music	**52**
Syllables	280 = 10 × (8 + 8 + 8 + 4) = 10 × **28**	84 = **12** × 7	**364**
Rhymes	10	2	**12**
Words	124 = 96 + 28	35 = 29 + 6	159

Two Sample Passages

Two extended passages especially demonstrate the intricate interplay of text and music, here chosen to counterbalance the frequent claim in older literature that motet word-setting was casual or barbaric. It may not conform to our aesthetic, but observable features invite us to try to understand theirs.

Passage 1. B46–B83 (mid-*taleae* III–V; sound clip ⊕ 9.21) span the words *jaces* ('you lie'; motetus line 3) to *penis jaces* ('you lie in torments'; triplum line 23). The passage includes the irregular cadence at B47–B49 (Ex. 9.8b above) and (as just mentioned) the unique and symmetrical rhythm ♩♩ ♪♪♪ ♪♪♪ ♩♩ for the adjacent and alliterating superlatives at *ferocissimo/judice justissimo* (B51–B52), followed by the central triplum word *obviatum*.

The triplum touches its topmost *c″* in only three places in the motet. One is at *Lucifer* at B6; the other two echo this at B52 and B93.

A musical near-recapitulation of triplum B51–B54 'ferocissimo a judice justissimo obviatum' at B92–B95 as 'actibus . . . et bonis omnibus obviare' centres on a musical rhyme for the central word, *obviatum* (triplum line 16) with *obviare* (triplum line 27). (These two passages can be heard at the end of sound clip ⊕ 9.10.)

At the low words *abyssos* (IV, B63–B65) and *speluncis* (V, B79–B80), the triplum dips below the motetus for two identical passages (triplum, breves 63–65 = breves 77–79; they can be heard at the beginning of sound clip ⊕ 9.10); the two parts also cross at III, B47–B48, for the motetus's high setting of its 'low' word *jaces*; all three cases descend to the triplum's lowest note *c* (or *c♯*). This audible concentration of activity is achieved by verbal and rhythmic highlighting, alliteration, extremes of range and voice-crossing.

Passage 2. The passage from B91 to B115 spans *talea* VI to mid-*talea* VII. It is bounded by the only two places where the motetus dips below the tenor, both with its lowest note, *f* (or *f♯*), which is also the lowest tenor note. The motetus thus encompasses the range of both triplum and tenor, touching both their extremes of range. Such voice-crossings may be masked when listening only to the complete three-voice texture without seeing (or knowing in advance) how it is scored. Sound clip ⊕ 9.22 gives the motetus line (alone) from B91–B115, showing the wide range and extreme leaps that are masked by the voice-crossings. Sound clip ⊕ 9.23 pinpoints two identical motetus progressions a full octave apart at breves 100–102 and 111–114.1. Sound clip ⊕ 9.24 sets this passage in its three-voice polyphonic context (see B91–B115 of ⊕ Ex. 9.1).

This passage spans a structural join of both textual and musical importance: the juncture of *taleae* VI–VII is exactly two-thirds of the way through the motet (excluding the introduction), and it coincides with the third and last cycle of two *colores* to three *taleae*. The unusual distribution of the motetus text, as already noted, confines the entire second half of that text to the final third of the piece. Thus the second half of the motetus text is declaimed at double the rate of the first half. This is a textual application of a device commonly used in motet tenors, where musical acceleration is used for a final section; in this case the acceleration is in the rate of text declamation, not the speed of musical notes.

The motetus words that start the second text half, 'retro pungit' (stings from behind), also signal the point from which the rhyme scheme is reversed (i.e. retrograded) in the second half of the motetus text. In the triplum text the midway point similarly marks the division from *supernis* to *ymis* and *infernis*; high to low in the triplum, back to front in the motetus, as stated earlier. Musically, it is not uncommon for structural joins in motets to be signalled by words signifying cutting, division, direction or measure. Here, 'retro pungit' is placed in the repeating tenor at the hinge point of a pattern that is both inverted and retrogradable (see Ex. 9.10, notes 7–11 and 12–14). *Pungit* is also interrupted by a tenor rest; and *pun-* at B110 falls on the centre of a musical palindrome in the tenor, B105–B115, in addition to the word-puncturing and musically graphic hockets; see Example 9.10, notes 9–12 and 1–4. At B112 the syllable *-git* joins with *stigos* for what sounds to us like a double leading-note cadence (*f♯–g* and *c♯–d*), whose resolution is strikingly and tortuously delayed.[27]

Ex. 9.10 Motet 9: inversion (upper brackets) and retrograde (lower brackets) patterns in the tenor *color*

At B94–B102 the motetus (at 'affatur dulcius') rises for the only time to its highest note *c′* (it occurs during sound clip ▶ 9.22), which is as high as the highest note of the triplum, a pitch previously heard at triplum B6–B9 (sound clip ▶ 9.25) and in the passages just mentioned at B52 and B93, touching the same top *c* for Lucifer flying high before his descent—a perfect musical expression of overweening pride. The Lucifer phrase in turn receives a musical near-recapitulation in motetus B109–B111 at 'retro pungit' (sound clip ▶ 9.26). An unsettling dissonant moment at the end of the passage in B112–B115 has already been discussed (Ex. 9.9 above; sound clip ▶ 9.20).

A Parallel with Motet 15

Finally, there is a parallel between the solo opening of Motet 9 and the opening of Motet 15 (*Amours qui ha le povoir/Faus samblant/Vidi Dominum*). We have also seen some affinities between tenors of different Machaut motets, but other suggestive musical relationships between motets in this period are less often recognised. Only three of Machaut's motets start with this rhythm; the others are Motet 10 (Ch. 12) and Motet 15 (Ch. 10), closely linked in other ways, which makes an allusive relationship between them and Motet 9 all the more intriguing. The first few bars of Motet 9 and Motet 15 have an even closer identity than is apparent on paper (see Ex. 9.11, which is laid out to show further parallels in the continuation; sound clip ▶ 9.27); the closeness depends on both upper parts being heard.

---

[27] See Ch. 29 for a comparable example given by Johannes Boen, the *Se grace/Cum venerint/Ite missa est* of the Tournai Mass.

Ex. 9.11 Similarities between openings of Motet 9 and Motet 15:
(a) Motet 15, triplum and motetus, opening;
(b) Motet 9, introitus, B1–B5, all of whose notes are present in the triplum or motetus of (a);
(c) continuation of the introitus, aligning rhythmic parallels, with ▶ sound clip 27

The rhythm ♩♩ ♩♩♩ occurs only this once in Motet 9 (see Table 9.4 above), and thus stands out strikingly from the limited rhythmic vocabulary with which Machaut works. That this is not part of the established vocabulary of Motet 9 might also indicate the direction of the quotation, namely, that Motet 15 antedates it, though other considerations (the extensive iambic rhythms) suggest a later date for Motet 15. By confining the choice of rhythmic and melodic patterns within any one piece, any departures can be made to sound more striking and purposeful—significant phonemes that stand out from the background language established for the piece.

Moreover, the tenor of Motet 15 is yet again from a Matins responsory, for the preceding (second) Sunday in Lent. The text *Vidi Dominum* is likewise from Genesis: Jacob has wrestled with the angel and seen the Lord face to face. The motet is *Faus samblant*; its subject is deception and duplicity, it uses mirror retrograde, and it has forty tenor notes, perhaps corresponding to the forty Lenten triplum lines of Motet 9.[28]

Conclusion

Such things as are pointed out here cannot all be heard in a single performance or by an unprepared listener. But the experienced listener who, like Boethius's *musicus*, 'exhibits the faculty of forming judgements according to speculation or reason', will be drawn to considerations and reflections outside the time it takes to perform the music, just as Dante demands longer and more multi-dimensional reflection than is possible in the time it takes to recite passages from his *Commedia*. As with all informed listening, whether as basic music appreciation or advanced analysis, discovering what subtleties have been planted by the composer may increase understanding and pleasure when the piece is heard as an entity. Repeated hearings will yield up many other features than those singled out here, including overall rhythmic structure and tenor repetitions, sonic

---

[28] See Brownlee, 'Machaut's Motet 15', and Bent, 'Machaut's Motet 15' (= Ch. 10).

verbal aspects such as alliteration, use of musical ranges and voice-crossing, hockets and verbal planning according to musical rests, local rhythms and exceptions to the basic rhythmic vocabulary, verbal links between triplum and motetus, long-range verbal and musical repetitions.

The sound of modern performances and recordings may beckon us into the realm of early music, but it is only when we recognise performance sound to be a modern construction, however beautiful, that we may penetrate beyond it, to the intrinsic content of the music independently of performance, and learn new ways of listening to unfamiliar musical styles. We cannot recover the sounds of medieval music as it was heard then, but we can recover much of its sense and particularity. Music only happens when it sounds, but works of music exist independently of individual performances. It is by this paradox that we are empowered to understand much about medieval music, as we can of ancient literatures, even lacking any recoverable notion of its original sound. Armed with a deeper understanding of how the music works, performers of music, as of poetry and drama, are liberated to communicate that understanding in more fulfilling ways than simply following instructions or 'singing the dots'.

10

Deception, Exegesis and Sounding Number in Machaut's Motet 15

↬The original version of this chapter on M15 (*Amours qui a le pouoir/Faus Samblant m'a deceü/Vidi dominum*) was published under the same title, together with, and designed to complement, a paper on the motet's texts by Kevin Brownlee, 'Machaut's Motet 15', in *Early Music History* (10) 1991, a welcome addition by a leading literary scholar to then-current studies that apply literary, textual and historical insights to fourteenth-century motets. This pair of articles followed seminar presentations we had made jointly on several of Machaut's French-texted motets. What follows is a slightly revised version of my contribution to our collaboration on M15. In general, I now draw back from what was perhaps an earlier overemphasis on the golden section relationship in textual–musical construction, but have retained those references here where I think they do carry some weight.

Motet 15, *Amours qui a le pouoir/Faus Samblant m'a deceü/Vidi dominum*, is given as Example 10.1 in an annotated copy based on Leo Schrade's edition.[1] One of the striking features of this motet as printed by Friedrich Ludwig, Schrade and Jacques Boogaart is the dissonant appoggiatura at the end of the triplum. Although confirmed by all sources, it is hard to accept, even as a deliberate piece of word-painting of *desconfiture* and *nonchaloir*, the final triplum and motetus words, when we can point to so few uses of dissonance that bypass grammatical convention in the service of depiction.[2] An alternative ending is provided in Example 10.1, making the last triplum notes ♩ ♩ ♦ ♮ instead of ♦ ■ ♮. This small violation of the isorhythmic correspondence imposes a choice between musical conformity and formal congruence, but the final notes of the upper-voice isorhythm are truncated anyway. It respects the *-ure* feminine rhyme and matches the corresponding point at the cadential arrival.

M15 is 120 breves long. The tenor consists of one *color* (melodic iteration) disposed in four equal *taleae* (rhythmic iterations) each of ten perfect longs, here numbered Ia, Ib, IIa, IIb. 10 longs × 3 = 30 breves; 4 *taleae* × 30 = 120. Peter's threefold denial and the 30 pieces of silver paid for Judas's betrayal have associations of deceit; the choice of these numbers for a motet about deceit may be far from accidental.[3] The tenor has 40 notes, 10 in each *talea*, 20 in each half. The 10s of the tenor, whether counted as notes or breves, when multiplied by 12 produce 120.

---

[1] PMFC 2. For a new edition based on **MachautA**, with excellent commentary and manuscript variants, see now Machaut, *The Motets*, ed. Boogaart.

[2] Non-coincident endings are considered in Ch. 1 and Exx. 1.1 and 1.2. See also Ch. 14: *desconfiture* is also the final word in M8, but has no such dissonant suspension.

[3] For the 'deceitful' use of 30 in a *Fauvel* motet see Arlt, 'Triginta denariis', and Ch. 12 n. 18. Johannes Boen's *Ars* [*musicae*] discusses tenor disposition, taking as his example the number of 30 tenor notes in two motets on *Alma redemptoris mater* that have been attributed to Vitry: *Impudenter circumivi/Virtutibus* and *Apta caro/Flos virginum*.

The Motet in the Late Middle Ages. Margaret Bent, Oxford University Press. © Oxford University Press 2023.
DOI: 10.1093/so/9780190063771.003.0011

Ex. 10.1 Machaut, Motet 15, *Amours qui a le pouoir/Faus Samblant m'a deceü/Vidi dominum*

Ex. 10.1 Continued

Ex. 10.1 Continued

Ex. 10.1 Continued

The Texted Parts

The music of triplum and motetus is disposed in two rhythmically identical *taleae* each of 60 breves, each spanning two 30-breve tenor *taleae* (Ia + Ib = IIa + IIb); the motet falls into two rhythmically identical halves. The midpoints of those halves are marked by the second and fourth tenor *taleae* (Ib, IIb) and also by the four divisions of the motetus text. Georg Reichert coined the term *Großtalea* for where an upper-voice *talea* spans multiple tenor *taleae*, as in Motets 12, 15 and 21.[4] But viewed another way, triplum and motetus can both be divided into two pairs of varied *taleae* (Ia = IIa, Ib = IIb), coinciding with the equal *taleae* of the tenor. In each of these four 30-breve periods the first three breves (actually four in the triplum), and the last 15 (the entire second half), are rhythmically identical. (These passages are shaded in Ex. 10.1.) Thus a total of just over 18 bars out of each 30 are rhythmically the same.[5] Such large and systematic deviations within otherwise identical sections in the upper voices may be considered part of the deceptive programme of the motet.

The texts (see Table 10.1) differ hierarchically in length, as triplum and motetus normally do, and each is differently patterned. They are distinct as are their subjects, *Amours* and *Faux Semblant*, which Brownlee shows to be presented in an apparent opposition that is in fact false.[6] The triplum text's 38 lines divide by line count, metrical and rhyme scheme only at the middle, its 19 + 19 lines matching the two musical periods of both upper parts. Each half follows the same rhyme scheme but with only the 'b' rhyme (-*ure*) maintained throughout both halves. The twelve b-lines each have six syllables, all other lines seven:

$$a^7 \, a^7 \, \mathbf{b^6} \, a^7 \, a^7 \, \mathbf{b^6} \, c^7 \, c^7 \, c^7 \, \mathbf{b^6} \, c^7 \, c^7 \, \mathbf{b^6} \, c^7 \, \mathbf{b^6} \, c^7 \, c^7 \, c^7 \, \mathbf{b^6} \mid$$

$$d^7 \, d^7 \, \mathbf{b^6} \, d^7 \, d^7 \, \mathbf{b^6} \, e^7 \, e^7 \, e^7 \, \mathbf{b^6} \, e^7 \, e^7 \, \mathbf{b^6} \, e^7 \, \mathbf{b^6} \, e^7 \, e^7 \, e^7 \, \mathbf{b^6} \mid$$

The parallel duplication makes regularity out of these two irregular forms. Similarly irregular but paired stanzas in Machaut's lais are also subjected to a similar rhyme discipline.

The motetus text has twelve lines, arranged in four groups of three lines, each of which has abc rhyme and 7–8–7 syllables.

$$a^7 \, b^8 \, c^7 \mid a^7 \, b^8 \, c^7 \mid a^7 \, b^8 \, c^7 \mid a^7 \, b^8 \, c^7$$

The four three-line groups correspond to the four *taleae* of the tenor; they thus encourage an interpretation of the upper parts as four *taleae* with deviations, whereas the textual structure of the triplum favours a division into only two strictly repeating halves. Just as false-seeming may go in either of two directions, so the *Faus Samblant* motetus

---

[4] Reichert, 'Das Verhältnis', 202. I now prefer to reserve the term *talea* for iterations that are either exact or homographic, 'period' where there are deviations; further on this and related terms see Ch. 12 n. 17. See also notes to the table in Besseler, 'Studien II', 222–24; Günther, 'The 14th-Century Motet', 30, 37.

[5] The golden section of 30 falls at 18.54.

[6] Reichert, 'Das Verhältnis', gives valuable analyses of the text forms of Machaut motets; M15 is one of only eight motets with clear strophic forms (Reichert, p. 202). Motets 4, 7, 8, 9 10, 15 are among those where both voices have strophe/*talea* alignment.

could have adapted its structure either to the four equal musical *taleae* of the two-faced tenor ('facie ad faciem') or to the two parallel textual halves of the triplum.[7] In fact, the music of both upper parts does both; they can be interpreted either as two strict or as four varied *taleae*. The composer's duplicitous and ambivalent strategy is reflected in such a reading.

Counting elided words as two, the triplum's 83 + 85 words are so arranged that the *Et* that begins line 20 just anticipates the musical midpoint; the triplum thus has 84 words in each musical half of the piece.[8] The coincidence of the midpoint of the music with the midpoint of the triplum word count makes possible a strict correspondence between word and note in the rhythmic repetitions. Musical overlapping of structural joins is often found in motets; here we find textual construction following the same procedure by a slight dislocation of line count and word count.

In similar fashion, and by word count, the first half of the motetus text has 30 words and the second half 32. The central thirty-first word is *Las!*, and there are 31 words after it, starting with the parallel to line 1. This may be heard as an *He-las* spanning the musical midpoint, with the triplum's *Et* that starts line 20, word 84, preceding and aurally linked to *Las!* in the motetus.[9] The midpoint by word count in both triplum and motetus thus falls after the first word of the second half of the text as defined by lines and syllables, again at the musical middle, coinciding in both texts, and joined together.

The Tenor

The words of the tenor beyond the incipit, *Vidi dominum*, are not supplied in the manuscripts but can be reinstated to the slightly varied chant. The notes for the final *anima mea* are left off, leaving unstated what it is that is saved. Nine syllables fall in each half of the motet, with one of the two 'faces' mirrored in each half around the midpoint of both text and music, the second (*faciem*) following the musical golden section:

Vidi dominum facie ad |

faciem [et] salva facta est ...

[7] Zayaruznaya, 'She has a Wheel', 206–9, adds some excellent supplementary observations. She is not quite right to say (p. 208) that M15's voice-crossings have never been commented upon: Boogaart is the only previous analyst to have noted the extent and importance of such crossings. Here, he argues that they depict the reversals that form the heart of the biblical history of Jacob and Esau: '*O series summe rata*', 108. When I wrote the original version of this article on M15 I had not yet given full attention to voice-crossings as I did in the study of M9 which is now Ch. 9, aspects of which were to bear fruit in Zayaruznaya's dissertation and beyond.

[8] The triplum has 268 notes, 38 lines and 168 words (counting elided words, transcribed with apostrophes, as two words). The motetus has 188 notes, 12 lines and 62 words.

In the following, x + y means: x is the number of words counting elided words, transcribed with apostrophes, as single words; y is the number of words with apostrophes; x + y is the word count reckoning *M'a* as two words:

   triplum, 78 + 5, 78 + 7 in the two halves (83, 85)
   motetus, 27 + 3, 28 + 4 (30, 32).

[9] Other striking instances of meaningful verbal play between triplum and motetus include the second *color* of *Vos/Gratissima* (see Ch. 8).

204 MACHAUT

Table 10.1 Texts of Machaut's Motet 15

Translations are taken from Brownlee, 'Machaut's Motet 15', 3.

	Triplum	Translation	Rhyme	Syllables	Words
	Amours qui a le **pouoir**	Love, who has the power	a	7	5
	De moy faire **recevoir**	to make me receive	a	7	4
	Joie ou mort obscure,	either joy or dark death,	b	6	4
	Ne fait par sa grace **Avoir**	does not, through his grace,	a	7	6
5	A ma dame tel **voloir**	give my lady the desire	a	7	5
	Qu'elle m'ait en cure.	to care for me.	b	6	6
	Durer ne puis longuement,	I cannot last for long,	c	7	4
	Car pour amer loiaument	because neither from loyal loving,	c	7	4
	Ne pour servir liement,	nor from gracious serving	c	7	4
10	Sans penser laidure,	(without an ugly thought),	b	6	3
	Ne pour celer sagement	nor from discreet concealing,	c	7	4
	N'ay confort n'aligement	do I have comfort or relief	c	7	5
	De ma dolour dure;	from my harsh pain.	b	6	4
	Einsois com plus humblement	Rather, the more humbly	c	7	4
15	La sueffre et endure,	I suffer and endure it,	b	6	4
	De tant est plus durement	the more harshly	c	7	5
	Traitiés mes cuers, que briefment	is my heart treated, so that I shall shortly	c	7	5
	Morray dolereusement	sadly die	c	7	2
	De dueil et d'ardure,	of grief and burning desire,	b	6	5/83 (midpoint)
20	Et tant sui plus eslongiés	and the farther I am removed	d	7	5
	De merci et estraingiés	from favour and the more I am distanced	d	7	4
	De ma dame pure.	from my pure lady.	b	6	4
	Mais aveuc tous ces **meschiés**	But with all these misfortunes,	d	7	5
	Sueffre **Amours** qui est **mes chiés,**	Love (who is my lord) allows	d	7	6 *Amours*: word 103
25	Que **Raison**, Droiture,	Reason, Equity,	b	6	3
	Douçour, Debonnaireté	Sweetness, Good Nature,	e	7	2
	Franchise, Grace et Pité	Openness, Grace and Pity	e	7	4
	N'ont pouoir à Cruauté,	to have no power against Cruelty	e	7	5
	Ensois regne et dure	Instead, there reigns continuously	b	6	4
30	En corps d'umblece paré	in a body adorned with humility	e	7	5
	Cuers qui est pleins de durté	a Heart which is completely hard	e	7	6
	Et de couverture,	and closed,	b	6	3
	Refus qui d'espoir osté	Refusal who has taken	e	7	5
	M'a la morriture,	the food of hope away from me,	b	6	4
35	Et Dangiers qui despité	and Resistance who has spurned me	e	7	4
	M'a sans cause et si grevé	without cause and has so injured me	e	7	7
	Qu'il m'a par desdaing mené	that he has led me, through disdain,	e	7	7
	A desconfiture,	to my ruin.	b	6	2/85

	Motetus				
1	Faus Samblant m'a deceü	False Seeming has deceived me	a	7	5
	Et tenu en esperance	and has held out the joyful hope	b	8	4
	De joie merci **avoir;**	of my obtaining favour.	c	7	4

MACHAUT'S MOTET 15   205

Table 10.1 Continued

	Motetus				
	Et je l'ay com fols creü	And I like a fool believed him,	a	7	7
5	Et mis toute ma fiancé	and put all the trust	b	8	5
	En li d'amoureus **vouloir**.	of my loving desire in him.	c	7	5/30
	Las! or m'a descongneü	Alas! now he has undeceived me,	a	7	5
	Quant de **moy** faire aligence	after having had the time and the	b	8	5
	Ha heü temps et **pooir**;	power to win my allegiance;	c	7	5
10	N'en riens n'a recongneü	In no way has he rewarded	a	7	6
	Ma dolour ne ma grevance,	my pain and my suffering,	b	8	5
	Eins m'a mis en **nonchaloir**.	rather he has treated me badly.	c	7	6/32

As already pointed out, triplum and motetus divide musically at the middle into two rhythmically identical arcs (breves 1–60 = 61–120), each of which encompasses two rhythmically identical tenor *taleae*. This structure perfectly accommodates the triplum text,
whose rhyme structure is suited only to a division at the middle, and is compatible with
the motetus text, which divides into quarters. It is also possible to interpret the triplum
and motetus as constituting four periods with deviation between breves 4 and 15.[10] Not
only are the opening rhythms of both triplum and motetus repeated at the beginnings of
the second and fourth tenor *taleae* (Ib, IIb, bars 31, 91) as well as the first and third (Ia, 1;
IIa, 61); in addition, at the second (Ib, bars 31–33) both triplum and motetus strikingly
maintain identical pitches for three breves' duration, so that bars 1–3 are, quite exceptionally, fully identical with bars 31–33, an added false-seeming, since not even rhythmic
identity is maintained between the fourth and fifteenth breves. The listener is thereby
deceived into expecting that the triplum and motetus are going to have not two but four
regular *taleae*, corresponding to the four of the tenor. The deceit is further signalled here
(at the second tenor *talea* Ib) by the triplum words *pour celer saigement*, and the motetus's
et je l'ay com fols creu. Indeed, all four tenor *taleae* are initiated with words of deceit in
the motetus, the voice of Faux Semblant: in addition to these words at *talea* 2 (Ib), *talea* 1
(Ia) starts with *deceu*, *talea* 3 (IIa) with *descongneu*, 4 (IIb) with *recongneu*. At *talea* 3 (IIa)
the beginning of the more concealed 'real' repeat, it is least conspicuous, indeed, 'wisely
concealed', and lasting only one breve. Thus, in the motetus, the two parallel halves of
the music open with the very close textual parallel 'Faux Semblant has deceived', 'he has
undeceived'. The 'deceitful' musical repetition occurred in the first half (we were deceived
at Ib); it is not maintained (hence undeceived, *descongneu*) at *talea* 3 (IIa, the true repeat),
to which the revelation to Jacob (tenor *faciem*) is also linked. At *talea* 4 (IIb, bar 91), the

---

[10] I now reserve the term *talea* for identity of upper-part rhythms, though I used it more freely in the
earlier publication of this chapter, as does Zayaruznaya, *Upper-Voice Structures*. See above n. 4, and
Ch. 12 n. 17.

second 'deceptive' repeat, Faux Semblant fails to reward (*n'a recongneu*); here, moreover, the triplum figure of the opening (*a aga*) appears a fifth lower (*d dcd*), changing places with the motetus as Jacob had with Esau, in disguise, a further false-seeming that abases itself in a downward transposition to the words *corps d'umblece*. This inverts a formal device of Machaut's lais, where the twelfth stanza climactically duplicates the first a fifth higher. The middles of the middles (the beginnings of *taleae* 2 and 4, bars 31 and 91) thus become nodes of deception or ambiguity.

In sense, too, the true middle of the piece is signalled by the self-conscious measuring of time and distance. 'Briefment morray dolereusement de dueil et d'ardure' brings us to the middle of the triplum, while the second half starts off by the author measuring his distance, 'Et tant sui plus eslongiés'.[11]

The four motetus groups end respectively with the words *avoir, voloir, pooir, nonchaloir*. Three out of these four words are shared in the *-oir* rhyme of the triplum (lines 1, 2, 4, 5): *pouoir, recevoir, avoir, voloir*; all these triplum words are heard within the first half of *talea* Ia, and are then heard, with the order of the pairs reversed, to end each of the four tenor *taleae*, thus underscoring, through the only shared rhymes between the texts, the rhythmic identity of the four musical endings. This could also be seen as applying a musical conceit to the verbal form.

The first five lines of the triplum form an acrostic: ADINA.[12] Adina, in Jewish tradition, is the mother of Rachel and Leah, and David Howlett reminded me that Jacob and Leah's youngest daughter was named Dinah (Genesis 30: 21), another Genesis reference relating to Jacob.[13] The first note of the triplum is *a*, sung to a word beginning with A; the phrase for the last A of Adina begins and ends on *a* and the whole five-line passage is set off by a rest after the first rhyme, *voloir*, perhaps confirming that the b-rhyme of line 6 belongs in structure, if not in sense, with what follows, as is more clearly the case after the corresponding line 24. All other major rests in the triplum follow the b-rhymes of lines 6, 10, 15 and 19 and fall correspondingly in the second half of the motet. So the acrostic lines are isolated; their somewhat special treatment might encourage belief that the acrostic is intentional rather than accidental. Concealment of various kinds may be signalled by the prominent long note given near the beginning to *obscure* (triplum, line 3; bars 7–9), as well as by the hiding of structural joins by musical and textual overlapping.

The final lines of the paired poems, in which the speaker bemoans his ruin (triplum) and bad treatment (motetus) are opposed to Jacob's wrestling with the angel that lead to his blessing and re-naming as Israel, after which he says 'I have seen the Lord face to face; and my soul is preserved' (Genesis 32: 30). Just as the ambiguities of the upper-voice texts are presented as two faces or facets of the same tenor foundation, so are they reconciled in disparity both musically, and with respect to textual form. This supports Brownlee's claim that his first opposition, between Amours and Faux Semblant, is indeed only apparent.

---

[11] One recalls Gurnemanz's midday exposition to Parsifal in the middle of Act 1: 'Zum Raum wird hier die Zeit'.

[12] Although the motet is full of betrayed faith, I hesitate to make too much of the acrostic FEDE that begins the motetus.

[13] Adina also has vowel rhyme with *anima*, the thing that is saved in the tenor's full phrase, though the tenor music stops short of the passage containing that word.

As to the second, 'true' opposition, that between 'the world of human seeming and the world of divine being', I suggest that the choice of Jacob's words for the tenor is less straightforward than 'divine being' implies. The biblical Jacob who utters the tenor words 'Vidi Dominum facie ad faciem, et salva facta est anima mea' is the musical and symbolic foundation of the motet. The tenor's *facie ad faciem*, face to face, advertises itself (to the initiated) as a two-faced seeing; the words follow Jacob's re-naming as Israel—two names. Jacob is yoked to its false seeming by his own earlier 'two-faced' deception of his father Isaac (by cheating his older twin brother Esau both of his birthright and of his father's blessing), as he was in turn deceived by Laban when he served seven years for Rachel and was then instead given her sister Leah. The first deception was promoted by his mother Rebekah, the second by her brother Laban, another sibling relationship in this complex of sibling pairs. Jacob's twinned relationship to deceit, as both a perpetrator and a victim, is implicit in the choice of his words; his two-faced history is now resolved in his face-to-face encounter with his God. The motet's startling alignment of the God of Jacob and the god of love is highlighted in the triplum text by the false-seeming pun on mischief, *meschies*, and my lord, *mes chies*. The tenor is here being recruited to underscore a double meaning, in both its biblical and liturgical setting; it opposes the god of love (who has deceived the lover) to the God of Jacob, and it parallels, by simultaneous presentation, the deceptions of which Jacob was perpetrator and victim with those of Amours and Faux Semblant. Faux Semblant is 'accepted into the army of the god of love'; the treacherous Jacob is accepted, renamed Israel, and sees his God after combat with the angel.

The opening triplum word, *Amours*, makes one other appearance in that text, in line 23. The twenty-fourth line is 'Sueffre Amours qui es mes chies' (with its critical pun on mischief and 'my lord', the god of love).[14] The key word *Amours* is here preceded by 'mischief' and followed by 'my lord', and is thus flanked by the two punned appearances of mischief in lines 23 and 24. (Machaut's Motet 10 also includes the line 'Amours qui est mes chies', and precedes *Amours* symmetrically with *meschies*: see Ch. 12.) The opening word *Amours* recurs as word 103, at the golden section of the triplum's 168 words; *Amours* is not only situated between the bad and good faces of the mischief pun, but functions as both the herald and the pivot of the entire triplum text to separate bad and good things in general. Line 24, in turn, directly precedes the musical golden section at bar 75, a turning-point that is preceded by bad things and followed by the list of seven virtues (in lines 25–27, and with the rhythmic recurrence).[15] That the golden section of triplum text by lines and words just anticipates the musical golden section gives structural weight to a turning-point of textual sense. The first-person motetus words 'moy faire aligence' span the mischief pun in the triplum, tying the motetus text to the music at this point; the golden section word itself is *moy*, the thirty-eighth of 62. The tenor word at this same point is, appropriately, *faciem*. The *je* of both upper parts is paralleled by the first person of the tenor, *Vidi*, in the voice of Jacob; he has seen the face of God,

---

[14] The 38 lines divide by golden section at 23.48 and 14.52. This line just precedes B74; the 120 breves of music divide by golden section at 74.16 (i.e. in B75) and 45.84.

[15] The seven virtues immediately following the musical golden section are headed by *raison*; Jeffrey Dean pointed out in conversation that this also meant a mathematical relation, from *ratio*, in which sense it is used in Boethius's *De institutione arithmetica*. This could therefore be another instance of a punning word of measurement made to coincide with a significant structural point.

has loved, deceived and been deceived. Brownlee shows that the *je* of the triplum has been moved by love while the *je* of the motetus has been deceived by Faux Semblant. The two 'contrasting self-presentations' are here made simultaneous, two-faced. Faux Semblant speaks in his own voice in the *Roman de la rose*; he is introduced into the poem by the god of love. We might add that Jacob in the tenor speaks in his own voice, setting up a simultaneous presentation of the *Dominus* he saw, in the tenor, with the god of love, 'Amours qui est mes chies', in the triplum. In the motetus Brownlee finds 'a contrastive self-presentation of the speaking subject as an unwitting victim of Faux Semblant, who has purposefully and successfully deceived him (by means of his lady's appearance) before openly revealing his deception'. The clothing of the lady deceives; the clothing of the music deceives. 'Faux Semblant's clothes and his words deceive qua signs.'[16] Faux Semblant wants to conceal his whereabouts. False-seeming is, after all, exactly what Jacob had earlier undertaken by means of clothing in deceiving their blind father Isaac and stealing Esau's birthright, even to the extent of changing his exterior by wearing Esau's clothes and feigning hairiness with the kid skins that were the byproduct of his mother Rebekah's fake venison.

The tenor not only opposes the divine being, represented by liturgical chant, to the human loving of the upper parts; it itself embodies many layers of duplicity. As well as being presented simultaneously, the music and text of tenor, triplum and motetus are in completely parallel symmetry, face to face. Of the two 'faces' in the tenor, one falls in each half of the motet. The two faces of the tenor are matched, feigned or avoided, and matches in turn are made, feigned or avoided with the upper parts in matters of metrical and musical structure. Many other promising aspects, such as phonic coordination of vowel and consonant sounds between the triplum and motetus, and the full extent of verbal reference between their texts, have not been explored here. This richly suggestive counterpoint of musical and textual structures and symbolism invites a parallel examination of other Machaut motets.[17]

---

[16] Brownlee, 'Machaut's Motet 15', 8.

[17] Since the original published version of this article in 1991, insightful work along these lines includes Boogaart, 'Love's Unstable Balance'; Boogaart, 'Encompassing Past and Present'; Boogaart, 'O series summe rata'; Machaut, *The Motets*, ed. Boogaart; Zayaruznaya, *The Monstrous New Art*; and Zayaruznaya, 'She has a Wheel'.

11

The 'Harmony' of the Machaut Mass

At least two studies of the 1990s affirmed the continuing and active reception of Machaut's Mass since its composition. Anne Walters Robertson demonstrated from their epitaph in Reims cathedral that Guillaume de Machaut and his brother Jean, both canons, had endowed a foundation for a Saturday Lady Mass that was to become a Requiem after their deaths.[1] Despite the unusual provision of a specifically polyphonic mass in such a bequest, supporting evidence comes from congruence between regional chant features and Machaut's cantus firmi, a reconstruction of Machaut's will, and a new transcription of the brass epitaph commemorating the brothers. Her essay and subsequent book provide a rich context that enhances the Mass's historical importance well beyond its significance as a purely musical survival. The other work specifically devoted to the Mass is Daniel Leech-Wilkinson's commentary and edition, which at last made it readily available to scholars and performers.[2] His publishers have allowed him to defend every editorial decision at length, a luxury to be envied by all who have been held by procrustean editorial policies in past decades to produce—and to read—dense and cryptic commentary. These two publications stand for different ways, neither opposed nor separable, of approaching a musical work of the past. One anchors the historical, liturgical and institutional context of the Mass's creation and early use, and the other scrutinises the musical text itself for evidence of Machaut's compositional process and intentions. Both in principle take account of all evidence that might bear on the fullest understanding of the work in its historical context. Both are valuable and complementary, without exhausting all possibilities for furthering such understanding.

In the spirit of dialogue envisaged for the volume in which this essay was first published, I here set out a view different from Leech-Wilkinson's, a view not so much of the unknowable mysteries of Machaut's creative process as of their observable consequences, reciprocally diagnosed against underlying assumptions. I discuss here the texted body of the Gloria, with a brief glance at the Credo, but excluding the Amens. The similarities between these two movements have perhaps been stressed more than the differences; they are superficially alike in their more-or-less simultaneous style and texting, the tenor–contratenor interludes and sustained-note passages, the four-part texture spiced with *Pulcinella*-like 'wrong notes' and austere 'parallel-leading-note' cadences. The melismatic Amens differ from the texted bodies of these movements in range and disposition of voices. Although observations about the body of the Gloria

---

This essay was first published in Leach (ed.), *Machaut's Music* (2003). This revised version is published with the permission of the Boydell Press. For a thoughtful critical evaluation of the present proposals, see Maw, 'Machaut and the "Critical" Phase', 264–67.

[1] Robertson, 'The Mass of Guillaume de Machaut', and subsequently, Robertson, *Guillaume de Machaut*, 272, suggesting that the brothers made their endowment and probably their wills in the early 1360s.

[2] Leech-Wilkinson, *Machaut's Mass*. Machaut studies would be much the poorer without Lawrence Earp's indispensable *vade mecum* (*Guillaume de Machaut: A Guide*), which draws together magisterially a century of accumulated scholarship. In this case, see 540, 581, 344–46.

210 MACHAUT

need adaptation for the different procedure and disposition of the Credo, similar general conclusions stand for both movements.[3] A starting point for the present investigation was this challenge, laid down by Leech-Wilkinson as a central hypothesis:

> If the four voices of the Gloria and Credo have consistently independent functions, if, in other words, the Tenor behaves as a referential line for Triplum, Motetus and Contratenor, each making correct counterpoint with it (if not necessarily with one another), if the Contratenor behaves as a conventional contratenor, making counterpoint against the tenor, and so on; then it may be said that the parts could have been written successively. At least, there is no absolute necessity for them to have been composed together.
>
> But in the Gloria and Credo the four voices do not consistently have these functions. Dissonances (most significantly, fourths) occur in every combination of upper and lower voices.[4]

Although Leech-Wilkinson's goal is to reconstruct compositional procedure rather than to disqualify historically informed analysis, he here categorically denies that these movements can be understood in terms of fourteenth-century counterpoint principles. While accepting the principle of a cantus–tenor framework, he repudiates what he sees as its implications for chronological or conceptual priority.[5] But the problem lies not with the cantus–tenor model, rather with too simple a view of what that model implies. While temporal priority unquestionably applies for some pieces that survive in different states, it is by no means a necessary assumption for what, for want of a better term, is called 'successive composition'. Aristotle in *Categories*, chapters 12 and 13, deals with concepts of non-temporal priority and non-temporal simultaneity, models that fit such musical situations rather well.[6] Kevin Moll describes as conceptually or referentially pre-eminent such a qualitative priority that is not necessarily chronological.[7] Whatever we call it, it no more demeans the musicianship or creative capacity of a composer to isolate layered structures than it does to parse the grammar of a literary work. 'Counterpoint is successive in principle, though a composer could conceive more than two parts together in such a way that they still reflected an underlying "successive" dyadic grammar',[8] and:

> It is not a corollary of dyadic procedure that it limits what can be heard or conceived in the mind. The order of conception is not confined by the grammar. When a native speaker utters a complex and grammatically correct sentence, he surely did not start by thinking of it as a simple subject-verb-object sentence, only then expanding it, even though the sentence can be parsed in an order other than that of its devising. Internalised grammar

---

[3] Moll, 'Structural Determinants', 345–46 argues that there could indeed be a chronological separation between the Gloria and Credo.

[4] Leech-Wilkinson, *Machaut's Mass*, 56–57.

[5] Leech-Wilkinson, 'Machaut's *Rose, lis*', 11. Bent, 'Grammar', develops at greater length some of the principles applied here, and might usefully be read in conjunction with the present chapter.

[6] I am grateful to Myles Burnyeat for locating this passage.

[7] Moll, 'Voice Function', and 'Texture and Counterpoint'.

[8] Bent, *Counterpoint*, 56.

THE 'HARMONY' OF THE MACHAUT MASS 211

permits correct articulation of a complex thought, whether in words or music, without violating or necessarily consciously invoking that grammar. As with speech, we need not assume that musical ideas occurred to a composer in grammatical order. While 'successive' composition should not necessarily be taken to mean that the piece was composed in that order (although sometimes it almost certainly was), it does mean that the piece was conceived in such a way that the grammatical skeleton was not violated. Exceptions and anomalies can then be isolated, will take on greater interest, and lead to extended formulations of the rules; grammars have irregular verbs or idioms and tolerate exceptions, and advanced accounts of them take account of such experience in usage. 'Successive' in music should refer to the procedure uncovered by analysis and inherent in its grammar, and not necessarily to the order of working or compositional process of a native-speaking composer. To talk in terms of triadic harmony no more means that we cannot cope with the five components of a dominant ninth (or the seven or eight of a dominant thirteenth), than dyadic counterpoint means that medieval composers could not conceive sonorities of three, four, five parts as extensions of the underlying dyadic grammar. A dyadic basis doesn't confine composers to hearing only two parts at a time any more than triadic harmony means that its practitioners cannot hear polychords.[9]

Gilbert Reaney set out in 1953 an eminently sensible account of fourteenth-century 'harmony', the term he used as a modern equivalent to medieval understandings of 'counterpoint'.[10] Although I would now adjust his emphases and make qualifications, this article importantly delineates some of the background expectations against which Machaut's usage is defined. Leech-Wilkinson is severe in judging that Reaney's article 'still deserves admiration for the courage with which it sets out to support a widely held but hopelessly illogical view', when his own account fails to define an alternative musical procedure.[11] He reported Richard Crocker as an 'early challenge' to Reaney's position, apparently without recognising that Crocker staunchly championed the same contrapuntally based dyadic procedures:

> If . . . the two-part framework was not linear counterpoint in the first place, then the third voice may not be either. Here we must avoid the false dichotomy between linear counterpoint and (triadic) harmony. . . . If the first step is the composition of a progression of two-note chords, then the third voice is added not as a third melody but as an enrichment of those chords.[12]

---

[9] Bent, 'Grammar', 33. Fuller, 'Contrapunctus Theory', 117–18, strongly criticises my approach. She is not quite correct to say that I advocate approaching these repertories *solely* through dyadic counterpoint; I argue that to understand it as the background grammar to composed music is a necessary prerequisite to analysis, from which there may be many deviations and extensions in practice. See also Ch. 29.

[10] Reaney, 'Fourteenth-Century Harmony', 129 n. 1. Hughes, 'Some Notes', supplies further evidence for the contratenor being added to a prior discant–tenor duet. 'Successive' composition is also presumed by Aldrich, 'An Approach'. The suggestion that composers' capacities are thus limited does sometimes occur in the older literature, such as Ulrich and Pisk, *A History of Music*, 79. See also Bent, 'Notes on the Contratenor', and Westerhaus, 'A Lexicon of Contratenor Behaviour'.

[11] Leech-Wilkinson, 'Machaut's *Rose, lis*', 23 n. 2, and Reaney, 'Fourteenth-Century Harmony'. Leech-Wilkinson, *The Modern Invention of Medieval Music*, especially chs. 2 and 3, make it clear how his view of medieval 'harmony' has been shaped by the bright, sharp, *a cappella* sonorities, with simultaneous texting, cultivated by Christopher Page's Gothic Voices.

[12] Crocker, 'Discant, Counterpoint, and Harmony', 12.

212 MACHAUT

This is surely the view that Leech-Wilkinson rejects. Crocker went on to unpick another false dichotomy, namely the assumption that 'if the renaissance bass was "non-functional", then everything over it must be linear'; 'the medieval sense of function resides . . . in the progression of concords, especially in the progression sixth-to-octave'.[13] Medieval counterpoint was not linear and it was not triadic. If functional dyadic formulas, when fleshed out, sound to us a bit like the functions of triadic harmony, it is because the latter eventually evolved from them, but later, and into something with a quite different basis of explanation. *Pace* Leech-Wilkinson, Crocker is an unabashed 'historicist': 'For it is the medieval view that we want to understand. We know how we conceive it. What we want to know is how they conceived it. To do this, we must take hold of their theory books in both hands and read. . . . The discant authors from the 13th to the 16th centuries provide a clear, consistent, and pertinent account of medieval—and Renaissance—polyphony.'[14]

The reasonable quest for appropriate methods of analysis, methods that are necessarily historically informed, is sometimes confused with another related but impossible enterprise, to which no one to my knowledge now subscribes: a restriction of analysis to contemporary resources only, in the belief that those resources suffice to provide the only acceptable reading. The latter straw-man position is demolished at the outset of Leech-Wilkinson's pioneering and provocative analysis of *Rose, lis* (R10):

> In attempting to talk about medieval music we face, among several ideologically imposed restrictions, two which are particularly effective in inhibiting attempts to come to grips with anything more than the surface of the music. The first is the view that the only acceptable reading (or 'interpretation') of a work of music is that current at the time it was produced. The second is the belief that polyphony was constructed successively, one part at a time, and that, as a result, vertical relationships within the music are of very much less significance than is the integrity of horizontal lines.[15]

His concerns about 'successive' composition have been addressed above. For present purposes 'interpretation' is not at issue, except at the level of establishing text. Even Putnam Aldrich, to whom a restrictive position has been ascribed, quite rightly advocated greater use of chronologically appropriate tools to the extent available, though his proposals for analysis by mode and solmisation now appear incomplete. He rightly warned against the view that 'since they sound like chords to us today they can and should be treated as such in analysis'.[16] As I have written:

> To prefer contemporaneous terms and concepts where available is not by any means to exclude useful modern extensions of them. Early theorists have sometimes been set aside as inconsistent with practice because they have been misread. Increasingly precise understanding of how relevant theoretical prescriptions are qualified, or their application confined, brings apparently contradictory theory back into play.[17]

---

[13] Ibid., 14.
[14] Ibid., 2.
[15] Leech-Wilkinson, 'Rose, lis Revisited', 9.
[16] Aldrich, 'An Approach'.
[17] Bent, *Counterpoint*, 3.

THE 'HARMONY' OF THE MACHAUT MASS   213

Kevin Moll makes a similar point: 'the descriptive tools of the period are more adequate to the task of analysis than has often been supposed, and . . . modern criticism is better served by extending them, wherever possible, than by ignoring or replacing them',[18] a view which has been well articulated by Roger Bowers with respect to Leech-Wilkinson's hypothesis about the genesis of Machaut's Gloria, in an otherwise rightly favourable review of his edition:

> The question is that of the identification of a vocabulary of analytical concepts and terms that is appropriate to the music, in its inalienable and indissoluble context in time and place. One school of analytical thought would contend that in so far as the objective of analysis is the revelation of transcendental internal musical processes and procedures created by, and perceptible by human intuition irrespective of superficial considerations of mere time and place, then any analytical languages and vocabularies will do, notwithstanding the boundaries of the contexts they were first coined to serve. The contrary view would state that any resort to non-contemporary and anachronistic vocabulary and concepts is inevitably a debilitating and vitiating solecism, requiring that analysis of fourteenth-century music be undertaken only in terms of contemporary values, objectives, concepts and vocabulary. .
>
> . . . before we can analyse music of the fourteenth and fifteenth centuries in any depth and with any validity, we have to devise an appropriate vocabulary from contemporary writing and from perusal of the music itself. The gratuitous and facile borrowing from terminologies devised for later periods and alien styles, uncritically applied to features of earlier music which superficially bear a beguiling but fortuitous and ultimately deceptive similarity, fails to meet legitimate needs.[19]

These statements are diametrically opposed to this: 'To suppose that medieval composers were to a large extent incapable of controlling their material is but one of a series of absurd consequences of this theory; and it has continued in currency amongst scholars only because it arises out of the writings of medieval theorists',[20] and to Peter Schubert's further conclusion that an analysis might not merely go beyond what can be historically supported but may legitimately contradict such evidence: 'Given the limits of Renaissance treatises, one way to "explain" large- and small-scale pitch organization is through analogy to tonal music. At worst such analyses are inconsistent, inefficient or unpersuasive, but never *a priori* wrong. Even if they contradict what historical evidence we have, they may be intellectually viable.'[21]

Leech-Wilkinson now claims that

> medieval studies in music . . . are still largely devoted to a belief in the possibility of recovering the past as it was. Indeed, if anything, attitudes have been hardening recently. I am thinking particularly of Margaret Bent's recent article which speaks of 'valid' and 'invalid' approaches to analysis in a way that clearly shows that for her there are moral

---

[18] Moll, 'Voice Function', 26–27.
[19] Review by Roger Bowers, *M&L* 74 (1993), 54–59.
[20] Leech-Wilkinson, 'Machaut's *Rose, lis*', 10.
[21] Schubert, 'Authentic Analysis', 17.

obligations on analysts to work 'historically'—'pre-conditions' as she calls them. From this point of view, abiding by medieval modes of musical thought is an essential qualification for scholarship in the field.[22]

This statement involves a fair degree of misreading. In particular, it conflates methodological questions with moral prescriptions, whereas the kind of validity and invalidity at issue is clearly epistemological in nature, not moral, and concerns matters critical, historical and scholarly. Ironically, the objection to moralising comes from Leech-Wilkinson, who himself introduces morality as an issue in taking exception to the appeal to validity and invalidity simply because *he* finds it somehow morally inappropriate to invoke these categories.

No one believes, certainly not I, that the past can be recovered 'wie es eigentlich gewesen'. The quest to which I and others subscribe reopens an important line of investigation that has been marginalised in some recent writing. As with ancient literature and drama, we cannot recover the sounds of medieval music, but we can recover much of its sense as a text. The word 'hardening' might be better applied to the manifest and repressive hostility towards any scholarly investigation which dares to pursue historical concerns about musical works and repertories rather than, or even alongside, the sensuous and sounding aspects of modern realisations. I identify not valid or invalid analyses, but rather validity in 'etic' pre-analytical assumptions relevant for these repertories, such as are widely assumed for other and later musics, in uncovering the grammar and sense of musical and other languages whose literatures have come to us likewise only in writing. Our frankly modern performance of that music is a different, vital, but fundamentally related issue; it stands only to gain from deeper understanding of music's language-like features, alongside the many other kinds of skill and knowledge that inform our re-creation of old music today. Leech-Wilkinson makes his choice, a different one from the earlier *Rose, lis* article, and different again from his concerns in *Machaut's Mass*:

> whatever kind of moral obligation you might feel we should have to the past, the fact remains that Machaut is dead and has been for over 600 years; we cannot owe him anything anymore. The only issue of any interest is what the music means to us. One can confine that meaning within a rigorous attempt at a historically constrained view if one so chooses; but one can choose not to, and there is no way to show that one choice is right and the other wrong.[23]

Far be it from us to judge each other's choices. My identification of analytical preconditions was directed to understanding the internal workings of Machaut's musical *language* in terms as close as possible to his own, given that the *sounds* of his performances are irrecoverable. Those preconditions are not just a matter of piety,

---

[22] Leech-Wilkinson, '*Rose, lis* Revisited', 248–49. The article of mine referred to is Bent, 'Grammar'. It should be clear by now that this is a serious misrepresentation of my position. Similarly, in his *The Modern Invention of Medieval Music*, 208–9, he misunderstands my view of counterpoint as the grammar of medieval polyphony as 'rules which composers follow'.

[23] '*Rose, lis* Revisited', 249.

certainly not of defining a debt, but of wanting to understand what this musical work had to say to us, being maximally open to its unexpected and foreign content, just as we may strive to understand the language of Beowulf or Chaucer and fully register its difference from modern English. Until Leech-Wilkinson, 'Rose, lis Revisited', I had assumed that this was his goal too, even if we agreed to differ about just what that language was and how it might be defined.[24] What this music means to us as scholars is what we imagine it meant to them, as far as we can ascertain that, through empathetic extrapolation from our research-based knowledge, in full awareness that the results are provisional and incomplete. But Leech-Wilkinson's new concern with 'not "what is right?" but rather "what is interesting?" ' (p. 249) sets a radically different agenda. To decline to distinguish sense from nonsense, to deny music's grammar-like features, removes any basis for critical editing, critical listening or analysis, and critical judgement.

There are many different ways of approaching 'the music itself'. Instead of considering aspects of the work that transcend individual performances, Leech-Wilkinson, 'Rose, lis Revisited', analyses one quite widely available commercial recording and a live performance less widely available. The work as documented in its notated forms has features and implications that remain constant irrespective of changing performance preferences, and may be over- or under-interpreted in any one performance. Analysis of modern performance may yield a perfectly interesting and indeed valid approach, within current interest in the reception of medieval music in the past two centuries, but it is a different enterprise, neither to be confused with text-based endeavours nor to replace them, and certainly not the only valid approach. To hear this music as a succession of chords composed from the bottom up carries assumptions about bass function imported from a later period, assumptions which demonstrably do not apply here. It imposes alien hierarchies while neglecting to recognise others that have long been accepted and can be clearly determined. All educated listening is in some way hierarchical, but some hierarchies are more appropriate than others to the music in question. In the seventeenth century, the governing relationship may be the treble–bass polarity of a continuo work, for a Josquin motet it may be the combination of a sustained cantus firmus in the middle of the texture with paired duets, while the primary scaffolding of a Du Fay song will be the underlying dyadic counterpoint of its discant–tenor relationship, with or without contratenor. None of these hierarchies necessarily implies temporal priority, though most do not exclude it; none endangers the composer's imaginative status.

Machaut's Gloria

The texted portion of the Gloria, transcribed as Ex. 11.1, may serve as a test case for the enterprise of bringing fourteenth-century music and fourteenth-century theory into mutual dialogue.[25] It is an inescapable fact that Machaut's Mass does contain dissonances

[24] See, for example, Leech-Wilkinson and Palmer, *Guillaume de Machaut: Le Livre Dou Voir Dit*, whose editorial introduction is largely concerned to anchor the letters of the poem in historical reality.

[25] Voice names are given in **MachautA**, but with Tenor and Contratenor reversed. In **Ferrell(Vg)** only the Amen of the Gloria is labelled, correctly.

Ex. 11.1 Gloria of Machaut's mass, excluding Amen

Ex. 11.1 Continued

218 MACHAUT

Ex. 11.1 Continued

Ex. 11.1 Continued

forbidden by the rules of counterpoint, fourths, sevenths and ninths. Reaney rightly observed that some of the ninths are superimposed fifths resulting from two separate relationships with the tenor. He perhaps goes too far in implying that Machaut nodded, or that the right hand did not know what the left was doing. Rather than discounting medieval theory just because it seems not to provide for these dissonances, the attempt to isolate and account for the extra-regular features is where the real interest starts. In Leech-Wilkinson's accounts of Machaut's careful calculation and purposeful intent with respect to many factors in his compositional process, there is rather less attempt than in Reaney's 1953 article to define the harmonic language itself that purportedly underlies Machaut's chordal conception, and in terms of which dissonance and voice leading are evaluated:

> the way in which contrapuntal lines are distributed amongst the voice-parts in the Gloria and Credo indicates that Machaut began with an approximate mental image of the whole texture, and then separated its constituent pitches into lines, finalizing details (especially melodic decorations) as he went. Several criteria governed the allocation of pitches to voice-parts, including (a) sonority, especially the desire to avoid the same voice disposition in repeated chords, (b) the need to nudge singers into producing the desired solmizations however unconventional the harmonic results, and (c) the traditional virtue of linear continuity. The part-writing that results from this technique is often far from conventional, but so is the harmony. The voices have no fixed functions. Structural consonances (sixth to octave progressions, for example) and dissonances (fourths and sevenths especially) are to be found in all possible voice pairings. There is a constant migration of contrapuntal lines between the notated parts, with the result that progressions may be resolved in voices other than those in which they began.

and

> other late works of Machaut were not composed in a similarly 'successive' manner, since if they were one would expect their lower voices to be more chordal and less linear in character. This of course reverses common assumptions about the results of composing parts successively or simultaneously.[26]

He claims that this was how Machaut conceived the 'harmony'; that, in the simultaneously texted Gloria and Credo, there is evidence of an underlying harmonic conception that was only later separated out into four parts of undifferentiated function. That is one version of the creation story, but it is not the only possibility. Despite paying some lip service to the incontrovertible dyadic contrapuntal basis of medieval polyphony ('Machaut's *Rose, lis*', 11), he has waged a sustained campaign against it:

> [Related works in the *Voir Dit*] help us to understand how he conceived a polyphonic song, imagining a whole and then working out the details into parts, and this has implications for the way we hear and study and perform this music. If its vertical

---

[26] Leech-Wilkinson, '*Le Voir Dit*', 56–57; 49. See also Leach, 'Machaut's Balades', 58–65.

THE 'HARMONY' OF THE MACHAUT MASS   221

coherence is fundamental (because it is the first aspect which Machaut designed) and if its horizontal laying-out is artificial (a matter of convenience and convention) then in our performances we should be aiming for coherence of sound, not contrasting instrumental colours, and in our listening and our analyses we should be focusing on harmony and on harmonic direction, rather than fruitlessly searching for integrity in the written voice-parts. *La Messe de Nostre Dame* and *Le Voir Dit* show us that the written parts have no such integrity: they are a set of instructions for performance, not a representation of the musical argument.[27]

Clearly, anyone who has more than a passing acquaintance with Machaut's artfulness as a composer will wish to rescue him from the trumped-up charge of being capable of hearing only two parts at a time. Leech-Wilkinson's demonstration that a harmonic conception preceded distribution into parts seems to have convinced at least Earp but, as Ernst Apfel noted in 1961, the texted parts of the Gloria and Credo do show clear evidence of the 'successive' procedures that Leech-Wilkinson claims are absent.[28]

Leech-Wilkinson claims that the Gloria is loosely based on chant. While it is possible that this chant was in Machaut's head and shaped some of the lines, so many cadences wilfully depart from it that its status as a compositional given cannot be deemed proven. It is not clear that we or they were meant to recognise it, but the only issue that affects the present argument is that the chant (if any) is not in the contratenor part that Leech-Wilkinson alleges is the foundation of the harmony.[29] He finds no distinction of function between pairs of parts, asserting that they result from distributing a harmonic conception into separate parts, and that this corresponds to the way Machaut conceived the texture. This is a bold claim: not only is there no medieval support for such a view of musical pedagogy, either from theorists or from internal evidence within the music, but the claim is contrary to what we can and do know about the basic syntax of medieval composition.

Reductive analysis assists grammatical parsing; the piece is reduced to two parts at a time, and to note-against-note successions. Such reduction does not necessarily reconstruct the compositional process. A first stage is to discount the contratenor, not because it is musically inessential or insignificant, but because the contrapuntal syntax can be most simply grasped without it, as the verbal grammar of a sentence may be stripped of adjectives that nevertheless complete its sense. The tenor–contratenor relationship can be evaluated separately. A second stage is to consider each of the remaining or upper parts alone with the tenor. In a florid piece, a further stage of reduction would be to identify essential and ornamental notes in the added voice, but this stage hardly needs to be considered in the largely note-against-note movement of Machaut's Gloria and Credo.

[27] Leech-Wilkinson, '*Le Voir Dit*', 64.

[28] Earp, review of Leech-Wilkinson, *Machaut's Mass*, in *JAMS* 46 (1993), 295–305; Apfel, 'Über den vierstimmigen Satz', translated as 'Four-Voice Composition in the Fourteenth and Fifteenth Centuries', in Moll, *Counterpoint and Compositional Process*, 257. See also Bent, 'Grammar', 47–48. Leech-Wilkinson correctly reports (*Machaut's Mass*, 131) that **MachautA** erroneously reverses the labels for contratenor and tenor for the Gloria only, but without acknowledging that the correct labels can be diagnosed from voice functions.

[29] This was what Besseler claimed for pieces including Du Fay's *Helas ma dame*, in Besseler, *Bourdon und Fauxbourdon*, 41, ex. 9; Bent, 'Grammar', 40–42.

Analysis

In the analysis that follows I use modern terms (such as appoggiatura and passing note) where there seems to be no medieval term for concepts that observably extend the rudiments of medieval counterpoint teaching. Conversely, medieval terms need to be used with some care where their modern cognates have different connotations. It is to be hoped that future work will propose improvements on these default solutions.

In Machaut's Gloria, the relationship between tenor and triplum is largely conventional in terms of fourteenth-century note-against-note dyadic counterpoint, allowing for some ornamental turns, passing notes and appoggiaturas, and with the exception of a few fourths and parallels. There are no sevenths or ninths. Dissonant accented appoggiaturas occur, for example, on the first beats of bars 26 and 27 and the second breve beats (at the half-bar) of bars 6 and 33. There are just five simultaneous fourths between tenor and triplum, all in passing or auxiliary positions approached and quitted conjunctly, at bars 10, 32, 76, 81 and 86. All are weak-beat neighbour-note coincidences (i.e. on the second or fourth crotchet—original semibreve—of the bar), which, like those appoggiaturas classified by Leech-Wilkinson as inessential, are not structural. The parallel fifths will be discussed below. Of other dissonances, only one (at b. 101) is so striking as to be a possible candidate for either an extension of the rules or for emendation of the tenor g to f (or even, less likely, to a). This is the only dissonance of its kind: the manuscripts could well present a reading that would have seemed obviously in error to those who had a native understanding of Machaut's contrapuntal practice. In addition, it makes a fourth with the contratenor, though that is not a primary disqualification.

Next to be considered is the discant–tenor relationship between motetus and tenor. Except for the very first sonority, a simultaneous fourth to which we shall return, the counterpoint is again entirely regular. There are only five other fourths, all likewise in passing or auxiliary positions approached and quitted by step, at bars 40, 42, 76, 79 and 91. There are some dissonant accented appoggiaturas (for example at b. 23) and several weak-beat passing dissonances (for example at b. 41). The parallel fifths, again, will be discussed below. The sonority on the first beat of bar 32 is unusual in having a sixth between tenor and motetus that does not resolve to an octave. Could that motetus d be intended as c? Even more unusual is the dissonance at bar 39.1, which is not approached conjunctly. The e might be emended to d; otherwise it must be treated as a dissonant appoggiatura resolving upwards, and not approached by step. However, we have come to know and maybe to like this dissonance as part of the spicy flavour of this Mass. Those who hear these movements as assimilated to tonal chordal progressions, unaware of their internal hierarchies, and without distinguishing the motetus–tenor relationship from the general level of undifferentiated dissonance, may not appreciate just how the unique dissonance stands out at bar 39.1.

The fourth in bar 1 stands out even more acutely from the normative counterpoint that follows. Why is it followed here by a double bar (representing its separation in the manuscripts, from what follows, by single bar lines through the staff)? Given the concentration of apparent exceptions in such places, it could be that sustained-note passages and the untexted interludes may have been open to more or different contrapuntal licence than normal successions. Did the tenor perhaps originally have d, adjusted for

THE 'HARMONY' OF THE MACHAUT MASS   223

the sake of sonority after the contratenor was in place, or was this chord—but only this chord—tacked on at the beginning, and indeed conceived as a whole sonority? Leech-Wilkinson's hypothesis of chords-awaiting-arrangement also posits the notion of subsequent adjustments, but with such adjustment starting from the chordal conception as a whole, undifferentiated as to voice functions. For me, the starting point for any adjustment necessitated by composition is the layers of contrapuntal dyads that are successive at least in principle and pre-eminence, if not in order of conception. For him, subsequent arrangement can modify what already exists to the point that 'simultaneous or successive composition loses all significance', whereas I would maintain that the underlying dyadic grammar is violated only in particular and exceptional circumstances, here perhaps only in bar 1. The motetus, on the whole, is placed purposefully in spaces left by the triplum, and these two parts move in parallel while the tenor moves largely in contrary motion to them both. The tenor, motetus and triplum at least must have been written in knowledge or anticipation of each other.

Once ornamental and weak-beat passing notes have been recognised, other contrapuntal dissonances between the upper parts themselves (excepting fourths) are minimal. This relationship seems to have been managed with some care. The exceptional dissonances at bars 39 and 101 have already been considered as possible candidates for emendation. Although the short c/d dissonance between the triplum and motetus on the last beat of 88 could similarly have been avoided with a motetus a instead of c, it might be regarded as a cadential licence in approaching the following long note. Otherwise the relationships are completely consonant, except for the fourths mentioned above. The triplum and tenor throughout the Gloria and Credo make near-perfect discant–tenor counterpoint, indeed, each of the two upper parts makes almost completely accountable dyadic counterpoint with the tenor (allowing for some fourths, appoggiaturas and parallels) following principles clearly stated in medieval treatises, which can be extended and qualified by observation. To superimpose these duets, both upper voices relating to the tenor, yields a smooth, self-contained three-part texture that has close counterparts in several quite unremarkable three-part fourteenth-century mass movements in simultaneous style, with the tenor at the bottom: what Alejandro Planchart would have called a 'mouse-brown' piece.

The Role of the Contratenor

It is the contratenor that gives this movement its special harmonic flavour and seems to set the Machaut Mass apart. Whereas most contratenors in fourteenth-century music make their cadences a fifth above the tenor, the contratenor of the Gloria is unusual (and different from the Credo) in having a very narrow range and staying close to the tenor, often cadencing with it from a third to a unison, giving a thick sound at the bottom of the texture. The closest comparand is probably the Credo 'Bonbarde' (**Apt** 40; CMM 29, 55; PMFC 23B, 51) by Perrinet (Perneth), a four-part movement whose contratenor is often dissonant with the upper parts. This contratenor differs from Machaut's in being more often above the tenor, thus making it harder to imagine that it forms a compound functional 'bass' with the tenor, such as Leech-Wilkinson claims for Machaut's contratenor. The layered dissonance treatment and hierarchy of voices of this movement are discussed in exemplary fashion by Reinhard Strohm.[30] The three-part Credo by Tailhandier (**Apt** 44; CMM 29, 51; PMFC 23B, 54) has a detachable contratenor that is mostly above the tenor, especially at cadences, where it makes a fifth with it. Three-part homophonic movements comparable to the upper parts of Machaut's Gloria include the Kyrie of the Barcelona Mass (CMM 29, 19; PMFC 1), the Graneti Kyrie *Summe clementissime* (**Apt** 35; CMM 29, 12; PMFC 23A, 22), the Susay Gloria (**Apt** 37; CMM 29, 35; PMFC 23A, 32), all plainer in texture than Machaut, the Gloria **Ivrea** 63 (CMM 29, 37; PMFC 23A, 38), with more ornamental embellishment of the basic structure, and untexted interludes in one or two parts. Machaut's untexted bridge passages for tenor and contratenor might argue in favour of a four-voice (but not therefore chordal) conception, as in the (evidently earlier) Tournai mass. Although two-breve interludes, for the tenor only, punctuate Ciconia's motets, such solo passages are rather rare in earlier mass settings. Single-breve examples occur in Machaut's *Voir Dit* ballades, B32, B33 and B34. A texture like that of the Machaut Gloria invites us to listen in layers, from the inside out, just as we need to adopt appropriate listening habits for a fugue subject, a harmonised chorale, a cantus-firmus mass, to discern serial procedures, or *Haupt-* and *Nebenstimmen*. The core of Machaut's music is audibly and clearly present in these duos and their superimposed combinations, and partly implies the full texture. It is the heart of the musical substance, even though the composer must have had in mind, specifically or generally, what other parts would be doing.

Anomalies and Irregularities

The few emendations tentatively suggested here result not from an attempt to impose norms, but rather from isolating and evaluating exceptional usage that may either be retained as such, or normalised. A hierarchical approach, like grammatical parsing, seeks to make sense of the received text against the background of an appropriate understanding, and ends up with a smaller number of specific anomalies, and indeed different ones, than would be produced by an undifferentiated evaluation of dissonance against less specific criteria. The irregularities are evaluated in the first instance according to medieval counterpoint theory and in the second instance by supplementary norms derived from the composition itself. In other words, historically appropriate analysis, as understood here, has greater explanatory power than approaches that ignore contrapuntal features peculiar to individual repertories.

Contrary motion is conspicuously cultivated between the tenor and each of the upper parts, but there are some exceptions, occurring at a few definable points in the texture that invite unwritten extensions to insufficient statements by contemporary theorists. The apparent conflict between theoretical prohibitions of parallel perfect intervals and their plentiful occurrence in fourteenth-century music has sometimes been used to discredit the relevance of what little the theorists do say. But as I have pointed out (in 'Grammar'), a ready explanation has escaped general notice, namely, that theorists confine the prohibition to 'in counterpoint': the rules of counterpoint are formulated for two parts at a time and forbid parallel perfect intervals between the

---

[30] Strohm, *The Rise*, 26–35; see also Moll, 'Texture and Counterpoint', fig. 5.8.

THE 'HARMONY' OF THE MACHAUT MASS   225

voices of a contrapuntal pair, and in this case between each upper part and the tenor. Parallel perfect intervals between the two upper parts may involve ligatures (as at bb. 3–4), or they may form part of an ornamental figure as at bars 6–7; they are not strictly speaking forbidden, as only their respective relationships with the tenor are in the strict sense contrapuntal. There is patently no objection in practice at this date to parallels between the 'added' voices of notionally successive pairs, in this case the triplum and motetus. Parallels between triplum and motetus are thus almost a corroboration of underlying successive grammar.[31] A distinction needs to be maintained between the status of parallels in different contexts; as with fourths, the 'normal' or acceptable ones may be classified before unexpected or inexplicable ones are isolated for further consideration (possibly for emendation, or for an extension of 'exceptional' usage).

Parallels between the upper parts are unproblematic, not because the composer could not hear them but because, not being 'in counterpoint' (as defined above), they are not ungrammatical. Parallels between the tenor and another voice, however, would be 'in counterpoint'; the tenor participates in only very few parallels, all of which will extend our analytical understanding of exceptional usage, as they seem to occur in unusual (and by inference extenuating) circumstances. Where there are octaves with the tenor at bars 14–15 and 61–62, the parallel spans two phrases, in each case *following* a perfect-interval cadential arrival on a long. We may infer from this, as a provisional extension to the rules, at least in Machaut's usage, that a parallel interval with the tenor is somehow annulled by the occurrence of the cadential articulation. At bars 42–43, 45–46, 51–52, 92–93 the parallels occur in transition to or from a long, or within a long-note passage, suggesting that these areas too were liable to exemption. Parallel octaves occur fleetingly between all three parts, tenor and motetus, tenor and discantus, at bars 52–53, perhaps a solecism, but affecting a melisma with ligatures, another area where exceptions tend to be concentrated. At bars 68 and 78–79 the parallels could be considered as arising from accented passing notes. Only the progression at bar 13 seems to occur outside those areas that have been proposed as extensions of the rules; here the parallel fifths between triplum and tenor fall between a weak beat and the next main beat. Maybe only the main breve beats were bound by the prohibition, and some licence was accepted within them?[32] Although there is a general avoidance of parallels with the tenor, to find the exceptions thus concentrated in definable places suggests that long notes and interludes, and junctions with them, may have been construed less strictly, as if these situations were not bound by the rule. Rather than being too ready to dismiss theorists as worthless because they failed to make all these provisions themselves, our first task is to reconstruct those things that theorists did not spell out because they took them for granted. Observations such as those made here may enable us gradually to build a collection of provisional extensions and complements to what the theorists say.

Nothing corroborates the primacy of the upper trio more clearly than the distinction between the grammatical role of the tenor and the role of the lowest voice, in this case mostly the contratenor. This corresponds to Moll's distinction between the referential voice and the referential pitch respectively.[33] First to be observed is that the

---

[31] Kevin Moll pointed out to me that such parallels are symptomatic of Apfel's 'multiple two-voice counterpoint', as are seconds and unisons (even consecutive ones) between the upper parts.

[32] Reaney, 'Fourteenth-Century Harmony', 132, explains some parallels in a similar way.

[33] Moll, 'Voice Function', 53–57, explains his distinction between the referential voice and the referential pitch.

226 MACHAUT

tenor–contratenor relationship is on the whole unexceptional, apart from some striking and sustained fourths. We have seen Machaut's use of mostly off-beat auxiliary or passing fourths between members of the other discant–tenor duets, but the fourths here are both qualitatively and quantitatively different. Between tenor and contratenor they are necessarily at the bottom of the texture, often strong and sustained. There are tenor–contratenor fourths of a breve or longer at bars 8, 15, 27 (all on *e*). The fourth at bar 49 could be corrected (on the first beat, to *a*, following manuscript **MachautE**, thus avoiding not only the dissonance with the *f* and *a* of the upper parts in Leech-Wilkinson's reading, but also the fourth between the lower parts, despite the resulting parallel fifths with the tenor; or even to *f* (despite the parallel with the triplum). The contratenor fourths at bars 17 and 78 are slight. We have seen above that bar 101 may call for emendation on other grounds.

Andrew Hughes ('Some Notes') cites the fifteenth-century theorist Anonymous XI as evidence that the contratenor was normally composed after the discant and tenor; he adduces theoretical support for its character as a voice added to a grammatically complete core, even if its presence was musically anticipated by the composer. But in Machaut's case, as in some other fourteenth-century works, the contratenor must be following different (or at least differently weighted) criteria from those that govern the tenor's relationship with the other parts. If we learn to hear tenor–discant relationships as central, we must necessarily hear the contratenor as adding a different or even bifocal dimension. If we are to remove the benefit of doubt from a phenomenon not yet fully understood, Machaut's competence will be called into question. Conversely, if we assume that everything in the received version makes sense, we have removed all criteria for detecting basic transmission errors. Clearly, neither of these extremes will do; more work is needed. Simultaneous fourths are irregular in counterpoint, but Machaut's handling of fourths invites us to classify some usages to which he subscribed. We clearly cannot claim, for the Gloria and Credo, that fourths between the lowest parts were outside his vocabulary, but if the contratenor was indeed the foundation of the 'harmony', by what harmonic system are such chords with fourths at the bottom imagined? Durationally and metrically strong parallel motion is greatly increased overall by the addition of the lowest voice, and falls between the contratenor and the upper parts. Often by going in parallel octaves with the triplum, the contratenor also makes parallel fifths with the motetus. There are very few tenor–contratenor parallels, and these occur in bars with other anomalies at bars 10, 86, 88, and in 49 as emended, and in three places following interludes: bars 20, 66, 99.

Most of the dissonances other than fourths (i.e. sevenths and ninths) occur between the contratenor and one of the two upper parts. Apart from readily explainable appoggiaturas, dissonances are sounded at bars 10, 13, 49, 50, 54, 68, 72, 78, 81, 88, 100. All of these except bar 49 sound a third below the tenor while an upper part sounds a fifth above, or a fifth below the tenor while an upper part sounds a third above, or a fifth below the tenor while an upper part sounds a fifth above. We might call them bifocal superimpositions. The tenor is the regulator of all the parts individually and in coordination, and needs to be heard from the inside out or even bi-dimensionally. Only the dissonance at bar 49 does not fit this model; here, the contratenor invites emendation of *g* to *a* in accordance with **MachautE**, as discussed already.

THE 'HARMONY' OF THE MACHAUT MASS   227

A similar examination of the Credo shows that it and the Gloria, so often linked to-gether and alike in superficial sound, differ in some striking ways, although many of the same observations and all the same criteria apply. The Gloria's contratenor lies closer to the tenor, making most of its cadences as a third contracting to a unison, rather than by thirds to fifths as in the Credo. The Gloria therefore has closer spacing at the bottom of the texture, more thirds and indeed fourths between the lowest parts, and more chords with sevenths; the sevenths are a consequence of superimposing thirds and fourths. The Credo is written in a different way. Its contratenor is far more normal by comparison with the relationship of other fourteenth-century contratenors to their tenors, with a wider range, remaining mostly higher than the tenor and having very few of the fourths that make this part so problematic in the Gloria. Only the motetus at bar 119 (and briefly at b. 78) has a problematic relationship with the tenor, like the first note of the Gloria. The Credo is written with two equal top voices, as opposed to the higher triplum and lower motetus of the Gloria. In the Credo, the upper voices share range and roles much as they do in a fourteenth-century Italian motet (Ch. 26).

A different but related issue in the texted movements of Machaut's Mass concerns *cadentia* or cadence, which, as defined by Jacobus, is no more than and no less than the two-part progression of an imperfect to a perfect interval, articulated with a semitone progression above or below.[34] Many current performances treat all long notes in the Gloria and Credo, the chords held for a full long, as if they were points of closure. But there are clear distinctions between them, which in some cases become all the clearer if the cadence (or *cadentia*) is considered without the contratenor. Some of them indeed conclude a phrase, with an arrival on a perfect interval. But others sustain an imperfect sonority, usually doubly imperfect, that demands resolution. Sometimes this demand is satisfied quickly, sometimes it is delayed and sometimes it is even subverted or tempo-rarily denied before an eventual resolution. These distinctions are indicated on Ex. 11.1 and explained in the commentary.

Not one of the ten or so recordings of the Gloria which I had to hand makes any distinction in performance between such different qualities of long-note sonorities; all are treated as closural, at least in the short term, as if they were respectively the perfect and imperfect cadences of a later era. This suggests that the modern performance tra-dition, however varied by individuals or however parasitic on other performances, has not even considered distinguishing these functions. In turn, the ears of a generation of listeners have been mistrained to hear imperfect sonorities as legitimate points of rest.

To examine the music in this way reveals a hierarchy of relationships and of disso-nance, of contrapuntal rules based on dyadic successions and their extensions, and of yet-to-be-explained contratenor behaviour. Only four possible emendations of pitch are suggested here, and those are to restore sense inferred from terms suggested by the music; normative impositions would be much more invasive and would necessitate second-guessing Machaut and implying that either he or the scribes were highly in-competent. Some dissonance can be seen provisionally in our terms (for want of theirs) as passing or auxiliary, rather than pertaining to the primary contrapuntal relation-ship. Some of these extra-regular moments occur in specifically delimited places within

---

[34] *Speculum musicae*, IV.5, 122–23. For the authority of this term as a possible alternative to the now widely used 'directed progression', see Chs. 1 and 29.

228 MACHAUT

the movement (for example at junctions with interludes, or in long-note passages), permitting the inference of 'special licence' for such passages and an extension to (not a contradiction of) the theorists' rules. Some dissonance can be explained as bifocal collisions between parts that individually go with the tenor. We can learn to hear these as independent but tolerable, indeed exciting, as the superimposition of apparently incompatible cadence formulas may be in later music. They need to be heard from the inside out rather than from the bottom up, inexorably logical, but moving in different planes or dimensions. The view presented here is the diametrical opposite of Leech-Wilkinson's belief that Machaut conceived in chords and teased out the parts later; but he stops short of defining the harmonic language against which we should judge Machaut's criteria of consonance and competence. The present study offers one step towards such a definition.

Out of what first seemed a jungle of arbitrary dissonance, and still seems so even after Leech-Wilkinson's explanation, a diagnostic examination of voice functions has enabled an entire part to be considered as the cause of irregularities, and a few single notes to be identified as candidates for emendation. Whether it makes the Mass a better piece is another matter. It is not the composer's creative process that is under examination here, but the musical rudiments common to the training and experience of composers and singers. What gives these dyadic procedures and dissonances interest is not the trivial fact of their use, but precisely the ways in which they are extended, distributed, controlled, or turned aside.

Music Commentary

The musical text printed in Ex. 11.1 largely follows the readings adopted by Leech-Wilkinson, except for *ficta* choices.[35] The accidentals proposed here are closer to those in the edition by Lucy E. Cross (Cross, *Messe de Nostre Dame*) than to Leech-Wilkinson's. Cross's explanations are more solmisation-driven than mine, and though differently rationalised, there is significant common ground. I believe that inflections are determined by counterpoint, not by solmisation, and that solmisation is a *post facto* pedagogic tool. Boxed notes are discussed in the text. At bars 32, 39, 49 and 101 they mark notes to be considered for emendation.

Accidentals suggested above the staff have been marked primarily to inflect imperfect-to-perfect progressions between each upper part and the tenor. Accidentals in parentheses are judged optional—most involve balancing the choice to inflect a cadence against singing an augmented or other awkward melodic interval, usually when this takes place within a group of short notes. More accidentals of this kind could be considered: ♯ signs could be applied to *g* in the tenor–contratenor interludes at 19, 47, 65 and 98. Contratenor accidentals take account primarily of the relationship with the tenor, secondarily to accommodate to the upper parts. But as stated above, this is not as straightforward a discant–tenor relationship as the tenor has with the upper parts.

Double bar lines through single staves represent manuscript bar lines. Cadential arrivals onto long notes are followed in this transcription by a single bar line through

---

[35] See *Machaut's Mass*, 131–36, for his report.

THE 'HARMONY' OF THE MACHAUT MASS   229

the upper three staves after the perfect interval (as at 4, 16, 18, 29, 56, 75, 87, 97 and 104). In some cases (14, 60, 64 and 71) these arrivals are undercut or weakened by the contratenor. That in bars 60–61 is weakened anyway by the difficulty of arranging a semitonal approach. Long notes so marked are arrivals on imperfect sonorities; they are not completed *cadentie* and require resolution, the long notes notwithstanding. These are either resolved directly, satisfying the most obvious expectation (solid horizontal arrow), or after a delay, withholding immediate resolution, or indirectly after an interruption, detour or denial (dotted arrow for indirect, delayed or diverted resolution).[36] Different degrees of resolution are not distinguished in Ex. 11.1 but are roughly classified here:

- Direct resolution occurs at 12–13 (*Laudamus te—Benedicimus*), 34–35 (*celestis—deus*), 38–39 (*omnipotens—domine*), 74–75 (*no-stram*), 77–78 (*sedes—ad*), 102–3 (*Gloria—dei*).
- Resolution is still straightforward but slightly delayed at 54–55 (*filius—patris*) and 69–70 (*mundi—suscipe*).
- The progression is somewhat irregular at 51–52 (*dei—filius*), which reaches its true cadence at 56.
- Resolution is even more strongly denied or even subverted, by following the *mi* with a presumed *fa* (or a sharp with a natural), before an eventual arrival, at 24–25 (*tibi—propter*), arriving at 29; 80–81 (*patris—miserere*) arriving at 83, and 92–93 (*altissimus || Jesu*) arriving at 97.

The last two resolve the same unusual sonority in the same somewhat irregular way, in both cases with parallel octaves. The notion of arousing expectations and then playing with, or delaying, their satisfaction, can be amply illustrated from analytical literature more generally; it is not the fact of such strategies which is singled out here, but the particular musical norms within which they operate.[37]

---

[36] For a more permissive view of the status of these imperfect sonorities, see Bain, 'Theorizing the Cadence'.
[37] A classic study, centred on the introduction and prompt denial of *e* natural in Schubert's *Moment musical* in A flat, Op. 94 No. 6, is Cone, 'Schubert's Promissory Note'.

12

Machaut's Motet 10 and its Interconnections

‧Kevin Brownlee and I gave a joint presentation on M10 (*Hareu! hareu! le feu/ Helas! ou sera pris confors/Obediens usque ad mortem*) in Oxford in 1991 and again in 2001. His contribution addressed not only the verbal intertextuality within the motet texts, but also its external literary context in the *Roman de la Rose* and the *Ovide moralisé*. It was published in a *Festschrift* kindly presented to me in 2005, where he announced my contribution as forthcoming; see Brownlee, 'Fire, Desire, Duration, Death'. Mine, lightly edited for this volume, was finally published in 2018.[1]

Meanwhile, Jacques Boogaart has independently completed a number of highly perceptive studies of the motets. Some of the present material, drafted long ago, overlaps with his observations, which I have tried to signal where appropriate; for M10 see Machaut, *The Motets*, ed. Boogaart, the bibliography there cited, and for an excellent edition in modern notation with manuscript variants. I am grateful to Jacques Boogaart, Jared Hartt and Sean Curran for valuable comments on an earlier draft. Brown, '*Flos/Celsa*', makes connections between that motet and M10.

Choice of Tenor

The musical foundation of a motet is a tenor that underpins the structure with a melody usually taken from chant. The treatise usually attributed to Egidius de Morino famously prescribes that the tenor should be taken from an antiphon, responsory or other chant, and that the words should concord with the *materia* about which the motet is to be made.[2] While the tenor is the musical foundation, it is not the only building block; the author at least implies that the verbal content of the upper parts has already been decided in outline, whether or not the texts, or indeed any musical features, have been worked out in detail.[3] This substance (*materia*) precedes and determines the choice of tenor. In nearly all of Machaut's motets (and in many by other composers) the words and chant excerpt of the tenor are not those of the beginning of the chant, often pointing up a deliberate choice to isolate a word or phrase especially suited to the—perhaps already planned—upper-part texts.[4]

---

[1] 'Machaut's Motet 10 and its Interconnections', in Hartt (ed.), *A Critical Companion to Medieval Motets*, 301–19. Reused here with permission from Boydell.

[2] See Ch. 1 for the proposal that the treatise revert to anonymous status; also Ch. 16. Leech-Wilkinson, *Compositional Techniques*, 1, 18–20, provided a revised version of this text, now in a fuller version in Zayaruznaya, *Upper-Voice Structures*, appendix, 110–16.

[3] See Ch. 4 for the argument that in *Tribum/Quoniam* the verbal 'citations' are as much building blocks as is the tenor chosen to go with them. See also Zayaruznaya, *Upper-Voice Structures*, 6, 46–47.

[4] Especially in M1, 2, 3, 4, 5, 6, 7, 8, 9, 10, 12, 14, 17, 19, 21, 22, 23. M15 is the only one to use a chant beginning, *Vidi Dominum*. See Clark, '*Concordare cum materia*'. Sean Curran (pers. com.) reminds me that tenors

---

The Motet in the Late Middle Ages. Margaret Bent, Oxford University Press. © Oxford University Press 2023.
DOI: 10.1093/so/9780190063771.003.0013

232 MACHAUT

This has often made it harder (and sometimes impossible) to identify the source chant, especially if it is unlabelled.

But it is not only in the disposition of the tenor as a skeleton or ground-plan for the motet that the tenor shapes its musical material. Machaut clearly also chose his chant excerpt for its musical qualities, important among them its potential to serve as the grammatical foundation for counterpoint; not only would the composer assess the number of tenor notes for its divisibility into *talea* units, but also its cadencing potential at tenor rests or *talea* divisions, especially at the end, at least in the three-part motets.[5] Nearly all of Machaut's three-part motets end with a stepwise descent in the tenor, which serves the final cadence. The exceptions are the three whose tenors are secular melodies (M11, M16 and M20), and whose final discanting ascents would once have formed counterpoint against the songs' own stepwise descending tenors, if any.[6]

The four four-part motets are also exceptions to final stepwise tenor descent; they all share the tenor role with an *essential* contratenor (and would thus have been candidates for composition with the aid of a solus tenor).[7] M5 and M23 are the only Machaut motets with (interlocking) coloration in tenor and contratenor.[8] The tenor of M21 does make a stepwise cadence, but in M22 and M23 the final stepwise descents are made not by the tenor, but by the contrapuntally essential contratenor.[9]

The extent to which tenor melodic material is integrated into the upper parts of *ars nova* motets has been under-recognised; Machaut's habitual use of that material must have influenced him in the choice of a tenor to suit the material of the texts. The dark textual content of M9, for example, is reflected in the conjunct and serpentine contour of its tenor, and by the use of motives derived from the tenor in the upper parts.[10] Conversely, for the uncertainties of *Fortune* in M8, Machaut chose a tenor with intervallic leaps which are echoed in the upper parts and reinforced with uncertainly swaying syncopations (see Ch. 14). Such relationships between music and text will be

---

of early 13th-c. motets were normally based on a single word from within a chant; the discant sections from which motets often derive are built on melismas which are usually embedded deep in a chant's structure.

[5] Hartt, 'Tonal and Structural Implications', also addresses these questions. See Ch. 10 for more on significant 30s.

[6] On the song tenors, see now Clark, 'Machaut's Motets on Secular Songs'.

[7] Essential, in that it underpins otherwise unsupported fourths. See Bent, 'Some Factors', updated in Bent, *Counterpoint*, 38–46, and Bent, 'Notes on the Contratenor'.

[8] See Ch. 22 for a special use of interlocking coloration in paired lower parts, and other instances there cited.

[9] The lower parts of M5 are extremely problematic, with many dissonances and unsupported fourths. See Machaut, *The Motets*, ed. Boogaart. I would suggest emending the worst such solecism, the first coloured tenor note (b. 9 and corresponding positions) from *a* to *bb*, as it appears in **MachautC**, **Ferrell(Vg)**, **MachautB** and **MachautE**, though in this *color* statement only. Although the tenor ends with a stepwise descent, it does so non-cadentially, and ahead of a final irregular cadence in the contratenor. See Boogaart, 'Encompassing Past and Present', 56–72 (also 23–26), for extensive discussion of this motet, and *passim* for the extent of Machaut's quotations, especially from trouvère songs. Dunstaple makes an unusual choice in his most famous motet, the four-part *Veni sancte spiritus/Veni creator*, choosing a tenor excerpt that ends with a falling fifth, producing a quite exceptional cadence at that time.

[10] See Ch. 9 on Motet 9 and the associated music examples. The serpentine character of the tenor of M9 and the relation of the tenor to upper-part motives in M4 has also been pointed out in Boogaart, 'Encompassing Past and Present', 9–10 and 22–23. See Ch. 14 below.

examined below as they apply to M10; some connections with other motets will also be noted.

If Machaut had decided in advance to include hockets, as he often does in isorhythmic passages that clearly mark *talea* joins (M9), or in a final diminution section (M10), and if he had further decided to adopt the discipline of not breaking words by rests (as in the hockets of M18 and M9), the texts had to be planned with monosyllables in positions which made this possible.[11]

Machaut's chant tenors are mostly plucked from a liturgical and hence usually also a biblical context which they implicitly carry with them, all the more strongly if better known and easily identified. Friedrich Ludwig identified the tenor melody of M10 as taken from the middle of the Maundy Thursday fifth-mode Gradual *Christus factus est pro nobis* **obediens usque ad mortem**, *mortem autem crucis* (Philippians 2: 8–9: 'Obedient unto death').[12] Jacques Boogaart reminds me that this chant concludes all three *Tenebrae* services, *mortem autem crucis* being an extension used on Good Friday. He proposes, rather, an identical antiphon from the same day that is associated with the liturgical action of extinguishing the fire of the candles.[13] Death and loyalty (= obedience?) are primary ingredients of this motet, which is transcribed as ⏵ Example 12.1.[14] The texts are transcribed in Table 12.1.[15]

Table 12.1 Verses lined up with *taleae* in Machaut, Motet 10

Talea		Triplum	Rhyme	Motetus	Rhyme
T I	1	Hareu! hareu! *le feu, le feu, le feu*	a	1 Helas! où sera pris confors	a
	2	*D'ardant desir*, qu'ainc si *ardant* ne fu,	a		
	3	Qu'en mon cuer ha espris et soustenu	a	2 Pour moy qui ne vail nès que *mors*?	a
	4	*Amours*, et s'a la joie retenu	a		
	5	*D'espoir* qui doit attemprer celle *ardure*.	b	3 Quant riens garentir ne me puet	b
	6	Las! se le *feu* qui ensement l'art dure,	b		

(continued)

[11] Unsignalled changes of mensuration occur in the motetus of M4 (Ch. 14), and by a different disposition within the modus in the second *color* of M6, whose tenor is written out only once, with repeat sign. Its concluding rest places the first breve of the second *color* as an 'upbeat' to the perfect modus, thus requiring different breves to be altered, or not, in the restatement. To a modern reader, this looks like a re-rhythmicisation of the *color*, but it is in fact derived from homographic notation. Boogaart, 'Encompassing Past and Present', 25, ingeniously construes this as overlapping telescoped *taleae*, removing the need to accept the fourth 'fragmentary' *talea* of Schrade's edition. The changes of mensuration in Rondeau 10 (*Rose lis*) are also unsignalled.

[12] Ludwig, *Machaut*, 2: *60 and 3: 40 (144). Variant melodies from appropriate liturgical sources are assembled in Clark, 'Concordare cum materia', 194 and 244.

[13] *Christus factus est pro nobis obediens usque ad mortem*. Fer. V in Coena Domini; Fer. VI in Parasceve; Sabbato Sancto; Invent. S. Crucis; Exalt. S. Crucis. *CAO* III, nr. 1792; IV, nr. 7983, *Cantus* ID 830399. Boogaart, 'O series summe rata', 242.

[14] The motet as it appears in **MachautC** is provided as figure 8.6 in Haines and Udell, 'Motets, Manuscript Culture'. The **Ferrell(Vg)** version is published in Earp, *Ferrell-Vogüé*.

[15] Italicised here are words associated with love, fire, burning, hope, despair, loyalty, death, desire (*Amours, ardure/feu, espoir/desespoir, loyauté, mors, desir*). Note how the *-oir* rhymes also highlight *espoir* and *desespoir* in non-rhyming positions. Brownlee, 'Fire, Desire, Duration, Death', 81–82, pointed out the unique triple statement of *le feu* in tr line 1, and the emphatic repetition of *ardant* in line 2.

Table 12.1 Continued

Talea		Triplum	Rhyme		Motetus	Rhyme
T II	7	Mes cuers sera tous bruis et estains,	c	4	Fors ma dame chiere qui vuet	b
	8	Qui de ce *feu* est ja nercis et tains,	c			
	9	Pour ce qu'il est fins, *loyaus* et certains;	c	5	Qu'en *desespoir muire*, sans plus,	c
	10	Si que *j'espoir* que deviés y ert, ains	c			
	11	Que bonne *Amour* de merci l'asseüre	b	6	Pour ce que je *l'aim* plus que nuls,	c
	12	Par la vertu *d'esperance* seüre.	b			
T III	13	Car pour li seul, qui endure mal maint,	d	7	Et Souvenir pour enasprir	d
	14	Pitié deffaut, où toute biauté maint;	d			
	15	Durtés y regne et Dangiers y remaint,	d	8	*L'ardour* de mon triste *desir*	d
	16	Desdains y vit et *Loyautés* s'i faint	d			
	17	Et *Amours* n'a de li ne de moy cure.	b	9	Me moustre adès sa grant bonté	e
	18	Joie le het, ma dame li est dure,	b			
T i	19	Et, pour croistre mes dolereus meschiés,	e	10	Et sa fine vraie biauté	e
	20	Met dedens moy *Amours*, qui est mes chiés,	e	11	Qui doublement me fait *ardoir*.	f
T ii	21	Un *desespoir* qui si mal entechiés	e	12	Einsi sans cuer et *sans espoir*,	f
	22	Est que tous biens ha de moy esrachiés,	e	13	Ne puis pas vivre longuement,	g
T iii	23	Et en tous cas mon corps si desnature	b	14	N'en *feu* cuers humeins nullement	g
	24	Qu'il me convient *morir* malgré Nature.	b	15	Ne puet longue durée avoir.	f

Tenor: Obediens usque ad mortem

Triplum: Help! Help! The fire, the fire, the fire of burning desire, which has never before been so burning, which Love has in my heart ignited and maintained, and thus has taken away the joy of Hope which should temper this burning heat. Alas! if the fire which consumes it completely continues!

Then my heart will be entirely burned up and extinguished; my heart, which is already blackened and charred by this fire, because it is pure, loyal and faithful; so that I expect that it will be dead before good Love assures it of Mercy through the power of reliable Hope.

Because Pity fails only for my heart, which suffers many pains, [Pity] in whom all Beauty dwells; Harshness rules there and Refusal there remains, Disdain lives there, and Loyalty grows weak; and Love does not care for my heart or for me; Joy hates it; my Lady is harsh towards it.

And, to increase my painful sufferings, Love, who is my commander, places within me a despair which is so ill disposed that it has pillaged all my goods from me; and in every case it so de-natures my body that I must die in spite of Nature.

Motetus: Alas! where will comfort be found for me, who am worth no more than if I were dead? When nothing can protect me except my dear Lady who wants me to die in despair, nothing more, because I love her more than anyone.

And Memory—in order to stir up the burning of my sad desire—shows me continually her [= my Lady's] great goodness and her refined true beauty, which makes me burn twice as strongly.

Thus, without heart and without hope, I cannot live for long, nor can a human heart survive for long in fire.[16]

Tenor: Obedient unto death.

Tenor Disposition

Machaut's tenor chant excerpts range in length from a *color* of 10 notes (M14) to 48 (M23). M15 has 40 notes (in a single *color*); M10 with 30 is close behind, but this is doubled by *color* repetition. Its 30-note chant segment begins and ends on *f*, and has the rather narrow compass of a 6th up to *d*. Example 12.2 numbers the chant notes, and shows how they are grouped in six rhythmically identical paired *taleae* or *ordines* each of five notes as Ia, Ib; IIa, IIb; IIIa, IIIb into three (10-note) double *taleae*, each of which corresponds to a period of the upper parts, as laid out in Example 12.2.[17] It is surely not accidental that 30 notes from a Holy Week chant suggest the 30 pieces of silver by which Christ was betrayed 'usque ad mortem' (even unto death).[18]

Ex. 12.2 The tenor of Motet 10

Melodically, this tenor is not as rich in symmetries as some others.[19] But segments Ia and IIIb are close to mirroring each other, and segments IIa and IIb are so nearly identical as to have caused the omission of IIb (in the first *color* only) by haplography in **MachautB** and **MachautE**. Each five-note *talea* (*ordo*) is palindromic: ▪ ▪ ▪ ▪ ▪, followed by a B rest. In the diminution section this becomes ♦ ▪ ▪ ▪ ♦. This palindromic rhythm appears with inverted values as ♦ ♩ ♩ ♩ ♦ (Ex. 12.3a and 12.3b), as a dominant rhythm in the upper parts.

---

[16] Translation by Kevin Brownlee (2005, 88–89), revised incorporating suggestions from Leofranc Holford-Strevens (pers. com., 2001) and Jacques Boogaart (pers. com., 2016).

[17] The following partially overlaps with what was reported in Ch. 2. This feature is what Reichert, 'Das Verhältnis', 202, called a *Großtalea*. Boogaart, 'O series summe rata', 107, refers to it as a 'supertalea', a term now adopted by Zayaruznaya; see Zayaruznaya, *The Monstrous New Art*, 81, and more recently Zayaruznaya, *Upper-Voice Structures*, calls them blocks. 'Double *talea*' works well where a pair of identical tenor *taleae* serve a single upper-voice *talea*, as adopted by Clark, '*Super omnes speciosa*'. Where the rhythmic correspondence is only partial, I prefer the term 'period', which avoids the connotations of rhythmic identity carried by *talea*, though the partial isorhythm in such periods serves as a powerful articulation. In M10, each pair of tenor *taleae* corresponds to a period of the upper parts, as also in M15. This also happens in M8, which has three short (four-note) *taleae*, more like 13th-c. *ordines*, in the time of one upper-voice *talea*, and four of these short *taleae* per *color*.

[18] Although M10 is not about deceit it is certainly about what leads to death. M15, however, is about deceit; I suggested that its 30-breve *taleae* might also have resonances of Judas's betrayal; see Ch. 10, and Arlt, 'Triginta denariis'.

[19] As demonstrated in Ch. 9 on Motet 9.

Ex. 12.3 Prominent motives in Motet 10

In *color* 1, each double *talea* occupies 24 breves, in the diminution section, *color* 2, 12 breves, where the same melody is written out at the next note level down. Both *colores* are internally isorhythmic but, because of the reduction, not with each other. The second substitutes ■ for ■, ♦ for ■, *resulting* in a 2:1 reduction (*per semi*, as sometimes specified for other pieces), as counted out in the minim values of the upper parts. But although the note values often appear to be straightforwardly halved, the operation of duple and/or triple divisions at different mensural levels can make it misleading to describe an asymmetrical *process* as a 2:1 reduction; but when only duple mensurations are affected, the diminution can be so described, and often was by contemporaries. The new values here are in fact derived by a light but unsignalled mensural transformation which changes the status of the notes. In the first *color*, the longs are perfect, with imperfect breves and major prolation, and they coincide with the upper-part breves. In the diminution section, the perfect longs become perfect breves, but with major semibreves (which thus do not directly mirror the corresponding imperfect breves of *color* 1). This also happens commonly in fourteenth-century motets by Machaut and others, as in the reduced sections of M18 and M2.[20] The now-perfect breves of the accelerated tenor undercut the clear duple tempus of the continuing imperfect breves in the upper parts, setting up an audible tension. The upper parts are in imperfect modus (i.e. with imperfect longs), while the first *color* of the tenor is in perfect modus, syncopated: the opening breve is not an upbeat but a 'downbeat' syncopating agent, made up to a perfection with the breve and breve rest that end each short *talea*.[21] Within each *color* the syncopations wrap around to the next *talea* ■ ɪ || ■, but the displacement remains. A literal reading of the tenor at the final cadence results in a dissonant delay, for which an alternative solution is suggested in ⏵ Example 12.1. Anomalous endings occur in several motets, including five by Machaut; these are discussed in Chapter 1.

Machaut plays with the mensural status of this opening: the opening melody and rhythm of the triplum (Ex. 12.3a, *c c b c a*) are echoed at the beginning of double *taleae* 2 and 3 (respectively a step lower, Ex. 12.3b, *b b a b g* at B26 and at the opening pitch at B50), but they are delayed by a breve, emphatically recapitulating the opening motive

---

[20] For M2, see Ch. 13. Up to a point, the diminution in M10 fits the brief prescription of Muris in the *Libellus*: 'Tertio nota, quod quando tenor est de modo perfecto et tempore imperfecto, diminutio etiam fit directe per medium, sicut pro longa valente tres breves ponitur brevis valens tres semibreves.' (Third, note that when the tenor is in perfect modus and imperfect tempus, diminution is also made by halving directly, so that for a long worth three breves is placed a breve worth three semibreves.) *Ars practica mensurabilis*, ed. Berktold, 76–77. Although Muris has allowed for substitution at all levels (including minim for semibreve), he does not address the fact that in cases such as this the same relationships of twos and threes do not apply obliquely at the next level down (prolation); see Bent, 'The Myth', 207–8.

[21] This offsetting has since been described by Desmond, *Music and the moderni*, 232–34. It is one of the resources often exploited in motets, also occurring in *Vos/Gratissima* (see Ch. 8) and elsewhere.

over the first tenor long rather than the initial breve that syncopates it, creating a playful ambiguity as to where the *talea* starts, and whether that breve might after all be an upbeat. Thus, short passages of upper-voice isorhythm, even where present, are not always aligned.[22] The first full statement of the opening triplum motive is followed by the second in displaced isorhythm (B26), which in turn is in aligned identity (pitch and rhythm) with the third (B50). An expectation is set up at the beginning, and then the same rhythm, also with similar melody, signals the beginnings of the new *taleae*, but a breve later. As here, oblique or displaced rhythmic correspondences create subtle asymmetries; this displacement pretends to challenge the modus status of the tenor notes by making the status of the first note ambiguous (as to whether it is an upbeat to the perfect-modus tenor or a syncopating agent). Such passages are far from simplistic views of isorhythm that applaud mechanical and regular repetition as if they embodied the mature perfection of the motet.[23]

Motives Derived from the Tenor Integrated into Upper Voices

The extent to which the tenor generates the melodic material of the upper parts varies between different motets; but this little-explored use of tenor material, in addition to the tenor's well-known symbolic and structural contributions, provides a musical counterpart to the perhaps more obvious semantic textual relationship between tenor and upper parts, weaving the sacred melody into the non-liturgical musical fabric in parallel to the simultaneous presentation of related sacred and secular texts.[24]

There is a textual relationship between the 'death' and 'obedience' of the tenor (*Obediens usque ad mortem*) and the upper parts (see Table 12.1 above), notably in *mortem*: *mors–muire–morir*, and *obediens*: *loyaus–Loyautés*, though such relationships are perhaps less abundant in M10 than in some other motets (for instance, M7, M9, M15). Musically, however, the chosen but pre-existent pitches of the tenor and its compositionally determined rhythms are pervasive in the upper parts of M10.

I have mentioned the inverse derivation from the tenor of the palindromic rhythm ♦ ♦♦♦ ♦ (Ex. 12.3a), the opening triplum motive. Its frequent occurrences are always prominently placed, at significant points on *c*, nearly always with the same melodic shape, a falling third at the end. The motive is sometimes shortened to the complementary forms ♦ ♦♦♦ (Ex. 12.3c) or ♦♦♦ ♦ (Ex. 12.3d), but in all cases the three minims (which occur twenty-four times) always have the same melodic shape (Ex. 12.3e).[25] These are derived (see the boxed notes in Ex. 12.2 above) from tenor notes 11–14 *cbca*, 24–27 *agaf*, descending a third; tenor notes 8–11 *dcdc*, descending a step. Tenor notes 14–17, *agab*, rising at the end, recur in tr B79, B85, B103, mo B88. The first box covers a fifth note: see Example 12.3 *g* (and *f*, transposed).

[22] In M17, a brief long-note isorhythmic passage in the motetus anticipates the subsequent *talea* joins by a breve with a similar displacement.

[23] In M7, three tenor *taleae* are imposed on two *colores* both in the first and the diminution sections. The second and third *taleae* in the first section are isorhythmically displaced by a breve from the opening statement, as in M10.

[24] For other instances see M9 (Ch. 9), M8 (Ch. 14), and the *Fauvel* motets *Tribum/Quoniam* and *Aman/Heu*: see Chs. 4 and 5.

[25] These motives are also set out by Boogaart, 'O series summe rata', 682.

238 MACHAUT

The three minims of these figures mostly take a single syllable in *color* 1, except where they mark the double *talea* joins with syllabic setting at B22, B46, B70; in *color* 2, due to the more condensed text setting, more of these minims are syllabic. The duple-time alternations of the complementary rhythms (Exx. 12.3c and 12.3d: ♦ ♩♩♩ and ♩♩♩ ♦), subsets of the larger group, coincide with imperfect breve groups throughout. The consequences of this for the perfect breve groups of the second *color* were noted above.

Most of these melodic motives also occur with the rhythm ♦♩ ♦♩. Melodic derivation from the chant is ubiquitous, though some characteristic intervals in the chant are not used, notably the rising fourth *f–b♭* (unless one counts the rising fourth *c–f* in mo B5–B7).[26] However, the motetus descent to its lowest notes in B7–B11 emphasises the progression *f b♭ a*, and although with a descending fifth—*f* is heard in the tenor at this point—strongly recalls the *f b♭ a* of the tenor notes 22–24.

The motive *c dcd* occurs both in the tenor (notes 7–10) and very conspicuously in the triplum at B35 around the middle of the first section. The first imitative appearance of ♩♩♩ ♦♩ appears in the motetus on *a* and, imitating it, in the triplum on *d*, B34–B35: Examples 12.3f and 12.3g. This figure is indeed a Machaut cliché, in rhythm and melodic shape, but what singles it out in this motet are its particular placements and derivation from the tenor pitches: see the first boxed group in Example 12.2 above. The tenor notes 8–10, *dcd*, give the same minim figure at mo B8, tr B35 (as *d c d*), mo B100, notes 11–13, *cbc* (*a*), at tr B1, B22, B50, B80, B97, B98 (each beginning on *c*), notes 24–26, *aga* (*f*), at mo B34, tr B46, mo B64, tr B70, mo B76, tr B91 (each beginning on *a*). The figure also occurs on *ede* (mo B3, B40, tr B103), *b a b* (tr B26), *gfg* (tr B79, mo B80, tr B85, mo B88), and in other rhythms.

The tenor-note progression *cbc* or *aga* followed by a falling third is a frequent feature of the upper parts: see mo B64, tr B70, and elsewhere, transposed to *dcd b* at tr B35. ♩♩♩ ♦, *cbca* (Ex. 12.3d), appears somewhere in each *talea*, nearly always at the beginning:

C1: T I tr B1 as *cbc a*
    T II in tenor (and transposed to *bab* g in tr B26)
    T III tr B50 (against *Souvenir* in mo B50)

C2: t i tr delayed to B80 (density area)
    t ii in tenor
    t iii tr B97–B98 (twice with *desnature*, the first time curtailed to ♩♩♩ ♩)

It also occurs at tr B14 and B76 as ♦♩ ♦♩. Given the motet's emphasis on death, and the prominent placing of this motive, might we also hear *cbca* as an allusion to the *Dies irae*?

D is the highest note of both the triplum and the tenor, at their respective octaves. B35 is the first of only two triplum occurrences of this peak note (on *fins, loyaus*, on the minim figure *d c d*, giving emphasis to loyalty = obedience?) while the motetus at the

---

[26] Boogaart, 'O series summe rata', 683, sets out the derivation of triplum motives based on the outlined descending fourth of tenor notes 13–15, 18–20.

same place has *muire*, thus linking the death and loyalty of the tenor's *Obediens usque ad mortem*.

The other appearance of the triplum's top note *d* is at B62, also on *Loyautés*. These two passages are also the only occurrences in the first section of the group ♦♦♦ ♦♦ (Exx. 12.3f and 12.3g) outside the *talea*-ends, creating particular emphasis. *Mors* coincides with the only occurrences of the lowest note of the motetus (B10–B11). Thus the extremes of range correspond to key concepts in the tenor (loyalty is high, death is low) and are emphasised in the upper-part texts: *Obediens usque ad mortem* literally runs the gamut.

Voice-crossing is not as prominent a strategy here as it is in some other motets, though the extremes of range are cultivated especially within the motetus, which goes below the tenor at B18 ('nothing can heal me').[27] It rises briefly above the triplum at B30, and more significantly at B51 for *souvenir* (memory), hitting its own highest note, the triplum pitch *c* which it recalls with the same motive—a souvenir.

The tenor notes 3–6 *fgac* occur up an octave in tr B5–B7 and at B79–B80, the motet's principal density point. Subsets occur as *ga c* in tr B13–B14, B42–B43, as the third *a c* in tr B33–B34 and B37, and the rising third emphatically in all three voices (*fa, cè, a c*) at the start of the second *color*, B73–B75.

What I have just called the main density point (B79–B83), three-quarters of the way through the motet, is marked by the first minim hockets (from tr B78), the coincidence of tr *Amours* with mo *ardoir* (love and burning), on the highest tenor note, *d*, a direct verbal and musical cross-citation with M15 (*meschiés*: see below), and mo *doublement* (doubly) marking the only place in the motet where the three-minim figure is heard twice in immediate succession within the same breve (B80 in mo, then tr), one of many local departures from the isorhythmic ground plan of the second *color*.

The tenor also contains the sequence of notes *abcagf* (notes 16–21 in Ex. 12.2), which from mo B50 is shadowed in ornamented form: *a ga b* | *c b c b* | *a b a g* | *f* (Ex. 12.3h) simultaneously with the triplum repeat of the opening (i.e. a *souvenir*). Here at B50 the motetus rises for the only time to the high *c* that is next-but-one the triplum's highest note. The prominent *abc* motive (tenor notes 16–18) is picked up in the tr ending *a a b b c* (B104–B106).

The tenor chant segment ends with a repeated *f* (tenor notes 29–30, but also 21–22, and on *c* notes 6–7); this is reflected in the repeated semibreve spondees at **B1** (mo), tr B9, B20, B24, mo B42, tr B44, **B48**, **B68**, **B72**. There are fewer in the second *color*, except, conspicuously, at tr B104 and in both parts at B105 (bold = on *f*). These include the ends of each of the first three *taleae* (their breve numbers are underlined).

Each triplum period spans two tenor *taleae*. The ends of each of the three periods in the first *color* contain both verbal rhyme (-*ure*, twice each, lines 5–6, 11–12, 17–18; see Table 12.1 above) and exact and aligned musical isorhythm (B14–B24, B38–B48, B62–B72). These serve as clear markers of the *talea* ends. The motetus is less consistently isorhythmic here, but mo B17–B23 and B65–B71, the ends of double *taleae* 1 and 3, have the same notes and rhythms.[28] In some motets (notably M9) the *talea* endings

---

[27] Notably in M9, Ch. 9. This idea was developed especially in Zayaruznaya's 2009 article, ' "She has a Wheel that Turns . . . " '.

[28] Sanders, 'The Medieval Motet', demonstrated the counting of periodicity in upper parts between rests. Such periods sometimes conform to a set of numbers different from the recurring periods themselves, but they are far from being the only criterion of tidy structure.

are signalled by hockets: that happens here (but less insistently) in the diminution section. But in the first *color*'s three double *taleae* the structure defined by the tenor is highlighted by this textual and musical rhyme in the upper parts. All six of the *-ure* feminine rhymes (the only feminine rhyme in both texts) from the first three stanzas are set to repeated-note semibreve spondees, which makes the setting of the final *-ure* couplet all the more striking: *desnature* is broken ('denatured') by rests, and the final cadence on 'malgré Nature' places the feminine syllable on the final long.[29] While there is strict aligned isorhythm only in the triplum at the end of each of the first three double *taleae*, there are many shorter rhythmic correspondences, sometimes between two but not all three periods, or not in both parts, and there are several lateral displacements, most strikingly that of the opening triplum phrase in *taleae* II and III.

Upper-Voice Rhythm

The twentieth-century term 'isorhythm' has shifted application in the course of the last century and is now commonly but improperly used to cover identity in both pitch and rhythm, and diminished or mensurally transformed iterations that are therefore not 'equal', *iso* (see Ch. 2). We do less than justice to the music by applying 'isorhythm' as a monolithic strait-jacket rather than being open to composers' inventiveness at drawing on a wide range of techniques to arouse our expectations and to satisfy or side-step them. Repetition is a fundamental, perhaps the most fundamental, musical form-building device. But fourteenth-century composers often chose to exercise subtlety and *varietas* by avoiding exact and regular repetitions. In motets, as elsewhere, it behoves us to celebrate diversity of structures and strategies—with and without isorhythm—rather than attempting to force conformity on them.

A full statement of the rhythm of the opening phrase (♦ ♪♪♪ | ♦ ♪♪ | ♪♪ ♪♪) occurs at tr breves 1–3, 26–28, mo breves 8–10, tr 50–52; it occurs partially at mo breves 3–4, 56–58, tr 80; of these, tr breves 1, 50 and 80 are at the opening pitch on *c′*. Smaller fragments of this imitated motive (Ex. 12.3c, ♦♪♪♪) are at mo B40, B56, and in the echo of the opening at pitch at tr B80. After B80 we no longer hear this rhythm in its full form, but its complement Ex. 12.3d, ♪♪♪ ♦ (already heard at breves 34, 35, 64, 70, 76), and in tr B80 the last statement on *c* of ♦ ♪♪♪.

Just as the upper-part melodic material is disciplined, with significant derivations from the chant tenor, so too is the rhythmic vocabulary. Each Machaut motet sets up its own vocabulary of rhythmic norms, exercising restraint even within a palette that is already quite restricted. A motet might, for example, use trochaic rhythms almost exclusively, with one or two isolated iambs at significant points, such as the pointed iambics that anticipate the *talea* joins in M14 and M15, or it might make a feature of iambic rhythms so that departures from them become significant, as in Vitry's *Petre clemens*. The norms thus set up may then be observed, frustrated, or played with, reserving different rhythmic formulas for special effect or for verbal or structural emphasis.[30]

---

[29] The striking treatment of feminine rhymes in M10 is reported in Earp, 'Declamatory Dissonance in Machaut', 114–15 and ex. 9.11.

[30] This feature has not been much noted, but see as demonstrated in Ch. 9, Table 9.4.

MACHAUT'S MOTET 10   241

Text Distribution

Machaut's motets show a full spectrum from even spacing of the text throughout the motet, or of stanza–*talea* correspondence (for example, the triplum of M9), to regular but spectacularly uneven spacing (as in the motetus of M9).[31] Such spacing is often purposefully contrived to bring about verbal coincidences, such as, here, tr *Amour* with mo *aim* in B42, tr *Amours* and mo *ardoir* in B80–B81, or in order to make a word like *souvenir* in the motetus punningly coincide with a pitch repetition at triplum B50.

The twenty-four ten-syllable lines of the triplum fall into four six-line stanzas with rhymes aaaabb ccccbb ddddbb eeeebb (Table 12.1 above); the recurrent b-rhyme is -*ure*, and no rhyme syllables are shared between triplum and motetus. One six-line stanza is allocated to each of the first three double *taleae*, the final stanza to the entire diminution section; in other words, the last three double *taleae* have just two lines each, an uneven distribution. The fifteen eight-syllable lines of the motetus fall into seven rhymed couplets, plus a final line. Three lines are allocated to each of the first three double *taleae*, two each for the last three. This cuts across the rhyming couplets by assigning three lines to each of the undiminished double *taleae*, in a way directly analogous to a three-on-two *talea–color* relationship (as in M9 and M4), or as here, the three-beat perfect breves of the diminished tenor set against the two-beat imperfect breves of the upper parts.

Thus the distribution of the text between the two *color* statements in the triplum is 18:6 (3:1), and in the motetus 9:6 (3:2). For each of the first three double *taleae* the tr–mo distribution is 6 lines to 3, i.e. 2:1, but for the last three double *taleae*, two lines each, i.e. equal text distribution in both parts. The second *color* includes some minim hocketing, which does not exploit this equal texting between the parts; upper-part isorhythm is maintained for only a few breves including this hocket.[32] Machaut here does not embrace the discipline of syllabic hockets without breaking words. The final 'odd' line of the motetus repeats the penultimate rhyme -*oir* (of the couplet lines 11–12), integrating the last three couplets with a rhyme-scheme of their own (abbccb) which coincides with the second *color*. The ratio of lines between tr and mo is 24:15 = 8:5, and the ratio of syllables 240:120, 2:1 (24 × 10:15 × 8), one of few cases in Machaut of such a neat proportion.[33]

Relation to Other Motets

Vitry's *Douce/Garison* has a strong literary connection to M10, and indeed may have been a model for it. This was demonstrated in a detailed comparison by Boogaart.[34]

---

[31] Reichert, 'Das Verhältnis', has explored this aspect in some detail for other motets.

[32] The equality of text between the upper parts is not exploited as fully for hockets here as in some other motets, such as Vitry's *Vos/Gratissima*.

[33] Or nearly so: see M6. M4 (Ch. 14) also has 15 motetus lines. See the 240 + 120 syllables of *Apollinis*, discussed in Howlett, '*Apollinis*', and here Ch. 16.

[34] Boogaart, 'Encompassing Past and Present', 51–52, who kindly noted that I had pointed out this connection in an earlier conference paper. Also, *Je respons* occurs at the junction to *Douce/Garison*'s second *color*, which, like those of Vitry's motets *Vos/Gratissima* and *Adesto/Firmissime Alleluya*, is newly rhythmicised, not a diminution or homographic transformation of the first. *Respons* is another instance of signalling a musical structural point with an appropriate word (cf. *souvenir* in M4, Ch. 14, *simili* and *vulnere* in *Vos/Gratissima*, Ch. 8). Boogaart, 'Encompassing Past and Present', 56–72, discusses the relation of Vitry's tenor to Machaut's M5.

242 MACHAUT

But apart from a few three-minim groups, some syllabic, there is little obvious musical connection between the two motets. Boogaart also pointed out M10's strong tie with M4, 'inspired by Thibaut's *Tout autresi*', and with M1.[35] Thomas Brown remarked that the triplum text of M10 also alludes to a few verses around the mid-point of the *Roman de la Rose*, with significance for its place in the ordering of the motets.[36]

The strongest links, however, are to M15. *Amour* is of course not an uncommon word in these motets, but the way in which it is recapitulated, with a musical allusion and a direct verbal cross-reference, suffices to establish a deliberate connection between M10 and M15. *Amours*, the first word of M15, recurs in line 24 of its triplum. It is the opening subject of M10, though the word appears there first in triplum line 4, and thereafter once in each of the four stanzas. In both motets it is placed between *meschiés* and *mes chiés* ('misfortunes' and 'my lord'), recapitulated at the centre of a pun on *meschiés*:

M15, lines 23–25:

Mais aveuc tous ces *meschiés*
Sueffre *Amours qui est mes chiés* |
Que Raison, Droiture, . . .

(But with all these misfortunes, Love who is my lord allows Reason [= ratio], Equity, Sweetness, Good Nature, Openness, Grace and Pity [a list of seven good things] to have no power against cruelty.)

M10, lines 19–20:

Et, pour croistre mes dolereus *meschiés*,
Met dedens moy *Amours, qui est mes chiés*,
Un *desespoir* . . .

(And, to increase my painful sufferings, Love, who is my commander, places within me a despair . . .)

Immediately striking is the musical setting in M10 of this *Amours* (at B80) to the same phrase, a third higher, that *Amours* receives at the beginning of M15 (Ex. 12.4). No other Machaut motet besides these two starts with this rhythm, let alone with a similar melodic shape, except M9.[37] This motive (M10, B80) refers back to its own full exposition at the beginning of M10, and to its full recapitulation at B50. As we saw above, there are several further repetitions at other pitches that are just rhythmic, or partial, but only these three (B1, B50 and B80) are on *c*. None is on *a*, the opening pitch of M15, though the M10 tenor contains the phrase *agaf* at notes 24–27.[38]

---

[35] Boogaart, 'Encompassing Past and Present', 52, 55, and Boogaart, 'Love's Unstable Balance', 3, 28–30.

[36] Brown, 'Another Mirror'. M4 also has a strong link to M9 because the shorter tenor of M9 (*Fera pessima*, an evil beast) is in fact identical with notes 3–14 of the 18 tenor notes of M4 (*Speravi*, I hoped), although drawn from within different chants; both are serpentine and completely conjunct, with a range of only a fourth and, despite their very different textual significance, afford considerable comparative interest for Machaut's use of the same melodic material. See Ch. 9 n. 13 and Ch. 14 on Motet 4.

[37] See Ch. 9 and Ex. 9.11.

[38] M15's melodic material is less closely related to its tenor than some, but it does several times have the tenor's *aga*.

Ex. 12.4 Openings of Motets 15 and 10 and the 'Amours' motive

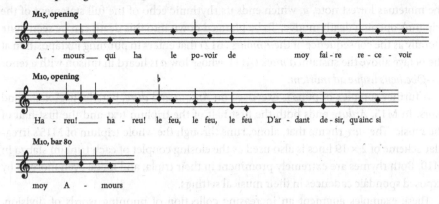

Recall that this motive, ♦ ♦♦♦ ♦ (Ex. 12.3a), is always prominently placed and usually falls a third. We might identify it as standing for *Amours*. The other motive, complementary and of secondary prominence, places the three minims in the rhythmically inverse position, ♦♦♦ ♦♦ (Ex. 12.3f and 12.3g), sometimes shortened in the *color*-2 hockets to ♦♦♦ ♦. Its first two occurrences are for the words *Las* (tr B22) and *muire* (mo B34, echoed immediately by tr B35), its last on *me convient morir* (tr B103); it might therefore be considered to have at least some rhetorical association with trouble and death. Its first statement, in the triplum on *Las*, is at the pitch of the opening *Amours* motive (*c b c*), where it coincides in B1 with the *las* of the motetus's opening word *Helas*. In addition, another significantly placed word linkage between the two motets connects *Helas*, the opening word of the M10 motetus, and the middle words *Et* and *las* of both M15 texts: in M15 the middle words of the triplum (*Et*, 84th of 168) and motetus (*Las*, 31st of 62) respectively are hooked together and exposed so that one hears *Et las* (= *Helas*) precisely straddling the mid-point of the music (the 60th breve of 120). Again, love tends to be higher in pitch than death.

The *amour* words in the first two stanzas are linked thematically in the first two double *taleae* (at B13 and B42), with the phrase *c c g a* (over tenor *c* and with a unison on *g*). The triplum's second-stanza *Amours* coincides with the only *amour* word in the motetus, *je l'aim* at B42. The third stanza's *Amours* at B66 coincides with *grant bonté* in the motetus, which is set in long notes to an exact repetition (pitches and rhythms) of what the motetus had at this point in *talea* 1. The fourth stanza's *Amours* (B80), as we have seen, alludes to the opening, at pitch, has verbal identity with M15, and presents the *Amours* motive that opens M15. An example of deceptive musical non-repetition in M15 occurs, appropriately, with *Faux Samblant*, the opening words of the motetus in M15, where at the final *talea* (B91) triplum and motetus usurpingly change places as did Jacob (the subject of the tenor), false-seemingly, with Esau.[39]

Both M15 and M10 are centrally concerned with love and death. The first triplum line of M15 tells of 'love who has the power to make me receive joy or death'. The first-person emphasis is confirmed by placing *moi* as the middle word of its motetus. M10 laments the fiery burning, *Ardour*, of love, *Amours* (note the assonant punning), which

---

[39] M15; see Ch. 10 for further observations on symbolic and text–music relationships in M15.

244   MACHAUT

leads to death, *mors*. *Mors*, as noted above, is set to a long on the only appearance of the motetus's lowest note, *a*, which ends its rhythmic echo of the full statement of the triplum's opening death motive. To be plunged down into this death can be seen quite literally as the consequence of the *Amours* (B12) that enters in punning juxtaposition at the octave above the sustained *mors* (B11), whose low *a* is heard in unison with a tenor *a—Obediens usque ad mortem*.

A further complex of puns is exercised on *Ardour* and *dure*, parallel to *Amours* and *mors*. In M15, *Ardure* ends both the first half of the triplum text and the first half of the music. The -*ure* rhyme that, alone, runs through the whole triplum of M15's irregular scheme of 2 × 19 lines is also used as the closing couplet of each triplum stanza in M10. Both rhymes are extremely prominent in their tripla, and made even more so by exposed spondaic cadences in their musical settings.

These examples augment an increasing collection of punning words of division, measurement or proportion occurring at significant structural points, such as 'beyond measure', *longue durée* etc. Such words in other motets include *medio*, *meta*, *iterum*, *bis*, *rursus*, as well as cutting or 'hard' words (here *dure*, punning on *talea = taille*). In *Musicorum* (Ch. 18), *bis acuto gladio*, *incidere* ('twice-sharp sword', 'cut'), and in *Vos* (Ch. 8), *vulnere*, *simili* ('wound', 'similar') coincide with structural joins. Words signifying repetition such as, here, *souvenir* and *doublement* are also often found at *talea* or *color* repetitions (see too M4, Ch. 14) as markers of actual verbal and musical recapitulations. In this case, *doublement* also comes soon after the *color*'s doubling of time (mo B79–B80).

I have drawn attention to 'word-painting' and intertextuality of a kind little noticed in this repertory; it is often richer and subtler than the more obvious madrigalisms to which we are accustomed from later music, and at least as pervasive. Because both the music and texts of motets are self-consciously structured in counted or proportioned ways, they offer opportunities to mark structural points by making them coincide musically with appropriate words or puns that Machaut has placed with equal deliberation in the texts. We have seen how the musical material of the tenor can permeate the upper parts just as their textual material determines the choice and disposition of the tenor *color*, and invites an intricate web of musical and textual conjunctions. Text–music relations in fourteenth-century motets have not been favourably received, largely because of the presumed incomprehensibility of simultaneously enunciated texts. But this is not the only genre which benefits from, and indeed invites, preparation and study. It is time to rethink that prejudice in the light of these connections, freed from the assumption that these pieces were designed for instant comprehension by an unprepared passive audience or, now, that motets are best heard in succession on a CD or playlist rather than being studied individually through repeated immersion in a single piece. Above all, these connections demonstrate (in this case as in others) that motet composition of this sophistication involves very complex planning and interaction between textual and musical components in individual and original conceptions, a very different picture from the idea of a rigid isorhythmic blueprint by which the maturity of a motet is judged according to how closely it conforms. The 'incomprehensibility' of simultaneously delivered texts has indeed earned motets a bad press; the intricacies of these compositions demand reflection and attention outside an unprepared hearing.

13

Motet 18: *Bone pastor Guillerme/Bone pastor, qui pastores/Bone pastor*

In the original publication of Chapter 9, on Motet 9 (*Fons tocius superbie/O livoris feritas/Fera pessima*), I included observations on Motet 18, *Bone pastor Guillerme/ Bone pastor, qui pastores/Bone pastor* (henceforth M18), which I have relocated to and extended in the present chapter in order also to address questions of its context and dating. The motet is here reproduced as ⊙ Example 13.1 from the excellent modern-notation edition by Jacques Boogaart.[1]

My observations concerned the careful arrangement of syllables so that no words are broken by rests. This practice was advocated in the text of the musicians motet *Musicalis scientia* (Ch. 17), showing that it was an issue around 1330; but that anonymous composer gave himself an easy time by making the hockets textless. M9 exemplified the discipline of not breaking words with hockets, and M18 is the closest comparand in Machaut. Other instances include the hockets with monosyllables in *Vos/Gratissima* (see Ch. 8). All those motets may date from *c.* 1330 or earlier. Two later English motets (*c.* 1400) follow this discipline: *Carbunculus ignitus lilie* (**OH** no. 143, Ch. 25 and Ex. 25.1) is a strictly syllabic setting without hockets but with carefully placed breaks; and in *O amicus/Precursoris* (Ch. 22, Ex. 22.3) the triplum is syllabic, the motetus only slightly less so, and although there are no hockets as such, short syllabic, conspicuously rhymed motives are tossed between the two texted parts.[2]

Of Machaut's six motets with two Latin texts (listed in Table 9.2 above), M9 and M18 are the only two that follow this discipline, in both cases with syllabic text on the hocketed notes. Two further motets, also listed there, have a French triplum and a Latin motetus. One of these, M12 (*Helas! pour quoy virent/Corde mesto cantando/Libera me*), is the only other Machaut motet with a French triplum and hockets that do not break words, unless one counts one melismatic continuation of a word over a rest. There are no opportunities for word-breaks in the motetus. In any case, as in many of the French-texted parts, the syllabification and text setting are looser than in the Latin texts of M9 and M18. The other of the two, M17 (*Quant vraie amour/O series/Super omnes speciosa*), has no hockets and (for that and other rhythmic reasons) may be one of Machaut's earliest motets.

The Texts

For the texts and translations see Table 13.1.[3] Note the change of metre for the last four triplum stanzas and last two motetus stanzas, both coinciding with *color* 3. A similar

---

[1] Machaut, *The Motets*, ed. Boogaart, 148–53. See ibid., 231–33 for details of manuscript variants. I am grateful to Jacques Boogaart and Medieval Institute Publications for permission to use his edition here.

[2] This phenomenon in *Vos/Gratissima*, and the precepts of *Musicalis*, were subsequently discussed in Zayaruznaya, 'Hockets', 463–64.

[3] For an extended and illuminating discussion of the texts and the institutional and liturgical context of Motet 18, see Robertson, *Guillaume de Machaut*, 53–68.

The Motet in the Late Middle Ages. Margaret Bent, Oxford University Press. © Oxford University Press 2023.
DOI: 10.1093/so/9780190063771.003.0014

Table 13.1 Texts of Machaut, Motet 18; translations by Leofranc Holford-Strevens

Colores		Triplum		Translation
C1 TI		Bone pastor Guillerme,	7a	Good shepherd Guillaume
		Pectus quidem inerme	7a	a defenseless breast
		Non est tibi datum;	6b	was not given to you,
		Favente sed Minerva	7c	but with the help of Minerva
	5	Virtutum est caterva	7c	it is strongly armed
		Fortiter armatum.	6b	with a host of virtues.
T II		Portas urbis et postes		You guard the gates and doors
		Tue munis, ne hostes		of your city, lest the enemy
		Urbem populentur,		destroy the city,
	10	Mundus, demon et caro,		The world, the devil and the flesh
		Morsu quorum amaro		with whose bitter bite
		Plurimi mordentur.		many are bitten.
C2 T III		Mitra que caput cingit		The mitre that crowns your head
		Bino cornu depingit		with its two horns signifies
	15	Duo testamenta,		the two testaments,
		Que mitrifer habere		which the mitre bearer
		Debet tanquam sincere		must have as ornaments
		Mentis ornamenta.		of a pure mind.
T IV		Et quoniam imbutus		And because you are imbued
	20	Et totus involutus		and wholly enveloped
		Es imprelibatis,		in purity,
		Ferre mitram est digna		Your neck is worthy to bear
		Tua cervix, ut signa		the mitre, so that the signs
		Sint equa signatis.		equal what is signified.
C3 Ti	25	Curam gerens populi,	7x	In caring for the people,
		Vis ut queant singuli	7x	you wish that individuals should strive
		Vagos proficere	6y	to help those that stray,
		Prima parte baculi	7x	and with the upper part of your staff
		Attrahere;	4y	to draw them in;
T ii	30	Parte quidem alia,		With the other part,
		Que est intermedia,		which is the middle,
C4 T iii		Morbidos regere;		you know how to minister to the sick;
		Lentos parte tercia		with the third part
		Scis pungere.		you know how to spur on the sluggards.
T iv	35	Oves predicamine		You feed your sheep with preaching
		Et cum conversamine		and with discourse
		Pascis laudabili,		that is praiseworthy,
		Demum erogamine		and finally with
		Sensibili.		observable gifts.
	40	Det post hoc exilium		After earthly exile
		Huic rex actor omnium,		may the King, maker of all,
		Qui parcit humili,		who spares the humble,
		Stabile dominium		grant a stable dominion
		Pro labili.		instead of this unstable one.

MACHAUT'S MOTET 18   247

Table 13.1 Continued

		Motetus		
		Bone pastor, qui pastores	8a	Good shepherd, who excels
		Ceteros vincis per mores	8a	other shepherds in morals
		Et per genus	4b	and in lineage
T II		Et per fructum studiorum	8c	and in the fruits of your studies
	5	Tollentem mentes ymorum	8c	raising the minds of those laid low
		Celo tenus,	4b	up to heaven.
C2 T III		O Guillerme, te decenter		O Guillaume, suitably
		Ornatum rex, qui potenter		adorned, the King who powerfully
		Cuncta regit,		rules all
T IV	10	Sue domus ad decorem		has predestined you
		Remensium in pastorem		to grace his house as shepherd
		Preelegit.		of the people of Reims.
C3 T i		Elegit te, vas honestum,	8x	He has chosen you, an honorable vessel,
(metre change)		Vas insigne,	4y	a distinguished vessel,
T ii	15	De quo nichil sit egestum	8x	let nothing issue from it
		Nisi digne.	4y	unless it be worthy.
C4 T iii		Dedit te, vas speciale		He gave you, a special vessel,
		Sibi regi;		to himself to be ruled,
T iv		Dedit te, vas generale		He gave you as a general vessel
	20	Suo gregi.		to his flock.

change, tailored specifically for the accelerated section, is found in the stanzas of M1, also of *Vos/Gratissima*. The significance of this will become clear.

> Triplum (44 lines)
>
> *Colores* 1 and 2: 4 stanzas of 7 7 6 7 7 6 (4 × 40 syllables = 160)
>
> *Colores* 3 and 4: 4 stanzas of 7 7 6 7 4 (4 × 31 = 124) = total 284
>
> Motetus (20 lines)
>
> *Colores* 1 and 2: 2 stanzas of 8 8 4 8 8 4 (2 × 40 syllables = 80, half of the triplum syllables)
>
> *Colores* 3 and 4: 2 stanzas of 8 4 8 4 (2 × 24 = 48) = total 128

Like much poetry demonstrably designed for motet composition, indeed for a specific musical partnership, the motetus has fewer words than the triplum, corresponding to its fewer notes. In most of Machaut's motets with stanzaic texts, stanzas and *taleae* correspond.[4] Less common is for the stanzas in both triplum and motetus in a second, musically reduced section to be shorter than the first section (and differently structured from it) to fit the new musical constraint, as they are in M18, in Vitry's *Vos/Gratissima*, and in

---

[4] Exceptions include the tripla of M2, 3 and 5 and the motetus parts of M19 and 22. Reichert, 'Das Verhältnis', and Machaut, *The Motets*, ed. Boogaart, 11–12.

248   MACHAUT

the second section of M1 (*Quant en moy/Amour et biauté/Amara valde*).[5] Such an arrangement, however, provides further corroboration of closely coordinated planning. In M1 the textual reduction is particularly striking as the music reduces 3:1: the fully perfect long ($3 \times 3 \times 3 = 27$ minims) is reduced in the second section to a perfect breve of just nine minims.

Text–Music Relationship of the Hocket Section

The poems of M18 are intact, purpose-made for the music, or together with it, and tightly coordinated: words tailored for music, and music for words, in a highly specific way. Several of Vitry's motet texts survive independently of their music, though in some cases with voice labels signalling their musical status. Of all Machaut's poetic works, the motets are the only genre whose texts are not also widely preserved without music.[6] The different poetic form of the last stanzas for the accelerated section, as also in M1 and Vitry's *Vos/Gratissima*, is evidence of words for music already designed for, or together with, M18's two pairs of *colores* of different lengths. The coordination of textual and musical composition in M18 is virtuosic. Machaut maintains regular verse structures (changing metre and stanza structure for the reduced section), rhymes, and syllable count in the poems, while combining them with each other, and with a regularly repeating isorhythmic pattern in the upper parts with coordinated hockets, having preplanned, hand in hand, the locations of monosyllables in both texts to be flanked by rests in those isorhythmic hockets.[7] There is limited, sporadic isorhythm in the upper parts of the first section; it is strict and consistent in all voices only in the *taleae* of the second section.

The hocket section of M18 is particularly interesting. As in M9, the triplum is straightforward and regular in *talea*–stanza correspondence, and arranges regularly placed one- and two-syllable words between rests. (See Fig. 13.1 and Table 13.2.) The motetus text is also metrically entirely regular, but here the few monosyllables are regularly placed in the isorhythmic iterations but not in the poetic structure. Upbeats in the motetus's hocket section are displaced in order to avoid breaking words and to isolate monosyllables (just one in each *talea*: *te*, *sit*, *vas*, *vas*), resulting in slightly irregular numbers of syllables in the groups between rests. This syllable distribution was contrived to enable one-syllable anticipations of *taleae* ii–iv, and to respect the discipline whereby a note flanked by rests would receive a monosyllable. This must in turn have been contrived with the predetermined and completely regular musical structure in mind.

[5] Besseler, 'Studien II', 200 observed this feature in Machaut M1 and Vitry's *Vos/Gratissima* as 'early' characteristics. The change of poetic structure in M1 and M18 has no poetic overlap into the new section. In *Vos/Gratissima*, however, the poetic change anticipates the structural join of the music.

[6] For one exception, M8, see Earp, *Guillaume de Machaut: A Guide*, 114 and 367, and here Ch. 14. A majority of the other 14th-c. motet texts that survive independently have at some time been attributed to Vitry; see Wathey, 'The Motets of Vitry'.

[7] The hockets exchange between the parts, but are not in rhythmic canon, as they are in *Vos/Gratissima*. They could be thought of as the standard ♦ ♦ ♦ pattern split between the voices.

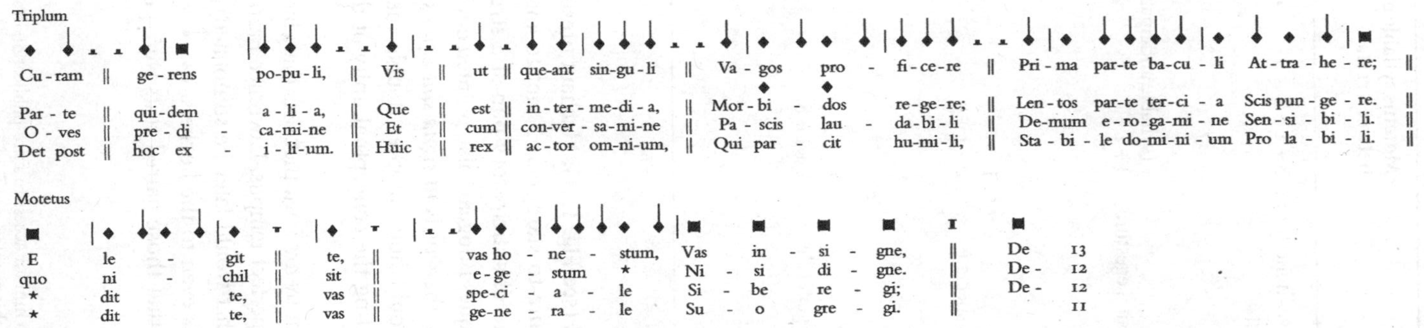

Triplum

Cu-ram	ge-rens	po-pu-li, ‖	Vis	‖ ut ‖	que-ant	sin-gu-li ‖	Va-gos	pro -	fi-ce-re ‖	Pri - ma	par-te	ba-cu-li ‖	At-tra-he-re;
Par-te	qui-dem	a - li - a, ‖	Que	‖ est ‖	in-ter-me-di-a,	‖	pro	- dos	re-ge-re; ‖	Len-tos	par-te	ter-ci - a ‖	Scis pun-ge-re.
O - ves	pre-di -	ca-mi-ne ‖	Et	‖ cum ‖	con-ver-sa-mi-ne	‖	lau		da-bi-li ‖	De-mum	e-ro-ga-mi-ne	‖	Sen-si-bi-li.
Det post	hoc ex -	i - li-um. ‖	Huic	‖ rex ‖	ac-tor om-ni-um,	‖	cit		hu-mi-li, ‖	Sta-bi-le	do-mi-ni-um ‖		Pro-la-bi-li.

Motetus

E	le -	git	te, ‖	vas ho -	ne -	stum,	Vas	in -	si -	gne,	De-	13
quo	ni -	chil	sit ‖	e - ge -	stum	*	Ni -	si -	di -	gne.	De-	12
*	dit	te,	vas ‖	spe-ci -	a -	le	Si -	be -	re -	gi;	De-	12
*	dit	te,	vas ‖	ge-ne -	ra -	le	Su -	o	gre -	gi.	De-	11

Fig. 13.1 Texts with hockets in Machaut, Motet 18. Word breaks coinciding with rests are shown by ‖

Fig. 13.1 shows the rhythm of the texts by musical correspondence from b. 97 to the end. These can be heard in sound clips ⊙ 13.1–13.3, which illustrate the triplum (sound clip 13.1); the motetus (sound clip ⊙ 13.2); all three voices (sound clip ⊙ 13.3). These were recorded in 2003 by members of Musick's Feast, a professional ensemble based in Iowa City: Elizabeth Aubrey, director, Barbara Evans O'Donnell and Marvin Bergman, for which Professor Aubrey has given permission.

Asterisks (*) are placed in the motetus of Fig. 13.1 to show where a syllable present in *talea* C3.i is dropped from subsequent *taleae* to manage the rests and the syllable count:

De of stanza 3 line 2 ends *talea* C3.i, making 13 syllables, not 12.
De of stanza 3 line 4 ends *talea* C3.ii.
De of stanza 4 line 2 ends *talea* C3.ii, but the melisma on *egestum* loses a syllable, making 12 for this *talea*. It continues with melisma to *talea* C4.iii.
De of stanza 4 line 2 ends that *talea*, and again continues with melisma to *talea* C4.iv, the final *talea* with 11 syllables. 13 + 12 + 12 + 11 = 48. The displacements, marked in each case with *De*, are cunningly arranged around the monosyllables.

250 MACHAUT

Table 13.2 The hocket passage laid out by stanzas in Machaut, Motet 18

Monosyllables isolated by rests (||); the number of syllables between rests is indicated.

Motet 18, final section	Triplum	Motetus	Motetus syllable groupings between rests
C3.i	Curam || gerens populi, || Vis || ut || queant singuli || Vagos proficere || Prima parte baculi Attrahere;	Elegit || te, || vas honestum, Vas insigne, ||	3 + 1 + 8
C3.ii	Parte || quidem alia, || Que || est || intermedia, || Morbidos regere; || Lentos parte tercia Scis pungere.	De quo nichil || sit || egestum Nisi digne. ||	1 (syllable anticipates new *talea*) 3 + 1 + 7
C4.iii	Oves || predicamine || Et || cum || conversamine || Pa[s]cis laudabili || Demum erogamine Sensibili.	De- dit te, || vas || speciale Sibi regi; ||	1 2 + 1 + 8
C4.iv	Det post || hoc exilium Huic || rex || actor omnium, || Qui parcit humili, || Stabile dominium Pro labili.	De- dit te, || vas || generale Suo gregi.	1 2 + 1 + 8

Preelegit is the last word (= line) of stanza 2 (see Fig. 13.1); Machaut presumably wanted *Elegit* initiating the new stanza structure to start *color* 3, not to anticipate it: *Preelegit* ('predestined') thus provides a kind of anticipatory pun at a structural join, such as we have noted in other motets. Jacques Boogaart also pointed out that in the triplum, just before the diminution section, the words *ut signa sint equa signatis* ('so that the signs equal what is signified') could hold another double meaning, signalling the diminution, thus further cementing the conceptual unity of the text with its music.[8]

The rhythms mainly follow the defaults set out by *ars nova* theorists that clarify the stemless semibreves in the *Fauvel* motets in imperfect tempus. Lawrence Earp posits the substitution of a pair of minim rests (or what would later be so notated) for an absent minor semibreve, to apply these defaults even to the hockets: ♦♦ ⌐ ♦ = ♦♦ ♦♦ and ♦♦♦ ⌐ ♦ = ♦♦♦ ♦♦ and so on.[9] He suggests that those paired rests were perhaps

---

[8] Email of 27.1.2021.

[9] This distinction is finely set out by Earp. I am grateful to him for access to a pre-publication draft of his 'Tradition and Innovation', for comments on earlier drafts of this chapter, and for ongoing discussion. Based on Machaut's use of default rhythms and use of paired, not single, minim rests, and on other criteria, and

originally indicated by a distinctive minor semibreve rest, though such rests are consistently notated only in some mid-fourteenth-century English sources, as rests hanging from the line rather than intersecting it. Exceptions to the default rhythms were gradually introduced by composers from the 1320s onwards, requiring clarification by minim stems, though even after stems came into regular use, the default rhythms often persisted.

One such exception in M18 is the lone minim rest at triplum bar 100 and isorhythmically corresponding places (⌐♦ ⌐♦♦), which Machaut seems not to have used again in his motets in imperfect time, major prolation [𝄴] until M13, and considerably later in M22 (*c.* 1358–59), though it appears in other works. Earp is very reluctant to accept this single rest in M18 at the early date that has been proposed for it, although he counts ♦♦ ⌐♦♦ as = ♦♦ ♦♦♦, a common variant of the default ♦♦♦ ♦♦.[10] It is not the rhythmic substitution that troubles him, but the need for a solitary minim rest. Minim stems were obviously necessary for the hockets, but although the full and explicit notation of rests may not yet have been in place, a general-purpose rest could have served for both the paired minim rests and the occasional single rest. We will return below to short rests, and the role of this rest in dating the motet.

Relationship of 'Early' Motets to the Notation and Dating of *Fauvel*

Except for some discreet downstems confirming that a note is not short (but not necessarily longer than it would have been if unstemmed), even the most advanced motets in *Fauvel* are notated with unstemmed semibreves, to be evaluated according to default patterns, as set out in treatises and confirmed by later sources with minim stems. It had been argued that these motets could be dated from as early as 1314, when Philip IV was still alive;[11] but I later suggested that a complex narrative fiction places the Marigny motets in or soon after 1317.[12] They follow the default patterns, using no rests shorter than a breve, let alone hockets with minim rests. Extension beyond the rhythmic defaults was gradual, and stems were in place well before those patterns receded.

Daniel Leech-Wilkinson could write in 1995 that *Flos/Celsa*, for the canonisation of St Louis of Toulouse in 1317, and M18 for Guillaume de Trie's elevation to the archbishopric of Reims in 1324, were 'the only reasonably certain dates for motets between *Fauvel* and Vitry's *Petre/Lugentium* [1342]'.[13] He also discussed the fragmentary *Per grama/Valde honorandus est beatus Johannes*, whose tenor for St John and apparently papal language in the surviving motetus led him to accept the coronation

---

moving in a tentative chronological order, Earp there places motets 11, 17, 6, 5, 1, 3, and 2 in the 1320s; and motets 9, 18, 16, 8, 7, 12, 10, and 19 in the 1330s. See below for M2, Ch. 9 for M9, Ch. 12 for M10.

[10] Earp, 'Tradition and Innovation', appendix 5.
[11] Sanders, 'Vitry', 36; he dates *Firmissime/Adesto* 'by mid-1314'.
[12] Bent, 'Fauvel and Marigny'; here Ch. 3.
[13] Leech-Wilkinson, 'The Emergence of *Ars Nova*', 285 n. 3.

252 MACHAUT

date of Pope John XXII in 1316.[14] These two motets, unlike those in *Fauvel*, required notated minim stems and some form of notated minim rests. Both have hockets with paired, but not single minim rests. At that time assuming a slightly earlier date for *Fauvel*, the 1316–17 datings led Leech-Wilkinson and Karl Kügle to place most of the early *ars nova* motet repertory between 1316 and *c.* 1325.[15] This now seems too early, though the 1324/5 date for M18 sat quite comfortably in that scenario. It now invites re-examination.

The copying window for the completion of *Fauvel* can be set quite generously between 1317, the date of the latest datable motets, and the death of Philip V in 1322. It was probably finished sooner, by *c.* 1320. And in any case, musical and notational advances beyond *Fauvel*, perhaps in early works by Machaut, need not all be later than the completion of *Fauvel*. Newer initiatives in practice, especially by younger men (perhaps including Machaut), could have overlapped the concluding stages of the *Fauvel* project. Indeed, innovations beyond *Fauvel* are attested in Muris's *Notitia* (with *Conclusiones*) of 1319/21. Taken together with the dating of the latest *Fauvel* motets, and even allowing for the coexistence of different stages and types of notational development, the proposed dates for *Flos/Celsa* and *Per grama* stood out as worryingly precocious, leading to attempts to overturn them or explain them away. *Flos/Celsa* is the easier to deal with; Louis of Toulouse continued to be venerated throughout the century, and the motet need not be as early as his canonisation. *Per grama* and its unresolved dedicatee and possible datings are discussed in Chapter 30: the motetus acrostic PETRUS, hitherto assumed to refer to the first pope, St Peter, has been proposed instead by Anna Zayaruznaya for Pierre Roger, who became Clement VI, a known associate of Vitry and a patron of the arts.[16] This attractive suggestion, however, does not explain the St John tenor, and at present I see no alternative but to associate it with St Peter and Pope John XXII, therefore before 1334, the year in which both he and Guillaume de Trie died, thus presumably a terminal date for compositions addressed to either of them.[17] I challenged the dates of those first two motets, but not that of M18, whose advanced features now look more exposed, including its use of hockets requiring stems on minims, and rests which at least by later convention would have been precisely notated as paired or single minim rests.[18]

The Dating of *Bone pastor* (Motet 18)

We know nothing about Machaut's early years except that he may have been born in the village of Machault, near Reims, and it is hypothesised that his early education could well have been at the cathedral school before his first known employment

[14] Ibid., 315, and transcription of the incomplete *Per grama*, with the suggestion that both are by Vitry. See here Ch. 30.

[15] Kügle, *The Manuscript Ivrea*, 124.

[16] Zayaruznaya, *Vitry*, and Zayaruznaya, 'Reworkings'.

[17] See the discussion of *Per grama* in Ch. 30 below, revised from Bent, 'Early Papal Motets', 10, taking account of a recent proposal by Zayaruznaya.

[18] There is an isolated minim rest in some sources of *Apollinis*. See Ch. 16 and Appendix; alternative readings are given for ▶ Ex. 16.1, B85.

MACHAUT'S MOTET 18   253

in the service of John of Luxembourg, King of Bohemia, from 1323.[19] Celebrating 'Guillermus' as archbishop of Reims, with a text which may imply that it is inaugural, M18 has long been dated to the appointment (1324) or investiture (1325) of Guillaume de Trie, the only archbishop of Reims named 'Guillaume' in the fourteenth century. The later date fits the text better, as the mitre is already on his head (triplum, line 13). The texts praise Guillaume's high morals: 'Oh you, Guillermus, so fittingly adorned | the King who powerfully | ordains all things | has, especially, chosen you | to grace his house as shepherd | of the people of Reims'. He is addressed in the vocative, which probably implies that he is alive. Although Guillaume remained archbishop until his death in 1334, his relationship with the canons of Reims quickly deteriorated to such a point that any local celebration of him would be highly unlikely after 1325, a date that would make M18 Machaut's earliest datable motet.[20] The 1324–25 date is most recently accepted by Boogaart.[21]

Some have long been uneasy about this early date; the motet has some notational features that are more advanced than anything else securely datable in the 1320s. Even if, as has been suggested, it was reused for later archbishops of Reims, Guillaume must have been the first bishop it celebrated, and the name was not changed after his death.[22] Earp (in 1995) accepted the early date, following 'student works' but, given that Machaut's Reims canonry (expectative from 1333) was not realised until 1338, he placed the motet outside Reims, in the Paris entourage of Machaut's then patron, John of Luxembourg, and the French court, Charles of Valois and his son Philip (the future Philip VI).[23] This overcame both the absence of a direct association of Machaut with Reims in the 1320s, and the problem of the archbishop's local troubles with the canons. More recently, Earp still proposed that M18 was composed in Paris, but now in celebrations which would have followed Philip VI's coronation in Reims in 1328 by his former tutor Guillaume de Trie, by then Archbishop of Reims, an occasion when Machaut's patron was also present. Paris celebrations might have taken place at the hôtel de Bohême (formerly de Nesle) which Philip VI had given to John of Luxembourg.[24] In work as yet unpublished, which Earp has generously shared with me, he now argues powerfully for its

[19] It has been observed that some of Machaut's identified motet tenors are from Reims or the surrounding region, suggesting that he probably encountered these in his early formative years. See Robertson, *Guillaume de Machaut*, 4; Clark, 'Concordare cum materia', 27–34 and 'Tracing the Tenor', 66. No exact chant match for the tenor of M18 has been found, though various similarities have been recorded, including by Robertson, *Guillaume de Machaut*, 63. See Machaut, *The Motets*, ed. Boogaart, 231, and Cuthbert, 'Hidden in our Publications'.

[20] The early date was accepted by Fuller, 'Modal Tenors', 302, Fuller, 'On Sonority'; Hartt, 'Rehearing Machaut's Motets', 197; and Robertson, *Guillaume de Machaut*, ch. 2, pp. 60–61, who accepted the possibility of an early composition date (55, 63–64) without challenging it on notational grounds, but finds occasions for the motet's repeated use in a liturgical and institutional context as admonitory rather than celebratory.

[21] Machaut, *The Motets*, 16, and Boogaart, 'Sound and Cipher', 377 n. 2. He notes that, as well as occupying rhyme position in the text, 'his name is emphasized by an ascending triad, first right at the beginning in the triplum (Bone pastor Guillerme), then in talea III (at bar 51) in the motetus (O Guillerme); the motive returns at the beginning of the diminution section at bar 97 in ascending and descending form in the triplum and motetus respectively. Even in the fourth section there is some echo of that motif, in descending form.'

[22] Leach, *Guillaume de Machaut*, 28–29, favours viewing the motet as an admonition for future bishops, even suggesting a possible composition date after Guillaume de Trie's death.

[23] Earp, *Guillaume de Machaut: A Guide*, 9–11, 296.

[24] Earp, 'Introduction', in Earp and Hartt (eds.), *Poetry, Art, and Music*, 34–36: 'around 1328, or towards 1332'. It is not clear why the officiant at a coronation would get a commemorative motet without some reference to the occasion or the king.

254 MACHAUT

composition in a royal context in Paris in 1332, when Guillaume de Trie presided at the collège des Pairs assembled at Paris for the trial of Robert III d'Artois.[25] In a famous miniature, Machaut's patron, John, King of Bohemia, is seated just below Philip VI. This proposal would remove the anomaly either of a precocious dating of notational features, or of placing the motet in Reims after the archbishop had fallen from favour there, while locating it in a context which included Machaut's patron, who may have awarded him the expectative Reims canonry in 1333.[26]

Later datings have recently been proposed for some *ars nova* theory texts;[27] these later dates have since been challenged, restoring them to the early 1320s.[28] But practice does not have to wait for theoretical codifications, as in the case of the stemless but unambiguous semibreves in *Fauvel* whose default values are corroborated in subsequent treatises as well as in later stemmed sources. For some time, it has been clear that Book VII of the *Speculum musice* of Jacobus need not antedate the famous bull *Docta sanctorum patrum* of John XXII of 1324/5.[29] But recent authors have not foregrounded the well-known fact that the pope's musical advisor complained, in precisely the years in which M18 might have been composed, that disciples of the new school (*novellae scholae discipuli*) were concerned with measuring out breves in new notes; that ecclesiastical chants are sung by the moderns in semibreves and minims, and that everything is struck through (punctured, *percutiuntur*) by little notes; that they cut across (*intersecant*) the melodies with hockets, they make them slippery with discants, they even stuff the tripla and moteti with vernacular texts. Although the small notes are not directly specified as minim hockets, I find it hard to read this passage other than as encouraging the belief that such hockets were already cultivated in the early 1320s. The word *percutiuntur* is not far from the *pungit* used so graphically in M9 to puncture the melodic line with hocket rests, but not to break words; it also appears in M18 as *pungere* (triplum, line 34). 'Scis pungere' seems punningly to announce: 'you know how to hocket'. Such details may further attest tight coordination between texts and music, precisely *this* music.

Later stemmed copies of originally unstemmed *Fauvel* motets attest a lively practice of notational updating when their copying alongside newer motets requiring rests and stems made it necessary to avoid ambiguity (see Table 7.2 above). Machaut had presumably been composing for at least thirty years by the time of his first surviving compilation in **MachautC** (*c.* 1350, when he was about fifty), a period of intense notational and stylistic evolution. His own notational practices must have evolved over that period, and it is therefore highly likely that the earliest versions as transmitted reflect

---

[25] Earp, 'Tradition and Innovation'. He pointed out (email of 9.12.2020) that the reference in the text (triplum stanza 2) to defending the city was not an issue until the 1330s, when Robert d'Artois was banished because of a forged will.

[26] On Machaut and Reims see Robertson, *Guillaume de Machaut*, 3–4 and *passim*; Bowers, 'Machaut', *passim*.

[27] Desmond, *Music and the* moderni, and Zayaruznaya, 'Old, New, and Newer Still'.

[28] Witkowska-Zaremba, 'Johannes de Muris's *Musica speculativa*', and Bent, '*Artes novae*'.

[29] See Bent, *Jacobus*, 54–55, and literature there cited (where I wrongly placed it in the first year of John's pontificate, correct elsewhere in the book), also 2 n. 5, 14; and here Ch. 30. Zayaruznaya, 'Old, New, and Newer Still', again affirms the disconnection. For different reasons for an early dating, see the works cited in n. 28 above.

some degree of notational updating and editorial standardisation. Karen Desmond indeed proposes that some level of notational revision of Machaut's earliest works was likely before their first surviving copy 'at least a couple of decades' later.[30] So even by her criteria, we need not assume that, if M18 was composed in 1325, the later notation in which we have it in **MachautC** was fully developed by that earlier date. **Paris571** contains two *Fauvel* motets in notation that, apart from some inconsistently applied stems, is barely updated and did not need to be, either for notational reasons (the music required no more) or for its demonstrated context.[31] Its dating to 1326 does not preclude more notationally advanced compositions by other composers from antedating it or, as suggested above, even from overlapping with the latest motets in *Fauvel* before 1320. It is just possible that a precocious Machaut in the, and his, late teens, might for a while have appeared to experiment more boldly than Vitry, ten years his senior. Many instances throughout the later Middle Ages attest that different notational states could be in concurrent use; this is even true within Machaut's own works, in the very conservative notation of the late David hocket, and where lais in longa notation sit alongside others in shorter values.

While I find Earp's case for a 1332 dating of M18 persuasive, in terms of Machaut's patronage at the time, some arguments in favour of the earlier dating remain, and I do not entirely exclude it on notational grounds. Musical and notational developments rarely proceed in a single linear progression, and should not be presumed to do so. While there are clear connections and responses between motets by Vitry and Machaut, for example, highly individual motets by them or anyone else cannot necessarily be reliably arranged, either in combination or separately, on an amalgamated line of development, solely on grounds of a chronology of notational usage in the often later sources which transmit them. An early date for a particular notational usage by Machaut should not be ruled out because it was not immediately picked up in other compositions. And if he indeed had juvenile associations with Reims cathedral, he might just possibly have been asked to compose an inaugural motet for the new archbishop.

In a recent study, Desmond accepts that the motet text must indeed be for Guillaume de Trie between 1324 and 1334, but her late dating of the *ars nova* treatises leads her to reject the possibility of an early dating of the diminution section of M18. She has focused on that section's notational features that were known to and castigated by Jacobus, whether or not he knew this motet, but dates Book VII of the *Speculum musice* in the 1330s or later.[32] More recent work points to its completion in the 1320s, thus attesting theoretical recognition of those practices well before 1330.[33] They include remote imperfection of the duplex long by one or two breves, the duplex long in ligature with a breve, and the simultaneous operation

---

[30] 'Traces of Revision', 428.

[31] Wathey, 'The Marriage'. The upstems in **Paris571** are erratic and inconsistent; groups of four 'minims' do not necessarily imply minor prolation, as sometimes in the same part major prolation is made explicit with up- and downstems.

[32] Desmond's first thoughts on M18 were presented in a paper which I heard at the Medieval and Renaissance music conference in Maynooth in July 2018. I am grateful to her for sharing this paper prior to its publication as Desmond, 'Traces of Revision'.

[33] See n. 28 above. This approximately restores Michels's dating, but for different reasons.

256 MACHAUT

of imperfect modus in the upper parts against perfect modus in the tenor.[34] As for a possible *terminus post quem*, Desmond finds some of the notational practices of M18 uncommon before *c.* 1350 or later, especially remote imperfection of the long by semibreves in its diminution section. Imperfection of both long and breve by a minim occurs in *Apollinis*, which must be dated around 1330 (see Ch. 16), though Desmond now seems to favour a dating of this motet towards 1350.[35] But such remote imperfection is already permitted in the fourth and fifth *Conclusiones* to Muris's *Notitia* of 1321 and, as David Maw has pointed out, a duplex long imperfected by a breve in ligature is used in a rondeau by Adam de la Halle (*Or est baiars*) in a manuscript dated to the early 1290s.[36] Simultaneous use of imperfect and perfect mensurations at the modus level occurs in a number of early motets, but of imperfect and perfect tempus in fewer, besides M18 including *Tuba/In arboris* and Machaut's M5 and M10, all of which have been judged relatively early works. This usage does not necessarily argue against an early dating for M18, as different simultaneous mensurations in motets that may date from *c.* 1320 now include simultaneous perfect and imperfect tempus in the texted upper parts of the aforementioned fragmentary motet on f. 79ᵛ of **Paris934**.[37]

However, as with all motets of the period, the tenor of the diminution section of M18 is written out in full, in this case with two pairs of *colores* (each pair with repeat signs), each of two *taleae* in each of the motet's two sections. The tenor for the second section is in strict diminution (i.e. all note values are substituted at the next level down), which means it could have been (and arguably was, in its originally conceived form) derived from the first section without the need for renotation or renaming of the shorter note-values, and it is those which Desmond finds problematic for remote imperfection at the early date.[38]

But what gives Earp most serious pause about the early dating of M18 are the minim hockets in the second section, especially the use of a single minim rest. I suggested above that short rests may have been present but perhaps graphically undifferentiated in the 1320s. Earp indeed cites the interesting case of *O/Nostris lumen* in **Br19606**, which has undifferentiated rests, some of which must stand for a minor semibreve equivalent to two minims, and some for a major semibreve, worth three. This notation in **Br19606** surely reflects an earlier (or much more conservative) notational stage than the most recent dating of this rotulus to 1335.[39] Encouraged by this

---

[34] *Speculum musicae*, Book VII, chs. 25, 28. I cannot agree that the phenomenon she identifies in the first section of M18 can count as semibreve hockets, nor with her proposal that, despite their current notation, the upper voices of the first section were originally conceived in perfect modus to align with the tenor.

[35] Desmond, *Music and the* moderni, 4 n. 7.

[36] Desmond, *Music and the* moderni, 34, 157, 238 for the *Conclusiones*, which she places in the later 1320s or 1330s. See now Bent, 'Artes novae', and Maw, review of *Music and the* moderni, p. 499.

[37] Dated thus by Earp, in Dudas and Earp, *Four Early* Ars nova *Motets*. They argue that this motet may be Vitry's *Thoma tibi*, cited in *ars nova* treatises for the features this motet exhibits.

[38] The tenors of Machaut's motets with diminution are written out in full in the surviving manuscripts, but all could have been conceived homographically, the reduced section to be derived by diminution or mensurally from a single notated form. The notation in full may have been an editorial decision taken for the complete-works manuscripts by Machaut or his compilers, as for all works of the period where the notation may have been updated in later manuscripts.

[39] Kügle, 'Two Abbots and a Rotulus', 151.

Fig. 13.2 Paris, Bibliothèque nationale de France, fr. 146, Lescurel, f. 58ʳ: rests in *Belle com loiaus*. © BnF

usage, Earp suggested (above) that what were later notated as paired minim rests may earlier have been distinguished as minor semibreve rests, or by some kind of undifferentiated short rest. Indeed, as noted in Chapter 30, although *Fauvel* motets use no rests shorter than the breve, the ballade *En chantant* (ff. 23ᵛ–24, p.mus. 56) has short rests that sit on the line and have the value of a semibreve.[40] A few instances in the songs of Lescurel in **Paris146** have short rests: *Amours que vous*, f. 57ᵛ, has a hanging semibreve rest (♦⊤); and *Belle com loiaus* on f. 58ʳ has several instances of a semibreve followed by a rest, indiscriminately hanging or sitting (♦⊤· ♦⊥), as in Fig. 13.2, where both must be major semibreve rests. And if such rests were imprecisely notated at this stage for paired minims, why not also for the occasional single minim? Could it not be that Machaut, faced with the need in M18 to accommodate an extra syllable in his complex and craftily contrived musico-textual conception, was here driven to find an ad hoc solution within the syllable-rest discipline he had set himself (⊥♦♦ instead of the more usual ⊥♦)?

Practice usually precedes theory, and the use of such a rest did not necessarily require prior formulation in a treatise. The minim rest is however attested in the early 1320s. Doubt has been cast on the illustration of short rests in Muris's *Notitia* because they seem precocious, and the sources containing them are later. However, single minim rests are clearly illustrated in the *Tractatus* of Petrus de Sancto Dionysio, written apparently not long after the *Notitia*, which Petrus cites and critiques extensively. He gives an explicit form for the single minim rest, simplifying short rests from what he sees as Muris's over-complicated and unpractical gradations, and thus corroborating their authentic presence in the *Notitia*.[41] With the restoration of dates in the early 1320s for treatises that attest minim rests, I still think a 1325 dating possible for M18 on notational grounds; there are arguments for and against both a 1325 and a 1332 dating.

---

[40] Signalled by Earp (email of 8.2.21). Early motets outside *Fauvel* that also have rests shorter than a breve include **Karlsruhe82** recto, where the S rests in *fa fa mi fa* are suspended between the staff lines; in **Troyes1949** S rests preceding or following a S are written interchangeably as hanging or sitting (on ff. A and B, and strip bʳ).

[41] CSM 17, 147–66, p. 39 for dating, 156–68 for minim rests. Cook, 'Theoretical Treatments of the Semiminim', 314–16.

A Proposal for Revision

Anna Zayaruznaya has drawn attention to a very interesting case of hocket revision in Vitry's *Cum statua/Hugo*, from semibreve hockets in **Ivrea** to minim hockets in **Ca1328**, but this does not affect the overall structure of the motet.[42] Variant versions of the *introitus* to *O Philippe/O bone dux* stand outside the structured part of that motet. Her proposals that hocket sections were added to other motets by Vitry remain hypothetical; but none of her instances are as radical as the recomposition now proposed by Desmond for M18.

Desmond finds a disjunction between the first and the accelerated sections of M18. She is prepared to accept the 1325 date for the first section of the motet, but finds it too early for the second section, on account of its various notational features—remote imperfection of the long (reduced from the maxima of the first section), simultaneous use of perfect and imperfect tempus (both allowed in the *Conclusiones* of Muris's *Notitia* in 1321 and found in some early *ars nova* motets), and its minim hockets, all features which she finds theorised mainly in the 1340s or later.[43] She observes that complete isorhythm as found in the accelerated section of M18 is unusual before 1350.[44] But *Vos/Gratissima*, with its similarly syllabic isorhythmic hockets in the accelerated section, has been dated to the early 1330s by Desmond (in my view it dates from the mid to late 1320s: see Ch. 8), and *Musicalis*, certainly of the early 1330s, has relentlessly isorhythmic hockets, though without a reduced section. (Some have even placed *Musicalis* earlier than *Apollinis*, but this cannot be so: see Ch. 17.) It has semibreve hockets and ⨪♩ but no single minim rests. Desmond proposes that M18 was revised at a date commensurate with her late dating of *ars nova* treatises, but offers no convincing occasion for such a revision. She proposes either an original setting of the first section only, or that what we now have is an ingenious adaptation which retains the original verbal text but replaces an older second section with the present hocket section. The tenor of this older section might have been newly rhythmicised (I avoid the term pseudo-diminution), as in Vitry's motets *Firmissime/Adesto*, *Douce/Garison* and *Vos/Gratissima*; though the last of these has minim hockets which would fall outside her dating. She rejects my claims that the music and text demand consideration as a single conception, and that the shorter texts for the second pair of *colores*, with monosyllables for hockets, were specifically tailored to the plan for the musically accelerated section.[45] I argued that the poems are intimately associated with specifically this musical setting, and reject her proposal of either a truncated or an alternative version. In further support of the unity of the poems, I would claim that the number and sequence of monosyllables in any case almost *prescribes* isorhythmic hockets, just as the reduced stanzas of the poetic structures prescribe an accelerated second section. Rhythms for this diminution section and its isorhythmic hockets could indeed be composed from the carefully calculated syllabic text of the triplum alone, with very

---

[42] Zayaruznaya, 'Reworkings'. See Lerch, *Fragmente aus Cambrai*, vol. 1, 80f; vol. 2, 129–36 (No. 16).

[43] Desmond, 'Traces of Revision', 413.

[44] Citing Günther, 'The 14th-Century Motet', 30–31. Desmond's late datings are governed by the chronology and late treatise datings set out in *Music and the moderni*. Motet 18, and others like it, must date from well before 1350 to have been included in **MachautC**.

[45] Desmond, 'Traces of Revision', 427.

MACHAUT'S MOTET 18   259

slight adjustments in the motetus. This argues against these texts ever being designed or set without hockets, *these* hockets. And against the idea that these stanzas could have been added later are the way the last words of the first section seem to point forward. Given the frequent verbal signalling in motets of musical structural joins (see Ch. 18, *Musicorum*; Ch. 8, *Vos*; Ch. 14, M4; and many other places), the last words of the first section may be significant: the triplum's 'Scis pungere' might be construed as announcing the ensuing hocket section (as noted above), and *Preelegit* as anticipating ('pre-') the next word, *Elegit*.

There is no direct evidence here or in any fourteenth-century motet for such major sectional replacement as Desmond proposes, as she herself admits.[46] It is a central premiss of the present book that at least the most sophisticated motets are finished and rounded constructions of text and music, often with the mutually reinforcing integrity of a Chinese puzzle or a crossword, leaving no room for addition, subtraction or substitution, as attested by densely packed structural, numerical, melodic, rhythmic, citational and symbolic text–music relationships.[47] There is no evidence of any such revisions in Machaut's motets. Added voices, usually contratenors, or (in the case of *Apollinis*) additional triplum parts, occur in other fourteenth-century motets, but these do not affect the overall durations and structures of the body of the motet, or its text–music relationships.

Contrafaction is rare, and it can be discounted in this case. Two documented instances are both later fourteenth-century English adaptations in Latin of French motets.[48] There are very occasional name replacements (*Ludowice* in **Paris571** for *Fauvel's O Philippe*), but here Guillermus in rhyme position makes a name replacement unlikely. And in any case, textual alteration would work the wrong way round. The name of the discredited Guillaume should have been replaced by a successor, but it is Guillermus's name alone that appears in the earliest transmission of the motet in **MachautC** together with the allegedly revised hocket section. The suggestion of a revision still does not explain why Machaut would have retained a text with inaugural or current connotations for an archbishop who would have been out of favour or dead by the time of those revisions, and indeed is no easier to explain than a later dating of the whole motet. Why would anyone want to revise M18 musically and not change the dedicatee? Indeed, the index of **MachautA** emphasises the dedicatee by citing this motet, exceptionally, by its triplum: *Bone pastor Guillerme*.[49]

---

[46] Indeed, Desmond admits that 'In the case of *Bone pastor*, there really is not much of this sort of evidence in the manuscript sources. The hypothesis here relies on the stylistic incongruity of the two sections, the likely updating of the upper voices in the *integer valor* section into imperfect modus, and the assemblage of advanced notational and technical features that cluster in the diminution section' (p. 430). In fact, there is no such evidence or incongruity; this change of pace and texture is normal in motets with a second section with tenor reduction and hockets, as in *Vos/Gratissima*.

[47] A view also subscribed to by Machaut; *The Motets*, ed. Boogaart, 8. But Zayaruznaya, 'Reworkings', has challenged the stability of motet transmission.

[48] *Se päour/Diex tan desir* becomes, in **Ox7**, *Domine quis habitabit/De veri cordis* (PMFC 5, nos. 16b and 16a). *Are post libamina*, **OH** no. 146, is a self-declared contrafact. Other unica in **Durham20** and **Ox7** could also be contrafacta of French motets.

[49] As a counter-example, it could be pointed out that Ciconia's motets for long-dead doges and bishops (Ch. 28) were recopied two decades after his death with added contratenors (musical updating) but no change of name. But these are not authorial changes. For Earp's later dating of M18, see above, and his 'Tradition and Innovation'.

Postscript on the Tenor of Motet 2,
Tous corps/De souspirant cuer/Suspiro

Much has been written about the sighing announced in the tenor and motetus of M2 and its onomatopoeic representation in all voices in rests of varying length. The lover must 'interrupt and syncopate his words by deep sighs, making him mute and silent'.[50] The text setting is almost the opposite of M18, in that words seem to be broken to achieve precisely that effect. Another instance of a word of division or puncture is the triplum's *Souffre la | morsure* (suffer the bite) at the junction to *color* 2, and of word-painting, a notated $g\sharp$ in the motetus against $g\natural$ in the tenor at *male pointure* (with a malicious sting). Fourteenth-century tenors with diminution, including Machaut's, are written out in full, even if the diminution could in all cases have been derived without renotation. The second *color* of M2 looks like a straightforward diminution section, the notes of the first *color* being substituted by those of the next level down.

There are no instructions, but the tenor's mensuration and coordination are clear empirically. The first *color* is in perfect modus. Ludwig and Schrade transcribed the second *color* in perfect tempus, as would be expected in a straightforward diminution, but requiring an awkward imperfection and an anomalous rest. Boogaart rightly recognised that the second *color* must be construed in imperfect tempus, not only a much more elegant solution, but notationally more correct: perfect long rests in the first section become imperfect breve rests in the second. So this is not simple diminution, but an early instance of mensurally transformed reduction.[51]

There is one irregularity in the notation as written; the penultimate note of each *talea* is a breve in both statements. In the first *color*, this has to be altered before the maxima, irregularly, because the maxima is not the next note-level up. In the second statement in imperfect tempus, this note is a straightforward imperfect breve preceding a long. There is no reason to presume perfect modus, and that breve could not in any case be altered if the modus is imperfect. Rather than treating the irregularly altered breve before a maxima in the first, undiminished section as a notational licence, I suggest that it was originally conceived as a long, imperfected by the preceding breve and legitimately preceding the maxima. There would then be no need to assume any irregularity when that long is notated as a breve in the written-out diminution. See Fig. 13.3. This is actually the opposite of Boogaart's diagnosis, which was that Machaut compromised the diminution. He assumed that in a true diminution from perfect modus to perfect tempus, the penultimate note ought to be an altered semibreve, corresponding to the altered breve of the first section. But as he recognised, the second *color* is not in perfect tempus, so alteration is neither possible nor called for. The penultimate note of the second *color* is correctly notated as an imperfect breve. It is the penultimate note of each *talea* of the first *color* that ought to be

---

[50] Boogaart, '*Folie couvient avoir*', 23–31. This section was drafted in response to Boogaart's reading of the tenor of this motet in Machaut, *The Motets*, ed. Boogaart. Desmond, 'Traces of Revision' (on M18) includes a short section agreeing with Boogaart's solution to M2.

[51] Boogaart, in Machaut, *The Motets*, 191, says that 'the second *color* is diminished partly to one-half, partly to one-third'; this is too complicated a way of expressing it; 'diminution with mensural change to imperfect tempus' obviates the need to posit variable reduction.

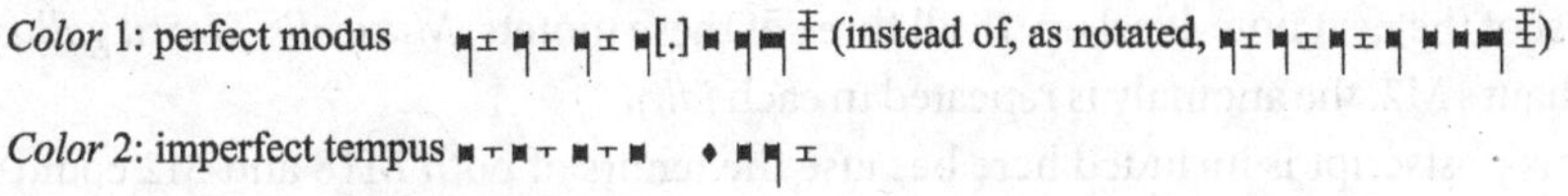

Color 1: perfect modus ◗ɪ ◗ɪ ◗ɪ ◗[.] ◼ ◗◗ ‡ (instead of, as notated, ◗ɪ ◗ɪ ◗ɪ ◗ ◼ ◼ ◗ ‡)

Color 2: imperfect tempus ◼┬◼┬ ◼┬◼ ◆ ◼◗ ɪ

Fig. 13.3 Proposed original notation of the tenor of Machaut, Motet 2

a long imperfected by the breve that precedes it. Then the notation of the two *colores* would correspond exactly, increasing the elegance of the mensural transformation and enabling them to have been derived from a single notated form. This restoration of an original homographic form of the tenor weighs for me more heavily than the irregular—but not unprecedented—alteration of a breve before a maxima, but both anomalies are resolved by the solution proposed here. About half of the *Fauvel* motets with exactly repeating *color* (eight motets) notate the tenor only once, and in all but one of those cases (*Ihesu, tu dator/Zelus familie*, f. 44) with a repeat sign ('&c').[52] All of Machaut's diminishing tenors could (and surely therefore must) have been conceived homographically, although they are fully written out in their earliest transmission in **MachautC**, as with all other motets of the period. An interesting case is M6, *S'il estoit nulz/S'Amours/Et gaudebit cor vestrum*, where the tenor is notated only once, with repeat signs, but where the second *color* is differently rhythmicised because the altered breves fall at different places in the perfection due to an initial rest.[53] That is the only Machaut motet where the second *color* requires different rhythmicisation but is not written out. That tenor is (correctly) neutrally notated without dots of division in **MachautC** and **MachautA**, but in **Ferrell(Vg)**, a dot of division has been added at the end of the third perfection for each of the first-*color taleae*, but this is incorrect for the second *color* to be read from the same notation.[54] The present proposal for M2 removes what may be a rare anomaly in Machaut's otherwise elegant dual-purpose tenor notations, even if in editing them for **MachautC** (as noted above) most tenors were written out in full, and to remove ambiguity by (in this case) compromising the homographic status. Dots of division are in most cases accidental (i.e. helpful but optional); in Fig. 13.3, the clarifying dot I have added in brackets could not be notated in a homographic presentation, because it would have been misleading in the second *color* to be derived from the same notation, as it would then appear as an unwanted dot of augmentation in imperfect mensuration.[55]

For the notation as it stands, a similar irregular alteration is in *Musicalis*, where a breve is preceded by a pair of minims, the second of which has to be altered (see Ch. 17). Another instance where alteration is required other than before the next higher adjacent value occurs in the tenor of *Garrit gallus*, where a breve is altered before a coloured breve (see Ch. 4). In that case, there is a dot, occasionally at this period causing alteration. By the later part of the century, good notational practice did not allow dots to cause alteration; the only criterion was that the note to be altered should precede a note

---

[52] *Ludowice* in **Paris571** also notes the tenor just once.

[53] Perhaps embodying Franco's statement: 'Et nota pausationes mirabilem habere potestatem; nam per ipsas modi adinvicem transmutantur' (CSM 18, 55). Rerhythmicisation without renotation also occurs in the *Super omnes speciosa* tenor of **Paris934**, f. 79ʳ.

[54] **MachautC**, ff. 210ᵛ–211, **MachautA** ff. 419ᵛ–420, **Ferrell(Vg)**, ff. 265ᵛ–266.

[55] A similar adjustment of dots for mensurally changed diminution in perfect and imperfect mensurations is found in *Alma polis*, Ch. 19.

262   MACHAUT

or rest of the next note-level up. In all three of these motets, *Musicalis, Garrit gallus* and Machaut's M2, the anomaly is repeated in each *talea*.[56]

This postscript is included here because the tenors of both M18 and M2 could have been notated only once, the diminutions read from the notation of the first section. Both tenors, I believe, were conceived in a single notated form, even if written out *ad longum*. In the case of M18, an earlier notation of the tenor *color* only in the longer values of its first statement would overcome Desmond's objection that remote imperfection is not documented for the lower level of note-values, because the reader would be thinking in the larger values, but accelerated. Moreover, in the case of M2, the removal of an irregular alteration enables both statements, including the mensurally altered diminution, to be read from the same notation in the form in which Machaut conceived it.

[56.] Admittedly, there are occasional irregularities. Earp, 'Scribal Practice', 306, discusses irregular instances of alteration other than before the next value up. In an email of 21.3.22 he notes the alteration of a breve before a duplex long in the tenor of **Mo**, 8.332, f. 380 (*Je cuidoie/Se j'ai/Solem*). The anonymous author of *De musica mensurabili* (CSM 13, formerly known as Theodoricus de Campo) disapproves of breve alteration before the duplex longa in the tenor of the *Fauvel* motet [*Super*]/*Presidentes*, and of semibreve alteration before a long. In the present case, this irregularity is the only impediment to a homographic notation that would serve both statements of the *color*. For documentation of remote imperfection already in Muris's *Conclusiones* (1321), see n. 36 above.

14

Text–Music Relationships in Motets 4 and 8

✠This chapter has its origins in seminars on Motets 4, 7 and 8 given jointly with Kevin Brownlee in Oxford in the early 1990s at All Souls College, and in presentations for interdisciplinary audiences on verbal and musical polyphony.[1] My challenge to Brownlee was to a reader highly alert to intertextuality who had read every word of poetry written by Machaut except the motets: what did he make of the unique form of intertextuality offered by the simultaneously presented texts of the motets, with words and even syllables precisely placed in relation to each other? He rose splendidly to the challenge, and we concentrated on motets whose literary texts invited reading against each other and particularly in dialogue with the *Remede de Fortune*, in addition to the ubiquitous influence of the *Roman de la Rose*. This was all before the appearance of Lawrence Earp's *Guide* in 1995, Anne Walters Robertson's *Guillaume de Machaut* in 2002 and the series of important studies by Jacques Boogaart (from 1993, and particularly from 2001 onwards).[2] While both motets have since received many insightful comments within broader studies, few or no studies have been devoted principally to them.

Motet 4. *De Bon Espoir/Puis que la douce/Speravi*

For the music, see ▶ Example 14.1 and for the texts and translation see Table 14.1.

Tenor

The slow-moving tenor, the bottom line of the score (▶ Ex. 14.1), is the foundation of the musical structure, though it was chosen to fit the previously established *materia* of the motet, as prescribed in the treatise *De modo componendi tenores motettorum* (usually attributed to Egidius de Morino, but see Chs. 1 and 16), in one of the very few motet procedures attested by a contemporary theorist. In this

---

[1] Brownlee, 'Textual Polyphony in Machaut's Motets 8 and 4' was his contribution to a Study Session which I convened at the 1992 annual meeting of the International Musicological Society in Madrid. See also his 'La Polyphonie textuelle dans le Motet 7'. The present section on M4 was the basis for a paper I gave at Kalamazoo in 2005. Images of these two motets can be seen as follows: **MachautA** https://gallica.bnf.fr/ark:/12148/btv1b84490444.image, M4, ff. 417ᵛ–418; M8, ff. 421ᵛ–422. **Ferrell(Vg)** https://www.diamm.ac.uk/sources/3774/#/images, M4, ff. 263ᵛ–264; M8, ff. 267ᵛ–268. For an excellent modern edition and full listing of variants, see Machaut, *The Motets*, ed. Boogaart, 195–98.

[2] For M4 see, among others, Boogaart, 'Encompassing Past and Present', 19–23, 33–35; Boogaart, '*O series summe rata*', 391–419; Hartt, 'Rehearing Machaut's Motets'; Fast, 'God, Desire, and Musical Narrative'. For M8 see Boogaart, '*O series summe rata*', 132–37, within a chapter on the related aspects of Motets 8, 12, 14, and 15, including a shared *talea* rhythm (pp. 636–37), and three dealing with Fortune. Boogaart, 'Sound and Cipher', discusses symbolism in both Motets 4 and 8. M8 has received scrutiny from Clark, 'Machaut Reading Machaut'; Earp, '"The spirit moves me"', 284–88. See Machaut, *The Motets*, ed. Boogaart, for excellent editions of both motets in modern notation with full details of manuscript variants.

The Motet in the Late Middle Ages. Margaret Bent, Oxford University Press. © Oxford University Press 2023.
DOI: 10.1093/so/9780190063771.003.0015

264   MACHAUT

Table 14.1 Texts and translation of Machaut, Motet 4

Talea		Triplum		Motetus
C1, I	1	De *Bon* **Espoir**, de t*res Dous* **Souvenir**	1	*Puis qu'*en la *douce* rousee
	2	Et de *tres Dous* **Penser** contre **Desir**		
	3	M'A bonne **Amour** maintes fois secouru	2	D'*umblesse* ne vuet florir
	4	Quant il M'A plus aigrement sus couru,		
	5	Car quant **Desirs** plus fort me destreingnoit,	3	**Pitez,** tant que meüree
	6	Moult *doucement* **Espoirs** M'asseüroit		
II	7	Et **Souvenirs** ME moustroit la **biaute,**	4	Soit **mercis** que tant **desir,**
	8	Le scens, l'onneur, le pris et la bonte		
	9	De celle dont li *amoureus* **penser**	5	JE NE PUIS avoir *duree,*
C2	10	MON dolent cuer venoient conforter.		
	11	**Las!** or M'assaut **Desirs** plus qu'il ne suet.	6	Car en MOY s'est engendree,
	12	Mais *durement endurer* le M'estuet,		
III	13	Car JE SUI pres de perdre le confort	7	Par un **amoureus desir,**
	14	De *Bon* **Espoir** dont je ME desconfort;		
	15	Et **Souvenirs** ME fait toudis **penser**	8	Une ardeur *desmesuree*
	16	Pour MON las cuer faire **desesperer,**		
	17	Car **Grace, Amour, Franchise, Loyaute,**	9	Qu'**Amours**, par son *dous* plaisir,
	18	**Pite, Doctrine** et **Debonnairete**		
C3, i	19	Sont pour MOY seul si forment endormi	10	Et MA dame **desiree,**
	20	Que **Dangiers** est souvereins de **Merci**		
	21	Et que MA dame, a qui JE SUI rendus,	11	Par sa **biaute** coulouree,
ii	22	Croit a **Durte** et orguilleus **Refus,**	12	De **grace** y ont fait venir,
	23	Pour ce, sans plus, que M'**amour** ne MON cuer		
C4	24	N'en vueil ne PUIS departir a nul fuer.	13	*Mais puis qu'*einsi leur agree,
iii	25	*Mais puis qu'*estre ne puet ore autrement,	14	JE vueil *humblement* souffrir
	26	Face de MOY tout son commandement,		
	27	Car maugre li l'**AMERAY** loyaument.	15	Leur voloir jusqu'au morir.

Tenor: Speravi

Triplum: With Good Hope, with Very-Sweet Memory and with Very-Sweet Thought, good Love has many times helped me against Desire, when it has most sharply pricked me; for when Desire held me most tightly, Hope very sweetly reassured me, and Memory showed me the beauty, the sense, the honour, the value and the goodness of her from whom the amorous thoughts came to comfort my piteous heart. Alas! now Desire attacks me more than it used to. But I must firmly [harshly] endure it, for I am ready to lose the comfort of Good Hope, which discourages me; and Memory continuously makes me think [of it] in order to make my weary heart despair, for Grace, Love, Honesty, Loyalty, Pity, Doctrine and Elegance are for me alone so deeply asleep that Resistance rules over [is the lord of] Mercy and my lady, to whom I belong, believes in Harshness and prideful Refusal, so that she does not want my love or my heart nor can I leave at any price. But because it can now not be otherwise may her entire commandment be done to me, for in spite of her I will love her loyally.

Motetus: Because in the sweet dew of humility Pity does not want to flower, until mercy (which I desire very much) be ripened, I am not able to last, for within me is engendered by an amorous desire, an excessive ardour which Love, through his sweet pleasure, and my desired lady, through her ruddy beauty, have mercifully made to come here. But because this situation pleases them, I want humbly to endure their wishes until my death.

Tenor: I hoped.

case the tenor is the Introit usually assigned to the first Sunday after Pentecost, *Speravi*, 'I have hoped', thus linking it firmly with *Espoir*, hope.[3] The text is from Psalm 12: 6: 'ego autem in misericordia tua *speravi*: exultabit cor meum in salutari tuo ... et psallam nomini Domini altissimi' (But I have hoped in thy mercy; my heart shall rejoice in thy salvation, and I will praise the name of the Lord most high). The Introit antiphon, however, uses the past tense, *exultavit cor meum*, parallel to the tenor's *speravi*, instead of the future *exultabit* of the psalm. The tenor *Speravi* is thus a first-person authorial comment on the triplum and motetus treatments of *Espoir*. The tenor is also authoritative and fundamental, providing, as it does, biblical authority for the text and, via the liturgical chant, the raw material for the music of the entire motet, including some of the melodic material for the upper parts. (Other motets where this happens include M8, this chapter; *Tribum*, Ch. 4, also Chs. 9, 12 and elsewhere.) In this way, as Brownlee signalled, it undergirds the corrective overwriting of courtly *Espoir* by spiritual Hope (*spes*, *speravi*) by using French and Latin words respectively.[4] These tenor melodic motives are made prominent in the upper parts with long notes, or with distinctive rhythms (♩♩♩ ♩♩), on key words such as *douce*, *Amours*, *dame*, the emphatic first person *je*, and even for the important and repeated conjunction *car*, just as the musical structural joins are clearly pointed. Even the rhythmicisation of the tenor also provides, in much longer values (♩♩♩ and ♩♩, ♩♩♩ and ♩♩) the rhythms ♩♩♩ and ♩♩ prominent in the upper parts; a projection of the (prior) tenor rhythms into those of the upper parts. Similar cases have been pointed out, as for example in M10 (Ch. 12).

As is often the case, Machaut has selected his tenor not from the beginning of the chant, but within it, in order to link its keyword *Speravi* directly to the opening *De Bon Espoir* of the triplum. He must also have chosen this excerpt for its musical properties, which he exploits both contrapuntally and in deriving material from it for the upper parts. The version used by Machaut differs in one small detail from most of the melodies for this Introit; he fills in the leap of a third (between notes 4 and 6,

[3] Identified in Ludwig, *Guillaume de Machaut*, ii. 60*; this Introit is sometimes assigned to a later Sunday after Pentecost. Melodies assembled in Clark, 'Concordare cum materia', 189.

[4] See Leach, *Guillaume de Machaut*, ch. 4, for the central role of Hope as a creative force in Machaut's works, especially in the *Remede de Fortune*.

$b\flat$–g) to achieve an entirely conjunct melody.[5] It is serpentine, like the tenor of M9 (Ch. 9), with a range of only a fourth. The shorter tenor of M9 (*Fera pessima*) is from a different chant, but in fact its twelve notes are precisely and entirely embodied in the tenor of M4; they are identical with notes 3–14 of its eighteen notes, creating a bond of shared material between the two motets. Example 14.2 shows how the notes of the tenor of M9 recur here (cf. Ex. 9.3), and how in M4 the two melodic statements are superimposed on the three rhythmic statements (or, vice versa), creating different intertextual permutations at a musical level.[6] The conjunct-motion tenor (like that of M9) is very rich in melodic palindromic material and symmetries, both within one *color* statement and taken together with its link to the next iteration. *Face de moy* at B143 enters on the end of one of these large palindromes. Note the number of words marking negatives or opposites: *destreingnoit, desmesuree, desesperer, desconforter*. Some opposites are signalled by *contre*.

Ex. 14.2 The tenor *color* of Motet 4, showing its overlap with that of Motet 9 (*Fera pessima*) and its articulation by *talea* repetition

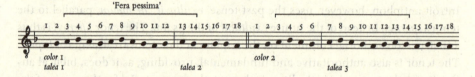

The phrase from which the Introit chant tenor comes, *In tua misericordia speravi*, links it further with *Merci* (= *misericordia*). The tenor *Speravi* is a first-person authorial comment on the—likewise first-person—triplum and motetus treatments of *Espoir* (= hope). However much the choice of tenor was conditioned by verbal considerations and liturgical context, Machaut also cared about the pliability and character of the musical material, in this case its conjunct serpentine quality.

Tenor Disposition, Notation and Upper-Voice Structures

In the first *color*, the maximodus is wonderfully ambiguous (▶ Ex. 14.1). The 34 breves of each *talea* divide neither by four nor by six. The tenor starts with three clear perfect maximodus groups, 3 × 3 = 9L, through B18. Another count of three could take us up to B24; thereafter the tenor can be counted in twos, though it dissolves into syncopation. The tenor modus is also unambiguously imperfect up to B18, but the syncopations thereafter bring strong coincidences with the upper parts which destabilise regular groupings. The upper parts are in imperfect tempus and major

---

[5] Clark, '*Concordare cum materia*', and 'Tracing the Tenor', 66; she also notes the possibility that Machaut made this slight alteration. Many of Machaut's tenor chants seem to have originated in or near Reims: see Ch. 13 n. 19.

[6] The phenomenon of shared or borrowed tenors between different motets is reviewed in Clark, 'Machaut Reading Machaut'.

prolation throughout; modus is imperfect, at least to start with. The triplum remains in imperfect modus; not so the motetus. It starts off in unmistakable duple modus groupings, appearing to follow the tenor's imperfect modus through B16; but then we are taken by surprise by the unsignalled need to alter B17 before the single dotted long at B19. The dot, by hindsight, is therefore not a dot of addition, but confirms its perfect status. An unsignalled shift to perfect modus, in the motetus alone, must start in B16, and therefore by further hindsight from B13, whose rest coincides with a strong tenor maxima. Motetus B23 likewise must be altered before the long at B25; but from B25–B34 the motetus falls into groupings of two breves to the long, setting up a tension with the syncopated tenor notes of its modus and maximodus, ambiguous at this point. This is repeated at the corresponding places in the other *taleae* of *color* 1, where the upper parts are partially but not wholly isorhythmic. Because of these ambiguities, some places in ⊙ Example 14.1 have been non-committally barred. The altered breves are marked in ⊙ Example 14.1 by swallowtails. Like many notational ambiguities and unsignalled changes, this one has to be construed empirically. Under-prescriptive notation is not necessarily faulty notation. There is no comparable shift in the fully isorhythmic diminished section, though the now short-term syncopations are heard as playful complements to the hockets that occupy the second half of each *talea*.

The tenor is stated twice, each statement embodying two *colores* (C1–2, C3–4), the second time in written-out diminution at the next note-level down, which in imperfect modus and tempus results in 2:1 proportion. Each of the motet's two sections contains three tenor *taleae* which overlap with the two differently rhythmicised *color* statements (C1–2, C3–4). Because the recurring pitches in C2 and C4 are attached to different rhythms, these statements differ in length from C1 and C3. The motet is 153 breves long; the first two tenor *colores* total 102 breves (53 + 49), the second two 51 breves (26½ + 24½).[7] The *talea* length is 34 breves in section I, 17 breves in diminution. Thus the tenor has altogether four melodic *color* statements asymmetrically mapped onto six rhythmic *talea* statements (three undiminished, three diminished), which avoids simple coincidence of the same notes with the same rhythms.

The ending is anomalous, as in several motets by Machaut and others, discussed in Chapter 1. The end of each undiminished tenor *talea* of M4 is ▅ ▅ ɪ, which in regular written-out diminution is ▅ ▅ ⊤ as in **Ferrell(Vg)** and **MachautG**, arriving a semibreve later than the upper parts, as in Example 1.1b above. But **MachautA** and **MachautE** have (irregularly) ▄ ▄ ⊤ for the final two tenor notes of the diminished *color*, thus arriving at the final cadence a semibreve ahead of the upper parts (as in ⊙ Ex. 14.1, B151–B53).[8] An alternative ending is provided in ⊙ Ex. 14.1 to align the cadential arrival. Other motets with non-coincident endings as notated are M10 (Ch. 12 and Ex. 1.1c), M17, M9 (Ch. 9, ⊙ Ex. 9.1), where the tenor arrives later, and M15 (Ch. 10 and Ex. 1.1d),

---

[7] The strikingly unmusical number of 153 (a multiple of 17) is the number of the miraculous draft of fishes (John 21: 1–14), and the length in breves of a perhaps surprising number of motets: *Sub Arturo*, Ch. 20; *Floret*, Ch. 6, Dunstaple's motet 28, *Gaude virgo salutata*, and the Cyprus motet 28 (*O rex*), Ch. 32. It is more common for motets to use numbers like 120 or 144, so it is surprising that several use 153.

[8] This may indicate some editorial initiative to rectify the cadence. The Ferrara Ensemble recording elongates the upper parts in order to end with the 'late' tenor ending (see Ch. 1 n. 14).

268 MACHAUT

where the triplum is delayed.[9] In these cases, the tenors could have been conceived and notated homographically, perhaps with the intention that an adjusted ending would be provided in performance, but which was not among any editorial adjustments made to Machaut's copies for their first surviving transmission in **MachautC**, and thence to the other complete-works manuscripts. The misaligned endings appear to be prescriptive because the diminutions are fully and mechanically written out; however, derivation by performers from a single notated form might have carried a common-sense expectation of adjustment.

Use of Chant in Upper Voices

The peak notes of the chant, *a bb a*, occur eight times in the tenor: twice in each tenor *color*, at breves 9 and 22, and their subsequent restatements. This peak also occurs three times in the motetus, an octave higher, in long notes; the *bb* is made very prominent, audibly and structurally, as the highest motetus note, occurring only in long notes, at B53–B58, punning, on the word *duree*, at the join of the first two *color* statements (C2), then at the *melodically* corresponding position B104–B6 and the *rhythmically* corresponding B121–B23 on *De grace*, each time crossing over and rising above the triplum. The *a bb a* figure occurs once in the triplum, at B72, with the triplum's only notated *bb* coinciding with a tenor *bb*. Such integration of the chant melody into newly composed upper voices is more often cultivated than has usually been noticed, and confirms tenor priority in relation to the melodic composition of the upper parts.[10] The highest triplum note *d* is at *amoureus penser*, B49–B50, on a descending scale down a fifth, as for the opening *Espoir*.

There is considerable play with voice-crossing, and with calculated use of the extremes of the ranges, though it is rather more understated here than, for example, in M9 (Ch. 9), where the depths are literally plumbed and the parts depictively crossed for *cavernis* and *speluncis* (caverns and pits). At B24–B25 of M4, to the triplum words in line 4, 'Il m'a sus couru' ('he runs above me'), the motetus goes above the triplum.[11]

Texts

Table 14.1 above shows how the verbal texts are distributed between the twice three *talea* statements for triplum and motetus. Unlike the striking case of M9 (Ch. 9), the text distribution is here fairly even, with two triplum lines to every one of the motetus in *colores* 1 and 2, and three triplum lines to every two of the motetus in the shorter *colores* 3 and 4. In *colores* 1 and 2, each *talea* takes six triplum and three motetus lines; in *colores* 3 and 4, three

---

[9] See especially Ch. 1; also Ch. 12, 'Endings', for discussion of whether these dissonant endings should be observed; Machaut, *The Motets*, ed. Boogaart, 15; and Ch. 12 n. 11 for the tenor of M6, whose differently rhythmicised second *color* is marked for repetition but not written out. It has no diminution, but the *talea* overlaps the join in such a way that the notes of the second *color* fall on different parts of the perfection, resulting in different application of imperfection and alteration. See Dudas and Earp, *Four Early Ars nova Motets*, for a comparable instance there on f. 79ʳ of **Paris934**. An instance where an adjusted ending seems to be prescribed is in *O amicus*, Ch. 22.

[10] It is a prominent feature of *Tribum*, Ch. 4.

[11] See more recently Zayaruznaya, 'She Has a Wheel'.

triplum and two motetus lines. 3:2 is also fundamental to the musical structure; each of the two sections contains two *colores* to three *taleae*.

The tenor, *Speravi*, was chosen to go with *De Bon Espoir*, combining Latin and French, sacred and secular hope. All three texts use the first-person singular pronouns (*moy* and *je*); the registers of the texts complement and reinforce each other. The contrastive challenges of the genre are instead fulfilled in other ways. Motetus texts are nearly always shorter and their music sparer than in the triplum; but here the line-lengths are also different (decasyllables, heptasyllables), as are the rhyme schemes, thirteen different couplets in the triplum, just two alternating rhyme syllables in the motetus.[12]

The 27:15 lines easily fall into 24 + 3: 12 + 3, i.e. a 2:1 ratio of lines (24:12) plus an *envoi* of three lines in each text. That this is the intended structure is confirmed by each *envoi* starting with the same words: *Mais puis que . . .*, which signal and initiate, in the triplum, the last *talea*, and in the motetus, the last *color*. This is followed by, respectively, *moy* and *je*, then love and death, knitting the texts together. *Puis que* recapitulates the opening of the motetus text.

Jacques Boogaart has noted several aspects of these texts in relation to a chanson by the trouvère Thibaut de Champagne, *Tout autresi con l'ente fet venir/Li arrousers de l'eve qui chiet jus*. Not only does Machaut's motetus start with the nature topos, fairly common in trouvère poetry, but it also has the unique conceit of bringing forth fresh growth by sprinkling water on a tree graft (*enté*: a striking reference also to the procedure of the *motet enté*), an image which Machaut uses to express the rejuvenation of his love: *umblesse*, the stance of the lady towards the aspiring lover, is compared to the dew which should bring forth the flower of Pity and the fruits of Mercy. Machaut knew the song, whose imagery is paraphrased in the second and third strophes of his *Lay de Plour*.[13] Boogaart demonstrates the detailed relationship between Thibaut's text and M4. The *abag* motive (tenor notes 3–6), so prominent in M9 (Ch. 9), is shown by Boogaart to allude also to Thibaut's song.[14] In the motetus this motive sounds three times in long note values (breves 53–58, 104–6 and 121–23). In the triplum it appears once, in shorter note values, at B73 (in TIII), at 'perdre le confort', but in this voice the ♭ sign is conspicuous because used only here.

Love and desire are threaded through both texts. The triplum alternates *Desir*, *Amour*, *Desir*, *amoureus*, *Desir*, then three forms of *Amour* in the second half of the text. In the motetus, *Desir*, *amoureus*, *desir*, *Amours*, *desiree*. *Grace*, *pite*, *merci* also occur in both texts. The motetus is chiastically structured at a literal level around the central line 8, *une ardeur desmesuree*, whose prolonged punning measuring significance we will see below. Musically the phrase spans B82–B94 and is flanked by *Amour*, *amoureus*, amorous desire in various combinations.

Whereas in some motets (M9 triplum, M8) the apportionment of text to music is evenly distributed, regular and predictable,[15] here there is some slight but purposeful local displacement, allowing different nodal points to be ingeniously brought together, perhaps to ensure that *amoureus desir*, motetus line 7, just before the midpoint of the

---

[12] The text forms are analysed exhaustively from this aspect, as for other motets, in Reichert, 'Das Verhältnis'.

[13] Boogaart, 'Encompassing Past and Present', 19–23.

[14] Ibid.: 'The motif also appears in the *Lay de plour* at a textually significant place, although not corresponding with the same words as in Thibaut's chanson.'

[15] See also Reichert, 'Das Verhältnis'.

text, is prolonged over the middle of the music from B71–B80. The crucial word *desir* is extended (the desire prolonged) over five breves (76–80) and given prominence, with no audible competition; indeed, the *de* of *desir* coincides with the *de* of the triplum's *desconfort* (a 'word chord'). *Desir* is nearly aligned across the first three *taleae*; triplum B8–B9, motetus B43–B46 and B76–B80. It is also contrived that the important word *Amours*, that follows the textual midpoint in the motetus, coincides with triplum *Amour* at B95, the golden section of the music.[16]

The midpoint of the music, centred around B77, is not the main structural join, which because of the diminution of C2 occurs at the two-thirds point, at C3, breve 103 of 153. Although it does not coincide with a *talea/color* shift or a musical structural point of any kind, this midpoint is marked by verbal and musical density. It is flanked by the recapitulation in the triplum of the opening words *De Bon Espoir* at the middle triplum line 14, B74, to their opening rhythm (♦ ♦ ♦♦ ♦♦), just anticipating the midpoint of the music (B77). That triplum opening rhythm (♦ ♦ ♦♦ ♦♦) occurs twice in succession in the first four bars, for *De Bon Espoir* and *de tres Dous Souvenir*; it is used in turn for the repeat of the word *Souvenirs* at B80–B82, a 'reminder', in case we missed the verbal recapitulation. Here at B80, instead of the opening *c c cbag f*, *Souvenirs* inverts the opening downward scale to a rising scale, *g g fgab c*.

The triad of words *Espoir, Souvenir, Penser*, comes three times, always in the same order, with *Souvenir* as the central term, in triplum lines 1–2, then at 6–9, where *Souvenir* punningly initiates the second *talea*, TII, B35, again, as if to nudge: 'remember?', also with ♦♦ ♦♦; and thirdly at lines 14–15, B80, around the musical and textual midpoint, as just noted. *Et souvenirs me*, plus a verb, begins lines 7 and 15, and line 1's *De Bon Espoir* is recapitulated at the middle line (14). Both textual and musical markers guide the ear to the formal layout by verbal and musical recapitulations. Note the play of different combinations of adjectives with these nouns—*amoureus penser, amoureus desir, tresdous penser, tresdous souvenir, bon espoir, bonne amour*—and of the interplay of the numerous first-person words.

Meanwhile in the motetus, the moisture and the heat identified as crucial by Brownlee (*rousee*, dew, and *ardeur*, heat), appear in lines 1 and 8, 8 being the middle line and *ardeur* the central word. 'Ardeur desmesuree' (beyond measure) invites and gets a multiple punning position, from its measured location and long notes B85–B93, a passage within the unsignalled switch to perfect modus. The corresponding passage in *talea* 2 also puns on measure: 'Je ne puis avoir duree' (B48–B60). The motetus words 'Une ardeur desmesuree' are introduced, in the triplum B80–B81 on the word 'Souvenirs' (memories), by the recapitulation of the opening triplum rhythm for 'De bon espoir', ♦ ♦ |♦♦ ♦♦ ♦, but with the syllables slightly realigned. Occupying B82–B94, 'Une ardeur desmesuree' fills the space between the midpoint of the music at B77 and the main structural join of the motet at B103, contributing to the audible density there, with *desmesuree* (excessive, beyond measure) punningly marking the shift to perfect modus on this *talea*, showing once again a close connection in the micro-planning of music–text relationships.[17]

---

[16] Instances of significant words calculated to coincide are ubiquitous. Examples are given for *Vos/Gratissima* in Ch. 8.

[17] In M1, 'Mais elle attent trop longuement' (But she waits too long) begins the diminution section, signalling the now speeded-up tenor.

The twelve-bar duration of the unsignalled switch to perfect modus in the motetus (B13–B24 and corresponding places)[18] coincides with *Je ne puis avoir duree* (I'm unable to last) in *talea* II B47–, and *Une ardeur desmesuree* (heat beyond measure) in *talea* III B81–, puns on duration. As noted for M10 in Chapter 12, and elsewhere, words for wounding and cutting, measurement and proportion and similar, are commonplace puns for structural joins in motets; not only does the music underline the text but the text also underlines the musical structure in mutual reinforcement. Memory (*souvenir*), also contributes to that function in M4. The motetus metre shifts back just before B95, where it is contrived that the important word *Amours*, immediately following the midpoint of the motetus text, coincides with triplum *Amour*, a point of dense activity marked by a list of seven virtues. The list shows a striking similarity to M15 (Ch. 10), where there is a marked switch from bad things to good, starting with a similar and similarly placed list of seven virtues, with four in common between the two lists, starting in M15 with *raison* (= *ratio* = proportion):

> M4: Car Grace, Amour, Franchise, Loyauté, Pité, Doctrine et Debonnaireté;
> M15: Que Raison, Droiture, Doucure, Debonnairete, Franchise, Grace et Pite.

D'umblesse is the seventh word from the beginning (in motetus line 2), and *humblement* the seventh from the end (in the penultimate line); both occurrences of these words get the motetus's lowest note, *c*, which points up the symmetry as well as depicting the abasement of their 'low' sense.[19] At triplum B9, the words are *contre desir*; to the equivalent of an interrupted cadence, frustrating the 'desired' resolution; and literally 'against desire', we hear in motetus B9–B11 a phrase that recurs at the same point in the following two *taleae*, identical in both notes and music, though over different tenor notes, both of them together with the word *desir* in the motetus. This is emphasised too by the distinctive and sparingly used rhythm ♦♦♦♦♦ and its more frequent inverse, ♦♦♦ ♦♦, which stand out against the predominant rhythms creating the neutral background of ♦ ♦ and ♦♦ ♦♦. We might call this the 'desire motive'; it occurs also at B27, literally 'contre pité', to the same rhythm ♦♦ ♦♦♦ ♦ *e d ede f*: here too the word *desir* is in the triplum, but the motive is set to *pité* in the motetus. (*Desir* is also set to ▪ ♦ | ♦ ♦ ♦ ♦ | ▪, *e d edec d* at motetus B109–B10.) Desire is emphasised in the texts, but musical reinforcing devices here draw attention to words or concepts, to place them significantly against words in other parts, and to imply them musically even in the absence of the word, like *Leitmotive*. Similarly, a tenor tag can imply more tenor text than is stated in the manuscript or even more than is used in the given segment of chant. The technique is both affective and structural.

The opening notes and rhythm of the motetus (B1–B3), *f fefg a* ▪ | ♦ ♦ ♦ ♦ | ▪ are identical with, and possibly an allusion to, the opening of the motetus of Vitry's

---

[18] It is not until the need to alter the breve at 17, 51 and 85 that perfect modus is confirmed, but the three-breve grouping is then projected back to B13, B47 and B81.

[19] Boogaart, 'Encompassing Past and Present', 19–23, also notes the symmetrical placement of *umblesse* and *humblement*: the lady's dew of *umblesse* enables the graft of Pity to flower, and then at the end, the lover subjects himself *humblement* to her will.

Garrit gallus/In nova, a passage also quoted in the related Marigny motet *Tribum/ Quoniam* (Ch. 4 and Ex. 4.6). In *color* 1, the upper parts, especially the triplum, deviate from strict isorhythm, especially at the beginnings and last breve of the first three *taleae*. Both upper parts are strictly isorhythmic in the three *taleae* of the second section. It is striking that the sixth breve of the motetus in all six *taleae* has the rhythm ♩♩♩ ♩♩. It also occurs at corresponding places in motetus B48 and B82, B61 and B95, but its only occurrence in the triplum is at B34, linking the end of TI to TII.

The following passages have the same pitches and rhythms in the motetus at the following places aligned in ⏵ Example 14.1: B39–B40 = B73–B74, B57–B61 = B91–B95; and B103–B9 = B120–B26. In both upper parts B112–B13 = B129–B30 except for the *g* minim pitch in B129, which could be emended to *f*.

Dating, and Absence from MachautC

There has been considerable debate about the absence of M4 from the earliest Machaut MS, **MachautC**, which otherwise presents the first twenty motets in what remained their standard order. Earp put this down to a codicological accident when recopying of the first six motets (by the same scribe) was necessary to integrate it with some later, less orderly additions but has more recently conceded that the motet could post-date that compilation.[20] Jared Hartt has recently summarised the dating considerations and makes the case for a later composition date on grounds of sonority, suggesting, on grounds of several appearances of her name (*bon, bonne*) in the text, that it could have been a memorial to Bonne of Luxembourg.[21]

Motet 8. *Qui es promesses/Ha! Fortune/Et non est qui adjuvat*

For the music see ⏵ Example 14.3 and for the texts and translation Table 14.2.

Motet 8 is one of the few motets that circulated outside the complete-works manuscripts, in **Ca1328**, **Ivrea** and **Trém**, and is the most widely transmitted of all Machaut's motets.[22] It was known to Chaucer, who paraphrases the triplum text in the *Book of the Duchess*. It is the only Machaut motet whose text is also preserved without music, in Stockholm, Kungliga Biblioteket, MS V.u.22, f. 138[v].[23] It is cited for imperfect time and prolation in the **Paris14741** version of the *Ars nova* treatise, interestingly by its triplum text, not by the more usual motetus as in the **Trém** index.

[20] Earp, 'Scribal Practice, Manuscript Production', 140–42. For a later concession, see Earp, 'Isorhythm', 100 n. 78. On the copying of the motets, see also Smilansky, 'Creating MS C', 288–92.

[21] Hartt, 'Approaching the Motets', 369–75.

[22] The accompanying transcription, ⏵ Ex. 14.3, mainly follows **MachautA** and **Ferrell(Vg)**. For an excellent modern edition and full listing of variants, see Machaut, *The Motets*, ed. Boogaart, 208–11.

[23] The Chaucer and text manuscript references are reported in Earp, *Guillaume de Machaut: A Guide*, 367. See also Machaut, *The Motets*, ed. Boogaart, commentary to M9, 211; Chaucer mentions the scorpion present in that motet, which was also in **Trém**.

MACHAUT'S MOTETS 4 AND 8 273

Table 14.2 Texts and translation of Machaut, Motet 8

Taleae	Line	Triplum		Line	Motetus	
PI C1	1	Qui es promesses	de **Fortune** se fie	1	Ha! **Fortune**	trop SUI mis loing de port,
	2	Et es richesses	de ses dons s'asseüre,			
	3	Ou cils qui croit	qu'elle soit tant s'amie	2	Quant en la mer	M'AS mis sans aviron
	4	Que pour li soit	en riens ferme ou seüre,			
	5	Il est trop fols,	car elle est non seüre	3	En un batel	petit, plat et sans bort,
PII	6	Sans foy, sans loy,	sans droit et sans mesure,	4	Foible, pourri,	sans voile; et environ
	7	C'est fiens couvers	de riche couverture,			
C2	8	Qui dehors luist	et dedens est ordure.			
	9	Une ydole est	de **fausse** pourtraiture,	5	Sont tuit li vent	contraire pour MA **mort**,
	10	Ou nuls ne doit	croire ne mettre cure:	6	Si qu'il n'i a	confort ne garison,
PIII	11	Sa convenance	en vertu pas ne dure,	7	Merci n'espoir,	ne d'eschaper ressort,
	12	Car c'est tous vens,	ne riens qu'elle figure			
	13	Ne puet estre	fors de **fausse** figure			
C3	14	Et li siens sont	toudis en aventure	8	Ne riens de bien	pour MOY, car sans raison
	15	De trebuchier;	car par droite nature,	9	JE voy venir	la **mort** amere a tort
PIV	16	La desloyal	renoïe, parjure,	10	Preste de MOY	mettre a destruction;
	17	**Fausse, traître,**	perverse et mere sure			
	18	Oint et puis point	de si **mortel** pointure			
	19	Que ceaus qui sont	fait de sa nourriture	11	Mais celle **mort**	reçoy JE par ton sort,
	20	En **traïson** met	a desconfiture.	12	**Fausse Fortune**	et par ta **traïson**.

Tenor: Et non est qui adjuvat

P = upper-part periods, each comprising three tenor *taleae*. The tenor's C3 starts during the lines marked, not at their beginning. Verbal relationships are typographically distinguished by boldface, italics and underlining.

Triplum: He who trusts Fortune's promises and counts on the riches of her gifts, or he who thinks that she might be his friend, that for him she might be stable or secure in anything, he is quite mad, for Fortune is uncertain, without faith, without law, without right, without decorum [*mesure*: but also moderation or 'measure']. She is excrement covered with a rich covering, which shines on the outside and inside is trash. She is an idol deceitfully shaped in which no one should believe or trust; her compact with virtue does not last, for it's all wind, and nothing it [= her countenance; or perhaps Fortune herself] represents can be anything except counterfeit signs [false figures]; and her followers are always at risk of stumbling; for according to [her] true nature, the disloyal one disavows and perjures; false, treacherous, mother of bitter milk, she anoints and then pricks with such a fatal prick that those whom she has raised she treacherously undoes.

Motetus: Ah! Fortune, I put myself too far from port when you put me into the sea oarless in a small boat, flat and without board, weak, rotten and without sail. And around me all the winds blow unfavourably [*contraire*] for my death, so that there is no comfort or healing, no mercy or hope, no way to escape, nor anything good for me, for unjustly I see bitter death advance wrongly, ready to destroy me, but I receive this death by your decision, false Fortune, and by your treachery.

Tenor: And there is no one who helps.

Tenor

Et non est qui adiuvet is from the Verse of the Responsory *Circumdederunt me* for Passion Sunday (CAO 4:6287); it is also sometimes specified for other Lenten occasions. The biblical source is Psalm 21: 12: 'quoniam tribulatio proxima est, quoniam non est qui adiuvet'. All the Machaut MSS have *adiuvat* (who helps), except **Ferrell(Vg)**, where *adiuvet* has been changed from *adiuvat* by erasure, to conform with the liturgical sources. **Trém** and **Ivrea** have *adiuvet*.[24]

The relation between the tenors of Motets 9 and 4 has been discussed, above and in Chapter 9. The tenor of M8 is a short segment from the end of the much longer chant used as the tenor of the longer and later M21. The relationship is fully discussed by Alice Clark, who also enumerates other cases of shared tenors, within and outside Machaut's own corpus, and offers interesting comparisons between the two motets. Earp has analysed the tonal implications of the tenor and commented on ways in which the instability of Fortune is emphasised.[25]

Tenor and Structure

The tenor *color* consists of 16 notes of the chant, stated three times, without dimunition. Modus and maximodus are both perfect, tempus and prolation imperfect. There are 12 very short tenor *taleae* of four notes, each consisting of three perfect longs (= 9 imperfect breves): ◼ ◼ ⊥ ◼ ◼, thus falling into perfect maximodus as well as perfect modus. At a total of 106 fully imperfect breves, it is one of the shortest motets. The tenor *color* occupies four of these *taleae*, 36 breves for each of the three tenor *color* statements. But these *colores* do not coincide with the three-*talea* periods of the upper parts. ⏵ Example 14.3 aligns not the three tenor *colores*, but four periods governed by the upper parts that have some rhythmic correspondences but not complete isorhythm. (The tenor *colores* could have been aligned instead, but this would have obscured the correspondences of the upper-voice *taleae*.) Three of the short tenor *taleae* make up one of these periods, as I shall call them, marked I abc, II abc, III abc, IV abc. The four aligned 27-breve periods are superimposed on the three tenor *colores* (4 × 3) each of 36 breves. These upper-part periods have been called 'Großtalea' (Reichert) and 'supertalea' (Boogaart). Anna Zayaruznaya prefers the neutral 'block' to designate spans of music that are articulated by, but not fully made up of, *taleae*.[26] Since the upper-voice periods may be only

---

[24] Boogaart notes (email of 7.2.2021) that **Ferrell(Vg)** made the change after **MachautB** had copied it, and **MachautE** copied *adjuvat* from **MachautB**, whereas the other later versions have the *e*. For the copying relationship between these manuscripts see Bent, 'The Machaut Manuscripts *Vg*, *B* and *E*' and Earp, *Ferrell-Vogüé*, 44–46.

[25] Earp, 'Declamatory Dissonance in Machaut'. Earp, '"The spirit moves me"', 284–88, explores the tonal implications of the tenor in relation to unstable Fortuna. Boogaart, '*O series summe rata*', 134, and Boogaart, 'Sound and Cipher', 389–90, suggest that cadences occurring at an earlier point in each *color* reflect the contrary motion of Fortune's double wheel, the fickleness of Fortuna being the subject of the motet.

[26] See Zayaruznaya, *Upper-Voice Structures*, for a recent highlighting of the phenomenon of upper-voice *taleae*. A number of the motets in which she identifies this phenomenon are discussed in the present book: *Tribum/Quoniam* (Ch. 4) as well as Machaut M15—all managed in a slightly different way from M8. See Ch. 4 on the term 'block', which I used for *Tribum* for the 2 × 3 blocks of music identical in pitch and rhythm in all parts, and which also works well for M20, where irregularly placed isorhythmic blocks of 3–4 breves in both upper parts only are irregularly spaced over differing tenor notes. The term is less well suited to M8, where there is partial isorhythm—hence 'periods'. 'Double *talea*' accurately describes a pair of identical tenor *taleae* that is spanned by a single upper-part *talea*.

partly isorhythmic, as here, I prefer to avoid the term *talea*, which has connotations of rhythmic identity, and will call them periods.

Both upper parts are strictly isorhythmic for just the last four perfect L of each period (L6–L9, B16–B27 and aligned corresponding places), starting with the striking syncopes of B16–B24 and corresponding places. While caution is in order about identifying word-painting or symbolism in an aesthetic and affective world so different from ours, there can be little doubt here that they represent the rocking of the rotten leaky boat and the instability of Fortune, built in the longer term on the shifting sands of a *color* staggered asymmetrically against non-coincident upper-voice periods. The duple time and prolation of the upper parts which constitute the audible surface of the motet are particularly well suited to this effect. Triplum and motetus come together in equality and in number of notes and syllables for these sections, accounting for the uneven distribution of text between triplum and motetus. In period I, triplum lines 4–5 align with motetus lines 2–3, and similarly in periods II–IV, while motetus lines 1, 4, 7 and 10 each stretch over three triplum lines for the first half of each period. Similar equality of notes and texts, especially at *talea* ends, is often achieved in other motets with hockets; here, instead, the choice of syncopes is particularly well suited to imperfect time and prolation as well as to reflecting the text.

For the first five perfect longs of each section, the triplum has much more isorhythmic correspondence than the motetus; see the aligned beginnings of periods II, III and IV, but not I. Brownlee defined the third-person triplum text as being concerned with logical proof, a clerkly warning of the nature of Fortune and the consequences of that nature. The motetus is a lament addressed to Fortune. He showed it to be contrastively rhetorical, which may be consistent with its lower incidence of isorhythm. Its emphatic first-person forms are distinguished in Table 14.2 by small capitals. The different registers he identified in the texts, more strongly so than in M4, are vividly reflected in the musical setting within a very tightly unified whole. Musically, the triplum register or range is literally narrower (a seventh), perhaps a function of its clerkly voice, while the motetus (range of a tenth) plays around it, appearing much less tightly disciplined in pitch and rhythm.[27] The voice-crossings (discussed above for M4, and for M9 in Ch. 9) cannot easily be heard from outside, because the wide range of the motetus is masked by its simultaneity with the triplum, which cancels out these extremes of range. But it is only by considering the qualities of each musical part separately, as also for the verbal texts, that these differences become apparent. There are very few rests in the upper parts. Apart from a minim rest in each to create the semibreve syncopations, both have a breve rest only at the end of each period; the rest in the triplum in each case precedes an identical refrain-like upbeat bridge to the next *talea*: four minims *a g f e* at the end of each system in ⓟ Example 14.3.

Derivation of Upper Parts from the Tenor

The melodic material of the upper parts is—yet again—derived closely from the tenor, with its conjunct motives, rising fourths, and especially the falling fifths. The whole motet is an essay in tightly disciplined permutations: the same pitches are placed over

---

[27] Machaut, *The Motets*, ed. Boogaart, 9–10, remarks that the less 'disciplined' and unruly nature of motetus parts is what makes them so interesting.

different tenor notes, different pitches over the same tenor notes. The top parts often work out in micro-motives the note-successions of the tenor's melodic content, here in forward, inverted and retrograde versions. Example 14.4 shows how many of the four-note minim formulas of the top parts are derived from the chant and used at various pitches. The most obvious ones are those marked x and y in Example 14.4. Both are used directly and in retrograde and inversion, and the last four tenor notes are y in retrograde. The retrograde of x is the inversion of y, and the retrograde of y is the inversion of x. Motive x, *a g a b* (tr B3), recurs at a different pitch in breves 31, 35, 57, 85, but then at the same pitch only in B61, followed by three statements in close succession at different pitches. Other combinations derived from the chant tenor are ubiquitous.

Ex. 14.4 Tenor of Motet 8, showing leaps of 4ths and 5ths, the x and y motives and their retrogrades and inversions, and the derivation of four-note minim formulas of the top parts from the chant

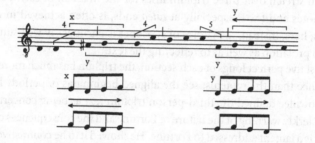

A different motive *a g g f* at triplum B4, for *Fortune*, recurs in the motetus for *Fausse Fortune* at B102, four breves from the end, where it rises above ('usurping') the triplum to the motetus's highest pitch *a*. The only other motetus occurrences of this motive are in the parallel places in periods 2 and 3.

Words for Music

The occurrences of *Fortune* in both texts at the beginning announce the theme unmistakably and make the word coincide musically at B4; the midpoint (end of system 2) brings together the synonymous words *garison* and *cure*; *traison* is nearly aligned in both the last lines, in close proximity to *Fausse Fortune* (bold in Table 14.2 above), finally conjoined at the end of the motetus as a culmination of several separate occurrences of *Fausse* and *Fortune*. *Contraire* and *sans raison* both have unusual octave leaps; comparable depictive musical responses to musically pregnant terminology can be multiplied in Machaut's motets. The opposites that characterised M4 have their counterparts in M8 in the strong use of *contraire* and the repeated use of *sans*, with their musical leaps.

Boogaart refers to the famous contrary wheels of Fortune, which I also invoked in Chapter 3 (especially there n. 26), in demonstrating the contrary motion of the double agenda of *Fauvel*. He points out that the estimated proportions of those wheels have been shown to give Fortune a mechanical advance of approximately 4:3; this is precisely the relationship between the tenor *color* (of four tenor *taleae*) to the upper-voice periods (of three tenor *taleae*).[28] Even the tenor has a negative: *Et non est*. The linking of *Merci* and *n'espoir* in M8 reflects two central words of M4. *Fortune* gets the only perfect long in the upper parts, motetus B7–B9, immediately followed, perhaps punningly, by 'trop . . . loing de port' at B10–B13, which also gets the lowest point of the motetus ('too far from port').

The triplum words of the first syncope passage emphasise instability: 'en riens ferme ou seüre, Il est trop fols, car elle est non seüre' (spanning lines 4–5). The threefold *sans* that ends motetus lines 2, 3, 4 ('sans aviron', 'sans bort', 'sans voile') immediately preceded the most negative triplum line 6 ('Sans foy, sans loy, sans droit et sans mesure') spanning periods I and II. There is much play between the voices with alliteration and assonance: *Que/quant* at B15, *Foy/foible* at B28, *pour/pour* at B46, *riens/sien/bien* at B70. The words are exploited for such sound qualities, perhaps even chosen for them. The distribution and spacing of key words in the texts is telling; they are used musically as sonic objects (in such alliterations) as well as for their meaning. Key words are so qualified by their frequency of occurrence or prominence of appearance, or both, and also by providing links between the two texts. Here they include *Fortune*, *fausse*, *mort*, *traison*, *vens/vent*—and the negative *sans*, typographically distinguished above in Table 14.2. *Fausse* at triplum B45 has a notated 'fictive' $f\sharp$ (punning on *musica falsa*) against the tenor *color*'s one notated $f\sharp$.

The Midpoint

One emendation requires comment. The motetus at B55 has *a* in all the main manuscripts, emended in **MachautE** to *g*, and by Friedrich Ludwig and Leo Schrade to *b*, which creates a strikingly high note on *Merci* at the midpoint, but takes the motetus outside its range. I adopt an emendation to $f(\sharp)$.[29] Most manuscripts have a clef change at this point which arguably leaves the pitch of this note as *a* or *f* ambiguous. But this solution creates unmitigated parallel fifths with the tenor, otherwise absent in this motet (though narrowly avoided at B100–B1). Neither *f* nor *b* is an ideal solution.

The area around the midpoint of a motet is often a centre of gravity or density. There is intense activity around B61–B67, just following the textual and musical midpoint (indeed, between the midpoint and the musical golden section of the motet, sometimes a significant node). Three bars, B61, B62, B64, all have four minims in both upper parts together; only otherwise at the beginning does this happen in two consecutive bars. The motetus motive *f e d e* at B61 otherwise occurs exclusively in the triplum. The motetus at B62–B65 is an almost exact recapitulation of its music for *Fortune* at B4–B7: Fortune is the present but unspoken sequel to the negative *Merci n'espoir*. This passage has a strong resonance with the melody used for love = fire = death in M10, as shown in Example 14.5. It also marks the junction between the two demonstrations about Fortune, an intense moment, bridged by *fausse figure* into the syncope section. The first triplum appearance of *Fortune* at B4 gets exactly the same notes in the motetus *Fortune* in B102, another recapitulation. None of this is simple motivic equation, but the music does serve to underpin many verbal subtleties in such ways.

---

[28] Machaut, *The Motets*, ed. Boogaart, 209; see also Zayaruznaya, 'She has a Wheel'.
[29] As proposed by Leach, *Guillaume de Machaut*, 213 n. 32.

Ex. 14.5 Similar phrases leading to death in Motet 10 and Motet 8

Relationship to Other Motets

The relationship between M8 and M21 (including their tenors) has been well expounded by Alice Clark.[30] The tripla of M8 and M15 both end with the same word, *desconfiture*, and on the same progression.[31] In M15 it receives a suspended dissonant appoggiatura at the final cadence which, if thought too 'discomforting', might have to be emended against the testimony of the manuscripts (see Chs. 1, 10 and 12). There is no such dissonant suspension on this final word in M8.

The motetus of *Aman novi*/*Heu Fortuna* in *Fauvel* is also a first-person reproach to Fortune, who has betrayed the speaker and caused his death, in both cases with watery metaphors for Fortune's instability—the leaky boat in M8 and, in *Aman*, 'sunk in the lake of tears', a watery end like that of Phaeton and Icarus in the triplum. In the motetus of each motet, the Latin *Heu Fortuna* in *Aman* is mirrored here by the French *Ha Fortune*. In *Fauvel*, the motet is introduced like a set piece, an aria within the narrative. The words of the motetus are put in Fauvel's mouth—'ha fait le motet qui s'ensuit'—while the triplum is in a different, mostly more impersonal, narrative register and fulfils a different role in the context of the *Fauvel* story (see Ch. 4).

This chapter has drawn attention particularly to further aspects of musical structure and detail with depictive text–music relationships, signalling structural points (*mesure*), low pitch for low words, contrary motion for contrary textual syncopes for the rocking instability of *Fortune*. The upper parts here, as elsewhere, are suffused with melodic and rhythmic ingredients drawn from the tenor—a pre-existent segment of melody chosen for its key word(s), and often its suitability to the prior concept of the *materia*, as expressed in the texts, corroborating yet again the tenor's musical priority over the organisation of the upper parts. The chapters of Part III have drawn together aspects of Machaut's motet composition in different ways, together with the Gloria

---

[30] Clark, 'Machaut Reading Machaut'.
[31] Boogaart, '*O series summe rata*', devoted a chapter (with examples III 4–5, pp. 636–37) to the relationship of M8, 12, 14 and 15; they share the same *talea* rhythm (in M12 with a little variation) and three deal with Fortune, M15 with False seeming, which is comparable to Fortune's falsity.

of the Mass, for different readerships (pedagogical and advanced) and with different concerns (contrapuntal, notational, rhythmic organisation). Above all I have attempted to show different ways in which text and music work together with musical structuring devices within each of the motets discussed, and in many instances between motets, to create rich compositions densely laden with meaning—literal, depictive, referential, symbolic and numerical.

PART IV
MUSICORUM COLLEGIUM:
THE MUSICIAN MOTETS

The motets discussed here celebrate music and musicians of the fourteenth and early fifteenth centuries. The five complete motets have long been recognised as a group, though their composition dates spread over more than half a century. They have in common the listing of musicians' names in the triplum, and are related to each other in various ways by ingenious musico-poetic construction and citation. They stand apart as a group both from earlier and later motets that name musicians. The purpose of Part IV is to investigate the sources, texts and music of each motet in turn, the possible identities of the musicians named, and to uncover some of the interrelationships, allusions and citations between the motets that demonstrate their membership of a subgenre with its own conventions, and that their composers, in contributing to it over a remarkably long time-span, were fully aware of the antecedents.

15

Apollinis eclipsatur, its Progeny and their Sources

The triplum voices of four late thirteenth-century French-texted motets recorded in fascicles 7 and 8 of the Montpellier codex (**Mo**) open by listing the names of musical companions. *Entre Adan et Hanikel* and *Entre Jehan et Philippet* are closely related texts describing the drunken musical activities of four young friends.[1] *Entre Copin et Bourgeois* identifies five student companions in Paris, and at least two of these characters reappear in the text *A maistre Jehan Lardier*,[2] which addresses eleven individuals by name in addition to other 'bons compaignons' within a Parisian community, possibly a confraternity.[3] Like the fourteenth-century motets, their tradition is interconnected and cross-referential, apparently stemming from one widely disseminated piece (*Entre Adan et Hanikel*), and the composers sign the texts. In the fifteenth century, Du Fay's rondeau *He compaignons* (CMM 1/6, no. 49) celebrates his colleagues in similar vein, greeting them informally by their familiar names. He drinks to 'Huchon, Ernoul, Humblot, Henry, Jean, Francois, Hugues, Thierry et Godefrin', in a register similar to those of the thirteenth-century motets. In both cases these are very different from the more elevated intellectual tone, the mostly formal naming, Latin texts, and absence of drink in the fourteenth-century musician motets. Jacopo da Bologna twice set the text of *Oseletto selvaggio* (various spellings), as a madrigal and as a canonic madrigal or caccia. The third terzina appears thus in the edition of Giuseppe Corsi: 'Pochi l'hano e tuti se fa magistri, | fa ballate, matrical e muteti, | tut'èn Fioràn, Filipoti e Marcheti', and in an alternative version: 'Pochi l'hanno e tutti si fan maestri, | fan ballate, madriali e mottetti, | fansi Fioràn, Filippotti e Marchetti.'[4] The named composers of *ballate*, madrigals and motets, with whom modern imitators are unfavourably compared, are assumed to be Floriano da Rimini, Philippe de Vitry, and Marchettus de Padua. Some ballades and other non-motet forms that deal with music, but do not list named musicians, are listed in Chapter 21. Binchois's *Nove cantum melodie* enjoins named colleagues to celebrate the baptism of Philip the Good's son Anthony, Count of Charolais in 1431; *Romanorum Rex*, by Johannes de Sarto, lists colleagues who are to mourn the death of King Albrecht

---

[1] On the relationship between these texts and the possible importance of Adam de la Halle in instigating an 'Entre' motet tradition, see Bradley, *Authorship and Identity*, ch.3. I am grateful to Catherine Bradley for access to her work before publication, and for a discussion of these texts. Most of the 'followers', as with the 14th-c. musician motets, are *unica*.

[2] On the identification of these names, see Ludwig, *Repertorium*, i/2, p. 599.

[3] See Everist, 'Montpellier 8', 24–28. Also commented by Gómez, 'Une Version à cinq voix du Motet *Apollinis*', 13–15, treating the **Mo** motets as antecedents for the 14th-c. group.

[4] See *Poesie musicali*, ed. Corsi, 42–43. The first version uses the reading of **Fp26** and **Lo29987**; the second is collated with other manuscripts. Corsi rejects the majority manuscript reading for both the madrigal and the canonic madrigal, 'Tuttenfioran' for 'Tutti infioran', as adopted by Li Gotti and Trucchi, avoiding the personal name.

The Motet in the Late Middle Ages. Margaret Bent, Oxford University Press. © Oxford University Press 2023.
DOI: 10.1093/so/9780190063771.003.0016

284   THE MUSICIAN MOTETS

II in 1439; Compère's celebratory *Omnium bonorum plena* probably of the 1470s includes a famous enumeration of 'greats', and Josquin's *Nymphes des bois* lists those solemnly enjoined to mourn the death of Ockeghem. All four works follow the pattern of listing colleagues in the second half of the motet, and in all those cases, those listed are known or assumed to be living at the time. The fourteenth-century group thus differs in tone and register from its predecessors and successors, with which there seems to be no direct connective tradition. Those motets celebrate musicians, sometimes over a long chronological spread, and not necessarily personally known to each other. For a start, they are in Latin, celebratory and formal in tone, ostentatiously, self-consciously clever constructions of text and music with citation and reference between them. They name a striking total of over sixty mostly unknown musicians within their texts— singers, theorists and composers, including authorial signatures—against a background of almost entirely anonymous manuscript transmission in that century, Machaut's self-promotion being the notable exception.[5] The subtle and abstruse interconnections be-tween the motets suggest a competitive culture. Since three of the five are *unica*, more compositions from this nexus may have been lost.

Four of the motets had been published in PMFC 5 (1968) and a fifth, from an English source, in PMFC 15 (1980). The five were published together in a Oiseau-Lyre reprint of 1986, with an introduction and tables listing the musicians referred to in motets already available in PMFC 5 and 15.[6] Further possible candidates for inclusion in this group in-clude two incomplete motets and one or more fragments, or titles of non-extant motets, though none of these have lists of names in the surviving portions (see Ch. 21). Ursula Günther had pointed out connections between *Apollinis*, *Alma polis* and *Sub Arturo* in her edition of the latter two motets.[7]

Attention was earlier drawn to two of the motets by Brian Trowell's ingenious unmasking in 1957 of the Latinised names of fourteen English musicians in the triplum of *Sub Arturo plebs*.[8] Trowell's article antedated both Günther's (1965) and Frank Ll. Harrison's (1968) editions of that motet;[9] indeed, the only other motet in this group that Trowell had access to was *Apollinis eclipsatur*, which he judged to be a response to *Sub Arturo* and not the other way round, as must be the case.[10] At the time Trowell wrote, almost none of the relevant repertory was available, and his early dating now needs to be revised. The order in which Harrison reprinted the motets in 1986 does not take account of the chronology suggested by their interrelationships, the order in which they are considered here, nor of the influences which constitute a network of compositions responding to and playing off each other. Harrison already

[5] Exceptions in the preceding century are the monophonic songs of troubadours and trouvères, culminating in the ascribed polyphonic rondeaux of Adam de la Halle.

[6] Harrison, *Musicorum collegio*, observes that in *Musicorum* and *Sub Arturo* the composers explicitly praise their fellow choir members; he goes on to list the musicians named in the other motets.

[7] CMM 39, pp. lii–liv and xlv–xlvi, enumerate connections and give chant identifications and comparisons (see further below).

[8] Trowell, 'A Fourteenth-Century Ceremonial Motet'.

[9] CMM 39 (1965), PMFC 5 (1968). The five motets were reproduced from PMFC 5 and 15 with an intro-duction in Frank Ll. Harrison, *Musicorum collegio: Fourteenth-century Musicians' Motets* (Monaco, 1986).

[10] Trowell, 'A Fourteenth-Century Ceremonial Motet', writes of 'average' dates, but it must be the latest date that determines the date of the composition. It quickly becomes obvious that while a particular occasion may have prompted the composition in each case, some of the motets, and especially *Sub Arturo*, are extensively retrospective. Bowers, 'Fixed Points'.

APOLLINIS ECLIPSATUR: PROGENY AND SOURCES 285

knew and published (as PMFC 5, no. 9a) the five-part expansion of *Apollinis* in **Stras** as transcribed by Coussemaker, with an additional texted triplum *Pantheon abluitur* and a textless fifth voice labelled 'Quadruplum sive triplum de Apollinis'. Although his edition of the base motet used **Barc853**, he made no mention of its additional voice(s), already known to Besseler, although he could not have anticipated the subsequent discovery of further sources, including **LoTNA**. In a valuable biographical study, Richard Hoppin and Suzanne Clercx treated *Musicalis sciencia*, with its twenty named musicians, as the primary composition, recognising the considerable overlap of names with the twelve of *Apollinis*.[11] Because of this overlap, these two motets must be closer in date to each other than to the other motets, but as Günther showed, though for different reasons, and quite apart from its wide circulation, *Apollinis* must come first. This is evident in a number of exchanges, citations or borrowings involving other motets in the group, notably *Sub Arturo plebs* and *Alma polis*, some already pointed out by Günther. *Apollinis*, *Musicalis* and *Musicorum* probably date in that order, between the 1330s and 1350s, *Alma polis* and *Sub Arturo* from the years on either side of *c*. 1400, when the added voices to *Apollinis* can probably also be dated. Support for these approximate datings will be offered in the chapters of Part IV. What is clear is that all the motets took *Apollinis* as their starting point, and that, despite the evidently narrower circulation of subsequent compositions, the composers knew and responded to the motets that preceded their own works. With fifteen musical attestations and at least four mentions in theoretical treatises, *Apollinis* with fifteen sources is by some distance the most widely circulated fourteenth-century motet, and over a long period well into the fifteenth century. *Sub Arturo* has three sources, but the other three (*Musicalis, Musicorum, Alma polis*) are all *unica*.

The motets which form this interrelated subgenre have lacked a full study hitherto. Work on them has received inspirational input from David Howlett and his readings of the texts. His imaginative counting of verbal dimensions had implications for the counting that is intrinsic to musical analysis, and the combined power of words and music emerges as much richer as a result. We worked fruitfully together on the motets and presented the results in seminars in Princeton, Oxford and elsewhere in the late 1980s and early 1990s. Because it proved hard to coordinate differing views on the lengths to which we were each prepared to take number symbolism, gematria and proportional counting, that work has not reached print, except in Howlett's brilliant contribution to a Festschrift offered to me in 2005.[12] He plans to explore in a separate publication the triple mythological bases for these compositions, a fusion of Classical legend with Christian symbolism from Plato, the Bible, and Boethius, together with a study and analysis of the verbal texts, with special attention to their ingenious numerical constructions (including letter counts), gematria, symmetries, chiasmi and anagrams. Some of the more striking cases are reported and credited here, and I remain grateful to him not only for the use of his text editions, but for the stimulus which has enriched my own work. More colleagues are thanked in the Preface and Acknowledgements.

[11] Hoppin and Clercx, 'Notes biographiques'.
[12] Howlett, '*Apollinis eclipsatur*'.

286 THE MUSICIAN MOTETS

Apollinis eclipsatur/Zodiacum signis/In omnem terram
and Related Motets

The progenitor of the group of musician motets is *Apollinis eclipsatur/Zodiacum signis/ In omnem terram*.[13] It is not only the first, the oldest technically and notationally of this group, the only one to have been present in both **Ivrea** and **Trém**, and the only one to have attracted the composition of additional parts in at least three of its later sources, but also more widely disseminated and cited than any other fourteenth-century motet. It occurs or is attested in no fewer than fifteen mostly fragmentary musical sources, from Spain, France, England, Italy, Germany and eastern Europe. In addition there are at least four citations in theory treatises, some of which overlap or are mutually dependent. *Sub Arturo* is known from three sources, one treatise citation and one archival mention, but the other three motets are *unica* and not otherwise attested. One continental and two English fragments, all unique, discussed in Chapter 21, appear to have come from further musical motets, with elements that relate to others of this group, though none list musicians' names in the surviving portions, and their status remains provisional. Given the unique or limited transmission of most of the motets later than *Apollinis*, others could very well have existed.

The only other contemporary motets whose circulation comes close to that of *Apollinis* are *Impudenter circumivi/Virtutibus laudabilis* in eleven sources, *Colla iugo/Bona condit* in nine, *Flos ortus/Celsa cedrus/Quam magnus pontifex* in eight, *Apta caro/Flos virginum*, *Degentis vita/Cum vix artidici/Vera pudicitia* and *Rex Karole/Leticie pacis* each in seven. All of these except *Degentis vita* and *Colla iugo* are in **SL2211**. *Colla iugo* and *Apollinis* were adjacent in **Tarragona2** and were also the first two pieces in **Trém** (see Ch. 31). Of that 'liber motetorum' only the outer bifolio of the first gathering survives, with an extensive list of contents, divided into motets and 'balades et rondeaus'; the bifolio contains music for four motets including *Colla iugo*.[14] Several of these have been attributed to Vitry with varying degrees of confidence. The wide circulation of these few motets is also reflected in the recurrence of many of them in treatise citations. For example, Johannes Boen's *Ars* of the mid-century cites *Impudenter/Virtutibus*, *O canenda/Rex quem metrorum*, *Tuba sacre/In arboris*, *Apta/Flos* (probably all by Vitry) but not *Apollinis*; his *Musica* refers to specific places in *Floret/Florens*, *Se grace/Cum venerint* (see here Ch. 29) and (again) *O canenda/Rex quem metrorum*. An appendix to the *Ars* of later but uncertain date in the late fifteenth-century manuscript **Venice24** also names *Rex Karole/Leticie* by its triplum incipit (those in the body of the treatise are cited by motetus, as normal in the fourteenth century). Its dedicatee, Charles V, did not come to the throne until 1364, and Boen died in 1367, which further confirms this as a later addition.[15] *Apta* and

---

[13] Hoppin and Clercx, 'Notes biographiques', treated *Musicalis* as primary, perhaps because it named more musicians.

[14] Although Machaut's songs had quite wide circulation in the anthology manuscripts, very few of his motets are found outside the complete-works manuscripts, and those are mainly in **Ivrea**, **Ca1328** and **Trém**.

[15] See Boen, *Ars*. **Venice24** also contains a version of Boen's *Musica* with the music examples that are lacking in the older MS **Paris14741**. *Rex Karole* is also cited in *Ars cantus mensurabilis*, ed. Balensuela, where the author erroneously refers to *Rex Karole* to demonstrate the process of diminution, which does not occur in this motet. See Hamilton, 'Philippe de Vitry in England', 35–36.

Tribum are cited by their tripla in the late fourteenth-century *Tractatus figurarum*.[16] Other treatise mentions of *Apollinis* are noted above.

One of the two youngest of the musician motets, *Sub Arturo*, is now known from three sources, one of them English (**Yox**), where it is also a near neighbour of the internationally widely distributed motet *Degentis vita*; both flank the very clever (unique) motet on John the Baptist, *O amicus/Precursoris* (Ch. 22). The other three complete musician motets are also *unica*, *Musicalis sciencia/Sciencie laudabili* in **Pic**, *Musicorum collegio/In templo Dei posita* in **Durham20**, *Alma polis religio/Axe poli* in **Chantilly**; the two fragments are each known from a single source only. Most are the only ones of the series in their (often fragmentary) source(s), but **Chantilly** contains both *Sub Arturo* and *Alma polis*, and **LoTNA** preserves in fragmentary form both *Apollinis/Psallentes/Zodiacum* and *Arta/Musicus* (Ch. 21).

Relationships between the Motets

Because of the interrelationships between the motets and the way they play off each other, this must have been a mutually engaging or even a competitive genre. Subsequent poet-composers variously attached their works to *Apollinis* as well as to one or more of the other companion pieces, by numbers (of text lines, syllables, breves, musicians, etc), recurring vocabulary, and citations or partial citations of various combinations of text, melody and rhythm, usually with two of those elements but not all three, and sometimes with slight variations that might escape digital searching. *Apollinis* is the source of quotations and other forms of reference in the later motets, and there is evidence of interplay between the later compositions. *Apollinis* is not only the oldest of the motets, but it had an exceptionally long shelf life into the fifteenth century, perhaps because of its iconic and self-fulfilling status in theoretical as well as practical sources. It is the only one of the musician motets to have acquired additional composed voices, and it stands alone among widely disseminated fourteenth-century motets in having attracted so many independently added parts; these include tripla rather than (as in most other cases of added voices) being restricted to contratenors. Although other motets have alternative contratenors, only one other motet from the period has a version with five voices: **OH** gives an additional textless fifth voice for *Are post libamina* (see Ch. 24). Yet *Apollinis* ranks low on a mapping of less to more upper-voice isorhythm. We should not be too ready to see this ancestral composition as less developed only because, by evolutionary standards hitherto applied, it seemed to be more free. The wide dissemination in music manuscripts and treatises, and the discovery of so many allusions to it in later motets in this group, challenge an older evolutionary view of the fourteenth-century motet that sees greater skill and later dating in more exact repetition, and immaturity in greater freedom. Ways in which later motets acknowledge the earlier one(s) will be addressed as they arise.

---

[16] *Apta* is judged to be more subtle than the older *Tribum*. See Desmond, *Music and the moderni*, ch. 2; and Bent, 'Artes novae'.

Anonymity and Authorial Signatures

Most fourteenth-century music has come down to us anonymously in the manuscripts that preserve it. The towering exception is Machaut, who oversaw the assembly of his poetical and musical output in complete-works manuscripts. A very few attributions were made by theorists, and a few more on circumstantial and stylistic evidence by modern scholars, mostly to Vitry. All the more precious, therefore, are the names of over sixty-five musicians (including composer signatures) recorded in these motets, many of whom we have never heard of, or names which lack any other attestation of musical activity. It is reassuring that some of those known to us as important for musical practice and theory are prominent: Johannes de Muris, Philippe de Vitry and Guillaume de Machaut. But what of the others? Whether the named musicians were singers, instrumentalists, theorists or composers is not usually specified, except to some extent in *Sub Arturo*. But at least three of the motet texts (most explicitly *Apollinis*, *Alma polis*, *Sub Arturo*) carry composer signatures, self-promotions with similar formulations, all with mock modesty, or what is now called humblebragging. In *Apollinis*, the author B. de Cluny names himself at the beginning of the second half of the motetus: 'shining with practical and theoretical art he commends himself to all': *recommendans se subdit omnibus*. He is referred to in modern studies as Bernard but, although his twelfth-century namesake makes that a likely choice for a man from Cluny, there is no confirmation that he was Bernard rather than, say, Bertrand or Bartolomeus. In *Sub Arturo plebs* (Ch. 20) J. Alanus appends himself as the last and least on his list of 'greats' at the end of the motetus: 'Illis licet infimus | J. Alanus minimus | sese recommendat'. At the midpoint of the motetus of *Alma polis/ Axe poli* (Ch. 19) the composer is identified as Egidius de Aurolia (Giles of Orleans), the poet as J. de Porta: 'Egidii de Aurolia, | manant a quo cantamina | pariter cum hac musica. | Carmineus J. de Porta | se commendat per omnia.' The anonymous author of *Musicorum* (Ch. 18) subjects himself to the service of all: 'obsequium | actoris, qui seruicio | se totum subdit omnium', but this time in the triplum. The mysterious Leouns, at the end of the motetus of the incomplete *Arta/Musicus* (Ch. 21), may also be its composer. The shared diction in these formulations is obvious. None of these is otherwise known as a composer, despite claims that J. Alanus was the singer who bequeathed a roll of polyphonic music to St George's Windsor in 1373; his candidacy will be evaluated below. An Alanus (without initial) was the author of four songs in **Stras**; the **OH** composer was probably a W. Aleyn. None of these works has anything to connect them to *Sub Arturo plebs* except a very common name with no initial J.

These are not the only fourteenth-century composers to identify themselves in the texts of their motets. Marchetto da Padova's *Ave regina celorum/Mater innocencie* has the explicitly authorial motetus acrostic *Marcum Paduanum*, which may be the earliest such authorial signature; most acrostics in fourteenth-century motets are for dedicatees.[17] Composer signatures become habitual in the Italian tradition; we find 'me

---

[17] For Marchetto's motet see Ch. 26. The author of the *Speculum musicae* names himself as Jacobus in an authorial acrostic. The 15th-c. Polish composer Petrus Wilhelmi signed the texts of all his compositions with an authorial acrostic; they all begin with P. See Gancarczyk, 'Petrus Wilhelmi'.

franciscum' in Landini's incomplete motet *Principum nobilissime* in **Pad1106**, and 'tua ciconia' or 'me ciconiam' at the end of five motet texts by Ciconia. Vitry signs himself in *Cum statua/Hugo* with 'hec concino Philippus publice', possibly also as *Phi millies* in the triplum of that motet, and perhaps as (Petrarch's) 'Gallus' in *Garrit gallus* and *Tribum*.[18] Although it had been doubted that *Gratiosus*, the first word of the motet *Gratiosus fervidus*, signalled the Paduan composer Gratiosus, as composer signatures do not usually occur at the beginning of a text, much speaks in favour of it being an authorial signature.[19] Manon Louviot's stunning discovery and decoding of a motet signed and dated in an acrostic has recently been brought to light, and David Catalunya has reported another signed composition, neither of these by composers otherwise known.[20] Machaut's motets are never signed in this way. Just about the only other composers' names we have for French or English fourteenth-century motets are those named in these musician motets, where we are dealing with musicians, most of whose names would not otherwise be known at all because of the almost entire absence of composer ascriptions in contemporary music manuscripts. Compositions by Machaut preserved in the so-called repertory manuscripts are often recorded there anonymously,[21] only known to be his from their inclusion in the composer's complete-works manuscripts; and works which may be by Vitry are attributed to him by contemporary theorists or modern scholars on a variety of grounds other than manuscript ascriptions. The group of musician motets, therefore, greatly extends the repertory of named musicians, including composers, for the generation preceding **Chantilly** and **OH**, which are among the first polyphonic sources, in the early fifteenth century, to provide significant numbers of composer ascriptions.

One anecdotal reference to *Apollinis/Zodiacum* is of a different kind from the other treatise references to be enumerated below as illustrations of particular mensural features. It will now be addressed here.

Heinrich Eger von Kalkar

Kalkar (1328–1408) was a Carthusian mystic who had studied in Cologne and Paris, where he became *magister artium* in 1356 and taught at the Sorbonne until 1363, when he accepted canonries in Cologne and Kaiserwerth. He entered the Carthusian order in 1365 and was successively prior in several houses, achieving high office, but from 1396

---

[18] See *Tribum*, Ch. 4.

[19] Cuthbert, 'Trecento Fragments', 140, asks: 'Is it possible that in a motet with a retrograde tenor [*Gratiosus fervidus/Gratiosus/Magnanimus*], even this tradition would be put in reverse? To read the acrostic, "Georgius miles," one must read every other line of the triplum and then every line of the duplum.' See Hallmark, 'Some Evidence for French Influence', 214.

[20] Presented by Manon Louviot in a seminar at All Souls College on 20.11.2020. See Louviot, 'Uncovering the Douai Fragment'; the text of the motet *Ferre solet* in **Douai74** is internally signed and dated as by Frater Johannes Vavassoris, 1373. The text of the solmisation piece *Fa fa mi fa* is signed in **Karlsruhe82** as by 'cantore Leodiensi Johanne qui in Rupis Amatore hoc compilavi', i.e. Rocamadour (Rupes Amatoris); see Catalunya, 'Nuns, Polyphony', 105.

[21] Ballades 18 and 34 are ascribed in **Chantilly**, Motet 8 and Rondeau 20 in the text manuscript Stockholm, Kungliga Biblioteket, MS V.u.22 (see Ch. 14). There are two erroneous ascriptions (in **Fribourg260** and **Stras**).

290 THE MUSICIAN MOTETS

until his death lived as a simple monk. He is known for his writings in various fields, notably with an ascetic-mystical focus, including his treatise on music (*Cantuagium*, dated 1380).[22] This carries a testimony of striking chronological precision, specifying events 'fifty years ago, around the year 1330' which has been seized on in recent scholarship.[23] However, since he was two years old at the time, his 'recollection' must depend on hearsay or transmitted wisdom, and may not be as precisely datable as it has been taken to be.

Sed quia ex notulis hiis non redactis ad mensuram cantari contigit olim satis discorditer Ideo quidam magni artiste Parisius quorum nomina in quodam discantu ponuntur qui incipit Zodiacus si bene recolo—et unum vidi episcopum *ante annos circiter quinquaginta circa annum videlicet domini M^mCCC^m Tricesimum*—specialiter dederunt se musice certis mensuris temporum ipsam regulantes sub notis quadratis et quadrangulis simplicibus et colligates punctis eciam et pausis . . . [Desmond, *Music and the* moderni, 5–6, stops here] quibus iam religiosi utuntur communius [MS communis] propter concordanciam servandam in cantibus et mensuras in discantibus. [Kügle, 'Die Fragmente Oxford', 319, stops here] Erat eciam maximus Cantor quidam Magister Franco de Colonia qui pulchrum de arte illa edidit librum quem et alios si perlegeris mensuras mirabiles notarum et pausarum in cantibus multis per ipsos regulatis et compositis perpendere poteris.[24]

Since it used to happen that one sang rather discordantly from notes not reduced to [temporal] measure, therefore certain great artists in Paris, whose names are listed in a certain *discantus* with the incipit 'Zodiacus', if I remember correctly (and I saw one as a bishop), about fifty years ago, namely around the year 1330, especially devoted themselves to music, regulating it according to the specified time values given to square, quadrangular, simple and composite notes, dots and rests, which monks were already using in order to keep concords in chant and measures in *discantus*. There was also the greatest singer, a certain Magister Franco de Colonia, who compiled

---

[22] Hüschen, *Das Cantuagium des Heinrich Eger von Kalkar*, 44–45. For an excellent survey and assessment of the treatise, see Meyer, 'Le Cantuagium de Heinrich Eger von Kalkar', which shows extensive parallels with Anonymous I such as to suggest a common source. The *Cantuagium* was a companion work to his so-called *Loquagium*, a treatise on rhetoric, for which see Hüschen, p. 12. There are three manuscripts of the *Cantuagium*: (1) Berlin, Staatsbibliothek Ms. Mus.theor. 1325, ff. 18–37ᵛ; (2) Darmstadt, Hessische Landes- und Hochschulbibliothek MS 705, ff. 140–71; both of these are late 14th c. and from the Cologne Charterhouse; (3) Mainz, Stadtbibliothek, MS II 375, late 15th c., from the Benedictine abbey in Mainz. Three further MSS are attested but not extant. I am grateful to Elżbieta Witkowska-Zaremba for sharing her knowledge of the sources and discussing the interpretation of these passages. Meyer points out the often faulty nature of Hüschen's edition; only the Berlin MS was known when he edited the text in 1952.

[23] For recent citations by musicologists, perhaps attaching more importance to Kalkar than he may deserve, see Kügle, 'Die Fragmente Oxford, All Souls 56', 317; Desmond, *Music and the* moderni, 5–9 and 202; Rico, 'Music in the Arts Faculty', 232f and Zayaruznaya, 'Old, New, and Newer Still'. Fuhrmann, 'Rhetorik der Verinnerlichung', discusses other important aspects of Eger's formation and his *Cantuagium*. He lists the sources (p. 499 n. 23); I echo his plea for a critical edition, which might help to clarify the sometimes-garbled syntax.

[24] Hüschen, *Das Cantuagium des Heinrich Eger von Kalkar*, 44–45 (italics added). Shorter excerpts are given by Rico, 'Music in the Arts Faculty of Paris', 232 n. 147; Desmond, *Music and the* moderni, 6; Kügle, 'Die Fragmente Oxford, All Souls 56'; and Kügle, 'Vitry in the Rhineland'. The first part of this passage is translated by Leofranc Holford-Strevens (email of 23.4.2017), who acknowledges that the text has *redactis* not *reductis*, 'but when Cicero speaks de iure civili in artem redigendo' we render 'of reducing civil law to a system'.

a beautiful book about that art. If you read him and others, you will be able to understand the admirable measures of notes and rests in the many pieces which are regulated and composed by them.

Anyone who hastens to this text hoping for more will be disappointed. Eger's treatise is quite conventional: it deals with the origins of music, the place of music in the seven liberal arts, the monochord, consonances, intervals, neumes, psalm tones, and ecclesiastical chant. As Wolfgang Fuhrmann has pointed out, the intended audience for the treatise is unclear and uneven. Although explicitly addressed to children (*pueri*), it lacks elementary aids such as solmisation instruction and a tonary, while writing extensively on the modes.[25] The importance that has been attached to it as a chronological marker for notational developments of the *ars nova* is undermined by the continuation in which Eger goes on to give a rudimentary but inaccurate account of Franconian notation.[26] Besides neumes and chant notation, his notational characterisation ('sub notis quadratis et quadrangulis simplicibus et colligates punctis eciam et pausis') gives no hint of acquaintance with *ars nova* innovations (including minims) such as would indicate any familiarity with the musical notation of the motet. He confines his limited notational palette to what monks do 'to keep concords in chant and measures in *discantus*', probably implying no more than fairly simple homophonic singing.

It has proved tempting to take such a dating literally because it seems so precise: but for dating what? The word order and lack of punctuation make it unclear precisely what Eger is setting at *c.* 1330; the bishop, the motet, the activity of those named in it, or their innovations. But in fact Denis le Grant became bishop of Senlis only in 1350 (he died in 1352), Vitry bishop of Meaux in 1351. Only because we know these dates can we say that Eger's text, despite the misleading word order, cannot apply the 1330 date to either of them; and that he probably only knew about one, the better-known Vitry, about whom he may have heard in Paris in the 1350s; I have therefore put that phrase in parentheses in the translation. His text cites the motetus *Zodiacum* (calling it the discantus), but the musicians (his *artistae*) are in fact named in the triplum, *Apollinis*.

Eger tells us that, as a monk, he did not deal with or approve of polyphony or instrumental music. This gives some discount value to his testimony. In fact the now-famous passage above is the only one in the whole treatise to suggest that he may have had some acquaintance with (Franconian) polyphony, but its authority is undermined by the patent gap in his knowledge; this part of his treatise appears to be imperfectly understood hearsay. The final paragraphs of the treatise are:

Ecce, carissime, feci quod promisi, aperiens vobis![27] Hostium musicae praecipue ecclesiasticae, si cui autem placuerit, intrare longius ad musicam speculativam vel

---

[25] Fuhrmann, 'Rhetorik der Verinnerlichung', 502.

[26] As noted within the Latin text above, recent citations by Kügle and Desmond stop short of the sentence about Franco, and its further continuation into a perfunctory account of older notation, which gives some context to his comments about later music, reducing his credibility as an informed witness.

[27] This is Hüschen's text and presumably his punctuation. I have ignored the first exclamation mark and modified the punctuation of the next sentence.

292 THE MUSICIAN MOTETS

practicam legat libros et studeat Boetii, Augustini, Hieronymi [de Moravia] et aliorum musicorum ecclesiasticorum, qui cantus corrigunt, qui differentias tonorum in diversis tonis dividunt et multa exempla de cantibus ecclesiasticis ponunt. Discantus autem discere vel musicis instrumentis insistere, licet multum esset pro juvenibus, non audeo persuadere, quia religiosus sum, ne forte occasionem dem lasciviae. Sufficiat ergo saltem hoc scire cantuagium ad laudem Dei et omnium sanctorum, ut post hanc miseriam det nobis gloriam idem ille, quem laudant mille milia angelorum per omnia saecula saeculorum, amen!

Behold, dear one, I have done what I promised, opening to you the door of music, mainly ecclesiastical [chant]. If, however, one wishes to enter further into music, let him read and study the theoretical and practical books on church music by Boethius, Augustine, Jerome [of Moravia] and others, which correct melodies, divide the *differentiae* of the tones in the various tones, and give many examples of ecclesiastical chant. However, because I am a monk, I dare not encourage the learning of discant or musical instruments, although it means much for the young, lest it give rise to lasciviousness. At least let this *Cantuagium* suffice, therefore, for the praise of God and of all the saints, and to know that after this misery he may give us the same glory which a thousand thousand angels praise, world without end, Amen!

If Eger had had direct knowledge or understanding of the music of *Apollinis/Zodiacum*, he would know that its musical style and notational innovations go well beyond Franco. He probably knew or understood only the verbal text, and had seen the names in the triplum. His repudiation of polyphony, on grounds of being a monk, reduces the credibility of his testimony as a witness of *ars nova*. As he simply reiterates respect for Franco and his teaching, it would be rash to accept Eger von Kalkar as a reliable witness to the dating of subsequent notational developments or musical genres that he neither understood nor claimed to know about. His account has little more status than hearsay; it seems to have been chronologically misinformed about the relationship between Franco and the Paris 'artistae' who are at least one if not two generations younger.[28] In short, it is unclear whether we should assume he intended 1330 as the date of the bishoprics (wrong), of the innovations of these 'artistae' (too late), of the motet (possible), or whether his testimony is too confused or ill-informed to be useful for setting chronology.

Sources of the Motets and References in Treatises

The five complete motets and two fragments under consideration are listed below with their sources, and theoretical mentions in the case of *Apollinis* and *Sub Arturo*.

---

[28] Eger studied in Paris in the 1350s, obtaining the doctorate in theology in 1362, and was a *magister regens* in the faculty of arts; he might well have picked up hearsay in Paris, both about Franco and about the musicians named in the motet.

Apollinis eclipsatur/Zodiacum signis/In omnem terram

Editions: PMFC 5, no. 9; Bent, *Two 14th-Century Motets*, 8–13; Harrison, *Musicorum collegio*, no. 2, and ⊙ Example 16.1.

Manuscript sources

Ivrea, ff. 12ᵛ–13: complete *a*3

Barc971, ff. 11ᵛ–12: complete *a*3[29]

Barc853, f. 1ʳ: motetus and tenor, followed by a textless triplum which fits. There is also a 'Contratenor *per sanctam civitatem*' claimed as a fifth voice by Gómez, '*Apollinis*', which even with drastic adjustments does not fit. (See ⊙ Ex. 16.2.)

Stras, ff. 64ᵛ–65: *a*5, including the additional texted triplum *Pantheon abluitur* and a textless 'Quadruplum sive triplum de Apollinis', both with pseudo-imitative beginnings following *Apollinis*. (See ⊙ Ex. 16.3.)

Tarragona2, f. 2ᵛ: this was an original recto (contains mo and T, *Zodiacum* and tenor); tr of *Colla jugo* on recto (original verso).

Leiden2515, f. 1ʳ: triplum only, original verso.[30]

Leipzig223, recto: end of triplum, and the motetus and tenor; the verso is blank.[31]

Pad658, f. Bᵛ: most of the triplum only.

LoTNA, f. 2ʳ.[32] Five-part version with additional texted triplum ([*P*]*Sallentes zinzugia*) and contratenor; followed by *Musicus est ille* (Ch. 21). The core three-part version is not preserved, just the two new additional parts. (See ⊙ Ex. 16.4.)

OxAS56, f. Aʳ: tenor and triplum, fragments.

SL2211, ff. R188ᵛ–189 (no. 215; A 69ᵛ, 79ʳ): a version *a*3, not contrapuntally viable, with *Pantheon* and *Apollinis* presented as Italianate equal-range cantus parts, and tenor, omitting the essential low motetus. (See ⊙ Ex. 16.3.)

Trém (index only): *Apollinis/Zodiacum* was on the missing recto of the first opening, presumably complete, facing the complete *Colla jugo* on the verso of the index page.

Brno, rear pastedown: contains a lightly ornamented version of about two-thirds (104 breves) of the triplum.[33]

---

[29] For the most recent work on the Barcelona and Tarragona fragments, see Catalunya, 'Polyphonic Music'.

[30] The verso of this fragment (original recto) carries the end of the triplum and the motetus and tenor of an otherwise unknown motet which has textual resonance with *Apollinis eclipsatur nunquam*. It may have been another musician motet: see Ch. 21.

[31] This new source was reported by Eva Maschke at the Medieval and Renaissance music conference in Maynooth, July 2018, and is now published as Maschke, 'Entfernte Einbandfragmente . . . Leipzig', at 272–74. She presented additional material in a seminar at All Souls College, Oxford, 12.3.2020.

[32] Not a motetus contrafact, as stated in Zayaruznaya, 'Form and Idea', 377.

[33] Described with facsimile and transcribed in Horyna, *A Prague Fragment*, 78–86, and Horyna, 'Ein Brünner Fragment'.

294 THE MUSICIAN MOTETS

Vienna922, f. 2ʳ: fragment containing the end of the motetus, and the tenor.

Vienna5094, f. 158ᵛ⁻ʳ: instrumental version in German tablature, 'rundellus'; triplum and motetus only.[34]

The three versions with added voices:

Barc853 with added textless triplum.

Stras with added triplum *Pantheon abluitur* (also in **SL2211**) and *Quadruplum sive triplum.*

LoTNA with added triplum [*P*]*Sallentes zinzugia* and contratenor.

Treatise citations of *Apollinis*

The contents of items 1–3 below are closely related in that they draw on the same core repertory of motet titles, with only slight variations. Of these, *Apollinis* with fifteen sources and *Degentis vita* with seven are among the most widely circulated motets of the fourteenth century, followed by *O Maria*, with at least three sources.[35] *Ave coronata* can be identified as the motet with that triplum incipit in **Speciálník**, pp. 420–21 and **Franus**, ff. 345ᵛ–346; it shares the mensural description of *Apollinis*, which both are cited to illustrate, namely perfect modus, imperfect time, major prolation. The motetus is texted *Alma parens regem glorie*. The tenor in both sources (truncated and incomplete in **Speciálník**) is broken up and rhythmicised into repeated notes to carry the triplum text, but was reconstituted by Jaromír Černý into its original values and identified as *Ave regina celorum*.[36] These corrupt late transmissions of *Ave coronata/Alma parens/Ave regina celorum* obscure the original simple isorhythm, with three five-note *taleae* per *color*, and four *color* statements without diminution. The wide citation of *Apollinis* in related theoretical sources and the sharing of examples between these treatises give rise to the suspicion that this motet took on a life of its own in

---

[34] Identified by Strohm, 'Native and Foreign', where he names the voices as motetus and contratenor. *Rondellus* or *rundellus* was a common term in Germanic and eastern European sources for a cantilena with a lively texted upper voice and slower-moving tenor (and sometimes a contratenor), in this case an adaptation of the motet. **Stras** no. 166, f. 94ᵛ, preserves the composition *Musicorum inter collegia* (transcribed in CMM 53/3, no. 299, p. 205), a title suggesting some connection to this group of motets (Strohm, *The Rise*, 116, states that the opening 'quotes *Apollinis*' but only a verbal similarity is involved). Widely cited in eastern European theoretical sources, and here headed *Rex rondelorum*, it is in three evenly active parts with a central structural break, suggesting a *forme fixe* rather than a motet adaptation. There is no list of names, but it surely once had more text than the minimal amount here provided.

[35] Only eight of the fifteen sources of *Apollinis* were known to Harrison for PMFC 5. *Degentis vitá*, another motet whose title is widely cited in eastern European theoretical sources, is in **Yox, Chantilly, Barc971, Brussels5170, Nuremberg9, Stras, Trém**: PMFC 5, no. 23. *O Maria* is in PMFC 12, no. 41; its three sources have strikingly different endings. See Ch. 1.

[36] For this motet, and for more on the central European treatises, see Gancarczyk, 'Memory of Genre'. The motet is transcribed in *Vícetextová moteta 14. a 15. století*, ed. Černý, 131–37, and *Historická antologie*, ed. Černý, 144–50. I am indebted to Paweł Gancarczyk for a copy of the motet. Černý had hypothesised that *Ave coronata* was composed around 1400 by a local musician, despite its unique status as a motet with isorhythm from eastern Europe, but in this more recent publication he identifies the tenor as *Ave regina celorum/Mater regis/O flos* (*LU* 1864, WA 405), a chant unknown in Bohemian sources. That melody is the same as *Ave rex gentis Anglorum* (PM 270), the tenor of the English motet *De flore martirum/Deus tuorum militum/Ave rex gentis*, which leads Černý to ask if *Ave coronata* could be an import from England. The rhythms mostly follow the defaults for stemless semibreves except that (as in *Apollinis*) some breves are imperfected by a single minim; and both ♦ ♦ ♦♦♦ and ♦♦♦ ♦ ♦ are used for groups of five.

APOLLINIS ECLIPSATUR: PROGENY AND SOURCES   295

theoretical transmission independently of knowledge of the motet, rather as the late thirteenth-century motet *Aucun ont trouvé* ascribed to Petrus de Cruce appears to have done.[37] However, unlike *Aucun ont trouvé*, the motet itself had wide circulation over many decades, and still invited the composition of added parts into the early fifteenth century.

1. **Wrocław16:** Anonymous, *Tractatus de musica mensurabili* (Breslau, now Wrocław).[38] After citing *Musicorum inter collegia* with a music example that seems not to relate to the composition of that name preserved in **Stras** (see below, Ch. 21), and '*Monachant*' [= *Mon chant en plainte*?], *Apollinis* twice heads lists of examples, first in company with *Ave coronata*, *Degentis vita* and *O Maria* for mensural properties, and then with the first two of these for motet definition.[39] *Apollinis* is correctly cited for perfect modus, imperfect tempus, major prolation. A motet is there defined as that in which each part has text, and which has no general pause except at the end (i.e. it is not sectional like a song form):

(I)tem propter maiorem euidenciam priorum est sciendum, quod in numero canticorum quidam sunt modi perfecti temporis perfecti et maioris prolacionis. Et illorum pauca inveniuntur ut: *Monachant de morte wilhelmi*.

Quidam sunt modi perfecti temporis imperfecti et maioris prolacionis, ut *Appollinis*, *Aue coronata*, *Fenix arabie* et sic de aliis.

Quidam sunt modi perfecti et temporis imperfecti et minoris prolacionis ut *Degentis vita*, *O Maria*.

Quidam sunt de modo imperfecto, de tempore perfecto et minori prolacione, vt *Virginem mire pulcritudinis*, *Deo gracias papales*. Quidam sunt modi imperfecti de tempore perfecto et maioris prolacionis, ut *Deo gracias conclamemus*, *Par ma[i]ntes foys*.[40]

Quidam sunt modi imperfecti, temporis imperfecti et minoris prolacionis ut *Demonis astuto* et communiter alie probationes.

Item sciendum: differencia est inter mutetum, rondellum, piroletum, baladum, stampaniam sive stampetum, katschetum et rotulum. Unde mutetus est, qui nullam habet pausam generalem nisi finem cuius quelibet pars habet textum, verbi gracia: *Appollinis*, *Aue coronata*, *Degentis vita*, *Fenix arabie* et sic de aliis.

---

[37] See Bent, *Jacobus*, ch. 2. On some problematic transmissions of motet examples in treatises see Hamilton, 'Philippe de Vitry in England', 35–36 and Leitmeir, 'Types and Transmission of Musical Examples'.

[38] Wolf, 'Ein Breslauer Mensuraltraktat', 335–36; now **Wrocław16**.

[39] The text continues with definitions (by section and clausula) for *mutetum, rondellum, piroletum, baladum, stampaniam* [BOZ1 adds *trumpetum*], *katschetum* and *rotulum*. *Monachant* may well be the refrain of a ballade from Jean de Le Mote's *Regret Guillaume* of 1339, *Mon chant en plainte*, and in turn related to the triplum of the **Ivrea** motet *Mon chant/Qui doloreus*, no. 39 (**Trém** no. 43); see Plumley, *The Art of Grafted Song*, 231–49, and Ch. 32 n. 51.

[40] The motetus of *Deo gracias conclamemus* is in **Mu3223**, recto, and **Cortona2**, f. 1. *Deo gracias papales/ Deo gracias fidelis/Deo gracias salvator* is in **Nuremberg9** and was in **Gdańsk2315**; *Fenix arabie* is not known. For the identification of *Virginem mire pulcritudinis* as a contrafact of *Adiscort* see Ward, 'A Central European Repertory'. Other unfamiliar titles may also be sacred contrafacta, a practice well attested in **MuEm**. For Cortona see Di Bacco and Nádas, 'Papal Chapels', at 82–86. I thank Lawrence Earp for pointing out that *Par maintes foy* must refer not to the Vaillant virelai but to the motet (triplum and tenor only) in **Ca1328** and **Würz**.

296 THE MUSICIAN MOTETS

2. **Melk950:** Anonymous, *Tractatulus de cantu mensurali seu figurativo musice artis.*[41] Again, *Degentis vita*, *Apollinis* and *Ave coronata* head the list, suggesting a derivational relationship between these theory texts. F. Alberto Gallo dates the content to mid-fourteenth century, the manuscript to the fifteenth century:

> Ulterius sciendum, quod de numero cantilenarum que sunt cantus mensuralis quedam sunt in modo perfecto et tempore [im]perfecto, ut *Degentis vita*, *Apollinis*, *Ave coronata*; alie sunt tam de tempore perfecto quam de modo perfecto, ut *Yelangis* [*Je languis*]; alie sunt de modo imperfecto et tempore.

3a. **BOZ1**, p. 508.[42] Closely related to the **Wrocław16** treatise, this version was copied into the codex after 1467, when an index was entered. A paragraph on genres, almost identical to Wrocław and including *mutetus/motetus*, again defines it as that in which each part has text, and which has no general pause except at the end. The examples cited are *Apollinis*, *Ave coronata*, *Degentis vita*, *Linor aula* (of which the last is unknown).

3b. **BOZ2**, p. 527 gives examples of motets, here defined having a texted discantus and medius, and a tenor. *Apollinis* is distinguished as having a texted tenor (this may refer to the motetus *Zodiacum* below the middle-voice tenor, which is, however, often given with its chant text), *Degentis vita* an untexted tenor. The tenor of *Degentis vita* is the unidentified *Vera pudicitia*, often unlabelled, whose music is cited in **BOZ1** (p. 503) as an example of modus perfectus.

4. **Pra103** (unpublished excerpts kindly provided by Martin Horyna).[43]

> F. 74ʳ: Propter clariorem evidenciam predictorum sciendum, quod de numero cantuum quidam sunt in modo perfecto et tempore imperfecto sicut *degentis vita*, *Appollinis*, *Ave coronata*. Alii sunt de tempore perfecto et de modo imperfecto sicut *musicorum inter collegia*. Alii tam de modo imperfecto quam de tempore imperfecto sicut *Gelagwis* [*Je languis*], *Schag melodie*. Alii tam de modo quam de tempore perfecto ut *nequicie peniteo*, *post missarum solennia*, et illorum pauca inveniuntur. Sequitur figura supradictorum de valore notarum.
>
> F. 84ᵛ: Mutetus est, cuius omnes partes sunt una indistincta pars ut *degentis vita*, *Appollinis*, *Beacius* etc.[44]

Thus, of the above treatises, (1) cites *Appollinis*, *Ave coronata*, *Degentis vita* and *O Maria*; (2) cites *Degentis vita*, *Apollinis*, *Ave coronata*; (3a, **BOZ1**) cites *Degentis vita*,

---

[41] CSM 16.

[42] For these Warsaw sources, see Witkowska-Zaremba (ed.), *Notae musicae artis*. Vitry's *Tuba sacre fidei* is cited in **BOZ1** for red notation in the tenor to vary the modus, as it indeed does (505) along with the tenors of the unknown *Hedroys* and *Heres unica* (505), both of which may be the same as *Hedwiges heres unica* (528). Other motets cited in these treatises but not known at all include *Linor aula zeli* and *Fenix arabie*, and the two motets *Nicolai solempnia* and *Martine sancte pontifex*.

[43] Cf. Horyna, 'Ein Brünner Fragment', 2 n. 1. There are close similarities to **BOZ2**; cf. Witkowska-Zaremba (ed.), *Notae musicae artis*, 516 and 527.

[44] This is the only known theoretical reference to what must be *Beatius/Cum humanum*, a motet reconstructed in Zayaruznaya, 'Quotation, Perfection'. It is listed in **Trém**. See also Ch. 4 n. 42 and Ch. 16 n. 26 below.

Appollinis, Ave coronata; (3b, **BOZ2**) cites *Degentis vita, Appollinis*; (4) cites *Degentis vita, Appollinis, Ave coronata, Musicorum inter collegia, Nequicie peniteo, Post missarum solennia, Beatius*. All these motets were in **Stras** except *Ave coronata*, which circulated in eastern European sources, and the last three cited in (4).

Musicalis sciencia/Sciencie laudabili/[Alleluia Dies sanctificatus]

Pic, f. 67[v]: see ⓟ Example 17.1 and Figure 17.2.

Musicorum collegio/In templo Dei posita/Avete

Durham20, ff. 338[v]–339: see ⓟ Example 18.1.[45]

Alma polis religio/Axe poli cum artica/[Et] in ore eorum

Chantilly, ff. 67[v]–68: see ⓟ Example 19.1.

Sub Arturo plebs/Fons citharizancium/In omnem terram

See ⓟ Example 20.1.

Manuscript sources

Yox, f. i: black notation, red coloration [anon.]; motetus and tenor only. J. Alanus (in mo text); *c.* 1410? This is the only English source.

Chantilly, ff. 70[v]–71: black notation, six-line staves, red coloration. J. Alani (in mo text). 1410s or later. 'Tenor De sub archuro' (not labelled 'in omnem terram').

Q15, no. 218 (f. 225[v])–R226, A254[v]–255: black notation, void coloration, and **Q15**, no. 328, f. R225[v], A342[v]. Ff. R225[v]–226 were originally facing pages, early 1420s. The original f. R225 is now at the end of the manuscript as A342. The present A254[v] in the body of the manuscript is a later recopy, early 1430s, of A342[v] (= R225[v]) with no independent authority but now facing the original recto. Both copies headed Jo. Alani (J. Alanus in mo text). The original facing pages, now as end flyleaves A342[v]–A255, were originally R225[v]–226.

References in theoretical and archival sources

There are two Italian references to *Sub Arturo*, both evidently of the early fifteenth century. One is to the tenor of *Sub Arturo* in a vernacular Italian treatise, the anonymous

---

[45] Not to be confused with the similar incipit of the rondeau *Musicorum inter collegia*; see Ch. 21.

298 THE MUSICIAN MOTETS

Notitia del valore delle note del canto misurato, the date of whose unique source is not established. Although dated by its editor to the fourteenth century, the script rather suggests the early fifteenth; it seems to have enough humanistic features to be datable probably to the second quarter of the fifteenth century. The treatise itself, however, could well be earlier.

> Onde colore nella musicha pratica sara un processo di piu note con sincope, <et> con spirationi, et poi, ripreso un' altra volta o piu, le medesime sincope et spirationi et valore, dissimili le voci. Niente di meno taglia ancora é medessimo modo. Ma usasi ne' tenori artificiali, partendo il tinore in certe parti, si come el tinore di certi motetti, cioe LUCE CLARUS o SUB ARTURO o OMNI HABENTI.[46]

After 'Luce Clarus' is given the first eight-note *talea* of the tenor [*In omnem terram*], with the accompanying text: 'SUB ARTURO a tre taglie di valore; ma in voce sono differentiate';[47] in other words, in a rare description of what we call isorhythm, the three *taleae* apply the same rhythms to different pitches within each *color*, which indeed is the case. The fact that *Sub Arturo* is named from its triplum makes it likely that the other two are also triplum incipits, as they do not correspond to known chants; and the fact that it is not named from its motetus suggests a later rather than an earlier date; most fourteenth-century motets (as in the **Trém** index; see Ch. 31) are named by their motetus parts, in the fifteenth century (as in **ModB**) by triplum. This is further discussed in the Introduction.

The other reference, kindly communicated by John Nádas in an email of 2009, is in an Augustinian inventory dated Rome, 1432, now housed among the Augustinian materials at the Rome State Archives, under the heading 'Libri cantus', where the third entry refers to the 'contratenor' of *Fons citharizancium*:[48] 'Liber quidam cantus figurati in papiro cuius princ' 1 Contratenor fons cytharicantium finis vero Et ascendit.' This is interesting in that the part specified is not a contratenor, as stated, but the motetus incipit. The motet has no contratenor and did not need one to support the harmony. This could indicate an added part, such as the additional ones supplied for *Apollinis*.

It is hard to imagine what format could lead to this being on the first recto of a manuscript unless the perhaps unbound book started incompletely, and had this voice on the

---

[46] *Anonymous, Notitia del valore delle note del canto misurato*, ed. Carapetyan (CSM 5), 57 (**Redi71**, f. 24ʳ). The tenor is given accurately, except that the first rest is omitted, and the first note should be a long, not a breve.

[47] The tenor is not that of the 14th-c. English motet *Omnis terra/Habenti dabitur* (**Ox7**, no. 12, ff. 266ᵛ–267; PMFC 15, no. 22). See now Colton, 'Making Sense of *Omnis/Habenti*'. The entries before and after *Sub Arturo* are:

> LUCE CLARUS a tre taglie di valore a questo modo; ma in voce sono differentiate. [As stated for *Sub Arturo*.] *c d f f g a b a g f*
> Tenor OMNI HABENTI a due taglie, non in medesma voce. Pero che se fossono le taglie in valore et in medesima voce, una compositione di note piu volte repetuta parebbe, et non altro (i.e. two *taleae* attached to different notes): *g f e f e d e d | d f e f g a g a*.

[48] Rome, Archivio di Stato, Agost. busta 34, f. 147ʳ. Nádas comments that all entries are of some interest (and the poetry collections allow for an identification in entry no. 2). The inventory was brought to musicological attention by Morelli, 'Musica e musicisti', 326, citing the complete edition of the inventory published in Gutiérrez, 'La biblioteca di Sant'Agostino', particularly 46–47; Pieragostini, 'Anglo-Italian Musical Relations', ch. 1, pp. 57–58; Pieragostini, 'Augustinian Networks'. *Alma polis* (Ch. 19) celebrates twenty Augustinians, so the presence of *Sub Arturo* in an Augustinian inventory might be suggestive.

first surviving recto, where a motetus part would normally be. No binding is described, as it is for the two preceding entries. Perhaps it was a manuscript of large format, like **Trém**, which could accommodate an entire motet on a single page.

Between them, these two Italian testimonies attest the presence of copies of *Sub Arturo* in Italy perhaps contemporaneously with those in **Q15** in the 1420s and 1430s.

Fragments, Possibly of Musician Motets

The surviving portions of three fragments lack names of musicians.

Arta/Musicus est ille qui perpensa racione

LoTNA, f. 2^r, written *c.* 1400 (see ▶ Ex. 21.1 below).

Non eclipsis atra ferrugine

Leiden2515, f. 1^v, original recto, contains the end of the triplum, and the motetus (*Non eclipsis atra ferrugine*) and tenor of an otherwise unknown motet. On the other side is the triplum of *Apollinis*: see above and n. 30. It may have been another musician motet: see Chapter 21.

Fons origo musicorum

Cu4435, fragment 16b^r, possibly belongs together with 16c^v. Part of a fragmentary royal choirbook of the 1420s.[49] The fragments of surviving text, and further candidates, are given in Chapter 21.

---

[49] Facsimiles and a reconstruction of the choirbook (RC) are in EECM 62; for the contents see Ch. 25 and ▶ Table 25.1.

16

Apollinis eclipsatur/Zodiacum signis/ In omnem terram and Later Versions with Added Parts

This widely circulated motet, transcribed in ▶ Ex. 16.1, was the progenitor of the network of motets which quoted and played off it and each other over many decades. These relationships are explored in the chapters of Part IV. Commentary notes to the transcription are in the Appendix to this chapter.

The Texts of *Apollinis eclipsatur/Zodiacum signis/ In omnem terram*

Texts and translations by David Howlett. The named musicians are in boldface.

Triplum		Rhymes	Words	Syllables
Apollinis eclipsatur		a	2	8
nunquam lux cum peragatur		a	4	8
signorum ministerio		b	2	8
bis sex, quibus armonica		c	4	8
fulget arte basilica	5	c	3	8
musicorum collegio		b	2	8
multiformibus figuris,		d	2	8
e quo nitet **J. de Muris**		d	6	8
modo colorum uario,		b	3	8
Philippus de Uitriaco	10	e	3	8
acta plura uernant a quo,		e	5	8
ordine multiphario;		b	2	8
noscit **Henricus Helene,**		f	3	8
tonorum tenorem bene,		f	3	8
Magno cum Dionisio,	15	b	3	8
Regaudus de Tiramonte,		g	3	8
Orpheÿco potus fonte,		g	3	8
Robertus de Palacio		b	3	8
Actubus petulancia		h	2	8
fungens, gaudet poetria	20	h	3	8
Guilhermus de Mascaudio,		b	3	8
Egidius de Morino		i	3	8

The Motet in the Late Middle Ages. Margaret Bent, Oxford University Press. © Oxford University Press 2023.
DOI: 10.1093/so/9780190063771.003.0017

THE MUSICIAN MOTETS

baritonans cum **Garino**,		i	3	8
quem cognoscat Suëssio,		b	3	8
Arnaldus Martini, iugis	25	j	3	8
philomena, **P. de Brugis**,		j	4	8
Gaufridus de Barilio;		b	3	8
vox quorum mundi climata		k	4	8
penetrat ad agalmata;		k	3	8
doxe fruantur bravio!	30	b	3	8
		11	93	240

Motetus

Zodiacum signis lustrantibus		a	3	10
armonia Phebi fulgentibus		a	3	10
musicali palam sinergia		b	3	10
Pictagore numerus ter quibus		a	4	10
adequatur preradiantibus	5	a	2	10
Boetii basis solercia.		b	3	10
B. de Cluni nitens energia		b	5	10
artis practice cum theoria		b	4	10
Recommendans se subdit omnibus		a	4	10
presentia per salutaria;	10	b	3	10
musicorum tripli materia		b	3	10
noticiam dat de nominibus.		a	4	10
		2	41	120

Tenor: In omnem ter[ram exiuit sonus eorum et in fines orbis terre uerba eorum]

Triplum: The light of Apollo (i.e. the sun) is never eclipsed while it is brought through its course in the service of the twice six signs (of the zodiac; but the same words may mean 'The light of Apollo, i.e. music, is never eclipsed while it is executed in the service of the twice six signs'), by which (sunlight or music) the church shines with harmonic art from the company of musicians with multiform figures; from among which (company) Jehan des Murs is brilliant in the varied mode of colours, Philippe de Vitry, from whom spring many accomplished things in multifarious order, Henri d'Helène knows well the tenor of tones with Denis le Grant, Regaud de Tirlemont, drunk from the Orpheic fountain, Robert du Palais, executing his achievements with boldness, Guillaume de Machaut rejoices in poetry, Gilles de Thérouanne, singing low with Guarin, whom Soissons ought to know, Arnaud Martin, the eversinging nightingale, Pierre de Bruges, Godefroy de Baralle, of which men the voice penetrates to the cardinal points of the world, to their honour. May they enjoy the prize of glory!

Motetus: With signs circling round (and irradiating) the zodiac, shining with the harmony of Phoebus, manifestly in musical cooperation, by which, radiating out, three times the number of Pythagoras (i.e. 3 x 10 = 30) is made equal with the cleverness of the basis of Boethius (i.e. 12). B. de Cluny, shining with the active power of the practical art joined with theory, recommending himself introduces himself to all by these present greetings. The subject matter of the triplum gives notice of the names of musicians.

Tenor: Into every land their sound has gone forth and their words to the limits of the land of the world.

Much of the following paragraph is indebted to David Howlett's unlocking of the ingenuity of these texts.[1] The name of the author B. de Cluny begins the second half of the motetus *Zodiacum*; the central, twenty-first, word is 'Cluni'. He states, just before the mid-point of the motetus text, that 'Pictagore numerus ter quibus | adequatur preradiantibus | *Boetii basis solercia*': 'three times the number of Pythagoras is made equal with the cleverness of the basis of Boethius'. The thirty-line triplum (thrice ten) and the twelve-line motetus are made equal by the musical setting, which causes them to begin and end together. In *De institutione arithmetica* II.XLII Boethius attributes the perfection of the number 10 to Pythagoras's observation that it was the sum of 1 + 2 + 3 + 4 (the tetraktys). The number 12 is referred to as the *Boetii basis* because in *De institutione musica* II.X Boethius explains musical proportions from it. The thirty octosyllabic lines of the triplum comprise 240 syllables, and the twelve decasyllabic lines of the motetus 120 syllables, a ratio 2:1, together 360, so that the total number of syllables in the motet equals the number of degrees in the circle. For a motet about the circling of earth, sun and zodiac signs this could hardly be more appropriate. The beginning of the triplum states that 'the light of the sun . . . is brought through its course in the twice six signs (of the zodiac)'; the beginning of the motetus recounts the 'signs circling round the zodiac'. *Musicali* in the motetus coincides with *musicorum* in the triplum at B31, serving to emphasise the phrase *musicorum collegio*, whose words and rhythm were to exercise such generative power on subsequent motets. *Musicali* is the seventh word from the beginning, *musicorum* the seventh word from the end. Thus *musicali* is preceded by six words that outline the twice six signs of the zodiac, and *musicorum* is followed by six words that allude to the twice six musicians named in the triplum. The opening of the triplum may allude to Ovid's *Metamorphoses*, Book 13, verses 618–19: 'cum sol duodena peregit | signa . . .'. 'Twice six' musicians (*bis sex*) are named in twelve of the thirty lines; they are aligned with the twelve signs of the zodiac which open the motetus, *Zodiacum signis*, forming a kind of celestial monochord mirroring the earthly musicians Pythagoras and Boethius.[2] Both names for the Greek god of the sun, Phoebus and Apollo, appear respectively in motetus and triplum, in both cases standing for the sun and for music. Twelve musicians are praised in a triplum whose mythological and cosmological programme is announced

---

[1] Howlett, '*Apollinis*'. Among the textual variants in **Brno** the most striking is at the beginning: *Apollinis eclipsatur | lux, quo peragatur | signorum sub emisperia | bis sex*. In this case, the crucial omission of 'nunquam' means that the sun sets (rather than *never* sets) when it passes below the hemisphere of the zodiac: Horyna, *A Prague Fragment*, 76, 86; 'Ein Brünner Fragment', 11. This is clearly a corruption which disrupts the octosyllabic lines and the presentation of the musicians as inextinguishable luminaries. The scribe was presumably trying to mend a corrupted text.

[2] The author of *Musicorum* reinterprets the twelves as monthly-calendrical as well as Apocalyptic. Canto X of Dante's *Paradiso* links twelve wise souls (named or implied) to twelve heavenly lights.

304 THE MUSICIAN MOTETS

by the first word: Apollo, son of Zeus and leader of the nine muses (sometimes considered their father, hence the fount of music and poetry) and god of the sun. The last lines of the motetus refer to the musicians listed in the triplum: 'musicorum tripli materia noticiam dat de nominibus'. The triplum (line 4) refers to the representation of these twelve by the twice six zodiac signs of the motetus. A similarly unusual cross-referencing between triplum and motetus texts occurs in other motets of this group: in *Sub Arturo*, Alanus refers in lines 29–30 of his motetus to the names in the triplum, 'quorum numen nominum triplo modulatur', and the motetus text also elucidates the tenor proportions. By sealing the links between text and music, such measures tend to make a motet proof against contrafaction, another manifestation of artful *sinergia* or 'working together'.[3] The words of the tenor also imply that the twelve musicians, representing the twelve apostles, spread their message to the ends of the earth, as in the Apocalypse, and as recounted in *Musicorum*—over a different tenor and with seven musicians representing the seven stars and apocalyptic sevens.

'Johannes de Muris is brilliant in the varied mode of colours': there are no statements in his early treatises about coloration—red notation—an innovation widely attributed to Vitry in the various testimonies to a treatise that he appears to have written and in the motet(s) widely attributed to him, especially *Garrit gallus*.[4] One name that is absent from all these motets is the theorist Jacobus. His enormous treatise (which survives in only one complete copy) never achieved the kind of circulation and reception enjoyed by Muris and Vitry—which ironically resulted in their treatises surviving in much more problematic form than the *Speculum musicae*.

The Music

The well-known text of the tenor *In omnem terram* has multiple liturgical placements and different melodies. Its source is Psalm 18, *Caeli enarrant gloriam Dei*, verse 5: 'in omnem terram exivit sonus eorum et in fines orbis terrae verba eorum', quoted in Romans 10: 18. The choice of tenor text, with its biblical contexts, is obviously appropriate for a motet about the light of the sun irradiating the signs of the zodiac. Verse 6 indeed refers to the sun: 'in sole posuit tabernaculum suum'. Ursula Günther argued that this tenor and the similar but unlabelled tenor of *Alma polis* related freely to the same chant source, the Offertory for the Mass of the missionary

---

[3] The balance of *sinergia* with *energia* implies the authenticity of *sinergia*, but the readings of this unfamiliar word as *sinsagia, sinsurgia, sinzugra, sinzigra* respectively in **Ivrea, Barc971, Barc853** and **Tarragona2** attest a variant which appeared early enough in the transmission of this text to influence the text of *Psallentes zinzugia* (see below), and now **Leipzig223** has *zinzugia*, indicating a possible link with the English added triplum.

A number of words or phrases in the triplum are echoed in the motetus: *Apollo—Phebus; signorum bis sex—Zodiacum signis; armonica—armonia; arte—artis; musicorum—musicorum; nitet—nitens*. Some of these occur nearly simultaneously (*signorum—signis, armonica—armonia, musicorum collegio—musicali*).

[4] Red notation was also used in *In virtute* (attributed to Vitry by Leech-Wilkinson, 'Related Motets', 5–8, 18; transcribed and discussed in Zayaruznaya, *The Monstrous New Art*, ch. 2 and appendix 1; and now in a motet in **Paris934** where it is used in the way described for *Thoma tibi* (see Dudas and Earp, *Four Early* Ars nova *Motets*). On Vitry's theoretical writings see Desmond, 'Ars vetus et nova'. For early English uses, see Ch. 4 n. 38.

saints Peter and Paul,[5] but Kévin Roger has now identified the tenor of *Alma polis*; see Chapter 19 and Ex. 19.2.

Apollinis stands out as unusual in the fourteenth-century repertory with its middle-voice tenor (see Ch. 1) and contrapuntally essential texted motetus *Zodiacum*, which lies mostly below the tenor, the main contrapuntal foundation, although it provides structural and melodic foundational material. Triplum and motetus form a largely but not wholly self-sufficient duet which takes account of the tenor pitches. The tenor provides essential support only at breve 37 when it dips below the motetus, and it rises above the triplum to form a fifth with it at breves 26 and 122. At breves 85, 133, and at 43, 91 and 139 the tenor goes below a self-contained triplum–motetus interval. The low motetus, *Zodiacum*, supports consonances, providing essential underpinnings to what would otherwise be fourths between triplum and tenor on strong beats, turning the sonorities into acceptable octaves and fifths.[6] This function was misunderstood by at least two of its medieval transmitters (in **SL2211** and **Barc971**) and by Frank Ll. Harrison, who mislabelled this part 'Contratenor'. Although the *In omnem terram* tenor of *Sub Arturo plebs* (a different chant) is not a middle voice, that piece is composed in such a way that triplum and motetus, while not entirely contrapuntally self-sufficient, largely work together as a pair.

Apollinis is 144 breves in length. As the theoretical citations note, it is in perfect modus, imperfect time and major prolation. The tenor *color* of sixteen perfect longs is stated three times, each consisting of two *taleae* (six altogether), each of eight perfect longs, each containing 3B = 24B.[7] Each *talea* has eight perfect longs = 24 breves = 144 minims. There are eleven notes per *talea*, 6 + 5, divided and followed by a rest. The tenor is also arranged in regular groups bounded by rests that cut across the *taleae* but correspond to them. The entire tenor has seven perfect longs between each rest, offset by placing five at the beginning and two at the end: 5 | 7 | 7 | 7 | 7 | 7 | 2. This pattern creates a displacement (i.e. syncopation) of periods at the beginning and end of the motet, creating a structural counterpoint with the outer parts.

Music: Texted (Outer) Parts and Number

Both triplum and motetus fall into periods of twenty-four breves, each period ending with a breve rest in the triplum, two breves rest in the motetus. These periods are not co-incident with the tenor *taleae*, but flanked in the triplum by periods of twenty-nine and nineteen breves, in the motetus by periods of twenty-seven and twenty-one breves, thus setting the triplum and motetus periodicity off from each other.[8] The twenty-four-breve

---

[5] GR [90]. CMM 39, p. LIV; p. XLVI compares the tenors of *Alma* and *Apollinis* with the Offertory chant. *Sub Arturo*, however, uses a different chant of the same name, which Günther identified as an adaptation of the first antiphon for the first Nocturn for Common of Apostles. See Ex. 20.2 below.

[6] At breves (bars) 13, 23, 47, 55, 59, 67–71, 73, 76, 115, 119, 141, 143.

[7] I use the words *color* and *talea* here in their received meanings to indicate respectively the melodic and rhythmic qualities of the tenor. See Ch. 1. It has long been known that medieval theorists are less consistent in applying these terms. The relevant passages have been usefully assembled in Zayaruznaya, *Upper-Voice Structures*, appendix.

[8] Nineteens are a multiple for *color* I of *Alma* (9 × 19), and for the whole of *Sub Arturo* counted in upper-part breves (152, 8 × 19) as opposed to the 144 of its nominal tenor breves. The lunar cycle of nineteen years yields the golden numbers used for finding Easter, and corresponds to nineteen places on the calendrical or musical hand.

first *color*, 16 perfect L

triplum periods bounded by B rests															
motetus periods bounded by imp L rests															
Tenor periods bounded by L rests	1	2	3	4	5	–	1	2	3	4	5	6	7	–	1	2
Tenor *taleae* 2 × 8L	1	2	3	4	5	6	7	8	1	2	3	4	5	6	7	8

second and third *colores*, each 16 perfect L

triplum cntd															
motetus cntd															
Tenor rests	3	4	5	6	7	–	1	2	3	4	5	6	7	–	1	2
Tenor *taleae* 2 × 8L	1	2	3	4	5	6	7	8	1	2	3	4	5	6	7	8

Fig. 16.1 Staggered periods in *Apollinis*

periods correspond to those identified by Ernst Sanders in some Vitry motets as the motet's modular number of twenty-four.[9] The central periods in each voice are thus the same length as the tenor *talea*, but are overlapped and staggered in relation to the tenor by two breves. Periods bounded by rests are in all three parts offset against the tenor *taleae* (see Fig. 16.1).

Apollinis has no tenor reduction, no upper-voice isorhythm, no recurrent local rhythmic patterning, no hockets, and in those respects stands early in what has often been considered an evolutionary spectrum from simple to complex.[10] The old habit of equating non-isorhythmic upper parts with less developed musical thinking confronts us immediately in this motet. Writers on music of all periods have often taken the identification of sameness, the recognition of repetition, as primary for form-building and foremost in interest. Much that can be said about the music of *Apollinis* will come in discussion of the later pieces that quote from it and make play with the material it provides. But as well as likeness and quotation, the congruences also have to do with structure such as the longer-range periods recounted above, with number, placement and order, with quotation and allusion, with symbolic representation, with the textual and musical interrelationship between parts, many of these in ways that have thus far been little noted, and which therefore give us a quite new access to the intellectual aesthetic of this repertory. Words, melody and rhythm are often quoted or alluded to separately, or quoted by two of those dimensions but not all three. Such quotations are often signalled as significant moments by being placed in prominent or neatly proportioned positions within the piece. While individual claims of such placement might seem forced, their accumulation is compelling.

As noted, the motet is 144 breves long, 12 squared, reflecting the twelve zodiacal signs and the cosmic ambition of the motet. Twelves underpin other motets in this group. The tenor *talea* length is the same in four of the musician motets: 24B of ℂ in *Apollinis*,

---

[9] Sanders, 'The Early Motets of Philippe de Vitry'.
[10] Notably Günther, 'The 14th-Century Motet'.

Musicalis, Musicorum (12B in the second *color*) and *Sub Arturo*, and in the second *color* of the fifth motet, *Alma polis*. The total length of *Apollinis* and *Musicorum* is 144 breves in each case, which is also the length of the tenor of *Sub Arturo* (although there the breves are of different lengths by mensural reinterpretation, and the count differs for the upper parts). In *Musicorum* the 144 is explicitly Apocalyptic, implicitly by punning with *Apollinis*; *Alma polis* would later join this game.[11] The second *color* of *Alma polis* is 144 semibreves (here on the accompanying transcription counted in semibreves to accommodate the different mensurations in the two texted parts). *Apollinis* and *Sub Arturo* each have three statements of a single notated *color*, *Apollinis* without change, *Sub Arturo* with mensural reinterpretation; *Musicalis* has a single *color*, so its seven *taleae* are fully written out, the seventh *talea* taking it beyond the 144 breves of the first six. In that sense, too, it goes one beyond the six *taleae* of *Apollinis*. These are just some of the ways in which the subsequent motets acknowledge *Apollinis* and each other. The second *color* of *Musicorum* in straightforward diminution is fully written out, though it could have been read from the first statement; the second *color* of *Alma polis* is mensurally reinterpreted without rewriting.

Music–Text Relationships

Although *Apollinis* has no repeating isorhythm in the upper parts, there are distinct melodic gestures whose recurrences articulate the form. Falling and rising fifths (*d–a*, *a–d*, *g–d*, *d–g*) are prominent in the motetus throughout, sometimes as solmisation vowel-rhyming puns: motetus 97–100 *a–d*, *la–re*: theori**ca R**ecommendans, and the slow enunciation of *basis* in the motetus on *bb–a*, *fa–mi*, at B70–71. Other descending *a–d* fifths occur at the opening *Zodiacum*, for the author's name *B. de Cluni* B77, and at *numerus ter* B46, rising *d–a* fifths for *musicorum* at B28 and B124; rising and falling fifths, sometimes in palindromic configuration, at *musicali* B31, *sinergia* B38, *adequatur* B55, *artis practice* B85, *musicorum tripli materia* B124. *Zodiacum*'s initial descent of the fifth *a–d* precedes an octave ascent followed by the descent down through a seventh, features which will be taken up in *Musicorum collegio, Alma polis* and *Sub Arturo*. In the triplum, all three *colores* begin with a descending scalar fifth outlining *a–d*.

No borrowings from earlier pieces have yet been detected in *Apollinis*, though *Apollinis* is itself the source of borrowed—and often dismembered or separated—verbal, rhythmic and melodic units in *Musicalis, Musicorum collegio, Alma polis* and *Sub Arturo plebs*. Breves 30–32 and triplum line 6 of the text of *Apollinis* have the words *musicorum collegio*, later to provide both words and rhythm (but not pitches) for the opening of *Musicorum collegio* and an important building block throughout that motet. Their rhythm provides the opening of *Musicalis*, repeated in each *talea*. Two striking passages in *Apollinis*, both involving a double presentation of the *musicorum collegio* rhythm, occur at breves 98–104 and 129–135. They correspond neither in their position

---

[11] As well as *Alma polis, Apollinis, Apocalipsis*, the English motets *Alma proles* and *Are post libamina* may nod at the same tradition. Connections between motets outside this group may be signalled by shared opening words: *Orbis orbatus/Vos pastores*, Ch. 7; *Vos/Gratissima*, Ch. 8; and the **Durham20** motet *O vos omnes* which might be English, or possibly by Vitry. See Ch. 1. See Ch. 6 for *Floret/Florens*, Ch. 30 for **Flos**/*Celsa*, Alís Raurich, 'The *Flores* of *Flos vernalis*' for **Flos** *vernalis/Fiat*. See also Ch. 25 for a lost motet *Flos mundi*.

308 THE MUSICIAN MOTETS

in the tenor *talea* nor, hence, in their own twenty-four-breve cycles. This is one of many instances of rhythmic recapitulation outside what would be the expected corresponding locations in an isorhythmic structure.

Robertus de Palacio and Philip de Vitry are presented in both *Apollinis* and *Musicalis* in melodic and rhythmic parallel (*Apollinis* B51 and 84: ♦ ♩♩♩ ♦ *e efe d* and ♦♦ ♩♩♩ ♦ *e d efe d*; *Musicalis* B41–42 and 65–66: ♩♩♩ ♦♦ ♦♦ ♦ *eee cd ec d*). *Philippus de Vitriaco* at B43–B52 of *Apollinis* straddles the junction to the second *color* (B49), starting at B43–B44 with emphatic parallel octaves on *Phili-*. While not presenting an exact melodic or rhythmic quotation, the triplum starts the second *color* with a clear allusion to the opening, thus setting Vitry's name parallel to that of Apollo. Vitry is the first musician named in the second *color*, Machaut in the third, which is introduced with the *musicorum collegio* rhythm. The musical mid-point coincides with the midpoint of the motetus text (by lines), between 'Boetii basis solercia' and 'B. de Cluni nitens energia', both text lines starting with the letter B and ending with *-ia*.

Interesting harvests can be expected from the—hitherto little-remarked—ways in which tenors provide melodic material integrated into the newly invented parts whose texts in turn determined the choice of tenor.[12] Here, the opening notes of the chant *In omnem terram*, *a c♯ d*, also recur in long notes in the motetus for *artis*, B82–85, where they coincide with the name of Robertus de Palatio in the triplum, while the tenor sounds its other non-conjunct progression with the descending fourth *c d a g*.[13] Transposed to *e g♯ a*, an octave above their pitch in most versions of the chant, they emphasise *Morino* at tr 106, also in long notes. In all three cases, the second note is signed as *mi* (thus the second and third notes are *mi–fa*), and in all three statements of the tenor *color c♯* is contrapuntally called for.[14] Uninflected, *a c d* set to *solerci(a)* in mo 71–72 ends the first half of both text and music. The descending fourth of the largest non-conjunct interval in the tenor is picked up several times in the texted parts. It announces *theorica* at mo 91–94, transposed at tr 38–39 for Muris. Its melodic fourths abound, as do the unmediated descent of this fifth and its ascending inversion, a rising fifth, throughout the tr and mo. The notes are varied to *a g d c♯* with rising fifth for *musicali* at mo 28. Melodic leaps of fourths and fifths are unusually prominent in this motet.

Triplum, motetus, and tenor all begin on the note *a*. The A of *Apollinis* and the Z of *Zodiacum* recall the 'alpha et omega', *principium et finis* of Revelation, anticipating the reverse span from the invocation of Genesis in *Sub Arturo* responding to that of the Apocalypse in *Musicorum*. The triplum range is from *a* up to *b′* (sometimes flattened); the *bs* are all rather prominent as the top note, at the beginning B1, at *musicorum collegio* 31, *actubus* 86, and *agalmata* 139 (emended by Howlett from *algamata*). The range of the later triplum *Pantheon* is *c* up to *d′*. The words *musicorum collegio* in *Apollinis* mark the first return to the opening highest note *b*, which is 'never exceeded' (*nunquam eclipsatur*).

---

[12] Chant citations worked into the texted parts: I have given further examples in Chs. 4, 12, 14.

[13] The same three notes *g a c d c* also end the *color*. The tenor thus sounds *a c d* six times, twice in each of the three *colores*. At B124–127 in **Ivrea** it occurs on the word 'musicorum', but all other sources have *b* in B127 (see commentary), which has been preferred, to avoid the crashing octaves with the tenor.

[14] See Ch. 20 and Ex. 20.2 for chant affinities and connections with on *Sub Arturo* and an erroneously signed *mi* in the tenor in **Yox**.

APOLLINIS ECLIPSATUR AND LATER VERSIONS 309

In the motetus *Zodiacum signis*, the twelfth note (the number of the zodiacal signs) is the first note of *signis* (coinciding with *signorum* in the triplum, B12–14), while the entire first text line, *Zodiacum signis lustrantibus*, occupies the first six perfect longs of the motet. It starts with a melisma, so that the opening triplum words *Apollinis eclipsatur nunquam* are heard with no textual competition. The triplum then starts the second group of six longs, punningly, with the words *bis sex* ('twice six'), which occur after six tenor notes and after six perfect longs.[15]

The Notation of *Apollinis*

The notational and musical style suggest a date of *c.* 1330, though all the surviving sources are at least several decades younger. The priority given in the listing to Muris and Vitry over the younger Machaut could reflect the greater fame of the older men at this date. Vitry is given emphatically slow notes in all parts at B43–49 (sounding together with *numerus ter*), as is Boethius at B67–73, ending the first half of both text and music. The nature of some of the many variants suggests that they may go back to a model that was less notationally precise; and the considerable variation in melodic details (see commentary in the Appendix) is, moreover, what might be expected from performerly interventions in such a widely circulated composition.

Despite the music being attested in fifteen sources, only two are complete: **Ivrea** and **Barc971**. **Stras** was also complete but survives only in the copy made by Coussemaker before the fire of 1870, with the original three-part version, plus two added voices.[16] Further nearly complete or legible versions of the triplum only are **Leiden2515**, **Pad658**, **Brno**, and of the motetus **Barc853**, **Tarragona2** and **Leipzig223**. The commentary does not attempt to report damaged or illegible passages or very fragmentary witnesses; it gives variants in dots or ligatures only where these seem to be significant. Witnesses to interesting or troublesome readings are reported where they can be discerned.

Given that *Apollinis* was reported in the theoretical treatises noted in Chapter 15 as a model example of perfect modus, the musical sources show a surprising degree of vacillation between perfect and imperfect modus:

1. Some longs are dotted where, in perfect modus, a dot is not needed: **Ivrea** needlessly dots the first two longs of the motetus; **Barc971** and **Leipzig223** dot those and all other perfect longs, including those in the tenor.
2. The two perfect long rests in the notated first tenor *color* (16–18 and 40–42) cover three spaces in **Ivrea**, **Barc853**, **Tarragona2**, **Leipzig223**, **Vienna922**, **Brno**, but

---

[15] The expression of 12 by *bis sex* also has a calendrical resonance; it recalls the denomination of what we call leap years as bissextile because the letter for 6 Kal. Mar. (24 Feb.) was repeated, yielding two dominical letters for those years. The tenor of *Apollinis* has three *c*s in the seventh perfect L, coinciding with the triplum's *bis sex*. The tenor of *Sub Arturo* has five consecutive occurrences of the note *c* towards the end of each *color*. Indeed, each *color* contains 12 *c*s, exactly half of its 24 notes. 9½ out of 24 perfect longs sound *c*. 9½ is the imperfect brevial length of the internal *talea* repetitions in *Alma*.

[16] While we must be grateful for Coussemaker's transcription, it cannot be assumed to be a faithful representation of the lost source. Assuming the bar divisions marked in the copy are his own, his command of the notational conventions was not perfect.

310   THE MUSICIAN MOTETS

Barc971 notates the first rest as an imperfect long and a breve, covering two plus one spaces.

3. The rule of *similis ante similem* is mostly observed. In all sources of the tenor, alteration of a ◾ before the ▮ is necessary, and those breves are never misnotated as longs, even in **Barc971**, which in other respects appears to construe the motet at least partly in imperfect modus: rests, dots, and what would, if perfect, be an infringement of *similis ante similem*. At triplum B106–108, **Ivrea's** ◾ ◾ ligature now, properly, requires alteration of the second breve before the ensuing ▮ at B109. This ligature originally had a downstem to the right, making the second note a long, improperly imperfect before the following ▮. The ◾ downstem is (improperly) present in **Leiden2515**. It is correctly notated as a breve (to be altered) in **Stras**, and in **Barc971**, surprisingly, given that source's other implementations of imperfect modus. At motetus 31–33, **Ivrea** and **Stras** correctly require alteration of the second ◾ before the ▮; **Leipzig223**, **Barc853**, **Barc971** and **Tarragona2** notate it as a long, again improperly if construed in perfect modus. **Leipzig223** and **Barc971** thus waver between perfect and imperfect modus. All of **Leipzig223's** 'perfect' longs are dotted, which they would not need to be if perfect modus were in force. In **Barc971** tenor 73–78 is notated improperly as ◾ ◾ (in ligature) followed by a separate ▮, although the corresponding place in the first *talea* (1–6) is correct with ◾, alt ◾, ▮. Some of these anomalies could possibly go back to an exemplar that was spelt out in duple modus (*ad longum*). The tenor is mislabelled 'Contra' in **Barc971**, apparently misunderstanding its status as a middle-voice tenor.[17]

The intact survival of the **Ivrea** version does not confer preferential status on its readings. Where **Ivrea** seems to have a less good reading, and where there is some degree of unanimity between other sources in favour of one I judge preferable, I have used that. There remain many passages where equally valid alternatives exist in one or more sources. Given the fragmentary state of most of the sources, and the high level of notational corruption, I make no apology for offering a transcription with some elements of conflation, a version which seeks to remove some of the anomalies which may have crept in over a decades-long transmission. The triplum has a wide range of melodic and ornamental variants in its various sources, the most striking being in **Brno**, which introduces many more minim groups, often to fill in disjunct intervals; it is more ornamented even than the organ intabulation in **Vienna5094**.[18] There is some notational hesitancy in **Brno**; a few S groups are left unstemmed, perhaps indicating uncertainty about their values. Some of the rhythms are unclear, perhaps requiring minim alteration, though scribal uncertainty is more likely. One minim stem points down (B88). Some longs and breves at the ends of ligatures are incorrectly notated, a feature not uncommon in late Germanic and eastern European sources in which the niceties of French *ars nova* notation were often simplified.[19]

---

[17] See Ch. 1 on middle-voice tenors. **Stras** labels the tenor of *Rex Karole* 'Contratenor'.

[18] Those two versions are transcribed alongside **Ivrea** in Horyna, 'Ein Brünner Fragment', 11 and Horyna, *A Prague Fragment*, 78–86.

[19] See Ward, 'A Central European Repertory' for documentation of east European adaptations of French notational practices.

To place the use of shorter note-values in *Apollinis* in context, we should recall that the stemless semibreves in the *ars nova* motets in *Fauvel* and others of only slightly later date lend themselves to interpretation according to the default specifications for unstemmed semibreves in imperfect time and what would later be called major prolation (rhythmic groupings of values below the breve) given by theorists (see CS iii: Anon III):

For several *Fauvel* motets, notated there without minim stems, these default values are confirmed by stems in later sources.[20] Occasional downstems on the first of a group affirm a longer rather than a short value; they are accidental, and do not necessarily make the note longer than it would be if unstemmed. Any other dispositions of rhythms within the breve outside those defaults require notated stems. Although the unsigned minim value exists in the advanced *Fauvel* motets, only when departure from the default values is required did stemming become necessary, earlier by downstems confirming longer notes, later by upstems for shorter values.[21] When groupings other than the defaults were wanted, or minim rests, it gradually became necessary to stem all minims, whether using the default rhythms or not. While the minim value already existed in the 1310s, only from the 1320s does it become an independent notated value. Its place in the hierarchy is clear in the gradus system of Muris's *Notitia* of 1319, though major and minor prolation is not so formulated and named until the treatise of Petrus dictus palma ociosa of 1336, and the *Libellus* attributed to Muris usually dated in the 1340s, when the semibreve–minim relationship took its place in the theoretical hierarchy (*mutatis mutandis*) parallel to long–breve and breve–semibreve, similarly subject to alteration and imperfection. This had applied in practice long before the theoretical formulations, though not always with absolute consistency. For the motets attributed to Vitry, observation of defaults provides partial corroboration of a chronology for his motets that can sometimes be proposed on other grounds. Indeed, the very term 'prolation', meaning performance, or bringing forward, hints at a tradition of performance practice preceding its theoretical codification, and it was used in a more general sense before it took on the specific meaning of the semibreve–minim relationship.

While all the musician motets show some departure from the default values that applied to stemless semibreves during the earliest stage of *ars nova*, *Apollinis*, the earliest of the musician motets, has only a very few variant sub-breve groupings. The only

---

[20] *Garrit gallus* in **Pic**, *Tribum/Quoniam*, *Firmissime/Adesto* and *Super/Presidentes* in **Br19606**, *Firmissime/Adesto* and *Orbis/Orbatus* in **Koblenz**. In some cases later sources (especially **Koblenz**) show some uncertainty, due probably to being transcribed from a stemless source with dots (some of which are retained).

[21] Some sources (mostly of the earlier 14th c. in France, also later in England) distinguish major semibreve rests intersecting the staff line from minor semibreve rests worth two minims, suspended from the line. Earp, 'Tradition and Innovation', sets out clearly the distinction between, on the one hand, motets whose hockets are or could have been notated with minor semibreve rests, where the rest simply replaced a note within the same rhythmic framework and, on the other hand, notation requiring single minim rests in interlocking hockets which are later developmentally and probably chronologically. See Ch. 30 n.20.

312   THE MUSICIAN MOTETS

non-default combinations used are: for three notes 2 1 3 (♦♦ ♦);[22] for four notes: 1113, 3111 (♦♦♦ ♦ and ♦ ♦♦♦);[23] for five notes: 2 1 111 (♦♦ ♦♦♦).[24] The motet could therefore originally have been notated with mainly unstemmed semibreves, requiring stems only in the fifteen bars with departures from the default values. *Apollinis* also exceeds the defaults by imperfecting breves (in B1, 6, 10, 59, 71, 73, 74, 112) and a long (in B137–138) by a single ensuing ♩, known as imperfection by a 'remote' or non-adjacent note-value.[25] Most or all of these could originally have been notated as plicas. Works attributed to Vitry, including late and recently reconstructed works like *Phi millies* and *Beatius/Cum humanum*,[26] never imperfect the breve in ℭ by a minim, except by using a plica, a usage which could be an authorial marker for Vitry, or at least a reason for doubting his authorship of motets with imperfect breves further imperfected by minims (see Chapter 7).

Other departures from the defaults involve rests and altered minims. In most sources, *Apollinis* has a single minim rest in B85 (♦ ⌐♦♦ | on *Palatio*). There are not even any semibreve rests (the one at **Barc971** B29 is in error for a breve rest), so that a single minim rest may seem suspicious and anomalous, resulting in a rhythm which stands outside the rhythmic vocabulary of this motet.[27] I have treated the rest as an alternative reading placed above the staff, adopting the main reading from **Brno** and **Vienna5094**. See the Appendix to this chapter for variants for multi-source motets.

The evidence is mixed as to whether B. de Cluny used an altered minim before a semibreve. On balance, I suspect that there were no altered minims in *Apollinis* as originally notated. If **Barc971**'s few altered minims are discounted in a transmission with evident corruptions, it would be the case that neither *Apollinis* nor *Musicorum* has altered minims. A single anomalous instance of alteration in *Musicalis* (repeated in each *talea*) is discussed below. At triplum 7–8 **Pad658**, **Stras**, **Barc971** all have ♦ ♦♦, requiring alteration of the second minim. (**Leiden2515** is cut off and **Brno** has ♦♦ ♦♦♦ *d e fef* twice, typical of its ornamental variants.) **Ivrea** originally had stems on both second minims; but these have been erased, a deliberate correction resulting in the rhythm used here (2 1 3, ♦♦ ♦). There is only one other place in the motet apparently requiring an altered minim, the single iambic pair in Harrison's transcription and present only in **Ivrea**: the last minim in triplum 118 (*Suessio*): ♦ ♦♦ | ♦♦♦ | ♦ ♦ *g a a* | *g gf* | *a e*, requiring alteration of the second M preceding the S. All other sources of B117–118 have a less awkward reading: **Barc971** and **Leiden2515** read ♦ ♦ | ♦♦ ♦♦ | ♦ ♦ *g a* | *a gfg* | *a e*, which has been used here. **Stras** has ♦ ♦♦ | ♦ ♦♦♦ | ♦ ♦ *g a a* | *g gfg* | *a e*; **Pad658** *g a* | *a g gf*, all of which make better sense, requiring no minim alteration in what was presumably the original version. It seems more likely that there is a minim missing here in **Ivrea** than that it is a unique instance of an altered minim in this transmission. **Barc971** has a pair of altered minims on *actubus* at B88, and a missing stem on the third note of the following group. Apart from these there are no other iambic progressions in the entire motet (♦♦ ♦ or ♦♦

---

[22] At tr 7, 8 (if the reading of 7–8 is correct: see below on altered minims), 28, 124.

[23] ♦ ♦♦♦ at tr 32, 51, 104; and ♦♦♦ ♦ at tr 55.

[24] At tr 9, 27, 37, 84, 123; mo 24, 120.

[25] Such remote imperfection is already allowed in the *Conclusiones* of Muris's *Notitia* (1321), as is imperfection of a breve by a single semibreve in perfect tempus. See Bent, 'Artes novae'.

[26] See also Ch. 4 n. 42.

[27] The presence of a single minim rest (in each of the final four triplum *taleae*) has been used to cast doubt on the 1325 dating of Machaut's Motet 18. See Ch. 13.

APOLLINIS ECLIPSATUR AND LATER VERSIONS   313

alt), which is resolutely trochaic. The anomalies may arise from corrupted transmission, possibly from a less prescriptive original notated form; given the absence of any other iambic formulations, or of alteration of values below the breve, iambic minims with alteration, whether in B7–8 or B118, may have lain outside the predominant style of this composition. If the altered minims and the minim rest are judged to be corruptions, the original form of this motet could well date to *c.* 1330 or even back into the 1320s, only needing stems for the few exceptions to the default values.[28]

Other Versions of *Apollinis*: Added Parts

The sources listed in Chapter 15 include three versions of *Apollinis* with an added triplum, the only fourteenth-century composition for which such arrangements or glosses exist. Two of these also have a fifth voice: as well as an additional triplum in both, there is a 'Quadruplum sive triplum' in **Stras**, and a contratenor in **LoTNA**, both textless, making them the only Continental examples of five-part motets during the entire fourteenth century, notwithstanding theoretical references to five-part composition (see Ch. 1). These additions are apparently later, probably dating from around 1400. They add no new names.

Although the two five-part versions seem not to be interrelated, it can be no accident that they each perform a similar double exercise on the same foundational composition, and each begins with 'P' (though **LoTNA** spells the opening word *Sallentes*). This also corroborates the primary status of *Apollinis*; like the *Roman de la rose*, it became a model for *remaniement*, for reworkings. These versions are treated under *Apollinis* because they are dependent on it; however, they may not antedate the other musician motets, which will be discussed in what appears to be their chronological order. Of the three additional triplum parts in later manuscripts, **Barc853**'s is textless and two are texted, *Pantheon* and *Psallentes*.

The Textless Triplum in **Barc853**

Barc853[29] (see ⏵ Ex. 16.2). Folio 1ʳ contains the motetus *Zodiacum signis*, the tenor *In omnem terram*, and in the same hand a textless 'triplum' and a 'Contratenor *Per sanctam civitatem*'.[30] Like *Pantheon abluitur* and the textless 'Quadruplum sive triplum' in **Stras**, the new extra triplum has no repeating or regular structure. As noted above, the 'Contratenor *Per sanctam civitatem*', claimed as a fifth voice by Gómez, cannot belong to *Apollinis* and has no textual connection; this is a four-part version. Gómez acknowledges the problems but maintains nevertheless that it contributes to a five-part version. The presence of this contratenor, however, is unexplained; there may have been insufficient space on this opening for other voices of the motet to which it

---

[28] See Appendix to this chapter.

[29] See Gómez, 'Une Version à cinq voix du motet *Apollinis*'.

[30] Variants in the triplum: 9–10 ambiguous; 10.1 ♩? in which case 10.2 is alt; 24, 28–30, 53–55, 61, 91, 112, 114 uncertain; 50 *d*; 62 ■? no stem visible, but must be ♦ lig.; 83 ◾; 114.4 ■? Gómez, 'Une Version à cinq voix du motet *Apollinis*', remarks on the exceptional nature of an upper motet voice without text.

314 THE MUSICIAN MOTETS

presumably belonged. It is indeed hard to explain the format, taking into account the missing facing verso, which presumably contained the triplum *Apollinis*, leaving little space for the other parts of a different motet. Gómez sets out style-related chronological arguments, presumed manuscript datings, presumptive dates of the musicians mentioned, and adds to the list of interconnections between the compositions.[31] The new triplum was clearly composed to fit the motetus–tenor pair (the low motetus being the contrapuntal foundation) but with only erratic regard to its consonance with the original triplum *Apollinis*, with which it has some doublings and parallel seconds, and much incidental dissonance. Occasional anomalies with the motetus include parallel ninths at B120. It is strongly dissonant with the tenor at B87 (but so is *Apollinis*), 128 and 131, less so at 79 and elsewhere. Groups of six semibreves (with some variation), punctuated by a few minim rests, recur at corresponding places B7–9, 55–57, 103–105, but there is no other regular periodicity. Those single minim rests create expectation of hocket, but there is none. There are many rhythmic and melodic echoes of the triplum *Apollinis* (notably at B29–30), which was clearly known to the later composer, who often took account of any available contrapuntal positions that avoided doubling, for example at B11–12, even if he allowed free incidental dissonance. The rhythmic vocabulary is very similar to *Apollinis*, but even closer to the defaults; the only exceptions are breves imperfected by minims, semibreves by minim rests, and the group ♦♦ ♦♦♦ instead of ♦♦♦ ♦♦ at B21, 29, 70, 94, 120, 139. (B3. 4–5 could be sharpened.)

Pantheon abluitur in **Stras** and **SL2211**

Stras contains a five-part version with the texted upper voice *Pantheon abluitur* and an additional textless upper part labelled *Quadruplum sive triplum de Apollinis*.[32] *Pantheon abluitur* is also now in **SL2211**. See ▶ Ex. 16.3. Commentary notes to the transcription are in the Appendix to this chapter.

Text and translation by David Howlett:[33]

	Rhyme	Words	Syllables
Pantheon abluitur	a	2	7
templum pseudodeorum;	b	2	7
[hodie] construitur	a	2	7
ecclesia sanctorum;	b	2	7

---

[31] Gómez uses stylistic arguments drawn from Günther, 'The 14th-Century Motet', and also adds to Günther's list of linking characteristics between the two pieces the repetition of three notes (*c*) in the tenors of *Apollinis* and *Sub Arturo*. *Sub Arturo* actually has five consecutive cs in each of its three *colores*.

[32] PMFC 5, no. 9a.

[33] 6 *mutaui*; 11 *confinitas*; 12 *iore* over *maiestate*; 14 *posi deces*; 22 *decorantur*; 24 *fruetur*; 27 *iubetur*; 29 *honoris*; 34 *lauato*. The first two syllables, *maies-* of *maiestate* 12 and *ier-* of *ierarchias* 13, must be elided to produce heptasyllabic lines. **SL2211**: large portions of the text are illegible, but where they can be deciphered they seem to confirm the above readings. One exception is in lines 2–3, where there is no room for a word between *pseudodeorum* and *construitur*; *criste* seems to be between *construitur* and *ecclesia*, but this fits neither the rhyme scheme nor the heptasyllabic count.

plus error destruitur	5	a	3	7
muta[tus] ui bonorum.		b	3	7
Prima Sancta Trinitas		c	3	7
ibidem ueneratur,		d	3	7
gratiam Diuinitas		c	3	7
ut plene largiatur;	10	d	3	7
hinc laudum concinitas		c	3	7
maiestate collocatur		d	3	7
ierarchias complete		e	3	7
post decem uenerari;		f	3	7
laus sequitur prophete	15	e	3	7
Johannes tam preclari.		f	3	7
Duodecim athlete		e	3	7
tunc debent collaudari;		f	3	7
martirum uibratio		g	2	7
consequenter laudatur,	20	d	2	7
confitens flagratio		g	2	7
uicissim decoratur,		d	2	7
uirginum fragratio		g	2	7
laude simul fruatur;		d	3	7
nos ubique locorum	25	h	3	7
his festum celebrare		i	3	7
iubemur singulorum.		h	2	7
Si non constat seruare		i	4	7
ius[ta] supplent honorum		h	3	7
quos contigit peccare;	30	i	3	7
nunc Caput deprecentur,		j	3	7
istius membra festi		k	3	7
corda nostra lauentur;		j	3	7
sic lauate celesti		k	3	7
ne nobis dominentur	35	j	3	7
proditores scelesti.		k	2	7
		11	93	252

The Pantheon, temple of false gods, is cleansed; [today] it is built as a church of saints; moreover error is destroyed, changed by the power of good men. On the first (day, i.e. Sunday) the Holy Trinity is worshipped there, that Divinity may bestow grace fully; afterwards from all sides a harmony of praises should be conferred with majesty to worship entirely the Ten Hierarchies (of Angels); praise of the Prophet so radiant John (the Baptist) follows; then the Twelve Contestants (i.e. Apostles) ought to be praised together; the Brilliance of Martyrs should be praised in succession, the Confessing Fire (i.e. the Company of Confessors) should be honoured in turn; the Fragrance of Virgins should enjoy praise together. We of particular places everywhere are bidden to celebrate the feast with them. If one does not agree to keep (the feast) those whom it has suited to sin will supply the dues of honours. Now let the members of this feast beseech

316   THE MUSICIAN MOTETS

the Head that our hearts may be washed. So wash [us] for heaven that evil traitors may not dominate us.

The texted voice *Pantheon abluitur* and untexted *Quadruplum sive triplum de Apollinis* were copied as additional voices to *Apollinis eclipsatur* in **Stras** and survive in Coussemaker's transcription, fortunately made before the manuscript was burnt, but of sometimes questionable reliability. According to his note, the two added parts are written on a separate folio pasted to the bottom of f. 64ᵛ. The quadruplum is labelled 'f 65 milieu de la page'. The presumption is therefore that the three-part motet filled an opening, and the two added parts were on a loose leaf pasted in; whether by the same or a later scribe is not known.[34]

This voice was unique until identified in the San Lorenzo palimpsest **SL2211**, the only added part that occurs in more than one source and thus attests more than local circulation. In the absence of overwriting, it is musically more legible than many pages of the palimpsest manuscript, especially in the most recent multi-spectral images, and offers variant readings which are in some cases improvements, as well as (from the spacing of notes) some guidance on text underlay, despite the largely illegible state of the verbal text.[35] The present edition uses the text as restored by David Howlett from **Stras**; it mends the syllable count, even though both sources suggest that the composer worked with a defective text. (*Maie-sta-te* has to be elided, B39, line 12.) Curiously, this added triplum is presented in **SL2211** on a single opening together with only the triplum, *Apollinis*, and the tenor, omitting the contrapuntally essential motetus. I have suggested that the compiler of **SL2211** may have been trying to give it the texture of an Italian motet, with two more or less equal upper voices and tenor, without realising that in this case it is the motetus and not the tenor that supports the counterpoint.

The text is tied to its model in many ways. There are exactly as many rhymes and words in this text as in *Apollinis eclipsatur*, eleven rhymes and ninety-three words, evidence of modelling that is also reflected in musical imitations. Like all voices of the original three-part *Apollinis*, both these added voices begin on the note *a*. Both the texted new voice *Pantheon* and the textless 'quadruplum sive triplum' have pseudo-imitation at the beginning and enjoy rhythmic imitations throughout. There are many reminiscences of the *Apollinis* triplum, showing a clear attempt to integrate the added parts, though there are (inevitably in a five-part texture) many parallel perfect intervals with the original parts and each other, and free dissonance. *Pantheon* mainly uses the rhythmic vocabulary of its model; apart from one anomaly noted in the commentary, none of the groupings requires minim alteration, which has therefore been avoided in cases of ambiguity. (Quadruplum 47 imperfects a breve by two following minims.)

The quadruplum fits almost perfectly with the motetus and tenor (dissonance with the motetus may invite further emendation at B113). At B122 the triplum supplies the support for what would otherwise be a fourth between quadruplum and tenor. At B73–74 there are incidental parallel sevenths between the two new parts, and *Pantheon* B64–65 is dissonant with the quadruplum. There are many corruptions in the **Stras**

---

[34] See the reconstructions in Welker, *Musik am Oberrhein*, 74–76.
[35] Nádas and Janke, *The San Lorenzo Palimpsest*, ii, ff. R188ᵛ–189.

quadruplum, some of which are wrongly resolved by Harrison, who also made some transcription errors in relatively unproblematic passages. The guiding principle here has been to establish how the added parts were formed. Both seem to have taken the motetus as their starting point, and with corrections to Harrison's transcription they mostly form reasonable counterpoint with it and usually also with the tenor. The price of this five-part effort is a residual high level of incidental dissonance, and a large number of parallel unisons of both parts with the motetus and with each other. The two new parts have parallel unisons at B33–34, B69–70, B81–82 (also with *Apollinis*), B90–91, B136–137.[36]

Psallentes zinzugia in **LoTNA**

LoTNA has a new texted triplum [*P*]*sallentes zinzugia* and a new contratenor (see ⏵ Ex. 16.4). The fragmentary bifolio **LoTNA** was rediscovered by David Howlett and the music identified by Andrew Wathey.[37] It has a new contratenor and yet another new triplum, this time texted.

[*P*]*sallentes zinzugia* is known only from **LoTNA**, where it is followed directly by a *Contratenor de Apollinis*, making a second five-part version, and then by the fragmentary motet [*Arta*]/*Musicus est ille*, two adjacent motets about music and musicians. All these added voices appear in manuscripts datable around 1400 and later, but they do not include names, as do the tripla of the core motets of the group, and are not easily datable on musical grounds, especially when (at least in *Pantheon*) they are clearly accommodating to the older model. Despite surviving only in an English source, this text seems to be addressed to implicitly compatriot Frenchmen. *Musicorum collegio*, also unique to an English source, appears to celebrate musicians at the exiled French court in England. Its tenor of greeting, *Avete*, is echoed here by *Gallici salvete*.

Text and translation by David Howlett:

		Rhyme	Words	Syllables
[P]Sallentes zinzugia		a	2	7
monocordo musa		b	2	6
nos illus[tre]t gracia		a	3	7
Domini diffusa		b	2	6
normulis ypocritis,	5	c	2	7
r[ith]mis emiolicis,		c	2	7
formis epogdoicis		c	2	7
sol[l]erter ela[tos]		d	2	6
diesisque commatis		c	2	7
tinnulis ornatos.	10	d	2	6

[36] See Appendix to this chapter for commentary to ⏵ Ex. 16.3, web transcription of *Apollinis* with additional triplum *Pantheon*.

[37] Wathey, *Manuscripts . . . Supplement 1 to RISM*, 54–57.

318 THE MUSICIAN MOTETS

Perstrepent tum [y]paton		e	3	7
menti musicorum		f	2	6
flosque diesum[e]non		e	2	7
licanos tenorum		f	2	6
fig[uris] cromaticis	15	c	2	7
modis enarmonicis		c	2	7
odis ypoyasticis;		c	2	7
sic qui [il]lustrati		h	3	6
ypermixolidia		a	1	7
iam plaudant elati	20	h	3	6
resulta[ntes] musica		i	2	7
muse preparata		j	2	6
necnon yperbolica		i	2	7
rudibus inflata		j	2	6
flatus scenophegici	25	k	2	7
pulsus ypophregici		k	2	7
practicique pistici		k	2	7
musici discrete		l	2	6
psallatis armoniam.		m	2	7
Gallici saluete!	30	l	2	6
		13	63	198

Let the diffused grace of the Lord illuminate us making music in combination on a monochord with the Muse (either 'the Muse' of poetry or 'the bagpipe'[38] or both), [us] expertly uplifted with norms for performers, with hemiolian rhythms, with epogdoic forms, and embellished with the jingling commas of the diesis.

Then the flower of the lowest notes of the tetrachord and of the disjunct tetrachord, the second highest note of the tetrachord of the tenors will resound to the mind of musicians, in chromatic figures, in enharmonic modes, in hypoiastic odes. Thus those who have been illuminated, uplifted, should now beat out in hypermixolydian, resounding with music prepared for the Muse and hyperbolical, inflated for the uninstructed (or 'prepared for the bagpipe and inflated by the sticks', i.e. the ribs in the bag), reed-devourers [should mark] breaths, beats of the hypophrygian (mode), and practical musicians who understand, may you make music discretely in harmony. Frenchmen, greetings!

The text of [P]sallentes zinzugia is a tour de force which parades the poet's knowledge of Greek theoretical terminology. David Howlett has shown that the many words of Greek derivation, twenty-nine out of sixty-three, are nearly all known from Boethius, De institutione musica, Martianus Capella, De nuptiis philologiae et Mercurii and Isidore of Seville's Etymologiarum libri. The triplum text Psallentes has the same number of

---

[38] The Summa Musice, ed. Page, 143: 'musica dicatur a musa quoddam simplicissimo instrumento quod a pastoribus gregum circa mundi principium primo fuit inventum'. I thank Bonnie Blackburn for this reference.

lines, thirty, as the primary composition *Apollinis eclipsatur; Pantheon abluitur* exhibits the same number of rhymes (11) and words (93) as *Apollinis*.

Pantheon, Apollinis, Zodiacum, In omnem terram and *Psallentes* all begin on the note *a*. Just as *Apollinis/Zodiacum* plays with the extremes of the alphabet, *A–Z, Psallentes* does the same in reversed order, *Z–A*:[39] lines 1 and 29, *psallentes zinzugia* and *psallatis armoniam*, recall from *Zodiacum signis* the first words of the first two lines, *zodiacum* and *armonia*, and the variant readings of line 3: *sinsagia* **Ivrea,** *sinzurgia* **Barc971,** *zinzurgia* **Leipzig223,** for *sinergia*; these may be the sources for use of that word in the **LoTNA** text—which could even be the source of that corruption. The presence of this motet in relatively late Germanic or east European sources (**Stras, Leipzig223, Brno**) attests a circulation that could account for its citation in theoretical treatises from those areas.

Notationally, this new texted triplum is more advanced than the other added voices detailed above, with frequent use of syncopation within the breve of $\mathbb{C}$ (♩ ♪♪♪, here notated without dots, but not implying alteration) and more syncopation at B72. There is only one altered minim, at B30, which could invite emendation. It appears to be in perfect modus on the strength of the apparently undotted three-beat L at B19, but otherwise has no clear modus indications, and no isorhythmic structuring. This voice again appears to have been composed to the motetus, with which it forms good counterpoint, but it is often strongly dissonant with the other parts, including most places where the tenor descends below the motetus, at B82–91, 133, 139 (and less so at 37), and it has some dissonance and parallelism with the new contratenor. It clashes strongly with the *Apollinis* triplum at B42 and generally has some roughnesses and parallels. Unlike the other added voices, the contratenor is isorhythmically structured, with four 36-breve *taleae* superimposed on the three 48-breve *color* statements of the tenor, each of two 24-breve *taleae*. It forms good consonant counterpoint with the foundational motetus and, unlike the triplum *Psallentes*, with the tenor, except at B91, where it only goes with the tenor.[40] It provides a third in the final chord, as in occasional English compositions of the early fifteenth century, a feature absent or vanishingly rare in French works, but—surprisingly—present in *Musicalis*.

De modo componendi tenores motettorum

Egidius de Morino is named in the texts of both *Apollinis* and *Musicalis*. A man of this name (also spelt Murino) has been associated with two treatises, *Tractatus figurarum* and *De modo componendi tenores motettorum*, linked in the sources in which both appear. Chapter 1 reviews their authorship and sources. The *Tractatus figurarum* is thought to date from the end of the century, and should probably be deemed anonymous.[41] Although Philipoctus and Egidius are rejected as authors, Egidius's name has

---

[39] A similar reversal is the later echoing of *Musicorum*'s 'testatur Apocalipsis' in *Sub Arturo*'s 'Genesis testatur'. See also below.

[40] Music variant: breve (in the isorhythm) is here split into two semibreves on *a*. Because of the extensive textual emendations and completions, the musical transcription has not been encumbered with square brackets: see the text above.

[41] See *Tractatus figurarum*, ed. Schreur, for the case for and (largely) against the authorship of Philipoctus; compositions ascribed to him do not use the note-shapes advocated in the treatise.

320 THE MUSICIAN MOTETS

stuck to the motet treatise, though the source situation leaves his authorship extremely dubious. I proposed there that the treatise revert to anonymous status. In any case, its author is very unlikely to be the Egidius named in these much earlier motets.

As noted in Chapter 1, the treatise is specifically directed to the teaching of children (*ad doctrinam parvulorum*). After the more-often-quoted elementary instructions, and after a peroration which may identify what follows as an addition, the author describes 'another way of writing motets', with a central tenor:[42]

Est autem alius modus componendi motetos quam superius dictum est, videlicet: quod tenor vadat supra motetum et sic ordinabis:	There is, however, another way of composing motets than that given above, namely when the tenor goes above the motetus, and you arrange it thus.
Accipe tenorem de antiphonario, sicut superius dictum est, quem colorabis et ordinabis, et stat in gamma bassa; et tu potes eum mittere in gamma alta; et quando est ordinatus bene, tunc facias discantum sub tenore, sicut melius scis. Et potes ipsum colorare et de modo perfecto facere si vis. Hoc facto facias triplum concordare supra motetum sicut melius scis et potes.	Take a tenor from the antiphoner as stated above, order and colour it.[43] [If] it stands in gamma bassa, you can place it in gamma alta [i.e. transpose it up]. And when it is well ordered, make a discant below the tenor as well as you know how. And you can colour [here, rhythmicise] it and make it in perfect modus if you wish. Then make the triplum concord above the motetus as well as you know how and are able.
Et si vis ipsum facere cum quatuor, tunc debet ibi esse contratenor. Sed oportet quod contratenor sit primo et concordet cum tenore, aliter non posset colorari.	And if you wish to make it in four parts, then the contratenor must be there [composed] first, and be consonant with the tenor, otherwise it cannot be coloured.[44]

This description perfectly fits the three-part original version of *Apollinis*, one of the rare French motets with a middle-voice tenor.[45] The central tenor of *Apollinis* is indeed in perfect modus, and transposed up an octave from most chant sources, a fourth or fifth from others.[46] It is very striking that a purportedly elementary treatise should advocate such an uncommon usage, and that the description fits *Apollinis* better than any other known motet of the period. The author of the treatise almost certainly knew *Apollinis*; since he is unlikely, decades later, to be the Egidius de Morino named in it, could

---

[42] Source: CS iii. 124–28. Electronic version prepared by C. Matthew Balensuela, Oliver B. Ellsworth, and Thomas J. Mathiesen for the TML, 1990. Partial edition and translation in Leech-Wilkinson, *Compositional Techniques*, i. 18–24 and appendix I, collated with variants from the five sources. Now a fuller text with translation is in Zayaruznaya, *Upper-Voice Structures*, appendix. *Tractatus figurarum*, ed. Schreur, gives full descriptions of the manuscripts containing both treatises.

[43] *In omnem terram* has many liturgical placements. The tenor of *Apollinis*, however, is not from the antiphoner, but from the gradual, though the different *In omnem terram* tenor of *Sub Arturo* is from the antiphoner. Leech-Wilkinson, *Compositional Techniques*, says there are no examples where the cantus firmus is placed in gamma alta; perhaps Egidius simply meant that the cantus firmus can be transposed up.

[44] This does not apply to inessential later-added contratenors. Of the other musician motets only the four-part *Alma polis* has a contratenor, in that case contrapuntally essential.

[45] On middle-voice tenors see Ch.1. *Zodiacum* is one of the rare motetus parts in the French repertory that lies below the tenor; *Tribum/Quoniam* may have been the first.

[46] See Clark, 'Concordare cum materia', H9.

his name have become attached to the treatise because of its presence in this widely circulated motet?

Again surprisingly for an elementary treatise, the author goes on to the rare case of composition in five parts:

Item si vis facere motetum cum quinque, per hunc modum potest fieri: fac primo tenorem, sicut dictum est, et fac [motetum] discantari subtus tenorem et concordare; hoc modo fac triplum discantari insuper motetum, sicut melius scis. Adhuc potes facere alium discantum qui ibi circumsonat triplum fulgendo ipsum triplum. Et iste quintus cantus vocatur quadruplum, et sic erit motetus totaliter plenus. Et credo quod non possint fieri plures cantus insimul.	If you want to make a motet in five parts, first make the tenor, then a [motetus] in discant below the tenor, then a triplum above the motetus. Then you can make another discantus sounding around that triplum [= in the same range?] and embellishing it. And this fifth cantus is called quadruplum, and then your motet will be full. And I think you cannot make more parts simultaneously.

Apollinis is not named, but not only does it fit the prescription for a three-part motet with motetus below the tenor in both passages; its adaptations fit the prescription for five-part composition to be on the basis of a three-part composition with low motetus and central tenor. The description, however, accounts for only four parts, though five are promised. Perhaps the author was assuming a contratenor, as prescribed earlier in the treatise. Two of the adaptations of *Apollinis* with later-added upper parts are indeed the only five-part motets from the entire period, and they too precisely fit this description. The terminology (*circumsonat, fulgendo*) resonates with the shared vocabulary of the motets forming the *Apollinis* constellation. The fifth textless part in **Stras** (*Pantheon*) does indeed 'sound around' the triplum in the same range, and is called *quadruplum*; as in the **Stras** version, no contratenor is mentioned here. I would go so far as to say that this description, both of the middle-voice tenor in a three-part motet, and of five-part composition, can apply only to *Apollinis* and its satellite added parts. Those added parts, however, invite datings close to 1400. If that becomes a *terminus post quem* for the treatise, it becomes even less likely that the Egidius de Morino named in *Apollinis* and *Musicalis* perhaps seventy years earlier can be its author. The treatise should revert to anonymous status, as proposed in Chapter 1. For possible identities for the Egidius named in the motets, see Chapter 17.

Appendix
Commentaries to Web Transcriptions for the Pieces with Multiple Sources

In the editions on the web for the chapters of Part IV, poetic lines are divided by | and each starts with a capital letter to signal lineation; u is changed to v when a consonant. An accidental present in any source is on the staff, above if editorial, and applies to adjacent notes of the same pitch.

322 THE MUSICIAN MOTETS

In the commentaries, notes relate to the numbering of the upper parts: usually (and here) in breves.

Variants to *Apollinis* (⊙ Ex. 16.1)

Triplum: 7–8 **Ivrea** all apparently originally minims, as in all other sources, reading ♦ ♦♦ ♦ ♦♦ requiring alt minims in both bars. **Ivrea's** correction to ♦ ♦ ♦ is used here; 3.4–5 **Barc971** *ddc* ♦♦♦; 9.2 **Leiden2515** *a*; 10.2 **Pad658** *f*; 19 **Stras** breve; 22.4 **Ivrea** *f*; preferred *g* in **Barc971**, **Stras**; **Pad658** *aga fg* ♦♦♦ ♦♦; 24.1 and 3 **Ivrea** M stems erased; 24.2 **Ivrea** *e*; *d* in **Barc971**, **Pad658**, **Stras** preferred; 26 **Stras** om.; 27.3 **Stras** *a*; 29 **Barc971** S rest, wrongly; 31 **Pad658** *bagf*; 33 **Barc971** *f e g* ♦ ♦♦, stems erased on the two S; 36.4 **Leiden2515**, **Pad658** *f*; 37 **Stras** *gfef* ♦♦ ♦♦; **Pad658** *g gef* ♦ ♦♦♦; 50.3 **Barc971** *g*; 50.4–5 **Ivrea** ♦ ♦ stem on 4 erased; 51.1–3 **Leiden2515** *efg* ♦♦♦; 50–51 **Barc971** *agg e dee efe* ♦♦♦ ♦ ♦♦♦ ♦♦♦; 54.2 **Ivrea** *f*; **Barc971**, **Leiden2515**, **Stras**, **Pad658** *g*, preferred; 58 **Barc971** ▪ ▪; 62.3–4 **Ivrea** *ag*; **Barc971**, **Leiden2515** *g e*; **Pad658**, **Stras** *gf*, preferred; 72 **Barc971** *g f* ▪ ♦; **Pad658** *ge* ▪ ♦; 74 **Pad658** *eee* ♦ ♦♦; 75 **Barc971** *eeed* ♦♦ ♦♦♦; **Leiden2515** *eee eee* all M; **Stras** *eeee* ♦♦ ♦♦; 79 **Barc971**, **Leiden2515** *agaa* ♦♦ ♦♦; **Ivrea**, **Pad658**, **Stras** *a a a a* ♦♦ ♦♦ preferred; 84 **Leiden2515** *efgef* ♦♦ ♦♦♦; 85 M rest in most legible sources, here above the staff, main reading ♦♦ follows **Brno** and **Vienna5094**; 88–89 **Ivrea** *b b baa*|*g gff* ♦♦ ♦♦♦ | ♦ ♦♦♦; **Barc971** *b b b* | *a g g gf* ♦ ♦♦ | ♦♦ ♦ ♦♦♦; **Pad658** *bbb*| *ag gf* ♦♦ | ♦♦ ♦♦; **Stras** *bbba*|*aggf* ♦♦ ♦♦ ♦♦ ♦♦; **Leiden2515** *b ba*| *ag gf* ♦ ♦♦ | ♦♦ ♦♦ preferred; 99.2 **Leiden2515** *g*; 99 **Pad658** *ed efe* ♦♦ ♦♦♦; 105 **Stras** ♦ ♦ ♦♦; 106–108 **Ivrea** L stem on ligature erased, enabling alt B; L stem in **Leiden2515** and **Pad658**; 111.2 **Pad658** ♦♦; 117–118 **Ivrea** *g a a* |*g gf* ♦ ♦♦ ♦ ♦♦ alt; **Leiden2515** 117–118 *gg*|*agfg*; **Barc971** *ga agfg*; **Stras** *g aa*| *ggfg* ♦ ♦♦ ♦ ♦♦♦; **Pad658** *g a* | *aggf* preferred; all except **Ivrea** avoid alt M; 120 **Stras** *fedc*; 122 **Stras** *e*| *f g aba*|*fe e* ♦ | ♦♦ ♦♦♦ | ♦♦ ♦; 123–124 **Ivrea** *e f g gf* | *fe e* ♦♦ ♦♦♦ | ♦♦ ♦; **Leiden2515** *efgf* | *fee* ♦♦ ♦♦ | ♦♦ ♦; **Leipzig223** 124 *fee*; **Barc971** 123–124 *e f gfg* | *ae e* ♦♦ ♦♦♦ | ♦♦ ♦ preferred; 127 **Stras**, **Leiden2515** *f f f f* ♦♦ ♦♦; **Barc971** *f f f e* ♦♦ ♦♦; **Pad658** *fgef* ♦♦ ♦♦; 133 **Ivrea** *eee*; 134.4 **Stras** *f*; **Pad658** lost from 134; 136–137 **Stras** *af g a* ♦♦ ♦ ▪ (not L); 139 *bb* **Ivrea**, **Stras**; 141.4 **Leiden2515** *d*. In **Leiden2515** some breves have downstem to the left: 52, 60, 90, 137.

Motetus: 1–6 **Ivrea**, **Barc971**, **Leipzig223** the first two longs are dotted; 4 om. (i.e. the second L) **Stras**; 22 **Stras** ♭; **Ivrea** no ♭; 24 **Stras** *agfe* ♦♦ ♦♦; 32 **Stras** L; **Ivrea** alt B, **Barc971** imp L precedes 34 L, therefore assuming imp modus; 34 **Ivrea**, **Stras** ♯; **Barc971** no ♯; 34 cut off, 37 an extra S (♦♦ ♦ ♦♦); 43 ♭ **Barc971**, **Ivrea**, **Stras**; no ♭ **Tarragona2**, **Leipzig223**; 63.4 **Stras** *b*; 70 ♭ **Ivrea**, **Stras**, **Barc853**, **Tarragona2**; no ♭ **Barc971**; 72 cut off **Tarragona2**; 83 ♯ **Ivrea**, **Stras**, **Barc853**, **Tarragona2**; no ♯ **Barc971**; 88–92 one lig **Tarragona2**; 94 ♭ **Stras**, **Barc853**; no ♭ **Barc971**, **Tarragona2**; 105 **Stras** ▪; 111 *ddd* ♦ ♦♦ **Stras**, 111.1 cut off **Tarragona2**; 111.2 *c* **Barc971**; 112 ▪ no ♦ **Barc971**; 118 ♭ **Barc853**, no ♭ **Barc971**; 120 *agfe* ♦♦ ♦♦ **Tarragona2**; 125 **Ivrea** *c*♯, approaching *d* in 127, also necessitating *c*♯ in tenor 124, reading rejected; 127 **Ivrea** *d*, rejected; all other sources (**Barc971**, **Tarragona2**, **Barc853**, **Leipzig223**, **Vienna922**, **Vienna5094** and **Stras**) have *b*, **Vienna5094** with *bb*, **Barc971**, **Barc853** with sharps before *b* and for 131 *c*; **Stras** ♮ before *b*, on *c*, could be meant for 127 or 131; **Ivrea** (alone) has a ♭ on *b* before the *c* in 131; 134 **Tarragona2** *a* in error; 136 ♭ **Barc971**, **Stras**, **Tarragona2**, no ♭ **Ivrea**; 137–138 ♦ ♦ not ■ ■ end torn out from 142 **Tarragona2**. **Leipzig223** has no accidentals.

Tenor: 2 ♯ on *b* in **Barc971**, **Barc853** and **Stras**; 20–21 are a long in **Barc971**; for rests see above.

Variants to *Apollinis/Pantheon* (▶ Ex. 16.3)

Readings are taken from **Stras** unless stated. The palimpsest **SL2211** is only partly legible; visible variants are recorded here.

14.1–2 **Stras** *g a* (*a b* **SL2211** used here); 11–15 **SL2211** *a* |*b a* |*g f* |*a b g*| *a g gf* ♦ ⊤| ■ ♦| ■ ♦|♦ ♦ ♦|♦ ♦ ♦; 28–29 *e* |*a b* ♦ ⊤ | ■ ♦; 33.4–5 **Stras** ♦♦; rendered here as ♦♦ as the second ♦ cannot properly be altered before the ensuing breve; **SL2211** 34–35 *a c* ♦ ⊤ | ■; 36.2 **Stras** *b*; **SL2211** *d* used here; 54–55 *b c*|*d b c* ■ ♦| ♦ ♦ ♦; 60 both sources ♯; 70–71 *d* |*a b* ♦⊤| ■ ♦; 74.3–4 bracketed in **Stras** but needed; 75.5 ♦; if the bracketed notes are omitted, the rhythm of 74–76 would be ♦♦ ♦♦ | ♦ ♦ ♦| ■ ♦; 74.4 **SL2211** *b*; 75.5 S; 77–79 *a* |*ag*| *fed* |*ag* ■ |⊤♦ ♦|♦ ♦ ♦|⊤♦ ♦; this passage in **SL2211** appears to be a breve longer than **Stras**, and may be compensated by the breve in 88 (instead of **Stras**'s ■), but this does not fit, and both sources seem to be corrupt; the passage between 76 and 90 is problematic in both added parts. Adjustments have been made to allow (mostly) consonance on the first perfect long of the combined motetus and tenor parts, though not with each other; 91–93 *gabc*|*a*| *c* ♦ ♦♦ ♦| ♦⊤|■; 104 **SL2211** breve; 109 2–3 one S; 124 ♦ ♦♦ *a ab*; 134 *a d* ♦♦ ligature.

Quadruplum: The present transcription of the quadruplum differs from Harrison's in many places, including at 38–39, 48, 57, 61, 68. Longs are imperfect; thus it does not respect the perfect modus of the tenor, though the barring in this transcription coincides. 4.4–5 ♦♦ resulting in an iambic pair with ♦ improperly preceding the following ♦; I have preferred to retain the imitation and assume an error for ♦♦ rather than a *similis ante similem* impropriety; 8 ♯ precedes *g*; 18 *c* ■; 19 ⊥ drawn long; 29.5 *f* and *d* both present vertically; 74 ■ dotted; 78.4 M; 80.2–3 absent; 82 ■; as in the upper part, the passage between 76 and 90 is problematic; 113 *g*; 123 redundant *f* precedes ■ bracketed in **Stras**; 137 ■ stem crossed, but it must be a ■.

17

Musicalis sciencia/*Sciencie laudabili* and the Musicians Named in *Apollinis* and *Musicalis*

Musicalis sciencia/*Sciencie laudabili*

The musicians named in *Musicalis* overlap with those of *Apollinis*, from which *Musicalis* also borrows formal and musical material, cementing their relationship. Unlike *Apollinis*, with its many sources, *Musicalis*, the second motet of the group, is known only from a single source, **Pic**: see Figure 17.1.[1] Fortunately, and fortuitously, f. 67 was cut from the rotulus in such a way as to preserve the complete music and text on the verso. For the edition see ⊙ Example 17.1.

Texts and translation by David Howlett. Named musicians are in boldface and *talea* ends are shown by |:

Triplum		Rhymes	Words	Syllables
Musicalis sciencia		a	2	8
qua regitur melodia		a	3	8
rethoribus uniuersis		b	2	8
arte suaque practicis,		b	3	8
specialiter dilectis,|	5	c	2	8
subscriptis suis subiectis —		c	3	8
de Douacho dicto Thoma		d	4	8
cuius fama fuit Roma,		d	4	8
Johanni de Muris quoque,		e	4	8
de Uiteri Phillippoque;|	10	e	3	8
Normanno Dyonisio,		f	2	8
de Burces et Egidio;		f	4	8
Gaudefrido de Baralis,		g	3	8
Ualquero de Ualencienis,		g	3	8
de Palacio Roberto|	15	h	3	8
atque **Louchart Ingelberto;**		h	3	8
dicto de **Soissons Garino,**		i	4	8
Egidio de Morino,		i	3	8
Reginaldo de Tyremont,		j	3	8
G. d'Orbendas et **Jo. du Pont;**|	20	j	7	8

[1] It can also be viewed (in black and white) on Gallica at https://gallica.bnf.fr/ark:/12148/btv1b10033904t/f212.item. MS variants: tr 167 *d*?; mo 28 *e* for *d*.

The Motet in the Late Middle Ages. Margaret Bent, Oxford University Press. © Oxford University Press 2023.
DOI: 10.1093/so/9780190063771.003.0018

THE MUSICIAN MOTETS

Guisardo de Cameraco,		k	3	8
et de **Bailleul Reginaldo**,		k	4	8
atque de **Machau Guillelmo**;		k	4	8
Petro Blauot et **Matheo**		k	4	8
de Luceu, d'Arras **Jacobo** —	25	k	5	8
salutem et obseruare		l	3	8
sua precepta mandare		l	3	8
uestrum cuilibet cupio,		f	3	8
ne sit erroris motio		f	4	8
in dominam rethoricam,	30	m	3	8
neque contra grammaticam;		m	3	8
lingua secans incomplexa		n	3	8
sit in silentio nexa;		n	4	8
cuncta uicia cauete;		o	3	8
in melodia ualete.	35	o	3	8
		15	117	280

Motetus				
Sciencie laudabili,		a	2	8
musice uenerabili,		a	2	8
rethorica sciencia		b	2	8
cum omni reuerencia		b	3	8
salutem, O dulcissima	5	c	3	8
subiectisque gratissima,		c	2	8
tali conquerens nuncio		d	3	8
quod maxima corrupcio		d	3	8
fit a multis canentibus		e	4	8
in nostris dictaminibus	10	e	3	8
nam diuidunt simplicia,		f	3	8
faciendo suspiria.		f	2	8
Quare pietate rogito		g	3	8 pie-ta-te
remedium his audito.		g	3	8
		7	38	112

Source: **Pic**, f. 67ᵛ

Triplum: Musical science, by which melody is ruled, to all rhetors practising in her art and to her specially beloved subjects written below—Thomas called de Douai, whose fame was in Rome, Jehan des Murs also and Philippe de Vitry, Denis le Normand and Gilles de Bruges, Godefroy de Baralle, Volquier de Valenciennes, Robert du Palais and Ingelbert Louchart, Guarin called de Soissons, Gilles de la Thérouanne, Réginald de Tiramont, G. d'Orbendas and Jehan du Pont, Guisard de Cambrai and Réginald de Bailleul, and Guillaume de Machaut, Pierre Blavot and Mathieu de Luxeuil, Jacques d'Arras—greeting, and I desire to command each of you to observe his precepts, lest

MUSICALIS/SCIENCIE AND NAMED MUSICIANS 327

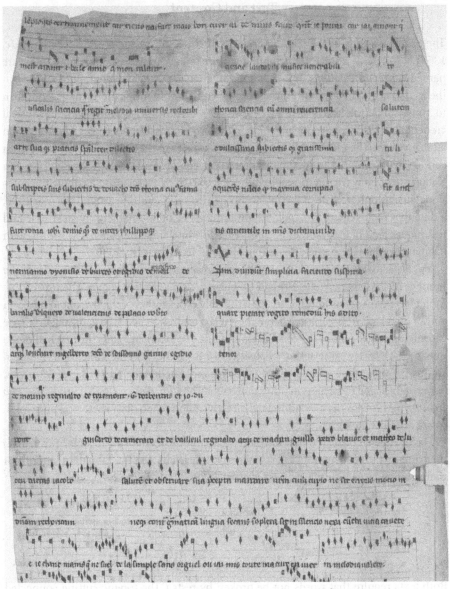

Fig. 17.1 *Musicalis sciencia* in Paris, Bibliothèque nationale de France, Collection de Picardie 67, f. 67ᵛ. © BnF

there be movement of error against Lady Rhetoric or against Grammar. The tongue cutting connected things should be bound in silence. Avoid all vices. Flourish in melody.

Motetus: To the praiseworthy science, venerable Music, Rhetorical science with all reverence (sends) greeting, O most sweet, and most pleasing to your subjects, lamenting such a message, that the greatest corruption is made by many singers in our poems, for they divide single elements, making breathings; wherefore in piety I ask, listen to the remedy for these things.

Text and Content

The first two words of the triplum are also the first two words of the later *Musica* (*c.* 1355) of Johannes Boen.[2] The triplum text lists twenty musicians, of whom nine were named earlier in *Apollinis* out of its total of twelve. Summary biographical notes on the musicians named in both motets are given below. Identifications range from firm to conjectural (the latter with little more than identity of surname without musical credentials). The large overlap of names in the two motets probably dates *Musicalis* soon after *Apollinis*. The identifiable musicians had careers in the first half of the fourteenth century, with most of the documents dated between 1316 and 1352. Heinrich Eger von Kalkar's testimony (of questionable authority; see Ch. 15) appears to attribute the notational inventions of some of the musicians named in *Apollinis* to around the year 1330, a date that seems likely for *Apollinis*, on grounds of notational and musical style and techniques, and of biographies of candidates for the named musicians; *Musicalis*, with its many overlapping names, then probably dates from the early 1330s.

Twenty is twice ten (*bis decem*), perhaps chosen to echo *Apollinis*'s 'three times the number of Pythagoras' (3 × 10) and its *bis sex* (twelve zodiac signs). The text of this motet has no direct authorial signature; the only other motet of the five not to name an author directly is *Musicorum*, where at best it is obscurely veiled. The name of Egidius de Morino, however, falls in the central triplum line (18 of 35) and ends the first half of the music (B84); this was the authorial position for B. de Cluny in the motetus of *Apollinis*, so this Egidius, whoever he was, could be a candidate for the composer of *Musicalis*. Some of the listed musicians in other motets may be spread over a long period, as in *Sub Arturo*; in *Musicalis* they are addressed directly and urged to obey rhetorical principles, so are presumed to be living.[3]

David Howlett observed that the motet is cast in the form of an epistolary exchange, the triplum a letter from musical science to rhetoricians and the motetus a letter from rhetorical science to music:

Musicalis sciencia   *Rethorica sciencia*

rethoribus dilectis   *musice uenerabili*

salutem   *salutem*

Both texts require that words not be broken by rests ('The tongue cutting connected things should be bound in silence', and 'the greatest corruption is made by many singers in our poems, for they divide single elements, making breathings'). The text–music relationship is so managed that not only are words not broken by rests (in accordance with the precepts of the text), but that rests only occur between lines of text.[4] The challenge

---

[2] *Johannes Boens Musica*, 32.

[3] Noted by Gómez, 'Une Version à cinq voix du motet *Apollinis*'. She observes that as Jean de Muris died *c.* 1350, *Musicalis* could be earlier than *Apollinis*. That seems to assume a later date for both motets than is here proposed.

[4] See Ch. 9 for discussion of the compositional choice whether or not to break words with rests. Machaut's Motet 18 and **OH**'s *Carbunculus* are there cited as examples. See also Chs. 8, 13, 25. This discipline is more recently referenced in Zayaruznaya, 'Hockets'.

MUSICALIS/SCIENCIE AND NAMED MUSICIANS   329

of not breaking words is avoided altogether in the textless hockets that occupy the last quarter (six breves) of each *talea* in both upper parts. The text distribution and underlay are identical in each *talea*, and apart from the opening motetus ligature of each *talea*, the setting is completely syllabic. The text is evenly distributed, reflected above by gaps in the text: of the thirty-five triplum lines, five are assigned to each of the seven *taleae*; of the fourteen motetus lines, two occupy each *talea*. The texts are not stanzaic; the motetus is rhymed in couplets throughout; the triplum is rhymed in couplets at lines 1–20 and 26–35. Only one rhyme (*-io*) is repeated, apart from lines 21–25, which are all *-o*. Machaut is named in the middle of those five lines. The total number of lines of triplum and motetus, 35 + 14, is 49, 7^2. This motet's insistence on sevens goes one beyond the sixes (*bis sex*) of *Apollinis*, and possibly acknowledges the seven liberal arts, of which music and rhetoric are invoked in the first lines.

In four places, while musicians are being named in the triplum, a single sound is being held over from preceding bars in the motetus, over a rest in the tenor. This happens first at B10, 'de Uiteri Phillippoque', second after four more lines at 15, 'de Palacio Roberto', third after four more lines at 20, 'G. d'Orbendas et Jo. du Pont', fourth after four more lines at 25, 'Matheo de Luceu, d'Arras Jacobo', allowing those six names to be sung—or heard—without competition from other sounds.

Music: Tenor

The tenor of *Musicalis* consists of a single *color* disposed in seven *taleae* of 8 longs in perfect modus, imperfect tempus, 6 breves (coloured) in imperfect modus, a total of 24 breves. The perfect modus and *talea* length are the same as in *Apollinis*, on which it is obviously modelled. Six *taleae* come to 144 breves, then there is an extra one, bringing the total length to 168 breves, another instance of sevens. Just as some of the motets outdo their predecessors in the number of musicians celebrated, so do they sometimes exceed the number of *taleae*, or the *talea* length, or some other measurable unit, by a unit comparable to that of a preceding piece. *Apollinis* boasts *bis sex*, then in *Musicalis* there are seven *taleae*, and in *Musicorum* seven musicians. *Sub Arturo* has fourteen musicians—twice (*bis*) the seven of *Musicorum*, nodding also at the *bis sex* of *Apollinis* and, as we shall see, it also goes one better in overall length. The single-*color* tenor of *Musicalis* is unlabelled but was identified as the full neuma (but not the verse) of the Alleluia *Dies sanctificatus* for the third Mass for Christmas, where it is preceded (unstated context) by *Viderunt omnes fines terre*, a resonance for *In omnem terram*.[5] *Musicorum*'s tenor is from an Easter Alleluia verse. 'Nam dividunt' begins the sixth *talea*: one of a number of instances noted in this book where a word of division coincides with a musical structural join, as we shall also see in *Musicorum*.

---

[5] Anderson, 'Responsory Chants', 122, identifies the tenor as 'Alleluia: the full neuma and its jubilus, but not the verse: *Dies sanctificatus* (*LU*, 409, MMMA, VII, 118)'. Note also the motet *Omnis terre*. Meanwhile Zayaruznaya, 'Hockets', at 498 calls the 'heretofore unidentified' tenor 'a mode 2 Alleluia of the type *Dies sanctificatus*. Due to the near-identity of the multiple chants in this family, we can never know which Alleluia it was. But perhaps the best semantic match is the *Alleluia Hic est discipulus* . . . It may well be that the tenor is pointing fingers as well, whether at a specific composer or at each of Music's disciples in turn: *hic est ille!*'

330   THE MUSICIAN MOTETS

Music: Upper Parts

Musicalis opens with the rhythm of *Apollinis* B30–B32, line 6, where the words were *musicorum collegio*: ♦ ♦♦ |♦♦ ♦♦ |∎. The same rhythm also occurs in *Apollinis* at B98–B100 for *fungens gaudet poetria* and at B102–B104, on the name of Machaut. In *Musicalis*, this rhythm is repeated obsessively three times in each triplum *talea*: 7 × 3 = 21, perhaps standing for twenty musicians plus the anonymous author. This is followed by ♦ ♦| ∎ |♦♦ ♦♦|∎ |♦♦♦ ♦♦|♦♦ ♦, rhythms which are conspicuous in *Apollinis*. The motet *Musicorum collegio* strikingly takes as its opening not only this same rhythm, over fully ten breves, but also the same words from *Apollinis* B30–B32, suggesting that its composer may have known not only *Apollinis* but also *Musicalis*. Figure 17.2 compares the openings of *Musicalis sciença* and *Musicorum collegio*.

Musicalis is musically the mōst straightforward and least ingenious of the musician motets. Richard Hoppin and Suzanne Clercx ('Notes biographiques') treated it as primary, perhaps because of its more simplistic style, or because it names more musicians. If *Apollinis* ranked low with respect to upper-voice isorhythm, *Musicalis* ranks high. But because of the close links between them, and their shared names, they must be fairly close in date to each other. Gómez ('Une Version à cinq voix du motet *Apollinis*') also thought *Musicalis* came first, because of the presumed respective dates of the first transmission of each motet, but these are not necessarily informative about composition dates. The upper parts observe strict and mechanical isorhythm corresponding to the tenor periods, each *talea* ending with six breves of wordless hocket with minim rests, a more advanced notational feature than *Apollinis*. The final cadential progression is unusual and surprising, especially the third in the final chord.

Pic contains the only instances known to me of a scribe's attempt to align isorhythmic repetitions (Fig. 17.1).[6] The alignment here is not perfect, but when writing the triplum in a single (left-hand) column, the ends of each of the first three *taleae* fall at the ends of alternate staves. That this was deliberate is shown by compression or extra space to preserve this distinction. The text was written before the music, in this case with a regular correlation between text-line and upper-voice *talea*. The syllable-note relationship is precisely indicated; the short column width gives ample opportunity to test this at line ends. At the end of the first staff of the motetus, two notes have been erased (B30.1–2) and transferred to the new line, to place them over the correct syllables. (As usual, the text was written first, but this is confirmed by these changes.) A text-copying error required a few notes to be erased and relocated: when writing 'dyonisio de burces et egidio de mori-. . . de', the scribe was evidently looking ahead (eye-skip) to 'egidius de morino' in triplum line 18, but added *gaufrido* over 'de mori-'

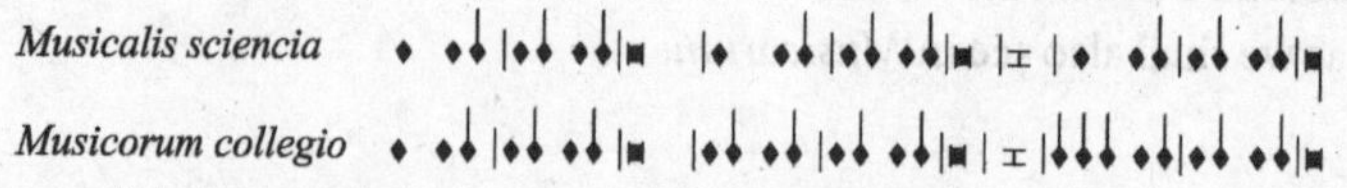

Musicalis sciencia   ♦ ♦♦ |♦♦ ♦♦|∎ |♦ ♦♦ |♦♦ ♦♦|∎ |⊡ | ♦ ♦♦|♦♦ ♦♦|∎

Musicorum collegio   ♦ ♦♦ |♦♦ ♦♦ |∎ |♦♦ ♦♦ |♦♦ ♦♦|∎ | ⊡ |♦♦♦ ♦♦|♦♦ ♦♦|∎

Fig. 17.2 Opening rhythms of *Musicalis sciencia* and *Musicorum*

---

[6] **Dorset**, *Ascendenti/Viri*, aligns section beginnings of a voice-exchange motet. See Bent, Hartt and Lefferts, *The Dorset Rotulus*.

MUSICALIS/SCIENCIE AND NAMED MUSICIANS 331

and erased the *d c* (B57.3–4), replacing those notes on the next line in order to accommodate *Baralis*.[7]

Each *talea* ends with six untexted breves with hocket. The fourth *talea* ends on the first staff of full-width copying, and is followed by a gap before the fifth *talea*. The ends of *taleae* 5 and 6 are more or less aligned with that of *talea* 4, and the final notes of *talea* 7 had to be tucked in at the end of a staff on which the next composition begins. The motetus is entirely contained in the right-hand column. The visually striking four-note ligature that begins each *talea* occurs at the beginning of staff 1, then at the end of staves 1, 2, 3, 4 for the first five *taleae*, and at the beginnings of staves 6 and 7 for the last two *taleae*. There was space for the scribe to have continued to align this ligature with the ends of the previous staves, but it may be that by then he recognised that the beginning of the *talea* should start the staff. The short tenor *taleae* are not lined up. They contain two strange double-stemmed symbols for the first two breves following the initial maxima.

There is a similar lining up for *Amer amours/Durement/Dolor meus* on **Pic**, f. 67ʳ. This is especially striking in the tenor, whose two identical *taleae* are fully written out; space is left at the end of the line in order to start each one on a new line. The rhythmic repetitions in the upper parts are only partial. Those in the triplum at the beginnings of most *taleae* are more or less aligned by alternate lines when the copy is still in two columns, but when it goes to the full page width, the last three *taleae* are more or less aligned by line. Interestingly, though, the line beginnings do not coincide with the *talea* beginnings. The motetus has less rhythmic repetition, but the three surviving line beginnings coincide approximately with the tenor *taleae*.

Pic, f. 67ʳ contains the *Fauvel* motet *Garrit gallus/In nova fert*, which has no upper-voice repetition, so there is nothing to be lined up (Ch. 4). *Musicalis* on f. 67ᵛ is flanked by two *chaces*, where such repetition likewise does not apply. The tenors of *Garrit gallus* and *Musicalis* both have tenor sections in coloration to denote imperfect modus; as is often the case in the earlier part of the century, tempus and prolation are not affected. (Later coloration for imperfection tends to fix notes at their minimum imperfect value at all levels of the notational hierarchy.) Both motets are given in **Pic** with void coloration (possibly the earliest known use), even though the scribe had red ink available for the staff lines. The copy of *Garrit gallus* in *Fauvel* famously displays the first recorded mensural use of red notation. In each of its six *taleae* (two *colores* each of three *taleae*), four longs of perfect modus (plus a final rest) notated in black flank four longs of imperfect modus plus a central rest, notated in red.[8] In each of the seven *taleae* of *Musicalis*, four longs of perfect modus in black precede six longs of imperfect modus notated in void (probably likewise originally red, and so shown in the present transcription in ⏵ Ex. 17.1).[9] As in *Garrit gallus*, the coloration passage also includes an imperfect long

---

[7] Motetus 124–25: the ligature originally ended with *b*, erased; *c* is attached to the erased note and clearly intended to belong to the ligature. 64, 130, 160 ▪, not dotted, probably confirming perfect modus throughout. Other undotted longs at the end of motetus *taleae* are imperfected from in front.

[8] See Ch. 4 and Fig. 4.2 for the notation of each *talea* as a nominal palindrome, and for the notational anomaly whereby a breve has to be altered before a dot, and before another (albeit coloured) breve. Neither condition sufficed to cause alteration later in the century.

[9] This is also suggested in Kügle, 'The Notation', 236, where he also cites examples from **Ivrea** of the fairly widespread practice of outlining, in void, notes intended to be filled in red. In many manuscripts, intended rubrication was not completed, and void notation may have originated in this way.

332 THE MUSICIAN MOTETS

rest. The **Pic** copy of *Garrit gallus* provides the unstemmed semibreves of *Fauvel* with stems in accordance with the default values with which they would originally have been evaluated. *Musicalis* uses a very limited rhythmic vocabulary, with the *musicorum collegio* rhythm from *Apollinis* predominating. It follows the default values except for the rhythm ♦♦ ♦ (instead of ♦ ♦♦) at B18 and corresponding places, and in the following respects. At B15 and all corresponding places in each *talea* (breves 39, 63, 87, 111, 135, 159) it has the rhythm ♦ ♦♦ ◣, where the second ♦ has to be improperly but inevitably altered before the long; improperly, because the minim does not precede a note of the next value up, a semibreve.[10] I suspect that the original may have been ♦♦, considering the first minim in each case as an error for ♦, restoring the trochaic norm; but this rhythm is repeated in each *talea* in its unique source, possibly reflecting an erroneous repeating template for the isorhythm in the process of composition. The isolated iambic rhythm is retained here. *Musicalis* also includes 'complementary' hockets with paired and single minim rests in the last six textless breves of each of its seven rhythmically identical *taleae*, and therefore belongs to a later notational stage than *Fauvel* and slightly later than *Apollinis*. Early in the century, rests shorter than a breve are often not distinguished, and short strokes of various kinds are used for major and minor semibreve rests and minim rests. These gradually gave way to more explicit and systematised rests, paired minim rests in France, the hanging rest being used exclusively for the perfect semibreve. Especially in England, a distinction is often found between major semibreve rests intersecting the staff line, and minor semibreve rests (worth two minims) hanging from the line without intersecting it.[11] *Musicalis* notates major but not minor semibreve rests, and uses single and paired minim rests for the interlocking hockets, as became normal. The adjacent *chace Se je chant* likewise has major semibreve rests intersecting the staff line and paired minim rests.[12] Karl Kügle has convincingly attributed this *chace* to Denis le Grant: Gace de la Buigne refers unmistakably to a *chace* by him about hunting with falcons, as this does.[13] It occurs anonymously in **Ivrea** and **Pic**, and is listed under motets as no. 9 in **Trém**. Further new testimony to Denis as a composer of mass movements is offered in Chapter 31. Denis is named in both *Apollinis* and *Musicalis*; in **Pic**, the unique source of *Musicalis* is immediately followed by *Se je chant*. The *chace* also links to earlier sources, starting with a refrain that matches the text (but not the music) of the motetus of **Mo**, fascicle 7, no. 277, *Coument se poet/Se je chante/Qui prendroit* (also like the *chace*, with interesting hockets). The opening and close of the *chace* also cite the text of the first two lines of a balette (without music) in **Ox308**.[14] The beginning is also cited (text and music, but without ornamentation) as the final refrain line of *Pour ce que mes chans fais*, Machaut's Ballade 12.

---

[10] Vitry's motet *Petre/Lugentium* in **Ivrea** often requires minim alteration before a breve or long.

[11] For example in **Durham20**, where *Musicorum collegio* has these rests; see Ch. 18 and also *Vos/Gratissima* in the same source: Ch. 8 n. 14, and Earp, 'Tradition and Innovation'.

[12] The *chace* is in **Ivrea**, no. 69, f. 52ᵛ and **Pic**, f. 67ᵛ, and listed in **Trém**. It is extensively discussed in Leach, *Sung Birds*, 221–29.

[13] Kügle, 'The Manuscript Ivrea', 277–78, Kügle, *The Manuscript Ivrea*, 159–60, *Manuscript Ivrea . . . facsimile*, 26. On the refrain *Se je chant* see also Plumley, 'Intertextuality', 363–64, Stone, 'Music Writing and Poetic Voice' and Leach, 'Singing More about Singing Less', 111–13, a view revised in Leach, *Guillaume de Machaut*, 118 n. 85, where she now thinks it likely 'that Machaut took this refrain from the anonymous balette rather than from its occurrence in Denis le Grant's *chace*', although 'Machaut probably also knew' the *chace*.

[14] That the second line of the balette is also quoted was reported by Maw, 'Machaut and the "Critical" Phase', 290.

This rotulus fragment has many other interesting aspects, not least its juxtaposition of two motets on the same tenor, *Dolor meus*, the final words of the Good Friday Responsory *Caligaverunt oculi mei*: *Amer amours/Durement/Dolor meus* and *Fortune, mere a dolour/Ma doulour ne cesses pas/Dolor meus*. Only the first line of the motetus survives for the latter. Points of notational interest are signalled above, as is a possible affinity of *Musicalis* with *Garrit gallus*: the tenors of both motets are in minor maximodus, perfect modus, with coloration indicating imperfect modus.

It follows from this notational description of *Apollinis* and *Musicalis* that both could have undergone some notational updating. Even without making allowance for this, the musical style and the surviving notated form suggest a date for *Musicalis* in the early 1330s, not much later than *Apollinis*. **Pic**, the unique source of *Musicalis*, has been dated around the middle of the century.[15] There were no strong reasons for earlier suggestions that dated **Pic** later in relation to **Br19606**, especially now that Brussels has received a surprisingly late dating of 1335, given its conservative notation and musical style.[16] **Pic**'s use of void notation does not in itself require a later dating; I see no reason to date anything in **Pic**, compositionally or notationally, later than the first half of the 1330s.[17]

Notes on the Musicians Listed in *Apollinis* and *Musicalis*

Andrew Wathey makes the interesting observation that, in terms of networks and identities, the two lists of names in *Apollinis* and *Musicalis* seem different.[18] The *Apollinis* names are more identifiable and, if there is a point of intersection, it is in the French court and those of near family (in Bohemia, Navarre, Flanders) with which it intermingled. Those in *Musicalis* look much more local—nine of the eleven unique to that text are toponymics, a compact northern group, with several in Artois/Hainault. Few of these are identifiable, but see below on Blavot, and further suggestions on Arras musicians from Brianne Dolce. Wathey wonders if some of these names could even be historic (late thirteenth-century trouvères or similar), but against that suggestion is the fact (noted above) that the musicians listed are addressed as if they are still living. He suggests that the list of names in *Musicalis* could be a deliberate local reframing of that in *Apollinis*, adding local worthies to a more famous set of names. He notes that the overlaps with *Apollinis*, in bold below, present two groups of three, the first (nos. 2–4) consisting of established masters, the second (nos. 10–12) perhaps as would-be

---

[15] Günther, 'Problems of Dating', 292, dated **Ivrea**, probably the earliest source of *Apollinis*, to after 1365. Gómez, 'Une Version à cinq voix du motet *Apollinis*', accepts this, and places *Musicalis* earlier, as **Pic** is generally dated to mid-century on grounds of script and notation (Hoppin, 'Some Remarks a propos of Pic'). This fails to take into account differences in dates of composition and transmission, but above all the now overwhelming evidence that *Apollinis* was the first composition of this group. Kügle dates the Ivrea repertory as mostly completed by 1359, the copying to the 1380s or 1390s. *Manuscript Ivrea . . . facsimile*.

[16] Kügle, 'Two Abbots and a Rotulus'.

[17] Hoppin, 'Some Remarks a propos of Pic', presciently commented: 'The notation of Br suggests that the scribe was deliberately and completely modernizing a notational system which he understood but which he felt to be inadequate and out of date. The scribe of Pic, on the other hand, may have been copying, perhaps for purposes already somewhat antiquarian, a notation which he knew how to modernize but whose basic principles he no longer completely understood' (p. 106). See Ch. 8 for the use of void notation *c*. 1330 in **Esc10** for the tenor of *Vos/Gratissima*.

[18] Email of 27.6.2020, and further correspondence at that time.

successors, with Egidius centrally placed, some of the others alternating. Wathey further notes that the court of Philippe III, King of Navarre, alongside that of John, King of Bohemia, has significance for three of those named in *Apollinis*.[19] Muris has been documented by Lawrence Gushee, and now by Karen Desmond.[20] Denis le Grant's 1329 canonry was granted with the support of Philippe III.[21] Wathey adds Guerrinet de Soissons [= Garinus de Soissons], a clerk of unspecified function in Philippe III's service 1337–43, appearing alongside Muris in the lists in BnF, MSS fr. 7855 and Clairambault 833. All of that points broadly to the 1330s. Machaut's subordinate position in both groups might support this rather than a later date.

Hoppin and Clercx provided the basis for most of what is known about the musicians named in some of the other motets; they start with *Musicalis sciencia/Sciencie laudabilis*, treating it as the oldest motet of the group, although it can no longer be taken as the progenitor.[22] Clercx and Hoppin's work, though admirable for the period in which it was done, now looks thin and includes several near-random identifications, for example, on the basis of a shared forename. But they reasonably assert (pp. 65–66) that the named musicians, at least in *Musicalis*, appear to be still living, and that most of them are composers, as befits the injunctions to 'music' for compositional practice in the triplum.[23] Nine of the twelve names in *Apollinis* recur in *Musicalis*. Both motets appear to date from well before the middle of the century, as the first and second compositions of the group, not vice versa, as Hoppin and Clercx assumed. They extended the search to the musicians named in the later motet *Alma polis* (for these see Ch. 19). Muris disappears and is assumed to have died in the late 1340s, perhaps of the plague. Assuming that those addressed are still living, *Apollinis* and *Musicalis* would have to date from before the mid-1340s; notational reasons are given above for placing them closer to 1330. But personal identifications are in many cases uncertain (notably for Egidius) and piece datings must depend on the latest, not the average datings.[24] Many musicians strongly praised are names we have never heard of, a salutary caution against assuming that only the names known to us were famous to them.

These are the twelve musicians of *Apollinis*, with their corresponding positions in *Musicalis*:

1. Muris (*Musicalis* 2)
2. Vitry (*Musicalis* 3)[25]
3. Henricus Helene
4. Denis le Grant (= Normannus? *Musicalis* 4)
5. Regaudus de Tiramonte (= Reginaldus: *Musicalis* 12)

---

[19] Further comments attributed to Wathey are from email correspondence in late 2020.

[20] Gushee, 'New Sources', 26; Desmond, *Music and the moderni*, ch. 3.

[21] Gushee (ibid., 26): Philippe d'Evreux, king of Navarre, not Philippe VI, king of France.

[22] They divide the names of *Musicalis* into three groups, of which the first group is not also in *Apollinis*, and assumed to be from an older generation. The ten names shared between the two motets are treated as a central generation, and the remaining two, Henricus Helene and Arnold Martini, deemed younger. Hoppin and Clercx, 'Notes biographiques', at 68–69. See also Hoppin, 'Some Remarks a propos of Pic'.

[23] In *Musicorum* (Ch. 18) the musicians are still living, or at least known to the author.

[24] See the discussion of *Sub Arturo plebs* (Ch. 20), where the chronological spread prevents a similar assumption that the musicians are still living, and where the identity of J. Alanus is in question.

[25] See *Benoit XII, Lettres communes*, ed. Vidal, ii (1903), 482, no. 5119, for Vitry in 1337; Hoppin and Clercx, 'Notes biographiques'.

MUSICALIS/SCIENCIE AND NAMED MUSICIANS 335

6. Robertus de Palacio (*Musicalis* 8)[26]
7. Machaut (*Musicalis* 17)
8. Egidius de Morino (*Musicalis* 11)
9. Garinus de Soissons (*Musicalis* 10)
10. Arnaldus Martini
11. Petrus de Brugis
12. Gaufridus de Barilio (*Musicalis* 6)

Others in *Musicalis*:

1. Thomas de Douacho
5. Egidius de Burces
7. Valquerus de Valencienis
9. Ingelbertus Louchart
13. G. d'Orbendas
14. Jo. du Pont
15. Guisardus de Cameraco
16. Reginaldus de Bailleul
18. Petrus Blavot
19. Matheo de Luceu
20. Jacobus d'Arras

The musicians appear in the following order in *Musicalis*; those also in *Apollinis* are in boldface:

1. Thomas de Douacho
2. **Muris**
3. **Vitry**
4. **Denis le Grant**
5. Egidius de Burces
6. **Gaufridus de Barilio**
7. Valquerus de Valencienis
8. **Robertus de Palacio**
9. Ingelbertus Louchart
10. **Garinus de Soissons**
11. **Egidius de Morino**
12. **Regaudus de Tiramonte**
13. G. d'Orbendas
14. Jo. du Pont
15. Guisardus de Cameraco
16. Reginaldus de Bailleul
17. **Machaut**

[26] Roberto de Palatio and Machaut, adjacent here, are named on adjacent days in petitions to the pope by John of Bohemia. Benedict XII, *Lettres communes*, ed. Vidal 1903: no. 749, Robert, for Meaux on 16.4.1335, no. 751, Machaut, expectative for Reims on 17.4.1335. See n. 32 below.

336 THE MUSICIAN MOTETS

18. Petrus Blavot
19. Matheo de Luceu
20. Jacobus d'Arras

The musicians most famous to us are: Muris (*Apollinis* 1, *Musicalis* 2), Vitry (*Apollinis* 2, *Musicalis* 3) and Machaut (*Apollinis* 7, *Musicalis* 17): these three are fully documented elsewhere and need no detail here. Vitry was born in 1291, became bishop of Meaux in 1351 and died in 1361. Muris was born 1290–95 and died after 1344. Machaut's dates are *c*. 1300–77.

Six musicians besides those three are listed in both motets:

Denis le Grant, 'Dionisius Magnus' in *Apollinis* (4), and possibly the 'Normanno Dyonisio' of *Musicalis* (4). A chapel clerk in 1328 of Philippe III of Navarre (reigned 1328–43), he received an expectative benefice from the king in 1329.[27] At this time Vitry was in royal service to King Philippe VI of France, to whom Denis is named as first chaplain in 1349. He was rewarded with a bishopric, the see of Senlis, in 1350 (promoted 23 Dec. 1349), and was succeeded as chaplain by his colleague in the French royal chapel Gace de la Buigne, who praised him in 'Le Roman des Deduis'.[28] Kügle's attribution to Denis le Grant of the *chace Se je chant*, and a further attribution in **Trém**, have been mentioned above. Denis was an acquaintance of Vitry and borrowed astronomical book(s) from Johannes des Muris.[29] A collection of nativities in the library of Charles V started with Denis; this was probably a quite detailed astrological judgement and not a simple horoscope; it was followed by two 'nativities' of distinguished earlier men, Henry Bate of Malines and Baudouin Courtenay, the last emperor of Constantinople, another indication of Denis's status in such company.[30] Denis died in 1352. Given the Normandy connections of Gace and Muris, he may well be the Dionysius Normannus named in the triplum of *Musicalis*, and is so listed above, though Senlis (of which Denis le Grant became bishop) is not in Normandy. Gace followed Jean le Bon into his English captivity until 1359, and could provide a link from *Apollinis* and *Musicalis* to *Musicorum*, which seems to be associated with John's English sojourn.

Reginaldus de Tyremont, Tyro Monte (*Apollinis* 5, *Musicalis* 12) is documented in the service of Philip VI for a financial transaction in 1349, but is not described as a musician.[31]

---

[27] Wathey, 'Philippe de Vitry'.

[28] Hoppin and Clercx, 'Notes biographiques', 71–72.

[29] Gushee, 'New Sources'. Wathey, 'Philippe de Vitry', 227–28 records legal cooperation between Vitry and Denis le Grand in 1351.

[30] Boudet, 'Jean des Murs', at 127–28; Boudet, 'La Science', 144.

[31] Wathey, email of 22.12.2020, reports that Reginald de Tyremont turns up as master of the song school (*scole cantus*) at Bayeux, appointed by a papal letter of 20.4.1344, where he is described as a married clerk from the diocese of Lisieux. The petition behind the letter reveals the appointment was sponsored by John, Duke of Normandy, and that Reginaldus had earlier been provided to the song school at Meaux, for life. Bayeux is the second of two options set out in the petition: the first, which did not materialise, is the [song?] school, founded by the late Cardinal 'of Auxerre', possibly Pierre Mortuomari, d. 1335, at the Benedictine Nunnery of Montivilliers, Rouen diocese. The connection to John Duke of Normandy may strengthen the case for the Reginald de Tyro Monte paid by Philip VI in 1349 being the same person. This nicely pulls him earlier— and earlier than 1344, since he was already established at Meaux—and draws *Apollinis* more closely into the orbit of the French royal and dependent courts. And his juxtaposition in *Apollinis* with Denis le Grant, both Normans, may be telling.

Robertus de Palatio is named in both motets (*Apollinis* 6, *Musicalis* 8), next to Machaut in *Apollinis*. This Robert was accorded a canonicate at Meaux on 16 April 1335, the day before Machaut was granted his at Reims (see above and n. 26). Both men were clerks, familiars and secretaries to John of Bohemia (Robert also a notary) on dates between 1332 and 1335, one on 1 May 1334 signed by both on the same day and place. They clearly had a close personal, clerical and musical association.[32]

Egidius de Morino (*Apollinis* 8, *Musicalis* 11). There is no firm identification among the several fourteenth-century musicians called Egidius. The place name Morino or Murino refers to the diocese of Thérouanne in northern France. The likeliest candidate, in my view, for the Egidius de Morino of *Apollinis* and *Musicalis* is Egidius de Flagiaco, of the diocese of Thérouanne, a man of the generation of Vitry and Machaut, already a senior cleric, and attested in 1336 as a musician, 'skilled in the art of music and master of the boys of the king's chapel'.[33] This man could well be the Egidius named in these motets. He is generally credited with the authorship of the variously titled treatise *De modo componendi tenores motettorum*, usually thought to date from the mid-century, but see Chapters 1 and 16 for arguments that the treatise must be too late for a man named in motets of *c.* 1330. Egidius de Flagiaco would probably have been too senior to write a treatise at the end of the century. Hoppin and Clercx noted an Egidius Morini who was a bachelor in civil law and student at the University of Orléans who received a canonicate with expectation of a prebend at Le Mans in 1337 on the initiative of the same king in whose service Egidius de Flagiaco was.[34] Another man of the same name, from Amiens, received a canonicate at Nivelles in the Liège diocese in 1378.[35]

Garinus of Soissons (Hoppin and Clercx, 'Notes biographiques', 77–78) is named in both motets (*Apollinis* 9, *Musicalis* 10). He may be the subject of a supplication by Robert, Bishop of Thérouanne, the future Clement VII, addressed to Urban V in favour of his *socius* Garinus de Arceys, doctor of law at the university of Orleans.[36] He received several benefices and in 1370 became chaplain to the pope. He was no longer there in January 1371 when he became bishop of Chartres, and died in August 1376. He is nowhere named as a musician, and may not be the same as the Garinus named as the composer of **Chantilly**, no. 51.

---

[32] Hoppin and Clercx, 'Notes biographiques', 72, citing John XXII, *Lettres communes*, ed. Mollat. The 17.4.1332 letter is adjacent in Mollat to Machaut's presentation to Arras, of the same date and with the same executors. Both letters are discussed in Herzblick, *Exekutoren*, 403–4, and 404–10 for John of Luxembourg's clerks and their benefices. The most recent account of links between Robert and Machaut between 1332 and 1335 is Earp, 'Introduction', in Earp and Hartt (eds.), *Poetry, Art, and Music*, 39–40, and table 3. Both signed a document together on 1.5.1334 at Noyon.

[33] Benedict XII, *Lettres commmunes*, ed. Vidal, no. 2895, 16.3.1336: 'In eccl. S. Petri Arien, Morinen. di., **Aegidius de Flagiaco**, in arte musicae perito, mag. puerorum capellae regis, qui perpet. capellanias de Athies, et de Villaribus Carbonelli, ac S. Mariae de Soysiaco supra Sequanam, Noviomen, et Parisien di. dim. tenetur. In e. m. abb. monast. s. Joannis in Monte juxta Morinum, et decano s. Donationi Brugen., ac cantori s. Bartholomaei Bethunien., Tornacen et Atrebaten' (A 50, f. 185; V, 122 n. 166). Hoppin and Clercx, 'Notes biographiques', 85–86, also suggest further possible identifications up to around 1350. Clark, '*Concordare cum materia*', 5, also favours this candidate. See also now Cook, *Music Theory in Late Medieval Avignon*, 61–64.

[34] 'In eccl. Cenomanen., consid. Philippi regis Franciae, **Aegidio Morini**, bac. in j.civ., Aurelianis in dicto jure studenti. –In. e.m. ep.o Colimbrien., et abb. monast. s. Vincentii Cenomanen., ac Bertrando Chausardi, can.'

[35] Hoppin and Clercx, 'Notes biographiques', 85.

[36] Doubted in Kügle, 'Die Fragmente Oxford, All Souls 56'.

338 THE MUSICIAN MOTETS

Gaudefridus de Baralis (*Apollinis* 12, *Musicalis* 6) received a canonicate in expectation of a prebend in Cambrai cathedral in 1342.[37] He already had three benefices with prebend at Courtrai, Saint-Quentin and Saint-Pierre of Lille. Two years later he calls himself secretary of Louis, Count of Flanders, and messenger from the count to the pope in Avignon.[38] His will of 10 June 1368 is preserved among the documents from Saint-Pierre of Lille, and he seems to have died in early January 1369. An earlier Joffroi de Barale, author of two songs in the thirteenth-century Chansonnier du Roi, is dismissed on chronological grounds.

Just three musicians are named only in *Apollinis*:

Henricus Helene is named in third place in *Apollinis* but is not listed in *Musicalis*. He was a music theorist, the author of a *Summula* in **Venice24**. He could be the Henricus signed in the text as the composer and poet of the motet *Portio nature/Ida capillorum* in **Ivrea**, **Chantilly**, **Trém** and **Stras**, whose motetus ends: 'Hoc tibi cantamen et dictionale gregamen offert laudamen Henricus, ovans rogitamen mortis in examen, anime quod sis relevamen, post exalamen ut tecum regnitet. Amen.' In **Stras** the motetus was headed 'Magister Heinricus', with 'Egidius de Pusiex' entered just below it and to the side. There is nothing more than the shared first name and attested musical competence to support the identification with Henricus Helene. That man received a canonicate in expectation of a prebend in the diocese of Sens on 12 February 1335, and received the prebend from 1337. He and Denis le Grant both appear in the Sens accounts for 1340, but Denis appears to have been largely absent thereafter, though he remained a canon until he became a bishop, and was dead by 3 May 1352.[39] The man identified as Egidius de Pusiex by Hoppin and Clercx died in 1348, though his connection with the motet is unclear, since the motetus text seems to attribute both text and music to a Henricus. Although both Helene and Egidius were active at the earliest date that has been suggested for the motet, the 1342 elevation to the cardinalate of St Ida's descendant Guy of Boulogne, this seems much too early for the music, which must, however, have been composed by 1376 because it was included in the **Trém** index by that date. (See Ch. 31.)

Two weeks later than Helene's expectative document, on 26 February 1335, **Arnoldus Martini** (also named in *Apollinis*, 10) received an expectative, likewise from Benedict XII. Martini is there specified as a Benedictine from the church of Alet (Aude, near Limoux).

P. de Brugis (*Apollinis* 11) is identified with a Petrus 'nato Goedanen de Brugis', clerk and familiar of Robert d'Anjou, king of Sicily (d. 1343). He received several benefices in the dioceses of Tournai and Liège between 1324 and 1332. Robert was the dedicatee of Marchetto's *Pomerium* and was honoured by Vitry in the acrostic of *Rex quem*

---

[37] Information on him, again, from Hoppin and Clercx, 'Notes biographiques', 73–74.

[38] Andrew Wathey reports (email of 27.6.2020) that Gaudefridus de Barilio may already have been in the service of the Count of Flanders, as several letters of the same date as that of his canonry at Cambrai (21.11.1342) were for servants of Louis, Count of Flanders.

[39] The prebend is recorded in *Fasti Ecclesiae Gallicanae*, 11: Diocèse de Sens, 292. His death is not recorded there but in AAV, Collect. 288, f. 145. Thanks to Andrew Wathey for these references. On this motet see now Zazulia, 'A Motet Ahead of its Time?'. See also Ch. 19 on the double attribution.

metrorum. Karen Desmond suggests that 'P. Philomena' of Bruges may be the astronomer and mathematician Peter of Dacia, known as Peter the Nightingale, a prolific astronomer active in Paris *c.* 1300. Pedersen indicates that three works of a 'Peter of St Omer' may also be by Peter of Dacia, although the connections of Peter of Dacia to St-Omer are not yet known.[40] Strohm suggests that the speaker named as Petrus in the motetus of *Comes Flandrie/Rector creatorum/In cimbalis* might be the composer Petrus Vinderhout, who might in turn be the P. de Brugis of *Apollinis.*[41]

Eleven musicians are named only in *Musicalis*:

Thomas de Douai (*Musicalis* 1). Thomas de Douai is the first-named in *Musicalis.* Hoppin and Clercx, 'Notes biographiques', propose a possible identity with the Thomas de Diciaco documented in letters of John XXII between 1327 and 1329, when he receives a canonicate at Arras under the protection of Philip VI, of whom he is named a clerk the previous year. But Andrew Wathey points out (email of 27 June 2020) that Diciaco is Dicy/d'Issy, not Douai. An alternative candidate, canon of St-Amand at Douai, obtained a canonicate at St-Géry in Cambrai in 1325. Neither of these has musical credentials, but that is not to be expected. A third candidate from the accounts of John XXII, one Thomas 'Gallus', not linked to Douai, is cited as 'cantor domini nostri', and as 'Thoma de capella', between 1317 and 1334.

Egidius de Burces (Bruges) is separately named as a musician in *Musicalis* (5); although sometimes identified as the Egidius de Morino of both motets, there seems to be no reason to connect them. The most promising of the candidates offered by Hoppin and Clercx is Egidius Belwardi de Bruges who in 1324 obtained a canonicate in expectation of a prebend at Bruges at the request of King John of Bohemia, who was also a patron of Robertus de Palatio and Machaut. Candidates from later in the century will be considered in relation to *Alma polis*, all of whose named musicians are claimed as Augustinians. Men called Egidius known as composers include Magister Egidius Augustinus, the author of several rhythmically complex ballades, and Magister Frater Egidius, who collaborated with Guilielmus de Francia in the composition of five ballades in **Sq**. These may be the same man; see Chapter 19.

Engelbert Louchart (*Musicalis* 9). The Louscharts are a numerous and prominent Arras family, and many are called Engelbert (Englebert). The likeliest candidate is the Englebert Louchart who was a monk of the abbey of St-Vaast in Arras. He became *suppraepositus* (sub-prior?) in 1304, *magnus praepositus* (prior?) in 1316, and again *suppraepositus* in 1338. He is included in a list of names in the statutes of the Confraternity of Jongleurs and Bourgeois in 1338; Guesnon's edition of the statutes calls Engelbert a *maieur des bourgeois*, indicating that he was or had been an elected leader (*maieur*) of the bourgeois portion of the confraternity, but not himself a

---

[40] Desmond, *Music and the moderni*, 4. St-Omer is about 100 km west of Bruges. A Peter of Dacia was rector of the University of Paris in 1327, although Olaf Pedersen believes this was not the same man as the astronomer Peter of Dacia. If Pedersen is correct, it is still possible that B. de Cluny has confused or conflated the two Peters. Pedersen, 'Peter Philomena'.

[41] Strohm, *Music in Late Medieval Bruges*, 42, 104 and Cuthbert, 'The Nuremberg and Melk Fragments', 10 n. 8.

340 THE MUSICIAN MOTETS

jongleur. In 1340 he is listed in the confraternity's register, possibly upon his death, confirming his membership of that organisation.[42]

Jo. du Pont (*Musicalis* 14). In April 1330 and April 1333, Johannes 'nato Oldrati de Ponte', canon of Tournai, requested leave of absence to pursue his studies in law and letters. Later, he is documented as singer and chaplain of Annibaldus, cardinal-bishop of Tusculum. He received an expectative in the diocese of Arras, where he already held two chaplaincies. In 1339 he acquired a canonicate in expectation of a prebend at St-Omer (diocese of Thérouanne).[43] Given the links with Arras, Brianne Dolce notes a possibly likelier identification: a Jehan du Pont was a monk at the Arras abbey of St-Vaast, who became *receptor* and *suppraepositus* in 1326.[44]

Reginaldus de Bailleul (*Musicalis* 16). Reginaldus de Bailleul received a benefice in the diocese of Arras in 1334, although he already held two chaplaincies in the dioceses of Arras and Tournai.[45]

A **Pierre Blavot** (*Musicalis* 18) is a clerk (function unspecified, but dealing with gifts of robes) in the service of Eudes IV, Duke of Burgundy, in 1346–48.[46]

Jacobus d'Arras (*Musicalis* 20). Given the connections with Arras and music, and the motet dating *c.* 1330, Brianne Dolce speculates whether this might possibly refer to Jacobus Louchart, a member of this very numerous Arras family, and a canon and cantor at Arras Cathedral, hence a musical connection. Jacques was the son of Audefrois Louchart the trouvère, as well as a moneylender to both the Countess of Flanders and the city of Ghent. He is listed in the confraternity's register in 1310.[47]

No suggestions are forthcoming for Valquerus de Valencienis (*Musicalis* 7), G. d'Orbendas (*Musicalis* 13), Guisardus de Cameraco (*Musicalis* 15) or Matheo de Luceu (*Musicalis* 19).

At least eight and maybe eleven of the musicians named in these two motets are documented in papal letters of John XXII, Benedict XII and Clement VI between 1316 and 1352, which points to careers mainly in the second quarter of the fourteenth century, and is consistent with the naming of the young Machaut in both motets. There may also be connections with Reims, as reported above for Robertus de Palatio as well as for Machaut. Senlis, where Denis obtained his bishopric, is in the ecclesiastical province of Reims. The possibilities of contact between Machaut and some of these other musicians are high. Vitry's procurator at Avignon, Nicholas de Hermondivilla, was also a canon of Reims, as briefly was a Jean de Vitry who was a notary of John, Duke of Normandy, and who may be one of Vitry's brothers.[48] Jehan de Vitry is named as a sommelier of the royal chapel in the document which names

---

[42] Guesnon, *Statuts et règlements*. I am grateful to Brianne Dolce for confirmation of this summary, based in turn on her 'Making Music and Community'.

[43] Hoppin and Clercx, 'Notes biographiques', 73, and see Wathey, 'The Peace of 1360–1369'.

[44] Dolce, 'Making Music and Community', 293; Van Drival, *Nécrologe*, 36.

[45] Hoppin and Clercx, 'Notes biographiques', 73, citing *Lettres de Jean XXII*, iii, no. 3580.

[46] Information and references from Andrew Wathey (email of 27.6.2020): Arras, AD Pas-de-Calais, A 653, pièce 18–19; A 658, pièce 35; see also Courtel, 'La Chancellerie', at 50.

[47] For this information with documentation see Dolce, 'Making Music and Community', 237–38, 288, and Berger, *Littérature et société Arrageoises*, 379–83.

[48] Andrew Wathey, email of 27.3.2017, and see Wathey, 'Philippe de Vitry', 246.

Gace as first chaplain in succession to Denis. Although many of the above identities are far from certain, there are enough potential connections between some of them, especially at the court of the Valois King Philip VI, and with benefices in dioceses in northern France, especially Thérouanne, to suggest that some of them may have known each other as colleagues or at least acquaintances.

18

Musicorum collegio/In templo Dei/Avete

The text of *Musicorum* seems to place the French court somewhere other than its usual location, at the 'court of the French people'. The motet survives uniquely in an English manuscript (**Durham20**) which was in the possession of the monks of Durham by the end of the fourteenth century. As Frank Ll. Harrison suggested, this probably places the motet during the English captivity of the French king John II between 1357 and 1360. He accepted a date of *c.* 1350–60 for the manuscript, close to the presumed date of composition, a generation later than *Apollinis* and *Musicalis*. As we shall see, it relates to *Apollinis* not only by naming musicians and by direct quotation, but also by the ways in which it plays with significant numbers. For the edition see ⓟ Example 18.1.

Texts and translation by David Howlett. Named musicians are in boldface:

Triplum		Rhymes	Words	Syllables
Musicorum collegio		a	2	8
in curia degencium		b	3	8
Gallicorum zelo pio		a	3	8
Dei tantum zelancium		b	3	8
in sancto desiderio	5	a	3	8
Xpisti matris officium		b	3	8
quater in mense — preuio		a	4	8
Hugone, quem propicium		b	3	8
largum quoque cunctis scio,		a	4	8
Robertum, fidum socium	10	b	3	8
huic adiungens **de Hoÿo**,		a	4	8
Johannem et **Nichasium**,		b	3	8
.J., speciali socio		a	3	8
dicto Pallart, quem preuium		b	4	8
cordetenus inspicio,	15	a	2	8
.J. Anglico, largum, pium		b	4	8
circumscribere nescio,		a	2	8
Stephanoque — sit gaudium		b	3	8
hiis salus et deuocio		a	4	8
cum crescant ac obsequium	20	b	4	8
actoris, qui seruicio		b	3	8
se totum subdit omnium.		b	4	8
.O. quanta delectacio		a	3	8
horum simul canencium!		b	3	8
.O. mira modulacio	25	a	3	8
sonorum musicalium!		b	2	8

The Motet in the Late Middle Ages. Margaret Bent, Oxford University Press. © Oxford University Press 2023.
DOI: 10.1093/so/9780190063771.003.0019

.O. dulcis altercacio		a	3	8
acutorum et grauium		b	3	8
mediorumque uicio		a	2	8
discordie carencium!	30	b	2	8
Xpistus, pro cuius proprio		a	4	8
zelo canunt, salarium		b	3	8
det eis ut consorcio		a	4	8
iungantur celi ciuium.		b	3	8
		2	106	272

Motetus

In templo Dei posita		a	4	8
miro modo composita		a	3	8
uidi septem candelabra,		b	3	8
quorum nemo cum dolabra		b	4	8
nec quisque ferri genere	5	c	4	8
unum posset incidere,		c	3	8
cum silice horum quia		d	4	8
inpressit in materia		d	3	8
formam Celestis Opifex,		e	3	8
Summus Sculptor et Artifex,	10	e	4	8
ambulans horum medio		f	3	8
cum bis acuto gladio,		f	4	8
septem gerens in dextera		g	4	8
stellas, ut inter cetera		g	4	8
testatur Apocalipsis.	15	h	2	8
Sic ego spero de ipsis		h	5	8
que uidi quorum nomina		i	4	8
sunt scripta tripli pagina.		i	4	8
		9	65	144

Tenor: Auete

Triplum: To the company of musicians living in the court of the Frenchmen (or 'musicians in the court of Frenchmen spending time [where they ordinarily do not]'), being zealous with the devout zeal of God in holy desire for the very great office of Christ's mother four times in a month—with Hugh as leader, whom I know as favourable and generous to all, adding to him his faithful colleague Robert from Huy, John and Nichasius, to J. the particular colleague called Pallart, whom I look on from the heart as a leader, to J. Langlois, I don't know how to write about him, generous, devout, and to Stephen—may there be joy for these men, health and devotion as they grow, and the deference of the agent (i.e. the one who is making this go, the author), who subjects his entire self to the service of all. O how great is the delight of these men singing together! O wondrous modulation of musical sounds! O sweet altercation of high-pitched and low-pitched and middle (notes) lacking the vice of discord! May

MUSICORUM COLLEGIO/IN TEMPLO DEI   345

Christ, for whose own zeal they sing, give them reward, that they may be united to the community of heaven's citizens.

Motetus: I saw seven candlesticks placed in the temple of God, composed in wondrous fashion, of which no man with an axe nor anyone with a sort of iron tool will be able to cut one, because with a hard stone on material the Heavenly Craftsman, the Highest Sculptor and Artist, has impressed their form, walking in the midst of them with a twice-sharp sword, bearing in His right hand seven stars as the Apocalypse states, among other things. Thus do I hope concerning those things which I have seen, about which words are written on the page of the triplum.

Tenor: Hail!

Context and Date

The French *curia* referred to in the text includes at least one Englishman, J. Anglicus, and singers engaged for the weekly Lady Mass. Harrison plausibly suggested that the motet was 'written for the court devotions of Jean II' while he was a prisoner in England between 1357 and 1360.[1] John II, 'le bon', king of France, was captured at the Battle of Poitiers on 19 September 1356, brought to Plymouth on 5 May 1357 and on 24 May over London Bridge and through the City to Edward III's palace at Westminster.[2] He was detained in some style at the Savoy, west of the Temple in London, and held for a ransom to be paid before St Martin's Day, 11 November.[3] This was not paid, and he remained at the Savoy, though he was not confined there all the time.[4] King John's accounts, kept from Christmas 1358, while he was at Hertford and Somerton, 'par moy Denys de Collors son chapellain', show that he kept a chapel establishment, in which new work was performed: 'Le Roy, pour offerands faicte par li à la messe nouvelle que le Chapellain, maistre Guillaume Racine, chanta lors devant le Roy, x nobles, valent lxvi s. viii d'. Among several items for the *Chapelle*, there is a payment in December 'Pour asporter les orgues en Savoie, vi d.', and again later 'Climent, clerc de Chapelle, pour ii varlet qui apportèrent les orgues du Roy de Londres à Erthford, iiii s'. In addition to the chaplains already named,

---

[1] Harrison, *Musicorum collegio*, p. iv.

[2] Roland Delachenal, *Histoire de Charles V* (Paris, 1909–31), ii, ch. II, 47–88, 'Jean II en Angleterre' and works there cited. *Chronica Johannis de Reading*, 124–27, 197–206.

[3] *Chronica Johannis de Reading*, 206. Howlett reports an item dated 17.8.1357 recording 'protection, until Christmas, for ministers and servants of the king's adversary of France deputed to provide and bring to London hay, oats, butter, meat, fish, corn and other victuals for the expenses of the household of the said adversary'. Patent Rolls, TNA MS C.66/252 m. 7 (*Calendar of the Patent Rolls, Edward III:* x. 1354–1358, p. 597), and *Chronica Johannis de Reading*, 128, 208.

[4] *Chronica Johannis de Reading*, 129. His presence at *hastiludia solempnia in Smythfelde Londoniis* is recorded at the end of the account of the year 1357. If John of Reading states correctly that David King of Scotland also attended, the event must have preceded his release in October. John of Reading further relates an anecdote about John II at a banquet at Windsor on St George's Day, 23.4.1358 (ibid., 130). An item among the Close Rolls dated 3.12.1358 refers to '4 tuns of wine . . . for the maintenance of certain of the king's servants whom he has appointed to stay there [at the castle of Somerton] to a certain date upon the safe custody of his adversary of France'. Close Rolls, TNA MS C.54/196 m. 4 (*Calendar of the Close Rolls, Edward III:* x. 1354–1360, 482).

346   THE MUSICIAN MOTETS

Denys de Collors and Guillaume Racine, the accounts mention Messire Jehan Roussel, *chapellain*, and with the clerk Climent three others, Caletot, Barbatre and Baudement.[5] None of these names corresponds to those in *Musicorum*, but the motet nevertheless appears to date from the period of John's captivity in England in the late 1350s, the only time when a French court was in England. The treaty of Brétigny (1360) imposed an enormous ransom for his release. He was liberated in order to raise the necessary funds, in exchange for his second son, Louis Duke of Anjou, who was retained as a hostage. Louis escaped, upon which John voluntarily returned to England from motives of honour, and died there in 1364.

The end flyleaves of **Durham20** present French motets, including five that have with varying degrees of certainty been attributed to Vitry. Harrison hypothesised that this and other motets in the Durham flyleaves were copied from a French manuscript in use in John's London chapel. However, the use of a Sarum chant, the reference to an Englishman within the text, and the English source all tend to confirm an origin in England, as could fit with the period of captivity. Vitry was present on John's campaigns when he was Duke of Normandy, and shortly after he was crowned king in 1350 acted as his representative at Avignon. Vitry's appointment as bishop of Meaux in 1351 had royal support. Harrison implies that John's exile may have been responsible for the transmission of Vitry motets to England, although this came during a period of intense hostilities, vituperatively reflected in Vitry's later motet *Phi millies ad te/ O creator/Iacet granum/Quam sufflabit* and in his ballade text *De terre en grec Gaulle appellee*, which styles England 'de Dieu maudite'.[6] If John's exile was indeed a path of transmission, it could account for the presence of two Vitry motet transcriptions in **Robertsbridge**, which on grounds of notational usage I date in the second half of the century rather than older datings in the 1320s.[7] But an English theorist's knowledge of two Vitry motets it cites must have happened before John's exile, as the *Quatuor principalia* carries the date of 1351.[8] However, the end flyleaves of **Durham20** present not only French motets, but also *O vos omnes* and *Virginalis concio*, which may well be English, as well as *Musicorum*; the notation of these motets is basically that of the fully developed French *ars nova*, but with some insular characteristics, notably the distinction between major and minor semibreve rests.[9]

[5] I am grateful to David Howlett for these references: Orléans, *Notes et documents*, 129, 90, 120, 118, 131, 137.

[6] Most of the triplum now survives for *Phi millies*, previously known only from its separately preserved texts: Zayaruznaya, 'New Voices', and *The Monstrous New Art*, appendix 3. The text calls for an end to English perfidy ('et cessabit horum perfidis, nec plus erit hoc nomen: Anglia') and the salvation of the French nation. A satirical ballade without music, *De terre en grec Gaulle appellee* (?1337–38), styles England 'de Dieu maudite'. Comment on England in Vitry's poetic output almost certainly dates from after the outbreak of hostilities with England in 1337. Vitry's part (the *sentencia judiciis*) of a jeu-parti, *Ulixea fulgens facundia*, written with Jean de Savoie (d. 1353) and Jean de le Mote, survives in an important 15th-c. literary collection (**Paris3343**) that also includes the triplum text of Vitry's motet for Pope Clement VI, *Petre clemens* (see Ch. 30). Vitry may also be the author of an episode describing the treachery of Edward I in 1301 that he copied into his copy of Guillaume de Nangis's *Chronicon*; in the same manuscript Vitry commented on the danger posed to Paris by the English in 1346. On *Ulixea*, see Wathey, 'Jean de Savoie'; on *Petre Clemens*, Wathey, 'The Motets of Vitry' and Zayaruznaya, *The Monstrous New Art*; on Nangis (Vatican City, Biblioteca Apostolica Vaticana, Reg. Lat. 544) and the English in 1346, Wathey, 'Philippe de Vitry's Books'.

[7] See now Alís Raurich, 'The *Flores* of *Flos vernalis*'.

[8] Aluas, 'The *Quatuor principalia*'.

[9] See Ch. 8 n. 14.

Texts

The triplum of *Musicorum* sets out a calendrical programme from the start, many ingredients of which are woven into both text and music, with counts of 7 (for days of the week), 4 (weeks in a month), 12 (months of the year), and 52 (weeks of the year). The triplum relates in line 7 (a week of lines) that the college of musicians sings the *Xpisti matris officium*, the office of the mother of Christ, the Saturday votive Mass of the Virgin Mary, *quater in mense* (four times in a month, i.e. weekly), i.e. on the seventh day. The number of lines in the triplum (34) and motetus (18) total 52, the number of weeks in a year.[10] The sevens and twelves are Apocalyptic numbers; the Apocalypse is specifically referenced in the motetus, as are its seven candelabra and seven stars. The sevens may be a deliberate nod at those of *Musicalis*. The seven churches of Asia are not specified in the motet, but accord with the missionary theme of the *In omnem terram* tenors of *Apollinis* and *Sub Arturo*, and the cosmic ambition of *Alma polis*.[11] The triplum text of 34 lines is arranged in 17 pairs using only two (double) end rhymes, *-io* and *-ium*. The motetus has nine couplets rhyming in disyllables, some of which extend also to the vowel of the antepenultimate; both texts have extensive internal vowel rhyme and alliteration. Uniquely and strikingly in this motet, both texts are written mostly in the first person; the *-io* verbs account for several of the rhymes, notably the contrast *scio–nescio*, but the author does not name himself. In the triplum he claims personal knowledge of the seven named musicians, but does not identify as one of them. They all appear to be still alive and active, something otherwise explicit only in *Musicalis*, where the musicians are enjoined to follow the rules of rhetoric and rhetoricians the rules of music. Some of the other motets, notably *Sub Arturo*, seem to have too wide a chronological spread to refer only to contemporaries, as will be seen.

Self-commendation, Puns

Authorial self-recommendations have been noted in the other motets. Here they are brought together with punning references to words of division or cutting which are quite often placed at numerically or structurally significant points in text or music. In *Musicorum*, triplum line 21 may refer anonymously to the author (*actor*), unusually (within this mainly first-person text) in the third person. The triplum words *obsequium | actoris, qui seruicio | se totum subdit omnium* ('the deference of the author, who subjects his entire self to the service of all') straddle the musical transition to the second *color* statement in diminution at B97. The point of juncture between the two *color* statements, two-thirds of the way through the music, falls in the triplum after *actoris*: *actoris | qui seruicio* and in the motetus after *acuto*: *cum bis acuto | gladio*; the *ac* of *actoris* and *acuto* coincide,

---

[10] David Howlett observed the extent of this programme. He also noted that the golden section of 52 falls at 34 and 18, precisely the division of lines between triplum and motetus, a relatively rare case of an incontrovertible division thus proportioned.

[11] Revelation also has seven seals, four angels, four horsemen, four winds, four beasts. The musical articulation of twelves will be dealt with below. Other instances of specific reference of this kind in these motets are to Genesis in *Sub Arturo* and to Boethius in *Apollinis* and *Musicus est*.

348 THE MUSICIAN MOTETS

as do the two final *-io* rhymes. This point is thus heralded by *bis* (twice) and the verbal phrase is cut with the twice-sharp sword at the musical juncture. This motetus text reference to cutting, *cum bis | acuto gladio*, is anticipated by the earlier reference to cutting, *nemo . . . unum posset incide-| re cum silice*, where the word *incidere* (cut) is itself cut by a musical structural division; it flanks the start of the third *talea* of the first *color* at B49, one-third of the way through the music. This falls at the midpoint of the forty motetus words, between words 20 and 21: *nemo . . . unum posset | incidere cum silice*. Thus different significant numerical or proportional structural points in text and music are brought into alignment, and in the case just mentioned reinforced by puns and vowel rhyme.

In *Apollinis* and *Alma polis* the authors are named immediately past the midpoint of the motetus text. At the midpoint of the *Musicorum* motetus text, in the two central lines 9–10, it is not the human but the heavenly creator who is named, as *celestis opifex, summus sculptor et artifex; sculptor* is the central, thirty-third word. This passage straddles the mid-point of the music (B75).[12] The trinity of names is mirrored in the triple anaphora of the triplum's *O quanta, O mira, O dulcis* (lines 23, 25, 27) which musically mark the junction between *taleae* 1 and 2 of the second *color* (B105–B10).

There is further punning on the calendrical numbers. Line 7, *Quater in mense previo*, refers to the weekly ritual and has four words; the musical phrase rises to a fourth and spans four breves. It occupies B27–B29, covering the twenty-eight days of the lunar month. As in *Apollinis* and *Sub Arturo*, the end of the motetus refers directly to the musicians named in the triplum; the word *tripli* spans a third. *Unum* in line 6 (B45–B46) is on a unison of pitch (*c*) and syllable (*-um*). There are musical solmisation puns: strange, indeed illegitimate dissonances are contrived at the words *mira modulacio* and *discordie carencium*. *Mi-ra* is rhyme-punned as *mi–fa*, with the *fa* signed; in *Sub Arturo plebs*, the similar line *mire vocis modulo* has a signed *mi* but no *mi–re* pun.[13] At *acutorum et gravium* (*Musicorum*, B120–B21), the triplum crosses from above the motetus to below it, high to low.

Music: Tenor

The tenor's *Avete* is the first word spoken by Jesus after the Resurrection, the middle word (7th of 13) of the Sarum Easter Alleluia verse *Surrexit dominus* (for the Mass for *feria iv post pasche*) set melismatically in the chant: 'Surrexit dominus et occurrens mulieribus ait **avete** tunc accesserunt et tenuerunt pedes eius.' This melisma is used for the motet tenor, which follows the Sarum version of the melisma with a few variants: see Example 18.2.[14] It has the unusually wide range of an octave, with striking leaps.

---

[12] David Howlett commented: 'The word *sculptor* occurs only once in the Vulgate, at Exodus 28: 11, in a verse about inscribing the names of God's people. The word *opifex* occurs only once in the Vulgate, in Acts 19: 25, in association with *artifex*. In Hebrews 11: 10 the *artifex* of the heavenly city is identified as God.' Howlett notes that 'other words recur at arithmetically fixed intervals. There are ten words before *zelancium*, and the tenth word from the end is *zelo*. There are fourteen words before *Xpisti*, and the fourteenth word from the end is *Xpistus*.'

[13] II 110; *bb* is possible, but the long-term resolution favours *b♮*, as does the *mi–fa* pun on *mira*. Editorial sharps at the final cadence (141) have been suggested, again because of the 6/3–8/5 progression, but also because the motetus ends with another *mi–fa* rhyming pun, *pagina*. Leach, 'Interpretation and Counterpoint', 331, points out a rare need in Machaut for *d♯* over *b♮* on the syllable *mi* (*d'amie*) in Ballade 5, *Riches d'amour*.

[14] Harrison misnames it the Gradual, but prints the Alleluia from *GS*, pl. 120; the Roman version in *GR* 251 differs in both text and music. *Musicorum* is among those compositions that, evidently for verbal and

Ex. 18.2 Chant melisma on *Avete* (*GS* 120) and the tenor of *Musicorum*

Harrison gives the Sarum version of the chant (*GS* 120) but does not comment on the use of an English chant—the Roman version is different in text and music. This raises the interesting possibility that it could be an English composition (also hinted at in the notational features just mentioned), or at least that King John's Lady Mass devotions in England involved English musicians who used their own chants. The fact that it refers to the court of the Frenchmen could also suggest that its composer may not have been French.

The tenor *color* is written out in full, twice, the second time in diminution (i.e. at the next note-level down). Each *color* contains four *taleae*, each of eight pitches and twelve longs duration (12 breves in diminution). The maximodus is ambiguous (it becomes modus in diminution); 12 divides either way, and there are no notational clues as to whether it is perfect or imperfect. In the accompanying transcription, I have arbitrarily grouped the longs as for perfect maximodus (three longs to a maxima), which in diminution becomes perfect modus. Modus and tempus in the upper parts are imperfect throughout, with major prolation.

The tenor has several links with the other motets: the major feast of Easter responds to the Christmas chant of the tenor of *Musicalis*, the melisma from the Alleluia *Dies sanctificatus*, for the third (main) Mass for Christmas. The notes *g a c* of *color* 3 anticipate the opening of the *In omnem terram* chant used in *Sub Arturo*. The greeting *Auete* of the tenor of *Musicorum* rhymes with and seems to mirror the final couplet of farewell of the earlier motet *Musicalis sciencia*: *cuncta uicia cauete | in melodia ualete*.

The music of *Musicorum*, like *Apollinis*, is musically based on units of twelve. Both motets are 144 breves in length (12^2), but differently disposed.[15] Here, each *color* statement has four *taleae*, four again being a calendrical and apocalyptic number. In the first tenor *color* of 96 breves there are four *taleae* each of 24 breves, of which one-third (8 breves) are rests. It totals 32 notes, eight in each *talea*. As noted above, this *color* is stated (and written out) twice, the second statement a diminution of the first, resulting in the ratio 2:1, a total of 48 breves. Put another way, the *talea* length of twelve (monthly) longs diminishes in the second *color* to 12 breves.

symbolic reasons, do not use the beginning of the chant, but an internal portion with the desired word. This is true of *Caput*, *O amicus*, *Omni tempore* and many other compositions, probably including hitherto unidentified tenors.

[15] *Apollinis*, three *colores* each of two *taleae*, *Musicorum*, two unequal *colores* each of four *taleae*. The tenor of *Sub Arturo* is also 144 breves, but with a difference which will be set out below.

350 THE MUSICIAN MOTETS

Music: Upper Parts

All five motets except *Apollinis* have some isorhythm in the upper parts. Of those, *Musicorum* is the least strict and complete. Upper-part isorhythm in any case occurs only between the four *taleae* of each *color*, not between the unequal *colores*. Repetitions in the upper parts are not exact at the beginnings of *taleae*, though they become so by the eighth breve if not sooner. In *color* 1, B8–B24 of each *talea* correspond rhythmically, with slight variations; in *color* 2, breves 4–10, 4–10, 4–9, 4–9 of the respective *taleae* correspond. In *color* 1 the aligned transcription shows that B5–B6 of the triplum, for example, correspond rhythmically over the four *taleae*, but that these breves in the motetus correspond only in *taleae* 2–4, while B4–B6 are occupied with a statement of the opening *musicorum collegio* rhythm. Many deviations from isorhythmic regularity occur at points of quotation or symbolic word-painting, thus drawing attention to them as purposeful irregularities, such as a slightly irregular placement of recurrences of the *musicorum collegio* rhythmic motive in relation to the underlying rhythmic scheme. Despite the presence of isorhythm, the texts are not regularly distributed; in some cases, this seems to be in order to make certain significant words occur at significant or structural points.

As is often the case with partial isorhythm, hocketing occurs especially at points of conspicuous rhythmic repetition, often around *talea* joins. Here there is no interlocking complementary hocketing, but the range of intrabrevial rhythms used goes beyond the rhythmic vocabulary of *Apollinis*:

in color I triplum:[16]

in color II triplum:

in color II motetus:

Relationship to *Apollinis*

Musicorum collegio emulates *Apollinis* at many levels. They and other motets in the group share the musical and cosmic subject with named musicians, a total length of 144 apocalyptic breves,[17] musical and textual borrowings, and each its own multiple

[16] The imperfect S rests in *color* I are notated thus instead of as paired minims ( ) as explained below under 'Notation'.

[17] A few other pieces also have this length, but with a less clear apocalyptic significance than that which unites these two musician motets. These include *Febus mundo* (another motet dealing with the sun and the Zodiac) and *L'amoureuse fleur*; *Garrit gallus* has 144 breves plus the final long. Its related *Tribum/Quoniam/ Merito* is 13 not 12 × 12 units, but the intended relationship is clear, and the extra, 13th, unit is introductory, without the tenor, and standing outside the main structural scheme. We have seen that *Musicalis sciencia* has 7 × 24-breve *taleae*; six would have been 144 breves; that the second *color* of *Alma* is 144 semibreves; and we shall see how the tenor of *Sub Arturo*, if not the whole motet, has 144 breves. *Omnis terra* would be 144 breves without its extra half-*taleae*, q.v. *Zolomina*, with 108 perfect breves, is equivalent in minims to 144 imperfect breves. *Degentis vita* appears to be 141 breves long, but the first *color* (72 breves) ends, in the tenor, with a long rest which, if observed in counting the second *color*, would bring it to 144 breves. It can be argued that some of these represent acknowledgements of or deliberate deviations from a count of 144 breves.

MUSICORUM COLLEGIO/IN TEMPLO DEI 351

counterpointing of musical, textual and biblical symbolism and number. *Musicorum* begins with the temple of God; the Apocalypse (21: 15, 17) measures the city of Jerusalem at 144 cubits. *Musicorum* (like *Apollinis*) is 144 breves long; its motetus has 144 words, which specifically cite the Apocalypse. Perhaps the *templum pseudodeorum* of *Pantheon abluitur* acknowledges the *templum Dei* in *Musicorum*, and the *basilica* of *Apollinis*, whose tenor source in Psalm 18 continues *et in sole posuit tabernaculum suum*, as noted above. In *Apollinis*, the number twelve is zodiacally referenced. In *Musicorum*, as well as the calendrical features just noted, and the Apocalyptic sevens, the citing of the Apocalypse implicates its twelve tribes multiplied to 144,000.

Besides links with the tenors of other motets, there are even stronger links in the upper parts. The triplum of *Musicalis scienca* begins with three statements of the rhythm ♦ ♦ ♦|♦ ♦ ♦ ♦ |■ derived from B30–B32 of *Apollinis*. *Musicorum* acknowledges *Apollinis* even more strikingly by taking the words *musicorum collegio* as its opening words, and to the same rhythm; the words and rhythm of triplum of B30–B32 of *Apollinis* are set to different pitches. Often a quotation, as here, will be varied by using just two out of the three parameters of text, pitch and rhythm. In *Musicorum collegio* the musicians are named between B32 and B80; *Musicorum* begins to name its musicians at the same point from which it took the quotation from *Apollinis*.

The words and rhythm borrowed from *Apollinis* that open the triplum of *Musicorum collegio* are set to a striking descending seven-note scale that literally runs the gamut from *g* down to *a*, and stands for the seven members of the *musicorum collegio* who are named in the triplum. This descent is also borrowed from *Apollinis*; after its initial descent of a fifth, the motetus *Zodiacum* rises an octave in order to delineate the seventh from *d* down to *e*. *Musicalis sciencia* also starts with the same rhythm, at the same pitch, and with the same first four notes. Both *Musicalis* and *Musicorum* have a tenor that starts on low *c* and enters at the beginning with the texted parts. The words 'vidi septem candelabra' are set to a second descending seven-note scale in the motetus from *g* down to *a*. The new context in *Musicorum* appropriates the quotation uniquely to the number of musicians celebrated here (seven), as opposed to the twelve in *Apollinis*, giving new significance to phrases borrowed from the parent motet. Seven literal statements of the *musicorum collegio* rhythm occur in *Musicorum*, six in the triplum (breves 1, 28, 76, 111, 123, 135) and one in the motetus (B5). A seventh triplum statement may be allowed if we count the striking scalar octave descent for *Johannem et Nicasium* with an interpolated breve between their names (B51–B54). Thus this rhythm may also have been used to stand for the seven lights (stars, candelabra) and seven musicians, as the Zodiac signs stand for the twelve of *Apollinis*. An unmediated octave descent occurs at triplum B25–B27; compare the direct octave ascent at the beginning of *Zodiacum*. The descending fifth *a–d* that opens *Zodiacum* finds an echo in the same descending fifth in the passage of chant chosen for the tenor of *Musicorum* (B59–B60). The motetus of *Musicorum* also features a prominent rising fifth *c g* for *vidi* (at B19) and *ego* (at B118), crossing above the triplum, two of the first-person authorial word markers mentioned above. Similar leaps of fifths in both directions have been remarked in *Apollinis*. The seven stars and seven candelabra are thus fixed to the musicians and to the musical substance of the motet; the motetus and triplum texts are counterpointed to each other as intricately as is their music. The seven stars, heavenly lights standing for men, and the

352　THE MUSICIAN MOTETS

seven candelabra/musicians, earthly lights standing for heavenly ones, are aligned in the two simultaneous texts.

Notation

If it originates from the composer rather than the copyist, an interesting notational feature may further point to an English origin for the motet. Major (perfect) semibreve rests intersect the staff line; these are used in the motetus. Minor (imperfect) semibreve rests (equivalent to two minims) hang from the line ⊤. The first *color* of the triplum uses these minor semibreve rests. In the second *colores* of the triplum and motetus, paired minim rests ⊥ are used instead; thus both systems appear in the same motet. This change of rest notation for the same value was prompted (if not actually necessitated) to clarify the triplum syncopation at breves 103, 115, 127, 139 and the related hockets. The triplum of *Apta caro/Flos* on the same manuscript opening has exclusively paired minim rests. Its motetus *Flos virginum* has (and needs) only major semibreve rests. In ⊙ Example 18.1 the minor semibreve rests in *color* 1 have been normalised to paired minim rests, but the notation switches to paired minim rests for the hockets in *color* 2. This change between the triplum *colores* may be partly explained by the syncopated (dotted) major ◆ in *color* 2.

There is no evidence in French sources of a distinction between major and minor semibreve rests, though Earp has drawn attention to undifferentiated rests in **Br19606** which include the value of a minor semibreve. French practice settled to a single type of semibreve rest (hanging from the line, always perfect in major prolation), and paired minim rests for a two-minim rest or imperfect semibreve in major prolation.[18] The distinction between major (perfect) and minor (imperfect) semibreve rests was retained in some English sources (including **Fountains**) up to around 1400.[19]

These notational features, taken together with the relationships between the motets, confirm the status of the three motets *Apollinis*, *Musicalis* and *Musicorum*, in that order, as a considerably earlier chronological group than *Alma polis* and *Sub Arturo*, a status borne out by biographical identifications, with *Apollinis* and *Musicalis* probably in the 1330s and *Musicorum* in the late 1350s. Since the added triplum parts of *Apollinis* try, with varying success and skill, to match their rhythms to the original triplum, they cannot be dated on grounds of notational and rhythmic vocabulary; all probably date from around 1400.

---

[18] See Ch. 8 n. 14.

[19] Earp, 'Tradition and Innovation', has importantly drawn attention to the use of rests of the value of two minims when hockets follow the default rhythms for stemless semibreves, substituting equivalent rest(s) for the minor semibreve. Both the motets on this opening, *Musicorum* and *Apta caro*, have hockets of this type. See also Ch. 8 nn. 2, 14, Ch. 17 n. 11.

19

Alma polis religio/Axe poli cum artica/ [Et] in ore eorum and its Named Musicians

Alma polis, like *Musicalis* and *Musicorum*, is another *unicum*, preserved in **Chantilly**, a manuscript compiled after 1400 which also contains one of the sources of *Sub Arturo*. It is the only four-part motet of the group, with an integral contratenor and an ingenious rhythmic conception. Its named musicians seem to have been active in the latter part of the fourteenth century, suggesting that it is separated in date from *Musicorum* by approximately a generation, as *Musicorum* was similarly separated from *Apollinis* and *Musicalis*. For the edition see ⏯ Example 19.1. Commentary notes to the transcription are in the Appendix to this chapter. This transcription is counted in semibreves because of the different simultaneous mensurations.

Texts and translation by David Howlett. Named musicians are in boldface:

Triplum		Rhymes	Words	Syllables
Alma polis religio,		a	3	8
doctrine pollens radio		a	3	8
fratrum Sancti Augustini.		b	3	8
Ydidi sunt hii celibes		c	4	8
cuncti uiginti cirices	5	c	3	8
musicique precipui.		b	2	8
Uno promo hinc peritos,		d	4	8
in neüma doctissimos		d	3	8
armonia sub pantrana:		e	3	8
breuiter ex quis modulo	10	f	4	8
P. de Sancto Dionisio		f	4	8
melos, plures uigent quia,		e	4	8
Johannis Foreastarii,		g	2	8
cum **Nicholao Bichomui**,		h	3	8
professores theorici;	15	h	2	8
camena **J. Struteuilla**,		i	3	8
Augustini de Florencia,		i	3	8
Johannis Desiderii;		g	2	8
Mutuilos, Theobaldus,		j	2	8
Taxinus de Parisius	20	j	3	8
Orpheico fonte poti;		h	3	8
ac uterque **Ydrolanus**		k	3	8

modulator **Ciprianus**,		k	2	8
Guillermus Caualerii,		h	2	8
Girardus de Colonia,	25	i	3	8
cum **Clemente de Berria**,		i	4	8
Petrus quoque Amatori,		h	3	8
tenorem preminet **Gratro**,		f	3	8
cum **Galterio de Gardino**,		f	4	8
Jeronimus Parisii.	30	h	3	8
Quorum fuit melodia		i	3	8
ac dulcior armonia		i	3	8
in canore et cantamen,		l	4	8
modulamen hoc carmine:		m	3	8
A solis ortus cardine	35	m	4	8
et usque terre limitem.		l	4	8
		13	110	288

Motetus

Axe poli cum artica		a	4	8
Ydam gerit extatura		b	3	8
architipi in figura;		b	3	8
antarticus a natura,		b	3	8
forma cuius est sperica	5	a	4	8
uallat uercia diaphana:		c	3	8
religio ita ista,		d	3	8
zodiaca, siderea,		d	2	8
ambit cosmum industria		e	3	8
atque antonomasia	10	e	2	8
cunctos cellit armonica		a	3	8
auroratque solercia		e	2	8
Egidii de Aurolia,		e	3	8
manant a quo cantamina		c	4	8
pariter cum hac musica.	15	a	4	8
Carmineus J. de Porta		d	4	8
se commendat per omnia:		e	4	8
uobis istis iure oda		d	4	8
debetur, que ad oria		e	4	8
plauza, dignaque dulcia,	20	e	3	8
canent ergo cum latria		e	4	8
uoce cuncti dulcisona:		c	3	8
O gloriosa domina,		c	3	8
beata nobis gaudia.		e	3	8

Syllables elided to maintain octosyllabic lines: tr: 4 **hii**, 11 **Dio**nisio, 13 **Fore**astarii, 14 **Nicho**lao, 17 Floren**cia**, 29 Gal**te**rio; mo: 6 uer**cia**, 13, Egi**dii**

Triplum: [O] life-giving (or 'nurturing') religion exerting power by the ray of the teaching of the brothers of St Augustine (i.e. the Austin Friars or Austin Canons) at the poles. They are knowable (i.e. famous) celibates, twenty altogether, criers (i.e. singers or preachers) and exceptional musicians. Above all I bring to notice hence the knowledgeable, most learned in neuma under all-bright (or 'entirely distinct') harmony. Because many flourish I sing briefly from among them a song of Pierre de St Denis, of John Forester, with Nicholas Bichomus (? Beauchamp, Beecham), professors of theory; the poetry of J. Struteville, Augustine of Florence, [and] J. Desiderii; Mutuilos, Theobald, Taxine de Paris, drunk from the Orpheic fountain; and each modulator Hydrolanos ('water trough') [and] Cyprian, Guillermus Cavalerii; Girardus de Colonia with Clement de Berry, also Petrus Amatori; Jerome de Paris surpasses the tenor with Gratrus [and] Walter de Gardino. Theirs was the melody and sweeter harmony and chanting in their song and measure in this poetry: 'Risen from the pole of the sun and as far as the end of the earth'.

Motetus: As the arctic, bound to stand out from the axis of the pole, bears Ida in the figure of an archetype, the antarctic by its nature, the form of which is spherical, walls the diaphanous veils, so that religion (i.e. the Augustinian), zodiacal, starry, goes round the world with its industry, and by antonomasia it surpasses all and 'shines like the sunrise' with the harmonic cleverness of Giles of 'Orleans' (playing on *aurorat* and *Aurolia*, though 'Aurelia' is normal for Orleans), from whom flow chants together with this music. 'Poetic John of Port' (or by hypallage 'John of the Carmentine Gate') commends himself through all these things: to you from those men by right an ode is owed, which as seasonable compositions, worthy and sweet, all will sing with worship in sweet-sounding voice: 'O glorious lady' [and] 'Blessed joys to us'.

Authors and Musicians

The motet claims to celebrate twenty Augustinian friars, celibate clerics. The naming of twenty musicians links *Alma polis* to the twenty musicians of *Musicalis sciencia*, eight or nine of whom were named earlier in *Apollinis*. After specifying 'uiginti cirices' in the twentieth bar of *Alma polis*, eighteen are named in twenty lines of the triplum and two in two lines of the motetus. The explicit collaboration of a poet and a composer uniquely distinguishes this motet in the group, as does the inclusion of the composer (Egidius de Aurolia) and poet (J. de Porta) in the motetus among the total of twenty; in *Apollinis* and *Sub Arturo* the authorial name in the motetus stands outside the count of names in the triplum.[1] J. de Porta was reported by Frank Ll. Harrison and earlier writers

---

[1] This also applies to *Musicorum*, if we accept *actor* in triplum line 21 as an anonymous indication of the author. Another co-authored motet, internally declared, is *Argi vices Poliphemus/Tum Philemon*, explicitly for John XXIII, either his election as pope in 1410 or the opening of the Council of Constance in 1414, but

356 THE MUSICIAN MOTETS

as the sole author of this motet. Ursula Günther pointed out some of the connections between *Alma polis religio* and *Apollinis*,[2] and was surely right to suggest (then followed by Harrison) that the double attribution signals Egidius de Aurolia as the composer of the music and J. de Porta of the texts. Their possible identities are considered below. The first person is used in the triplum, but the composers of texts and music are named in the motetus in the third person, as in *Apollinis* and *Sub Arturo*, and possibly also in *Musicorum*, if the composer is indeed referred to there.

Texts

The triplum begins with a reference to 'the poles', and ends with a reference to 'the pole of the sun', giving as its last couplet the first two lines of Sedulius's abecedarian hymn *A solis ortus cardine Et usque terre limitem*.[3] This widely known hymn is used for Lauds in the Christmas season; *Musicalis* uses a Christmas chant, and *Musicorum* one for Easter. *Usque terre limitem* recalls the tenor of *Apollinis*, *In omnem terram exiuit sonus eorum et in fines orbis terre*, also used for *Sub Arturo* (with a different chant), more powerfully than a still uncertain tenor identification (see below). The motetus begins with references to 'the axis of the pole', 'the arctic', 'the antarctic', and ends with the first lines of two other hymns, *O gloriosa domina* for the Virgin Mary, and *Beata nobis gaudia* for Whitsun.[4] Both voices begin with the letter A, and the music—yet again—begins on the note *a*. The first lines of both triplum and motetus include syllables from *Apollinis*: **Alma POLIs** religio and **Axe POLI** cum artica.[5] These in turn have vowel rhyme with *A solis*. Similar play on *Apollinis* was noted in the *apocalipsis* of *Musicorum*.

---

in any case before his discrediting that year. It is preserved in a late copy in **Ao**, ff. 4ᵛ–7 (PMFC 13, no. 49). The motetus ends: 'Hec Guilhermus dictans favit |Nicolao, qui cantavit, | ut sit opus consummatum.' There is no strong reason to identify the composer with Nicolaus Frangens de Leodio (d. 1433 in Cividale), as was suggested in PMFC 13, rather than some other Nicholas; see Ch. 30.

[2] CMM 39, p. xlv. See Marchi, 'Traces of performance', especially 9–10, for an interesting hypothesis that some of the secondary names in the double attributions in **Chantilly** may signal a performer or rearranger. The present cases are different, as the double names are integral to the text and appear to be explicit in distinguishing composer and poet.

[3] Leofranc Holford-Strevens maintains a poor view of the Latinity of these poets. He comments that 'the "religio" (i.e. order) would indeed seem to be Augustinian. Not finding a main verb in ll. 1–3, but observing that a new sentence starts in l. 4, I suppose we must understand "est" in l. 1, Life-giving for/at the poles [a recognized metonymy for "heaven", but we might expect "on earth"] is the order mighty in the ray of the learning of St Augustine's brethren. Granted that the sentence is grammatically detached from what follows, it would make sense as a general statement made specific by the following list of twenty celibates. Otherwise what is it doing there at all?' (email of 4.12.2018).

[4] The cosmological description implies the global spread of Augustinian religion. The etymological and geographical description serves at the same time to imply the dissemination of the music of Egidius de Aurolia and the poetry of J. de Porta.

[5] The opening words also evoke the later Old Hall motet by Cooke, *Alma proles regia*, which has been associated with the post-Agincourt celebrations in London. That motet also shares its rare 9:6:4 proportion with the English motet from this group, *Sub Arturo plebs*, but in a simpler execution. **OH** is closely related to the partially reconstructed royal choirbook (see EECM 62), which preserves the fragmentary motet *Fons origo musicorum*. See Chs. 21 and 25.

Although the rhyme scheme does not suggest a regular stanzaic structure, each *talea* of the thirty-six-line triplum takes six poetic lines, of which four are set to the undiminished part of the *talea*, two to the reduced section. There are some slight overlaps at the sectional joins. Each *talea* takes four poetic lines of the twenty-four-line motetus. The text is set out above to show these divisions. The assigning of the same amount of text to each *talea* results in a faster rate of text setting in the shorter second *color*. This slightly uneven distribution contrives to place the textually central *solercia* and name of Egidius (the first-named author) at the juncture with the second *color* in the music, which falls beyond the middle of the piece (the two *colores* occupy 171 + 144 semibreves); it must be taken as yet another strong instance of the deliberate setting in parallel of different proportions. Egidius here occupies the same authorial position established for B. de Cluny in *Apollinis/Zodiacum*. Like B. de Cluny's, his name stands where the heavenly creator stands in *Musicorum*. In *Apollinis*, the first half of the motetus text ends 'Boetii basis solercia'; in *Alma polis*, 'Auroratque solercia' ends the first half of the motetus text and the first of the two *colores*. *Apollinis's Zodiacum* is echoed here by *zodiaca* (motetus line 8). 'Carmineus J de Porta' is presented melodically as a descending seventh from *g* down to *a* as in *Musicorum collegio*, perhaps alluding to that motet if not also to the different descending seventh of 'Zodiacum signis' (*d* down to *e*), to which *Musicorum collegio* undoubtedly refers (because of its twinned quotation of those words and their rhythm from *Apollinis*). Between the names of the collaborators (Egidius and J. de Porta) are heard the words *uterque* ('and each') in the triplum and *pariter* ('equally') in the motetus.

The text contains even more Greek and Greek-derived words than *Psallentes zinzugia*. Many words link triplum and motetus.[6] *Apollinis*, triplum line 17, 'Orpheÿco potus fonte', recurs as *Alma polis*, triplum line 21, 'Orpheico fonte poti'. The Orphic word occurs at nearly the same position roughly halfway through each of these texts. The musical placings of this line also correspond, in *Apollinis* starting at breve 80 out of 144, in *Alma polis* at semibreve 186 out of 315. The Orphic line quoted in *Alma polis* from *Apollinis* links to the beginning of the motetus of *Sub Arturo* (*Fons citharizancium*), which names Orpheus's instrument (as a *cithara*), as well as anticipating the initial word *Fons* (see further below).

Just as *Alma polis* takes up the global idea in the hymn quotation *A solis . . . usque terre limitem*, so does *Musicorum* in the Apocalyptic motetus, which takes the Word to the seven churches of Asia. The A to Z of *Apollinis–Zodiacum* is picked up by 'I am the first and the last' (Apoc. 1: 17), beginning and end, alpha and omega (1: 18, 1: 11) as well as by *Sub Arturo's* reference to Genesis and *Musicorum's* to the Apocalypse. The use of hymn beginnings to end the texts of *Alma* is another play with beginnings and ends.

---

6 The triplum is linked to the motetus by many shared words. In the triplum, *polis, religio, cuncti, musicique, armonia, dulcior, cantamen, carmine*, corresponding in the motetus to *poli, religio, cunctos, cuncti, musica, armonica, dulcisona, cantamina, carmineus*.

Music: Lower Parts

Until very recently, the tenor had not been identified. Günther (in CMM 39, p. xlvi) noted the similarity of its opening notes ($d\,f\,g\,a\,g\,f\,g$) to those of the *In omnem terram* tenor of *Apollinis* ($a\,c\,d\,e\,d\,c\,d$) and proposed that a version of that chant might also underlie *Alma polis*. (Notes 2–4, $d\,f\,g$, of the tenor of *Musicalis*, a Christmas Alleluia neuma, might also be suggestive.) The tenor of *Alma polis* is not so labelled, as are the different chants of that name used for *Apollinis* and *Sub Arturo*.[7]

I had written: 'Until such a chant turns up, the matter must rest there. Identification will have been impeded if it comes from the middle of a chant. That the texts allude to the sense of *In omnem terram* there can be no question'. But at a late stage in the preparation of this book, a brilliant and wholly convincing identification by Kévin Roger came to my attention.[8] Indeed it is not from the beginning of a chant. The motet tenor corresponds with only minor variants to a passage from the Responsory for the Dedication of a church: *In dedicatione templi decantabat populus laudem. Et **in ore eorum dulcis resonabat sonus*** (words of the relevant passage in boldface). They are compared in Example 19.2, which is reproduced with Roger's permission from his

Ex. 19.2 Comparison of the tenor of *Alma polis* with chant melody from Fribourg (Freiburg) MS 2. Reproduced from Roger, 'La composition du tenor', 402, with his permission

thesis.

The words of the chosen chant excerpt ('a sweet sound resonates in their mouth') are, as Roger pointed out, well suited to the musicians celebrated in the triplum, and almost a paraphrase of its penultimate lines: *Quorum fuit melodia| ac dulcior armonia| in canore et cantamen| modulamen hoc carmine*. Tenors of the other musician motets relate to their subjects in similar ways. In addition, the 'templum' of the Responsory resonates with the motetus of *Musicorum collegio/In templo* (Ch. 18).

---

[7] *Omnis terra/Habenti dabitur* (**Ox7**, pp. 530–31, PMFC 15, no. 22) has some suggestive verbal links with the group, but does not list named musicians. Lefferts suggests the possibility that it could be a contrafact from the French, but that would not help with a connection. See now Colton, 'Making Sense of *Omnis/Habenti*'.

[8] Roger, 'La composition du tenor', 402–3, where he gives the version of the chant from the Franciscan Antiphoner Switzerland, Fribourg (= Freiburg), Bibliothèque des Cordeliers, MS 2, f. 244v (**Fribourg2**), accessible at https://www.e-codices.unifr.ch/fr/fcc/0002/244v. The Cantus database, https://cantus.uwaterloo.ca/chant/689756 (Cantus ID 006897), cites 110 concordances, some of which may hold a version even closer to the *Alma* tenor, perhaps a source of Augustinian provenance.

As to the mensural plan, here we are in a different world from the three earlier motets, and several decades later, towards 1400. *Alma polis* and *Sub Arturo plebs* are musically the most complex of the group.[9] Both use notational and mensural complexities that were not cultivated until the last quarter of the century. The lower-part canons read: 'Tenor cantatur bis, primo de modo perfecto cum diminucione eiusdem per semi. Secundo de modo imperfecto cum diminucione eiusdem per semi. Contratenor dicitur eodem modo sicut Tenor.' The instruction for internal diminution simply describes what has been implemented in the notated *color*. Both lower voices have a repeat sign for two iterations, and could not have been more compactly notated, as there is no melodic repetition for the internal diminution within each *color*. Each of the two *color* statements is interpreted according to the different mensurations specified; the instructions for the tenor apply also to the contratenor. The two lower parts are complementary and designed together both rhythmically and contrapuntally. The contratenor supplies a few contrapuntally essential notes (for example at S25.2, S146, but generally improves the sonority) and must be classed as essential. The *color* is divided into three isorhythmic *taleae*, each of which is in fact a pair of *taleae* embracing two unequal statements, with the tenor (and ancillary contratenor) first as written, and then written out in notes of the next level down (i.e. diminution), with long replaced by breve, breve by semibreve.[10] These *talea* pairs will here be called *taleae* C1.I, i, II, ii, III, iii; C2.I, i, II, ii, III, iii within each of the two *color* statements, as labelled in ▶ Example 19.1. Each *talea* has eight notes in both T and Ct, so each *talea* pair has twice eight notes. The whole *color* statement therefore has 48 notes and contains three *talea* pairs. The two *color* statements each have three double *taleae*, a total of 6 × 2 (12) *taleae*. Similar mensural transformation occurs in *Arta/Musicus*; see Chapter 21 for its explicit epogdoic relationships. In *Alma polis* 171: 144 is 0.8 (divided by 9 = 19:16), very close to the epogdoic 9:8. *Sub Arturo* presents simultaneously (152 = 8 × 19), *Alma polis* successively, a nineteen-based multiple in conjunction with 144. Nineteen is the number of places on both the musical and the astronomical hand.[11]

The first tenor *color* statement is in perfect modus and (unstated) imperfect time, major prolation; the immediately following diminution within each of the three *taleae* is in perfect tempus, major prolation, written out in full. A breve is altered before a long, the corresponding semibreve before a breve. Each unreduced *talea* has a duration of 38

---

[9] The transcription of *Alma* is correctly solved by Günther, but not by Harrison, whereas *Sub Arturo plebs* is correctly transcribed by Harrison and not by Günther. There is still a problem in the contratenor of *Alma*, around S41, to which there is no obvious or elegant solution, involving as it does a rhythm whose notation is fixed for six statements in each of two mensurations.

[10] Examples of diminution within a *color* or *talea* before a *color* or *talea* repeat are rare, but occur in Ciconia's *Petrum Marcello*. See Ch. 26 on *Povero zappator*. Other motets with complex arrangements include *Alpha vibrans/Cetus, Portio nature/Ida capillorum, Almifonis/Rosa*.

Other motets for which collaboration appears to be claimed include *Portio nature/Ida capillorum* in **Ivrea**, **Chantilly**, **Leiden342A**, **Trém** and **Stras**, where in **Stras** the motetus was headed 'Magister Heinricus' (also mentioned in the text, apparently as poet and composer) and 'Egidius de Pusiex', thought perhaps to be the poet but whose status is uncertain (PMFC 5, no. 5, and commentary). See Zazulia, 'A Motet Ahead of its Time', and here Ch. 17. **Ivrea** and **Chantilly** reverse the status of triplum and motetus parts, but **Stras** and the testimony of **Trém** (which always lists motets by motetus) affirm the correct status; *Portio* is longer and more triplum-like. Zazulia, 'Verbal Canons', writes that the only other 14th-c. motets besides *Portio nature/Ida capillorum* to feature mensural reinterpretation are *Inter densas* and *Sub Arturo* (p. 349). She overlooks *Alma polis* which, like *Portio/Ida*, also uses diminution as well as mensural reinterpretation, albeit more simply; and the status at least of *Sub Arturo* is here questioned.

[11] Fritz Reckow, in *HMT*, s.v. clavis.

major S, each reduced *talea* 19 major S (a total of $57 \times 3 = 171$ per *color*). These irregular numbers are exploited in syncopations in the tenor and contratenor, displaced in relation to each other within the perfect modus: in the first *color*, the contratenor's three-breve groupings are offset by a supernumerary breve rest at the beginning (1–2) of the unreduced *talea*, the tenor's by a supernumerary breve rest at the end (37–38); both are similarly offset by semibreve rests in the reduced section, bringing each double *talea* in *color* 1 (C1) to the irregular count of $38 + 19$ (= 57) semibreves. The first tenor long (which becomes a breve in diminution) is confirmed as perfect by a dot. The ensuing breve (a semibreve in diminution) displaces the next two perfect longs (breves in diminution), and makes up its perfection group with the next two breve rests. Although the reduced *taleae* are effectively in halved values, as prescribed by the rubric *per semi*, they could equally well, and perhaps more correctly, have been described as being in diminution, reading the notes at the next level down, as the relationships of twos and threes are not exactly parallel for the diminution: perfect modus with *imperfect* time is not directly parallel to perfect tempus with *major* prolation. Medieval notators seem to have been as ready as modern scholars to take this imprecise shortcut (halving rather than diminution); it just needs to be recognised that the two procedures will usually but not always yield the same results. The tenor's first perfect long is worth 18M, the first *imperfect* breve 6M (2×3). At the rhythmic diminution the perfect breve is worth 9M, the first major (*perfect*) semibreve 3M.

The lower parts of the second *color* are read from the same notation, but in straightforward imperfect modus (without displacement), followed in diminution by imperfect tempus in each *talea*, thus now with no alteration of the breve (then of the semibreve, in the reduced sections, lower-case i, ii, iii). The breves remain imperfect, with major prolation. Each double *talea* contains $32 + 16 = 48$ major S, a total of 144 for the three *taleae* of the second *color*. The dots are ingeniously managed so that what served as dots of perfection or division in the first *color* become dots of addition in the second.[12] This may sometimes result in dots that would have been helpful in perfect mensurations being omitted so that they do not have to be read as dots of addition in imperfect ones. See Chapter 13 for an instance of this in Machaut's Motet 2.

Figure 19.1 shows the tenor and contratenor parts as they appear in Chantilly. Example 19.3 shows the first *talea* pair of each *color* in simplified modern notation, aligned to show the syncopations. Altered notes in the triple-mensuration reading are marked 'alt'. The first note in each *talea* (except one) is dotted; the dots are for perfection in triple measure, for addition in duple. See ⊙ Example 19.1 for a full transcription in original note values.

Music: Upper Parts

Reference to the musical scores on the linked website is usually by bar or breve. Here the calculation is in semibreves to facilitate reference and to take account of the fact that the triplum is in C throughout, the motetus in $\odot$, with breve lengths of two and three semibreves respectively. In *color* 1, three breves of C coincide with two of $\odot$ and,

---

[12] The first dot is omitted in contratenor, *talea* II.

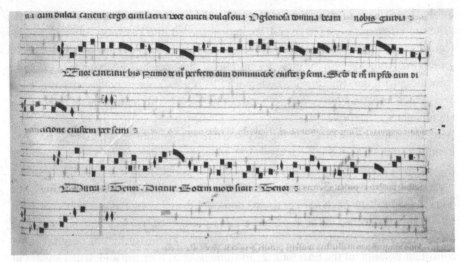

Fig. 19.1 Tenor and contratenor of *Alma polis* in Chantilly, Bibliothèque du Château de Chantilly, MS 564, f. 68. Cliché CNRS-IRHT © Bibliothèque du château de Chantilly–Musée Condé, reproduced with permission

Ex. 19.3 The first *talea* pair of each *color* of *Alma polis* in simplified modern notation

THE MUSICIAN MOTETS

but for the syncopations in the lower parts, would coincide with their perfect longs. (The supernumerary rests in *color* 1 are here absorbed into a regular pattern.) The irregular extra beats in the lower parts are noted above. In *color* 2, pairs of triplum breve groups in ℭ coincide with the imperfect modus of the tenor, but the motetus in ☉, while coinciding with the triplum with each pair of its breves, only coincides with the tenor every three imperfect longs, or every four of its breves. This should be clear from the alignment in ⓑ Example 19.1.

In the triplum of the first *color* the fifty-seven major semibreves of each *talea* proceed in imperfect time, with a half-bar at 51, 108, 165 to accommodate the odd total number ($57 \times 3 = 171$ semibreves). The motetus proceeds in perfect tempus with a displacement syncopation: the two semibreves at 34–35 (91–92, 148–49) are made up to three with one at 56 (114, 171). Each *talea* of the second *color* contains 48 major semibreves, with no adjustments needed to the imperfect-time triplum or the perfect-time motetus. The overall length of $171 + 144 = 315$ semibreves is clear from the isorhythm, despite the inconsistent notation of the final longs.[13] In *Alma polis*, *Sub Arturo* and *Arta*, changes of mensuration mean that the breves are of different lengths.

There is no hocketing in the upper parts, but the second *color* contains passages of rhythmic canon (S193–S200 and corresponding places). The upper parts have a consistently high level of incidental dissonance with the lower parts; this has not been edited out.

Within each of the two *colores*, the upper parts have almost completely strict isorhythm between the three *taleae*; in two of the three places where ambiguity or minor variation occurs, it has been assimilated to the majority reading: tr S139 ♪ ♦ has been changed to conform with S25 and S82; mo S206 ♪ ♪ (the second minim altered) has been changed to ♦♪ to conform with S254 and S302, where an accident could have happened over the line end in **Chantilly**. One anomaly remains: tr S44 ♪ is not present in the other iterations. Mo S273: a redundant ⊤ after *d* was perhaps mistranscribed from a dot. A few omissions have been supplied editorially in [].

In the upper parts in major prolation plentiful minim alteration is required, altered semibreves in the perfect-time motetus (marked by swallowtails); and several passages in syncopation are marked by dots. Some ambiguity in the smaller note-values may be clarified by dots in one but not all of the rhythmic replications, or by groupings. Only dots present in the MS are marked in the transcription. (For variants, see the Appendix to this chapter.)

Possible Identities of the Musicians Named in *Alma polis*

Hoppin and Clercx offered a number of tentative identifications, mostly from papal documents from Urban V and Clement VII.[14] The musicians in the triplum are named in six groups of three: three professors of theory, Pierre de St Denis, John Forester, and Nicholas Bichomus; three poets: J. Struteville, Augustine of Florence, and J. Desiderii.

---

[13] The triplum has a final ■, the motetus ◄, the contratenor ×, and the tenor ♦ and ⊤, consistent with the corresponding preceding *taleae*.

[14] Hoppin and Clercx, 'Notes biographiques', 81–88.

The areas of musical competence of the others are not specified. Three more are drunk from the Orphic fountain: Mutuilos, Theobald and Taxine de Paris; another three unspecified: Hydrolanos, Cyprian and Guillermus Cavalerii; three more: Girardus de Colonia, Clement de Berry and Petrus Amatori; and finally Jerome de Paris, Gratrus and Walter de Gardino.[15] The list lacks the familiar names of Vitry, Muris and Machaut present in *Apollinis* and *Musicalis*, perhaps because they were not Augustinians. Hoppin and Clercx have associated many of the musicians named in *Alma polis/Axe poli* with clerics traceable in Avignon or in papal documents from 1379 to the 1390s.[16] Günther plausibly dates the motet during the papacy of Clement VII, 1378–94. The 'professor of theory' who heads the list might be the Frater Petrus de Sancto Dionisio named in two manuscripts as the author of a treatise comprising a *musica theorica* and a *musica practica*.[17] The theoretical part is identical with the first part of the treatise of Coussemaker's Anonymous VI in **Newberry**, and draws heavily on the *Notitia* of Johannes de Muris. The transmission of the practical part is more complex, and is fully discussed by its modern editor. One might suspect an Augustinian link with *Alma polis*; the author has imported into the *Notitia* frequent references to St Augustine, the source of the treatise's opening line 'Musica est scientia bene modulandi', which in turn recalls the texts of the motet *Musicalis sciencia/Sciencie laudabili*.[18] Because of the Augustinian connection, he is almost certainly the 'Petrus de Sancto Dionisio, Ordinis fratrum Heremitarum Sancti Augustini' named as a beneficiary in a letter of 13 September 1332 from John XXII to Guilelmus, chancellor of Paris.[19] Even earlier, the Neapolitan chapel of Robert of Anjou included in 1317 and 1318, together with Marchetto, an Augustinian monk by the name of Petrus de Sancto Dionysio.[20] Not only does this open up a fascinating window on Franco-Italian music-theoretical contacts in Robert's chapel at this crucial time, perhaps accounting for the knowledge of French theory displayed in Marchetto's *Pomerium*, but this Petrus now becomes a strong candidate to be the Augustinian music theorist praised in a motet of perhaps seventy years later. Most of the other hypothetical identifications of names in this motet are for men active in the second half of the century; the composition itself cannot be much earlier than the 1390s.[21] It is possible, therefore, that *Alma polis* took a long view of the musical achievements of Augustinians, and did not confine its praise to contemporaries. In that, it is comparable to the long historical perspective of *Sub Arturo*'s roll-call of English musicians dating back to the mid-fourteenth century. However, few of the twenty can be positively identified, either from other musical activity or from dated documents. Only Augustinus is specified as 'de Florencia'. The provenance of the other names, where unambiguous, is overwhelmingly French, as is the compositional technique of the motet, preserved uniquely as it is in **Chantilly** along with other advanced French repertory.

[15] He names the composer and the poet by *antonomasia*, with word play on their compositions and their places of origin.

[16] *Colloques de Wégimont* II, 1955 (Paris, 1959).

[17] The late 15th-c. **WashingtonJ6** and **Siena30**. The treatise of Petrus is edited by Ulrich Michels in CSM 17 (Johannes de Muris, *Notitia*).

[18] *Johannis de Muris Notitia*.

[19] This could be the same man as the Petrus de Sancto Dionysio who was listed as regent in the faculty of theology in 1305 and 1330. Courtenay, *Parisian Scholars*, 201–2.

[20] Vivarelli, 'Di una pretesa scuola napoletana', 289–92.

[21] Hoppin and Clercx, 'Notes biographiques', 81.

364   THE MUSICIAN MOTETS

For Egidius de Aurolia, Günther argues for a strong connection with Avignon, based on the identification of some of the names with Augustinians documented there, and especially of the Egidius de Aurolia (Orleans), named in the motetus of *Alma polis/ Axe poli* as the composer of the music, with Magister Egidius Augustinus, composer of three ballades in **Chantilly**, **ModA** and **Reina**. These include *Courtois et sages*, with an acrostic 'Clemens', honouring the schismatic Avignon pope Clement VII as rightful pope, and was therefore composed after 1379, one reason for Günther's suggestion that *Alma polis* might be in honour of Clement or at least date from his reign.[22] The ballade *Franchois sunt nobles* is ascribed to 'Magister Egidius ordinis heremitorum Sancti Agustini'. Another ballade, *Roses et lis*, ascribed to 'Magister Egidius Augustinus', is associated with the festivities in Avignon for Jeanne de Boulogne preceding her marriage to Jean duc de Berry in 1389.[23] He may also be one of the composers of five two-voice ballatas in the section of the Squarcialupi codex (**Sq**) devoted to 'M. frater Egidius et Guilielmus de Francia'. In the miniature representing both composers, Guilielmus, at least, is dressed as an Augustinian. Two of the ballatas are attributed in **Paris568** to Guilielmus alone.

An Egidius of Orleans with no known musical or Augustinian credentials studied theology in Germany, Italy and Paris, receiving a doctorate on 3 December 1379 from Clement VII, entitling him to call himself 'magister'. He was entrusted with papal tasks in 1379, 1385 and 1393 which took him to Rouen, Reims, Cambrai and Paris (an Egidius de Aurelianis is recorded in Paris in 1385 and 1393). He continued a close relationship with the papal court at Avignon from 1394 under Benedict XIII.[24] This distinguished cleric may or may not be the musician named in the motet, and he may or may not be responsible for the three ballades mentioned above. But the Augustinian connection of the song composer makes it possible that he was indeed also responsible for the motet; the connection of documented papal servant and song text with Clement VII increases the likelihood that they are the same man. There is no connection with the earlier Egidius de Morino named in the texts of both *Apollinis* and *Musicalis* and to whom the little motet treatise *De modo componendi tenores motettorum* is usually attributed. Doubts are here cast on his authorship (Chs. 1, 16).

De la Porte is not an uncommon name in the fourteenth century, and there can be no certain identification. Several clerics named J. de Porta are documented in the second half of the century, and it is not always clear whether the references are to the same man. Hoppin and Clercx propose two candidates: one is a request on 5 January 1363 from Marguerite, daughter of the king of France, for a benefice for a Johannes de Porta from the diocese of Arras and clerk of her chapel.[25] The other is the conferral on 20 February 1379 by Clement VII *motu proprio* of a canonicate with prebend at the cathedral of Chartres on a Johannes de Porta, priest of the diocese of Saint-Malo, and secretary to the pope's 'devoted son', the Breton soldier Olivier de Clisson.[26] This secretary with a papal connection was from another diocese. There is no reason to think he is the

---

[22] CMM 39, pp. xliii–xlv. For a differently texted concordance in **Leiden2720** see Ch. 30 n. 55.
[23] Details in CMM 39, p. xliv. All three songs are similar in style and published in CMM 53/1.
[24] Hoppin and Clercx, 'Notes biographiques', 87ff., further discussed by Günther in CMM 39, p. xliii.
[25] Hoppin and Clercx, 'Notes biographiques', 82, citing Fierens, *Suppliques d'Urbain V*, no. 495.
[26] Valois, *La France et le Grand Schisme*, i. 251 and n. 5. Hanquet, 'Documents', no. 2335, vacant by the death of the cardinal of Thérouanne; this was Gilles de Montaigu; see below.

ALMA POLIS /AXE POLI   365

Johannes de Porta who became the parish priest of Annecy in the diocese of Langres when his rectorship of the parish of S. Maria de Noseriis in the diocese of Vienne passed to one Matheus Gralhonis on 16 February 1363.[27] A Johannes de Porta is listed as a canon of Laon 1331–70, but he had already died when he was succeeded by Petrus de Bouconvilla (1371–95) on 29 September 1369.[28] This man was too old, and died too early, to be identified as the poet of a motet of a decade or two later.

None of these is as well documented as a Johannes de Porta de Annoniaco (Annonay) in the diocese of Vienne, who was chaplain, domestic familiar and, evidently, secretary to the French cardinal and diplomat Pierre Bertrand de Colombier (1299–1361), nephew and namesake of Cardinal Pierre Bertrand of Annonay.[29] He is a tempting candidate for the poet of *Alma polis* because of his literary associations as a diarist and associate of Petrarch. The younger Pierre Bertrand was promoted cardinal of Santa Susanna by Clement VI in 1344, and became Cardinal Bishop of Ostia in 1353. He was sent on a number of important missions, including peace negotiations with England, and on 9 February 1355 was sent to induce Charles IV of Germany to come to Rome for coronation as emperor.[30] Johannes de Porta kept a lengthy diary of this expedition, including reporting the cardinal's meeting with Petrarch, and the fact that Petrarch had earlier been crowned with the laurel wreath.[31] He may have come to the attention of the Cardinal through their shared origin in Annonay (Ardèche), perhaps as a young man. He is last documented as an executor and beneficiary of the cardinal's will of 5 July 1361, so he died after that date.[32] After the death of his cardinal, he would have needed other employment. He could have known Petrarch during his period in Avignon up to June 1353. One of Petrarch's closest friends, the Roman nobleman Angelo Tossetti, his Lelio, was (together with Porta) in the entourage of the cardinal sent to organise the coronation of Charles IV, as coordinator of the trip to Italy and of relations with the Roman authorities. Porta witnessed and described the coronation with the laurel wreath of the Florentine poet Giovanni Zanobi da Strada by the emperor Charles IV in Pisa on 24 May 1355. Zanobi was a grammar teacher who then exercised various public functions in and around Florence; he was in Naples with Niccolò Acciaioli, but in 1357 he was in Montecassino as vicar of the Florentine republic. In 1359 Zanobi moved to Avignon,

---

[27] *Urbain V . . . Lettres Communes*, iii, no. 1978.

[28] Millet, *Les Chanoines*, 515, 400–1. *Urbain V. . . Lettres communes*, viii, ed. Hayez, no. 24230 of 29.9.1369 confirms that this Johannes de Porta was dead by that date.

[29] I am grateful to Elena Abramov-van Rijk for locating this promising candidate and alerting me to these references to him, now published as Abramov-van Rijk, 'The Roman Experience'; to Julian Gardner for more sleuthing and bibliography, and to Andrew Wathey for confirming the interpretation of some documents.

[30] These included negotiating the marriage of the duke of Normandy (later John the Good) with Bonne of Luxembourg. In 1335 he became bishop of Nevers and in 1339 of Arras.

[31] Page 5 of the diary of J. de Porta: '1354 scriptus per me Iohannem Porta de Annoniaco Viennensis dyocesis, capellanum et familiarem domesticum commensalem reverendissimi in Christo patris et domini domini Petri [Bertrandi de Columbario Viennensis dyocesis] miseratione divina Ostiensis et Velletrensis episcopi [and cardinal]'. Johannes Porta de Annoniaco, *Liber de coronatione*. Pages 115–16 report the poetic coronation of Petrarch, which took place in the Campidoglio in Rome in 1341 by Robert of Anjou: 'Florentie florem verum et toto in terrarum orbe notabilem, ymo verius unicum singularem poetam, qui nullus maior natus umquam esse creditur, dominum scilicet Franciscum Petrarcam.'

[32] 'Quo anno natus sit, ignoramus; mortuus est post 1361. lul. 5, quo die eius ut inter vivos existentis mentio fit in testamento cardinalis [i.e. Pierre Bertrand de Colombier] domini sui.' Duchesne, *Histoire de tous les cardinaux*, 359ff. Against this identification is the absence of any documentation after 1361, which is too early for the motet; but in other respects he is well qualified. Reports that he died in 1369 seem to represent a confusion with the canon of Laon.

366 THE MUSICIAN MOTETS

becoming a papal secretary, responsible for relations with Florence, and died there in 1361 during the plague. Thus two Florentine poets strongly bound to the Avignon court may both have been personally known to this Johannes de Porta. Moreover, Petrarch's connections with Augustinians have been documented, and his *Secretum* was written in Avignon between 1347 and 1353 in the form of dialogues between the poet and St Augustine.[33] But in order to be a poet for a motet not earlier than the 1380s, he would have to have served the cardinal as a very young man. This is possible if he was born in the early 1330s.

Hoppin and Clercx identify Johannes Desiderii as the author of a short mensural treatise in **Seville25**, and further identify him with a Johannes Desiderii de Latines.[34] They failed to note, as Karen Cook has now shown, that the author of this treatise is identified within the text as 'Magister Johannes Pipudi, canonicus Sancti Desiderii avinionensis' (canon of Saint Didier in Avignon). The name of Johannes Desiderii de Latines seems to derive from his father, Désiré de Latines, not from a canonicate held in Avignon. Cook observes that Pipudi is unlikely to have been referred to as Johannes Desiderii rather than as Johannes Pipudi. Moreover, Johannes Pipudi or Pipardi was a cleric from the diocese of Cambrai, and in 1378 was in the household of Cardinal Johannes de Blauzac, formerly Bishop of Sabina. Johannes Desiderii de Latines, on the other hand, was from the diocese of Liège, and in the same year recorded in the household of a different cardinal. On 15 November 1378 Gilles de Montaigu, Cardinal of Thérouanne, addressed a supplication to Clement VII in favour of his 'dilectorum sociorum et capellanorum ac clericorum, familiarum suorum domesticorum continuorum commensalium'; these include Johannes Desiderii, 'dilecto suo', a cleric from the diocese of Liège, who already held a canonicate with prebend at Namur. On 6 May 1410 he is still mentioned as canon-singer of Notre Dame de Dinant.[35] As Cook points out: 'If the Johannes Desiderii of the motet is in fact Johannes Desiderii de Latines, then neither can also be the theorist Johannes Pipardi.'[36] It is this Johannes Desiderii de Latines, and not Pipardi, who would be a strong candidate for identification with the musician named in the motet, but for the fact that he has no known Augustinian affiliation.

Two teachers named 'Johannes Forestarii' are named on 9 November 1403 in a roll presented to Benedict XIII by the masters of the faculty of arts of the university of Paris, but no firm identification is possible.[37] Harrison vernacularises him as Jehan de Vorst.[38]

Günther leans towards accepting Hoppin and Clercx's suggestions of an Avignon cleric 'petro tenoro' who resigned a benefice in 1362 for Petrus Amatori, and of Theobaldus Furnerii, a singer for Urban V in 1367 and Gregory XI in 1371.[39] She notes

---

[33] Mariani, *Il Petrarca*.

[34] Hoppin and Clercx, 'Notes biographiques', 81 n. 7.

[35] Ibid., 81, cited from the records for Sainte-Croix of Liège.

[36] Cook, *Music Theory in Late Medieval Avignon*, 65–67. He may have been related to Henri Desiderii (Dezier) de Latinia (Latunna) or de Latines (d. by 1423), also from Liège, a singer in the chapel of Pope Boniface IX in Rome, possibly also of Urban VI. Henricus succeeded another singer of Boniface IX, the Carthusian Joannes Sapens of Malines (d. 1391), to a canonry at Liège cathedral in about 1374, when he was described as a 'familiaris commensalis' of cardinal Petrus Corsini, bishop of Florence, and is also reported as a canon and singer at the collegiate church of Saint-Paul in Liège, where he composed an office for the Visitation. Di Bacco and Nádas, 'Papal Chapels', 89. See also Nádas and Cuthbert, *Ars nova*, 51–55.

[37] Hoppin and Clercx, 'Notes biographiques', 82.

[38] *Musicorum collegio*, p. xii.

[39] CMM 39, p. xliv. On Furnerii see also Di Bacco and Nádas, 'Verso uno "stile internazionale"', 9 n. 5.

that he held the same position in 1373–74. No further convincing identifications have been put forward.

All these tentative identifications are consistent with a dating of *Alma polis* towards the end of the century. Günther also pointed out a few of the more obvious textual connections between *Alma polis* and *Apollinis* while suggesting that imitation of the older work might not have been intentional;[40] those connections are here taken further in support of a highly purposeful relationship of the younger to the older motet.

Appendix
Commentary Notes to ⊙ Example 19.1, *Alma polis religio/Axe poli cum artica/[Et] in ore eorum*

In the commentaries, notes relating to the numbering of the upper parts are usually in breves, but here in semibreves because of the different mensurations between the parts.

Triplum: 39–42, 96–99, 153–56 ♦♦ |♦♦♦ ♦♦ read as 3 3 | 1 1 1 2 1. The same rhythm occurs at 47–50, 104–7, 161–64 (neutral) transcribed as suggested by some groupings; but both passages could be read as 3 2 1 |1 2(alt) 2 1. 42–44 ♦♦ ■ ♦ read as 2 1 | 5 1, but it could be 3 | 1 5 1. The last ♦ is not present at the corresponding places 101 and 158. 174–76, 222–24, 270–72 ♦♦ ♦ ♦♦♦ read as 2 1 3 | 1 1 1 but it could be 2 1 2 1 |1 2alt. The grouping of 174 is neutral; 223 is grouped ♦♦ ♦♦ ♦♦, suggesting the latter reading, but in 271 the *b♭* is written after the *d* ♦, suggesting the grouping used here. 191–92, 239–40, 287–88 ♦ ♦♦♦ actual 3 | 1 1 1 but it could be 2 1| 1 2alt. The groupings of 191–92 and 239–40 are neutral, but 287–88 has a clear gap after the S, suggesting the grouping used here.

Motetus: 4–9, 61–66, 118–123 ■ ♦ ♦ | ■ ♦ ♦ here treated as 5 1 3 | 5 1 3; space after the ♦ at 5, 62, 65, dot after 119, eliminating 6 1 2 | 6 1 2; 31–33, 88–90, 145–47 ♦ ♦♦ . ♦ ♦ ♦; although only present at 31–32, the dot prevents 1 2 1 1 1 3. Treating it as a dot of syncopation yields 1 3 1 . 1 1 2, the reading used here, further encouraged by the grouping at 145. It would have been clearer with a second dot after the first ♦. An alternative reading would be for the dot to start a new group, requiring alteration of the last minim: 1 2 1 · 1 2alt 2. ♦ ♦♦ · ♦ ♦ ♦ In either case the last ♦ is imperfect, which is possible, as it is followed by ♦.

---

[40] CMM 39, p. xlv.

20

Sub Arturo plebs/Fons citharizancium/
In omnem terram and its Musicians

Sub Arturo is the only motet of the group that is unmistakably English, and it has attracted more scholarly attention than the others. It is a brilliant and exuberant piece, extremely cleverly constructed, and with a kind of earthy energy more characteristic of English than of French composition at the time.[1] For the transcription, see ▶ Example 20.1. Commentary notes are in the Appendix to this chapter. Although the use of isorhythm between *taleae* has long been associated with the importation of French influence into England, this motet differs in several respects from anything known in England or France from the fourteenth century. This exceptional and unquestionably English motet names fourteen English musicians in the triplum and seven heroes from the history and mythology of music in the motetus, including, with mock modesty, last, lowest and least, its composer, J. Alanus.[2]

Texts and translation by David Howlett (slightly adapted):

Triplum		Rhymes	Words	Syllables
Sub Arturo plebs uallata		a	4	8
plaudat melos; laus ornata		a	4	8
psallatur Altissimo.		b	2	7
Anglis conferentur grata		a	3	8
euentu piissimo.	5	b	2	7
En milicia cum clero		c	4	8
floret; musicorum uero		c	3	8
chorus odas iubilat,		d	3	7
e quibus modo sincero		c	4	8
J. de Corbe emicat,	10	d	4	7
cuius non preuisas posco		e	4	8
res, quas **J. de Alto Bosco**		e	6	8
reserat theorica,		f	2	7
qua fulgens uernat, ut nosco,		e	5	8
T. Marconi practica.	15	f	3	7

[1] It was recorded by Musica Reservata on Philips (1969), now available on YouTube, a performance in my view unsurpassed by more recent (and more sedate) performances on Hyperion by the Orlando Consort (CDA68132) and the Binchois Consort (CDA68170).

[2] *Alani* is given within the **Chantilly** text in the genitive but in **Q15** as *Alanus*. In both appearances of the triplum in **Q15** the composer heading is given as *Jo Alani*.

The Motet in the Late Middle Ages. Margaret Bent, Oxford University Press. © Oxford University Press 2023.
DOI: 10.1093/so/9780190063771.003.0021

THE MUSICIAN MOTETS

Piis placent ac tirannis		g	4	8
res **Ricardi Blith, Johannis**		g	4	8
necnon **de Exonia,**		h	3	7
arte cuius multis annis		g	4	8
fulsit Cantuaria.	20	h	2	7
Sed **G. Mughe,** radix florum,		i	5	8
det generibus melorum;		i	3	8
Edmundus de Buria		j	3	7
basis aurea tenorum		i	3	8
est, quem fouet curia.	25	j	4	7
Princeps bellicus probauit		k		8
quas **Oxwick G.** res creauit,		k	5	8
rutilantes oculo,		l	2	7
Episwich J. quas gustauit		k	4	8
mire uocis modulo.	30	l	3	7
Flos Oxonie miratur		m	3	8
Nicholaus, qui uocatur		m	3	8
de Uado Famelico;		n	3	7
E. de Miresco iungatur		m	4	8
his triplo mirifico.	35	n	3	7
Prepollet **G. de Horarum**		o	4	8
Fonte lira; uox non parum		o	5	8
mulcet aures **Simonis**		p	3	7
Clementis, os cuius clarum		o	4	8
manus nitet organis.	40	p	3	7
Practizat **Adam Leuita**		q	3	8
precellenter. Quorum uita		q	3	8
sana diu uigeat,		r	3	7
ut et illis, qua finita,		q	5	8
porta celi pateat.	45	r	3	7
		18	157	342

Motetus

Fons citharizancium		a	2	7
ac organizancium		a	2	7
Tubal predicatur,		b	2	6
musice primordia		c	2	7
sculpans ut historia	5	c	3	7
Genesis testatur.		b	2	6
Pondera Pictagore		d	2	7
numerorum decore		d	2	7
artis uernant legem,		e	3	6

quam rimans Boecius	10	f	3	7
propalauit latius		f	2	7
regum laudans Regem.		e	3	6
Doctrina Gregorii		g	2	7
gesta Dei Filii		g	3	7
canit omnis ordo;	15	h	3	6
Guido fons inicia		i	3	7
lineas et spacia		i	3	7
dedit monocordo;		h	3	6
sed Franco theorice		j	3	7
dat mensuram musice	20	j	3	7
quam colores ligant.		k	3	6
Fontes hi sunt seculi		l	4	7
adhuc quorum riuuli		l	3	7
cuncta regna rigant.		k	3	6
Huius pes triplarii	25	g	3	7
bis sub emiolii		g	3	7
normis recitatur,		b	2	6
ut hi pulsent dominum		m	4	7
quorum numen nominum		m	3	7
triplo modulatur.	30	b	2	6
Illis licet infimus		n	3	7
J. Alanus minimus		n	3	7
sese recommendat,		o	2	6
quatenus ab inuidis		p	3	7
ipsum sonis ualidis	35	p	3	7
horum laus defendat.		o	3	6
			18	97	240

Triplum: Let the people protected by Arthur (also 'under the North Star', near the seven-starred constellations *Ursa Major* and *Ursa Minor*, 'the Bear', which is the etymological root of the name 'Arthur') applaud song; let embellished praise be sung to the Most High; pleasing things will be conferred on the English in a most holy result. Lo, the military flourishes with the clergy; the chorus of musicians, moreover, shouts its odes, from whom John of Corby shines out in unblemished fashion, whose unprecedented compositions I invoke, which John Hauboys unlocks in his Book of Theory, from which the radiating practice of Thomas Marcon springs, as I know. The compositions of Richard Blithe please holy people and kings, also those of John of Exeter, with whose art Canterbury radiated for many years. But let William Mugge, the root of the flowers, contribute to the types of songs; Edmund of Bury is the golden foundation of the tenors, whom the court favours. The warlike prince approved the compositions which William Oxwick created, glowing golden to the eye, which John Ipswich savoured with the melody of his wonderful voice. The flower of Oxford is

THE MUSICIAN MOTETS

wondered at, Nicholas who is called 'of Hungerford'. Let Edmund de Miresco be joined to them in a wondrous threesome (or triplum). William of Tideswell excels on the lyre. The voice of Simon Clement soothes the ears not a little, the bone of whose hand shines bright upon the organ. Adam the Deacon performs excellently. May the healthful life of these men flourish for a long time, so that for them, when (this life is) finished, the gate of heaven may lie open.

Motetus: Tubal (*recte* Jubal) is proclaimed the source of harp-playing and organ-playing, fashioning the beginnings of music as the story of Genesis relates. The weights of Pythagoras by the beauty of numbers make the law of art spring, which Boethius examining opened out more widely, praising the King of kings. By the teaching of Gregory every order sings the deeds of the Son of God. Guido (of Arezzo) the source gave principles, lines, and spaces to the monochord. But Franco (of Cologne) gives to the theory of music measure which the colours bind. These are the springs of the age, whose rivers still water all the realms. The foot (*pes*) of this three-part piece is (sung once and) repeated twice under the rules of hemiolus so that those, the majesty of whose names is sung in the triplum, may importune the lord. To them the lowest, least, J. Alanus recommends himself so that the praise of these men may with mighty sounds defend him from envious men.

General Remarks

Musicorum celebrated seven musicians: here twice seven, surely going one better not only than *Musicorum*, but than the *bis sex* ('twice six') of *Apollinis*, and nodding at the seven *taleae* of *Musicalis* which go one better than the six of *Apollinis*. The nature and dating of *Sub Arturo* depends on the possible identification of the most recent musicians named in the triplum. Dates between 1358 and the early 1370s have been suggested, but even the 1370s now seems to me too early.

At the time the edition in PMFC 5 was made, *Sub Arturo* was known only from two Continental sources dating from forty to fifty years later than the 1370s. If the motet was indeed that old, this would be an exceptionally long transmission life: first, **Chantilly**, now thought to have been copied in the 1410s,[3] where *Sub Arturo* takes its place in a choice collection including the most sophisticated and arcanely constructed motets then current (compositionally at least a generation beyond Machaut), and second, **Q15**, where it was first copied in the early 1420s. If dating from the 1370s, it would be by several decades the oldest composition in the first layer of that manuscript and, moreover, was still valued and kept alive there in a partial recopy as late as the 1430s, and that by a compiler ruthless in discarding music that was no longer in use. **Chantilly** is in most respects less reliable than **Q15** with respect to pitches and rhythms. *Sub Arturo* turned up more recently in **Yox**, a fragmentary English manuscript of *c.* 1400 or the very early

---

[3] Plumley and Stone, *Codex Chantilly*, 179–82, carefully consider Günther's suggestion of a possible Parisian origin *c.* 1415, but offer an alternative possibility of copying in the orbit of the Pisan popes between 1408 and 1419.

fifteenth century, on a recto containing the motetus and tenor.[4] This may be the oldest source. The motet is perhaps tellingly absent from earlier sources of fourteenth-century motets, **Ivrea**, **Cambrai** and **Trém**.

The Motetus Text

Playing not only on the wide-ranging A–Z of *Apollinis/Zodiacum*, but also on the explicit Apocalyptic content of the motetus of *Musicorum collegio/In templo Dei*, Alanus's motetus gives a unique and long-range potted history of music, beginning with 'Tubal'. All three manuscripts give Tubal, following a long-standing medieval confusion between Jubal, 'father of singing to the cithara and organ' and his brother Tubalcain, the hammerer who came to be conflated with Pythagoras's alleged discovery in the smithy and associated with music as the *fons citharizancium ac organizancium*, aligned with the words of the psalmist.[5] The line 'Genesis testatur', the authority for the mythical origins of music, names the first book of the Bible in response to a previous motet's invocation of the last book: line 15 of the motetus of *Musicorum collegio* is 'testatur Apocalipsis'. Pythagoras and Boethius appear in the same order as in *Apollinis*.

Alanus's roll of honour of seven 'greats' praises, in chronological order, 'Tubal', Pythagoras, Boethius, Gregory the Great, Guido of Arezzo,[6] and Franco of Cologne, culminating outrageously with himself, albeit with mock modesty. As the only authority still living, he casts himself as the seventh and last of the great authorities since earliest times.[7] He does so ('infimus J. Alanus minimus sese recommendat') borrowing the authorial form of self-reference of B. de Cluny, composer of *Apollinis eclipsatur/Zodiacum*: 'recommendans se subdit omnibus'. In both cases (as also in *Alma polis*) this formula is in the motetus. In three of the motets, *Apollinis*, *Musicorum* and *Sub Arturo*, the motetus in each case cross-refers to the names listed in the triplum. All this suggests that the composers wrote their own texts or at least closely controlled them.

---

[4] For **Yox** see Ch. 22 and Wathey, *Manuscripts . . . Supplement 1 to RISM*.

[5] Genesis 4: 21–22: 'Iubal ipse fuit pater canentium cithara et organo. Sella quoque genuit Thubalcain qui fuit malleator et faber in cuncta opera aeris et ferri.' Since it was Jubal and not Tubalcain who is named in Genesis as the source (there 'father', here 'fount') of 'citharising' and 'organising', there can be no doubt who is meant; however, the legend was confused in popular transmission, and in view of the strong tradition in favour of Tubal, especially in sources known to musicians, 'Tubal' is retained here. Jacobus, *Speculum* I.VI attests that the confusion goes back to Isidore, also citing Petrus Comestor and Josephus: 'Moyses, secundum Isidorum, repertorem musicae artis dicit fuisse Thubal de stirpe Cain ante diluvium. Hic enim Genesis [4: 20–22] dicitur fuisse pater canentium in cithara et organo, non quia dicta repererit instrumenta, ut ibidem dicit Magister in Historiis, quae longo post tempore reperta sunt, sed quia aliquas repererit musicales consonantias illis applicatas postmodum instrumentis.'

[6] Cf *Quatuor Principalia* 2, ch. 3: 'Deinde fuerat Guido monachus, qui compositor erat gammatis, quod monacordum nuncupatur; voces vero in eo continentes, in lineis et spatiis distribuit' (Aluas, 'The *Quatuor principalia musicae*'). Alanus's six authorities are listed in the same order in chs. 2–3, except for Gregory, who is added before Guido in *Principale* 3, ch. 4.

[7] David Howlett observed that the poet 'widens the range of mythological reference by alluding in the first line of the triplum to King Arthur, for knowledge of whom the primary source was Geoffrey of Monmouth's *Historia Regum Britanniae*. The diction of the motetus derives in part from Geoffrey's preface, in which he hopes for protection from *inuidis*.

374 THE MUSICIAN MOTETS

Stanza 5 of the motetus states the proportions resulting from applying three successive mensuration signs to the tenor: the tenor or *pes* (a word used for older medieval English motet tenors) is to be repeated twice by hemiola (3:2): 'Huius pes triplarii | bis sub emiolii | normis recitatur', that is, the three statements are to stand in the geometric proportion 9:6:4, reducing by a double hemiola. But this describes the resulting overall proportions, not the method by which they are arrived at; the three statements are derived not by diminution (which would require the longs and breves to be substituted by values at the next level down) but by mensural reinterpretation of a homographic tenor under the mensuration signs $\odot$, $\mathbb{C}$, C, yielding respectively breves of 9, 6 and 4 minims of the upper parts, which are in $\mathbb{C}$ throughout.[8] The mensural procedure yields the proportioned result here only because the composer has taken care to notate the tenor entirely in (imperfect) breves and longs, avoiding semibreves or minims, the values below the level of the breve that would have required alteration and imperfection at the levels of tempus and prolation, resulting in mensural discrepancies between statements in perfect and imperfect mensurations, and possibly in overall proportional inexactness. Only because no value shorter than the breve is used do no relative internal differences of rhythm arise from the tenor of these mensural rereadings (unlike Dunstaple's mensural tenors with overall 6:4:3 proportion; see Ch. 25).

Text–Music Correspondence

Sub Arturo is the only one of the five musician motets whose texts are unambiguously stanzaic.[9] The triplum comprises nine five-line stanzas each with syllables and rhymes 8a, 8a, 7b, 8a, 7b. Nines are important here. There are nine *taleae* (3×3), and nine triplum stanzas. The six motetus stanzas, albeit of different length, stand in hemiolic relationship to the nine of the triplum, again reflecting the motet's hemiolic underpinnings. The total number of lines, $45 + 36$ ($5 \times 9 + 4 \times 9$), is 81 (9^2, compared to the 12^2 of *Apollinis*, *Musicorum* and, by one count, of *Sub Arturo*: see below). The triplum and motetus lines thus relate 5:4, which add to nine; 45 exceeds 36 by 9.

There is a close *talea–stanza* correspondence: despite the successive reductions between the three *color* statements, each of the nine *taleae* receives one of the nine (equal, five-line) triplum stanzas, with no overlaps or anticipations. This results in an audible acceleration of text delivery in the second and third *colores*, which adds to the excitement produced by the faster tenor and the consequently increased pace of harmonic movement. Of the six motetus stanzas, the first three are assigned one each to the first

---

[8] The tenor's 144 (3×48) variable breves are equivalent to the 153 breves of $\mathbb{C}$ of the upper parts, a paradoxical juxtaposition; see further below. For other examples of compositional/performance instructions embedded in the text see *O amicus* (Ch. 22); for descriptions of the skill and completeness of the work see *Zodiacum* (three times the number of Pythagoras, i.e. 3×10, the number of triplum lines, is made equal to the basis of Boethius, i.e. 12, the number of lines in the motetus; the texts of Tr and motetus take up the same musical time) and *Musicorum collegio* (take nothing away, add nothing).

[9] The voice *Psallentes zinzugia* added to *Apollinis* is also stanzaic, unlike the existing texts of *Apollinis*, and is probably likewise English in origin. Günther presents *Alma polis* also as stanzaic, CMM 39, p. xlv (its motetus, *Axe poli*, rightly, in couplets), and with emendation this is indeed possible, perhaps corroborated by the close correspondence of *talea* and stanza in that motet, as in *Sub Arturo*.

three *taleae* of *color* 1, also with no overlap or anticipation.[10] The remaining six *taleae* (*colores* 2 and 3) receive half a stanza each, with an anticipatory syllable at the end of each *talea*, thus making for slight irregularity in matching corresponding syllables in successive isorhythmic *taleae*. The setting is largely syllabic, though there is some room for alternative placements; some discrepancies seem deliberate, as between motetus breves 75–76, 91–92, to avoid breaking a word with a rest. All parts are strictly iso-rhythmic throughout the three *taleae within* each *color* statement. There is only one small deviation, at the end of the final triplum *talea*: for *porta celi* (at triplum B150) a semibreve of *taleae* 1 and 2 is broken into two minims in *talea* 3.[11] This enables the two words to be pronounced without splitting *ce-li* with a rest. Interruption of words by rests is largely but not entirely avoided, but increases in the final *color*, where the fast syllabic setting on minims with hockets is often punctuated by minim rests.

The motet was made virtually contrafact-proof by the tight and ingenious fit of words to music, largely syllabic; by the composer's self-naming in the motetus, its cross-reference to the names in the triplum; and by the statement of the resulting tenor proportions ('twice by hemiola'). Solmisation puns have been noted in other motets, sometimes with notated signs, as in *Musicorum*, where *mira* falls on *mi–fa* (Ch. 18). Sub Arturo's *mire* has a signed *mi*, but the pun is not continued. Rhyming *mi–fa* solmisation puns also occur here on 85 *ligant*, 40 *rimans* [*sic*].

Music: Tenor

In omnem terram ('into all the earth') are the tenor words of both *Apollinis* and *Sub Arturo*, as noted already. But despite the same words, each tenor uses a different chant. *In omnem terram* has many liturgical placements and different melodies (at least for the apostles Thomas, Simon and Jude) but, because of a long melisma, the only words associated with the portion used are *In omnem ter-*, suggesting also a pun on 'three' (cf. *numerus ter* in its motetus text) and the three *color* statements of each tenor. The tenor chant of *Sub Arturo* was identified by Günther as a slightly shortened and transposed version of the first antiphon for the first Nocturn for the Common of Apostles, those ambassadors sent out to the ends of the earth.[12] The tenor *color* corresponds to a more extensive passage from this well-known psalm, whose words are given more fully in **Q15**: 'In omnem terram exivit sonus eorum et in fines orbis [terre verba eorum]' (Their sound is gone out into all lands and

---

[10] The conspicuous tribrachic group of six syllabic minims at the end of each of the first motetus *taleae* perhaps reflects a similar verbal rush before the hockets in each *talea* of *Musicalis*.

[11] This introduction of an extra minim near the end, if compositional and not editorial-scribal, may contribute to the minim play in this motet (*J. Alanus minimus*). Is it, in part, a repayment of the minim dropped from the opening rhythmic quotation from *Apollinis* (Fig. 20.1 below)? Is that dropped minim also or instead reflected in the foreshortening of the final triplum *talea*? Minim puns might be at work here (also in *Sub Arturo*'s neighbour in **Yox**, *O amicus/Precursoris* (Ch. 22), in turn punningly related to the verbal form of the authorial signature, 'J. Alanus minimus sese recommendat', itself borrowed from *Apollinis*: 'recommendans se' (*minimus* is set to the first three notes of ♦ ♦ · ♦ ■ ♦): an error here in Bent, *Two 14th-Century Motets*.

[12] Günther, CMM 39, pp. liii–iv, gives four versions, none of which corresponds closely. Alice Clark, 'Concordare cum materia', H31 (228) gives more chants, but this confirms Günther's assessment that the chant has been adapted. The *taleae* are so arranged that each ends with a stepwise descent to facilitate cadence formation.

[their words] to the ends of the earth). In **Yox** the tenor is labelled not 'In omnem terram' but its continuation, 'exivit sonus eorum', and in **Chantilly** the tenor is labelled 'Tenor de sub archuro', without reference to the chant. Günther suggested that it might be a hitherto untraceable melody to *In omnem terram*,[13] but the tenor chant has now been identified by Kévin Roger: see Chapter 19.

The mode II chant tenor of *Sub Arturo* on *d* has its recitation tone on *f*. In the motet it is transposed up a fifth with recitation on *c*, where both tenors end; several melodic cells are common to the two chants, in addition to the repeated *c*s. See Example 20.2.[14]

Ex. 20.2 Tenors of *Apollinis* and *Sub Arturo*. Shared notes are bracketed and *taleae* are labelled

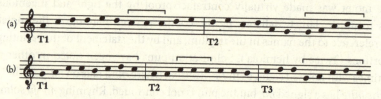

The last note-group of the *Apollinis* tenor, *g a c d c* (uninterrupted by rests), is contrived also to be the last five notes of the portion of the different chant selected for the *Sub Arturo* tenor. In both motets, this note-group ends each of the three *color* statements, and hence the whole piece, making a striking and audible piece of quotation and connection. In addition, the first *color* of *Sub Arturo* presents the same group, interrupted by the notes *c b*. Although both chant segments end on *c*, the *Apollinis* tenor is its middle voice, and the final sonority is *f c f*, whereas in *Sub Arturo* it is the lowest voice, and the final sonority is *c g c*. Comparable affinities between the tenors of *Apollinis* and *Alma* were noted in Chapter 19, yet another way in which these motets nod at each other and their predecessors.

The tenor *color* of *Sub Arturo*, notated only once, is to be stated three times. Each *talea* consists of eight notes, four longs and four breves, plus four breves rest, yielding a total of eight imperfect longs (16 breves). Three 16-breve *taleae* in each of three *colores* yield a total of 144 breves (16 × 3 = 48; 48 × 3 = 144). These breves, however, are of successively reducing length, as prescribed by successive mensuration signs, requiring breves of respectively 9, 6 and 4 minims. This is not diminution, because the tenor notes retain their status as longs and breves throughout; diminution as strictly defined in fourteenth-century terms involves substitution of the next note-level down.[15] The acceleration is achieved by mensural redefinition: in **Q15** by vertically aligned mensuration signs ☉, ℂ, C, and in **Chantilly** by the equivalent verbal canon: 'Canon primo de tempore perfecto maioris, secundo de tempore imperfecto

---

[13] CMM 39, p. xlvi compares the tenors of *Alma polis* and *Apollinis* with the Offertory. The source chant of the *Apollinis* tenor exists in many variant versions and on various pitches, from which it is transposed up an octave, fourth or fifth. Clark, 'Concordare cum materia', H9.
[14] Cf. **Paris279**, which starts *cd*; the others start *dd*. Shared notes are bracketed and *taleae* are labelled.
[15] Bent, 'The Myth'.

maioris, tertio de tempore imperfecto minoris.' This is written by the main scribe at the foot of the page. A later hand has added in cursive the same canon under the tenor itself, but supplying *prolacionis* after each clause. In all three manuscripts the tenor is marked with :|||: for threefold repetition; in **Q15** these strokes are written as dragma-like forms.

Music: Upper Parts

The counterpoint is ingeniously managed throughout, achieving a higher level of consonance at the minim level than in most compositions of around 1400. Each upper part makes good counterpoint independently with the tenor, as do the two parts with each other. The motetus occasionally underpins what would otherwise be an exposed fourth with the tenor.[16] Parallel seconds at B76 are in both sources and the voices have a certain individual logic. However, they stand out, without obvious purpose, and I have emended triplum *b a* to *c b*. Some ambiguities surround the final cadence. A breve rest is notated in **Yox** and **Chantilly** before the final breve of the motetus (in **Chantilly** the final is a maxima), completing the motetus *talea*, and sounding the final *g* after the triplum and tenor have made their final cadence on *c*. This rest and breve are replaced in **Q15** with a coloured (void) long, so that the motetus coincides with the tenor at the final cadence. In the triplum, **Chantilly** (but again, not **Q15**) follows the last (necessarily perfect) semibreve of its truncated *talea* with a minim rest at B152. This appears to imperfect the final S, but it cannot do so without (unacceptably) making the final triplum *c* coincide with the motetus $f\sharp$.[17] The rest enables the triplum to cadence with the tenor; otherwise **Q15**'s penultimate triplum note would need to be extended by a minim.

The total tenor length of 144 breves connects it to *Apollinis* and *Musicorum*. But in *Sub Arturo* the tenor breves are of different lengths, whereas the triplum remains in C throughout, in the transcription with 154 numbered breves including the final long, but since 131 and 142 are half-bars, the final count for the triplum is actually 153 breves, which is satisfyingly divisible by 3, and the number of the miraculous draft of fishes (John 21: 1–14). The final *color* has an unusual and highly ingenious lateral displacement of the triplum against both other parts, a 'creeping' shift of alignment: the three iterations of the triplum *talea*, still strictly isorhythmic within that *color*, are successively shorter by a minim (63 minims = 9 × 7) than those of the motetus and tenor (64 minims = 8^2). It progressively gains on those parts by a minim in each *talea*. The motetus coincides with the triplum in the first *talea* of the final *color* before this foreshortening. Its *taleae* continue to be coterminous with the tenor's, but while it remains in C against the tenor's C, there is considerable disturbance from syncopation, caused mainly by coloration, and by dint of the final

---

[16] At breves 17, 65, 84, 109, 116, 146.

[17] Commentary in Appendix to this chapter. The final sonority of motetus and tenor is notated as eight minims, the triplum technically with twelve minims, a minor and allowable untidiness given the virtuosic combination of mensurations in the final section. Such anomalies in the length of a final note are quite common; see also *Alma polis*, and on endings in Ch. 1.

378 THE MUSICIAN MOTETS

coloration group in each *talea*, which exceeds a ¢ count by four minims, to align it with the imperfect tempus of the tenor.[18]

Not only do we hear the interplay, in excited cross-rhythms, of the major prolation triplum with the coloration syncopations of the motetus and the minor prolation of the tenor, but the triplum relates differently to the two other parts at each iteration. No other fourteenth-century motet even approaches this complexity. Something comparable occurs in the mensuration canon in **OH**, Credo no. 75, and the complete void-notation Credo *Omni tempore* (in **Yox**, the same manuscript as the English source of *Sub Arturo*: see Ch. 23), where equal-length segments in the upper parts are combined with non-coincident mensural transformation and diminution in the lower parts.[19] The effect is to heighten excitement towards the end, to demonstrate virtuosity, and to develop with minims the minim pun ('J. Alanus minimus'). At the very point where the composer is about to play with time by foreshortening the triplum by one minim at the end of the first truncated *talea*, he announces this emphatically with the words 'triplo modulatur' in the motetus, and 'his triplo mirifico' directly preceding the first triplum *talea* statement in its new alignment. The now displaced second *talea* starts with the anticipatory syllable '**Pre**-pollet G. de horarum fonte', 'Tideswell', again playing on *fons*, and on time (*horarum*). It ends with Simon Clemens's shining hand on the organ and coincides with the motetus signature of 'J. Alanus minimus'. Other fourteenth-century motet tenors subject to mensural reinterpretation combine perfect and imperfect tempus between the parts, but usually in such a way that there is a regular coincidence of bars, as there is in *Alma polis* despite the irregularities. Even *Inter densas*, with the extreme mensural manipulations of its tenor (see Ch. 1), achieves more regular coordination than in the artfully contrived last *color* of *Sub Arturo*.

Grammatically, the triplum and motetus of *Sub Arturo* are mostly self-contained, but at a few places (for example, breves 17–18, 65, 84, 109, 116, 129, 146) the motetus rather than the tenor underpins the counterpoint. Consonance is handled very deftly, much more so than in *Alma polis*, and conspicuously so at the minim level in the rhythmically complex third *color*. Even the most complex first-layer Old Hall compositions rarely achieve such precisely calculated consonance. There is a conspicuous punning on 'A', letter and note, between some of the motets, and *Apollinis* starts on the note *a*. Triplum and motetus of *Sub Arturo* start on a unison *g*, before the tenor entry on *g*, which might be regarded as starting 'Sub A . . .', i.e. on *g*, the note below *a*.

Notation

In *Apollinis* the breve is imperfected, but by no more than a single minim, and there are no altered minims.[20] In *Sub Arturo plebs* the breve is imperfected from both sides by minims, and by a minim and minim rest, as well as by a single minim. *Sub Arturo* alters minims before semibreves, which places it notationally beyond *Apollinis*. The

---

[18] Wrongly transcribed in CMM 39, correctly in PMFC 5.

[19] The notationally redundant syncopation dots strike an archaic note in this highly sophisticated composition.

[20] In **Ivrea** two minims in breve 118 require alteration, but this seems to be an error.

younger work, unlike *Apollinis*, also has minim hockets with paired as well as single minim rests.

Coloration in the fourteenth century was mostly confined to tenor and contratenor parts of a handful of motets by Vitry and Machaut and a few pieces in **Ivrea**.[21] In earlier instances, it was usually confined to modus change. If *Sub Arturo* is as early as has previously been suggested, the motetus coloration would represent one of the earliest instances of coloration to effect mensural change to imperfection (in this case minor prolation) in a voice other than the tenor or contratenor, and at a sub-breve level. *Sub Arturo* uses imperfection coloration in the motetus in a very subtle way. The three mensurally different tenor statements ☉, ℭ, C are pitted against the ℭ of the upper parts, as explained above.

The coloured notes (void in **Q15**) must have originally been red, because of their associated rests, as they are in **Chantilly** and **Yox**, needing no change of signature to colour-code the shift to imperfect time and minor prolation. **Chantilly** adds redundant (and anomalous) ℭ signatures for the red coloration passages. **Q15** presents the void notes with a C signature, which in this case is necessary in order to ensure that the rests are imperfect, as they cannot be distinguished in monochrome notation: void rests are not possible.

The dating of **Yox** is uncertain (see Ch. 22). Of the two pairs of flyleaves preserved in that volume, the motet bifolio containing *Sub Arturo* is in black notation, the other (with mass movements) in void. *Sub Arturo* is followed on what was a centre gathering by a motet of different but comparable ingenuity. The void notation of the Credo bifolio would normally suggest a date after 1400. Despite the different scribes and notation, it seems likely that the bifolios are from the same original manuscript, on grounds of format and their survival in the same binding, as well as by the advanced nature of the compositions in both. A date between 1400 and 1410 seems likely. But **Yox** also has some notational Anglicisms: atavistic major semibreve rests intersecting the line, and swallowtailed minims for alteration before both red and black semibreves, which would have been old-fashioned by 1410. **Fountains**, a paper manuscript using void notation, probably dates from soon after 1400; it also has swallowtails and major semibreve rests, though these and other English notational particularities have been eliminated in **OH** (whose scribe took a number of editorial initiatives), and are not found in any later manuscripts.

The placing of the coloration passages in relation to the text has often been managed playfully: the word *colores* falls at a change from red to black; *normis* straddles another return to black notation. The striking and audible syncopating coloration in the motetus (*color* II, 1a) reflects the reference to Franco in the motetus text: Franco gave measure to music 'which the colours bind', though not as far as we know did he introduce red notation. Coloration also coincides with 'huius pes triplarii', which announces the mensurally achieved proportional relationship in a passage of red imperfect semibreves, three imperfect in the time of two perfect notes, the second group of which starts at *bis*. *Recitatur* also embodies the idea of repetition and heralds the third *color*. The motetus coloration and the tenor mensurations may be considered to realise the 'modo colorum vario' of *Apollinis*, triplum line 9. The reference in *Sub Arturo* to Guido's invention of the

---

[21] And one Machaut ballade, B4, with tenor coloration.

380 THE MUSICIAN MOTETS

lines and spaces (motetus lines 16–18, B64–B72) is accompanied by eight successive notes in spaces and then eleven lines in the original C clefs, not a result likely to occur by accident.

Relation to Earlier Musician Motets

Sub Arturo responds virtuosically, in both texts and music, to other members of this interconnected, international and, indeed, competitive group of musician motets, of which the earliest is *Apollinis*, *Sub Arturo* perhaps the latest. Many of those interconnections have already been noted. *Apollinis* and *Sub Arturo* are both underpinned by a tenor with the same words of the psalmist, singer and 'citharist' King David, *In omnem terram* (Their sound is gone out *into all lands*, even unto the ends of the earth), from Psalm 18, whose unquoted first line 'Celi enarrant gloriam Dei' ('The heavens are telling the glory of God') resonates with the pun in the first line of *Sub Arturo* 'under the North Star'. The double meaning of Arthur for English kingship and Ar[c]turus the star echoes the strategy of *Apollinis*, where Apollo stands for both the sun and music.

In *Sub Arturo*, the tenor accompanies a triplum that aligns King Arthur (a young warrior king like Henry V) with the words of another young warrior, King David the psalmist, with a northern star (Arcturus) and with what it is that the heavens are telling. However, *In omnem terram* has, as shown above, several different liturgical placements and melodies: the two motets are based on different chants to these words; this is just one instance of how motets cite or acknowledge each other with creative variation. Much of the vocabulary is shared with *Apollinis*/*Zodiacum* and with *Musicorum collegio*/*In templo Dei*. The stanzaic structure of both triplum and motetus may echo that of the—probably English—additional voice for *Apollinis*, *Psallentes zinzugia* (Ch. 16).

Apollinis praises Apollo and Orpheus, and in *Sub Arturo*'s motetus the Orphic fount of *Apollinis* becomes the Jubal of Genesis 4: 21 (by medieval tradition given erroneously as Tubal; see above, n.5), a biblical *Fons citharizancium*. As we saw, the words 'Orpheÿco potus fonte' in *Apollinis* recur as 'Orpheico fonte poti' in *Alma polis*, making as direct a quotation as we find between any of the texts, and at nearly the same midpoint position in each of them. *Fons* in the two earlier motets referred to the spring of the Muses as a source of artistic inspiration; the Muses were presided over by Apollo, the teacher of Orpheus. What was Orpheus' instrument, or indeed Jubal's? If J. Alanus thought it could be called a cithara, we might treat *Fons citharizancium* as a direct reference to that Orphic line already quoted in *Alma polis* from *Apollinis*. The reference to the Orphic topos and the line borrowed in those two motets suggests that the author of *Sub Arturo*/*Fons* knew *Alma polis* as well as *Apollinis*. Apollo, Orpheus and Jubal, like King David, were all *citharistae*. 'Cithara' at this period is a general-purpose word for any plucked string instrument, often translated as 'harp' or 'gittern'. But the instruments of Apollo and Orpheus could also be referenced in *Apollinis*, and that of David in the common source of their tenor texts in Psalm 18. Perhaps even more to the point is the position of *fons*, which occurs likewise just after the textual midpoint in *Apollinis* and *Alma polis* in the three-word Orphic line and is the opening word of the motetus of *Sub Arturo*/*Fons citharizancium*. *Fons* is recapitulated twice; in line 16 as *Guido fons inicia*, and at the beginning of line 22 as *Fontes*. *Fonte lira* starts line 36 of the 45-line triplum of *Sub Arturo* (the motetus has 36 lines). In *Sub Arturo*, the main (line-beginning) recapitulation of *fons/fontes* occurs just after the midpoint as it does in *Apollinis* and *Alma polis*. *Fons* is also the first word of the later, fragmentary motet *Fons origo musicorum* (Ch. 21), and a reason for tentatively attaching that fragment to the group. In *Apollinis*, ⊙ Example 16.1, triplum line 14, the words 'tonorum **tenorem** bene' coincide with 'Boetii **basis** solercia' in the motetus, straddling the midpoint of the music at B72. The triplum of *Sub Arturo* links those simultaneous words successively in '***basis** aurea **tenorum**'* (line 24, B99).

The connection of both *Alma polis* and *Sub Arturo* to *Apollinis* is certain, for reasons given above. The composer of *Alma polis* knew not only *Apollinis* but also *Musicorum collegio*, to which references are strong. *Axe poli* ends with the line 'usque terre limitem', which provides a paraphrase of the continuation of the *In omnem terram* text beyond the point used in either tenor (*Apollinis* and *Sub Arturo*), defining the limits of the earth. Beyond the Jubal–Orpheus–cithara link, the evidence for direct knowledge of *Alma polis* by the composer of *Sub Arturo* is oblique. Both motets are among the most complex in **Chantilly**. The polar aspects of *artica* explored in *Alma polis/Axe poli* might be reflected in Ar[c]turus (in the northern constellation Boötes) with or without the later piece having knowledge of the earlier. Certainly the play on words and the letter 'A' is striking, perhaps also taken up punningly in *Arta/Musicus est ille* (Ch. 21) and other uses of the word *ars*. There may be a further correspondence. In *Alma polis* the next line is 'ac uterque Ydrolanus'. *Ydrolanus* is a water trough, but *ydraulis* could also denote water organs; [*or*]*ganizancium* in *Sub Arturo* is set to the same descending fifth in the same rhythm as *ydrolanus* in *Alma polis*, where it is a fourth higher. This phrase in turn is part of the descending seventh mentioned above that derives from *Zodiacum*, and appears in spectacular and prominent form at the beginning of *Musicorum collegio* at the same pitch used also for *Fons citharizancium*.

As noted above, *Sub Arturo*'s Genesis ('genesis testatur') responds (with a stronger rhythmic tribrach) to *Musicorum collegio*'s Apocalypse ('ut testatur apocalipsis'), creating another elliptical beginning and end, A–Z. In *Sub Arturo*, Tubal (*recte* Jubal) fashions the beginnings of music, 'sculpans ut historia', at the beginning of the Genesis-based motetus, implying the beginnings of creation more generally; *Musicorum* gives *sculptor* as one of the three central creative names in its Apocalyptic first-person motetus (as noted). *Apollinis* referred in the motetus to the names listed in the triplum, 'musicorum tripli materia': both *Musicorum collegio* ('nomina sunt scripta tripli pagina') and *Sub Arturo* ('quorum nominum tripli modulatur') do likewise. In any case, *Musicorum* and *Sub Arturo* are related to each other even as each derives more directly from *Apollinis*. *Musicorum* names seven and *Sub Arturo* twice seven musicians.

Sub Arturo has many verbal echoes of *Apollinis* and *Musicorum collegio*, as well as striking musical cross-references. Just as *Musicorum collegio* quotes its opening words and rhythm from within the triplum of *Apollinis*, *Sub Arturo* takes its opening triplum rhythm from the opening of the triplum of *Apollinis*, with only one minim variant in a passage of sixteen notes, seventeen in *Apollinis* (see Fig. 20.1).

Fig. 20.1 Opening triplum rhythms of *Apollinis* and *Sub Arturo*

382   THE MUSICIAN MOTETS

The variant is due to the alteration of a minim; see above for the argument that this was not yet in the rhythmic vocabulary of the composer of *Apollinis*.

Because there are three *taleae* to each *color*, with exact upper-part isorhythm within each, this opening triplum rhythm is repeated at the beginning of each of the first three *taleae* (3 × 12 notes). The second *talea* opens, in both triplum and motetus, with a transposition up a tone of the first four breves of the opening—only the first two triplum pitches are different. Moreover, just as this triplum quotation ends, the motetus *Fons citharizancium* has a descending seventh from *g* down to *a* on 'ac organizancium'. This descending scale refers to the opening of *Musicorum collegio*, which quotes words and rhythm from *Apollinis* to the notes of that same descending seventh *g* to *a*, which in turn derives from the prominent descending seventh from *d* down to *e* at the beginning of *Zodiacum*. Thus, in pitches and rhythms a correspondence of *Sub Arturo* to the parent motet is established as strongly as it is for *Musicorum collegio*. Among additional reasons for believing that the composer of *Sub Arturo* knew *Musicorum collegio* are the choice of the same pitches for the descending seventh at the beginning and *Sub Arturo's* 'genesis testatur', balancing *Musicorum's* 'testatur apocalipsis'.

Bis occurs in three of the motets. In *Apollinis*, the number 12 is presented as *bis sex*. In *Musicorum*, 'bis acuto gladio' 'cuts' the main structural join between the two *color* statements. In *Sub Arturo*, 'bis sub emiolii' prescribes or describes the three *color* statements that stand in a hemiolic relationship, 9:6:4. *Sub Arturo* doubles (*bis*) the number of musicians in *Musicorum* from seven to fourteen.

The later motet thus recognises its predecessors, and particularly *Apollinis*, as both in different ways celebrate the cosmic sound of music. We noted that twelves underpin the words and music of *Apollinis*; the Pythagorean numbers from which the musical ratios derive, 6, 8, 9 and 12, are all factors of 144 (12^2) and are conspicuously exploited in these motets, and of course not only these. Pythagoras is named in Alanus's review of music theory, as well as in *Apollinis*. We saw that the triplum of *Musicorum collegio* names seven musicians at the French court, linking them to the seven stars and candelabra of the Apocalypse (which also records the spreading of the gospel to the seven churches of Asia). The number of English musicians praised in the triplum of *Sub Arturo*— fourteen—is twice that number, perhaps going one better than the twelve (*bis sex*) musicians of *Apollinis*. It continues the astral references of these predecessors, Arcturus being the brightest star in the northern constellation Boötes, as well as referring to Arthur, king of a northern nation.

The Musicians Named in *Sub Arturo plebs*

This strikingly unusual composition had been noted for nearly a century before Brian Trowell brought it into prominence in 1957 with his ingenious unmaskings of Latinised versions of English vernacular names, and a series of archival identifications for many of those celebrated, mostly in English royal household chapels (of Edward III, Richard II, John of Gaunt, the Black Prince, and St George's, Windsor).[22] These

---

[22] Brian Trowell noted: 'The texts of *Sub Arturo*, naming the composer and several other musicians, enjoy a long historiography as literary curiosities, beginning with Coussemaker's edition of 1869' (*Les Harmonistes*,

identifications led him to date the motet for the Garter celebrations at Windsor in 1358 following the victory at Poitiers. Because of this early dating, Trowell thought that *Sub Arturo* was earlier than the clearly related *Apollinis eclipsatur*, whose text 'is so close to the English motet in some respects that it appears to be an answer to Aleyn's challenge'.[23] Writing before modern editions of most of these motets had been published, he had not seen a transcription of *Apollinis*, and it is now clear that the relationship must have been the other way round. Indeed, at that time, little was known of the fourteenth-century French repertory, let alone of English motets, but discomfort was soon expressed by others with such an early date for the advanced musical style of this apparently isolated work.[24]

As knowledge of English fourteenth-century music increased, especially with the publication of PMFC, volumes 14–17, Trowell's dating of 1358 came to seem too early. Already in 1986 Harrison wrote that the advanced structure of *Sub Arturo* is the only thing that argues against Trowell's 1358 dating, though even there the spread of dates makes it unlikely that only 'fellow choir members' are named.[25] In 1990 Roger Bowers revised and extended some of the identifications and their archival anchorage, pointing up their wide chronological span—the earliest candidate proposed is documented in 1341 and the latest died in 1420—and arguing that some of the datings must be retrospective. Bowers gives the triplum spelling variants; the presentation of the names differs considerably between the sources.[26] He moved the date forward to the early 1370s, still treating the *terminus ante quem* as the death in late 1373 of the royal chaplain

---

12ff.); Trowell, 'A Fourteenth-Century Ceremonial Motet', 74. Some of the musicians named in *Sub Arturo* are completely obscure to us, and at a distance of two or three generations must have been equally so to the compiler of this text. But this is just a reminder of something already familiar from other sources: some of the names on Loyset Compère's famous musical roll-call in the motet *Omnium bonorum plena*, alongside the names of Du Fay, Ockeghem, Busnois, Caron and Josquin, are equally unknown to us. See Wathey, 'The Peace of 1360–1369', 150.

[23] Trowell, 'A Fourteenth-Century Ceremonial Motet', 74.

[24] Including by Günther in CMM 39 (pp. li–lii), and more strongly in Bent, 'Transmission', 70–72, and in Bent, *Two 14th-Century Motets*. I would now disown the performative concessions I made there in barring the lower parts to fit with the regular 6/8 of the triplum, and seek a layout that better reflects the interplay of the simultaneous mensurations; see ⊙ Ex. 20.1. Günther's transcription (CMM 39) is wrongly aligned in the final section. Harrison's (PMFC 5) is correctly aligned, and he gives tables of the musicians in this group of motets. When Trowell was writing in 1957 he had access only to the facsimile of **Chantilly** in Wolf, *Musikalische Schrifttafeln*, pll. 30–31, and the edition in Ficker, *Sieben Trienter Codices*, 9–11.

[25] Harrison, *Musicorum collegio*, p. v.

[26] Bowers, 'Fixed Points', at 321–22, 327–29. At p. 322, citing Trowell: 'For the fifteen named musicians he was able to propose identifications that have proved convincing for no fewer than eleven, almost all of whom were active at some point in their careers as members either of the Chapel Royal of Edward III and Richard II or of the chapel of Edward, Prince of Wales (the Black Prince), between the 1340s and the 1380s. On the grounds that all the named musicians must have been alive when the text and music were written, Trowell gave late 1358 as the *terminus non post quem* for the composition of the motet and, indeed, proposed Edward III's extravagant congregation of the Knights of the Garter at Windsor Castle in April 1358.' In a 1999 supplement to 'Fixed Points', Bowers dates *Sub Arturo* before the death of John Aleyn in late 1373, to the early 1370s 'on the grounds that it would not have been possible for that particular collection of names to have been made any earlier than about 1370'. I doubt if his dating would have been so constrained without a death date for Aleyn; he does not consider that it might be later. Bowers shows that at the end of his life (1372) Aleyn withdrew from court to live as a canon residentiary at Exeter, of which he had held an absentee prebend since 1370. Bowers interprets this as a 'disastrous' falling out with the king, but it could have a much more innocent explanation, such as old age. He also interprets the motet as an act of propitiation for this hypothesised disaster, in which Alanus 'urges the list of musicians (or the potency of their memory, in the case of those deceased) to defend him from the malice of the envious and to prevail upon their lord in Aleyn's favour'.

384 THE MUSICIAN MOTETS

and canon of Windsor, Johannes Alanus (or Aleyn), who owned 'unus rotulus de cantu musicali', and assumed by both him and Trowell to be the composer.[27]

In an article published in 1990, Andrew Wathey substantially extended the documentation of many of the men named in the triplum.[28] He strengthened the musical credentials of some of them, including William Mugge, dean of St George's Chapel, Windsor, who participated in the services of the royal chapel in the mid-1360s, and the Benedictine monk Edmund de Bury (*alias* Bokenham), described in the text of the motet as 'the golden foundation of the tenor', who was in charge of the boys of the royal chapel by 1368 and presumably responsible for their musical instruction.

But despite the evidence of names and death dates that underpins even that later dating to the early 1370s, the motet still seems problematically precocious, both on grounds of musical technique and of the manuscripts in which it is transmitted, given the greater knowledge we now have of English and international musical styles in the decades around 1400. Even a dating *c.* 1370 stands out as earlier by at least a full generation than the motet's nearest musical comparands, English or otherwise, all of which date from after 1400.[29] I have noted above the late datings of sources containing this motet, all of which suggest a date closer to 1400 than a generation earlier.

There are two men named Excestre or Exeter, John and William. Trowell thought that William was a likely identity for the **OH** composer, but Harrison pointed out that his initial there is J.[30] John served as a chaplain of the chapel royal *c.* 1374–96, largely under Richard II. It is reported that John de Excestre held the prebend of Pratum Minus at Hereford by royal grant 1389–96, in which year on 18 October he exchanged it with Walter Trote for a prebend in the collegiate church of St Chad, Lichfield.[31] Since there is no later trace of him, he may have died soon after 1396. Earlier in the same year, on 19 July 1396, William de Exeter was collated to the prebend of Stotfold in Lichfield cathedral,[32] and held it until his death before 20 August 1419 when his will (dated 1 October 1416) was proved.[33] William served in John of Gaunt's chapel in 1383 and was rewarded with many benefices including a canonry at Wells cathedral; he served in the

---

[27] Trowell, 'A Fourteenth-Century Ceremonial Motet', 69, refers to 'our Aleyn'. The dating problems are reviewed by Wathey, 'The Peace of 1360–1369' at 150–53, where he cites a pre-publication version of Bowers's 'Fixed Points' as dating the motet '*c.* 1380, although he too acknowledges the problems that this date presents for the identity of John Aleyn'. Bowers evidently withdrew this dating in the final version. I have no new archival information to add to the excellent work of Trowell, Bowers and Wathey. However, Bowers continues to insist on the death of a John Aleyn in 1373 as a *terminus ante quem* for the motet, regardless of musical stylistic considerations and the anomaly of a late dating for Blithe, most recently in Bowers, ' "Goode and Delitable Songe" '. He does not address my questioning of this early date, most recently formulated in Bent, 'The Earliest Fifteenth-Century Transmission'.

[28] Wathey, 'The Peace of 1360–1369' at 150–55 and 167–74.

[29] I have signalled this issue in Bent, 'Transmission', Bent, *Two 14th-Century Motets*, and Ch. 22. David Fallows agrees: 'but an even later date becomes possible once it is accepted that the composer may not have been the man who died in 1373 and that some of the musicians were already dead when the work was written' and 'Bent, "Transmission" drew attention to its classical 15th-century structure, . . . three levels of diminution, and rhythmic overlapping between upper voices and tenor in the final section' (*NG1*, 276; Grove online, s.v. Alanus). Lefferts, 'Motet in England', 28, observes: 'The discrepancy in suggested dates for the composition of the motet *Sub Arturo plebs* reaches 50 years.'

[30] Harrison *Music in Medieval Britain*, 22.

[31] *The register of John Trefnant*, 190; *Fasti ecclesiae anglicanae*, ii, Hereford, 43. Stow, 'Richard II's Interest in Music', cites CPR 1391–96, p. 664 and CPR 1396–99, p. 17.

[32] *Fasti ecclesiae anglicanae*, x, Lichfield, 56. Not 'John' (as Bowers, 'Fixed Points', 326).

[33] As Stow reports ('Richard II's Interest in Music'), *Somerset Medieval Wills*, 75–76. See also Ford, 'Some Wills', 82.

SUB ARTURO/FONS CITHARIZANCIUM 385

Chapel Royal from 1392 and was a clerk of the chapel under Henry IV in 1402–3.[34] In either case, there is a long gap between the last recorded documentation before his death, and the matter must remain uncertain. A date much before 1400, and a formation in the 1360s, seems too early for the musical style, with its consonant counterpoint, tripartite structure, ingenious rhythms and extensive coloration; the fact that both careers started so early may cast doubt on either being the **OH** composer. If either J. Excestre or W. Excestre was the composer, their service respectively under Richard II and John of Gaunt increases the possibility that Pycard and Mayshuet are indeed to be identified with the French musicians hired by John of Gaunt in that decade, and that the compositions of this group around and after 1400 could have formed the nucleus of the **OH** repertory. (See Ch. 24.)

Because Bowers assumed that it was John of Exeter who died in 1419, he thought that 'he could well have been of the same youthful generation as Richard Blithe, with whom the text of the triplum closely associates him'.[35] 'Ricardi Blith' was already identified by Trowell as Ricardus Blithe, a member of Henry V's chapel, who lived until 1420, though Trowell and Bowers admitted he would have had to be very old by then if praised in a work of 1370, let alone of 1358.[36] He is named together with Excestre in stanza 4; but the names do not seem to be in any kind of chronological order.[37] A younger Blithe would fit well with a later compositional date: the motet's roll of honour is already recognised as historicising, and a later dating simply extends the period of retrospection.[38] The fact that the motetus of *Sub Arturo* covers such a long range gives some credence to a long-range retrospective reading of the identities of the musicians named in the triplum text. That the triplum names are largely unfamiliar to us is hardly an objection to such an interpretation.

By contrast with the earlier musician motets, which were often unspecific about whether the musician being praised was composer, theorist, singer or instrumentalist, *Sub Arturo plebs* is highly specific. It names 'J de alto bosco', a latinisation of J Hauboys, presumably as the theorist we know (probably mistakenly) as Hanboys (active *c.* 1375).

[34] Stow, 'Richard II's Interest in Music', cites TNA E.101/404/21, f. 50.

[35] Exeter and Blithe post-date the focus in the 1360s of Wathey, 'The Peace of 1360–1369' article. Wathey (email of 28.12.2016) reports new material on Richard Blithe (or Blich) relating to the payment of his pension from the parish of West Kington, Wilts., which he was granted on 9.4.1419 (as noted in Trowell, 'Later Plantagenets'). The payment suggests that Blithe died after Easter 1420, and—as was already known—before 8 September that year. The new material consists of entries in the Wiltshire Sheriff's accounts in the Pipe Rolls (National Archives, E 372) and a set of letters in the King's Remembrancer Memoranda Rolls (E 159) instructing the Exchequer to make allowance in the Sheriff's accounts for these sums. Wathey further clarifies: 'The pension was payable by either the Sheriff of Wiltshire or the Vicar of West Kington, and it may be that they alternated (there is no entry in the Sheriff's accounts for Michaelmas term 2019).'

[36] Long before Trowell and Bowers, Bukofzer, *Studies*, 76–77, had already pointed out that the John Aleyn who died in 1373 was too early to be the composer. Trowell, 'A Fourteenth-Century Ceremonial Motet', 65.

[37] Stanza 2, John of Corby; stanza 3, John Hauboys; Thomas Marcon; stanza 4, Richard Blithe, John of Exeter; stanza 5, William Mugge, Edmund of Bury; stanza 6, William Oxwick, John Ipswich; stanza 7, Nicholas 'of Hungerford', Edmund de Miresco; stanza 8, William of Tideswell, Simon Clement; stanza 9, Adam the Deacon.

[38] See Bowers, 'Fixed Points' and Wathey for summary identifications. David Fallows makes the point of generational spread in 'Alanus', *NG2*, i. 276. Fallows notes that four songs ascribed to him in **Stras** are hard to compare with the motet. The virelai *S'en vous pour moy* and *Min herze wil all zit* (also with the contrafactum text *O quam pulchra*) 'could just be aligned stylistically with the English song repertory of the years around 1400; but *Min frow, min frow es tut mir we . . .* seems thoroughly German in style and its text fits the music well. Of the fourth song only an untexted incipit survives.' For another example of retrospective historicising see Ch. 3.

386 THE MUSICIAN MOTETS

As composers it names John of Corby, royal chaplain 1358–66, who may be too early; Richard Blithe, clerk of the Chapel Royal 1406, 1413–19, d. in 1420, adding another composer to the chapels of Henry IV and V; John of Exeter, royal chaplain 1372–1402, d. by 1419, who may be the **OH** composer William Oxwick (past tense, last referred to in 1363); and maybe Thomas Marcon, Chapel Royal chaplain, 1384–1403, 1405, d. 1407.[39]

J. Alanus

Certainly, most of the musicians named can still be plausibly identified with the fourteenth-century candidates proposed by Trowell and amplified by Bowers and Wathey, though these may not in all cases be the only possibilities; but it is the latest, not the average dates that must count, and the retrospective character of the listing may have to be extended forward over a longer period.[40] The fact that the named musicians do not include those we would have thought of as front runners is surely a reminder of how little we know and how much has been lost. I would now go further than Bowers, set aside the Alanus who died in 1373, argue that the motet was retrospective from the position of its latest named musicians and, on grounds of compositional techniques and comparands, move the composition date forward to *c.* 1400 or into the early fifteenth century. Bowers indeed showed that some of the musicians were already dead when it was composed, not still living, as Trowell had assumed; a later date becomes possible if the composer was not the man who died in 1373.

If the composer J. Alanus is correctly identified with the Chapel Royal member and King's clerk John Aleyn who died in 1373, *Sub Arturo* can be no later. As a canon of St George's Chapel, Windsor in 1363 he went to Salisbury together with one of the vicars choral to correct the Windsor chant books against Salisbury exemplars, and at his death in 1373 he bequeathed 'unus rotulus de cantu musicali' to St George's.[41] Despite these musical credentials, there are no compelling reasons to identify the composer with this rather than some other, later, J. Alanus, such as (but not necessarily) the John Aleyn who became a minor canon of St Paul's Cathedral and died in 1437, or some other undocumented Alanus, as suggested by Manfred Bukofzer.[42] Even a proposed identification

[39] Using datings from Bowers, 'Fixed Points', it requires more than a stretch to assume that Marcon (d. 1407), Blithe (d. 1420) and the John Exeter who died in 1419 had made their reputations in time to be praised by a man who died in 1373. G. de Horarum Fonte could alternatively (although the translation is less literal than 'Tideswell') be the William Bonetemps documented as a chorister in the chapel of Richard II from 1384, a fellow of King's Hall 1388–94. He served in the chapels of Henry IV and V and held a number of benefices, including a canonry at Windsor until his death in 1442 (Stow, 'Richard II's Interest in Music', 40–41).

[40] Bowers, ' "Goode and Delitable Songe" ', 211, asserts that 'Although there may be anomalies, it appears that this aggregation of names could not have been compiled much later than the early 1370s, and that the motet was composed toward the end of his life by one John Aleyn, a chaplain of the Chapel Royal of Edward III from 1360 × 1362 until his death at the end of 1373.' Anomalies indeed! Bowers leans to an earlier identification for Exeter, without taking into account that the later man is specified as a composer, which surely favours him as a candidate for the **OH** composer.

[41] Bond, *Inventories*, 34, 103; Wathey, 'Lost Books', 13, no. 133. Wathey, 'The Peace of 1360–1369', 167–68. Bowers, ' "Goode and Delitable Songe" ', 333.

[42] Bukofzer, *Studies*, 76f. Trowell, 'A Fourteenth-Century Ceremonial Motet', 65: 'Now Dom Anselm Hughes had tentatively identified Aleyn with John Aleyn, canon of Windsor, who on his death in 1373 left "unus Rotulus de Cantu musico" to St George's Chapel there. Bukofzer brushed this aside: it would not tally well with the other known dates concerning **OH** composers; and furthermore, *Sub Arturo* names a certain

SUB ARTURO/FONS CITHARIZANCIUM 387

with the Old Hall composer Aleyn can probably be discounted, not only because of the impossibility of cross-generic comparisons with the simple style of Aleyn's Old Hall pieces, but also because his (erased) initial there seems to be 'W' not 'J'.[43] Alanus/Allen is a very common name, and musical style gives no reason to link the two composers. Four songs in Strasbourg ascribed to 'Alanus' without initial are likewise rather simple in style. Roger Bowers himself has warned against assuming that identity of names can be aligned with composer identity,[44] and the recently uncovered multiple owners of the name John Dunstaple should serve as a caution. The motet surely cannot be the only clever and exciting piece by J. Alanus, but we know of no others. In any case, if he were the Old Hall composer, this would have dating implications for the motet.

Comparands and Dating

Everything about the musical style and technique of *Sub Arturo* suggests a dating in the early fifteenth century. Only two other motets, both English, both in **OH**, have the unusual overall proportions 9:6:4, likewise achieved by mensural change: Cooke's *Alma proles regia* (**OH** 112) and the anonymous and incomplete motet *Carbunculus ignitus lilie* (**OH** 143; see Ch. 25), of which only the triplum survives. The latter is in the main corpus of **OH** (composed before *c.* 1413), the former a later addition by one of Henry V's chaplains to that manuscript when it came into their hands. In both of these, the texted parts change mensuration to accommodate the tenor changes and do not attempt the ambitious mensural conflict or artful irregularity of *Sub Arturo*. For these other motets, see Chapter 25.

Rather than casting doubt on the younger identifications, I challenge the proposal that the composer was the Alanus who died in 1373. The 1370s now carry some precious datings around which chronological proposals can be suggested. The motet *Ferre solet* carries the date 1373 within its text;[45] the main body of the **Trém** index carries a *terminus ante quem* of 1376; and the motet *Rex Karole* celebrating Charles V (d. 1380) is dated by Günther 1375, by Carolann Buff 1378 (see Ch. 27 n.8). *Sub Arturo* would be inconceivably precocious to be earlier than these. I am therefore suggesting that *Sub Arturo* sits most comfortably after 1400, perhaps even as late as 1410, on grounds of musical style and notation, comparands, its latest identifiable named musicians, and the dates of its sources.[46]

"Ricardus Blich", whom Bukofzer equated with Richard Blithe, a member of Henry V's Chapel Royal in 1419—forty-six years after the death of John Aleyn of Windsor. Bukofzer then repeated the reference to Jean Alain quoted above, and went on to identify the composer with the John Aleyn who became a minor canon of St Paul's Cathedral, London, in 1421, and who died in 1437. Here the matter has been allowed to rest.'

[43] For the jolly but rather simplistic Gloria **OH** no. 8 only 'Aleyn' is visible; but for an erased Agnus on f. 102, no. 128, the initial seems to be W.

[44] Seminar on Dunstaple, All Souls College, 21.2.2019.

[45] Louviot, 'Uncovering the Douai Fragment'.

[46] If it were even a few years later than that, the valiant fights of the English under 'Arthur' could possibly be added to the number of motets that refer to the military successes of that decade, with 'Arthur' referring to Henry V, though such a suggestion probably stretches the dating of **Chantilly** and **Yox** too far.

388 THE MUSICIAN MOTETS

Appendix
Variants in *Sub Arturo plebs/Fons citharizancium/In omnem terram*

Except as noted, dots of division and ligatures are entered from any source where they appear, but are not individually specified. The delayed arrival of the motetus at the final cadence is not dissonant, but an adjustment in **Q15** nevertheless makes the motetus coincide with the tenor; it omits the rest and breve, and gives the last two notes as void (coloured) longs, the stem on the first of which appears to be partially erased; this solution to the ending is given in ⊙ Example 20.1. On non-coincident endings, see also Chapter 1.

Triplum: **Q15** has ligatures at 73.2–3 and 74.1–2; but the word *ac* is omitted; that syllable needs to be accommodated, so the ligature in 73 is not indicated in the transcription; **Chantilly** triplum 5.2 *d*; 22.4 *g*; 32.2 *d*; 49.2 *c*; 54.1 f; 60.3 M; 70.4 *g*; 73–4, 90, 97–8 ♦ ♦ ■ ; 99.2 *b*; 102.2 *b*; 109.1 f; no ligs; 115 ♯; 121 ♯; 121.2 f; 141 ♯; 143.1 *a*; 121 dot in **Chantilly**. **Chantilly** 121.2–3 *ff*; 152 ♦ and no rest; rest in **Chantilly** only, no dot, so it appears to imperfect the ♦. Both sources at 76 have *b a*, which I have emended to *c b* to avoid the uncharacteristic parallel seconds with the motetus.

Motetus: C3 clef; 9, 33, 57 **Q15**'s void coloration is preceded by (redundant) C, and **Chantilly**'s red coloration is preceded by (incorrect) v; 113 **Yox** and **Q15** *c*: **Chantilly** *e*; **Chantilly** 6-line staff; *bb* signature first three staves; 2 no ♯; 3.4 *g*; 4 erased S stem on ligature?; 11, 20 **Chantilly** ♯; 19.2 *d* minim erased above *g*; 40 ♯ placed before f; 42 dot misplaced after rather than before rest; 6 dot moved from after to before rest; 68 no ♯; 73–74 *g e f d*; 85 ♯ present; 89–91.1 *a d c d d*; 93.3 *g*; 95.1 *e*; 102 L; 104 no ♯; 113 ♯; 115–18 a third too high; 125.3 *e* ♦ omitted; 146 f♯; 151 no f♯; final ■ written as ■. In **Yox** most altered minims have swallowtails; 11 no ♯; mo 19.2, 43.2, 67.2: red; 20 ♯; 24 clef change to C2 to end of line, C3 restored at 35.2; 40 ♯; 42 dots before and after rest; 60.1 *a* instead of *g*; 13, 37, 61, major S rest, intersecting the line; 72.2 *d*; 85 ♯; 102 f; 113 *c*; 125 ♯; 146 ♯; 151 ♯. **Q15** 11 no ♯; 40 ♯; 49 ♯; 68 no ♯; 85 ♯; 104 ♯; 113 *c*; 125 ♯; 146 ♯; 150 *b*♯; 151 f♯ and no rest; final notes are two void longs *f*♯ *g*; ligs. 73.2–3 and 74.1–2; but the word *ac* is omitted and that syllable needs to be accommodated; 152 S and no rest; 113 **Yox** and Q15 *c*: **Chantilly** *e*.

Tenor: 13 **Q15**, **Chantilly**, *b*♯; **Yox** *c*♯, here treated as applying to preceding *b*, but it is cancelled on the next *c* (22) by letter 'c'.

21
Fragmentary Motets and Other Possibly Linked Compositions

1. *Arta/Musicus est ille*

All that survives of this highly intriguing work in the English fragment **LoTNA** is the motetus, *Musicus est ille*, and its 'Contratenor de Arta'. *Arta* must refer to the first word of the missing triplum. These two surviving voices directly follow, on the same page, *Psallentes zinzugia* (see above, Ch. 16), an additional triplum to *Apollinis*, together with a new contratenor to that motet, so labelled, making a unique five-part version.[1] This cements the connection between the two motets as progeny of the original version of *Apollinis*. The text of *Psallentes zinzugia* refers to hemiolian rhythms and epogdoic forms, a preoccupation with proportions present also in the text of *Musicus est ille* and its musical realisation. See ⊙ Example 21.1.

Text and translation by David Howlett:

MVsicus est ille qui perpensa racione non tantum cognouit opus sed qui speculari gaudet et arte magis /splendet quam uoce serena limite supremo libri primi canit erus do[. . .]mira uirtute boecius ista carmen /epogdoice cane presens artis.[..]inde emioli prodasquam dulci ter istius odas sicque leouns fieri iubet hortator nisi /ueri. contratenor de Arta.

It can be laid out thus:

Musicus est ill*e* qui perpensa racion*e*		6	14
non tantum cognouit opus sed qui speculari		7	14
gaudet et arte magis splendet quam uoce serena;		8	15
limite supremo libri primi canit erus		6	14
doctrina mir*a* uir-|- tute Boecius ist*a*.		5	14
Carmen epogdoice cane presens artis et ind*e*		7	16
emioli pr*odas*—quam dulciter—istius *odas*		6	15
sicque Leouns fi*eri* iubet hortator nisi u*eri*.		7	16
			total 118 syllables

---

[1] This and *Pantheon abluitur* in **Stras** are the only five-part versions.

The Motet in the Late Middle Ages. Margaret Bent, Oxford University Press. © Oxford University Press 2023.
DOI: 10.1093/so/9780190063771.003.0022

Contratenor de Arta.

> A musician is that man who by carefully assessed rule
> has not only learned a work but who rejoices to observe closely (i.e. to theorise)
> and shines more from art than from a serene voice;
> in the last limit of the first book the noble Boethius sings
> those things with power in his wondrous teaching.
> Sing the present song of epogdoic art, and thence
> you may uncover—how sweetly—odes of that man's hemiolus,
> and so Leouns the inciter orders that there be nothing except of the truth.

Instead of Genesis, Apocalypse or the psalms, the author of this motetus directly cites the first book of Boethius' *De institutione musica*, giving the precise location for the definition of a musician, I.xxxiv (the last chapter of the first book):

> Is uero est musicus qui ratione perpensa
> canendi scientiam non seruitio operis
> sed imperio speculationis adsumpsit.

The *Arta/Musicus* text consists of two sentences in eight lines of dactylic hexameter verse, with one false quantity in *ille*. David Howlett has uncovered several instances of ingeniously counted proportions in this text, which I hope he will report elsewhere. Most simply, the eight lines are divided into two sentences of which the first, ending at *ista*, occupies five lines, and the second, beginning at *carmen*, occupies three lines.[2] Ratios at or close to the golden section are not uncommon in textual composition, as Howlett has shown in some incontrovertible divisions between triplum and motetus syllables, as in *Musicorum*.[3] As in *Apollinis* and *Sub Arturo* explicitly, elsewhere implicitly, Boethius is placed in the motetus, as is the Apocalypse in *Musicorum* and Genesis in *Sub Arturo*. He is named at the end of the fourth line (just before the midpoint), exactly as in *Apollinis*, pointing again to *Apollinis* as the model. 'Leouns' may be an authorial signature, placed at the end of the motetus, as J. Alanus is in *Sub Arturo*. 'Leouns' is a little too far from 'Leonel' to permit a confident attribution to Leonel Power of what would be his only extant motet with isorhythm. The name is placed at the epogdous (8:9) by word count (46.6 of 52 words) in this 'song of epogdoic art'.

Ex. 21.2 *Arta/Musicus est ille*: contratenor with three isorhythmic *taleae*

---

[2] As tenth and last in a list of means, Boethius, *De institutione arithmetica*, II. 53, 168–69, gives the three terms 3: 5: 8, which form part of what would later be defined as the Fibonacci series, where each number is the sum of the two preceding ones, or extreme and mean ratio. In this case: 'medius terminus ad parvissimum comparatur, quali extremorum differentia contra maiorum terminorum differentiam proportione coniungitur'. The ratio of the middle to the smallest number (5:3) is the same as the ratio of their sum to the larger of the two (8:5).

[3] See Ch. 18 n. 10.

FRAGMENTARY MOTETS AND OTHER COMPOSITIONS 391

The music presents a most intriguing concept. The upper parts are in imperfect tempus throughout. The contratenor notation with its three isorhythmic *taleae* is shown in Example 21.2, a modern-notation transcription of the two surviving parts in ⊙ Example 21.1. As with *Alma polis*, the two *colores* are to be read in different mensurations. If there were instructions applying to both lower parts, they are lost with the missing tenor. Their mensurations cannot be unambiguously explained, but clearly involve syncopation.

The maxima is hard to explain. Everything would be simpler if it were a dotted long. The upper-voice *talea* is 14 breves in *color* 1, 17 semibreves in *color* 2. With a normal interpretation of the maxima, the *talea* length in *color* 1 would be 15 breves, 18 semibreves in *color* 2. The parts only fit together if these are reduced to 14 breves and 17 semibreves; a creeping shift as in *Sub Arturo* does not work. In *color* 1, the maxima must be imperfected by the breve rest before or after it; breves and longs are imperfect. In *color* 2, the now-reduced longs are perfect, the breves imperfect, and the maxima must again be imperfected, this time to the same length as the longs. *Color* 1 thus has, in both voices, three *taleae* (each of 14 breves), *color* 2 three *taleae* (each of 17 semibreves). 14:17 = 0.8, or 8/9, consistent with the text identifying this song 'of epogdoic art', an echo of the proportional statement 'bis sub emiolii' in *Sub Arturo*, and here applied to both text and music. The setting is strictly syllabic, with 118 syllables, 118 notes, 63 in C1, 55 in C2, divided between the *colores* again at the epogdoic ratio of 9:8. Some words are broken by rests. In order to fit the parts as in ⊙ Example 21.1, only one pitch correction was needed. In C1, T2, breve 2, *e* appears against the written *d*, but the *e* is in fact written high, almost above the line, so I have emended it to *f*.

The irrational relationship between the two *colores* amounts in minim count to a total of 271 minims, divided between the *colores* 168:103. There is an extra minim at the end of the final *talea* to accommodate the final syllable. Since the composer is playing with ratios that are not whole numbers, it is just possible that this extra minim was also introduced in order to bring the relationship between the two *colores* as close as possible to the golden section of 271, which is 167.47: the first *color* has 168 minims, the second 103 (102 + 1). This irrational proportion is much rarer in a musical than a textual relationship. No doubt even more proportional art would emerge from the complete piece.

To add *Arta/Musicus* to the group of musician motets assumes that the missing triplum would have listed names of musicians; but the subject matter, the placement of Boethius, the apparent authorial signature, and the careful proportioning all appear to echo the earlier compositions. I have not reconstructed an identifiable tenor, but it would likewise be subject to mensural transformation of its second statement, as in *Alma polis* and *Sub Arturo*, and it shares the 'irrational' nature of its *talea* length with *Alma polis*, possibly referring to that motet. *Musicalis sciencia* opposes art and science, not in quite their modern understandings, but stressing science, and mentioning art only once. Both *Apollinis* and *Sub Arturo* refer to art once and only once each in both triplum and motetus; the motetus *Musicus est ille* uses *ars* twice (in the forms *arte* and *artis*), at carefully spaced intervals. While *arta* derives from *artus* rather than *ars*, a punning intent would be well within the toolbox of these motets, as it is for *tribum* and 'three' in *Tribum/Quoniam*

392 THE MUSICIAN MOTETS

(Ch. 4).[4] The status of *ars* here may echo the choice of *artifex* as one of the central names for the Creator in the motetus of *Musicorum*, *artica* opposed to *antarticus*, in the first lines of *Axe poli*, and *Arturo* in *Sub Arturo plebs*.

There is still much to be done in the matter of tenor reconstruction, identification and choice. The investigation often rests at just that point where much of the interesting work should begin. Just which and how many notes, to which and how many syllables, from precisely which point in which chant, may carry rich significance.[5]

2. *Non eclipsis atra ferrugine*

Only the motetus, *Non eclipsis atra ferrugine*, the tenor *Quorum doctrina fulget ecclesia*, and the end of the triplum of an otherwise unknown motet survive on the verso (original recto) of **Leiden2515**, f. 1ᵛ: see ⓟ Figure 21.1. This motet has not to my knowledge received scholarly notice, but its cosmic reference and other features have strong textual resonance with *Apollinis*, whose triplum is on the other side of the leaf (see Chs. 15 and 16), and affinity with other musician motets. Here is the text as emended and translated by Leofranc Holford-Strevens, with his footnotes (nos. 6–12):

End of triplum	Translation
... eluminant dum g ...	... when/while they shine out ...
...	...
ecclesie sacrum celum	the holy heaven of the Church (?)
et quorum dirigit velum	and those whose sail it steers (?)
iustorum sunt tutamentum,	are the protection of the just,
firmi tanquam firmamentum.	who are firm as the firmament.
hinc vox laudet canencium	Hence let the voice of the singers praise
empireum palacium.	the empyrean palace.

Motetus	Translation
Non eclipsis atra ferrugine	Let these luminaries not be enshadowed
tenebressent hec luminaria,	by the black stain of eclipse,
qui rimantur dei sublimia	who search out the sublime things of God
dum prepollent sensus accumine;	being outstanding for acuity of mind;
albi celum docte cristallinum	white?[6] let them expertly make the shape of
effigiant speramque stellatam	the crystalline heaven and the starry sphere
dum virtutum stellis trabeatam	while leading a life robed by the stars of the virtues
vitam gerant iubarque divinum.	and (bearing) a divine gleam.

[4] Other occurrences of the word *ars* in the motet group are as follows: 'fulget arte basilica' (*Apollinis*, line 5); 'artis practice cum theoria' (*Zodiacum*, line 8); 'arte suaque practicis' (*Musicalis sciencia*, line 3); 'arte cuius multis annis' (*Sub Arturo*, line 19); 'artis uernant legem' (*Fons*, line 9).

[5] See Chs. 22 and 23.

[6] *Albus* means 'matt white'; in principle *albi* might be genitive singular agreeing with *sensus* (across a rest!) or nominative plural agreeing with the subject of the plural verbs, but neither seems to make any sense.

hiis saturni gravitas est morum,	They have Saturn's gravity of conduct,
mira[7] iovis in hiis benignitas,	in them is Jupiter's wondrous kindness,
in hiis martis viget strenuitas,	in them is the strenuous vigour of Mars,[8]
in hiis phebi decor radiorum	in them the beauty of Phoebus' rays
exuperat[9] in pulcritudine,	exceeds in beauty,
suptiles[10] sunt velut mercurius,	they are clever as Mercury,
qui dyana micabunt apcius,[11]	they will gleam more aptly than Diana [the moon],
non eclipsis recti ferrugine.	not by the darkness of the eclipse of righteousness.[12]

Although the final surviving lines of the triplum contain no names, 'hinc vox laudet canencium empireum palacium' echoes a prayer for the singers' heavenly afterlife similar to that at the end of the triplum of *Sub Arturo*, 'ut et illis, qua finita, porta celi pateat'. The opening words of *Apollinis*, 'Apollinis eclipsatur nunquam' are echoed in the negation of eclipse at the beginning and end of the motetus, 'non eclipsis'. There are many other instances of shared vocabulary or imagery with the complete musician motets. Most significant is a listing of heavenly bodies which in the other motets stand for a specific number of musicians named in the triplum. This motetus names six planets: Saturn, Jupiter, Mars, Phoebus (the sun is also thus referred to in *Apollinis*, where Phoebus and Apollo stand both for the sun and music), Mercury and Diana (the moon); Venus is absent, but would have made seven. *Apollinis* matched twelve named musicians ('bis sex') to the twelve zodiac signs, *Musicorum* the seven named musicians to the seven stars and seven candlesticks of the Apocalypse. *Sub Arturo* placed its twice seven singers under the constellation Arcturus, and *Alma polis/Axe poli* ranges through the poles to the heavenly bodies. Shining or gleaming is common parlance for praise in those texts, as in this motetus. 'These luminaries', I suggest, might be six named musicians in the missing voice who are the singers at the end of the triplum praising the empyrean palace, and with whose doctrine, in the tenor, the church shines ('Quorum doctrina fulget ecclesia'; cf. *Apollinis*: 'quibus armonica fulget arte basilica'). Given the tenor *talea* length of seven longs (see below), and the cultivation of symbolic numbers within this group, it is just possible that a seventh name might be in play, perhaps of the composer, perhaps for Venus; but without the triplum this can only be conjecture.[13] Richard Dudas calculated that with even text distribution as in the motetus, the triplum would have had 40 octosyllabic lines. This leads me to note that the motetus has 16 decasyllabic lines and that the proportion of

---

[7] The scribe wrote *mina*, which makes no sense.

[8] Literally: 'the strenuousness of Mars is vigorous', but that is hardly English.

[9] The scribe absurdly wrote *utesperut*, which is here emended.

[10] The scribe first wrote *suptiles*, then adjusted the spelling to *subtiles*. The sense is unaffected.

[11] In the line 'qui dyana micabunt apcius', the future seems out of place and *apcius* is hardly apt. Holford-Strevens is tempted to suggest 'micant apercius', 'twinkle more openly', understood as 'shine more brightly', supposing the crossbar on the p of *ap(er)cius* to have been overlooked in copying and *micant* changed to *micabunt* to make up the syllable count, but all that before the music was notated.

[12] This is highly obscure, and does not make a complete sentence.

[13] The anonymous motet in **Chantilly**, *Pictagore per dogmata/O terra sancta, suplica/Rosa vernans caritatis* (*c.* 1375) for pope Gregory XI, also names six out of seven planets, this time omitting Saturn. The sun is also referred to as Phoebus. See Ch. 30, n. 45. But there is no linkage to musicians.

394   THE MUSICIAN MOTETS

syllables was therefore 320:160. This must surely be a response to *Apollinis*'s 240:120 syllables: its triplum has 30 octosyllabic lines, the motetus 12 decasyllabic lines, yielding the significant total of 360 (the number of degrees in the circle), the syllable count likewise proportioned 2:1 (see Ch. 16).

The chant excerpt chosen for the tenor text, *Quorum doctrina fulget ecclesia*, may have been selected precisely to echo those words in *Apollinis* ('quibus armonica fulget arte basilica'). It is the repetendum of the Responsory *Isti sunt viri sancti quos* for the Common of Apostles, perhaps likening the musicians to the apostles as well as matching them to the planets, as in the other musician motets. In the Sarum Antiphoner BnF lat. 12044, f. 227v, this Responsory follows the Verse *In omnem terram*, which ends with the cue to the repetendum, 'Quorum'.[14] The different *In omnem terram* tenors of *Sub Arturo* and *Apollinis* are for Apostles, often with a global missionary emphasis, which further strengthens the case for this motet being related to *Apollinis*.

Whereas *Apollinis* is in French notation in **Leiden2515** as in its other sources, this motet is notated in what looks at first sight like Italian notation, but could possibly reflect a post-*Fauvel* stage of French notation. Both texted parts are in perfect time, and use semibreves and minims in breve groups marked off by dots, which are also used for addition in the triplum. Breves or longs in initial positions are sometimes imperfected by semibreves or semibreve rests. Most breves have downstems to the left. Altered semibreves preceding breves are shown as downstemmed major semibreves. The tenor is in imperfect modus, notated entirely in breves and longs, and consists of two *color* statements written out in full, each of four *taleae* of seven longs, without diminution, and with an extra breve-plus-breve-rest at the beginning. This compensates for the omission of the imperfect long rest from the *talea* at the final cadence. Thus the total length of the motet is 2 x (7 x 4) = 56 imperfect longs or 112 breves. The motetus follows the tenor's seven-long *taleae* in periods of fourteen breves; in the upper parts, breves and longs, and many recurrent motives, appear in the same place in each tenor *talea*. The minims and semibreves are not strictly isorhythmic but are varied in order to achieve a nearly syllabic setting of the words on semibreves, and sometimes on minims. Musically, this seems more simplistic than the other musician motets, and there are no obvious musical allusions or citations to set beside the striking verbal links. The text script has Italian features, and the provenance is uncertain. Without more evidence it is not yet possible to place it chronologically or geographically. *Apollinis* was clearly the starting point for the other four complete motets. Its wide circulation stands in contrast to the sole and incomplete survival of *Non eclipsis atra ferrugine*. I have here assumed that the affinities with *Apollinis* are derived from it, but it is just possible, given its early and unrelated style and notation—all the other musician motets have upper parts in major prolation— that it could have preceded *Apollinis*, its six planets (and presumably six musicians) prompting the 'bis sex' of *Apollinis*, just as the fourteen of *Sub Arturo* respond to the seven of *Musicorum*. If an earlier motet, the other influences noted between the two would also work in the reverse direction. Was it known to B. de Cluny, who took the

---

[14] I am grateful to Richard Dudas for this observation and for refining the chant identification. In *AS* plate P the Responsory follows a different Verse.

FRAGMENTARY MOTETS AND OTHER COMPOSITIONS   395

idea of attaching musicians to heavenly bodies, and of cosmic reference, and developed it into his much more successful and influential motet?

3. *Fons origo musicorum*

The following two fragmentary texts in **Cu4435** may belong together:

> Fons origo musicorum, laus et decus|
>
> qui das sanos de insanis et|
>
> languidum dites fugas dotas ..|

and:

> -ent musice|
>
> ta fragran|
>
> vibrancia et per|
>
> estas tua qua|
>
> dulces pho|

Although the fragments of the putative triplum part, and of a motetus that might possibly belong with it, have no sign of musicians' names, this might well be related to the complex, especially if it took its opening triplum word *Fons* from the motetus of *Sub Arturo*, which must have been known to its author.[15] It starts (like *Sub Arturo*) on the *g* above middle *c*; see Example 21.3. Its opening rhythm differs from that of *Fons citharizancium* by one extra minim only, just as the opening of the triplum of *Sub Arturo* differs by having only one minim fewer than the opening of the triplum of *Apollinis* (See Fig. 20.1). This is suggestive, given the borrowing of openings and other motifs we have seen within this group.

Ex. 21.3 Opening rhythm in motetus of *Sub Arturo*/*Fons citharizancium* and triplum of *Fons origo musicorum*

Fons citharizancium: ◼ ◆ ◆ ◆ ↓ ↓↓ ◆ ◼ ◆

Fons origo musicorum: ◼ ◆ ◆ ◆↓ ◆ ↓ ◆ ↓↓ ◆ ◼ ◆

Too little survives to say more, but this may well be a lost musician motet of *c.* 1420, closely related to *Sub Arturo*, though no musicians are named in the surviving fragment. *Sub Arturo*'s opening motetus word *Fons* is recapitulated at line 22 of that motet, giving it particular prominence.

---

[15] Cf. Tinctoris, *Proportionale*, 10 gives prominence to *fons*: 'novae artis fons et origo apud Anglicos quorum caput Dunstaple exstitit, fuisse perhibetur, et huic contemporanei fuerunt in Gallia Dufay et Binchois . . .'.

4. Other compositions

Other compositions, all unique, mostly on Latin texts, mostly song-like, with possible textual linkage or allusion, but lacking listed musicians, include:

- *Musicorum inter collegia*, **Stras**, no. 163, f. 94[v] (CMM 53, iii, no. 299)[16] This low-cleffed three-part composition, labelled *Rex rondellorum*, is a rondeau, not a motet, and despite the suggestive opening words has no further connections to the motet group. The entire text is: 'Musicorum inter collegia | musica nobilis;|| Praxi melos musa, theoria | vox variabilis'. It survives only in a corrupt copy in Coussemaker, *Strasbourg*. It is cited in east European treatises for perfect tempus and imperfect modus, which does not adequately describe its alternating sections in perfect and imperfect time.[17] It is in minor prolation throughout. Apel notes its interesting use of patterns of 2 + 3 + 3 units.[18]

- *Musicorum decus et species*, **Ox213**, f. 70. Fallows, *Catalogue*, p. 586, describes it as being in praise of a musical patron. It is an anonymous three-voice ballade, published in *Polyphonia Sacra*, ed. van den Borren, 232.

- *Arte psallentes*, **ModA**, ff. 37[v]–38 (CMM 53, iii, no. 294), not in Fallows, *Catalogue*, is ascribed to frater Bartolomeus de Bononia. The text indicates that it was sung before a pope ('Patre summo pontifex coram [cantemus]'), for whom Apel suggests either of the last two Avignon popes or the last two Roman ones before the councils of Pisa and Constance.

- *Veri almi pastoris musicale collegium*, **ModA**, f. 36[v] (CMM 53, iii, no. 304); Frater Coradus de Pistorio. The text celebrates a papal *collegium musicum*.

- *Ore Pandulfum modulare dulci*, **ModA**, f. 33 (CMM 53, iii, no. 300); a ballade celebrating music and a journey to Jerusalem by Pandolfo III Malatesta in 1399.

- *Furnos reliquisti quare?* **ModA**, ff. 35[v]–36 (CMM 53, iii, no. 295), Egardus (MS *furnis*); laden with musical terminology, addressed to the singers' absent singing companion Buclare, who has gone to the Black Sea. The cantus is in canon; cantus and tenor have different texts, all rhyming in -*are*. At least one of the texts can be presumed to be in the voice of the poet-composer, Egardus.

- *Letificans tristantes*, **Leiden2720**, f. 1[v] (CMM 53, iii, no. 298); includes musical terminology: 'Astent armonizantes, Discordias vitantes' (recalling the 'discordie carencium' of *Musicorum collegio*).

- *Febus mundo oriens* is rich in astronomical, astrological and zodiacal references, as recently discussed by Kévin Roger.[19] Like *Apollinis*, the motet is 144 breves long and has three non-reducing tenor *taleae*: *Apollinis* has three non-reducing statements of the tenor *color*, but *Febus mundo* lacks other features that would qualify it for attachment to the core group.

---

[16] Not in Fallows, *Catalogue*. The music example in **Wrocław16** (Wolf, 'Ein Breslauer Mensuraltraktat', 384) bears little relation to the composition preserved in **Stras**.

[17] For example in **Pra103**: 'Alii sunt de tempore perfecto et de modo imperfecto sicut *musicorum inter collegia*'. See Ch. 15.

[18] CMM 53, p. xxix.

[19] Roger, 'Références astronomiques et astrologiques'. *Febus mundo/Lanista vipereus/Cornibus equivocis*, unique to **Ivrea**, is published in PMFC 5, no. 3.

FRAGMENTARY MOTETS AND OTHER COMPOSITIONS   397

- *Deus compaignouns de Cleremunde*, **Washington1400**, f. 2.[20] Incomplete triplum (upper half of a leaf, verso, with the motetus of *Rex Karole* on the recto) of what was presumably a motet. RISM suggests French provenance, but the text is macaronic (Anglo-Norman and Latin), and the script English, as is the host volume. This composition has been little noticed. As just two companions from 'Cleremunde' (Clermont), Gwillelmus 'Malcharte' and his brother Alebram, are specified and named and praised, we are presumably not lacking a further listing in this triplum. The presence of two companions suggests some analogies with *Furnos reliquisti quare?*. The first-person voice of the text is reminiscent of *Musicorum collegio*, but otherwise there is little to link it to the core group.

The last-named compositions stand outside the close-knit motet tradition to which the chapters of Part IV have been devoted. The remarkably tight network of links between the five motets of the core group affirms their ingenuity, the conception of text and music together, and the playing out of ludic elements in related compositions over many decades. The way in which all the motets echo the text and music of *Apollinis* supports its primacy, as does its widespread and long-term dissemination, rather than that of *Musicalis*, as has been claimed. In addition, the extent to which they allude to each other identifies this as a possibly competitive genre. Given the unique preservation of three of the five motets, we may well be lacking other members of the genre, and other factors which could link them even more closely.

[20] See now Bent, 'Washington, Library of Congress, M2.1 C6 1400 Case'.

PART V
ENGLISH MOTETS C. 1400–1420

400 ENGLISH MOTETS C. 1400–1420

Part V addresses English motets from around and after 1400. My work on earlier English motets has been incorporated in or superseded by Bent, Hartt and Lefferts, *The Dorset Rotulus: Contextualizing and Reconstructing the Early English Motet* (2021). Chapters 22 and 23 describe the Yoxford fragment and its two remarkable *unica*; Chapter 24 revises an essay on two motets in the Old Hall manuscript (**OH**) and their composer, Mayshuet; Chapter 25 surveys the other motets in **OH** and revisits its topical motets and dating, affirms the identity of Roy Henry as Henry V and reviews the place of Dunstaple in a reconstructed fragmentary choirbook that may have been produced for the Duke of Bedford.

22

The Yoxford Manuscript and the Motet
O amicus/Precursoris

Among the significant English manuscript discoveries of recent decades is a fifteenth-century archival volume from Yoxford, Suffolk, whose parchment endpapers include one bifolio of chant and two of polyphony. Each polyphonic bifolio was a centre gathering, and contributes a new complete composition of major interest to the English repertory *c.* 1400: the motet *O amicus/Precursoris* (this chapter), and a Credo included here (Ch. 23) for its motettish ingenuity. But first, a short description of the source is in order. The host volume is a manuscript Extent of the manor of Yoxford, Suffolk, dated 11 Edward IV (1471–72).[1] The front bifolio ('I', ff. i–ii) has twelve red staves per page, each of 14 mm gauge, and contains three motets in full black notation, the middle one new and complete. The rear bifolio ('II', ff. 159 and 162, flanking a bifolio from a thirteenth-century noted breviary, ff. 160–61) has three Credos in black void notation, the middle one likewise new and complete. It has the same rastrum gauge as the motet bifolio, but the staves are brownish. Each bifolio was therefore at the centre of its gathering; they now measure 320 × 230 mm but have been trimmed and were originally larger. There is a slight difference in the written area, which is wider for 'II', but given the similar size and rastrum, and despite their different genres (motets, Credos), script (textura, cursive), and notation (black, void), it is likely that the two bifolios came from the same original manuscript, perhaps respectively from a slightly earlier corpus of motets in black notation and later additions to it of mass movements in void notation. That two polyphonic bifolios were available for a local binding of a local manuscript suggests common rather than independent provenance, especially as their musical sophistication is anything but provincial.

Both bifolios combine music of the highest ingenuity with old-fashioned (and partly redundant) notational elements. Both of the new complete or completable pieces (the second of three Credos and the present motet) have a solus tenor and a mensural scheme of considerable complexity; both invite a compositional dating around 1400. These two new compositions considerably expand our knowledge of complex compositional activity in England at that period, outside but parallel to the repertory that is in **OH** or sources related to it by concordance.

The original version of this chapter was published (with David Howlett) as '*Subtiliter alternare*: The Yoxford Motet *O amicus/Precursoris*', in Peter M. Lefferts and Brian Seirup (eds.), *Studies in Medieval Music: Festschrift for Ernest Sanders*, Current Musicology 45–47 (New York, 1990); this revised version is published with the permission of the editors of *Current Musicology*.

[1] **Yox**: Ipswich, Suffolk Record Office, HA30: 50/22/13.15. Andrew Wathey originally drew my attention to **Yox**, and Adrian Bassett sent me a copy of his unpublished paper delivered in 1983 to the Research Students' Conference in Manchester. **Yox** has been at the Suffolk Record Office in Ipswich from 1952, and was on deposit at Keble College, Oxford in 1983–90. It has meanwhile been described in Wathey, *Manuscripts . . . Supplement 1 to RISM*, 31–33 (facs.) and now in EECM 62, with colour facsimiles. Images are also on DIAMM at https://www.diamm.ac.uk/sources/374/#/images. In Lefferts, *Motet in England*, 300–1, it is wrongly described as 'not the center of a gathering'; the four items listed should be reduced to three.

The Motet in the Late Middle Ages. Margaret Bent, Oxford University Press. © Oxford University Press 2023.
DOI: 10.1093/so/9780190063771.003.0023

402 ENGLISH MOTETS C. 1400–1420

Contents of **Yox**:

I: three motets in full black notation

1. f. 1ʳ: Motetus and tenor of *Sub Arturo plebs/Fons citharizancium* (Ch. 20). The (English) *cauda hirundinis* (swallowtail) is used for minim alteration. Red imperfection coloration is used in the motetus.

2. ff. iᵛ–iiʳ: *O amicus sponsi primus/Precursoris preconia. Unicum*, the subject of this chapter. The upper parts are in imperfect time and minor prolation; with lower-voice 'reverse' coloration, red for perfect, black for imperfect.[2]

3. f. iiᵛ: Triplum and tenor of *Degentis vita/[Cum vix artidici]*, one of the most internationally widely circulated motets of the later fourteenth century. In imperfect time and minor prolation, its presence in an English source at this time is striking and may raise questions about its origin.

II: Three Credos, all *unica*, in void notation. They are listed in Curtis–Wathey as C[redos]8–10. Nos. 1 and 3 are edited as nos. 42 and 41 in EECM 55. No. 2 is EECM 55, no. 8, based on the transcription in Bent, 'Yoxford Credo', slightly modified here as ⊙ Example 23.1.

1. f. 159ʳ: Credo in unsignalled perfect time, minor prolation, with many syllabic repeated notes. An isolated upper part, probably the second, of a setting in three parts, whose tenor must have been stated three times (see Ch. 23).

2. ff. 159ᵛ–162ʳ: Credo *Omni tempore*: complete, the subject of Chapter 23.

3. f. 162ᵛ: Credo in [ℭ] with flagged semiminims, changing to O at *Et resurrexit*; two cantus parts in score, probably the upper parts of a four-part setting. Black full coloration.

Ursula Günther, in her edition and study of the **Chantilly** and **ModA** motets, and Harrison in his editions of motets of French and English provenance, both defined the fourteenth-century motet largely by French standards.[3] Ernest Sanders and Peter Lefferts, in a series of editions and writings, developed a case for an expanded definition of the motet in England.[4] The English motet, long neglected, is now attracting more attention. PMFC largely excludes incomplete pieces; the number of complete English motets, especially from the late fourteenth century, is still relatively modest, though there are many fragmentary compositions.[5] Any addition to their number deserves study, especially when, as in this case, it has been fashioned with high ingenuity. Datings are uncertain: Chapter 20 and the chapters of Part V (22–25) attempt to situate some of these compositions in relationship to their comparands, and to suggest datings closer to 1400 for some compositions that have been dated earlier.

Subtiliter alternare: The Motet *O amicus/Precursoris*

O amicus/Precursoris occupies the centre of the bifolio that now serves as the first pair of flyleaves in **Yox**.[6] It is transcribed as Example 22.1 in the Appendix to this chapter. It

---

[2] Although first signalled in print as two pieces (Lefferts, *Motet in England*, 300–2) it is in fact a single motet.

[3] Günther in CMM 39 and Günther, 'The 14th-Century Motet'; Harrison in PMFC 5 and 15.

[4] Sanders, 'The Medieval Motet'; Lefferts, 'Motet in England' (1983) and Lefferts, *Motet in England* (1986).

[5] See Lefferts, 'The Motet in England' and Bent, Hartt and Lefferts, *The Dorset Rotulus*.

[6] This part of the chapter is revised from the original version published as Bent (with David Howlett), '*Subtiliter alternare*' (1990) in a Festschrift for Ernest Sanders, and adapted here with permission from *Current*

qualifies as a motet by even the most rigorous of French standards, with its tenor diminution, two different texts, and chant tenor. In addition, it undertakes many further subtleties, to be set out below.

Lower Parts
The Plainsong Tenor and Its Text

In outward and most immediate appearance, *O amicus* is a motet about John the Baptist. A cursory search of chants for John's Nativity (24 June) and Decollation (29 August) failed to yield any melodies beginning with the material of the present tenor, which, although labelled 'tenor', is otherwise undesignated. The sharp eyes of John Caldwell, however, noted the similarity of this tenor to a portion (beginning in the middle of a word) from the Introit for the Nativity of John the Baptist, *De ventre matris*: see Example 22.2.[7]

Ex. 22.2 Comparison of tenor of *O amicus* with proposed chant

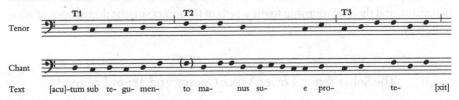

Taken together with its psalm verse, *Bonum est*, the tenor excerpt is drawn from approximately the middle of the Introit (italic), whose full text is:

> De ventre matris mee vocavit me dominus nomine meo: et posuit os meum ut gladium acu*tum: sub tegumento manus sue prote*xit me, posuit me quasi sagittam electam. Ps. Bonum est confiteri domino et psallere nomini tuo altissime.

> The Lord called me by name from my mother's womb: he made my mouth like a sharp sword: he protected me under the shelter [*tegumentum* also means a roof] of his hand, and made me like an arrow shaft. It is good to give thanks to the Lord and to praise your name, O most high.

Two variants of pitch in such a short excerpt, coupled with the derivation of the tenor from the middle of a chant, might discourage this identification. However, an intriguing web of musical techniques and affinities within these associated bifolios gains

Musicology, where it was simultaneously published. David Howlett contributed the textual edition, translation, and commentary. The performance instructions embedded in the text were teased out in collaboration. Images are on DIAMM and in EECM 62. The first modern performance was given by members of the Queen's College, Oxford, on 20 May 1988 in the chapel of All Souls College, on the occasion of the 550th anniversary of the College's foundation charter.

[7] *GS*, pl. l; *GR*, 570.

404 ENGLISH MOTETS C. 1400–1420

further substance from the unusual relationship of the tenor to its plainsong model in each of the two complete compositions. In the case of the tenor of the Credo (Ch. 23), the first two notes of its named chant are omitted; then textually pertinent words and their associated notes are drawn from the middle of the chant, and subjected to further liberties to the extent of casting doubt on the identification. But for its label *Omni tempore*, that chant would never have invited a match with the tenor of the Credo but, whether or not the identification stands, it provides a timely pun for the manipulation of the tenor through six temporal permutations. Caldwell's identification for the motet tenor looks secure by comparison and gains strength by a similar appropriateness of the words to the goal of the motet, in this case the solicitation of protection by a patron. Perhaps this is a temporal patron John as well as the saint, who may also be the namesake of the author, presumably called John, and possibly the petitioning composer, like J. Alanus in the adjacent motet *Sub Arturo plebs* (Ch. 20). The passage selected from the chant includes the words most consistent with votive appeal for a patron's protection: 'he protected me under the shelter of his hand'. The tenor is taken from the middle (the protective *tegumentum* or roof-pitch) of the chant *De ventre matris*: *ventre* is a bodily middle. The words of the derived tenor, the location of words and notes in that chant, and their relationship to the words of the motet suggest dimensions of symbolic play.

The Solus Tenor, Lower-Voice Canon, and Tenor Lacuna

There are two *colores*, each of three *taleae*. The short *talea* consists of only six notes. The second *color* is derived directly from the first statement at the next note-level down; it was not strictly necessary to write out the diminution. Since the breves and semibreves are imperfect, the result in this case is the same as if the repetition had been described as duple proportion, or halving of values, as often found in such descriptions, then and now. The motet is provided with a solus tenor as well as a tenor, but lacks the expected contratenor, although there is room for one on the page. A solus tenor is a conflation of two lower parts where the composition has an essential contratenor, always giving the lower note that provides necessary contrapuntal support.[8] Here, the tenor, on its own, provides an incomplete support for the upper parts. There must have been a contrapuntally essential contratenor, whose missing notes are embedded in the solus tenor part. I shall here call it a contratenor, though it is likely, as we shall see, that it was considered a second tenor to be derived from the notated one, and hence not lacking. Instructions for the derivation or performance of two lower parts often call them *tenores* even when one is labelled 'contratenor'.[9] The solus

---

[8] I have made the case for the solus tenor being a compositional aid. Bent, *Counterpoint, Composition, and Musica Ficta*, Introduction, 38–46 and chs. 8 and 9. See also Ch. 1.

[9] **Paris14741**, one source for Vitry's *Ars nova*, refers in the plural to the 'tenors' of *Thoma tibi*, i.e., they must have been equal tenors or tenor and contratenor. The lower parts of the incomplete motet in **Paris934** f. 79ᵛ fit this description and are labelled Tenor and Contratenor. See Dudas and Earp, *Four Early Ars nova Motets*.

THE YOXFORD MS AND *O AMICUS/PRECURSORIS*   405

tenor permits a simplified but grammatically complete performance of the motet with a single accompanying voice that leaves no unsupported fourths or other solecisms. Its ungainly line is due to telltale upward leaps during tenor rests to provide notes from the missing derived part, all higher in range than the tenor, and sounding while the tenor rests (see Ex. 22.3a below).

The extent of those notes supplied during the lengthy tenor rests takes us most of the way towards reconstructing the contratenor. When the solus tenor coincides with the tenor, the tenor must be the lowest part. When the tenor is resting, the solus tenor reproduces the contratenor, which occupied a range consistently higher than the tenor. The three consecutive contratenor notes embodied in the solus tenor in the middle of each *talea* are notes 3–5 of the tenor, but a fifth higher. The solus tenor also yields note 1 during another tenor rest; thus fully four of the six tenor notes can be accounted for in the solus tenor, transposed up a fifth. The general outline of the contratenor can thus be recognised as being in canon with the tenor a fifth higher, but artfully timed to avoid simultaneously occurring parallel fifths, although the parts begin and end simultaneously. I use canon here in the modern sense; it would then have been called *fuga*. This may be the earliest known lower-voice canon on a pre-existent chant. To construct such a canon poses considerable constraints, here assisted by plentiful rests. By the standards of modern notation the canon appears to be rhythmically free, but not by theirs: it is a mensuration canon, the two voices reading the notation according to different ground rules. Most significantly, the contratenor is indeed not missing: it is to be derived from the homographic tenor and does not require separate notation.[10]

This is also one of the earliest known examples of canon at the fifth; canons at the unison and octave are much more common. Landini's madrigal *De dimmi tu*, in which the two lower parts are in canon at the fifth above, competes with the present piece for the status of being the earliest canon at an interval other than unison or octave, as well as being perhaps the only precedent for a lower-voice canon other than voice-exchange tenors of the kind found in the Summer canon, a *pes* possibly based on the *Regina celi* chant.[11] The present instance in *O amicus* may thus be the first use of a plainsong presented in canon as the foundation of a motet; it is one of very few combinations of canon and isorhythmic structure, and perhaps the earliest; it is one of the earliest canons

---

[10] Another canon on a chant from this period is Pycard's incompletely preserved Sanctus (**OH**, no. 123). In that case it is an upper-voice canon for two voices, which squeezes its chant rhythmically into repeating segments that can be reconciled as harmonically constant over the free tenor. Canonic lower parts of any kind are not common. Landini's madrigal *De dimmi tu* is mentioned in the text below. There is one such mass movement in Old Hall (Gloria no. 27, ff. 22ᵛ–23; see CMM 46, i, pt. 1, 70), which is actually a double canon. See Bent, 'Pycard's Double Canon'. The **OH** double canon carries for the lower canon the instruction 'tenor et contratenor fugando quinque temporibus', indicating that the canonic parts could be thought of (at least in England) as a tenor–contratenor pair derived from a single notated part. Lerch, *Fragmente aus Cambrai*, no. 13, i. 49–52, ii. 88–108, gives a very rare combination, also in a mass movement, of a canonic motetus with isorhythm in all parts. In Du Fay's canonic songs the upper-voice canonic parts function mutually as discant–tenor. No part is labelled tenor, and further added parts are called contratenor(s).

[11] Then there is Ciconia's canonic *Quod jactatur*, presumably from the first decade of the 15th c., evidently intended by its clefs and rubric as a canon 3 in 1 at the fifth. It only works in two parts and is still not satisfactorily solved despite various published attempts and an ingenious proposal by Martin Just, Review of PMFC 24 in *Die Musikforschung* 41 (1988), 193–95.

406 ENGLISH MOTETS C. 1400–1420

at an interval other than the unison; and it may be one of the earliest mensuration canons. *O amicus* is certainly the first known piece to do all those things. Its lower parts share with other canons mentioned here, and with the mensurally transforming tenor of *Sub Arturo*, its neighbour in **Yox**, the capacity to be read from a single notated part; the challenge of the present piece is to reconstruct a solution that permits such a derivation, either with or without verbal instructions.

All pieces that are provided in one or more manuscripts with a solus tenor have a contrapuntally essential contratenor; these include the few compositions with lower-voice canon.[12] In *O amicus*, the powerful constraints of chant and canon in the lower voices determine that they must have been worked out first, then collapsed to a solus tenor as a scaffold or *basso seguente* upon which the upper parts could be erected.[13] As confirmed and corrected in the solus tenor, a major lacuna renders the tenor unperformable as it stands. The omission of the equivalent of two longs (breves in reduction) at the same point in all of the six tenor *taleae* must be interpreted as rests of that value. This omission is all the more striking because, as noted, the tenor is written out in full to show the *color* repetition in reduced note values. It is unlikely that the replication of this omission can be explained by the copying of the tenor rhythm from a single notated pitchless *talea* which was then reproduced for the two subsequent *taleae* that make up the *color*.[14] More likely, the repeated error results from a misunderstanding or omission of coloured rests. Either the scribe assumed that his exemplar had an error of duplication (successive red and black rests) which he consistently eliminated, or he misunderstood the performance instructions. But is the tenor lacuna in fact an error? As noted above, the piece could be musically complete as it stands. All that is missing are clear instructions.

Texts

But are the performance instructions in fact missing? By hindsight it may be possible to scent them, albeit camouflaged in obscurely formulated hints, hiding in plain sight in the text of the motetus. Both texts and David Howlett's translations are given in Table 22.1, the double meanings in the motetus glossed by both of us.[15] The triplum text gives a fairly straightforward biography of John the Baptist: the biblical references are also in Table 22.1, which italicises the rhyme words, and shows where rests fall (always between words). The rhyme scheme is further discussed below. The repeated final rhyme *-ota* ends both triplum and motetus.

---

[12] See n. 10.

[13] Although not involving canon, the ingenious construction of the second **Yox** Credo (Ch. 23) also needed the crutch of a solus tenor, fashioned from its tenor and essential contratenor.

[14] Another instance of an anomaly repeated in each tenor *talea* is the pair of minims requiring 'improper' alteration in *Musicalis*, Ch. 17. Whether such cases shed any light on compositional procedure has yet to be investigated.

[15] His further commentary, together with my transcription, Example 22.1, and its musical commentary, are in the Appendix to this chapter.

Table 22.1 Texts and translation of *O amicus/Precursoris*

Talea	Line	| = musical rest; || = stanza end; rhymes italicised	Translation	Gospel references
		Triplum text, *color* 1		
Ia		[O A]micus sponsi pr*imus*,[a]	O, the first friend of the Bridegroom,	John 3: 29
		en zakarie fil*ius*,	Lo! the son of Zacharias,	Luke 1: 5–13
		baptista domini | p*urus*,	the pure baptiser of the Lord,	Matthew 3: 1
		ut dic*am* | quod finit *ausus*.	that I may tell the crime that ended his life.	
Ib	5	Antequ*am* | puer nasc*itur* |.	Before the boy is born	Luke 1: 41–44
		renatus ipse cred*itur*, |	he is believed reborn	
		sed et propheta dic*itur* |	but he is also called a prophet	
		cum dat pl*ausus* | alvo cl*ausus*. ||	because he gives applause enclosed in the womb.	
IIa	9	Senex mutus substit*uit*	The old man, mute, cut short his speech	Luke 1: 18–22
		ac propheta[b] conval*uit*	and regained his health as a prophet	Luke 1: 67
		ex quo circums*isus* | *fuit*	from the time when the little boy was circumcised	Luke 1: 59
		parv*ulus*, | qui in des*ertum*[c]	who into the desert,	Luke 1: 80
IIb	13	sed*ulus* | iam a ten*ero* |	attentive now from a tender age,	
		cum victu cultu asp*ero* |	with rough food and clothing	Mark 1: 6, Matthew 3: 4
		dirigit rege[d] sup*erno* |	directs his certain journey towards Him	Luke 1: 79
		in exp*ertum* | iter c*ertum*. ||	who has been tested by the Supernal King.	

(*continued*)

Table 22.1 Continued

Talea	Line	| = musical rest; || = stanza end; rhymes italicised	Translation	Gospel references
IIIa	17	plusquam propheta *merito* fit, agnum promens *digito*, quem baptizat, et sic | *sito* *sonitum* | patris *audivit*.	More than a prophet deservedly he becomes, pointing out with his finger the Lamb, whom he baptises and thus quickly heard the sound of the Father.	Luke 7:26 John 1:36 Mark 1:9–11, Matthew 3:16–17, Luke 3:21–22
IIIb	21	*spiritum* | sanctum *meruit* | videre quod nullus *fuit* | maior, Christus *asseruit*, | ut qui *scivit* | *diffinivit*, ||	He deserved to see the Holy Spirit because none was greater, Christ asserted, so that the who knew stated definitively,	Luke 3:22 Matthew 11:11, Luke 7:28
Triplum text, color 2				
i	25	Forciorem *prophetavit* venturum, et *increpavit* | quam plures, | et quos | *vocavit* limpha, verbo, | *lavit*, | *pavit*. ||	He prophesied and roared out that a stronger man was to come and very many people whom he called he cleansed with water and fed with his word.	Mark 1:7, Matthew 3:11, Luke 3:16, Luke 3:2–8
ii	29	tandem quod dampnat *incestum* non licere, non $honestum_2$, puelle | caput | in *questum* dat abscisum | *festum mestum*. ||	Finally because he judges that incest is not allowed, not honest, an ill-omened feast gives his head cut off on the request of a girl.	Mark 6:17, Matthew 14:3–4, Luke 3:19 Mark 7:22–28, Matthew 14:6–8
iii	33	O Johannes, cum *devota* mente cano voce *tota*, | precando | pro me | *scemata* labe sume | *nota vota*. ||	O John, with a devout mind I sing, with my whole voice praying for myself, take my compositions, my noted offerings with their defect(s).	
	36			

(continued)

Table 22.1 Continued

		Motetus text, *color* 1	Translation	Comments
I		[P]recursoris | precon*ia* | mellison*a* | concord*ia* | uti pron*a* | memor*ia* |	Let the preachings of the precursor, in sweet-sounding concord as from a ready memory.	It is hard to make any other sense of this line; *pronus* is literally 'prone', and *memoria* can also mean historical tradition or a monument.
		promant | gaud*ia* | prev*ia*, ‖	make known the harbinger joys	This alludes to John the Baptist's announcement of the coming of the Messiah as foretold by the Prophets. But as the rest of the text bristles with musical terminology it might also be construed: Let the declaimings of the one who runs ahead (the canonic *dux*) bring out from concealment (i.e. the hidden conceit of the musical canon (*fuga*) notated in a single statement and expressed in hidden language) delights that lead the way from sweet-sounding concord (the fifth that starts the canon) as from a ready memory.
II	5	alternatis[e] | color*ibus*, | epogdois | plenis tr*ibus* |	with alternating colours in three full *epogdoi*	Perhaps whole tones? There may be a further pun on 'colour'; red and black colours/*colores* alternate, as do the alternating *colores* in the canonic statements. There are three *taleae* in each *color* but nothing about them suggests 9:8.
		atque scemo | scandent*ibus* |	and by a scheme with accelerating modi	Presumably meaning the tenor *color* repetition in diminution.[f]
		modis | par*ibus* | pas*cibus*. ‖	and with paired [foot]steps	Tenor and contratenor mutually reversing the order of notes and rests, red and black; *passibus* may also include a play on the English usage of *pes* for tenor, especially when there are two *pedes* on equal terms.

(*continued*)

Table 22.1 Continued

		Motetus text, *color* 1	Translation	Comments
III	9	Alternare[g] | subtil*iter* |	one of two [i.e. each] can alternate subtly	This stanza does not make grammatical sense. It could refer to the alternation of notes and rests, of black and red notation, or canonic alternation.
		possit duum | viril*iter*,|	in manly fashion	
		currens suum | simpli*citer* |	running his own course simply	
		cursum | vel *iter* | brev*iter*.	or his journey briefly	With musical play on brevially, at the transition from the simple statement as notated, to the diminution of *color* 2.

		Motetus text, *color* 2		
i	13	Sic patron*um* | me*um* | tota |	Thus do my noted offerings.	Noted: both written and famous.
ii	14	vi laudare | laudis | nota |	demand by right to laud my patron	Patron saint John and possibly also a temporal lord.
iii	15	iure poscunt | mea | vota. ‖	with the whole power of praise.	

[a] O as well as A is needed for the syllable count.

[b] MS *prophetas*

[c] MS *deserto*

[d] MS *regi*

[e] MS *alternensis*.

[f] Thomas Walker suggested treating *scemus* as an alternative spelling of *semus* (= imperfectus): by imperfection with accelerating *modi*. The acceleration of the diminution section, however, does not particularly involve imperfection.

[g] MS *Alternatibus*.

Coloration

The modus relationship of red to black notes and rests throughout the motet is 3:2, perfect to imperfect longs, a reversal of the more common relationship of black to red, whether connoting perfection to imperfection, or a hemiolic proportion. Tempus and prolation are imperfect throughout. A red (perfect) long is worth three (imperfect) breves, a black long two. The scribe not only spelt out the rhythmic reductions of the second *color*; he also provided dots of addition after each red note in the tenor and solus tenor (long and maxima in *color* 1, breve and long in *color* 2) to confirm the note values as being, unusually, half as long again as their black counterparts. This proliferation of dots violates the elegance of the notation and renders the redness of the notes, though not of the rests, redundant—a clumsy expedient.

The original notation surely used both black and red, as now, and as the different rest evaluations require, but without dots. The red notes meant what dotted (black) notes would have meant, that is, they were perfect, and needed no dots. In the first (and originally the only) notated *color*, red notes would yield:

> imperfect maximodus (maxima = 2 perfect longs)
>
> perfect modus (long = 3 imperfect breves; perhaps the 'plenis tribus' of motetus line 6)
>
> imperfect tempus (breve = 2 imperfect semibreves [of the upper parts]).

Black notes are imperfect throughout; it is only at the modus level that red signals perfection. This reconstruction is supported by the rests; both red and black rests are required. Rests cannot receive dots of addition except, paradoxically, in some English practices lamented by the author of the *Quatuor principalia*.[16] The scribe failed to make the adjustment that would have been necessary (if inelegant) for his spelling out in duple values (which could as well have been monochrome), namely, to give the tenor rests that were originally red as perfect long rests spanning three not two spaces each. Breves, being duply subdivided, are not affected, hence the red–black tenor–contratenor hocket upbeat to each new *talea* statement (perhaps another representation of 'paribus pascibus', set illustratively to equal rhythms, in motetus line 8).

This projected use of red corresponds to one of the alternative meanings given in the earlier Vitriacan *ars nova* treatises, whereby red notation can change modus or tempus (or both) to become imperfect *or* perfect. The normal practice by around 1400 was for red imperfection coloration to yield minimum imperfect values for all levels within perfect black notation (as in the motetus of *Sub Arturo plebs*, which immediately precedes *O amicus* in **Yox**). *O amicus* uses so-called 'reverse' coloration, but not all levels are affected; in the first *color*, only the modus relationship (long to breve) is made triple (perfect) by red coloration.[17] Maximodus, tempus and prolation remain imperfect (in relation to the wholly imperfect upper parts) whether red or black. The red maximas

---

[16] Anonymous, *Quatuor principalia*, quartum principale, ch. 37, CS iv. 271b, and Aluas, 'The *Quatuor principalia*'.

[17] Imperfection coloration by *c.* 1400 usually reduces all coloured notes to their minimum imperfect value; here the coloration applies only to modus. Most coloration is of this type, but by the later 14th c. coloration was also used for sesquialtera proportion 3:2, applied at duple levels, imperfect time, minor prolation. See examples in the **OH** motets in Ch. 25.

412   ENGLISH MOTETS C. 1400–1420

contain two perfect longs; the red longs contain three imperfect breves. This usage corresponds to that described for a Vitry motet: '*In arboris empiro*, nam in tenore illius moteti de rubeis tria tempora pro perfectione sunt accipienda, de nigris vero duo'.[18] *In arboris* differs only in using major prolation; *O amicus* is in minor prolation throughout. **Yox** furthermore spells out the second *color* statement in diminished values, thereby at this level making just the tempus relationship (breve to semibreve) triple by red coloration. (It could have been derived by diminution without renotation.) *In arboris* is again cited at the end of the short coloration chapter in the *ars nova* treatises not only for using red notation to yield a perfect (triple) red long before another, but also a perfect red breve before another such. In other words, it spells out for the second section of that motet the same translated diminution (in terms of the lower note values) that is written out in *O amicus*. The other examples in the *ars nova* treatises of at least partially reversed coloration (in which some but not all levels in red notation are perfect) include the lost motet *Thoma tibi obsequia*, in whose *tenoribus* black notes were to be sung in perfect modus, imperfect tempus, and red notes in imperfect modus, perfect tempus. Although lacking its beginning, the second anonymous motet in **Paris934**, on f. 79ᵛ, now provides an anonymous instance of the same usage, where black notes are in perfect modus, imperfect tempus, and red in imperfect modus, perfect tempus.[19] Lawrence Earp has suggested that this could be the missing motet; however neither the tenor chant (Offertory *Ave Maria*) nor the surviving portions of the texts (which include an amorous French triplum) seem to relate to Thomas, whether Thomas of Canterbury or the apostle. Another non-extant motet, *Plures errores*, is cited as the converse usage of *Douce/Garison*, in turn one of the few surviving pieces cited to illustrate the use of black for perfection and red for imperfection in both modus and tempus.[20]

The unique motet by Johannes Vavassoris in **Douai74**, *Ferre solet/Anatheos*, dated 1373, offers an unprecedented instance of alternating blocks of partly reversed coloration. The lower parts are notated only in longs and breves. In the tenor, black and red notes are in perfect modus, but in *color* I red notes are sung at half the notated values. This is reversed in *color* II, with the black notes at half values. In the contratenor red notes are in perfect modus, black in imperfect. In *color* I, both sing at half values. In *color* II, the black sing at notated values, the red at half their previous values (i.e. one quarter).[21]

The motetus texts of both *Sub Arturo* (Ch. 20) and *O amicus* include hemiola in their musical indications. Yet another hemiolic relationship is present in *O amicus*: the first

---

[18]   See CSM 8 (Vitry, *Ars nova*), 28–29, also for the larger discussion of coloration on which this paragraph draws. The early treatises describing coloration to change modus allowed for reversibility of black and red meanings on equal terms.

[19]   Dudas and Earp, *Four Early* Ars nova *Motets*.

[20]   *Thoma tibi obsequia* and *In arboris* are listed in the 1376 index of the largely lost **Trém**. See Bent, 'Trémoïlle', here Ch. 31, and Dudas and Earp, 'Paris 934'. The only one of the three **Yox** motets to be cited in that index is the widely copied *Degentis vita/Cum vix artidici*, which follows *O amicus* in **Yox**. Machaut's Motet 23 specifies that the black tenor notes are perfect, the red imperfect. This yields imperfect modus and tempus but aligned with the major prolation of the upper parts. Other use of 'reverse' coloration, licensed by early *ars nova* theorists, include Vitry's *Tuba/In arboris*, *Alpha vibrans/Cetus venit*, and *Alme pater* in **Fountains** (see Ch. 30).

[21]   Presented by Manon Louviot in a seminar at All Souls College on 20.11.2020. See Louviot, 'Uncovering the Douai Fragment'.

four reconstructed contratenor notes occupy eighteen breves to the corresponding twelve of the tenor, leaving respectively twelve and eighteen breves for the remaining two notes.

Reconstruction of the Original Notation

Example 22.3a gives the first *talea* of the solus tenor, Example 22.3b that of the tenor, as now notated. Disregarding rests for the moment, the contratenor can be assigned the same note values as the tenor but with the colours reversed, as in Example 22.3c. Its colours are consistent with those of its embedded notes in the solus tenor, saving only the first *a*, left black in the solus tenor to reflect that it is the continuation of an already sounding note.

Ex. 22.3 Solus tenor, tenor and contratenor of *O amicus*: (a) *Talea* 1: solus tenor, with redundant dots removed. Tenor notes marked *; (b) *Talea* 1: tenor. The two black long rests following the red rests are omitted; (c) Contratenor: derived from the tenor by reverse coloration prior to solution of the rests; (d) Contratenor: as derived from the tenor, with rests, and showing the reverse coloration. Brackets show reversals of note and rest in relation to the tenor; (e) Tenor in its presumed original form, with black not red long rests, permitting contratenor derivation with reversed colours

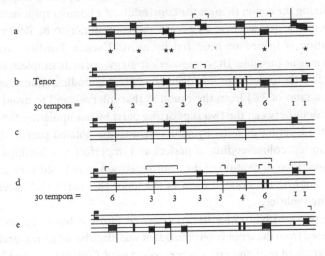

Ex. 22.4 Contratenor and tenor in *talea* 1. The red rests in T 5–6 have no counterpart in the Ct; they should probably have been the omitted black rests in T 7–8, realised as red in the Ct 9–10

414   ENGLISH MOTETS C. 1400–1420

The adjacence in the solus tenor of notes 3–5 (*b g a* in *talea* 1, up a fifth from the chant) of the six canonic pitches shows that no rests can have intervened in the contratenor at a point where the tenor has red rests and where a like pair of black rests must also be inserted.[22] This appears at first to be an insuperable obstacle to achieving a notation from which both parts can be derived. If, however, the canon that is so clearly embedded in the solus tenor is to remain strict with respect to its pitches, notes 2, 5 and 6 of the contratenor must be *followed* by the rests that *precede* them in the tenor.[23] Ignoring for the moment the omitted pair of rests necessary to complete the tenor, this proposed reversal of the order of notes and rests for the derived contratenor removes the obstacle posed by the 'restless' adjacence of notes 4 and 5 in the solus tenor and therefore in the reconstructed contratenor, shown in Example 22.3d.

It is clear from this example that everything that is black in the tenor is red in the contratenor, and vice versa, with the exception of the pair of long red rests, which are red in both parts. Given the omission of a needed pair of long black rests in the tenor, I suggest that the red tenor rests at Example 22.4 bars 5–6 should be black, as at 7–8, enabling them to be reversed as the red contratenor rests at 9–10, and that the tenor was required to insert a pair of black rests that are not needed in the contratenor. (These would probably have preceded the red rests, but I have placed them after, to simplify transcription.) This would achieve a perfect reversal of colours in the canonic parts.

The contratenor must have been spelt out in notated form at some point, its colours thus made tangible, and the solus tenor derived from it, presumably by the composer after fixing the canon to meet the constraints of a homographic notation. None of the refinements devised here to permit the contratenor to be derived from the tenor's notation is helped or hindered by musical sense. Further variations and refinements may be possible. The composer's strategy, put at its simplest, was to create a harmonic foundation of sounding fifths (his 'sweet-sounding emiolic concord', the fifth having a ratio of 3:2) from the canon at that interval, and to avoid direct parallel progressions between the two supporting parts by manipulating their mensural values and the location of rests. By assuming a single notated part as the basis for the canon, dotless colour-coding of perfect and imperfect relationships in red and black, and unwritten derivation of the *color* repetition in reduced values, we can restore an elegant original notated form to the tenor that earns the motet's textually self-proclaimed subtlety.

There are two possibilities for the contratenor. Either it has to be imagined with colours reversed from the tenor (everything that was black becomes red, and vice versa) and with reversals of rests and notes as prescribed here. (This is suggested by the notation of the solus tenor, which uses red for what would be red in such a reversal in the derived part; i.e. the solus tenor is notationally consistent in making red longs perfect and black imperfect.) Or are the meanings of the coloration to be reversed, as in a mental derivation? This yields the more elegant solution of a presumed rubric that would reverse the meanings of black and red in the contratenor.

---

[22] On contrapuntal grounds the contratenor needs no rests. Each note as reconstructed could be sustained through the ensuing rest. Such a solution, however, defies a rendering in original note values that can be accommodated to those of the tenor.

[23] Not a necessary assumption for note 2, but applied for consistency.

Missing Performance Instructions?

The original instructions to derive the canon from the notated tenor and to make the tenor itself performable may have gone something like this:

> The contratenor is in *fuga* with the tenor, beginning together with it at the fifth above. Red notes and rests in the tenor are in perfect modus, black are imperfect. In the contratenor the colours are reversed. Tempus and maximodus are imperfect throughout. (Assuming that the tenor's red rests should have been black), the tenor (but not the contratenor) must insert two red long rests after (or before) the black rests. The contratenor should sing all notes before and not after the rest(s) following them.[24]

This may seem an excessive number of qualifications for a six-note canon, but they are certainly shorter and less extreme than some surviving examples of verbally qualified canon that permit performance from a single notated part, notably the extraordinary three-part mensuration canon of the Credo **OH**, no. 75; or what would have been necessary for the unexplained tenor of *Inter densas* (see Ch. 1) had it not been solved by the provision of a tenor *ad longum*.

The rests omitted from the tenor are needed only in the tenor and may therefore have been prescribed verbally to enable the same notation (without them) to serve both tenor and contratenor. But the **Yox** scribe may have compounded our confusion by mistaking the instruction and inserting the red rests in place of the black rests which must directly have preceded note 5. These red rests preceding the (omitted) black rests were not needed for the contratenor; they may have been instructed to be inserted mentally by the tenor. Thus note 5 in the tenor should be a red maxima immediately preceded by two black (not red) long rests, as in Example 22.3e. The solus tenor shows that note 5 in the contratenor was not preceded by rests; it must have been a black maxima *followed* by two red (not black) long rests.

From this point to the end of each *talea* there is a very straightforward, and not so subtle, alternation (*subtiliter alternare*) both of sound and silence and of red and black within and between the two 'virile' parts (low-pitched? *viriliter*, motetus lines 9–10). Example 22.4 shows how the parts fit together in *talea* 1. The solution to note 6 also reverses note and rest in order to maintain the alternation; the tenor is reconstructed as red rest plus breve, the contratenor as black breve plus rest. The colour difference is here cosmetic because the breve value is not affected by coloration, the breve (tempus) being imperfect throughout the first *color*.

The Final Cadence

Tenor and contratenor must obviously end on the fifth, *f* and *c*. The solus tenor approaches the final *f* stepwise at the end of the first *color* with two semibreves *a g*.

---

[24] Rendered in Latin by David Howlett: 'Contratenor incipit cum tenore, fugando in diapente (3:2) super tenorem. Rubee note et pause in tenore debent cantari de modo perfecto, nigre de imperfecto; in contratenore e converso. Tempus et maximodus semper imperfecti. Tenor (sed non contratenor) debet inserere duas pausas longas rubeas post quartam notam. Contratenor debet cantare omnem notam ante pausam que se sequitur et non post.'

416 ENGLISH MOTETS C. 1400–1420

In the second *color* these are replaced with a semibreve rest and semibreve *g*, to be hocketed between tenor and contratenor, but these cannot be accommodated in the canon at the final cadence.[25] While the concluding figure of each *talea* in *color* 1 of the solus tenor does not match the canon, it is, on the other hand, appropriate to the adaptation needed (and supplied in this transcription) for the final cadence, whose resolution lies outside the canonic and rhythmic structure. The inconsistency between the two written-out *colores* within the solus tenor part is no less problematic than that between both of them and the reconstructed contratenor. All this could simply be due to a late compositional decision about placing the last note of the canon; such anomalies in solus tenor parts sometimes suggest that they were made from a premature version of the conflated parts.[26]

It could even have been applied to the internal cadences by a copyist who did not realise that what he was looking at was in fact a draft for the end of the piece. The rests in the first two *taleae* of *color* 2 coincide, in the motetus, with notes that duplicate the pitch of the canonic contratenor. No attempt has been made here to prescribe the final cadence in the proposed qualifying verbal canon.

The necessity of a final chord on *f c f* is corroborated by the solus tenor, which makes the rhythmic adjustment needed for a final cadence outside the canonic and rhythmic structure, while the diminution in the tenor is written out literally, with no provision either for the final chord or for a satisfactory approach to it. The reconstructed contratenor must and can have *c* on the antepenultimate semibreve, but the tenor needs an interpolated *g* on the penultimate, not *f* as notated in the tenor (consistently with the canon), descending to its final resolution on *f*, as in the solus tenor. If the tenor must bend to approach the cadence, so may the contratenor. The final note of the canon, a fifth apart, is thus delayed in both lower voices for the final simultaneous cadential arrival. Non-coincident final cadences occur in some Machaut motets (Ch. 12), and in Vitry's *Vos/Gratissima* (Ch. 8) and are also discussed in Chapter 1; I suggest that such final cadences often required initiatives from performers.[27] Some of these dissonant endings have been claimed as intentional, but I am inclined to see most as the result of a diminution written out too mechanically from a homographic tenor, failing to adjust the final cadence to consonance as would have been obvious to performers accustomed to making such adjustments. The explicitly adjusted notation of the present solus tenor encourages some scepticism about allegedly intentional dissonant endings. The adaptation required to the cantus and tenor as written and the contratenor as reconstructed could have been devised by the performers, as it has been at the end of Example 22.1 following the clues of the cadential formulas of the solus tenor and cantus II.

The triplum has a ligature of two semibreves, *a e*, and no resolution, where strict isorhythm would demand a semibreve and a semibreve rest. At least one part, possibly two, must supply *b–c* in a four-part cadence whose tenor proceeds from *g* to *f*. This need

---

[25] On the penultimate breve or semibreve of each *talea*, except the last time, the motetus sounds the contratenor note a fifth above the tenor. The only anomalous place, where the upper parts do not go well with the reconstructed contratenor, is at the end of the first *color*, b. 45, which is only marginally acceptable with the solus tenor. Given the exact correspondence of the motetus at the end of *talea* 1, I have emended the triplum in bars 44–45 from *gabb fgaa* down a step to *fgaa efgg*. Both triplum and motetus now correspond to bars 14–15.

[26] Notably in Bent, 'Pycard's Double Canon', reprinted in Bent, *Counterpoint*, ch. 9.

[27] *Sub Arturo plebs* likewise has to be 'fixed' at the end, but no dissonance is involved; see Ch. 20.

can be addressed by a cadential adjustment in the reconstructed contratenor. The top part's *a e* must be followed by [*f*] (♦ ♦ ◼). Musically more pleasing, but hard to defend by manuscript evidence or part range, would have been a triplum reading that doubles the contratenor progression at the octave, *a* [*b c*] (♦ ♦ ◼). Readings are given in the musical commentary at the end of this chapter.

Upper Parts

The tenor of *color* 1 is laid out in three *taleae* each of fifteen imperfect longs (= thirty imperfect breves), in *color* 2 in three *taleae* each of fifteen imperfect breves, following the tenor's simple diminution to the next level down (which at imperfect levels is indistinguishable from duple proportion). The upper parts operate in duple tempus and minor prolation throughout, though they partake in the triple shift that is fundamental to the lower-voice design, a shift (of meter, not of mensuration) that is made prominent and audible in the second *color*. The upper parts maintain strict duple time with minor prolation throughout, and have no coloration. Even when, at each *talea* midpoint, the supporting tenor and contratenor assert a triple pattern (bb. 7–9 and corresponding places), the duple regularity of the texted upper parts is not only maintained but given deliberate sequential emphasis. This is, of course, especially noticeable in the second *color*, where the reduced values claim attention more aggressively.

At the end of each *talea* of the first *color* (bb. 14–15, 29–30 and 44–45), the insistently duple pattern of mensuration and syllabification is broken in two ways which serve to prepare the next *talea*: the clearly audible sequence ('cum dat plausus | gaudia | alvo clausus | previa') is in both texted parts 'displaced' so that two groups are presented, each of three semibreve beats, while at the same time the eight-syllable lines of the motetus are at this moment divided not by fours but (again audibly) as words of 2 + 3 + 3 syllables ('promant | gaudia | previa'). The effect of rhythmic repetitions at corresponding positions in the *talea* repetitions is intensified by rhythmic and melodic sequence and by alternating dialogue between the two texted parts. Within *color* 1, both upper parts have an exact rhythmic repeat across the middle of the *talea* at triplum bars 6–8 = 9–11, motetus bars 5–7 = 8–10, and at the corresponding places in the subsequent two *taleae*.[28] In *color* 2 at the corresponding points a different device is used. The shorter musical span of each *talea* would have been overwhelmed by a comparable rhythmic repetition. Instead, the composer juxtaposes the two audibly perfect lower-voice breves, produced by the *color* diminution, with the continuing duple tempus of the top parts. The triplum maintains duple measure throughout. After the spondee on (*incre-*)*pavit* (and corresponding places) come three rhythmically identical groups of minims separated by rests.[29] The motetus, although still subject to duple mensuration,

[28] One could also count this simply as a repetition of both parts in bb. 6–8 and 9–11, but this cuts across words and is a cruder way of counting.

[29] Although these are actually each of three, two, and three minims = syllables, the second group is notated with two minim rests preceding the two minims, instead of the semibreve rest used elsewhere, which would have sufficed here. This apparent notational anomaly (unlike the others) must be taken not as a coarsening by the scribe but as expressing the compositional intent of presenting this second group also as a unit of three minims (i.e. syllables), the first of which is, in this case, silent, though signalled by its visual separation.

418 ENGLISH MOTETS C. 1400–1420

has breves 7–9 of the *talea* (bb. 49–50 and corresponding) arranged in two equal triple groups. In addition, many local repetitions contribute to a sense of careful planning and economy. These include repeated notes,[30] a falling fourth figure,[31] falling fifths,[32] and sequences.[33]

Relationship of Words and Music: Priority and Order of Composition

The two texts of *O amicus/Precursoris* were clearly designed as a related pair, not as a single text to be divided. There is some alliteration, notably at the motetus's opening *Precursoris preconia*, but this English predilection is less pervasive than in some other motets. Here the sonic concentration is more obviously on the end-rhymes, often in adjacent words and treated with musical rhyme. The lines are octosyllabic throughout. In what order might we suppose the texts and music to have been conceived and united?

The adjacent Yoxford motets *Degentis vita* and *O amicus* belong to a small number of motets in imperfect time, minor prolation, that observe a strict relationship between notes and syllables, characterised by a patter at the minim level with many repeated notes, also a feature of the Credo *Omni tempore* (Ch. 23). Here, the triplum is entirely syllabic, the motetus likewise but for a few short melismas and isolated textless notes. The two texts of *O amicus* were surely written at the same time by the same person, who must have known already the intended details of the musical construction in order to be able to build the descriptive wording, albeit not precisely prescriptive, into the motetus text. Certainly the texts here are very closely tailored to each other and to the musical plan by:

1. Relentlessly syllabic setting in the triplum, and in the syllabic portions of the motetus. The motetus has some short melismas, whose notes were ligated where possible. The sounding of different text at the same time in those two parts is kept to a minimum; presentation of syllabic text in one part against melismatic ligatures in the other contributes to text audibility, as does the *cursiva* technique used for the Yox Credo (Ch. 23). Syllabic text setting is almost a commonplace in

---

[30] *Color* 1, triplum: repeated notes: *ut dicam* (*fff*); *parvulus* (*eee*); *sonitum* (*ggg*); *nascitur* (*eee*); *tenero* (*ggg*); *meruit* (*aaa*): ('puer nascitur is the *inversion* of 'iam a tenero'). *Color* 1, motetus: b. 7, *mellisona* (*eddd*); b. 22, *epogdois* (*aggg*); b. 37, *possit duum* (*feee*); b. 10, *uti prona* (*eccc*; emend to *dccc*?); b. 25, *atque scemo* (*eddd*); b. 40, *currens suum* (*feee*); bb. 14–15 *gaudia previa* (*ffc fff*); bb. 29–30, *paribus pascibus* [rhythmically this can be treated as word painting, linked by *iter* in the triplum, even if not in pitch 'equal' steps (*ccb* and *eee*)]; bb. 44–45, *vel iter breviter* (*ffc fff*).

[31] Falling fourth figure: *antequam* (*ggd*), *creditur* (*aae*), *sedulus* (*aae*).

[32] *Color* 2, motetus: melisma-hocket at end of each *talea* is *ad, gc, ad*, falling fifths, mirroring the descending fifth heard in the canonic lower parts.

[33] Sequences: 'sed et propheta dicitur, dirigit rege superno' (but 'maior Christus asseruit' is different rhythmically as well as melodically). Sequences also end each triplum *talea*: 'cum dat plausus alvo clausus' (*fgaa efgg*); 'in expertum iter certum' (*efgg deff*); 'ut qui scivit diffinivit' (*gabb fgaa*), starting respectively on *f*, *e*, and *g*, exact sequences to point the section ends. The first and third of these are over the same tenor note but a step apart; the first and third *taleae* in the motetus ('gaudia brevia, vel iter breviter') respond at the same pitch (*ffc fff*), a clever correspondence. *Color* 2, triplum: 'vocavit limpha verbo lavit pavit' (*aaae defga ag*); 'in questum dat abscisum festum mestum' (*gggd cdefg gf*); 'scemata labe sume nota vota' (*aaae defga ba*).

English fourteenth-century composition.[34] The dotted semibreves in the second *color* (motetus, bb. 52–53) are evidently intended to have no text, despite the manuscript underlay to them of *vi laudare*, here matched to the second and third *talea* statements.

2. Most of the many word breaks that fall at textually and musically corresponding places in successive *taleae* are articulated by a musical rest. And conversely, not only is the triplum strictly syllabic, but no word is broken by a rest; this requires close coordination of text and music.[35] The triplum rhythms ♦♦♦♦ ♦♦♦♦ and the motetus rhythms ♦♦ ♦ ♦♦ ♦ at the end of each of the first three *taleae* required two groups, respectively, of words of four (2 + 2) and of three syllables, given prominence by double rhymes, similarly planned. The texts must have been planned together with the music, written with a syllabic discipline that would fit rest placements in the intended stanza–*talea* correspondence. Although there are no hockets as such, short syllabic motives, conspicuously rhymed, are tossed between the two texted parts.

3. A secondary rhyme scheme which receives musical prominence in conjunction with some word-breaks. Some other subsidiary rhymes are not maintained in each *talea*. Not only are musical rhythms exactly and prominently matched to each other but also to the text rhymes *subtiliter*, *viriliter*, and *simpliciter*. In addition, interestingly, those same rhythms, in the diminution section, are used for *vel iter* and *breviter*, interspersed with similarly matching music for *possit duum* and *currens suum*. The obsessive repeating rhymes are given musical emphasis, often occurring before rests.

4. Text lengths that are exactly tailored to the musical requirements. The final motetus stanza has only three lines, one for each *talea* of the second *color*, breaking for a compelling musical reason the otherwise observed four-line integrity of the texts. Although to us an obvious thing to attempt, the rigorous correspondence of stanza to *talea* found here was by no means ubiquitous. Each of the half-stanzas of the first triplum *color* is set to fifteen breves (half the *talea*). The stanza division (without a musical break after *ausus*, *desertum*, and *audivit*) occurs exactly at the midpoint of the *talea* (bar 7½), just as the two 'full threes' (*plenis tribus*) of the contratenor red notes are audibly exposed to straddle the middle three units of the *talea*. *Plenis tribus*, moreover, is set in the motetus to three imperfect breves.

The text of the motetus both advertises the compositional conceit and adumbrates, sphinx-like, how the performer is to retrieve it from the notation. This text must postdate the construction of the lower voices; it is a more complex case than the 'bis sub

[34] Examples include *Patrie pacis* in PMFC 15, and the majority of settings in PMFC 16 and 17. Tight syllabic tailoring is present in many Latin-texted motets of French provenance, less so in French and French-texted motets of the later 14th c.

[35] In few other pieces does this kind of planning occur in such a sophisticated way. The English motet *Suffragiose virginis* (PMFC 17, no. 54), for example, has twenty units each of six breves all rhythmically identical, overlapped with seven *colores*. The text of the upper parts is in simple rhythmic canon throughout, with alternating five- and three-syllable groups punctuated by rests. Other motets that avoid breaking words with rests include *Musicalis* (Ch. 17), following the advice in its own text. Instances noted in Ch. 13 include Machaut M9 (Ch. 9) and M18, *Carbunculus ignitus lilie* (**OH**, no. 143, Ch. 25), and *Vos/Gratissima* (Ch. 8). In those cases, the syllabification of the texts was planned precisely for, or together with, the music that would clothe it.

420 ENGLISH MOTETS C. 1400–1420

emiolii' of *Sub Arturo plebs*, whose stated proportions could have been decided ahead of their implementation. The simpler explanation for *O amicus* is that the musical composition proceeded hand in hand with the composition of the texts. First, a clever constructional conceit was in place together with its notated form—the chant-based lower-voice canon. Then a solus tenor was drawn from that foundation, and the upper voices erected upon it: either their strictly patterned rhythmic figures and repetitions provided a straitjacket into which the words were chosen to fit syllabically or, more likely, words and music were planned together, as suggested above.

Such close interconnection of words and music leads to the unavoidable conclusion that text and music are by a single author and conceived as an entity (as in *Sub Arturo* and others of the musician motets, Part IV; also Machaut M9 and M18, Chs. 9 and 13, the Marigny motets in *Fauvel*, Chs. 3–5, *Carbunculus ignitus lilie*, Ch. 25, and Vitry motets including *Vos/Gratissima*, Ch. 8). Indeed, the author of this text seems to identify himself as the musical composer by first-person formulations such as *mea nota* and *cano*. The mutual accountability of text and music, and a concomitant reconstruction of the disciplines of construction faced at each stage by the creator, give us access to an authorial intent that we as editors may have recovered more fully, and may value more highly, than did the scribe through whose dim glass we see—and recover—the verbal and musical text.

The 'fore-running' choice of subject predetermined the chant tenor and the symbolism of its manipulation. The entire motetus text, starting with the word *precursoris* to denote both John the Baptist and the canonic *dux*, plies an elaborate double meaning in counterpoint with the canonic tenor on an Introit for this saint, introductory if not precursive. Clearly loaded with musical terminology as well as allusions to John the Baptist, it appears by hindsight to contain performance instructions—albeit vague ones—for unlocking the concealed riddle of the double tenor, whose mutually prefiguring constituents play out graphically, audibly, and differently, the complementary, harmonious roles of the prefiguring Baptist and the prefigured Christ. The four-voice piece is supported on the symbolic structure of a chant-based canon two in one; the texts of its upper parts (permeated by fourfold counts of lines, rhymes, syllables, and musical rhythms) are a *cento* drawn from all four Gospels (as noted in Table 22.1), that counterpoints the Baptist story, in the triplum, with the musical performance indications (framed by Baptist allusions *Precursoris* and *patronum*) in the motetus.

Neighbouring Compositions

The unique copy of *O amicus* is sandwiched in **Yox** between two possibly significant neighbours, both of which are known from other sources. The first recto of the first bifolio contains the motetus and tenor of *Sub Arturo plebs*, not hitherto known from an English source. The last verso contains the triplum and tenor of the motet *Degentis vita*, hitherto widely distributed in Continental sources only, which now for the first time comes under suspicion of an English career if not of English origin.[36] The succession

---

[36] *Degentis vita* is in **Chantilly**, **Barc971**, **Nürnberg9**, **Brussels758**, **Stras** and **Trém**, as well as being cited in a number of treatises. See Ch. 15.

THE YOXFORD MS AND *O AMICUS/PRECURSORIS*   421

of these three pieces in **Yox** is highly suggestive. *O amicus* has (different) affinities with each of the others that may point to mutual knowledge, common provenance, or at least shared technical concerns.

We have already observed that *Degentis vita* shares with *O amicus* the feature, less common in French motets, of a strictly syllabic text in imperfect time and prolation.[37] *Degentis vita* further shares with *Sub Arturo plebs* some syncopes, albeit in 'easier' duple mensuration, like those in the **Yox** Credo *Omni tempore* (Ch. 23). It is structurally simpler, with two non-reducing *color* statements, each of two *taleae*. *Degentis vita* does not appear to be 'signed', despite some first-person references. It must antedate the main body of the 1376 **Trém** index in which it appears (Ch. 31); its presence there, and in eastern European circulation, make an English origin less likely. Neither of its two companions in **Yox** is in that index; I believe both date closer to 1400.

The use of **Yox** in the binding of a local administrative document may betoken local origin. The superficial appearance of awkward script and the unpractised musical notation and its inconsistent ductus conspire with textual and musical infelicities to show that the scribe was out of his depth, or at least at the limits of his understanding. The text includes spelling errors and obvious grammatical slips, though this is not unusual in transmitted motet texts.[38] *Sub Arturo plebs* is provided in the **Yox** copy with redundant swallowtails to confirm minim alteration, an Anglicism that died out soon after 1400 and was purged from the **OH** repertory, although present in some of its concordant sources, including the important **Fountains** fragment. Similarly redundant are the addition of dots to the red notes in the tenor of *O amicus* and the superfluous dots of syncopation within wholly duple mensuration in the **Yox** Credo *Omni tempore* (Ch. 23), although copied in another hand. It is quite surprising that compositions of the highest sophistication, stylistically consistent with a date close to 1400, are here furnished with superfluous elementary reading aids in a manuscript of provincial appearance. *O amicus*, moreover, uses the major semibreve rest, a distinctive form peculiar to English fourteenth-century sources which, equivalent to a 'dotted' rest, straddles its staff line; it is not here always graphically distinguished from the minim rest, but musical sense and regular rhythmic repetitions leave no ambiguity in its evaluation. Such rests are usually associated with major prolation, but here, unusually, it stands for a semibreve plus minim rest in minor prolation. (See Ch. 8, n. 14.)

O amicus shares with *Sub Arturo plebs*, its immediate predecessor in **Yox**, mensurally significant coloration, unusual in English music before **OH**.[39] There is strict correspondence between stanzas and *taleae*; a motetus text that embodies information about the musical technique of its lower parts, and a personal statement by the poet/

---

[37] The overwhelming majority of French 14th-c. motets are in major prolation. One exception in minor prolation is the *Post missarum* in **Ivrea**, which, however, is less syllabic than the **OH** setting. Another with minor-prolation syllabic patter is *Alpha vibrans/Cetus venit* (only in **Chantilly**), not as completely syllabic as *Degentis vita*; it respects word divisions by virtue of textless hockets, as in *Musicalis* (Ch. 17).

[38] For example, *tripharii* for *triplarii*, and *gwydo* in *Sub Arturo plebs*, *prehenda* for *prebenda* in *Degentis vita*. It has not been established whether they (a) give support to any of our emendations, or (b) suggest that the three motets, or at least the first two, had been copied from a source that habitually made the same kinds of errors. The latter would suggest that they might have been copied from the same source, thus firming up by a notch their claims to sibling pedigree.

[39] An early exception is in **Lwa12185**: see Ch. 4 n. 38, and for **OH**, Bent, 'Principles of Mensuration and Coloration'.

422 ENGLISH MOTETS C. 1400–1420

composer, in both cases with self-conscious cleverness. Musically, their styles seem different because their mensurations are different; *Sub Arturo* is musically a more brilliant piece, though the technical verbal–musical challenges posed are of different but parallel ingenuity. Both are so different from anything else in England at the time that the personalisation of both texts by their makers, the likelihood that the author wrote text and music in both cases, that the author of *O amicus* seems to be saying in the text that he wrote the music and that his name is John, and that he has a barely concealed if unctuous pride in his own work—all this suggests that *O amicus* might be considered in some ways a companion piece to its neighbour *Sub Arturo plebs*, though there is insufficient evidence to suggest common authorship.[40] Each is a unique, cleverly posed and brilliantly solved technical essay that exceeds in self-conscious hubris (signed and advertised in the text) any known English work and most non-English works of the period around 1400. *O amicus* is an important addition to a small but significant repertory; it certainly calls for revisions to existing views of the English and Anglo-French motet at this time.

---

[40] See Ch. 20 for the date, authorship and musical technique of *Sub Arturo plebs*.

THE YOXFORD MS AND O AMICUS/PRECURSORIS   423

Appendix
Musical Transcription of *O amicus/Precursoris* (Ex. 22.1), with Musical and Textual Commentary

Ex. 22.1 Transcription of *O amicus sponsi primus/Precursoris preconia*

Ex. 22.1 Continued

Ex. 22.1 Continued

426 ENGLISH MOTETS C. 1400–1420

Ex. 22.1 Continued

Ex. 22.1 Continued

428 ENGLISH MOTETS C. 1400–1420

Musical Commentary (by MB)

Voices are referred to as I, II, T, Ct, and ST. The references in the left column are to bar, voice, and note of the bar when applicable.

2.1.5	minim
4.II.2	*a* not *g*
6.I	rest and dotted semibreve are missing
7–9.T	The rests are omitted here and in all corresponding *taleae*, as discussed above
10.II.1	*e*; all appearances of this figure are now given as intervallically stepwise
12–13, 27–28, 42–43.II	the first two pairs of semibreve ligatures are written close together to indicate single syllabification
13.I.2	*e* (emendation to the triadic figure used elsewhere)
18.II.4	followed by extra minim *d*
29.I	last semibreve rest omitted?
37.T	clef changes to F4, with custos
42.ST	dot present?
44–45.I	was a step higher. Its first note appears to have been changed in the manuscript from one a step lower, leading to scribal confusion
46.ST	breve should be long (other *taleae* are correct)
58.II	minim rest after 58.1 omitted
62.T	*c, recte d*

Final cadence:

ST   After dotted maxima, semibreve rest and semibreve *g*, respecting isorhythm; final long *f* outside the structure, correctly.

I   Final long omitted; semibreve ligature *a e* makes parallel octaves with II. II correctly provides a final long outside the structure.

T   Last note omitted; *f* semibreve mechanically reproduced from *color* I, its pitch here transferred to the final long outside the structure. Cadential approach *a g* supplied from the corresponding ST place at 45. The Ct must have provided *c b c* at this cadence.

Textual Commentary (by David Howlett)

Text I has (for *color* 1) three (double) stanzas each of 8 lines × 8 syllables, then (for *color* 2) three stanzas each of 4 lines × 8 syllables. Text II has (for *color* 1) three stanzas each of 4 lines × 8 syllables, then (for *color* 2) a stanza of 3 lines × 8 syllables.

In text I *color* 1, the last line of each a-stanza is linked to the first line of each b-stanza by rhyme in the third syllable or the second and third syllables. The first three lines

THE YOXFORD MS AND O *AMICUS/PRECURSORIS*   429

of each a-stanza share end-rhyme, and the first three lines of each a-stanza share end-rhyme. One rhyme at the end of each a-stanza is echoed twice at the end of each b-stanza. In *color* 2, by a simpler scheme, one feminine rhyme, which ends the first three lines of each stanza, is echoed twice in the fourth line. The last two lines of the third stanza share a further rhyme in -*me*.

Text II *color* 1 has the same rhyme scheme as text I *color* 2, five feminine rhymes in each four-lined stanza, but two lines in each stanza share a further rhyme. In *color* 2, the end-rhyme -*ota* is repeated from the last stanza of text I *color* 2, and the rhyme -*um* is repeated from the last stanza of text II *color* 1. More than one-third of the syllables of the entire composition belong to rhyme schemes.

In text I there are 144 words, 88 in *color* 1 and 56 in *color* 2, arranged in the ratio 11:7. In text II there are 33 words in *color* 1 and 12 in *color* 2, arranged in the ratio 11:4. The numbers 88 and 56 are the major and minor parts of the Golden Section of 144.

In text I John the Baptist is described as *baptista* in Ia3, who *circumcisus fuit* in IIa3, who *baptizat* in IIa3, and *limpha lavit* in the fourth line of *color* 2. Note *propheta* in Ib3, IIa2, IIa1, and *prophetavit* in the first line of *color* 2. The Baptist is *filius* in Ia2, *puer* in Ib1, *parvulus* in IIa4, *a tenero* in IIb1. But in IIa1 he is *plusquam propheta, nullus maior* in IIb2–3, who *forciorem prophetavit* in the first line of *color* 2.

23

The Yoxford Credo

The musical flyleaves of the Yoxford manuscript were described in the preceding chapter, as was the motet on John the Baptist on the front flyleaves. The central opening of each of the two bifolios contains a complete, unique and ingenious composition. The bifolio at the end of **Yox** contains three Credos in void notation, all so far unique.[1] Both in composition and copying, they must be slightly earlier than or roughly contemporary with the **OH** and **Fountains** manuscripts. Musically, they are innocent of many stylistic and technical features that mark the mature work of Leonel and Dunstaple of the first two decades of the fifteenth century, but they exploit to the full the musical language of the immediately preceding generation, less in evidence after **OH**, whose repertory they extend. Similar compositions are found neither in contemporary English fragments nor in Continental sources of English music. The first recto of the end flyleaves (f. 159^r) presents an isolated texted upper part (presumably a second cantus), in unsigned perfect time and mostly in C3 clef. This part is in nine sections (abc abc abc), which can be aligned in such a way that the same tenor *color* must have been repeated once for each equal-length third (abc) of the piece.[2] Several anomalies of rhythm and pitch in one or other of these three iterations need to be accommodated to each other and to the demands of the missing tenor. It seems that the repeating sections have been freely and somewhat roughly adapted to their differing text; both the cleffing and the number of minims provided are erratic. The last verso of the bifolio contains two upper parts of another unknown Credo, in unsigned ℭ mensuration with flagged semiminims, changing to (signed) O time. The parts are in approximately aligned score with the text under the lower part. In extent it is nearly complete, lacking only from 'regni non erit finis' to the end. The cadences are to a unison; the texture is nearly complete as a two-voice piece as it stands but, as Peter Wright points out in his edition,[3] a number of unsupported fourths require at least one and possibly two lower parts. In addition, only alternate sections of text are set. The text provided corresponds to that in telescoped Credos by Dunstaple, implying completion from other parts; but this unique and puzzling presentation of two upper parts in score with implicitly the same text discourages a similar solution.[4]

Original version published in 1990 as 'The Yoxford Credo'. The present adaptation is published with permission from the American Musicological Society.

[1] Meanwhile these have been published in EECM 55, respectively nos. 42, 8, 41, with commentary.

[2] Such a repeating form has English precedents. These include two Glorias in score, in various fragmentary versions, first reported in Bent, 'Transmission', 69, and now published in PMFC 16, the first as nos. 39 and 40, the second as no. 35. The first has the form aax, bbx, ccy, ddy (in **Lo36579**, **Ox27**, **Lo24**, and more recently in RC, no. 2). The second (in **Lo40725**): abb' cc' dd' ee' ff' gg. Similar forms with sectional repetition occur in some north Italian compositions, notably Ciconia's Gloria, PMFC 24, no. 8 (abcbd) and a possibly spuriously attributed Credo, no. 11 (abc def bcg).

[3] EECM 55, no. 8.

[4] The missing text could have been provided in chant, though this is early for an alternatim setting. See Peter Wright's commentary to EECM 55, no. 41, and Wright, 'A New Attribution', 213 n. 47.

The Motet in the Late Middle Ages. Margaret Bent, Oxford University Press. © Oxford University Press 2023.
DOI: 10.1093/so/9780190063771.003.0024

432 ENGLISH MOTETS C. 1400–1420

The complete Credo to be described here is on the central bifolio ff. 159^v and 162^r (the music on ff. 160^v–161 bound between them is not polyphonic). It is not technically a motet, although the strategy of this Credo places it high on the panoply of individual motets that follow no existing template. The six statements of its tenor and contratenor reduce successively in paired iterations by mensural reinterpretation within each pair and by diminution between each pair. It is also a striking and ingenious instance of upper-voice structures whose periods are quite independent of the tenors.[5]

It shares with the motet *O amicus* a compositional procedure (essential contratenor) requiring or required for a solus tenor, and a degree of mensural ingenuity found otherwise at this time only in **OH**. It alternates text and melisma between equal upper voices (a technique known as *cursiva*; see below); because of this equal range and activity the upper voices are here called cantus I and cantus II. The tenor is structured to this individual movement rather than designed to support a unified cycle, and it makes advanced use of mensural transformation and diminution. The majority of English polyphonic Credos up to and including **OH** are homophonic settings in score. **OH** and **Fountains** between them present almost the only surviving examples of more elaborate essays in setting the two longer-texted Ordinary movements, the Gloria and Credo. The only hitherto known Credos not notated in score from the period around 1400, in the **Fountains** and **Princeton103** fragments, have **OH** concordances, while the present three do not—a notable absence. Credos are grouped in succession, as in **OH** and RC, not presented in pairs or cycles. (RC is a reconstructed fragmentary royal choirbook of the early 1420s; see Ch. 25 and ⏵ Table 25.1, adapted from the full discussion in EECM 62.)

The script, and the appearance of the void notation, are similar to **Fountains**; this bifolio can hardly be dated much later or earlier than the first decade after 1400, a judgement of the script confirmed orally by Malcolm Parkes. The new Credo is provided with syncopation dots, redundantly, since they are here used with wholly duple and unambiguous mensuration. (Redundant dots also appear in *O amicus*; see Ch. 22.) Comparable provincial or accidental notational signs, including the *cauda hirundinis* for alteration in **Fountains** and in the **Yox** copy of *Sub Arturo*, are absent from **OH**, and virtually disappear thereafter.

This long and ambitious Credo, transcribed in modern notation as ⏵ Example 23.1, deploys unique structural strategies. With its compact text setting, duple time throughout the upper parts, transparent texture, and absence of mensurally florid writing, it does not at first seem to match the ingenuity of the more complex settings in **OH**. In fact, it combines the apparently irreconcilable elements of mostly equal-length segments in the upper parts with non-coincident mensural transformation and successive diminution in the lower parts. Imaginative use is made of audible accelerations and palindromic elements. ⏵ Figure 23.1 shows some of the main features in diagrammatic form.

---

[5] Tucked away in a Festschrift for Alvin Johnson, the original publication of this essay has been little noticed; it provides a virtuosic instance of the independence of upper-voice structures, a subject which is the focus of Zayaruznaya, *Upper-Voice Structures*.

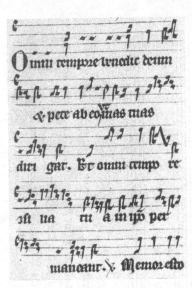

Fig. 23.2 Responsory *Omni tempore*, AS, pl. 317

Tenor Chant

The tenor on the recto (f. 162) is not so designated, but is labelled *Omni tempore* (through all time). These words replace a longer, erased inscription that cannot yet be deciphered, but presumably gave instructions for the tenor iterations. The words open the second Matins responsory of the first nocturn for the Sunday following 11 September, a week known as 'Peto Domine', from the first responsory of Sunday Matins, or 'Tobias', from the source of the daily readings; see Figure 23.2.[6] In the spirit of directives to take for a motet an appropriate tenor from the Antiphoner (in the treatise attributed, perhaps wrongly, to Egidius; see Chs. 1 and 16), this choice of tenor text might have been harnessed to do double duty as a generalised instruction to perform the tenor in all mensural permutations.

Other identified tenors of English Gloria and Credo settings of this period are mostly antiphons, several of them for Lauds. But for the manuscript designation, this responsory would not have been a candidate for identification with the Credo tenor, as it differs extensively from available versions of the chant. The Credo tenor is notated with *b♭*, begins and ends on *f* without returning to that note in between, and remains entirely within the soft hexachord; the chant is a clear mode 8. It appears at present that the Credo *color* may have been more freely derived from the Salisbury version of the chant than would qualify as an identification. Until a closer match is found, we might attribute the very substantial differences to compositional intervention by the composer (see Ex. 23.2).

---

[6] AS, 317; also in WA, 176. There are slight variants between these two, and our Credo is different again; its tenor seems to be somewhat closer to the Salisbury version of Fig. 23.2.

Ex. 23.2 Tenor of Yoxford Credo, with relevant portions of chant

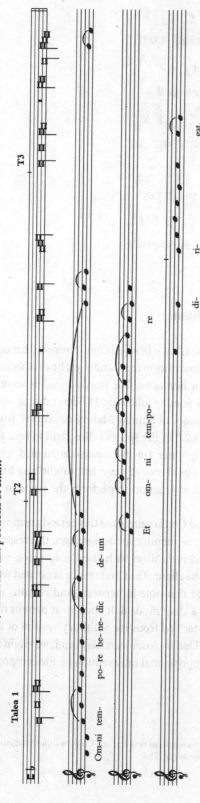

Talea 1: some correspondence to the first phrase of the responsory *Omni tempore benedic deum*, but omitting the first two notes (*d d*, for *Omni*);
Talea 2: freely based on the beginning of the repetendum ('Et omni tempore'), but omitting the first two notes (for *Et*). The verbal association with *omni tempore* is the same as for the first *talea*. In addition, only this part of the responsory rises to the upper *d* used in the tenor;
Talea 3: attempts to show a derivation from the chant are forced and unconvincing. However, the third *talea* is, unlike the chant, a retrograde form of the first, and save for the changed position of its first *g*.

The end of *talea* 2 and the beginning of *talea* 3 might be seen as a free play on forward and retrograde elements of *dirigat*, the melismatic phrase directly preceding the repetendum. The retrograde of *talea* 3 is underlined by the restraint of confining *f* to the beginning and end of the *color*. Other palindromic aspects of the Credo will be discussed below. Another retrograde manipulation of a Credo tenor is in **OH**, no. 90 (f. 77ᵛ, completed in **Fountains**), where the *color* (comprising three *taleae*) is to be stated three times, of which the second is to be read in retrograde, prescribed by a verbal canon, and then the entirety has to be repeated in unspecified diminution. The retrograde reading in that case, unlike the present, can be derived from the same notated part, albeit with improper brevial alteration in both forward and backward readings. No chant tenor for that Credo has been identified; without a label, it would be hard to do so if it had undergone a manipulation similar to *Omni tempore*.

For the moment, we must conclude that the composer, for symbolic reasons, took his starting point from the chant words that would serve his purpose, whose number and arrangement of pitches he then shaped freely for his own purposes. The tenor notes are selected in a highly capricious way from the chant, using mainly the notes that go with two appearances of the words *omni tempore*, presumably to signal his mensural games with time. Other chant-like but unidentified tenors may well be similarly camouflaged.

Tenor Disposition

The tenor *color*'s thirty notes are arranged in three *taleae* of ten notes each, disposed in eight *modus* units (i.e. longs), and notated in longs and breves only. The six *color* iterations are read from the single notated statement and grouped in three pairs, each pair consisting of one in perfect (triple) and one in duple (imperfect) mensuration, derived by different mensural interpretations of the same notation.[7] Diminution then takes place between each of the three pairs, read at the next note-level down. The method of derivation is not proportional, but the combination of mensural change and diminution results in the unprecedented overall proportions 12:8, 6:4, 3:2. Tenor, contratenor and solus tenor are each followed by a custos and six vertical strokes, diminishing in size from two spaces on the staff to a mere intersection of the middle line, a graphic indication of the number of accelerating repeats. The sixth *color* statement is one-sixth the length of the first (see Fig. 23.3).

The main tenor divisions fall between the three pairs of *color* statements as follows:

Section I, bb. 1–60: $(3 \times 12) + (3 \times 8) = 60$

Section II, bb. 61–90: $(3 \times 6) + (3 \times 4) = 30$

Section III, bb. 91–105: $(3 \times 3) + (3 \times 2) = 15$

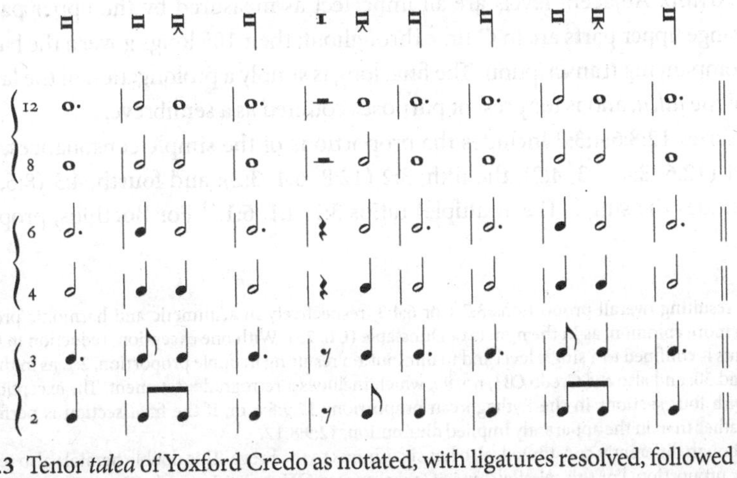

Fig. 23.3 Tenor *talea* of Yoxford Credo as notated, with ligatures resolved, followed by the reducing derivations

---

[7] The Glorias **OH**, nos. 19 and 23 have alternation of text and melisma in irregular periods, only one level of diminution, 2:1, and mensural change within, not of, the *color*, effected by coloration. Alteration marked here by swallowtails applies only to the triple mensurations.

436 ENGLISH MOTETS C. 1400–1420

As determined by the tenor, the overall proportions are thus 60:30:15 = 12:6:3 = 4:2:1, a geometric series of twice duple proportion. Although many motets have a single diminution that is most often duple, occasionally triple, a resulting double diminution in geometric proportion is rare, and unprecedented before *c.* 1400.[8] Depending on a resolution of its date, one of the earliest motets with two levels of acceleration is also a neighbour of *O amicus* (Ch. 22) in **Yox**: *Sub Arturo plebs* (Ch. 20). Although its motetus text embodies the resulting tenor proportions *bis sub emiolii*, twice applying the proportion 3:2 to yield the harmonic proportion 9:6:4, the acceleration is achieved in that motet not by diminution (to the next note-level down) but by a succession of tenor mensurations (⊙ ℂ C) in which the breve is worth respectively 9, 6 and 4 minims, the full range of minim units represented by the 'quatre prolacions'.[9] Technical kinship of various kinds adds interest and perhaps significance to the survival of all three compositions in flyleaves of the same manuscript. There is even a verbal kinship, and possibly play, between the tenors of *Sub Arturo plebs* (*In omnem terram*) and the Yoxford Credo (*Omni tempore*).

In the Credo, the unaltered breve remains constant within each pair of statements: relative breve value for all statements can be expressed as 4:4:2:2:1:1. The different lengths of paired *colores* based on those equal breves are due to the operation of alteration and perfection upon the same notated symbols in perfect mensuration, or their absence in imperfect, and account for the different overall proportions within each pair (3:2) and between pairs (2:1). The three pairs of *colores* could have been notated *ad longum* respectively in the modus, tempus and prolation corresponding to the upper-part values, with a shift to the next note-level down for each pair. These relationships had to be discovered empirically from the single notated *color*, unless they were prescribed in the line of now illegible erased text below the tenor. Since the tenor *color* uses only two adjacent note-values, breve and long, only one level of mensural relationship operates at any given time within the tenor itself, reducing the variables that would arise if combinations of modus and tempus, tempus and prolation, or all three, were in simultaneous effect.[10] This was also the strategy for the mensural acceleration of the tenor of *Sub Arturo*. Adjacent levels are all imperfect as measured by the upper parts. The equal-range upper parts are in C time throughout; their 105 longs govern the barring of the accompanying transcription. The final long is simply a prolongation of the last semibreve of the *talea*, and is for present purposes counted as a semibreve.

The series 12:8:6:4:3:2 includes the proportions of the simple consonances, the octave, 2:1 (12:6, 8:4, 6:3, 4:2); the fifth, 3:2 (12:8, 6:4, 3:2); and fourth, 4:3 (8:6, 4:3). It also includes the simple (i.e. multiple) ratios 3:1, 4:1, 6:1.[11] For Boethius, proportions

---

[8] The resulting overall proportions 3:2:1 or 6:4:3, respectively in arithmetic and harmonic proportion, are much more common, as in the motets of Dunstaple (Ch. 25). With one exception, reduction in **OH** mass movements is confined to a single level and to diminution resulting in duple proportion, 2:1, as in the Glorias nos. 23 and 30; and also the Credo **OH**, no. 90, which includes a retrograde statement. The exception is **OH**, no. 28, with four sections in the Pythagorean proportions 12:9:8:6 or, if the final section is performed as notated rather than in the apparently implied diminution, 12:9:8:12.

[9] ⊙, though differently constituted, also has six minims to the breve. This double hemiola also results in a geometric proportion. For this relationship in Cooke's motet, **OH**, no. 112, see Ch. 25.

[10] Such an exploration of multiple mensural combinations is the primary strategy of the late 14th-c. motet *Inter densas*, uniquely preserved in **Chantilly** and edited in CMM 39, no. 15. See Ch. 1.

[11] For a different example of such a series, see Boethius, *De institutione musica*, II.xvi. With the addition of 9 to the series, the epogdoic whole tone (9:8) could have been added to these basic intervals. That interval is musically emphasised elsewhere, as for example in *Psallentes zinzugia*, Ch. 16, and *Musicus est/Arta*, Ch. 21.

proceed from equality; equal proportion, 1:1, is followed most closely by 2:1 and then by 3:1. Our progression yields several proportioned series using the three means Boethius favoured for music: the *arithmetic* mean, with equal differences: 12:8:4, 3:2:1, 8:6:4:2; the *geometric*, with terms in equal proportion: 12:6:3, 8:4:2, 9:6:4, 4:2:1; and the *harmonic*, where the proportion of the outer terms equals the proportion of their differences from the mean: 6:4:3, 12:8:6, 6:3:2, 12:6:4. The series also includes, adjacently, the disjunct geometric proportions 12:8 = 6:4 = 3:2, and 8:6 = 4:3.

Contratenor and solus tenor follow the tenor; their structure is not separately described here. The contratenor provides harmonically essential support to the upper parts when it descends below the tenor; see bars 12, 14, and corresponding places. The solus tenor has no irregularities; it is a simple *basso seguente* conflation of contratenor and tenor, presenting the lower-sounding voice at all times. As such, it offers no further evidence for or against the view that solus tenor parts were a convenient aid in the composition of complex pieces without the visual control of aligned score. While incidentally providing an alternative to tenor and contratenor for reduced performance, it should be omitted when they are performed.

Text and melisma alternate between the twin upper parts in a manner that has come to be known as *cursiva*, a term known only from the index of **Ox213**, where it is applied to a Gloria by Loqueville whose distinctive feature is that the text, as Hans Schoop explains it, 'runs' from one voice to the other.[12] The alternating sections in the few Continental examples neither follow an obvious numerical scheme nor are combined with tenor repetition. In the English repertory, on the other hand, alternation is fundamental to the fourteenth-century voice-exchange motet, where the paired sections, having the same content, are necessarily identical in length. The texture facilitates audible projection of the text over one, or more usually two, slow-moving lower parts, because only one of the two upper voices at a time is texted, albeit often densely, while the other recedes from prominence with slower-moving melisma.

Some mass movements of the **OH** period extend such alternation of equal-length sections to a number of successive statements coordinated with tenor repetition. Their musical content may no longer be identical, but is sometimes matched by rhythmic parallels or by pitch content so as to fit *color* repetition. This Credo adopts the established English voice-exchange texture of two upper voices sharing text, arranged in balanced sections of equal length and parallel rhythm that alternate text and melisma, supported by two untexted lower ones. It boldly combines this model with an ambitious scheme of mensurally reducing tenor statements, unknown in earlier voice-exchange motets. When a tenor is repeated in either equal or duple proportion, it is easy, indeed obvious, to arrange things so that upper-part sections corresponding to one or two tenor repetitions will themselves be rhythmically similar, if not identical. Queldryk's Gloria (**OH**, no. 30) has a tenor to be restated in diminution,[13] and is so

---

[12] Folio 68ᵛ, CMM 11/3, no. 8. Schoop, *Entstehung*, 49–51. See *Oxford, Bodleian Library MS Canon. Misc. 213*, ed. Fallows, and Fallows, *Dufay*, 13 and n. 24 for further adoption of the term, also Bent, 'The use of cut signatures in sacred music by Binchois', 295 n. 25.

[13] This Gloria punctuates the ends of *taleae* with short passages texted *a2*. There are some delays and overlaps in making the transition from one sub-segment to the next. There is some motto allusion, especially at beginnings of the melismatic phrases, though cantus I's characteristic rhythm differs from that of cantus II. The diminution is unspecified; there is only a repeat sign. The notes are read at the next level down, but because the mensuration is wholly duple, this results in a 2:1 reduction.

438 ENGLISH MOTETS C. 1400–1420

arranged that the alternating texted and melismatic periods of the upper parts coincide with one unreduced or two reduced tenor statements. The first two *taleae* each contain two double segments (each of 2 × 9 breves); then the two duply reduced *taleae* each contain one double segment (of 2 × 9 breves). The closest parallel to the Yoxford Credo, albeit a much simpler design, is **Fountains** Gloria no. 1.[14] One of the remarkable features of the **Yox** Credo is the non-coincidence of the upper- and lower-part periods.

The number of reducing sections is unprecedented, except in the presumably French anonymous motet *Inter densas* (Ch. 1), which must probably be dated before the death of Gaston Phebus in 1391, making it as worryingly precocious as the debate on the dating of Machaut's Motet 18 (Ch. 13). But the **Yox** combination of paired mensural transformation applied to three levels of diminution may be unique in mass composition.[15] One branch of its pedigree surely lies in the interest of late fourteenth-century English theorists in an extended panoply of note-values, in one case from the irreducible *minima* through the *minuta*, *semibrevis*, *brevis*, *longa* and *larga* to the *largissima*.[16] Another derives from the purely English fourteenth-century tradition of large-scale voice-exchange motets, pieces with two slow-moving lower parts that support a pair of upper parts with alternating text and melisma, now augmented by the discovery of **Dor**.[17] It is a small compositional step from that to bond members of the pair by texture and rhythm, and to extend the procedure to a strophic continuation without exact musical repetition.

Not only does the plan for the upper voices need to be distinguished from that for the tenor, but also from its own realisation. Just as a labelled chant is strikingly departed from, so the structure of the upper parts has a clear underlying strategy, but one with calculated irregularities of execution. Up to the Amen, the upper parts were planned as nine non-reducing double periods, notionally each of ten longs duply divided into two

---

[14] The **Fountains** Gloria no. 1, f. 9, ed. Kershaw and Sandon in *The Fountains Fragments*, is tentatively attributed by its editors to Pennard. The upper voices alternate text and melisma in periods of 2 × 7 breves (of perfect *tempus*, major *prolatio*) that coincide with the fourteen-breve tenor *talea* length. The untexted portions of the upper parts use only breves and breve rests while the Gloria text is present (first two *colores*); the note values of both upper parts in the melismatic Amen are matched, with semibreves and minims. Two non-reducing tenor *color* statements of three *taleae* each accommodate the Gloria text; the Amen presents the same double *color* statement in diminution. The first *color* is in imperfect modus, perfect time and major prolation; the diminution section is in imperfect time, major prolation. This results in 3:1 reduction. The upper parts of this Gloria are isoperiodic and only isorhythmic for the Amen, where the three upper part periods coincide with pairs of tenor *taleae* but overlap with the two *colores*. Pennard's Credo **OH**, no. 89, also in **Princeton103**, has twenty non-reducing statements, each of eight breves of ₵ time, supporting upper-part alternation in periods of the same length.

[15] The second section of Machaut's Motet 2 is in diminution as well as with mensural transformation from perfect to imperfect (Ch. 13). Mensuration and diminution are also applied in *Portio/Ida capillorum*, present in **Ivrea**, **Chantilly**, **Stras**, and the main part of **Trém**, therefore datable before 1376. The tenor is read first in perfect modus, then in imperfect modus, then 'per semi' of those statements. Zazulia, 'A Motet Ahead of its Time?', highlights its precocity. Günther, 'The 14th-Century Motet', 38, noted that it is the only motet in **Ivrea** to use semibreve syncopation in major prolation. Despite having four sections it has only one level of reduction. Mensural transformation apart, no motet clearly datable before 1400 has more than one such level. *Sub Arturo* has three levels of mensural reduction, and *Omni tempore* may be the earliest to have three levels of diminution. Zazulia (p. 349) also discusses an anonymous motet-style Gloria in **Ivrea**, no. 47 (ff. 28ᵛ–29, CMM 29, nos. 21, 23–25) with a homographic tenor that must be interpreted in a similar manner to *Portio/Ida*, except that its upper voices change mensurations at the same time as the tenor, whereas the upper voices of *Portio/Ida* remain in imperfect tempus, major prolation throughout. The upper parts of *Omni tempore* remain in imperfect time and minor prolation, pitted against changing mensurations in the lower parts.

[16] See Reaney, *Willelmus*.

[17] For extensive discussion of the early 14th-c. voice-exchange repertory, see now Bent, Hartt and Lefferts, *The Dorset Rotulus*.

THE YOXFORD CREDO   439

segments of five longs. These are relentlessly counterpointed against the reducing proportional scheme and paired threefold structure of the tenor, whose only tenfold feature is that each *talea* contains ten notes. The underlying plan for the upper parts would have related to the tenor as follows:

Section I, bb. 1–60: six double segments of ten longs, spanning the first pair of tenor *colores*, $(3 \times 12) + (3 \times 8) = 6 \times 10$;

Section II, bb. 61–90: three double segments of ten longs, spanning the second pair of tenor *colores*, $(3 \times 6) + (3 \times 4) = 3 \times 10$;

Section III, bb. 91–105: Amen, occupying the last pair of tenor *colores*. These two sections are fully melismatic and isorhythmic within each *color*, with full coincidence between the parts, and complementary hocketing of upper and lower parts, $(3 \times 3) + (3 \times 2)$.

However, this was not what happens. The composer chose to sacrifice the rigorous neatness of this underlying scheme to the gratuitous flourish of a structural 'rubato'. See again Figure 23.1. The ten-long segment that would have occupied bars 41–50 (*Et resurrexit*) was shortened to nine longs, dividing in half at four and a half longs and ending in bar 49; the segment bars 50–59 (*Et iterum*) is again ten longs, causing the following ten-long segment at bars 60–69 (*Qui cum patre*) to anticipate and camouflage, rather than to reinforce, the structural tenor join that falls between bars 60 and 61. The 'robbed' long is recovered in the eleven-long segment bars 80–90 (*Et vitam*; itself further subdivided, as we shall see), allowing the two patterns to coincide for the Amen starting in bar 91.

Why did the composer avoid bringing the upper and lower parts together at bar 61? The irregularity serves no apparent formal purpose. Rather, it seems to meet an extranumerical consideration that we might call aesthetic: while respecting the underlying numbers and acknowledging their force, the composer saved the full power of their simultaneity for the beginning of the climactic Amen (b. 91). Dynamic considerations of sounding energy were allowed to bend the numbers. At bars 60–61, a sustained tenor *f* bridges two tenor *colores* that are still in relatively long notes; momentum would have been lost if the rhythmic hiatus that divides the upper-voice segments fell at just the same point. Nowhere else does a similar stasis of tenor pitch and upper-voice rhythm threaten to coincide. That is no longer a problem for the juncture with the Amen, where the strategy for the upper parts is different and the tenor *f* is of shorter duration. Examples of demonstrable deviations that invite such explanations are rare indeed; and the rarity is compounded in this case by the inevitability of the ground plan.

One effective strategy in this Credo is the graduated acceleration of the melismatic part towards the texted voice's motion in minims and semibreves until, in the final *color*, the two upper voices as well as the tenor operate simultaneously. Although structurally and numerically yoked to the non-diminishing text-bearing voice rather than to the lower parts, the melismatic voice speeds up in a way that echoes the diminution in the lower voices. The upper-part ten-long double segments are maintained without external diminution until bar 90, but diminution is present or simulated internally, always occurring stepwise with a new segment and never changing within it.

440 ENGLISH MOTETS C. 1400–1420

This diminution is accomplished in part by the discipline of restricting note-values. Not only does the tenor confine itself to longs and breves, but no single segment in the upper parts uses more than two adjacent values. The first twelve single melismatic segments (bb. 1–59) use only breves and longs, flanked by two breve rests; the next four (bb. 60–79, *Qui cum patre*) only breves and semibreves, flanked by semibreve rests; the next four (diminished, bb. 80–90, *Et vitam*) only semibreves. Meanwhile, the texted sections and the Amen use exclusively semibreves and minims, except for the breve that comes at the cadence of each of the first twelve segments.

The first stage of diminution just anticipates the start of section II, at bar 60 (*Qui cum patre*). The upper parts' first two double periods of ten longs are arranged as they were in section I, alternating text and melisma in five-long segments, with the difference that the accompanying (textless) upper voice now starts and ends each statement not with a breve but a semibreve rest, followed by syncopated breves and semibreves. To simulate duple diminution by this means at the audible beginning of each phrase gives a clear sense of accelerated motion, although the segment itself is not yet shortened.

The next diminution occurs within section II at the third segment (bb. 80–90, *Et vitam*); its ten bars are extended to eleven (compensating for the long dropped in bb. 41–49, *Et resurrexit*), and the segment is divided not only in half but in half again; thus, each of the two five-and-a-half-long periods is itself a diminutive form of a whole double segment with its own alternation of text and melisma. In each of the four 'melismatic' segments, each of eleven semibreves, nine semibreves are flanked by two semibreve rests—a 2:1 diminution of the opening melismatic segments, where eight breves are flanked by two breve rests—while the 'texted' part has a chain of syncopated semibreves initiated by a minim rest, which prepares for the full diminution effect of minim hockets, minim rests, and successive minims in the Amen. In cantus II from bars 80–90 the 'melismatic' segments are both eleven semibreves; the 'texted' segments start alike with semibreve–semibreve–minim rest, followed by a syncopated semibreve that continues to simulate diminution.

The originally sharp distinction between text and melisma, which defined the upper-part periods, begins to blur at bars 80–90. At first sight, too little text seems to have been left for this section; *Et vitam venturi seculi* is stretched over eleven longs. Despite scribal confusion, the intention (as shown in the transcription) is clearly that *Et vitam venturi* should be even-handedly repeated successively in each voice for the first half of this section and *seculi* for the second, thus maintaining the alternation.[18] There is no other textual duplication in the Credo. Each of these five-and-a-half-bar segments is divided into diminished versions of the text and melisma alternation, grouped in cantus I in four strictly alternating phrases of eleven semibreves each, but playfully dislocated and overlapped in the second voice as eleven semibreves of melisma, twelve semibreves texted, eleven semibreves of melisma, and ten semibreves texted. The rhythms of cantus I segments for this passage in ⓑ Example 23.1 are marked x and y (from b. 80), each of 11 semibreves; x + y is isorhythmically repeated. Cantus II has rhythmically identical y sections of 11 semibreves while cantus I is doing x, a kind of voice exchange, for which

---

[18] In cantus I, *Et vitam* was placed too early, in bb. 77–80; only *venturi* was moved, correctly, to b. 81, and the 'A' for Amen to b. 91. In cantus II, *Et vitam* was originally placed earlier; it has been erased and respaced, still not quite accurately.

THE YOXFORD CREDO   441

there is a long English tradition. In addition, the rhythm of the syncopated passage within x ($\llcorner$ ♦ ♦ ♦ ♦ ♦ ♦ ♦) is repeated within the intervening Cantus II segments not of 11 semibreves, but of 12 semibreves and 10 semibreves. This non-functional irregularity provides a kind of camouflaging syncopation or rubato to the eleven-semibreve units that avoids tidy joins, analogous to the long that is dropped in bars 41–49 and made up in the *Et vitam* section.

The acceleration gets seriously under way once textual constraints recede, as they do partially in *Et vitam* and wholly in the Amen. As the melismatic voice accelerates towards synchrony with the faster-moving texted voice, the latter loses its text and thus permits full mutual assimilation of their initially contrasting characters. The tenor finally matches the duple mensuration that the upper voices have maintained throughout, while the upper voices accommodate to the threefold dimensions and strict rhythmic repetitions that have been constant in the tenor.

By these means the texture is progressively transformed from the opening, where a single, fast-moving textual patter of minims and semibreves is projected against a slow-moving harmonic support, until the extremes of motion are mutually assimilated and resolved in the Amen. Each of these accelerating stages is dovetailed to avoid simultaneous structural joins. We have already observed this in the relation of the upper voices to the lower, and suggested that deviation from the plan was motivated by dynamic considerations. Structural coincidence is also avoided tonally: because the repeating temporal units of the upper parts are independent of the reducing proportions of the lower, the upper parts' tonal adaptation to the repeating pitch cycle and cadential opportunities of the lower parts is independent of that temporal cycle. Only for the Amen, once again, are the cycles synchronised.

In the upper parts, rhythmic motto tags are used to mark or to punctuate periodic repetition, even to simulate rhythmic duplication. Changes in the motto figure often mark major structural changes. The tags define and punctuate the segments audibly, anticipating the full rhythmic repetitions of the Amen. Each of the first nine texted sections begins ♦ ♦ ♦ and ends with ♦ ♦ ♦ ■, or slight variations thereof, creating musical rhyme. The beginning motto is sometimes maintained even when it does not fit the text very well, such as at bar 11 for *Et ex patre*, as if the supratextual aspects of the motto are given priority. At other times declamation seems to evoke a variant, as at bar 21 (♦♦♦♦), for *Genitum non*, bar 45 for *Et ascendit*, and bar 60 for *Qui cum patre*. Bars 45 and 60 have considerable structural weight. Bar 45 is close to the midpoint (at it in theory, just anticipating it in practice) of the texted first two pairs of *color* statements, bars 1–90. Its rhythm (first in cantus II), ♦ ♦ ♦♦♦, commands attention by its novelty. This is the first appearance of a figure that is then used with significance in bars 75, 80 and 85; in the last two instances it forms part of a pattern where voice I is strictly isorhythmic. Bar 60 heralds the juncture of the first and second *color* pairs; it divides the whole composition at the proportion 4:3, as well as bridging two *color* statements that are related in 4:3 proportion. Its ♦ ♦ ♦ is the first appearance of a figure that also takes on increasing palindromic importance from this point to the end.

The motto that ends most texted sections is ♦ ♦ ♦ ■, which occurs in that form, or a close variant of it, in each of the first twelve segments, up to bar 59. In the next six segments (i.e. in bb. 64, 69, 74, 79, 82 and 87), the breve consistently becomes two ligated semibreves. Sometimes the first minim is extended from a preceding syncopating

442 ENGLISH MOTETS C. 1400–1420

semibreve (at bb. 15, 20, 44, 74, 82 and 87), or expanded to ♩♩ ♩♩ ▪ (bb. 25, 35 and 54). None of these minor variants weakens the effect of cadential rhyme. Sometimes the ♩ ♦ ♩ figure is extended backwards, as at bars 4–5 in cantus I and bars 57–58 in cantus II, to set an extended three-minim pattern of alternating semibreves and minims (♦ ♩ ♦ ♩ ♦ ♩ ♦) against the prevailing two-minim grouping of minor prolation. Again, it is at structurally significant points that the end motto is noticeably changed. ♩ ♦ ♩ ▪ is replaced in the texted voice of bar 79 by ♦ ♩♩ ♦ ♦, closing a segment and preparing the new section. Cantus I at bar 80 starts and cantus II at bar 90 ends with the ♦ ♦ ♩♩ ♦ figure, so that bars 80–90 are framed by the retrograde of the new figure from bar 79, and a link between opening and closing mottoes is forged. The figure is immediately turned around again in bar 91, to start the Amen with ♦ ♩♩. In the final *color*, each *talea* in cantus I and II and the tenor is framed by this same rhythmic palindrome, ♦♩♩ – ♩♩ ♦. The entire Credo thus ends with the retrograde of its opening rhythm, ♦♩♩. This is in turn a diminution of the tenor's opening ▪ ▪ ▪, which is retrograded to ▪ ▪ ▪ to frame each *talea*, ensuring that the third *talea*'s melodic retrograde of the first is also a rhythmic retrograde. (The only two tenor occurrences of the pitch *f* frame the *color* and reinforce the retrograde.) Nested palindromes in local segments, spanning the whole piece and further linking the lower and upper parts, thus contribute powerfully to the unifying strategies.

Calculated noncoincidence of rhythmic periods between upper and lower voices happens on a microscopic level in the final section of *Sub Arturo plebs*, which pits the 16 breves (= 64 minims) of each duple-time tenor *talea* in c against the 21 major semibreves (= 63 minims) of the ℂ triplum, creating a creeping difference between them of a minim in each of the final three *taleae*. This slight difference enhances excitement and surprise in the final *color*, whereas in the Credo the irregularity is effected and recovered before the Amen (from b. 91), achieving climax by synchronisation, all parts moving at a similar rate, jubilant hocketing, and an audible pitting of c in the upper parts with minim equivalence against the lower parts, now reduced to ℂ. However, the upper parts of *Sub Arturo plebs* are isorhythmically organised within each *color*, while the Credo's alternating periods invoke the very different tradition of voice exchange.

Descendit descends; *de celis* ascends. There are no other obvious responses to directional mimetic opportunities. The text distribution, shown in summary in Figure 23.1, is fairly even up to bar 79; the amount of text allocated to each section conditions the distribution of semibreves and minims. Far from miscalculating the amount of text for bars 80–90 (*Et vitam*), it seems that the composer used this section as a bridge from the brisk textual patter of the preceding sections to the melismatic Amen, in which all distinction between text and melisma is finally dissolved. At the same time, the melismatic sections have, through the steps outlined above, approached by graduated steps the motion in semibreves and minims of the texted part, so that there is little distinction between the upper voices in bars 80–90 and none in the Amen. At the opening, one upper part projects compact and clear textual declamation soloistically against its slow-moving partner as well as against the slow-moving harmonic support of the lower voices; this extreme contrast to the equal motion and textless homogeneity of the Amen is gradually reduced both by increased motion in the melismatic voice and by the systematic acceleration of the tenor statements. The seams are camouflaged until the Amen, where we are faced with a perfect and perfectly timed coming together, not only of coincident rhythmic repetition in all parts, but also with the tenor, by its own inevitable

THE YOXFORD CREDO   443

plan, having speeded up to match the motion of the voice that was texted. At the same time, the melismatic voice accelerates towards the texted voice as the tenor sections become shorter. By the time these voices, in their different ways, have approached the motion of the texted voice, that voice has passed beyond text and textual constraints in favour of joining a purely musical jubilation governed by the final tenor diminutions.

Each tenor *talea* contains ten notes, but that is, as already noted, its only 'tenfold' feature. The underlying arrangement of the paired upper parts in periods of ten longs (duply divided, 2×5, and non-diminishing up to b. 80) is boldly pitted against the tenor, with its three *taleae* to each *color* and the threefold diminishing structure (twice 2:1) of the paired *colores*. Each of the three final *taleae* contains ten notes not only in the tenor, but also in each of cantus I and II; in all voices, each *talea* contains five notes in each of its two imperfect longs. The tenor has come to match both the duple time and the motion in semibreves and minims with which the upper texted part opened; the upper parts, in their turn, have adopted the scheme of the tenor and even its number of notes. The first and last three notes of each *talea* in cantus I, II, and the tenor are not only palindromic, as noted (♦♦♦ – ♦♦ ♦); they pick up and resolve two of the most distinctive rhythmic mottoes of the earlier texted segments, as well as mirroring the palindromic elements of the tenor *color* itself. This final *color* is a brilliant summation of the numerical strategy that is the ultimate aesthetic goal of the piece, a true symphony of numbers within the decad, devised to reconcile tens and fives with the more conventionally musical combinations of twos and threes, while rounding off both rhythmic and melodic palindromes in upper and lower parts.

I know of no other piece that so cunningly avoids any alignment of upper-voice *taleae* with those of the lower parts.[19] Only in the Amen, the final two *colores*, do the *taleae* come into alignment, giving a sense of resolution and climactic arrival. This Credo joins *Sub Arturo plebs* and some of the mensural, proportional and canonic *tours de force* in **OH** as another beacon of English achievement and adventure, belying the impression, drawn from some simpler music of the period, that English composers cultivated sonority at the expense of structure and intellectual challenge.[20]

Appendix
Notes to Credo Transcription (▶ Ex. 23.1)

The syncopation dots throughout are redundant in this mensuration. The following minims, all in cantus I, are flanked by syncopation dots: 14.1; 24.3, 5; 34.1, 3; 71.7; 72.1, 8. The semibreve 73.1 in cantus I is preceded by a redundant minim with dots.

Oblique ligatures are often carelessly drawn; such cases are not noted here unless clearly wrong. Ligature brackets are not marked in the lower parts, but occur for the following notes of each *talea*: Ct: 2–3, 4–6, 8–9; T: 3–4, 5–6, 8–10; ST: 3–4, 5–7, 9–11.

Accidentals:
Cantus I: 9–10 f♯ for *c*; 48.2 g♯ for *f*; 51.6 c♭ for *b*; 81 ♭ for 82.2 but no rest; 92.2 c♭ intended for 92.3 (*b*); 98 c♯ at beginning, intended for *b* or for 98.3.

---

[19] But see the discussion of *Carbunculus*, Ch. 25, for a possible instance.

[20] This chapter as originally published concluded at this point with a section on isorhythm, an early formulation of the reflections that came into sharper focus in the essay now in Ch. 2.

444 ENGLISH MOTETS C. 1400–1420

Cantus II: 21 e♯ for f; 69.3–69.4 b♯ for f.

Contratenor: 23 c♭ meant for b♭; 8 c is preceded by large letter C, perhaps for 'c natural'. The following flat signs are provided with a serif: II.23; I.51.6; I.81.

Note in bb. 41–42 the progression b♭–e.

Underlay:

II.8 *filium dei*: MS underlay has been adjusted to one minim later; I.33 *natus est* added; I.76 The words *Et vitam* have been moved; see above.

Manuscript readings:

5 ST has c, Ct has d; parallel passages show that d must be correct. In view of this, the e in II is emended to f; 16 II.4 d for e; 27 I.1 b for c; 53 I.3 oddly formed S with apparently added stem looks like a ♭ but must be ♦; 61 II.1–3 coloured without significance; also I 66.1–3; the corresponding II.71 and I.76.1–3, however, are not coloured; 72 I.8 followed by an extra ♦ c; 75 I.1 written ambiguously: g or a; 79 II.5 g for f; 81 I no rest, but c♭, c perhaps mistaking exemplar; 83 II.1 is followed by S rest, not M; 95 I first rest is S, not M; 96 I last rest is S, not M; 98 I first two rests are S, not M; 103 II second rest is B, not M; 105 II S + L.

24

Mayshuet and the *Deo gratias* Motets in the Old Hall Manuscript

The last two motets in **OH** declare themselves in their last lines as *Deo gratias* substitutes for the end of Mass; they were almost certainly the final works in the manuscript. The composer of the first one, *Are post libamina/Nunc surgunt in populo*, is named as 'Mayshuet'. The two motets are so nearly identical in form and style that the same composer is probably also responsible for its anonymous neighbour *Post missarum sollennia*. Only the triplum and contratenor of *Post missarum sollennia* survive in **OH**; the facing recto of *Post missarum* there is lost.[1] Judging by the contratenor, the missing tenor also shared its formal structure with *Are post libamina*. After publication of the **OH** edition (CMM 46), the two motets turned up anonymously on both sides of an English half-leaf, **Ox32**, that belonged to RC, a fragmentary royal manuscript, apparently copied partly from **OH** in the 1420s, and with newer added repertory.[2] Although likewise adjacent, the motets are in reverse order. The recto of the leaf contains most of the missing motetus of *Post missarum sollennia*, enabling an almost complete transcription of that motet, leaving only the tenor to be reconstructed; the verso contains most of the triplum of *Are post libamina*.

Mayshuet, *Are post libamina/Nunc surgunt in populo*

This motet has rightly attracted attention on account of the striking claims of its verbal texts:[3]

Revised and expanded from 'Bent, 'Mayshuet and the *Deo gratias* Motets in the Old Hall Manuscript', in Kirnbauer (ed.), *Beredte Musik: Konversationen zum 80. Geburtstag von Wulf Arlt*, Schola Cantorum Basiliensis Scripta, 8 (Basel, 2019), with permission from Schwabe Verlag. This version differs mainly in expanding on the relationship between the **Ivrea** and **OH** motets, in taking account of more recent work by Anna Zayaruznaya and Zoltán Rihmer, and in proposing a little more confidently a possible identity for the composer.

[1] CMM 46, i, pt. 2, nos. 146 and 147.

[2] RC has been pieced together over many decades. A revised and updated evaluation of this fragmentary choirbook together with inventory and facsimiles is now given in Bent, 'Towards the Reconstruction', in EECM 62, including evidence for the direct copying of some pieces from **OH**. A simplified inventory is given as ▶ Table 25.1. **Ox32** was briefly described among 'Notable Accessions' by B. C. Barker-Benfield in *Bodleian Library Record*, 11 (1982–85), 187 and an account of the musical yield up to that point given in Bent, 'The Progeny'. The Hilliard Ensemble recorded this motet from the then-superseded editorial reconstruction in CMM 46, but did not pick up this already published improved version using the new source.

[3] Translation by Leofranc Holford-Strevens. Textual emendations and commentary by Leofranc Holford-Strevens (LHS), incorporating suggestions by David Howlett (DRH); 9: Andrew Hughes translated this as 'it may be accompanied by stringed instruments'; 10: DRH suggests emendation to

---

The Motet in the Late Middle Ages. Margaret Bent, Oxford University Press. © Oxford University Press 2023.
DOI: 10.1093/so/9780190063771.003.0025

446 · ENGLISH MOTETS C. 1400–1420

Triplum OH, f. 111ᵛ, Ox32 verso	Syllables	Translation
Are post libamina	7	After the oblations of the altar
odas atque carmina	7	let us sing odes
laudis iubilemus.	6	and songs of praise.
Cuius finis bonus est	7	Him whose end is good
5 ipsum bonum superest	7	it remains for us to praise,
totum ut laudemus.	6	the All-good.
Vocis modulacio,	7	Let the music-making of the voice,
sicut iubet racio,	7	as reason orders,
concinat cum corde.	6	be in harmony with the heart.
10 Prevalet ignorancia,	8	Ignorance prevails,
ceca arrogancia	7	blind arrogance
involuta sorde;	6	wrapped up in filth;
cantatores sunt plerique	8	there are very many singers
quorum artes sunt inique;	8	whose skills are unequal [to the task];
15 vanam querunt gloriam.	7	they seek vainglory.
Libens cane,—non inane,	8	Sing willingly, not worthlessly,
propter deum,—ut in evum	8	to the glory of God, so that in eternity
ducaris in patriam.	7	you may be led into your [heavenly] fatherland.
Armonias mellicas	7	Let us give forth honeyed harmonies,
20 demus, yperliricas,	7	highly lyrical,
tono cum iocundo.	6	with joyful tone.
Nullus nostrum properet	7	Let none of us hasten
aut sonum anticipet,	7	or sing his note too soon,
sed semper ascultando.	7	but always listening.
25 Practicus insignis	6	A skilled distinguished
gallicus sub gallicis	7	Frenchman composed this song
hemus hunc discantavit	7	on French verses;
cantum, sed post reformavit;	8	but afterwards he revised it;
latina lingua anglis (**Ox32** angelis)	7	the Latin language is more often
30 sepius fit amena	7	pleasing to the English (or angels)
reddendo Deo gracias.	8	in rendering thanks to God.

preest; 21: **Ox32** *cito*, which would mean 'nor swiftly race ahead', but this is grammatically impossible. DRH suggests emendation to *toto*; 27: **Ox32** *henus*, but neither is a Latin word. What may be intended is *neniis*, though it does not fit the music; the Latin word has various meanings, not all complimentary, but Horace applies it to poems, and that seems to be the sense here. LHS cannot make any sense of *hunc*, masculine singular accusative; DRH suggests emendation to *themis*: sang (= composed) this song on Gallic themes; 29: **Ox32** has *angelis*, and an extra syllable to go with it, demonstrating scribal adjustment. It seems more likely that the English prefer Latin because they are losing their French, than that the angels prefer it because it is one of the three sacred languages; 31: DRH suggests emendation to *dando*.

MAYSHUET AND THE *DEO GRATIAS* MOTETS 447

Motetus[4] OH, f. 112		Translation
Nunc surgunt in populo	7	Now there arise in the people
viri mercatores;	6	mercenary men;
aurum mutant optimum	7	they change the best gold
in stannum, et flores	6	into tin, and sweetly
5 odorantes dulciter	7	fragrant flowers
in pravos fetores.	6	into evil smells.
Hi dicuntur (ni fallor)	7	These men (unless I am mistaken)
plerique cantores.	6	are mostly called singers.
Cum vident in medio	7	When they see in the middle [of the church]
10 aliquem magnatum	6	some great person
cantum querunt optimum,	7	they seek their best song,
sibi valde gratum.	6	intensely pleasing to him.
Notulas multiplicant	7	They multiply the notes
et reputant cantatum	7	and they think it was sung
15 non amore domini,	7	not for the love of God,
puto sed magnatum.	6	I believe, but of great persons.
Vos, tales ypocrite,	7	You, such hypocrites,
numquid aspexistis	6	have you never paid attention
sanctum evangelium,	7	to the Holy Gospel,
20 [in] quo perlegistis	6	in which you have read
vere dictum domini	7	the true word of God
loquentis de istis?	6	speaking about these matters?
Amen, vobis dicitur—	7	Verily, you are told—
mercedem recepistis.	7	you have received your reward.

The triplum text complains of singers who are incompetent but vainglorious; it stresses the importance for singers to listen in order to keep in time together; and most significantly, it is a self-declared contrafact. The text announces that it has been Latinised from a (non-extant and perhaps entirely different) French original by its French composer, which, together with the jaunty tenor (see below, Ex. 24.3), may imply that its *Deo gratias* status was associated only with the contrafact (see lines 25–31).[5]

---

[4] 10: LHS: literally, 'some one of the great persons'; 12: LHS: Classically, it would be 'to themselves', but in medieval Latin it may also be 'to him'; 13: LHS: *Notulas* is not necessarily diminutive; 14: DRH suggests omission of *et*; 20: LHS: *In* makes better sense, also of the syllable count, but there is no note for it; 24: DRH suggests emendation to *cepistis*.

[5] Contrafaction is quite rare in this repertory. The French motet *Se päour d'umble astinance/Diex tan desir estre amés de m'amour/Concupisco*, in **Ivrea** and **Ca1328**, expressing ceaseless love-longing, is retexted in Latin in its English source, **Ox7**, as *Domine quis habitabit/De veri cordis adipe/Concupisco* (PMFC 5, nos. 16, 16a). The tenor is the verse of the 8th respond at Matins on the feast of St Agnes. It presents prayers to God, virtues required for heaven (Ps. 15), and requests to Jesus for help. But this is an earlier motet of the mid-14th c., a

448 ENGLISH MOTETS C. 1400–1420

The motetus is even more scathing about singers who show off to important people. The thirty-one triplum lines of *Are post libamina* are metrically irregular. Its first twenty-four lines are arranged in six-line stanzas with somewhat irregular syllable count. The final sentence, here lines 25–31, is more like rhyming prose, and might equally well be so construed. The motetus has three eight-line stanzas, with alternating lines mostly of seven and six syllables. David Howlett produced an emended form of these texts correcting the syllable count. Even if these were the original forms of the texts, they were not the ones set by our composer, as can be shown from the almost entirely syllabic setting, and the care with which the few intended two-note melismas are notated. There is not even a note to accommodate the editorially suggested *in* in line 20 of the motetus; **Ox32** provides a note for the extra syllable in the variant *angelis* for *anglis*. This is an old confusion: *anglis* in **OH** is no doubt correct, English rather than angels. If the text was indeed a contrafact it has been very carefully tailored to the existing music.

Does the syllabic setting mean, then, that the original French text of *Are post libamina* was similarly irregular, or that it had fewer repeated notes to accommodate a different text? The two versions of the triplum are musically very close, and the few variants are not such as to sustain or disprove a claim of direct copying from Old Hall. The only text variants between the two sources occur in the last few lines. The upper parts are in unsigned c throughout, though the notation is cunningly managed to coordinate with the tenor rhythms, especially when these are diminished to the equivalent of ₵ in the final statements. The setting is almost entirely syllabic at the minim level. Indeed, the duple-time patter with many repeated notes of both *Are post libamina* and *Post missarum sollennia* has a strong affinity with the similar writing in the triplum of *O amicus*, except that here words are broken by rests. The alignment of text and music by the main scribe of **OH** is slightly better than **Ox32**, which, however, is not unclear, and has at least one clearly shown difference of placement.

Post missarum/Post misse: The Ivrea Motet

Before giving a further account of the similarities between the Old Hall pair of motets, a precedent needs consideration. The texts of *Post missarum sollennia/Post misse modulamina* are adapted from an earlier motet in **Ivrea**, which is also listed in the index of the mostly lost **Trém**. News of a new source in **Aachen** was published in 2001, but overlooked by other musicologists until Anna Zayaruznaya drew wider attention to this important fragment.[6] There can be no doubt that the **Ivrea** texts were

---

pious exhortational contrafaction of a motet on secular French texts over a suitably texted albeit chant tenor. It is not impossible that other Latin-texted motets in England may have been similarly adapted from French originals. Kügle, *The Manuscript Ivrea*, has written extensively about the grouping and dating of motets in **Ivrea**. He accepts Wathey's identification of the **OH** composer with Matheus de Sancto Johanne (p. 86). He does not give musical reasons for the presumably text-based claim that the **OH** motets were modelled on the Ivrea *Post missarum*.

[6] *Post missarum sollempnia* is in **Ivrea**, ff. 7ᵛ–8. The triplum and solus tenor are now in **Aachen**, f. 2ᵛ, in company with three motets attributable to Philippe de Vitry. See Lüdtke, 'Kleinüberlieferung' and Zayaruznaya, *The Monstrous New Art*, 177–89. The edited texts in her appendix 4 (pp. 256–57) take account of the Aachen

designed as a pair, and that the **Ivrea** motet came first. Here is its triplum text from **Ivrea** and **Aachen**.[7] Boldface in this and the **OH** triplum (following) indicates shared diction between them:

Triplum Ivrea f. 7[v]; Aachen f. 2[v]	Translation
Post missarum sollempnia **divina post eulogia:**	After the solemnities of masses, after the praises of God,
Presul, gregem rege tuum speculo bonum actuum, 5 rectos unire **studeas**, malos pie coherceas.	bishop, may you rule your flock by the mirror of good actions, strive to unite the righteous, dutifully constrain the wicked.
Rex, apex **fulgens apice**, **habenas rei publice** modereris **eximie** 10 **canendus** pater patrie;	King, peak gleaming at the peak, may you excellently command the reins of state, to be hymned as the father of your country.
Sana detis ut dogmata principi, strategemata historica revolvite, proceres stirpis inclite.	That you may give sound opinions to the prince, scroll through the stratagems in history, you nobles of a famous race.
15 Miles, predis non inhiya, percipis qui stipendia, nec fuge nec dedecore te dedas tecto corpore.	Knight, be not greedy for plunder, you who receive pay, neither flee nor disgracefully surrender with armoured body.

source. See also Zayaruznaya, 'New Voices'. In Bent, 'Mayshuet', I was only able to mention this in a footnote. Of the four motets represented on the two leaves of **Aachen**, the other three are all on good authority attributed to Philippe de Vitry, which raises the question whether this might be also. This suggestion lacks any authority other than adjacence in that fragment; there are no clear Vitriacan markers and no strong reason to consider an attribution.

[7] Variants and alternative modern readings: 1–2, 7–9 and other words in bold are also in **OH**; 5 *rectos* **Ivrea**, *sectes* **Aachen**; *unire* **Aachen**: *unice* **Ivrea**; 8 *rei publice* **Aachen**, **OH**: *zey pliblite* **Ivrea**; 9 *moderer*[*is*] **Aachen**: *moderaris* corr. from *moderans* **Ivrea** (cf. *moderans* **OH**); 12 *principi* **Aachen**: *precipi* **Ivrea**; 15 *inhiya* **Aachen**: *inhyna* **Ivrea**; 16 *percepis* [*sic*] **Ivrea**: *principis* **Aachen**; 17 *dedecore* **Ivrea**: *decore* **Aachen**; 18 *te dedas* **Aachen**: *de detas* **Ivrea**; 19 *uis* **Ivrea**: *vis* **Aachen**; *lantibus* **Aachen**, corr. Rihmer: *laudibus* **Ivrea**; 21 *imbecillibus* **Ivrea**: *investilibus* **Aachen**, Rihmer.

Spelling variants (the better first, which is not necessarily the poet's): 6 *coherceas* **Aachen**: *choerceas* **Ivrea**; 11 *dogmata* **Aachen**: *docmata* **Ivrea**; 16 *percepis*: a common medieval spelling; corrected by Rigg, Rihmer, LHS. 22 *sed* **Ivrea**: *set* **Ivrea**, also a good classical spelling (LHS); 24 *gratias* **Aachen**.

Commentary (LHS): Both **Ivrea** texts (tr and mo) are in regular octosyllables. 4 The sense seems inescapable, but *bonum* genitive plural is a pre-classical form one would not expect to find at this date except in a very affected author. It is also the only instance in these texts of final -*m* before a vowel, though that was not unusual; emendation to the normal *bonorum* would require either an extra syllable at the start of the verse or elision of -*um*, neither of which is to be expected outside classicizing quantitative verse. [MB: While there are enough notes to accommodate trisyllabic *bonorum*, this would be the only exception to the completely regular octosyllabic lines of both **Ivrea** texts.] 7 i.e. head of the people, with a gleaming crown on your head; 19–20 Literally: 'share in equal scale-pans'; 21 Rihmer adopts **Aachen**'s *investilibus*, translating it 'the unclothed [poor]'; this is ingenious, but I await evidence that an adjective *investilis* exists; 23 'Whoever you are' is not to be understood as the insult it often is in English (though not Latin); the sense is simply 'whatever your station in life.'

450 ENGLISH MOTETS C. 1400–1420

20	Iudex, equis ius lancibus utris partire partibus, ac inbecillibus fave, set ab iniuria cave.	Judge, dispense justice fairly to both parties and favour the weak, but beware of injustice.
	Quisquis es, recte sentias post datas **Deo gracias**.	Whoever you are, may you think rightly after thanking God.

Below are the texts of the triplum of the English motet *Post missarum* from **OH**, and of the motetus as in both **Ivrea** and **Ox32**.[8] A transcription of the reconstructed Old Hall motet is given as Example 24.1.[9]

Triplum text of *Post missarum sollenia* (**OH**):[10]

Triplum: OH, f. 112ᵛ	Syllables	Translation
Post missarum sol[l]ennia	8	After the solemnities of masses,
divina post eulogia:	8	after the praises of God,
voce cum dulciflua	7	let us sing songs
5 decantemus cantica,	7	with sweetly fluent voice,
flagitantes dominum,	7	beseeching God,
fontem bonorum omnium,	8	the fount of all good things,
ut nostrum gregem visere	8	that He be willing to visit
velit et dirigere,	7	and guide our flock,

[8] English translations of the texts of the two Old Hall motets by Andrew Hughes in the only source available at the time were given in CMM 46. The **Ivrea** texts were presented with a short commentary and English summary by A. G. Rigg for Harrison's edition of the **Ivrea** *Post missarum/Post misse* in a Supplement to PMFC 5. When the **Ox32** motetus text came to light, Professor Rigg kindly provided a tentative translation, given in Bent, 'The Progeny', 10. Improvements by Leofranc Holford-Strevens to the texts and translations of the Old Hall and Ivrea motets were then incorporated in Bent, 'Mayshuet', which was written before access to Anna Zayaruznaya's book, in which she discussed the Ivrea motet and signalled Joachim Lüdtke's overlooked 2001 publication of **Aachen** (Lüdtke, 'Kleinüberlieferung', and Zayaruznaya, *The Monstrous New Art*). In appendix 4 to that book she published Zoltán Rihmer's excellent edition and translation of the texts of the Ivrea motet, with the benefit of the **Aachen** readings. Leofranc Holford-Strevens accepts most of Rihmer's readings, but his emendations and translations differ in a few respects and are given here with his commentary (LHS), together with his editions of the Old Hall texts.

[9] Music commentary to Ex. 24.1: No emendations. Notes cut off in **Ox32** and supplied editorially are in small type, as is the reconstructed tenor.

[10] Variant readings: 7 *vitere*; 8 *velud*; 10 *cavenda* makes sense here, but may have been adapted from **Ivrea** line 10's *canendus*; 19 *moderans*, thus in **Ivrea** 9, there in error for *moderaris*, but sense is made of *moderans* here; 20 *patile*.

Commentary (LHS): Irregular metre: syllable count by line is shown. 9: *doruma* is not a Latin word; if as Andrew Hughes's translation ('the gifts of virtue') implies the author had some notion of Greek δώρημα, 'gift', the gifts would be those of the Spirit listed more than once by St Paul. But the line as transmitted contains a syllable too many; 16: I have translated what the text says, nonsense as it is; one might emend *ditamine* to *dictamine*, understood as the Word of God, but even then we should be missing a verb; 22: A confusing transition from an earthly to the heavenly king.

MAYSHUET AND THE *DEO GRATIAS* MOTETS 451

	in nos dorumas inserere	9	to implant in us the gifts of the Spirit,
10	et ne nos abradere.	7	and not to rub us away.
	Pie **presul, studeas**	7	Holy bishop, take pains
	deliros ut corigas,	7	to direct those who have strayed,
	obstinatos mollias,	7	soften the obstinate,
	conversos et foveas,	7	and strengthen the converted,
15	et privatos lumine	7	and those deprived of light
	caro ditamine.	6	by a dear enrichment.
20	**Rex, fulgens in apice,**	7	King, gleaming at the peak,
	habenas reipublice	8	excellently commanding
	moderans eximie,	7	the reins of state,
	cavenda docens patule.	8	plainly teaching the things to be avoided.
	Qui das iustis dindima	7	Who givest the heights of Heaven
	salvatis agalmata,	7	to the just, and joys to the saved,
	da nos ita psallere	7	grant us to sing
	et laudis musas prodere	8	and bring forth the muses of praise
25	per odas iperliricas,	8	through highly lyrical odes,
	ut demus **Deo gracias.**	8	so that we may give thanks to God.

Motetus of both motets (**Ivrea** and **Ox32**): *Post misse modulamina:*[11]

Ivrea, f. 8, Ox32, recto	Translation
Post misse modulamina,	After the music of the mass,
post verbi dulcis (**Ox32**: *divini*) semina,	after the deeds of the sweet Word:
5 Cives graves, politia	grave citizens, lest the well-ordered state
ne vel aristogarchia	or the rule of the best
cedat, prodeste liberis	should be lost, be of profit to your children
et moribus et literis.	in both morals and letters.
Mercator, emas utile	Merchant, may you buy what is useful,
neque fuca vendibile;	nor adulterate what is saleable;
pondere, metro, precio,	in weight, measure, and price
10 periusta sit vendicio.	let your selling be thoroughly fair.

[11] Variants and alternative modern readings: 2 *dulcis* Rigg: *dulci* **Ivrea**: *divini* **Ox32**; 3 *graves* **Ox32**: *gemes* **Ivrea**; *politia* Rihmer, *spolicia* **Ox32**, *ploica* **Ivrea**; 4 *aristogarchia* Rihmer: *aristogorgia* **Ox32**: *arcato garchia* **Ivrea**; 5 *cedat* **Ivrea**: *cedas* **Ox32**; 7 *emas* Rigg: *emat* **Ivrea**: *ei vas* **Ox32**; 8 *fuca* LHS: *fusca* **Ox32**, Rihmer: *fusta* **Ivrea**, Rigg; 11 *vel* **Ox32**: *nec* **Ivrea**; 13 *peracue* **Ox32**: *per acrie* **Ivrea**; 14 *strenue* **Ox32**: *stranue* **Ivrea**; 15 *sulca* Rigg: *sulfa* **Ox32**, *fulca* **Ivrea**, *sere* **Ivrea**, *sege* **Ox32**; 16 *lege* **Ivrea**: *le* **Ox32**, which breaks off here; 19 *quivis* Rihmer: *qui vis* **Ivrea**; 10 *venditio*, 20 *gratias* **Ivrea**.

Text commentary (LHS): 2 Hypermetric *divini* instead of *dulcis* has been retained. It makes sense, it has its own note in this nearly syllabic setting and seems intentional, reflecting the *divina* of triplum line 2. Both OH motets have a high level of metrical irregularity. 3 Rihmer is right to discern *politia* = πολιτεία here, but I suspect it has here not its general meaning of 'state' but the specific meaning Aristotle gives it in his sixfold classification of constitutions, a blend of aristocracy and democracy (*Politics* 4. 9).

Architector vel opifex,	Architect or workman,
esto fidelis artifex;	be an honest craftsman;
ingenium peracue,	thoroughly sharpen your wits,
manibus age strenue.	work hard with your hands.
15 Agricola, sulca, sere,	Farmer, plough, sow,
mete, puta lege terre,	harvest, prune by the law of the soil,
prout congruit tempori,	as suits the season,
nec parce duro corpori.	and do not spare your hardened body.
Tu quivis, bonum facias	Whoever you are, do good
20 post datas Deo gracias.	after thanking God.

Both texts of the Ivrea motet are in entirely regular octosyllabic lines; the twenty-four triplum lines are disposed in five four-line stanzas, the twenty motetus lines in four four-line stanzas, in both cases framed by a couplet at the beginning and end. Both texts begin with *Post miss-* . . . . and end . . . *Deo gratias*, as do those of the Old Hall *Post missarum sollennia*. The Ivrea triplum exhorts that, after Mass, the bishop (lines 3–6), king (lines 7–14), knight (lines 15–19), and judge (lines 19–22) should go forth and perform their high offices fairly. The motetus text parallels the triplum, one stanza shorter, but is addressed to social ranks of the middle and lower classes: citizens, merchant, builder, and farmer are urged to work well and justly. Both texts devote a four-line stanza to each addressee (except to the king, who gets two stanzas). Zayaruznaya has contextualised the social hierarchies of the powerful figures invoked in both texts as instances of 'estates satire', a well-known literary topos, even a genre, also suggesting a link between this motet and the peasant uprising (the Jacquerie) of 1358, and a possible connection with *Se grace/Cum venerint*, the *Ite missa est* motet which ends the Tournai mass, and which outlines a more limited social hierarchy.[12] She shows how the relation of the categories to each other in the Ivrea motet is managed in the mutual placement of the simultaneous texts, the four estates of each voice coinciding approximately with the four *taleae*, so that the higher and lower strata are presented simultaneously, as if equal. In an interesting musico-textual analysis, she demonstrates how syllable and semantic 'rhyme' between the parts reinforces this potentially subversive message, also by bringing the beginning and end of each part together as musical and textual unities. Similar coordination of motet texts occurs quite frequently, for example in the musician motets discussed in Part IV.

Musically, the Ivrea motet is in four parts including a contrapuntally essential contratenor. It has been proposed that the tenor may be a hitherto unidentified *Ite missa est*

---

[12] Kügle, *The Manuscript Ivrea*. A primary reason is given as it having a middle-voice tenor like *Tribum*, but since this is true also of later motets like *Apollinis*, it is not a strong argument for such an early dating. Middle-voice tenors are reviewed in Ch. 1 and, for *Apollinis*, in Ch. 16. Kügle also suggests the possible dependency of the Marchetto motet *Ave regina/Mater innocencie* on *Cum venerint*, which would therefore be earlier; but the dating and even the authorship of that motet is uncertain (Ch. 26). Having said that, the notation and style of *Cum venerint* are entirely compatible with a dating alongside the most advanced motets in *Fauvel*. Kügle, *The Manuscript Ivrea*, 163–67, dated *Cum venerint c.* 1315. In reporting my earlier reconstruction of the **OH** *Post missarum* motet, Zayaruznaya, *The Monstrous New Art* (178 n. 10), wrongly states that it is adjacent to *Se grace/Cum venerint* in two sources, rather than that it is adjacent to *Are post libamina*.

Ex. 24.1 Transcription of *Post missarum sollennia/Post misse modulamina* (**OH**)

454 ENGLISH MOTETS C. 1400–1420

Ex. 24.1 Continued

MAYSHUET AND THE *DEO GRATIAS* MOTETS 455

Ex. 24.1 Continued

456 ENGLISH MOTETS C. 1400–1420

Ex. 24.1 Continued

or *Deo gratias* chant.[13] A solus tenor conflation of tenor and contratenor is provided in **Ivrea** and **Aachen**. I have argued that solus tenors may have played a part in the compositional process, as they survive exclusively for works where the contratenor shares the contrapuntal foundation with the tenor, as here, as a *basso seguente* on which upper parts could then be erected in a compositional process without recourse to visually aligned score.[14] The **Ivrea** motet (with two *color* statements, each of two *taleae*, and no diminution) is in perfect modus with imperfect time and prolation. If Kügle is right, it dates presumably, and plausibly, before *c.* 1360.[15] There are many dissonances and parallels between the texted parts, which are nearly equal in range. Zayaruznaya observes that the upper voices cross occasionally, though, in this case, without special textual significance.[16]

The **Ivrea** motet has two identical lower-voice *colores* of twenty-eight perfect longs (each of three imperfect breves in minor prolation), each comprising two *taleae* of fourteen longs. There is no regular isorhythm in the top parts, but a six-breve isorhythmic repetition in the triplum at the same place in each of the four *taleae* includes a hocket that is briefly complemented in the motetus but not fully interlocked at the minim level.[17] In the first case it serves to separate the opening couplet from the stanzas devoted to the bishop in the triplum and the citizens in the motetus, as Zayaruznaya has pointed out. The social hierarchy is also reflected in the fact that the triplum, with its loftier addressees, is higher in range (clef C1) than the motetus (C2).

Post missarum in Old Hall and Ivrea

The triplum of the Old Hall motet *Post missarum* adopts the Ivrea motet's first two lines, the final two words (*Deo gratias*), and much intermediate diction, especially in the four lines beginning *Rex*. But otherwise the triplum text differs significantly and is only loosely based on the Ivrea original. It makes no attempt to retain Ivrea's metre or structure, abandoning the stanza form. It is metrically irregular: its twenty-six lines have mostly seven syllables, sometimes eight, and in one case each six and nine.

It eliminates Ivrea's knight and judge and concentrates on the bishop and king, in a much altered form which disrupts the hierarchy and parallelism of the paired Ivrea texts. The Old Hall composer clearly knew the older French motet, but chose to

[13] Harrison in PMFC 5, and Clark, '*Concordare cum materia*', report it as unidentified.

[14] It is often the case, as in *Vos/Gratissima* (Ch. 8) and in Dunstaple's *Veni sancte/Veni creator* (MB 8, no. 32), that a chant tenor cannot also fulfil the function of supporting the counterpoint of the upper parts, so that an essential contratenor (and therefore a solus tenor, actually in *Vos*, potentially in *Veni*) is needed.

[15] The most recent work on **Ivrea** suggests that the repertory was frozen in 1359, though copied later, in the 1380s and 1390s, with only a few (unspecified?) compositions dating from those later decades. See Kügle, *Ivrea*. The Ivrea motet is in perfect modus, imperfect time, minor prolation, like the opening of the Old Hall motet; but there the musical resemblance ends, except that both cadence on *f*. For other uses of texts from older motets in newer ones, see two by Hubertus de Salinis: *Psallat chorus/Eximie pater*, which adapts St Nicholas texts for St Lambert, and *Si nichil/In precio*, whose texts are taken from a 13th-c. conductus. See Reaney in CMM 11/7, 62–64 and **Q15**, no. 247, with commentary in Bent, *Q15*, i. 222–23. For more on Salinis, see Ch. 27.

[16] On voice-crossing, see Ch. 9, also taken up in Zayaruznaya, *The Monstrous New Art* and Shaffer, 'Finding Fortune'.

[17] As well as alternating semibreves and rests in opposite phase between the upper parts, the triplum has ♩ ♦ ♩ ♦ hockets against motetus semibreves without rests.

adapt its texts and emphases to a new (or differently texted) musical setting. By contrast, the now-discovered **Ox32** motetus of the **OH** motet, *Post misse modulamina*, is textually identical to that of the Ivrea motet, with only minor variants. Its fragmentary half-leaf breaks off before the end, but the text can be confidently completed from **Ivrea**.[18]

Musically, the two *Post missarum* motets are quite different in style, though there are a few parallels. Most conspicuously, both motets are in perfect modus with (unsigned) imperfect time and minor prolation. The final *color* of the **OH** motet is in signed ℭ time (in both the **OH** triplum and the **Ox32** motetus) to align with the tenor; in this it differs from *Are post libamina* whose upper parts remained in [C]. The **OH** *Post missarum* follows **Ivrea** in having *colores* of twenty-eight units each of two *taleae* of fourteen units. It differs in that there are three *colores*, not two, and that those are in successive diminution, whereas **Ivrea** has no diminution. In the case of other related motets (notably those of the musician group, Part IV), later motets find comparable ways of going beyond their models. In both motets, the twenty-eight perfect longs of the first *color* each consist of three imperfect breves in minor prolation. But the second *color* of the **OH** motet is twenty-eight perfect breves and the third twenty-eight major semibreves, with corresponding changes of mensuration in the upper parts. Unlike the **Ivrea** motet, each of the three pairs of *taleae* is fully isorhythmic in all parts within each pair, but there is of course no isorhythm *between* the diminishing *colores*. The upper parts are equal in range, in C1 clefs, again unlike **Ivrea**. Both motets are tonally on *f*, and both have contrapuntally essential contratenors. The reconstructed tenor of the **OH** motet is unidentified (see Ex. 24.2). Even if some alternative pitches are proposed, it is hard to turn the *Post missarum* tenor into either a piece of plainsong or a popular tune, though it has periodic phrases of 5 + 5 + 4, 5 + 5 + 4 units.[19]

Ex. 24.2 Reconstructed tenor of *Post missarum*

The tenor of the other **OH** motet, *Are post libamina*, appears to have been a secular trochaic tune, popular in character, shorter, 2 × 7 units, and with *overt* and *clos* endings in the paired *talea* statements (see Ex. 24.3). This tenor is similar to that of a motet in **Durham20**, *Herodis in pretorio/Herodis in atrio/Hey, hure lure*, which has units of 6 + 6 + 5 and is texted

---

[18] See n. 3 above for the readings, and ▶ Table 25.1 for an inventory of RC.
[19] Other 14th-c. motets of English provenance with French tenors are *Solaris ardor Romani/Gregorius sol seculi/Petre tua navicula/Mariounette douche*; *Triumphat hodie/Trop est fol – Si que la nuit*; *Deus creator omnium/Rex genitor/Doucement mi reconfort*; *Pura placens pulcra/Parfundement plure Absolon*. Of these, the first two have similar short, irregular phrases. *Mariounette douche* has unit groups of 7s and 4s; it is a virelai with a Latin contrafact in the motetus of *Caligo terre/Virgo mater*. *Triumphat hodie* in **OxNC362** and **Lo24198** divides the profane French song between the tenors: *Trop est fol ky, Si que la nuit*; the tune has the form aabb abba aa, with irregular units (also 7 + 4). The other two French tenors, *Doucement mi reconforte* and *Parfundement plure Absolon*, are longer-breathed tunes. All these motets are in PMFC 15, and the tenors are unidentified. *Domine quis habitabit* in **Ox7** is a contrafact of a French original (PMFC 5, nos. 16 and 16a), but the tenor is Latin and liturgical.

with secular French words (see Ex. 24.4).[20] All three motets attest a lively tradition of secular tenors which retain their merry rhythms, albeit slowed down for use in motets.

Ex. 24.3 Tenor of *Are post libamina*

Ex. 24.4 Tenor of *Herodis in pretorio/Herodis in atrio/Hey, hure lure* from **Durham20**

The texts of the Old Hall *Post missarum* were thus adapted from an older French motet with Latin texts, presumably, like the ascribed motet, *Are post libamina*, adjusted for an English constituency. Whether the original texts of *Post missarum* were Latin or French cannot be determined. We have seen that a different kind of adaptation, from a French vernacular original, applied to *Are post libamina*. We might guess that the French composer who adapted or contrafacted his motet from French into Latin as *Are post libamina* could also have made the verbal adaptation of *Post missarum*, in view of their comparable metrical insouciance: just as the triplum lines of *Are post libamina* are metrically irregular, so is the adapted triplum of *Post missarum*. In both Old Hall motets, the poet was unconcerned with regularity, in contrast to the wholly regular octosyllables of the Ivrea texts of *Post missarum*. It is also possible that *Are post libamina*'s near-twin, *Post missarum*, likewise a *Deo gratias* substitute on a non-chant tenor, might have been composed to secular French words, and a contrafaction contrived by borrowing and adapting the ready-made texts, but this cannot yet be proven.[21] Both **OH** motets include the unusual word *iperliricas/yperliricas*.

They share a similar tenor/contratenor structure. *Are post libamina* has, and the missing tenor of *Post missarum* would have had, a homographic tenor whose longs and breves are to be repeated in two successive levels of diminution at the next note-level down, as breves and semibreves, then as semibreves and minims. *Post missarum* thus has three tenor and contratenor iterations in successive diminution. Each *color* statement comprises a pair of *taleae* which are isorhythmic in all parts. The first *color* statement is 2 × 14 perfect longs, the second 2 × 14 perfect breves, the third 2 × 14 major semibreves (14 units being the *talea* length). The lower parts of the shorter motet *Are post libamina* are in fact marked for four iterations; the fourth tenor/contratenor statement is without further diminution from the third. The four *color* statements of *Are post libamina* each have a pair of *taleae*, also isorhythmic in all parts within each pair, and as in both the *Post missarum* motets, based on units or multiples of seven.[22]

---

[20] I made this comparison in Bent, 'Transmission', 67. See now for another instance *Plausu querulo*, Ex. 31.2 below.

[21] The tenor of *Are post libamina* must indeed be a catchy secular tune, quite similar to the mid-century motet tenor in **Durham20**, f. 1, *Herodis in pretorio/Herodis in atrio/Hey hure lure* (Ex. 24.4 above). This would seem to leave the shared basis of all three motets in units of seven unexplained, but they exist in *Are post libamina* independently of any dependence on the Ivrea motet.

[22] The *color* and *talea* length of the Ivrea *Post missarum* (28 and 14) recur in **OH**'s *Post missarum*.

460 ENGLISH MOTETS C. 1400–1420

The first *color* statement is 14 (2 × 7) perfect longs, the second 2 × 7 perfect breves, the third and fourth 2 × 7 major semibreves; as there is no further diminution between these last two, their four *taleae* can be, and are, isorhythmic in all parts.[23] In both Old Hall motets the equal-range texted upper parts for each successive tenor reduction have no changes of mensuration. They are computed entirely in imperfect tempus and minor prolation, but they fall into groups compatible with the mensural diminutions of the tenor (in perfect time and then major prolation) with minim equivalence throughout, and are so aligned in the accompanying transcription of the **OH** *Post missarum*, Example 24.1. In *Are post libamina* the contratenor is contrapuntally in-essential (i.e. it does not underpin any otherwise unsupported fourths), so it could have originated as a three-voice motet. In *Post missarum* the Old Hall contratenor evidently provided essential support to the missing tenor. The two motets thus differ in that respect. *Are post libamina* has an optional added fifth voice in **OH**. That voice is unlabelled, textless, and low-cleffed, with plentiful minim movement, and is quite dissonant. With some deviations, it follows the isorhythm of the other parts within each *talea* pair.[24]

Mayshuet, the Composer

Ursula Günther wrongly reported that Old Hall gives the composer's name of these two motets as M. or Matheus de Sancto Johanne. The **OH** ascription of *Are post libamina* is to 'Mayshuet'; *Post missarum* is anonymous.[25] She, Gilbert Reaney, and others following them, had assumed on the basis of similarity of names that these are one and the same composer. 'Mayhuet de Joan' is named in **Chantilly** as the composer of a Latin-texted three-stanza ballade *Inclite flos orti Gebenensis* for Clement VII as pope, referring in its opening line to Robert's Geneva origin; the tenor in **Chantilly** is labelled 'pro papa Clemente'.[26] This composer is assumed to be the Matheus de Sancto Johanne credited with three French-texted songs in **Chantilly**.[27]

A supplication for a canonry to Pope Clement VII in November 1378 by presumably the same Matheus de Sancto Johanne names him as a familiar of Louis I, duke of Anjou.[28] He may have joined Louis's expeditions in 1377, and was still with his chapel

---

[23] See Ch. 2. Isorhythm is used here to designate exactly replicated rhythms to different pitches, and not applied to any form of diminution or mensural manipulation.

[24] As the fragmentary concordance in **Ox32** preserves only the top half of the verso with nearly all of the triplum, it cannot be determined if this source had the optional extra part, which is on f. 112ʳ in **OH**. It seems to me likelier that this voice is unique to **OH**.

[25] Günther in *NG1*, and Günther, 'Zur Biographie', 180–85: 'sein Name in lateinischer Form als M. bzw. Matheus de Sancto Johanne', citing Reaney, 'The Manuscript Chantilly', 71–72: 'He is also the only French composer named in **OH**, which contains two works by him.' Thus Reaney assumes the identity but does not actually cite the less explicit form of the name ('Mayshuet') in Old Hall.

[26] In **Chantilly**, f. 41ʳ, and in **ModA**, f. 15ʳ, where it is anonymous. See Ch. 30.

[27] The rondeaux *Je chante ung chant*, f. 16 and *Fortune faulce*, f. 59ᵛ, also in **Ivrea**, f. 21, and the ballades *Sans vous ne puis*, f. 35, also in **ModA**, f. 15ᵛ, and *Sience n'a nul annemi*, f. 57. The songs are quite unlike the Old Hall motets, but cross-genre comparisons are dangerous.

[28] For the biographical summary which follows, see Ursula Günther, 'Matheus de Sancto Johanne', *NG1*, ix. 820, and 'Zur Biographie'; Andrew Tomasello, *Music and Ritual*, 252–53; Wathey, 'The Peace of 1360–1369', 144–50; Di Bacco and Nádas, 'Papal Chapels', 47; Andrew Wathey in *NG2*; Nádas, 'Secular Courts', 194–95; reprinted in Nádas, *Arte Psallentes*, 382–83. I am grateful to John Nádas and Andrew Wathey for checking my reporting of their work.

at Avignon in 1380.[29] Louis had been one of the group of noble hostages who sailed to England in 1360 as guarantors of the ransom of his captured father King John II, but he escaped, incurring the displeasure of the French king, who voluntarily returned to captivity to redeem his honour.

The same document also indicates that Matheus had indeed previously served Cardinal Robert of Geneva. John Nádas dates this service at some time between 1371/2 and 1378, possibly for Róbert's legation in Lombardy 1376–78, and preceding his service with Louis of Anjou. In 1379 John, duke (subsequently king) of Aragon instructed his agents to seek good singers in Avignon for his chapel. They were to be young, unmarried, preferably able to play an instrument, and not to have been in the service of the duke of Anjou (see Ch. 30). Whether this was intended as an *ad hominem* exclusion of Matheus we cannot tell. By 1382 Matheus was a papal singer for Clement VII; thus, apart from his time with Louis, Matheus de Sancto Johanne (also known in the documents as 'Mahuetus') was almost continuously (with a gap of two to three years) in the service of Clement, both before and after his election to the papacy, as one of his singing chaplains in Avignon up to at least 1387 and probably until his death, which occurred by June 1391. The 1378 supplication names him as from the diocese of Thérouanne, but of all the documents reported by Nádas it is the only one to do so; all others state his diocese of origin as Noyon.[30]

Andrew Wathey reports that 'The "Mahiet" who was a clerk in the chapel of the duchess of Anjou from September 1370 cannot be identified with Matheus de Sancto Johanne'.[31] Nádas cites another document of November 1378, in which a Matheus, *clericus* of Noyon, is reported as the duchess's first chaplain. Despite the coincidence of names, neither Wathey nor Nádas claims positive identification with Matheus de Sancto Johanne; he appears to be just another clerk named Matheus from the diocese of Noyon with no stated connections to music. There are indeed several clerics called Matheus who lack further identification or beneficial overlaps with Matheus de Sancto Johanne, who in turn may not be the composer of all the music attributed to him, or to someone named Matheus but lacking further specification.

Wathey reported the presence of Matheus de Sancto Johanne in England, Anglicised as 'Matheu Seintjon', in the chapel of the English queen Philippa during the mid-1360s and perhaps earlier; there was some blurring of the distinction between the king's and queen's chapels. Nádas suggests that he may have arrived at the English court of Edward

---

[29] He may therefore also be the composer of an unascribed ballade on Louis I of Anjou, *Los prijs honeur*. He would have been a colleague in Avignon of the distinguished cleric Egidius de Aureliana, also favoured by Clement VII in 1379–93, who may perhaps be the composer thus named in the text of the motet *Alma polis religio/Axe poli*. See Ch. 19. For a documented account of what can be known about Louis and music, see Clark, 'Music for Louis of Anjou'.

[30] Based on this document, Wathey gives his origin as the diocese of Thérouanne ('The Peace of 1360–1369', 147 n. 46), but reported in *NG2* the conflicting view that he came from the diocese of Noyon. The one instance in which Thérouanne (*Morinensis*) is given as his origin is the supplication of November 1378 (cited from Hanquet, 'Documents relatifs au Grand Schisme', 109, no. 347). John Nádas persuasively explains the anomaly in favour of Noyon: 'the papal singer is in every case but one cited as coming from (or at least ordained in) the diocese of Noyon (*noviomensis*). I believe the scribe made a mistake in reading from his exemplar, given the close similarity in the orthography of the Latin names of those two dioceses' (email of 17.1.2018: *morinensis*). Wathey argued that a Thérouanne origin could help to explain his English connections in view of the English exercise of ecclesiastical preferments in northern France and of the Duke of Anjou's recruitment of musicians who, like Mathieu, had previously served English nobility, but this Thérouanne origin is now not favoured for the papal singer.

[31] Citing Paris, BnF, MS fr. 11863, f. 26, and *Analecta Vaticano-Belgica*, 8 (1924), 175.

462 ENGLISH MOTETS C. 1400–1420

III in the 1360s with Enguerrand de Coucy, in whose service he is reported as a clerk in 1366, in a document which names him as a canon of Laon. Matheus held preferments at various French collegiate and parish churches, including further canonries between 1378 and 1391 at Soissons, Noyon, Cambrai, Narbonne and Tournai.[32] Enguerrand was also in England as one of the noble hostages who arrived in 1360. He married Edward III's daughter Isabella in 1365 and remained neutral during the Hundred Years' War, travelling widely, perhaps with Matheus, who left in May 1368 for France and did not return again to England.[33]

Although there is no evidence of English contacts for Matheus after 1368, Wathey considers that a past period of service in the 1360s could strengthen his claim for identity with the 'Mayshuet' of Old Hall, a claim I have questioned.[34] He makes the case that his English connection could have forged links which led to repertory being selectively passed on through a succession of royal chapels before **OH**. That does not necessarily require a dating of the motet during his English period in the 1360s; it could have been produced after he left England. If the motets are by the Matheus de Sancto Johanne who died in 1391, both motets, as well as the original and the contrafaction of *Are post libamina*, must date from no later than the 1380s, but even a dating in the 1380s seems to me too early on musical grounds, a dating in the 1360s much too early. The 1380s is not entirely impossible, as they would not be the only innovatively structured motets from that decade, though they would then be the earliest motets anywhere, and the only ones clearly before *c.* 1400, to have three levels of tenor reduction.[35] The presence of three such levels is new in four first-layer Old Hall motets including these two (for the others, see Ch. 25); no other fourteenth-century motet has more than two levels (that is, just one diminution section). I have made the case elsewhere (Ch. 20) that the one apparent exception, *Sub Arturo plebs*, might in fact date from after 1400. In any case, its reducing sections do not involve diminution, but are rereadings of the same notation in different mensurations.[36] The corresponding upper parts of the **OH** *Deo gratias* motets are successively in C, O, ℭ (unsigned except for the final ℭ in the triplum of *Post missarum*). Both motets use syncopated minor prolation rhythms in a way reminiscent

---

[32] Nádas, 'Secular Courts', 194–95. The Cambrai benefice was reserved for him but became available only after his death, which must have occurred by 12 July 1391 (Wathey, 'The Peace of 1360–1369', 147). From another document, Nádas, 'Secular Courts', 194, establishes a slightly earlier death date, by 10 June 1391 'outside the Roman curia'. Nádas offers the cautionary note that the Belgian Academy, because of its highly nationalistic filter, regularly left out of its Vatican reporting documents that did not include reference to one of the old dioceses now in present-day Belgium—such is the case generally with, for example, the many English clerics contained in supplications and papal letters of the late 14th c., and here in the specific case of the two Enguerrand de Coucy documents in RS 45 cited on p. 383 of his *Arte Psallentes* reprint.

[33] Wathey, 'The Peace of 1360–1369', 144–45. There, Matheus would have met the musicians in the chapels of King Edward III and the Black Prince, including some cited in what Di Bacco and Nádas call 'the contemporary motet' *Sub Arturo plebs*, Nicolas Hungerford and Simon Clement; John Nádas and Giuliano Di Bacco, 'The Papal Chapels', 44–92 at 47.

[34] Bent, 'The Progeny', 6; Bent, 'Towards the Reconstruction', 10–11, here superseded, and in EECM 62.

[35] See Ch. 23. Diminution, reinterpretation of note-values at the next level down, is not to be confused with mensural rereading. See Bent, 'The Myth'. Even the precocious motet *Portio/Ida* (in **Trém**, before 1376) only has one level of diminution; it states each *color* in perfect and then imperfect time before the entire tenor is repeated at the next level of note-values down. For *Inter densas/Imbribus* see Ch. 1.

[36] The first piece in **ModA**, Matteo da Perugia's motet *Ave sancta mundi*, presumably after 1400, is on an *Agnus dei* tenor notated once, to be stated three times in successive diminution. The equal-range upper parts are on the same text, but it shares few other features with Italian motets as defined in Ch. 26. The tenor is notated as if unmeasured, all 'breves', and prescribed to be sung in second (iambic) mode.

of Machaut, but on grounds of formal technique and rhythmic language, they seem to be at least a generation later than the **Ivrea** motet.

There are no obvious stylistic connections with the songs in **ModA** and **Chantilly**. Mathieu's documented English involvement was so much earlier than a plausible musical dating that it offers no direct reason for him to have made a Latin adaptation of one of his French motets a generation later. The triplum text of *Are post libamina* does appear to attribute the contrafaction to the composer of the French original, though if it is by this Mathieu, the later composition or adaptation of a motet to please the English might depend on the strength of the personal connection and how long it endured. Is it even possible that Mathieu was the composer of the anonymous Ivrea motet, and that his name wrongly became attached to the later, textually related anonymous composition in Old Hall and its ascribed stylistic twin? I think not, and will explain why.

Wathey reports other candidates who have been implausibly identified with Matheus solely on the basis of similar names or presumed compositional activity.[37] Yet previous authors have assumed, on a basis no stronger, that this composer can be identified with the Frenchman Mayshuet who composed one and probably both of the last two motets in Old Hall. None of the various forms of Matheus (Mahiet, Mahuetus, etc) contains a central 's'. The question remains open. Without the biographical information attached to this proposed candidate, I would have dated these motets around or a little after 1400, rather than twenty, let alone forty years earlier. A dating of *Sub Arturo plebs* before the death of another of Queen Philippa's chaplains, John Aleyn, in 1373, would seem to make plausible an early dating for the Mayshuet motet(s), assuming they are by Matheus de Sancto Johanne, but if my arguments for a later dating of *Sub Arturo plebs* stand (Ch. 20), and for doubting that a John Aleyn who died so early could be the composer J. Alanus, it no longer provides supporting corroboration for an earlier dating of the Mayshuet compositions.[38] In this case, as with J. Alanus, I propose to set aside a weakly supported identification on the basis of similarity of names in favour of a dating around or after 1400 of the compositions so attributed, even though in the case of Mayshuet this leaves us without a candidate to be the composer, unless he be the Jacob Musserey documented in the early 1390s as one of a group of five French singing-men in John of Gaunt's chapel, a long but chronologically plausible shot that has I think not yet been suggested.[39] Roger Bowers reports that Gaunt must have recruited these

---

[37] Several identities that have been proposed for medieval composers remain questionable for lack of supporting evidence. Of English composers soon after 1400, we have significant information for Leonel Power and John Dunstaple, both blessed with distinctive names. There is also documentation in varying quantities for the chapel royal composer-chaplains Burell, Cook, Damett and Sturgeon, where their contextual situation in the royal chapel, both archivally and in the Old Hall MS, corroborates the identifications. For more on these men, see Ch. 25. Likely identifications also exist for Chirbury, Tyes, Typp, among others. Identification is harder for composers with a common surname and no Christian name or initial, as in the cases of Forest and Pycard. The identification of Forest with John Forest, Dean of Wells, is plausible but has no corroboration from a Christian name in the manuscripts or a musical office in archival sources. Wathey, 'John of Gaunt', proposes that Pycard may have been the singer Jean Pycard in the chapel of John of Gaunt in the 1390s, an identification confidently reasserted by Roger Bowers (paper at the Medieval and Renaissance Music Conference, Prague, 6.7.2017). But although Pycard could equally well be one of a number of other men, including the Thomas Pycard who witnessed a charter with the royal chaplain Thomas Damett in 1420, I now lean towards agreeing with Bowers that Gaunt's chaplain is a strong candidate, for further reasons given at the end of this chapter. As for the composer of *Sub Arturo plebs*, Alanus is not an uncommon name, J not an uncommon initial.

[38] Bent, 'The Earliest Fifteenth-Century Transmission', 86–88, and Ch. 20.

[39] Wathey, 'John of Gaunt', 35.

464 ENGLISH MOTETS C. 1400–1420

men before returning to England from France in 1389. Each has a French name: Jean (John) Pycard, Jean (John) Housy, 'Peryn' (Pierre) de Arcomonte, 'Jacomyn' (Jacques) Mucherye, and Ivo de Bonefoye; this last man was successively replaced by others. They were well rewarded, and the other four probably remained in Gaunt's service in England until his death in February 1399. Bowers proposes that the Pycard who heads these lists may be the Old Hall composer of that name.[40] The association may in turn strengthen the candidacy of Musserey or, even closer in the form Mucherye, to be the phonetically plausible Mayshuet of Old Hall, a Frenchman living in England who adapted and Latinised one of his French-texted motets in order to accommodate to English taste (as *Are post libamina*), and who adapted the Latin texts of the companion motet, *Post missarum*.[41]

Although we cannot be certain, composers active as young singers in the 1390s could have continued to compose after Gaunt's death into the early 1400s. Moreover, the young future King Henry V and his brother John the future duke of Bedford lived in Gaunt's household from 1392 to 1394, which would have exposed them to his chapel musicians, where they could have formed both the tastes and personal contacts reflected in the Old Hall repertory and the slightly later fragmentary royal choirbook (RC), which may have been prepared for Bedford, and perhaps developed the skills underlying the **OH** compositions by 'Roy Henry', Henry V.

Another name comes into play, a French musician known and loved in England. In a little-explored fragmentary motet datable *c.* 1400, with a macaronic text in Anglo-Norman and Latin, two fine singers from Clermont are affectionately praised by the English writer: Gwillelmus nicknamed 'Malcharte' and his brother Alebram.[42] It is to be hoped that future discoveries may resolve the identity of this most intriguing composer.

---

[40] Bowers, '"Goode and Delitable Songe"'. Bowers further reports that 'from Easter 1392 until Easter 1394 Bolingbroke's first and third sons, Henry (later King Henry V) and John (later duke of Bedford), were nurtured together in Gaunt's household. Evidently the boys made a favourable impact on their grandfather, being the sole two among Bolingbroke's six children to whom later he made bequests in his will; and while resident in his household doubtless they experienced the conduct of service by the staff of his chapel.'

[41] I ended the previously published version of this paper: 'On balance, I prefer to treat the composer as not yet identified.' I now advance this hypothesis with more confidence.

[42] See Bent, 'Washington, Library of Congress, M2.1 C6 1400 Case'.

25

Old Hall, the Agincourt Motets, and Dunstaple

Dating the Main Compilation of Old Hall

Before turning to the motets in the Old Hall manuscript, we need to revisit its dating. I originally proposed that the principal layer was compiled c. 1413–15 for an unknown but probably royal institution; that the compilation was interrupted when the book was sent for illumination; and that it did not return to the original scribe, who was therefore unable to enter the specific compositions for which he had prescribed illuminated initials or, in one case, even a text incipit. At that stage it came into the hands of Henry V's singer-chaplains who, instead of continuing the compiler's intentions, entered their own compositions, some of them autograph (where scribal and composer identifications coincide), in 1415–19, when they were all together in Henry's chapel; we will return to the reasons for this dating. Roger Bowers then discovered documentation that Leonel Power, the most strongly represented composer in **OH**, had served in the chapel of Thomas Duke of Clarence in 1419, and probably since c. 1411.[1] I readily concurred that the original layer had very probably been prepared for Clarence, and still do. But I now think I was wrong to accept his further proposal that the interruption was occasioned by Clarence's death in 1421 or his removal in 1419.[2] This imposes much too tight a timing for the later additions, which must have been made while those chaplains were still serving in Henry V's chapel. I therefore now revert to my original proposals for the dating, but now with knowledge of the Clarence association. The organisation and consistency of the original layer of copying suggests that most of the material was assembled and planned before copying began, most of it composed in the first decade of the new century (the more old-fashioned pieces perhaps in the preceding decade) and that because of the prior organisation, it could all have been copied in the space of a year or two. In short, the first layer was probably compiled in the first two years of Henry V's reign, 1413–15, presumably in and for Thomas's chapel. The two compositions ascribed to 'Roy Henry' must be by his brother King Henry V, probably also composed in that first decade. It is barely conceivable that the ailing Henry IV could have had the energy and ability to compose in an up-to-date style by then, even if he had shown

---

Much of this section is new. Parts have been updated and expanded from Bent, 'Sources of the Old Hall Music', 'The Old Hall Manuscript', and *Dunstaple*. Some (on RC) has recently been set out in more expanded form in Bent, 'Towards the Reconstruction' (in EECM 62), where the dating of **OH** is reviewed.

[1] Bowers, 'Lionel Power'. The Duke of Berry loaned Clarence **MachautE** in 1412 (it was back with the Dukes of Burgundy at least from 1467). *Guillaume de Machaut*, ed. Ludwig, ii. 10*–11*, and 11* n. 1, and Earp, *Guillaume de Machaut: A Guide*, 93.

[2] Bent, 'The Progeny'. I thank David Fallows for prompting me to revisit the issue of dating and to revert to something closer to my original proposal.

The Motet in the Late Middle Ages. Margaret Bent, Oxford University Press. © Oxford University Press 2023.
DOI: 10.1093/so/9780190063771.003.0026

466 ENGLISH MOTETS C. 1400–1420

musical talent in his youth. His sons (Henry V and his brothers Clarence, Bedford and Gloucester) all have at least some credentials as practitioners or patrons of music or musicians. The inscription must, I believe, date from early in the reign of the new king. He need not have been king when he composed them, only when the copy was made. In a manuscript so close to the crown, Henry must have been 'Roy', king, when the scribe made his ascription.[3]

Some English motets of this period have been discussed here, in other chapters or sections: *Sub Arturo* among the musician motets in Chapter 20, *O amicus* in Chapter 22, *Are post libamina* and *Post missarum* in Chapter 24. I have given reasons for dating all those motets closer to 1400 (or even after) than had previously been suggested, notably for *Sub Arturo*.

The Motets in the Original Layer of Old Hall

Only five motets from the original compilation survive at the end of **OH** (nos. 143–47) in a depleted section (gathering XVII) that originally held at least one more motet. We can be sure, however, that the section began and ended with the motets currently in those places: the first because it immediately follows the last Agnus setting and carried a decorative initial (later cut out) of the type found only at section beginnings, and ended with two adjacent motets for the end of Mass. Both the first and last of these are incomplete due to lack of a facing page but, as was shown in Chapter 24, no. 147 can be nearly completed from another source. The motets are:

No. 143, f. 109[v]: *Carbunculus ignitus lilie*, on St Thomas (triplum only);

No. 144, f. 110: motetus (*Mater munda*) and tenor (*Mater sancta Dei*) only, on the Virgin;

No. 145, ff. 110[v]–111: *En Katerine solennia/Virginalis concio*, on St Katherine, by Byttering, complete;

Nos. 146 (*Are post libamina*) and 147 (*Post missarum*) are the two motets by Mayshuet for the end of Mass that were the subject of Chapter 24.

We will first deal with nos. 144 and 145, before a lengthier discussion of no. 143.

No. 144: the motetus is texted *Mater munda*. The unidentified tenor melody is labelled *Mater sancta Dei*, but as there is no known chant of this name, this is probably the incipit of the missing triplum. A text beginning with these words is in AH 24: 179, and was used in CMM 46. This motet has just two sections. The long tenor *color* is divided into two *taleae* each of 24 longs of perfect modus; the motetus starts in C, its imperfect breves aligned with the tenor's.[4] The tenor is marked for repetition, the second statement in (unspecified) diminution, at which point the motetus changes to O, its perfect tempus semibreves aligned with those of the diminished tenor. The red coloration in both surviving parts is for imperfection.

---

[3] Roger Bowers ('"Goode and Delitable Songe"', 223) agrees that the main compilation was made in the reign of Henry V, but maintains that Henry IV was the royal composer.

[4] Including a syncopation which gives three periods of seven (3 + 4) breves.

No. 145, ff. 110ᵛ–111: *En Katerine solennia/Virginalis concio*, on St Katherine, by Byttering; this and *Are post libamina* (no. 146) are the only motets of this group in **OH** surviving complete, and the only two with composer ascriptions.[5] The tenor is the verse of the responsory *Virgo flagellatur* for the second nocturn at Matins on the feast of St Katherine (25 November), with slight variants from the chant in *AS*, pl. Y. Encouraged by St Katherine and the tenor *Sponsus amat sponsam* (deliciously mis-written as *sponsum*), Bukofzer suggested that it could have celebrated the wedding of Henry V and Katherine in 1420; but that is too late, given its position in the main compilation of **OH**. This mensurally virtuosic motet survives here complete in three parts. The tenor *color* is disposed in two *taleae* of 27 breves, with syncopation, alteration and coloration, and is marked to be stated three times, the successive reduction unspecified. Coloration most commonly denotes imperfection, but here, unusually, it is for sesquialtera proportion, three in the time of two; the second breve in each case has to be altered before the final long of the group, which would not happen in imperfection coloration.[6] The dots (of division) also indicate the triple grouping, and the proportional (as opposed to mensural) interpretation of the coloration is confirmed by alignment with the upper parts. Figure 25.1 gives the numerical values of the notes in breves (albeit breves of different lengths; the numbers for the red notes in sesquialtera are in italics). The three '1's in bold make up a split syncopation group; the first tenor breve and its rest form a perfection with the last breve before the coloration. The semibreve count for each *talea* in relation to the upper parts is 9 9 3 3 9 9 3 6 9. 3 for the black notes (three semibreves to the breve, rests italicised), followed by 4 2. 2 4 6 for the red notes (two semibreves to the breve).

Fig. 25.1 Tenor of Byttering, *En Katerine*, tenor *Sponsus amat sponsum* [sic] in London, British Library, Add. MS 57950 (**OH**), f. 111. Reproduced with permission of the British Library. Number values of red notes are in italics

The first tenor *color* is in perfect modus and, although notated only in longs and breves, must be construed in the perfect tempus and minor prolation of the upper parts, to which its values correspond. The second *color* is to be read at the next note-level down (as if in breves and semibreves), in perfect time, but now assuming major prolation to match that of the upper parts. The third *color* does not undergo a further diminution of note-levels, but is mensurally (not proportionally) reduced to be read in perfect time, now coordinated with the minor prolation of the upper parts. This requires the coloration (unusually) to be construed as triplets against the duplets in the upper parts, i.e. it is still for sesquialtera, not imperfection. The three sections all have

---

[5] The motetus text (*Virginalis concio*) is known from the motetus voice of an earlier incomplete St Katherine motet in **Durham20**, f. 336. Its contratenor *De sancta Katerina* shows that the lower parts had two *colores*, the second in written-out diminution, each of four *taleae* with coloration.

[6] On coloration usage in **OH** see Bent, 'Principles of Mensuration and Coloration'.

468 ENGLISH MOTETS C. 1400–1420

different mensurations between the two texted upper parts: in I, triplum C is set against motetus O; in II triplum ⊙ is against motetus ₵; in III, triplum C is against motetus O.[7] The coloration in the upper-part major prolation sections is for imperfection, not sesquialtera; red notation thus has different meanings within the same composition. Although there is no temporal overlap at these sectional signature changes, it is clear that minim equivalence applies horizontally, and that the upper-part minim values control the tenor evaluations and successive reductions, even though the tenor contains no notes shorter than a breve. The overall proportions of the sections are 6:3:2.

OH, no. 143 (f. 109ᵛ), *Carbunculus ignitus lilie*, is the triplum part of a motet on St Thomas Becket. That a motet with this dedication heads the motet section (its elaborate initial was cut out), could add support to the destination of the manuscript as the chapel of Duke Thomas. Two mass movements on Thomas chants lend further support: the Credo OH, no. 84, on *Opem nobis*, ascribed to Leonel, who is almost certainly the composer of its twin, the anonymous Gloria no. 24, on *Ad Thome*. These are the only other Thomas compositions in Old Hall, both with irregular isorhythmic elements very different from the regularity of the motet triplum. Although the only documentation of Leonel Power's membership of Clarence's chapel is later (the single surviving account applies from 1418 to Clarence's death in 1421), we have noted Bowers's view that it probably dates back to *c.* 1411, and at least to the beginning of Henry's reign, when Thomas increased his chapel, probably recruited in 1411–13, during which time he was created Duke of Clarence and became heir to the throne.[8] This would be further supported by Leonel's composition of the Thomas mass movements by that earlier date, in time for inclusion in the first layer of OH.

In November 1419 he is named as Lyonell and, as clerk and instructor of the choristers, Lionell Power. He is listed second, so may have been quite senior.[9] He is the only composer in OH whose works are ascribed exclusively by a first name, usually as 'Leonel', but in the second-layer ascription of a Credo, no. 73 (f. 61ᵛ), by an otherwise unrepresented scribe, as 'Lyonel', closer to the spelling in the Clarence accounts, and perhaps his own, as it is also the spelling found in the authorial attribution at the end of his vernacular treatise 'upon the Gamme' in Lo763: 'Quod Lyonel Power'. The two mass movements on Thomas chants were already mentioned. Taken together with the strong likelihood that OH was compiled for Thomas's chapel, and the placing of a Thomas motet in pride of place at the decorated head of the motet section, these factors all point to Leonel's possible authorship of *Carbunculus*. This would be his only surviving periodic motet with isorhythm; he must surely have composed others.

Only the triplum of this motet survives. Its texting is entirely syllabic and, because it strictly observes the discipline of not breaking a word with a rest, the words and music must have been planned together, in order to make monosyllables fall in the right places for the isorhythmic repeats (not in this case hockets), even though the number of syllables is not reduced for the musical reduction between the first two sections, and just from four lines to

[7] I now repent the standardised barring adopted in CMM 46.
[8] The personnel of Thomas's chapel when he became heir to his brother's throne is unknown. Might it still have included some of the members of John of Gaunt's chapel? The young French singers recruited by Gaunt, including Pycard and Mucherey/Musseret (possibly = Mayshuet? see Ch. 24), may have been the OH composers of those names, though this is highly conjectural. If so, they may have continued under some kind of royal patronage after Gaunt's death, perhaps already recruited by Clarence soon after 1400, and thus accounting for their presence in OH.
[9] Bowers, 'Lionel Power', 106–7.

three in the third. See Figure 25.2. The text consists of thirty-three decasyllabic lines. A minority of line-breaks coincide with rests, but most rests occur at other points in the lines, differently placed in the three sections (*colores*), but always, however, at a word break:

In C1 each of the three *taleae* has a four-line stanza, all rhyming *-ie* (12 lines). The number of syllables between rests in each line is 10, 6, 9, 8, 7 = 40;

in C2 likewise, each rhyming *-ium* (12 lines). The number of syllables between rests in each line is 22, 4, 4, 10 = 40;

in C3 each of the three *taleae* has a three-line stanza, all rhyming *-ia* (9 lines). The number of syllables between rests in each line is 15, 5, 3, 7 = 30.

The location of rests in the first stanza of each *color* of *Carbunculus* is shown by vertical lines:

C1, T1
Carbunculus ignitus lilie |
Flammas vibrans lucis | eximie
Noctis latebris | fulgor Anglie
Lucerna | decoris ecclesie.| (× 3: different texts, same word divisions)

C2, T1
En propter Cristi testimonium
Ecclesie quoque zelum pium
Durum| fastigium| obprobrium|
Archi presul mentis absinthium.| (× 3: different texts, same word divisions)

C3, T1
Sed hec reproborum nequicia
Comitans sancti | desideria |
Mensura | propter temporalia.| (× 3: different texts, same word divisions)

Musically, the three sections are in [☉], ℂ and C. Each section contains 12 × 3 = 36 breves; the breves are of different lengths according to the mensuration, resulting in the overall proportions 9:6:4 based on those breve lengths. Each upper-voice *color* is divided into three isorhythmic *taleae* of 12 breves each, 12 × 3 breves, a total of 108 breves of different lengths (equivalent to 114 breves of ℂ). This suggests that the missing tenor may also have been mensurally redefined for each section, but I have not yet been able to reconstruct a tenor *color* that fits all three upper-part sections, let alone to identify it with a Thomas chant. I have to conclude that there is no tidy coincidence with the structure of this upper part, but rather that there must either have been a single tenor color or some clever overlapping mensural scheme, perhaps more extreme than the non-alignment in *Sub Arturo* (see Ch. 20). It awaits an ingenious solution. I know of only three motets which have the overall proportions 9:6:4: *Carbunculus*, Cooke's *Alma proles/Christi miles* (**OH**, no. 112), and *Sub Arturo plebs*.[10] All three are English, and all

---

[10] *Sub Arturo plebs* (Ch. 20) redefined the tenor mensurally for each section in ☉, ℂ and C, resulting in the same 9:6:4 proportions, but there the upper parts remained in ℂ throughout.

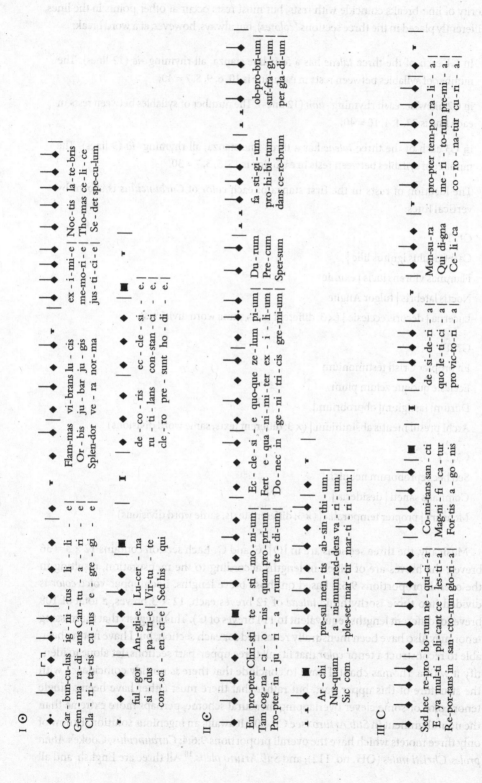

Fig. 25.2 Text of *Carbunculus ignitus lilie*, with aligned isorhythm, showing that rests never divide words

date from around 1400 or within the two following decades. The accelerating proportion in each case is achieved not by diminution, but by mensural reinterpretation of the same notation, as if they are acknowledging each other, though doing so in different ways. I have linked Cooke's St George motet *Alma proles/Christi miles* to the peace process preceding Agincourt in 1415, and its possible use in the aftermath of that victory (see below). But neither it, nor anything else attributed to the royal clerks or chaplains Burell, Cooke, Damett and Sturgeon, made its way across the Channel. Conversely, the assertively patriotic *Sub Arturo* was until recently known only from Continental sources (now also in an English source, **Yox**; see Chs. 20, 22). Its absence from **OH** is surprising, when that manuscript offers a range of other motets including, as later additions to be discussed below, patriotic and Agincourt-related pieces and, anonymously, Dunstaple's *Veni sancte spiritus/Veni creator*, which I date to 1416 or before. *Alma proles regia*, like *Sub Arturo*, states the tenor three times, in ⊙, ℂ and C. The upper parts for the first section are ambiguously in ℂ or ⊙; the two following sections are in C and ℂ, respectively against ℂ and C in the tenor, with ingenious tricky alignment and split coloration not unlike the final section of *Sub Arturo*. The mensural affinity between *Sub Arturo* and *Alma proles regia* also suggests a possible alliterative relationship of the latter motet with the musician motet *Alma polis religio* (Ch. 19) and in turn with *Apollinis* (Ch. 16), although it stands outside the musician motets group. Such play on similarity of verbal incipits between motets is a feature of that repertory.

A further pointer to possible authorship of *Carbunculus* by Leonel is that the overall proportions of Cooke's motet may be a homage to Leonel, if the motet is indeed by him; they are two of the only three known motets with this proportion. They are the only two composers represented in both layers of **OH**; Cooke's Gloria no. 36 in the main layer is closely modelled on Leonel's Gloria–Credo pair nos. 21 and 77, likewise with alternating sections in two and four parts, a final five-part section, with even a third in the final chord (like Leonel's no. 21). Cooke and Leonel share the apparently personal habit of using little letter names to cancel notated sharps; although not exclusive to them, it is far from universal, even in their circle. Cooke's *Stella celi* (no. 55) is so heavily provided with cadential sharps that it may have been a pedagogic exercise or demonstration. It is a simple piece, essentially a succession of cadential formulae with notoriously explicit accidentals including $d\sharp$ and $g\sharp$. All this could indicate that Cooke was a disciple or pupil of Leonel; and as a bridge between the layers could have been instrumental in removing the manuscript in the mid-1410s from Clarence's chapel, in which Leonel served, to that of Henry V, in which Cooke served. If Cooke's motet was in any sense modelled on *Sub Arturo*, we might see it as a homage to another highly talented composer.

Motets nos. 143–45 all change mensuration in the upper parts at each structural section (with horizontal minim equivalence), coinciding with a tenor *color* repeat in nos. 144 and 145, but possibly not in no. 143 (*Carbunculus*). The upper parts of the two motets by Mayshuet (nos. 146 and 147, discussed in Ch. 24) do not change mensuration with the tenor diminutions, with the one exception that the *Post missarum* triplum in **OH** and the motetus in **Ox32** change from C to ℂ for the final *color* to align with the major prolation of the final tenor diminution.

Apart from no. 144, *Mater sancta Dei/Mater munda*, with only two *color* statements, all five motets thus have three statements in successive reduction, whether achieved

472 ENGLISH MOTETS C. 1400–1420

mensurally or by diminution, and in that respect they have no English precedents apart from the Yoxford motet *O amicus* (Ch. 22) and *Sub Arturo* (Ch. 20). Alongside and very soon after the **OH** compositions, the three-section pattern with two levels of reduction became standard in England, with either two or three *taleae* per *color*. Some of these (including *Sub Arturo* and some by Dunstaple) involve mensural transformation and not diminution strictly defined. Whether composed before or after 1400, English motets, or motets preserved in England, seem to be the first to have three successively reducing sections. They include the Mayshuet motets in **OH**, at least one of which could, as stated in Chapter 24, be a contrafact from the French, and nos. 143 and 145. Nor does any fourteenth-century Continental motet have as many as three sections in successive reduction. Only the special case of *Inter densas* in **Chantilly** has more sections. It apparently dates from before 1400; its apparent dedicatee died in 1391. It does not apply diminution, but is entirely a mensuration motet, of the most extreme kind, perhaps a demonstration piece (see Ch. 1); the sections are not arranged in descending order of length.

The Later Additions to Old Hall: The Agincourt Motets

At some point in the 1410s, the compilation of **OH** was interrupted, and the book came into the hands of Henry V's clerks and chaplains Damett, Cooke, Sturgeon and Burell.[11] Compositions by these men were entered piecemeal at various times, probably soon after composition. Various scribes are involved in compositions ascribed to them, some apparently the composers themselves, others possibly also members of Henry's chapel.[12] If some of Cooke's contributions are indeed autograph, they must have been entered by *c.* 1419, when he is last documented and may have died. At any rate, he is no longer listed in 1421 as a member of Henry's chapel.[13] His autograph contributions would have required his presence together with the other chaplains; even if he was alive and present after 1419, but not by 1421, this would still require a dating of the second layer within the reign of Henry V. The reason for the interruption remains unknown.[14] It does not require a specific occasion, such as Clarence's death or removal. The book which originated in his chapel could have been loaned or given to the king's chaplains, or simply appropriated. The

---

[11] Much of this section has been updated and extended from Bent, 'Sources'. The same sources were used and commented on in Nosow, *Ritual Meanings*, with some differing interpretations, some of which are taken into account here.

[12] The autograph claim for some pieces rests on the alignment of scribal identifications with composer ascriptions, and the evidence of compositional revisions by the same scribes in some of those pieces. These were reported in Bent, 'The Old Hall Manuscript'.

[13] Roger Bowers, email of 25.6.2019: 'The next list of Chapel Royal employees following 1419 is that made for the supply of livery in anticipation of the coronation of Katherine of France as Queen of England on 24 Feb. 1421 (TNA, E 101/407/4, f. 36ʳ). It contains no John Cook.' Andrew Wathey (email of 9.4.2022) provided me with a copy of the document London, The National Archives, C 81/1365/11, dated 25 July 1419, granting to Thomas Gyles 'the prebende whiche John Cooke late clerc of our saide Chapelle, hadde within oure free chapelle of Hastynges'.

[14] I now strongly reject the suggestions I made ('The Progeny', 27) that the Zacara Gloria could have been transmitted at Constance and that (following Bukofzer) Byttering's St Catherine motet could be for the wedding of Henry and Catherine in 1420; both are too late if, as I now believe, those compositions were in place by 1415.

royal brothers and the chaplains of Henry's chapel royal were regularly travelling to and from France at this period.

The port town of Harfleur was besieged by the English from 18 August 1415 and captured on 22 September, followed by the victory at Agincourt on Friday, 25 October 1415 (St Crispin's day, as immortalised by Shakespeare). On 23 November 1415, Henry returned to London in triumph, received by elaborate pageants, as reported by chroniclers.[15] Three motets by his chaplains Damett, Cooke and Sturgeon seem particularly well suited to the English situation before and following Agincourt. Thus *c.* 1415–19 is the likely period within which the interruption took place, the manuscript changed hands, and the later (partly autograph) additions were made.

The motets by these Chapel Royal composers have attracted attention on account of the topical references in their texts. Albeit less explicit than the anonymous Agincourt carol, they offer our only internal clue for dating any of the music of the second layer. They are:

Damett, *Salvatoris mater pia/O Georgi Deo care/Benedictus Marie Filius qui ve-* (no. 111, ff. 89ᵛ–90);

Cooke, *Alma proles regia/Christi miles inclite/Ab inimicis nostris defende nos Christe* (no. 112, ff. 90ᵛ–91);

Sturgeon, *Salve mater Domini/Salve templum gratie/-it in nomine Domini* (no. 113, ff. 91ᵛ–92).

Their texts supplicate for peace and for delivery from affliction with prayers for the safeguarding of Henry and England, and may relate to the continuing peace negotiations before and after Agincourt and to the post-Agincourt celebrations themselves. The saints addressed in all the texts are Mary and George, the two most commonly invoked and thanked by the English at the time of Agincourt, as attested in the *Gesta Henrici Quinti*.[16] St George literally figured large at Henry's arrival. A verse account of the pageant formerly attributed to Lydgate reports thus:

> To londonn Brigge thanne rood oure Kyng
> The processions there they mette hym ryght
> 'Ave Rex anglorum' thei gan syng
> 'Flos mundi' thei seide, 'goddys knyght' [i.e. *miles Christi*]

[15] *Gesta Henrici Quinti*; the introduction gives an account of the various chronicles covering these events and their status. *A Chronicle of London*, ed. Tyrell et al., 100–4, reports ceremonies of thanksgiving in London when news of the Agincourt victory arrived on 29 Oct.: *Te deum* was sung, and a procession from St Paul's to Westminster made offerings at the shrine of St Edward; thanksgiving was made to Christ, Mary and George, with *Hec est dies quam fecit dominus*. For Henry's return to London in November, and Sigismund's visit the following year, a short report adds no new information. Given-Wilson, *The Chronicle of Adam Usk*, 256–65, describes the Agincourt victory and gives a detailed description of Henry's triumphant reception in London, including the figure of St George, but without naming the titles that could denote musical items. Sigismund's visit (and return to Constance) is briefly mentioned in conjunction with Bedford's naval victory, but there is no musically relevant information.

[16] The *Gesta*, also known as the chaplain's account, was compiled between Nov. 1416 and July 1417 (pp. xviii and xxiv) and is the earliest and most authoritative account of the events of 1415–16. The author was an eyewitness and an unnamed royal chaplain, which may account for the precision and detail of his account of Henry's liturgical mandates, for which see below.

474 ENGLISH MOTETS C. 1400–1420

> To londonn Brigge whan he com right
> Upon the gate ther stode on hy
> A gyaunt that was full grym of syght
> To teche the frensshemen curtesy.
>
> And at the drawe brigge that is faste by
> To toures there were upright
> An Antelope and a Lyon stondyng hym by
> Above hem seynt George oure lady knyght
> Besyde hym many an angell bright,
> 'Benedictus' thei gan synge
> 'Qui venit in nomine domini', 'goddes knyght'
> 'Gracia dei' with yow doth sprynge.[17]

Compare the version of a related prose chronicle:

> Where as he was riolly receyvet with precession and song *ave anglorum, flos mundi, miles Christi*, and when he come to Londonn brigge whereas were ij turrettes on the drawbrige, & a gret Geaunt and on the turrettes stonding a lyon and a antelope with many angeles syngyng *Benedictus qui venit in nomine domini*. And so rode he forth in to london.[18]

As the king turned into Cornhill, he was greeted with the arms of St George, Edward the Confessor, Edmund and England. Cooke's motetus text petitions George, then Mary, then both together, for victory and for peace, and to protect the king from his enemies. The opening words address St George as *Christi miles*, soldier of Christ. Both the above accounts of the London pageant hail Henry with these very words, as *miles Christi*, thus endowing him with the attributes of St George, whose feast-day (23 April) was formally proclaimed a greater double feast after the Agincourt victory.[19] *Ave [rex gentis] anglorum, Flos mundi* and *Miles Christi* may either denote separate items, or the three texts of a non-extant polytextual motet.[20] Motets of this type are hardly suited to outdoor performance in a popular ceremonial context, but they could nevertheless have played a part in the

---

[17] This follows **Lo565**, f. 112ᵛ, corrected from *Gesta Henrici Quinti*, Appendix IV, 191–92. There are four and a half more stanzas. The whole poem is printed in Nicolas, *History of the Battle of Agincourt*, 327; see also *A Chronicle of London*, ed. Tyrell et al., 231, 327–28, and Appendix IV of *Gesta Henrici Quinti*. A different version of the same poem in **Lo12** perished in the Cottonian fire; for this we are dependent on *Thomæ de Elmham Vita & Gesta*, 359–75; this account is now known as pseudo-Elmham, as Elmham is no longer thought to be its author.

[18] **Lo53**, f. 157ᵛ. This 15th-c. manuscript preserves one of the continuations in English of the *Brut* chronicle (up to 1436); see Brie, *The Brut*, ii. 558 and Brie, *Geschichte und Quellen*. An older account of the chronicles relevant to Henry V is in Kingsford, *English Historical Literature*.

[19] *The Register of Henry Chichele*, III. 6, on 20 Nov. 1416. *Benedictus* and *Miles Christi* might refer to two different but related extant motets, as suggested here, or they could be two texts of a single motet that has not survived. *Miles Christi* is a responsory for Edward the Confessor, but no known chant for St George begins with these words.

[20] Nosow so interprets them (*Ritual Meanings*, 40), but does not make it entirely clear that this motet does not survive, nor why he designates *Flos mundi* the triplum text (ibid. 41). He could have brought into play several fragmentary English motets with potentially royal connotations that have not yet received much attention, notably the incomplete motet *Ave miles triumphalis* which is on the verso of **Cant128/6**, the Canterbury source of *Preco*.

celebrations, perhaps in a more reflective and less public continuation which allowed the chronicler (albeit imperfectly) to note the Latin titles. The tenor of Cooke's motet uses the words and music of the rogation litany for peace: *Ab inimicis nostris defende nos Christe*.[21] The rogation days in 1415, 6–8 May, occurred at the most anxious time in the peace negotiations between the French and the English. Talks had broken down, and the truce, due to expire on 1 May, had been extended to 8 June in a last effort to avert war. This would have been one of several appropriate times to write a motet of supplication for peace, glossed in the upper parts by appeals to Mary and George to secure victory for England. Particularly suited to the previous truce negotiations, Cooke's motet would have become topical again at and after the celebrations.

The two motets by Damett and Sturgeon display a rare and deliberate kind of collaboration, since they share a plainsong, dividing it between them at the mid-point. The plainsong is *Benedictus qui ve- | (n)it in nomine Domini* ('Blessed is he that cometh in the name of the Lord'), with the Sarum Sanctus trope *Marie Filius*.[22] Could this refer to the angelic song welcoming Henry to London, as reported above? The tenors of all three motets, Cooke's *Ab inimicis*, as well as the *Benedictus* chant for Damett's and Sturgeon's motets, might allude to the chronicle reports. Damett's portion is *Benedictus Marie Filius qui ve-*, Sturgeon's *[n]it in nomine Domini*. While the texts of the upper parts do not correspond directly to anything in the accounts of the pageant, Damett's motetus text, again addressed to St George, has the right ingredients for the occasion:

O Georgi Deo care	O George, dear to God,
salvatorem deprecare	pray to the Saviour
ut gubernet Angliam.	that He may guide England,
Ipsam teque commendare	and that we may be worthy
valeamus et laudare	to entrust it to thee,
deitatis graciam.	and to praise the grace of God.
Tu qui noster advocatus	May you, who are our advocate,
es ius tui patronatus	defend from enemies the rights
defendas ab hostibus.	of your status as [our] patron,
Et Anglorum gentem serva	and preserve the race of the English
pace firma sine guerra	with constant peace, without war,
tuis sanctis precibus.	by your holy prayers.
Miles fortis custos plebis	Strong soldier, guardian of the people,
sis Henrici nostri regis	be present at the deliberations
presens ad consilium.	of Henry our king;

---

[21] The tenor of this motet is a processional antiphon specified in *Liber regie capelle*, ed. Ullman, of 1448, for the daily procession and litany of the chapel royal 'to be sung through solemnly as in the Processional'. This wording implies chant rather than a polyphonic setting in which the chant is long drawn out and not readily heard as such. This source is a generation later, and it is a bit of a stretch to take it, with Nosow, *Ritual Meanings*, 8, as licence for assuming that the motet, rather than the chant, was sung in this processional context.

[22] Damett uses the Sarum plainsong 3 transposed down a tone; Sturgeon uses it untransposed. This is hardly an obstacle to linked performance, since there is no evidence that written pitches were tied even to approximate standards of sounding pitch. Use of high clefs does not necessarily imply performance by trebles at this date.

476   ENGLISH MOTETS C. 1400–1420

Contra hostes apprehende
arma scutum archum tende
sibi fer auxilium.

Gloriosa spes Anglorum
audi vota famulorum
tibi nunc canencium.
Per te nostrum ut patronum
consequamur pacis donum
in terra vivencium.

warn against enemies, offer
arms—the shield, the bow;
bring help to him.

Glorious hope of the English,
hear the praise-offerings of thy servants
now singing to thee,
so that, through thee as our patron,
we may attain the gift of peace
in the land of the living.

This text expresses confidence in the strength and superiority of England and of Henry, combined with supplication to preserve the peace, to preside over the treaty negotiations, and to warn Henry if his enemy started to re-arm; presumably composed during the prior negotiations whose continuation still required humble prayers for peace, in the spirit of pious humility which Henry himself displayed.[23] The text refers to the bow, literally the instrument of victory at Agincourt, and the deliberations of Henry, which may well refer to the long-drawn-out treaty negotiations which followed. The explicit references place this text during the reign of Henry V.

Damett's triplum text is a known Marian sequence (*Salvatoris mater pia*), the last part of which has been replaced by lines requesting eternal life for Henry.[24] The first three stanzas show only minor variations from the standard text, but the last two (below) differ significantly to include topical reference to Henry:

Standard text:

Regi nato adhaesisti
Quem lactasti et pavisti
More matris debito:
Quae coniuncta nunc eidem,
Es regina facta pridem
Operum pro merito.

Reis ergo fac, regina
Apud regem, ut ruina
Relaxentur (or relaxetur) debita
Et regnare fac renatos,
A reatu expurgatos
Pietate solita.

OH:

Tutrix pia tui gregis
Memor sis Henrici regis
Pro quo pete filium:
Ut exutus carne gravi
Vite scriptus sit suavi
Post presens exilium.

Regis nostrique regina
Ora natum ut ruina
Relaxetur debita
Et regnare fac renatos,
A reatu expurgatos
Pietate solita.

---

[23] *Gesta Henrici Quinti*, 150–55 and Jacob, *The Fifteenth Century*, 123–24. Harrison, *Music in Medieval Britain*, 246–47, associates *Alma proles* and *Salvatoris* generally with Henry's campaigns. Bukofzer, *Studies*, 70, suggested that the motets by Damett and Sturgeon (with upper-voice texts beginning *Sa-* and using a Sanctus plainsong) 'can be regarded as elaborately troped settings of the Sanctus'. After the Sanctus was one of the places prescribed for polyphony; these motets were interpolated in a group of first-layer Sanctus settings.

[24] AH 54: 280. For sources see https://cantus.uwaterloo.ca/search?t=salvatoris+mater+pia (consulted 10.4.2023). The standard text is also in **Cu710**, the Dublin troper.

Translation of Old Hall text:

Holy guardian of Thy flock, be mindful of King Henry, for whom beseech Thy Son that, stripped of heavy flesh, he may be enrolled for everlasting life after his present exile on earth. And, O Queen of our king, pray Thy Son with Thy usual faithfulness, that the down-fall due to us may be alleviated and that, reborn and cleansed from sin, we may reign [with Thee in heaven].

The third motet, by Sturgeon, is simply votive to the Virgin and contains no topical references, but it is linked by the continuation of its tenor plainsong to the motet by his chapel royal colleague Damett. The points of contact with the chronicle accounts would have made all three highly suitable both before and after Agincourt, with the prominence they give to Mary and George. The Damett/Sturgeon pair could possibly relate to the *Benedictus qui venit in nomine domini* which the angels sang to greet him, and Cooke's rogationtide motet, with one part beginning *Christi miles*, might reflect the *miles Christi* reported by the chronicler. Both Damett's motet and Cooke's address the patron of Agincourt: 'O George, dear to God, pray to the Saviour that He may guide England, . . . and preserve the race of the English with constant peace, without war' (Damett), and 'holy George, most brilliant of soldiers', who 'guards the realm of England' (Cooke). Even if these motets by Henry's own chaplains were not sung in the streets, they catch much of the vocabulary of the chroniclers' accounts. Bowers has proposed that they could be associated with any period during the wars with the French.[25] Because of the probable timing of the interruption to Old Hall, and the date constraints for the copying of the autograph compositions (i.e. by 1419), the political situation around 1415, including the victories at Agincourt and Harfleur, seems to offer the most likely context for the composition of the three motets.

Mensural and Structural Features of the Agincourt Motets

No. 111: Damett, *Salvatoris mater pia/O Georgi Deo care/Benedictus Marie Filius qui ve-*

Each of the four tenor *colores* has two *taleae*, each of six perfect longs in perfect modus, including a split coloration group of three imperfect red longs. The tenor as notated uses longs and breves only. The overall notated proportions are 12:8:6:2 = 6:4:3:1, but they appear to disagree with the specifications of a later informally written *Canon tenoris*, which replaces a series of erased mensuration signs for the tenor: $\odot$ O O O:

P⁰ sicut iacet de modo perfecto temporis imperfecti

2⁰ per dimidietatem

---

[25] Bowers, email of 5.5.2005, does not accept the Agincourt connection: 'There are indeed some pieces whose texts and tenors appear to imply that they were composed in time of war; but between 1409 and 1461 there were not many years when the English were not engaged in warfare.' I agree that the motets are not purely celebratory, but also piously reflective and supplicatory. But they must date from the reign of Henry V, and therefore refer to the political situation before and after Agincourt.

478   ENGLISH MOTETS C. 1400–1420

3° per terciam partem
4° per sextam partem

These, however, yield the proportions 6:3:2:1, which are accomplished by mensuration signs in the upper parts which override the notated values, as explained below. The notated values of the tenor *color* correspond to the upper parts neither at the values of the first nor the last statements, but at those of statement 3.

The first tenor statement (*color* 1) is prescribed for perfect modus, imperfect tempus. Although specified as *sicut jacet*, an imperfect breve of the tenor corresponds to two perfect breves of the upper parts, i.e. a tenor semibreve equals a perfect breve of the top parts; *sicut jacet* therefore denotes, here and elsewhere, a non-equivalent relationship, contrary to the common understanding of this term. In *color* 2, in imperfect modus and tempus, a tenor breve equals two imperfect breves of the upper parts, which would relate (by semibreves) 6:4 to *color* 1. But the upper parts are signed ↄ (= 4:3, sesquitertia), achieving the halving specified in the verbal canon, 6:3. *Color* 3 is specified *per terciam partem*, which defines its relationship neither to 1 nor 2. But its note values are read in diminution, down a level from *colores* 1 and 2, in perfect modus, perfect tempus, so that their notated values now correspond to those of the upper parts. If they were signed with a black o, this would reverse the v of the preceding section, yielding 3:4 of the 6:4:3 notated values. But the o is red, here taken to reduce what follows by a third, i.e. by sesquialtera. (The reduction is by a third, not to a third.) Thus the first three sections relate not 6:4:3 as notated, but 6:3:2 as prescribed verbally, and modified by mensuration signs. The final section (*color* 4) is in diminution in relation to 3, down a level, in perfect time, minor prolation, again relating with semibreve equivalence to the upper parts. A black O sign undoes the sesquialtera of the preceding section, resulting in a 2:1, not 3:1 relationship between *colores* 3 and 4, overall 6:3:2:1. This is a very unusual instance of precise tempo instructions being built in to override the (otherwise presumed) semibreve equivalence of the notated values, in the form of proportional indications or modified mensuration signs in the upper parts. Although the red mensuration sign causes an overall proportional reduction, the notational coloration is for imperfection throughout, with split groups causing syncopation.

No. 113: Sturgeon, *Salve mater Domini/Salve templum gratie/-it in nomine Domini*

As noted, Sturgeon's motet continues Damett's *Benedictus* tenor. There are three statements of the eight-note *color*, which contains two *taleae*, each of two red notes and two black notes. (See Fig. 25.3.) The upper parts are in [O] throughout and follow the tenor structure isorhythmically. The tenor is marked 'De modo perfecto', and the three *color* statements are specified mensurally as ☉ O ℭ. The numerical values are in semibreves as they correspond to the upper parts. The first semibreve rest, followed by a syncopating dot, offsets what follows.

Fig. 25.3 Tenor of Sturgeon, *Salve mater/Salve templum* in London, British Library, Add. MS 57950 (**OH**), f. 92. Reproduced with permission of the British Library

The asterisks in Figure 25.3 indicate the following:

* The B would normally be worth 3S, but it is altered to 6 before the following L, and then imperfected to 5 by the second S rest (the rest after the dot).
** The L would normally be worth 9S, but is imperfected to 6 by the first (offset) S rest and the two S rests that follow the L.
*** The B has to be altered (from 2 to 4S) before the L; this must therefore be coloration for sesquialtera, not for imperfection (as also in *En Katerine solennia*). The numerical values given here are as for the upper parts, but the red B rest is therefore technically 3S in the time of 2, the altered red B that follows it 6S in the time of 4, the red L 9S in the time of 6. Thus both the black and the red L are in the prescribed perfect modus.

The tenor is written with semibreve equivalence between upper and lower parts only for *color* 3. The prolation signatures imply that the tenor is being construed in augmentation for *color* 1; for each perfect tenor semibreve under ☉, the upper parts have a perfect breve (tenor M = upper S). For each imperfect tenor semibreve under O in *color* 2, the upper parts have an imperfect breve, again, augmentation. But for each perfect tenor semibreve under ℂ, in *color* 3, the upper parts have a perfect breve, so if the tenor's major prolation is here counted in minims, it is now in diminution in relation to the upper parts (tenor M = upper parts' S). The mental gymnastics of the imperfection, alteration and syncopation of this tenor are virtuosically conceived and have to be solved empirically.

No. 112: Cooke, *Alma proles regia/Christi miles inclite/Ab inimicis nostris defende nos Christe*

This motet is altogether more straightforward. The tenor is again prescribed mensurally, as ☉ O ℂ; the upper parts change signature at each *color* [ℂ] C ℂ, though they align major and minor prolation between the tenor and upper parts. Its mensural affinity with *Carbunculus*

480 ENGLISH MOTETS C. 1400–1420

and *Sub Arturo* has been discussed above, together with the suggestion of a possible mentor-pupil relationship between Leonel and Cooke. There are three *color* statements, each of two *taleae* of 18 longs. The tenor is in imperfect modus; unlike the other two motets, it corresponds straightforwardly with the upper parts according to the signatures in each section. Successive tenor statements reduce mensurally; there is no diminution.[26] Thus, despite some superficial similarities, each of these three motets employs a very different strategy, attesting a high degree of competence in manipulating mensural complexity.

The Events of 1416, and the Motets of Dunstaple

The English had held Harfleur since September 1415, when the town surrendered after the above-mentioned siege, which was followed by the victory at Agincourt in October. But in 1416, the small English garrison had difficulty defending the town, and a series of encounters in the first half of the year finally resulted in the victory of John Duke of Bedford at the Battle of the Seine on 15 August (the feast of the Assumption). This occurred during the visit to England of the Emperor Sigismund; he and Henry had signed the treaty of Canterbury on that day.[27] News of his brother's victory reached Henry on 21 August on his return from Smallhythe to Canterbury, where the Emperor was preparing his departure. Both attended a service in the cathedral, probably on that same day or the next when, according to the *Gesta Henrici Quinti*, they gave thanks with the *Te Deum* 'and other [unspecified] offerings of propitiation' ('et aliis placacionum libaminibus deo dederunt gloriam et honorem').

Titus Livius reports, following Bedford's victory, that

Rex autem ut fratrem cum tanta victoria vidit redeuntem, cognito prius quo fuerat ordine pugnatum, & quid in omnibus gestum erat, gratias agens immortali Deo, quoniam ea fuerat obtenta victoria feriis assumptionis beatae Mariae Virginis, mandavit ut singulis diebus vitae suae in sacrario suo Antiphona cum versiculo & Collecta in commemoratione prefatae Virginis semel a capellanis & sacerdotibus suis decantaretur.

The king, however, when he saw his brother returning so victorious, having first learned of the course of the battle, and what in all was accomplished, gave thanks to immortal God. Since the victory was gained on the day of the Assumption of the Blessed Virgin Mary, he ordained that on every day of his life in his chapel an antiphon with versicle and collect should be sung by his chaplains and priests in commemoration of the said Virgin.[28]

[26] Nosow, *Ritual Meanings*, 31 computes the proportions of Cooke's motet by counting section II twice, adding the number of minims in sections I and II to those in Sections II and III, to make the numbers come out the same as for Dunstaple's *Veni* and *Preco*, where he counts each section separately. Those two motets have overall proportions of 3:2:1, achieved by successive diminution. *Alma*'s sections relate 9:6:4, an overall proportion which it shares with *Sub Arturo plebs* and *Carbunculus*. The tenor of *Carbunculus* is missing, but *Alma* and *Sub Arturo* both interpret a homographic tenor under different mensuration signs: this is neither diminution nor a proportional process.

[27] Sigismund was at this time King of the Romans, in effect the Holy Roman Emperor, though not so crowned until 1433. The *Gesta* already calls him emperor.

[28] Titus Livius, *Vita Henrici Quinti*, 26. Similar wording occurs in a version of the Latin *Brut*. Nosow, *Ritual Meanings*, 19, suggests that 'decantaretur' might imply polyphony. He later quotes (pp. 34–35) a similar account from *Thomæ de Elmham Vita & Gesta*, 83, no longer accepted as being by Elmham, seeming to imply that the two accounts refer to different points in the narrative.

OLD HALL, THE AGINCOURT MOTETS, AND DUNSTAPLE 481

Following this news, Henry indeed promptly mandated daily memorials augmenting the liturgy of his chapel, and presumably its music. His direct personal interest is reported at this point in the *Gesta Henrici Quinti*, chapter 22, which sets out the provisions in striking detail. New memorials are prescribed for each daily litany and procession: three memorials at High Mass for the Trinity, for the Assumption (the date of the recent naval victory), and for St George, 'our champion and protector', and six daily memorials after compline. The *Gesta* account is complemented by that in Elmham, *Liber metricus* (partly derived from the *Gesta*) which sets out the psalms and responds for the daily litany and procession in tabular form:[29]

day	dominica	feria ii	feria iii	feria iiii	feria v	feria vi	sabato	
psalm	**Cantemus**	**Iubi**late	**Confi**-temini	**Lauda**te nomen domini	**Bene**-dicite	**Lauda**te dominum de celis	**Exul**tavit cor meum in domino	in ordine psalle
respond	**Summe** trinitati	**Bene** dictus	**Quis** deus	**Gloria** patri	**Honor** virtus	**Tibi** laus	**Benedi**camus patrem	dabis his

These agree with the prescriptions of the *Gesta*. The three Mass memorials are reported in the next few lines, and are likewise compatible with the *Gesta* account. Up to this point, there is no reason to assume that anything other than chant is intended. Then finally the post-compline memorials are set out in tabular form. The upper line identifies the feast, with the addition, in a remarkable graphic coupling, of text incipits that in at least one and probably more cases imply polytextual motets:

Sunday	Monday	Tuesday	Wednesday	Thursday	Friday	Saturday
Trinitas	[not specified; traditionally the Requiem]	**Spi**ritus sanctus	**Rex** Edwardus [the Confessor]	Johannes baptista **Preco**	Sanctus Georgius **Miles**	Sancta Maria **Regina beata**
Libera nos		**Veni** sancte spiritus	**Rex** gentis &c (**Lo13**: Rex sancte Edwarde) **Confer ave iungis**	**Inter** natos	**Hic** est vere martir	**Placet hec** ad placitum chori

These additional texts are not given in the *Gesta*, but Elmham's account is so closely aligned with it that there is no reason to doubt that the additional incipits are integral. The lower line gives one or more further text incipits, this time for chants that in some cases may be motet tenors. The divisions between upper and lower lines may not always be consistent in what they depict, but where the uppermost line specifies the saint, the remaining one or two incipits (on either line) can be taken to indicate either chant or

---

[29] There are slight differences between the sources (**Lo4**, article 4, and **Lo1776**). The versions here are transcribed from **Lo4**. Bold type distinguishes larger, heavier script in **Lo4**. Attempts to show the tabulations in the edition, Elmham, *Liber metricus*, 140–41, are somewhat garbled. Nosow, *Ritual Meanings*, 20–21, sets out the comparative statements clearly in Table 1.1; Table 1.2 (p. 24), transcribes from the varied alignments in the other manuscripts, **Lo13** and **Lo861** (the latter possibly a less careful copy of **Lo4**).

482 ENGLISH MOTETS C. 1400–1420

polytextual polyphony, most likely a polyphonic motet when two texts are given and one is not chant.[30]

The most suggestive candidate for identification is *Preco*, the unique non-liturgical text of a known motet, coupled with the tenor of that motet, the John the Baptist chant *Inter natos*, prescribed for Thursday; there can be little doubt that Dunstaple's motet on that tenor is indicated: *Preco preheminencie/Precursor premittitur/Inter natos* (MB 8, no. 29).[31] This motet's more famous musical twin, *Veni sancte spiritus et emitte/Veni sancte spiritus et infunde/Veni creator spiritus* (MB 8, no. 32), may be intended by *Veni sancte spiritus*. This is slightly less secure, since the well-known sequence of that name is not a new text like *Preco*.[32] But the context, in suggestive company with *Preco*, and their very similar musical styles and structures, encourages the suggestion that Dunstaple's four-part motet is indeed meant. At least, if a polyphonic interpretation is contested, the specification of these mostly liturgical texts in a royal context could have encouraged composition of the motets. The other saints with double incipits are Edward (the Confessor) and George. Taken alone, *Miles*, on Friday for St George, could imply the **OH** motets by Cooke or Damett addressed to him but, coupled with a different chant, *Hic est vere martir*, probably refers to a non-extant motet on that tenor.[33] It could also refer to the *miles Christi* incipit in the excerpt from the English extension of the *Brut* chronicle and the pseudo-Lydgate poem cited above. For St Edward, *Rex gentis* most nearly corresponds in known liturgical manuscripts to *Ave rex gentis Anglorum*, a motet in **Ox7** (from Bury St Edmunds), which refers not to St Edward but to St Edmund.[34] But our text is specified not for Edmund but for Edward, for which the *Rex sancte Edwarde* of the **Lo13** version seems closer: *Ave sancte rex Edwarde* is a sequence known from **Worcester160**, f. 99[v]; this text or a variant of it could have served as a motet voice. The status of *Ave jungis* is not known.

Henry's liturgical programme in both sources is sandwiched between the same datable events in August 1416, Bedford's victory and Sigismund's departure, together with the motets signalled only in the *Liber metricus*. Although that programme has longer-term implications, its inclusion at precisely this point in the chronicle narrative suggested to its editor, and to me, that some of these titles might also be associated with that service. Robert Nosow rightly states that 'there is no solid justification for the

---

[30] Both accounts have long been known; Nosow has tabulated them in combination. He ingeniously proposes extant polyphonic settings for these items, but the kinds of composition identified as having known musical settings are so heterogeneous that no clear picture emerges.

[31] Colton, *Angel Song*, 90–91, demonstrates that a line in Wheathamstead's epitaph, 'melior vir de muliere nunquam natus erat', referring to John the Baptist both biblically and liturgically, reflects Dunstaple's motet and its tenor, thus showing knowledge of the motet and applying Christ's appraisal of the one John to another.

[32] The motetus text *Veni sancte spiritus et infunde*, otherwise unknown, is a trope or calque on the known triplum text. *Spiritus sanctus* designates the feast; if it were taken as a text incipit, Dunstaple's other motet for the Holy Spirit (MB 8, no. 33), the differently constructed three-part *Veni sancte spiritus/Consolator optime/Sancti Spiritus assit*, could be intended. Account could not be taken here of work in progress by Roger Bowers, based on his new scrutiny of the *Gesta*, which redates its reports of Henry's memorials to the beginning of his reign, and seeks to loosen any connection of the incipits with the Dunstaple motets. Their dates however remain plausible because of the **OH** context.

[33] Another possible *Miles Christi* is the setting of a different text in **OxS26**. This is not addressed to St George, but is an antiphon of St Thomas of Lancaster (d. 1322): Greene, 'Two Medieval Musical Manuscripts', 3.

[34] Bukofzer, *Studies*. The *Ave anglorum* reported earlier, conflated with this *rex gentis*, would yield *Ave rex gentis Anglorum*, the title of the St Edmund motet.

OLD HALL, THE AGINCOURT MOTETS, AND DUNSTAPLE   483

supposition that any motets were sung at the Mass . . . for which the only music specified [in the *Gesta*] is the Te Deum'. But mention of the Te Deum does not necessarily exclude other music; indeed, in this case the *Gesta* adds 'and other offerings of propitiation', as noted above. Whether or not either motet was performed then, their position at this point in the *Liber metricus* at least provides a hypothetical *terminus ante quem* of August 1416 for the titles listed.[35]

Veni sancte spiritus in **OH** and *Preco* in a fragment probably of Canterbury provenance (**Cant128/6**) are the only two Dunstaple motets with isorhythm preserved in any English source, *Veni* the only one to survive complete in England. They are also the only two such Dunstaple motets to appear in Continental sources in addition to the much later **ModB** (*c.* 1440). On the verso of the Canterbury leaf is a motet triplum, *Ave miles triumphalis*, followed by what seems to be the start of a low-range motetus part, *Cristi morte nato mundo vite reserato . . . interdicti hostis*. This sounds very much like another Agincourt-related motet, and would tend to corroborate the dating to 1415–16 here proposed for *Preco*. Addressed to a *miles*, St George would seem an obvious choice, but Edward is another possibility.[36] John the Baptist and George are celebrated on adjacent days in the provisions (Thursday, Friday), possibly reflected in the adjacence of these motets in **Cant128/6**.

Elmham's testimony is the clearest we could have that Dunstaple's *Preco preheminencie/Precursor premittitur*, and probably its structural and almost certainly chronological twin, his *Veni sancte/Veni creator*, were composed in or before 1416, if indeed they are the titles cited in the chronicle at this point.[37] The composition of *Veni*, at any rate, cannot be much later in date because of its presence, copied anonymously by a scribe otherwise unrepresented, among the later additions to **OH** in the second half of the 1410s. The script does not correspond to known Dunstaple autographs. Although not bound by the latest date that the four composer–chaplains were together, it occupies the central bifolio (ff. 55^v–56) of the interpolated gathering IX, making it likely that it was in place before its neighbours were copied around it. This location in the manuscript suggests that it was more or less contemporary with the other second-layer additions, which would again corroborate an early dating, not later than 1419; earlier if it was indeed associated with the documentation of 1416.

---

[35] I proposed these datings for the two Dunstaple motets in Bent, *Dunstaple*, 8–9. I would now withdraw the direct association I made with the Canterbury service itself, but still find their position in the narrative persuasive for dating them by 1416, specified in conjunction with Henry's *memorie*. The case that had been made for Elmham's authorship not only of the *Liber metricus* but of the prose *Gesta* is set out clearly by the editors in *Gesta Henrici Quinti*, pp. xviii–xxviii. Nosow uses Elmham's testimony to propose incorporating these large-scale motets, extant or lost, into the prescribed ritual setting. I would limit them to the post-compline observances, rather than the litanies, processions and Mass.

[36] **Cant128/6**. Sandon, 'Fragments of Medieval Polyphony', 41–44, suggests this motet may be for St Bartholomew because of its apparent mention of Armenia; but he is not known as a soldier saint. The reading of *Armenie* is doubtful, and I wonder if it could be *Armonie*. Another text mentioning Edward is the motet fragment **Cu4435**, b^v: 'a serva regnum Anglie virtute . . . ndorum lilii rosa sine spina. Edwardus . . . ne miles vigorosus. Insignis in . . .'; but this also appears to be a triplum part, like the Canterbury verso. Maybe this text addresses George, Mary and Edward? This fragment is part of RC: see Bent, 'Towards the Reconstruction' in EECM 62 for facsimile and commentary, and inventory as ⏯ Table 25.1.

[37] MB 8, nos. 29 and 32. Nosow, *Ritual Meanings*, has proposed a different interpretation of *Preco*, seeing Bedford (as John the Baptist) as the precursor of his brother Henry V (as Christ): see the review by Bent in *PMM*, 22 (2013), 107–13.

484 ENGLISH MOTETS C. 1400–1420

Dunstaple and the Duke of Bedford

There have long been several candidates for identification with the composer, but only recently has it become clear that some of the existing references to a John Dunstaple in service to various members of the royal family may not all be to the same man. Lisa Colton proposed a new candidate who died in 1459, which turns out to be the death date of a different but probably related John Dunstaple.[38] The composer's epitaph famously describes him as an astronomer and musician; its date is non-negotiable, so the one secure fact is that the composer died in 1453. It has long been known that an astrological treatise in St John's College, Cambridge, MS 162, f. 74[r], is headed with an inscription describing him as 'musician with the Duke of Bedford'.[39] Other astronomical treatises associated with Dunstaple, some (notably in **Ce70**) in his autograph, are also well documented, though they remain under-investigated.[40] Rodney M. Thomson discovered the erased name of Dunstaple in a Boethius manuscript in Corpus Christi College, Oxford (**OxC118**), from which it became clear that annotations to the *De institutione musica*, and the entire *De arithmetica*, were in his hand, as well as prompting further speculations about his possible studies in Oxford and connection to the Merton calculators.[41] Further biographical work by Lisa Colton, Andrew Wathey and Roger Bowers is ongoing.[42] It necessitates disentangling existing archival references that have been thought to apply to the same man, though it does seem that much of the archival documentation associating Dunstaple with Bedford, uncovered by Wathey and others, indeed applies to the composer.

The presence in the 1433 inventories of the Duke of Bedford's property of a 'book of motets in the French manner' has been widely reported. It is assumed that these were motets with isorhythm such as the impressive body of such works left by Dunstaple and preserved mostly in **ModB**.[43] The stronger his ties to Bedford, the more likely it is that this book included Dunstaple's motets, but it is nevertheless interesting that they would be identified as 'in the French manner', since their distinctive characteristics were in place at an earlier date than the motets of Du Fay, which by the mid-1430s might stand as typical 'French' motets.

The dating of at least *Preco* and *Veni* to the mid-1410s raises the possibility that all of Dunstaple's similarly structured motets could be relatively early, perhaps between

---

[38] Colton, *Angel Song*, 86–115.

[39] 'Iste libell*us* pertinebat Joh*ann*i dunstaple, *cum* duci Bedfordie musico' (This booklet used to belong to John Dunstaple, musician with the Duke of Bedford). The treatise is a separate libellus containing the *Introductorium in principiis iudiciorum* of the ninth-century astrologer, astronomer and mathematician known as 'Zael', and contains annotations in Dunstaple's hand.

[40] Summarised in Bent, *Dunstaple*.

[41] Thomson, 'John Dunstable'. The Merton association was already mentioned in Bent, *Dunstaple*, 4. Elżbieta Witkowska-Zaremba is currently working on the annotations to the Boethius MS **OxC118**, owned and partly written by Dunstaple, and on other instances of his hand, notably the partly autograph astrological treatises in **Ce70**.

[42] Colton, *Angel Song*; Wathey, 'Dunstable in France'; Stell and Wathey, 'New Light'; Wathey, *Music in the Royal and Noble Households*; Bowers, 'Choral Institutions', and Bowers, ' "Goode and Delitable Songe" '. Ongoing work by Bowers and Wathey is as yet unpublished, but was presented in seminars at All Souls College respectively on 21 Feb. ('Composer biographies – the cases of John Dunstable and "Roy Henry" ') and 14 Nov. 2019 ('John Dunstaple, Lionel Power and the mid Fifteenth Century').

[43] 'Item ung livre de motez a la maniere de France couvert de cuir blanc': See Stratford, *Bedford Inventories*, 20, 66–67.

the mid-1410s and the 1420s (*c.* 1415–30). David Howlett proposed that *Albanus roseo rutilat* might be dated 1426, on the occasion of a splendid visit to St Albans by the Duke of Bedford.[44] This hypothesis is strengthened by the increasing likelihood that the composer was in Bedford's employ at least by the 1420s if not before. Bowers has cleared away possibly conflicting royal patronage by showing that he was not the same John Dunstaple who was richly rewarded by the dowager Queen Joan in 1427–28 and 1436.[45] He proposes that the composer was probably in Bedford's service until the duke's death in 1435, implying frequent travels to France; and that he was with Bedford not only from 1422, but perhaps from as early as 1414, when Bedford was elevated to his dukedom with a consequent presumed upgrading of his household and chapel personnel, thus opening up the possibility of a twenty-year association for the composer.[46]

Bowers has contributed a further important discovery relating to Dunstaple's motet *Dies dignus decorari/Demon dolens*, on St German. Neither text specified which of two northern French bishop–saints was honoured. It was assumed to be St Germanus of Auxerre (*c.* 378–*c.* 448) because of Dunstaple's association with St Albans, where this saint was specially venerated. But Bowers was able to show by relating the motet texts to the saint's hagiography that the motet honours St Germanus of Paris (*c.* 496–576), who miraculously cured a supplicant in the manner described in the motetus text, prompting his translation to a finer tomb. The saint's relics and shrine were preserved in the abbey church of St-Germain near (and now in) Paris. That John Duke of Bedford was one of this saint's fervent devotees is documented around the time of the illness and death of his wife Anne in 1432, when he caused the saint's relics to be carried in solemn procession through the city. She did not recover, but Bedford appointed the monks of St-Germain to escort her coffin to its tomb at the Célestins; the ducal chapel was in attendance at the funeral. The motet further cements Dunstaple's connection with both Bedford and Paris. But the identification of a different St German in no way detracts from his association with St Albans, not only because of the St Alban motet, but also on grounds of the attribution to Abbot Wheathampstead of one or both of Dunstaple's funerary verses.[47] Humfrey Duke of Gloucester also had strong associations with Wheathampstead and St Albans, and apparently employed the composer after the death of Bedford in 1435: a John Dunstaple, probably the composer, was recorded in 1438 as his 'serviteur et familier domestique'.[48]

Bowers also finds 'oblique hints that Bedford's chapel may have been joined by Lionel Power following Clarence's death in 1421'.[49] Bedford was next in line to the throne after the infant King Henry VI, following the deaths of both his elder brothers.

---

[44] Howlett, 'A Possible Date'. Dunstaple is assumed to have had dealings with St Albans at some date, partly through his later connection with Duke Humfrey, but more particularly because his two surviving epitaphs are attributed to Abbot John Whethamstede of that abbey.

[45] Bowers, ' "Goode and Delitable Songe" ', 228. See also Bent, 'Towards the Reconstruction'. A similar early dating of the upgrading of Clarence's chapel was proposed above.

[46] Seminar paper, 'Composer biographies – the cases of John Dunstable and "Roy Henry" ', All Souls College, 21 Feb. 2019.

[47] Bowers, at the same seminar. For the epitaphs, see Bent, *Dunstaple*, 1–3. Wathey, 'Dunstaple, Power', suggests that it could have been performed at the Paris coronation of Henry VI in 1431.

[48] Wathey, 'Dunstable in France', 21–23, 28–29.

[49] Bowers, ' "Goode and Delitable Songe" ', 227 and Bowers, *English Church Polyphony*, pp. ix, 111, 'Commentary and Corrigenda', 10–11. See also Wathey, 'Dunstaple, Power', for new biographical information there on Power in the late 1430s, and his potential link with John Duke of Bedford through the duke's former household officers.

486 ENGLISH MOTETS C. 1400–1420

If indeed there was contact between Power and Dunstaple through Bedford in the 1420s, this could have led to a degree of mutual influence to account for so many conflicting attributions between them of music composed probably in the later 1420s, especially for the mass cycles *Rex seculorum* and *Sine nomine*, and perhaps even for their joint role in initiating the cyclic mass, as well as the composition of antiphon settings in 'song' style.[50]

Dunstaple: Musical Discoveries since MB 8, and Dating

Dunstaple is central to our understanding of English music in the first half of the fifteenth century, and of why it was so highly regarded and influential on the Continent.[51] Musical discoveries made since MB 8 and included in MB 8rev are the missing Kyries (anonymously transmitted in an English source, **Ce300**) of three mass cycles: *Rex seculorum* (with majority ascriptions to Leonel), *Sine nomine* (with conflicting ascriptions to Leonel and Benet), and Dunstaple's *Da gaudiorum premia*, parts of the Gloria *Da gaudiorum premia*, and a reworking (not necessarily by Dunstaple) of the Magnificat. There is also a four-voice setting of *Descendi in ortum meum*, of which two voices are ascribed to him in **Lo54324**; the other two are anonymous in **Maidstone** and enable a full reconstruction (see ⓑ Ex. 25.1). This is one of two works which evidently belong to Dunstaple's late period, in the 1440s; the other is a setting of *Gaude flore virginali*, in five parts with a range of twenty-one notes, ascribed to Dunstaple in the index of the Eton Choirbook, but now missing from that source. An anonymous and incomplete setting in **Lo54324** meets these criteria; this may be all we have of a late work by Dunstaple. ⓑ Example 25.2 gives what survives of the first section in O time, including a small portion in which all five parts are present. The more fragmentary second section in C time is not reproduced, being on the next opening of which only the verso survives. The lost Eton setting is less likely to be a two-opening setting of *Gaude flore virginali* in **Cu4435**, part of RC, which may have been in five parts but of which too little survives to establish its range.[52] All three compositions survive in fragmentary form in English fragments containing other works by Dunstaple.[53]

Another subsequent addition is a three-voice Kyrie of which the isolated but ascribed lowest voice was published as MB 8, no. 65. Parts of the other voices were recovered and transcribed in Bent, *Dunstaple*, 72–73. The late Peter Wright, whose close knowledge of this repertory was unparalleled, more recently attributed to Dunstaple a three-voice Credo transmitted anonymously ('Anglicanum') in two sources of the 1430s, **Ao** and **Tr92**. His fine-grained stylistic and source-based study is based on links with the

---

[50] The *Alma redemptoris* cycle (EECM 42) is ascribed to Leonel in **Ao**. The Credo and Sanctus have recently turned up alongside the Gloria *Rex seculorum*, all anonymously, in the English fragment **Norwich6** (see EECM 62).

[51] Testimonies of Tinctoris and Martin le Franc are discussed in Wegman, 'Martin Le Franc' and Bent, 'Martin le Franc'.

[52] Bent, 'Towards the Reconstruction', and facsimile in EECM 62.

[53] In **Lo54324**. Partially transcribed in Bent and Bent, 'Dufay, Dunstable, Plummer', where mention of its chant cantus firmus, *Ad nutum [domini nostrum]*, was inadvertently omitted.

OLD HALL, THE AGINCOURT MOTETS, AND DUNSTAPLE   487

Credos MB 8, nos. 8 and 5, and further illuminated by his identification of a differently notated English concordance to the latter in **Philadelphia658**.[54]

RC is an assemblage of eighteen leaves, now widely scattered, that once formed part of a royal choirbook. It must have been copied in the early to mid-1420s, because some direct copying into it from **OH** occurred while that manuscript was still in use and before some corrections were made.[55] ▶ Table 25.1 gives a simplified inventory of RC. Its royal credentials are its very interesting decorative initials, with heraldically significant animals, and especially its direct access to and direct copying from **OH**, then in the hands of the chaplains of Henry V who had stayed on to serve his infant son; some of their works were included in the main body of RC. This royal connection was established before a Dunstaple component was discovered in **Tallinn**. Just as the quest for a likely royal patron of Old Hall led to Clarence, a similar quest for RC leads to Bedford, in any case the likeliest royal patron in the early 1420s, a proposal further encouraged by the prominence given to Dunstaple: two adjacent works by him head the Gloria section. The first is a unique and remarkable Gloria, an accompanied canon 4 in 1, reproduced as ▶ Example 25.3.[56] Following it on the verso is the Gloria of the four-part Gloria–Credo pair hitherto known only from **Ao** (MB 8, no. 11, presumably contemporary with its paired Credo, no. 12). These works can all now be dated no later than the early 1420s. I have thus taken the opportunity to reproduce here for convenience (as ▶ Exx. 25.1, 25.2 and 25.3) three compositions by or probably by Dunstaple (in addition to the three-voice Kyrie just mentioned) which I have been able to reconstruct (for Ex. 25.2 only partially), and which are not otherwise conveniently available. We must assume more later works are lost, or hiding in anonymity.

The first layer of the Veneto manuscript **Q15**, completed by 1425, included English compositions probably acquired during the Council of Constance (1414–18). A Credo by Dunstaple (MB 8, no. 8) is in the first stage of **Q15** (*c*. 1420–25), so this too must date from *c*. 1415–20.[57] **Q15**'s first stage contains none of his structured motets with isorhythm, but it does include the English motet by Alanus, *Sub Arturo plebs* (Ch. 20), as well as two works by Leonel, his *Salve regina* and the Credo **OH**, no. 83, as well as works by Gervase (an **OH** composer) and Benet.

Dunstaple's other works in **Q15**, all antiphon settings, were copied in the early 1430s, and are not known from earlier sources. They are the *Regina celi*, MB 8, no. 38, and *Sub tuam protectionem* (no. 51). Three more have conflicting ascriptions in their various manuscripts: *Alma redemptoris* (no. 40) to Power and Binchois, the *Beata dei genitrix* (no. 41) to Binchois, and *Quam pulchra es* (no. 44) to 'Egidius' (Binchois is probably intended).[58] The compilation dates of other Continental sources (**Trent**, **Ao**, **ModB**) in

---

[54] P. Wright, 'A New Attribution'. His edition of the Credo is in EECM 55, no. 10. The presentation of no. 5 in **Ao** has been notationally changed from what was obviously the English original. His subsequent discoveries will be reported in Bent, 'New concordances'.

[55] A full account is given in Bent, 'Towards the Reconstruction', together with facsimiles, in EECM 62.

[56] This reconstruction / transcription was first published in my article 'A New Canonic Gloria and the Changing Profile of Dunstaple'.

[57] Bent, 'Constance'; Bent, *Q15*; P. Wright, 'A New Attribution', 222.

[58] *Regina celi*, MB 8, no. 38; *Quam pulchra es*, MB 8, no. 44; *Sub tuam protectionem*, MB 8, no. 51; *Alma redemptoris*, MB 8, no. 40, with conflicting ascriptions to Leonel Power and Binchois; *Beata dei genitrix*, MB 8, no. 41, ascribed in **Q15** to Binchois. Wright, 'Binchois and England', evaluates and mostly rejects the conflicting ascriptions to Binchois.

488   ENGLISH MOTETS C. 1400–1420

the 1430s and 1440s are too late to offer useful *termini ante quos*, though it is in those manuscripts that we find the first unified English tenor mass cycles. In the absence of earlier datable manuscripts, we might tentatively place the mass cycles and antiphons in the late 1420s and into the 1430s. If not only Dunstaple but also Power (as has been tentatively suggested) was associated with the Duke of Bedford in the 1420s, the opportunity for mutual influence could account for some of the conflicting attributions between them for works that may date from this period, some of which have been mentioned above: the *Alma redemptoris* setting in **Q15** (the authorship of Leonel's mass on this chant is uncontested), the *Rex seculorum* mass (of which only the Gloria is ascribed to Dunstaple, all other movements to Leonel), and the *Sine nomine* mass also ascribed to Benet and Leonel.[59]

Dunstaple's absence from **OH** except as an anonymous later addition may simply be due to him being probably about ten years younger than Leonel Power, not yet active in the first decade of the century, outside the circle that constituted Clarence's chapel, having enjoyed different patronage, and that his absence from the main round of additions to **OH** may be explained by the fact that he was not one of Henry V's chaplains. Most of the **OH** music was probably composed in the first decade of the fifteenth century. If Dunstaple was born no earlier than *c.* 1390, he would still have been in his teens in that decade, perhaps too young for the main compilation *c.* 1413–15. His motets would then be works of his twenties and thirties. The later the main **OH** compilation is placed, the harder it would be to account for his absence from it. As already noted, the best-represented composer, responsible for some of the most striking music, is Leonel Power, a member of the chapel of Thomas Duke of Clarence for which the main layer of **OH** was apparently compiled. I estimate that Leonel (d. 1445) was probably born *c.* 1380–85, to allow for him to have written so many works of such compositional sophistication in his late teens and twenties.

If the music of the second layer of **OH** was largely composed and compiled *c.* 1415–19, it could be that a considerable quantity of Dunstaple's music, beyond the few pieces just mentioned, could date from the later 1410s and into the 1420s, while he was in Bedford's service, when his works would presumably have been copied into a manuscript of Bedford's chapel, rather than added to **OH**, which by then was in the hands of the chaplains of Henry V and the infant Henry VI.

Dunstaple's Motets with Isorhythm

Bukofzer included in MB 8 as 'Isorhythmic motets' Dunstaple's nine 'regular' periodic motets. He also included three motets that fall outside the predominant pattern: *Specialis virgo* (MB 8, no. 31) has an irregular tenor in which the rhythm of two two-note segments is repeated; MB 8, no. 34 is a textless piece on a short tetrachord tenor stated four times, a step higher each time; and the three-part motet *Veni sancte Spiritus* (MB 8, no. 33), whose tenor is repeated in inversion and retrograde.

---

[59] Several conflicting ascriptions between Dunstaple and Binchois, Leonel Power and John Benet, have yet to be resolved. P. Wright, 'A New Attribution', 196–97, also refers to issues affecting the attribution of songs and a carol. On carols see now Fallows, *Henry V and the Earliest English Carols*.

OLD HALL, THE AGINCOURT MOTETS, AND DUNSTAPLE   489

The motetus text of the better-known four-part no. 32 is an otherwise unknown paraphrase of the sequence, *Veni sancte spiritus, et infunde*, with three double stanzas. In no. 33 the stanzas of the complete *Veni sancte Spiritus* sequence are divided between the upper parts. Its tenor is another Pentecost sequence, *Sancti spiritus assit*, stated first as written, then in inversion, and then in retrograde a fifth lower. The first two sections have some isorhythm in the upper parts, stricter for the opening duets. See Table 25.2.

Table 25.2 Distribution of the sequence texts in Dunstaple's motets nos. 32 and 33

No. 33, by section	Sequence stanza		No. 32, tr and mo by *color* and *talea*	No. 32, motetus text distribution (by complete lines only)	Sequence stanza
triplum, I	1a	Veni, Sancte Spiritus, et emitte celitus lucis tue radium.	C1.T1	Veni, Sancte Spiritus, et infunde primitus rorem celi gratie.	1a
	1b	Veni, pater pauperum, veni, dator munerum, veni, lumen cordium.		Precantibus humanibus	1b
motetus, I	2a	Consolator optime, dulcis hospes anime, dulce refrigerium.	C1.T2	salva nos divinitus a serpentis facie.	
motetus, II	2b	In labore requies, in estu temperies, in fletu solatium.		In cuius presentia ex tua clementia	2a
	3a	O lux beatissima, reple cordis intima tuorum fidelium.			
motetus, III	3b	Sine tuo numine, nihil est in homine, nihil est innoxium.	C2.T1	tecta sint peccata.	
triplum, II	4a	Lava quod est sordidum, riga quod est aridum, sana quod est saucium.		Nostraque servitia corda penitentia tibi fac placata.	2b
	4b	Flecte quod est rigidum, fove quod est frigidum, rege quod est devium.	C2.T2	Languidorum consolator et lapsorum reformator, mortis medicina.	3a
triplum, III	5a	Da tuis fidelibus, in te confidentibus, sacrum septenarium.	C3.T1	Peccatorum perdonator esto noster expurgator	3b
	5b	Da virtutis meritum, da salutis exitum, da perenne gaudium.	C3.T2	et duc ad divina.	

490 ENGLISH MOTETS C. 1400–1420

Table 25.3 The Dunstaple motets classed by Bukofzer as isorhythmic

No.	Composition	Tenor	Subject/saint
	motets *a*3		
23	*Albanus roseo / Quoque ferendo*	*Albanus* (antiphon, 6th couplet)	Alban
24	*Ave regina / Ave mater*	*Ave mundi* (sequence)	BVM
25	*Christe sanctorum / Tibi Christe*	*Tibi Criste* (hymn)	Michael
26	*Dies dignus / Demon dolens*	*Iste confessor* (hymn)	German of Paris
27	*Gaude felix / Gaude mater*	*Anna parens* (verse of respond)	Anne
	motets *a*4		
28	*Gaude virgo salutata / Gaude virgo singularis / Virgo mater*	[*Ave gemma*] (sequence: stanza 5 of *Ave mundi*)	BVM
29	*Preco preheminencie / Precursor premittit* / textless	*Inter natos* (antiphon)	John the Baptist
30	*Salve scema / Salve salus* / textless	*Cantant celi* (respond, end of repetenda)	Catherine
32	*Veni sancte spiritus et emitte / Veni sancte spiritus et infunde / Veni creator*	*Mentes tuorum* (hymn, line 2)	Pentecost
	irregular forms		
33	*Veni sancte spiritus / Consolator*	*Sancti spiritus assit* (sequence)	Pentecost
31	*Specialis virgo*	*Salve parens inclita* (sequence, stanza 5)	BVM
34	textless	solmisation exercise	

Adapted from Bent, *Dunstaple*, 64–65.

Table 25.3 Continued

Overall reduction of tenor	Tenor notated values	Tenor *taleae* and notes	Overall length, and *talea* unit	Upper parts in ModB
6:4:3; notated as for *color* 3 (16B)	L, B	3C T **3** × 8	176 (16) last statement foreshortened because of rests	[O] ¢·O
6:4:3; notated as for *color* 3, with altered S	B, S	3C T **2** × 9	128 (16)	[O] ¢·O
3:2:1	L, B	3C T **2** × 11	120 (12)	[O] C φ
6:4:3; notated as for *color* 3, with altered S	L, B, S	3C T **2** × 9	143 (18)	[O] ¢ O
3:2:1	L, B	3C T **2** × 18	180 (18)	[O] C O
6:4:3; notated as for *color* 3, with altered S	L, B, S	3C T **3** × 7	153 (8) each *color* contains two differently rhythmicised melodic statements each of 11 notes	[O] C O
3:2:1	Mx, L, B	3C T **2** × 12	150 (15)	[O] ¢ O
3:2:1	Mx, L, B	3C T **2** × 18	180 (18)	[O] C O
3:2:1	Mx, L, B	3C T **2** × 11	150 (15)	[O] C O
3:3:2 I as written; II inverted; III retrograde, 5th lower	L, B	12		[O] O C
none	ℂ L, B	13		upper parts φ
none	ℂ B, S	5		upper parts O

492 ENGLISH MOTETS C. 1400–1420

For motets nos. 23–32, the mensural pattern for the upper parts is standard: [O] C O, with isorhythmic repeats between each of the two or three *taleae* within each *color*. Whether there is or is not a stroke through a signature in the various manuscripts has no mensural significance. These strokes occur only in Continental manuscripts and are inconsistently applied.[60] All those motets, except the three 'irregular' ones, have three *color* statements, three reducing sections, most with two *taleae* per *color*, two with three *taleae* (nos. 23, 28); both of those have overall 6:4:3 proportions. Table 25.3 lists their overall proportions as 3:2:1 (five) or 6:4:3 (four). The tenors of all Dunstaple's '3:2:1' motets are notated in values corresponding to the upper parts for the first statement, the subsequent two statements to be read in diminution, at the next note-level down. 3:2:1 is an arithmetic proportion, though the result is achieved not proportionally but by diminution. The rhythms of the tenor statements are successively the same but faster.[61]

But the tenors of all the motets with the overall (harmonic) proportion 6:4:3 are notated in the shorter values that correspond to the third *color* statement, in perfect tempus. Where the tenor includes semibreve pairs preceding a breve (only in nos. 24, 26 and 28), the second one is altered, in that final statement only. In other words, there is mensural transformation.[62] It is more often the case that subsequent tenor statements are diminutions of the first, but here the first and second *colores* are read in augmented values from the third, both up a single level to fit with the upper parts. The breve of the third *color* is read in the first *color* as a long in imperfect modus, perfect tempus, in the second as a long in imperfect modus, imperfect tempus. The semibreves are now read as breves in imperfect modus, which precludes the alteration required in the third *color*.

Afterword to Part V

The texts of the English motets reviewed in Chapters 22–25 are more resolutely sacred than most of their French counterparts. They seem to afford less opportunity for the detailed verbal play and word-painting that permeates the motets of Vitry and Machaut. There are, however, topical deviations from standard texts, as in Damett's *Salvatoris mater pia*; polemics about vainglorious singers in a self-declared contrafact in *Are post libamina*; cryptic statements of compositional technique in *O amicus/Precursoris*. Words and rhymes are exploited as sonic objects, as in *O amicus*, where a long-standing English predilection for alliteration is lightly present. Numerical symbolism seems to be less in evidence than in French motets; but in motets other than those by Dunstaple the notational sophistication is at a very high level, equal to anything in **Chantilly**. Dunstaple's own motets come closer than those of his lesser-known contemporaries

---

[60] See Bent, 'The Early Use', and related articles.

[61] See Ch. 2 for the distinction between this statement, and equal rhythm, i.e. without diminution, which is what the term isorhythm implies. Ch. 23 recounts the distinction between arithmetic, geometric and harmonic proportions.

[62] The Dunstaple motets here referred to are no. 23, *Albanus roseo rutilat*; no. 24, *Ave regina celorum*; no. 26, *Dies dignus decorari*; and no. 28, *Gaude virgo salutata* (MB 8, 1953, and MB 8rev, 1970). No. 23 is also proportioned 6:4:3, but no semibreves are used and alteration at the tempus level is not involved. No. 23 uses longs and breves only; no. 24 uses breves and semibreves; nos. 26 and 28 use longs, breves and semibreves.

to following a standard template, though with music of the highest quality. With little more than *Sub Arturo* (Ch. 20) as an international ambassador (the only unmistakably English motet that circulated on the Continent in the first quarter of the fifteenth century), the conundrum remains as to how English and French composers at that time developed similarly ingenious constructions without leaving more signs of access to each other's repertories.

PART VI
ITALIAN MOTETS

496 ITALIAN MOTETS

These chapters, devoted to Italian motets and motets in Italy, originated with my 1984 paper (publication delayed until 1992), which sought to reinstate the Italian motet as a distinctive genre alongside the madrigal, ballata and caccia. The neglect of motets was largely due to their absence from the retrospective anthologies, most famously the Squarcialupi codex (**Sq**), which assembled works in those other genres grouped by composer, and to very fragmentary survival until their culmination in the intact motets of Johannes Ciconia (mostly composed in Padua *c.* 1400–1411), which I edited for PMFC 24. As well as updating that earlier work in Chapter 26, Chapters 28 and 29 consider various aspects of his motets, both repertorially and analytically, and Chapter 27 evaluates the presence of motets in the palimpsest MS **SL2211**.

26
The Fourteenth-Century Italian Motet

In both general histories of music and specialist studies, French criteria have tended to govern accounts of the motet in trecento Italy. To consider the Italian motet an offshoot of the French tradition may be more valid for its origins than for its continuing history.[1] The motet is indisputably French by origin and definition, but that need not bind the subsequent, divergent traditions of other countries, notably England and Italy, to negative definition by French standards.

The Italian motet is a poor hunting ground for the features accepted as those of the French motet as defined, for example, by Ursula Günther and Frank Ll. Harrison. One of the few surveys of native Italian motet composition, when this paper was first given, presented the older received view:

> Before the early fifteenth century, motet production in medieval Italy had been negligible; the extant pieces number fewer than half a dozen and demonstrate a fundamental distrust of the species. Even more than the 13th-century English composers the Italians shied away from the cantus firmus and evidently tended to mould their motets into non-isorhythmic secular forms, like madrigals. All of Ciconia's dozen motets have tenors with bass-like support quality . . . All but two are tonally unified . . . Their clear sectional articulation is produced by various means, such as isomelic endings of taleae, structurally placed melismas and cadential arrest of motion preceded by climactic acceleration. Furthermore, the composers active in northern Italy evidently were the first to transfer the technique of imitation from monotextual duets, where it was at home, to the motet. Since monotextual motets were now written more frequently and the poems of a polytextual composition were usually of the same length and had similar versifications and related subject matter, the two upper voices, which had already occupied the same range in many 14th-century French motets, were now assimilated by melodic cross-references, by similar rhythmic facture and by declamation.[2]

These are distinctive features which can be expanded in substance, further distanced from French practices, and extended by subsequent discoveries. My 1984 paper sought

---

Original version published as Margaret Bent, 'The Fourteenth-Century Italian Motet', *L'Ars nova italiana del Trecento*, 6. *Atti del Congresso internazionale 'L'Europa e la musica del Trecento', Certaldo, 19–21 July 1984* (Certaldo, 1992). This revision is published with permission from the Centro Studi sull'Ars Nova Italiana del Trecento, Certaldo. Following the Certaldo presentation, I had supplied Kurt von Fischer at his request with a copy of my paper, of which Fischer, 'Bemerkungen', published in the same year, includes a German digest. I have taken the opportunity to add to this chapter one of the more recent post-Ciconian discoveries, as ▶ Ex. 26.3, my reconstruction of *O Antoni expulsor demonum*.

[1] The cultivation of the older motet in Italy was reviewed by Ziino, 'Una ignota testimonianza'. Gallo, 'Mottetti del primo trecento', reports the early Florentine motets in **Ox42**. Cuthbert, 'Trecento II' gives an excellent recent overview of the repertory.

[2] Ernest Sanders, 'Motet', in *NG1*, xii. 627. Similar definitions were widespread, as for example in Günther, 'The 14th-Century Motet', and Harrison in PMFC 5.

The Motet in the Late Middle Ages. Margaret Bent, Oxford University Press. © Oxford University Press 2023.
DOI: 10.1093/so/9780190063771.003.0027

498 ITALIAN MOTETS

to reinstate the Italian trecento motet as a distinctive genre in its own right, alongside the madrigal, caccia and ballata. Principal reasons for neglect or non-recognition of the genre were its largely fragmentary survival, and its exclusion from the main retrospective anthologies of Italian music, an omission which remains puzzling.

Because of the parlous source situation, studies of the fourteenth-century motet necessarily consider the cultivation of the French motet in Italy, and have overwhelmingly done so. Manuscript fragments and references in treatises attest the circulation of French motets south of the Alps. They were certainly available for emulation by native Italians, whose adoption of specifically French techniques was largely delayed until the early fifteenth century, when the so-called international style brought northern repertories and their notation together with Italian compositions in the same anthology manuscripts. Almost the same is true of England, where, despite exposure to French music and French music theory from the mid-fourteenth century onwards, English composers assimilated current French techniques only towards the end of the century. In both countries, strong indigenous traditions persisted.[3]

One of the very few contemporary theoretical accounts of the motet is the short treatise *De modo componendi tenores motettorum* usually ascribed to Egidius de Morino, whose identity and date remain obscure, though he presumably originated from Thérouanne.[4] In Chapter 1 I argued that this ascription is unsafe and proposed restoring the treatise to anonymous status. In its manuscript sources, the treatise is usually linked with, or even treated as a continuation of, the *Tractatus figurarum* ascribed variously to Philipoctus and to Egidius.[5] The author of the motet treatise provides for pre-existent chant, tenor priority and contratenors, all of which have more place in the French than the Italian motet. This treatise can be counted a further witness to the cultivation of the French motet in Italy, and not to the indigenous Italian motets assembled here, notwithstanding the author's instructions for text distribution. Although the 'four sections' are not stated to be equal, the fact that the division is made first in the text rather than the music evidently made no allowance for the smaller amount of text often required for reduced-value second sections common in French but almost never found in Italian motets.

Those fourteenth-century French motets with Latin texts that were known to Italian scribes and theorists, however, do happen to include the ones that most clearly approach Italian features in aspects of mensuration, equality or near-equality of cantus parts, and

---

[3] Concordances for French motets occur in the English manuscripts **Durham20**, **Robertsbridge** and **Ox7**; titles are also mentioned in English theory manuscripts from the mid-14th c. For the motets of **SL2211** see Ch. 27. Bent, 'Continuity and Transformation', reflects on the simultaneous cultivation of different musical cultures in Italy in the early 15th c.

[4] Egidius de Morino is thus named in the texts of both *Apollinis* and *Musicalis*. For possible identities of that musician, for the motet treatise and a challenge to authorship by Egidius, see Chs. 1, 16 and 17.

[5] Arlt, 'Der *Tractatus figurarum*' evaluated the sources for these treatises, which are overwhelmingly of Italian provenance. He cautioned against making a premature identification of Philippus/Philipoctus as 'de Caserta', and concluded that the authorship at least of the *Tractatus* had best be left unresolved. Against authorship by Philippus is that the note-shapes set out in the treatise do not correspond to those used in his compositions. The *Tractatus* was discussed in Leech-Wilkinson, *Compositional Techniques*, i. 160–62, then edited and translated in *Tractatus figurarum*, ed. Schreur, and further evaluated together with the other treatise attributed to Philipoctus in Di Bacco, 'Original and Borrowed'. See also Stone, 'Lombard Patronage'. Despite its promising title, the treatise entitled *Compendium artis motectorum Marchecti editum a Fratre Petro Capuano de Amalfia* (in *Mensurabilis musicae tractatuli*, ed. Gallo, 41–47) is entirely concerned with mensuration. Petrus Picardus, *Ars motettorum*, is a short treatise on mensural notation which gives no motet-specific precepts. For sources and authorship of *De modo componendi tenores motettorum* see Ch. 1.

THE FOURTEENTH-CENTURY ITALIAN MOTET   499

presence of an *introitus* or introduction (for these, see Ch. 1).[6] Some solo and two-part introductions exist in the French repertory; a high proportion of the motets that were known in Italy have such introductory duets before the tenor entry, though none has extended imitation like the Italian ones of later date. Most of the French motets in Italian sources other than **Ivrea** and **Chantilly** are exceptional or unusual in various respects. Further, motets in **Chantilly** may have circulated in Italy not long before 1400; that manuscript is now dated after 1400. The contents of the later manuscripts **ModA** and **Q15** cannot be shown to have circulated in Italy prior to the second and third decades of the fifteenth century. Possible reasons for the choices of motets in **SL2211** are explored in Chapter 27.

There are two outliers in the presumably French motet repertory, both datable to the late 1370s. One is the well-known *Rex Karole*, the other a very interesting and little-known unique motet preserved in two Basel fragments and further discussed in Chapter 30. **Basel71** preserves *Gaudeat et exultet . . . Papam querentes*, celebrating the French antipope Clement VII and damning the Roman pope Urban VI, therefore probably datable to 1378 or soon after. The verso of **Basel72** has what appears to be its contrafact, *Novum sidus orientis . . . De scintilla*, in a different script. The motet is still incomplete, but both sources make essential contributions to a reconstruction. On the recto of that leaf, directly preceding *Novum sidus*, is the last page of a two-opening presentation of *Rex Karole/Leticie pacis*. It celebrates Charles V, a strong supporter of pope Clement VII. If *Novum sidus* was indeed a contrafact of the pro-Clement, anti-Urban *Gaudeat et exultet . . . Papam querentes*, why would the compiler of these motets have needed to change its text?[7]

Both *Rex Karole* and *Gaudeat et exultet* have many features strongly associated with Italian motets: perfect time with minor prolation, imitative solo introductions and interlocked hockets. But since one celebrates a French king, dated *c.* 1375 by Günther, 1378 by Carolann Buff, and the other a French antipope, from 1378, there is no reason to consider them Italian. *Rex Karole* is the only French motet in O time from this entire period, perhaps joined now by *Gaudeat et exultet*. The picture is further complicated by discoveries of motets from northern and eastern Europe that share some features with Italian motets (including O time), in turn highlighting some common ground between Italian and Germanic motets.[8]

Ursula Günther claimed on the basis of **Chantilly** and **ModA** that composition of the [French] motet declined around 1400.[9] Although she refers in that study to Matteo da Perugia's *Ave sancta mundi* as a motet, she excluded it from her motet edition in CMM 39, presumably because its tenor is an *Agnus Dei* chant (which therefore qualifies it by

---

[6] Ch. 1 notes the imitative introduction to *Petre clemens/Lugentium* reconstructed in Zayaruznaya, 'New Voices for Vitry'.

[7] Reasons are given in Ch. 30 for believing the contrafact to be in this direction, though the converse remains a possibility.

[8] Cuthbert, 'The Nuremberg and Melk Fragments', gives commented transcriptions of *Celice rex regum/Ingentem gentem* from **Mu3223**, *Deo gracias papales/Deo gracias fidelis/Deo gracias salvator* from **Nuremberg9** and **Gdańsk2315**, and *Tu venerandus presul Amandus* from **Belfast**, a fragment which also preserves *Gratiosus fervidus*, bringing that motet's Italian status into question (see also Cuthbert, 'Trecento II', 1103), and notes the presence of *Comes Flandrie* also in an Italian source. Cuthbert, 'A Postscript', transcribes excerpts of the isorhythmic motets *Mater digna Dei* and *Presulum quo tantus* from the very damaged **Montefortino** fragment.

[9] 'The motet with its long tradition as an art-form of the first rank had to give way before the more modern polyphonic song': Günther, 'The 14th-Century Motet', 47.

500   ITALIAN MOTETS

some definition as a Mass setting) and because both upper parts have the same text.[10] In different ways, two editions presenting complete compositions (Günther's French motet edition in CMM 39, with its exclusive generic boundaries, and PMFC 12 and 13 with Italian motet sections inclusive of simple homophonic pieces) had combined to obscure recognition of the Italian motet proper.[11] *Ave sancta mundi*, the first piece in **ModA**, has little in common with what is here defined as the Italian motet style, beyond having two equal-range top parts with the same text. The tenor is notated in breves, which, however, have no mensural meaning, but are instructed to be performed in iambic pairs (breve–long). Against this triple modus, the upper parts are in imperfect time and prolation throughout. The tenor is notated once, but specified to be repeated in two stages of diminution (i.e. three reducing statements), a feature not found anywhere before *c.* 1400. The first tenor *color* has two *taleae* in the upper parts, one of which spans the entire second tenor *color* (although that tenor statement is half the length of the first). The same upper-voice *talea* is diminished to fit the final tenor *color* (half the length of the second), consequently with very short note values. For motets with two or more levels of reduction, see Chapters 24, 25 and 20.

The large retrospective Florentine collections of Italian-texted repertory give no encouragement to believe that the motet, whether French or Italian, was highly valued at the time of their compilation. A payment to 'Francisco' (Landini) in 1379 by Andreas de Florentia 'pro quinque motectis' remains tantalising; it has even been suggested that these were not really motets—presumably because Italians were not thought to have cultivated them.[12] **SL2211** of around 1420 appears to modify this picture somewhat, with its gathering of French and Italian motets (Ch. 27). But even here, the motets seem to form an appendix of miscellaneous provenance rather than a homogeneous collection like the other genre and composer groupings. Given the often topical texts of the Italian motet, it is strange that it did not commend itself more to the historical consciousness of the compilers of those monumental retrospective trecento anthologies, and that in this one instance when motets were included it was a small, motley and largely international group. The general neglect has been perpetuated in modern scholarship, an example of the way in which exceptional early patterns of collecting and therefore of survival (the trecento collections, the Machaut manuscripts) can narrow or distort our view of the period's musical culture as a whole.

In setting out the case for treating the Italian trecento motet as a genre alongside the madrigal, ballata and caccia, although not included in the retrospective manuscripts, I did not yet know of an informative testimony probably of the 1360s, a fascinating list in the composite manuscript **Seville25** of some thirty-five titles, some attached to named composers.[13] It appears to list the contents of a lost or prospective book of polyphony,

---

[10] This piece, in **ModA**, is printed in Cesari and Fano, *La cappella musicale*, 191. See now PMFC 13, no. 46.

[11] Issues of generic classification were raised in my review of PMFC 12 (*JAMS* 32 (1979), 561–77). The subsequent publication of PMFC 13 in 1987 filled some of the gaps and separated motets from simpler liturgical settings; motets are distributed between the two volumes.

[12] See Ch. 27 n.6 for the documentation of this payment. '"Motecti" are probably not to be understood here as motets, but rather, in the wider sense of the word, as songs': thus Kurt von Fischer, *Landini*, in NG1, x. I do not see why their status should be doubted. In Simone Prodenzani's *Il Saporetto*, *c.* 1415, some of the Latin titles might also refer to lost motets. The jongleur Solazzo performs many genres, but these do not include motets. See Nádas, 'A Cautious Reading', and Ch. 27 n. 2.

[13] **Seville25**, f. 23ᵛ, palimpsest and very hard to read, was the subject of Michael Scott Cuthbert, 'Trecento Theory in Italian and Italian Theorists as Composers', paper presented at the Medieval and Renaissance Music Conference, Prague, 5 July 2017, and in 2018 at a conference at Yale University. It was independently studied

THE FOURTEENTH-CENTURY ITALIAN MOTET   501

interspersed with a few items that may be treatises. The parchment bifolio 23–39 serves as a wrapper for the paper folios 24–38. The front of the wrapper is inscribed 'Liber cantus i[d est] rationum', an odd way to refer to the music treatise that forms the main present contents of the wrapper. It seems to refer neither to some palimpsest music nor to the list; f. 23v is upside down in relation to f. 23r, the outside of the wrapper. Nearly all the titles are in Latin, either of liturgical items or probably independently texted motets, and three Sanctus settings, none identifiable with known compositions. Most are ascribed to named composers known and unknown, including four works by Marchetto, twelve unknown mostly Latin works by 'Magister Ja' and one by Magister Petrus; Cuthbert is cautious about identifying these with Jacopo da Bologna and Magister Piero. Just three of the Italian texts are known, two of which (a madrigal and a caccia) can be matched to extant compositions.[14] Thus only a couple of the Italian works that form the bulk or the entirety of the later collected-works manuscripts are represented in the Seville list. Other hitherto unknown composers, some of which were added later, include: frater Terencinus de Verona He[remitarum], [frater] Michael de Pad[ua]. It is exceptional not only in attesting to a significant body of Latin-texted trecento works, hinting at a largely lost Latin repertory, but also in the fact that at this early date almost all of them are ascribed to composers. Even such an early source of naming does not solve the puzzle as to what kinds of sources furnished the later manuscripts of trecento secular repertory with so many ascribed compositions; only a couple of the Italian works that form the bulk or the entirety of those manuscripts are identifiable here.

Q15 is a unique document of fifteenth-century *Rezeptionsgeschichte*, in this case, reception by its creator. Since the scribe worked on it for a period of at least fifteen years, the nature of his substantial changes enables us to discern how he adapted, edited and criticised what he copied.[15] It is possible to detect not only how he changed his models by addition or renotation, but also how his own tastes changed. The eight complete motets by Ciconia from the first decade of the fifteenth century have been viewed as isolated and original utterances; as their background becomes clearer, these motets still stand out for their superb quality, but are revealed as exceptional not so much in their generic innovation as in their survival. Most of them were selected for copying into **Q15** from about 1420, together with distinctly later repertory, a circumstance which also serves to highlight their unusual features. The scribe who copied them made no changes in their texts, even though those texts were intended for long-dead Veneto bishops and dignitaries. He did, however, make substantial musical changes to their texture and notation, principally by the addition of contratenors and the transformation

---

in Zimei, 'Un elenco veneto'. On the structure of **Seville25**, see Cuthbert, 'Palimpsests, Sketches, and Extracts'. The list includes many titles which may be motets, some ascribed to composers. This testimony to lost works and otherwise unknown composers falls outside the remit of Cuthbert, '*Tipping the Iceberg*', a statistically based study of lost repertories similar to works that survive, and the incidence of concordances in approximately the two decades either side of 1400, which concluded that 'Scholars now need have little worry that they are viewing only a small, possibly unrepresentative sliver of the original written repertory'. Cuthbert excludes older works, Latin-texted motets and sacred music, and composers not represented in the retrospective anthologies, thus conceding 'a larger lost repertory of music from mid-century and earlier'.

[14] The caccia *In forma quasi* is here attributed to an unknown Frater Enselmus, in **Sq** to Vicenzo da Rimini, and anonymous in **Lo29987**.

[15] See now Bent, *Q15*.

502 ITALIAN MOTETS

of Italian into French notation, changes which had the effect of making them look and sound more French. If we strip off these changes, we are left with eight complete and well-made three-part Italian motets by Ciconia that are very close to the norm that we are about to propose on the basis of earlier pieces. Within the assembly of currently known Italian motets from the fourteenth century, there are elements of a recognisable tradition, functional and musical, to which most of the pieces from the later part of the century conform.

Sources and Repertory

The number of motets of Italian origin preserved in manuscripts earlier than **Q15** has now risen to at least sixteen, a significant increase on the half dozen noted by Ernest Sanders. Many of these pieces are incomplete because the sources are fragmentary. Of the motets listed in Table 26.1, nos. 1–16 are distributed in twelve sources, of which the most significant is **Pad1106** (see Ch. 28), the surviving leaves from a motet section in PadD, surely originally more extensive, and the only clear example of what must have been an Italian motet anthology. Five of the motets have concordances. The last three listed items in Table 26.1 could qualify as motets by a liberal definition; they do, however, stand somewhat outside the norm defined by the others. No. 26, *Laurea martiri*, probably by Matteo da Perugia and in **ModA**, has a chant tenor with diminution; the prevailing cadences are the Italianate 10/6–12/8.[16] Likewise no. 27, the *Ave sancta mundi salus* by Matteo already mentioned and the first piece in **ModA**, has a chant tenor (*Agnus Dei*) with diminution, but with 6/3–8/5 cadences in the prevalent French manner. No. 28, *Cantano gl'angiol lieti*, in **Lo29987**, has a single Italian text in both of the two equal top parts, 6/3–8/5 cadences, and a tenor which is not chant despite being labelled 'Sanctus'. It has a 'madrigalian' change to triple time for the final section. An Italian motet listed in Table 26.1 that stands somewhat outside the core features is no. 29, *Argi vices Polyphemus/Tum Philemon rebus*, for Pope John XXIII, possibly for his election in May 1410, but no later than 1414; it is discussed in Chapter 30.[17] It shares many features of other Italian motets: O time, two top parts equal in range and activity (but with different texts), with syllabic patter and some rhythmic canon, and with a final 10/6–12/8 cadence. Less characteristic are that the unidentified tenor may be chant; there is a contrapuntally essential contratenor; the final cadence is on the less common pitch *g*, and there are four sections, isorhythmic in all four parts and without diminution. The motet is unique to **Ao** in a copy much later than its date of composition.

---

[16] The Matteo fascicles of **ModA** were dated by Günther 1410–18; gatherings 2–4 have been placed in Bologna *c.* 1410, with repertory from Avignon, Genoa, Milan, and the Council of Pisa 1409–10. Stone, *The Manuscript Modena*, dated **ModA** to *c.* 1420. A later date is now accepted by Stone, 'Lombard Patronage', perhaps as late as 1425–30, and Andrés Locatelli in an unpublished paper at the Basel Medieval and Renaissance Music conference (6 July 2019) even proposed a dating into the 1430s. The recognition that Matteo's disappearance from the archives after 1418 does not necessarily mean his death opens the way to later activity, and potentially later datings for his compositions and for **ModA**.

[17] Published in PMFC 13, no. 49. The division of the text into four corresponds to a precept of *De modo componendi tenores motettorum*: after an introductory quatrain, each of the four musically equal sections gets 13 lines of triplum text, 11 lines of motetus. On the text, see Holford-Strevens, 'The Latin Poetry'.

THE FOURTEENTH-CENTURY ITALIAN MOTET   503

To these we add the motets of Ciconia composed in the first decade of the fifteenth century but preserved mainly in **Q15**, in later copies dating from between *c.* 1420 and *c.* 1435. The total of at least twenty-five items yields a repertory of the same size as the twenty-six surviving caccias.[18] Given the different survival patterns for French and Italian music, this is a more significant body of motets than its neglect has led us to believe. The list, however, could be extended to over forty pieces belonging to a coherent and continuing tradition of north Italian motet composition, were we to add about twenty motets by Ciconia's followers, notably Antonius de Civitate (Cividale), Antonius Romanus and Christoforus de Monte, all of which date from the second and third decades of the century and are found in **Q15** and **Ox213**.[19] The table excludes Latin-texted homophony of the so-called 'simple' or *Ars antiqua* kind, as well as contrafacta.[20] For the status of *O Petre Christi discipule* (no. 25) as a two-part motet without tenor, see Chapter 28.[21]

Table 26.1 is very approximately chronological by manuscripts or by datable pieces. With little effort it can be divided into three main chronological layers. The first three items date from the early part of the century, and combine several technical and constructional features of the French tradition, from which they branched off after Franco, with new Italianate features of notation and surface style. The large middle group (nos. 4 to 16) represents the later fourteenth-century Italian motet as Ciconia must have encountered it. Of these, only nos. 8 and 9 are less strongly marked with features of the standard Italian model, as are the anomalous (and possibly later) nos. 26–29, discussed above. These six pieces happen to survive complete, but otherwise only nos. 1, 2 and 7 of the listed motets are complete until we reach the Ciconia group. Such accidents of preservation, which have rendered unperformable and for most purposes unpublishable the most relevant precursors of Ciconia, have conspired to delay generic recognition. Without the retrospective anthologies, we would be in no better state with the rich vernacular trecento repertory.

Marchetto's motet *Ave regina/Mater innocencie* has several features that link it to early fourteenth-century developments, including its semibreves with some downstems, in groups separated by dots. Marchetto subsequently displayed his familiarity with the French rhythmic innovations attributed to Vitry in the *Pomerium*. A 'Marchetus' was documented as a choirmaster in Padua in 1305–6. F. Alberto Gallo suggested that the motet was composed in association with the 1305 dedication of the Scrovegni chapel, and Eleonora M. Beck associated it even more closely with the Giotto frescoes.[22] The

---

[18] These are listed in Fischer, *Studien*. The newest critical edition, of 19 caccias, is *La caccia nell'Ars Nova italiana*, ed. Epifani. His introduction, 'Caccia e mottetto' (pp. lvii–lxi) extends the parallels between caccia and motet suggested below.

[19] Nosow, 'Equal-Discantus' and 'Florid and Equal-Discantus Motet'.

[20] It excludes eight of the fifteen 'motets and other sacred pieces' printed in PMFC 12; inclusion of these pieces dilutes the flavour of the Italian motet as presented in that volume, as does its necessary exclusion of fragmentary pieces. Also excluded from this discussion are 'simple' motets in square notation listed in PMFC 12, appendix II (2).

[21] I did not include it in my 1984 paper, but recognised it as a motet in 'Papal Motets', revised as Ch. 30, in *Q15*, and in Ch. 28. See also Buff, 'Ciconia's Equal-Cantus Motets'. Ch. 28 also addresses how the recto or verso status of the leaves of **Pad1106** bears upon whether the voices they preserve are judged to be cantus I or cantus II parts. It reports some challenges to judgements made in PMFC 24 on the basis of codicological examination by Cuthbert, 'Trecento Fragments', 104–5 and 189–93.

[22] Marchetto was a singer and teacher of the boys at Padua cathedral in 1305 and is still documented there in 1307. Gallo, 'Marchettus de Padua', suggested that he wrote the motet for the opening ceremonies of the

504 ITALIAN MOTETS

Table 26.1 Italian motets *c.* 1310–1410

No.	MSS	Texts	Composer	Dedicatee or occasion	Date
1	**Ox112**	*Ave regina/Mater innocencie*	'Marcum Paduanum' (acrostic)	B.V.M. Probably not Scrovegni 1305	
2	**SanGiorgio**	*Ave corpus/Protomartiris/T.Gloriosi Stefani*		Francesco Dandolo St Stephen	doge 1329–39
3	**SanGiorgio**	*Cetus inseraphici/Cetus apostolici*		B.V.M., Apostles	—
4	**Egidi GR224**	*Marce Marcum*		Marco Cornaro	doge 1365–68
5	**Egidi SL2211**	*Florentia mundi speculum/Marce pater pietatis*		Marcus of Viterbo, minister general of Franciscans from 1359, led chapter general in Florence 1365	1365 (d. 1366)
6	**Egidi**	*Leonarde, pater inclite*		Leonardo Rossi da Giffoni	1373–79
7	**Pad1475 SL2211**	*Lux purpurata/Diligite*	'M. Jacobi de Bononia' (Pad1475)	'Luchinus Vicecomes' (acrostic, L. Visconti)	1346–49
8	**Pad1475 ModA**	*Gratiosus/ Magnanimus*	[Gratiosus de Padua?]	'Georgius miles' (acrostic)	1390s?
9	**Q15 MuEm Pad1106**	*O Maria/O Maria*		B.V.M.	—
10	**Pad1106**	*Padu…serenans/ (Pastor bonus)*	[Ciconia?]	Andrea Carrara, abbot of S. Giustina	1402–4
11	**Pad1106**	*Principum nobilissime*	('me Franciscum' in text; Landini?)	Andrea Contarini	doge 1368–82
12	**Pad1106**	*Hic est precursor*		John the Baptist	—
13	**Pad1106**	*Laudibus dignis*	[Jacopo da Bologna?]	'Luchinus dux' (acrostic: L. Visconti)	1346–49
14	**Pad1106**	*O proles Yspanie*	[Ciconia?]	S. Anthony of Padua	

THE FOURTEENTH-CENTURY ITALIAN MOTET   505

Table 26.1 Continued

Parts surviving	Voices	Rhythmic plan	Mensuration*	Texts	Final cadence
complete I T II	T chant? middle T	T: 2 *colores*, 6 *taleae*	[p]	2	g 6/3–8/5
complete I T II Ct	T chant? middle T	T: 2 *taleae*	[p]	2	g 6/3–8/5
end, I II T	T chant [*Salve regina*]		[p]	2	d 10/6–12/8
nearly complete I II T	free T, equal top voices	—	[i] p	1	d 10/6–12/8
incomplete I II?T	free T? equal top voices	—	[p]	2	f 10/6–12/8
I	free T? equal top voices?	—	[n]	?	c 10/6–12/8
complete I T II	free T, nearly equal top voices	—	[i]	2	d 10/6–12/8
complete I T II	T chant? middle T	top voices 2 × 2 *taleae* (AABB) over 3 T statements, second in retrograde	[i]	2	c 6/3–8/5
complete on 1ʳ I II Ct T and Solus T	T chant? equal top voices. Pad T & Ct, others Solus T only	T: 2 *colores*, 4 *taleae*, top voices also repeat × 4	[i]	2	f 10/6–12/8
on 1ᵛ; cadence suggests II, but verso, therefore I and T (lacks II)	free T, equal top voices?	2 statements all voices	[p]	2?	d 10/6–12/8?
II, on 2ʳ, lacks I and T	equal top voices?	—	[s.i.]	?	f 10/6–12/8?
on 2ᵛ, I and T (lacks II)	free T? equal top voices?	—	[p]	?	f 10/6–12/8?
on 3ʳ; cadence suggests I, but recto, therefore II (lacks I and T)	equal top voices?	—	[i]	?	f 10/6–12/8?
on 3ᵛ; cadence suggests II, but verso, therefore I, and T, lacks II	free T; equal top voices?	2 statements, all voices	[p]	?	f 10/6–12/8?

* Mensurations for earlier motets are given in Italian style; from Q15 onwards with 'French' mensuration signs.

(continued)

506 ITALIAN MOTETS

Table 26.1 Continued

No.	MSS	Texts	Composer	Dedicatee or occasion	Date
15	**Ox16**	[*Cristina*]	[Ciconia?]	S. Cristina	
16	**Houghton122**	*Trinitatem*		threefold schism	1409
17	**Q15** **Ox213**	*O felix templum*	Ciconia (in text and ascribed)	Stefano Carrara, bp. of Padua	1402
18	**Q15**	*Venecie mundi/ Michael qui Stena*	Ciconia (in text I and ascribed)	Michele Steno Venice and doge 1400	1406
19	**Q15**	*Albane misse celitus/ Albane doctor maxime*	Ciconia (in text II but not ascribed)	Albano Michiel bp. of Padua, 1406–9	1406
20	**Q15**	*Petrum Marcello/O Petre antistes*	Ciconia (in text II and ascribed)	Pietro Marcello bp. of Padua 1409	1409
21	**Q15**	*O Padua*	Ciconia (in text and ascribed)	City of Padua	
22	**Q15**	*Doctorum principem/ Melodia suavissima/ Vir mitis*	Ciconia (ascribed)	Zabarella	
23	**Q15** **Ox213**	*Ut te per omnes/Ingens alumnus Padue*	Ciconia (ascribed)	Zabarella	
24	**Q15**	*O virum omnimoda/ O lux et decus/*	Ciconia (ascribed)	S. Nicholas of Trani	possibly 1394 (too early?)
25	**Q15**	*O Petre Christi discipule*	Ciconia (ascribed)	For St Peter, Pietro Filargo, and perhaps also Pietro Emiliani; see Ch. 28	1409?
26	**ModA**	*Laurea martiri/ Conlaudanda est/ Proba me domine*	[Matteo da Perugia?]	St Laurence	
27	**ModA**	*Ave sancta mundi/ Agnus Dei*	Matteo	Eucharist	
28	**Lo29987**	*Cantano gl'angiol lieti*			
29	**Ao**	*Argi vices Polyphemus/ Tum Philemon rebus*		Pope John XXIII; see Ch. 30	

THE FOURTEENTH-CENTURY ITALIAN MOTET 507

Table 26.1 Continued

Parts surviving	Voices	Rhythmic plan	Mensuration*	Texts	Final cadence
incomplete, I, II, T	free T; II slightly lower	?	[i]	2	*f* tenor final on verso, despite *d* tonality of first section
recto; II, T; second half?		?	O C	2?	*f* 6–8
complete I II T + optional problematic Ct	free T; equal top voices, Ct added later, then withdrawn	—	[O]	1	*f* 10/6–12/8 (*d* tonality of first section)
complete I II T	free T; equal top voices (I has one higher note)	—	[O]	2	*f* 10/6–12/8
complete I II T + optional Ct	free T; equal top voices (I has one higher note)	2 statements, all voices	[C]	2	*f* 10/6–12/8
complete I II T + optional but integrated Ct	free T; equal top voices	2 statements, all voices, each with T–Ct repeat with dim; T *ad longum*	[O]	2	*f* 10/6–12/8
complete I II T	free T; equal top voices	—	[C]	1	*c* 10/6–12/8
complete I II T + optional Ct	free T; equal top voices	Three T/Ct statements successively in ℂ O C	ℂ O C	2	*f* 10/6–12/8
complete I II T + optional Ct	free T; equal top voices	2 statements all voices	[O]	2	*d* 10/6–12/8
complete I II T + optional Ct	free T; equal top voices (I has one higher note)	—	[O]	3	*f* 10/6–12/8
I II	2 equal voices, no T	—	[ℂ]	1	*d* 6–8
I II Ct T; inessential Ct but Solus T present	T *Proba me* unidentified; equal top voices	3 tenor *colores* reduced by ½ then ⅓. Each *color* = 2 *taleae*	[C]	2	*d* 10/6–12/8
I II T	T: Agnus IV; equal top voices (I has one higher note)	3 T statements, successive dim. by ½; I and II 4 statements, the last in halved values for *talea* 3	[C]	1	*g* 6/3–8/5
I II T	equal top voices: final section madrigal-like in O	—	[C] O	1	*d* 6/3–8/5
I II Ct T essential Ct		long texted canonic introduction then four sections isorhythmic in all parts	[O]	2	*g* 10/6–12/8

508 ITALIAN MOTETS

proposed date is more than a decade earlier than the traditional datings of the complex of *ars nova* treatises associated with Philippe de Vitry, and than Marchetto's own theoretical writings, which are dated *c.* 1317–19.[23] The music fits with Marchetto's notational teachings; a date closer to his treatises around 1320 would be more credible, further encouraged by a 1325 date within **Ox112**, the only source of his one extant motet.

The main contents of **Ox112** are the *Speculum vitae* and *Legum moralium* of Belinus Bixolus (ff. 1–59ᵛ), copied by one scribe who signs himself on f. 58ᵛ in red as Prosdocimus de Citadella, *custos* of Padua cathedral, with the date of 1325.[24] The main text is interspersed with prayers, tables and jottings, and plainsong insertions on ff. 35ʳ–36ᵛ.[25] The highly important polyphonic composition at the end is catalogued simply as a hymn to the Virgin with musical notes. In fact it is probably the oldest extant motet of the Italian *ars nova*. The middle-voice foundational tenor of the musical setting is an *Ite missa est* chant for the end of mass. Stated twice in slow notes, each statement is divided into three rhythmically identical segments (thus $2 \times 3 = 6$ *taleae*) which determine the overall structure and length of the motet. The two faster-moving outer voices have different texts simultaneously: *Ave regina celorum* and *Mater innocencie*. The top part starts each line with a word from the *Ave Maria gratia plena*:

Triplum	Motetus
AVE regina celorum, pia virgo tenella.	[M]ater innocencie,
MARIA candens flos florum, Christi[que] clausa cella	A ula venustatis.
GRACIA que peccatorum dira abstulit bella.	R osa pudicicie,
PLENA odore unguentorum, stirpis David puella.	C ella deitatis.
DOMINUS, rex angelorum te gignit, lucens stella.	V era lux mundicie,
TECUM manens ut nostrorum tolleret seva tela.	M anna probitatis.
BENEDICTA mater morum, nostre mortis medela.	P orta obediencie,
TU signatus fons ortorum manna [das dulcicella,	A rca pietatis.
IN te lucet] lux cunctorum quo promo de te mella.	D atrix indulgencie,
MULIERIBUS tu chorum regis dulci viella,	V irga puritatis.
ET vincula delictorum frangis nobis rebella.	A rbor fructus gracie,
BENE[DICTUS futurorum ob nos] potatus fella.	N ostre pravitatis.
FRUCTUS dulcis quo iustorum clare sonat cimella.	V irtus tue clementie
VENTRIS sibi parat thorum nec in te corruptella.	M E solvat a peccatis.
TUI zelo fabris horum languescat animella.	

Scrovegni Chapel in 1305, but he does not repeat this suggestion in his introduction to PMFC 12, where the motet is edited, and from which the reconstructions bracketed in the text below are taken. Beck, 'Marchetto da Padova', defends the early date by reference to the frescoes, and partly on numerological grounds.

[23] For a model account of this fragile transmission, see Fuller, 'A Phantom Treatise', now revisited in a series of articles by Karen Desmond (including 'Did Vitry Write an Ars vetus et nova?', and '*Omni desideranti*') with important contributions to the Vitriacan theoretical corpus.

[24] Folio iiiᵛ also has a note dated 1325 in a different hand, referring to Florence and Tuscany. There are different (informal) hands on f. 60ʳ⁻ᵛ and the final verso of f. 64ᵛ, where later jottings include the date 1431, part of the two nested bifolios ff. 61–64 containing the motet.

[25] Kyrie, Alleluya, *Adiuva nos*, Alleluya, *Veni sancte spiritus*, Sanctus, Agnus, what the catalogue calls hymns to the Virgin. These appear to be by the same text hand as the main text; music and text *may* be in the same hand, that of Prosdocimus, the *custos* at that date, albeit slightly less formal, and with a finer nib.

The text of the motetus has the acrostic 'Marcum Paduanum', which signals the composer as the music theorist Marchettus of Padua, the unique source of his only surviving composition. Authorial acrostics within musical compositions at this period are less common than acrostics honouring dedicatees.[26] Here, the accusative form of the acrostic is integrated with the final line, the first-person request for absolution (*me solvat*) confirming that it is in this case authorial: *Virtus tue clementie | Me solvat a peccatis*. That he was a composer as well as a music theorist is also attested from the list of compositions in **Seville25** headed with his name, and in the text of Jacopo da Bologna's canonic madrigal *Oseletto salvagio*.[27]

But although the roots are shared with late-thirteenth-century France, the Italian trecento motet soon departs from French models, just as the Italian notational system diverges. In fact, the first three items on the list, dating from the first half of the century, do not yet have the distinctive features of the later Italian motet, but they are certainly Italian and in some ways they do anticipate it. Tenor repetition is present in the first two; Marchetto's *Ave regina* has two identical *colores* of three *taleae* each, and the anonymous *Ave corpus sanctum/Protomartiris/Gloriosi Stefani* has two *taleae* but no *color* repetition. Such repetition is unusual in the later trecento motet, and diminution in particular is exceptional, occurring only in no. 20 and the anomalous nos. 27 and 28. The motets that look most like precursors of Ciconia are nos. 4–7 and 10–16. Of these eleven, only no. 7 is fully complete, 4 and 5 nearly so.

In reporting the Venice fragment (**SanGiorgio**) containing nos. 2 and 3, Gallo noted that the series of motets in honour of doges attests the existence of a secular motet tradition, thus inviting its further investigation.[28] All the doge motets except the very early no. 2 fit our model (nos. 4, 11, and 18); more, not listed here, date from after Ciconia's death in 1412.[29] Seven motets survive in honour of six of the fourteen Venetian doges inaugurated between 1329 and 1423,[30] four of them earlier than 1412, and there is an almost unbroken succession for the doges inaugurated from 1365 to 1423. The two simultaneous texts of *Venecie mundi splendor/Michael qui Stena domus* (no. 18) honour Venice and the doge Michele Steno. If it were not for Ciconia's association with Padua, the most obvious suggestion—sometimes adopted—is that this motet dated from immediately after the doge's election in 1400. Some such occasional pieces are overtly inaugural, but this one is not. Padua was conquered by Venice in 1405; in view of Ciconia's association with the Carrara lords of Padua, his motet can more readily be explained

---

[26] Jacopo's motet *Lux purpurata/Diligite justitiam* (complete) and the single voice *Laudibus dignis merito* (probably also by Jacopo) bear acrostics of the Visconti dedicatee *Luchinus*, followed by *vicecomes* and *dux* respectively, both published in PMFC 13. A few non-acrostic authorial signatures appear directly within motet texts. Elena Abramov-van Rijk informs me (email of 8.4.2021) that Zoltán Rihmer reads the tenth line not as *verus amator efficax*, but *iuris amator efficax*, which restores the word *vicecomes* in the acrostic, making much more sense than the hitherto accepted *vucecomes*.

[27] 'tutti si fan maestri: | fan ballate madrial'e motetti | tutt'en Fioran, Filippotti e Marchetti'; and in Niccolò de Rossi's sonnet *Io vidi ombre e vivi al paragone*: 'Marchetto e Confortino, Agnol cum ello, | Blasio, Floran, Petro mastro garçone'. On **Seville25** see n. 13 above, and on *Il Saporetto*, n. 12.

[28] Gallo, 'Da un codice italiano', with facsimile and transcriptions; also reproduced in *I più antichi monumenti*, ed. Gallo and Vecchi, plates CXXXII–CXXXV. This fragment from San Giorgio can no longer be found.

[29] See Nosow, 'Florid and Equal-Discantus Motet'.

[30] **Q15**, no. 243, *Ducalis sedes*, by Antonius Romanus, is in honour of doge Tommaso Mocenigo, elected in 1414. Nos. 206, *Carminibus festos*, and 215, *Plaude decus mundi*, respectively by Antonius Romanus and Christoforus de Monte, are both in honour of Francesco Foscari, elected doge in 1423. See *Antonii Romani Opera*.

as an expression of Paduan acceptance of the new regime. Suzanne Clercx suggested 1407 as a likely date, when privileges were granted to Padua cathedral in recompense for confiscated Carrara goods. But a more likely occasion might be that when Francesco Zabarella, the archpriest of Padua Cathedral, in the name of the *comune* of Padua, made an oration and presented the doge with the emblems of the Signoria before the doors of San Marco on 3 January 1406. (Ciconia's patron Zabarella was the dedicatee of two of his motets.)[31] Venice responded officially on 30 January with the 'Golden Bull' acknowledging the surrender of Padua, and promised to respect the privileges, customs, statutes and wool trade of the city.[32]

Numbers 7 and 13 incorporate acrostics of the dedicatee's name; in addition, no. 1 has the authorial acrostic *Marcum Paduanum*, discussed above. Numbers 11, 17 and 18 incorporate a personal signature or composer's name in the text itself; the words *me Franciscum* in the text of no. 11, *Principum nobilissime*, may or may not refer to Magister Franciscus, better known to us as Landini. Ciconia's name is embedded authorially in the texts of nos. 17–21.[33]

In all Italian motets there is either no musical repetition at all (apart from tenor *color* and *talea* restatements, as in Marchetto's motet), or else the second half of the motet is a straightforward rhythmic duplicate of the first; any such repetition is in all voices, not only the tenor. Two other motets (that stand apart from the later fourteenth-century Italian norm in several other respects) are *Gratiosus fervidus* and *O Maria*, which have rhythmic repetitions both in the tenor and the upper parts, as does no. 29, *Argi vices*. The same is true of three motets by Ciconia (nos. 19, 20 and 23) and two fragmentary motets in **Pad1106** (**PadD**; nos. 10 and 14), all of which may date from after 1400. It is not the motet but rather two madrigals, Lorenzo's *Povero zappator* and Landini's *Sì dolce non sonò* that document the adoption of 'French' isorhythm in Italy.[34] The tenor of *Sì dolce non sonò* has three *color* statements, each of three *taleae* (i.e. a total of nine rhythmic statements), and in the ritornello two identical statements, in which *color* and *talea* coincide. There is no diminution. *Povero zappator* has three *talea* statements in the tenor. Each of these statements has the rhythmic form ABAA, where each letter represents two perfect longs (two bars) followed immediately by their rhythmic diminution (two breves, one bar). The ritornello in C time has two *color* statements, the second a diminution of the first. This internal diminution scheme, although on a very local scale, provides a precedent for Ciconia's procedure in *Petrum Marcello*. The rarity of diminution perhaps qualifies it as a special experimental device, like the use of retrograde tenor statements in the earlier *Gratiosus fervidus*, and like the mensural reinterpretation of successive tenor statements in *Doctorum principem*, previously used in French and English motets, but here originally devised in Italian notation and adapted in its unique source (**Q15**).[35]

[31] See Ch. 28 and n. 64 for Jason Stoessel's proposal to link Ciconia's *O Petre Christi discipule* to another oration by Zabarella.

[32] As suggested in PMFC 24. See Simioni, *Storia di Padova*, especially 566, 611–12.

[33] On Ciconia's texts, see now Holford-Strevens, 'The Latin Poetry'.

[34] CMM 8/III, no. 9, and PMFC 4, no. 15. Fischer, 'Philippe de Vitry', discusses these two pieces and argues that the latter honours Vitry. See now Abramov-van Rijk, 'Povero zappator'.

[35] Cuthbert, 'The Nuremberg and Melk Fragments', 18–19 suggests that *Gratiosus* might have been a foreign import into Italy. Hallmark, 'Some Evidence', draws a possible connection between its use of retrograde motion and Machaut's *Ma fin* preserved in **PadA**, which of course uses retrograde. I was wrong to

Tenors

In the Italian repertory, unlike the French, chant tenors are the exception; no. 3, the incomplete *Cetus inseraphici/Cetus apostolici*, has a *Salve regina* tenor. Marchetto's *Ave regina/Mater innocencie* is on the same tenor as the *Ite missa est* of the Tournai mass (*Cum venerint*), but even it has not been otherwise identified. Several other tenors that look like chant have not been convincingly identified. These include the anonymous no. 2, *Ave corpus*; no. 9, *O Maria*; no. 8, *Gratiosus fervidus*; and even Ciconia's *Petrum Marcello*.[36]

Kurt von Fischer judged Vitry's *Tribum/Quoniam* an important herald of the Italian motet, since it has an introduction, a middle-voice (chant) tenor (like Marchetto's motet), and repeating *taleae* with no diminution. These features are by no means confined to Italian motets. But beyond this, *Tribum* has no close link to the more distinctive features of the later Italian motet, where few of the tenors look or behave like chant, and almost none have been identified. At least some of them, written as accompaniments to the primary upper parts, may have been fashioned as pseudo-chant but are not in fact pre-existent. Marchetto's tenor has been mentioned above. We can at least say that from the start the Italian motet was less bound to tenor priority than was the French, and that any such dependency receded further during the century. Three items have the tenor as the middle part, in each case unidentified chant-like melodies. This may be true of Marchetto's motet (no. 1), *Ave corpus* (no. 2), and the later *Gratiosus fervidus* (no. 8). In addition to these, three further motets have unidentified tenors which are chant-like but are not middle parts. Of these, the tenors of *O Maria* and *Laurea martiri* are completely unidentified, and *Ave sancta mundi* is based on an *Agnus Dei* chant which, in being drawn from the Mass Ordinary, may place it as much outside the tradition of the Veneto as of the French motet.[37] The practice of placing the tenor as the middle voice is common in the English motet, and found in some French motets.[38] It is not, however, a normal feature of Italian motets in the later fourteenth century.

Top Parts

The top two parts were normally of equal or nearly equal range and activity. Unfortunately for purposes of generalisation, nos. 5 and 7, *Florentia mundi* and *Lux purpurata*, are almost the only two instances before Ciconia for which both upper parts survive complete, and in both pieces the second cantus is a little lower than the first. But in nos. 4 and 15, *Marce Marcum* and *Cristina*, enough survives to show that they

---

classify *Doctorum principem* as isorhythmic; its tenor is subject to mensural rereading. See Bent, Q15, and Ch. 28. For other motets where a *talea* is followed immediately by its diminution before the next statement, see Chs. 12 and 19.

[36] See CMM 39, p. xlviii, and Anderson, 'Responsory Chants'. S. E. Brown, 'A Possible Cantus Firmus', 8, proposed a possible chant for *Petrum Marcello*.

[37] No. 27, *Cantano gl'angiol*, as stated already, has an unidentified tenor marked 'Sanctus'.

[38] Of motets discussed here, notably in *Tribum/Quoniam* (Ch. 4) and *Apollinis* (Chs. 15, 16 and n. 43); and see Ch. 1. Another unidentified middle-voice tenor is the recently reconstructed *Flos vernalis/Fiat intencio* of c. 1320. See Alís Raurich, 'The *Flores* of *Flos vernalis*'.

ITALIAN MOTETS

indeed were truly equal. They may also be somewhat later in date than *Florentia mundi* and *Lux purpurata*, whose upper parts are in other respects equal—in length, function, rhythmic activity, and amount of text. The eventual equality of upper voices might well have been the natural outgrowth of an earlier type having two active parts forming a partly self-contained duet around or above a tenor.

Contratenors

I maintain a distinction between a second cantus such as described above and a true contratenor in the French manner, as also between contrapuntally essential and non-essential contratenors, while acknowledging that some intermediate cases defy definition.[39] The true contratenor evidently had no part in the typical Italian motet. Contratenors (always fourth voices in motets) that survive from the fourteenth century up to Ciconia are all in some way problematic, even if not all are demonstrably later additions. The contratenor of no. 2, *Ave corpus*, is clearly redundant in its copious doubling of the top voice. The tenor and contratenor of no. 9, *O Maria*, are present only in the earlier source, **Pad1106**, whereas two later sources, **Q15** and **MuEm**, replace them with a solus tenor. In this motet, the contratenor is at some points the lowest but nevertheless inessential voice; at other points it is essential, underpinning simultaneous fourths between the tenor and an upper part. No. 26, *Laurea martiri*, has a true contratenor, but it is a motet in French style with no detectable Italian features. Ciconia's *Ut te per omnes* survives in both a three-part and a four-part version; Besseler declared the latter to be inauthentic, but he never went on to apply the same scepticism to motets that happen to survive in only one version with a contratenor.[40] None of the surviving Italian motets with contratenors before Ciconia fits the Italian model; the ones that have them are to varying degrees influenced by French practice in other respects, as were editorial initiatives taken by the scribe of **Q15**, who converted Italian notation to French, and both added and removed contratenors. The evidence is particularly compelling in the case of the added contratenor, published for the first time in PMFC 24, of Ciconia's *O felix templum* (see Ch. 29 and Fig. 28.1 below). Consequently, the authenticity of many unique contratenors appearing in **Q15** for motets by Ciconia and his Veneto followers comes into question. Some of these parts are associated with only a single version of each piece, or are in later manuscripts that may be to some extent dependent on **Q15**; without them, these pieces are much more easily recognised as typical late fourteenth-century Italian motets.

Characteristics of the Italian Motet

I shall now attempt to characterise the typical Italian motet as it crystallised around the middle of the fourteenth century. From then on it became as distinct from the French tradition as from the English; the same is true of the nationally distinct notational traditions that conditioned the musical thinking of composers both on a large

---

[39] Some parts added to Italian madrigals are labelled 'Contratenor' in the manuscripts, but do not behave as contratenors. See Bent, 'Notes on the Contratenor', and *Counterpoint*, Introduction, 38–46 on contratenors and the solus tenor.

[40] Besseler, *Bourdon und Fauxbourdon*, 81, table and n. 6.

THE FOURTEENTH-CENTURY ITALIAN MOTET   513

scale and at local levels. The Italian motet is represented almost exclusively in sources from the Veneto; its main features lasted at least until the death of Ciconia, and continued beyond, including in early motets by Du Fay. Except for pieces like *Florentia mundi speculum* (whose text might nevertheless find more than an accidental echo in *Venecie mundi splendor*), it might indeed be more appropriate to refer to this type as the Veneto motet, and to see in this civic distinction a principal reason for its neglect by Florentine anthologies. The two Italian motets in **SL2211** are among the few that do not refer to Veneto subjects, which may be why they are there, although a celebration of the Lombard Luchino Visconti in Jacopo's *Lux purpurata* might have been even less acceptable to the Florentines than the Venetians.[41] However, the musical characteristics, though more assiduously cultivated in the Veneto, are also abundantly present in these few non-Veneto examples, so I shall not further localise the term here. The possibly earlier dating of *O virum* is addressed in Chapter 28.

The most characteristic examples of the Italian motet have some if not all of the following features:

1. A primary duet for upper parts that are either equal or nearly equal in range, normally pitched high, with C1 or C2 clefs. The parts are usually equal in length, function, rhythmic activity and amount of text.
2. These upper parts may have either the same or different texts.
3. The composer's name or that of the dedicatee may appear in one of the texts, occasionally as an acrostic.
4. The accompanying tenor is freely composed, often with semibreve motion, leaps of fourths and fifths, rests of two breves while the upper parts continue, interludes of two breves while the upper parts rest, and held longs in all parts.
5. The clearest examples of this style have no contratenor. If a contratenor is present it can usually be diagnosed as a later addition and may be musically anomalous.
6. Use of hocket, imitation, syncopation, rhythmic canon and sequence, often requiring participation by the tenor, is common.
7. There is little use of French techniques of rhythmic diminution or mensural reduction.[42]
8. The prevailing mensuration is often .p. (= *tempus perfectum*), sometimes adapted to its French equivalent O (transcribed as 3/4) but with the characteristic Italian rhythms associated with its renunciation of breve imperfection.[43]
9. Changes of mensuration within a piece are found in nos. 16 and 22, *Trinitatem* and *Doctorum principem*, both dating (on grounds of their texts) from after 1400. Such changes earlier than 1400 seem to follow the model of the madrigal

---

[41] See Ch. 27 and n. 4.

[42] True isorhythm, rhythmic replication for the second half of the piece, where present, is usually in all voices. This did not require the precompositional planning that diminution demands. *Petrum Marcello* is exceptional in having diminution within the *color*; but see *Alma polis/Axe poli* (Ch. 19), and similarly complex motets listed there in n. 10. See n. 34 above on *Povero zappator*.

[43] All of Ciconia's motets seem to have been conceived in Italian notation, and some of them display direct evidence of notational translation; details are given in the Critical Commentary to PMFC 24. *O felix templum* is the only one that actually survives in both notations in its two sources, but its typically Italian rhythms are shared by others, and the process of transformation can be detected in erasures and adjustments within **Q15**. Imperfect time, together with Italian triplet rhythms at the semibreve level, are found in nos. 19 and 21, *O Padua sidus* and *Albane misse celitus*. The only French motet in O time from this period is *Rex Karole*, one of the motets that was known in Italy.

514　ITALIAN MOTETS

ritornello, as in no. 4, *Marce Marcum*, which changes from octonaria [.o.] to .p, and the undated *Cantano gl'angiol lieti*, which changes from [C] to O for a true madrigalian ritornello.

10. Tenor coloration occurs in **Pad1106**, in the anonymous no. 10, *Padu...serenans/ Pastor bonus*, and in some motets ascribed to Ciconia, all after 1400. No imperfection coloration occurs in any upper parts. Sesqualtera minim triplets are sometimes flagged, sometimes void.

11. Typical cadences are 10/6–12/8, on *f*, *d* or *g*, and extreme 'tonal stability' is often cultivated. After Ciconia, the hitherto predictable roles of voices I and II at the final cadence are occasionally reversed.

12. The subject matter is often civic or honorific: dedicatees include doges, bishops, and other public figures. Where cities or saints are addressed, they may be coupled with topical worthies. Although some motet texts are sacred or at least reverent (none is frivolous or amorous, and all except the hybrid no. 28, *Cantano gl'angiol lieti*, are in Latin), it would be a mistake to regard the motet, the Italian no more than the French, as primarily sacred, let alone liturgical. Even the pieces that might appear to be liturgical (because honouring a saint) could have been intended for secular ceremonial use. Madrigals that carried civic or honorific function are better preserved and known, owing to their inclusion in the large vernacular anthologies.

Stylistic Roots

Where are the stylistic roots of this characteristic texture of two equal top parts with a free accompanying tenor? In the three-voice madrigals of Jacopo da Bologna the upper voices do have equal ranges, but they are different from the upper voices of a motet. In particular, the two-part madrigals (and the primary duet of the few three-voice madrigals) characteristically cadence with a third converging on a unison (3–1), while the ballatas (mostly *a*3), in common with a very few motets, have closer spacing between the voices, reflected in their characteristic 6/3–8/5 cadence. The motets, on the other hand, most often cadence 10/6–12/8, with parallel fifths between the top parts (see the last column of Table 26.1 above). This feature they share with some caccias and with Jacopo's canonic madrigal *Oseletto salvagio*; among Jacopo's three-voice works this formula occurs otherwise only in his motet *Lux purpurata*. We might thus look to the caccia for parallels and precedents for this disposition of voices. Other features of the caccia most easily recognisable in the motet are the accompanimental character of the tenor, which is almost never based on chant, and the effect of canonic techniques (extended canon in the caccia, canonic unison imitations in the motet), which tend to foster precisely the kind of tonal stability just mentioned. Other surface features, such as imitation, declamation, clichés and melodic interplay, are clearly related to madrigal idioms. Just as caccia techniques were used in madrigal and ballata settings, so they left their mark on the motet. The text of the canonic madrigal *Oseletto salvagio* names the musical genres as *ballate, matricale e muteti* and, as mentioned above, **Trém** lists French *chaces* together with motets (but see Ch. 31 for a possible explanation). In **Egidi**, three motets appeared in company with Zacara's caccia.

One manuscript of the Paduan judge Antonio da Tempo's well-known treatise of 1332, the *Summa artis rithmici vulgaris dictaminis*, has an anonymous addition

THE FOURTEENTH-CENTURY ITALIAN MOTET   515

entitled 'Capitulum de vocibus applicatis verbis', now dated after 1332.[44] It discusses *ballade, rotundelli, motteti, cacie, mandrigalia* and *sonetti*; the motet thus takes its place alongside these other genres, whose descriptions have more often been related in recent literature to the surviving music. Little account, however, had been taken of the section on motets:

Motteti sunt cantus applicati verbis (sive dictionibus vel parabolis). Fiunt etiam ad unum et ad plures cantus. Non habent ita ordinem in verbis sicut ballade et rotundelli; possunt esse de tempore perfecto et etiam mixti, et de italica et gallica, ita quod tempora unius correspondeant ad tempora alterius et sit simile alteri. Et si primum, secundum et tertium de uno cantu sit de uno tempore, scilicet perfecto, ita de alio cantu primum, secundum et tertium esse volunt simili perfecto, ut in mensura similiter concordent, et de aere debent esse ad invicem et assimilari. Vult etiam in compositione mottetorum haberi hec regula generalis, videlicet quando unus cantus ascendit, alter descendat et non se inveniant in dissonantia in pluri quam in uno tempore, quia nimis foret asperum in auditu.

Caveat etiam, ne tritonum componat, quia, sicut dictum est, fit auribus nimis durum; et quando unus rumpit, alius utatur brevibus vel longis et e converso. Et sic diversificando completi fiunt de illis circa fines: Unus pausat, alter cantat, et postea pausat, qui cantavit, et alter cantat. Utimur in eisdem mottetis pausis unius temporis et pauciores. Quare sic utendo uchettis et pausis videntur mottizando cantare.

Cacie (sive incalci), a simili per omnia formantur ut motteti, salvo quod verba caciarum volunt esse aut omnes de septem, aut omnes de quinque syllabis.

Motets are melodies (*cantus*) applied to words or narratives or allegories. They are furthermore made for one and for more voices (*cantus*); they thus do not have a verbal form like ballatas and *rondeaux*. They can be in perfect tempus, and even mixed tempus, and in [senaria] italica or gallica, so that the breves of one correspond to the other and are similar to it. And if the first, second and third breves of one melody (*cantu*) are perfect, so in the other melody the first, second and third [breves] should also be perfect, so that in measure they may concord in similarity, and that in melody they should be adjacent and assimilated. This general rule applies in motet composition, namely, that when one cantus ascends the other descends, and they should not be dissonant with each other for more than a breve, because it sounds harsh.

Beware also lest you compose a tritone, because it sounds hard to the ear, as we have said. And when one voice has small notes (*rumpit*), the other uses breves or longs and vice versa. And thus diversifying they are filled with these towards the conclusions: one rests, the other sings, then the one who sang rests while the other sings. In these motets we use rests of a breve and shorter, because using hockets and rests they thus seem to sing 'motetting'.

Caccias, or *incalci*, are in all respects composed similarly to motets, saving that the verses (poetic lines) of the caccias should be either all of 7 or all of 5 syllables.

---

[44] **Venice97**; see Debenedetti, *Un trattatello*, 79, newly edited in Burkard and Huck, 'Voces applicatae verbis'. Their edition, helpfully punctuated, is used here, but without classical diphthongs. Abramov-van Rijk, 'Evidence for a Revised Dating', convincingly dates the *Capitulum* after 1332, when da Tempo completed his *Summa*, rather than, as previously dated, between 1313 and 1332.

516   ITALIAN MOTETS

This is at least as remarkable for what it does not say as for what it does. We are not told about constraints on motet composition, such as versification (prominent in the other genres discussed), pre-existent tenors, or contratenors, let alone isorhythm. More important is that the cantus parts (with one or two texts?) should complement each other, and that dissonance should be avoided. The use of hocket, of breve rests, contrary motion, and a preference for tempus perfectum are all mentioned. All of these are normal features of the trecento motet as described here. Motets are likened to caccias except for textual constraints which, however, are not spelt out for the caccia. The description of the caccia goes on to describe alternation of voice roles, apparently referring both to caccia and motet, and prescribes that the voices end some on the fifth, some on the octave. This of course would be true not only of motets and caccias, but, in conjunction with role alternation between the equal-range parts, it surely implies the widely spaced cadences typical of both forms.

New Additions in Bent, 'The Fourteenth-Century Italian Motet'

Trinitatem

Trinitatem (no. 16), is named as the tenor of what seems to be the second half of a motet preserved on a pasted-down flyleaf bifolio (**Houghton122**) that could not be lifted to display the other side.[45] Its text possibly refers to the period of threefold Schism between 1408 and 1415; the music could conceivably be by Ciconia, whose patron Zabarella was active in efforts to resolve the Schism and in fact died at Constance, but it lacks strong stylistic markers for Ciconia.

A revised description of the bifolio follows:

f. 1ʳ (pasted down), first half of a Credo; f. 1ᵛ (exposed), verso with the second half of the same Credo from *Et in spiritum* (left-hand side cut off), two texted voices, a cantus I part and Tenor, to be continued on the facing page together with cantus II. Identified by Michael Scott Cuthbert as **Q15**, no. 64 (Salinis), where it is also texted in all three parts and occupies two openings (there dividing at *Et resurrexit*): see Chapter 27, Table 27.2.[46]

f. 2ʳ (exposed); probably the second opening of a motet, Tenor *Trinitatem*, not chant, therefore perhaps the incipit of either or both voices on a preceding lost opening; cantus II starts [*de*] *qua cordis* (reading uncertain; *qua* looks more like *pia* or *pra*, but the '2' form of letter 'r' is used nowhere else on this fragment, only one syllable is required, and ink is lost from the left side of the descender). Neither musically nor textually does this appear to be a beginning. For an Italian motet it is unusual

---

[45] **Houghton122**. A first account was given in Bent, 'New Sacred Polyphonic Fragments', including my transcription, which was also used in PMFC 13, no. A17. Some revision to the description is in Bent, 'Motets Recovered'. I now deplore the Houghton library's initiative (not mine) to use a chemical in an attempt to make the reverse side more legible. Minimally greater visibility was achieved, with allegedly no lasting damage. Cuthbert, 'Trecento Fragments', 283, questions whether this is fact an Italian manuscript. The script and orthography seem to me Italian ('*babtisma*', and '3' form of final 'm').

[46] Cuthbert, 'Hidden in Our Publications'.

in changing mensuration from O to C. The hockets in C time are unusual, but the short passages in rhythmic canon, presumably tossed between the two cantus parts, are typically Italian.

On f. 2ᵛ (pasted down), is apparently a Marian motet.

A Motet on Santa Cristina

Another fragmentary motet (no. 15) is preserved on a flyleaf (**Ox16**) that was cut from a bifolio of music, most of which has been erased.[47] (See Ex. 26.1 for a tentative transcription.) A significant legible portion survives complete in three parts on the bifolio which is now f. 97ᵛ (= Aᵛ–Bʳ of the original), and the motet is completed overleaf on f. Bᵛ, where one or two of the three parts remain in currently illegible form; it can be hoped that new non-invasive techniques will one day make them legible. Only isolated words and syllables of the two texted cantus parts can be made out, enough to confirm elements of the saint's legend, but insufficient to determine the form of the text. The legible text of the topmost part includes the words 'baptizari virgo Cristina post tua sancta dissipavit et fornacem sprevisti . . . -cem ubera tua et lingua Julianus . . . sit', and of cantus II: 'prole tue gens se . . . -samus . . . sunt equales tuorum ne iaspes es de . . . redolens . . ', leaving no doubt that it refers to the legend of Santa Cristina (feast day 25 July). The legend amalgamates elements from two different stories for saints of this name from Tyre and Bolsena. The story of the Roman virgin martyred for maintaining her Christian belief in disobedience to her father relates how, when thrown into Lake Bolsena, she was baptised by Christ himself; how when her tongue was cut out she threw it at the Judge Julianus, thus causing him to lose the sight of one eye; how she 'spurned the furnace' and was then further (presumably in the missing portion of the text) tormented by serpents and finally killed by arrows. The manuscript, like many in the Canonici collection, appears to be of Veneto provenance. There were naturally various claimants to the remains of the saint, but of relevance to this case is the fact that the Benedictine nuns of San Marco di Ammiano, an island in the Venetian lagoon, believed that they had acquired her in 1252, from which time they were known as the nuns of SS. Marco and Cristina of Ammiano. During the fourteenth century, physical conditions on the island deteriorated. Fetid air and rising water are reported, and eventually the nuns moved to Murano with their relic. Reprimanded for an unauthorised translation of the saint, they were instructed to return the relic to San Marco, which they did in 1340, with much ceremony. This date is probably too early for the motet. The nuns remained on the sinking island until only one nun was left, when the relic was officially translated in the 1430s to St Anthony of Torcello. This date is too late, stylistically and notationally, for the composition of the motet. Meanwhile, the Scuola Grande della Misericordia in Venice erected a chapel in honour of the Virgin and Santa Cristina, which was moved and renovated some time after 1386. It is reported that the Scuola tried to acquire the relic

---

[47] **Ox16**, flyleaf. Andrew Wathey kindly alerted me to this fragment, which he subsequently described in Wathey, *Manuscripts . . . Supplement 1 to RISM*.

Ex. 26.1 Excerpt from fragmentary motet on S. Cristina in Ox16

Ex. 26.1 Continued

from St Anthony of Torcello in 1442. Since the likeliest time for the composition of the motet, on grounds of style and script, is around 1400, it is tempting to speculate that it may have formed part of a bid on behalf of the Scuola for the relic during that same period of growing veneration for Santa Cristina.[48]

Even superficial comparison of the music of this fragment with Ciconia's *O felix templum* shows strong points of similarity.[49] It is in pure Italian notation with *pontelli* (dots separating brevial groups, down-stemmed major semibreves, oblique-stemmed 'dotted' notes and successive paired semibreve ligatures requiring 'alteration' (by *via naturae*) of the second note, even when not preceding a breve. Tonally, in rhythm, range, imitations and so on, it clearly draws upon the same stock vocabulary as the motets of Ciconia, and so it is possible that we have here the remains of an otherwise unknown motet by him. While the most legible section with all three parts suggests a '*d* minor' tonality, the final 10/6–12/8 cadence on the verso is on *f*. These features it shares with the securely attributed *O felix templum*.

The total length can be estimated at around one hundred breves, but the complete three-part texture is preserved only for a very short section. There is no rhythmic repeat. Like all Ciconia's motets, it has two equal top parts, was conceived without a contratenor and contains imitation sequences, hocket with participation by the freely composed tenor, held longs, and two-bar tenor interludes. But are we in any position to make a claim of authorship? I have tried to review the profile of Ciconia in relation to the Italian tradition from which his motets seem to have grown. The premise of a typical Italian motet, of which Ciconia's are the main surviving complete but late examples, lessens certainty about his personal individuality and discourages the attribution of anonymous works. However, the features of surface style in *Cristina* do fall more fully within Ciconia's known style than do the two incomplete motets in **Pad1106** that appear in PMFC 24 (nos. 10 and 14) as *opera dubia*; these are discussed in Chapter 28. The comparison group of named composers is too small to permit certainty, given the hazards of comparison between different genres.

Florentia mundi speculum / Marce pater pietatis

This motet is perhaps the most significant yield: the full extent of the two upper parts can be recovered, leaving the tenor to be editorially reconstructed. Having said that, the transcription in Example 26.2 remains tentative. Many aspects—pitches, rhythms and simultaneity—are open to revision. Two different sources are here conflated. One is a barely legible image of a lost manuscript, the other a heavily overwritten palimpsest. Staff lines and note stems are partly invisible. Some measures that appear simultaneously may be successive and vice versa; pitches may be a step up or down from those given, and rests are often uncertain.

---

[48] The amalgamated legend of Santa Cristina is given in *Acta Sanctorum*, v. 495–534. Sources for her office in AH XXV, 193–96, include a 15th-c. breviary from San Niccolò of Padua. She is represented in the procession of virgins in S. Apollinare Nuovo, Ravenna. Most of the other details reported here are drawn from Corner, *Notizie storiche*.

[49] PMFC 24, no. 12, discounting the contratenor which is a later addition by the scribe of **Q15**.

Ex. 26.2 *Florentia mundi/Marce pater*, transcribed from **Egidi** and **SL2211**

Ex. 26.2 Continued

Ex. 26.2 Continued

524 ITALIAN MOTETS

Ex. 26.2 Continued

THE FOURTEENTH-CENTURY ITALIAN MOTET 525

Ex. 26.2 Continued

526 ITALIAN MOTETS

Egidi has been lost since the death of its owner,[50] and survives only in a very poor microfilm copy provided by Kurt von Fischer, slightly enhanced on DIAMM.[51] As well as the cantus *Florentia mundi speculum*, **Egidi** also contains *Marce Marcum* in honour of Marco Corner, doge of Venice 1365–68 (ff. 1ᵛ–2; no. 4 in Table 26.1, completable from **GR224**), and cantus I of the motet *Leonarde, pater inclite* (no. 6 in Table 26.1) in honour of Leonardo Rossi da Giffoni, d. 1405, master of theology, head of the Friars Minor in Campania in 1372, and the general head of the Franciscan Order in 1373. It celebrates his appointment as cardinal by Clement VII in December 1378, an honour he had recently declined from Urban VI, who also removed him as head of the Franciscans. Clement reinstated him as General and rewarded him for having opposed the Roman pope.[52] He was from Salerno, a subject of Queen Joanna of Naples, who is thanked for her support of the Avignon pope. **Egidi** also contains on f. 1ʳ the tenor of Zacar's caccia [*Cacciando per gustar*]/ *Ay cinci ay toppi*.

On the basis of the opening imitation, I was able to identify that the then recently discovered **SL2211** contributes a complementary cantus II, previously transcribed as *Parce pater pietatis*, to the single cantus I voice *Florentia mundi speculum* in **Egidi**, yielding two voices of an Italian-style motet and lacking only the tenor. Folio 69ʳ (R188) in the palimpsest **SL2211** preserves this cantus II, very difficult to read when I made the provisional transcription published with the original version of this article. But enough imitation could be detected between the two differently texted voices that the transcription of each can benefit from knowledge of the other. In 1984 I informed the editors of PMFC 13 (published in 1987) of the discovery that the two motet voices belong together, and provided them with my transcription.[53]

My readings remain provisional, especially for **Egidi**, where much remains doubtful, but my transcription was largely vindicated by the now more legible images in Nádas and Janke, *The San Lorenzo Palimpsest*, which fortunately is on one of the pages that has responded well to multispectral imaging. Some revisions are incorporated here in Example 26.2. From bars 121–26 the two parts seem to have different versions of the hocket, cantus II being one breve longer than cantus I (**SL2211** is clear here); hence the curious alignment in Example 26.2. The important new finding is that the colour separation of the multispectral images of **SL2211** shows that what had been taken as an initial P by all previous writers is in fact part of the overwriting, and that a guide letter 'm' for the intended initial is in the margin, as spotted by the sharp

---

[50] See Egidi, *Un frammento*.

[51] John Nádas meanwhile achieved different improvements with the aid of the University of North Carolina Computer Science Department.

[52] Di Bacco and Nádas, 'Papal Chapels', 67, where the text is transcribed from **Egidi**, f. 1ᵛ. This corrects and extends my report in Bent, 'Italian Motet'.

[53] The editors published fragments (PMFC 13, no. A 14, pp. 246 and 288), disconnected and misfitted, rejecting my transcription, evidently able to read less than I had, and presuming that I had invented the readings of **SL2211**. The editors report: 'Margaret Bent tried to transcribe also other fragmentary passages based on the principle of imitation. These are not included in the transcription.' It would be more correct to say that my transcription was based on what I could read, the coordination of the parts being confirmed by identifying points of imitation. Now that multispectral images of **SL2211** are available (Nádas and Janke, *The San Lorenzo Palimpsest*), readers may offer their own improvements.

eyes of Bonnie Blackburn, so the motet can now be known as *Florentia mundi speculum/Marce pater pietatis*.[54] I have also been able to transcribe more of the verbal text of *Marce pater*, of which even Leofranc Holford-Strevens has been able to make only limited sense.

The cantus I, *Florentia mundi speculum*, refers to Florence and the Franciscans. I suggested in the earlier form of this article that this pointed to the Chapter General of the Order held in Florence in 1365, presided over by Marcus of Viterbo, who was elected minister general of the Franciscan Order in 1359, made a cardinal by Urban V in 1366, and died of plague on 4 September 1369. A monument to him is in the Chiesa di S. Francesco in Viterbo. It is now clear that he is the Marco addressed and honoured in cantus II, and that the motet can therefore be dated 1365, the year of the Florence Chapter. Thus **Egidi** contained three motets for named individuals, two of them Franciscan leaders; all three of its motets can now be dated 1365–78.

Further Recent Additions
O Antoni expulsor demonum

Vienna661, two bifolios from the same original Veneto manuscript as **Mu3224**, contains a unique motet, *O Antoni expulsor demonum*.[55] Although trimmed, it can be editorially completed, as ⓟ Example 26.3. It is a strange little piece, shorter than most of the Italian motets in the generation after Ciconia referred to above, from which it probably dates, therefore falling outside Table 26.1. But it has many features of the Ciconian motet: both upper parts have the same ranges and the same text, a short prose text with some internal rhyme (*-um*). There are also some declamatory chordal passages for all four parts simultaneously. The saint addressed is the widely venerated St Anthony Abbot ('the Great', 3rd–4th c.), known not only for resisting temptations, but also for expelling demons from his cave and for protection against sickness, notably 'Saint Anthony's fire', which has been thought to describe various afflictions, notably those of the skin. The ingenious interlocking hockets are Ciconia-like, if not quite up to Ciconia's standard. The accompanying tenor is freely composed. The inessential contratenor has octave doublings and rhythmic duplication of cantus II, also some dissonances, and could be a later addition.

New since that publication is the discovery by Alberto Rizzuti of this text as an Alleluia verse for the Commemoration of St Anthony in a beautifully illuminated missal of local use for S. Antonio di Ranverso (Torino) dating from around 1420, now Lausanne, **Lausanne8076** f. 178[r].[56] Rizzuti reports later survivals of this text, previously known in a missal printed in Lyon in 1527 for the church of Viviers, and in a psalter/book of hours from the late fifteenth century, now Brive, Bibliothèque

---

[54] On **SL2211** see Ch. 27. Cantus II variants: 85.3 *f* (here corrected to *g*); 105 ♪ for major S; 108 oblique-stemmed S; 131–32 oblique ligature LL.

[55] See Bent and Klugseder, *A Veneto Liber cantus*. Discovered by Klugseder, and identified by Bent as belonging with **Mu3224**.

[56] Rizzuti, 'Margaritae ante porcos'. This substantial study provides artistic and documentary context for the cult of St Anthony at Ranverso. It builds on the discovery of the motet in Bent and Klugseder, *A Veneto Liber cantus*, and reproduces Bent's reconstruction and transcription of *O Antoni*, here ⓟ Ex. 26.3.

528 ITALIAN MOTETS

municipale, MS 1, f. 173^r, with the variant (from the Brive version) 'languorum' in line 2. These sources otherwise agree, and show the motet text to be corrupt in lines 3 and 4:

Text of Vienna661

O Antoni, expulsor demonum,
liberator languidorum hominum,
qui es spes fidelium,
deprecare dominum,
ut det nobis celorum gaudium.

Text of Lausanne8076, f. 178^r

O Anthoni, expulsor demonum,
liberator langorum hominum,
qui es spes et dux fidelium,
deprecare tu Dei filium
ut det nobis celorum gaudium.

Other Fragmentary Motets

A damaged bifolio used as the cover of **SienaRavi3** contains two incomplete motets.[57] The text of *Gaude felix parens Yspania nove prolis* on f. 67^r is a version of the first Vespers antiphon for St Dominic.[58] The second cantus and apparently free tenor are preserved, but damaged and hard to read. Pitched on *d* and apparently in duple time, minor prolation, with some hocketing, it shared a manuscript opening with the motet *Sanctus itaque patriarcha Leuntius* by Antonio da Cividale, known from **Q15** no. 247 (ff. R272v–273, A301v–302). Another fragmentary motet on this bifolio is *Katerina pia virgo purissima* (f. 70^r). The second cantus and apparently free tenor are preserved, pitched on *f* with a 6–8 cadence, and in perfect tempus with passages in imperfection coloration. There are two rhythmically identical halves, and some hocketing. Both motets are untranscribed in print and are possible candidates for attachment to this group although, like *O Antoni*, they may be rather later than the focus of this chapter, and belong with the post-Ciconian motets preserved in **Q15** and elsewhere.[59]

Quire guard strips in **Perugia2** contain fragments of motets. In addition to the well-known *Rex Karole/Leticie pacis* (strips I and IX), text fragments of hitherto unidentified motets include, on strip II, A^r [*Ve*]*netia iustitia mannas mannas et*; B^r *nutritorem hoc debet nos docere . . .-are proditorem . . . di . . .*; A^v *. . . ditis Bononia statuti tullis . . . fit ducisbus amen*; B^v *. .quoque facto . . .*; on strip X, A^r *. . .-is integer vir gratia pacis et mare tutum numina posseas*; B^r *marique signifer defende tibi supplices yllustra bonis moribus adsis pris favoribus*; A^v *et Cripsti passi retollens sepe comitis prelia, agarenis crudelia. Ortus occasus*; B^v *. . . tuosa plena fraude vulpina. Et veneni sentina et scorpionis stracta fa . . .*[60]

Conclusions

Given our dependence on such fragments, it is striking that as many as five of the pre-Ciconia motets, *Marce Marcum*, *Gratiosus*, *O Maria*, and now *Florentia mundi speculum*

---

[57] Mecacci and Ziino, 'Un altro frammento'.
[58] Cantus database (https://cantus.uwaterloo.ca/), Cantus ID 201900: *Gaude felix parens Hispania novae prolis dans mundo gaudia sed tu magis plaude bononia tanti patris dotata gloria lauda tota mater ecclesia novae laudis agens sollemnia.*
[59] Those motets are reviewed in Nosow, 'The Equal-Discantus Motet Style after Ciconia'.
[60] Text fragments as given in Brumana and Ciliberti, *Frammenti Musicali*, 51–54.

and *Lux purpurata*, recur in more than one manuscript, thus suggesting a finite repertory of limited circulation. Conversely, the absence of Ciconia motets from **SL2211** may offer further evidence of the narrow circulation of his motets, which, apart from *O virum omnimoda* in **Siena36**, was apparently confined to the Veneto; most are *unica*.[61] There are apparently no contratenors in the two truly Italian motets in **SL2211**. In cases where only one page of an opening survives, this can sometimes be assessed by practical constraints of spacing and layout, an observation which offers further support for the addition of contratenors as a particular peculiarity of **Q15**. A northern ingredient in Ciconia's musical education had been presumed because of his use of isorhythm. But his simple replication in three motets (literal isorhythm) is very different from French motets with diminution or otherwise varied restatements. To put it over-simply, his motets are, rather, composed from the top down, as in other Italian instances (Ch. 29 refines this statement). It is true that Ciconia was born in Liège, but he evidently spent his entire adult career in Italy. An earlier view that he was born in the 1330s has long been discounted on grounds of having confused a father and son of the same name. The now-accepted dating for Ciconia's life, with a birthdate in the 1370s, is compatible with a hypothesis that he travelled south at an early stage, and there encountered and adopted an established Italian motet style.[62] Despite his northern birthplace, there is none of the Franco-Italian fusion with which he has been credited by most scholars. Rather, we should now see Du Fay as the composer responsible for fusing French structural techniques with a number of features typical of the Italian ceremonial motet. This gives a new slant to the view that such motets are essentially rooted in French isorhythm. There is nothing French about Ciconia's motets, and the Italian influences that have been pointed out in Du Fay have not hitherto conspicuously included that of the Italian motet. It seems possible that Du Fay came to know Ciconia's music in versions with added contratenors such as those in **Q15**. The pseudo-chant also became 'real' chant for him (*Vasilissa*, with its chant tenor and 'Ciconian' isorhythmic replication for the second half of the motet), and the detail of the rhythmic surface sounds similar, even if Ciconia and Du Fay were conditioned by different traditions. When the scribe of **Q15** dressed up Ciconia's Italian motets with French notation and contratenors in the French manner, he may thereby have pointed the way to a marriage consummated in the works of Du Fay.

As a tradition with its own definable features and constants, the Italian motet provides us with:

1. A means of diagnosis and of understanding a piece like *Hic est precursor*, which can now be claimed as a motet lacking its second upper part rather than as a complete two-voice piece.[63]
2. Some possibility of chronological sorting of the repertory around datable pieces.
3. A purely Italian background for the motet repertories of Ciconia and **Q15** which no longer compels us to subscribe to the older view that the isorhythmic motet with a freely invented tenor represents an innovation of considerable magnitude.

---

[61] They occur only in **Ox213**, **Q15**, **BU2216**, **Siena36**, and perhaps **PadD**. Details are given in PMFC 24.

[62] Fallows, 'Ciconia padre e figlio'. See also the preface to PMFC 24.

[63] PMFC 12, no. 42. Not everything, of course, fits the prototype: of Ciconia's two equal-voiced pieces in **Q15**, *O Petre Christi discipule* (Ch. 28) is now counted as a tenorless motet.

530 ITALIAN MOTETS

Many of the features of Ciconia's motet that do not fit the French model have Italian and specifically Veneto antecedents that put his apparently striking personal originality into a fresh perspective. We no longer need to view the Italian caccia as a mere derivative of the French *chace*, and may be able to make a similar claim for the autonomy of the Italian motet.

4. *Petrum Marcello/O Petre* is unusual in presenting each *talea* first as is, then in diminution before proceeding to the next one. The isorhythmic replication includes these diminutions which are not themselves isorhythmic. The advent of the integral contratenor comes relatively late in Italian compositions and may be influenced by French practices.

5. A new recognition of Du Fay as the merger of French and Italian traditions. The older picture of Ciconia as an epoch-maker and international innovator is flawed, and is already much changed by the subsequent recognition that Ciconia was a younger composer.[64] The motets of Ciconia and his followers can now be seen as the culmination of an Italian tradition. They both followed its normative conventions and at the same time transcended them. How central Ciconia himself was in this process cannot be known as long as the surviving competition is so scanty and the surviving pieces remain unattributed. To look at them all, including Ciconia's, without their contratenors, and to compare them with the survivals in **Egidi, SL2211** and the Padua fragments, makes it very clear that Ciconia was, with his seemingly original creations, crowning a tradition that already existed and had many conventions of its own. Whatever the young (maybe very young) Ciconia brought to Italy from the north, it certainly included a greater readiness to adopt the Italian motet than to impose a northern model upon it. It is with Du Fay rather than Ciconia that the traditions of the French and Italian motet are brought together. Ciconia remains—if only by accidents of survival and the taste of the **Q15** scribe—an isolated, excellent, original and mature surviving witness to a well-established and purely Italian motet tradition.

---

[64] The epochal claim is made by Besseler, 'Hat Matheus de Perusio Epoche gemacht?', the demonstration that Ciconia was a younger composer in Fallows, 'Ciconia padre e figlio'.

27

The Motet Collection of San Lorenzo 2211 (SL2211) and the Composer Hubertus de Salinis

The magnificent reconstruction of the gathering structure and contents of the San Lorenzo palimpsest by John Nádas and Andreas Janke will long be the starting point for new work on its repertory.[1] Like some other manuscripts of trecento repertory, **SL2211** is mostly organised by composer. The five caccias, however, unlike in the other anthologies, are separated from the composer sections and presented together in Gathering XVI,[2] apparently all anonymously, and together with other additions of international French repertory from Gathering XIV onwards. **SL2211** is also the only manuscript of trecento repertory to include a group of motets. This might at first suggest that these, like the caccias, are segregated not by composer but by genre, and that they represent an Italian trecento genre otherwise absent from the repertory manuscripts.[3] Surviving in similar numbers to caccias, albeit mostly in fragments, motets are absent from the composer groupings in those sources. But, in fact, the choice of Italian and international motets in **SL2211** is idiosyncratic, largely non-Italian, presented anonymously, and does not herald a change of policy from the failure of other retrospective anthologies to include motets. The ten motets in **SL2211** are all in the final gathering, XIX (see Fig. 27.1), and together with other French repertory and additions from Gathering XIV onwards they form additions to the main retrospective Italian corpus of madrigals and ballatas, arranged by composer. The motets follow the French songs added anonymously in Gatherings XIV and XV (along with compositions by Paolo) and the even later Gathering XVII with works by Piero Mazzuoli; they are additions which were never planned as part of the core repertory composer groupings. The **SL2211** scribe had access to songs by Machaut that circulated outside the Machaut manuscripts, but not to his motets, which, with few exceptions, did not circulate. Except

---

The original version of this paper (Bent, 'The Motet Collection of San Lorenzo 2211' in Calvia et al., *The End of the Ars Nova in Italy*, 43–68) and its present revision are dedicated to John Nádas. Reuse of the material was permitted by Sismel – Edizioni del Galluzzo (Florence).

[1] Nádas and Janke, *The San Lorenzo Palimpsest*, and Janke, 'Die Kompositionen'. See my review in *PMM* 26 (2017), 186–98. The title was garbled after proofs and corrected in the next issue, 27 (2018), 99 and online. I thank colleagues at Certaldo and by email for helpful comments, especially Elena Abramov-van Rijk and Michael Scott Cuthbert.

[2] The three-part *Oseletto salvagio* in Gathering III is listed as a caccia but, despite similar musical techniques, Elena Abramov-van Rijk (email of 2.12.2017) reports that it is usually now defined as a canonic madrigal, not as a caccia or a caccia-madrigal. Its poetic text is not at all that of a typical caccia, and it was not included with the other caccias in Gathering XVI.

[3] Motets are linked to caccias in the *Capitulum*: 'Cacie (sive incalci), a simili per omnia formantur ut motteti, salvo quod verba caciarum volunt esse aut omnes de septem, aut omnes de quinque sillabis.' Burkard and Huck, 'Voces applicatae verbis', 16.

The Motet in the Late Middle Ages. Margaret Bent, Oxford University Press. © Oxford University Press 2023.
DOI: 10.1093/so/9780190063771.003.0028

532 ITALIAN MOTETS

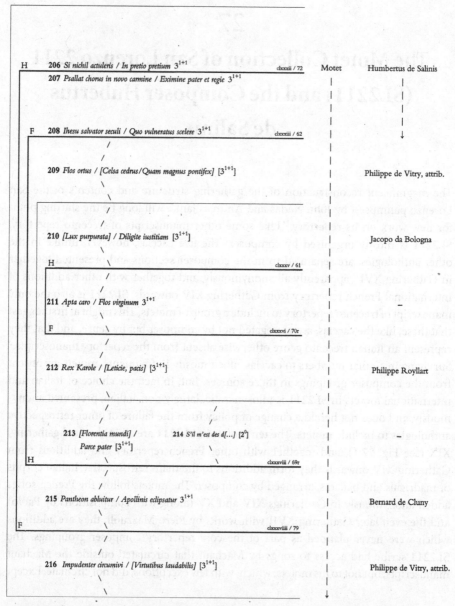

Fig. 27.1 The structure of Gathering XIX in Florence, Archivio del Capitolo di San Lorenzo, MS 2211. Reproduced with permission from John Nádas and Andreas Janke (eds.), *The San Lorenzo Palimpsest: Florence, Archivio del Capitolo di San Lorenzo, Ms. 2211*, i. 47 (Libreria Musicale Italiana, Lucca, 2016) and Schwabe Verlag, Basel

for two of the three by Salinis, all the **SL2211** motets are presented anonymously, even the two Italian ones.

Five of the ten motets are widely circulated international pieces. Although Italian motets (predominantly from the Veneto) are now recognised as a distinct genre, they are not included in the main collections of trecento repertory (Ch. 26). Indeed, it was the absence of motets from the anthologies and their often fragmentary survival that led to this genre being overlooked for so long. But only two of the **SL2211** motets are Italian (nos. 210, *Lux purpurata/Diligite iustitiam* and 213, *Florentia mundi/Marce pater*), and even they lack obvious Veneto connections—one is by Jacopo da Bologna and the other is about Florence.[4] All earlier accounts of the contents of **SL2211** (including Fig. 27.1) read the title of cantus II as *Parce*; the colour separation of the new multispectral images enabled Bonnie Blackburn to read the intended initial as M, as noted in Chapter 26. The motet thus honours Marcus of Viterbo, who presided over a Chapter General of the Franciscans in Florence in 1365, which can now be taken as the date of the motet.[5] But even this Florentine compilation does not include the incomplete motet *Principum nobilissime* known only from **Pad1106** and attributed to Landini on the basis of the text (*me Franciscum*), nor any others of the five non-extant motets for which he was paid nine shillings (*pro quinque motectis*) by Andrea da Firenze in 1379.[6] As this text is in praise of Andrea Contarini (Venetian doge 1367–1382), it is unlikely to be one of those unnamed Florentine motets; and there is no obvious reason for Landini to have celebrated a Venetian doge. The two missing bifolios in Gathering XIX are mostly accounted for by projected completions of works on their facing pages. At most, three more short motets could have been accommodated on the missing pages, and only if each occupied a single side.

The ten motets in **SL2211** include five of the most widely circulated international motets of the mid-fourteenth century or later, each of which is preserved in from five to fourteen further sources (see Table 27.1): 209, *Flos ortus/Celsa cedrus/Quam magnus pontifex*; 211, *Apta caro/Flos virginum*; 212, *Rex Karole/Leticie pacis*; 215, *Pantheon abluitur/Apollinis eclipsatur*; 216, *Impudenter circumivi/Virtutibus laudabilis*.[7] Three of these, nos. 209, *Flos ortus*; 211, *Apta caro*; 216, *Impudenter circumivi*, have been attributed to Vitry with varying degrees of confidence. Three (nos. 209, *Flos ortus*; 211, *Apta caro*; 215, *Apollinis eclipsatur*) are listed by their motetus parts in the **Trém** index of 1376 (Ch. 31). Four are in **Ivrea** or **Trém**; *Rex Karole* (212) is in neither, and may therefore be later, though probably from before 1380.[8] The added triplum *Pantheon* voice of *Apollinis eclipsatur*, hitherto known only from Coussemaker's copy made from the destroyed **Stras** manuscript, may also be later; it raises questions to be discussed below. It is now the only one of the additional parts to *Apollinis* to survive in more than one source. I shall tentatively suggest reasons for these particular choices, though they may simply represent what was available to the compiler.

---

[4] Elena Abramov-van Rijk points out (email of 8.4.2021) that the celebration of the Lombard Luchino Visconti (d. 1349) in Jacopo's *Lux purpurata* would have been even less acceptable for the Florentines. But, a generation later, both of Jacopo's madrigals for Luchino, *O in Italia* and *Lo lume vostro*, appear in all the important Florentine trecento anthologies, including **SL2211**.

[5] See Ch. 26 and Ex. 26.2.

[6] The source of this payment is Archivio di Stato di Firenze, Conv. ss. Annunziata, vol. 841, f. 23, cited in Taucci, 'Fra Andrea dei Servi', 102. Landini is never so called in the sources; Magister Franciscus is a more appropriate appellation. In his 1980 *NG1* article on Landini, Kurt von Fischer attributed three anonymous motets to him as doubtful works: *Florentia mundi speculum* (**SL2211** and **Egidi**; the motetus or second cantus in **SL2211** presented here was not yet known), *Leonarde, pater inclite* (**Egidi**), and *Marce Marcum* (**Egidi** and **GR224**). Von Fischer's attributions were retained in the *NG2* revision by Gianluca D'Agostino. I see no reason to support them, nor to assume that these were among the five motets specified.

[7] Other widely circulated motets not present here include *Colla iugo/Bona condit* and *Degentis vita/Cum vix artidici*.

[8] *Rex Karole*, dated *c*. 1375 by Günther (CMM 39, pp. xxix–xxxi), 1378 by Carolann Buff ('Ciconia's Equal-Cantus Motets', 142–51), is dedicated to the French King Charles V (1364–80): CMM 39, pp. xxix–xxxi.

Table 27.1 Motets in SL2211

SL	Title	SL2211 contents	Other sources
206 R182ʳ	*Si nichil actuleris/ In precio precium*	tr, T, mo on recto	**Q15**, no. 278, ff. R275ᵛ–276, A304ᵛ–305; recopied stage III on II
207 R182ᵛ	*Psallat chorus in novo carmine/ Eximie pater et regie*	tr, T, mo on verso	**Q15**, no. 247, ff. R250ᵛ–251, A279ᵛ–280. Ct in **Q15** only (*a*4); **Utrecht37**, f. Vᵛ identified by Michael Scott Cuthbert[a]
208 R183ʳ	*Ihesu salvator seculi/Quo vulneratus scelere*	tr, T, mo on recto	**Q15**, no. 213, ff. R220ᵛ–221, A249ᵛ–250; verso recopied at stage II; **Ox213**, f. 81ʳ, black notation; **Stras**, ff. 97ᵛ–98 mo, T; no tr
209 R183ᵛ	*Flos ortus/Celsa cedrus/Quam magnus pontifex*	tr on verso; recto missing	**Ivrea**, ff. 9ᵛ–10; **Ca1328**, f. 14ᵛ (tr, mo, T; frag); **Paris2444**, f. 49ʳ; **Trém**; **Würz**, f. 2ʳ, end of mo; **Paris22069**, f. 158ᵛ ᵇ; **Darmstadt521**, f. 235ʳ⁻ᵛ text only
210 R185ʳ	*Lux purpurata/ Diligite iustitiam*	C2 and T on recto; C1 lost with f. 184ᵛ	**Pad1475**, f. 50ᵛ
211 R185ᵛ–186ʳ	*Apta caro/Flos virginum*ᶜ	mo and T on verso; tr on recto [*sic*], incomplete. Either a 10th system was intended on f. 70ʳ, or the scribe intended to complete on the facing verso but did not do so. A clef of uncertain pitch is indeed visible on the verso.	**Ivrea**, ff. 5ᵛ–6 with Ct; **ModA**, ff. 17ᵛ–18; same Ct as **Ivrea**; **Chantilly**, ff. 60ᵛ–61; different Ct; **Ca1328**, ff. 10ᵛ–11 (T and beginning of tr); **Durham**, ff. 338ᵛ–339; no Ct; **Trém**
212 R186ᵛ	*Rex Karole/Leticie pacis*	tr on verso; recto missing	**Chantilly**, ff. 65ᵛ–66; tr, mo, T, Ct, solus T; **Basel72** recto, mo, solus T; **LoTNA**, f. 1ʳ; mo, Ct, and new Ct; **Stras**, ff. 7ᵛ–8; tr, T and solus T, but labelled Ct and T; **Washington1400**, f. 2ʳ; mo only, frag.; **Perugia2**, f. Cᵛ–Dʳ (strips 1 and 9), Ct and solus T, frag.
213 R188ʳ	*Florentia mundi/ Marce pater*	mo only	**Egidi**, f. 2ʳ – original verso? (tr only)
215 R188ᵛ–189	*Pantheon abluitur/ Apollinis eclipsatur*	lacks contrapuntally essential motetus (*Zodiacum signis*); *Pantheon* is otherwise only in **Stras** *Apollinis* (original tr) and T on verso, *Pantheon abluitur* on recto	**Stras**, ff. 64ᵛ–65; 5 voices including additional triplum *Pantheon abluitur*. For thirteen other sources of all or part of *Apollinis*, without this added part, see Ch. 15
216 R189ᵛ	*Impudenter circumivi/ Virtutibus laudabilis*	tr on verso, not overwritten; recto missing	**Ivrea**, ff. 4ᵛ–5 with Ct and solus T; **Apt**, ff. 13ᵛ–14, tr, mo, Ct, T; **Bern**, f. 18' Ct only, unique, against solus Tᵈ; **Brussels5170**, Tr frag., mo, solus T; **Br19606**, no. 6 with Ct and unique solus T; **Leiden342A**, f. 1ᵛ tr frag.; **Stras**, ff. 20ᵛ–21 tr, mo, solus T; **Troyes1397**, f. [230ʳ] frag.; **Würz**, f. 1ᵛ; **Tarragona1**ᵉ Plus two text-only sources: see Wathey, 'The Motets of Philippe de Vitry', 123.

ᵃ Further discussed in Fankhauser, 'Recycling Reversed', 57–58.
ᵇ Identified in Cuthbert, 'Monks, Manuscripts', 122–23, with a contratenor in **Paris22069**, on which see Everist, 'A New Source'.
ᶜ This motet was once contained in a lost codex in the former ducal library, Pavia (item 84 of the inventory drawn up in 1426; Milan, Biblioteca Braidense, MS AD XV.18.4). See Kügle, *The Manuscript Ivrea*, pp. xvi, 212.
ᵈ Discussed in Steiger, 'Das Berner Chansonnier-Fragment', 57–60.
ᵉ After the pastedown was lifted, this motet was identified by David Catalunya on Facebook, 29.10.2013.

Table 27.1 Continued

Attributions	Comments
Q15: hubertus de salinis **SL2211**: Imbert' d' Salinis	2 × C2, with 10/6–12/8 final cadence on *d*, ₵ void col.
Q15: Hubertus de salinis **SL2211**: no attribution	2 × C1, with 10/6–12/8 final cadence on *g*. ₵ void col. On St Lambert, patron saint of Liège
Q15: hubertus de salinis **Ox213**: Ubertus depsalinis **SL2211**: Hu'bert' d' Salinis	2 × C1, with 10/6–12/8 final cadence on *f* C time, no col. On the passion of Christ, or Holy Week. II paraphrases stanza 2 of the hymn *Vexilla regis*; T quotes the beginning of the hymn melody.
SL2211: no attribution attrib. Vitry by Leech-Wilkinson and Kügle on grounds of structure and style[f]	Equal-cantus motet 2 × C1 with 10/6–12/8 final cadence on *f* On St Louis of Toulouse. Vitry generally avoids breaking words with rests, either by matching hockets and text or by leaving hockets untexted; this motet does not do so, which might argue against his authorship.[g]
SL2211: no attribution Jacopo da Bologna (**Pad1475**)	Nearly equal cantus parts C1, C2, with 10/6–12/8 final cadence on *d*
SL2211: no attribution	Final cadence on *f*
SL2211: no attribution **Stras**: Philippus Royllart	The only tempus perfectum minor prolation motet in the 'French' repertory: final cadence on *f*
Egidi: anon. **SL2211**: no attribution	Transcribed in Bent, 'Italian Motet', and here Ch. 26. Lacks tenor. Equal cantus parts 2 × C1 with 10/6–12/8 final cadence on *f*
SL2211: no attribution 'B. de Cluni' in text; no other attributions in any source	Perhaps copied thus because compiler was looking for equal-cantus motets and mistook the 2 × C2 parts with opening imitation as 'essential'. Original motet (*Apollinis eclipsatur/Zodiacum signis*) has 10/6–12/8 final cadence on *f*, but **SL2211** version lacks proper cadence.
SL2211: no attribution attrib. Vitry in Coussemaker's transcription of **Stras**[h]	Equal-cantus motet 2 × C1 with 10/6–12/8 final cadence on *f*

[f] Leech-Wilkinson, 'Related Motets', 11; Kügle, *The Manuscript Ivrea*, 124–25.
[g] See Zayaruznaya, 'Hockets', 493.
[h] For his index and partial copy of **Stras** see Coussemaker, *Strasbourg*.

536   ITALIAN MOTETS

Of the other five motets, only two are Italian—nos. 210, *Lux purpurata/Diligite iustitiam*, and 213, *Florentia mundi/Marce pater*—interspersed with the 'international' ones. Each is known from just one other source. Jacopo's *Lux purpurata/Diligite iustitiam* survives complete in the Padua fragments (**Pad1475**), and **SL2211**'s *Marce pater* complements the cantus *Florentia mundi* from **Egidi**.[9]

The group is headed by the three known motets by Hubertus de Salinis (nos. 206–8), copied consecutively in what is now their earliest source.[10] All three are also in **Q15** a few years later.[11] In **Q15** *Psallat chorus in novo carmine/Eximie pater et regie* (207) has an inessential and presumably added contratenor that is not in **SL2211**. Unlike some **Q15** contratenors, it was not added at stage II but copied integrally at stage I before 1425.[12] *Ihesu salvator seculi/Quo vulneratus scelere* also appeared anonymously in **Stras** and is Salinis's only motet in **Ox213**, ascribed, and in pride of place at the beginning of Gathering V, the original starting point of that manuscript. I shall return to Salinis.

Six of the ten motets—*Psallat chorus/Eximie pater* (207); *Flos ortus/Celsa* (209, in **Paris22069**), *Apta caro/Flos virginum* (211, with a contratenor in **ModA** and **Ivrea**, and a different contratenor in **Chantilly**); *Rex Karole* (212); *Apollinis eclipsatur* (215); *Impudenter circumivi* (216)—survive elsewhere with one or more contratenors, and (in the case of *Apollinis*) optional added triplum parts. None of those contratenors is in **SL2211**, which (as far as can be judged, taking missing folios into account) confines itself to three-part versions. None of the motets is given with more than three voices, although one combination, for *Apollinis*, is anomalous. *Apollinis* has no fewer than three different added tripla in three different sources, all hitherto unique: a textless triplum in **Barc853**,[13] *Psallentes zinzugia* in **LoTNA**, and *Pantheon abluitur* in **Stras**. It is that **Stras** voice which appears here together with the original triplum *Apollinis*, but the piece is unperformable as presented in **SL2211**: it gives the central tenor voice, but lacks the grammatically essential motetus *Zodiacum signis* that (unusually, in this and very few other motets) provides the contrapuntal foundation below the tenor.[14]

No fewer than four of the motets (*Apollinis, Rex Karole, Impudenter*, and Salinis's *Ihesu salvator*) were in **Stras**, a collection thought to have conciliar links to the 1410s (the date 1411 appeared within the main compilation). A possible connection here, direct or indirect, gains significance from the fact that **Stras** was hitherto the unique source of *Apollinis*'s added triplum part *Pantheon abluitur*.[15]

---

[9] I identified the connection from the opening imitation. See Ch. 26 n. 51 and Ex. 26.2.

[10] Nosow (*NG2*) calls them 'an uneasy appropriation of Italian 14th-century motet style'.

[11] One (*Psallat chorus/Eximie pater*) was identified in **Utrecht37** by Michael Scott Cuthbert. He also identified Salinis's Credo no. 4 (**Q15**, ff. R79ᵛ–81) in **Houghton122**; both in Cuthbert, 'Hidden in Our Publications'.

[12] At least two of these motets date from **Q15** stage I (*Psallat chorus* entirely, and *Ihesu salvator* partly recopied at stage II; the hitherto unique *Si nichil*, now in what is probably a stage-III recopy on stage-II paper and parchment, was probably also present in stage I), but they do not appear consecutively. For these placements see Bent, *Q15*, i. **Q15** compositions were sometimes recopied in order to add a contratenor, but the only one of Salinis's motets with a contratenor is wholly in stage I, and the recopies in this case were not for that purpose. Both rectos of the Gloria *Jubilacio* have the text incipit following cantus II for a contratenor that was not entered (**Q15**, no. 54, R62ᵛ–64, stage I).

[13] Although claimed in Gómez, '*Apollinis*', as a five-voice version, it seems to be in only four parts. Even with drastic adjustments, a contratenor on the same opening marked *Per sanctam civitatem* does not fit: see Ch. 16.

[14] See Ch. 1 for middle-voice tenors.

[15] The triplum only of *Apollinis* also survives in **Pad658**; whether this source had an added part for *Apollinis* is unknown, but unlikely. Jacopo's motet is in **Pad1475**.

A picture begins to emerge of the possible reasons for the choice of motets in **SL2211**:

- The number of voices, three, appears to have been one of the bases for selection. No optional contratenors are included, even where they exist in other sources.
- All have different texts for triplum and motetus, as in all international motets and most Italian motets, though some Veneto motets—the doge motet *Marce Marcum* and some by Ciconia and later composers—have a single text in both voices.
- Some French motets have texted voices that are differentiated in range, though most are equal or nearly so; all the **SL2211** motets have two equal- or very nearly equal-range texted upper parts plus tenor.[16]
- The **SL2211** compiler has chosen motets where the two upper parts have fairly equal activity as well as range. This is particularly striking in the case of *Apollinis*, where the true motetus *Zodiacum*, which is slower-moving and contrapuntally essential, has been sacrificed in favour of an inessential additional triplum part. The compiler's preference for motets with equal cantus parts seems to have resulted in his misunderstanding of that composition.
- Nearly all motets in the Italian repertory have 10/6–12/8 final cadences on f ('major') or d ('minor'), rising parallel fifths in the upper part over a stepwise descending tenor. About half the French fourteenth-century repertory has 6/3–8/5, half 10/6–12/8 cadences, with a few irregular endings. None of the ten motets in **SL2211** has a 6/3–8/5 cadence; all have some form of 10/6–12/8 final cadence, one on g, two on d, seven on f.
- The choice of motets in **SL2211** seems to favour echo openings. *Rex Karole* has opening echo imitation and, like many Italian motets (including *Florentia mundi*), is in perfect time; it sounds superficially a bit like an Italian motet.[17] Salinis's *Ihesu salvator* and *Psallat chorus* have opening echo imitation; the added triplum *Pantheon abluitur* briefly echoes in imitation the opening of its true triplum *Apollinis eclipsatur*; *Impudenter circumivi* and *Apta caro* have spaced but not echo openings, as does Jacopo's *Lux purpurata/Diligite iustitiam*.
- The absence of Ciconia from this manuscript during the decade after his death again suggests that the circulation of his motets may have been mainly limited to the Veneto.

All these choices favour characteristics of the Italian motet, albeit in the case of *Apollinis* misunderstood by the compiler. It may be that these motets were selected not only because they were widely available, but because they were more like Italian trecento motets or could be made to appear more like them. That raises the unanswerable question why Italian motets that better meet these criteria were not included. Do the motets in **SL2211** represent choices by the compiler, or did he simply copy what happened to be available to him?

---

[16] I have called these second voices mo[tetus], but it would usually be equally or more appropriate, as with Ciconia's and other Italian motets, to call the equal upper voices cantus I and II (C1 and C2 in the tables).

[17] This is the only French motet in PMFC 5 in perfect tempus with minor prolation. In CMM 39 Günther labels as contratenor a voice found only in **Chantilly**; the parts she labels solus tenor and [tenor] are correctly labelled in **Stras** as tenor and contratenor.

538 ITALIAN MOTETS

Various dates have been given for the compilation of **SL2211** and additions to it in relation to **Sq**. The additions cannot be very much later than the corpus if indeed the scribe is recognisably the same throughout, as Nádas and Janke assert, though this is very hard to ascertain, given the state of damage. The difficulty of making judgements about script and ink colour is also an impediment to determining whether the song-fillers within the main corpus were entered at the same time as the main items on those openings, or over how long a time spread. John Nádas's identification of the scribe of **SL2211** with that of the Gloria and Credo added later on ff. 82ᵛ–85ʳ of **Lo29987** invites further exploration of a possible Medici connection.[18] Some of the contents of **Lo29987** have Visconti associations, but the first folio of the surviving portion of the divided manuscript bears a Medici coat of arms.[19] This, but especially the scribal connection, could bring the chronology of those two manuscripts together in Florence in the Medici orbit at an earlier date than hitherto suggested for **Lo29987**. Since San Lorenzo was the parish church of the Medici, it cannot be ruled out that the music manuscript reused for the Campione had indeed been associated with them, though Nádas and Janke prudently do not commit to a Medici provenance.[20] These relationships deserve further exploration; there seems no reason to challenge the judgement that this scribe was working in Florence.

Another possible point of reference for the compilation could be the employment of Ugolino of Orvieto as a singer at Florence Cathedral in 1417–18.[21] An earlier assumption that a whole gathering might have been devoted to him was tempered by the discovery of other ascriptions within that gathering, notably to Salinis, as noted above. But he was accorded at least a grouping if not a whole gathering of his own, perhaps reflecting his late arrival and short tenure in Florence. Ugolino and Piero must be the youngest composers represented, reflected in their position after the French section.

The main corpus was not terminated by the provision of capitals, which were anticipated by guide letters, so there was no hard break between the core repertory and the added gatherings; the manuscript was never completed as intended. Indeed, as can be demonstrated for other manuscripts, it may have remained unbound for a while, presumably as a growing collection, at least as far as the additions are concerned, but within a shorter time-span than, for example, **Q15** or **Ox213**.[22] The relationship between **Sq** and **SL2211**, and indeed between **Lo29987** and **SL2211**, and their order of compilation, is one of the most pressing and interesting questions for future work.

---

[18] Nádas, 'Some Further Observations', 147. He there refers to the 'main' scribe of **SL2211**, perhaps implying others, but in the latest publication a single scribe is favoured (Nádas and Janke, *The San Lorenzo Palimpsest*, i. 18 and 22: 'a single hand'). That, and most other studies by Nádas referred to here, are reprinted in Nádas, *Arte Psallentes*. The scribal characteristics of **Lo29987** are described in Di Bacco, 'Alcune nuove osservazioni', 191 and 195, and Gozzi, 'Alcune postille'. **Lo29987** was part of a larger manuscript of at least 185 folios, as the surviving leaves were originally numbered 98–185. The question of scribal identity in **SL2211** is crucial for assessing the later additions, though certainty may never be possible.

[19] Opinion has been divided as to whether this coat of arms is of the 15th or the 19th century, perhaps added to enhance its sale to the British Museum in 1876. Michael Scott Cuthbert judges it to be 19th-c. Stefano Campagnolo has suggested that the dating could be resolved with a simple scientific examination of the blue pigment, and prefers to see the stemma as a mark of ownership rather than of patronage (email of 2.1.2018). See Campagnolo, 'Il Frammento Brescia 5', 82 n. 62. He reveals further highly significant scribal interconnections between Florentine manuscripts.

[20] For San Lorenzo in this period, see Gaston and Waldman (eds.), *San Lorenzo*, especially Gardner von Teuffel, 'The Altarpieces of San Lorenzo'.

[21] D'Accone, 'Music and Musicians', 106.

[22] As suggested in Nádas and Janke, *The San Lorenzo Palimpsest*, i. 18.

Hubertus de Salinis

Hubertus de Salinis occupies a special position in **SL2211** as the only named composer of any of the motets (two of the three) and French-texted songs (three), and the only non-Italian to be named anywhere in the manuscript.[23] (See Table 27.2.) The little we know about his biography is due to the fundamental researches of John Nádas and Giuliano Di Bacco, who were able to reconstruct part of his ecclesiastical career from two papal documents of 1403 and 1409.[24] I am very grateful to John Nádas for sending me the documents and his readings, on which the following summary is based.

In a papal response dated 29 May 1403 to a supplication from Ubertus de Salinis, the Roman Pope Boniface IX greeted him as a canon of Braga, referring to an earlier supplication in which he had been allowed to proceed to minor orders, despite being the illegitimate son of a priest and a single woman, and to a single benefice *sine cura*, after which time he would be given permission to attain full holy orders and receive all forms of benefices. In fact, he was eventually promoted to the diaconate and was able to receive the canonicate with prebend at Braga that he now held. He also exchanged a benefice at the church of St Peter de Torrados for one (presumably more lucrative) at the parish church of Sanctus Salvator in Taagilde in the diocese of Braga.[25] With this letter the pope allows Hubertus to increase his beneficial portfolio by receiving greater favours, and assures him that no one can deny him this privilege.[26] His naming as a deacon in 1403 has led to a presumption that he was then below the canonical age of twenty-five for the priesthood, though this cannot necessarily be assumed. The letter is crossed out, but a marginal note explains that the corrected letter is entered again, in the first year of Gregory XII's reign; this revised letter has not been found. John Nádas believes that the corrections were needed simply due to an error in the original reading; lines 6 and 7 did not correctly represent his clerical status and the beneficial career already attained. Nothing in this document indicates that Salinis was in Italy in the period from 1403.

The second papal letter is from Alexander V, dated 10 July 1409, three days after his inauguration at the Council of Pisa. It names Humbertus [*sic*] de Salinis, still a canon at Braga cathedral, as a familiar of the newly elected pope and singer in the papal chapel ('familiari nostro . . . in capella nostra cantor existis').[27] The letter grants him an

---

[23] The article by van den Borren in *MGG1* records him as 'Hubertus de Salinis', without giving alternative spellings at the head of the article, though he does note the **Chantilly** ascription to 'Hymbertus'. He points to various corresponding place names in France and Walloon Belgium, favouring Slins near Liège, as noted above. *MGG2* (Robert Nosow) follows its predecessor in prioritising 'Hubertus de Salinis', but gives alternative forms.

[24] The first document is Archivio Segreto Vaticano, Registra Lateranensia (AAV, RL), vol. 111 (Boniface IX, 1403, anno 14, lib. 158), f. 182ᵛ, dated from Rome, 4 Kl. Junii Anno XIV (29 May 1403). The letter was briefly reported by Di Bacco and Nádas, 'Papal Chapels', 71–72, and anticipated in more detail (but with some ambiguities) by Nosow, 'Florid and Equal-Discantus Motet', to whom they had communicated it in advance of their publication.

[25] Or Tuagilde = Tagilde, south of Braga (not the small community of Tangil north of Braga, as Nosow suggests in *MGG2*).

[26] A copy of the letter goes to the archbishops of Vienne and Braga.

[27] A letter from Alexander V to Salinis, dated Pisa, 10 July 1409, AAV, RL, vol. 138 (Alexander V, anno 1, lib. 5), ff. 105ʳ–106ʳ: 'dilecto filio Humberto de Salinis canonico Bracharensi, familiari nostro, . . . in capella nostra cantor existis'. See Di Bacco and Nádas, 'Papal Chapels and Italian Sources', 71–72 n. 77. According to Nosow the letter also appears to name the bishop-elect of Silva, also in Portugal, as Salinis's legal representative. See Nosow, 'Florid and Equal-Discantus Motet', 89. Nosow (*NG2*) takes this document to imply that he was a priest (aged twenty-five or more) and that his birthdate can therefore be set between 1378 and

540 ITALIAN MOTETS

Table 27.2 Mass music and motets by Hubertus de Salinis

Composition	Q15	Ox213
Gloria *Jubilacio*, a3	54: R62ᵛ–64 | A63ᵛ–65	
Gloria, a3	63: R78ᵛ–79 | A79ᵛ–80	
Credo, a3	55: R64ᵛ–66 | A65ᵛ–67; pair, *unicum*	
Credo, a3	64: R79ᵛ–81 | A80ᵛ–82; irreg. paired	
Salve regina, 'Virgo mater ecclesie', a3	232: R236ᵛ–237 | A265ᵛ–266, *unicum*	
Ihesu salvator seculi/Quo vulneratus scelere, a3	213: R220ᵛ–221 | A249ᵛ–250	**Ox213**, no. 179, f. 81,[a] full black notation, Ubertus de psalinis
Si nichil actuleris/In precio precium, a3	278: R275ᵛ–276 | A304ᵛ–305	
Psallat chorus in novo carmine/ Eximie pater et regie, a3, on St Lambert	247: R250ᵛ–251 | A279ᵛ–280	

[a] This is his only piece in **Ox213**, and was the original beginning of the collection, gathering V, the earliest gathering to be copied. In **SL2211** the three Salinis motets (206, 207, 208) have voices below each other on a single page, but in all cases the Motetus follows the tenor: Tr T Mo. Salinis is the only non-Italian composer to have pieces attributed to him in **SL2211**.

MOTETS IN SL2211 AND HUBERTUS DE SALINIS 541

Table 27.2 Continued

SL2211	Venice145	Other
	Venice145, ff. 15ᵛ–19	**Utrecht37**, III (Strohm, *The Rise*, 100)
		Q1 verso (I and first staff of T only), black notation [anon.]
		Houghton122, identified by M. Cuthbert [anon.]
208, R183, black notation Hu'bert' d' Salinis		**Stras**, ff. 97ᵛ–98 (not transcribed in Coussemaker, *Strasbourg*) [anon.]
206, R182, black notation Imbert d' Salinis		
207, R182ᵛ, black notation (anon. here)		**Utrecht37**, f. Vʳ; identified by M. Cuthbert [anon.]

542 ITALIAN MOTETS

additional lucrative canonicate and prebend at Lisbon Cathedral, implicitly *in absentia*, worth 80 *livres tournois* annually, vacated on the promotion of its holder Fernando to the archbishopric of Lisbon. That he succeeded an archbishop (albeit just to a benefice) might imply that Salinis was in fact already quite senior, or at least specially favoured. His benefices at Taagilde and Braga also amount to 80 *livres tournois*. In addition, he holds an expectative benefice at Coimbra (worth 50 *livres tournois*) and one at Evora, which he must relinquish in order to take the Lisbon benefice. These benefices confirm his previous Portuguese career, and have led to a presumption that he had come to the council with the king of Portugal's large embassy. Salinis is not in the first full listing of the chapel of John XXIII, dated 18 March 1413, where Antonio Zacara heads the list and is called 'magister', here and in the April list.[28] It is therefore assumed that Salinis was by then no longer in the papal chapel; there is no further record of him.

The name Hubertus or Humbertus appears both with and without an 'm', but these are not simple variants; there are distinct traditions for the two names.[29] Hubert was a venerated eighth-century bishop of Liège; the name in various forms but without the 'm' is rare in southern Europe. Humbert is a name particularly associated with Savoy and south of the Alps, so 'Hubert' might well have been assimilated to 'Humbert' or Umberto in Italy and Iberia. The Veneto manuscripts **Ox213** and **Q15**, accustomed to migrants' names from the Low Countries, unanimously call him Hubertus or Ubertus, without 'm'. The Italian scribe of **Chantilly** uses the—perhaps for him—more familiar 'Hymbert'. The San Lorenzo ascriptions are hard to read, but both forms appear to be present.[30] Given that all archival or musical sources of the name are Italian, the presence in some of those Italian sources of the almost uniquely northern form without 'm' may count as a *lectio difficilior* favouring Hubert, and thence a Liège origin. Nádas and Janke standardise his name to 'Humbertus' in their inventory of **SL2211**; the first papal document calls him Ubertus, the other Humbertus.

Charles van den Borren named the composer only as Hubertus in his article in *MGG*1, though noting the **Chantilly** variant. He had no biographical documents, but he made the case for the composer's origin in Slins (Salinis), a demesne that belonged in the fourteenth century to the cathedral chapter of St Lambert of Liège, a few kilometres

---

1384, but as the document does not name him as a priest this cannot be taken for granted; many men older than twenty-five were still described as deacons or subdeacons, having never reached the priesthood (including cardinals).

[28] Nádas, 'Further Notes', 175–76, reports the three surviving accounts volumes from the papacy of John XXIII, preserved among the Strozzi papers in the Biblioteca Nazionale in Florence: Magl. XIX. 80 (1410), Magl. XIX. 79 (1410–12), Magl. XIX. 81 (1413–14), citing Waldmüller, 'Materialien'. Nosow (*NG*2, s.v. Hymbert de Salinis) says that he was no longer in the chapel by Jan. 1413, but that list is not a full one. Zacara then heads the list and may have been *magister cappelle*, though not so named. See Nádas, 'Further Notes', and Di Bacco and Nádas, 'Zacara e i suoi colleghi'.

[29] Leofranc Holford-Strevens observes that Humbert (Germanic, 'warrior-bright') is a name particularly associated with Savoy (and thence, as Umberto, with the Italian royal family); the Dominican Humbert of Romans was from Romans-sur-Isère in south-eastern France. Hubert ('mind-bright') was a bishop of Liège, whose name in various forms (for example, Hupperts) became widespread in northern Germany and the Low Countries.

[30] Ascriptions in the musical sources are as follows: Q15, H de Salinis or Hubertus de salinis; Ox213, Ubertus de psalinis; Ch, f. 46, *En la saison* carries an ascription to Hymbert de Salinis, but for a song that may be spurious anyway. SL2211, Nádas and Janke, *The San Lorenzo Palimpsest*, i. 20, read two of the ascriptions as 'Imbert*us*' (R177r and R182r), and another as 'Hubertus' (R183r); in the other cases it is not clear (to me) whether there is an abbreviation sign over the 'u'. They report for R175v M' Hu, R177 Imbert, R179 Hu t' d' S, R182 Imbert' d' Salinis, R183 Hu'bert' d' Salinis.

MOTETS IN SL2211 AND HUBERTUS DE SALINIS   543

from that known musical centre. The Latinisation of Slins as 'de salinis' or 'de psalinis' is documented in Liège archives.[31] Van den Borren noted the dedication of *Psallat chorus* to St Lambert, as well as the name Hubert being relatively restricted in the Middle Ages to that area. Additional support for a *liégeois* origin comes from the texts of the motets. Two of Salinis's three motets are based on older works. Both texts of *Psallat chorus/Eximie pater* are adapted to celebrate St Lambert, the patron saint of Liège, from a widely circulated St Nicholas motet on the tenor *Aptatur*.[32] '*Aptatur*' (= 'fitting', or 'adapted') ends triplum and motetus parts in both motets, though the Salinis motet is no longer on that tenor. The words *Domine Nicholae* and *Hac die, Nicholae* in the two original texts are here replaced by *Sancte Lamberte*; other variants are minor. In **Q15**, tenor and contratenor join the upper voices between the fermatas with the emphatic words *sancte Lamberte*, the only text in those parts.[33]

Like those of *Psallat chorus/Eximie pater*, the texts of *Si nichil/In precio* are taken from a thirteenth-century composition, in this case two stanzas of a three-part conductus in score, which starts with Salinis's motetus underlaid to the music, followed by the triplum stanza.[34] In Salinis's setting, the equal cantus parts set the two texts with nearly simultaneous syllabification over a free accompanying tenor in the Italian manner. These short texts, taken from thirteenth-century models, lead to motets that are exceptionally short for the early fifteenth century, even where the music is extended with textless canonic or sequential interludes, as here. *Ihesu salvator/Quo vulneratus* is another strikingly short motet. Since two of Salinis's three motets use older texts, could these texts also be pre-existent, although not yet identified? Although many texts start with these words, I could not find elsewhere the version that mentions Judas.

Nádas and Giuliano Di Bacco collected some twenty references in papal documents to clerics called 'de Salinis', nearly all explicitly from the Besançon diocese.[35] Nosow places his birth categorically in Salins-les-Bains near Besançon.[36] The Besançon affiliation is lacking, however, in both documents affecting our Hubert, which could support

[31] I am grateful to Catherine Saucier, email of 19.2.2017, for the following references:
- Four payments from the Cathedral of Liège, Compterie des Anniversaires, register numbers 80 (1418); 83 (1426); 84 (1432); and 87 (1442) for the celebration of the anniversary of Hermannus de Salinis (also spelt 'Psalinis' in register 87) in the month of February.
- One payment from the collegiate church of Sainte-Croix, accounts of the grain, register number 206 (1354?) to Jacobus de Salinis (possibly a canon of Sainte-Croix?) for singing a responsory on the feast of St Lambert.

[32] The older motet, with both texts, is in **Mo**, fascicle 4, no. 51 (60), ff. 98ᵛ–100; **Bamberg**, no. 30; **Darmstadt3471**; **Paris11411**; and **Lwa33327**. On *Aptatur* see now Bradley, 'Choosing a Motet Tenor', and Bent, Hartt and Lefferts, *The Dorset Rotulus*. The texts of the anonymous motet *O Maria virgo/O Maria maris stella* in **Q15**, **MuEm** and **Pad1106** are likewise adapted from an older motet, also in **Mo** fascicle 4 and elsewhere: see Bent, *Bologna Q15*, I, 217, and here Chs. 1, 26, 28.

[33] **Mo** variants include the following: Tr: *tuo tegmine* (**Q15** has the metrically less correct *tuo regimine*); *domine Nicholae* (**Q15** *Sancte Lamberte*); *aptatur* (**Q15** wrongly *optatur*). Mo: *hac die Nicholae* (**Q15** *Sancte Lamberte*); *nos doce* (**Q15** *doce nos*). Nosow (*NG2*) suggests that 'Salinis seems to have travelled provided with ready-made texts, which explains the re-use of 13th-century French motet or conductus texts'.

[34] The motetus imagines a contemporary reception of Homer and Croesus; Homer's literary prowess would now mean nothing, while Croesus' wealth would bring him friendship, praise, and honour. See CMM 11/VII. Reaney reports text in other sources including Dahnk, *L'Hérésie de Fauvel*, 34. *In precio precium* is in *Fauvel*, p.mus. 16; the first lines are from Ovid, *Fasti* I. 217. **Florence29** no. 652, f. 227ʳ⁻ᵛ, two stanzas of a conductus, has *In precio precium* underlaid in one voice, with Salinis's triplum text *Si nichil* following as a second stanza.

[35] Di Bacco and Nádas, 'Papal Chapels', 71–72.

[36] See Nosow, *Hubertus de Salinis*, in *MGG2*. In his earlier dissertation ('Florid and Equal-Discantus Motet', 98 and 87), however, because of prepublication access to the information about his beneficial career in Portugal, he called him a 'Portuguese composer' and 'from the diocese of Braga, in northern Portugal'.

544   ITALIAN MOTETS

him not being from that diocese. Nothing else associates the composer with Besançon, which seems not to have had a significant musical tradition at the time. Northern musicians were in demand in Italy and the Iberian peninsula, as evidenced by the careers of Ciconia, the Lantins and, only a little later, Du Fay. The name Hubert, and the motet texts for St Lambert, make it in my view more likely that he was from Slins near the known musical centre of Liège, given that Salinis is a documented Latinisation of that place-name.[37]

Doubt hangs over the attribution of what was hitherto his only song, *En la saison*, unique to **Chantilly** (f. 46[r]; and see Ch. 30). There is also doubt about the dedicatee and date, despite Ursula Günther's careful heraldic work. In an ingenious and wide-ranging study, involving heraldry, genealogy and historical connections, Günther associated two ballades with members of the du Guesclin family.[38] *Bonté de corps* (**Reina**, f. 55) is unambiguously tied to Bertrand du Guesclin (d. 1364) by an acrostic as well as by the heraldic content of the text. The ballade *En la saison* specifically refers to the du Guesclin family heraldry and contains references to an 'olivier' and a 'pierre'.[39]

Günther concluded that the ballade was in fact written in the early 1390s for the son of Thomasse le Blanc, dame de la Roberie et de la Bouverie ('la pierre', she female, 'pierre' the name of her father, 'blanche' the family name), wife of Bertrand and mother of Olivier du Guesclin, who from 1386 was seigneur of Brisarte. He died before 1397 but seems to have been alive in the early 1390s. Günther leaves open the possibility that the ballade could instead refer to a younger grandson of Thomasse called Olivier, about whom nothing is known, but would place *En la saison* at the latest before 1398. The younger candidate might have to be considered if a later date for the song became necessary to reconcile with authorship by Salinis.

The ballade carries an ascription to Salinis at the head of the page in **Chantilly**, but the name of Jo. Cuvelier (or Cunelier; u and n are often indistinguishable) appears under the tenor in the same hand. Gilbert Reaney assumed that just the tenor was by Cuvelier, but Günther rightly thought this unlikely. Cuvelier may well be Jean le Cuvelier, chronicler of Bertrand de Guesclin, the high-ranking Constable of France, buried with royalty in St-Denis. The *Règles de la seconde rhétorique* refer to a poet Jacquemart le Cuvelier from Tournai, possibly the author of that chronicle, completed *c.* 1387, and thus well placed to be the author at least of the text of the ballade honouring a member of that family, perhaps Bertrand's son. 'Jo. Cunelier' is the composer of another **Chantilly** ballade, on Gaston Febus, *Se Galaas* (f. 38), which, as Günther points out, has strong stylistic and notational affinity with *En la saison*, both of which use full and void forms of both black and red notation. Other works in **Chantilly**, anonymous or with cryptic ascriptions, have been linked to this composer on stylistic and notational grounds.[40] Without the

---

[37] Strohm, *The Rise*, 100, calls Hubertus de Salinis 'a contemporary of Ciconia from the diocese of Liège'.

[38] Günther, 'Zwei Balladen'. The heraldry is discussed in great detail, 'a la barre vermeille' at 23.

[39] Günther offers a corrected version of the text and music, which was taken over by Reaney in CMM 11/VII. She calls it one of the latest works in **Chantilly**, by a very young Salinis ('Zwei Balladen', 38).

[40] *Lorsques Arthus* (**Ch**, no. 61, f. 40[v]) and *Se Geneine* (**Ch**, no. 63, f. 41[v]) have cryptic superscriptions, which Gilbert Reaney reads as 'Jo Cun[elier]' ('The Manuscript Chantilly'), and Günther as Jo Cuvelier ('Zwei Balladen'), a reading adopted in Reaney's edition. It is hard to share their confidence; Plumley and Stone (*Chantilly Codex*) are more cautious and read it as 'J.O.'. However, the stylistic and notational usage between all four pieces and the anonymous *Medée fu* (**Ch**, no. 26, f. 24[v]) is so strikingly similar that the same composer is quite possible.

MOTETS IN SL2211 AND HUBERTUS DE SALINIS 545

subsequent documentary evidence for Salinis in 1403 and 1409, Günther thought *En la saison* must be a very early work, under the influence of Cuvelier. In linking the marginal drawings in **Chantilly** f. 37 to artist(s) associated with Boniface IX, Francesca Manzari raises the possibility of a relationship of the manuscript to the court of Boniface, who signed Salinis's first surviving documentation in 1403.[41] Other considerations point to a later dating of **Chantilly** in the 1410s, with these artists working after the pope's death in 1405, possibly for a different patron.

Günther's sense of Salinis's likely age was based on the span between a ballade written before 1398 and his presence in the later manuscripts **Ox213** and **Q15**, and the assumption that his Gloria *Jubilacio* was written as a prayer for the end of the Schism in 1417. Since Günther's article, the above-reported biographical documentation of Salinis in the first decade of the century has come to light. It now seems more likely that this Gloria was composed in 1409, referring as it does to a newly elected pope (Alexander V) who will bring the Schism to an end.[42] As Salinis's career can now be documented only in the first decade of the fifteenth century, if the assumptions that he was still young are correct, and if the identity proposed for Cuvelier holds, Cuvelier seems the likelier author for a piece dedicated to someone who died before 1398. Accepting that the date is too early for Salinis to be the composer, Lucia Marchi suggests that he could be the performer responsible for its transmission into **Chantilly**.[43]

Yolanda Plumley and Anne Stone question the Salinis ascription of *En la saison* and favour attributing the entire piece to Cuvelier on grounds of context, musical style and notational links to his other ascribed composition (*Se Galaas*) and perhaps to the two other **Chantilly** songs that may be by Cuvelier. They note that Salinis has no known connections 'to the Avignon papacy or to the French circles in which so many **Chantilly** composers appear to have been active'.[44] His status as a deacon in 1403 has suggested that Salinis could still have been relatively young (even though succeeding an archbishop-elect to a benefice, as noted above), perhaps born in the early 1380s. If that were so, he cannot be the composer of a notationally and heraldically complex composition dating from the early 1390s, probably composed closer in time to Cuvelier's activity, in the 1380s, and much more elaborate notationally and stylistically than anything else

[41] Manzari, 'The International Context', 31.

[42] Lacking biographical guidance, van den Borren associated the Gloria *Jubilacio* with the election of Martin V in 1417, which ended the Schism (as reported in Reaney CMM 11/VII, p. ix). Now that Salinis is known to have been associated with Pietro Filargo around the time of his election as Pope Alexander V, documented as a familiar of the new pope and singer in his chapel, a date in 1409 seems likelier, even if the hope that this election would end the Schism proved premature. This earlier dating was first proposed in print by Strohm, *The Rise*, 100). Without access to the new documents, Strohm proposed that he was active in Florence around 1410. This redating was affirmed at a conference held at the Library of Congress on 1–3 Apr. 1993, later published as Di Bacco and Nádas, 'Papal Chapels', 71 n. 77 and Bent, 'Early Papal Motets', 29 (here Ch. 30). For the Gloria, see CMM 11/VII, vii, ix, and xxv, and *Il Codice T.III.2*, ed. Ziino, 50. The trope text is in AH 47, 279 and is set by Salinis as duets. The trope is as follows: 'Gloria, jubilacio | uni Deo et simplici, | vero Christi vicario, | nostro summo pontifici. || Laudet chorus ecclesie | unum Christi vicarium; | benedicat, glorificet, | adoretque non dubium. || Gratias tibí ferimus | quia, excluso scismate, | sacro dedisti pneumate | verum papam quem credimus. || Fili patris obediens, | agnus Dei purissime, | carisma sanctum tribuens | unionis sanctissime. || Tu tulisti de medio | scisma donante flamine | ut esset pax et unio | sub veri pape culmine. || Patris sedens ad dexteram, | solus sanctus et dominus, | regeque sponsam dexteram, | papam nostrum quem colimus.'

[43] Marchi, 'Traces of Performance', 14.

[44] Plumley and Stone, *Codex Chantilly*, 133–34 and 150.

546   ITALIAN MOTETS

attributed to Salinis.[45] The **SL2211** songs by him appear to be much simpler in style—as are his mass movements and motets, which casts further doubt on his authorship of the complex ballade. Style alone would not necessarily discount his authorship; *Sus un fontaine*, for example, is an essay in proportional and mensural subtlety found nowhere else in Ciconia's works. But I agree that *En la saison* is probably by Cuvelier; it seems very unlikely that, as a young composer with an early beneficial career in Portugal, Salinis had contacts with, or reasons to honour, the du Guesclins.

However, the fact that Salinis was known as a composer to the **Chantilly** compiler favours a date of compilation of that manuscript around and after 1410, whether or not he composed the ballade. It is indeed because of the ascription of the ballade *En la saison* to 'Hymbert de Salinis', who was apparently already in the service of Pietro Filargo at the time of his election as Alexander V in 1409, that Plumley and Stone associate the later parts of the **Chantilly** repertory with the circles around this pope; they suggest that the actual compilation may have started under his aegis and continued after his death, and that **Chantilly** was compiled between *c.* 1409 and 1420, later than previous datings and in the same decade as **SL2211**.[46] All Salinis's other works—three motets, four mass movements, and his *Salve regina*—are in **Q15**, hitherto all *unica* except the motet *Ihesu salvator* and a concordance in **Houghton122** for the Credo **Q15**, no. 64, discovered by Michael Scott Cuthbert. Most of them (probably all originally) are in the old layer before 1425.[47]

Four of the added French songs in Gathering XVIII of **SL2211** (all *unica*) are the only pieces in void notation, though they again appear to be by the same scribe.[48] These are nos. 198 (R175[v]); 200 (R176[v]); 201 (R177[r]); and 204 (R178[v]–179). (See Table 27.3.)

Table 27.3 Songs by or possibly by Salinis

Song	SL2211	Chantilly
En la saison que toute riens (ballade), *a*3; *opus dubium*? J. Cuvelier?		f. 46 *unicum*: Hymbert de Salinis Tenor Jo. Cuvelier
Con plus (rondeau?), *a*2	198, R175[v]: 'M Hu', void notation	
J'ai . . . (rondeau?), *a*2	201, R177[r]: Imbert, void notation	
unidentified ballade, *a*3	204, R178[v]–179[r]: Hu't d' S, void notation	
Other possible candidates:		
Las. . . (virelai), *a*3	199, R176[r]: anon. in same group	
T . . . (rondeau?), *a*3	200, R176[v]: anon., void notation	
unidentified virelai, *a*3	202, R177[v]: anon. in same group	
Adieu plaisir (ballade), *a*3	205, R179[v]–180	

[45] Plumley and Stone, *Codex Chantilly*, do not cite this chronological problem as a reason for discounting the ascription to Salinis.

[46] Plumley and Stone, *Codex Chantilly*, 181.

[47] Nosow observes (*NG2*) that the troped *Salve regina* '*Virgo mater ecclesie*' is otherwise set only by English composers; it reflects the international milieu at the Council of Pisa, and was probably composed in the *divisi notation current in papal circles*'. See Bent, '*Divisi* and *a versi*'.

[48] Reported by Janke, 'Die Kompositionen', 33.

MOTETS IN SL2211 AND HUBERTUS DE SALINIS 547

This is particularly striking given that Salinis's motet *Ihesu salvator* is one of only four pieces in black notation in **Ox213**. It was the showpiece at the beginning of the original compilation (the current Gatherings V–VIII), the first recto of Gathering V, with an enormous capital I and monogram 'YHS'. A more formal script was used at the comparable place at the beginning of **Q15** (f. R1); and Bartolomeo da Carpi prescribed *bona nota* for the black notation in which the Lamentations he requested for his memorial volume were copied.[49] Another black-notation piece in **Ox213** is Ciconia's *O felix templum*, in what I presume to be its original Italian notation. Salinis's motet in its presumably original full-black French notation contrasts interestingly with his void-notation songs in **SL2211**. All the contents of **Q15** (except the later-added textless song no. 109) are in black notation. The (full) clefs and (void) *custodes* of the **SL2211** songs appear to be consistent with those of the black-notation pieces, so there is no *prima facie* reason to challenge the claim that all are by the same scribe, even though the void note-bodies are larger than and differently formed from full-black notes. Three of the four void-notation songs in **SL2211** are ascribed to Salinis. These ascriptions are very striking, as all the other French songs (apart from one by Ugolino) are the fifty-four anonymous *unica*, or the anonymously presented known songs of international circulation by Machaut, Senleches, and others. It is possible that the fourth void-notation song, the three-voice rondeau no. 200, could also be by Salinis—perhaps reflecting an authorial notational preference—and the other anonymous songs appearing consecutively with them are also candidates. So at least three songs in **SL2211**, nos. 198, 201 and 204, are attributed to him, and possibly four (the void-notation songs) or more (nos. 199 and 202) may be by him. They remain untranscribed and incompletely decipherable. In positing void notation as a possible authorial preference, we should remember that his only motet in **Ox213** is in full black notation. But that could well have been because it was the first piece, and presented conservatively, not uncommon for opening pages or pieces, as just mentioned for the opening recto of **Q15**.

The two ascribed rondeaux (nos. 198 and 201) are both for two equal texted voices.[50] No. 203, ascribed to Ugolino, is also a two-voice piece (but a ballade with differentiated ranges) and adjacent to a three-voice ballade by Salinis with macaronic text (no. 204). But the other items in this consecutive group, nos. 199, 202, 205, and the fourth void-notation piece, no. 200, all directly precede his three motets (nos. 206–8) and may also be candidates for authorship by Salinis. The recto for no. 205 is not overwritten and contains the contratenor. These songs seem to be much simpler in style and notation than *En la saison*, hitherto his only ascribed song, further bringing his authorship of that ballade into question.

It is perhaps noteworthy that no works by Salinis are preserved in **ModA** together with those of Matteo da Perugia, since both composers were in the service of the Pisan Pope Alexander V (Pietro Filargo).[51] Although Filargo must be suspected of strong musical persuasions and tastes, corroborated perhaps by the connection with his supporter, the music-loving Pietro Emiliani, whom he promptly promoted to the bishopric of

---

[49] Bent, 'Pietro Emiliani's Chaplain'.
[50] The then-known repertory of equal-voice songs was catalogued by Fallows, 'Two Equal Voices'.
[51] Stone, 'Lombard Patronage', addresses Filargo's patronage of Matteo da Perugia.

548   ITALIAN MOTETS

Vicenza,[52] no motets survive for that new pope by Salinis or Matteo. However, Salinis's troped Gloria *Jubilacio*, referring to a newly elected pope who will bring the Schism to an end, and formerly associated with the Council of Constance, has now more plausibly been associated with Alexander V and the Council of Pisa.[53] This new dating is also consistent with his disappearance from archival records by 1413; he is then no longer listed when Zacara is named. But Constance could account for the transmission of his music to the Veneto manuscripts **Ox213** and **Q15**.

Salinis's three short motets are in **SL2211** and all were copied in **Q15** a few years later than **SL2211**. *Si nichil actuleris/In precio precium* is so far known from no other source. *Ihesu salvator seculi/Quo vulneratus scelere* is in **Ox213** and **Stras**. *Psallat chorus/Eximie pater* was recently identified in **Utrecht37** by Cuthbert.[54] In **Q15** it has an inessential and presumably added contratenor, apparently unique to that source. The layout of all three of his motets in **SL2211** is highly unusual, each complete on a single page: triplum, then tenor, followed by the motetus below the tenor. *Ihesu salvator* also appears with the parts in this unusual order on its single side in **Ox213** for his only motet in that manuscript. **Q15** uses the normal layout across an opening. No other motet in **Ox213** with two cantus parts occupies only one side, so there is no precedent there for this layout.[55] It may have been chosen as the original opening piece of **Ox213** because it could be contained on a single page, the opening recto of the manuscript.[56] As mentioned, it has a huge initial letter and the monogram 'YHS'; the choice of an opening motet addressed to Jesus can perhaps be read as a salutation of new beginnings through Church councils; we know Salinis was at Pisa, which could also have been the conduit for **SL2211**'s acquisition of international repertory.[57]

All three Salinis motets are short, respectively only 64, 64 and 56 breves in length, with freely composed tenors and no rhythmic or structural repetition; all have simultaneous and equal or nearly equal text in the texted portions of both voices. *Ihesu salvator* is in imperfect time, with 64 breves of C. There is a short (five breves) opening echo imitation at the unison, between equal top parts over a free tenor, and it ends with a 10/6–12/8 cadence on *f*. Two lines of text are set simultaneously in the upper parts, followed by an untexted interlude, then two more lines, then another untexted interlude, then two final lines of text. There are some parallel fifths with the tenor and between voices I and II.[58]

---

[52] Bent, 'Early Papal Motets', 27–28.

[53] Strohm suggested that Ciconia's Gloria *Suscipe Trinitas* might be associated with post-Pisan conciliarism around the election of John XXIII in May 1410 (*The Rise*, 17). Instead, Di Bacco and Nádas, 'Papal Chapels', 70–77, argue that the Trinity is invoked as a statement of faith, symbolic of unity of differences, and, above all, that it would be blasphemous to equate it with the very division that was tearing the church apart. Starting from a careful exegesis of the text, they reject the claim associating the Trinity invocation with threefold schism, i.e. after 1409, that was suggested by Michael Connolly and reported in PMFC 24. It has always felt uncomfortable to have to place this Gloria in the final years of Ciconia's life. Di Bacco and Nádas point to Ciconia's patron Philippe d'Alençon's role in trying to mediate the Schism, and find the text suited to the intellectual climate surrounding debates starting with the Jubilee year in 1390 and attempts in 1395 to force Benedict XIII's abdication. They argue for a date for this Gloria between 1390 and Philippe's death in 1397, placing it in Ciconia's Roman years that they have so persuasively documented.

[54] Cuthbert, 'Hidden in Our Publications'.

[55] There is another layout anomaly for no. 211: *Apta caro/Flos virginum* in **SL2211** has motetus and tenor on the verso, triplum on recto. There is no obvious explanation for this except the weak one that the motetus (*Flos virginum*) starts without rests, or that it was confused with the triplum *Flos ortus*.

[56] Gatherings I–IV with newer material were added in front of the original starting point, now Gathering V, the present Gathering I being the last to be copied. See *Oxford, Bodleian Library MS Canon. Misc. 213*, ed. Fallows.

[57] Di Bacco and Nádas, 'Papal Chapels', 71–72; Bent, 'Early Papal Motets', 29, and here Ch. 30.

[58] The complete motets from which these examples are adapted are published in CMM 11/VII.

These untexted interludes are quite ingenious. The first (Ex. 27.1) presents rhythmic canons ♩♩♩♩ in all three parts in bar 10 at a semibreve's distance (crotchet in this transcription), four and a half times. The next (Ex. 27.2) has rhythmic repetition and melodic sequencing in the upper parts only: ♩♩♩ (five times) then ♩♩ ♩ (three times), strictly melodically sequential; in II: ♩♩♩ (four times) then ♩♩♩♩ (three times).

Ex. 27.1 Salinis, *Jhesu salvator*, first textless interlude with strict rhythmic canon (8-minim unit) in all three voices (CMM 11/VII, pp. 60–61, bb. 8–15)

Ex. 27.2 Salinis, *Jhesu salvator*, second textless interlude, with two strict rhythmic canons (of 4- then 6-minim units) between the upper voices, also strictly melodically sequential in I (CMM 11/VII, pp. 60–61, bb. 20–26)

Psallat chorus is the only one of Salinis's motets with a contratenor, which may have been added by the **Q15** compiler in accordance with his habit. Unlike some **Q15** contratenors, it was not added at stage II but was copied integrally at stage I. *Psallat chorus* also has 64 breves, this time of ₵, and 11 breves of echo opening.

Again, there are different simultaneous texts, alternating with interludes of textless rhythmic sequencing in the upper voices. The first four text lines are followed by just such an interlude of five breves (Ex. 27.3); two more lines take us to 'Sancte Lamberte' in all (four) parts with fermata chords at bars 38–42, then three lines followed by five breves of textless rhythmic sequencing reversing the roles of I and II. **Q15**'s added contratenor makes parallels, and forms tenor cadences below the unison cadences of triplum and tenor, before a final line. The even shorter motet *Si nichil* has 56 breves of ₵ again with simultaneous texting throughout, but no echo opening, and no textless interludes.

Ex. 27.3 Salinis, *Psallat chorus*, first textless rhythmic sequential passage. Each voice has a different rhythm. The integrated contratenor is present only in Q15 (CMM 11/VII, pp. 62–64, bb. 27–31)

In conclusion: a closer examination of the choice of motets in **SL2211** and the possible reasons for those choices leads to an extension of the comments I made in an article drawing attention to the contemporaneous copying of the retrospective trecento anthologies and the new international style represented in **Q15**.[59] The comments should also be extended to include the simultaneous cultivation of Italian- and French-texted pieces evident in the Padua fragments and to a striking extent in **SL2211**. What I perhaps failed to stress sufficiently in that article was that the core repertory of **SL2211** follows the normal pattern for trecento manuscripts, but that additions including French songs and motets stand outside that core. (**Fp26** of course also contains added French songs but no motets.) The prominent inclusion of Salinis but not Ciconia in a conciliar collection is noteworthy, as is the absence of motets by Landini in a Florentine anthology. **SL2211** is indeed an exception among the trecento anthologies in its inclusion of a group of motets, albeit as an afterthought; but apart from not being typically Italian, they hardly change the still-unexplained exclusion of Italian motets from those anthologies and of all but two in **SL2211**.

---

[59] Bent, 'Continuity and Transformation'.

28

The Motets of Johannes Ciconia

The inclusion of Ciconia in the series Polyphonic Music of the Fourteenth Century (PMFC) was planned well before the appearance in 1976 of an article by David Fallows establishing that Ciconia was not a canon of Liège born *c.* 1330, as had previously been claimed, but was the illegitimate son of that canon, born *c.* 1370, and only by marginal definition a fourteenth-century composer.[1] Since then, we learned that he left Liège as a young man, accompanying the cardinal and papal legate Philippe d'Alençon from Liège to Rome around 1390, where he probably spent a few years, but it is very likely that he spent at least part of the later 1390s at the court of Giangaleazzo Visconti in Pavia; the madrigal *Una panthera* has been dated to mid-1399, for the visit of Lazzaro Guinigi of Lucca to Pavia to secure an alliance with Giangaleazzo.[2] Other works (*Le ray au soleyl* and *Sus une fontayne*) display advanced French-Italian musical features that show Ciconia's mastery of current styles associated with that court, before he was recruited to Padua.[3] Thus his composing career unfolded in the 1390s in Rome, then probably in Pavia, and finally, most importantly, in Padua from 1401 until his premature death there in 1412. He thus stands right on the edge of classification as a composer even of the long fourteenth century, and his inclusion in a fourteenth-century series now looks anomalous. The older view promulgated by Suzanne Clercx that an elderly Ciconia was responsible for marrying Italian lyricism to French structural principles was based on faulty biographical premises, on a misplaced assumption that motets were inherently 'French', and on too narrow an understanding of the fragmentarily preserved motet genre in Italy.[4] The time was ripe for a new edition following her pioneering biographical study and edition, since when much new biographical and musical material had come to light from which a new attempt could benefit. Following the publication of PMFC 24 in 1985, yet more new material has become known, important new biographical material, a few new sources and some new ascriptions or attributions, and other updatings, not to mention the advent of digital images, whose manipulation can sometimes produce better readings.[5]

This chapter was originally written in 1991 as part of an introduction intended for a reprint for Oiseau-Lyre of *The Works of Johannes Ciconia*, PMFC 24. The reprint, alas unrealised, was planned for three paperback volumes (Mass music, Songs, Motets) with new introductions. The numbers in this chapter are those of the motets in PMFC 24. This chapter was intended for the motets volume; an abbreviated version formed part of my contribution on Ciconia's works in NG2. Here it is in revised form, with updates (including some revisions to the commentary notes in PMFC 24) in the light of more recent thinking by myself and others, including Robert Nosow, Michael Scott Cuthbert, Leofranc Holford-Strevens and Jason Stoessel. I am grateful to Cuthbert for his comments (email of 6.3.2016) on an earlier draft of this chapter, prompting me to several clarifications. I have not attempted to take account of everything that has been written about Ciconia's motets since first drafting this essay, and apologise to any authors whose work I have neglected.

[1] Fallows, 'Ciconia padre e figlio'.
[2] *The Lucca Codex*, ed. Nádas and Ziino, and Di Bacco and Nádas, 'Verso uno "stile internazionale"'.
[3] See Hallmark, 'Johannes Ciconia'.
[4] Clercx, *Johannes Ciconia*.
[5] Most strikingly, *Deduto sey* now has an authoritative attribution to Zacara from the Vercelli treatise: see Cornagliotti and Caraci, *Un inedito trattato*; and *Merçe o morte* has an ascription to Ciconia in the further

552 ITALIAN MOTETS

As stated in Chapter 26, earlier studies of the fourteenth-century motet had concentrated on the French at the expense of the different Italian and English motet traditions. Ciconia's motets are as much influenced by Italian precedents as by whatever French influences he absorbed in his youth, a view consistent with the establishment of his birthdate at *c.* 1370, and with his early move to Italy.

The recognition of a distinctively north Italian tradition of motet composition in the fourteenth century has provided a context and background for Ciconia's motet style, as well as placing the Italian motet alongside the previously recognised genres of madrigal, ballata and caccia, despite the absence of motets from all the retrospective trecento anthologies except **SL2211**. Even there, the motet section did not represent the typical Italian motet but rather is dominated by international repertory that was in wide circulation (Ch. 27).

Chapter 26 spelt out characteristics of the typical Italian motet, mainly associated with the Veneto, as two upper voices of equal or very nearly equal range, with the same or different texts, and with imitation and interplay between them. Some have initial echo imitation. Table 26.1 listed those motets including those by Ciconia. Table 28.1 lists Ciconia's motets, with more detail, and will be referred to in what follows. Only two of them, PMFC 24, nos. 12 (*O felix*) and 15 (*O virum*), start with wide-spaced non-overlapping echo imitation, each statement differently accompanied, in both cases starting with cantus I and tenor and with rests in cantus II.[6] In all motets but no. 16 (*Albane*) the upper parts are accompanied by a tenor from the beginning. The final cadence is typically 10/6–12/8, in a piece oriented on *f* ('major') or *d* ('minor').[7] These motets are typically conceived from the top parts down, anticipating the addition of a— usually essential—supporting tenor. These tenors are freely composed accompanying parts; despite some attempts, none has convincingly been shown to derive from pre-existent chant, even in the motet (*Petrum Marcello*, no. 18) that is least like the others in having a slow-moving tenor that looks like chant but has not been so identified.[8]

The style of a fragmentary motet on Santa Cristina in **Ox16**, f. 97[v], strongly suggests authorship by Ciconia, as discussed in Chapter 26 (Ex. 26.1).[9] It has strong affinities

---

leaves of Mancini published in Nádas and Ziino, 'Two Newly Discovered Leaves'. Fallows has also reviewed (and augmented) Ciconia's song attributions and their datings in Fallows, 'Ciconia's Earliest Songs', and 'Fallows, 'Ciconia's Last Songs'.

[6] Nos. 12 and 13 are analysed in Ch. 29. For further on the repetition strategy of these motets see Buff, 'Ciconia's Equal-cantus Motets', 69–78; despite generous references to my work elsewhere in the dissertation, she takes no account of my analyses in her chapter discussing the same pieces.

[7] Only one of Ciconia's ascribed motets, *Ut te per omnes*, ends on *d*; *O Padua* unusually ends on *c*, but with the same cadential progression. One of the few complete older motets, an antecedent forty years earlier, is *Marce Marcum*, for the doge Marco Corner (1365–68), ed. in PMFC 13, no. 44. See Ch. 26 and Caffagni, 'Omaggio a Johannes Ciconia'. It has a single text, equal-cantus parts over a free tenor, triplet figuration and opening echo imitation. In that imitation, however, cantus I continues singing during cantus II's echo, and the final cadence is not 10/6–12/8, but 6/3–8/5 on *g*. Another motet in the Padua fragments with features that place it outside the 'Italian' type (including a 6/3–8/5 cadence, chant tenor and a cantus II below the central tenor) is *Gratiosus fervidus/Magnanimus opere*, PMFC 12, no. 43, p. 153. On candidates for the tenor of *Gratiosus*, see Roger, 'La composition du tenor', 401. On the solus tenor and its criteria, see Bent, *Counterpoint*, Introduction, 38–46.

[8] Despite Brown, 'A Possible Cantus Firmus'.

[9] A portion where all three parts are mostly legible was transcribed in Bent, 'Italian Motet', 120–21, and here, revised, as Ex. 26.1, up to the end of the first opening of what was a two-opening presentation: **Ox16**, f. 97[v] is part of a centre-gathering bifolio, severely trimmed at top and left, and barely legible on the recto. Ultraviolet photography since my transcription makes a few more notes available.

THE MOTETS OF JOHANNES CICONIA 553

with *O felix templum* and is in the pure Italian notation which I have proposed as original for at least some of Ciconia's motets.

Omitted from this list is *Regina gloriosa* (PMFC 24, no. 24) which must be a Latin contrafact of a virelai or ballata, as the provision of open and closed endings and a strong terminal cadence at the midpoint show. Without its contratenor, it invites comparison with the virelai *Aler m'en veus*, contrafacted as *O beatum incendium* (no. 22), though no vernacular version of *Regina gloriosa* is known. But having rejected Clercx's proposed connection between the Gloria–Credo pair (PMFC 24, nos. 3–4) and this anonymous 'motet', no good reason remains to attribute it to Ciconia, though his authorship cannot be excluded.[10] In its unique source, **Warsaw8054** (*olim* Krasiński 52), it appears as a page-filler after Credo settings by Radom and Ciconia. Uncoupled from the mass pair, it was nonetheless included in PMFC 24 to facilitate review of the relationship proposed by Clercx, which rested too heavily on the use of a cliché common to many works of the period. David Fallows has proposed the addition to the Ciconia canon of two Latin-texted works, but neither bears any resemblance to any contemporary motet.[11]

The motets listed as nos. 12–19 present no problems of authenticity and share distinctive style traits. All eight except *Albane misse celitus* (no. 16) are ascribed to Ciconia in **Q15** (the unique source for *O Padua, Venecie mundi splendor, Albane misse celitus, Doctorum principem* and *Petrum Marcello*, nos. 13, 14, 16, 17 and 18). *Albane*, together with *O felix templum, O Padua, Venecie mundi splendor* and *Petrum Marcello*, have the further authorial corroboration of incorporating Ciconia's name within their texts as supplicant and composer, presumably of both text and music; those are here described as 'signed'. Six motets (nos. 13, 14, 16, 17, 18, 23), are unique to **Q15**. *O felix templum* and *Ut te per omnes* (nos. 12 and 19) are also in **Ox213**, *O virum omnimoda* (no. 15) in **BU2216** and **Siena36**. The five signed motets are all in **Q15**. *O Padua, Venecie, O virum omnimoda, Petrum Marcello, Ut te per omnes, O beatum incendium* and *O Petre* are all in stage I of that manuscript. *O felix templum* was in stage I, subsequently discarded and recopied in an unprecedented three-stage transmission within a single manuscript (see Fig. 28.1; ▶ Fig. 28.1 appears additionally on the website to facilitate magnification).[12] *Albane misse celitus* and *Doctorum principem*, although now only in later copies, were probably also in stage I, though earlier presence is not supported by direct evidence.

Thus, all of Ciconia's ascribed motets are preserved in **Q15**, several of them uniquely. But that manuscript does not contain two anonymous and incompletely preserved motets that have been attributed to Ciconia as *opera dubia*, *O proles Yspanie* and *Padu[a] . . . ex panis . . . serenans* (nos. 21 and 20).[13] These are in **Pad1106**, part of the

---

[10] See PMFC 24, pp. xi–xiii, and bibliography there cited.

[11] One is the French rondeau *Ave vergene* (**Lucca 184** and **Perugia3065**, the Mancini codex, f. 54) of which only the lower parts survive; it is quite unlike any other song of the 14th or 15th cc. and Fallows suggests a possible context among his motets, though those parts are also quite unlike any motet, Italian or other. But as he points out, Pirrotta's argument that it is too late in style falls away if we accept Nádas and Ziino's dating of Mancini in Ciconia's lifetime in the first decade of the century (*The Lucca Codex*, ed. Nádas and Ziino). The other piece is the macaronic *Sancta Maria regina celorum* (**Venice**, ff. 25ᵛ–27), with a faster-moving cantus accompanied by tenor and contratenor. Both are of uncertain status (possibly contrafacta?) and are discussed and transcribed in Fallows, 'Ciconia's Last Songs'. See also Fallows, 'Ciconia's Earliest Songs'.

[12] These are set out in Bent, *Bologna Q15*, 145, also 98 and 138.

[13] Published in PMFC 24 as *Padu. . . serenans*; a few more letters have since been deciphered by Cuthbert, 'Trecento Fragments' and Holford-Strevens, 'The Latin Poetry'. The first line is problematic and hard to read. PMFC 24 gave it as *Padu . . . serenans*. Cuthbert, 'Trecento Fragments', reads *Paduas ex panis serenas*, but

554 ITALIAN MOTETS

Table 28.1 Ciconia's motets (numbered as in PMFC 24)

PMFC 24 no.	Title	Sources[a]
12	*O felix templum jubila*	Q15-[I], no. 216, R223ᵛ-(224), A252ᵛ-253, 'Jo ciconie', and no. 341, f. R224/A341, anon; was in stage I; **Ox213**, no. 33, ff. 22ᵛ-23, 'Magister Johannes Ciconia de leodio'
13	*O Padua sidus preclarum*	Q15-I, no. 256, R257ᵛ-258, A286ᵛ-287; stage I, no contratenor, 'Jo ciconie'
14	*Venecie mundi splendor/Michael qui Stena domus* Tenor *Italie mundicie*	Q15-I, no. 257, R258ᵛ-259, A287ᵛ-288, stage I, no contratenor, 'Jo ciconie'
15	*O virum omnimoda veneracione/ O lux et decus tranensium/O beate Nicholae*	Q15-I, no. 254, R255ᵛ-256, A284ᵛ-285, stage I, 'Jo ciconie'; **BU2216**, no. 55, pp. 72–73, ff. 36ᵛ-37, 'Jo Cichonia'; **Siena36**, ff. 25ᵛ-26, anon.
16	*Albane misse celitus/Albane doctor maxime*	Q15-III, no. 273, R271ᵛ-272, A300ᵛ-301, stage III copy, was possibly in I; anon., but signed within the text
17	*Doctorum principem/Melodia suavissima/Tenor Vir mitis* [plus canon]	Q15-III, no. 272, R270ᵛ-271, A299ᵛ-300 (stage III or II, was possibly in I), 'io ciconia'.
18	*Petrum Marcello venetum/O Petre antistes inclite* T, Ct	Q15-I, no. 245, R248ᵛ-249, A277ᵛ-278 (stage I), 'Jo. ciconie'
19	*Ut te per omnes/Ingens alumnus Padue*	Q15-I, no. 259, R260ᵛ-261, A289ᵛ-290 (stage I), 'Jo ciconie': Ut per te omnis', *a3*; **Ox213**, no. 277, ff. 119ᵛ-120 (*a4*, with Ct in Ox only), 'M. Johannes ciconia De leodio conposuit'. Incipit reverses two words: 'Ut te per omnes'
22	*O beatum incendium*	Q15-I, no. 255, R256ᵛ-257, A285ᵛ-286, stage I), 'Jo ciconie'. Latin contrafactum *a2* of the virelai *Aler mèn veus*, of which cantus I only survives in **Pad1115** (PadB), no. 3, f. Aᵛ, 'Johes' [Ciconia]
23	*O Petre Christi discipule*	Q15-I, no. 258, R259ᵛ-260, A288ᵛ-289, stage I, *a2*, 'Jo ciconie'
	Opera dubia:	
	Santa Cristina motet	**Ox16**, f. 97ᵛ, anon., *a3*
20	*Padu[a]... ex panis... serenans/* Tenor *Pastor bonus*	(**Pad1106**, f. 1ᵛ), anon., cantus and tenor
21	*O proles Yspanie/Tenor O proles nobile depositum*	(**Pad1106**, f. 3ᵛ), anon., cantus and tenor

[a] For **Q15**, see Bent *Q15*. **Q15** piece numbers are as given in Bent, *Q15* (and earlier in the inventory of De Van). A[rabic] folio numbers are the modern foliation which runs through the entire manuscript, and corresponds to the numeration on the DIAMM images. R[oman] numbers are those of the latest of the original series of foliations, referring to the first stage, in part to the second, but it is absent in gatherings added at stage III. Both systems are used in the scholarly literature, usually without specification. There is no original foliation in stage III, though Gulielmus Musart added a few local numbers in portions he indexed. Here, (224) is a later substitution for that roman folio which is now one of the rear flyleaves. For **Ox213**, see *Oxford, Bodleian Library MS Canon. Misc. 213*, ed. Fallows. For **BU2216** see Gallo, *Il codice musicale 2216*. For all the Padua fragments, including **Pad1106**, see Cuthbert, 'Trecento Fragments', and Cuthbert, 'Groups and Projects'.

THE MOTETS OF JOHANNES CICONIA   555

Table 28.1 Continued

Ciconia's name 'signed' authorially within the text?	Equivalent French mensurations	Tonality	Comments[b]	Date, dedication
one text, signed in both	[O]	(d) final f	echo imitation; later Ct added and then withdrawn	1402, Stefano Carrara, bishop of Padua
one text, signed in both	C	c	a3	before 1405; possibly 1401
2 texts, signed in I	[O]	f	a3	January 1406: submission to Venice and Doge Michele Steno
3 texts, not signed	[O]	f	echo imitation; Ct all sources, with variants	possibly 1394, 300th anniversary of St Nicholas of Trani, but this seems early
2 texts, signed in II	[C]	f	+ Ct; isorhythmic; upper parts have 12B introduction before T/Ct entry	1406, Albano Michiel, bishop of Padua 1406–9
2 texts, not signed	₵ O C	f	+ Ct; three tenor statements in different mensurations	Zabarella
2 texts, signed in II	[O]	f	tenor and contratenor coloration; + Ct. Dim. within each half; isorhythmic	1409, Pietro Marcello, bishop of Padua 1409–28
2 texts, not signed	[O]	d	+ Ct in Ox only. On St Francis, Francesco Zabarella and Franciscans; isorhythmic	Zabarella
not signed	[O]	d	a2, equal voices, contrafact	
not signed	[O]	d	a2, equal voices	1409? (St Peter and Filargo and/or Emiliani; see below); or 1406
2 texts	[i]	d	fragment, anon., but with strong Ciconian features	
not signed	[p]	d	I (or II) and T; tenor coloration; 'tenores'; isorhythmic	1402? Andrea Carrara, abbot of Santa Giustina
not signed	[p]	f	I (or II) and T; isorhythmic	

[b] + Ct: contratenor probably added. 'Isorhythmic' means two rhythmically equal halves in all parts. Hypermetric [O] added in PMFC 24 to both texted voices of *Doctorum principem* for the initial melisma.

group of Padua fragments known as PadD copied by Frater Rolandus of Santa Giustina, probably in the first decade of the fifteenth century. Dating from Ciconia's lifetime and the same city, these copies seem to be not only older but potentially more authoritative than the more complete survivals in **Q15** and even later sources, which often show signs of reworking—notational translation and added contratenors. But the Padua fragments give us only approximate dating clues for the few fragmentary pieces they contain. Despite their incomplete state, a wide range of composers is represented, and even if Ciconia was foremost, he cannot be the only candidate for compositions celebrating Padua in the early 1400s. All the sources of Ciconia's ascribed and completely surviving mass and motet compositions date from ten years or more after his death, and there-fore have no value in establishing a chronology of composition. They also need to be viewed with scepticism where there is reason to think they present changed versions, as is most apparent in the motets. This may seem a strange claim for a source of such central importance and proven reliability as **Q15**, which must have been used by singers who had known and sung with Ciconia. However, the compiler of that manu-script intervened in two major respects: he added (and in one demonstrable instance withdrew) contratenors, and he changed the notation of at least some of his exemplars from Italian to French.

Contratenors

I have shown that at least some of the contratenors to motets by Ciconia and other composers in **Q15** were or may have been later additions.[14] By characterising them as 'inessential' I mean grammatically inessential, i.e. where a contratenor does not pro-vide essential support to otherwise unsupported fourths between the tenor and the top parts, and can be omitted without damage to the musical sense.[15] In some cases it can be argued that these contratenors make a musical contribution by enlivening the texture; equally often, they flatten it by crossing the tenor so that the lower parts together form a drone (as in the opening of *Doctorum principem*, no. 17), or obfuscate what was a clean, clear texture, and introduce anomalies of superimposed fifths and other dissonances. These contratenors often go well with the tenor but not with the upper parts, while the upper parts go well with the tenor, as when, for example, the upper parts have a fifth above the tenor, the contratenor a fifth below it; I call these conflicts 'bifocal'.

Unstable transmission and later addition are most abundantly documented for *O felix templum* (no. 12, Fig. 28.1 above); it has no contratenor in **Ox213**, whose Italian notation I believe reflects its original state. The composite copy of this motet now in the body of **Q15** (no. 216, ff. A252ᵛ–253) contains cantus I and tenor on the left (the stage-II

Paduas is not a word and makes no sense. The letters are as read, except that there is a macron over the last word, making *serenans*. Holford-Strevens reads the opening hexameter as *Padu<a> ... ex vanis serenans*. The problem is in the two letters preceding *ex*, which may be *as*. Even the first two letters '*Pa*' are now partly cov-ered by a restorer's patch and no longer easily legible. In view of the uncertainty, the title will be given here as *Padu[a] ... ex panis serenans*.

[14] See Bent, *Q15*, i. 147, and Westerhaus, 'A Lexicon of Contratenor Behaviour'.
[15] See Bent, 'Notes on the Contratenor'.

Stage I
Capital #84, reused
at stage II (below)

Capital #92, flipped: end of
first staff of stage-I copy

Stage II
Originally facing pages, now separated; f. A341ʳ was moved to the end, forming a composite bifolio with the stage-I f. A342

f. A252ᵛ

f. A341ʳ

 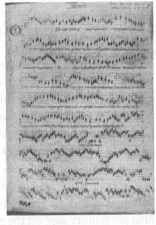

Stage III
Not recopied; the stage-II
f. A252ᵛ now faces f. A253ʳ

f. A253ʳ, now *in situ*

Fig. 28.1 The three stages of *O felix templum* in Bologna, Museo Internazionale e Biblioteca della Musica, MS Q.15 (Q15). Reproduced with permission from the Museo internazionale e biblioteca della musica di Bologna. ▶ Fig. 28.1 is also on the companion website in colour

558 ITALIAN MOTETS

verso), facing cantus II on the right (the late stage-III recto). The stage-II recto that originally faced the stage-II verso was relegated to serve as one of the rear flyleaves (f. A341, no. 326), and includes an inessential and problematic contratenor added at that stage and then rejected for the stage-III recopy of that page now *in situ*. A few notes of music from near the end of the first staff of the recto of *O felix templum* on the back of pasted capital no. 92 attests that this piece existed in a stage-I copy, whose more generous spacing would have left no room for a contratenor on that opening. R223[v] (= A252[v]), the left-hand page (verso) of the copy now in the body of the manuscript, uses pasted capital no. 84, which was cut from the stage-I verso of this piece; pasted capital no. 64, also cut from the stage-I copy, faced it on the recto.[16]

Thus *O felix templum jubila* went through no fewer than three copying stages in **Q15**. The first of these was without contratenor, the second was evidently made in order to accommodate a new contratenor originating from the compiler, who in a final third stage thought better of it and recopied that recto page without contratenor, a positive rejection rather than a passive omission. While such a tortuous and instructive process cannot be documented for other motets, there are indications that this scribe took similar initiatives elsewhere, thus placing all the Ciconian contratenors under suspicion. No contratenors earlier than those in **Q15** survive for any Italian motet, with the exception of *O Maria virgo davitica/O Maria maris stella* in **Pad1106**, which is also an outlier in the Italian repertory (if indeed it is Italian) in having an essential contratenor and a solus tenor.

By any standards we can now understand, there is no obvious reason to forfeit the satisfactory (and, I believe, original) texture of two cantus parts plus tenor that is basic to all Ciconia's motets (except *O Petre Christi discipule*, for two equal parts without tenor; see below), in order to enjoy whatever dubious musical gains the contratenors may bring, however interesting they are for the near-contemporary reception of this music. This view challenges Heinrich Besseler's claim that tenor and contratenor parts in the fifteenth century support the harmony as a foundational duo; that claim can apply only to those pieces with essential contratenors, but to none by Ciconia.[17] The type of dissonance introduced by these contratenors (a pedal or drone, or 'bifocal' superimposed fifths) has an idiomatic quality of its own which, while very different from that of the primary parts, often looks worse on paper than it sounds in performance. The contratenors were printed in PMFC 24 on small staves to draw attention to their optional character. Performers are nevertheless encouraged to experiment by performing the four-part motets with and without contratenors, and perhaps to programme performances of both versions in succession: the two sound very different.

O virum omnimoda (no. 15) stands apart from Ciconia's other ascribed motets in several ways. It is the only one with prose rather than verse texts, with three texts (one of them a texted tenor), and with more than two sources, **Q15**, **BU2216** and the non-Veneto source **Siena36**.[18] The contratenor is present in all three sources, but with

---

[16] For the pasted capitals, see Bent *Q15*, i, ch. VIII. For *O felix*, see 145–46.

[17] See Bent, 'Grammar'. It is possible that the contratenor of *Petrum Marcello*, though still inessential, may be original, because of the way it works together with the tenor. See below on *Padu[a] . . . ex panis* (no. 20).

[18] It is one of the minority of his motet texts that are unsigned by Ciconia. The two monotextual motets nos. 12 and 13 are both signed; of those with more than one text, no. 14 is signed in cantus I, 16 and 18 in cantus II. The two Zabarella motets nos. 17 and 19 are unsigned. This pattern may lightly challenge the authenticity of nos. 20 and 21.

interesting variants. It fits perfectly with the tenor, but creates some problems with the upper parts, most notably at bars 65 and 80, where two fifths are superimposed. The contratenor sounds a fifth below the tenor while an upper voice is a fifth above it; the resulting bifocal sonority can only be rescued by omitting the contratenor.[19] See Example 28.1.

Ex. 28.1 Final systems of *O virum omnimoda* (PMFC 24, p. 84). Reproduced from Éditions de l'Oiseau-Lyre, with permission from The University of Melbourne

* See Critical Commentary for this imitation.

PMFC 24 followed **Q15** in giving five exact and one inexact limbs of the imitations in bars 75–80 (asterisked at b. 75 in the edited score), which involve the three primary voices (excluding the contratenor, which does not participate in the imitations), and start on an unusually wide range of pitches (g, d, f, c). Neither of the other two sources is prior to **Q15**, and both may depend on it; both begin the imitation with $g f e f$ in the tenor, followed by $d c b c$ in the two upper parts, before adopting the version as printed for the last two entries. Did these other sources soften an imitation that was felt to be too

---

[19] Not by turning the lower fifth into a fourth, as on several recordings. Pedro Memelsdorff has refined and amplified interpretations and classifications of contratenors in a series of luminous articles, notably in Memelsdorff, 'Lizadra donna'.

560 ITALIAN MOTETS

bold, or did the compiler of **Q15** seize an opportunity to take Ciconia's own imitation a step further?

The contratenors of two Ciconia motets copied early in **Q15** stage III are both grammatically inessential. The contratenor of *Doctorum principem* (no. 17, **Q15**, no. 272) neutralises the leaping tenor part, turning the lower-voice pair into a sort of drone, as mentioned above. The contratenor of *Albane* (no. 16, **Q15**, no. 273), albeit integrated into the rhythmic and melodic repetition scheme, is problematic in that it introduces actual and narrowly avoided dissonance and parallels uncharacteristic of the three principal parts.[20] Contratenors were probably added to both motets at that late stage, which occasioned their recopying, probably from copies without contratenors that were discarded from stage I, to judge by the uniquely documented case of *O felix templum*. Those two motets are excellent instances of the copying of Ciconia's celebrations of long-dead dignitaries, twenty years after their and his own death, with some musical updating, but with no recycling of the dedicatees' names—a fascinating indication of that compiler's priorities.

The tenor of *Petrum Marcello* (no. 18) bears the rubric: 'Canon tenores dicuntur sic: primo usque ad secundam talliam ut iacent; 2º diminuuntur resumendo et sic successive alie talie procedant.' The contratenor is marked *ad modum tenoris*; although it is grammatically inessential and causes several anomalies of superimposed fifths, for example at bar 24, where it is integrated into the rhythmic structure and accompanies the brief opening duet before the tenor entry. In this case, the contratenor may be original, if not grammatically essential. The two lower parts are referred to as tenors (plural), as also in no. 20, *Padu[a] . . . ex panis*, even if they do not have tenor function contrapuntally. (The plural usage *tenores* often applies in rubrics for complex pieces with twinned lower parts, implicitly treating an essential contratenor as a second tenor.) The slower-moving undiminished tenor and contratenor here necessarily relate to the paired upper voices somewhat differently from most other motets. In both tenor and contratenor, the first statement is to be followed immediately by one in diminution; the second half of the motet is then a rhythmic replication of the first, each half in full values followed by a statement in diminution. Possibly the only Italian precedent for this highly unusual procedure, albeit in much shorter segments and a very different style, is the madrigal *Povero zappator* by Lorenzo da Firenze.[21] There is no indication within the motet's tenor and contratenor parts as to where the diminution is to be inserted; this has to be inferred from the point at which the tenor's rhythm repeats. For the diminution, notes of the next value down are substituted, which means in this case (where perfect modus becomes perfect tempus) that the breve becomes a semibreve, resulting in the relatively unusual reduction 3:1.[22] The contratenor has been artfully integrated with the diminution. Its harmonic anomalies, albeit fewer, are similar to those of the other contratenors (as at b. 22) and it must also be considered suspect. Both tenor and contratenor are in addition written out as *ad longum* parts of some notational interest, fully notated rather

---

[20] Brown, 'The Motets', 104.

[21] See Abramov-van Rijk, '*Povero zappator*'. This also occurs in more complex form in the **Chantilly** motet *Alma polis/Axe poli*; see Ch. 19.

[22] This diminution relationship is not common in the French motet (*pace* Machaut Motet 1) but is also found in **Fountains**, *Humane lingua/Supplicum voces/Deo gratias*, and in Cyprus motets 8 and 14 (Ch. 32).

THE MOTETS OF JOHANNES CICONIA   561

than being left for derivation by repetition and diminution, respelt in imperfect modus (with imperfect longs instead of altered breves), but with the diminutions written out in perfect tempus, with altered semibreves. These *ad longum* parts (not to be confused with solus tenors) represent not merely a respelling but a reconstruing of the compactly notated tenor and contratenor forms, from which they seem to derive; unless they too were an aid to the compositional process, simply spelt in unambiguous values after a more complex mensural conceit had been worked out.[23]

Besides *Petrum Marcello* (no. 18), the only other motet possibly by Ciconia with tenor coloration is no. 20, *Padu*[a] . . . *ex panis*, where it is specified 'Canon tenorum: Rubee dicantur de modo perfecto et tempore e converso; nigro vere e contra' (red L = 3 imperfect B, black L = 2 perfect B). Since the hockets at the end of each section of *Padu*[a] . . . *ex panis* span four-semibreve phrases, this would allow a complex interlocking of four hocketing parts, the two cantus parts and the plural *tenores*. Both motets have rubrics referring to 'tenors' in the plural, which may indicate that they have or had integral and original contratenors and were conceived in four parts, the plural referring to a twinned tenor and contratenor, both with coloration; in *Petrum Marcello* the contratenor is conspicuously different from those of Ciconia's other motets. While the references to tenors in the plural (as noted above) might be thought to imply equal supporting status for the lower parts, the contratenor does not have this role in *Petrum Marcello* and probably did not for *Padu*[a] . . . *ex panis*, though there remains a chance that the rubrics could have been provided later or rewritten. None of the fragmentary motets in **Pad1106** preserves a contratenor, though evidently *Padu*[a] . . . *ex panis* may have had one because of the plural *tenores*.

While at least in *O felix templum* and in some works by other composers there is evidence that contratenors were later additions and not integral to the original composition, or that they are unstably transmitted or exceptionally problematic, it may well be the case that a few of these contratenors are indeed part of the original conception. This is most likely for *O virum omnimoda* and *Petrum Marcello*. However, in all Ciconia's motets including these, a contratenor (if any) can be omitted without grammatical damage.

Compositions in **Q15** by other composers appear similarly to have been provided by the compiler with added contratenors at stages II or III (*c*. 1425–35). **Q15**, no. 242, the motet *Pie pater* by Antonius de Civitate, was copied at stage I, but an unlabelled, untexted contratenor was added late in stage III (with the fine pen of the latest additions) on f. R246/A275. I have shown that the Du Fay Gloria and Credo **Q15**, nos. 107–8 (CMM 1/1, pair no. 5), originally each on a single opening, must have been recopied at stage III over two openings each, in order to make space for added contratenors, and also to unite this musically matched pair. The contratenors of two motets by Antonius Romanus (*Aurea flammigeri*, **Q15**, no. 219, on f. R227/A256, and *Ducalis sedes*, no. 243, on f. R247/A276) were present at stage I, but their more compressed recopying at stage II (after the manuscript had been trimmed for binding) suggests that even at stage I the contratenors were an afterthought, added to motets originally composed without

---

[23] In PMFC 24 the pair of *ad longum* parts are transcribed on small staves below the main score and are not intended for performance. The contratenor of *Petrum Marcello* is printed on a normal-sized staff. See Allsen, 'Tenores ad longum'.

them.[24] Other pieces in **Q15** to which contratenors may have been added later, on similar grounds of spacing and stage-II recopying, include Grenon's motet *Plasmatoris humani generis/Verbigine mater ecclesia*, no. 223 (ff. R230ᵛ–231, A259ᵛ–260), the Hugo de Lantins Credo no. 68 (ff. R95ᵛ–86, A86ᵛ–87), and the Gloria no. 76 (ff. R97ᵛ–99, A98ᵛ–100) by Antonius Romanus.[25]

Notation

The transmission and presentation of Ciconia's music reflect the notational fluidity current in northern Italy *c.* 1400. It is possible to reconstruct with some confidence the original form of notation in which certain pieces, since changed, were conceived; this is especially true of the motets, but also of Ciconia's Gloria PMFC 24, no. 3.[26] All of Ciconia's motets survive in **Q15** in French notation, but use characteristically Italian rhythmic configurations (usually within the breve of tempus perfectum, and including duplet and triplet minims), which strongly suggest, with the further supporting evidence of erasure or change, that they are transcribed from Italian originals.[27]

Most striking in this regard is the homographic tenor of *Doctorum principem* (no. 17), composed in such a way that it could be notated just once (in Italian notation), and performed in three successive mensurations (₡, O and C) for the three sections of the motet (see Fig. 28.2). By the rules of Italian notation it works perfectly, where in perfect time the lengthening of a semibreve by *via naturae* (the second semibreve of a ligated pair) does not require it to precede a breve; but a rubric had to be added to this homographic tenor to override French alteration rules for the perfect-time section, to permit the improper alteration of a semibreve before another semibreve: 'Et dicitur primo inperfecto maiori 2° perfecto minori semper ultima semibrevis alteratur 3° imperfecto

Fig. 28.2 Tenor of *Doctorum principem* in Bologna, Museo Internazionale e Biblioteca della Musica, MS Q.15 (Q15), f. A299ᵛ. Reproduced with permission from the Museo internazionale e biblioteca della musica di Bologna

---

[24] In the case of *Ducalis sedes*, **BU2216** has no contratenor, while the **Q15** version does have an added and inessential contratenor. **Q15** names the doge as Tommaso Mocenigo; **BU2216**, although an earlier version, substitutes 'N' for his name, indicating that it was copied after his death but not explicitly recycled for his successor. **Q15** also implements a notational translation of the upper part from ₡ to O.

[25] Bent, *Q15*, i. 140, 146–47.

[26] This is possibly also true of Gloria no. 6, whose 4:3 relationships in the upper parts may reflect the influence of Italian notation as expounded by Prosdocimus for .i.–.o. (senaria imperfecta to octonaria), and where the layout on the second opening suggests that the long Amen may be an addition post-dating the contratenor. See Honisch, 'The Transmission of Polyphonic *Amens*', and Bent, *Q15*, i, commentaries to individual pieces.

[27] See the commentary comments in PMFC 24 for affected pieces, and those in Bent, *Q15* for all the pieces here named.

THE MOTETS OF JOHANNES CICONIA 563

minori.' Contrary to its classification in PMFC 24, I now emphatically withdraw the
isorhythmic designation from this motet. (See Ch. 2 for isorhythmic definition.) This
motet and Ciconia's Gloria **Q15**, no. 74 (PMFC 24, no. 3), require reinterpretation of
the same notated tenor in imperfect and perfect mensurations, with a similar anomaly.
Both must originally have been conceived in Italian notation.[28]

Ciconia's four Italian-texted madrigals in **Lucca184** and **Perugia3065** and some
of his *ballate* are in Italian notation with *pontelli*, but this is true of none of his mass
music. Other ballatas are in French notation, even in early sources including **Lucca184**
and the Padua fragments, and even alongside Italian-notated pieces. Nevertheless,
most if not all of his motets may have been conceived in Italian notation, as the
upper-part triplet passages and the rhythms of the tenor parts in perfect time suggest.
Notational evidence supports this in several ways. The **Ox213** copy of *O felix templum*
(no. 12) is actually in full-black Italian notation with downstemmed major semibreves
(instead of imperfected breves) and oblique stems, though without *pontelli* and therefore suggesting a newer stage. Extensive erasures in triplet passages in some of the
Q15 motets suggest that the scribe had trouble with how best to renotate these typically Italian gestures, or at least that he had second thoughts.[29] Only three of Ciconia's
ascribed motets, *O felix templum*, *O Padua*, *Venecie mundi splendor* (nos. 12, 13, 14),
have minim triplet passages. The only pieces copied in **Q15** at stage I with upper-part
minim triplets, *Venecie* and *O Padua*, have full-black triplets whose flags and filled
bodies were laboriously erased and replaced with the void unflagged forms that the
scribe preferred at stage II; the stage-II copy of *O felix templum* has void minim triplets
with no such alteration; the scribe evidently had a settled preference by this time. Many
internal indications and anomalies indicate that the—albeit older—French-notated
copy in **Q15** is an adaptation of the Italian-notated version in **Ox213** and not vice
versa. Similar anomalies in other motets for which we depend on the French-notated
versions in **Q15**, and sources related to it, strongly suggest that their originals, too,
were in Italian notation. The Santa Cristina motet in **Ox16** (Ex. 26.1) is in pure Italian
notation, with characteristic rhythms and imitations; if it is indeed judged to be by
Ciconia, this would provide further support.

Isorhythm

Isorhythm is a term coined by modern scholarship primarily for French motets using
repetition with diminution, organised around or over a tenor and requiring pre-
compositional planning. I have meanwhile sought to disqualify diminution and mensural manipulation from inclusion in this term, which means '*equal* rhythm' (i.e. not
'the same but faster'), and to reserve it for passages that are rhythmically identical
(Ch. 2). The only Ciconia motet to have any diminution in the lower parts is *Petrum
Marcello* (no. 18). As stated above, it is unusual in following each half of the tenor (and

---

[28] Michael Scott Cuthbert reminds me that the two Ciconia songs (*Aler m'en veus* and *Dolçe fortuna*) in
Pad1115 (PadB) show no signs of Italian notation, although that is probably the earliest source of his music
and contains other pieces in pure Italian notation. My case for the motets is genre-specific, though it seems to
apply also to the Gloria no. 3 in PMFC 24.
[29] See Bent, *Q15*, i. 148–49.

contratenor, called *tenores* in the rubric) by its own repetition and in an unusual (3:1) diminution because the perfect modus diminishes to perfect tempus. The two halves of the motet are rhythmically identical in all parts, as are Ciconia's two other ascribed isorhythmic motets, *Albane misse celitus* and *Ut te per omnes*, and the two anonymous incomplete motets nos. 20 and 21, *Padu[a] . . . ex panis* and *O proles Yspanie*. Ironically, these motets with exact replication are more truly isorhythmic than the more complex structures which have enjoyed a blanket application of the term to motets with tenor diminution or mensural transformation and which ranked higher on the status spectrum of 'the isorhythmic motet'. *Albane* starts with the two cantus parts before the lower parts enter, but this introduction is included in the isorhythmic scheme, unlike no. 20 (*Padu[a]*), whose introduction (presumably for two upper parts of which one survives) stands outside the isorhythmic structure.

Texts

Some motets have a single Latin text for both upper parts, some two; and one, *O virum omnimoda veneracione/O lux et decus tranensium/O beate Nicholae* (no. 15), also has a third text, a differently texted tenor (see Table 28.1 above). The texts were edited and translated for PMFC 24 by M. J. Connolly. The verse texts have now been authoritatively evaluated and annotated in a magisterial study by Leofranc Holford-Strevens, who writes: 'Ciconia presents himself in his treatise *Nova Musica* as a musical humanist anxious to rescue the true ancient theory of music from the corruption of the *Guidonistae*. Nevertheless his Latinity is far from humanistic, and reaches a pinnacle of pretentious incompetence in the dedication of *De proportionibus*.'[30]

The texts signed with Ciconia's name strongly suggest that they as well as the music are by Ciconia. All the texts are in rhythmic verse with three exceptions: the three prose texts of the unsigned *O virum* (no. 15); with three sources, this is his most widely distributed and possibly his earliest motet. Two texts, *Ut te* and *Padu[a] . . . ex panis* (nos. 19 and 20) 'aspire to be *metra*, poems in classical quantitative meter'.[31] All texts appear to be originally composed except the *opus dubium O proles Yspanie* (no. 21), in honour of St Anthony of Padua. This text by Julian of Speyer was later used by Du Fay for his motet *O proles Hispanie/O sidus Hispanie*; one of its sources is a fourteenth-century Franciscan breviary from Padua.[32] If this motet is by Ciconia, it would be his only use of a pre-existent text. Probably not by Ciconia, on grounds of their greater competence, are the three texts of *O virum omnimoda* (no. 15), not covered by Holford-Strevens, but which he rates as ornate prose rather than rhymed doggerel, and having 'a fluency both in language and versification that Ciconia lacks'. Also judged too competent to be by Ciconia are the texts of *O Petre Christi discipule* (no. 23) and *O beatum incendium* (no. 22), by 'the cleric at home in devotional Latin who contrafacted a verse hymn for Ciconia's virelai *Aler m'en veus*'.[33]

[30] Holford-Strevens, 'The Latin Poetry', 437–38.
[31] Ibid. 438.
[32] See PMFC 24, 208.
[33] Holford-Strevens, 'The Latin Poetry', 454, 453.

Chronology and Datings

Most of Ciconia's motets are dedicatory or occasional pieces referring to Padua or Venice. *O felix templum jubila* (no. 12) honours Stefano Carrara, illegitimate son of Francesco Carrara 'il Novello', administrator of the Paduan see from 1396. Clercx suggested that this motet was written to celebrate the dedication of an altar to St Stephen in Padua Cathedral by Stefano Carrara in 1400,[34] but several allusions in the text suggest that it must either celebrate or post-date his assumption of the bishopric on 10 April 1402. This would place the motet first in a sequence of three by Ciconia honouring successive bishops of Padua, perhaps for the installations of the next two Venetian bishops of Padua, Albano Michiel (8 March 1406: *Albane misse celitus*, no. 16) and Pietro Marcello (16 November 1409: *Petrum Marcello Venetum*, no. 18).[35] The incomplete and unascribed motets are also clearly Paduan, no. 21 *O proles Yspanie* in honour of St Anthony of Padua, and no. 20, *Padu[a] . . . ex panis*, for Andrea Carrara, nominated abbot of Santa Giustina in 1398, a post he held in the period 1402–4.

O Padua, sidus preclarum (no. 13) refers to Antenor, the mythical founder of the city. Absence of reference to Venice suggests that it precedes the 1405 conquest; on the other hand, the 'bright flowering garland' of stanza 1 might be the constellation of Venetian-dominated cities thereafter.[36] The motet for St Anthony, *O proles Yspanie* (no. 21), and the two for Francesco Zabarella, *Doctorum principem* and *Ut te per omnes* (nos. 17 and 19), presumably date from 1401–12 when Ciconia was in Padua.

The two texts of *Venecie, mundi splendor/Michael, qui Stena domus* (no. 14) honour Venice and Michele Steno, doge from 1400 to 1413. Some but not all motets for doges and bishops are overtly inaugural. But for Ciconia's known association with Padua, the most obvious dating would fall in the period of or immediately following the doge's election. Padua was conquered by Venice in 1405, and the motet can be more readily explained as an expression of Paduan acceptance of the new regime. More likely than Clercx's dating of 1407, based on the granting of privileges to the Cathedral in that year in recompense for confiscated Carrara goods, is the occasion of Padua's formal surrender to Venice on 3 January 1406, when Ciconia's patron Francesco Zabarella delivered an oration and presented the doge with the emblems of the Signoria before the doors of San Marco, in the name of the Comune of Padua. Venice responded officially on 30 January with the 'Golden Bull' acknowledging the surrender of Padua and promising to respect the privileges, customs and statutes of the city, the university and the wool trade.

Francesco Zabarella was archpriest of Padua from 1398 until his appointment as bishop of Florence in 1410.[37] He presented Ciconia to his first Paduan benefice on 11 July 1401, and Ciconia's close association with him is cemented by the survival of two

---

[34] Clercx, *Johannes Ciconia*.

[35] Holford-Strevens, 'The Latin Poetry', 451, notes: 'There is no excuse for *Marcello* instead of *Marcellum*, but whether the error be the scribe's or the poet's is impossible to determine.'

[36] Stoessel, 'Music and Moral Philosophy', 111–15, suggests a chronology for Ciconia's motets (table 1), with a date of 1401 or soon after for *O Padua*, based on an undoubtedly correct reading of the second text line, 'boece' instead of the meaningless 'bocce', referring not to Boethius but to the constellation of Boötes, permitting the association of this motet with the astronomical emblems of the Carraresi of Padua and their political circumstances in 1401, which he had previously discussed in 'Arms, a Saint', 32–34.

[37] See Hallmark, 'Zabarella'.

566 ITALIAN MOTETS

motets in his honour. No. 19, *Ut te per omnes celitus*, addressed to Zabarella's patron saint Francis, intercedes for him as a great teacher and Paduan lawyer, and prays also for the Franciscan order. *Doctorum principem* (no. 17) praises Zabarella directly as 'prince of teachers' and 'nourisher of the clergy', alluding to music. No reason remains for Clercx's datings of these pieces at 1390–97 and 1406–9 respectively, though as the outer limits of Zabarella's teaching career in Padua (1398–1410) the motets must also fall within Ciconia's nearly co-terminous Paduan career.

One possible exception to the general pattern of the genesis of the motets in Padua in the years 1401 to 1412 is *O virum omnimoda* (no. 15) honouring St Nicholas of Trani.[38] It had been assumed that 'Trani' was an error for the nearby city of Bari, and that the saint referred to was the more famous bishop whose remains were retrieved from Myra in the eleventh century and installed at Bari. Although rival claimants to the honour of housing St Nicholas brought about a certain degree of confusion in his legend, that of Nicholas of Trani does have separate features clearly identifiable in the text of this motet. Also known as Nicholas Pilgrim ('Nicholaus peregrinus' in the motet text), he was a pious and simple-minded Greek shepherd boy who crossed the Adriatic from Greece (by one account, on the back of a dolphin) and wandered throughout Apulia, collecting and distributing alms and fostering the Kyrie eleison, which he continuously intoned (translated as the 'Miserere nobis, Domine' obsessively repeated in the version of the motet in **BU2216**). He died in Trani in 1094 at the age of nineteen, from the combined results of his own asceticism and of the persecutions which he attracted. Miracles were reported, his Life was written, and he was canonised by Urban II in 1097. Accounts of his cult outside Trani are scarce, and it remains something of a mystery how Ciconia came to celebrate him. His feast day is given as 2 June, but a different date of 30 May north of the Alps suggests that the observance was more than local.

A possible occasion for the composition of Ciconia's motet was proposed as the 300th anniversary of the saint's death in 1394.[39] In the early 1390s, before his Paduan career a decade later, Ciconia was in the household of Philippe d'Alençon in Rome; a letter of Boniface IX dated 27 April 1391 gave him a dispensation for illegitimacy, opening the way for an expectative prebend in Liège.[40] Giuliano Di Bacco and John Nádas were able to show that the saint's anniversary coincided with the presence in Rome of curialist associates of d'Alençon, one of whom (Richardus de Sylvestris) was bishop of Trani from 1390 to 1393; they suggest that the election of the new bishop, Jacobus Cubellus, coinciding with the 1394 anniversary, could have occasioned the composition of the motet, which may therefore be older by about eight years than the earliest of the Paduan motets (datable 1402–9). This early dating has unexplored implications for the dissemination of a motet style hitherto associated with the Veneto.[41] But more recently, David Fallows in a study of Ciconia's earliest songs, has challenged this early dating. He sets out a careful argument for Ciconia's early works by a young man in his twenties in the 1390s experimenting with many styles from the existing repertory, including the madrigals and some of the *ballate* in the so-called Mancini codex (dated before 1410 by Nádas

[38] Jones, *Saint Nicholas of Myra*, 207–8, and *AASS, Junii, tomus primus* (Paris and Rome, 1867), 229–54.
[39] In PMFC 24, p. xiii this anniversary is suggested but offered no answer to the puzzle of how Ciconia came to write a motet for him.
[40] Di Bacco and Nádas, 'Verso uno "stile internazionale"', 31–32.
[41] Among those who accepted this date is Buff, 'Ciconia's Equal-cantus Motets', 54–68.

THE MOTETS OF JOHANNES CICONIA   567

and Ziino), and *Sus un fontayne*, before finding 'his own highly distinctive style' in the next decade. Even allowing for the dangers of cross-genre stylistic comparisons, Fallows judges that *O virum* does not fit this pattern and is inclined to place it after 1400, finding little support for placing it so long before the other motets dating from 1402, and I tend to agree. So we are back to lacking an occasion, but this is a much more comfortable conclusion stylistically.[42]

Pad1106 and *Opera dubia*

The only two motets listed here that are not in **Q15** are the incomplete and anonymous *Padu*[a] ... *ex panis* and *O proles Yspanie* (nos. 20 and 21). Both are unique to **Pad1106** (part of PadD) and to different degrees rubbed, faded, and difficult to read. No. 21, *O proles Yspanie*/Tenor *O proles nobile depositum*, in honour of St Anthony of Padua, uses (as mentioned earlier) a pre-existing Franciscan text.[43] No. 20, *Padu*[a] ... *ex panis*, honours Andrea Carrara, brother of Stefano, as Abbot of Santa Giustina in Padua, a post to which he was nominated in 1398 but held effectively from 1402 until his death in 1404, a year before the fall of the Carrara at the Venetian conquest. Since there is no evidence of Ciconia's presence in Padua before 1401, a date *c.* 1402 seems more likely, if this could indeed be by him, albeit not the only composer in Padua at the time. His first two Paduan motets would then be for these two clerical Carrara brothers. Although musical style and the Paduan context remain strongly suggestive of Ciconia's authorship, and recent work has accepted them more confidently than I did for PMFC 24, I will review some arguments for and against.

Both motets have two sections which are fully isorhythmic in both surviving parts. *Padu*[a] ... *ex panis* in addition has a sixteen-breve melismatic (but not self-contained) cantus introduction which stands outside that scheme, unlike any motet ascribed to Ciconia; the two-voice twelve-breve introduction of Ciconia's *Albane* before the tenor and contratenor enter is included in the isorhythmic scheme of that motet.[44] Tenor coloration is found otherwise only in *Petrum Marcello*. The hockets are texted, whereas in Ciconia's ascribed motets, and in *O proles*, they are untexted.[45]

Range, tonality, and some melodic features of *Padu*[a] ... *ex panis* are shared with the other Carrara motet, probably of the same year, *O felix templum*; the sequences, hocketed cross-rhythms and isorhythmic replication are typical. The text is very corrupt and/or incompetent; Holford-Strevens, 'The Latin Poetry', diagnoses it as an unsuccessful attempt at elegiac couplets; otherwise only the texts of *Ut te per omnes* are in a classical metre, iambic dimeters. This may provide a Ciconian link. The texts of *O virum*, no. 15 are in prose of a higher quality, as noted earlier.

Both nos. 20 and 21, *Padu*[a] ... *ex panis* and *O proles*, have links to Padua during Ciconia's lifetime and share features of his style. They were included in PMFC 24 as *opera*

---

[42] Fallows, 'Ciconia's Earliest Songs'.
[43] See PMFC 24, Commentary, p. 208.
[44] On *introitus* as a term for self-contained introductions, see Ch. 1.
[45] The text is transcribed very incompletely in Plamenac, 'Paduan Fragment' and analysed more or less in this form by Holford-Strevens, 'The Latin Poetry'. Its plural tenor rubric ('tenorum', implying also a contratenor) has been discussed above.

568 ITALIAN MOTETS

dubia because of their topical links to Padua, their presence in the Padua fragments that include other pieces by Ciconia and were compiled there while he was present in that city, and because they seemed to share stylistic traits with the ascribed motets. In view of the now-uncovered precedents for features that are typical of the Italian motet rather than personal to Ciconia, it might seem riskier to ascribe these two motets to him on purely stylistic grounds; he may not have been the only composer in Padua who could have written topical motets.

At stake is my earlier designation of the surviving cantus parts of nos. 20 and 21, *Padu*[a] . . . *ex panis* and *O proles*, as cantus II parts; in both cases, the surviving voices appeared to be a cantus II and tenor, therefore probably on a recto. This raises awkward questions of format about the recto–verso status of the leaves of PadD preserved as **Pad1106**, of which the signed copyist is the Santa Giustina monk Rolandus de Casale. Both motets have a 6–8 final cadence, which occurs in all of Ciconia's motets between cantus II and tenor; they were presumed to lack their cantus I parts in equal or nearly equal range, which would have cadenced 10–12 with the tenor. However, Cuthbert has made the case on stylistic and codicological grounds that the surviving voices are in both cases cantus I parts with tenor. The stylistic argument is that echo imitation, when present, always starts in cantus I, and that these voices have no initial rests, as would be expected for a cantus II participant in echo imitation.[46] However, of the attributed Ciconia motets, only nos. 12 and 15 start with echo imitation, and in both those cases the tenor enters together with cantus I. In no. 20 (*Padu*[a] . . . *ex panis*), the tenor enters only after sixteen breves, so the introduction must have involved both upper parts, therefore not with echo imitation. Although the surviving voice opens with a brief similarity to that of *O felix templum*, its opening phrase is not followed by rests such as would be needed for a spaced opening echo imitation, and such an imitation cannot be made to fit in canon here.[47] In most of Ciconia's motets, the tenor enters at or near the beginning (though in *Ut te* the first tenor long is followed by five breve rests, as in no. 21, *O proles Yspanie*, where the opening tenor long is followed by eight breves rest). *Albane misse celitus* opens with a non-imitative duet, and the tenor enters after twelve breves, in a duet that is within the isorhythmic structure. I suggest that something similar could have happened in *Padu*[a] . . . *ex panis*. The absence of initial cantus rests and the unlikelihood of initial echo imitation, therefore, do not compel us to assume on stylistic grounds that it is a cantus I part. But for codicological evidence about the status of the surviving parts, we need to turn to the three leaves that constitute **Pad1106**.

Folio 1 was a pastedown at the front of the host volume.[48] The faded contents of f. 1ʳ are complemented by its reverse image on the board to which it was glued; it contains all five notated voices of the anonymous *O Maria virgo/O Maria maris stella*, namely the two cantus parts, tenor, contratenor and solus tenor, all on one page. This is of particular interest, as **Q15** preserves only the solus tenor as a supporting lower part.[49]

---

[46] Cuthbert, 'Trecento Fragments', 190–92.

[47] The older motet *Marce Marcum* (PMFC 13, no. 44) is unusual in that in the opening echo imitation cantus I does not have rests while cantus II echoes its opening.

[48] The foliation is that used by Plamenac, RISM B IV⁴, and Cuthbert's inventory of the Padua fragments, 'Trecento Fragments', 98–111.

[49] **Q15** and **MuEm** do not give the tenor and contratenor parts, only the solus tenor (so labelled in **Q15**, tenor in **MuEm**). PadD (**Pad1106**) gives all five parts. The tenor has two *color* statements without diminution; all parts have four isorythmic *taleae*. The tenor, possibly liturgical, has not yet been identified. A transcription

THE MOTETS OF JOHANNES CICONIA 569

On f. 1ᵛ are the badly rubbed and partly illegible cantus and tenor parts of *Padu*[*a*] . . . *ex panis* (no. 20). I designated this a cantus II part because it takes what would be the lower note (6–8) of two cantus parts for the standard final cadence, as in all the ascribed Ciconia motets. But cantus II would normally be on a recto. In this case it would have had to precede *O Maria virgo*, which is complete on one page. It often happened that the first recto of a new gathering presents a motet such as this that was short enough to be accommodated on a single page, so that f. 1ʳ is very likely an original recto.[50] If that was the case, the surviving voice of *Padu*[*a*] . . . *ex panis* would be on its verso, and hence probably cantus I, despite taking the lower note at the final cadence. Since the cantus parts were almost certainly equal in range or very nearly so, and the opening here must have been a duet for the cantus voices before the tenor entry, that does not help to determine its status.

The tenor is labelled 'Tenor *pastor bonus*'. If this were the incipit of a cantus part, one would expect it to denote the incipit of cantus I. But the incipit of the surviving cantus I part is not *Pastor bonus*. It is more likely to be an epithet for the dedicatee, as was apparently the case for Francesco Zabarella in the tenor label of *Doctorum principem/ Melodia suavissima*, as 'Tenor *Vir mitis*'. This would also explain its nominative case. If *Pastor bonus* was the incipit of a missing cantus part, one might expect a vocative form of address to the dedicatee. The plural *tenorum* in the tenor rubric suggests that there was a contratenor. Thus if this was a verso, it would have contained cantus I and the tenor, leaving cantus II and the contratenor for the missing recto, a more normal arrangement than placing the contratenor on the verso. It is not known if there were one or two texts but, if *Pastor bonus* was not a text incipit, either is possible. It is clear in this case either that the expected recto–verso status was reversed, or that cantus I did not take the upper note at the final cadence.

Folios 2–3 were pasted down at the rear of the volume. Cuthbert diagnosed that they formed an intact bifolio (but not a centre gathering); this would fix the recto and verso status of the two leaves.[51] All four pages contain some of the characteristic note shapes and *pontelli* of Italian trecento notation, which are not found on f. 1.

Folio 2: the recto and verso status of both sides of f. 2 is what would be expected from its contents. The recto contains the sole surviving voice part of *Principum nobilissime*, thought to be by Landini on grounds of the text words *me Franciscum peregre canentem*. Because of its initial rests, and because it takes the lower note at the final cadence (6–8), this appears to be a cantus II part, lacking the cantus I and tenor on the missing facing verso.

---

from **Pad1106** is in PMFC 12, no. 41, p. 147; this version has an unsatisfactory and non-coincident ending; bar 82 of cantus I should be omitted. Cox, 'The Motets of Q15', ii. 323–29 follows **Q15** (no. 227, R233ᵛ–234, A262ᵛ–263), which completes the isorhythmic repeat with (texted) repeated notes on *c* for bars 82–85, thus ensuring a convincing cadential arrival, albeit an unusual rhythmic extension. **Q15**, however, inverts the two penultimate notes of cantus II as *e d*; the *d e* of **Pad1106** makes a more normal cadence for an Italian motet. **MuEm**, no. 97, ff. 56ᵛ–57 rhythmically adapts the ending in order to ensure an appropriate cadence. See Ch. 1 and Ex. 1.3 for the anomalous ending(s) of this motet.

[50] Examples of one-page compositions on a recto include Dunstaple's canonic Gloria in **Tallinn** (part of RC), Ex. 25.4, and Salinis, *Ihesu salvator* in **Ox213**.

[51] Cuthbert notes that the distinctive hair spotting pattern on staff 6 of the folio containing *Hic est precursor* continues onto staff 6 of the folio containing *Laudibus dignis*, showing that the folios form a bifolio, resolving the caution he expressed earlier about their status (Cuthbert, 'Trecento Fragments', 190 n. 132).

570   ITALIAN MOTETS

Folio 2ᵛ has a cantus part and tenor of *Hic est vere martir*, with the upper note at the final cadence (10–12), suggesting cantus I. Rather than a two-part piece as published in PMFC 12, this is surely an incomplete motet lacking cantus II on the missing facing recto, very much in the Italian tradition. There are no particular reasons to attribute it to Ciconia.[52] Thus the recto and verso status of both sides of f. 2 is as expected. The problems arise with f. 3. In what follows, I accept Cuthbert's judgement, but I would be happier if it could be shown that the join had resulted from a modern restoration, enabling the status of the sides of f. 3 to be reversed.

Folio 3ʳ, one of the pages scribally signed by 'Frater Rolandus monachus', contains the cantus part *Laudibus dignis merito* tentatively attributed to Jacopo da Bologna on grounds of the Visconti dedicatee acrostic: lines 1–11 of its sixteen lines make the acrostic 'Luchinus dux'.[53] This has been designated a cantus I part because it takes the upper note at the final cadence (10–12), but if ff. 2–3 are indeed a bifolio (though not a centre gathering), it has to be on a recto and must probably, and with some reluctance, be treated as a cantus II, with cantus I and the tenor on the missing facing verso.

Folio 3ᵛ contains *O proles Yspanie* (PMFC 24, no. 21). Here again, much of the musical content can be retrieved from the offset on the back board of the volume. Despite it taking the lower note at the final cadence (6–8), I equally reluctantly concede that this too may after all be a cantus I part. This would place *O proles Yspanie* on a verso, with the tenor beneath it, making the **Pad1106** motets inconsistent as to whether the tenor is placed below cantus I on the verso or cantus II on the recto. The tenor label is followed by the words *O proles nobile depositum*. These do not indicate a different text for the other cantus part,[54] for the words *nobile depositum* occur later in the surviving cantus part and are therefore not the incipit of a missing cantus part. The text *O proles Yspanie* is, as already noted, from a rhymed office for St Anthony of Padua; it would be the only text in a Ciconia motet with a known earlier derivation. It is likely to have been either a monotextual motet, or the second cantus may have inserted *nobile depositum* as a cue during a rest. If bitextual, cantus II may have used another known text, perhaps *O sidus Hispanie*, the text paired in Du Fay's motet with *O proles Yspanie*. That text, according to Alejandro Planchart, is an imitation of Julian of Speyer's work that was attributed to Simon de Montfort, so if this text was used by the earlier composer it would increase the likelihood of Du Fay having known it, and of using them as a pair.[55]

My earlier assumption that f. 3 was reversed (because on both sides the final cadence is contrary to expectation) would have to be abandoned if ff. 2–3 are indeed an intact bifolio, fixing the recto–verso status of f. 3 with a reversal of cantus I and II parts

---

[52] Another more recent discovery is the post-Ciconian motet *O Antoni expulsor demonum*, ⊙ Ex. 26.3, as reconstructed in Bent and Klugseder, *A Veneto Liber cantus*, 154–56. It is in triple time, with equal cantus parts, wide-spaced echo imitation, a contratenor that is contrapuntally problematic but integrated into the four-beat hocket limbs, so clearly part of a four-part conception. It is unusual in that the final cadence is reversed, cantus I taking the lower part of the 10/6–12/8 cadence; but see the preceding discussion of recto-verso status in PadD.

[53] Jacopo's complete and ascribed motet *Lux purpurata/Diligite justitiam* bears the acrostic 'Luchinus', followed by *vicecomes*, in its cantus I part. Both motets are in PMFC 13. On the correction of the acrostic to *vicecomes*, see Ch. 26 n. 26.

[54] As suggested in Cuthbert, 'Trecento Fragments', 191.

[55] Planchart, *Du Fay*, 409. See Ch. 27 for Salinis's use of older texts.

THE MOTETS OF JOHANNES CICONIA   571

between recto and verso. It goes against Ciconia's normal practice of giving cantus I the upper note at the final cadence. But cantus II seems to end on top here on f. 1ᵛ, for *Padu[a] . . . ex panis* (no. 20). All these factors, including the use of an existing text, slightly weaken the case for Ciconia's authorship of these two motets, even with the status of *opera dubia*.

O Petre Christi discipule

Two two-part Latin-texted pieces are presented in PMFC 24 as contrafacta, *O beatum incendium* and *O Petre Christi discipule* (nos. 22 and 23).[56] *O beatum incendium* is preserved in **Q15** with this contrafact Latin text. Its top part survives in the Padua fragments as a French-texted virelai *Aler m'en veus* (separately edited in PMFC 24 as no. 44). *O beatum incendium* retains *ouvert–clos* endings and was therefore not a motet proper. Both pieces share a texture of two equal low-cleffed voices on six-line staves without the need for a supporting tenor, which places them outside anything known from the Latin motet repertory, but they have little else in common. *O Petre* is a different matter. There is no evidence that it is a contrafactum other than its anomalous style and superficial kinship with the demonstrable contrafact *O beatum incendium*, and I withdraw the contrafact classification. Fallows, however, believes the two are a pair, and that *O Petre* can be divided in two halves to resemble a virelai, just like *Aler m'en veus*, whose contrafact status is corroborated by survival in both forms.[57] It likewise has a single sacred Latin text. In musical style *O Petre* is more like a madrigal, but in imperfect time, major prolation and without a change of mensuration for a ritornello. It lacks the telltale repeat indications that mark *O beatum incendium* as a contrafact, but even if these could have been obliterated by an arranger, none of its many cadences clearly stands out as an undisputed midpoint. The commentary to PMFC 24, no. 23 already casts doubt on its contrafact status, and in the years since that publication I came to agree with Robert Nosow that this must indeed be an original composition.[58] Unlike the motets nos. 12–14, 16 and 18 it lacks an authorial signature within the text, though it is ascribed in its only source, **Q15**, and is entirely consistent with Ciconia's musical style. The text is as follows, with translation by Leofranc Holford-Strevens, who judged the verbal text too proficient to be by Ciconia ('The Latin Poetry'):

Voices I, II	Translation
1 O Petre, Christi discipule,	O Peter, Christ's disciple,
prime pastor ecclesie,	shepherd of the first church [Rome: the Pope]
funde preces quotidie	pour forth prayers every day
pro Petro nostro presule.	for Peter our bishop.

[56] Due to an unfortunate error in the database that generated the indexes and tables, this title is in several places in Bent, *Q15*, misspelt as *O Petre, Christi discipuli*.

[57] Fallows, 'Ciconia's Earliest Songs', 120.

[58] Nosow, 'Florid and Equal-Discantus Motet', and Nosow, 'Equal-Discantus'. I classified it as a motet in Bent, *Q15*, before Buff, 'Ciconia's Equal-Cantus Motets' reached the same conclusion.

ITALIAN MOTETS

2 O princeps apostolice, O prince of the apostles [St Peter:
  turbe Cephas dominice, Cephas = Peter], rock of the Lord's multitude,
  pastorem nostrum dirige, guide our shepherd,
  quem omni malo protege. protect him from all ill.

3 Da sit in cunctis providus, Grant that he be foresighted in all things,
  corpus et mentem candidus, fair in body and mind,
  omni virtute splendidus, resplendent in all virtue,
  in bono semper fervidus ever eager in what is good.

4 O Christi ductor ovium, O leader of Christ's sheep,
  perempne presta gaudium; grant eternal joy;
  pastorem, clerum, populum save thy shepherd, clergy, and people
  salva per omne seculum. throughout all ages.

Various occasions and honorees for *O Petre* have been proposed. The text invokes 'Peter, Christ's disciple', on behalf of 'Peter our bishop (or prelate, 'presul'), so at least two Peters are involved. Disagreement arises as to which Peters are referred to. Clercx attempted to associate the second Peter with the Avignon Pope Benedict XIII, Pedro de Luna, from the records of whose chapel at the time of his election in 1394 and in the surrounding years Ciconia is absent; but the more recent references associating Ciconia with Rome and with Roman obedience, while removing the need to place him in Avignon, make this unlikely, and in any case Ciconia's biography has meanwhile been revised in a way that excludes Avignon. Zacara and Ciconia were present in Rome in the early 1390s, Ciconia perhaps until the death of his patron Philippe d'Alençon in 1397.[59] Then he may have spent some time at the Visconti court in Pavia, accounting for his Visconti pieces from that period before he is documented in Padua from 1401. Zacara had initially followed Gregory XII but switched to Pisan obedience in 1409.

In the commentary to PMFC 24 I presumed that it was 'votive to St Peter, and is probably in honour of Pietro Marcello, Bishop of Padua (1409–1428), hence composed between 1409 and Ciconia's death in 1412'.[60] Di Bacco and Nádas, followed by Nosow, then recognised that three Peters were involved, and that Filargo was addressed as protector of a bishop Peter. They accepted my suggestion that this was Pietro Marcello, bishop of Padua (for whom Ciconia's *Petrum Marcello* was written), and that the Peter of stanza 2 was Saint Peter (Cephas, rock).[61] I followed with the revised suggestion that, as Marcello was appointed in 1409 by a different pope, the third Peter was more likely to be Pietro Emiliani, appointed by Filargo to the bishopric of Vicenza soon after his election as pope in 1409: 'The text addresses Saint Peter, protector of Peter the new Pope,

---

[59] Di Bacco and Nádas, 'Papal Chapels', 50–58.
[60] PMFC 24, no. 23 and p. 209.
[61] Di Bacco and Nádas, 'Verso uno "stile internazionale"', 33 n. 63: 'Il testo si articola in tre invocazioni successive; a Pietro Filargo (prima stanza: perchè vegli su Pietro Marcello, protetto di Filargo, eletto nello stesso 1409 vescovo di Padova); la seconda a S. Pietro (seconda e terza stanza: "Cephas"—come Cristo chiama Pietro nel Vangelo—perchè protegga il nuovo papa "candidus" ovvero Pietro da Candia); la terza a Cristo "ductor omnium" perchè assicuri la prosperità alla cristianità nel suo complesso, nella sua organizzazione a tre livelli "pastorem, clerum, populum").'

who in turn watches over our Bishop Peter, that is, Filargo and Emiliani respectively.'[62] Holford-Strevens accepts the reading of Nádas and Di Bacco as addressing three Peters, and the identity of the third as Emiliani.

A revised 'three-Peter' reading addresses, first, not St Peter, but Pietro Filargo, the Conciliar Pisan Pope Alexander V, elected 1409, as 'Peter, Christ's disciple, shepherd of the first church' (1. 1–2), the first church being Rome, first in dignity, not chronology. He is requested to pray daily for Peter our bishop (Emiliani, appointed by Filargo: l. 3–4.) The second stanza addresses St Peter as prince of the apostles (a higher form of address to the saint than that used for Peter the pope in stanza 1), requesting guidance and protection for our shepherd ('our' bishop Emiliani). Stanza 3 may refer to him as 'our bishop', though 'candidus' could also refer punningly to Filargo's origin from Candia, i.e. Crete. Stanza 4 invokes St Peter to grant 'our shepherd, clergy and people' eternal life and salvation, and to look after the bishop and his flock.[63]

It could be asked why Ciconia, established in Padua, would have composed a motet for the bishop of Vicenza. If, as hinted by his Visconti-linked compositions, he was in Pavia in the late 1390s, he may well have encountered Filargo there, and possibly also Emiliani. There is no direct evidence to associate Ciconia with Filargo, but by 1409 his connections with Vicenza were well established through his close friend Giovanni Gasparo, canon and singer at Vicenza, and almost certainly thence with the polyphony-loving bishop Pietro Emiliani, promoted to that bishopric by Filargo in Pisa that year. This could have led to a commission for a composition in honour of Emiliani. Emiliani spent at least as much time in Padua as in Vicenza, and surrounded himself with singers; both he and Filargo were documented patrons of polyphonic music.

This three-Peter reading has been challenged by Jason Stoessel, who proposes a different interpretation. He reports a visit to Padua by Cardinal Pietro Filargo, then bishop of Milan, on 6 March 1406, which occasioned a fulsome oration by Francesco Zabarella, comparing Filargo to an angel and to the apostle Peter, pointing out that Filargo was also cardinal and papal nuncio in 1406, and a citizen of the Venetian republic. He notes parallels between Zabarella's speech and Ciconia's motet, and dates *O Petre* to that occasion. He reads this as a votive piece to St Peter in honour of Filargo, declaring that 'the motet text is concerned with not three Peters, but only two: Saint Peter and another Peter, a prelate of the church. No one else is named.'[64] Stoessel is right (in continuation) to point out that there is some ambiguity as to whether two or three Peters are meant, but ambiguous it remains, and both readings have merit. I am not sure why anyone in Padua would have referred to Filargo in 1406 as 'our prelate'; he was then cardinal-archbishop of Milan. But by drawing attention to this visit, Stoessel provides an opportunity for Ciconia to have come to Filargo's attention through his patron Zabarella, which could have paved the way for a musical tribute in 1409 when Filargo had become pope and his protégé Emiliani bishop of Vicenza. He also makes the interesting suggestion that the higher quality of this text noted by Holford-Strevens could mean that it was written by Zabarella. The 1406 occasion would provide a reason for him to collaborate with Ciconia on this tribute, whether in 1406 or 1409. A 'two-Peter' reading,

---

[62] Bent, 'Early Papal Motets', 24–26, revised here as Ch. 30.
[63] Holford-Strevens, 'The Latin Poetry', 451–53.
[64] Stoessel, 'Johannes Ciconia and his Italian Poets', 228–33. See Ch. 30 n. 66.

574 ITALIAN MOTETS

as originally proposed by me and revived in a different form by Stoessel, still has some traction. In that case, St Peter would be the addressee of all four stanzas, and the prelate and shepherd to be prayed for could be either Filargo or Emiliani. Holford-Strevens judges Emiliani to be more likely, in that case, but in favour of Filargo is the above-mentioned possible pun in stanza 3 on his native Candia (*candidus*).

I still incline to the 'three-Peter' reading, and favour a dating to 1409 rather than 1406, after the appointment of Filargo as pope and Emiliani as bishop of Vicenza. Either reading, but especially the three-Peter one, could also relate to Emiliani's will and the iconography of his funerary chapel in the Frari in Venice, where (over the portal) God the father blesses St Peter, who in turn stands above the Emiliani arms, and (over the tomb) St Peter with key and papal tiara surmounts Emiliani's effigy. Filargo is not directly represented, but Emiliani invoked him in his will of 1429, where Pope Alexander (Pietro Filargo) 'who made me a bishop' is the only non-family member for whom prayers are mandated.[65] Emiliani was uniquely aware of his three-stage Petrine lineage: St Peter the apostle, Pietro Filargo as pope, and himself, Pietro Emiliani. Thus, there is still room for interpretation with respect to the date and destination of *O Petre*; and the balance of evidence now points slightly away from Ciconia for the two 'Paduan' motets in **Pad1106**.

---

[65] Bent, 'The Emiliani Chapel in the Frari', and Girgensohn, 'Il testamento'.

29

Ciconia, Prosdocimus, and the Workings of Musical Grammar as Exemplified in *O felix templum* and *O Padua*

The understanding of musical practices within any given repertory, in all their particularity, depends primarily on readings of the musical works themselves in the written texts transmitted to us, however much those readings are enriched by the knowledge we have built up about performance practices and contexts. By 'readings', I mean the spectrum of understanding that reaches from textual criticism and diagnosis of error, through analytical recognition of *cadentie* or sense breaks and their appropriate inflections, to the rhetorical projection of unnotatable nuance in performance. Since we are no longer native speakers of old musical languages, our readings can be helped by recourse to whatever contemporary testimony seems helpful and relevant.[1] Elementary pedagogy reminds us, for example, that musical grammar around 1400 is fundamentally dyadic, not triadic, an orientation that has greater explanatory power than alternatives lacking contemporaneous anchorage. Readings that take this as their point of departure can in turn confirm, amplify, revise, refine, extend the elementary but vitally important guidance derived from counterpoint treatises, evidence to which the notated examples stand in symbiotic relationship. This is no more and no less a circular process than the acquisition and use of language, or indeed many other arts that combine practice with internalised theory, such as cooking or dancing, whose notations (where they exist) tend to be even less prescriptive than that of late medieval music. Just as the understanding of a verbal sentence depends on knowing (usually intuitively) the grammar in terms of which it was formulated, so musical sense can be communicated and understood in terms of its own background grammar, rather than of the intuitions of a modern listener which have been developed through later music. All musical texts are incomplete or underprescriptive by some standards; for old music we lack not only the irrecoverable life-blood of performance conventions affecting unknowable things like vocal timbre, use of dynamic change and tempo, but also some partly knowable things like pitch and rhythm. Further aspects of performance practice that are totally lost to us are the rhetorical nuances by which performers communicate the sense and direction of the music as

---

Originally published as 'Ciconia, Prosdocimus, and the Workings of Musical Grammar as Exemplified in *O felix templum* and *O Padua*', in Vendrix (ed.), *Johannes Ciconia* (2003). I am grateful to Bonnie Blackburn, Jan Herlinger, Leofranc Holford-Strevens, Pedro Memelsdorff and Theodor Dumitrescu for helpful comments and corrections to that earlier publication. This revised version is published with permission from the Centre d'études supérieures de la Renaissance, Tours, together with the music examples beautifully set by Vincent Besson.

[1] For the dyadic basis of counterpoint see Bent, 'The Grammar of Early Music'; for *cadentia* see Ch. 1.

The Motet in the Late Middle Ages. Margaret Bent, Oxford University Press. © Oxford University Press 2023. DOI: 10.1093/so/9780190063771.003.0030

they understand it, its articulations, forward motion and resting points. This involves more than simply following editorially supplied accidentals, let alone imposing later criteria of tension and resolution. The notated text of any music can be taken literally, at face value, as a basis only for certain kinds of analysis-on-paper, and then with many limitations.[2] Contemporary theorists, moreover, are incomplete witnesses; they are silent about many of the things we most want to know, either because these were so obvious that they did not need saying, or because they were not the concern of a particular treatise, where they might be hinted at, if at all, only in tantalising asides. Absence of mention by a theorist cannot be taken to prove that something was not the case.

In seeking to understand our musical texts, allowance must also be made for individual usage and local dialects. For most purposes, theoretical help brings us little closer to specific repertories than to state the generalised rules of counterpoint, whose lowest common denominators remained fairly constant over some time, with only gradual change, as a basis both for composition and for the construal of notation by performers—the analytical activity that guided their performance choices—in turn communicating this understanding to listeners.

In musical styles involving highly disciplined part-writing, whether by Bach or Ciconia, criteria for judging dissonance are context-dependent and not necessarily equated with local dissonance, or with the actual sonority at any one moment. Such dissonant events may exist only at surface level, needing to be construed against their presumed harmonic or grammatical background, from which the surface sonorities may be displaced or ornamented. For pedagogical purposes, which are the foundation of trained intuition, progressions can be reduced to their essentials. In thus reducing a Bach chorale harmonisation, dissonant notes as heard will be eliminated in favour of the consonances to which they relate as appoggiaturas or passing notes. The structure is parsed back to a skeleton that uses legitimate progressions where possible, avoiding solecisms such as parallel fifths, just as a verbal sentence is in the first instance construed in terms of legitimate grammatical norms or expectations. If it proves impossible to construe the sentence or the musical progression in such terms, we then have to judge whether the irregularity is an original stroke of precocity, stretching or advancing the musical language, or whether it is simply idiosyncratic, local, personal, anomalous, barbaric, or erroneous. The same procedure applies to older music, taking due account of different harmonic language. Any momentary dissonance needs to be judged by reference to its context, function, or lateral displacement. I see no problem in referring to appoggiaturas and passing notes, given that there is no contemporary terminology for these and other usages. The strict contrapuntal background cannot, by definition, contain dissonance. We should always be open to seeing such anomalies as possible surpassings of the norms, but may be forced to judge a reading as an error of transmission or an anomaly of composition. Many analyses of early music have not yet made such distinctions against any defined background. I have tried to do this for Machaut in a study of the Gloria

---

[2] See, for example, the important observations in Leach, 'Interpretation and Counterpoint'.

CICONIA, PROSDOCIMUS AND MUSICAL GRAMMAR   577

of the Mass (Ch. 11), reading the music against its background counterpoint and recognising layers that are superimposed grammatically, not necessarily chronologically. Here I propose to read Ciconia's motets against the background of contemporary Paduan theory, as stated in treatises and, crucially, extended by observation of surviving compositions.

In the case of Ciconia, we are in the fortunate position of having a theoretical point of reference that is not only close to him in time and place, but offers quite a good fit with his own music. Unfortunately, this is not his own treatise, *Nova musica*, a massively learned work presumably written some time after his first documented appearance in Padua in 1401. Later, in December 1411, he revised book III as the separate treatise *De proportionibus*, directing it to his singer-colleagues to save them from error, and dedicating it to the singer Giovanni Gasparo da Castelgomberto, described as Ciconia's *frater carissime*, a canon of Vicenza and *preclarus cantor*.[3] *Nova musica* is by far the most substantial of the flurry of treatises attributed to composers dating from around 1400; it is a speculative work, largely eschewing practical or elementary pedagogy. Even *De proportionibus* with its avowedly practical aim does not resolve the mysteries of different transmissions of the proportional and mensural signs in Ciconia's *Sus une' fontayne*.[4] *Nova musica* contains no discussion of hexachordal solmisation, nor does it discuss counterpoint in any way that bears on our present enquiry. It sheds little direct light on the contrapuntal craft of Ciconia's own compositions, but nevertheless gives some encouragement to the present view of how music was construed. I have invoked grammar as an analogy for the parsing and delivery of under-prescriptively notated music. I have developed this line of thought to show that many medieval theorists use the same range of models, invoking grammar, rhetoric and dialectic, in some cases going so far as to equate musical procedures with those of grammar or rhetoric.[5] For present purposes it suffices to note that Ciconia, in the most original part of his treatise, invokes Aristotelian 'accidents' for the orderly classification of 'songs' (*cantibus*) in 'declensions' (*declinationibus*), and notes that

> sicut grammatica de partibus nominum vel litterarum disputat, ita quoque de declinationibus accidentium cantuum musica tractat.

> just as grammar reasons out the parts of names or letters, so also music treats of the declensions of the accidents of songs.[6]

Practical testimony of the kind we seek, however, is forthcoming from another Paduan treatise written in the year of Ciconia's death, Prosdocimus's *Contrapunctus*.[7]

---

[3] Ciconia, *Nova musica*, ed. Ellsworth, 10.

[4] PMFC 24, no. 45, and Stone, 'A Singer at the Fountain'.

[5] Much of this work remains unpublished. It was set out in a series of public lectures for Royal Holloway, University of London, 2001–2, entitled '*Soni pereunt*: Sense and Nonsense in Early Music', and in lectures given in Montréal in 2010. Related published articles are Bent, 'The Grammar of Early Music', 'Sense and Rhetoric', 'Grammar and Rhetoric', 'Performative Rhetoric' and, especially, 'Reading, Memory'.

[6] Ciconia, *Nova musica*, 364–65.

[7] Prosdocimo, *Contrapunctus*.

578   ITALIAN MOTETS

Although there is no archival evidence of direct contact between Ciconia and the professor of quadrivial arts at Padua University, Prosdocimus de Beldemandis, it is not often that we can draw on relevant theoretical testimony with such a close fit in time and place. Although his short counterpoint treatise is still less detailed than we might have hoped, it does provide both a clear starting-point for analysis informed by contemporary theory, and also some striking specific observations. It is dated from Montagnana near Padua in 1412, the year of Ciconia's death, and the year following the dated *explicit* of Ciconia's revision of *De proportionibus*. Prosdocimus's treatise also exists in a revised form, dating from 1425–28, the last three years of his life, in which he amplifies some points and attacks Marchetto's use of the natural or 'cross' sign and his division of the whole tone into five equal parts.[8] Marchetto is dismissed as a mere *practicus*; one wonders what Prosdocimus thought of Ciconia's treatise, which long antedated Prosdocimus's sharpest criticisms of Marchetto. Is his silence significant? Paradoxically, Prosdocimus's *Contrapunctus* is unabashedly practical, and is one of the most important treatments of counterpoint between those of Johannes de Muris and Johannes Tinctoris, some sixty years earlier and later respectively. Prosdocimus admits that there is controversy, 'rejecting some things customary among modern writers'; it is unlikely that this could be an attack on Ciconia's treatise, which does not deal with counterpoint.

What follows is a summary of Prosdocimus's counterpoint teaching, with glosses, indicating how certain passages might be understood. With minimal modifications, I adopt the excellent edition and translation by Jan Herlinger. First, Prosdocimus's definition of counterpoint, quoted in full:

Quia igitur cantum contra cantum sumere duobus modis inveniri potest, scilicet quando plures note contra unicam solam notam sumuntur et supra vel infra ipsam scribi vel cantari habent, et quando unica sola nota contra aliam unicam solam sumitur et supra vel infra ipsam scribi vel cantari habet, est sciendum quod contrapunctus potest sumi dupliciter, scilicet comuniter sive large et proprie sive stricte.

Contrapunctus largo modo sive comuniter sumptus est plurium notarum contra aliquam unicam solam notam in aliquo cantu positio, et de tali non intendo hic determinare, nec talis vere contrapunctus nominari habet;

Because the phrase 'melody against melody' can be construed in two ways—when many notes are employed against a single note and are to be written or sung above or below it, and when a single note is employed against another single note and is to be written or sung above or below it—counterpoint can also be construed in two ways, in the ordinary or loose sense and in the proper or strict sense.

Counterpoint construed in the ordinary or loose sense is the placing of many notes against one single note in a melody, and this sort I do not intend to treat here; nor is this sort truly to be called counterpoint.

---

[8] Ibid., 54–57, 86–95.

contrapunctus vero proprie sive stricte sumptus est unius solius note contra aliquam aliam unicam solam notam in aliquo cantu positio, et de tali hic bene intendo determinare, cum hic vere contra-punctus nominari habeat, eo quod in ipso est vera contrapositio, quia scilicet contrapositio note contra notam, que contrapositio vere est interpretatio istius termini contra-punctus, cum contrapunctus dicatur quasi contrapositio note scilicet contra notam, quando scilicet nota supra vel infra notam scribi vel cantari habet, et est huiusmodi contrapunctus proprie sumptus alterius comuniter sumpti fundamentum, eo quod habita noticia huius, statim haberi potest noticia alterius, saltim apud usitatos circa cantum fractibilem.	Counterpoint construed in the proper or strict sense is the placing of one single note against another single note in a *cantus*, and this sort I do intend to treat here, since it is truly to be called counterpoint, because in it there is a true counterplacement of note against note. This counterplacement is the true meaning of the term counterpoint, which is defined as the counterplacement of note against note—one note to be written or sung above or below the other note. Counterpoint construed in the proper sense is the foundation of the other kind, construed in the ordinary sense, because by understanding the one, the experienced can straightway understand the other, the practice of florid composition (or song: *cantus*).[9]

This could not be clearer. Strict counterpoint is a two-part procedure which places single note against single note, point against point. It is the basis for counterpoint 'in the ordinary or loose sense', free counterpoint in which more than one note is set against another, and in turn for composed, contrapuntally based polyphonic music, of which those experienced in counterpoint (*apud usitatos*) are thereby vouchsafed immediate understanding. I suggest that this implies habits of analytical listening and construing, whether conscious or internalised. Not surprisingly, this process is implied in a number of fourteenth-century treatises, of which a few samples follow. The fourteenth-century Abbot Engelbert of Admont recognises the principle of analysis or construal for chant: 'Just as in the other senses the delight in what is perceived proceeds from perception and perception from observing distinctions, so in the hearing of song there will be no pleasure unless the song is clearly perceived, nor can it be clearly perceived unless correctly parsed (*distinguatur*).'[10] Arnulf of St Ghislain, writing around 1400, makes several references to the kind of musical understanding communicated by performers to listeners, perhaps most vividly thus: 'Who will not marvel to see with what expertise in performance some musical relationship, dissonant at first hearing, sweetens by means of their skilful performance and is brought back to the pleasantness of consonance?'[11] Johannes Boen most interestingly discusses a harsh but logical dissonance at the beginning of *Se grace/Cum venerint*, the *Ite missa est* motet of the Mass of Tournai (Ex. 29.1a): 'the harshness is covered over with the surrounding sweetness'. Example 29.1b shows the triplum–motetus reduction: the motetus here

[9] Prosdocimo, *Contrapunctus*, 28–31.
[10] GS ii. 366. See Fuller, '*Delectabatur in hoc auris*', at 467 and n. 6.
[11] Page, 'A Treatise on Musicians', 16, 20.

usurps the tenor's contrapuntal function. Example 29.1c reduces motetus and tenor to their essential progressions. The disturbing sonority remarked by Boen arises from superimposition of these two pairs of voices, and from appoggiaturas between them. He allows for auditory expectation, describing how imperfect consonances attract and allure the ear towards their resolution in perfect intervals.[12]

Ex. 29.1 Johannes Boen, *Musica*, example from *Se grace/Cum venerint*, Mass of Tournai: (a) transcription of the opening; (b) triplum–motetus reduction; (c) motetus–tenor reduction

Prosdocimus undertakes to deal with counterpoint only in the proper or strict sense, the placing of a single note against another single note of an [existing] melody—*in aliquo cantu*. Thus, while the existence of a cantus prius factus is, as usual, acknowledged, the technique of counterpoint itself stresses the succession of dyads. Only indirectly does counterpoint result in placing melody against melody; the melody resulting from the contrapuntal operation is secondary to the principles governing the succession of dyads. Counterpoint in its proper or strict sense is not concerned with multiple-part writing, nor does it include *cantus fractibilis*, florid writing with several notes set against a single note. Like the grammatical base of a verbal utterance before it has been

---

[12] *Johannes Boens Musica*, 158–59, discussed by Fuller, '*Delectabatur in hoc auris*', 475–76. I disagree with Fuller's c♯ in motetus, b. 1, and with PFMC 1, p. 129, where Schrade suppresses the tenor c♯. The manuscript accidentals are unambiguous: see the facsimile (f. 33ᵛ) in *La Messe de Tournai*, but those editors also introduce c♯ in the motetus (p. 104). See also Fuller, 'Contrapunctus Theory', 144–47. **Ivrea**, f. 21ᵛ has b♭ at the beginning of the motetus, apparently applying to both bs, and c♯ in the tenor, thus corroborating the reading of **Tourn27**.

clothed in rhetoric, strict counterpoint is stylistically neutral. Note that he calls this clothing process not *cantus fractus* but *cantus fractibilis*, not already fractured, but with that potential.

Prosdocimus's precepts pertain both to vocal and written counterpoint; these he distinguishes as two distinct types, treating neither type as a consequence, or a different presentation or format, of the other. He affirms the practical mastery of plainsong as the basis and prerequisite of counterpoint, and promises to confine himself to essentials. He defines intervals as major and minor, expressed in hexachord syllables, and using what he calls the 'modern names'—generic numerical designations such as fifth and second, rather than the older size-specific Greek names (ditone, diapente, etc.). He feels the need to define these: 'the discrete quantity of tones and semitones consists of the number by which that interval is named, less one', so that the second, minus one, yields one, since a second consists of either a tone or a semitone. He acknowledges octave equivalence for purposes of interval discernment and treatment. The unison, fifth and octave are perfect consonances. The status of the octave is counted like the unison, and therefore given slight pre-eminence over the fifth; thirds and sixths are consonant but not perfectly so. The second, seventh, diminished fifth and diminished octave are discords, not to be used 'in counterpoint'. In other words, they are not to be used between any two parts that are at that time in a strictly note-against-note dyadic contrapuntal relationship with each other, or whose florid relationship must be reduced to such progressions. To determine how parts are related, one may need not only to strip away a grammatically inessential part, perhaps a contratenor, but also to reduce florid counterpoint to its underlying dyadic progressions.

I have referred several times to reduction. Far from being a modern term, it is used by Petrus dictus Palma Ociosa in his surprisingly early demonstration of florid counterpoint (1336), making explicit that for him the rhythmic elaboration of simple counterpoint was to be understood against just such a background as I find implicit in Prosdocimus. It is clear that for Petrus, too, surface dissonance even on strong beats of florid counterpoint (by appoggiaturas, etc.) was not counted as part of the background counterpoint:

Dicunt enim flores musicae mensurabilis, quando plures voces seu notulae, quod idem est, diversimode figuratae secundum uniuscuiusque qualitatem ad unam vocem seu notulam simplicem tantum quantitatem illarum vocum continentem iusta proportione reducuntur.[13]	They are called flowers of measurable music when several pitches or notes, which is the same thing, notated in various ways according to the quality of each, are reduced to a single pitch or note containing the full value of those notes in due proportion.

For purposes of counterpoint, the fourth is counted among the dissonances, but is 'less dissonant than the other dissonant intervals'; Prosdocimus mediates its anomalous

---

[13] Petrus dictus Palma Ociosa, *Compendium*, 516–17. Petrus's account of florid counterpoint is discussed insightfully in Leech-Wilkinson, 'Written and Improvised'.

582   ITALIAN MOTETS

position (as having acoustic perfection, but the status of a dissonance requiring resolution in counterpoint) by placing it between true consonances and dissonances. In the revised version of this passage, he adds the familiar observation that inexperienced singers easily confuse the fourth with the fifth (still today a common error), and goes on to distinguish the fourth from the 'exceedingly dissonant' tritone (augmented fourth). The augmented and diminished forms of the octave are truly discordant, he says, but he gives no parallel for the inflected unison or fifth.[14]

Prosdocimus then gives six rules for counterpoint (ch. 4):

1. Dissonances are excluded from counterpoint (here understood as the underlying dyadic relationship) but may occur fleetingly in florid writing, where they are excused because they are so quickly over that they are not perceived as dissonances—an interesting and rare early reference to duration in relation to dissonance treatment. However, he does not explain longer dissonances, which would have to be treated either as licences or as a consequence of the composing-out process based on the contrapuntal skeleton. Such sustained fourths sometimes occur between lower parts, as in the Gloria and Credo of Machaut's Mass and in some four-part motets by Ciconia, but in these cases it is always the contratenor which causes the fourth.

2. Counterpoint should begin and end only with a unison, fifth or octave; the listener ought to be charmed at the beginning and sent away at the end with sweet harmony, a perfect interval, a unison, fifth or octave.

3. No parallel perfect intervals are permitted in counterpoint. Here again, the prohibition is qualified, and I take it to apply to any two voices that are in contrapuntal relationship. For example, in the normal Italian motet cadence 10/6–12/8, there are parallel fifths between the upper parts, but those parts are not in contrapuntal relationship with each other, as defined here (Ch. 26). Each is related to the tenor, with which it cadences by contrary motion.

4. Counterpoint should not be made entirely of imperfectly consonant intervals (thirds and sixths) without inserting perfectly consonant intervals (unisons, fifths and octaves) between them; it would sound harsh, 'for no harmony whatever would be found in the counterpoint, and harmony seems to be the end of all music'. I understand this use of 'harmony' to be an aesthetic judgement, not a technical statement.[15]

5. He forbids *mi contra fa* (and vice versa) in perfectly concordant intervals, because the forbidden interval would make the perfectly consonant intervals minor or augmented. Although he does not say so directly, this prohibition also has

[14] For 'imperfect' perfect consonances, see Bent, 'On False Concords', where in ex. 3.5 (p. 101), the editorial g♯ in b. 45 is correct in version (a) but should be deleted in example (b), and the editorial b♭ in example (a) deleted.

[15] At least for this period, I see no need to posit any tradition other than counterpoint to explain combinations of notes. This point was eloquently made by Crocker, 'Discant, Counterpoint, and Harmony'. See also rule (2) above. Note that *armonia* here is a sonority of two notes, not a compositional technique or a means of regulating progressions. In a series of articles, Bonnie Blackburn has argued for the later use of *armonia* to refer to a codified tradition of harmony, as opposed to the counterpoint teaching which operates at this period. See Blackburn, 'On Compositional Process', 'Leonardo and Gaffurio', and 'The Dispute about Harmony'.

CICONIA, PROSDOCIMUS AND MUSICAL GRAMMAR   583

consequences for the approach to a perfect interval; solmisation expresses a linear contextual dimension as well as a simultaneous occurrence.[16]

6. Thirds and sixths are acceptable, whether of identical or different sizes in succession, but perfectly concordant intervals should be interspersed with them. Conversely, perfect intervals should be separated by, and hence approached by, imperfect consonances. The progression of a third to a fifth, a sixth to an octave, results in an 'extremely sweet way of singing', 'dulcissimus modus cantandi'. Indeed, Prosdocimus says, 'there are many such ways, which it would be difficult and perhaps impossible to write down, because they are infinite; a variety of compositional practices arises on account of them, but they are omitted here'.

Note that rule (4) was given on account of avoiding what sounds harsh, the related or complementary rule (6) on account of what is hard to write. Remember that he tells us that his precepts apply both to written and to vocal counterpoint. This is, I believe, where he sets the only (and significant) distinction between written and sung counterpoint. He surely intends here at least the cadential semitone approach, usually unmarked but necessarily sung, but he may well mean more than that. It is of course possible to signal cadential semitone inflections notationally, again, like punctuation in verbal text. But while it is necessary to inflect in performance ('delivery'), it is not always either necessary or possible to notate such inflections, in verbal or in musical texts. Just as punctuation was primarily a readerly rather than an authorial function in verbal text, fictive inflections have a parallel function in music, a means whereby performers communicate their understanding of sense breaks and articulations to the listener. The music may be set up in such a way that adept performers listening attentively to their colleagues can hear how the music should go, or is going in this particular performance, and respond accordingly.

Beyond the normal requirement for the major form of third or sixth, could he also be referring in rule (6) to unnotated practices such as those praised by Arnulf of St Ghislain? Women singers, deemed rather angelic than human, are said to divide 'tones into semitones with a sweet-sounding throat, and . . . semitones into indivisible microtones'.[17] Subtleties of rhetorical delivery and communication of sense defy notation both in verbal text and in music, and these may be among the kinds of infinite variety that Prosdocimus meant here, as they may continue to be implicit in the ongoing quotation of Isidore's famous 'nisi enim ab homine memoria teneantur soni pereunt, quia scribi non possunt'; the sounds themselves perish, even after the invention of musical notation to represent them.[18] Some aspects of both verbal and musical performance can never be notated.

Prosdocimus's tantalising nod at infinity leads on to his well-known final chapter, on *musica ficta*, defined as the feigning of syllables in places where they do not exist on the hand. The purpose of *musica ficta* is to colour consonances; it should be applied before the note whose syllable is to be changed in order to colour the consonance. In other words, once it has been decided which inflection is to be made, the sign should be

[16] Bent, *Counterpoint*, chs. 1 and 3.
[17] Page, 'A Treatise', 16, 20.
[18] The second clause of this statement is: 'sonus praeterfluit in praeteritum tempus imprimiturque memoriae' ('sound flows by as time passes and is imprinted on the memory').

written or imagined, and the hexachord changed, in time to accommodate the semitone cadential approach. He explains that, in rising intervals, ♭ ('round b') lessens the ascent and ♮ ('square b') augments it; in descent, ♭ augments the descent and ♮ diminishes it. Finally, he requires that octaves, fifths and their octave duplications should be made perfect if they would otherwise have been dissonant (augmented or diminished).

He advises choosing that form of the imperfect interval which, in the interests of *dulcior armonia*, is nearer to the intended destination. While he does not use the formulation *causa pulchritudinis*, this seems to be his way of describing approaches, whose melodic aspect sometimes seems to be equated with beauty, as opposed to the necessity of correct simultaneities. I increasingly believe that the frequent association of necessity with perfect simultaneities and beauty with melodic inflections might best be understood against a background of grammar and rhetoric respectively: the arts of writing or composing correctly (criteria of necessity) and of delivering or performing well (criteria of beauty).

He gives an example in order that that this may be better understood, the sole and notorious notated musical example in the treatise (Ex. 29.2).[19] He says neither that inflections must be notated, nor that the notation is complete, but perhaps his circumlocution implies that it is, here. Rather, he notates for purposes of demonstration what might otherwise not be notated, by drawing attention to the fact that the example is provided with signs. But note that he uses the square ♮ sign here, a sign usually reserved for treatises and not for practical notation in musical sources.

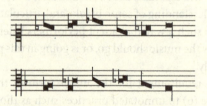

Ex. 29.2 Prosdocimus, *Contrapunctus*, example of *musica ficta*

After the example he goes further. He extends this rule of proximity to the antepenultimate, the sixth before the sixth immediately preceding the octave. He seems to justify the melodic augmented fourth in the tenor (without directly saying so) on the grounds that it makes the sixth *c♯–a*, the antepenultimate to the perfect interval that is the next dyad but one, adhere more closely to the penultimate sixth *d–b♭*, which tends to the perfect octave *a–a*. The rules are given not at all in melodic terms, but by the requirements of dyadic contrapuntal successions.

At the end of his revision of this treatise, Prosdocimus invokes the criterion of inflecting according to where the inflections sound better (not whether to use them at all).[20] I take 'applying the signs' to refer to implementing but not necessarily writing the inflections. If they sound better in the tenor, one should do that, if in the discant, that; if equal, give preference to the discant, lest it be necessary to apply one of the signs in parts

---

[19] Prosdocimo, *Contrapunctus*, 84–85. Note also the similar example in his monochord treatise, Prosdocimo, *Parvus tractatulus*, 106.

[20] Prosdocimo, *Contrapunctus*, 94–95.

CICONIA, PROSDOCIMUS AND MUSICAL GRAMMAR   585

other than the discant and tenor, i.e. to address the relationship between superimposed parts whose primary relationship is not with each other but with the tenor. At two points in the treatise he mentions the contratenor (also triplum and quadruplum), showing clearly that he has in mind the consequences of applying dyadic counterpoint teaching in a composed multi-voice context. But the context commends that this judgement of the ears should be applied only subject to respecting the more binding rules: taste can no more override those rules than it can in verbal grammar. There may not always be a choice; where there is, it may be a constrained choice, and Prosdocimus goes some way towards formulating bases for making such choices, thereby licensing us to do so. There are some non-negotiable locutions in this music, but there are also opportunities for alternative interpretations, both ones that could and ones that could not have been notated.

One aspect of Ciconia's style has been obfuscated in debates about the role of the tenor, and even indeed about whether there is or is not in late medieval composition a two-part core, a discant–tenor *Gerüstsatz*. Without completely denying it, Heinrich Besseler's theory of the *Harmonieträger* depends on subservience of the tenor to a contratenor, where the contratenor is lower.[21] But a contratenor does not necessarily become 'essential' by being lower than the tenor; many contratenors, including some of Besseler's examples, can be contrapuntally 'inessential' and still be lower than the primary harmonic support, a tenor which 'makes sense' with the upper parts without the contratenor.[22] The main criterion for an 'essential' contratenor is that it underpins otherwise unsupported fourths; it is 'inessential' if the tenor has no unsupported fourths with the upper parts.

The emphatic and characteristic final 10/6–12/8 cadences that conclude all Ciconia's motets establish a norm of finality within the genre of the Italian motet: the respective 6–8 and 10–12 *cadentie* of each upper part with the tenor are superimposed.[23] So when we hear the penultimate sound, what Sarah Fuller rightly calls the 'doubly imperfect' interval that arises from superimposing a sixth and a tenth above the tenor, a double resolution is called for, the sixth to the octave and the tenth to the twelfth. The parallel fifths between the cantus parts at the surface level in no way violate the theorists' proscription of parallel perfect intervals; the prohibition is presented in counterpoint treatises, or the prohibition is qualified as 'in counterpoint', that is, at the background level between parts that are in dyadic contrapuntal relationship, here, between each cantus part and the tenor. The parallels here are between the two cantus parts which are not so related, though on a musical level Ciconia calculated his imitations, hockets and interlockings in a very careful way, taking all three parts into account (see also below).

---

[21] Moll, *Counterpoint and Compositional Process, passim.* The reverse claim, that understanding of medieval music has been impeded by precisely the analytical stance that can be well grounded, albeit in a caricatured statement, is made in Leech-Wilkinson, 'Machaut's *Rose, lis*', 9. See the important classification of contratenor procedures in Memelsdorff, '*Lizadra donna:* . . . *Ars contratenoris*'; also Bent, 'Notes on the Contratenor'.

[22] These constraints are recognised by theorists who distinguished between tenor and *gravior vox*. In discussing the solus tenor, I have made allowance for multiple tenor functions: when it is carrying a plainsong, it may not also be functioning as the contrapuntal tenor. It is also possible for parts to be written in such a way (i.e. not completely self-contained, as in the canonic parts of a caccia or of an accompanied fugue) as to anticipate what will support it, recalling the architectural term 'toothing stone' (*pierre d'attente*). See Bent, *Counterpoint*, chs. 8, 9, and pp. 38–46.

[23] As in the cadences marked in Ex. 29.3. A section on *cadentia*, originally here, has been moved to Ch. 1.

586 ITALIAN MOTETS

Prosdocimus, like Boen, excludes thirds in final chords, and Ciconia's music offers no encouragement to think that he considered arrival on a third capable of defining closure, or that he would have considered this an acceptable way to end a piece or even a section. A third or sixth preceding a perfect interval at the level of the underlying counterpoint is always to be construed as a *penultima*. This sharper recognition of the status of the third in theory and practice invites a new evaluation of its arrival in the fifteenth century (in English music much earlier than elsewhere), sometimes even as a final sonority. It suggests that a different grammar is in play, just as the grammar governing contratenor-tenor relationships may differ from that governing the relationship between tenor and upper parts. The gradual establishment of the third as a legitimate point of rest is an example of gradual shifting of the rules as music evolves, just as, earlier, the fourth made a transition from the status of a perfect interval to that of a dissonance requiring resolution when used in counterpoint.[24] Fourths and fifths, similar in acoustic status, are thus differentiated in use. Something similar is true of thirds and sixths, which enjoy similar status as imperfect intervals: thirds gradually come to be admitted as final sonorities, as they can be combined with fifths and octaves; sixths cannot be so combined and are not so used. It is this differentiation in use that gradually leads to a distinction in contrapuntal status between thirds and sixths. In the motets of Ciconia, the status of thirds and sixths remains unquestionably imperfect, unquestionably expectant of resolution. In the last section of *Venecie mundi splendor*, the final cadence of the piece is anticipated at the juncture of the end of the texted section to the Amen, where *Ciconia* and *secula* (bb. 89–90) must be linked to *Amen* (see Ex. 29.3).[25]

This does not preclude a pause for sense or breath after bar 89 and at similar points between the imperfect interval and its resolution, but if a pause is taken, forward energy must be maintained, and any sense of closure on the imperfect interval avoided. In both cases a doubly imperfect interval (i.e. a simultaneous third and sixth above the tenor, superimposed dyads) resolves to a doubly perfect combination (octave and twelfth). The grammatical function is the same in each progression. The end is clearly an ending, bar 90 a transition, an arrival immediately redefined as a beginning, but one which prolongs the interval of arrival over an *f* pedal.

Even with the end of the verbal sense at bars 88–89, something has to be done to communicate that the held chord is not itself an ending, not resolved, but demanding resolution. The textual and musical sense do not coincide; the join is overlapped. The effect, in terms of rhetorical punctuation, must surely be that of a colon, maintaining energy even if there is a pause for breath, rather like the expectant 6/4 chord that launches a classical cadenza. I am here questioning not a choice of *ficta* articulation, but the musical sentence division, the construing of points of tension and resolution, which will determine that choice. As with parallel situations in speech, there is a range of literate possible ways to approach such a junction, and a wide range of illiterate or incorrect ways. Some recordings (misguidedly) make a polite or uncertain pause and then start the Amen as a new beginning. Others in different ways rightly

---

[24] See Prosdocimo, *Contrapunctus*, 40–41, for his definition of fourths as occupying a middle place between true consonances and dissonances, and his very interesting expansion of this point in the later revision of the treatise.

[25] A shorter version of this example is given in Bent, 'The Grammar of Early Music', 46–47, where it is misprinted with misaligned barlines.

Ex. 29.3 Ciconia, *Venecie mundi splendor*, bb. 85–end

connect bars 88–89 to what follows.[26] Whatever the sense of this held chord, it marks not closure, but rather expectancy, anticipation. The choice may be further conditioned by text sense and placement. In this case, the final vowel of *Ciconia* and *secula*

---

[26] In the former category are recordings by the Dufay Consort, Munich Capella Antiqua, and in the latter, the Huelgas Ensemble, Alta Capella, and Mala Punica. Mala Punica, interestingly, even repeats the entire motet as if it were the second limb of one of Ciconia's bipartite motets in which the second statement is in all voices a simple replication of the first.

588 ITALIAN MOTETS

could continue into *Amen*. One could breathe here before the Amen. One could creep into the Amen, conveying connection; or make a short breath-break before the Amen while maintaining energy, perhaps with an interrupted crescendo up to the hiatus. The one 'wrong' reading is to treat imperfection as though it were perfection, to treat anticipation as if it were closure, tension as resolution. The chord containing the imperfect interval should not sound like a point of arrival, but rather resolve onto the Amen, with or without a break.

The musical orator communicates expectations of closure or continuity by appropriate inflections (*musica ficta*) as well as by the infinite and often unnotatable means available to verbal orators—the equivalents of punctuation, dynamics, agogic accents, pauses, crescendos, variations of speed in delivery, all destined to communicate the sense, the continuities and discontinuities, of his literate reading of the composer's notated text. (He may of course also know the piece in performance, with or without the composer's authority.) The complementary role of the listener is to respond to performerly signals of closure or continuity, and to understand when those expectations are being met, delayed, or artfully side-stepped. A major third or sixth resolves outwards and/or upwards, with a semitone step to the ensuing perfect interval; if the semitone step is not, as usual, in the upper voice (*mi–fa*, a leading note), it will be in the lower (*fa–mi*). The interval is made major in order to achieve the nearest approach to a perfect interval; likewise, the listener expects the reader's voice to drop at the end of an English sentence, or to rise for a question or exclamation. A minor third or sixth, conversely, resolves inwards or downwards. This reflects Prosdocimus's spelling out of preferences: the semitone step in this case is more likely to be in the upper voice. Held chords, then, must be evaluated as to whether they have the status of arrival points or of anticipations, and if anticipations, which ones are directed, which ones are ambiguous, which are left hanging, perhaps for longer-term resolution, and which are deliberately softened or side-stepped.[27]

Prosdocimus's prescriptive procedure needs to be reversed for diagnostic purposes. As in a grammatical parsing, the florid composition is reduced to its underlying counterpoint, the note-against-note dyadic background against which an experienced ear construes the musical surface. The first step is to strip off any part that stands outside the main contrapuntal relationships, such as the contratenor of *O felix templum*, reserving it for separate consideration, as one would do with a subsidiary verbal clause. This contratenor is of dubious status and is not included here.[28] To remove it for analytical purposes in no way demeans its possible musical, stylistic and rhetorical contribution to the whole, though the unstable transmission of contratenor parts in general and this one in particular suggest that performance without them was common. Professional groups are sometimes reluctant to perform these pieces in anything less than the maximum number of surviving voices. As a result, we get to know the pieces in their thickest versions and come to like them that way, leaving the probably original ('reduced') versions sounding thin. A vicious circle of habituation is thus set up in our aural training.

---

[27] For this point, see also Ch. 11 above, on long held notes in the Machaut mass.
[28] On the status of this contratenor, see Fig. 28.1 and Bent, *Q15*, i. 145.

CICONIA, PROSDOCIMUS AND MUSICAL GRAMMAR 589

Such reductions are made in a way quite different from the Schenkerian reductions that some analysts have (inappropriately) applied to early music: the end product is defined in the treatises themselves, the procedure for achieving it inferred by us.[29] The reduction should normally retain adjacence of tenor notes: special cases of prolongation are discussed below. Reductions should avoid prejudging or imposing long-term tonal goals, the a priori assumption of which remains to be justified. Terms of approbation, such as 'coherence', need to be defined in relation to specific musical languages. Getting back to the essential counterpoint is one vital tool, if not the only one, for understanding the grammar and sense of the music as composed. The composer needs no more to have started with this contrapuntal skeleton than an articulate native speaker needs to construct a complex sentence by starting with a simple one. But the skeletal grammar can be extracted, as I believe both Prosdocimus and Petrus imply. A fledgling composer might use such a model as a chronologically prior stage, as allowed for by the pedagogy of two-part counterpoint; but for the experienced musician, conceptual pre-eminence does not necessarily entail temporal pre-eminence. An experienced speaker will have internalised the grammar and can use it correctly without consciously building up from, or even being aware of, its underlying grammatical structure. Likewise in music, an experienced composer could have conceived in his mind's ear a texture with a contratenor, one that never usurped the tenor function; and he could have controlled, by internalising the grammar of counterpoint, discant–tenor relationships that can be parsed back to that skeleton. Such reductions were not necessarily his procedural starting point, not even necessarily conscious; but they constituted a stage, like solmisation, easily elided by the experienced, and can indeed be counted as conceptually pre-eminent rather than chronologically prior. Analysis of this kind is not necessarily anachronistic, contrary to the claim that analysis is itself an anachronistic activity. They may not have called it that, but the singer has in effect to analyse in order to inflect appropriately. Ciconia would have been no more baffled than Petrus by the reduction of a composed piece, as of a Latin text, to its grammatical core, reversing the pedagogy of counterpoint.[30]

The superimposed duets formed by each equal upper part with the tenor are clear evidence, if any were needed, of composition conceived in three parts while being grammatically grounded in superimposed dyads. The intimate imitative, rhythmic and tonal relationships between the upper parts attest that they were conceived together, but each

[29] See Everist (ed.), *Models of Musical Analysis*, chs. 5 (Saul Novack) and 9 (David Stern). On the other hand, the historical grounding of Sarah Fuller's analytical work on this repertory has produced many valuable insights. She sets out her premises with admirable clarity in Fuller, 'On Sonority'. Her contrapunctus reductions, however, rather embody total sonorities (usually of three parts), than unpicking them to a two-part core. She admits some dissonance and parallels at the background level, which I think can usually be avoided by recognising lateral displacement and appoggiaturas. In 'Guillaume de Machaut: *De toutes flours*', she gives more consideration to dyadic pairings, but begins her analysis with linear motion, part by part, introducing counterpoint at a relatively late stage, whereas I view it as fundamental to the generation of those lines, not a consequence of them.

[30] Wegman, 'Das musikalische Hören', p. 452, n. 37, referring to Bent, 'The Grammar of Early Music': 'Similarly, it is unclear why the reader should accept her premise that analysis depends for its "validity" on the avoidance of anachronism, given that it is itself an anachronistic procedure to begin with.' I did not ask for 'avoidance of anachronism' but for the music to be approached on the basis of the appropriate musical grammar, the better to appreciate apparent deviations or innovations against that shared background, rather than an inappropriate one of, say, Riemannian tonal harmony (or even of Schenkerian *Ursatz*), which has led to so many misguided analyses.

590　ITALIAN MOTETS

of them relates perfectly and independently to the tenor. As stated above, the criteria for evaluating dissonance are the successions of intervals in the underlying counterpoint, not the actual sounding combinations at any one moment.

O felix templum

Two of Ciconia's motets have a widely spaced imitative introduction for the uppermost cantus part, accompanied by the tenor: *O virum omnimoda* and *O felix templum*. *O felix* has an unstably transmitted contratenor, which will here be excluded from consideration. Each introduction presents two separated imitative statements by the two top voices in turn; we will here consider *O felix templum*, whose first twenty-seven bars are given as Example 29.4.[31] A reduction is shown in Example 29.5.[32]

Sometimes there are alternative possibilities for the contrapuntal reduction (joined by angled lines in Ex. 29.4). These choices have consequences for how the sense of the piece is understood, and for how it is articulated by fictive inflections. Ambiguity arises when different rules compete for priority. Just as a literary text may lend itself to different readings and indeed to ambiguity, the composer may have contrived the piece in such a way that more than one understanding is possible, and still more ways of projecting those readings.

The two introductory statements begin at bars 1 and 10. Each is differently harmonised, yielding different background counterpoint. Excluded from that background counterpoint are (1) notes dissonant with the tenor and (2) choices that produce parallel perfect intervals. Some pre-performance analytical choices have to be made where there are legitimate alternatives as to what constitutes the background. To treat all the *cadentie* as points for inflection may seem to us to impede the flow too much, just as punctuation can be taken to excess; it may sometimes be decided to use less to improve the communication of a larger sense unit. I do not necessarily recommend taking every local opportunity for inflection, but I believe it is instructive to know where those opportunities are, so that a balanced choice can be made.

The cantus–tenor background reduction (Ex. 29.5) avoids parallel fifths in bars 3, 9, 12, 18. In bar 16, *a* may be preferred to *g* to avoid parallels. To parse the music in accordance with Prosdocimus's injunctions, I read the underlying counterpoint of *O felix templum*, bars 3, 18 and especially 12, and 50–51, not as a succession of coincident beats yielding a row of parallel fifths (as in Ex. 29.6 below), but rather have picked the underlying notes that make the best simple counterpoint with the tenor. The parallel fifths heard in the compositional surface between I and tenor on successive semibreve beats are prohibited 'in counterpoint', compelling the melody to be construed in some other way, namely, by not treating the parallels as belonging to the

---

[31] The boxed notes in I and II of Ex. 29.4 indicate notes in those parts that form the background counterpoint of those parts respectively with the tenor. They differ with the different harmonisations of the two statements of the introduction; it is not necessarily the note of simultaneous attack that carries the background progression, avoiding dissonance and parallel fifths. The caret joining two such notes indicates points where either of two notes could be interpreted as forming the background. Curved arrows show *cadentie*. Alternative readings are shown for 22–24, cadencing on 24.1 (main system) or 24.3 (above the staff).

[32] For bars 1–3 an alternative reading for I and tenor is given below the staff, and for 15–17 two further alternative versions for II are given above the staff.

Ex. 29.4 Ciconia, *O felix templum jubila*, bb. 1–27

592 ITALIAN MOTETS

Ex. 29.5 Ciconia, *O felix templum jubila*, contrapuntal reduction of bb. 1–27

background. The audibility of such surface parallels can be mitigated or neutralised by ornamentation. If there appear to be fifths on the surface between an upper part and the tenor, a first assumption would be to reconstrue them in such a way as to produce a grammatically correct result in the underlying counterpoint, irrespective of what happens on the surface. Parallels between the upper parts themselves, as often happens conspicuously at final cadences, are not 'in counterpoint' with each other, and are therefore not ungrammatical.

Commentary to Examples 29.4 and 29.5

Bar 2. If the cantus *f* were chosen for the reduction, essential counterpoint would require a tenor *b♭* against it (Ex. 29.5b). But in this case, the following unison cadence on *d* could not be easily accommodated without an augmented second in the tenor line. Such awkward melodic leaps are not excluded, and they clearly may be present in the background, if that is indeed what Prosdocimus's notorious examples are, here and the similar one in the monochord treatise. But Ciconia's elegant melodic clothing of that skeleton often avoids such angularity in the composed-out surface, if not in the tenor, which survives in the contrapuntal reduction. In what

I take to be his examples of strict or background counterpoint, Prosdocimus allows angular tenor progressions when they serve the higher priority of making correct cadential approaches. As noted above, he goes beyond what we would otherwise judge melodically acceptable in giving also to the antepenultimate 'closer adhesion' to the penultimate, even where this results in a melodic tritone. We today might choose to resolve such conflicts of priorities otherwise, perhaps by avoiding the melodic angularity that results from thus privileging the antepenultimate, preferring the reading represented by the version of the reduction at Example 29.5a, cantus g♮ with tenor b♮. In this case, the sounding of *f* against b♮ would not form part of the background counterpoint and can therefore simply be excused as a passing dissonance, not an illegal one; its normal melodic trajectory would not need to be adjusted by a sharp.

Assuming the last beat of bar 3 to be not *f* but *d* (avoiding parallel fifths from 3 to 4), the tenor *b* in bar 3 is flat because of the progression of third to fifth from bars 3–4 rather than because of the *f* sounding with it. There is no harm in perfecting such surface fifths where this can be done easily, even if they have no status in the background counterpoint.

Bars 4–5 and 13–14 are simply rhythmically animated prolongations of the same background sonority, both with simple repetition. What lies between the downbeats of bars 4 and 6, 13 and 15 could be regarded as ornamental emphasis or prolongation anticipating the *a–e* fifth, hence secondary to the underlying counterpoint and not governed by its rules of succession.

If the background of bars 6–7 were to be construed as a sixth proceeding to a fifth, with repeated *e* in I, only one part moves and the other repeats its note, resulting in very weak cadential status and no tenor g♯; in a strong *cadentia*, both parts move. The choice of *f* may be better for the first beat of bar 7, a succession of non-cadencing sixths, which in turn become candidates for inflection by Prosdocimus's criteria for 'closer adhesion' in antepenultimate approaches.

Bars 7–8, if treated as a third proceeding to a fifth, with *g–a* in I, invite a g♯ (major third); but this might seem over-punctuated, drawing too much attention to a fleeting local close. It also involves an angular augmented second if *f* is preferred to *e* in bar 7, avoiding repeating the *e* of bar 6. Although implicit in the counterpoint, we might therefore decide not to inflect this cadence at 7–8, also because of the strong movement towards the *d* cadence at bar 10. However, the melodic augmented second resulting from a g♯ reading in bar 7 would be rather like the augmented fourth in Prosdocimus's own treatise example (Ex. 29.2 above). If, however, *f* rather than *a* is read in I as the background for 8, avoiding the cadence, all awkwardness is avoided; it also makes a smooth cadential transition to 9, minor tenth to fifth.

In bars 15–16 *f* rather than *e* on the downbeat of 16 avoids interpreting the background progression with a repeated note *e*. Although not expressly mentioned, progressions in which one note remains stationary seem implicitly weaker.

In bars 16–17, note how the harmonisation of II differs from the parallel passage for I, bars 7–8. Tenor b♭ in the cadence 16–17 avoids the need for melodically angular sharps in II.

From this point on, we have to consider the effects of the two superimposed upper parts and their independent relationships with the tenor, an independence already set up in the different harmonisations of their identical material in the introduction. For the next stage, we consider passages where both upper parts are present. Each is taken as a counterpoint with the tenor; we see that each may imply a different underlying counterpoint, just as the two widely spaced imitations of the introduction were differently harmonised.

At bar 21, $c\sharp$ in II would resolve the overlapped cadence onto the first beat of 22, a third to a fifth between II and tenor; but this might be seen as an over-punctuation, given that the primary and sustained sonority at 22 is the imperfect interval in I demanding resolution. The two *cadentie* are superimposed. One of the parts (II) forms a perfect interval with the tenor and the other (I) an imperfect, as at bar 22, *g d b*. This of course sounds to our ears more like an arrival point than the 'doubly imperfect' penultimate of *Venecie* (Ex. 29.3 above), because here one of the intervals is a fifth and not a sixth. We should recognise the ambiguity of superimposed dyads where one interval is perfect and one imperfect, not treating such chords as wholly points of arrival.

Where is this sonority going (b. 22), and what are our options for interpreting it? In most performances, and indeed in PMFC 24, no $b\flat$ is suggested. But consider the underlying counterpoint. There are two possibilities. One is that there is a superior logic to $b\flat$ here, a minor tenth resolving to a perfect fifth with *fa–mi* in I. We may not like this at first, for no better reason than that we have always heard it performed with $b\natural$. What is the alternative? At bar 24, the top-part *a* could be treated as an auxiliary note, not a resolution, going on to define the approach to *c* on a weak beat, via $b\natural$, as a cadence, with $f\sharp$ in voice II. This involves making judgements about the relative strength of cadences; either interpretation can make sense.

Another area of choice is how early in a phrase an inflected cadential progression should be anticipated, which in turn raises the complementary question of how distantly a part may be considered to resolve an imperfect interval. This is surely another place where Prosdocimus's judgement of the ears comes into play. The listening singer may be encouraged or discouraged from anticipating a cadential sharp by what he hears in the other parts; this, as proposed above, may affect the decision.

In bars 50–51 (see Ex. 29.6), if we were to take the first sound of each group of triplets there would be consonance with the tenor, but, as in bar 11 and elsewhere, parallel fifths between the first beats. This again disqualifies them from being part of the underlying counterpoint; therefore they are to be construed as ornamenting notes other than the first one of each group. In this case, there is no resolution of *b–c* in I as there was at bar 24. The resolution could perhaps be treated (somewhat irregularly) as transferring to voice II, which rises to *c* at 60, but even this oblique resolution does not come soon enough to be persuasive, and the case for anticipating it with an expectant $b\natural$ at bar 55 seems weaker than the immediate resolution of a $b\flat$ (as performed by the Orlando Consort). At bar 22, $b\flat$ might therefore be preferred, by hindsight. At bar 54 II the last minim *c* is not part of a background progression, and therefore it needs no cadential inflection.

Ex. 29.6 *O felix templum jubila*, bb. 47–62

O Padua

Let us now look at an entire three-part piece: Ciconia's *O Padua*, given in full as Example 29.7. Here, there is no contratenor part to complicate matters. Some cadences are superimposed and some are not. Cadences between two of the three parts either coincide with, overlap with, or are not connected with, a cadence between two others. Inflections punctuate or articulate just such a range of cadences in the context of grammatical and rhetorical norms and expectations. Barring is by cadential arrival, marked between all three, or just two of the parts.[33] Momentary dissonance between the upper parts is often due to different lateral displacement of their essential counterpoint in relation to the tenor. Bars 9–10 are only mildly dissonant, but the essential notes do not

---

[33] For 12 II, alternative readings with sharp and natural are given, depending on how the resolution is construed. At 8 there should probably be no sharp, for the same reason that there should be no g♯ in 29–30 and 38.

Ex. 29.7 Ciconia, *O Padua*

Ex. 29.7 Continued

Ex. 29.7 Continued

Ex. 29.7 Continued

Ex. 29.8 Ciconia, *O Padua*, bb. 9–10, showing the contrapuntal reduction of each upper voice with the tenor

600   ITALIAN MOTETS

coincide: see Example 29.8. Prolongations (in addition to interludes where the tenor rests) occur at bars 4–7, 22, 44.

Several degrees of cadencing may be distinguished:

1. Cadences made by *both* upper parts with the tenor, either arriving onto or from (as penultimate) a breve or longer value in the tenor, are shown by a solid or dotted bar through the whole system, following the arrivals in bars 3 (*a*), 4 (*g*), 10 (*g*), 15 (*g*), 17 (*g*), 19 (*c*), 25 (*e*), 28 (*d*), 32 (*d*), 33 (*g*), 40 (*d*), 42 (*d*), 43 (*d*), 54 (*c*), 56 (*f*), 58 (*d*), 59 (*c*), 63 (*g*), 71 (*c*), 72 (*d*), and the end, 74 (*c*). The cadence on *d* in 38 could in principle be anticipated with inflected *g* and *c*, preparing the sound of the cadence at 40, but these inflections are discouraged by the unison imitation of *opum*, and impossible to implement on 38.1. The fleeting cadence at 42 could be inflected, but this is discouraged by surface angularity. To inflect the cadence on *d* at 72 is not only angular but arguably detracts from the preparation of the final cadence in 71. The irregular distribution of these *cadentie* is analytically suggestive.

2. *Cadentie* made by only *one* of the upper parts, from an imperfect to a perfect interval, always with the tenor, are shown by coincident bars through the affected parts only, at 24 (I); 34 (II), where *e♭* is rejected; 35 (I) *d*, with *b♭*; 36 (II) *a*, with *b♭*; 41 (I) *f*; 65 (II) *d*, 66 (I) *a*. Bars 65 and 66 can both have semitone resolutions in cantus I. Bars 34–35 show superimposed successive cadencing, with II and tenor resolving onto 34 and I and tenor onto 35. Similarly, II and tenor cadence onto 65, I and tenor onto 66.

3. Non-cadences: a succession of two perfect intervals. In rule (6), Prosdocimus says that perfect intervals should be separated and hence approached by imperfect consonances. Jacobus defines *cadentia* as the progression from an imperfect to a perfect interval, not the approach to a perfect from another perfect interval (see Ch. 1). Properly cadencing parts coincide with such non-cadences at 8 (I), 24 (II), 45 (I).

4. Delayed or avoided resolutions: 8 (II) *c*—possibly a long-term resolution to *d* in 10? If this is signalled by *c♯*, maintained in 9, it would be denied by the *c♮* of I in bar 9. In 12 (II) there is a choice: either *f♯* resolves melodically to the *g* of 13, albeit unsupported except by *c* in I, or *f♮* achieves delayed resolution in 14, with a semitone step in the resolution of the minor third to the fifth, interrupted by the tenor rest. At 45 (II) the resolution of *c♯* to *d* is implied but withheld: if the *c* is made ♯, it will imply *d*, and be heard to resolve at 48 (I) and 50 (II). Resolution is avoided at 21 (I): the *b* third with tenor is not resolved unless indirectly at 24 (II); 36 (I) is incomplete and unresolved. Some successions of perfect intervals are not *cadentie*, because they are not approached from an imperfect interval. Bars 12 and 21 are both preceded by a tenor rest, with no preparation. At 27, although I and II arrive together with the tenor *d*, the tenor is not approached by step from *e* but from *g*, and there is therefore no need to consider *g♯* and *c♯* in 26.

In all these cases, the performers' choice between a major and minor third prepares the listener to expect *how* they will resolve the cadence, and if the held note is itself a resolution, it will likewise have been prepared. They are informative about how Ciconia operates the basic grammar, and about the kinds of choices he passes on to us.

Conclusions

Counterpoint, analysis and *ficta* are all parts of the same process, just as grammar, parsing and punctuation are to verbal understanding. Counterpoint (in Prosdocimus's strict sense of note-against-note two-part combinations) underlies what we would call florid counterpoint, and it also underlies composition, which may of course be in multiple parts. Many analytical systems, including Schenker's, were initially driven by interpretative needs. The principal performance decisions that depend on analytical understanding of early music include *musica ficta*. If viewed merely as addition, *ficta* is a surface matter. But if viewed as an integral part of the engine of counterpoint, construing and parsing made audible, then it is not at all cosmetic. Prosdocimus's treatise is very concise, and he says he has not treated matters covered elsewhere, making it all the more striking that he devotes so much space to *ficta* at the level of background. *Ficta* articulates the performer's understanding of the musical sense as punctuation articulates grammatical structure and delivers it rhetorically. These analytical exercises therefore need to be undertaken before or during performance. Performers experienced in the style could have done this almost instantaneously. Today we are often exposed to 'white-note' performances without cadential inflection, another instance of circular mistraining of our aural understanding of the musical grammar.

The more under-prescriptive the notation, the greater an understanding it calls for on the part of interpreters. A reader of ancient Greek or Latin texts needs to understand sense and grammar in order to separate words that are written without breaks, as do readers of medieval texts with abbreviations and little punctuation, or of Semitic languages written without vowels. To enunciate and communicate anything beyond a very simple sentence in a language, one needs to understand its grammar; this understanding is communicated by pauses, emphasis, and by the rise and fall of the voice. The amount of written punctuation (or other markings) actually notated may vary. An experienced native speaker may need little help, while someone reading aloud a speech in a foreign language might mark it up heavily. This obvious point needs making for two reasons. First, the readings I have discussed here are not necessarily the heard surface simultaneities but go back to the underlying counterpoint, which can in some cases be construed in different ways, and needs to be invoked in defending alternative readings, just as grammar does for an ambiguously, wrongly, or under-punctuated sentence. The singer will communicate an understanding of the sense, of the structure, by pauses and *ficta*. Second, did composers intend a single version with respect to *ficta* choices, choices which singers were expected to second-guess, or did they envisage multiple solutions arising from different possible readings? I believe that the answer is a mixture, but not a random mixture. Some solutions are definitely right or possible grammatically, while others are wrong or impossible. Beyond that, there is some flexibility, some room for choice and judgement in rhetorical delivery. As with language, there is some but not infinite latitude for different interpretations

602   ITALIAN MOTETS

and inflections. In most musical situations, there is no choice but to perfect a written perfect consonance which is present in the underlying simple counterpoint. In other cases, as with reading verbal sentences aloud, there are different ways of articulating sense, bringing out ambiguities or even different meanings, but the ends of sentences or other major sense units will usually be clear and unambiguous, and inflected accordingly.

From all this one might perhaps begin to tease out a general grammar for a period and see what is specific to Ciconia in his use of that grammar. I tried to do this for music a century later by extrapolating, from Pietro Aaron's musical examples taken from real music, what were his underlying rules for the Josquin period.[34] Prosdocimus serves as a guide but not necessarily an arbiter. To bring him into dialogue with Ciconia suggests there is little or nothing they would have fundamentally disagreed about, which makes it all the more remarkable that neither mentions the other.

Such investigation may reveal significant differences between different repertories and composers in the management of the underlying grammar. Much more detailed investigation along these lines has the promise of producing analytical data that could give us more informative composer or repertory profiles than are yielded by surface features and descriptive analysis. For example, reductions of music roughly contemporary with Prosdocimus (Ciconia, early Du Fay) tend to yield backgrounds like those of Prosdocimus's examples, with more frequent insertion of perfect intervals, resulting in angularity when those intervals are correctly approached. Late fifteenth-century pieces usually reduce to less angular skeletons, more like those found in the counterpoint examples of Tinctoris, which have longer successions of imperfect intervals between cadential arrivals.[35] The difference was not in the way the reduction was made, but was inherent in the background interval successions themselves and in changing priorities in the basic teaching.

The result is certainly not to have solved all problems of *musica ficta*, inflection and caesura, nor necessarily to have offered firm prescriptions. I have suggested a basis from which to approach problems and their solutions, as well as setting *ficta* in a larger grammatical and rhetorical context. The hypothesis is grounded in the music and receives endorsement and encouragement from at least one authoritative contemporary theorist. Pre-performance analytical judgements may, indeed must, affect performances, while still leaving performers considerable freedom in how they communicate inherent musical sense, by strategies of grammar and rhetoric as well as by sonority.

[34] Bent, 'Accidentals, Counterpoint and Notation', reprinted in Bent, *Counterpoint*.
[35] Similar arguments about background counterpoint from Tinctoris are made in Bent, 'On False Concords'.

PART VII
MUSIC FOR POPES AND
THE COURTS OF BURGUNDY
AND CYPRUS

604 POPES, TRÉMOÏLLE AND CYPRUS

This final Part brings together revised versions of three previously published papers. Chapter 30 is a survey of music composed for popes from the early fourteenth to the mid-fifteenth century, updated from its earlier version on the strength of new insights and discoveries. Chapter 31 revises my earlier study of the **Trém** index with a number of new identifications and concordances. Chapter 32 updates my previous study of the Cyprus motets in **Turin**, from the first third of the fifteenth century, and considers recent suggestions about its compilation and provenance.

30
Early Papal Motets

The fourteenth and fifteenth centuries were perhaps the most protracted period of in-stability the papacy has ever suffered. For much of the fourteenth century the papal residence was not in Rome but at Avignon, with notably lavish cultural flowering, espe-cially under Clement VI (r. 1342–52). During the Great Schism from 1378 there were two popes, one in Avignon and one in Rome. Instead of ending the Schism, the election of a third pope at Pisa in 1409 ushered in a period of threefold division, since neither of the other popes was prepared to resign; but at least briefly it gave occasion for celebra-tion and optimism. This threefold Schism lasted until the election of Martin V in 1417 at the Council of Constance. He and his successors gradually re-established the papal seat in Rome, though not without continuing schismatic rumblings. Not until later in the fifteenth century could there begin the golden period of building and patronage that led to the sumptuous architecture, sculpture, painting, and manuscript collections that now constitute the Vatican galleries and library. The famous series of music books for the newly stabilised choir of the Sistine Chapel also started in the late fifteenth cen-tury but, as Alejandro Planchart pointed out, the emphasis in the preceding centuries was on a team of singing clerks who brought multiple general skills to the curia, rather than on a choir as such, let alone a team of composer-singers, an image fostered by a line of composers from Du Fay onwards.[1] In his essay, Planchart dealt with the standard repertory of the papal chapel in the period before and including Du Fay. Even then, oc-casional or ceremonial music written especially *for* popes or papal ceremonies seems to have been exceptional. Before Du Fay our knowledge of any such compositions is extremely sketchy and scattered. Moreover, very little time between about 1320 and 1420 was spent by any pope in Rome. The schismatic popes were of necessity itin-erant; travelling courts or communities are less likely to leave permanent monuments, whether architectural, artistic, or musical.

Various scholars have identified isolated polyphonic compositions between the early fourteenth century and the mid-fifteenth as being written for, or in honour of, popes. It is my purpose here to assemble this interesting and varied collection, which as a con-tinuing repertory or even genre has received little notice. It is on the texts of such pieces that we depend for a papal association, which they signal with varying degrees of ex-plicitness. In some cases, the text is reflected in aspects of the music, by choice of chant, or by some form of number or constructional symbolism; such evidence may support

---

An earlier version of this chapter was published under the same title: 'Early Papal Motets', in Richard Sherr (ed.), *Papal Music and Musicians in Medieval and Renaissance Rome* (Oxford, 1998), 5–43. It meets OUP's conditions for reuse without obtaining formal permission. It has been considerably updated, most signif-icantly to review possible circumstances for the composition of *Per grama* following suggestions by Anna Zayaruznaya, and to take account of her analysis of the recently found lower parts of *Petre clemens*. These in turn prompted revisions to parts of my earlier discussion and in some cases supersede them. The main discus-sion of *O Petre Christi discipule* is now in Ch. 28.

[1] Planchart, 'Music for the Papal Chapel', and now his monumental *Du Fay*.

606 POPES, TRÉMOÏLLE AND CYPRUS

a papal association but is never the primary evidence for it. The number of motets for popes surviving before Du Fay is rather small, and two of them are incomplete and unperformable. The longer list given here includes pieces other than motets—ballades, Gloria tropes, and pieces of anomalous form—that appear to be written specifically in honour of popes, named or unnamed. To this list could be added pieces that deal directly with the Schism, praying for or celebrating its end; for an interim list of all these pieces see the Appendix to this chapter.

I have not gone further to include other music written by papal chaplains and familiars, and music generally from papal circles, though some of it is mentioned in passing. Such a list would quickly become unmanageable, potentially comprising the known works of all composers who at some time in their careers appear to have served in any papal chapel or household. These composers include Philippe de Vitry,[2] Matheus de Sancto Johanne,[3] Magister Franciscus, Haucourt (= Altacuria), Johannes Symonis (= Hasprois), Pelisson (= Johannes de Bosco),[4] Antonio Zacara da Teramo,[5] Matteo da Perugia, Hubertus de Salinis,[6] Nicolaus Zacarie,[7] Guillaume le Grant (= Guillaume le Macherier),[8] Nicolas Grenon, Pierre Fontaine, Guillaume Modiator (= Malbecque), Barthélemy Poignare, Gautier Libert, Jean Sohier (= Fedé), Arnold de Lantins, Johannes Brassart, and Guillaume Du Fay.[9] Names of chaplains and singers attached to papal and cardinalate chapels have been splendidly augmented for the late fourteenth century by Giuliano Di Bacco and John Nádas, but with the striking exceptions of Ciconia and Zacara, few of the new names produced clearly identify composers of surviving works with chaplains listed for Popes Gregory XI, Urban VI, or Clement VII.[10] Matteo da Perugia is documented in the service of a prelate later elected pope (Pietro Filargo

---

[2] Vitry was a commensal chaplain to Clement VI (Tomasello, *Music and Ritual*, 26) and has been further tied, together with Petrarch, to cultural circles surrounding his court. See Coville, 'Philippe de Vitri'. Refinement of the context of Vitry's motet for Clement VI (*Petre clemens/Lugentium*) reinforces older claims linking him closely with papal circles in the 1340s. See Wathey, 'The Motets of Vitry', especially 121, and Tomasello, *Music and Ritual*.

[3] Matheus was a papal chaplain 1382–86. See, *inter alia*, Günther, 'Matheus de Sancto Johanne', *NG1*, xi. 820; Günther, 'Zur Biographie', 180–85; and Tomasello, *Music and Ritual*, 252–53. See also Wathey, 'The Peace of 1360–1369'. For a disambiguation with the 'Mayshuet' of **OH**, see Ch. 24, where I withdraw the identification of Mayshuet with Matteo de Sancto Johanne made in the earlier version of the present chapter.

[4] He served in the chapel of Clement VII (r. 1378–94).

[5] Zacara was a singer and papal secretary in the Italian chapels of Boniface IX (r. 1389–1404), Innocent VII (r. 1404–06), and Gregory XII (r. 1406–15); his presence in the chapel of Alexander V (r. 1409–10) is indirectly inferred, but he is documented as *magister capelle* to John XXIII (r. 1410–15). See Ziino, 'Magister Antonius dictus Zacharias'; Pirrotta, 'Zacarus Musicus'; Nádas, 'Further Notes'; and all contributions in Zimei (ed.), *Antonio Zacara*.

[6] Di Bacco and Nádas, 'Papal Chapels', summarised in Nosow, 'Florid and Equal-Discantus Motet', 87–92, and reported here, Ch. 26. His Gloria *Jubilacio* was copied into early layers of **Q15** in company with other music by Zacara and Salinis that may have formed part of the repertory of the papal chapels in Pisa and Bologna between 1409 and 1414.

[7] A papal singer in 1420–24 and 1434; it appears to be coincidental that the similarly named Antonio Zacara da Teramo was also a papal singer a generation earlier. Reaney's attempt to identify the two (*NG1*) must be set aside since the clarification of Antonio's biography by Ziino and Nádas; see above, n. 5.

[8] See Schuler, 'Zur Geschichte', 40, and Higgins, 'Music and Musicians'.

[9] For most of these names see Planchart, 'Music for the Papal Chapel', tables 3.1 and 3.2, also Planchart, 'Guillaume Du Fay's Benefices'; Planchart, 'The Early Career'; and now Planchart, *Du Fay*.

[10] Di Bacco and Nádas, 'Verso uno "stile internazionale"' and Di Bacco and Nádas, 'Papal Chapels'. Composers among these include Renzo da Pontecorvo (with Gregory XII), Nicolaus Ricci de Nucella Campli (with Boniface IX, Innocent VII, and Gregory XII), perhaps the 'Nucella' of **Stras**, Ugolino of Orvieto (with Gregory XII), Guido de Lange (with Gregory XI and Clement VII), composer of a number of songs in the Chantilly MS, and perhaps Richardus de Bosonvilla (with Clement VII), who might be the 'Richart' of **Apt** and **Stras**.

as Alexander V), but we lack evidence of his continuing service in the papal chapel. Hubertus de Salinis, on the other hand, is confirmed as a member of the papal chapel shortly after the election of the same pope, but no prior association is documented (see Ch. 27). Musicians could move freely between often rather short periods of papal employ and that of secular patrons, as the now well-documented case of Du Fay shows.[11] The church councils of Pisa, Constance and Basel have frequently been cited as opportunities for recruiting and exchanges both of personnel and repertory; this was undoubtedly the case, and in this respect the councils must have functioned like large present-day American meetings of professional and learned societies. The scattered remains of early papal pieces with ceremonial or political content reflect the itinerant condition of the chapel. Not until the papacy was securely re-established in Rome in the late fifteenth century, with adequate buildings and a stable establishment, can we point to a full and continuous series of associated polyphonic manuscripts.[12]

Most of the pre-Schism music gathered in this chapter survives only in a single source, and some of it is fragmentary. When there is no network of concordances to define circulation, it is hard to estimate what is lost, beyond the uncontested assumption that the highest polyphonic skills must always have been an elite preserve and their practitioners few in number. The number of pieces with papal associations increases in the late fourteenth and early fifteenth centuries, that is, from the latter part of the Avignon papacy and the period during and immediately after the Schism. Arguments of varying strength have been advanced to associate manuscripts and fragments with itinerant papal courts in the early fifteenth century, but any such associations have to be argued from the contents and composers represented, not from a known papal provenance for the source itself. If a general thesis emerges from this survey, it is that the number of individual cases in which such pieces are not or cannot be inaugural is sufficient to dislodge the common presumption of first resort that they are more likely than not to be inaugural. There was often little time between the election and coronation of a pope; customised compositions may have followed later.

Music for Avignon Popes before the Schism

After the death of Clement V on 20 April 1314 it took the cardinals over two years to elect the Dominican Jacques Duèse, which they did on 7 August 1316 in Lyon, where he was crowned in September as John XXII. This delay is among the events darkly chronicled, alongside the misfortunes of the French royal house, in the apocalyptic interpolations to the *Roman de Fauvel* in **Paris146** and the parallel chronicle and narrative *dits* in the same volume (see Chs. 3–6). The papal court had often been alienated from Rome and partly itinerant in the previous three centuries until established in Avignon by Clement in 1309, and retained there by John, beginning the period of so-called Babylonian captivity.

---

[11] For Du Fay's biography see Wright, 'Dufay at Cambrai'; Planchart, 'Guillaume Du Fay's Benefices'; 'The Early Career'; and *Du Fay*.

[12] Sherr, 'Music and the Renaissance Papacy'; pl. 147 shows the first list of singers for Eugene IV (1431) including Du Fay. For the state of the city of Rome and old St Peter's prior to the re-establishment of the papacy in Rome, see Grafton, 'The Ancient City Restored', and Reynolds, *Papal Patronage*.

Per grama protho paret: for John XXII?

Per grama protho paret had been considered the earliest papal motet, but questions have been raised, both in my original article and since, about its dating and its dedicatee. Motetus and tenor only are preserved in **McV**. The tenor, *Valde honorandus est beatus Johannes* (Blessed John is worthy to be honoured), is from a responsory for the feast of St John the Evangelist. The first line of the motetus announces an acrostic, to be resolved as *Petrus*: 'through the first letter [of each stanza] is revealed the name of the Romans' constancy, whereby the glory of the church now has lustre'.[13] The first two letters of the first stanza (PE) are required to give the name of Peter, hitherto assumed to refer to St Peter, the first pope, and the rock on which the Church is founded. The text goes on, apparently, to refer to the beloved disciple, i.e. John, and to make further unmistakable papal references ('he is raised up on high, worthy of papal dignity'). Taken together with the tenor for St John the Evangelist, the conclusion seemed inescapable that the motet must indeed be for John XXII, 1316–34; no other pope during this period had the Christian name John before election.

PEr grama protho paret	Through the first letter is revealed
onema[14] constancie	the name of the Romans' constancy,
romanorum quo claret	whereby the glory of the Church
iam decus ecclesie.	now has lustre.
Tellus ovans satorem	Let the cheering earth exalt
tollat sapiencie	the sower of wisdom,
catholicorum florem	the flower born of
genitum progenie.	Catholics' lineage.
Regi nato Maria	It pleased the King born of Mary
placuit sic mittere	thus to send,
largitione dya	by divine bounty,
radium phox supere.	the ray of heavenly light.
Vere manet electus	Truly he remains the elect,
non a kari nomine	not apart from the name of the dear one [i.e. John, the beloved Disciple],
omni bonoque tectus	and covered with all good things
propinanti numine.	by God's gift.
Summe vivens benignus	Living with supreme good will,
Christo sic opifice	Christ thus being his maker,
pontificali dignus	he is raised on high,
sublimatur apice.	worthy of the papal dignity.

[13] The motet with its tenor designation was first noted by Besseler, 'Studien II', 218, since when it has received little attention. Besseler claimed, not convincingly, that the illegible word at the top might be an ascription to Johannes de Muris. He missed the acrostic, which I reported in the 1993 conference paper eventually published in 1998 as 'Early Papal Motets' and from which the present chapter is revised; I was there able to take account of Leech-Wilkinson, 'Ars nova', where it was meanwhile independently reported with a discussion and transcription of the music. Leech-Wilkinson reads the 'illegible' word as *Invidie* and offers a comparison with Vitry's motet *Cum statua/Hugo, Hugo, princeps invidie/Magister invidie*.

[14] *Onema = onoma*; not *enema = aenigma*; this corrects the misreading of Besseler, 'Studien II', 218.

EARLY PAPAL MOTETS   609

Most motets are dated or placed on the basis of their texts, and this is no exception, though without the triplum we may lack a significant clue to its true destination. Daniel Leech-Wilkinson proposed *Per grama* as 'possibly celebrating the election of Pope John XXII and in that case dating from soon after 7 August 1316, or his coronation on 5 September 1316'.[15] This early date was encouraged by the similarly early dating that Leech-Wilkinson proposed for *Flos ortus/Celsa cedrus/Quam magnus pontifex*, for the canonisation of Louis of Toulouse in 1317, a motet similar in style, technique and notation to *Per grama*, both credibly attributed by Leech-Wilkinson to Philippe de Vitry.[16]

My earlier publication went on to express serious doubts about these early datings; those doubts still stand, and are addressed in the context of the disputed early dating of Machaut's Motet 18 in Chapter 13. That *Per grama* might have been written for a papal coronation is neither supported nor discouraged by the text alone. However, placing it at the beginning of John XXII's reign is irreconcilable with what we know about the rapid technical and notational developments in French music of that period. Given the accepted dating of the most advanced *Fauvel* motets in the mid- to later 1310s, these early datings now seem not merely precocious but impossible on notational and stylistic grounds. Both motets have features that place them so far in advance of the most progressive motets in *Fauvel* that a dating before *c.* 1320 is almost inconceivable, even if enterprising composers outside the *Fauvel* project, and perhaps away from the latest developments in Paris, such as the young Machaut, were experimenting independently at the same time.

1316–17 is precisely the time when musicians in Paris were adapting, assembling, and composing music for the massive *Fauvel* enterprise in **Paris146**, whose compilation Roesner had dated to 1317–18, but in the light of more recent work could have extended towards but not beyond the death of Philip V in 1322.[17] Its motets present for the first time some of the most advanced musical and notational usages then known, including imperfect time and the earliest appearance, in *Garrit gallus*, of mensurally transforming coloration. Its composers were pushing at the limits of what could be conceived in the current state of the notational art, and introducing innovations, both in musical structure and in the specification of details. But although the tenor of *Firmissime/Adesto* has a newly rhythmicised second *color* in shorter values, there are no real diminution sections in the *Fauvel* motets, no *color* and *talea* overlaps, no significant isorhythmic recurrences in the upper parts. *Per grama protho paret* has extensive isorhythmic recurrences in the surviving upper part over a cunningly overlapped *color* and *talea* in the tenor, another feature present in *Flos/Celsa*, but not in *Fauvel*, and found in only a few of Machaut's motets.[18] The tenor of *Flos/Celsa* has 3½ *taleae* imposed on 2 *colores*, which are then

---

[15] Leech-Wilkinson, 'The Emergence of *Ars nova*', 309.

[16] Indeed, Leech-Wilkinson described *Flos/Celsa* (1317) and Machaut's Motet 18 for Guillaume de Trie's elevation to the archbishopric of Reims in 1324 as 'the only reasonably certain dates for motets between *Fauvel* and Vitry's *Petre/Lugentium* [1342]' ('Ars nova', 285 n. 3). Louis was the second son of Charles II of Naples; he became a Franciscan and bishop and was canonised in 1317 (feast day 7 Apr.). Louis was the brother of Robert of Anjou, King of Naples (r. 1309–43), honoured in another motet by Vitry: see below. *Flos/Celsa* is published in PMFC 5, no. 7. For the dating, see Leech-Wilkinson, 'The Emergence of *Ars nova*', 309 n. 45. Kügle gives an account of 14th-c. motets and their chronology which accepts Leech-Wilkinson's early dating of *Flos/Celsa* and related motets: Kügle, *The Manuscript Ivrea*, 124. But see Ch. 13.

[17] See *Le Roman de Fauvel*, ed. Roesner et al., Introduction, 49; and now here the essays in Part II., especially Ch. 3.

[18] *Per grama protho paret* has three tenor *colores* of 15 notes each, a total of 45 notes, also patterned as 5 *taleae* of 9 notes each. Each *talea* is 12 longs, making a total of 60 longs. Machaut motets nos. 4, 7, 8, 9, 14, 19,

610 POPES, TRÉMOÏLLE AND CYPRUS

repeated in diminution. *Per grama* has 5 *taleae* imposed on 3 *colores* and no diminution. On any spectrum of style-based chronology these 'advanced' tenor patterns of irregularly overlapping *color* and *talea* would fall later, at least in the 1320s.

The *Fauvel* motets use two to five semibreves per breve of imperfect time, with almost no minim stems—indeed, none are necessary to deal with the rhythmic vocabulary of *Fauvel*, that is, what would later be notated as major and minor semibreves and minims, in standard groupings, but here with no minim rests or hockets. The conventional interpretation of unstemmed semibreves is confirmed in all cases where later concordances are more explicitly notated with stems, and conforms to the default groupings set out in treatises.[19] Between them, the theorists provide for up to three minims per semibreve in imperfect and perfect time—what was later called major prolation, though at that early stage without requiring stems when standard combinations were to be interpreted conventionally. Groups of five semibreves (mostly unstemmed) occur only in *Quare fremuerunt*, conspicuously placed on f. 1ʳ of *Fauvel*, and *Servant/O Philippe* (on King Philip V, r. 1316–22), one of the most modern motets and perhaps a kingpin in the planning of the collection.

Per grama makes use of the same groupings of two to five semibreves as the *Fauvel* motets, all in the standard default patterns for imperfect tempus. It also uses stems, not because those standard groupings needed them but because, by the time it was notated, other options were possible, necessitating the general introduction of clarifying stems for what had previously been standard, unambiguous default resolutions of unstemmed semibreves. However, there are two factors that mark the construction and notation of this motet as being more advanced than anything in *Fauvel*. *Per grama* must always have had some stems, because it also uses minim hockets, which cannot be notated without rests, either what came to be stabilised as paired minim rests, or their possible antecedents as general-purpose short rests, such as suggested in Chapter 13. *Fauvel* motets use no rests shorter than the breve, though the ballade *En chantant* (ff. 23ᵛ– 24, p.mus. 56) has short rests that sit on the line and have the value of a semibreve. The upper voices of both motets follow the default rhythms that would apply if their minims were unstemmed, and could thus fall relatively early in the 1320s. Both have minim hockets, *Per grama* throughout and *Flos/Celsa* in the reduced section. In both cases, these hockets involve paired but not single minim rests, which allows the default rhythm of ♦ ♦ to continue as ⏤ ♦ ·. This suggests that they were not yet dependent on a fully formulated prolation system, and earlier in date than when interlocked hockets needing single minim rests appear.[20] The upper parts of *Flos/Celsa* are isorhythmic in the diminution section with hockets. The motetus of *Per grama* has substantial passages of isorhythm at the beginning of each tenor *talea* and in the hocket sections, a feature

---

22 also have overlapping *color* and *talea*: Günther, 'The 14th-Century Motet', 30; and see now Guillaume de Machaut, *The Motets*, ed. Boogaart.

[19] Philippe de Vitry, *Ars nova* in CSM 8, which includes a re-edition of CS III, Anonymous III. See Fuller, 'A Phantom Treatise', and Desmond, 'Did Vitry Write an Ars vetus et nova', 'Texts in Play', and '*Omni desideranti*'.

[20] See Earp, 'Tradition and Innovation'. French sources, however, lack clear instances of the notated English distinction between major and minor semibreve rests (the latter interchangeable with paired minim rests) found in sources throughout the century, especially **Ox7** and **Durham20** (see Ch. 18 on *Musicorum* and Ch. 13 on Machaut's Motet 18). *O . . ./Nostris lumen* in **Br19606** has undifferentiated rests, some of which must stand for a minor semibreve, some for a major semibreve. See Ch. 13 and n. 9.

understated by Leech-Wilkinson and hardly present yet in most earlier motets of Machaut.[21] Taken together, these features of structure and detail point to datings in the years from the mid-1320s towards or around 1330.

It is thus clear that the two motets in question cannot date from as early as 1316–17. The date of *Flos/Celsa* is easier to move; it is indeed for Louis of Toulouse, but he was celebrated throughout the fourteenth century. The motet does not have to be for his canonisation in 1317 and could have been written at a later date.[22] Its attribution to Vitry is highly plausible on many grounds, including the separate survival of its texts in the tradition now documented by Andrew Wathey.[23] But the motets of Vitry it most resembles probably date from the late 1320s and early 1330s, present in the much later Ivrea manuscript, and in some intervening fragmentary sources, but not in *Fauvel*.[24]

The dating of *Per grama* is much more problematic, its occasion now uncertain. There are no explicitly inaugural references in the text; the missing triplum might have clarified the identity of the dedicatee, or given other textual clues to its original context.[25] With its hockets, small notes and rests, it is hardly a manifesto piece written to the austere prescriptions of a Cranmer or a Council of Trent. If John XXII is recognised in the tenor, could it even have been this piece that prompted the striking technically informed condemnations that he consented to promote in the famous bull *Docta sanctorum* of 1324–25?[26] It is more likely that the motet was written after the bull, either in negligence or nescience of the approved style guidelines. John or his musical advisors could hardly have been pleased by something that so plainly flouted his directive, unless the story, and his position, is much more convoluted than we have thought it to be. However, the bull seems not to condemn these stylistic features in themselves, but to proscribe them in liturgical observance, together with other features (such as secular texts in motets).[27] If this were to provide an oblique hint against the performance of these motets in a liturgical context, we might have good reason to dissociate them from papal coronation ceremonies. I concluded that a date closer to 1330 would be more musically acceptable, perhaps even from the mid-1320s, especially if either or both motets

---

[21] Leech-Wilkinson, 'The Emergence of *Ars nova*', 309 ff. Günther, 'The 14th-Century Motet'. Ten Machaut motets have diminution in the second section, all with hockets.

[22] Julian Gardner has generously provided me (email of 3.1.2021) with information derived from *Bullarium Franciscanum* V, of some of the occasions for which a celebratory motet might have been appropriate. In addition to the bull of canonisation *Sol oriens mundo* of 7 Apr. 1317 (no. 267, pp. 111–14), an indulgence was granted on 8 Nov. 1323 for the feast of the translation of Louis to the Franciscan church in Marseilles (no. 517, pp. 255–56). On 15 Jan. 1326 Philip I, Prince of Taranto, established a foundation in Louis's honour in Naples cathedral (no. 599, p. 296). Chapels in honour of St Louis were founded in Barcelona and Vienna in 1327. Payment survives from 30 Apr. 1338 for a reliquary in Naples which survives in the Louvre: Leone de Castris, 'Une attribution à Lando di Pietro', and Cioni, *Scultura e smalto*, 296–99, figs. 35, 36, 39–42. On 26 Nov. 1343 Clement VI granted to Louis equivalent privileges to those of SS. Francesco and Antonio. *Bullarium Franciscanum* VI (no. 182, p. 105).

[23] Wathey, 'The Motets of Philippe de Vitry'.

[24] Kügle now dates **Ivrea** in the 1380s and 1390s ('The Manuscript Ivrea', 130–33).

[25] Besseler, 'Studien I', 196.

[26] For the observation that the musical part suggests a different author from the rest of the bull, see Hucke, 'Das Dekret', 122.

[27] The bull complains that disciples of the new school, concerned with measuring out breves in new notes, prefer to fashion (*fingere*) their own music rather than sing the old songs; that ecclesiastical chants are sung by the moderns in semibreves and minims, and that everything is struck through (punctured? *percutiuntur*) by little notes. For they cut across (*intersecant*) the melodies with hockets, they make them slippery with discants, they even stuff the tripla and moteti with vernacular [texts]. See Hucke, 'Das Dekret'; Donella, 'La Costituzione'; Klaper, 'Docta sanctorum'.

are to be considered candidates for the authorship of Vitry. Assuming that the most advanced motets in *Fauvel* represent Vitry's then-current notational vocabulary, he could not have composed these other motets before *c.* 1320. That does not exclude the possibility of concurrent innovations in the late 1310s, outside the *Fauvel* orbit, by a younger composer such as Machaut.

Because of the apparently immovable connection with John, I did not then consider the alternative, now proposed by Anna Zayaruznaya, that the acrostic 'Petrus' of the surviving motetus part might refer not to the apostle Peter as first pope, but rather to Pierre Roger, who would be elected as Clement VI in 1342, and whose relationship with Vitry is established. She is right to observe that motetus acrostics more commonly celebrate dedicatees. However, she has not yet offered strong reasons for the choice of the St John tenor, and the possible reference within the motetus text to the beloved disciple. She observes that 'the fragment of chant actually excerpted for *Per grama* does not include the word 'Johannes'—the borrowed notes span only "Valde honorandus est." Only the tenor's liturgical context, then, and not the tenor *qua* tenor, implicates a Johannes'. If Johannes was not to be featured, one might ask, why is the full text *Valde honorandus est beatus Johannes* given in its only source, **McV**, when an abbreviated incipit could have avoided this? Rightly pointing out that the end of the poem could nearly as well signify an episcopal mitre as a papal tiara (though the poet could have written 'episcopali', and 'dignity' is perhaps a more prudent translation than any form of headgear), she goes on to suggest that 'if the motet celebrated one of Pierre Roger's promotions before 1334, then the papal authority elevating him would have been John XXII'.[28] She thus concedes that the motet could date from the reign of John XXII, which is more consistent with its musical style, though it would be rather unusual to combine a new bishop with his papal promoter in this way.[29] She also points to Pierre Roger's devotion to St John, which led him, as pope, to build a chapel dedicated to the saint; but this was after 1342, which is late for the style of the motet.

To distance *Per grama* from John XXII, however, would remove the apparently uncomfortable anomaly that he appeared to have been honoured by a motet exhibiting precisely the musical features castigated in *Docta sanctorum*, though as pointed out above, the prohibitions may have been restricted to their use in a liturgical context. The question, then, is whether a later dating must fall within the reign of John XXII for him to be the John honoured in the tenor, whether there is another explanation of that tenor, or whether *Per grama* could be late enough to be for Clement VI as pope. Having disqualified it from a dating a dozen years earlier than its style suggests, I am now reluctant to place it a dozen years later than a new notional style-based dating of *c.* 1330 or earlier.

In the absence of better explanations, I saw no alternative to accepting that John XXII was honoured in *Per grama*, but looked for an occasion as late in his reign as possible,

---

[28] Zayaruznaya, 'Evidence of Reworkings', 174 n. 41, and Zayaruznaya, *Vitry*. I am grateful to Anna Zayaruznaya for discussing this issue and for sharing her material before publication. One other link between John XXII and Pierre Roger—though hardly occasion for a motet—was a treatise that Roger wrote in 1325 condemning the anticlerical stance of Marsilius of Padua and defending John against the Holy Roman Emperor Louis IV.

[29] The possible combination of Pietro Filargo and Pietro Emiliani with St Peter is handled in a different way within a single text, *O Petre Christi discipule*. See Ch. 28.

especially one that also involved Pierre Roger. One such was 1333, when a successful case was made to the still very active Pope John XXII to authorise a crusade; the delegation was led by Pierre Roger, the future Pope Clement VI and a colleague and contemporary of Vitry.[30] Vitry was involved in crusade politics through his patron Louis of Bourbon, whose political relationships with Robert of Anjou, King of Naples, were close enough in the mid-1330s to have provided the occasion for Vitry's composition of the motet in honour of Robert, *O canenda/Rex quem*, on a tenor for St Louis (the French king Louis IX), and with full isorhythm, diminution, and minim hockets. Robert's name appears as an acrostic in the motetus, a normal place for a dedicatee, which could argue in favour of 'Petrus' in *Per grama* being for Pierre Roger rather than St Peter.[31] The same Vitry–Bourbon–Anjou link might also have occasioned the composition, at the same period, of *Flos/Celsa* for the king's saintly brother, Louis of Toulouse, and Vitry's composition of all three motets.

Looking for another John in connection with Pierre Roger, we find another—perhaps remote—possibility. When Pierre Roger was elevated to the archbishopric of Rouen on 14 December 1330, he was required to swear allegiance to his feudal overlord, the Duke of Normandy. But although Philip VI had promised the dukedom to his eldest son, later King John II, John was not installed as duke until 27 April 1332. The dukedom being vacant in 1330, Roger evidently made homage to the king, but was required to do so also to John as duke in 1332. He temporised, fearing that if someone other than a member of the French royal family might in future become duke, the archbishopric could then be detached from the French crown. His temporalities were seized, whereupon he negotiated an agreement that if the duchy of Normandy passed out of the royal line, the right to receive homage would revert to the king; this settlement of the matter is reported in documents of 1334. Roger acted as a conciliator between Norman interests and those of the French king, but otherwise enjoyed an uninterrupted good relationship with Philippe.[32] Could the resolution of this matter following the installation of duke John in 1332 have occasioned a motet celebrating both names? It seems impossible to take this further without the missing triplum.

However, circumstances in 1330 do suggest a possible occasion unconnected with Pierre Roger.[33] John XXII had refused to ratify the 1314 election of Louis of Bavaria as King of the Germans. In 1324 he excommunicated Louis, who was crowned king of Italy in 1327. In January 1328, Louis had himself crowned Holy Roman Emperor in Rome, which could in the circumstances show the opposite of the Roman constancy lauded at the beginning of the motetus of *Per grama*, and a reason for asserting it by an opponent. Later that year Louis declared John XXII deposed on grounds of heresy and, still under excommunication, installed Pietro Rainalducci in Rome as antipope

---

[30] For information on the crusade-related Bourbon–Anjou connections in the 1330s I am much indebted to Andrew Wathey (private communication of material in a paper delivered at the AMS annual meeting, New York, 1995), who proposed a mid-1330s date for *O canenda/Rex quem* on grounds quite independent of the stylistic ones included here.

[31] Kügle suggests the period 1319–24, when Robert was in the north ('The Manuscript Ivrea', 145), but Wathey's most recent suggestion makes a northern constraint unnecessary.

[32] Cazelles, *La Société politique*, 137. I am grateful to Andrew Wathey (email correspondence of Nov. 2020) for helping to untangle the chronology of these events, based on Fisquet, *La France pontificale*.

[33] Andrew Wathey should have the credit for developing this suggestion more strongly than stated in Bent, 'Early Papal Motets', in email correspondence of Dec. 2020.

Nicholas V. Support for Louis collapsed; both were driven from Rome in 1328 by Robert of Anjou, king of Naples, the dedicatee of Vitry's motet *O canenda/Rex quem metrorum*, as noted above, and brother of Louis of Toulouse. Nicholas was excommunicated by John XXII in April 1329 and, on making his confession to Pope John, was absolved in August 1330. This restoration of John's authority following the submission by Nicholas could be reflected in formulations in the motetus text: 'Truly he remains the elect, not apart from the name of the dear one'. John, carrying the name of the beloved disciple, is acknowledged as the true pope, on Petrine and Roman authority as set out in the first verse: 'Through the first letter [of the acrostic 'Petrus'] is revealed the name of the Romans' constancy'. The ideological victory is implicit in asserting the authority of St Peter and old Rome (the historical papal seat) at the beginning. At the end of the text, the affirmation that the dedicatee is 'worthy of the papal dignity' could be seen as a rebuttal of Louis's charge (in deposing him) that he was a heretic. In this way, nuances in the text could explain the combination of Peter and John and support a dating of 1330, when these crises were resolved; but the dating and circumstances of *Per grama* remain uncertain.

John XXII, an austere and elderly Dominican, was followed by the likewise ascetic Cistercian Benedict XII, pope from 20 December 1334 to 25 April 1342. Had we accepted for *Per grama* a dating as late as the 1340s for Clement VI as pope, no polyphonic music could have been associated with either earlier reign. We have tentatively suggested that the motet could be restored to John XXII. But with the election of Pierre Roger as Clement VI, a golden decade of cultural and artistic patronage, including music, was about to begin.

Clement VI: *Petre clemens/Lugentium* (Vitry)

Cardinal Pierre Roger, archbishop of Rouen, and previously chancellor to Philip VI, was elected pope on 7 May 1342, partly in reaction against Benedict's austere rule. As Clement VI he held the most brilliant court in Europe; it was he who did most to establish the luxurious image of the Avignon papacy. He exercised notable patronage of all the arts, cultivating contacts with the leading intellectuals of his day, including Petrarch. Among non-musical works dedicated to Clement are several by Johannes de Muris, including an astronomical calendar from the fifth year of Clement's pontificate, a set of prophetic prognostications referring to planetary conjunctions in 1357 and 1365, and a treatise in collaboration with Firmin de Belleval on the reform of the Julian calendar in 1344–45.[34]

Compositions that can be associated with him are, most significantly, the motet *Petre clemens/Lugentium/Non est inventus*; and with only slightly less confidence, a motetus text troping a Gloria, *Clemens Deus artifex tota clementia*, no. 45 in **Ivrea**, and possibly a related Kyrie, no. 71. The possible claim of *Per grama* as a work for Clement VI has been discussed above and, with some reluctance, cast into doubt.

---

[34] See *NG1*, s.v. Jehan des Murs, and Gushee, 'New Sources'. And more recently, Desmond, *Music and the Moderni*, ch. 3: 'Jean des Murs, Quadrivial Scientist'.

The most substantial and interesting of the tributes firmly associated with Clement is Philippe de Vitry's motet *Petre clemens/Lugentium*. The music was known and published as a three-voice motet from **Ivrea**, its unique musical source until the discovery of **Aachen**, which presents it for four voices, with a tenor, contratenor and solus tenor, which show the **Ivrea** 'tenor' to be in fact a solus tenor conflation, differing from the **Aachen** solus tenor mainly in providing an accompanying line to the upper parts before the entry of the contratenor and solus tenor in **Aachen**. What this source reveals about the motet has been set out by Anna Zayaruznaya, together with a full transcription.[35]

It is one of a number of motets for which texts survive separately in humanist collections. None of these texts is for any named fourteenth-century composer other than Vitry, and the anonymous texts belong only to those compositions that at least some modern scholars have suspected to be possibly his work.[36] Leo Schrade reported the presence of the triplum text in **Paris3343**, and its ascription to Vitry. Andrew Wathey reports no fewer than fourteen text-only sources, one of which, **Vienna4195**, was a new one for this motet in a collection of Clement's sermons copied in Avignon in the late 1340s.[37] It is therefore the earliest of the text-only copies of Vitry motet texts, made during the lifetimes of both Clement and Vitry.[38] The texts in the sermon volume are immediately preceded by a longer verse celebration of Clement's rule, beginning *Aperi labia mea*. They are followed by a tenor incipit, *Non est inventus similis illi*, and then by a brief colophon, added in a different but contemporary hand, which not only attributes the texts to Vitry but supplies a date for their composition: 'Magister Philippus de Vitrejo in laudem Pape Clementis vj^ti anno suo primo circa natalem domini' (i.e. around Christmas 1342; taking the confines of the feast literally, this could be narrowed to 24 December 1342–5 January 1343). There are two sermon cycles: the first includes sermons of Pierre Roger as Archbishop of Rouen preached in Avignon in the 1330s; the second consists exclusively of sermons by Clement dating from immediately before his coronation and from the early years of his pontificate. Most are associated with special occasions and special themes. The most important of these are for April 1343 and April 1346, and refer to part of his campaign against Louis of Bavaria, the pretender to the Imperial crown. There are bulls against Louis, and there is Clement's often-quoted reply of 27 January 1343 to the embassy of Roman citizens, discussed below.

The motet texts had been assumed to be for Clement's coronation, or just generally laudatory. There is nothing specifically inaugural in them, and with this new loosening of the—anyway weak—basis for assuming that motets are more likely to be inaugural than not, a primary function as propaganda to promote papal diplomacy can now be contemplated. At Christmas 1342 a Roman delegation came to Avignon to petition for the return of the papacy to Rome. Clement's reply included the famous

---

[35] Zayaruznaya, 'New Voices', brought to wider notice from a first report in 2001 by Lüdtke, 'Kleinüberlieferung'. *Petre clemens* is in **Ivrea**, ff. 37^v–38, **Aachen**, f. 2^r, and listed in the index of **Trém**. Another motet preserved in some sources with solus tenor alone is *O Maria virgo davitica//O Maria maris stella*, which survives complete with five voices including its solus tenor in **Pad1106** (see Chs. 1 and 28), but only with its upper parts and solus tenor in **Q15** and **MuEm**.

[36] The only known exception to this is the separate preservation of the text of Machaut's Motet 8 in a Stockholm MS; see Ch. 14 and Wathey, 'The Motets of Philippe de Vitry'.

[37] Wathey, 'The Motets of Vitry', 122 n. 7 and table 1.

[38] See Wood, *Clement VI*, and Wathey, 'The Motets of Vitry', including text and translation by David Howlett.

expression 'ubi papa ibi Roma'. He supported his refusal not only with practical reasons arising from the Anglo-French wars but also with doctrinal considerations. He upheld the independence of the papacy from the bishopric of Rome and the universal rather than the local character of papal power. In the words of the text: 'Petrus primus petrum non deseris, vices eius quia recta geris' (You first Peter [pope] do not abandon the rock [petrus, St Peter—i.e. of the church] because you guide it rightly in his stead). We might find here, also, an allusion to the rocky fortress of Avignon as a suitable seat for Peter's successor.

On the basis of the evidence placing *Petre clemens* several months into the new pope's reign and thus dissociating it from his coronation, Wathey argues that a single monofunctional association between motets and narrowly defined state purposes, royal and papal coronations in particular, no longer appears justifiable in all cases. Official festivity was indeed one, but not necessarily the only, performance context. This fits perfectly with later evidence for multiple use of occasional pieces, and may ease the dilemma outlined above for earlier ones. Many of the occasional motets in **Q15** were written in honour of dedicatees or occasions. In some cases they might have been inaugural, in others they clearly cannot have been. Some motets celebrating individuals were recopied long after the deaths of their dedicatees with musical updating but without verbal change.[39]

Petre clemens is anonymous in both musical sources. With 251 perfect breves of major prolation, it is Vitry's longest motet and, until some of the music was found for *Phi millies*, probably his latest surviving musical work.[40] If it seemed less compactly structured than his earlier works, that is partly due to the lack, until recently, of its true tenor, labelled in **Aachen** with the text provided in the text manuscript **Vienna4195**, 'Non est inventus similis illi'. These words are also echoed at the end of the motetus part: 'Non est inventus tuus similis' in **Ivrea**, and 'Non fuit inventus similis' in **Aachen**.[41] Earlier puzzlement about the only partial correspondence of the Ivrea tenor to the chant of this name can be laid aside now that the true tenor has been found to correspond to the entire verse, 'Non est inventus similis illi qui conservavit legem excelsi' of the Gradual *Ecce sacerdos*, making a very long single *color*.[42]

Little needs to be added to the analysis of the music given by Zayaruznaya.[43] All known instances of solus tenors involve compositions (mostly motets, but some mass movements) with essential contratenor parts, as here, and usually embed the lowest or contrapuntally essential note from whichever of the lower parts provides it. *Vos/Gratissima* is treated in Chapter 8; another striking but little-known instance is the lower-voice canonic pair of *O amicus/Precursoris* reconstructed in Chapter 22. Any lone tenor parts whose chants are unidentified, or which deviate significantly from a chant, invite interrogation in case they too are in fact solus tenors.

---

[39] See Bent, *Q15*, PMFC 24, p. xii, and Ch. 28 for the dating of Ciconia's *Venecie*.

[40] The texts of *Phi millies* were known to Schrade from **Paris3343**. Part of the triplum is now in **Aachen**, transcribed in Zayaruznaya, *The Monstrous New Art*, appendix 3.

[41] Might the past tense indicate that Clement VI was already dead, this copy therefore after 1352?

[42] Various attempts to explain the structure were reported in Bent, 'Early Papal Motets', but are omitted here, as that discussion is superseded by Zayaruznaya, 'New Voices'.

[43] 'New Voices'. However, she reads the tenor as in perfect, the contratenor in imperfect modus. But, as confirmed in correspondence with Lawrence Earp, both lower parts must be construed in perfect modus; the contratenor enters first, and the tenor's perfections are displaced by a breve.

Gloria *Clemens Deus artifex* and Kyrie *Clemens pater, conditor syderum*

This Gloria is unique to **Ivrea**, as no. 45, with the Gloria text in the triplum. The motetus text carries the trope 'Clemens Deus artifex tota clementia', assumed to embody punning on the name of the pope. The Gloria may be paired with a Kyrie with the triplum trope 'Rex angelorum' and the motetus trope 'Clemens pater, conditor syderum'. It may thus be a similarly punned companion piece to this Gloria, although it has no specific language that would invite associations outside the Kyrie.[44] The composition of both Gloria and Kyrie as bitextual motets is unusual; their common technique and opening word further encourage a pairing.

Clemens Deus artifex,		The merciful creator God,
tota clementia,		all clemency,
actuque specie		in deed and in appearance,
mirabilis essentia,		marvellous in essence,
carens carie	5	lacking decay
spurcitia,		and filth,
dux venie		commander of mercy
patriarcharum		sent for the justice
missus pro iustitia,		of the patriarchs,
pastor ecclesie,	10	shepherd of the church,
conservator fidei sanctie		preserver of the holy faith,
triumphator pro victoria.		triumpher for the victory.
extirpandi hostis tormenta varia		of wiping out various devices of the enemy
crucem mysterii previa.		with the cross of mystery going before.
o que spiritus incendia!	15	O what fires of the spirit!
o redemptor, o rex pie,		O redeemer, O merciful king,
splendor eterne glorie		splendour of eternal glory,
fac fidelium virtutem		cause the virtue of the faithful
resistere contra vitia		to hold out against vices,
ut mederi nullus valeat	20	so that none may heal one
iam infectum fecis sanie		already infected by the filth of dregs,
et dimittat ius profanum		and let him discard profane law,
venenosum et insanum		a poisonous and insane
errorem ad fidelia		error, for the faithful
perennis dona gratie	25	gifts of eternal grace,
constanter indefectivia.		constantly never-failing.
Amen		Amen

[44] The Gloria and Kyrie are published respectively in CMM 29, nos. 22 and 2. The Kyrie is in both **Apt** (no. 1) and **Ivrea** (no. 71), and a fragment in **Barc971**. This Kyrie is the opening piece in **Apt**, which also contains (no. 38, CMM 29, no. 12) a more normally troped Kyrie *Summe clementissime rex eterne glorie eleyson.*

In the Kyrie *Rex angelorum*, **Ivrea** (no. 71), the motetus trope is:

Clemens pater, conditor syderum.
Mundi rector datorque munerum,
Verax Deus, destructor scelerum, eleyson.
Kyrie eleyson.
Rex pie celi potens virtutibus,
Tremor factus cunctis demonibus,
Qui ruerunt ab altis sedibus, eleyson.
Christe eleyson.
Jesu Christe, nostra redemptio.
Fili Dei vera, dilectio,
A quo cuncta manat perfectio, eleyson.
Christe eleyson.
Sacrosancte amborum spiritus
Qui vocaris semper paraclitus
Placans omnis languentium genitus, eleyson.
Kyrie eleyson.
Sacrum flamen superna bonitas.
Ignis ardens zeli[que] caritas.
Una manens in tribus deitas, eleyson.

Gregory XI

Pope Gregory XI (1370–8) was Pierre Roger de Beaufort, a nephew of Clement VI. The Chantilly motet *Pictagore per dogmata/O terra sancta, suplica/Rosa vernans caritatis* must have been written for him. Ursula Günther (in CMM 39) places it early in 1375, certainly between 1374 and September 1376, when Gregory left Avignon in order to take up residence in Rome. The text is a plea to recapture the Holy Land, used here as a metaphor for the recapture of Rome.[45] There is play on the name Rosiers, Roger, for the tenor *Rosa vernans caritatis* alludes to the Roger arms, identical for Clement VI and Gregory XI, which bear six roses. Gregory's other paternal uncle, Hugues, had refused the papal tiara in 1362. This motet joins a cluster of orientation points in the 1370s: *Ferre solet* is dated 1373,[46] *Rex Karole* has been dated *c.* 1375 (1378 by Carolann Buff); most of **Trém** was compiled before 1376; Machaut died in 1377, and a Basel motet must date from soon after 1378 (see below, and the Introduction).

[45] Seven planets are referred to in the text, but only six named. Günther (CMM 39, pp. xl–xlii) believes the unnamed planet Saturn, before his fall from power as a god, is to be identified with Gregory. Tomasello, *Music and Ritual*, 26–30, disagrees, and points to the parallel ancestries of the Roman people and of Gregory XI. He is Mars, Clement VI his uncle was Phoebus. For planets, see also *Non eclipsis atra ferrugine* in Ch. 21.

[46] Louviot, 'Uncovering the Douai Fragment'.

The Great Schism

Throughout the Avignon period, attempts were made to secure a return of the papacy to Rome. Urban V was in Italy 1367–70, the first to re-establish the *sedes romana*, albeit temporarily. Gregory XI was in Rome with seventeen cardinals early in 1376, and remained there until his death in March 1378. Under pressure to choose an Italian, these same cardinals elected the Neapolitan canonist Bartolomeo Prignano, who was enthroned as Urban VI at Easter (18 April). Urban behaved with an authoritarianism that alienated the cardinals, whose lifestyle he tried to simplify and whose wish to return to Avignon he quelled. Violent outbursts, and impolitic and abusive behaviour, created difficulties that eclipsed the firmness of purpose and austerity that had helped his candidacy. Repelled by Urban's behaviour, the French cardinals defected under the leadership of Robert of Geneva, whom they elected pope at a new conclave in Fondi on 20 September 1378, thus opening the Schism. Taking the name of Clement VII, Robert remained in Italy at first, moving to Avignon in May 1379, where he died on 16 September 1394.

Clement VII: *Gaudeat et exultet* and ballades

Clement's election is celebrated in the first part, and Urban condemned as Antichrist in the second, in the texts of a motet discovered by Martin Steinmann and Wulf Arlt in two independent fragments (but still incomplete): a motetus *Gaudeat et exultet* in **Basel71** which fits with a triplum *Novum sidus orientis* in **Basel72** for the first *talea*.[47] The two fragments are in different scripts; the extant triplum part of the second *talea* starts in **Basel71** with the words *Papam querentes* and in **Basel72** with *De scintilla*, this time to identical music. Since only the texts in the same script in **Basel71** name the two popes, it seems that **Basel72**, from a different manuscript, may be a contrafact (*Novum sidus*) of the partisan papal motet (*Gaudeat et exultet*) in **Basel71**. The contrafaction may have been in the other direction.[48] As there is no overlap of triplum and motetus texts between the *taleae*, it cannot be established whether either version was a singly or doubly texted motet. In **Basel71**, lower parts are labelled Tenor solus, Contratenor cum solo tenore, Tenor and Contratenor. In **Basel72**, a part labelled Tenor corresponds to the Solus tenor of **Basel71**. The motet has many puzzling features of form and format, upper-voice status, lower-voice facture; it merits a full study.[49] This is the only known motet that refers so explicitly to two factions in the Schism; it presumably dates from

[47] Reported by Welker, *Musik am Oberrhein*, 77, who correctly identifies *Novum sidus* in **Basel72** as the triplum of *Gaudeat et exultet* in **Basel71**, as did Wulf Arlt, to whom, and to Michael Scott Cuthbert, I am grateful for sharing their transcriptions of this most intriguing composition. The promised study by Steinmann and Arlt never appeared.

[48] Johanna-Pauline Thöne, 'Papal Polyphony', will argue cogently for *Gaudeat et exultet* as a contrafact of *Novum sidus* mainly on grounds of its text distribution. I thank her for alerting me to Vlhová-Wörner, 'Novum sidus orientis', which gives two Bohemian sources for this Franciscan sequence on St Francis (transcription on pp. 462–63), permitting completion of the Basel text, which uses the first three double stanzas. There is no apparent musical relationship between the motet and the sequence melody.

[49] Thöne, 'Papal Polyphony', will seek to untangle the lower parts and their functions. The papal version has a third in the final chord, rare in the 14th c. Another instance is *Musicalis*, Ch. 17.

620 POPES, TRÉMOÏLLE AND CYPRUS

soon after 1378. The recto of **Basel72** preserves the end of *Rex Karole*, a motet in honour of the French king Charles V, who favoured Clement, but *Novum sidus* on the verso carries the non-papal text. *Rex Karole* shares with *Novum sidus* a perfect tempus and a spaced imitative introduction before the lower parts enter, features associated more with Italian than with French motets.

The musical culture of the Avignon chapel is as well attested as its other artistic manifestations. John, Duke (subsequently king) of Aragon, instructed his agents in 1379 to seek good singers in Avignon for his chapel. They were to be young, unmarried, preferably able to play an instrument, and not to have been (as was Matheus de Sancto Johanne) in the service of the Duke of Anjou. They were to bring a book of 'cant de la missa notat e un libre' (containing many) 'motets e rondels e ballades e virelay'.[50] This cannot be the later Chantilly manuscript, which contains no masses but a hundred songs and thirteen motets. Studies by Reinhard Strohm and John Nádas combined to eliminate Avignon itself and to advance Visconti circles in Pavia as a likely place of origin for **Chantilly** and as the centre from which French music of the so-called *ars subtilior* may have been disseminated in Italy.[51]

Clement VII's court continued and extended the sumptuous style established by Clement VI. Apart from *Gaudeat et exultet*, the three compositions directly associated with him are all in **ModA**, and two are in **Chantilly**, two French ballades and one in Latin. It is too rash to extrapolate a decline in popularity of motet composition from the particular case of **Chantilly** or from the particular ethos of his court. Moreover, many motets of this period were hardly less secular than ballades. They may have had symbolic tenors drawn from chant, and as such complied with the general restrictions of John XXII earlier in the century; but their newly composed texts were no less enthusiastically packed with classical allusions and sophistries.

Mayhuet de Joan's three-stanza ballade *Inclite flos orti Gebenensis* refers in its opening line to Robert of Geneva's origin, and the tenor in **Chantilly** is labelled Tenor *pro papa Clemente* [VII].[52] Matheus de Sancto Johanne received a canonry from Clement in 1378, while he was serving in the chapel of Louis I, Duke of Anjou. It could be that he was personally excluded on the instructions (above) of John of Aragon. He was one of the private chaplains of the pope in Avignon from 1382 until at least 1386. Because of the references in this text to Spanish acceptance of Clement's papacy, it has been thought that this piece must date from later in his reign. Early Spanish support for Clement was evidently undergirded by many more factors than the later confirmations suggest: Castille recognised Clement in 1382, Aragon in 1387, Navarre not until 1390.[53] However, *Inclite flos* and other compositions lauding the newly elected Pope Clement VII may have been composed while Clement and his musicians were still in Naples following the election, between September 1378 and May 1379, especially since Matheus was probably in Italy during those months, and he had previously served Clement.[54]

---

[50] Tomasello, *Music and Ritual*, 40.

[51] Strohm, 'Filippotto da Caserta', and *The Lucca Codex*, ed. Nádas and Ziino. See now Plumley and Stone, *Codex Chantilly*.

[52] **ModA**, f. 15, **Chantilly**, f. 41. On the 'Avignon repertory' of **ModA** see Stone, *The Manuscript Modena*, 90–99. For a disambiguation from the **OH** composer Mayshuet, see Ch. 24.

[53] Tomasello, *Music and Ritual*, 41.

[54] Di Bacco and Nádas, 'Papal Chapels', 46 and n. 7.

Magister Egidius's ballade *Courtois et sages* affirms the validity of the election and names 'Clemens' in an acrostic.[55] *Par les bons Gedeons*, a ballade by Filippotto da Caserta, has the refrain line 'le souverayn pape qui s'appelle Clement'.[56] In the Boverio manuscript in Turin, which has connections with the Pisan popes Alexander V and John XXIII, this same ballade appears with the variant *antipape* in this line.[57]

Popes named Clement of course invite punning salutations, and we must take care not to see them where they are not, for example in the invocation *O clemens* in the *Salve regina*. But another troped Gloria *Clementie pax* in the Padua fragments (**Pad1475**) cannot be excluded as a Clementine composition: *Clementie* is the first word of a trope that expands and further tropes the Gloria trope *Spiritus et alme*. Clement VII died in 1394; this is characterised as a Gloria for a late fourteenth-century Marian Mass.[58] The text mentions Esther, who is lauded in the motet *Argi vices* for John XXIII (see below), as she is invoked as a champion on both sides in several other English and French compositions during the Hundred Years War. But this Gloria is not included in the Appendix, the papal reference being insufficiently specific.

Abandoned in Rome by the cardinals who left for Fondi, Urban VI created twenty-five new cardinals, one of whom was the Valois Philippe d'Alençon, of whom more below. Although the papal entourage in Italy had to moderate considerably the luxurious style to which it had become accustomed in Avignon, even on a reduced scale the retinues of pope and cardinals included foreign musicians who had been in Avignon, thus starting a two-century tradition of northerners in Italy.[59] There is also a reverse direction: the musicians who had been in Rome but then returned to Avignon with Clement VII may have had some reciprocal influence.

Alme pater: Urban VI?

One of the most puzzling of papal motet survivals is another fragmentary work, *Alme pater*, of which triplum and tenor only (of originally four parts) are preserved in the English Fountains manuscript of around 1400, one of the earliest documents of void notation, and on paper.[60] Roger Bowers has proposed a convincing solution to the historical events dealt with in the motet.[61]

---

[55] A differently texted concordance in **Leiden2720** was identified independently by Hertel, *Chansonvertonungen*, 232, Cuthbert, 'Hidden in our Publications', and now analysed by Johanna-Pauline Thöne in a paper at the Conference on Medieval and Renaissance Music at Uppsala, 7 July 2022, and in Thöne, 'Papal Polyphony'.

[56] Published in CMM 53/I, nos. 21 and 82.

[57] See *Il Codice T.III.2*, ed. Ziino, f. 5ᵛ.

[58] PMFC 12, no. 9, p. 30. It is in **Pad1475** (PadA) from the older complex of Paduan fragments that also includes the Sanctus St Omer and the *Ite missa est* of the Machaut mass.

[59] Di Bacco and Nádas, 'Verso uno "stile internazionale"'. On the subject of northerners in Italy, see also Strohm, 'Filippotto da Caserta'.

[60] Bent, *The Fountains Fragments*, and *The Fountains Fragment*, ed. Kershaw and Sandon. The provenance remains uncertain. The host MS is an account book of Fountains abbey of the 1440s, but the music is mostly based on Sarum chants from the English lowlands.

[61] Bowers, 'Fixed Points', 317–20. He extends the similar conclusion of Lefferts, *Motet in England* (1986), 184, 348–49. The translation is by Bowers.

Alme pater, pastor vere	Kindly father, true shepherd
christicolarum omnium,	of all Christ-worshippers,
per te diu doluere	for you for a long time
mentes nostrorum omnium.	the minds of all our people have lamented.
....	
.... misera trucibus	You, captured,
sustulisti tam perversa	alas have suffered such miserable
heu, captivatus,[62] manibus	improprieties from brutal hands.
......	
.... neepolitani nobiles	The Neapolitan nobles,
quos diligebas tamen	indeed whom you highly esteemed,
heu, non fuerunt nobiles.	were alas no gentlemen.
Ulcissi tuum munere	With [due] reward, avenge your fate
egena illorum atria,	upon their beggarly halls!
repleverat innumere	Your ungrateful native land
ingrata tua patria.	had rewarded them inordinately.
Dudum profusis lacrimis	A little while ago our faces
nostre sunt uncte facies,	were anointed with copious tears
quod te dum malos comprimis	because, while you were restraining wicked men,
atrox obcedit acies	the cruel blade threatens you.
Intra suos vidit muros,	Within her walls, Luceria
omni cantanda feria.	(every day to be praised in song)
casus diu pati duros	has seen you for a long time
te flebiles luceria.	to suffer harsh, lamentable mischances.

What is such a text doing in an English manuscript? The motet may be English or French in origin, but neither side had much enthusiasm for Urban. The English were at least nominally on the side of the Roman pope at this time. The pope addressed must be Urban VI (1378–89), the events his misfortunes at the siege of Nocera (also called *Luceria christianorum*). Before his election the Neapolitan Urban had been Archbishop of Bari and vice-chancellor of the papal household. He was recognised by the English church and government against Clement VII as the Schism developed in 1378–79. To the anger of Urban, Queen Joanna I of Naples sided with Clement. With Urban's help, Charles of Durazzo deposed and murdered Joanna in 1381, but as king of Naples (Charles III) he failed to show gratitude to Urban, who then took up residence in 1384 at the castle of Nocera, where he was besieged (*captivatus*) and subjected to many indignities between March and July 1385.

Roger Bowers gives a masterly account of the competing claims and loyalties that led not only to the composition of this piece (perhaps by an Englishman, and probably in 1385). He also suggests how it may have come to be copied in a later English source, pointing out that few Englishmen had reason to favour Urban, especially as he

---

[62] An irregular abbreviation. I had originally read it as *captivarum*, which led me down a different but related path of investigation into the captivity of Queen Joanna and her female attendants.

EARLY PAPAL MOTETS   623

imprisoned and tortured the English Cardinal Adam Easton during the siege, a cardinal Strohm thinks may be responsible for the motet text.[63] Bowers identifies John of Gaunt as one of few Englishmen well disposed towards Urban; he recognised his counterclaim to the Castilian throne in 1381 and supported his military campaign of 1386. Bowers observes that after Urban's death in 1389 the motet can hardly have remained long in any live repertory, and offers parallel events in 1405–7 as a possible occasion for the motet's revival and recopying, the 1380s being too early a dating for **Fountains**, though 1405–7 is quite late for a *terminus post quem* for that manuscript. There are, however, instances, from *Fauvel* to Ciconia, of the later copying of pieces no longer topical, for reasons ranging from satire to musical interest, which should caution against over-literal assumptions about the topical life or the need for a specific occasion for the revival of such compositions (see Ch. 3 for *Fauvel*).

The motet has six stanzas—for Urban VI? As well as being an early example of void notation in England, the tenor uses coloration in the unusual reversed sense to provide perfect notes, the basic void notes being imperfect.[64] With some irregularities, it appears to have been isorhythmic in all voices.

The Pisan Antipopes

We move now to the events surrounding the Council of Pisa. The Veneto abandoned the Venetian pope Angelo Correr, Gregory XII, in favour of Pietro Filargo of Candia (Venetian Crete), who was elected Pope Alexander V (26 June, crowned 7 July 1409). The ranks of those who were to be his supporters had been augmented in the preceding few years by deserters from Rome, impatient at Gregory's nonfeasance. Briefly thought to have ended the Schism, this third papacy was of necessity itinerant, but based mainly in Bologna.

Two compositions, neither of them conventional motets, allude to Alexander, and *Argi vices* is for his successor John XXIII. The two pieces for the first Pisan pope are by two front-rank composers, neither of them directly documented in his service, Ciconia and, probably, Zacara.

Composers Serving Alexander V, and Works
by Ciconia and Zacara

Several possibilities have been put forward for the addressee and subject of Ciconia's *O Petre Christi discipule*.[65] These are set out at the end of Chapter 28 and are not rehearsed here, except to say that ambiguity remains as to whether the text celebrates two or three Peters. Jason Stoessel claims that just two Peters are referenced, St Peter and Pietro Filargo, elected as Alexander V at Pisa in 1409. He links it to an earlier 1406 oration by Zabarella in honour of Filargo, and dates it accordingly.[66] I agree with Di

---

[63] Strohm, *The Rise*, 16–17; the rest of his introduction gives more comments on this repertory.

[64] Also found in *Alpha vibrans* (PMFC 5, no. 25), Vitry's *Tuba/In arboris, O amicus* (Ch. 22) and *Ferre solet* of 1373 (see Louviot, 'Uncovering the Douai Fragment').

[65] Unfortunately, misprinted repeatedly in Bent, *Q15* as *discipuli*, due to an error in the database that generated the tables. Text and translation in Holford-Strevens, 'The Latin Poetry'.

[66] Stoessel, 'Johannes Ciconia and his Italian Poets', 228–33. See Ch. 28.

624   POPES, TRÉMOÏLLE AND CYPRUS

Bacco and Nádas that the text can be taken at three levels of invocation, first addressing the new pope Pietro [Filargo] who watches over another Pietro, then St Peter (*cephas*) who protects the new pope; then finally addressing Christ the leader of all, setting out the three levels *pastorem*, *clerum*, *populum*, St Peter, Filargo, and his protégé Pietro Emiliani, bishop of Vicenza.[67]

A newer addition to this two-equal-voice repertory, this time not a motet, is the ballata *Dime, Fortuna, poi che tu parlasti* in **Boverio**.[68] Both its manuscript neighbours and its musical and vivid autobiographical text style strongly suggest Zacara as the composer. It includes the words 'Se Alessandro a Roma gito fosse, Fortuna, al tuo despecto uscia de fosse'. This seems to express the speaker's frustration at Fortune that Alexander V had not returned to Rome; that is, that the Pisan election had not succeeded, and that the dependent speaker was thereby deprived of going to Rome with him. If both pieces were addressed to Alexander during his lifetime, they must date from the same nine-month period.

Alexander's short papacy was followed by that of John XXIII (the Neapolitan Baldassare Cossa, elected 17 May 1410). Before his election, he had been archbishop and papal legate in Bologna, a prime mover in the Council of Pisa, and one of those who helped get Alexander V elected. Together with Louis II of Anjou, he had led the successful siege and military campaign against Rome on behalf of Alexander V, finally taking the city in January 1410. When he was deposed and condemned by the Council of Constance, he was accused of having poisoned Alexander and his physician, and of all kinds of fraud and sexual misdemeanours.

Antonio Zacara da Teramo had been a singer and secretary in Rome under popes Boniface IX, Innocent VII, and Gregory XII from early in 1391 to at least 1407; his presence in Rome therefore overlapped with Ciconia's.[69] Di Bacco and Nádas have now pushed Zacara's Roman residence back to at least 5 January 1390, when he was paid for the writing, notation and illumination of an antiphonal for the hospital of Santo Spirito in Sassia, in a document that also reveals his patronymic: 'Magister Antonius Berardi Andree de Teramo alias dictus vulgariter Zacchara'.[70] Zacara's presence as *magister capelle* of John XXIII in Bologna in 1412–13 (after which he disappears) shows that he had transferred to the Pisan faction at some stage.[71] Indeed, an earlier association with Alexander V is attested by the new text in **Boverio**. However, his continued activity as 'scriptor litterarum apostolicarum' shows that he was in Rome up to the eve of Gregory XII's departure in June 1407. Here, if not before, he must have come into contact with Pietro Emiliani, who had served Gregory as clerk of the papal Camera from March of that year, and then as vice-chamberlain. Emiliani followed Gregory to Viterbo and Siena that summer, but left Gregory's retinue in October 1407, and was present in Pisa as a supporter and beneficiary of Filargo.[72] Zacara could

[67] Di Bacco and Nádas, 'Papal Chapels'. For Emiliani, see Bent, 'The Emiliani Chapel in the Frari'; 'Pietro Emiliani's Chaplain'; *Q15*, i, ch. I; and Girgensohn, 'Il testamento'.

[68] *Il Codice T. III.2*, ed. Ziino.

[69] Ziino, 'Magister Antonius', and Nádas, 'Further Notes'.

[70] Di Bacco and Nádas, 'Verso uno "stile internazionale"', 27, drawing on the 1390 document published in Esposito, 'Magistro Zaccara', 334–42, 446–49.

[71] Nádas, 'Further Notes', 178–79. See also Di Bacco and Nádas, 'Verso uno "stile internazionale"', 28, for the narrowing of Zacara's death date to between May 1413 and Sept. 1416.

[72] Girgensohn, 'Il testamento', 19.

EARLY PAPAL MOTETS   625

have done the same, or he could have left Gregory with other defectors in July 1408 to gather in Pisa in preparation for the Council.[73] The presence of Zacara's work in the Cividale fragments has been taken to imply that he may have been there for the abortive Council of Cividale called by Gregory XII from June to September 1409 where, deserted by most of his cardinals, he had fled with his remaining retinue. But there is no evidence that Zacara remained with Gregory after 1407 or that he accompanied him to Cividale; the presence of his and Filippotto's music in **Civ98** does not necessitate their physical presence there.

No motet survives for the new pope by Hubertus de Salinis or Matteo da Perugia, both known to be composer-singers in his retinue. Pietro Filargo must be suspected of strong musical persuasions and tastes, from the very fact of employing at least two notable composers. It has been suggested that the first stage of **ModA** may have been prepared for him by Matteo; the manuscript contains three essays by Ciconia in styles very different from each other, and each apparently unique in his output—*Sus un fontayne*, *Le ray au soleil*, and *Quod jactatur*.[74] But **ModA** preserves neither *O Petre Christi* nor *Dime Fortuna*, which are only in **Q15** and **Boverio** respectively. Given that Matteo merely disappears from the records but did not necessarily die in 1418, as previously reported, recent work proposes a later dating for **ModA**, after 1412, and for the later gatherings into the 1420s.[75]

Reinhard Strohm proposed that Pavia rather than Avignon was the main centre of cultivation of the French *ars subtilior*, and suggested that Filippotto and Antonello da Caserta, Ciconia, Matteo da Perugia, and Senleches may have been guests or clients of Giangaleazzo Visconti (ruled 1385–1402).[76] Anne Stone has pointed out that Filargo is known from later evidence to have had a house in Pavia, and convincingly suggests a possible genesis for **ModA** in his circle.[77] Matteo da Perugia had served in Filargo's chapel when he was archbishop of Milan, and Salinis was confirmed as a member promptly after the election. In the case of this conciliar election of a third pope, there was not an existing chapel for him to inherit, except insofar as deserters from Gregory were available in Pisa. **Q15** also presents the Paduan work of Ciconia, including the two motets for his patron Francesco Zabarella, who along with Jean Gerson and Du Fay's patron Pierre d'Ailly were noted supporters of music in addition to being the prime legal, theological and tactical movers in attempts to end first the twofold and then threefold Schism at the councils respectively of Pisa and Constance.

Matteo da Perugia is presumed to have followed his patron from Milan to Pisa and remained with him after his election as pope. His continuing service is not documented, but may be implied by his absence from Milan cathedral between 1407 and 1414.[78] Hubertus de Salinis appears as a papal familiar and singer on 10 July 1409,

---

[73] Nádas, 'Further Notes', 169.

[74] See Strohm, 'Magister Egardus', 59 for the suggestion that **ModA** originated in Filargo's circle, and that the pieces listed by Bartolomeo and Corradus may have been written for his coronation. For further development of this hypothesis see Stone, 'Writing Rhythm'.

[75] Stone, *The Manuscript Modena*, 101–6. An even later dating was proposed by Andrés Locatelli. See Ch. 26 n. 16.

[76] Strohm, 'Filippotto da Caserta', 65–74.

[77] Stone, 'Writing Rhythm', 15, 44–51.

[78] Maiani, 'Notes on Matteo da Perugia', 4–7.

626 POPES, TRÉMOÏLLE AND CYPRUS

three days after Alexander's coronation.[79] Boniface IX awarded his first papal benefice (as a deacon) on 29 May 1403 in a document indicating that he was at the time in Braga. This need not mean that Hubertus was Portuguese by birth; indeed his use of old texts known in the north and a motet for the Liégeois St Lambert strongly suggest that he, like so many other singers in receipt of high patronage, came from northern Europe. If he was too young to be a priest in 1403, there is one work which may be out of line chronologically, if indeed it is by him.[80] This is the ballade *En la saison* (**Chantilly**) for Thomasse le Blanc, the mother of Olivier du Guesclin. She died in 1406, but Gilbert Reaney says it could date from Olivier's lifetime, before 1397. The earlier date now looks less likely. Three Salinis motets are grouped together in **SL2211** (late 1410s); in the first layer of **Q15** they are scattered.[81] His Good Friday motet, *Jesu salvator*, heads the original opening page of **Ox213**; it can perhaps also be read as a salutation of new beginnings through Church councils. We know he was at Pisa; for Constance we have no evidence.

One other work, by Ciconia, is associated with this period and these events. Unlike the simultaneous texting of the Gloria with its trope *Clemens Deus artifex*, Ciconia's Gloria *Suscipe Trinitas* is troped in the more normal manner, with alternating sections, in three-part writing for the text of the Gloria of the Mass, and two-part sections for the added trope, otherwise unknown. The verses of the trope are addressed to the Trinity, to Mary, and to St Peter, the first pope and 'heavenly keeper of the keys'. The trinitarian references have contributed to the suggestion that the trope must date from the period of threefold Schism between the election of a third pope in 1409 and Ciconia's death in 1412.[82] Strohm suggests that it may have followed the election of John XXIII in 1410, 'whose support exceeded that of the other schismatic popes'.[83]

Salinis's troped Gloria *Jubilacio uni Deo* celebrates the end of the Schism, and has usually been dated to the election of a single pope, Martin V, in 1417. However, Salinis is no longer listed as a papal chaplain in 1413, when Zacara is named as *magister capelle* for John XXIII, and there is no evidence of his activity after that. It now seems more likely that the Gloria trope dates not from Constance (1417), but from Pisa (1409), when the election of Salinis's patron as Alexander V could well have been celebrated as ending the Schism, although that attempt turned out to be unsuccessful: for Salinis, see Chapter 27. Until the discovery of **SL2211**, all Salinis's mass music and motets were unique to **Q15**, except for one motet in **Ox213** and **Stras**, a newly discovered concordance in **Utrecht37** for another (see Table 27.1 above) and the Gloria *Jubilacio*, which also appears in **Venice145**. His mass music is transmitted together with Zacara's in **Q15**; we surely have here remnants of the repertory of Pisa–Bologna from the years 1409–14 as well as additions from Constance.

---

[79] On Salinis, see Di Bacco and Nádas, 'Papal Chapels', 71–72, and here Ch. 27.

[80] See Ch. 27. Günther calls it one of the latest works in **Chantilly**, by a very young Salinis ('Zwei Balladen', 38).

[81] See Boone, 'Dufay's Early Chansons', 29–31, and here Ch. 27.

[82] PMFC 24, p. xi.

[83] Strohm, *The Rise*, 17. But Di Bacco and Nádas, 'Papal Chapels', 70–77, argue for a date for this Gloria between 1390 and Philippe's death in 1397, placing it in Ciconia's Roman years that they have so persuasively documented. See Ch. 28.

Argi vices Polyphemus/Tum Philemon rebus: for John XXIII

The motet *Argi vices Polyphemus/Tum Philemon rebus*, unique to the manuscript **Ao** in a copy much later than its date of composition, is explicitly for John XXIII, possibly for his election in May 1410, but perhaps for the start of the Council of Constance, and at any rate before 1414, when he was discredited.[84] *Argi vices* joins the small number of compositions whose texts carry an indication that they were written by someone other than the composer.[85] Here the poet is named in the text simply as Guillermus, the composer as Nicolaus: 'Hec Guilhermus dictans favit | Nicolao, qui cantavit | ut sit opus consummatum' (William wrote these words as a favour to Nicholas, who sang them, in order for the work to be complete). Neither the poet nor the composer has been satisfactorily identified with any of the candidates of those names who have been put forward.[86]

Previous scholars considered both Nicolaus Zacarie and Nicolaus Grenon as possible candidates for this composer, but their candidacy has weakened in the absence of evidence of any connection with John's chapel. It has to be stated, however, that evidence for Nicolaus Frangens de Leodio, currently assumed by some to be the composer, is no more secure. Certainly the use of the verb *frangit* in triplum line 41 is insufficient: it is the clouds that are being broken through, and to attach this epithet to the composer involves special pleading of an unacceptable kind.[87] If he is to have written *Argi vices*, we have to assume a change of papal allegiance for which there is no evidence other than the wish to attribute the motet to him. This theory has him move to Bologna shortly after (putatively) leaving Gregory. He went to Cividale, moved to Treviso on 15 September 1411,[88] then returned to Cividale in 1414–18, where he died in 1433 after a time in Chioggia, 1419–21. His presence in Cividale, again, after the time when *Argi vices* must have been written, severely weakens the case for attributing it to him. In all, it must be concluded that a single Christian name, Nicholas, is much too fragile a basis for the attribution of this motet to any Nicholas not known to have been in John's chapel and not known to have been a musician, and the identity of the composer had better revert to unknown status.[89] The texts have many points of interest and are packed with classical and biblical allusions.[90]

---

[84] PMFC 13, no. 49. See also Allsen, 'Style and Intertextuality', 529–31. The motet is discussed at length by Cobin, 'The Aosta Manuscript'. Nosow, 'Florid and Equal-Discantus Motet', has pulled together this composer's biography and itinerary. Fischer, 'Bemerkungen', adds it to the list of Italian motets I published in Bent, 'Italian Motet' (now Ch. 26), thus vindicating Guillaume de Van's claims for the piece, which I had excluded because of its later transmission and because of an uncertain cut-off date for precedents for Ciconia.

[85] Other instances are *Alma polis/Axe poli*, Ch. 19, and *Portio nature/Ida capillorum*, for which see Zazulia, 'A Motet Ahead of its Time?'.

[86] For an authoritative edition and translation of the texts, see now Holford-Strevens, 'The Latin Poetry'.

[87] Holford-Strevens, 'The Latin Poetry', 462 n. 46, supports this view, showing 'Frangens' to depend on a false derivation. The PMFC editors reject attributions to Nicolaus Zacarie (favoured by Strohm, *The Rise*, 117–18) and Grenon and favour Nicolaus Frangens de Leodio (commentary, p. 285). A Nicolaus Simonis de Frangees de Leodio started his career in Avignon with Clement VII in 1380, though he is not identified as a singer. He was a mansionary at Cividale (Petrobelli, 'La musica nelle cattedrali', 467) in 1407; he joined the chapel of Gregory XII in May 1409 at Rimini and remained with him until Mar. 1410, by which time Gregory had withdrawn south to Gaeta. This is summarised in Nosow, 'Florid and Equal-Discantus Motet', 84.

[88] D'Alessi, *La Cappella musicale del duomo di Treviso*, 36–37.

[89] In the context of a magisterial survey of musical repertory and patronage of the conciliar period, Strohm, *The Rise*, 116–18, also draws attention to the motet's Italian features and seeks to reinstate an attribution to Nicolaus Zacarie, who first appears in the chapel of Martin V.

[90] Edited and translated in Holford-Strevens, 'The Latin Poetry', 461–69.

The Council of Constance and Martin V

The powerful Roman Colonna family had provided several fourteenth-century cardinals, but Martin V was its only pope. He had been a supporter of the Malatestas, for whom Du Fay wrote at least three pieces, of which the ballade *Resveilles vous* celebrates the wedding on 18 July 1423 of Carlo Malatesta, the brother of Cleophe and Pandolfo, to the pope's niece, Victoria Colonna, in a grand ceremony at Rimini. This not only cements the close bonds between Du Fay's patron families at this time, but provides a natural link for Du Fay's transition from Malatesta to papal patronage in the 1420s.[91] Hugo de Lantins, another Malatesta client, may have composed the rondeau *Mirar non posso* for the same occasion; it refers to the Colonna family.

We have seen that **Chantilly** represents a high point for celebratory pieces in Latin and French that include but are not confined to motets. The composition of ceremonial and topical ballatas and madrigals in Italy also reached its height around 1400, as represented in the repertory of the Modena and Lucca codices. This tradition is continued from the 1420s by the new generation of composers after Constance. Many of these vernacular pieces are for occasions connected closely to papal concerns or even driven by papal politics. Lantins's *Tra quante regione*, like Du Fay's motet *Vasilissa ergo gaude*, celebrates the wedding (or at least the nuptial journey) of Cleophe Malatesta to the despot Theodore Palaiologos of Mystra; she departed on 20 August 1420. This wedding was part of a post-Constance campaign to heal the rift between the Eastern and Western churches by marrying Italian princesses to Byzantine rulers. Du Fay's unique vernacular motet *Apostolo glorioso* was for Cleophe's brother Pandolfo Malatesta as bishop of Patras, an appointment with a similarly ecumenical (or even territorial) intent. It is rather striking that we have no compositions from Du Fay's pen that are overtly dedicated to Martin, in whose chapel he served from 1428, while we do have pieces by him for Eugene IV from his periods of service with that pope (until 1433, and 1435–37 in Florence). However, Alejandro Planchart has shown that Du Fay had already left Constance at the time of Martin's election, and was in Cambrai from at least late 1417 to early 1420, so he could not yet have been a papal singer.[92]

Nicolaus Zacarie's vernacular ballata *Già per gran nobeltà*, another two-voice piece (following *O Petre Christi discipule* and *Dime, Fortuna*), but not, this time, for equal voices, may date from 1420 when this composer first appears in Martin V's chapel; it immediately precedes Du Fay's Malatesta–Colonna ballade *Resveilles vous* in **Ox213**.[93] It is certainly a better piece than Nicolaus Zacarie's presumably later motet for St Barbara, *Letetur plebs fidelis/Pastor qui revelavit*, written (by internal signature) in Tarento, and strongly indebted to Ciconia's *O felix templum*. Despite the coincidences of name and cogent arguments on behalf of the various candidates,

---

[91] Schuler, 'Zur Geschichte'. For a new proposal that Du Fay's principal Malatesta patron, following Constance, was the clerical Pandolfo, brother of Cleophe and Carlo (of the Pesaro branch, all three with Du Fay dedications), see Bent, 'Petrarch, Padua, the Malatestas'.

[92] Planchart, 'The Early Career', 361.

[93] Schuler, 'Zur Geschichte'.

EARLY PAPAL MOTETS   629

I do not think he can be the composer Nicolaus of the motet *Argi vices* for Pope John XXIII, discussed above.

The motet *Clarus ortu/Gloriosa mater* for Martin V has been treated as anonymous because the author's name is cut off in its unique source: . . . *composuit*. Robert Nosow persuasively reads 'Fr[ater] Antonius de Civitato' by analogy with the attribution to this composer elsewhere in the same manuscript.[94]

CANTUS I

Clarus ortu, clarior opere		Illustrious in birth, more illustrious in achievement,
clarissimus regnans in ethere		most illustrious ruling in heaven,
digna laudum dignus suscipere		worthy to undertake things worthy of praise,
Georgius Capadox genere		George, Cappadocian by race,
tribunatum solitus agere	5	accustomed to fulfil the tribune's office,
Palestinam festinat subdere		hastens to subdue Palestine,
miserando Lydditas solvere		to free the wretched men of Lydda,
truculentem draconem cedere		slay the fierce dragon,
mesto regi filiam reddere		restore the sad king his daughter,
pro mercede thesaurum spernere	10	refuse a treasure for his reward,
nudam fide turbam induere		clothe the naked crowd in faith,
debis binis regem instruere		instruct the king in twice two things:
ecclesiam mente diligere		to love the church with his mind,
sacerdotum decus attollere		to exalt the honour of the clergy,
officio Dei persistere	15	to hold fast to God's service,
de misello compungi paupere		to take pity on the unhappy poor man;
Christianos lugens deficere		be wearied with weeping for Christians,
hos tormentis istos in carcere		some under torture, others in prison;
Dacianum videns succumbere		seeing the Dacian succumb, he offers
caput offert cruenti dextere	20	his head to the right hand of the bloodstained one
ut sit carnis excussus onere		that freed thus of the burden of the flesh
beatorum letetur munere.		he may rejoice in the rank of the blessed.
Felix Roma cujus in aggere		Happy Rome on whose hill
Georgius dignatur tollere		George deigns to exalt his happy name that,
felix nomen quod felix federe	25	happy in the covenant,
cardinalis levita prospere		the cardinal deacon auspiciously glories
gloriatur inceptum gerere		to carry on what he has begun,
velum gaudens aureum jungere		rejoicing to join the golden veil;
generose martyr amplectere		noble martyr, embrace
vota nostra sursum erigere.	30	the upraising of our prayers.

[94] **Ox213**, ff. 117ᵛ–118ʳ, published in *Polyphonia Sacra*, ed. van den Borren, no. 23. Nosow, 'Florid and Equal-Discantus Motet', 73–76. The comparable inscription is on f. 8ᵛ. The text has been emended by Leofranc Holford-Strevens and David Howlett, whose translation is used here.

CANTUS II

Gloriosa mater ecclesia	Glorious mother church,
orbem sacris alens uberibus	feeding the world with thy holy breasts,
pretiosa ducens primordia	drawing the precious beginnings
ex unici Christi visceribus	from the entrails of Christ the unique,
desponsari non amat pluribus 5	does not have to be betrothed to man,
sed tueri rite vicaria	but properly to preserve the successions
uno gaudet de stirpe regia	rejoices in one of royal stock
et Romanis imperatoribus	and the Roman emperors,
cuius amor	whose love
absterget lacrymam neque luctus 10	shall wipe away tears, nor shall there be weeping
erit neque clamor.	or crying.
De Columna fit Odo primitus	Oddo Colonna, who would then
tunc futurus basis justitie	be the basis of justice,
Georgius titulum meritus	first became George, having earned his title of grace,
cardinalis levita gratie. 15	a cardinal deacon.
Nunc Martinus lucerna glorie	Now he is Martin the lamp of glory,
dignitate papali preditus	possessing the papal dignity,
vita bonis malis interitus	life to the good, death to the bad.
ad jus ejus status pastorie	The state of the pastorship must be restored
redigendus 20	to its right;
hic tibi precipue sit pura mente	let this above all be honoured by thee
colendus.	with pure mind.
Verus pastor ut Deus colitur	The true shepherd is worshipped as a god
dum residet nixus in specula	while he dwells leaning on the watchpost;
lex Moysi per eum regitur 25	the law of Moses is governed by him,
archa Noe Petrina vicula	Noah's ark, Peter's skiff,
turris David vas implens vascula	the tower of David, the vessel filling smaller vessels;
lapis Jacob oleo tingitur	Jacob's stone is oiled;
vite mortalis divus efficitur	a mortal is made divine,
cuncta claudens sub ejus regula 30	enclosing all things under the rule
majestatis	of his majesty,
facit ut pateant celesti regna	and causes the celestial to be opened
beatis.	to the blessed.

The tenor is *Justus non conturbabitur*, an obsolete Gradual from the old office proper to St Stephen, celebrated as pope and martyr on 2 August.[95] The motet texts honour the Colonna family, especially its members who were church dignitaries, and above all Martin V, who before his election was Cardinal-Deacon at the church of S. Giorgio in Velabro in Rome, otherwise known as *Sancti Georgii ad Velum aureum*, and is thus referred to in both texts. Martin's strong connection with Rome (and even with the Roman emperors) is stressed: Cantus I refers to the eighth-century elevation

---

[95] *Le Codex 121*, 284; *Antiphonarium Tonale Missarum*, 179.

of the church within the walls of Rome as the seat of the cardinalate,[96] and Cantus II expresses hopes for a return of papal law (*lex moyse*), stresses Old Testament antecedents, and may also underlie the choice of tenor. A parallel is implied between St George's rescue of Christians from persecution at the hands of Dacian in Cantus I, and the position of Martin V at the end of the Schism. Nosow suggests performance on St George's day after Martin's eventual entry into Rome in September 1420, i.e. 23 April 1421.[97]

Musically, the motet has a long single *color* (like *Petre clemens*), but divided into two sections (like St Martin's cloak?). The tenor for the second division has a ꜱ signature, implying four new minims in the time of three preceding. Each section has three *taleae*. There is an untexted twelve-breve *introitus* in ℭ, with canonic imitation at two breves' distance, strict until the last two breves. This is the first known motet composed for Rome in the fifteenth century, celebrating the return of Martin V to his titular church as the sole legitimate pontiff.

The title *Martine sancte pontifex* is cited in fifteenth-century eastern European sources as being in the simple style of the *antiqui*; the text was set in central European sources over a long period. It must, however, refer not to the Colonna pope Martin V but to the much earlier bishop, St Martin.[98] A motet of the early fifteenth century, *Deo gracias papales/Deo gracias fidelis* in **Nuremberg9**, is named together with *Virginem mire pulcritudinis* in **Wrocław16** as using imperfect modus, perfect time and minor prolation, implying that they are modern works (see Ch. 15).[99]

Motets by Brassart

Johannes Brassart is recorded as a singer with Eugene IV (elected 3 March 1431) on 5 March and 24 April 1431, and remained until November. He was succentor at Saint-Jean l'Évangeliste, Liège, from 1422 to 1431 and celebrated his first Mass there in 1426, and from 1428 he also held a post at the Cathedral of St Lambert in Liège. He was admitted in his own right to the Council of Basel in 1433, was *rector capelle* to the

---

[96] Nosow, 'Florid and Equal-Discantus Motet', 74.

[97] The account of this motet by Nosow, 'Florid and Equal-Discantus Motet', enables us to set aside the suggestion by Schuler, 'Die Musik in Konstanz', 161–62, that it was for Martin's nephew Prospero Colonna, who was likewise Cardinal-Deacon at S. Giorgio in Velabro, from 8 Nov. 1430. It seems altogether right to recognise this as yet another papal motet with political and propaganda import, composed not for the papal coronation itself but early in the new pope's reign.

[98] Witkowska-Zaremba (ed.), *Notae musicae artis*, 536, citing treatises in **BOZ3** (before 1467) and the Prague MS of Petrus Besch, **Pra103**, which follows: 'Nam antiqui notis minimis vel semiminimis non utebantur, sed solum brevibus et semibrevibus interdum et valde raro simplicibus longis. Unde minime et semiminime postea per subtilitatem successorum sunt invente, ut patet in *Nicolai solemnia* vel *Martine sancte pontifex*, ubi solum plane vel simplices concordancie sunt ordinate et in talibus antiqui delectabantur. Sed moderni ingenio subtiliores et vocibus agiliores plures invenerunt concordancias et fracturas.' Although there is some ambiguity in the order of this account, it seems that both pieces were in the simple style of the *antiqui*, as opposed to the more elaborate music of the *moderni*.

[99] Text and music of *Deo gracias papales* are transcribed in Cuthbert, 'The Nuremberg and Melk Fragments', reporting (by clever sleuthing) that it was also in **Gdańsk2315**, lost since the Second World War, but partially transcribed by Hanoch Avenary, giving the incipit of a contratenor (or perhaps motetus), *Deo gracias salvator*. No specific pope is celebrated.

632   POPES, TRÉMOÏLLE AND CYPRUS

Emperor Sigismund from 1434, and remained in imperial service until at least 1443.[100] Two of his motets may refer to Martin V.

The texts of *Magne Deus potencie/Genus regale esperie* are problematic. They have been privately judged by no less a Latinist than Leofranc Holford-Strevens to be 'almost incomprehensible, with very little grammatical coherence, almost as bad as [the fourteenth-century motet] *Apta caro*'.[101] The texts are not given here, and must await further study. Ambros suggested that the motet was for a pope, but without venturing to say which one.[102] Brassart was a member of the papal choir in 1431, which has led several scholars to believe that *Magne Deus* was written for the election of Eugene IV.[103] Brassart's two motets *Ave Maria gracia plena/O Maria gracia plena* (also in **Tr87**, f. 51[v]) and *Magne Deus potencie/Genus regale esperie* (*unicum*) are both present in the original layer of **Q15** (Q15-I), which has a terminal date of *c.* 1425.[104] For this reason I reject the possibility that it could be for Eugene's coronation. If *Magne Deus* is for a pope, it cannot be for one later than Martin V, although there is not even a *columna* (Colonna) in the text to encourage that association.

Brassart did, however, spend time at the curia of Martin V.[105] On 16 May 1424 he was given permission to leave Liège to visit the Roman curia, and was paid his salary for the entire year before departing.[106] 1425 was a Jubilee year and Rome was thronged with pilgrims. He reappears in the Liège archives in 1426 when, now as *dominus*, he celebrates his first Mass. We cannot yet tell if this was an isolated connection with the curia or if the visit had musical antecedents or consequents. Brassart's papal visit could also have permitted the indirect transmission of this or other works to **Q15**, as well as opening the possibility that they acknowledge favours granted by Martin to Brassart or that they are supplicatory motets written by Brassart for Martin.

Musically, *Magne Deus* resembles other motets from papal circles in the 1420s, including *Clarus ortu* (discussed above), *Ad honorem* by Grenon, and *Apostolo glorioso* by Du Fay. There is no list of Martin's singers immediately prior to his death; but those confirmed by Eugene in a standard supplication on 5 March 1431, just two days after his election, surely include many of Martin's chaplains. Brassart is one of the fourteen singers listed; there is a strong probability that he had some previous connection with Martin's chapel.[107]

---

[100] *O rex Fridrice* celebrates the accession of Frederick III in 1440. The last document referring to him is dated 7 Feb. 1445 (Keith Mixter, *NG1*). For the most recent work on Brassart, see Wright, 'A New Attribution to Brassart?'; Saucier, *A Paradise of Priests*; 'Johannes Brassart's *Summus secretarius*', and 'Reading Hagiographic Motets'.

[101] Private communication.

[102] Ambros, *Geschichte*.

[103] For example Fallows, *Dufay*, 264. Lütteken, *Guillaume Dufay*, now rejects a dedication to Eugene IV (I agree, but for different reasons), as he rules out his own earlier suggestion that it could be for Amadeus V of Savoy, which is much too late to fit the motet's early transmission (pp. 286–87). The best summary of interpretations of this motet is given in Allsen, 'Style and Intertextuality', 430–32. Allsen concludes partly on the basis of stylistic affinity that this motet belongs with a group from the early and middle 1420s; I agree.

[104] The text erasures at the beginning of this motet seem to have been made solely to clarify the underlay and do not change the text itself. As Lütteken points out (*Guillaume Dufay*, 286), the common reading *decus* results from a misreading of this erasure.

[105] Mixter, 'Johannes Brassart', 40. Some discussions of the date of *Magne Deus* neglect this contact.

[106] 'Item xvi maii Jo. brassar de ludo pro gratia sibi facta per capitulum qui Ivit versus curiam Romanum . . .'; Mixter, 'Johannes Brassart', 40.

[107] Note the different case of Matteo da Perugia, who was a personal chaplain to Filargo and remained with him on his election as Pope Alexander V.

EARLY PAPAL MOTETS   633

This tentative dating of *Magne Deus* prompts a closer look at another motet by Brassart, *Te dignitas presularis*. The single text of this motet quotes at the end an entire antiphon for St Martin (*Martinus adhuc*):[108]

Te dignitas presularis		Thee the priestly dignity,
strenuitas militaris		military valour,
et fidei caritas		and the charity of faith
habilem reddunt pastorem		make an apt shepherd,
solertissimum tutorem	5	a most diligent guardian,
ovilis Dominici.		of the Lord's flock.
Decor nam si corporalis		For if you had corporal beauty,
tamen vita liberalis		yet you had generous life;
quem sanctorum paritas		whom equality with the saints
adornavit qua dilectus	10	has ennobled, where the beloved
Ihesu et mundo electus		Jesus is, and chosen by the world,
clarens rite magnificus.		glorious, duly magnificent.
O Martine exaudi nos qui dignus		O Martin, hear our prayer, who art worthy
audire Ihesum digne promere		to hear Jesus, worthy to take forth,
Martinus adhuc cathecuminus hac me	15	Martin while still a catechumen clothed me
veste contexit.		with this garment.

Oddo Colonna was elected on St Martin's Day, 11 November 1417, and took the name Martin. Given the other connections between Brassart and this pope, although they still lack archival anchorage apart from the 1424 visit, it seems very likely that this text to St Martin also addresses Pope Martin as the earthly type of the saint ('ovili dominici decor/solertissimum tutorem': glory of the flock of God, one and only protector). It may also represent a petition for protection by the composer to his employer, present or future: cover me with your cloak (St Martin).[109]

Nosow places *Te dignitas presularis* on St Martin's Day 1430, presumably because Brassart is assumed not to have been free to join the papal chapel until about this time.[110] The possibility must remain open that after his 1425 visit Brassart retained contacts, and a musical relationship, with Martin; we have stated that *Magne Deus* must be from the first half of the decade because of its presence in the first stage of **Q15**.[111] The fermata chords on *O Martine*, the treble-dominated style, and the single text are among stylistic features that make a dating around 1430 quite comfortable for *Te dignitas presularis*, as also for Feragut's *Excelsa civitas Vincencia* of 1433.[112]

Te dignitas presularis (also in **Tr87**, ff. 77^v–78^r) is one of two motets by Brassart copied into **Q15** at the second stage of compilation in the early 1430s. The other is *O flos fragrans* (also in **Ox213**, **Tr87**). *Gratulemur Christicole* (*unicum*) and *Summus*

---

[108] Both motets are published in CMM 35. For the antiphon, see *CAO*, no. 3712 and *AS*, pl. 594. The translation is by David Howlett.

[109] A similar petition is embodied in the John the Baptist motet *O amicus/Precursoris*. See Ch. 22.

[110] Nosow, 'The Florid and Equal-Discantus Motet', 116.

[111] *Pace* Lütteken, *Guillaume Dufay*, 286, 91.

[112] For the dating of *Excelsa* not in 1409 but in 1433, see Bent, 'A Contemporary Perception', and *Q15*, 90–99.

634   POPES, TRÉMOÏLLE AND CYPRUS

secretarius (also in **Ox213**) are added on second-layer openings but at the third stage (from *c.* 1434), which also includes mass settings by Brassart. It is likely that these latest works were collected and added by the Vicenza delegation to the Council of Basel, *c.* 1434.[113] Brassart's motet *Summus secretarius* was thought to be for an unknown papal secretary, but Robert Nosow claimed that we need look no further for a candidate than the Holy Ghost, thus removing it from the list of topical or potentially datable pieces.[114] More recently, Catherine Saucier has located the text within the medieval cult of St John the Evangelist and placed it at the church of Saint-Jean l'Evangéliste in Liège where Brassart served as a singer, chaplain, priest and canon.[115] We can now tentatively add *Clarus ortu* and *Te dignitas presularis* to the list of motets composed for a pope but not for his coronation, possibly also *Magne Deus potencie/ Genus regale esperie.*

Martin V died on 20 February 1431; Eugene IV (the Venetian Gabriele Condulmer) was elected on 3 March and crowned on 11 March. Promptly after his election he reinstated the members of Martin V's chapel (on 5 March), including Du Fay. Eugene offended the Colonnas by seeking to undo the territorial web set up by Martin for his nephews. His antagonism towards both the Colonnas and the Malatestas, two of Du Fay's patron families, led to some discomfort and a rapid exodus of the singers he had retained, despite efforts soon after his election to secure benefices for them. He also at the same time encouraged attention to both the fabric and the musical traditions of cathedrals.

Eugenius IV and Motets by Du Fay

Du Fay's grand and solemn motet *Ecclesie militantis* has invited many datings. Franz Xavier Haberl proposed a date of 1436, when Florence, Venice and Francesco Sforza formed a league against the Visconti, Milan and Genoa.[116] A further temptation to consider this date is provided by a bull of Eugene IV (24 November 1436) starting *Militantis ecclesie*, relating to the reformed congregation of S. Giustina and naming to office the Archbishop of Milan, the bishops of Castello and Rimini, and the Abbot of Montecassino.[117] *Ecclesie militantis* is the only possibly datable work by Du Fay that might fall within the repertory cultivated by the **Q15** scribe but was not included in that manuscript. It survives uniquely, and in an anomalous layout, in **Tr87**, probably copied in the late 1430s. A dating of the motet in 1436 would have helped to point to *c.* 1435 as the terminal date of work on **Q15** and a more mundane reason for the exclusion of *Ecclesie militantis.* But the church militant is too common a formulation to impose such an interpretation; and Julie Cumming, who gives the best recent summary of the debate about the motet's dating, has pointed to uses of *ecclesia militans* in other conciliar documents from Constance and Basel, describing Eugene's stand as a declaration of

[113] Bent, 'Bishop Francesco Malipiero' and 'Francesco Malipiero and Antonio da Roma'.
[114] Nosow, 'The Florid and Equal-Discantus Motet'.
[115] Saucier, 'Johannes Brassart's *Summus secretarius*'. See also Saucier, 'Reading Hagiographic Motets', on Brassart and Liège.
[116] Haberl, *Wilhelm Du Fay*, 88.
[117] Leccisotti, 'La congregazione benedettina', 461.

war.[118] The church militant was clearly in the air. The elegiac couplet of the contratenor confirms the militant spirit:

> Bella canunt gentes: querimur, Pater optime, tempus.
>
> The nations sing of war; we bewail, o best father, the time.

An even later date, 1439, has been suggested by David Crawford.[119] Heinrich Besseler and Guillaume de Van have won wider acceptance for their identification of the piece as a coronation motet for Eugene IV in 1431.[120] Charles Hamm's doubt, on mensural grounds, about a dating as early as 1431 for this piece assumes added interest in the context of its absence from **Q15**, whose later additions were completed by about 1435.[121] Alejandro Planchart has suggested that the motet might have been excluded from **Q15** because it would have 'appeared to many as a cruel joke, particularly in the years 1434–38. Eugene's moment of glory went by very quickly and, in fact, were it not for Philip the Good, he would probably be reckoned today as an antipope'.[122] The survival of the piece in the 'conciliar' Trent source **Tr87** makes good sense in the context of the diplomatic positions taken in relation to the Council of Basel between 1431 and 1433. The Council had been called by Martin V shortly before his death and it got off to a slow start. Eugene tried to dissolve it and failed to do so. It was not until 1433 that he officially supported it and, once he was himself persuaded of its value, applied pressure on bishops for their support. Stanza 3 refers to the pope's election, but in the past tense, and in sombre rather than celebratory mood. But the mention of the election with use of his previous name Gabriel [Condulmer] would tend to place it early in his reign.

Julie Cumming's argument is amplified with a musical analysis of the warring elements combined in this extraordinary work, and she accepts it as a political statement and propaganda on behalf of Eugene, likewise early in the new pope's reign, also recognising both his new and his papal name, but more concerned with the immediate (and in some ways parallel) political problems that the new pope had to address in the first year of his pontificate. *Ecclesie militantis* therefore probably dates from sometime after Eugene's election but before Du Fay's departure from Rome for Savoy in August 1433; he rejoined the papal chapel in Florence in 1435. Because of the prominent mention at the beginning of 'Rome seat of the Church Militant' it is presumably before Eugene was driven from Rome on 4 June 1434, not to return until 1443, unless it can be argued that the affirmation of Rome would be made precisely because of Eugene's exile.

Few if any of the papal motets here reviewed have any claim to be ceremonial coronation pieces. *Supremum est mortalibus* celebrates the meeting of Eugene and King Sigismund in Rome before Sigismund's imperial coronation (31 May 1433), and is

---

[118] Cumming, 'Concord out of Discord', ch. 10. For the manuscript format, see Welker, *Musik am Oberrhein*, 78–80.

[119] Crawford, 'Guillaume Dufay, Hellenism, and Humanism'. Cumming elegantly refutes his case (see previous note).

[120] Among those who have more recently affirmed this dating are Fallows, *Dufay*, 112, and Lütteken, *Guillaume Dufay*, 286, where he also speculates how Du Fay could have composed *Ecclesie militantis* in only a week by starting before the pope had chosen his new name.

[121] Hamm, *A Chronology*, 67–70; Bent, *Q15*.

[122] Private communication of 28.9.1980.

not a motet for the coronation itself. We should perhaps entertain the idea of their use as edifying and politically charged chamber music in private and semi-private contexts.

There is surprisingly little recycling, contrafaction, or even neutralising of occasional motets at this period. An isolated case is *Stirps mocinigo*, where **BU2216** substitutes 'N' for this doge's name. Rather the reverse: **Q15** gives us a unique example of repertory renewal within the detectable history of a single book. Many pieces were jettisoned, including, for example, textually neutral Magnificats; at the same time, occasional motets for long-dead patrons were recopied up to twenty years after their and Ciconia's death without textual change but often with musical modification. In some cases the circumstances of the commission and first performance can be inferred or guessed. But why were they recopied? There is strong evidence for the use of that manuscript for domestic performance for Pietro Emiliani, bishop of Vicenza, by his own familiars and by visiting musical canons of Vicenza and Padua cathedrals, depending on where he and they were at the time. This merely confirms what we thought happened anyway, but the evidence for it in Emiliani's case is particularly suggestive and multi-stranded. Bertrand Feragut's motet *Excelsa civitas Vincencia* was written close to the time of the election of Francesco Malipiero as bishop in 1433, and the text even makes it possible that it was in this case inaugural (though Malipiero's entry was made by proxy), but for Malipiero, not Emiliani; the scribe reassigned it posthumously to Emiliani (bishop 1409–33), helping to cement the view that the collection stands very close to the loyal household familiars of that music-loving bishop who were antagonistic to his successor.[123]

A dating of 1436 is secure for *Nuper rosarum flores*, which celebrates Pope Eugenius's rededication of Florence cathedral and Brunelleschi's new dome. The musical proportions and their significance have been much discussed, and need no further comment here.[124] With these and the other political and commemorative motets of Du Fay we enter well-trodden ground and more certain anchorage, a good point at which to end this survey. It has perhaps provided a framework and incentive for further discussion of connections and *topoi* that establish papal motets as a subgenre, albeit of a tradition fragile at first in identity and in preservation. Dating considerations presented here suggest that we should, again, be cautious in applying the default assumption that a commemorative motet is likely to be inaugural. That leaves open the question on whose initiative or commission such pieces were written, and may shift more of the responsibility from formal papal commission to individual initiative by composers, whether already within the curia or as supplicants from outside.

---

[123] See Bent, *Q15*, and earlier studies.

[124] Most notably Warren, 'Brunelleschi's Dome', Wright, '*Nuper rosarum*', and Trachtenberg, 'Architecture and Music'. I would only add that the text itself forms a kind of cupola, formed by what lies between the words *Eugenius* and *Florentie*, which are respectively preceded and followed by 28 words, the main number governing the motet's musical structure. From *Eugenius* to *Florentiae* inclusive are 25 words (the rededication took place on 25 Mar.) and flank praise of the *templum* and of the Virgin to whom it was dedicated. In the prose *Nuper almos rose flores* (Wright, p. 436), possibly also by Du Fay, the word 'Gabriel' (Eugenius's Christian name as Gabriele Condulmer) is also precisely placed at word 29, the same position that 'Eugenius' occupies in *Nuper rosarum*. See, most recently, Zazulia, *Where Sight Meets Sound*, ch. 3.

The crusades form an abiding theme, and aspects of the motet texts reflect the shift from the particular crusade politics of the 1340s, which provide the context for Vitry's *Petre clemens*, to those of a century later. Military elements are increasingly common in papal discourse in the fifteenth century, with more emphasis on reconciliation with or recovery of the Eastern church, crusades against the Turks, and eventually the fall of Constantinople in 1453. Indeed, connections with the crusades and their papal component have often been pointed out in discussions of the complex of *l'homme armé* compositions. In the fourteenth century there is naturally a stronger emphasis on the recovery of Rome, the historical Holy See. The secular alliances and military support that were needed before the papacy could be securely re-established in Rome mean that imagery of and allusions to the Church militant were never far away, culminating in Du Fay's *Ecclesie militantis/Sanctorum arbitrio/Bella canunt gentes*.

Appendix
Music for Popes John XXII(?) to Eugene IV

Composition	Composer	Pope	Sources
MOTETS AND MASS MOVEMENTS			
Per grama protho paret (mo)/*Valde honorandus est beatus Johannes* (T)	Anon.	John XXII? Possible connection with Pierre Roger has been suggested	**McV**, f. 26 (no. 1)
Petre clemens/Lugentium/Non est inventus	Vitry	Clement VI (Pierre Roger)	**Aachen**, f. 2^r; **Ivrea**, ff. 37^v–38; **Trém**; texts in **Paris3343** and **Vienna4195**
Gloria *Clemens Deus artifex*	Anon.	Clement VI	**Ivrea**, no. 45, ff. 27^v–28
Kyrie *Rex angelorum*; motetus trope *Clemens pater, conditor syderum*	Anon.	Clement VI?	**Ivrea**, no.71, ff. 53^v–54^v; **Apt**, 1^r–2^r; **Barc971**, f. 1^r
Pictagore per dogmata/O terra sancta/Rosa vernans	Anon.	Gregory XI, *c.* 1375	**Chantilly**, ff. 63^v–64
Alme pater (Tr/T)	Anon.	Urban VI, 1385?	**Fountains**, f. 14^v
Gaudeat et exultet . . . Papam querentes, with contrafact(?): *Novum sidus orientis . . . De scintilla*	Anon.	Clement VII and Urban VI, 1378 or soon after	**Basel71**, **Basel72** (contrafact?)
O Petre Christi discipule	Ciconia	Alexander V? Filargo, and possibly Emiliani	**Q15** (I), ff. R259^v–260
Gloria *Suscipe trinitas*	Ciconia	Schism	**Warsaw378**, ff. 25^v–27; **Pad675** (PadD), f. 2^v; **GR224**, ff. 9^v–10^v; **GRss**, f. 2^v
Benedicta viscera/Ave mater/Ora pro nobis	Velut	Schism; Virgn birth	**Ox213**, ff. 102^v–103
Eya dulcis/Vale placens	Tapissier	Prayer to Virgin for end of Schism	**Ox213**, ff.139^v–140
Venite adoremus/Salve sancta	Carmen	Schism; God and Trinity	**Q15** (III, I), ff. A353^v–354 and R224^v–225; **Ox213**, ff. 138^v–139
Argi vices Polyphemus/Tum Philemon rebus paucis	Nicolaus/ Guillermus	John XXIII	**Ao**, ff. 4^v–7
. . . de qua cordis/Trinitatem	Anon.	1409–15, threefold Schism?	**Houghton122**
Gloria *Jubilacio uni Deo*	Salinis	end of Schism	**Q15** (I), ff. R62^v–64; **Venice145**, ff. 15^v–19

*Clarus ortu/Gloriosa mater ecclesia/Justus non conturbatitur**	Antonio da Cividale?	Martin V, 1420?	**Ox213**, ff. 117^v–118
*Te dignitas presularis**	Brassart	Martin V	**Q15** (II), ff. R266^v–267; **Tr87**, ff. 77^v–78
Magne Deus/Genus regale	Brassart	Martin V?	**Q15** (I), ff. R253^v–254
*Balsamus et munda cera**	Du Fay	Eugene IV, 7 Apr. 1431	**Q15** (III), ff. R191^v–192
*Ecclesie militantis/Sanctorum arbitrio/Bella canunt gentes**	Du Fay	Eugene IV, 1431–33?	**Tr87** (I), ff. 85^v–86 and 95^v–96
*Supremum est mortalibus**	Du Fay	Eugene IV and Sigismund, 21 May 1433	**Q15** (III), ff. R190^v–191; **BU2216**, f. 28^v; **Tr92**, ff. 32^v–34; **MuEm**, ff. 107 ^{v}–109; **ModB**, ff. 66^v–67; **Cop17a**, f. 17
Nuper rosarum flores	Du Fay	Eugene IV; Florence, 25 Mar. 1436	**ModB**, ff. 67^v–68; **Tr92**, ff. 21^v–23
Sanctus ('papale')	Du Fay		**Tr92**, ff. 213^v–215; **Tr90**, ff. 277^r–279^v; **Tr93**, ff. 350^r–352^v; **Q15** (III), ff. A134^v–135
Agnus *Custos et pastor ovium*	Du Fay		**Tr92**, ff. 208^v–210

LATIN BALLADES AND VERNACULAR PIECES

*Inclite flos orti Gebenensis**	Mayhuet de Joan	tenor 'pro papa Clemente' [VII]	**ModA**, f. 15; **Chantilly**, f. 41
*Courtois et sages**	Magister Egidius	Clement VII (acrostic); validity of election	**ModA**, f. 35; **Reina**, f. 54
*Par les bons gedeons**	Filippotto da Caserta	'le souverayn pape qui s'appelle Clement' [VII]	**ModA**, f. 31; **Chantilly**, f. 45^v; **Boverio**, f. 5^v ('antipape')
Veri almi pastoris	Conradus de Pistoria	for a pope?	**ModA**, f. 36^v
Dime, Fortuna, poi che tu parlasti (ballata)	A. Zacara?	'Se Alessandro a Roma gito fosse' [Alexander V]	**Boverio**, f. 2
*Arte psalentes**	Bartolomeus de Bononia	musical collegium singing for a true shepherd, supreme pontiff [Alexander V or John XXIII?]	**ModA**, ff. 37^v–38
Mirar non posso	H. de Lantins	Colonna: Victoria or Martin V?	**Ox213**, f. 26
Gia per gran nobeltà (ballata)*	N. Zacarie	Martin V, 1420?	**Ox213**, f. 125^v

* Recorded by the Orlando Consort on 'Popes & Antipopes', MET CD 1008 on CD-SAR 49.

31
Trémoïlle Revisited

As the lone surviving bifolio from a large-format manuscript of fourteenth-century music, **Trém** (Paris, Bibliothèque nationale de France, nouv. acq. fr. 23190) has attracted scholarly attention in generous proportion to its modest extent because of the index to the lost collection that is inscribed on its first recto.[1] Many items listed can be identified with some certainty as pieces known from other manuscripts. **Trém** is routinely listed among the sources for editions of those pieces, although in nearly all cases the music is not preserved there. With about 70 motets listed, it is the largest documented motet collection of the century. It bears a note of ownership dated 1376 which had been taken to provide a *terminus ante quem* for the composition dates of all the pieces indexed; this interpretation will be refined here. The remainder of the bifolio contains in complete or partial form the music of four motets corresponding to the index numbers for those folios, giving not only a general sense of the appearance and quality of the manuscript and a sample of the scribe's work and procedures, but some basis for assessing how the index related to the lost volume. The intact parchment bifolio is of large format, measuring 50 × 32.5 cm, and must have been the outer bifolio of the first gathering. This adapted version of the earlier article includes a corrected transcription of the index with an updated list of concordant sources (in the Appendix to this chapter), three or possibly four new motet identifications (*Beatius/Cum humanum*, *Plausu querulo/Plausu querulo*, *Flos vernans/Fiat intencio* and *Thoma tibi*), and one or two new composer attributions to Denis le Grant.

Since the original publication (1990) I have become sensitised to the distinction between indexes and tables of contents. Indexes are in some way classified, whether alphabetically, by genre or some other criterion. A table of contents lists works in the order in which they appear in the manuscript or, in the case of a prescriptive table, the order in which they were intended to appear. I diagnosed the **Chantilly** 'index' as a case of the latter type: the pieces are listed in the order in which they appear, and the folio numbers supplied later.[2] Likewise prescriptive is the index of **MachautA**.[3]

An earlier version of this chapter was published as 'A Note on the Dating of the Trémoïlle Manuscript', in Gillingham and Merkley (eds.), *Beyond the Moon: Festschrift Luther Dittmer* (Ottawa, 1990), 217–42, a Festschrift in honour of Luther Dittmer, acknowledging his own work not only in 14th-c. studies but also in making fundamental scholarship available. I am particularly grateful for more recent additions provided in correspondence by Lawrence Earp, Michael Scott Cuthbert and Yolanda Plumley. This substantially revised version is published with permission from the Institute of Mediaeval Music.

[1] https://gallica.bnf.fr/ark:/12148/btv1b8451108d/#. Discovered by Charles Samaran (see Machaut, *Musikalische Werke*, ed. Ludwig, ii. 18* n. 2) and first described by Droz and Thibault, 'Un chansonnier', followed by Besseler, 'Studien II', 235–41, with a catalogue of contents in reconstructed manuscript order; then by Ludwig, ii. 18*–20*, who documents inventory references to **Trém** also used by later scholars. Most recently before my essay, Wright, *Music at the Court of Burgundy*. RISM B IV/2 (1969) still listed **Trém** as F-SERRANT, though recording it as being already in Paris.

[2] Bent, 'The Absent First Gathering'.

[3] Earp, 'Scribal Practice', 51–82, and *The Ferrell-Vogüé Machaut Manuscript*, ed. Earp et al., i. 2 n. 8. See also McGrady, *Controlling Readers*, ch. 3 ('Instructing Readers: Metatext and the Table of Contents as Sites of Meditation in BnF, MS fr. 1584').

The Motet in the Late Middle Ages. Margaret Bent, Oxford University Press. © Oxford University Press 2023.
DOI: 10.1093/so/9780190063771.003.0032

642 POPES, TRÉMOÏLLE AND CYPRUS

The main entries in **Trém** are consistent in script; later additions are distinguished by shifts in script presumably reflecting piecemeal copying order. **Trém**'s minimal classification barely qualifies it as an index, though it is conveniently so referred to. It has just two categories: 'Motez ordenez et escriz ci apres' (then, erased: 'selon le nombre', with an illegible continuation) and 'Balades et rondeaus ci apres par le nombre'. The motet listing is in strict numerical order for the original corpus (disturbed thereafter between 33 and 41), hence perhaps 'ordenez', to distinguish it from the songs, which are listed 'according to number' but not as 'ordenez'. This confirms the likely scenario that longer pieces were copied first, one or two on an opening, and were listed in the order in which they appear; and that shorter songs, evidently entirely page-fillers, were entered as space permitted. They were listed in order of copying, which was not necessarily the order they appear in the manuscript, as the non-consecutive numbers indicate. This is especially true for those page-filler songs, whose numbers are far from being 'ordered'. The motet list also includes at least three *chaces* and four mass ordinary movements (a Gloria and three Credos; five if *Kyri sponse* at 31 was a troped Kyrie). Did the canonic technique of *chaces* perhaps bring them closer to the qualifying length and complexity of the motet?[4] The list of ballades and rondeaux also includes at least one virelai and a hymn, and thus contained other short pieces that could be fitted in below the motets as space permitted. For neither column should we assume that the compiler considered these outliers to be classified respectively as motets, ballades or rondeaux. The partial classification probably had a practical rather than a generic basis: 'motets' include other long pieces which could not serve as page-fillers (though, given the large format, two motets could often be accommodated on an opening).[5] Although some manuscripts are arranged by composer (notably **Sq**), indexes at this time are never classified by composer, and rarely name composers. Those that do (including **Tr92**, **Ao**, **Q15**) do so only (or mainly) to distinguish different settings of the same text, usually Mass ordinaries; two instances in **Trém** will be given below.[6]

An original foliation presumably existed to correspond to the index numeration, but it is no longer present on the extant bifolio; the upper margin has been closely trimmed. Made known in 1926, it was used in 1512 as a cover for an account book of Georges de la Trémoïlle, to whom much of Charles the Bold's property was given by Louis XI in 1477, evidently including the musical manuscript, on which he can have set so little value that it was used for scrap. The bifolio remained in the Trémoïlle family until its acquisition by the Bibliothèque nationale de France around 1970.

Droz and Thibault identified many of the titles, the dated heading, and the manuscript as recorded in inventories of the Dukes of Burgundy. It is recorded in the 1420 chapel inventory of John the Fearless as: 'Item ung grant livre plat, noté, de plusieurs

---

[4] The anonymous author of the *Capitulum de vocibus applicatis verbis* likened the Italian caccia to the [Italian] motet, which in Italy it more obviously resembled by virtue of often equal-range and imitative top parts and similarly spaced cadences. The 'Capitulum' is an anonymous fourteenth-century addition to Antonio da Tempo's 1332 *Summa artis rithimici vulgaris dictaminis*. See Ch. 26, and also Burkard and Huck, '*Voces applicatae verbis*' and Abramov-van Rijk, 'Evidence for a Revised Dating'.

[5] The large-format **MachautE** similarly used songs as page-fillers sharing openings with motets.

[6] Guillelmus Musart, the indexer of **Q15**, listed only mass ordinaries, and often distinguished settings by composer names. See Bent, *Q15*, i. 89–95; Bent, 'The Trent 92 and Aosta Indexes' and Bent, 'Indexes'. **ModB**, however, has a wholly exceptional table of contents in manuscript order, with genre headings, and gives not only composer names, but text and thematic incipits for all compositions.

motez, virelaiz et balades qui commence: *Colla jugo fidere* [*sic*], et se fenit *Bis dicitur*.[7] The surviving bifolio gives on f. 1ᵛ the opening motet, *Colla iugo subdere/Bona condit*.[8] *Bis dicitur* was probably a tenor canon for the last listed (and unidentified) motet, *Nova stella*.[9] This might also be the larger of two motet books referred to in the 1404 chapel inventory of Philip the Bold. Craig Wright also reports the next item in the 1420 inventory, namely 'another book of motets, patrems, virelais, ballades, and other things, from which one sang in the chapel on the great feast days'. From this he infers that 'the motet books of the duke of Burgundy were used in the chapel *only* during the major feasts of the liturgical year' [my italics] and that the repertory was sung at the courts of both Philip the Bold and John the Fearless.[10]

The heading of the index page now reads: 'Iste liber motetorum pertinet capelle illustrissimi principis Philippi ducis Burgondie et comitis Flandrie'. The last six words (from *Philippi*) are not only in a later and apparently different hand, but over an erasure of the second half of that first line of writing. An entire second line has also been erased. The name which Philip's replaces, following *principis*, cannot be deciphered, but the continuation can be read in part with ultraviolet light as follows: '. . . quem scripsit Michael de . . . ia, ejusdem principis capellanus, millesimo trecentesimo septuagesimo sexto'. Wright endorsed Droz and Thibault's proposal that the scribe was Michael de Fontaine, first chaplain to King Charles V, who would therefore have been the first owner. Senior chaplain from 1370, Fontaine became cantor of the Sainte-Chapelle on the death of Charles in 1380 and remained there until his own death in 1403. Philip became Duke of Flanders in February 1384, and in July of that year bought 'for himself' a book of motets for 13 francs from Jean Mâçon, a priest of the Sainte-Chapelle. The heading was presumably changed at this time by a member of Philip's chapel. He purchased other service books from canons of the Sainte-Chapelle during the 1390s.[11] However, Reinhard Strohm reports that Wright now questions this identification on the grounds that ' . . . *ia* does not seem a possible desinence for a latinised version of "fontaine"'. Strohm further suspects that the codex did not belong to a king, because the heading refers to the owner as 'illustrissimus princeps' and the scribe as 'ejusdem principis capellanus'.[12] The issue of the original provenance cannot be resolved without more knowledge of the other dukes' chapel personnel. Andrew Wathey informs me that any of the sons of Jean II or Charles V, and perhaps even Robert of Geneva, may be considered candidates for ownership; and that there seems to be no Michael de . . .in the chapel of Louis, Duke of Anjou, in the early 1370s.

[7] Doutrepont, *Inventaire*, p. 28 No. 64.

[8] As **Trém** was also a royal manuscript, the identification is likely, though it may not have been the only manuscript to start with this widely circulated motet.

[9] It is tempting to propose a possible match with the triplum *Novum sidus orientis* in **Basel72**; see Ch. 30. However, it is not clear that *bis dicitur* applies to that tenor.

[10] Wright, *Music at the Court of Burgundy*, 140, 147, 149. Kirkman, *The Cultural Life of the Early Polyphonic Mass*, 151–57, draws attention to polyphonic books (probably including **Trém**) recorded in the 1420 Burgundian chapel inventory, others of which also contained songs and motets specifically reported as being sung in the chapel; he applies this also to **Trém**, which contains only four mass movements. This is admittedly a conundrum, given its large format and formal presentation. Early 15th-c. Italian mixed-repertory quarto manuscripts such as **Q15** (*libri de cantu*) may be a different matter. While their mass movements and some motets may have been used at Mass, I believe these personal compilations are more likely to have served mainly for highbrow chamber music in the sacristy or the bishop's palace.

[11] Wright, *Music at the Court of Burgundy*, 148.

[12] Strohm, 'The Ars Nova Fragments', 125.

644 POPES, TRÉMOÏLLE AND CYPRUS

An amalgamated inventory of books that belonged to Charles V and Charles VI was published by Léopold Delisle (and drawn on selectively by Droz, Thibault, Ludwig and Wright) from inventories compiled in 1373 (rev. 1380), 1411, 1413, and 1424. Passage of our manuscript to the Sainte-Chapelle, and its subsequent acquisition by the dukes of Burgundy, would have disqualified it for all but the later recension of the first of these inventories. In all but one case, the inventories record the beginning and end of the text; none is *Bona condit*. The exception (inv. 1231) appears only in 'another copy' of the 1373 (1380) inventory and is listed simply as 'Motez notés en françois et latin'. Four other entries combine motets with chançons, lais and even a bestiary.[13]

The present argument proceeds from the observation that the index is not written in a consistent script, even though most of the entries may well be by the same scribe. The first column, now visibly headed 'Motez ordenez et escriz ci apres' but formerly followed by the continuation, now erased: 'selon le nombre [. . .]', contains the pieces numbered for ff. 1–33, in a fairly consistent hand and probably at a single sitting. The heading of this column, now confined above column 1, originally extended over column 2, which contains entries for motets from f. 34 onwards. These are in varying script and ink colours, in groups of one to four pieces entered at the same time. Column 1 was evidently a retrospective listing in manuscript order of the original nucleus of thirty-two folios, presumably arranged in four quaternions. The numbers actually run to 33; I shall suggest that they mostly refer to openings rather than to folios.[14] Column 2 contains additions made to that nucleus in two further quaternions.

The heading of the third column, 'Balades et rondeaus ci apres escriz par le nombre', does not claim that they are *ordenez*, and has not suffered erasure. The entries have no numbers lower than for f. 10; songs were therefore added not in the first gathering but only in the second through fourth gatherings of the original compilation. The first set of entries and folio numbers for the songs is in the same script as the first column of motets, and likewise appears to have been written at the same sitting, no doubt listing items already copied. However, after the first thirteen items (ending with the two for f. 27), the given folio numbers remain in what is evidently the same hand, while the additions of items to those folios show enough differences to reflect successive stages of writing.

Another decisive break in the ballade list comes after f. 32, when a series of distinguishable hands made groups of additions, starting with ff. 25 and 23 within the existing gatherings, which could evidently still accommodate further additions, before going on to folio numbers after 33. It seems that at this stage a few available spaces in the existing collection were finally filled, followed by spaces beneath the primary motets in an added fifth and then a sixth gathering. While the corpus of the motet index proceeds in folio order (with anomalies only at the end of the first four gatherings, in changed folio numbers affecting ff. 32 and 33), the ballades and rondeaux, evidently added in most or all cases to folios already containing one or more motets, have entries for ff.

---

[13] Delisle, *Recherches*, inventory nos. 1229, 1230 (which may be the same book as 1231 despite the different description), 1232, and 793. Other collections of *chans royaulx, laiz, pastourelles couronnées, chançons* (mostly 'notées'), all with identifying text, are nos. 1226, 1227, 1228 and 1233–39. For more on the Delisle references, see Besseler, 'Studien I', 184 n. 4 and 'Studien II', 187 and Baltzer, 'Notre Dame Manuscripts', 396. On 1233, see Earp, *Guillaume de Machaut: A Guide*, 105 [29].

[14] See Bent, 'The Trent 92 and Aosta Indexes'.

TRÉMOÏLLE REVISITED 645

18–22, and then for ff. 10–16, then ff. 27–32. In other words, the ballades of gathering III were listed—and therefore perhaps copied—before those of gathering II, whereas the motet gatherings are listed in order. It looks as though the index was made before the gatherings were bound, and supports the obvious inference that they were listed after copying. It seems more than likely that all the entries after that initial retrospective indexing were recorded as the piece was copied, and therefore reflect the order of copying.[15] This offers the best explanation for the striking change in the motet index, for gathering V, to a non-consecutive order that could reflect the actual order of copying of an unbound gathering. The scribe may have anticipated such problems in indexing page fillers; the ballades are indeed less 'ordenez' than the motets.

The original heading, with the date 1376, was copied before, and probably at the same sitting as, the earliest form of the index, a retrospective listing of the contents of the first thirty-two folios. Scholars have accepted 1376 as the *terminus ante quem* for all the compositions listed. In fact, this terminus can probably only be applied to most of the music copied on the first thirty-two folios. Two gatherings, i.e. the contents of openings designated 34 through 49 (viz., ff. 33–48), were added, probably singly, at some time thereafter. As Craig Wright has shown, the continuing use of **Trém** is documented, at least obliquely, as one of two books of motets in the 1420 inventory. Demonstrable additions, the presumed extension of the indexed compilation into the time beyond 1376, and a continuing record of use into the fifteenth century, all make it possible that the book continued to receive additions during that period.[16] Fontaine lived until October 1403. If he was the scribe, and had no further access to the book after its sale to Duke Philip in 1384, that would be the terminal date of the indexed additions, if indeed their varying script can be shown still to include his hand. Also, in the autumn of 1403, Wright notes a payment to the composer Jean Carmen for adding 'hymns, Glorias and Patrems newly made' to the book of motets of the Duke's chapel.[17] It cannot be known whether this refers to either of the two inventoried books, and whether it was to this manuscript that Carmen made additions that do not appear in our index.

The index is in a stylish French secretary hand with some personal or self-conscious variation, some features of which connect, in turn, with the heading. The additions are in similar scripts which I believe to be all or mostly by the same scribe—some of them tend to the larger and more ornamental style of the heading to the index page. It is hard to find any points of secure identification with the Gothic book-hand used for the texts of the motets surviving on the bifolio. If, however, the index is mostly by the same scribe and was compiled over a period of time, it is likely that both index and contents are nonetheless the work of the man identified in the heading as the scribe of the book of motets.

All identified motets are listed by the text of the motetus voice. Certainly the indexer needed musical knowledge to select that incipit and to assign pieces to the correct

---

[15] Droz and Thibault assumed that the list reflected the order of copying, but without going on to consider its scribal layering.

[16] It may already have become detached before being used to cover a family account book in 1512; the last verso of the surviving bifolio has the text of a rondeau *Incessament* (with deletions, and neither the text set by Josquin nor that by Pierre de la Rue) upside down in a cursive hand of the period around 1500. It is not clear whether the rondeau was written while the musical status of the manuscript was still undisturbed, or whether it is coincidence that the rondeau text was written on a leaf that had earlier had a musical life of its own.

[17] Wright, *Music at the Court of Burgundy*, 158.

646 POPES, TRÉMOÏLLE AND CYPRUS

column. Some motets copied across an opening reverse the normal assignation of triplum to verso, motetus to recto, in order to balance the space for the second motet on an opening, as can be seen on the last recto of the surviving bifolio, which contains the shorter motetus (*Faux samblans*) and tenor of one Machaut motet (M15), and the longer triplum (*Qui es promesses*) and tenor of another (M8).[18] The facing verso must have started with the triplum of the first motet, followed by the motetus of the other. When there are two motets on an opening, such a complementary arrangement allows the space to be used efficiently by reversing the order of the shorter and longer (motetus and triplum) voices for the second piece on the opening, but in no case does this seem to have resulted in other than motetus parts being indexed. Identification by motetus part is standard in the fourteenth century, as here. Some Italian treatises, however, used triplum citations earlier in the century, perhaps thereby disclosing their different approach to the genre, and even central French sources at the end of the fourteenth century (such as the table of contents of **MachautE**) began to follow the general fifteenth-century practice of treating the triplum as primary. Several otherwise unknown motets cited by triplum in central and eastern European treatises cannot therefore be checked against **Trém**. Two **Trém** listings that appeared to be tripla can now be accepted as motetus parts; both have to do with concordances in **Stras**. One is *Ida capillorum*, often cited as the triplum voice, so presented in **Ivrea** and **Chantilly**, and so published by Frank Ll. Harrison in PMFC 5. Ursula Günther pointed out that **Stras** began with the longer and more triplum-like *Portio nature*, and convincingly presents it with *Ida capillorum* as the motetus, consistent with its listing in **Trém**.[19] The other is *Organizanter*, of which Coussemaker transcribed a verso incipit *Organizanter contine*; the matching and higher triplum, *Luceat laudis*, was on the recto. In this case, the evidence from **Stras** works in the other direction, and *Organizanter* was the motetus, as in **Trém**.

The motet *Rex Karole/Leticie pacis*, cited by its triplum in two treatises, is not listed in **Trém**. Günther has shown that 'Rex Karole' must be Charles V (1364–80) and argued for dating it to *c.* 1375; Carolann Buff has proposed 1378.[20] This absence of the one surviving piece that was written for the king who is supposed to have patronised the manuscript, even as an addition after 1376, is therefore surprising, and adds some weight to Strohm's suggestion (see above) that it may instead have belonged originally to any of the dukes of Anjou, Berry or Burgundy. The possibility that **Trém** was neither compiled for the king, nor that the Michael who copied it was his chaplain Fontaine, opens up many questions, and perhaps places its Sainte-Chapelle sojourn in question. While too much cannot be built on the absence of *Rex Karole* from our index, it is

---

[18] The minor variants reported for M15 in Machaut, *The Motets*, ed. Boogaart, are mostly unique to **Trém**, whereas most of those for M8 are shared with **Ivrea** and/or **Ca1328**, suggesting that that motet at least had more in common with a version circulating with the so-called repertory manuscripts than the complete-works manuscripts. Apart from M19, which is also in **Ivrea**, **Trém**'s six other Machaut motets are shared otherwise only with the complete-works manuscripts.

[19] CMM 39, p. lix. Contemporaries were confused about the status of these voices. *Ars cantus mensurabilis* (ed. Balensuela), normally refers to motets by their triplum voice, as in *Rex Karole*, but for this work 'in tenore *Portio nature* vel *Ida capillorum*' (256). Perhaps specifically for the motetus: 'in motecto *Ida capillorum* talem sincopam' (212). On this motet, see Zazulia, "A Motet Ahead of its Time?". Earp has reviewed the practices of listing by motetus or triplum in indexes and treatises in 'Scribal Practice', 65–66. Besseler, 'Studien II', 236, cites Du Fay's citation in his will of 1474 of his own motet *O proles/O sydus* as a late instance of citation by motetus incipit.

[20] Günther in CMM 39, pp. xxix–xxxi. Buff, 'Ciconia's Equal-Cantus Motets', 142–151 and Ch. 30.

possible that the indexed additions were indeed in place by the date of its composition. Was the collection already copied too early to include *Rex Karole*, or was that motet preserved in one of the several other motet books (attested by the royal inventories) to which this collection was complementary? Another conspicuously absent piece that has been dated to the early 1370s is *Sub Arturo/Fons*; its absence from **Trém** therefore does not rule out my proposed later dating of that motet: see Chapter 20. Twenty-eight of the **Trém** motets are in **Ivrea**, but only four are in the later **Chantilly**, all of which are in the original **Trém** compilation and can thus be dated before 1376: *Degentis vita/Cum vix artidici*; *Portio nature/Ida capillorum*; *Apta caro/Flos virginum*; *L'ardure qu'endure/ Tresdouz espoir*.

Droz and Thibault listed the contents of the index alphabetically. Craig Wright followed Heinrich Besseler by cataloguing pieces in manuscript order, blending motets and songs into a single sequence, and adding further concordances.[21] Appended to this chapter is a simple transcription of the index, this time in index order, preserving the two separate listings headed respectively as motets and songs. It gives the number of each piece as in the index, without translating it as referring to folio, opening, or recto/ verso occupancy. It provides the text incipit of the other (triplum) motet voice where known, and an updated listing of concordant manuscripts. The groups of additions, distinguished by script appearance, are separated by dotted lines.

I have estimated that the manuscript contained six quaternions, four original and two added, and that the index numbers generally refer to the opening on which that number would be visible; in the case of *O dira nacio/Mens in nequicia*, the whole piece is contained on f. 8ᵛ but is designated 9. Both the Machaut motets on f. 8ʳ are listed as 8. Hence, a piece at the end of a gathering, whether or not it uses the new recto, and whether or not the next folio was already present, will carry the new number. This would explain why 33 (for 32ᵛ) is the last listed number of the original four gatherings, and 49 (for 48ᵛ) the last of the indexed manuscript. Only f. 1 is then anomalous. If the index was on f. 1ʳ, then *Bona condit*, listed as 'i', is on its verso, not its opening. Was the index itself inconsistent in labelling by folio or by opening? If not, then we must posit that the 'foliation' started on the first opening of music, and that an extra, ninth folio was placed somewhere in the first gathering; this seems unlikely. Since we have the last leaf of the first gathering, which must have been numbered 8, all the following gatherings can be treated as multiples of eight and are not affected by any structural anomaly, if that is what it is.[22]

The first gathering was not only self-contained, it was the only one lacking additions of ballades and rondeaux. The motets seem always to have been primary, and there were often two on an opening. For some openings, one motet and a ballade are recorded. The index, however, shows some anomalies. The well-filled fifteen staves of f. 8ʳ, and the minimal amount of unused space on ff. 1ᵛ and 8ᵛ, make it hard to take at face value index entries that seem to list two motets *and* two ballades under a single number and

---

[21] Wright, *Music at the Court of Burgundy*, 149–57.

[22] If, however, the index numbers refer to folios and not openings, we would have to consider the surviving bifolio as representing ff. 1 and 9, with, again, an additional folio somewhere in between. That would leave *Bona condit* on f. 1ᵛ then requiring no explanation, likewise *O dira nacio/Mens in nequicia* on f. 9ᵛ, but it would then become harder to explain the two Machaut motets listed as 8, one of which would have had its motetus and tenor, the other its triplum and tenor, on f. 9.

648 POPES, TRÉMOÏLLE AND CYPRUS

apparently for a single opening, as for ff. 13 and 25, or, for f. 27, two motets, two rondeaux and a ballade. Except in gathering IV, where ff. 25, 27 and 31 each have at least four pieces, the other openings with four pieces would all have been the middle bifolio of their quaternions, assuming the numbers to refer to openings: 17, 21, 37, 45. If gathering IV had been, rather, two binions (i.e. two pairs of nested bifolios), its overfilled openings 27 and 31 would have been at the centre of each, but this seems unlikely. On the other hand, only a single motet is recorded for f. 38, a single ballade for f. 48. Later gatherings of the large-format pages may have been ruled in a much more compressed way to receive additional staves. Alternatively, but less likely, some pieces were perhaps not presented complete but as single voice parts, or else the numeration is misleading or wrong.

As can be seen in the Gallica images, and marked on the present transcription of the index in the Appendix to this chapter, the additions after f. 32 for both motets and songs fall into scribally compatible groups of, again, one to four titles. The folio numbers attached to these added motets, however, fall into two clear groups, each corresponding to a gathering (V, VI), and added after the titles. The motets of gathering V are listed in non-consecutive folio order, with numbers up to 41 (presumably for f. 40^v, the last page of gathering V). Folio numbers for gathering VI starting from 41 form a distinct and differently indented sequence, this time with few deviations from folio order. The Gloria, Credo and motet listed for 36, 37 and 41 form a scribally consistent trio of titles that bridges the junction of the gathering change, as seen in the folio numbers. After 27, from *Dame de qui*, the song entries appear to be added in groups of four, three and three, but the consistency of the folio numbers up to 32 suggests that this group still forms part of the original corpus, though perhaps the last additions within it. Song additions after 32 (from *En ma dolour*) show two for 25 (spanning gatherings III–IV?), another for 27 (gathering IV), one for 41 (spanning gatherings V–VI), two for 37 (V),[23] then six in gathering VI. Apart from the few numbers whose openings bridge two gatherings, each group of entries is confined to a single gathering. Even the numbers of openings that bridge joins may refer to pieces copied wholly in the gathering within which the other additions of that group occur. Gathering I was self-contained; others may have been too.

Gathering I began with five Latin motets, followed by nine with French texts (including five by Machaut); the gathering ends with the complete *unicum O dira nacio/ Mens in nequicia* on f. 8^v.[24] There were two motets per opening, either interlocked (as on ff. 7^v–8) or one on a side (as f. 8^v). Gathering II seems to have two motets on most openings, with added songs. Gathering II must have opened with the *chace Se je chant* on f. 9^r; in addition to French and Latin motets this gathering also filled unused space with ballades. Gathering III features a consecutive run of nine Latin motets (listed from 19 to 24); most of its added songs were indexed ahead of gathering II, perhaps further testimony that the gatherings were (at least originally) self-contained, and unbound when indexed. Three further songs added to this gathering (for ff. 25 and 23) are

---

[23] Droz, Thibault and Wright list *Quicunques vuet* as being on f. 37. Apart from further overloading an opening for which two motets had been listed, and to which two other songs further down the list are assigned, there is a problem about this number. Both previous inventories read it as xxxvii. However, the first two x's, if that is what they are, are graphically distinct from the third, which belongs together with the vii. It could even read *Quicunques vuet &c xvii*. At the very least, the number has been changed; it is uncertain where the rondeau was originally located.

[24] Published in PMFC 17, no. 55, as a possibly English motet. Its status remains uncertain.

listed after those for gathering IV; the script change places them with the subsequent additions. Gathering IV itself is again mixed.

Of the Machaut works, six motets but only two ballades and the rondeau are not otherwise recorded outside the Machaut manuscripts. The Machaut ballades 18, 23, 31, 41, 42 and the rondeau 9 all belong to that rather small group of Machaut works that survive with a triplum as well as (or as alternative to) a contratenor. The main corpus of **Trém**, gatherings I–IV, contained some of the most widely circulated motets and ballades of the fourteenth century. Particularly well represented are pieces that have come down to us (whether or not they were so presented in **Trém**) in versions with additional or alternative voices, partly but not wholly a function of wide circulation. Motets indexed in **Trém** known to have had additional voices, solus tenors, or alternative versions (none by Machaut) include *Apollinis eclipsatur/Zodiacum signis*,[25] *Portio nature/Ida capillorum*, *Vos quid/Gratissima*, *Post missarum/Post misse*, *Degentis vita/ Cum vix*, *Se paour/Diex tant desir*. The useful statistics by which Günther contrasts Machaut's preference for French motet texts with the decisive preponderance of Latin-texted motets in **Chantilly** and **Ivrea** are tempered somewhat by the balance in **Trém**, which lists (excluding a Gloria, Credos and *chaces*) 44 Latin and 27 French motetus parts (of which 13 Latin and 8 French are among the additions, a similar proportion).[26]

Of the 79 items listed in the motet columns (including a few mass movements and *chaces*), 53 works pre-date the 1376 inscription. Of these, 39 are known from outside **Trém** and 14 are otherwise unknown. Of the 26 added 'motet' items, on the other hand, only 13 are known and 13 are new.[27] Of the 35 items listed in the songs column, 21 date from the first stage, of which fully 20 have identifications (some questionable), not counting the duplication of *Phiton*. The 13 subsequent additions show the very different balance of 7 known and 6 unknown songs. Five rondeaux precede f. 33, and only one is later. Nine Machaut motets were included, of which only M9 was copied later than 1376, by far the greatest number outside the Machaut manuscripts. Machaut's secular songs had a wider circulation than the motets outside the Machaut manuscripts; seven Machaut ballades (plus one duplicate) and one rondeau were copied before 1376, one ballade (B4) afterwards.

Especially given the possibly later date of these additions, the overall shortage of concordances with the large song repertory of **Chantilly** is striking: there are only four in the main corpus (two of those by Machaut) and one among the additions. Only two works by Machaut were added after the main corpus, one motet (M9) and one ballade (B4), and both were early among those additions. The additions in both categories thus contain a much lower proportion of identified works than those in the original compilation. The observation that the index of **Trém** is temporally layered bears mainly on those unidentified pieces for which concordances may yet materialise, and which must now be considered exempt from the 1376 cut-off point for dating. It serves as a reminder that accidents of source preservation may distort conclusions based on surviving repertory. The sharply different concordance profile of the corpus and the additions may reflect, as often happens in manuscripts that were added to, a continuing pattern of collection

---

[25] See Ch. 16 for the voices added to *Apollinis*.

[26] Günther, 'The 14th-Century Motet'. Four mass movements bring the added 'motet' listing up to 26.

[27] These include titles known from the lost manuscript **Stras** and treatise citations. However, lost motets known to us only by citation of the triplum voice may include pieces listed here by their motetus, and hence inaccessible to identification.

650 POPES, TRÉMOÏLLE AND CYPRUS

closer to the patron's immediate circle than was the 'standard' repertory that makes up a substantial portion of the nucleus. Despite the books inventoried for Charles V, and those surviving manuscripts that affirm a tradition of mixed repertory manuscripts including motets and fixed-form songs (**Ivrea, Ca1328, Chantilly**),[28] the low proportion of identified pieces among the later additions to **Trém** may mean that the royal and ducal repertories up to 1376 included more widely known pieces than it did after that date.

Finally, we turn to the new identifications that have been made in recent years. Named in *Apollinis*, direct testimony to Denis le Grant as a composer was elusive until Karl Kügle convincingly attributed to him the chace *Se je chant mains*.[29] It occurs anonymously in **Ivrea** and **Pic**, and is listed under motets as no. 9 in **Trém**. Further testimony to Denis as a composer may be the name 'denis' (previously misread as 'decus') preceding the *Patrem omnipotentem* at no. 37, in a different hand.[30] Similarly placed, 'Sortes' precedes the *Patrem omnipotentem* at 45; a Credo ascribed to Sortes survives in many sources, a precedent for treating 'denis' also as a composer attribution, presumably here to distinguish like-texted entries, as often happens with mass movements in indexes. The 'Denis' Credo is immediately preceded by a Gloria, which therefore might possibly also be his. Both the Credos distinguished by composer are among the later additions. Besseler ('Studien II', 241) thought the two words, both misread, might be trope texts.

New motet identifications have been made on the basis of newly discovered sources:

1. *Beatius/Cum humanum* (f. 39, among the later additions) has been expertly reconstructed by Anna Zayaruznaya ('Quotation, Perfection'), from the three sources listed in the Appendix under '39', *Cum humanum*.[31]
2. *Flos vernans* has long been known from the intabulation in **Robertsbridge**, but only more recently have sources of the vocal original come to light. Fragments were identified in binding strips in **OxAS56** by Andrew Wathey.[32] Cristina Alís Raurich discovered **Karlsruhe82**, of which one side contains the triplum, notated in unstemmed semibreves. After the publication of Kügle's preliminary study of **Koblenz701** ('Vitry in the Rhineland') the pastedowns were lifted, revealing more music. A series of strips used as quire-liners turned out to contain a virtually complete copy of the motet, the *ars nova* rhythms now made explicit with notated stems. The hitherto missing motetus *Fiat intencio* enables the motet *Flos vernans/ Fiat intencio* to be identified with the incipit in **Trém**.[33]

[28] *Motez et chançons notées, partie en latin, partie en françois*; see nn. 7, 10 above.

[29] In 1993 and 1997. See Ch. 17 nn. 12 and 13.

[30] It was recently brought to my attention that Jason Stoessel had reported the correct reading in a blog of 2012: https://jjstoessel.blog/2012/01/11/a-new-composition-by-denis-le-grant/. I had noticed this independently, but after the publication of my original article.

[31] The motet still lacks tenor, or tenor and contratenor. '*Beacius*' is also mentioned in an unpublished treatise in Prague along with more commonly listed triplum titles: Horyna, 'Ein Brünner Fragment'. Central and eastern European sources often cite motets by triplum incipit, which in the case of otherwise unknown motets impedes identification in **Trém**, and would have done in the case of *Beatius/Cum humanum* but for its musical sources. See also Chs. 15 and 16.

[32] Wathey, *Manuscripts . . . Supplement 1 to RISM*. More recently, see Kügle, 'Die Fragmente Oxford, All Souls 56'.

[33] Kügle made images of the strips available to Cristina Alís Raurich, who has joined them up digitally to reveal the complete motet, enabling identification of the motetus text as that in **Trém**. See Alís Raurich, 'The *Flores* of *Flos vernalis*' (forthcoming), on which she presented in the All Souls College seminar series on 4 Mar. 2021. I am grateful to her for sharing these materials with me.

3. The two sources containing *Plausu querulo* have been known about for some time, but are not easily accessible or legible. **Cortona1** was described as long ago as 1981 by Agostino Ziino. It contains a complete texted voice and the tenor. Ziino provided a partial transcription of the text, in honour of St Thomas of Canterbury.[34] Its motetus status is confirmed by the presence of the triplum of *Almifonis* on the other side of the leaf. In 1998 Giuliano Di Bacco and John Nádas reported further on this fragment, with an improved transcription of the text of *Plausu querulo*, and an improved reproduction of the offset that complements the very damaged recto.[35] They note that three out of the four pieces in **Cortona1**, and all five of the motets in **Paris2444**, were also in **Trém**. A voice starting *Plausu querulo* in **Paris22069**, f. 158[r], led to expectation of another copy of the motetus.[36] But apart from the opening words, the music and text are different. The motetus of *Flos/Celsa* on the other side of that leaf (with up and down semibreve stems, and a unique contratenor) confirms the status of this voice as the (nearly) complete triplum of *Plausu querulo*, as does its higher range.[37] Both sources are very hard to read, and have not to my knowledge been deciphered meanwhile. Thanks to new photographic access, determination and ingenious manipulation, Richard Dudas has produced the accompanying provisional transcription of *Plausu querulo* which he has graciously allowed me to append to this chapter as ▶ Example 31.1. He has exercised digital magic on the two complementary sources, and achieved good musical sense. The verbal texts are much harder to decipher, and even Leofranc Holford-Strevens could only make slight improvements in the version presented here. The final cadence notes of the three parts are g♯–a, c♯–d, e–d. It is in perfect modus and tempus perfectum, with unstemmed semibreves, imperfected breves, semibreve hockets and semibreve rests. Both sources have the tenor of this nearly complete new motet (lacking the last few notes in **Paris22069**). The tenor is unlabelled, but the jaunty rhythm suggests a tune of secular origin. With tenor values reduced as in Example 31.2, it is comparable to the secular tenors of

Ex. 31.2 Tenor of *Plausu querulo*

[34] Ziino, 'Precisazioni', with faint reproductions of the leaf and the offset on the binding. Ziino was following an indication by Ghisi, 'Inno-lauda polifonica'.

[35] Di Bacco and Nádas, 'Papal Chapels', 84–86 and pl. 9. Their suggestion that the text might celebrate the fourth (fifty-year) jubilee of Thomas's martyrdom in 1370 is too late for a composition that can now be placed more appropriately in the 1320s. It could date as early as the third jubilee in 1320. Peter Lefferts had informed them of the **Trém** concordance. I am very grateful to John Nádas, who with characteristic generosity shared his wonderfully legible images of the offset.

[36] **Paris22069** was first announced in 2009 by Everist, 'A New Source', with reproduction and discussion of the two song folios. He reports on the history and the other musical contents of this disparate collection. The two sources of the motet, known to Cuthbert and Nádas, were reported by Stoessel, 'Revisiting "Aÿ, mare"', 467 n. 8.

[37] Cuthbert, 'Monks, Manuscripts', 122–23, reports that it was independently identified by himself, Giuliano Di Bacco and me.

Examples 24.2–24.4. There are three statements of this *color*, which consists of two *taleae*, without diminution.

4. *Thoma tibi* (f. 20) is cited in *ars nova* treatises for simultaneous use of perfect and imperfect tempus in the upper parts, and for the tenors (*sic*, plural) to have black notes in perfect modus and imperfect tempus, red notes conversely. Lawrence Earp has shown that the four-part motet on f. 79ᵛ of **Paris934** meets these criteria, and goes on to argue that this could be the lost motet. My hesitancy about accepting this tempting suggestion rests on the absence of any reference to Thomas (either the apostle or Thomas of Canterbury) in what survives of the Latin motetus, the amorous French triplum (for which Richard Dudas has now found a concordance with the incipit, *Bien doit amours*), and the choice of an *Ave Maria* rather than a Thomas tenor; but it certainly does, mensurally, what *Thoma tibi* is purported to do.[38] Pending further confirmation, this might be treated as a less secure identification.

In any case, **Trém** included at least two extant motets for St Thomas of Canterbury, *O dira nacio/Mens in nequicia* and *Plausu querulo*. I know of none for the apostle from this period. The widespread cult in France of Thomas Becket reduces the pressure to assume that those motets are of English origin.[39] They may be, but that case needs to be argued separately on stylistic grounds. Whether *Thoma tibi* was for Becket or the apostle is unknown in the absence of more text. If the identification with the motet in **Paris934** stands, it is not helped by the fragmentary texts there.

It is tempting to look for signs of grouping or ordering. There is no clear composer ordering, though there is some bunching of Machaut motets near the beginning, three plus two, interrupted by two non-Machaut motets. This may not be surprising if they were copied from one of the complete-works manuscripts, given how relatively few of Machaut's motets were in circulation outside those manuscripts. If that were the case, one could ask on what basis this scribe made his selection. *Thoma tibi* is tucked into a sequence of motets (ff. 18–23). It shared a manuscript opening with Vitry's *Rex quem metrorum/O canenda/Rex regum*, so it must have been short enough to fit alongside that fairly long motet. If indeed *Thoma tibi* is the four-part motet in **Paris934**, it shares an *Ave Maria* tenor (albeit a different one) with the preceding motet, and *Rex quem metrorum* shares a *Rex regum* tenor with the following motet. Most of the motets in this group have at some time or other been attributed to Vitry, with varying degrees of authority. All this may be suggestive, but there is not a sufficiently consistent pattern of groupings in **Trém** that we should assume such groupings as there are to be deliberate. A case can be made for suspecting Vitry's authorship of at least some of the motets cited in the *ars nova* treatises; the case for his authorship of *Thoma tibi* might be strengthened by its context in this apparent or possible Vitry grouping, together with 'similar' pieces.

The Appendix provides an updated transcription of the listing on the first recto of **Trém**. The state of completeness of concordant sources is not usually given.

---

[38] Dudas and Earp, *Four Early* Ars nova *Motets*; presented in their seminar at All Souls College, 22 Oct. 2020.

[39] See Slocum, *Liturgies in Honour of Thomas Becket*.

Appendix
Transcription of Incipits as Listed in the Trém Index, with Identifications and Sources

Because of the uncertainty about numbering by folio or by opening, marked gathering boundaries may differ by one piece or unit. Dotted lines separate scribally distinct entries between the later additions in gatherings V and VI.

Motez - ordenez et escriz ci apres (then, erased: *selon le nombre . . .* [illegible]).

Trém no.	Incipit as in **Trém**	Triplum	Tenor	Concordances	Composer
Gathering I					
1	Bona condit[40]	Colla iugo	Libera me	**Ivrea, Apt, Ca1328, Stras, Arras983, Wrocław411, Tarragona1, Tarragona2** text-only MSS: **Ber49, Jena105, Kremsmünster149, Vienna3244**	Vitry?
1	Zodiacum	Apollinis	In omnem terram	**Barc853, Barc971, Leiden2515, LoTNA, Ivrea, Pad658, SL2211, Stras, OxAS56, Tarragona2, Vienna5094, Vienna922, Leipzig223, Brno**	B. de Cluni
2	Yda capillorum	Portio nature	Ante thronum	**Chantilly, Ivrea, Leiden342A, Stras**	Henricus (Egidius de Pusiex also named in **Stras**)
2	Hugo princeps	Cum statua	Magister invidie (?)	**Ivrea, Ca1328, Leipzig431, Jena105** (motetus text only)	Vitry
3	Rosa sine culpe spina	Almifonis	[Tenor]	**Ivrea, Cortona1**	
3	Trop est la dolour	Dame plaisans	Neuma	**Würz**[41]	
4	Helas ou sera pris	Hareu! Hareu!	Obediens usque	**MachautA, B, C, E, G, Ferrell(Vg)**	Machaut M10
4	De ma dolour	Maugré mon cuer	Quia amore	**MachautA, B, C, E, G, Ferrell(Vg)**	Machaut M14
5	Se j'aim mon loyal	Lasse! comment	Pour quoy me bat	**MachautA, B, C, E, G, Ferrell(Vg)**	Machaut M16

[40] The complete motet is preserved on f. 1ᵛ. For further sources with text for a lost contratenor *Egregius labor*, see Wathey, 'The Motets of Vitry', 123 and 138, and Ch. 3, n. 4.

[41] See Lerch-Kalavrytinos, 'Ars Nova-Fragmente in Würzburg' for three strong identifications in **Würz** and one doubtful suggestion (see n. 58 below).

(*continued*)

Trém no.	Incipit as in **Trém**	Triplum	Tenor	Concordances	Composer
6	Puisque pites				
7	Dame d'onnour				
7	Durement au cuer	Amer amours	Dolour meus	**Durham20, Ivrea, Pic**	
8	Ha fortune[42]	Qui es promesses	Et non est qui	**MachautA, B, C, E, G, Ferrell(Vg), Ivrea, Ca1328**	Machaut M8
8	Faux samblans[43]	Amours qui ha	Vidi Dominum	**MachautA, B, C, E, G, Ferrell(Vg), Ivrea**	Machaut M15
9	Mens in nequicia[44]	O dira nacio	[Tenor]	*unicum* surviving in **Trém**	

Gathering II

Trém no.	Incipit as in **Trém**	Triplum	Tenor	Concordances	Composer
9	Se je chant mains[45]	[*chace*]		**Ivrea, Pic**	(Denis le Grant)
10	Organizanter[46]	Luceat laudis		**Stras**	
11	J'ai le chapelet[47]				
11	Hareu, hareu, je la	[*chace*]		**Stras**	
12	Post misse modulami[na][48]	Post missarum	[Tenor]	**Ivrea, Aachen**	
12	Biauté paree	Trop plus est belle	Je ne sui mie	**MachautA, B, C, E, G, Ferrell(Vg)**	Machaut M20
13	Lugencium	Petre clemens	[Tenor]	**Ivrea, Aachen, Paris3343** (tr text), **Vienna4195** (texts only)	Vitry
13	Vos leonis				
14	Diex tant desir	Se paour d'umble[49]	Concupisco	**Ca1328, Ivrea, Ox7** (Latin contrafactum)	

[42] F. 8 (9) recto contains the triplum and tenor of this motet in second position on the opening.

[43] F. 8 (9) recto contains this motetus and tenor at the top of the opening.

[44] Complete, and unique, f. 8ᵛ (9ᵛ).

[45] Attributed by Kügle; see Ch. 17, nn. 12 and 13.

[46] Although evidently on f. 14[ᵛ], *Organizanter contine* has a C2 clef in Coussemaker's index of **Stras**, whereas *Luceat laudis* on f. 15ʳ has the higher C1 and was probably the triplum. The incipits are compatible.

[47] Yoland Plumley points out (email of 19.2.2021) that several of the unidentified French incipits in the motet section are reminiscent of 13th-c. refrains. The refrain *J'ai un chapelet d'argent et bele amie a mon talent* (Boogaard, *Rondeaux et refrains*, 985) appears as an inserted song or carole in *La Court d'amours* and in a 13th-c. motet enté from **Paris844**, f. 4ᵛ.

[48] The motet on this text in **Ivrea** is the obvious candidate because of the date and the large number of concordances between **Ivrea** and **Trém**. For the motet on the same pair of texts in **OH/RC** see Ch. 24.

[49] The triplum and motetus of the English contrafactum are *De veri cordis, Domine quis habitabit*.

14	Cum venerint	Se grace n'est	Ite missa est	**Ivrea, Tourn27, Wrocław411**	
15	Plausu querulo	Plausu querulo		**Cortona1, Paris22069**	
15	Plains sui d'amere	Helas j'ay lonetamps	Infelix[50]	**Ca1328**	
16	En l'estat d'amere	L'amoreuse flour	[Sicut fenum arui]	**Durham20, Ivrea**	
17	[. . .]reo gencium				

Gathering III

17	Se j'ai par la vostre				
18	Garison selon	Douce playsance	Neuma quinti toni	**Ivrea**	Vitry
19	Nazarea que decora	Zolomina zelus	Ave Maria	**Barc853, Ivrea, Paris 2444** (catchword only)	
20	Thoma tibi			**Paris934?**	
20	Rex quem metrorum	O canenda vulgo	Rex regum	**Ivrea, Fribourg260, Paris2444, Durham20**	Vitry?
21	O Philippe[51]	Servant regem	Rex regum	**Paris146, Paris571**	
21	Petre petre				
22	Flos virginum[52]	Apta caro	Alma redemptoris	**Ca1328, Chantilly, Durham20, Ivrea, ModA, SL2211**	
23	Gratissima	Vos quid admiramini	Gaude gloriosa	**Ivrea, Ca1328, Durham20, Brussels758, Brussels5170, Aachen, Esc10**	Vitry
24	Diligenter	Martyrum gemma	A Christo	**MachautA, B, C, E, G, Ferrell(Vg), Ivrea**	Machaut M19
24	O que purificacio				
25	L'autre jour[53]				

[50] Michael Scott Cuthbert reports (email of 26.2.2021) that the *Infelix* tenor is from within the Responsory *Amicus meus*. See http://cantus.sk/image/6481.

[51] Usually identified, and with Besseler's blessing, as the *Fauvel* motet of which *O Philippe* is the motetus (as 'Ludowice' in **Paris571**) and *Servant regem* the triplum. *O Philippe Franci qui/ O bone dux*/[*Solus tenor*] (**Ivrea**, ff. 1ᵛ–2) would be another eligible candidate only if motetus and triplum have been reversed for this entry. Moreover, if there really were four pieces on this opening, some must have been shorter or incompletely presented.

[52] This is surely the widely disseminated motet whose triplum is *Apta caro*. It is a lost codex listed as item 84 in a 1426 inventory of the former ducal library in Pavia: Milan, Biblioteca Nazionale Braidense, MS AD XV 18.4, item 84. RISM BIV2 lists another motet in **Ca1328** with these words for its motetus incipit, but this is in fact the motet *Floret cum vana/Florens vigor* in **Br19606** whose triplum an adapted prose is also in **Paris146**. See Ch. 6.

[53] Yolanda Plumley (email of 19.2.2021) wonders if this could be a 13th-c. motet, either *L'autre jour par un matin* in **Bamberg**, f. 7ʳ⁻ᵛ, or *L'autre jour me chevauchoie* in **Mo**, no. 313.

(*continued*)

Trém no.	Incipit as in **Trém**	Triplum	Tenor	Concordances	Composer
Gathering IV					
25	Fiat intencio	Flos vernalis		**Koblenz701, Karlsruhe82, OxAS56, Robertsbridge**	
26	Cum vix	Degentis vita	Vera pudicitia	**Barc971, Brussels758, Chantilly, Nuremberg9, Stras, Yox**	
26	Prosapie				
27	Ve constat				
28	De tous les biens	Li enseignement	Ecce tu pulchra	**Fribourg260, Ivrea**	wrongly ascribed to Machaut in **Fribourg260**
28	Jure quod in opere (*recte*, opera)	Scariotis geniture	Supreme matris	**Paris146**	
29	Quant la pree				
31	Kyri sponse[54]				
32	Inviolant [= Inviolata?][55]	Felix virgo	Ad te suspiramus	**MachautA, B, G, Ferrell(Vg)**	Machaut M23
31	O livor	Inter amenitatis	Revertenti	**Paris146, YorkN3** (both without motetus), **Tr87**	
30	O admirabile				
33[56]	Ma dolour	Fortune, mere à	Tenor	**Ca1328, Ivrea, Pic**[57]	

[54] This could be a troped Kyrie; but it lies within the original compilation, and the four other Mass movements are all among the later additions.
[55] Number changed from 31. Schrade argues that this reference is not to the Machaut motet.
[56] Number changed from 32.
[57] A lost copy from a 1487 inventory of the dukes of Burgundy is reported by Kirkman, *The Cultural Life*, 245.

Gatherings V and VI

34	O livoris	Fons tocius	Fera pessima	**MachautA, B, C, E, G, Ferrell(Vg)**	Machaut M9
35	Et se je serai li secons	Je comence	Soulés viex	**Ivrea, McV, Ca1328**	
35	Adieu ma dame[58]				
36	Pater ave				
39	Cum humanum	Beatius se servans	[Tenor]	**Paris2444, Würz, Vienna123a**	
38	Karissimi[59]				
39	Decens carmen	In virtute	Clamor meus	**Ivrea, Paris2444**	
34	In arboris	Tuba sacre fidei	Virgo sum	**Ivrea**	Vitry?
40	Humblement	[*chace*]		**Ivrea**; texted *O pia Maria*, **Mu716, Vienna5094**; texted *Ju ich iag* **Vienna2856, Michaelbeuren10, Vat1260** (text only)	
41	Celsa cedrus	Flos ortus	Quam magnus	**Ca1328, Ivrea, Paris2444, Paris22069, SL2211, Würz, Darmstadt521** (texts only)	
33	O crux preciosa				
36	Et in terra[60]				
37	Patrem omnipotentem				(Denis le Grant?) 'denis' precedes 'Patrem' in a different hand

[58] Lerch-Kalavrytinos, 'Ars Nova-Fragmente in Würzburg', offers this as a possible motetus of *Par maintes fois/Ave Maria* in **Würz** and **Ca1328**, but solely on grounds of the subject matter, parting from the lady. See also Ch. 15 n. 40.

[59] A remote candidate not hitherto proposed is Zacar's Latin ballade *Summite carissimi*, which can hardly be so early.

[60] This item and the two following are in a script more different than most, but they could still be by the same scribe. Note the low top and long descender of 'f'.

(*continued*)

Trém no.	Incipit as in **Trém**	Triplum	Tenor	Concordances	Composer
41	Deo per confidenciam				
42	Tresdouz espoir	L'ardure qu'endure	Ego rogavi Deum	**Chantilly**	
43	Qui dolereux[61]	Mon chant en	Tristis est anima	**Durham20, Ivrea**	
44	Parfondement	Pura, placens	[*Tenor*]	**Ox7**[62]	
44	Patrem omnipotentem				
45	Patrem omnipotentem			**Apt, Barc971, Civ98, Ivrea, Ca1328, Leiden2515, Utrecht37, Fleischer, Toul94, Pad14, Solsona109, Vienna123a**	Steve Sort 'sortes' precedes 'Patrem' in a different hand
46	Loyelon loielete				
46	Ja couars n'ara[63]				
47	Rex beatus	Se cuers ioians	Ave	**Br19606, McV, Paris146**	
46	Dessus une fontenelle				
48	Pastoribus				
47	Mulierum				
49	Nova stella				

[61] A number of compositions quote texts composed in 1339 by Jehan de Le Mote, of which this is the only motet; this suggests it dates from after *c.* 1340. Plumley, *Grafted Song*, 231–39 and table 6.2. See her table 6.5 for quotations from Le Mote shared between this triplum and the ballade *Ne celle amour* in **Ca1328**. The motet is cited as an example of tempus perfectum, major prolation in the *Compendium totius artis motetorum* in **Paris14741**, in Wolf, 'Ein anonymer Musiktraktat', and also in **Wrocław16**.

[62] Besseler, 'Studien I', 184, 222 n. 1: this piece was the first in a now-lost manuscript.

[63] Cited as a refrain (Boogaard, *Rondeaux et refrains*, 898) in the *Tournai de Chauvency* and other texts from before *c.* 1300.

Balades et rondeaus ci apres escriz par le nombre[64]

Trém f. no.	Title as in Trém	Song type[65]	Concordances	Composers
18	Dame sans per	B	Reina	
19	Iste confessor[66]	hymn	Apt, Ber190, Ca29, Civ57, Paris196, Tr87	Machaut B38
19	Phiton le merveilleux	B	MachautA, E, G	Machaut B18[67]
21	De petit peu	B	MachautA, B, C, E, G, Ferrell(Vg), Chantilly, Ca1328, Ghent3360, Fp26, Paris568, ModA, Pra9, SL2211, Nuremberg9a, Brescia5	
21	De fortune	B	MachautA, B, C, E, G, Ferrell(Vg), Morgan396, Reina, Chantilly, Stras, SL2211	Machaut B23
22	De narcisus	B	Autun152, Chantilly, Paris568, Reina, SL2211, Bergamo589, Bud298	Franciscus
10	Amis dont ton vis	R	GR219, Ivrea, Paris568, Pra9, Stras (a second version not copied by Coussemaker), Cortona1 (with a unique contratenor)	Molins
10	De tous les biens[68]	B?	Ox213 (?)	
13	De ce que fol	B	Ca1328, Chantilly, Faenza, Gent3360, Fp26, McV, Mu15611, Paris568, Reina, Stras,[69] Faenza	Molins
13	De toutes flours	B	MachautA, B, E, G, Ferrell(Vg), Morgan396, Reina, Paris568, Fp26, ModA, Stras, Faenza	Machaut B31
16	En amer	B	MachautA, B, C, E, G, K, Ferrell(Vg), Pepys1594, Reina, Paris568, Fp26, Kassel1	Machaut B41
27	Revien espoir	R	Ca1328, Stras, Utrecht37; text in Philadelphia15	
	Espoir me fuit[70]			

[64] Wright lists all unidentified works from the Ballades and rondeaux column as ballades.

[65] B(allade), R(ondeau), V(irelai).

[66] It may be premature to assume that this must be the hymn, rather than a rondeau with a liturgical text or incipit; cf. *Quicunques vuet*. The hymn *Iste confessor* is, however, very widely disseminated. Its presence in **Ca1328**, a motet manuscript with many **Trém** concordances, a few added ballades, some Mass Ordinary movements, and no other hymns, encourages the present identification.

[67] B18, B23 and B31 are all named within the treatise in **Philadelphia614**, f. 207ᵛ.

[68] David Fallows (*A Catalogue of Polyphonic Songs*) believes that the ballade of this name in **Ox213** must remain a strong candidate despite the later date of that manuscript, where it appears in fascicle VII in company with some of the oldest pieces in the manuscript, including pieces concordant with **Ca1328**.

[69] 'De ce que fol pense' is presented on a scroll in an early 15th-c. tapestry from Arras in the Musée des Arts Décoratifs, Paris. Reproduced in Wangermée, *Flemish Music*, pl. 38. I thank Lawrence Earp for reminding me of this.

[70] Both incipits are listed, bracketed together as 27.

(continued)

Trém f. no.	Title as in **Trém**	Song type[65]	Concordances	Composers
27	Dame de qui	B	**MachautA**, **B**, **C**, **E**, **F**, **J**, **K**, **Ferrell(Vg)**, **Reina**, **Pepys1594**	Machaut B42
28	A maint biau jeu			
29	Merci ou mort	B	**Reina**, **Utrecht37**	
29	Phiton le merveilleux[71]	B	(duplicate: see above, **Trém** index number 19)	Machaut
30	He doux regars	V	**Ca1328**	
30	Honte paour	B	**MachautA**, **B**, **E**, **G**, **Ferrell(Vg)**, **Fp26**, **Faenza**, **SL2211**	Machaut B25
31	Jour a jour la vie	R	**Faenza** (twice), **Fp26**, **Lo36**, **Paris586**, contrafacta in **MuEm**, **Reina**, **Stras**, **WolkA** and **WolkB**	
31	Celle dont ma joye	B	**Stras**	
32	Tant doucement	R	**MachautA**, **B**, **C**, **E**, **G**, **Ferrell(Vg)**, **Morgan396**, **Pepys1594**. An apparently different virelai starting with these words is in **Ca1328**	Machaut R9
32	J'ai grant desespoir	B	**Reina**, **Faenza**, **SL2211**, **Stras**	
25	En ma dolour			
25	Danger refus			
23	Se Lancelot	B	**Gent3360**	
37	Quicunques vuet	R	**Ca1328**, **Fp26**, **Ivrea**, **Paris568**	
41	Biaute qui toutes	B	**MachautA**, **B**, **C**, **E**, **G**, **Ferrell(Vg)**, **Utrecht37**	Machaut B4
37	Cuers qui se sent			
37	Laissiez parler		**Turin10**[72] (text only)	
43	A celui dont sui ser[viteur]			
45	Caveus			
45	Comme le cerf	B	**Reina**	
48	Cuer gai			
37	Ma dame m'a conge	B	**Chantilly**	
45	Fuiez de moi	B	**Reina**, **Pra9**, **Stras**, **Civ98**, **Melk391**; contrafacta in **Todi**, **WolkA** and **WolkB**	Alain

[71] This is also listed under 19. It is either the only repeated item, or it reflects an indexing error confusing the numerals xix and xxix.

[72] *Laissiés parler chascun en son droit* is listed in the text manuscript **Turin10**, together with other Machaut song identifications in **Trém**: *Honte paour*, *De petit peu*, *Merci ou mort*. Identified in Plumley, 'Crossing Borderlines', 18.

32

Some Aspects of the Cyprus Manuscript and its Motets

Turin, Biblioteca Nazionale Universitaria J.II.9 (here, **Cyprus**) is a luxuriously produced and illuminated parchment manuscript of monumental scope, containing monophonic plainsong Offices followed by no fewer than 228 polyphonic compositions—mass settings, thirty-three Latin and eight French double-texted motets, and French ballades, rondeaux and virelais.[1] Although its 158 folios were separated and distorted in the Turin library fire of 1904, the musical contents survive more or less intact. With original dimensions of 390 × 283 mm, its large format is comparable to **Chantilly**. An inventory of the contents was first published by Heinrich Besseler, followed by an excellent complete edition of the polyphony and contextual studies by Richard Hoppin.[2] The manuscript has always held an isolated and puzzling position in that it bears no composer attributions. Its most remarkable feature is a complete lack of musical concordances with the mainland repertories in which its stylistic roots can be detected. Its music seems to have developed in isolation, with no interchange in either direction.

The plainsong Offices for St Hilarion and St Anne, together with several of the motet texts, led Besseler to infer the repertory's indisputable connections to Cyprus, and to conclude that the manuscript was produced there for the (Bourbon–)Lusignan court and brought to Chambéry in Savoy in preparation for the marriage in 1434 of Anne (1419?–1462), daughter of King Janus and Queen Charlotte, to Louis, Count of Geneva and son of Amadeus VIII of Savoy, whence it eventually came to Turin, along with other contents of the Savoy ducal library.[3] It has been widely accepted that the manuscript can be positively identified with an entry in a Chambéry inventory of 1498, which cites the opening words on the verso of the front flyleaf: 'ung livre de parchemin à grant volume, escript à la main en prose, et glosé en latin à une histoire, commençant Johannes episcopus servus servorum Dei etc.'[4] Thus begins the 1413 authorisation from Pope John XXIII for the rhymed office for St Hilarion. But at a conference in Turin 30 September–1 October 2021, Alessandro Vitale-Brovarone argued convincingly against this identification, on grounds that this opening formula was common to numerous papal documents, that the contents of the manuscript neither are in prose nor have

---

[1] Available in facsimile as *Il codice J.II.9 della Biblioteca Nazionale Universitaria di Torino*. In this chapter, the Cyprus motets will be referred to by number as M1, M7, etc. Elsewhere in this book (especially Part III), M numbers are used to refer to motets by Machaut. The present adaptation of Bent, 'Some Aspects of the Motets in the Cyprus Manuscript', is published with permission from the American Institute of Musicology.

[2] Besseler, 'Studien I', 209–17; CMM 21 (*The Cypriot-French Repertory*, ed. Hoppin); published in facsimile as *Il codice J.II.9*. I have been unable to consult Richard H. Hoppin, 'The Motets of the Early Fifteenth-Century Manuscript J.II.9. in the Biblioteca Nazionale of Turin' (Ph.D. diss., Harvard University, 1952), but see Hoppin, 'The Cypriot-French Repertory'.

[3] Besseler, 'Studien I', 210–11; on Anne, see below, n. 10.

[4] Giaccaria, 'Il codice franco-cipriota', 12.

The Motet in the Late Middle Ages. Margaret Bent, Oxford University Press. © Oxford University Press 2023.
DOI: 10.1093/so/9780190063771.003.0033

662 POPES, TRÉMOÏLLE AND CYPRUS

Latin glosses, and that music, its dominant feature, is not mentioned. Besseler's own description of the codex had suggested a scribal link to Italy,[5] but Hoppin continued to defend not only the repertory's strong roots in French musical culture before and after 1400, but its compilation in Cyprus between *c.* 1413 and 1420.[6] He suggested that the likeliest time for completion was before the death of Charlotte in 1422, rather than in the troubled times which followed; in a Muslim invasion of 1426, Janus was captured and his palace destroyed.[7]

King Janus of Cyprus (1375–1432) was born in Genoa in 1375 and was named after the mythical founder of that city, whose two faces, in this case, look one towards the sea, the other towards the land. The child was left there as a hostage from 1382 to 1392 when his father King James I returned to Cyprus. Janus's first wife, Anglesia, was a daughter of Bernabò Visconti of Milan; she had not provided him with heirs, and the marriage was annulled between 1407 and 1409. In 1409 he married his second wife, by proxy: Charlotte of Bourbon (1388–1422),[8] Anne's mother. She arrived in Cyprus in 1411, two years before the 1413 *terminus post quem* for work on the manuscript. The royal pair are portrayed in frescoes in the exquisite little Lusignan royal chapel of Ayia Ekaterina at Pyrga, built for them in 1421, the year before Charlotte's death.

Queen Charlotte's Musicians and Anne's Savoy Wedding

The contemporary chronicle of Leontios Makhairas reports some of the names of those who accompanied Charlotte in 1411 when she sailed from Venice to Cyprus.[9] Both sources of the chronicle have a lacuna; only nineteen names of her sixty-strong entourage survive. These include Jean Canel and Gillet Veliout.[10] Hoppin and subsequent scholars assume that Gillet Veliout was indeed Gilet Velut, composer of four songs, two mass movements and two motets in the Veneto manuscripts **Ox213** and **Q15**.[11] None of those compositions is in **Cyprus**. Karl Kügle further identified Jean Canel (or Kanelle) as Jean Hanelle who, like Velut, was a *petit vicaire* at Cambrai during the year 24 June 1410–24 June 1411: both had overlapped there with Du Fay's service as a choirboy, 1409–12.[12] Hanelle would meet Du Fay again in Savoy in 1434, when documents

---

[5] Besseler, 'Studien I', 211.

[6] One of very few hints of Cypriot musical activity apart from **Cyprus** is a Kyrie in **Apt** (f. 4ᵛ) headed 'Chipre' in the position where a composer's name might be expected.

[7] Hoppin, 'The Cypriot-French Repertory', 93.

[8] Charlotte was a daughter of John I, Count of La Marche and Catherine de Vendôme.

[9] Makhairas, *Recital concerning the Sweet Land of Cyprus.* Wikipedia's claim that 'Charlotte's lavish retinue ... included many musicians' seems to be based on supposition rather than documentation.

[10] It continues by reporting that he (presumably Verniet) committed some offence and was excommunicated; that he went to the pope and was released from the excommunication and came back to her company. It is not clear whether a reference to Gillet the secretary is a different person from Velliout. The chronicle does not mention Anglesia. It ends with the death of Janus and a brief section on King John. Makhairas, *Recital*, 625. The date of Anne's birth is given as 24 Sept. 1415 or 1418—the two manuscripts disagree—but it makes no mention of her marriage. Collenberg, 'Les Lusignan', reports that Anne was younger than Jean, therefore that she must have been born in 1419 rather than 1418, when John's birth is recorded. In any case, they were both minors at the time, respectively, of her marriage and his succession.

[11] *Summe/Summa* is also in **Tr87**. Velut's surviving works are in CMM 11/2.

[12] Kügle, 'Repertory'. For a comprehensive listing of Cambrai musical personnel at this period, see Planchart, *Du Fay*, appendices 1 and 2. For Hanelle see pp. 737–38, where he was documented in Cambrai as from Tournai, whereas Collenberg, 'Le Royaume et l'église de Chypre', cites him from Vatican documents as a cleric from Thérouanne.

describe him as singer (*cantor*) of the king of Cyprus, and in 1436 as 'mestre de chappelle du Roy de chippres'.[13] Jean Hanelle's brother was the better-known Mathieu Hanelle, a slightly older contemporary of Du Fay at Cambrai, likewise multiply beneficed, and a papal singer.[14] Charlotte's chapel thus appears to have been recruited at least in part from Cambrai; ten per cent of the surviving names are Cambrai musicians. In any case, it is clear that she had fostered a flowering of French culture at the Lusignan court until her death in 1422, and was evidently a patron of the musicians and musical culture she brought with her. The absent forty-one names may well have included more musicians and other clues that might help to explain the balance of French and Italian influences discernible in the manuscript.

A further document attests the continuing presence of Jean Hanelle in Cyprus: a papal letter of 4 August 1428 from Martin V appoints him to the *scribendaria* of Nicosia cathedral. He is there described as a 'clericus coniugatus'.[15] This attestation of his scribal as well as musical ability invites speculation as to whether he was one of the scribes of the manuscript, particularly the northern text scribe who was also the music scribe who copied all the polyphony.[16]

Velut is no longer documented in the 1430s, indeed not after 1411. Kügle interprets this silence to suggest that he returned to mainland Europe after a few years, in time to contribute a few songs and motets to Veneto manuscripts; however, he did not need to return to Europe to do so, as all his music in those sources, like that of Carmen, Cesaris and Tapissier (not documented after 1417), could have been written in the first decade of the fifteenth century, and transmitted to Italy from the north during the Council of Constance, or even in Venice before Charlotte's entourage set sail. Velut may have died before the 1430s.[17] Jean Hanelle, however, retained an attachment to the Lusignan court, and although by then in Savoy, is described as 'cantor regis chippri' in 1434 and as the king's *mestre de chappelle* in 1436. By then the new king was John II, Anne's brother. Documented continuity over twenty-five years in the career of this musician

[13] Kügle, 'Glorious Sounds', appendix B. Planchart (*Du Fay*, 737–38) gives the sources of the payment for 16 Aug. 1434 as TAS (= Turin, Archivio di Stato), Inventario 16, Reg. 79, f. 473ᵛ: [16 August 1434, Thonon] 'Libravit dicta die Hannelle cantori regis chippri donato per dominum sibi facto videlicet . . . . . . x ducatos auri ad xx'; and for November 1436 (usually cited as 16/17th, by Planchart as the 14th) as TAS, Inventario 16, Reg. 81, f. 207ᵛ. They were first reported by Bradley, 'Musical Life and Culture at Savoy', 535.

[14] Both Jehan and Mathieu Hanelle have multiple entries in Planchart, *Du Fay*, including pp. 16–17, 58–59, and appendices 1 and 2. See also Kügle, 'Repertory' and Kügle, 'Glorious Sounds'.

[15] AAV Reg. Lat. 278, ff. 299ᵛ–300. Collenberg, 'Le Royaume et l'église de Chypre', 697 (139). Planchart, 'Early Career', 357, citing the same AAV document, just says he is 'listed as a scribe'. Planchart, *Du Fay*, 737–38, reports (AAV, RS 228, f. 101ʳ) that Jean Hanelle was married and in the service of the king of Cyprus. Likewise married were Renaud Liebert and Richard de Loqueville, also *petits vicaires* at Cambrai, who each served as *magister puerorum*. Widaman, Wathey and Leech-Wilkinson ('The Structure') identify two expert text scribes; one Italian, one French, and a third scribe with Italian and French features who is also the main music scribe. Kügle's view of the scribes (set out in *Il codice J.II.9*, 21–39) differs from that of Widaman, Wathey and Leech-Wilkinson; his analysis makes it easier to suggest that the music scribe and the text scribe at least of the vernacular works was a northerner, possibly Hanelle.

[16] Kügle, 'Glorious Sounds', 643: 'Small corrections and amendments throughout the manuscript in what appears to be a single corrector's hand suggest that the Italians were working under the supervision of one principal scribe whose main contributions include all text and music of Fascicle V and much of Fascicle IV as well as, above all, the musical notation of *all* the polyphony. This hand was clearly northern-trained, as is visible from its angular ductus, its extended serifs, and the comparatively narrow and compressed spacing of the letters within a given word along the vertical axis.' The added mass cycle (ff. 139ᵛ–141ᵛ), without Agnus, is in a different hand, identified as probably Savoyard by both Strohm ('European Politics') and Kügle ('Some Notes').

[17] The surviving works of Carmen, Cesaris and Tapissier are in CMM 11/1.

664   POPES, TRÉMOÏLLE AND CYPRUS

is significant. Hoppin suggested that the repertory may have been largely the work of musicians Charlotte had brought with her to Cyprus: Velut is the only such musician who may be identifiable with a known composer, though neither of his two known motets, despite some similarities, closely fits the template of most of the Cyprus motets. Velut's eight ascribed works (rondeaux, mass movements and motets, all but one unique to **Ox213** or **Q15**) show considerable variety, so while it is not inconceivable that he went on to cultivate different styles, it is perhaps puzzling that his earlier works are not included in the new compilation. Kügle adds the candidacy of Jean Hanelle as a possible composer. Indeed it is very likely that he was also a composer, though no music is ascribed to him, and that either or both of Velut and Hanelle may be hidden amongst the entirely anonymous composers, whose musical style within each genre is more homogeneous than the known works by Cesaris, Carmen, Tapissier and Velut. In any case, it is clear that Charlotte fostered a flowering of French culture at the Lusignan court until her death in 1422. While there is no documentation of an Italian ingredient in the largely French culture she took with her, the internal evidence of this manuscript may attest it.

A Cypriot Repertory: A Manuscript for Anne

All considerations point to a repertory composed in and for Cyprus, in isolation from mainland developments, by highly skilled composers formed or active in the first decade of the fifteenth century. The repertory could certainly represent a continuation of Velut's and Hanelle's (otherwise undocumented) composing careers in isolation on Cyprus, and perhaps that of other unknown composers in Charlotte's retinue. The marriage of her daughter Anne to a prince of Savoy had been planned from 9 August 1431, by which time she had attained the twelve years necessary for such arrangements to be made. The first intended consort was Amadeus, son and heir of Amadeus VIII, the future antipope Felix V, but he died in August 1431 aged 19, and was replaced by his brother Louis. As his duchess, in addition to bearing nineteen (or eighteen) children, Anne was culturally active, nostalgic for her homeland of Cyprus, and a lavish entertainer of Cypriot visitors. Her father King Janus had died in 1432, when plans for Anne's Savoy wedding were already in place. He was succeeded by her brother John (born 16 May 1418), who may have cared less about music than Anne; it seems that John II retained (at least nominally) the chapel personnel of his parents, and allowed Hanelle to leave with Anne. He had, however, declined to pay the full dowry agreed for her.[18] If she had brought with her, together with Hanelle, an expensive and explicitly Cypriot music manuscript, this could well have been part of the show the teenage bride provided, along with other luxury goods. The period preceding her wedding seems the likeliest time for the compilation of a splendid manuscript containing the accumulated compositions of the Cypriot court composers from the 1410s onwards. It also contained specifically Cypriot chant, notably for St Hilarion, a Cypriot saint and St Anne, the

---

[18] Kügle, 'Glorious Sounds', 645 n. 24. Collenberg, 'Le Royaume et l'église de Chypre', reports of John II (1418–58) that he was obese, suffered from elephantism, was weak-minded and effeminate; that his first wife Medea died 1440, and that his second wife Helene Palaeologue was a daughter of Cleophe Malatesta, a cousin of Martin V known to us from Du Fay's motet in her honour.

namesake of the bride, both of whose offices are headed by miniatures of those saints, the only historiated initials in the manuscript. Although the period preceding her wedding seems a likely time for the compilation, repeated severe Ottoman attacks from the mid-1420s must have curtailed cultural enterprises in Cyprus.

A conference in Paphos in 1992 afforded an opportunity to reassess this large but isolated and under-studied repertory.[19] There was general agreement that the repertory was composed and gradually accumulated in Cyprus from the 1410s until it accompanied Anne on her marriage journey in late 1433, arriving in Savoy on 1 January 1434,[20] but less consensus among contributors to the volume resulting from that conference as to when and where the manuscript itself was prepared. Hoppin had declared the repertory to be entirely French. Kügle agreed, calling it 'the only source of the early fifteenth century housing an exclusively French or French-derived repertory'.[21] However, he raised the possibility that the unique manuscript containing this repertory was copied not in Cyprus but in Savoy or northern Italy as late as the mid-1430s; Giulio Cattin's essay in the same volume confirmed Besseler's observation that the main scripts are all Italian *rotunda*, while the French vernacular texts of section IV and the final six French motets are in the hands of professional French scribes.[22] However, the presence of an Italian scribe need not force the conclusion that the manuscript was copied and illuminated in Italy: Cyprus had constant contact with Venice through trade and pilgrimage, and the court was quite cosmopolitan. King Janus, as noted above, spent his childhood and adolescence in Genoa, and his first wife was a Visconti; this provides a ready explanation for continuing Italian as well as French contacts.[23]

Despite Kügle's proposed copying date as late as the mid-1430s, his cited art-historical authorities suggested an earlier dating of the decoration, in the years around 1425, by Italian artists, and that the miniature of St Hilarion on f. 1 was more archaic in style, which could in principle have placed the manuscript in Charlotte's lifetime.[24] There seems to be little trace of Cypriot book illumination at this period, though, again, foreigners were present at the Lusignan court. What is at stake is where and when the music was assembled and copied in the manuscript that has come down to us.

The Motets: Subjects and Groupings

The forty-one motets in the Cyprus manuscript, as outliers, have often been omitted from stylistic and statistical surveys of motets in general, although they constitute

[19] Günther and Finscher (eds.), *The Cypriot-French Repertory*.

[20] Kügle, 'Repertory', 175; 'Glorious Sounds', 641.

[21] Hoppin, 'The Cypriot-French Repertory'; Kügle, 'Repertory', 151.

[22] Cattin, 'The Texts of the Offices', 268–89, also raises the possibility of Italian compilation; see also Widaman, Wathey, Leech-Wilkinson, 'Structure'.

[23] Clément et al., *Poésie et musique*, includes valuable chapters on the historical context at the court of Cyprus, which reached me too late to be taken into account here. Especially relevant to Italian contacts are Gilles Grivaud, 'Résonances humanistes à la cour de Nicosie (1411–1423)', 27–39 and Clémence Revest, 'La rhétorique humaniste au service des élites chypriotes dans l'Italie septentrionale de la première moitié du XVᵉ siècle', 41–50. Interesting insights on some motets are in Fañch Thoraval, 'Dévotion, liturgie, performativité: "religion royale" et "géographie religieuse" dans les motets du manuscrit Turin J.II.9 et les offices du Saint-Sépulcre', 145–66.

[24] *Il codice J.II.9*, 33.

a significant proportion of the surviving motets of the period. The total absence of composers' names and of links through concordances with other repertories have conspired to leave them with the appearance of a self-contained repertory, perhaps influenced by but not seminal to other European collections. The Paphos conference provided a welcome opportunity to redress in this case a general neglect of such isolated and anonymous repertories; other conferences have occurred meanwhile. Here follows an outline of the motet corpus, both its stylistic and technical features and the scripts in which it was copied. Observations and emphases are added to Hoppin's published account and editorial commentary; subsequent observations by Kügle are incorporated, some of which overlap with my own.[25]

The motets comprise section III, made up of quinternions VII–X. The thirty-three Latin motets are M1–18, M20–34, the eight French motets are M19, M35–41. M8 and M15 are dedicated to St John the Baptist, M14 and M32 to St Katherine, a saint much honoured in Cyprus. There are other direct references to Cyprus in the motet texts. In M7 the word *Engadi* appears at the end of cantus II; Hoppin's critical commentary reported that a medieval tradition wrongly placed the biblical Engaddi in Cyprus, based on Song of Songs 1: 13: 'Botrus Cypri dilectus meus mihi in vineis Engaddi'; 'botrus cypri' refers to a cluster of cypresses, and Engaddi is a valley in Israel near the Dead Sea, with several biblical references. In addition to John the Baptist, M8 refers to Janus as King of Jerusalem, Armenia and Cyprus, coinciding with a melisma on *Janum* in cantus II.[26] Hoppin's commentary reported that the Macarius of cantus I may be a synonym for St Denis, and refer to a Greek or Hellenised Denis (Dionysius Ionicus) 'qui appellatur Macarius'. Kügle earlier argued that this further supports an association with Paris and the French royal family.[27] M17 is for the Cypriot saint Hilarion, and may celebrate the inauguration of his rhymed office, copied at the beginning of the manuscript, probably datable to St Hilarion's day, 21 October 1414; Janus and Cyprus are named in the texts. Hoppin enumerated these Cypriot references; none is precisely datable, though the two John the Baptist motets, M8 *Gemma florens/Hec est dies* and M15, *Hunc/Precursoris*, could celebrate the birth of Janus's son John, the future king.

None of the motets can be described as doctrinal or ceremonial. Over half the texts celebrate Christ or feasts of the Christian year, or the Virgin Mary, to whom seven Latin and six French motets are dedicated. The only motets on entirely secular themes, M39 and M40, both contained on ff. 95ᵛ–96, have cantus I texts about courtly love that have been partly erased, perhaps in preparation for sacred contrafaction.[28] All other French texts honour the Virgin Mary; M3 and M4 form an *Ave Maria* pair. M4 has both an acrostic and rhyme. M3 also has acrostics, not noted by Hoppin; the first letter(s) of each verse yield in cantus I *Ave Maria* and in cantus II *Gratia plena*. M18 is a Sanctus

---

[25] Hoppin, 'Cypriot-French Repertory', and CMM 21/2. See also Kügle, 'Repertory' and Kügle, 'Glorious Sounds'.

[26] Given the equality or near-equality in text, range and activity of the upper parts, they are here referred to as cantus I and II rather than triplum and motetus.

[27] Kügle, 'Repertory', 162–67, offers further amplification to some of these associations and possible datings.

[28] Anne Walters Robertson presented a paper at the Turin conference, 2021, to be published as 'Two French Secular Motets in the Cyprus Codex and a New Composer from Cyprus'. I am grateful to her for sharing her findings in advance of publication, which also include the discovery of 'Johannes Gallioctus' from the kingdom of Cyprus as the composer of a 'new mass' in 1453. This could add his candidacy to that of Velut and Hanelle as composers in the service of Charlotte and/or Anne and potential contributors to **Cyprus**.

THE CYPRUS MANUSCRIPT AND ITS MOTETS   667

substitute, and M33 and M34 are *Deo gratias* substitutes, each with an acrostic of *Deo gratias* in both texts (in the case of M34, *Deo gratias Amen*).[29] They close the sequence of Latin motets M1–34, which is interrupted only by the French motet M19.

Some approximate groupings by texts or subject can be detected, though the boundaries are not consistent.[30] The first and largest group is built mainly around some feasts of the Temporale (mostly M1–7), the Virgin Mary and other saints (mostly M8–21, ending with M22 for the Transfiguration); these are not in strict liturgical order, and include the isolated French-texted M19.[31] The clearest grouping consists of M23–30, which form a cycle of the eight Advent 'O' antiphons (within Kügle's second cycle *de tempore*), followed by M31 for the Nativity, M32 for St Katherine, and closing with the last two Latin motets, the two *Deo gratias* settings M33–34. These are followed by French-texted motets for the Virgin and the two secular motets just mentioned.

Each section of the manuscript shows some script differences unique to that section; these have been analysed in a co-authored study.[32] The texts of the Latin motets and two of the French motets are assigned to the main text scribe E, but the last six French motets (from f. 92[v]) are adjudged additions by scribe F, who together with scribe D is responsible for later additions which incorporate more French elements. The authors believe that, despite some superficial differences, the text hands identified as A, B, C, E are the work of a single scribe writing an Italian *rotunda* script, and working under different constraints of spacing. Sections IV and V, containing vernacular French *formes fixes*, are texted by two hands, the first a professional French scribe (G), the other (later) possibly Savoyard (H), writing a script which combines French and Italian elements, which could support Reinhard Strohm's suggestion that later additions (especially the mass cycle) were made in Savoy.[33] Text scribe H is also proposed as the single *music* scribe, responsible for sections I–V; he may also be the composer of some of the additional pieces.[34]

Musical Features

The motets are listed in the Appendix. All are *a*4, for two texted cantus parts, tenor and contratenor, except M11, M12, M14, M16, which are *a*3 without contratenor. In all cases, the trio of two cantus parts and tenor makes self-contained grammatical sense, and is therefore primary.[35] Without exception, the contratenors are contrapuntally

---

[29] *Deo gratias* motets in the French tradition are *Se grace/Cum venerint*, the *Ite missa est* motet of the Mass of Tournai, and *Post missarum/Post misse* in **Ivrea**. A pair of adjacent *Deo gratias* motets conclude both the Old Hall manuscript and its younger sibling, a fragmentary Royal Choirbook. See EECM 62, introduction, and Chs. 24 and 25. These two motets have less strict end-rhyme.

[30] Also tabulated by Kügle, 'Repertory', 158–59. There is some overlap of statements about the motets with mine. For new observations see ibid., 161–68.

[31] Kügle, 'Repertory', 158, table I, divides this cycle into feasts *de tempore*, a cycle *de Sanctis* and a second cycle *de tempore*. However, there are feasts of the BVM in both the first two series.

[32] Widaman, Wathey, Leech-Wilkinson, 'Structure'; also Kügle, 'Some Notes'.

[33] Strohm, 'European Politics', 317. Strohm presented a new paper on the mass cycle at the Turin conference, 2021, to be published as 'The earliest cantus firmus Mass? A challenge to historiography in the Turin Manuscript J.II.9'.

[34] *Il codice J.II.9*, ed. Kügle, 29–31, offers correctives to Hoppin's scribal designations, but apparently without taking Wathey, Widaman, Leech-Wilkinson, 'Structure' into account.

[35] I have made the case in Ch. 29 that such three-part conceptions are still dyadically based.

668 POPES, TRÉMOÏLLE AND CYPRUS

inessential, often causing dissonance; they are consequently expendable, their function secondary, even when they go below the tenor. There are no solus tenor parts; those known elsewhere are confined to cases where the contratenor contributes with the tenor to essential contrapuntal underpinnings. That is not the case here, so it is not surprising that solus tenors are absent from this largely four-part repertory.[36]

More than half of the motets follow a simple formal template. Motets 1–5, 19–30, 32–39 and 41 all have a single tenor *color* statement, divided into two or three *taleae*, complete isorhythm in the upper parts, and no tenor diminution. The cycle M6–18 includes all the exceptions: motets that have no isorhythm (M9), no upper-part isorhythm (M12 and M16), or only partial upper-part isorhythm (the remainder), the four three-part motets (M11, M12, M14, M16), and all but two of the musical forms that do not conform to the above template. Those non-standard forms are M7, with two (undiminished) *color* statements, and motets 8, 12, 14 and 18 with various kinds of tenor reduction. Only two motets outside this group (M31 and M40) have tenor diminution. It may be significant that the only French-texted motet that interrupts the Latin sequence is M19, immediately following the M6–18 group. M31 is a Nativity motet following the Advent cycle, and M40 may have ended the originally planned motet group. So at least two considerations may have been in balance here, on one hand the creation of loose liturgical groupings, and on the other, considerations of musical technique, with pieces distinct by language or technique set at the boundaries of these groups.

Both the tenor melody and the upper-voice texts of M1 are based on the sequence *Victime paschali laudes*. M1 was apparently copied later than the texts of M2–35 (though by the same scribe), and may have been added as a short motet to fill the otherwise blank recto at the beginning of the motet section, gatherings VII–X. (In all other cases of short motets, two are copied across the same opening rather than occupying a single page each: M33 and 34, M39 and 40.) Only two other motets, M12 and M16 (two of the four three-part motets), have tenors labelled for chant, both as Alleluyas. The M16 Alleluya tenor is closer to the version of *GR* than that of M12. Other tenor incipits (all unlabelled) could be chant-related, but none has been identified. Indeed, it seems that Hoppin was right to declare that the remaining tenors were free accompaniments—composed expressly for their motets. They were added to the paired upper parts, which anticipate the provision of tenor support by leaving some unsupported fourths for it to underpin, as in the Italian motets of Ciconia.

Most motets have one statement of a single *color* melody; only M7 has two *color* statements without reduction. Only six other motets have any repetition of the tenor *color*, M8, M12, M14, M18, M31 and M40, all with some kind of reduction for the repeated tenor *colores*. In M8 and M18 the repeat is written out, with red notation for the diminution in M8. In M12, M14, M31, M40 the tenor is accompanied by a verbal instruction, and (except for M31) by repeat signs. The term diminution is not used; the

---

[36] On the Solus tenor, see Bent, *Counterpoint*, 38–46 and Chs. 1 and 8 above. The motets of Carmen, Cesaris, Tapissier and Velut all have extensive rhythmic replication in all parts between three or more sections or between pairs of *taleae*. Two of Carmen's three motets (with solus tenor parts) and one of Velut's have essential contratenors; none of these motets applies diminution or halving, but they achieve difference between sections by purely mensural means, as in many of the Cyprus motets. Most have equal or nearly equal top parts, and (especially Carmen's quite complex *Venite*) use a range of mensurations.

THE CYPRUS MANUSCRIPT AND ITS MOTETS   669

reduction is expressed mensurally (by combinations of modus and tempus) or as by halving (*per semi*). Of the motets with *color* repetition, only M7, M31 and M40 follow a familiar French pattern whereby each of two statements of the tenor *color* comprises two *taleae*. The second tenor *color* statement is not written out; repeat signs are provided for M7 and M40 but not for M31. In those three cases the contratenor and upper parts do not repeat melodically and are necessarily fully written out. The second tenor statement is diminished in M31 and M40, and the tenor *colores* each also contain two *taleae*. The *colores* are to be repeated as instructed: M31: 'Tenor primo dicitur perfecte, secundo per semi de primo' (without repeat sign); M40: 'Tenor bis dicitur, primo ut jacet, secundo per semi' (with repeat sign). Although specified as a proportion rather than as diminution, the mensurations in both cases are such that the result is the same. In both motets, the contratenor and upper parts have two isorhythmic *taleae* within each tenor *color* for the undiminished first section, and two different isorhythmic *taleae* for the tenor's reduced section. However in M7, the *color* is repeated without diminution and is therefore identical in pitch *and* rhythm, so I would classify this as an identical repeat, not limiting the description to (iso)rhythm.[37] Each tenor *color* contains two isorhythmic *taleae* but the contratenor *talea* repeats only once, with the repeat of the tenor *color*. The upper parts of M7 are not wholly isorhythmic, but repeat the same rhythm over longs 7–8 of each of the four tenor *taleae*.

The single tenor *colores* of M8 and M18 are divided into two *taleae* of equal length and identical rhythm; each *talea* is stated and repeated immediately in diminution, at note-values down one level, before the same procedure is applied to the second *talea*.[38] In both cases, the tenor parts are written out in full, spelling out the diminution. In M8 all voices are written in red notation for the diminution section, as stated, but an overlap makes it clear that the coloration causes neither imperfection nor proportional change. Reading the notes down a level (the historically authorised definition of diminution) is not necessarily the same as halving values (*per semi*, or 2:1 proportion), because different combinations of modus and tempus may apply at the different levels.[39] The tenor of M18 is in imperfect modus and tempus, major prolation; when the breve is read as semibreve, it becomes imperfect tempus, major prolation, with divisions by 2 and 3 in both cases, and resulting in an overall proportion of 2:1. But M8's tenor is in perfect modus, imperfect tempus and major prolation; in diminution it becomes perfect tempus, minor prolation, therefore asymmetrically with 2 and 3, 3 and 2 divisions, and resulting in an overall proportion of 3:1. M12 (exceptional in many ways) presents its perfect-modus *color* of two *taleae* three times, the second in diminution (breve is read as semibreve), the third reverting to original values, resulting in overall sectional proportions 2:1:2.

---

[37] See Ch. 2.

[38] Ciconia's *Petrum Marcello* applies diminution to a *color* before restating it. Like nearly all the Cyprus motets, *Petrum Marcello* is in perfect modus and tempus, so a perfect long in diminution becomes a perfect breve in perfect tempus and minor prolation, resulting in a 3:1 proportion (PMFC 24, no. 18). The tenor of the **Fountains** motet *Humane lingua/Supplicum voces/Deo gratias* is likewise in perfect modus with perfect tempus. Its diminution section with perfect tempus and minor prolation likewise results in a relationship of 3:1 (C–W O246); Bent, *The Fountains Fragments*, f. 14. Editions: PMFC 15, no. 36; *The Fountains Fragments*, ed. Kershaw and Sandon, no. 17. *Alma polis* (Ch. 19) has a written-out diminution within each *color* statement.

[39] See Bent, 'The Myth'.

670   POPES, TRÉMOÏLLE AND CYPRUS

The unusual qualities of M14 are further discussed in the Excursus to this chapter. Its tenor, exceptionally, has five *color* statements that are varied mensurally; they are therefore not isorhythmic. The *color* is notated once with a five-stroke repetition sign, and the instruction: 'Primo dicitur de tempore et modo perfectis. 2° de modo perfecto et tempore imperfecto. 3° semi de 2°. 4° ut 2°. 5° ut prius'. Only the central third iteration is marked for a proportional interpretation, by half (*semi*), but because of the mensural configuration, the result is the same (2:1) as reading it in diminution at the next note-level down, as just shown for M18. The upper parts are in tempus imperfectum throughout, though lend themselves to irregular barring in sections 1 and 5 to coincide with the perfect tempus of the tenor. The overall palindromic structure, perhaps reflecting St Katherine's wheel, lends itself to substantial sections of upper-part isorhythm between sections 1 and 5, and 2 and 4, a fascinating and unprecedented structure.

Hoppin counted forty out of the forty-one motets as isorhythmic; even with the more restrictive definition of isorhythm which I have proposed, it is still true that all except M9 have some full or partial isorhythmic patterning in the tenor and/or the upper parts.

The seven exceptions with *color* repetition apart (M7, M8, M12, M14, M18, M31 and M40), the remaining thirty-four motets all have a single tenor *color* statement which is divided into either two or three *taleae*, with no mensural or proportional manipulation, and with varying degrees of isorhythmic correspondence in the upper parts and contratenor; rhythmic replication without diminution meets the stricter criteria for isorhythm (Ch. 2). Most of the contratenors are indeed 'contra' the tenor, of similar length and activity. Some are longer, with notably more short values; strikingly long and active ones include those for M28, M30, M31.

All but one motet have equal range and activity of the two cantus parts. In M12 with tenor Alleluia, exceptional in this as in other respects, the upper parts share the range $a'-c''$ but the tessitura of cantus II is, in this motet alone, distinctly lower than cantus I. All but one of the motets have final cadences made by the cantus and tenor intervals 10/6–12/8; M12 has the unusual final cadence 8/5–12/8.

The motets are presented as essays in various mensurations, with examples of all four combinations of tempus and prolation. There is a predominance of ₵ (18 motets) and O (14), mensurations respectively very common and quite rare in the French repertory. M8 uses ₵ and O, both unsigned; the shift of mensuration is shown (as mentioned) by a change to red coloration but without proportional significance. Four motets are entirely in the rare ⊙ mensuration, compared to four in PMFC 5 and two by Machaut. Five are in C. All but three (M11, M18, M40) are in perfect modus, and the tenors mostly follow the upper parts without setting up counter-patterns, except in M14, and in the diminution section of M31, where the perfect tempus of the tenor is pitted against the continuing imperfect tempus of the contratenor and upper parts. The maxima appears in only two motets (M18, M36). M36 is the only motet with perfect maximodus as well as perfect modus. There are no mensuration signs throughout the motets, except in M36, which has frequent changes between ₵, O and C in both upper parts, with almost constant juxtaposition of different mensurations at the same time, a veritable essay in mensural combinations.

The motets are also presented as essays in various tonalities, but within a very narrow band of choice, and with a predominance of finals on *f* ('major') and *d* ('minor'). Three motets cadence on *g* (M16, M29, M30) and only one, M14, on *c*. About two-thirds of the motets open with the same sonority as the final. All pieces with *f* final have a *bb* signature in the tenor, except M27, M28, M32, M35, M40, which have none; only pieces with *f* final have a flat signature. M41 in addition (and alone) has a signature of two flats in the contratenor. M14, exceptional in many ways, has a tenor signature of *eb* only, with corresponding *ebs* in the other voices, partly at staff beginnings, partly as accidentals.

M2 illustrates the standard pattern as well as any of the twenty-eight perfectly regular motets. It has two *taleae* of 60 breves each, or twenty perfect longs, and a single *color* of 120 breves. The second *talea* is a literal isorhythmic replication of the first. Modus and tempus are perfect, prolation minor. The tonality and final cadence (10/6–12/8) are on *f*; the tenor starts on *c* but is underpinned by contratenor *f*. The contratenor is nonetheless inessential, and causes a 'bifocal' sonority at bar 88 (fifths both above and below the tenor).[40]

French or Italian?

Hoppin considered the repertory to be entirely French. Indeed, not only the use of vernacular texts but many aspects of the notation encourage this view. There is extensive use of advanced applications of alteration and imperfection and of displacement coloration to create syncopation. This is carried through in an entirely literate French way, but as is well known, this notation was also mastered by composers active in Lombardy and the Veneto around and after 1400, such as Philipoctus de Caserta and Ciconia. But this is not the whole story. In addition to features usually associated with French notation and motet technique, there are many instances of the features I have identified as characterising the distinctive Italian motet style of the late fourteenth and early fifteenth centuries, heard at its finest in the motets of Ciconia.[41] These features were much cultivated by Du Fay (in his case truly blended with his early French training) and post-Ciconian composers from the north, and are not commonly found in French motets of the period up to 1400. This observation bears on the styles and techniques of composition, not on the compilation, and is therefore independent of the judgement that most of the manuscript's verbal text was copied by an Italian scribe. I now list those features of the Italian motet which are also conspicuous in the Cyprus motets:

1. Two high cantus parts that are equal or nearly equal in range and tessitura, activity and number of notes.
2. Two texts that are equal or nearly equal in amount of text, and often in metrical, stanza or rhyme scheme. In the Cypriot repertory the two cantus parts always have different texts, as in French motets; Italian motets are sometimes monotextual.
3. The predominant tonalities and finals are *f* 'major' (24 Cyprus motets) and *d* 'minor' (13).
4. Use of unison hocket, rhythmic sequence, conspicuous declamatory passages and close imitations between equal voices, as in the motets of Ciconia.

---

[40] For 'bifocal' see Bent, 'The Grammar of Early Music' and 'Naming of Parts'.
[41] See Chs. 26 and 28.

672 POPES, TRÉMOÏLLE AND CYPRUS

5. Mostly non-chant, freely composed, accompanying tenor parts, often with leaps of fourths and fifths.

6. Contratenor parts, where present, are contrapuntally inessential and are procedurally later, if not actually separated in intent or in time of composition.

7. Final cadences are formed of the intervals 10/6–12/8 between the essential three voices, the two cantus parts and tenor. This applies to all except M12, which parodies the texts of a motet by Vitry, and whose unusual cadence is 8/5–12/8 on *d*.

8. Limited use of tenor diminution. As noted above, only seven of the Cyprus motets have *color* repetition. Of these, M7 has no diminution, two (M31 and M40) repeat the *color* in halved values (*per semi*), two (M12, M14) re-augment after diminution. M8 and M18 diminish the first half of the *color* (in M8 written out using coloration) before presenting the second, which is then also diminished.[42] In the remaining single-*color* motets, the upper parts simply repeat isorhythmically at each new *talea*. M9 has no isorhythm; in M12 only the tenor is isorhythmic, and in M16 tenor and contratenor are isorhythmic.

9. Upper-voice rhythmic replication in the second half of a motet.

10. Senaria perfecta (.p.), equivalent to French perfect tempus with minor prolation (O), is one of the most characteristic mensurations of the Italian motet. While this mensuration does not prevail in the Cyprus motets, it is used for fully one-third of them (14), many more examples than in the fourteenth-century French repertory, where it is uncommon. Of the motets in PMFC 5, apart from two older-generation motets (nos. 14, *Les l'ormeile* and 22, *Clap, clap, par un matin*), it is used only in *Rex Karole* and *Trop ay dure/Par sauvage* (**Ivrea**, 57ᵛ–58; PMFC 5, no. 20), and in Machaut only in motets 11 (a rhythmically conservative piece), 19 and the inauthentic no. 24 (*Li enseignement/De touz les biens*).

Only M15 and M17 have an introduction (or *introitus*) before the tenor entry, a common but not universal feature of the early fifteenth-century Italian motet. That for M15 has a grandly wide-spaced imitation in the Ciconian manner; that for M17 is textless.[43]

Having said that, let us turn our attention to motets by French composers dating from the first decade of the fifteenth century. Here we find some features not so marked in the slightly older fourteenth-century repertory as transmitted in **Ivrea**. In fact, some of these features are present in a French motet dated *c*. 1375 or 1378, *Rex Karole* by Philippe Royllart (PMFC 5, no. 26). It stands out as almost the only French motet datable before 1400 to incorporate many of the features favoured by Italian motet composers: as just mentioned, exceptionally, among French motets, it is in triple time, but also has an echo opening (as does Vitry's *Petre/Lugentium*), equal range top parts with hocketing and 10/6–12/8 final cadence.[44] (It differs from the Italian model in other respects, having a chant tenor and essential contratenor. There are changes of signature, but no

---

[42] This also happens in Ciconia's motet *Petrum Marcello*. See PMFC 24, no. 18. The **Chantilly** motet *Alpha vibrans* presents each of four *color* segments first as written, then in retrograde and diminution, then *recte* and in diminution. See PMFC 5, no. 25.

[43] Such introductions are usually referred to as *introitus*; on this term see Ch. 1.

[44] A small majority of Machaut's motets have 6/3–8/5 cadences, but his motets 3, 4, 7, 10, 12, 15, 19 have 10/6–12/8 final cadence, and motets 5, 11, 16, 20, 23 have irregular cadence forms.

diminution, and there is no upper-part isorhythm.) This widely distributed motet could have been a conduit for some of these features adopted in northern motets of the first decade of the fifteenth century.

Some of this may be explained by tendencies in the few motets by northern composers dating from the first decade of the fifteenth century. These include some of the above Italianate features, notably upper texted parts of equal range and activity, *talea* pairs isorhythmic in all parts, use of a range of mensurations, some chant and some free tenors, some essential and some inessential contratenors, single *color* or replication without diminution.

Roots of the Repertory

Without detracting from the obvious French connections of the repertory, the links with the Italian motet, and especially the Veneto, are strengthened by the case made here for affinities between the Cyprus motets and the specifically Italian motet genre known mostly from the Veneto. Remembering Janus's Italian origins, trade and communications continued strongly between Cyprus and Venice, presumably including some cultural exchange, though evidently not of actual musical compositions in either direction.

Hoppin noted a 'similarity of textual construction' between motets in **Cyprus** and **Ox213**.[45] He also rightly pointed out connections, in the use of musical clichés, with works by Cesaris, Velut and others, including suggestive similarities between M4 and Velut's *Benedicta viscera/Ave mater gratie*.[46] Velut's motet, however, is unlike the majority of Cyprus motets in that it has a single *color* chant tenor and an essential contratenor as well as adapting each *color* statement to mensural changes in the upper parts. The other motet ascribed to Velut, *Summe summy* in **Q15**, is an equal-cantus motet with inessential contratenor, imitative introduction, *d* tonality and O time, but with a single text and no isorhythmic repeat. The differences between these two ascribed Velut motets provide an inconclusive basis for further attributions to him of the Cyprus motets, though they are not to be excluded as models. The compositions of the generation of Velut, Cesaris and Carmen must lie close to the point at which both French and Italian ingredients of the Cyprus techniques were borrowed and exported.[47] If Velut was responsible for taking them to Cyprus, why did he not take these existing compositions and build them into the repertory? His departure in 1411 is earlier than has hitherto been suggested for the exportation of this repertory to the Veneto manuscripts in which they were copied in the 1420s and 1430s, but now seems the likeliest *terminus ante quem*, since he had left the mainland, not apparently to return. To the influences of Velut and his contemporaries documented in that first decade, Carmen, Cesaris, Tapissier, we should add Ciconia as a probable source of many of the clichés identified by Hoppin as 'a common stock of melodic formulae', features also adopted by his subsequent Veneto imitators.[48] Ciconia's motets date from before his death in 1412,

---

[45] Hoppin, 'Cypriot-French Repertory', 99.
[46] CMM 11/2, no. 7. Leech-Wilkinson, 'Cyprus Songs', has gone considerably further in establishing common material and musical language between pieces of various genres within French vernacular song.
[47] Kügle, 'Repertory', 164, underlines the close connection of the Cyprus motets to these composers.
[48] Hoppin, 'Cypriot-French Repertory', 103.

674 POPES, TRÉMOÏLLE AND CYPRUS

and thus could have been known to the musicians who sailed to Cyprus from Venice in 1411, along with other northern repertory. The Cyprus composers have learned all the tricks and apply them with skill; they do not, however, except in a few cases, seem to pack the compositions with innovative devices to achieve truly individual works. If they did, then they are different enough from what we now know to look for that we have yet to find them. It is certainly possible that these are the works of Velut and his colleagues and apprentices who had absorbed by 1410 some of the clearest techniques of the French and Italian traditions that were beginning to merge around that time. My own sense of the style of the Cyprus motets is quite consistent with a composition date in the 1410s or early 1420s.

Texts

All the Latin texts are in verse of a fluent, competent but relatively conventional kind. No classical quotations have been identified. Much of the textual substance is patchworked from vocabulary and phrases familiar from well-known hymns, sequences and other liturgical items, but also from other known motets. Besseler and Hoppin pointed out direct textual paraphrasing in M12 (*Incessanter/Virtutibus*) of *Impudenter/Virtutibus*, a motet probably by Vitry. The poet of M12 knew Vitry's motet, though there is no apparent musical relationship.[49] The word *virtutibus* also occurs in the cantus II parts of M8, M9, M20.[50] *Lugentibus*, recalling his *Petre Clemens/Lugentium*, occurs in M13 cantus II; *altisonis* in M14 cantus II recalls the **Ivrea** motets *Altissonis/Hin [sic] principes* (no. 2) or *Almifonis/Rosa* (no. 21).[51] Kügle also notes textual paraphrasing in the cantus I parts of M39 (*Mon mal/Toustens*) of *Mon chant/Qui doloreus*—a weaker but possible candidate for Vitry's authorship.[52] Some of the texts, for example, M5, fall into regular sequence form, with double stanzas aabccb, 887, 887. Others, such as the triplum of M6, are not stanzaic, and quite irregular in line length and rhyme scheme. While Velut's motet *Benedicta viscera/Ave mater* has at least an approximate correspondence between stanza and *talea*, this is not always true of the Cyprus motets. In M5, for example, the thirty lines of both upper voices are very approximately allocated to the three *taleae*, close to ten lines each, but with no respect to the divisions between the five six-line stanzas in each part. The incipits of M5, *Iubar solis universa/Fulgor solis non vilescit*, on the Eucharist, recall the text of Du Fay's motet on the Virgin, *Fulgens iubar ecclesie dei/ Puerpera, pura parens*, written for Cambrai, and dated by Fallows to 1442, and to 1445

---

[49] Besseler, 'Studien I', 213; Hoppin, 'Cypriot-French Repertory', 98–99. The relationship between the two motets has also been studied by Welker, *Musik am Oberrhein*, 113–17.

[50] Kügle, 'Repertory', 163. Pp. 161–62 also list some verbal resonances with the French repertory. He drew attention to the sharing of stock Latin phrases, and to the feature, shared with both French and Italian motets, of concluding a motet with a prayer for intercession.

[51] PMFC V, 46–49.

[52] Hoppin, 'The Cypriot-French Repertory', 98, and see also Widaman, Wathey, Leech-Wilkinson, 'Structure' and Kügle, 'Repertory', who tabulates textual resonances with other 14th-c. motets on pp. 162–63, suggesting a strong association with French royal court culture. As Yolanda Plumley has shown, the anonymous motet *Mon chant/Qui doloreus* (**Ivrea** no. 39, also in **Durham20**, and **Trém** no. 43: see Ch. 31, Appendix, n. 61) cites in both voices a ballade written by Jehan de Le Mote in 1339 upon the death in 1337 of Guillaume I, count of Hainaut: *Qui dolereuse onques n'a conneü*, with the refrain *Mon cant em plaing, ma cançon en clamour*' (Plumley, *Grafted Song*, ch. 6). Also reported in Ch. 15 n. 39.

THE CYPRUS MANUSCRIPT AND ITS MOTETS   675

or 1447 by Planchart, all on the strength of the cantus II acrostic 'Petrus de Castello canta'.[53] There is no apparent further connection between the compositions, and the date of Du Fay's motet is by any standards too late to have served as a model for M5.

Many of the locutions are almost school exercises in ingenious acrostics, internal, crossed and chained rhymes, alliteration and other devices. Variety of metrical and rhyme schemes is actively cultivated, though many of the individual texts are in standard metrical and stanzaic patterns, regular, paired rhymes, octosyllables or alternating lines of seven and eight syllables rhyming abab, stanzas rhyming ababcc, or sequence-like double stanzas of 887 syllables. As for rhyme, nearly all the Latin rhymes are of at least double syllables. Occasionally the poet managed only a single-syllable rhyme. But elsewhere he sometimes contrives triple or even quadruple rhymes. There are many intricate schemes of internal rhyme.

All the motet texts are in syllabic verse except two, M14 and M18, which are in quantitative hexameters, for which their irregular syllable count is therefore irrelevant. Both of those motets have internal rhyme within each line, sometimes with neighbouring lines, either direct or obliquely crossed. Kügle overlooked M18 (*Sanctus in eternis/ Sanctus et ingenitus*) in reporting that M14 (*Personet armonia/Consonat*) shares its use of hexameters with internal rhyme *only* with the motet *Portio nature/Ida capillorum* (in **Ivrea** and elsewhere); both celebrate a female saint, Katherine and Ida respectively; M32 is also on St Katherine. Other texts in hexameters include Dunstaple's *Albanus roseo rutilat/Quoque ferendus* (John Dunstable, *Complete Works*, no. 23), the motetus of *Inter densas/Imbribus irriguis* (**Chantilly**), the fragmentary *Arta/Musicus est ille* (Ch. 21) and *Padu . . . serenans* (Ch. 28).

The texts of cantus I and II are rarely exactly the same in stanza or metrical make-up. Indeed, the most surprising aspect of the texts is the frequent and quite deliberate cultivation of difference—in length and other respects—between texts that are set to musically equal and twinned cantus parts. Only six motets (all Latin-texted: M1, 5, 9, 13, 32, 33) have absolutely twinned texts with respect to line and syllable count and rhyme scheme. M3 and M20 have the same number of eight-syllable lines in each part, but with different rhyme schemes in the two voices.

All the other thirty-two text pairs are in some way unequal in length, as if the poet anticipated that they would be composed with a hierarchy between the status of cantus I and II, or triplum and motetus, as in most French motets. M6 has twenty-four lines in each part, but differently arranged; cantus I has the so-called Sapphic arrangement in lines of 11 11 11 5 syllables. (Cantus I of M8 is 8 8 8 4.) Where the same metre is used in both parts, cantus I often has one more stanza than cantus II. This leads to simple proportional ratios between the text syllables in both parts. In M7 the proportion is 4:3 (24:18); in M21, 6:5 (24:20); in M23, 5:4 (20:16), also in M 25 (25:20). Such numbers are also achieved by varying the line length or metrical structure between them. Thus, of the Latin motets:

equal in line/syllable *and* rhyme scheme are nos. 1, 5, 9, 13, 32, 33

equal in line/syllable but with variant rhyme are nos. 3, 16, 20

---

[53] Holford-Strevens, 'Du Fay the Poet?', 145–50.

equal in syllable and rhyme (= stanza structure?) but with more lines in cantus I than cantus II are nos. 7, 21, 23, 25:

motet	Lines	proportion
7	24:18	4:3
21	24:20	6:5
23	20:16	5:4
25	25:20	5:4

This tendency to proportioned inequality sets these pairs apart from most equal-cantus Italian motets, which tend to have perfectly equal, twinned texts (and in some cases a single text). Of the two motets written in hexameters (M14, M18), the texts of M18 have twenty lines each, while M14 has 24:20. Each of these pairs of texts employs intense and purposefully varied strategies of chained and internal rhymes in a complete lattice—as we shall soon see. An elaborate pair of Sanctus tropes in M18 works in the words of the Sanctus text in a most ingenious way that stitches the texts together at many points.

Stanza to *talea* Relationship

Stanza to *talea* correspondence such as has been demonstrated for Machaut would be expected in motets that conform as strongly as these to archetypes. Such correspondence, however, is rather infrequent, and quite rarely follows a tidy pattern in both cantus parts. It is somewhat more common in cantus I than cantus II, but full correspondence is prevented when the second texts of such pieces are not equal but otherwise proportioned to the first. Relationships between texts of different motets offer another striking aspect. They are not only related outside but within this repertory. The texts of the 'O' antiphon cycle, for example, are related proportionally.

In writing about the grand cycle of eight Advent 'O' antiphons, M23–30, Hoppin noted that it was primarily the tripla that expand and paraphrase the antiphon texts. M27 omits the first words of the antiphon (*O oriens, splendor*) deliberately, as to restore them would break the alternation of 7- and 9-syllable lines.[54] None of these antiphons has truly twinned pairs of texts, but two other observations proved intriguing. First, *all* the cantus I texts of this group are constructed with 200-syllable patterns, either 25 octosyllabic lines (M25–30) or 20 decasyllables (M23, M24). All the texts with 25 octosyllabic lines are identical in rhyme scheme. Second, the second texts are all different from the first, but the cantus I:II relationship by syllable count is in most cases 5:4. See Table 32.1

Correspondence between stanza and musical structure (*talea*) is achieved for cantus I but not cantus II. The musical lengths and relationships between the motets of this group show no such clear cyclic goal, though their tonal and mensural plan is clearly

---

[54] Hoppin's editorial commentary notes that 'the omission of "Oriens" destroys the retrograde acrostic *Ero cras* that is formed by the first words of the antiphons (after the initial "O")'.

Table 32.1 The 'O' Antiphons

No.	Title, final, mensuration	Clefs/flat	Breves	Cantus I lines/syllables	Cantus II lines/syllables	Total syllables
23	O Sapientia (*d*), ☉	C2, C4	117	20 × 10	16 × 10	200:160
24	O Adonay (*d*), O	C2, C4	135	20 × 10	20 × 8	200:160
25	O Radix (*f*), ℭ	C1, C3, ♭	[138]	25 × 8	20 × 8	200:160
26	O clavis (*f*), C	C1, C3, ♭	171	25 × 8	18 × 8	200:144
27	[O oriens splendor] Lucis eterne (*f*), ☉	C2, C4	144	25 (× 7, 8, 9) tr stanza 1: 47 49; 2: 88; 3: 88 17	20 × 8	199 [*sic*]:160
28	O Rex (*f*), O	C2, C4	153	25 × 8	20 × 8	200:160
29	O Emanuel (*g*), ℭ	C1, C4	108	25 × 8	20 × 8	200:160
30	O sacra virgo (*g*), C	C1, C4	[192]	25 × 8	20 × 8	200:160

cyclic. The eight motets make four pairs with respect to tonal types if not indeed modes; and they rotate the four mensurations twice, in the same order. All eight have perfect modus; all have three *taleae* except M30, which has four, and a differently constructed contratenor.

Was there a plan to the collection? On evidence of arrangement, it appears so, but the motets seem to have been through-copied in gatherings VII–X (ff. 59–97), with none of the articulation points of the collection corresponding to a gathering or scribal break. All four motet gatherings (about a quarter of the manuscript) are quinternions, but a blank-staved folio has been removed from the end of gathering X following f. 97.

As stated above, it has been judged that one music scribe is responsible for the entire manuscript. Two scribes copied the motet texts, of whom the principal is the main text scribe of the preceding sections of the manuscript. The second text scribe copied the last six French motets.[55] Widaman, Wathey and Leech-Wilkinson identify him with the music scribe, on the evidence of a marginal correction on f. 76[r] in which this scribe adds music and text for a passage omitted by the main text scribe. Motets 36–41, however, are preceded by one French motet (M35) in the main hand, immediately following the two *Deo gratias* motets. The scribal break therefore comes one piece later than would be expected, after M35. The first motet, on *Victime paschali*, appears to be a later addition by the same scribes to the first recto of gathering VII and, as stated above, may have been designed precisely to occupy the first recto of the motet section. The fact that the parts are copied below each other in the order cantus I, tenor, cantus II, contratenor, suggests that it was copied from a source laid out across facing pages like all the other Cyprus motets, with the tenor below cantus I on the left, the contratenor below cantus II on the right. Thus the cycle of whole-opening motets may be said to begin with M2 (ff. 59[v]–60[r]). As the same authors observed, this would have brought the planned number of motets to the round number of forty.

---

[55] Widaman, Wathey, Leech-Wilkinson, 'Structure'. On the round number of forty motets, see their discussion on pp. 95–116.

678 POPES, TRÉMOÏLLE AND CYPRUS

The question of quality also arises. It is unlikely to be coincidence that the most interesting and diverse pieces seem to be those in the group M6–18 that show greatest variety of technical means and experiment, rather than the more numerous pieces that conform to a standard template and present a homogeneous impression. This homogeneity has been remarked on in all the genres in the manuscript.[56] That there seem to be so few individual creations in both text and music, so few that avoid signs of mass production, argues in favour either of a relatively short time-span for their composition, or of a close circle of composers, if not a single one, over a longer period. This judgement stands in sharp contrast to the individuality identified in most motets discussed in this book. In drawing attention to some technical aspects of text and music, I hope to have balanced French and Italian views of the repertory that may contribute to the continuing discussion of its origins and the date and provenance of the manuscript.

Excursus: M14 *Personet armonia/Consonat*

This motet stands out as exceptional in many ways, some of which have been noted above. Like the nearly contemporary Lusignan *chappelle royale* in Pyrga, Cyprus, it is dedicated to St Katherine. The motet shares the number of sections (five) and some rotary cyclic structuring with the—also exceptionally long—English St Katherine motet *Rota versatilis* of the early fourteenth century.[57] These musical features are the motet's most remarkable aspect, but they are underpinned by texts which also have striking symmetries and numerical correspondences.

Texts

This is one of only two of the Cyprus motets with texts in hexameters; these are coupled with unusual internal rhymes as shown in the Appendix. Cantus I has 140 words (12^2 minus 4) and cantus II 121 (11^2). The total duration of 396 semibreves, resolved to 132 perfect breves, is 12×11. Note the caesural rhyme in cantus I, with only -*orum* repeated; alliteration (f in lines 10–11, l in 12, d in 12–13), with extended play on *lux* and *dux*; and in cantus II the crossed double rhymes in different groupings. *Speculum* in cantus I marks the end of the first 'mirrored' passage (i.e. mirrored in *color* 5: see below), spanning from *color* 1 to *color* 2. In cantus II *Converti gaudet* 'turns' the text at the musical chiasm at the centre of the whole motet (as we shall see below); *gaudet* is the middle word. (Cantus I has *gaudia* in line 13, the first of the second half of the text.) The midpoint of the music is flanked on either side by the middle text words of each texted part. In cantus I the midpoint of words falls between *duxque* and *ducis*. Other links between the texts include: cantus I, lines 1–2: *Personet ... cantus ... laudis ... Katerine*; cantus II, lines 1–2 *Consonet ... laudes ... Katerine*. The final lines of both cantus parts each contain the words *fac nos* twice, and share (in cantus I) *virgo ... Katerina ... grata ... beatis*

---

[56] For example Leech-Wilkinson, 'Cyprus Songs'.
[57] See Bent, '*Rota versatilis*' and its revision in Bent, Hartt and Lefferts, *The Dorset Rotulus*, ch. 5.

THE CYPRUS MANUSCRIPT AND ITS MOTETS   679

and (in cantus II) *Katerine . . . virgo . . . gratos . . . beatos*. Her wheel is invoked by *radius, radians, radiavit* in cantus II, line 8.

Music

This is one of only three motets without a contratenor, one of only two in hexameters and, with 396 major semibreves, it is one of the longest, exceeded only by M27 with 432 major semibreves (144 perfect breves). It is the only motet with a *c* final, and it cadences with the tenor rhythm ▪ ▪ ▪ (3 2 1) at the end of each of the five *color* statements, all of which start on *g* and end on *c*. The tenor has a signature of *e♭* only, and several *e* flats are notated in the upper parts, confirming the intent and implying more.

Five *color* statements are disposed chiastically in the proportions 3 2 1 2 3. The mensurations are alternately ⊙ and ℂ: ⊙ ℂ ⊙ ℂ ⊙, with tenor diminution in the central *color*, where the perfect breve becomes a perfect semibreve, a reduction of 3:1. In breves, the lengths of sections are 36^3 36^2 12^3 36^2 36^3, altogether 84 perfect and 72 imperfect breves. In major semibreves, this yields 108, 72, 36, 72, 108, a total of 396. Sections 1 and 5 of the tenor are in major modus, perfect tempus; sections and 4 are major modus, imperfect tempus. Section 3 is marked '3° semi de 2°'.

The corresponding sections in the upper parts (*colores* 1 and 5, 2 and 4) have substantial isorhythmic correspondences, passages which are mostly occupied with extended and skilful rhythmic canon.[58] In *color* 1 the rhythm of bars 29–44 = *color* 5, 157–72; the 13-limbed rhythmic canon occupies 39 semibreves of ⊙. In *color* 2 the rhythm of bars 54–69 = *color* 4, 102–17; here there are two rhythmic canons, one of 14 semibreves followed by one of 12 semibreves, occupying 26 semibreves of ℂ. The division between the two canons falls at the midpoint of the *color* (bb. 62–63), which also divides the words *radium* and *rota* in the motetus in *color* 2, just before *Katerine magna rotarum* following the parallel place in *color* 4. In the short central *color* 3 (bb. 81–92) a new hocketed rhythmic canon at one minim's distance (with units of only ⌐ ♦♦) starts just after the midpoint of the *color*, also the centre of the whole motet, flanked by the central text words, and announced by the motetus words *Converti gaudet* which, as noted above, 'turns' the musical chiasm.

Each tenor *color* is perfectly chiastic in rhythmic result but not in notation (1 2 3, with second breve altered, 3 2 1 with second long imperfected: ▪ ▪ ▪ ▪ ▪ ▪ ▪ ▪ | ▪ ▪ ▪ ▪ ▪ ▪ ▪ ▪). That means that the entire tenor rhythm of the five *colores* is chiastic overall as well as within each *color*. The remarkable design of the whole motet, text and music, can therefore be seen as a vivid representation of the Katherine wheel.

Postscript: Where was the Manuscript Produced?

Until Kügle's article of 2012, the majority consensus was that the manuscript was copied in Cyprus and came to Savoy with Anne's retinue in 1434. Questions were raised about

---

[58] Cf. the rhythmic canons in motets by Salinis, Ch. 27 and Exx. 27.1, 27.2, 27.3, and similar passages in Carmen.

680 POPES, TRÉMOÏLLE AND CYPRUS

the Italian script of parts of the collection but, given the apparently cosmopolitan nature of the Cypriot court, those scribes could have worked in Cyprus. More challenging was the opinion of Italian art historians that the miniatures, initials and decoration were Italian. Given that there was little evidence of insular illumination, whether or not by Italian artists, this led to suggestions by art historians that the illumination was probably done in Italy, by Venetian or more probably Bolognese artists, leaving open the possibility that the manuscript could have been brought to Savoy unilluminated and probably unbound, and decorated there or in northern Italy. Kügle went further and, on the basis of the previously unidentified coat of arms in the border of f. 1, made the case that the entire manuscript was created in Italy in the 1430s for a Brescian aristocrat, Pietro Avogadro, using exemplars brought from Cyprus by Hanelle, who probably made the majority of the copies, both interim and final, some or many of them even his own compositions.

The original draft of the revision to this chapter expressed scepticism about Kügle's surprising hypothesis. If Avogadro was prepared to pay for an expensive new manuscript, why would he have wanted to take over a readymade and then rather old-fashioned repertory, rather than to commission a new manuscript that reflected local saints, tastes, composers, and current musical styles? What evidence is there that he was a patron of music or had the resources to perform this specialised foreign repertory, unknown to him and to any musicians in his employ?[59] The two years in which this is supposed to have happened (1434–36) are almost impossibly short for the copying and decoration of such an enormous codex, let alone the associated negotiations and organisation. The reason given by Kügle for Hanelle's conjectured hasty return to favour in Savoy with the completed manuscript (namely, that his status as a 'clericus coniugatus' was a moral contamination which also infected the manuscript) does not stand scrutiny.[60] But at the aforementioned 2021 Turin conference Kügle drew back from this hypothesis, as he now shared some of the misgivings I and others had expressed meanwhile. He presented a new hypothesis for the genesis of the manuscript, still involving Avogadro as patron, but with one of two Lusignan clerics, Lancelot, a nephew of Janus, as recipient. Both hypotheses assume that the entire manuscript was copied from exemplars brought from Cyprus by Hanelle, still with a probable role for him (among others) in the compilation.

A central question is whether indeed it *is* the Avogadro coat of arms. Kügle rejected Besseler's identification as the arms of the Bagarotti family of Padua, on grounds that the colours (blue and silver) are wrong.[61] Avogadro's arms at this time appear to have been red and silver, but the coat of arms in **Cyprus** is red and gold. In both Besseler's and Kügle's suggestions, one of the two colours is wrong, at least for the time period in which the manuscript was compiled. While rejecting Besseler's anomaly, Kügle seems to accept

---

[59] Diego Zancani, the only scholar to have written about Antonio Cornazzano's *Vita* of Pietro Avogadro in recent years, assures me that there is nothing in this *Vita*, or that he knows independently, that can even remotely connect Avogadro to Cyprus, or indeed to Savoy. Zancani, 'Un recupero Quattrocentesco', and email correspondence of Feb. 2020.

[60] For other instances of married clerics see n. 15 above; this was a canonically legitimate status for clerics in minor orders.

[61] *Il codice J.II.9*, 33 n. 20. Besseler, 'Studien I', 211.

THE CYPRUS MANUSCRIPT AND ITS MOTETS · 681

a similar one in his own identification.[62] The best hope for solving this puzzle would be the discovery of a better match for the coat of arms with the correct colours. Kügle was unaware in 2012 (as was I) of the 2004 suggestion, by Luisa Gentile to Giovanna Saroni, that the coat of arms corresponds to that of the noble Savoyard Beggiamo family of Savigliano, as also proposed by Alessandro Vitale-Brovarone at the Turin conference.[63] With respect to colours and chronology, the match is better than for Avogadro, the location likelier. The presence of a coat of arms belonging neither to Cyprus nor to the dukes of Savoy remains a conundrum.

I will not take these arguments further until Kügle has finalised a case that may yet undergo revision, but I find it impossible to believe that this isolated repertory would have been copied at the instigation of any Italian patron in the 1430s. If Avogadro was sufficiently interested in music to commission *this* manuscript, why did he not include the music he knew or which was then prestigious, for example that of Du Fay? Meanwhile, it is hoped that technical and stylistic work on the illuminations, initials and borders may answer some of these questions and produce a plausible explanation for the addition of these arms. Could the border to f. 1 (to which the arms are integral) have been added in Italy, long after the 'archaic' St Hilarion initial? That would allow the bound and partly illuminated manuscript to have been prepared in Cyprus and to have travelled to Savoy with Anne. These issues will be taken further in the proceedings of the Turin conference.

Meanwhile, Alberto Rizzuti has further explored the connection with the Beggiamo family, whose arms with red on gold provide a convincing match, with the correct colours, accompanied by the initials G.B., reported before the fire of 1904, and still faintly detectable. Moreover, Rizzuti has discovered traces of blue below the Beggiamo arms, which correspond to the arms of Anne of Lusignan, thus supporting the original hypothesis that the manuscript was indeed brought with Anne in 1434 and her arms subsequently overpainted. Rizzuti's thorough and complex argument is supported by extensive specialist photography and detailed research.[64]

---

[62] Kügle, 'Glorious Sounds', 651 n. 35.
[63] Giovanna Saroni, *La Biblioteca di Amedeo VIII*, reporting a suggestion of Luisa Gentile.
[64] His findings will be published as Rizzuti, 'Four Angels and a Coat of Arms'.

Appendix
The Cyprus Motets

The groupings are labelled as in Kügle, 'Repertory', 158–59.

No.	Folios	Texts	Comments	Final	Mensuration	*Taleae*
		First cycle *de tempore*				
1	59	*Victima laudum pascalis/Victimis in pascalibus/*Tenor: *Victime paschali/*Contratenor	Easter sequence	*d*	O	1C 3T; upper iso.
2	59ᵛ–60	*Qui patris atris honoris/Paraclite spiritus/*Tenor/Contratenor	Pentecost; Cyprus	*f*	O	1C 2T; upper iso.
3	60ᵛ–61	*Assumpta gemma virginum/Gratulandum mente pia/*Tenor/Contratenor	BVM; Assumption; acrostics	*d*	⊙	1C 3T; upper iso.
4	61ᵛ–62	*Aurora vultu pulcrior/Ave virginum flos et vita/*Tenor/Contratenor	BVM; acrostics	*f*	C	1C 3T; upper iso.
5	62ᵛ–63	*Iubar solis universa/Fulgor solis non vilescit/*Tenor/Contratenor	Eucharist	*d*	O	1C 3T; upper iso.
6	63ᵛ–64	*Nate regnantis super astra/Maria, proles regina/*Tenor/Contratenor	BVM; Cyprus and King Janus	*f*	₵	1C 3T; partial upper iso.
7	64ᵛ–65	*Natus in patris gremio/Apparuit sol hodie/*Tenor/Contratenor	Nativity; 'Engaddi'; Cyprus?	*f*	₵	2C × 2T; partial upper iso, × 4
		Cycle *de sanctis*				
8	65ᵛ–66	*Gemma florens militie/Hec est dies gloriosa/*Tenor/Contratenor	Denis, Macarius, King Janus. Cyprus; St John Baptist	*f*	₵ O	1C × 2T with internal dim. Aa Bb; upper parts fully iso. × 2
9	66ᵛ–67	*Porta celi fulgentibus/Assit deus huic domui/*Tenor/Contratenor	BVM; Dedication of a church	*f*	₵	1C × 1T; no iso.
10	67ᵛ–68	*Reverenter veneremur/Venerandum crucis lignum/*Tenor/Contratenor	True Cross; Cyprus?	*f*	O	1C 3T; partial upper iso.
11	68ᵛ–69	*Mater alma clementie/Deitatis triclinium/*Tenor	BVM	*f*	O	1C 2T; partial upper iso.

12	69ᵛ–70	*Incessanter expectavi/Virtutis ineffabilis/* Tenor: *Alleluya*	BVM; texts modelled on Vitry's *Impudenter/Virtutibus*	*d*	₵	3C × 2T; C2 dim. (*semi*); no upper iso.
13	70ᵛ–71	*Christe qui supra sydera/Christe nostra salvatio/* Tenor/Contratenor	Christe eleison tropes? Ascension	*f*	₵	1C 2T; partial upper iso.
14	71ᵛ–72	*Personet armonia dulcis cantus, melodia/ Consonet altisonis laudes notulis Katerine/* Tenor	St Katherine; Cyprus	*c*	₵ ☉ see Excursus above	1C 5T, mensural; partial upper iso.
15	72ᵛ–73	*Hunc diem festis celebremus hymnis/ Precursoris verbi solennia/*Tenor/Contratenor	St John Baptist; canonic introduction before T entry (*precursor!*)	*f*	O	1C 3T; partial upper iso.
16	73ᵛ–74	*Alma parens, nata nati/O Maria, stella maris/* Tenor Alleluya	BVM; Nativity	*g*	₵	1C 2T; no upper iso.
17	74ᵛ–75	*Magni patris magna mira/Ovent Cyprus, Palestina/*Tenor/Contratenor	St Hilarion; Cyprus. Introduction before T entry	*d*	C	1C 3T; partial upper iso.
18	75ᵛ–76	*Sanctus in eternis regnans, pater inque supernis/ Sanctus et ingenitus pater atque carens genitura/* Tenor/Contratenor	Sanctus tropes	*f*	₵	1C × 2T with internal dim.; Aa Bb; partial upper iso.
19	76ᵛ–77	*Certes mont fu de grant necessite/Nous devons tresfort amer/*Tenor/Contratenor	Rose; BVM; French texts	*d*	₵	1C 2T; upper iso.
20	77ᵛ–78	*Maria, mare gratie/O Maria, celi porta/*Tenor/ Contratenor	BVM	*f*	₵	1C 3T; upper iso.
21	78ᵛ–79	*Dulce melos personemus/Matrem Christi rogitemus/*Tenor/Contratenor	BVM	*f*	₵	1C 3T; upper iso.
		Second cycle *de tempore* M23–M30 are the eight 'O' Antiphons: see Table 32.1				
22	79ᵛ–80	*In talem transfiguratur/Iubar lustrat radiosum/* Tenor/Contratenor	Transfiguration	*d*	₵	1C 2T; upper iso.

(*continued*)

No.	Folios	Texts	Comments	Final	Mensuration	*Taleae*
23	80ᵛ–81	*O Sapientia incarnata/Nos demoramur, benigne rector*/Tenor/Contratenor	Advent, 17 Dec.	*d*	⊙	1C 3T; upper iso.
24	81ᵛ–82	*O Adonay, domus Israel/Pictor eterne syderum*/Contratenor/Tenor	Advent, 18 Dec.	*d*	O	1C 3T; upper iso.
25	82ᵛ–83	*O Radix Yesse splendida/Cunti fundent precamina*/Tenor/Contratenor	Advent, 19 Dec.	*f*	ℭ	1C 3T; upper iso.
26	83ᵛ–84	*O clavis David aurea/Quis igitur aperiet*/Tenor/Contratenor	Advent, 20 Dec.	*f*	C	1C 3T; upper iso.
27	84ᵛ–85	*Lucis eterne splendor/Veni, splendor mirabilis* Tenor/Contratenor	Advent, 21 Dec. Based on *O oriens, splendor lucis*	*f*	⊙	1C 3T; upper iso.
28	85ᵛ–86	*O Rex virtutum, gloria/Quis possit dign[e] exprimere*/Tenor/Contratenor	Advent, 22 Dec. Based on *O rex gentium*	*f*	O	1C 3T; upper iso.
29	86ᵛ–87	*O Emanuel, rex noster/Magne virtutum conditor*/Tenor/Contratenor	Advent, 23 Dec.	*g*	ℭ	1C 3T; upper iso.
30	87ᵛ–88	*O sacra virgo virginum/Tu, nati nata suscipe*/Tenor/Contratenor	Advent, 24 Dec.	*g*	C	1C 3T; upper iso.
31	88ᵛ–89	*Hodie puer nascitur/Homo mortalis, firmite*/Tenor/Contratenor	Nativity	*d*	ℭ	2C × 2T; dim. AB ab; upper iso. aa bb
		Supplementary repertory (saints, *deo gratias*, BVM)				
32	89ᵛ–90	*Flos regalis Katerina/Maxentius rex propere*/Tenor/Contratenor	St Katherine; Cyprus	*f*	O	1C 3T; upper iso.
33	90v–91	*Da, magne pater, rector Olimpi/Donis affatim, perfluit orbis*/Tenor/Contratenor	*Deo gratias*; acrostics. M33 and M34 are on the same opening	*d*	ℭ	1C 2T; upper iso.
34	90ᵛ–91	*Dignum summo patri/Dulciter hymnos*/Tenor/Contratenor	*Deo gratias Amen*; acrostics	*f*	C	1C 2T; upper iso.

35	91ᵛ–92	*Toustans que mon esprit mire/Qui porroit amer/*Tenor/Contratenor	BVM	*f*	ℭ	1C 3T; upper iso.
36	92ᵛ–93	*Coume le serf a la clere fontainne/Lunne plainne d'umilite/*Tenor/Contratenor	BVM	*d*	signed oℭ and c; upper parts juxtapose different mensurations; frequent change	1C 2T; upper iso.
37	93ᵛ–94	*Pour ce que point fui de la amere espine/A toi, vierge, me represente/*Tenor/Contratenor	BVM	*f*	O	1C 3T; upper iso.
38	94ᵛ–95	*Par grant soif, clere fontainne/Dame de tout pris/*Tenor/Contratenor	BVM	*f*	O	1C 3T; upper iso.
39	95ᵛ–96	*Mon mal en bien, en plaisir ma dolour/Toustens je la serviray/*Tenor/Contratenor	secular texts partially erased; M39 and M40 are on the same opening	*d*	☉	1C 2T; upper iso.
40	95ᵛ–96	*Amour trestout fort me point/La douce art m'estuet aprendre/*Tenor/Contratenor	secular texts partially erased	*f*	ℭ	2C × 2T; dim. AB ab; upper iso. aa bb
41	96ᵛ–97	*Se je di qu'en elle tire/Tres fort m'abrasa/*Tenor/Contratenor	cantus II: BVM	*f*	O	1C 3T; upper iso.

Bibliography

Abramov-van Rijk, Elena, 'Evidence for a Revised Dating of the Anonymous Fourteenth-Century Italian Treatise *Capitulum de vocibus applicatis verbis*', *PMM* 16 (2007), 19–30.

Abramov-van Rijk, Elena, 'Luchino Visconti, Jacopo da Bologna and Petrarch: Courting a Patron', *SM* NS 3 (2012), 7–62.

Abramov-van Rijk, Elena, 'The Non-Italian Ars Nova: How to Read the Madrigal *Povero zappator* by Lorenzo da Firenze', *EM* 48 (2020), 41–54.

Abramov-van Rijk, Elena, 'The Roman Experience of the Holy Roman Emperor Charles IV', *EMH* 37 (2018), 1–44.

Adler, Guido (ed.), *Handbuch der Musikgeschichte*, 2 vols. (Frankfurt am Main, 1924).

Adler, Guido (ed.), *Handbuch der Musikgeschichte*, 2nd edn., 2 vols. (Frankfurt am Main, 1930).

Aldrich, Putnam, 'An Approach to the Analysis of Renaissance Music', *MR* 30 (1969), 1–21.

Alís Raurich, Cristina, 'The *Flores* of *Flos vernalis*: Intabulation, Ornamentation and Diminution in the 14th Century', in preparation.

Alís Raurich, Cristina, 'Karlsruhe, Lichtenthal 82 and a Unique Polyphonic Setting of *Ave sidus lux dierum*', in preparation.

Allsen, Jon Michael, 'Style and Intertextuality in the Isorhythmic Motet, 1400–1440' (Ph.D. diss., University of Wisconsin, 1992).

Allsen, Jon Michael, '*Tenores ad longum* and Rhythmic Cues in the Early Fifteenth-Century Motet', *PMM* 12 (2003), 43–69.

Aluas, Luminita, 'The *Quatuor principalia musicae*: A Critical Edition and Translation, with Introduction and Commentary' (Ph.D. diss., Indiana University, 1996).

Ambros, August Wilhelm, *Geschichte der Musik*, 2nd edn. (Leipzig, 1881).

Anderson, Gordon A., 'Responsory Chants in the Tenors of Some Fourteenth-Century Continental Motets', *JAMS* 29 (1976), 119–27.

Anonymous, *Notitia del valore delle note del canto misurato*, ed. Armen Carapetyan, CSM 5 (n.p., 1957).

Antiphonarium Tonale Missarum. XIᵉ siècle. Codex H. 159 de la Bibliothèque de l'École de Médicine, Paléographie musicale, 1st ser., 7 (Tournai, 1901).

Antonii Romani Opera, ed. F. A. Gallo, Antiquae Musicae Italicae-Monumenta Veneta Sacra, 1 (Bologna, 1965).

Apel, Willi, 'Remarks about the Isorhythmic Motet', in *Les Colloques de Wégimont. II, 1955, L'ars nova: Recueil d'études sur la musique du XIVe siècle* (Paris, 1959), 139–48.

Apel, Willi (ed.), *Keyboard Music of the Fourteenth and Fifteenth Centuries*, CEKM 1 (n.p., 1963).

Apfel, Ernst, 'Über den vierstimmigen Satz im 14. und 15. Jahrhunderts', *AfMw* 18 (1961), 34–51.

Arlt, Wulf, 'Der *Tractatus figurarum* – ein Beitrag zur Musiklehre der "*ars subtilior*"', *SBM* 1 (1972), 35–53.

Arlt, Wulf, '*Triginta denariis* – Musik und Text in einer Motette des *Roman de Fauvel* über dem Tenor *Victimae paschali laudes*', in *Pax et sapientia: Studies in Text and Music of Liturgical Tropes and Sequences, in Memory of Gordon Anderson*, Acta Universitatis Stockholmensis: Studia Latina Stockholmensis, 29 (Stockholm, 1986), 97–113.

Ars cantus mensurabilis mensurata per modos iuris, ed. and trans. C. Matthew Balensuela, Greek and Latin Music Theory, 10 (Lincoln, NE, 1994).

Ars musicae mensurabilis secundum Franconem, ed. Gilbert Reaney and André Gilles, CSM 15 (n.p., 1971), 33–47.

Ars practica mensurabilis cantus secundum Iohannem de Muris: Die Recensio maior des sogenannten 'Libellus practice cantus mensurabilis', ed. Christian Berktold (Munich, 1999).

688 BIBLIOGRAPHY

Bain, Jennifer, 'Theorizing the Cadence in the Music of Machaut', *JMT* 47 (2003), 325–62.

Baltzer, Rebecca A., 'Notre Dame Manuscripts and their Owners: Lost and Found', *JM* 5 (1987), 380–99.

Barale, Elisabetta, and Daniele Valentino Filippi (eds.), *Il codice cipriota: origini, storie, contesto culturale* (Venice, forthcoming 2023).

Beck, Eleonora M., 'Marchetto da Padova and Giotto's Scrovegni Chapel frescoes', *EM* 27 (1999), 7–23.

Becker, Ph. Aug., 'Fauvel und Fauvelliana', *Berichte über die Verhandlungen der Sächsischen Akademie der Wissenschaften zu Leipzig*, Philologisch-historische Klasse, 88 (1936), ii. 5–45.

Benoit XII (1334–1342): Lettres communes, analysées d'après les registres dits d'Avignon et du Vatican, ed. J.-M. Vidal, Bibliothèque des Écoles françaises d'Athènes et de Rome, 2 bis (1902–11), ii (1903).

Bent, Margaret, 'The Absent First Gathering of the Chantilly Manuscript', *PMM* 26 (2017), 19–36.

Bent, Margaret, 'Accidentals, Counterpoint and Notation in Aaron's *Aggiunta* to the *Toscanello in Musica*', *JM* 12 (1994), 306–44.

Bent, Margaret, '*Artes novae*', *M&L* 103 (2022), 729–52.

Bent, Margaret, 'Bishop Francesco Malipiero, Music, and the Vicenza Delegation to Basel', in Matteo Nanni (ed.), *Music and Culture in the Age of the Council of Basel* (Turnhout, 2014), 161–69.

Bent, Margaret, *Bologna Q15: The Making and Remaking of a Musical Manuscript: Introductory Study and Facsimile Edition* (Lucca, 2008).

Bent, Margaret, 'Ciconia, Prosdocimus, and the Workings of Musical Grammar as Exemplified in *O felix templum* and *O Padua*', in Philippe Vendrix (ed.), *Johannes Ciconia* (Turnhout, 2003), 65–106.

Bent, Margaret, 'Composing in the late Middle Ages: Paradoxes in Anonymity and Attributions', in Anne-Zoé Rillon-Marne and Gaël Saint-Cricq (eds.), *Composers in the Middle Ages* (Woodbridge, forthcoming).

Bent, Margaret, 'A Contemporary Perception of Early Fifteenth-Century Style: Bologna Q15 as a Document of Scribal Editorial Initiative', *MD* 41 (1987), 183–201.

Bent, Margaret, 'Continuity and Transformation of Repertory and Transmission in Early 15th-Century Italy: The Two Cultures', in Sandra Dieckmann, Oliver Huck, Signe Rotter-Broman, and Alba Scotti (eds.), *Kontinuität und Transformation in der italienischen Vokalmusik zwischen Due- und Quattrocento*, Musica mensurabilis, 3 (Hildesheim, 2007), 225–46.

Bent, Margaret, *Counterpoint, Composition, and Musica Ficta* (London and New York, 2002).

Bent, Margaret, 'Deception, Exegesis and Sounding Number in Machaut's Motet 15 *Amours qui a le pouoir/Faus samblant/Vidi dominum*', *EMH* 10 (1991), 15–27.

Bent, Margaret, 'Diatonic *Ficta*', *EMH* 4 (1984), 1–48.

Bent, Margaret, 'Divisi and a versi in Early Fifteenth-Century Mass Movements', in Francesco Zimei (ed.), *Antonio Zacara da Teramo e il suo tempo* (Lucca, 2004), 95–137.

Bent, Margaret, *Dunstaple* (London, 1981).

Bent, Margaret, 'The Earliest Fifteenth-Century Transmission of English Music to the Continent', in Emma Hornby and David Maw (eds.), *Essays on the History of English Music in Honour of John Caldwell* (Woodbridge, 2010), 83–96.

Bent, Margaret, 'Early Papal Motets', in Richard Sherr (ed.), *Papal Music* (Oxford, 1998), 5–43.

Bent, Margaret, 'The Early Use of the Sign Φ', *EM* 24 (1996), 199–225.

Bent, Margaret, 'The Emiliani Chapel in the Frari: Background and Questions', in Carlo Corsato and Deborah Howard (eds.), *Santa Maria Gloriosa dei Frari: Immagini di devozione, spazi della fede (Devotional Spaces, Images of Piety)* (Padua, 2015), 177–86 and plates 74–81.

Bent, Margaret, 'Fauvel and Marigny: Which Came First?', in Margaret Bent and Andrew Wathey (eds.), *Fauvel Studies* (Oxford, 1998), 35–52.

Bent, Margaret, *The Fountains Fragments* [facsimile with introduction], Musical Sources (Clarabricken, 1987).

Bent, Margaret, 'The Fourteenth-Century Italian Motet', *L'Ars nova italiana del Trecento*, 6. *Atti del Congresso internazionale 'L'Europa e la musica del Trecento', Certaldo, 19–21 July 1984* (Certaldo, 1992), 85–125.

Bent, Margaret, 'Francesco Malipiero and Antonio da Roma—Another Musical Connection?', in Antonio Lovato and Dilva Princivalli (eds.), *Mondo latino e civiltà bizantina: Musica, arte e cultura nei codici del '400* (Padua, 2014), 225–38.

Bent, Margaret, 'The Grammar of Early Music: Preconditions for Analysis', in Cristle Collins Judd (ed.), *Tonal Structures in Early Music* (New York, 1998), 15–59.

Bent, Margaret, 'Grammar and Rhetoric in Late-Medieval Polyphony: Modern Metaphor or Old Simile?', in Mary Carruthers (ed.), *Rhetoric Beyond Words: Delight and Persuasion in the Arts of the Middle Ages* (Cambridge, 2010), 52–71.

Bent, Margaret, 'The "Harmony" of the Machaut Mass', in E. E. Leach (ed.), *Machaut's Music: New Interpretations* (Woodbridge, 2003), 75–94.

Bent, Margaret, 'Humanists and Music, Music and Humanities', in Raffaele Pozzi (ed.), *Tendenze e metodi nella ricerca musicologica. Atti del Convegno internazionale (Latina 27–29 Settembre 1990)* (Florence, 1995), 29–38.

Bent, Margaret, 'Indexes in Late Medieval Polyphonic Music Manuscripts: A Brief Tour', in James H. Marrow, Richard A. Linenthal, and William Noel (eds.), *The Medieval Book: Glosses from Friends and Colleagues of Christopher de Hamel* (Houten, 2010), 196–207.

Bent, Margaret, 'The Late-Medieval Motet', in Tess Knighton and David Fallows (eds.), *Companion to Medieval and Renaissance Music* (London, 1922), 114–19.

Bent, Margaret, 'The Machaut Manuscripts *Vg, B* and *E*', *Musica Disciplina* 37 (1983), 53–82.

Bent, Margaret, 'Machaut's Motet 10 and its Interconnections', in Jared C. Hartt (ed.), *A Critical Companion* (Woodbridge, 2018), 301–19.

Bent, Margaret, *Magister Jacobus de Ispania, Author of the* Speculum musicae, RMA Monographs, 28 (Farnham, 2015).

Bent, Margaret, 'Manuscripts as Répertoires, Scribal Performance and the Performing Scribe', *Atti del XIV Congresso della Società Internazionale di Musicologia [Bologna 1987]* (Turin, 1990), i [Round Tables], 138–48.

Bent, Margaret, 'Mayshuet and the *Deo gratias* Motets in the Old Hall Manuscript', in Martin Kirnbauer (ed.), *Beredte Musik* (Basel, 2019), 11–28.

Bent, Margaret, 'The Measurement of Time and the Structure of Motets', in Marcel Pérès and Catherine Homo-Lechner (eds.), *La Rationalisation du temps au XIIIe siècle*, Actes du colloque de Royaumont, 1991 (Royaumont, 1998), 133–44.

Bent, Margaret, 'Melchior or Marchion de Civilibus, *prepositus brixiensis*: New Documents', in Benjamin Brand and David Rothenberg (eds.), *Music and Culture in the Middle Ages and Beyond: Liturgy, Sources, Symbolism* (Cambridge, 2016), 175–90.

Bent, Margaret, 'The Motet Collection of San Lorenzo 2211 (SL) and the Composer Hubertus de Salinis', in Antonio Calvia et al. (eds.), *The End of the Ars Nova in Italy* (Florence, 2020), 43–70.

Bent, Margaret, 'Motets Recovered from a Binding (fMS typ 122)', in Rodney G. Dennis with Elizabeth Falsey (eds.), *The Marks in the Fields: Essays on the Uses of Manuscripts* (Cambridge, MA, 1992), 16–19.

Bent, Margaret, 'The Musical Stanzas in Martin le Franc's *Le Champion des dames*', in John Haines and Randall Rosenfeld (eds.), *Music and Medieval Manuscripts* (Aldershot, 2004), 91–127.

Bent, Margaret, 'The Myth of *tempus perfectum diminutum* in the Chantilly Manuscript', in Yolanda Plumley and Anne Stone (eds.), *A Late Medieval Songbook* (Turnhout, 2009), 203–27.

Bent, Margaret, 'Naming of Parts: Notes on the Contratenor, c. 1350–1450', in Gioia Filocamo, M. Jennifer Bloxam, and Leofranc Holford-Strevens (eds.), '*Uno gentile et subtile ingenio': Studies in Renaissance Music in Honour of Bonnie Blackburn* (Turnhout, 2008), 1–12.

Bent, Margaret, 'A New Canonic Gloria and the Changing Profile of Dunstaple', *PMM* 5 (1996), 45–67.

Bent, Margaret, 'New Concordances for Dunstaple, Cooke and Binchois Identified by Peter Wright in English Fragments', in James Cook et al. (eds.), a volume provisionally entitled *Music, Materiality, Manuscripts, and Movement: Essays in Honour of Peter Wright* (Lucca and Trent, forthcoming).

Bent, Margaret, 'New Sacred Polyphonic Fragments of the Early Quattrocento', *SMus* 9 (1980), 171–89.

690 BIBLIOGRAPHY

Bent, Margaret, 'A Note on the Dating of the Trémoïlle Manuscript', in Bryan Gillingham and Paul Merkley (eds.), *Beyond the Moon* (Ottawa, 1990), 217–42.

Bent, Margaret, 'The Old Hall Manuscript: A Paleographical Study' (Ph.D. thesis, Cambridge University, 1968). Available at https://www.diamm.ac.uk/resources/doctoral-dissertations/.

Bent, Margaret, 'On False Concords in Late Fifteenth-Century Music: Yet Another Look at Tinctoris', in Anne-Emmanuelle Ceulemans and Bonnie J. Blackburn (eds.), *Théorie et analyse musicales 1450–1650* (Louvain-la-Neuve, 2001), 65–118.

Bent, Margaret, 'Orfeo: *dominus presbiter Orpheus de Padua*', in Anna Zayaruznaya, Bonnie Blackburn, and Stanley Boorman (eds.), *'Qui musicam in se habet': Studies in Honor of Alejandro Enrique Planchart* (Middleton, WI, 2015), 231–56.

Bent, Margaret, 'Performative Rhetoric and Rhetoric as Validation', in Laura Iseppi De Filippis (ed.), *Inventing a Path: Studies in Medieval Rhetoric in Honour of Mary Carruthers*, Nottingham Medieval Studies, 56 (Turnhout, 2012), 43–62.

Bent, Margaret, 'Petrarch, Padua, the Malatestas, Du Fay and *Vergene bella*', in Fabrice Fitch and Jacobijn Kiel (eds.), *Essays on Renaissance Music in Honour of David Fallows: Bon jour, bon mois et bonne estrenne* (Woodbridge, 2011), 86–96.

Bent, Margaret, 'Pietro Emiliani's Chaplain Bartolomeo Rossi da Carpi and the Lamentations of Johannes de Quadris in Vicenza', *SaM* 2 (1995), 5–16.

Bent, Margaret, 'Polyphony of Texts and Music in the Fourteenth-Century Motet: *Tribum que non abhorruit/Quoniam secta latronum/Merito hec patimur* and its "Quotations"', in Dolores Pesce (ed.), *Hearing the Motet* (New York, 1997), 82–103.

Bent, Margaret, 'Principles of Mensuration and Coloration: Virtuosity and Anomalies in the Old Hall Manuscript', in Antonio Delfino and Francesco Saggio (eds.), *La notazione della polifonia vocale dei secoli IX–XVII. Antologia, Parte seconda: Secoli XIV–XVII* (Pisa, 2021), 73–95.

Bent, Margaret, 'The Progeny of Old Hall: More Leaves from a Royal English Choirbook', in Luther Dittmer (ed.), *Gordon Athol Anderson (1929–1981) in Memoriam*, Musicological Studies, 49 (Henryville, Ottawa, and Binningen, 1984), i. 1–54.

Bent, Margaret, 'Pycard's Double Canon: Evidence of Revision?', in Chris Banks, Arthur Searle, and Malcolm Turner (eds.), *Sundry Sorts of Music Books: Essays on the British Library Collections Presented to O. W. Neighbour on his 70th birthday* (London, 1993), 10–26; repr. in Bent, *Counterpoint*, ch. 9.

Bent, Margaret, 'Reading, Memory, Listening, Improvisation: From Written Text to Lost Sound', *BJHM* 34 (2010) [appeared 2014], 13–28.

Bent, Margaret, 'Reflections on Christopher Page's *Reflections*', *EM* 21 (1993), 625–33.

Bent, Margaret, '*Rota versatilis*—Towards a Reconstruction', in Ian Bent (ed.), *Source Materials and the Interpretation of Music: A Memorial Volume to Thurston Dart* (London, 1981), 65–98.

Bent, Margaret, 'Sense and Rhetoric in Late-Medieval Polyphony', in Andreas Giger and Thomas J. Mathiesen (eds.), *Music in the Mirror: Reflections on the History of Music Theory and Literature for the 21st Century*, Publications of the Center for the History of Music Theory and Literature, 3 (Lincoln, NE, 2002), 45–59.

Bent, Margaret, 'Some Aspects of the Motets in the Cyprus Manuscript', in Ursula Günther and Ludwig Finscher (eds.), *The Cypriot-French Repertory* (Neuhausen-Stuttgart, 1995), 357–75.

Bent, Margaret, 'Some Factors in the Control of Consonance and Sonority: Successive Composition and the Solus Tenor', in Daniel Heartz and Bonnie Wade (eds.), *International Musicological Society: Report of the Twelfth Congress: Berkeley 1977* (Kassel, 1981), 625–33.

Bent, Margaret, 'Sources of the Old Hall Music', *PRMA* 94 (1967–8), 19–35.

Bent, Margaret, 'Text Setting in Sacred Music of the Early 15th Century: Evidence and Implications', in Ursula Günther and Ludwig Finscher (eds.), *Musik und Text in der Mehrstimmigkeit des 14. und 15. Jahrhunderts: Vorträge des Gastsymposions in der Herzog August Bibliothek Wolfenbüttel, 8. bis 12. September 1980*, Göttinger Musikwissenschaftliche Arbeiten, 10 (Kassel, 1984), 291–326; repr. in Bent, *Counterpoint*.

Bent, Margaret, 'The Transmission of English Music 1300–1500: Some Aspects of Repertory and Presentation', in Hans Heinrich Eggebrecht and Max Lütolf (eds.), *Studien zur Tradition in der Musik: Kurt von Fischer zum 60. Geburtstag* (Munich, 1973), 65–83.

BIBLIOGRAPHY 691

Bent, Margaret, 'The Trent 92 and Aosta Indexes in Context', in Danilo Curti-Feininger and Marco Gozzi (eds.), *I codici musicali trentini del Quattrocento: Nuove scoperte, nuove edizioni e nuovi strumenti informatici* (Lucca, 2013), 63–81.

Bent, Margaret, 'Towards the Reconstruction of a Dismembered Royal Choirbook of the 1420s', in Margaret Bent and Andrew Wathey (eds.), *Fragments of English Polyphonic Music c. 1390–1475*, EECM 62 (2022).

Bent, Margaret, 'The Transmission of Music by English Composers and Du Fay at the Time of the Council of Constance', in Stefan Morent, Silke Leopold, and Joachim Steinheuer, *Europäische Musikkultur* (Ostfildern, 2017), 163–74.

Bent, Margaret, *Two 14th-Century Motets in Praise of Music[ians]* (Newton Abbot, 1977).

Bent, Margaret, 'The use of cut signatures in sacred music by Binchois', in Andrew Kirkman and Dennis Slavin (eds.), *Binchois Studies* (Oxford, 2000), 277–312.

Bent, Margaret, 'Washington, Library of Congress, M2.1 C6 1400 Case: A Neglected English Fragment', in Jared C. Hartt, Benjamin Albritton, and Tamsyn Mahoney-Steel (eds.), *Manuscripts, Music, Machaut* (Turnhout, 2022), 529–52.

Bent, Margaret, 'What is Isorhythm?', in David Butler Cannata, with Gabriela Ilnitchi Currie, Rena Charnin Mueller, and John Nádas (eds.), *Quomodo Cantabimus Canticum? Studies in Honor of Edward H. Roesner*, American Institute of Musicology, Miscellanea, 7 (Middleton, WI, 2008), 121–43.

Bent, Margaret, 'Words and Music in Machaut's Motet 9', *EM* 31 (2003), 363–88.

Bent, Margaret, 'The Yoxford Credo', in Lewis Lockwood and Edward Roesner (eds.), *Essays in Musicology: A Tribute to Alvin Johnson* ([Philadelphia], 1990), 26–51.

Bent, Margaret (with David Howlett), '*Subtiliter alternare*: The Yoxford Motet *O amicus/Precursoris*', in Peter M. Lefferts and Brian Seirup (eds.), *Studies in Medieval Music: Festschrift for Ernest Sanders* = *CM* 45–7 (New York, 1990), 43–84.

Bent, Margaret, and Ian Bent, 'Dufay, Dunstable, Plummer: A New Source', *JAMS* 22 (1969), 394–424.

Bent, Margaret, and Kevin Brownlee, 'Icarus, Phaeton, Haman: Did Vitry Know Dante?', *Romania* 137 (2019), 85–129.

Bent, Margaret, Jared C. Hartt, and Peter M. Lefferts, *The Dorset Rotulus: Contextualizing and Reconstructing the Early English Motet* (Woodbridge, 2021).

Bent, Margaret, and Robert Klugseder, *A Veneto Liber cantus (c. 1440): Fragments in the Bayerische Staatsbibliothek, Munich, and the Österreichische Nationalbibliothek, Vienna* (Wiesbaden, 2012).

Bent, Margaret, and Andrew Wathey (eds.), *Fauvel Studies: Allegory, Chronicle, Music and Image in Paris, Bibliothèque nationale de France, MS français 146* (Oxford, 1998).

Berger, Roger, *Littérature et société arrageoises au XIIIe siècle: Les chansons et dits artésiens* (Arras, 1981).

Besseler, Heinrich, *Bourdon und Fauxbourdon* (Leipzig, 1950).

Besseler, Heinrich, 'Hat Matheus de Perusio Epoche gemacht?', *Mf* 8 (1955), 19–23.

Besseler, Heinrich, 'Studien zur Musik des Mittelalters I: Neue Quellen des 14. und beginnenden 15. Jahrhunderts', *AfMw* 7 (1925), 167–252.

Besseler, Heinrich, 'Studien zur Musik des Mittelalters II: Die Motette von Franko von Köln bis Philipp von Vitry', *AfMw* 8 (1926–7), 137–258.

Blachly, Alexander, 'The Motets of Philippe de Vitry' (M.A. thesis, Columbia University, 1971).

Blackburn, Bonnie J., 'The Dispute about Harmony c. 1500 and the Creation of a New Style', in Anne-Emmanuelle Ceulemans and Bonnie J. Blackburn (eds.), *Théorie et analyse musicales 1450–1650* (Louvain-la-Neuve, 2001), 1–37.

Blackburn, Bonnie J., 'For Whom do the Singers Sing?', *EM* 25 (1997), 593–609.

Blackburn, Bonnie J., 'Leonardo and Gaffurio on Harmony and the Pulse of Music', in Barbara Haggh (ed.), *Essays on Music and Culture in Honor of Herbert Kellman* (Paris, 2001), 128–49.

Blackburn, Bonnie J., 'On Compositional Process in the Fifteenth Century', *JAMS* 40 (1987), 210–84.

Boen, Johannes, *Ars (Musicae)*, ed. F. Alberto Gallo, CSB 19 (Rome, 1972).

692 BIBLIOGRAPHY

Boethius, Anicius Manlius Torquatus [Severinus], *De institutione arithmetica*, ed. Gottfried Friedlein (Leipzig, 1967).

Boethius, Anicius Manlius Torquatus [Severinus], *De institutione musica libri quinque*, ed. Gottfried Friedlein (Leipzig, 1867).

Boethius, Anicius Manlius Torquatus [Severinus], *Fundamentals of Music*, trans. Calvin M. Bower (New Haven and London, 1989).

Bond, Maurice F. *Inventories of St George's Chapel, Windsor Castle, 1384–1667* (Windsor, 1947).

Boogaart, Jacques, 'L'Accomplissement du cercle: Observations analytiques sur l'ordre des motets de Guillaume de Machaut', *Analyse musicale* 50 (2004), 45–63.

Boogaart, Jacques, 'Encompassing Past and Present: Quotations and their Functions in Machaut's Motets', *EMH* 20 (2001), 1–86.

Boogaart, Jacques, '*Folie couvient avoir*: Citation and Transformation in Machaut's Musical Works—Gender Change and Transgression', in Yolanda Plumley, Giuliano Di Bacco, and Stefano Jossa (eds.), *Citation, Intertextuality and Memory*, i: *Text, Music and Image from Machaut to Ariosto* (Exeter, 2011), 15–40.

Boogaart, Jacques, 'Love's Unstable Balance, Part I: Analogy of Ideas in Text and Music of Machaut's Motet 6. Part II: More Balance Problems and the Order of Machaut's Motets', *Muziek & Wetenschap* 3 (1993), 1–33.

Boogaart, Jacques, '*O series summe rata*: De motetten van Guillaume de Machaut; De ordening van het corpus en de samenhang van tekst en muziek' (Ph.D. thesis, University of Utrecht, 2001).

Boogaart, Jacques, 'Playing with the Performer in Medieval Music: Machaut's Ideas on Love and Order in *Quant vraie Amour/O series summe rata/Super omnes speciosa* (Motet 17)', *Dutch Journal of Music Theory* 14 (2009), 32–41.

Boogaart, Jacques, 'Sound and Cipher: Number Symbolism in Machaut's Motets', in Lawrence M. Earp and Jared C. Hartt (eds.), *Poetry, Art, and Music* (Turnhout, 2021), 377–95.

Boogaart, Jacques, 'Thought-Provoking Dissonances: Remarks about Machaut's Compositional Licences in Relation to his Texts', *Dutch Journal of Music Theory* 12 (2007), 273–92.

Boone, Graeme MacDonald, 'Dufay's Early Chansons: Chronology and Style in the Manuscript Oxford, Bodleian Library, Canonici Misc. 213' (Ph.D. diss., Harvard University, 1987).

Boudet, Jean-Patrice, 'Jean des Murs, Astrologer', *Erudition and the Republic of Letters* 4 (2019), 123–45.

Boudet, Jean-Patrice, 'La Science des étoiles dans la librairie de Charles v', in Boudet (ed.), *Astrologie et politique entre Moyen Âge et Renaissance* (Florence, 2020), 135–62.

Bowers, Roger, 'Choral Institutions within the English Church: Their Constitution and Development 1340–1500' (Ph.D. thesis, University of East Anglia, 1975).

Bowers, Roger, *English Church Polyphony: Singers and Sources from the 14th to the 17th Century* (Aldershot, 1999).

Bowers, Roger, 'Fixed Points in the Chronology of English Fourteenth-Century Polyphony', *M&L* 71 (1990), 313–35, and supplement, *M&L* 80 (1999), 269–70.

Bowers, Roger, ' "Goode and Delitable Songe": The Elite Promotion of Sacred Music in England by the Chapel Royal and its Emulators Noble and Episcopal, *c.*1315–1485', in Christopher M. Woolgar (ed.), *The Elite Household in England, 1100–1550*, Harlaxton Medieval Studies, 28 (Donington, 2018), 204–36.

Bowers, Roger, 'Guillaume de Machaut and his Canonry of Reims, 1338–1377', *EMH* 23 (2004), 1–48.

Bowers, Roger, 'Some Observations on the Life and Career of Lionel Power', *PRMA* 102 (1975–6), 103–27.

Bradley, Catherine A., *Authorship and Identity in Late Thirteenth-Century Motets*, RMA Monographs, 39 (Abingdon, 2022).

Bradley, Catherine A., 'Choosing a Thirteenth-Century Motet Tenor: From the *Magnus liber organi* to Adam de la Halle', *JAMS* 72 (2019), 431–92.

Bradley, Catherine A., 'Perspectives for Lost Polyphony and Red Notation Around 1300: Medieval Motet and Organum Fragments in Stockholm', *EMH* 41 (2022), 1–92.

BIBLIOGRAPHY   693

Bradley, Catherine A., 'Origins and Interactions: Clausula, Motet, Conductus', in Jared C. Hartt (ed.), *A Critical Companion* (Woodbridge, 2018), 43–60.

Bradley, Catherine A., *Polyphony in Medieval Paris: The Art of Composing with Plainchant* (Cambridge, 2018).

Bradley, Catherine A., and Karen Desmond (eds.), *The Montpellier Codex: The Final Fascicle. Contents, Contexts, Chronologies* (Woodbridge, 2018).

Bradley, Robert J., 'Musical Life and Culture at Savoy, 1420–1450' (Ph.D. diss., City University of New York, 1992).

Brett, Philip, 'Facing the Music', *EM* 10 (1982), 347–50.

Brie, Friedrich W. D., *The Brut, or, The Chronicles of England*, 2 vols. (London, 1906–8).

Brie, Friedrich W. D., *Geschichte und Quellen der mittelenglischen Prosachronik The Brute of England, oder The Chronicles of England* (Marburg, 1905).

Brothers, Thomas, 'Vestiges of the Isorhythmic Tradition in Mass and Motet, ca. 1450–1475', *JAMS* 44 (1991), 1–56.

Brown, Elizabeth A. R., 'Rex ioians, ionnes, iolis: Louis X, Philip V, and the Livres de Fauvel', in Margaret Bent and Andrew Wathey (eds.), *Fauvel Studies* (Oxford, 1998), 53–72.

Brown, Samuel E., Jr., 'The Motets of Ciconia, Dunstable and Dufay' (Ph.D. diss., Indiana University, 1962).

Brown, Samuel E., Jr., 'New Evidence of Isomelic Design in Dufay's Isorhythmic Motets', *JAMS* 10 (1957), 7–13.

Brown, Samuel E., Jr., 'A Possible Cantus Firmus among Ciconia's Isorhythmic Motets', *JAMS* 12 (1959), 7–15.

Brown, Thomas, 'Another Mirror of Lovers? Order, Structure and Allusion in Machaut's Motets', *PMM* 10 (2001), 121–33.

Brown, Thomas, '*Flos/Celsa* and Machaut's Motets: Emulation – and Error', in E. E. Leach (ed.), *Machaut's Music: New Interpretations* (Woodbridge, 2003), 37–52.

Brownlee, Kevin, 'Dante's Transfigured Models: Icarus and Daedalus in the *Commedia*', in R. Howard Bloch, Alison Calhoun, Jacqueline Cerquiglini-Toulet, Joachim Küpper, and Janette Patterson (eds.), *Rethinking the New Medievalism* (Baltimore, MD, 2014), 162–80.

Brownlee, Kevin, 'Fire, Desire, Duration, Death: Machaut's Motet 10', in Suzannah Clark and Elizabeth Eva Leach (eds.), *Citation and Authority* (Woodbridge, 2005), 79–93.

Brownlee, Kevin, 'Machaut's Motet 15 and the *Roman de la Rose*: The Literary Context of *Amours qui a le pouoir/Faus Samblant m'a deceu/ Vidi Dominum*', *EMH* 10 (1991), 1–14.

Brownlee, Kevin, 'Phaeton's Fall and Dante's Ascent', *Dante Studies* 102 (1984), 135–44.

Brownlee, Kevin, 'La Polyphonie textuelle dans le Motet 7 de Machaut: Narcisse, la Rose, et la voix féminine', in Jacqueline Cerquiglini-Toulet and Nigel Wilkins (eds.), *Guillaume de Machaut: 1300–2000. Actes du Colloque de la Sorbonne 28–29 septembre 2000* (Paris, 2002), 137–46.

Brownlee, Kevin, 'Textual Polyphony in Machaut's Motets 8 and 4', *Actas del XV congresso de la sociedad internacional de musicologia, Madrid/ 3–10/IV/1992 = RM* 16 (1993), 1554–58.

Brumana, Biancamaria, and Galliano Ciliberti (eds.), *Frammenti musicali del Trecento nell'incunabolo Inv. 15755 N. F.* (Florence, 2004).

Buff, Carolann, 'Ciconia's Equal-Cantus Motets and the Creation of Early Fifteenth-Century Style' (Ph.D. diss., Princeton University, 2015).

Bukofzer, Manfred F., *Studies in Medieval and Renaissance Music* (London, 1951).

Burkard, Thorsten, and Oliver Huck, 'Voces applicatae verbis: Ein musikologischer und poetologischer Traktat aus dem 14. Jahrhundert. (I-Vnm Lat. Cl. XII.97 [4125]). Einleitung, Edition, Übersetzung und Kommentar', *AM* 74 (2002), 1–34.

Busse Berger, Anna Maria, *Medieval Music and the Art of Memory* (Berkeley, 2005).

Butterfield, Ardis, 'The Refrain and the Transformation of Genre in the Roman de Fauvel', in Margaret Bent and Andrew Wathey (eds.), *Fauvel Studies* (Oxford, 1998), 105–59.

La caccia nell'Ars nova italiana: Edizione critica commentata dei testi e delle intonazioni, ed. Michele Epifani, La Tradizione Musicale, Studi e testi, 20 (Florence, 2019).

694 BIBLIOGRAPHY

Caffagni, Claudia, 'Omaggio a Johannes Ciconia (ca. 1370–1412): Un modello per i mottetti di Ciconia. *Marce Marcum imitaris*', *Marcianum*, 8 (2012), 479–501 (with a new edition on 498–501).

Calvia, Antonio, Stefano Campagnolo, Andreas Janke, Maria Sofia Lannutti, and John Nádas (eds.), *The End of the Ars Nova in Italy: The San Lorenzo Palimpsest and Related Repertories* (Florence, 2020).

Campagnolo, Stefano, 'Il frammento Brescia 5 e le relazioni di copista tra i codici fiorentini dell'Ars nova', *SMus* NS 9/1 (2018), 47–85.

Das Cantuagium des Heinrich Eger von Kalkar, ed. Heinrich Hüschen, Beiträge zur Rheinischen Musikgeschichte, 2 (Cologne, 1952).

Caraci Vela, Maria, Daniele Sabaino, and Stefano Aresi (eds.), *Le notazioni della polifonia vocale dei secoli IX–XVII. Antologia–Parte Prima: Secoli IX–XIV*, Università di Pavia, Dipartamento di Scienze Musicologiche Paleografico-Filologiche, Centro di Musicologia W. Stauffer (Pisa, 2007).

Catalunya, David, 'The Customary of the Royal Convent of Las Huelgas: Female Liturgy, Female Scribes', *Medievalia* 20/1 (2016), 91–160.

Catalunya, David, 'Medieval Polyphony in the Cathedral of Sigüenza: A New Identification of a Musical Example Quoted in the Anonymous Treatise of St. Emmeram (1279)', *SMus* NS 5/1 (2014), 41–82.

Catalunya, David, 'Nuns, Polyphony, and a Liégeois Cantor: New Light on the Las Huelgas "Solmization Song"', *JAF* 9 (2017), 89–133.

Catalunya, David, 'Polyphonic Music of the Fourteenth Century in Aragon: Reassessing a Panorama of Fragmentary Sources', in Giovanni Varelli (ed.), *'Disiecta Membra Musicae': Studies in Musical Fragmentology* (Berlin, 2020), 117–63.

Cattin, Giulio, 'The Texts of the Offices of Sts. Hylarion and Anne in the Cypriot Manuscript Torino J.II.9', in Ursula Günther and Ludwig Finscher (eds.), *The Cypriot-French Repertory* (Neuhausen-Stuttgart, 1995), 249–301.

Cazelles, Raymond, *La Société politique et la crise de la royauté sous Philippe de Valois*, thèse pour le Doctorat ès Lettres (Paris, 1958).

Cesari, G., and F. Fano, *La Cappella musicale del duomo di Milano*, pt. I: F. Fano, *Le origini e il primo maestro di cappella: Matteo da Perugia*, Istituzioni e Monumenti dell'Arte Musicale Italiana, NS 1 (Milan, 1957).

Ceulemans, Anne-Emmanuelle, and Bonnie J. Blackburn (eds.), *Théorie et analyse musicales 1450–1650*, Musicologica neolovaniensia Studia, 9 (Louvain-la-Neuve, 2001).

Chronica Johannis de Reading et Anonymi Cantuariensis 1346–1367, ed. J. Tait (Manchester, 1914).

The Chronicle of Adam Usk, 1377–1421, ed. and trans. Chris given-Wilson (Oxford, 1997).

A Chronicle of London, from 1089 to 1483: Written in the Fifteenth Century, and for the First Time Printed from Mss in the British Museum . . ., ed. N. H. Tyrell et al. (London, 1827; repr. Felinfach, 1995).

Ciconia, Johannes, *Nova musica and De proportionibus*, ed. Oliver Ellsworth (Lincoln, NE, 1993).

Cioni, Elisabetta, *Scultura e smalto nell'oreficeria senese dei secoli XIII e XIV* (Florence, 1998).

Clark, Alice V., '*Concordare cum materia*: The Tenor in the Fourteenth-Century Motet' (Ph.D. diss., Princeton University, 1996).

Clark, Alice V., 'The Flowering of Charnalité and the Marriage of Fauvel', in Margaret Bent and Andrew Wathey (eds.), *Fauvel Studies* (Oxford, 1998), 175–86.

Clark, Alice V., 'Machaut Reading Machaut: Self-Borrowing and Reinterpretation in Motets 8 and 21', in Suzannah Clark and Elizabeth Eva Leach (eds.), *Citation and Authority* (Woodbridge, 2005), 94–101.

Clark, Alice V., 'Machaut's Motets on Secular Songs', *PMM* 29 (2020), 1–25.

Clark, Alice V., 'Music for Louis of Anjou', in Karl Kügle and Lorenz Welker (eds.), *Borderline Areas in Fourteenth- and Fifteenth-Century Music* (Münster and Middleton, WI, 2009), 15–32.

Clark, Alice V., 'New Tenor Sources for Fourteenth-Century Motets', *PMM* 8 (1999), 107–31.

Clark, Alice V., '*Super omnes speciosa*: Machaut Reading Vitry', in Tess Knighton and David Skinner (eds.), *Music and Instruments* (Woodbridge, 2020), 247–70.

Clark, Suzannah, '"S'en dirai chançonete": Hearing Text and Music in a Medieval Motet', *PMM* 16 (2007), 31–59.

Clark, Suzannah, and Elizabeth Eva Leach (eds.), *Citation and Authority in Medieval and Renaissance Musical Culture: Learning from the Learned. Essays in Honour of Margaret Bent* (Woodbridge, 2005).

Clément, Gisèle, Isabelle Fabre, Gilles Polizzi, and Fañch Thoraval (eds.), *Poésie et musique à l'âge de l'Ars subtilior: Autour du manuscrit Torino, BNU, J.II.9*, Épitome musical (Turnhout, 2021).

Clercx, Suzanne, *Johannes Ciconia, un musicien liégois et son temps*, 2 vols., Académie Royale de Belgique, Classe des Beaux-Arts: Mémoires: Collection in-4, II série, 10, fasc. 1a/1b (Brussels, 1960).

Cobin, Marian, 'The Aosta Manuscript: A Central Source of Early Fifteenth-Century Sacred Music' (Ph.D. diss., New York University, 1978).

Le Codex 121 de la Bibliothèque d'Einsiedeln, Paléographie musicale, 1st ser., 4 (Solesmes, 1894).

Il codice J.II.9 della Biblioteca Nazionale Universitaria di Torino (Codex J.II.9 of the National and University Library, Turin), Facsimile with introduction, ed. Karl Kügle in collaboration with Isabella Fragalà Data, Ars Nova: Colour Facsimiles of the Italian Sources of Ars Nova, 4 (Lucca, 1999).

Il codice T.III.2: Torino, Biblioteca Nazionale Universitaria, ed. Agostino Ziino (Lucca, 1994).

Cohen, David E., '"The Imperfect Seeks its Perfection": Harmonic Progressions, Directed Motion, and Aristotelian Physics', *Music Theory Spectrum* 23 (2001), 139–69.

Collenberg, Wipertus Rudt de, 'Le Royaume et l'église de Chypre face au grande schisme (1378–1417) d'après les registres des archives du Vatican', *Melanges de l'Ecole française de Rome/Moyen age, temps modernes* 94 (1982), 621–701 = *Epeteris*, 13–16 (1984–7), 63–193.

Collenberg, Wipertus Rudt de, 'Les Lusignan de Chypre: Généalogie compilé principalement selon les registres de l'Archivio Segreto Vaticano et les manuscrits de la Biblioteca Vaticana', *Epeteris* 10 (1979–80), 85–319.

Colton, Lisa, *Angel Song: Medieval English Music in History* (Abingdon, 2017).

Colton, Lisa, 'Making Sense of *Omnis/Habenti*: An Ars Nova Motet in England', in Tess Knighton and David Skinner (eds.), *Music and Instruments* (Woodbridge, 2020), 221–46.

Compendium musicae mensurabilis artis antiquae, ed. F. Alberto Gallo, CSM 15 (n.p., 1971), 61–73.

Cone, Edward T., 'Schubert's Promissory Note: An Exercise in Musical Hermeneutics', *19th Century Music* 5 (1982), 233–41.

Cook, Karen, *Music Theory in Late Medieval Avignon: Magister Johannes Pipardi*, RMA Monographs, 37 (Abingdon, 2021).

Cook, Karen, 'Theoretical Treatments of the Semiminim in a Changing Notational World c. 1315–c. 1440' (Ph.D. diss., Duke University, 2012).

Cornagliotti, Anna, and Maria Caraci Vela, *Un inedito trattato musicale del medioevo: Vercelli, Biblioteca agnesiana, cod. 11* (Florence, 1998).

Courtel, Anne-Lise, 'La Chancellerie et les actes d'Eudes IV, duc de Bourgogne (1315–1349)', *Bibliothèque de l'École des chartes* 135 (1977), 23–71.

Courtenay, William, *Parisian Scholars in the Early Fourteenth Century* (Cambridge, 1999).

Coussemaker, Charles Edmond Henri de, *Les Harmonistes du XIVᵉ siècle* (Lille, 1869).

Coussemaker, Charles Edmond Henri de, *Le Manuscrit musical M 222 C 22 de la Bibliothèque de Strasbourg, XVe siècle*, Thesaurus Musicus, 2, ed. Albert Vander Linden (Brussels, [1977]).

Coville, Alfred, 'Philippe de Vitri: Notes biographiques', *Romania* 59 (1933), 520–47.

Cox, Bobby Wayne, 'The Motets of MS Bologna, Civico Museo Bibliografico Musicale, Q 15' (Ph.D. diss., North Texas State University, 1977).

Cox, Bobby Wayne, 'Pseudo-Augmentation in the Manuscript Bologna, Civico Museo Bibliografico Musicale, Q 15 (BL)', *JM* 1 (1982), 419–48.

Crane, Frederick, '15th-Century Keyboard Music in Vienna MS 5094', *JAMS* 18 (1965), 237–43.

Crawford, David, 'Guillaume Dufay, Hellenism, and Humanism', in Carmelo P. Comberiati and Matthew C. Steel (eds.), *Music from the Middle Ages through the Twentieth Century: Essays in Honor of Gwynn S. McPeek* (New York, 1988), 81–93.

Crocker, Richard L., 'Discant, Counterpoint, and Harmony', *JAMS* 15 (1962), 1–21.

Crocker, Richard L., 'Musica Rhythmica and Musica Metrica in Antique and Medieval Theory', *JMT* 2/1 (1958), 2–23.

Cross, Lucy E., *Guillaume de Machaut: Messe de Nostre Dame* (New York and London, 1998).

Cullinane, Elizabeth A., 'Les *Dits entés* de Jehan de Lescurel, BNF fr.146: L'auditoire, l'auteur, et l'interprétation', Mémoire de Master Professionnel (Université Paris IV Sorbonne, 2017).

Cumming, Julie Emelyn, 'Concord out of Discord: Occasional Motets of the Early Quattrocento' (Ph.D. diss., University of California, Berkeley, 1987).

Cumming, Julie Emelyn, *The Motet in the Age of Du Fay* (Cambridge, 1999).

Curran, Sean, 'Hockets Broken and Integrated in Early Mensural Theory and an Early Motet', *EMH* 36 (2017), 31–104.

Curtis, Gareth, and Andrew Wathey, 'Fifteenth-Century Liturgical Music: A List of the Surviving Repertory', *RMA Research Chronicle* 27/1 (1994), 1–69.

Cuthbert, Michael Scott, 'Groups and Projects among the Paduan Polyphonic Sources', in Francesco Facchin and Pietro Gnan (eds.), *I frammenti musicali padovani tra Santa Giustina e la diffusione della musica in Europa: Giornata di studio Padova, Abbazia di S. Giustina-Biblioteca Universitaria 15 giugno 2006* (Padua, 2011), 183–214.

Cuthbert, Michael Scott, 'Hidden in our Publications: New Concordances, Quotations, and Citations in Fourteenth-Century Music', paper delivered to the American Musicological Society, Vancouver, 5 November 2016.

Cuthbert, Michael Scott, 'Monks, Manuscripts, and Other Peer-to-Peer Song Sharing Networks of the Middle Ages', in Lynn Ransom and Emma Dillon (eds.), *Cantus scriptus: Technologies of Medieval Song, 3rd Lawrence J. Schoenberg Symposium on Manuscript Studies in the Digital Age* (Piscataway, NJ, 2012), 101–23.

Cuthbert, Michael Scott, 'The Nuremberg and Melk Fragments and the International Ars Nova', *SMus* NS 1 (2010), 7–51.

Cuthbert, Michael Scott, 'Palimpsests, Sketches, and Extracts: The Organization and Compositions of Seville 5-2-25', *L'Ars nova italiana del Trecento* 7 (Lucca, 2009), 57–78.

Cuthbert, Michael Scott, 'A Postscript to the Montefortino Fragment with Transcriptions', *L'Ars nova italiana del Trecento, 8. Atti del Convegno internazionale 'Beyond 50 years of Ars Nova Studies at Certaldo 1959–2009', Certaldo, 12–14 June 2009*, ed. Marco Gozzi, Agostino Ziino, and Francesco Zimei (Lucca, 2014), 449–60.

Cuthbert, Michael Scott, '*Tipping the Iceberg*: Missing Italian Polyphony from the Age of Schism', *Musica Disciplina* 54 (2009), 39–74.

Cuthbert, Michael Scott, 'Trecento Fragments and Polyphony beyond the Codex' (Ph.D. diss., Harvard University, 2006).

Cuthbert, Michael Scott, 'Trecento II: Sacred Music and Motets in Italy and the East from 1300 until the End of the Schism', in *The Cambridge History of Medieval Music*, ed. Thomas Forrest Kelly and Mark Everist (Cambridge, 2018), vol. II, ch. 36: 1100–24.

D'Accone, Frank A., 'Music and Musicians at Santa Maria del Fiore in the Early Quattrocento', in *Scritti in onore di Luigi Ronga* (Milan, 1973), 99–126.

D'Accone, Frank A., 'Una nuova fonte dell'Ars nova italiana: Il codice di San Lorenzo 2211', *SMus* 13 (1984), 3–31.

Dahnk, Emilie, *L'Hérésie de Fauvel*, Leipzig romanistische Studien, Literaturwissenschaftliche Reihe, 4 (Leipzig, 1935).

D'Alessi, Giovanni, *La cappella musicale del duomo di Treviso* (Treviso, 1954).

Dammann, Rolf, 'Spätformen der isorhythmischen Motette im 16. Jahrhundert', *AfMw* 10 (1953), 16–40.

Dean, Jeffrey, 'The Occasion of Compère's *Sola caret monstris*: A Case Study in Historical Interpretation', *MD* 40 (1986), 99–133.

Debenedetti, Santorre, 'Un trattatello del secolo XIV sopra la poesia musicale', *SMed* 2 (1906–7), 57–82.

Delachenal, Roland, *Histoire de Charles V* (Paris, 1909–31).

Delisle, Léopold, *Recherches sur la librairie de Charles V*, 2 vols. (Paris, 1907).

De semibrevibus caudatis, ed. André Gilles and Cecily Sweeney, CSM 13 ([Rome] 1971), 65–79.

Desmond, Karen, 'Behind the Mirror: Revealing the Contexts of Jacobus's *Speculum Musicae*' (Ph.D. diss., New York University, 2009).

Desmond, Karen, 'Did Vitry Write an *Ars vetus et nova*?', *JM* 32 (2015), 441–93.

Desmond, Karen, *Music and the moderni, 1300–1350: The ars nova in Theory and Practice* (Cambridge, 2018).

Desmond, Karen, 'Notations', in Jared C. Hartt (ed.), *A Critical Companion* (Woodbridge, 2018), 103–29.

Desmond, Karen, '*Omni desideranti notitiam*: An Online Edition of a Fourteenth-Century Theory Treatise on Ars nova Notation Attributed to Philippe de Vitry', available at http://www.arsmusicae.org.

Desmond, Karen, '"One is the loneliest number . . .": The Semibreve Stands Alone', *EM* 46 (2018), 403–16.

Desmond, Karen, 'Texts in Play: The Ars nova and its Hypertexts', *MD* 57 (2012), 81–153.

Desmond, Karen, 'Traces of Revision in Machaut's Motet *Bone pastor*', in Lawrence M. Earp and Jared C. Hartt (eds.), *Poetry, Art, and Music* (Turnhout, 2021), 397–432.

Desmond, Karen, 'W. de Wicumbe's Rolls and Singing the Alleluya ca. 1250', *JAMS* 73 (2020), 639–707.

Di Bacco, Giuliano, 'Alcune nuove osservazioni sul codice di Londra (British Library, Additional 29987)', *SMus* 20 (1991), 181–234.

Di Bacco, Giuliano, 'Original and Borrowed Authorship and Authority: Remarks on the Circulation of Philipoctus de Caserta's Theoretical Legacy', in Yolanda Plumley and Anne Stone (eds.), *A Late Medieval Songbook* (Turnhout, 2009), 328–64.

Di Bacco, Giuliano, and John Nádas, 'Papal Chapels and Sources of Polyphony', in Richard Sherr (ed.), *Papal Music* (Oxford, 1998), 44–92.

Di Bacco, Giuliano, and John Nádas, 'Verso uno "stile internazionale" della musica nelle cappelle papali e cardinalizie durante il Grande Scisma (1378–1417): Il caso di Johannes Ciconia da Liège', in Adalbert Roth (ed.), *Collectanea*, 1; *Capellae Apostolicae Sixtinaeque collectanea acta monumenta*, 3 (Vatican City, 1994), 7–74.

Di Bacco, Giuliano, and John Nádas, 'Zacara e i suoi colleghi italiani nella cappella papale', in Francesco Zimei (ed.), *Antonio Zacara da Teramo e il suo tempo* (Lucca, 2004), 34–54.

Dillon, Emma, *Medieval Music-Making and the Roman de Fauvel* (Cambridge, 2002).

Dillon, Emma, 'The Profile of Philip V in the Music of *Fauvel*', in Margaret Bent and Andrew Wathey (eds.), *Fauvel Studies* (Oxford, 1998), 215–31.

Diverrès, Armel, *La Chronique métrique attribuée à Geffroy de Paris* (Strasbourg, 1956).

Dolce, Brianne, 'Making Music and Community in Thirteenth-Century Arras: A Study of the Confraternity of Jongleurs and Bourgeois' (Ph.D. diss., Yale University, 2020).

Donella, Valentino, 'La costituzione "Docta Sanctorum Patrum" di Giovanni XXII (1324–25): Una persistente attualità', *Rivista internazionale di musica sacra* 4 (1983), 353–77.

Doutrepont, Georges, *Inventaire de la "librairie" dePhilippe le Bon (1420)* (Brussels, 1906).

Droz, E., and G. Thibault, 'Un chansonnier de Philippe le Bon', *Revue de musicologie* 7 (1926), 1–8 and facsimile.

Duchesne, François, *Histoire de tous les cardinaux françois de naissance*, ii (Paris, 1660).

Dudas, Richard, 'Another Look at *Vos/Gratissima*', in Jared C. Hartt, Benjamin Albritton, and Tamsyn Mahoney-Steel (eds.), *Manuscripts, Music, Machaut* (Turnhout, 2022), 441–65.

Dudas, Richard, and Lawrence Earp, *Four Early Ars nova Motets in Paris, BnF, n.a.fr. 934*, in preparation.

Dunbabin, Jean, 'The Metrical Chronicle Traditionally Ascribed to Geffroy de Paris', in Margaret Bent and Andrew Wathey (eds.), *Fauvel Studies* (Oxford, 1998), 233–46.

Earp, Lawrence M., 'Declamatory Dissonance in Machaut', in Suzannah Clark and Elizabeth Eva Leach (eds.), *Citation and Authority* (Woodbridge, 2005), 102–22.

Earp, Lawrence M., *Guillaume de Machaut: A Guide to Research* (New York, 1995).

Earp, Lawrence M., 'Introduction', in Lawrence M. Earp and Jared C. Hartt (eds.), *Poetry, Art, and Music* (Turnhout, 2021), 21–55.

Earp, Lawrence M., 'Isorhythm', in Jared C. Hartt (ed.), *A Critical Companion* (Woodbridge, 2018), 77–101.

Earp, Lawrence M., 'Scribal Practice, Manuscript Production and the Transmission of Music in Late Medieval France: The Manuscripts of Guillaume de Machaut' (Ph.D. diss., Princeton University, 1983).

Earp, Lawrence M., '"The spirit moves me to speak of forms changed into new bodies"': Anton Webern, Philippe de Vitry, and the Reception of the Ars Nova Motet', in Tess Knighton and David Skinner (eds.), *Music and Instruments* (Woodbridge, 2020), 271–304.

Earp, Lawrence M., *Tradition and Innovation in the* Ars nova *Motet*: Senaria gallica *and* Gradus Structure, in preparation.

Earp, Lawrence M., and Jared C. Hartt (eds.), *Poetry, Art, and Music in Guillaume de Machaut's Earliest Manuscript (BnF fr. 1586)*, Epitome musical (Turnhout, 2021).

Eggebrecht, Hans Heinrich, 'Machauts Motette Nr 9', *AfMw* 19–20 (1962–3), 281–93; 25 (1968), 173–95.

Egidi, F., *Un frammento di codice musicale del secolo XIV. Nozze Bonmartini-Tracagni XIX Novembre MCMXXV* (Rome, 1925).

Elmham, Thomas, *Liber metricus de Henrico V*, ed. C. A. Cole, in *Memorials of Henry the Fifth, King of England* (London, 1858).

Elmham, Thomas, *Thomæ de Elmham Vita & Gesta Henrici Quinti, Anglorum Regis*, ed. Thomas Hearne (Oxford, 1727).

Esposito, Anna, '"Magistro Zaccara" e l'antifonario dell'Ospedale di S. Spirito in Sassia', in Paolo Cherubini, Anna Esposito, et al. (eds.), 'Il costo del libro', in Massimo Miglio et al. (eds.), *Scrittura, biblioteche e stampa a Roma nel Quattrocento. Atti del 2. seminario*, Littera Antiqua, 3 (Vatican City, 1983), 334–42, 446–49.

Everist, Mark, 'A New Source for the Polyphony of the Ars subtilior: Paris, Bibliothèque nationale de France, nouvelles acquisitions françaises 22069', in Yolanda Plumley and Anne Stone (eds.), *A Late Medieval Songbook* (Turnhout, 2009), 287–303.

Everist, Mark, 'Montpellier 8: An Anatomy of . . .', in Catherine A. Bradley and Karen Desmond (eds.), *The Montpellier Codex* (Woodbridge, 2018), 13–31.

Everist, Mark (ed.), *Models of Musical Analysis: Music before 1600* (Oxford, 1992).

Everist, Mark, and Thomas Forrest Kelly (eds.), *The Cambridge History of Medieval Music* (Cambridge, 2018).

Facchin, Francesco, and Pietro Gnan (eds.), *I frammenti musicali padovani tra Santa Giustina e la diffusione della musica in Europa. Giornata di studio Padova, Abbazia di S. Giustina-Biblioteca Universitaria 15 giugno 2006* (Padua, 2011).

Fallows, David, 'Alanus', *NG2*.

Fallows, David, *A Catalogue of Polyphonic Songs, 1415–1480* (Oxford, 1999).

Fallows, David, 'Ciconia padre e figlio', *RIM* 11 (1976), 171–77.

Fallows, David, 'Ciconia's Earliest Songs', in Martin Kirnbauer (ed.), *Beredte Musik* (Basel, 2019), 117–24.

Fallows, David, 'Ciconia's Last Songs and their Milieu', in Philippe Vendrix (ed.), *Johannes Ciconia* (Turnhout, 2003), 107–30.

Fallows, David, *Dufay* (London, 1982).

Fallows, David, Henry V and the Earliest English Carols: 1413–1440 (Abingdon, 2018).

Fallows, David, *The Songs of Guillaume Dufay: Critical Commentary to the Revision of Corpus Mensurabilis Musicae, ser. I, vol. VI*, Musicological Studies and Documents, 47 (n.p., 1995).

Fallows, David, 'Two Equal Voices: A French Song Repertory with Music for Two More Works of Oswald von Wolkenstein', *EMH* 7 (1987), 227–41.

Fankhauser, Eliane, 'A Collection of Collections: New Insights into the Origins and Making of the Utrecht Fragments, NL-Uu 37.1', *TKVNM* 64 (2014), 3–29.

Fankhauser, Eliane, 'Recycling Reversed: Studies in the History of Polyphony in the Northern Low Countries around 1400' (Ph.D. thesis, Utrecht University, 2018).

Fast, Susan, 'God, Desire, and Musical Narrative in the Isorhythmic Motet', *Canadian University Music Review* 18 (1997), 19–37.

Fasti Ecclesiae Anglicanae, 1300–1541, 2: Hereford Diocese, ed. Joyce M. Horn (London, 1962).

Fasti Ecclesiae Anglicanae, 1300–1541, 10: *Coventry and Lichfield Diocese*, compiled by B. Jones (London, 1964), *British History Online*, http://www.british-history.ac.uk/fasti-ecclesiae/ 1300-1541/vol10 (accessed 7 August 2021).

Fasti Ecclesiae Gallicanae, 11: *Diocèse de Sens*, ed. Vincent Tabbagh (Turnhout, 2009).

Ferreira, Manuel Pedro, 'Compositional Calculation in Philippe de Vitry', *SMus* 37 (2008), 13–26.

The Ferrell-Vogüé Machaut Manuscript, ed. Lawrence M. Earp with Domenic Leo, Carla Shapreau, and Christopher de Hamel, 2 vols. (Oxford, 2014).

Finscher, Ludwig, and Annegrit Laubenthal, '"Cantiones quae vulgo motectae vocantur": Arten der Motette im 15. und 16. Jahrhundert' 'Die Spätblüte der isorhythmischen Motette', in Carl Dahlhaus (ed.), *Neues Handbuch der Musikwissenschaft*, 3/2 (Lilienthal, 1990), 278–370.

Fischer, Kurt von, 'Bemerkungen zur Trecento-Motette: Überlegungen zu einem Aufsatz von Margaret Bent', in Herbert Schneider and Heinz-Jürgen Winkler (eds.), *Die Motette: Beiträge zu ihrer Gattungsgeschichte. Ludwig Finscher zum 60. Geburtstag*, Neue Studien zur Musikwissenschaft, 5 (Mainz, 1992), 19–28.

Fischer, Kurt von, 'Philippe de Vitry in Italy and an Homage of Landini to Philippe', in *L'Ars nova italiana del Trecento*, 4 (Certaldo, 1978), 225–35.

Fischer, Kurt von, *Studien zur italienischen Musik des Trecento und frühen Quattrocento* (Bern, 1956).

Fisquet, Honoré, *La France pontificale (Gallia Christiana): Histoire chronologique et biographique des Archevêques et Evêques de tous les diocèses de France, depuis l'établissement du christianisme jusqu'à nos jours, divisée en 18 provinces ecclésiastiques*, 17: *Rouen* (Paris, 1864).

Ford, Wyn K., 'Some Wills of English Musicians of the Fifteenth and Sixteenth Centuries', *RMA Research Chronicle* 5 (1965), 80–84.

The Fountains Fragments: Polyphony for Mass c.1400 from a Fountains Abbey Memorandum Book, ed. Edward Kershaw and Nick Sandon, Medieval Church Music, 2 (2nd edn., Newton Abbot, 1988).

Fuhrmann, Wolfgang, 'Rhetorik der Verinnerlichung: "Close listening" im Cantuagium des Heinrich Eger von Kalkar', in Fabian Kolb (ed.), *Musik der mittelalterlichen Metropole: Räume, Identitäten und Kontexte der Musik in Köln und Mainz, ca. 900–1400* (Merseburger, 2016), 491–517.

Fuller, Sarah, 'Contrapunctus Theory, Dissonance Regulation, and French Polyphony of the Fourteenth Century', in Judith A. Peraino (ed.), *Medieval Music in Practice: Studies in Honor of Richard Crocker* (Middleton, WI, 2013), 113–52.

Fuller, Sarah, '"Delectabatur in hoc auris": Some Fourteenth-Century Perspectives on Aural Perception', *MQ* 82 (1998), 466–81.

Fuller, Sarah, *European Musical Heritage 800–1750* (New York, 1987).

Fuller, Sarah, 'Guillaume de Machaut: *De toutes flours*', in Mark Everist (ed.), *Models of Musical Analysis* (Oxford, 1992), 41–65.

Fuller, Sarah, 'Modal Tenors and Tonal Orientation in Motets of Guillaume de Machaut', *CM* 45–47 (1990), 199–245.

Fuller, Sarah, 'On Sonority in Fourteenth-Century Polyphony: Some Preliminary Reflections', *JMT* 30 (1986), 35–70.

Fuller, Sarah, 'A Phantom Treatise of the Fourteenth Century? The Ars Nova', *JM* 4 (1985–6), 23–50.

Fuller, Sarah, 'Tendencies and Resolutions: The Directed Progression in Ars Nova Music', *JMT*, 36 (1992), 229–58.

Gallo, F. Alberto, *Il codice musicale 2216 della Biblioteca Universitaria di Bologna*, Monumenta Lyrica Medii Aevi Italica, 3.3, vols. 1 (facsimile) and 2 (commentary) (Bologna, 1968–70).

Gallo, F. Alberto, 'Da un codice italiano di mottetti del primo Trecento', *Quadrivium* 9 (1968), 25–35.

Gallo, F. Alberto, 'Marchettus de Padua und die "franco-venetische" Musik des frühen Trecento', *AfMw* 31 (1974), 42–56.

Gallo, F. Alberto, 'Mottetti del primo Trecento in un messale di Biella (Codice Lowe)', *L'Ars nova italiana del Trecento*, 3 (Certaldo, 1970), 215–45.

Gancarczyk, Paweł, 'Memory of Genre: The Polytextual Motet in Central Europe and its Two Traditions', in Karl Kügle (ed.), *Sounding the Past: Music as History and Memory* (Turnhout, 2020), 141–55.

Gancarczyk, Paweł, 'Petrus Wilhelmi de Grudencz (b. 1392) – a Central European Composer', *De musica disserenda* 2 (2006), 103–12.

Gardner von Teuffel, Christa, 'The Altarpieces of San Lorenzo: Memorializing the Martyr or Accommodating the Parishioners?', in Robert W. Gaston and Louis Waldman (eds.), *San Lorenzo: A Florentine Church*, Villa I Tatti Series, 33 (Florence, 2017), 184–243.

Gaston, Robert W., and Louis Waldman (eds.), *San Lorenzo: A Florentine Church*, Villa I Tatti Series, 33 (Florence, 2017).

Gesta Henrici Quinti: The Deeds of Henry the Fifth, ed. Frank Taylor and John S. Roskell (Oxford, 1975).

Ghisi, F., 'Inno-lauda polifonica all'Assunta ritrovata nell'Archivio comunale di Cortona', *Quadrivium* 16 (1974), 105–14.

Giaccaria, Angelo, 'Il codice franco-cipriota J.II.9 e le vicende del fondo manoscritto della Biblioteca Nazionale Universitaria di Torino', in Isabella Data (ed.), *Miscellanea di studi 4, in onore di Alberto Basso*, Il Gridelino, 17 (Turin, 1996), 7–12.

Gillingham, Bryan, and Paul Merkley (eds.), *Beyond the Moon: Festschrift Luther Dittmer*, Musicological Studies, 53 (Ottawa, 1990).

Girgensohn, Dieter, 'Il testamento di Pietro Miani ("Emilianus") vescovo di Vicenza († 1433)', *Archivio veneto*, ser. 5, 132 (1989), 5–60.

Göllner, Theodor, 'Notationsfragmente aus einer Organistenwerkstatt des 15. Jahrhunderts', *AfMw* 24 (1967), 170–77.

Gómez, Maria Carmen, 'Une version à cinq voix du motet *Apollinis Eclipsatur/Zodiacum Signis* dans le manuscrit *E-BCEN 853*', *MD* 39 (1985), 5–44.

Gozzi, Marco, 'Alcune postille sul codice Add. 29987 della British Library', *SMus* 22 (1993), 249–78.

Gozzi, Marco, Agostino Ziino, and Francesco Zimei (eds.), *Beyond 50 Years of Ars Nova Studies at Certaldo 1959–2009. Atti del Convegno internazionale (Certaldo, 12–14 giugno 2009)*, L'Ars nova italiana del Trecento, 8 (Lucca, 2013).

Grafton, Anthony, 'The Ancient City Restored: Archaeology, Ecclesiastical History, and Egyptology', in Anthony Grafton (ed.), *Rome Reborn: The Vatican Library and Renaissance Culture* (Washington, DC, 1993), 87–123.

Greene, Richard L., 'Two Medieval Musical Manuscripts', *JAMS* 7 (1954), 1–34.

Guesnon, A., *Statuts et règlements de la confrérie des jongleurs et bourgeois d'Arras aux XIIe, XIIIe et XIVe siècles* (Arras, 1860), https://gallica.bnf.fr/ark:/12148/bpt6k745373/f12.image.r=%22Englebert%20Louchart%22?rk=21459;2 (acc. 15 Jan. 2021).

Günther, Ursula, 'Bemerkungen zur Motette des frühen und mittleren Trecento', in Herbert Schneider and Heinz-Jürgen Winkler (eds.), *Die Motette: Beiträge zu ihrer Gattungsgeschichte. Ludwig Finscher zum 60. Geburtstag*, Neue Studien zur Musikwissenschaft, 5 (Mainz, 1992), 29–39.

Günther, Ursula, 'Datierbare Balladen des späten 14. Jahrhunderts', *MD* 15 (1961), 39–61; 16 (1962), 151–74.

Günther, Ursula, 'The 14th-Century Motet and its Development', *MD* 12 (1958), 27–58.

Günther, Ursula, 'Problems of Dating in Ars nova and Ars subtilior', *L'Ars nova italiana del Trecento*, 4 (Certaldo, 1978), 289–301.

Günther, Ursula, 'Zur Biographie einiger Komponisten der Ars subtilior', *AfMw* 21 (1964), 172–99.

Günther, Ursula, 'Zwei Balladen auf Bertrand und Olivier du Guesclin', *MD* 22 (1968), 15–45.

Günther, Ursula, and Ludwig Finscher (eds.), *The Cypriot-French Repertory of the Manuscript Torino J.II.9*, Report of the International Musicological Congress, Paphos 20–25 March, 1992, Musicological Studies and Documents, 45 (Neuhausen-Stuttgart, 1995).

Gushee, Lawrence, 'New Sources for the Biography of Johannes de Muris', *JAMS* 22 (1969), 3–26.

Gutiérrez, David, 'La biblioteca di Sant'Agostino di Roma nel secolo XV', *Analecta Augustiniana* 27 (1964), 5–58.

Haaß, Robert, 'Eger von Kalkar, Heinrich', in *NDB*, iv. 327.

Haberl, Fr. X., *Wilhelm Du Fay*, Bausteine für Musikgeschichte, 1 (Leipzig, 1885).

Haines, John, and Randall Rosenfeld (eds.), *Music and Medieval Manuscripts: Paleography and Performance* (Aldershot, 2004).

Haines, John, and Stefan Udell, 'Motets, Manuscript Culture, Mise-en-page', in Jared C. Hartt (ed.), *A Critical Companion* (Woodbridge, 2018), 175–92.

Hallmark, Anne, 'Gratiosus, Ciconia, and Other Musicians at Padua Cathedral: Some Footnotes to Present Knowledge', in *L'Ars nova italiana del Trecento*, 6 (Certaldo, 1992), 69–84.

Hallmark, Anne, 'Johannes Ciconia: Reviewing the Documentary Evidence', in Marco Gozzi, Agostino Ziino and Francesco Zimei (eds.), *Beyond 50 Years of Ars Nova Studies* (Lucca, 2013), 265–85.

Hallmark, Anne, 'Protector, imo verus pater: Francesco Zabarella's Patronage of Johannes Ciconia', in Jessie Ann Owens and Anthony Cummings (eds.), *Music in Renaissance Cities and Courts: Studies in Honor of Lewis Lockwood* (Warren, MI, 1997), 153–68.

Hallmark, Anne, 'Some Evidence for French Influence in Northern Italy, c.1400', in Stanley Boorman (ed.), *Studies in the Performance of Late Mediaeval Music* (Cambridge, 1983), 193–225.

Hamilton, Elina G., 'Philippe de Vitry in England: Musical Quotations in the *Quatuor principalia* and the *Gratissima* Tenors', *SMus* NS 9/1 (2018), 9–45.

Hamm, Charles, *A Chronology of the Works of Guillaume Dufay, Based on a Study of Mensural Practice* (Princeton, 1964).

Handschin, Jacques, *Musikgeschichte im Überblick* (Lucerne, 1948).

Hanquet, K. *Documents relatifs au Grand Schisme*, I: *Suppliques de Clément VII (1378–1379)* = *Analecta Vaticano-Belgica* 8 (1924).

Harrison, Frank Ll., 'Ars Nova in England: A New Source', *MD* 21 (1967), 67–85.

Harrison, Frank Ll., *Music in Medieval Britain* (London, 1958).

Harrison, Frank Ll. (ed.), *Musicorum collegio: Fourteenth-century Musicians' Motets* (Monaco, 1986), [reproduced from PMFC 5 and 15, with new introduction].

Hartt, Jared C., 'Approaching the Motets in MS C: Structure, Sonority, Sense', in Lawrence M. Earp and Jared C. Hartt (eds.), *Poetry, Art, and Music* (Turnhout, 2021), 343–75.

Hartt, Jared C., 'The Duet Motet in England: Genre, Tonal Coherence, Reconstruction', in Jared C. Hartt (ed.), *A Critical Companion* (Woodbridge, 2018), 261–85.

Hartt, Jared C., 'A Missing Middle-Voice Melody: Reconstructing the Tenor of *A solis ortus/ Salvator mundi Domine*', in Jared C. Hartt, Benjamin Albritton, and Tamsyn Mahoney-Steel (eds.), *Manuscripts, Music, Machaut* (Turnhout, 2022), 553–80.

Hartt, Jared C., 'The Problem of the Vitry Motet Corpus: Sonority, Kinship, Attribution', *Music Theory and Analysis* 4 (2017), 192–228.

Hartt, Jared C., 'Rehearing Machaut's Motets: Taking the Next Step in Understanding Sonority', *JMT* 54 (2010), 179–234.

Hartt, Jared C., 'The Three Tenors: Machaut's Secular Trio', *SMus* 38 (2009), 237–71.

Hartt, Jared C., 'Tonal and Structural Implications of Isorythmic Design in Guillaume de Machaut's Tenors', *Theory and Practice* 35 (2010), 57–94.

Hartt, Jared C., (ed.), *A Critical Companion to Medieval Motets* (Woodbridge, 2018).

Hartt, Jared C., Benjamin Albritton, and Tamsyn Mahoney-Steel (eds.), *Manuscripts, Music, Machaut: Essays in Honor of Lawrence Earp*, Épitome musical (Turnhout, 2022).

Hasselman, Margaret Paine, 'The French Chanson in the Fourteenth Century' (Ph.D. diss., University of California, Berkeley, 1970).

Hertel, Carola, *Chansonvertonungen des 14. Jahrhunderts in Norditalien: Untersuchungen zum Überlieferungsbestand des Codex Reina* (Hildesheim and New York, 2002).

Herzblick, Kerstin, *Exekutoren: Die ausserordentliche Kollatur von Benefizien im Pontifikat Johannes' XXII*, Spätmittelalter, Humanismus, Reformation: Studies in the Late Middle Ages and the Reformation, 48 (Tubingen, 2009).

702 BIBLIOGRAPHY

Higgins, Paula, 'Music and Musicians at the Sainte-Chapelle of the Bourges Palace, 1405–1415', in Angelo Pompilio et al. (eds.), *International Musicological Society, Report of the Fourteenth Congress, Bologna, 1987: Trasmissione e recezione delle forme di cultura musicale*, 3 vols. (Turin, 1990), iii. 689–701.

Historická antologie hudby v českých zemích (do cca 1530) = Historical anthology of music in the Bohemian lands (up to *c*.1530), ed. Jaromír Černý (Prague, 2005).

Hofmann, Klaus, 'Zur Entstehungs- und Frühgeschichte des Terminus Motette', *AM* 42 (1970), 138–50.

Holford-Strevens, Leofranc, 'Du Fay the Poet? Problems in the Texts of his Motets', *EMH* 16 (1997), 97–165.

Holford-Strevens, Leofranc, 'Fauvel Goes to School', in Suzannah Clark and Elizabeth Eva Leach (eds.), *Citation and Authority* (Woodbridge, 2005), 59–66.

Holford-Strevens, Leofranc, 'The Latin *Dits* of Geffroy de Paris: An *Editio Princeps*', in Margaret Bent and Andrew Wathey (eds.), *Fauvel Studies* (Oxford, 1998), 246–75.

Holford-Strevens, Leofranc, 'Latin Poetry and Music', in Mark Everist (ed.), *The Cambridge Companion to Medieval Music* (Cambridge, 2011), 225–40.

Holford-Strevens, Leofranc, 'The Latin Poetry of Johannes Ciconia and "Guilhermus"', in Anna Zayaruznaya, Bonnie Blackburn, and Stanley Boorman (eds.), *'Qui musicam in se habet': Essays in Honor of Alejandro Enrique Planchart* (Middleton, WI, 2015), 437–69.

Honisch, Erika, 'The Transmission of Polyphonic *Amens* in the Early Fifteenth Century', *PMM* 21 (2012), 41–72.

Hoppin, Richard H., 'The Cypriot-French Repertory of the Manuscript Torino, Biblioteca Nazionale, J. II. 9', *MD* 11 (1957), 79–125.

Hoppin, Richard H., 'Some Remarks a propos Pic', *RBM* 3 (1956), 105–11.

Hoppin, Richard H., and Suzanne Clercx, 'Notes biographiques sur quelques musiciens français du XIVe siècle', *Les Colloques de Wégimont* II, 1955 (Liège, 1959), 63–92.

Horyna, Martin, 'Ein Brünner Fragment der Motette Apollinis eclipsatur – eine Bemerkung zur Rezeption der Ars Nova in Mitteleuropa um 1400', *Hudební Věda* 57 (2020), 2–21 (English abstract, 123).

Horyna, Martin, *A Prague Fragment of Organ Tablature and the Earliest Attempts in the Middle Ages to Notate Organ Music (Pražský zlomek varhanní tabulatury a nejstarší středověké pokusy o zápis varhanní hudby)*, Association for Central European Cultural Studies, Clavis Monumentorum Musicorum Regni Bohemiae, Series A. VII (Prague, 2021).

Hornby, Emma, and David Maw (eds.), *Essays on the History of English Music in Honour of John Caldwell* (Woodbridge, 2010).

Howlett, David, '*Apollinis eclipsatur*: Foundation of the "Collegium musicorum"', in Suzannah Clark and Elizabeth Eva Leach (eds.), *Citation and Authority* (Woodbridge, 2005), 152–59.

Howlett, David, 'A Possible Date for a Dunstable Motet', *MR* 36 (1975), 81–84.

Hucke, Helmut, 'Das Dekret "Docta Sanctorum Patrum" Papst Johannes' XXII', *MD* 38 (1984), 119–31.

Hughes, Andrew, 'Some Notes on the Early Fifteenth-Century Contratenor', *MQ* 50 (1969), 376–81.

Hunt, Tony, 'The Christianization of Fortune', *Nottingham French Studies* 38 (1999), 93–113.

Jacob, Ernest F., *The Fifteenth Century, 1399–1485* (Oxford, 1993).

Jacobus Leodiensis, *Speculum musicae*, ed. Roger Bragard, 7 vols., CSM 3 (Rome, 1955–73).

Janke, Andreas, *Die Kompositionen von Giovanni Mazzuoli, Piero Mazzuoli und Ugolino da Orvieto im San-Lorenzo-Palimpsest (ASL 2211)*, Musica Mensurabilis, 7 (Hildesheim, 2016).

Johannes Boens Musica und seine Konsonanzenlehre, ed. W. Frobenius (Stuttgart, 1971).

Johannes de Grocheio, Ars musice, ed. and trans. Constant J. Mews, John N. Crossley, Catherine Jeffreys, Leigh McKinnon, and Carol J. Williams, TEAMS Varia (Kalamazoo, MI, 2011).

Johannes de Muris, *Notitia artis musicae et Compendium musicae practicae; Petrus de Sancto Dionysio Tractatus de musica*, ed. Ulrich Michels, CSM 17 (n.p., 1972).

BIBLIOGRAPHY 703

Johannes Porta de Annoniaco, *Liber de coronatione Karoli IV. imperatoris*, ed. Richard Salomon (Hannover and Leizig, 1913), available on available on https://archive.org/details/iohannispor tadea00port/page/n23.

John XXII, *Lettres communes*, ed. Guillaume Mollat (Paris, 1904–47).

John XXII, *Lettres de Jean XXII (1316–1334)*, ed. Arnold Fayen (Rome, 1908–12).

Johnson, Mildred, 'The Motets of the Codex Ivrea' (Ph.D. diss., Indiana University, 1955).

Jones, C. W., *Saint Nicholas of Myra, Bari and Manhattan* (Chicago, 1978).

Kingsford, Charles Lethbridge, *English Historical Literature in the Fifteenth Century* (Oxford, 1913).

Kirkman, Andrew, *The Cultural Life of the Early Polyphonic Mass: Medieval Context to Modern Revival* (Cambridge, 2010).

Kirnbauer, Martin (ed.), *Beredte Musik: Konversationen zum 80. Geburtstag von Wulf Arlt*, Schola Cantorum Basiliensis Scripta, 8 (Basel, 2019).

Klaper, Michael, '"Verbindliches kirchenmusikalisches Gesetz" oder belanglose Augenblickseingebung? Zur Constitutio Docta sanctorum patrum Papst Johannes' XXII', *AfMw* 60 (2003), 69–95.

Klugseder, Robert, *Ausgewählte mittelalterliche Musikfragmente der Österreichischen Nationalbibliothek. Codices Manuscripti* (Purkersdorf, 2011).

Knighton, Tess, and David Skinner (eds.), *Music and Instruments of the Middle Ages: Essays in Honour of Christopher Page* (Woodbridge, 2020).

Kreutziger-Herr, Annette, *Johannes Ciconia (ca. 1370–1412): Komponieren in einer Kultur des Wortes* (Hamburg, 1991).

Kügle, Karl, 'The Aesthetics of Fragments: Reading Pastedowns in Context or, Late Medieval Bookbinders, Readers, and their Choices', in Giovanni Varelli (ed.), *Disiecta Membra Musicae: Studies in Musical Fragmentology* (Berlin and Boston, 2020), 205–37.

Kügle, Karl, 'Codex Ivrea, Bibl. cap. 115: A French Source "Made in Italy"', *RM* 13 (1990), 527–61.

Kügle, Karl, 'Die Fragmente Oxford, All Souls 56 und die mensural notierte Mehrstimmigkeit in Köln um 1400: Ein Zwischenbericht', in Fabian Kolb (ed.), *Musik der mittelalterlichen Metropole: Räume, Identitäten und Kontexte der Musik in Köln und Mainz, ca. 900–1400* (Merseburger, 2016), 301–24.

Kügle, Karl, 'Frankreich und sein direkter Einflußbereich', in *Die Musik des Mittelalters: Die Musik des 14. Jahrhunderts*, Neues Handbuch der Musikwissenschaft, ii, ed. Hartmut Möller and Rudolf Stephan (Laaber, 1991), 352–84.

Kügle, Karl, 'Glorious Sounds for a Holy Warrior: New Light on Codex Turin J.II.9', *JAMS* 65 (2012), 637–90.

Kügle, Karl, 'The Manuscript Ivrea, Bibl. cap. 115: Studies in the Transmission and Composition of Ars Nova Polyphony' (Ph.D. diss., New York University, 1993).

Kügle, Karl, *The Manuscript Ivrea, Biblioteca Capitolare 115: Studies in the Transmission and Composition of Ars Nova Polyphony*, Musicological Studies, 69 (Ottawa, 1997).

Kügle, Karl, 'The Repertory of the Manuscript Torino J.II.9, and the French Tradition of the 14th and Early 15th Centuries', in Ursula Günther and Ludwig Finscher (eds.), *The Cypriot-French Repertory* (Neuhausen-Stuttgart, 1995), 151–81.

Kügle, Karl, 'Two Abbots and a Rotulus: New Light on Brussels 19606', in David Butler Cannata, Gabriela Ilnitchi Currie, Rena Charnin Mueller, and John Louis Nádas (eds.), *Quomodo cantabimus canticum? Studies in Honor of Edward H. Roesner*, American Institute of Musicology, Miscellanea, 7 (Middleton, WI, 2008), 145–85.

Kügle, Karl, 'Vitry in the Rhineland: New Discoveries', *EM* 46 (2018), 393–402.

Lavacek, Justin, 'Hidden Colouration: Deep Metrical Flexibility in Machaut', *PMM* 31 (2022), 143–67.

Leach, Elizabeth Eva, 'Adapting the Motet(s)? The Case of *Hébergier* in Oxford MS Douce 308', *PMM* 28 (2019), 133–47.

Leach, Elizabeth Eva, 'The Genre(s) of Medieval Motets' in Jared C. Hartt (ed.), *A Critical Companion* (Woodbridge, 2018), 15–41.

Leach, Elizabeth Eva, *Guillaume de Machaut: Secretary, Poet, Musician* (Ithaca, NY, 2011).

704   BIBLIOGRAPHY

Leach, Elizabeth Eva, 'Interpretation and Counterpoint: The Case of Guillaume de Machaut's *De toutes flours* (B31)', *Music Analysis* 19 (2000), 321–51.

Leach, Elizabeth Eva, 'Machaut's Balades with Four Voices', *PMM* 10 (2001), 47–79.

Leach, Elizabeth Eva, 'Singing More about Singing Less: Machaut's *Pour ce que tous* (B12)', in E. E. Leach (ed.), *Machaut's Music: New Interpretations* (Woodbridge, 2003), 111–24.

Leach, Elizabeth Eva, *Sung Birds: Music, Nature, and Poetry in the Later Middle Ages* (Ithaca, NY, 2007).

Leach, Elizabeth Eva, (ed.), *Machaut's Music: New Interpretations* (Woodbridge, 2003).

Leccisotti, Tommaso, 'La congregazione benedettina di S. Giustina e la riforma della chiesa al secolo XV', *Archivio della Deputazione Romana di Storia Patria*, 67 (1944), 451–69.

Leech-Wilkinson, Daniel, *Compositional Techniques in the Four-Part Isorhythmic Motets of Philippe de Vitry and his Contemporaries* (New York and London, 1989).

Leech-Wilkinson, Daniel, 'The Cyprus Songs', in Ursula Günther and Ludwig Finscher (eds.), *The Cypriot-French Repertory* (Neuhausen-Stuttgart, 1995), 395–431.

Leech-Wilkinson, Daniel, 'The Emergence of *Ars Nova*', *JM* 13 (1995), 285–317.

Leech-Wilkinson, Daniel, *Machaut's Mass: An Introduction* (Oxford, 1990).

Leech-Wilkinson, Daniel, 'Machaut's *Rose, lis* and the Problem of Early Music Analysis', *Music Analysis* 3 (1984), 9–28.

Leech-Wilkinson, Daniel, *The Modern Invention of Medieval Music: Scholarship, Ideology, Performance* (Cambridge, 2002).

Leech-Wilkinson, Daniel, 'Related Motets from Fourteenth-Century France', *PRMA* 109 (1982–3), 1–22.

Leech-Wilkinson, Daniel, '*Rose, lis* Revisited', in E. E. Leach (ed.), *Machaut's Music: New Interpretations* (Woodbridge, 2003), 249–62.

Leech-Wilkinson, Daniel, '*Le Voir Dit* and *La Messe de Notre Dame*: Aspects of Genre and Style in Late Works of Machaut', *PMM* 2 (1993), 43–73.

Leech-Wilkinson, Daniel, 'Written and Improvised Polyphony', in C. Meyer (ed.), *Polyphonies de tradition orale* (Royaumont, 1993), 170–82.

Lefferts, Peter M., *The Motet in England in the Fourteenth Century*, UMI Studies in Musicology, 94 (Ann Arbor, 1986).

Lefferts, Peter M., 'The Motet in England in the Fourteenth Century' (Ph.D. diss., Columbia University, 1983).

Leitmeir, Christian Thomas, 'Types and Transmission of Musical Examples in Franco's *Ars cantus mensurabilis musicae*', in Suzannah Clark and Elizabeth Eva Leach (eds.), *Citation and Authority in Medieval and Renaissance Musical Culture* (Woodbridge, 2005), 29–44.

Leone de Castris, Pierluigi, 'Une attribution à Lando di Pietro, le bras-reliquaire de saint Louis de Toulouse', *Revue du Louvre* 30 (1980), 71–75.

Lerch, Irmgard, *Fragmente aus Cambrai: Ein Beitrag zur Rekonstruktion einer Handscrift mit spätmittelalterlicher Polyphonie*, 2 vols., Göttinger musikwissenschaftliche Arbeiten, 11 (Kassel, 1987).

Lerch-Kalavrytinos, Irmgard, 'Ars Nova-Fragmente in Würzburg', Karl Kügle and Lorenz Welker (eds.), *Borderline Areas in Fourteenth- and Fifteenth-Century Music* (Münster and Middleton, WI, 2009), 121–24.

Lerch-Kalavrytinos, Irmgard, 'Die Notation in den Cambraier Fragmenten', in Maria Caraci Vela, Daniele Sabaino and Stefano Aresi (eds.), *Le notazioni della polifonia vocale dei secoli IX–XVII* (Pisa, 2007), 163–70.

Liber regie capelle: A Manuscript in the Biblioteca Publica, Evora, ed. Walter Ullmann (London, 1961).

Louviot, Manon, 'Uncovering the Douai Fragment: Composing Polyphony and Encoding a Composer in the Late Fourteenth Century', *EMH* 40 (2021), 85–166.

The Lucca Codex: Codice Mancini, Lucca, Archivio di Stato, MS 184, Perugia, Biblioteca comunale 'Augusta', MS 3065, Introductory Study and Facsimile Edition, ed. John Nádas and Agostino Ziino, Ars Nova, 1 (Lucca, 1990).

Lüdtke, Joachim, 'Kleinüberlieferung mehrstimmiger Musik vor 1550 in deutschem Sprachgebiet IV: Fragmente und versprengte Überlieferung des 14. bis 16. Jahrhunderts aus dem mittleren und nördlichen Deutschland', *Nachrichten der Akademie der Wissenschaften in Göttingen, philologisch-historische Klasse*, 6 (2001), 420–28 and 465–68 (plates).

Ludwig, Friedrich, 'Die mehrstimmige Musik des 14. Jahrhunderts', *SIMG* 4/1 (Nov. 1902), 16–69.

Ludwig, Friedrich, *Repertorium organorum recentioris et motetorum vetustissimi stili* (Halle, 1910).

Ludwig, Friedrich, 'Studien über die Geschichte der mehrstimmigen Musik im Mittelalter. II. Die 50 Beispiele Coussemaker's aus der Handschrift von Montpellier', *SIMG* 5/2 (Feb. 1904), 177–224.

Lütteken, Laurenz, *Guillaume Dufay und die isorhythmische Motette: Gattungstradition und Werkcharakter an der Schwelle zur Neuzeit*, Schriften zur Musikwissenschaft aus Münster, 4 (Hamburg, 1993).

McGrady, Deborah. *Controlling Readers: Guillaume de Machaut and His Late Medieval Audience* (Toronto, 2006).

Machaut, Guillaume de, *The Complete Poetry and Music*, ix: *The Motets*, ed. Jacques Boogaart, trans. R. Barton Palmer, TEAMS Middle English Texts Series (Kalamazoo, MI, 2018).

Machaut, Guillaume de, *Le Livre dou Voir Dit (The Book of the True Poem)*, ed. Daniel Leech-Wilkinson and R. B. Palmer, Garland Library of Medieval Literature, 106A (New York and London, 1998).

Machaut, Guillaume de, *Musikalische Werke*, ed. Friedrich Ludwig, 4 vols. (Leipzig, 1926–54; repr. Leipzig, 1954).

Maffioletti, Stefano, 'Il mottetto di musici fra Trecento e Quattrocento' (Tesi di laurea, Milan, 2019).

Maiani, Brad, 'Notes on Matteo da Perugia: Adapting the Ambrosian Liturgy in Polyphony for the Pisan Council', *SMus* 24 (1995), 3–28.

Makhairas, Leontios, *Recital concerning the Sweet Land of Cyprus, Entitled 'Chronicle'*, ed. and trans. R. M. Dawkins (Oxford, 1932).

Mann, Nicholas, 'In margine alla quarta egloga: Piccoli problemi di esegesi petrarchesca', *Studi Petrarcheschi* NS 4 (1987), 17–32.

Manuscript Ivrea, Biblioteca Capitolare 115: Introductory Study and Facsimile edition, ed. Karl Kügle, Ars nova NS 5 (Lucca, 2019).

Le Manuscrit musical M 222 C 22 de la Bibliothèque de Strasbourg, XVe siècle, ed. Albert vander Linden, Thesaurus Musicus, 2 (Brussels, 1977).

Manzari, Francesca, 'The International Context of Boniface IX's Court and the Marginal Drawings in the Chantilly Codex (Bibliothèque du Château, Ms. 564)', *Recercare* 22 (2010), 11–33.

Marchi, Lucia, 'Traces of Performance in Early Fifteenth-Century Musical Attributions', *Philomusica on-line* 18 (2019), http://philomusica.unipv.it.

Mariani, Ugo, *Il Petrarca e gli Agostiniani* (Rome, 1946).

Marinescu, Ruxandra, 'The Politics of Deception and the French Lais in the Roman de Fauvel, Manuscript Paris, Bibliothèque nationale de France, fonds français 146' (Ph.D. thesis, Utrecht University, 2014).

Markstrom, Kurt, 'Machaut and the Wild Beast', *AM* 61 (1989), 12–39.

Maschke, Eva, 'Entfernte Einbandfragmente aus Altzelle und Ars nova-Fragmente auf Papier und Pergament: Neue Entdeckungen in der Universitätsbibliothek Leipzig', in Martin Kirnbauer (ed.), *Beredte Musik* (Basel, 2019), 261–75.

Maw, David, 'Machaut and the "Critical" Phase of Medieval Polyphony', review of *Essays on Music and Poetry in the Late Middle Ages* by Marie Louise Göllner, and *Machaut's Music: New Interpretations*, ed. Elizabeth Eva Leach, *M&L* 87 (2006), 262–94.

Maw, David, 'Redemption and Retrospection in Jacques de Liège's Concept of *cadentia*', *EMH* 29 (2010), 79–118.

Maw, David, review of Desmond, *Music and the moderni*, *Revue de Musicologie* 106 (2020), 494—501.

Mecacci, Enzo, and Agostino Ziino, 'Un altro frammento musicale del primo Quattrocento nell'Archivio di Stato di Siena', *RIM* 38 (2003), 199–225.

706   BIBLIOGRAPHY

Memelsdorff, Pedro, '*Je ne sçay lequel m'a plus conturbée*: A Classification of Late Medieval Contratenors with a "New" Contratenor by Matteo da Perugia and a Reflection of his *Se je me plaing*', *BJHM* 34 (2010; published 2014), 29–60.

Memelsdorff, Pedro, '*Lizadra donna*: Ciconia, Matteo da Perugia and the Late Medieval *Ars contratenoris*', in Philippe Vendrix (ed.), *Johannes Ciconia* (Turnhout, 2003), 235–80.

Memelsdorff, Pedro, 'Siena 36 revisitata: Paolo da Firenze, Johannes Ciconia, e l'interrelazione di polifonia e trattatistica in fonti del primo Quattrocento', *AM* 76 (2004), 159–91.

Mensurabilis musicae tractatuli, ed. F. Alberto Gallo, Antiquae Musicae Italicae Scriptores, 1 (Bologna, 1966).

La Messe de Tournai, ed. Jean Dumoulin, Michel Huglo, Philippe Mercier, and Jacques Pycke (Tournai, 1988).

Meyer, Christian, 'Le Cantuagium de Heinrich Eger von Kalkar et ses sources', *Analecta Cartusiana* NS 1/2 (1989), 112–34.

Millet, Hélène, *Les Chanoines du chapitre cathédral de Laon 1272–1412*, Collection de l'École Française de Rome, 56 (Rome, 1982).

Mixter, Keith, 'Johannes Brassart: A Biographical and Bibliographical Study: I: The Biography', *MD* 18 (1964), 37–62.

Moll, Kevin N., 'Structural Determinants in Polyphony for the Mass Ordinary from French and Related Sources (ca. 1320–1410)' (Ph.D. diss., Stanford University, 1994).

Moll, Kevin N., 'Texture and Counterpoint in the Four-Voice Mass Settings of Machaut and his Contemporaries', in E. E. Leach (ed.), *Machaut's Music: New Interpretations* (Woodbridge, 2003), 53–73.

Moll, Kevin N., 'Voice Function, Sonority, and Contrapuntal Procedure in Late Medieval Polyphony', *CM* 64 (2001), 7–59.

Moll, Kevin N. (ed.), *Counterpoint and Compositional Process in the Time of Dufay*, Criticism and Analysis of Early Music, 2 (New York and London, 1997).

Morelli, Arnaldo, 'Musica e musicisti in S. Agostino a Roma dal Quattrocento al Settecento', in Renato Lefevre and Arnaldo Morelli (ed.), *Musica e musicisti nel Lazio*, Lunario romano, 11 (Rome, 1985), 325–48.

Morent, Stefan, Silke Leopold, and Joachim Steinheuer (eds.), *Europäische Musikkultur im Kontext des Konstanzer Konzils* (Ostfildern, 2017).

Morin, Joseph C., 'Jehannot de Lescurel's Chansons, Geffroy de Paris's Dits, and the Process of Design in BN fr. 146', in Margaret Bent and Andrew Wathey (eds.), *Fauvel Studies* (Oxford, 1998), 321–36.

Mühlethaler, Jean-Claude, *Fauvel au pouvoir: Lire la satire médiévale* (Paris, 1994).

Musicorum collegio: Fourteenth-Century Musicians' Motets, ed. Frank Ll. Harrison (Monaco, 1986).

Nádas, John, *Arte psallentes. John Nádas: Studies in Music of the Tre- and Quattrocento, Collected in Honor of his 70th Birthday*, ed. Francesco Zimei and Andreas Janke (Lucca, 2017).

Nádas, John, 'A Cautious Reading of Simone Prodenzani's *Il Saporetto*', *Recercare* 10 (1998), 23–38.

Nádas, John, 'Further Notes on Magister Antonius dictus Zacharias de Teramo', *SMus* 15 (1986), 167–82; 16 (1987), 175–76.

Nádas, John, 'Manuscript San Lorenzo 2211: Some Further Observations', in *L'Ars nova italiana del Trecento*, 6 (Certaldo, 1992), 145–68.

Nádas, John, 'Secular Courts during the Period of the Great Schism: Documentation in the Archivio Segreto Vaticano', in Bianca Maria Antolini, Teresa M. Gialdroni, Annunziato Pugliese (eds.), *Studi in onore di Agostino Ziino in occasione del suo 65° compleanno* (Lucca: Libreria Italiana Musicale, 2004), i. 183–206.

Nádas, John, 'The Transmission of Trecento Secular Polyphony: Manuscript Production and Scribal Practices in Italy at the End of the Middle Ages' (Ph.D. diss., New York University, 1985).

Nádas, John, and Agostino Ziino, 'Two Newly Discovered Leaves of the Lucca codex', *SMus* 34 (2005), 3–23.

Nádas, John, and Michael Scott Cuthbert (eds.), *Ars nova: French and Italian Music in the Fourteenth Century* (Farnham, 2009).

Nádas, John, and Andreas Janke (eds.), *The San Lorenzo Palimpsest: Florence, Archivio del Capitolo di San Lorenzo, Ms. 2211*, 2 vols., Ars Nova, NS 4 (Lucca, 2016).

Newes, Virginia, 'Early Fourteenth-Century Motets with Middle-Voice Tenors', in Ursula Günther, Ludwig Finscher, and Jeffrey Dean (eds.) *Modality in the Music of the Fourteenth and Fifteenth Centuries = Modalität in der Musik des 14. und 15. Jahrhunderts* (Neuhausen and Stuttgart, 1996), 31–52.

Nicolas, N. H., *History of the Battle of Agincourt*, 2nd edn. (London, 1832; repr. London, 1970).

Nosow, Robert, 'The Equal-Discantus Motet Style after Ciconia', *MD* 45 (1991), 221–75.

Nosow, Robert, 'The Florid and Equal-Discantus Motet Styles of Fifteenth-Century Italy' (Ph.D. diss., University of North Carolina, 1992).

Nosow, Robert, *Ritual Meanings in the Fifteenth-Century Motet* (Cambridge, 2012).

The Old Hall Manuscript, ed. Andrew Hughes and Margaret Bent, 3 vols., CMM 46 (n.p., 1969).

Orléans, H. d' (ed.), *Notes et documents relatifs à Jean, Roi de France, et à sa captivité en Angleterre*, Miscellanies of the Philobiblon Society, 2 (London, 1855–6).

Ovid, *Tristia; Ex ponto*, ed. A. L. Wheeler (Cambridge, MA, 1924).

Oxford, Bodleian Library MS Canon. Misc. 213, ed. David Fallows, Late Medieval and Early Renaissance Music in Facsimile, 1 (Chicago and London, 1995).

Page, Christopher, *Discarding Images: Reflections on Music and Culture in Medieval France* (Oxford, 1993).

Page, Christopher, 'Johannes de Grocheio on Secular Music: A Corrected Text and a New Translation', *PMM* 2 (1993), 17–41.

Page, Christopher, 'A Reply to Margaret Bent', *EM* 22 (1994), 127–32.

Page, Christopher, 'Tradition and Innovation in BN fr .146: The Background to the Ballades', in Margaret Bent and Andrew Wathey (eds.), *Fauvel Studies* (Oxford, 1998), 353–94.

Page, Christopher, 'A Treatise on Musicians from? c.1400: The *Tractatulus de differentiis et gradibus cantorum* by Arnulf de St Ghislain', *JRMA* 117 (1992), 1–21.

Palm, Konrad, *Italienische Ereignisse in den ersten Jahren Karl IV* (Göttingen, 1873).

Pedersen, Olaf, 'Peter Philomena of Dacia, also known as Petrus Dacus, Petrus Danus, Peter Nightingale', *DSB* 10, 540–42.

Peraino, Judith A., 'Monophonic Motets: Sampling and Grafting in the Middle Ages', *MQ* 85 (2001), 644–80.

Pesce, Dolores (ed.), *Hearing the Motet: Essays on the Motet of the Middle Ages and Renaissance* (New York, 1997).

Petrarch, *Bucolicum carmen*, ed., trans., comm. by Marcel François and Paul Bachmann, with François Roudaut, Textes de la Renaissance, 43 (Paris, 2001).

Petrobelli, Pierluigi, 'La musica nelle cattedrali e nella città', in *Storia della cultura veneta*, 5 vols. (Vicenza, 1976–), ii, pt. 2, pp. 440–68.

Petrus Comestor, *Scolastica historia: Liber Genesis*, ed. Agneta Sylwan, Corpus Christianorum Continuatio Mediaevalis, 191 (Turnhout, 2004).

Petrus dictus Palma Ociosa, *Compendium de discantu mensurabili*, ed. in Johannes Wolf, 'Ein Beitrag zur Diskantlehre des 14. Jahrhunderts', *SIMG* 15 (1913–14), 504–34.

Pieragostini, Renata, 'Aspects of Anglo-Italian Musical Relations in the Fourteenth Century' (Ph.D. thesis, Cambridge, 2009).

Pieragostini, Renata, 'Augustinian Networks and the Chicago Music Theory Manuscript', *PMM* 22 (2013), 65–85.

Picardus, Petrus, *Ars motettorum compilata breviter*, ed. F. Alberto Gallo, CSM 15 (n.p., 1971), 11–30.

Pirrotta, Nino, 'Zacarus Musicus', *Quadrivium* 12 (1971), 153–75.

I più antichi monumenti sacri italiani, ed. F. Alberto Gallo and Giuseppe Vecchi (Bologna, 1968).

Plamenac, Dragan, 'Another Paduan Fragment of Trecento Music', *JAMS* 8 (1955), 165–81.

Planchart, Alejandro Enrique, 'The Early Career of Guillaume Du Fay', *JAMS* 46 (1993), 341–68.

Planchart, Alejandro Enrique, *Guillaume Du Fay: The Life and Works*, 2 vols. (Cambridge, 2018).

Planchart, Alejandro Enrique, 'Guillaume Du Fay's Benefices and his Relationship to the Court of Burgundy', *EMH* 8 (1988), 117–71.

708 BIBLIOGRAPHY

Planchart, Alejandro Enrique, 'Music for the Papal Chapel in the Early Fifteenth Century', in Richard Sherr (ed.), *Papal Music* (Oxford, 1998), 93–124.

Plumley, Yolanda, *The Art of Grafted Song: Citation and Allusion in the Age of Machaut* (Oxford, 2013).

Plumley, Yolanda, 'Crossing Borderlines: Points of Contact between the Late-Fourteenth Century French Lyric and Chanson Repertories', *AM* 76 (2004), 3–23.

Plumley, Yolanda, 'Intertextuality in the Fourteenth-Century Chanson', *M&L* 84 (2003), 355–77.

Plumley, Yolanda, and Anne Stone, *Codex Chantilly: Bibliothèque du château de Chantilly, Ms. 564; Introduction*, Collection 'Épitome musical' (Turnhout, 2008) [published separately from the facsimile].

Plumley, Yolanda, and Anne Stone (eds.), *A Late Medieval Songbook and its Context: New Perspectives on the Chantilly Codex* (Turnhout, 2009).

Poesie musicali del Trecento, ed. Giuseppe Corsi (Bologna, 1970).

Polyphonia Sacra: A Continental Miscellany of the Fifteenth Century, ed. Charles van den Borren (University Park, PA, 1963).

Prosdocimo de' Beldomandi, *Contrapunctus = Counterpoint*, ed. and trans. Jan Herlinger (Lincoln, NE, 1984).

Prosdocimo de' Beldomandi, *Parvus tractatulus de modo monacordum dividendi*, ed. and trans. Jan Herlinger (Lincoln, NE, 1987).

Proverbia sententiaeque latinitatis medii aevi: Lateinische Sprichwörter und Sentenzen des Mittelalters, ed. Hans Walther, 5 vols., Carmina Medii Aevi Posterioris Latina, 2 (Göttingen, 1963–7).

Raitzig, Olaf, *Codex Ivrea: Studien, Gotische Polyphonie, Motetten der Ars Nova* (Berlin, 2011).

Rankin, Susan, 'The Divine Truth of Scripture: Chant in the *Roman de Fauvel*', *JAMS* 47 (1994), 203–43.

Reaney, Gilbert, 'Fourteenth-Century Harmony and the Ballades, Rondeaux and Virelais of Guillaume de Machaut', *MD* 7 (1953), 129–46.

Reaney, Gilbert, 'The Manuscript Chantilly, Musée Condé 1047', *MD* 8 (1954), 59–113.

Reaney, Gilbert, 'New Sources of *Ars Nova* Music', *MD* 19 (1965), 53–67.

Reese, Gustave, *Music in the Renaissance* (New York, 1954).

Regalado, Nancy Freeman, 'The *Chronique métrique* and Moral Design of BN fr. 146: Feasts of Good and Evil', in Margaret Bent and Andrew Wathey (eds.), *Fauvel Studies* (Oxford, 1998), 466–94.

The Register of Henry Chichele, Archbishop of Canterbury, 1414–1443, ed. E. F. Jacob, with the assistance of H. C. Johnson, 4 vols. (Oxford, 1938–47).

The Register of John Trefnant, Bishop of Hereford (A.D. 1389–1404), ed. William W. Capes (Hereford, 1914).

Reichert, Georg, 'Das Verhältnis zwischen musikalischer und textlicher Struktur in den Motetten Machauts', *AfMw* 13 (1956), 197–216.

Reynolds, Christopher A., *Papal Patronage and the Music of St. Peter's, 1380–1513* (Berkeley, 1995).

Rico, Gilles, 'Music in the Arts Faculty of Paris in the Thirteenth and Early Fourteenth Centuries' (D.Phil. thesis, University of Oxford, 2005).

Riemann, Hugo, 'Noch zwei verkannte Kanons', *Zeitschrift der internationalen Musikgesellschaft* 7 (1906), 137–42.

Rizzuti, Alberto, 'Four Angels and a Coat of Arms. The Case of MS I-Tn, J.II.9', in Elisabetta Barale and Daniele Valentino Filippi (eds.), *Il codice cipriota: origini, storie, contesto culturale* (Venice, forthcoming 2023).

Rizzuti, Alberto, 'Margaritae ante porcos: Musica per S. Antonio di Vienne nell'Europa del Quattrocento', *Philomusica on-line* 20 (2021), http://philomusica.unipv.it, 67–122.

Robertson, Anne Walters, *Guillaume de Machaut and Reims* (Cambridge, 2002).

Robertson, Anne Walters, 'Local Chant Readings and the *Roman de Fauvel*', in Margaret Bent and Andrew Wathey (eds.), *Fauvel Studies* (Oxford, 1998), 495–524.

Robertson, Anne Walters, 'The Mass of Guillaume de Machaut in the Cathedral of Reims', in Thomas Forrest Kelly (ed.), *Plainsong in the Age of Polyphony* (Cambridge, 1992), 100–39.

Robertson, Anne Walters, 'A Musical Lesson for a King from the *Roman de Fauvel*', in Benjamin Brand and David Rothenberg (eds.), *Music and Culture in the Middle Ages and Beyond: Liturgy, Sources, Symbolism* (Cambridge, 2016), 242–62.

Robertson, Anne Walters, 'Two French Secular Motets in the Cyprus Codex and a New Composer from Cyprus', in Elisabetta Barale and Daniele Valentino Filippi (eds.), *Il codice cipriota: origini, storie, contesto culturale* (Venice, forthcoming 2023).

Robertson, Anne Walters, 'Which Vitry? The Witness of the Trinity Motet from the *Roman de Fauvel*', in Dolores Pesce (ed.), *Hearing the Motet* (New York, 1997), 52–81.

Robertus de Handlo, the Rules, and Johannes Hanboys, the Summa, ed. Peter M. Lefferts (Lincoln, NE, and London, 1991).

Roger, Kévin, 'La composition du tenor dans le motet isorythmique français post-Machaut (1370–1420)' (Ph.D. thesis, University of Tours, 2021).

Roger, Kévin, 'Références astronomiques et astrologiques dans un motet du xive siècle: l'énigme de Febus mundo oriens', *Revue de musicologie* 108 (2022), 275–98.

Rohloff, Ernst, *Der Musiktraktat des Johannes de Grocheo nach den Quellen neu herausgegeben mit Übersetzung ins Deutsche und Revisionsbericht*, Media latinitas musica, 2 (Leipzig, 1943).

Le Roman de Fauvel in the Edition of Mesire Chaillou de Pesstain: A Reproduction in Facsimile of the Complete Manuscript Paris, Bibliothèque Nationale, Fonds Français 146, Introduction by Edward H. Roesner, François Avril, and Nancy Freeman Regalado (New York, 1990).

Le Roman de Fauvel par Gervais du Bus publié d'après tous les manuscrits connus, ed. Arthur Långfors, Société des anciens textes français (Paris, 1914–19).

Roman de la Rose, ed. Armand Strubel (Paris, 1992).

Rondeaux et refrains du XIIe siècle au début du XIVe, ed. Nico H. J. van den Boogaard (Paris, 1969).

Rondeaux, Virelais und Balladen aus dem Ende des XII., dem XIII und dem ersten Drittel des XIV. Jahrhunderts, mit den überlieferten Melodien, ed. Friedrich Gennrich, 3 vols., Gesellschaft für romanische Literatur, 43 (Dresden, 1921, Göttingen, 1927, Langen bei Frankfurt, 1963).

Rosen, Charles, *Sonata Forms* (New York, 1980).

Saint-Cricq, Gaël, 'Motets in Chansonniers and the Other Culture of the French Thirteenth-Century Motet', in Jared C. Hartt (ed.), *A Critical Companion* (Woodbridge, 2018), 225–42.

Salomon, Richard, 'Johannes Porta de Annoniaco und sein Buch über die Krönung Kaiser Karls IV', *Neues Archiv der Gesellschaft für ältere deutsche Geschichtskunde zur Beförderung einer Gesamtausgabe der Quellenschriften deutscher Geschichten des Mittelalters*, 38/1 (1913), 227–94.

Sanders, Ernest H., 'The Early Motets of Philippe de Vitry', *JAMS* 28 (1975), 24–45.

Sanders, Ernest H., 'English Polyphony in the Morgan Library Manuscript', *M&L* 61 (1980), 172–76.

Sanders, Ernest H., 'The Medieval Motet', in *Gattungen der Musik in Einzeldarstellungen: Gedenkschrift Leo Schrade*, ed. W. Arlt et al. (Bern and Munich, 1973), 497–573.

Sanders, Ernest H., 'Motet, I: Medieval', *NG*1, xii. 617–28.

Sandon, Nicholas, 'Fragments of Medieval Polyphony at Canterbury Cathedral', *MD* 30 (1976), 37–53.

Saroni, Giovanna, *La Biblioteca di Amedeo VIII di Savoia (1391–1451)* (Turin, 2004).

Saucier, Catherine, 'Johannes Brassart's *Summus secretarius*: Extolling the Evangelist', *JM* 34 (2017), 149–81.

Saucier, Catherine, *A Paradise of Priests: Singing the Civic and Episcopal Hagiography of Medieval Liège* (Rochester, NY, 2014).

Saucier, Catherine, 'Reading Hagiographic Motets: *Christi nutu sublimato, Lamberte vir inclite*, and the Legend of St. Lambert', *JAF* 6 (2014), 84–111.

Schipperges, Thomas, *Die Akte Heinrich Besseler: Musikwissenschaft und Wissenschaftspolitik in Deutschland 1924 bis 1949*, Quellen und Studien zur Musik in Baden-Württemberg, 7 (Munich, 2005).

Schneider, Herbert, and Heinz-Jürgen Winkler (eds.), *Die Motette: Beiträge zu ihrer Gattungsgeschichte. Ludwig Finscher zum 60. Geburtstag*, Neue Studien zur Musikwissenschaft, 5 (Mainz, 1992).

710 BIBLIOGRAPHY

Schoop, Hans, *Entstehung und Verwendung der Handschrift Oxford, Bodleian Library, Canonici misc.* 213 (Bern, 1971).

Schrade, Leo, 'Philippe de Vitry: Some New Discoveries', *MQ* 42 (1956), 330–54.

Schubert, Peter, 'Authentic Analysis', *JM* 12 (1994), 3–18.

Schuler, Manfred, 'Die Musik in Konstanz wahrend des Konzils 1414–1418', *AM* 38 (1960), 150–68.

Schuler, Manfred, 'Zur Geschichte der Kapelle Papst Martins V', *AfMw* 25 (1968), 30–45.

Seiferling, Steffen, *O felix templum jubila: Musik, Text und Zeremoniell in den Motetten Johannes Ciconias* (Berlin, 2004).

Shaffer, Melanie, 'Finding Fortune in Motet 13: Insights on Ordering and Borrowing in Machaut's Motets', *PMM* 26 (2017), 115–39.

Sherr, Richard, 'Music and the Renaissance Papacy: The Papal Choir and the Fondo Capella Sistina', in Anthony Grafton (ed.), *Rome Reborn: The Vatican Library and Renaissance Culture* (Washington, DC, 1993), 199–223.

Sherr, Richard (ed.), *Papal Music and Musicians in Medieval and Renaissance Rome* (Oxford, 1998).

Sieben Trienter Codices (Sechste Auswahl), ed. R. von Ficker, D.T.Ö. 76 (Vienna, 1933).

Simioni, Attilio, *Storia di Padova dalle origini alla fine del secolo XVIII* (Padua, 1968).

Six Historical Poems of Geoffroi de Paris, ed. Walter Storer and Charles Rochedieu (Chapel Hill, NC, 1950).

Slocum, Kay Brainerd, *Liturgies in Honour of Thomas Becket* (Toronto, 2002).

Smilansky, Uri, 'Creating MS C: Author, Workshop, Court', *EMH* 39 (2020), 253–304.

Somerset Medieval Wills, 1383–1500, ed. F. W. Weaver, Somerset Record Society, 16 (London, 1901).

Staehelin, Martin, 'Münchner Fragmente mit mehrstimmiger Musik des späten Mittelalters', *Nachrichten der Akademie der Wissenschaften in Göttingen*, 1, Philologisch-historische Klasse, Jahrgang 1988, no. 6, 167–90.

Steiger, Adrian V., 'Das Berner Chansonnier-Fragment: Beobachtungen zur Handschrift und zum Repertoire', *Schweizer Jahrbuch für Musikwissenschaft* 11 (1991), 43–65.

Stell, Judith, and Andrew Wathey, 'New Light on the Biography of John Dunstable?', *M&L* 62 (1981), 60–63.

Stevens, John, *Words and Music in the Middle Ages: Song, Narrative, Dance and Drama, 1050–1350* (Cambridge, 1986).

Stoessel, Jason, 'Arms, a Saint and *Inperial sedendo fra più stelle*: The Illuminator of Mod A', *JM* 31 (2014), 1–42.

Stoessel, Jason, 'Johannes Ciconia and his Italian Poets: Text, Image and beyond in Early Fifteenth-Century Padua', in Anna Alberni, Antonio Calvia and Maria Sofia Lannutti (eds.), *Polyphonic Voices. Poetic and Musical Dialogues in the European Ars Nova* (Florence, 2021), 211–36.

Stoessel, Jason, 'Music and Moral Philosophy in Early Fifteenth-Century Padua', in Jason Stoessel (ed.), *Identity and Locality in Early European Music 1028–1740* (Farnham, 2009), 107–27.

Stoessel, Jason, 'Revisiting "Aÿ, mare, amice mi care": Insights into Late Medieval Music Notation', *EM* 40 (2012), 455–68.

Stone, Anne, 'Che cosa c'è di più sottile riguardo l'*ars subtilior*?', *Rivista italiana di musicologia* 31 (1996), 3–31.

Stone, Anne, 'Lombard Patronage at the End of the Ars Nova: A Preliminary Panorama', in Antonio Calvia et al. (eds.), *The End of the Ars Nova in Italy* (Florence, 2020), 217–52.

Stone, Anne, *The Manuscript Modena, Biblioteca Estense, α.M.5.24: Commentary* (Lucca, 2005).

Stone, Anne, 'Music Writing and Poetic Voice in Machaut: Some Remarks on B12 and R14', in Elizabeth Eva Leach (ed.), *Machaut's Music* (Woodbridge, 2003), 125–38.

Stone, Anne, 'A Singer at the Fountain: Homage and Irony in Ciconia's *Sus une fontayne*', *M&L* 82 (2001), 361–90.

Stone, Anne, 'Writing Rhythm in Late Medieval Italy: Notation and Musical Style in the Manuscript Modena, Biblioteca Estense, Alpha.M.5.24' (Ph.D. diss., Harvard University, 1994).

Stow, George B., 'Richard II's Interest in Music' (unpublished typescript).

BIBLIOGRAPHY 711

Stowe, John, *The Annales of England: faithfully collected out of the most autenticall authors, records, and other monuments of antiquitie, lately corrected, encreased, and continued, from the first inhabitation vntill this present yeere 1600 By Iohn Stovv citizen of London* (London, [1600]).

Stratford, Jenny, *The Bedford Inventories* (London, 1993).

Strohm, Reinhard, 'The Ars Nova Fragments of Gent', *TVNM* 24 (1984), 109–31.

Strohm, Reinhard, 'The Earliest Cantus Firmus Mass? A Challenge to Historiography in the Turin Manuscript J.II.9', in Elisabetta Barale and Daniele Valentino Filippi (eds.), *Il codice cipriota: origini, storie, contesto culturale* (Venice, forthcoming 2023).

Strohm, Reinhard, 'European Politics and the Distribution of Music in the Early Fifteenth Century, *EMH* 1 (1981), 305–23.

Strohm, Reinhard, 'Filippotto da Caserta, ovvero i francesi in Lombardia', in Fabrizio Della Seta and Franco Piperno (eds.), *In cantu et in sermone: A Nino Pirrotta nel suo 80° compleanno* (Florence, 1989), 65–74.

Strohm, Reinhard, 'Magister Egardus and Other Italo-Flemish Contacts', *L'Ars nova italiana del Trecento*, 6 (1992), 41–68.

Strohm, Reinhard, 'Native and Foreign Polyphony in Late Medieval Austria', *MD* 38 (1984), 205–30.

Strohm, Reinhard, *The Rise of European Music 1380–1500* (Cambridge, 1993).

Strubel, Armand, *Le Roman de Fauvel*, Lettres gothiques (Paris, 2012).

The Summa musice: A Thirteenth-Century Manual for Singers, ed. and trans. Christopher Page, Cambridge Musical Texts and Monographs (Cambridge, 1991).

Suppliques d'Urbain V (1362–1370), ed. A. Fierens = *Analecta Vaticano-Belgica*, vii (Namur, 1924).

Taucci, Raffaele, 'Fra Andrea dei Servi: organista e compositore del trecento', *Rivista di studi storici sull'Ordine dei Servi di Maria* 2/2 (1934), 73–108.

Taylor, Jane H. M., '*Le Roman de Fauvain*: Manuscript, Text, Image', in Margaret Bent and Andrew Wathey (eds.), *Fauvel Studies* (Oxford, 1998), 570–89.

Thesaurus proverbiorum Medii Aevi: Lexikon der Sprichwörter des romanisch-germanischen Mittelalters (Berlin, 1996).

Thomson, Rodney M., 'John Dunstable and his Books', *MT* 150 (2009), 3–16.

Thöne, Johanna-Pauline, 'Papal Polyphony of the Great Western Schism (1378–1417)' (Ph. D. diss., University of Oslo, in preparation).

Tinctoris, Johannes, *Liber de arte contrapuncti*, ed. Albert Seay, Johannis Tinctoris Opera theoretica, 2, CSM 22 (Neuhausen-Stuttgart, 1975).

Tinctoris, Johannes, *Proportionale musices*, ed. Albert Seay, Johannis Tinctoris Opera theoretica, IIa, CSM 22 (Neuhausen-Stuttgart, 1978).

Titus Livius de Frulovisiis, *Vita Henrici Quinti, Regis Angliæ*, ed. Thomas Hearne (Oxford, 1716).

Tomasello, Andrew, *Music and Ritual at Papal Avignon 1309–1403* (Ann Arbor, 1983).

Trachtenberg, Marvin, 'Architecture and Music Reunited: A New Reading of Dufay's *Nuper Rosarum Flores* and the Cathedral of Florence', *Renaissance Quarterly* 54 (2001), 740–75.

Tractatulus de cantu mensurali seu figurativo musice artis (MS. Melk, Stiftsbibliothek 950), ed. F. Alberto Gallo, CSM 16 (n.p., 1971).

Tractatus figurarum/Treatise on Noteshapes, ed. and trans. Philip E. Schreur (Lincoln, NE, 1989).

Trowell, Brian, 'A Fourteenth-Century Ceremonial Motet and its Composer', *AM* 29 (1957), 65–75.

Trowell, Brian, 'Music under the Later Plantagenets' (Ph.D. thesis, Cambridge University, 1960).

Ulrich, H., and P. Pisk, *A History of Music and Musical Style* (London and New York, 1963).

Urbain V (1362–1370) Lettres communes, i, ed. M.-H. Laurent (Rome 1954–8).

Urbain V (1362–1370) Lettres communes, iii, ed. Michel Hayez (Rome, 1976).

Urbain V (1362–1370) Lettres communes, viii, ed. Michel and Anne-Marie Hayez, Bibliothèque des Écoles Françaises d'Athènes et de Rome, 3 ser.Vbis (Rome, 1982).

Valois, Noël, *La France et le Grand Schisme d'Occident* (Paris, 1896).

Van Drival, Eugene (ed.), *Nécrologe de l'abbaye Saint Vaast d'Arras* (Arras, 1878).

Vendrix, Philippe (ed.), *Johannes Ciconia, musicien de la transition* (Turnhout, 2003).

Vícetextová Moteta 14. a 15. století – Mehrtextige Motetten des 14. und 15. Jahrhunderts, ed. Jaromír Černý, Thesaurus Musicae Bohemiae, Series A (Prague, 1989).

712 BIBLIOGRAPHY

Vitry, Philippe de, *Ars nova*, ed. G. Reaney, A. Gilles, and J. Maillard, CSM 8 (n.p., 1964).

Vivarelli, Carla, '"Di una pretesa scuola napoletana": Sowing the Seeds of the *Ars nova* at the Court of Robert of Anjou', *JM* 24 (2007), 272–96.

Vlhová-Wörner, Hana, '*Novum sidus orientis*: New Identification Perspectives', in Martin Kirnbauer (ed.), *Beredte Musik* (Basel, 2019), 457–66.

Waldmüller, L., 'Materialien zur Geschichte Johannes XXIII (1410–1414)', *Annuarium Historiae Conciliorum* 7 (1975), 229–37.

Wangermée, Robert, *Flemish Music and Society in the Fifteenth and Sixteenth Centuries* (New York and London, 1970).

Ward, Tom R., 'A Central European Repertory in Munich, Bayerische Staatsbibliothek, Clm 14274', *EMH* 1 (1981), 325–43.

Warren, Charles, 'Brunelleschi's Dome and Dufay's Motet', *MQ* 59 (1973), 92–105.

Wathey, Andrew, 'Auctoritas and the Motets of Philippe de Vitry', in Suzannah Clark and Elizabeth Eva Leach (eds.), *Citation and Authority* (Woodbridge, 2005), 67–78.

Wathey, Andrew, 'Dunstable in France', *M&L* 67 (1986), 1–36.

Wathey, Andrew, 'Dunstaple, Power and the mid Fifteenth Century', in preparation.

Wathey, Andrew, 'John of Gaunt, John Pycard and the Amiens Negotiations of 1392', in Caroline Barron and Nigel Saul (eds.), *England and the Low Countries in the Late Middle Ages* (New York, 1995), 29–42.

Wathey, Andrew, 'Lost Books of Polyphony in England: A List to 1500', *RMA Research Chronicle* 21 (1988), 1–20.

Wathey, Andrew, *Manuscripts of Polyphonic Music, Supplement 1 to RISM B IV 1–2* (Munich, 1993).

Wathey, Andrew, 'The Marriage of Edward III and the Transmission of French Motets to England', *JAMS* 45 (1992), 1–29.

Wathey, Andrew, 'More on a Friend of Philippe de Vitry: Johannes Rufi de Cruce alias Jean de Savoie', *PMM* 28 (2019), 29–42.

Wathey, Andrew, 'The Motet Texts of Philippe de Vitry in German Humanist Manuscripts of the Fifteenth Century', in John Kmetz (ed.), *Music in the German Renaissance: Sources, Styles, and Contexts* (Cambridge, 1994), 195–201.

Wathey, Andrew, 'The Motets of Philippe de Vitry and the Fourteenth-Century Renaissance', *EMH* 12 (1993), 119–50.

Wathey, Andrew, *Music in the Royal and Noble Households in Late Medieval England: Studies of Sources and Patronage* (London and New York, 1989).

Wathey, Andrew, 'Musicology, Archives and Historiography', in Barbara Haggh, Frank Daelemans, and André Vanrie (eds.), *Musicology and Archival Research* (Brussels, 1994), 1–16.

Wathey, Andrew, 'Myth and Mythography in the Motets of Philippe de Vitry', *Musica e storia* 4 (1996), 81–99.

Wathey, Andrew, 'The Peace of 1360–1369 and Anglo-French Musical Relations', *EMH* 9 (1990), 129–74.

Wathey, Andrew, 'Philippe de Vitry, Bishop of Meaux', *EMH* 38 (2019), 215–68.

Wathey, Andrew, 'Philippe de Vitry's Books', in J. P. Carley and C. G. C. Tite (eds.), *Books and Collectors 1200–1700: Essays Presented to A. G. Watson* (London, 1997), 145–52.

Wathey, Andrew, 'Words and Music in the Motets of Philippe de Vitry', *RM* 16 (1993), 1548–53.

Wegman, Rob C., '"Das musikalische Hören" in the Middle Ages and Renaissance: Perspectives from Pre-War Germany', *MQ* 82 (1998), 434–55.

Wegman, Rob C., 'New Music for a World Grown Old: Martin Le Franc and the Contenance Angloise', *AM* 75 (2003), 201–41.

Welker, Lorenz, *Musik am Oberrhein im späten Mittelalter: Die Handschrift Strasbourg, olim Bibliothèque de la ville, C.22* (Habilitationsschrift, Basel, 1993).

Welker, Lorenz, 'Polyphonic Reworkings of Notre-Dame Conductus in BN fr. 146: *Mundus a mundicia* and *Quare fremuerunt*', in Margaret Bent and Andrew Wathey (eds.), *Fauvel Studies* (Oxford, 1998), 615–36.

Westerhaus, Andrew, 'A Lexicon of Contratenor Behaviour: Case-Studies of Equal-Cantus Italian Motets from the MS Bologna Q15', *PMM* 18 (2009), 113–40.

Widaman, Jean, Andrew Wathey, and Daniel Leech-Wilkinson, 'The Structure and Copying of Torino J.II.9', in Ursula Günther and Ludwig Finscher (eds.), *The Cypriot-French Repertory* (Neuhausen-Stuttgart, 1995), 95–116.

(Willelmus), *Breviarium regulare musicae*, ed. Gilbert Reaney, CSM 12 (n.p., 1966), 13–31.

Witkowska-Zaremba, Elżbieta, 'Johannes de Muris's *Musica speculativa* cited by Jacobus de Ispania', *PMM* 31 (2022), 37–63.

Witkowska-Zaremba, Elżbieta (ed.), *Notae musicae artis: Musical Notation in Polish Sources, 11th–16th Century* (Kraków, 2001).

Wolf, Johannes, 'Ein anonymer Musiktraktat aus der ersten Zeit der "Ars Nova"', *Kirchenmusikalisches Jahrbuch* 21 (1908), 34–38.

Wolf, Johannes, 'Ein Breslauer Mensuraltraktat des 15. Jahrhunderts', *AfMw* 1 (1918–19), 331–45 (= Anonymous, *Tractatus de musica mensurabili*).

Wolf, Johannes (ed.), *Musikalische Schrifttafeln für den Unterricht in der Notationskunde* (Bückeburg and Leipzig, 1923).

Wood, Diana, *Clement VI: The Pontificate and Ideas of an Avignon Pope* (Cambridge, 1989).

Woodley, Ronald, 'Minor Coloration Revisited: Ockeghem's Ma bouche rit and Beyond', in Anne-Emmanuelle Ceulemans and Bonnie J. Blackburn (eds.), *Théorie et analyse musicales 1450–1650, Music Theory and Analysis* (Louvain-la-Neuve, 2001), 39–63.

Wooldridge, H. E., *Early English Harmony*, i (London, 1897).

Wright, Craig, 'Dufay at Cambrai: Discoveries and Revisions', *JAMS* 28 (1975), 175–229.

Wright, Craig, 'Dufay's *Nuper rosarum flores*, King Solomon's Temple, and the Veneration of the Virgin', *JAMS* 47 (1994), 395–441.

Wright, Craig, *Music at the Court of Burgundy 1364–1419: A Documentary History* (Henryville, Ottawa, Binningen, 1979).

Wright, Peter, 'Binchois and England: Some Questions of Style, Influence, and Attribution in the Sacred Music', in Andrew Kirkman and Dennis Slavin (eds.), *Binchois Studies* (Oxford, 2000), 87–118.

Wright, Peter, 'Johannes Brassart and Johannes de Sarto', *PMM* 1 (1992), 41–61.

Wright, Peter, 'A New Attribution to Brassart?', *PMM* 3 (1994), 23–43.

Wright, Peter, 'A New Attribution to Dunstaple', *M&L* 100 (2019), 196–232.

Zancani, Diego, 'Un recupero quattrocentesco: *La vita di Pietro Avogadro Bresciano* di Antonio Cornazzano e il lavoro di un editore del Cinquecento (Remigio Nannini)', in *Libri, tipografi, biblioteche: Ricerche storiche dedicate a Luigi Balsamo*, Biblioteca di bibliografia italiana, 148 ([Florence], 1997), 145–67.

Zayaruznaya, Anna, 'Evidence of Reworkings in Ars nova Motets', *BJHM* 38 (2014 [published 2018]), 155–75.

Zayaruznaya, Anna, 'Form and Idea in the Ars Nova Motet' (Ph.D. diss., Harvard University, 2010).

Zayaruznaya, Anna, 'Hockets as Compositional and Scribal Practice in the Ars Nova Motet—A Letter from Lady Music', *JM* 30 (2013), 461–501.

Zayaruznaya, Anna, '[In]troitus: Untexted Beginnings and Scribal Confusion in the Machaut and Ivrea Manuscripts', *Digital Philology: A Journal of Medieval Cultures* 5 (2016), 47–73.

Zayaruznaya, Anna, '*Materia* Matters: Reconstructing *Colla/ Bona*', in Jared C. Hartt (ed.), *A Critical Companion* (Woodbridge, 2018), 287–99.

Zayaruznaya, Anna, *The Monstrous New Art: Divided Forms in the Late Medieval Motet* (Cambridge, 2015).

Zayaruznaya, Anna, 'New Voices for Vitry', *EM* 46 (2018), 375–92.

Zayaruznaya, Anna, 'Old, New, and Newer Still in Book 7 of the *Speculum musice*', *JAMS* 73 (2020), 95–148.

Zayaruznaya, Anna, 'Quotation, Perfection and the Eloquence of Form: Introducing *Beatius/ Cum humanum*', *PMM* 24 (2015), 129–66.

Zayaruznaya, Anna, ' "Sanz note" & "sanz mesure": Toward a Premodern Aesthetics of the Dirge', in Irit Kleiman (ed.), *Voice and Voicelessness in Medieval Europe* (New York, 2015), 155–75.

714   BIBLIOGRAPHY

Zayaruznaya, Anna, '"She has a Wheel that Turns . . .": Crossed and Contradictory Voices in Machaut's Motets', *EMH* 28 (2009), 185–240.

Zayaruznaya, Anna, *Upper-Voice Structures and Compositional Process in the Ars Nova Motet*, RMA Monographs, 32 (Abingdon, 2018).

Zayaruznaya, Anna, 'What Fortune Can Do to a Minim', *JAMS* 65 (2012), 313–81.

Zazulia, Emily, 'A Motet Ahead of its Time? The Curious Case of *Portio nature/Ida capillorum*', in Jared C. Hartt (ed.), *A Critical Companion* (Woodbridge, 2018), 341–54.

Zazulia, Emily, 'Verbal Canons and Notational Complexity in Fifteenth-Century Music' (Ph.D. diss., University of Pennsylvania, 2012).

Zazulia, Emily, *Where Sight Meets Sound: The Poetics of Late Medieval Music Writing* (New York and Oxford, 2021).

Ziino, Agostino, 'Una ignota testimonianza sulla diffusione del mottetto in Italia durante il XIV secolo', *RIM* 10 (1975), 20–31.

Ziino, Agostino, 'Magister Antonius dictus Zacharias de Teramo: Alcuni date e molte ipotesi', *RIM* 114 (1979), 311–48.

Ziino, Agostino, 'Precisazioni su un frammento di musica francese trecentesca conservato nell'archivio comunale di Cortona', in I Deug-Su and Enrico Menestò (eds.), *Università e tutela dei beni culturali: Il contributo degli studi medievali e umanistici* (Florence, 1981), 351–61.

Ziino, Agostino, 'Una sequenza mensurale per San Fortunato ed un "Amen" a tre voci nella Biblioteca Comunale di Todi (con un'Appendice sul frammento di Cortona)', *L'Ars nova italiana del Trecento*, 5 (Certaldo, 1985), 257–70.

Zimei, Francesco, 'Un elenco veneto di composizioni del Trecento con inedite attribuzioni a Marchetto da Padova e altre novità', *Recercare*, 30 (2018), 5–14.

Zimei, Francesco (ed.), *Antonio Zacara da Teramo e il suo tempo* (Lucca, 2004).

Index of Compositions

Most incidental mentions are not indexed. The distinction between composer assignations with and without '?' is not a firm one. Principal discussions are in boldface. For the benefit of digital users, indexed terms that span two pages (e.g., 52–53) may appear on only one of those pages. Where an item appears in a table, only the first page of that table is indexed (*t*). Where a figure or example extends over more than one page, only the first page is indexed (*f*).

. . . de qua cordis/Trinitatem, 506, 513, 516–17, 638

/[. . .]reo gencium, 655

A celui dont sui ser[viteur], 660

A maint biau jeu, 660

A maistre Jehan Lardier, 283–84

A solis ortus cardine Et usque terre limitem, 356

Adieu ma dame, 657

Adieu plaisir (Hubertus de Salinis), 546*t*

Agnus Custos et pastor ovium (Du Fay), 639

Albane misse celitus/Albane doctor maxime (Ciconia), 55, 504*t*, 513n.43, 553, 554*t*, 560, 564, 565, 567, 568

Albanus roseo rutilat/Quoque ferendus/Albanus (Dunstaple), 485, 490*t*, 675

Aler m'en veus (Ciconia), 553, 564, 571

Alma parens, nata nati/O Maria, stella maris/Alleluya, 683

Alma polis religio/Axe poli cum artica/[Et] in ore eorum, ▶ Ex. 19.1, 21, 53, 285, 287–88, 304–5, 306–8, 347, **353–67**, 373, 376, 378, 380–81, 391–94

Alma proles regia/Christi miles (Cooke), 307n.11, 356n.5, 387, 469–71, 473, 474–75, 477, **479–80**

Alme pater, 621–23, 638

Almifonis/Rosa sine culpe spina (Vitry?), 29, 653, 674–75

Alpha vibrans/Cetus venit, 359n.10, 412n.20, 421n.37

Altissonis/Hin [sic] principes, 674

Aman novi/Heu Fortuna/Heu me, tristis est anima mea (Vitry), ▶ Table 5.1, 67–81, 83–84, **111–29**, 133–35, 144–48, 278

    dating and relationship to *Garrit* and *Tribum*, **67–81**

Amer amours/Durement/Dolor meus (Vitry?), 20, 331, 333, 654

Amis dont ton vis (Molins), 659

Amor vincens omnia/Maria preconio/Aptatur, 46

Amour dont tele est la puissance, 141–42

Amour trestout fort me point/La douce art m'estuet aprendre/T/Ct, 685

Amours qui a le pouoir/Faus Samblant m'a deceü/Vidi dominum (Machaut, M15), 193, **197–208**, 278, 646, 654

    puns, 207–8

    relation to Machaut, M10, 242–44

    word-painting, 197, 205–6

Apollinis eclipsatur/Zodiacum signis/In omnem terram (B. de Cluni), 20–21, 50–51, **283–99**, ▶ Ex. 16.1, ▶ Ex. 16.2, ▶ Ex. 16.3, ▶ Ex. 16.4, **325–41**, 347, 348, 350–52, 353, 355–58, 364, 367, 372, 373, 375–76, 377–83, 389, 390, 392–95, 396, 397, 533–36, 653

    citations in treatises, 294–97

    date, 328

    named musicians, 333–41

    related motets, 286–87

    relation to *Musicalis*, 330

    relation to *Musicorum collegio*, 350–52

    sources, 293–94

    taleae, 329, 331

Apostolo glorioso (Du Fay), 628, 632

Apta caro/Flos virginum/Alma redemptoris (Vitry?), 10, 29, 97, 352, 532*f*, 533, 534*t*, 537, 632, 647, 655

Are post libamina/Nunc surgunt in populo (Mayshuet), 307n.11, **445–48**, 458–60, 459*f*, 462–64, 466, 467

Argi vices Poliphemus/Tum Philemon rebus (Nicolas/Guillermus), 355n.1, 502, 504*t*, 510, 621, **627**, 629, 638

Arta/Musicus est ille qui perpensa racione, ▶ Ex. 21.1, ▶ Fig. 21.1, 287, 288, 299, 359, 362, 381, **389–92**, 675

Arte psallentes (Bartolomeus de Bononia), 396, 639

Ascendenti sonet geminacio/Viri Galilei, quid vos admiramini?, 161

Assumpta gemma virginum/Gratulandum mente pia/T/Ct, 682

Aucune gent m'ont demandé/Qui plus aimme plus endure/Fiat voluntas tua/Ct (Machaut, M5), 33, 70n.15

Aurea flammigeri (Antonius Romanus), 561–62

716 INDEX OF COMPOSITIONS

*Aurora vultu pulcrior/Ave virginum flos et vita/*T/ Ct, 682

Ave [rex gentis] anglorum, 474–75

Ave coronata, 294–97

Ave corpus sanctum/Protomartiris/Gloriose Stefani, 20, 504t, 509, 511, 512

Ave Maria gracia plena/O Maria gracia plena (Johannes Brassart), 632

Ave miles triumphalis, 483

Ave regina/Ave mater/Ave mundi (Dunstaple), 490t

Ave regina/Mater innocencie (Marchetto da Padova), 20, 288, 503–9, 504t, 511

Ave sancta mundi/Agnus Dei (Matteo da Perugia), 462n.36, 499–500, 502, 504t, 508–11

Ave vergene, 553n.11

Avete (tenor of *Musicorum collegio*), 348

Balsamus et munda cera (Du Fay), 639

Beatius se servans/Cum humanum (Vitry?), 102–4, 296–97, 312, 641, 650, 657

Belle com loiaus, 257, 257f

Benedicta viscera/Ave mater/Ora pro nobis (Gilet Velut), 35, 638, 673–75

Biaute qui toutes (Machaut), 660

Bone pastor Guillerme/Bone pastor, qui pastores/ Bone pastor (Machaut, M18), ▶ Ex. 13.1, 245–59

  dating, 251–57

  hocket section, 248–51

  proposed revision, 258–59

  texts, 245–48

Bonté de corps (Hubertus de Salinis), 544

[Cacciando per gustar]/Ay cinci ay toppi (Antonio Zacara da Teramo), 526

Caligo terre/Virgo mater, 458n.19

Cantano gl'angiol lieti, 502, 504t, 514

Carbunculus ignitus lilie, 245, 387, 420, 466, **468– 71,** 470f

Carminibus festos (Antonius Romanus), 509n.30

Carnalitas, luxuria, 133–37, 146

  texts, 134t

Caveus, 660

Ce est la bele flour (Ugolino of Orvieto), 547

Celice rex regum/Ingentem gentem, 499n.8

Celle dont ma joye, 660

*Certes mont fu de grant necessite/Nous devons tresfort amer/*T/Ct, 683

Cetus inseraphici/Cetus apostolici/Salve regina, 504t, 511

Christe, qui lux es et dies/Veni creator spiritus (Machaut, M21), 28–29, 184t, 278

*Christe qui supra sydera/Christe nostra salvatio/*T/ Ct, 683

Christe sanctorum/Tibi Christe/Tibi Christe (Dunstaple), 490t

Clarus ortu/Gloriosa mater (Antonius de Civitate; Antonio da Cividale), 35, **629–34,** 639

Colla iugo/Bona condit/Libera me (Vitry), 40, 68n.4, 123, 643, 653

Comes Flandrie/Rector creatorum/In cimbalis, 339, 499n.8

Comme le cerf, 660

Con plus (Hubertus de Salinis), 546t, 547

*Coume le serf a la clere fontainne/Lunne plainne d'umilite/*T/Ct, 685

Coument se poet/Se je chante/Qui prendroit, 332

Courtois et sages (Magister Egidius Augustinus), 364, 621, 639

Credo (Pennard), 437n.13

Credo, a3 (Hugo de Lantins), **Q15,** no. 68), 562

Credo, a3 (Hubertus de Salinis) **Q15,** no. 55), 540t

Credo, a3 (Hubertus de Salinis) (**Q15,** no. 64), 540t

Credo Anglicanum (attr. Dunstaple), 486–87

Credo Omni tempore, ▶ Ex. 23.1, ▶ Fig.23.1, 12, 54, 378, 402, 418, 421, **431–44**

Credo Opem nobis (Leonel), 468

Credo, see also Patrem omnipotentem

Credos in **Yox,** 402

Cristi morte nato mundo, 483

[Cristina] (Ciconia?), 504t, 511–12, **517–20,** 518f, 552–53, 554t

Cuer gai, 660

Cuers qui se sent, 660

Cum statua/Hugo princeps/Magister invidie (Vitry), 44, 106, 151, 157, 258, 289, 653

*Da, magne pater, rector Olimpi/Donis affatim, perfluit orbis/*T/Ct, 684

Dame de qui (Machaut), 660

Dame d'onnour, 654

Dame plaisans/Trop est la dolour/Neuma, 653

Dame sans per, 659

Danger refus, 660

D'ardant desir/Se fus d'amer, 20

De bon espoir/Puis que/Speravi (Machaut, M4), ▶ Ex.14.1, 178, 178f, **263–72**

De ce que fol (Molins), 659

De dimmi tu (Landini), 405

De fortune (Machaut), 659

De narcisus (Franciscus), 659

De petit peu (Machaut), 659

De terre en grec Gaulle appelle (Vitry), 346

De toutes flours (Machaut), 659

De ventre matris, 403–4

Degentis vita/Cum vix artidici/Vera pudicitia, 20, 286–87, 294 –97, 402, 418, 420–21, 647, 649, 656

Demonis astuto, 295

Deo gracias conclamemus, 295

Deo gracias papales/Deo gracias fidelis/Deo gracias salvator, 295, 499n.8, 631

Deo gratias, 666–67

  Deo gratias motets in Old Hall, 445–63

Deo per confidenciam, 653

Descendi in ortum meum (Dunstaple), ▶ Ex. 25.1, 486

Desolata mater/Que nutritos/Filios enutrivi, 68

Dessus une fontenelle, 658

INDEX OF COMPOSITIONS 717

Detractor est nequissima/Qui secuntur castra/
Verbum iniquum, 68, 77n.29, 79–80, 139–
40, 142
Deus creator omnium/Rex genitor/Doucement mi
reconfort, 458n.19
Deus compaignouns de Cleremunde, 397
Deus in adiutorium, 140, 141t
Dies dignus decorari/Demon dolens/Iste confessor
(Dunstaple), 54, 485, 490t
Dies sanctificatus, 329, 349
Dignum summo patri/Dulciter hymnos/T/Ct, 684
Dime, Fortuna, poi che tu parlasti (Antonio Zacara
da Teramo?), 624, 625, 628–29, 639
Doctorum principem/Melodia suavissima/T Vir mitis
(Ciconia), 55, 61, 63, 504t, 510, 513, 553–56,
554t, 560, 562–63, 562f, 565–66, 569
Domine quis habitabit/De veri cordis adipe/
Concupisco (contrafact of Se päour d'umble
astinance), 259n.48, 447n.5, 458n.19
Douce playsence/Garison selon nature/Neuma quinti
toni (Vitry), 52, 72, 94, 131, 145, 155, 241,
412, 655
relation to Machaut, M10, 241–42
tenor, 131
Ducalis sedes (Antonius Romanus), 509n.30, 561
Dulce melos personemus/Matrem Christi
rogitemus/T/Ct, 68

Ecclesie militantis (Du Fay), 634–35, 637, 639
En amer (Machaut), 659
En chantant, 257, 610
En Katerine solennia/Virginalis concio (Byttering),
466, 467–68, 467f, 479
En la saison (Hubertus de Salinis? Cunelier/
Cuvelier, Jo.?), 542n.30, 544–47, 546t, 626
En ma dolour, 648, 660
Entre Adan et Hanikel, 283
Entre Copin et Bourgeois, 283
Entre Jehan et Philippet, 283
Espoir me fuit, 659
Et in terra, 653
Excelsa civitas Vincencia (Bertrand Feragut), 633, 636
Eya dulcis/Vale placens (Tapissier), 638

Fa fa mi fa (Johannes Leodiensi[s]), 257n.40, 289n.20
Febus mundo oriens/Lanista vipereus/Cornibus
equivocis, 350n.17, 396
Felix virgo/Inviolata/Ad te suspiramus (Machaut,
M23), 656
Fenix arabie, 295
Ferre solet/Anatheos de gracia/Ave Maria
(Johannes Vavassoris), 5, 104n.45, 289n.20,
387, 412, 618
Firmissime fidem teneamus /Adesto sancta trinitas/
Alleluya (Vitry), 51–52, 83, 94, 102n.42, 117,
125, 141t, 142, 144–45, 147–50, 155, 609
Florentia mundi speculum/Marce pater pietatis, 504t,
511–12, 520–27, 521f, 533, 532f, 533n.6, 534t,
536, 537

Floret cum Vana Gloria/Florens vigor/Neuma
(Vitry?), 72, 131–37
texts, 131–35, 134t
Flos mundi, 474–75
Flos ortus/Celsa cedrus/Quam magnus pontifex
(Vitry), 251–52, 532f, 533–36, 609–13, 657
Flos regalis Katerina/Maxentius rex propere/T/Ct,
684
Flos vernalis/Fiat intencio, 20, 135, 656
Fons citharizancium (motetus of Sub Arturo),
380–81, 382, 395
Fons origo musicorum, 299, 380–82, 395
Fons tocius superbie/O livoris feritas/Fera pessima
(Machaut, M9), ▶ Ex. 9.1, 24, 51,
171–95, 653
alliteration, 188–90
hockets, 180–81, 185
ranges and cadences 181–84
rhymes, 187–88
rhythmic groupings, 190
talea, 177–78
tenor melody, color, 175–76
texts, 173, 186t
triplum and motetus, 179–80
Fortune, mere à/Ma dolour/T, 653
Franchois sunt nobles (Magister Egidius
Augustinus), 364
Fuiez de moi (Alain), 660
Fulgens iubar ecclesie dei/Puerpera, pura parens
(Du Fay), 674–75
Furnos reliquisti quare? (Egardus), 396, 397

Garrit gallus/In nova fert/Neuma (Vitry), ▶ Ex. 4.5,
67–81, 97–109, 136–37, 140–42, 144–46,
147–48, 149–50, 303–4, 331–33, 609–10
dating and relationship to Aman and Tribum,
67–81, 118, 124–27
interplay with Tribum/Quoniam, 104–9, 108f
quotations from Ovid, 99, 127–28
Gaude felix/Gaude mater/Anna parens (Dunstaple),
490t
Gaude felix parens Yspania nove prolis, 528
Gaude flore virginali (Dunstaple), ▶ Ex. 25.2, 486
Gaude virgo salutata/Gaude virgo singularis/Virgo
mater/[Ave gemma] (Dunstaple), 490t
Gaudeat et exultet . . . Papam querentes (see also
Novum sidus), 5, 499, 619–20, 638
Gemma florens militie/Hec est dies gloriosa/T/Ct,
666, 682
Già per gran nobeltà (Nicolaus Zacarie),
628–29, 639
Gloria (Loqueville), 437
Gloria (Queldryk), 437–38
Gloria Q15 no. 76 (Antonius Romanus), 561–62
Gloria, a3 (Hubertus de Salinis), 540t
Gloria Ad Thome (Leonel Power), 469–71
Gloria Clemens Deus artifex, 617–18, 638
Gloria Clementie pax, 621
Gloria in canon (Dunstaple), ▶ Ex. 25.3

718 INDEX OF COMPOSITIONS

Gloria *Jubilacio uni Deo* (Hubertus de Salinis), 540*t*, 545–48, 626, 638

Gloria *Suscipe Trinitas* (Ciconia), 548n.53, 626, 638

Gloria, *see also Et in terra*

Gracieus temps est (Jehannot de Lescurel), 115, 142

Gratiosus fervidus/Magnanimus opere (Gratiosus de Padua?), 20, 289, 499n.8, 504*t*, 510–11

Gratulemur Christicole (Johannes Brassart), 633–34

Han Diex! ou pourai je trouver, 140–42

Hareu! hareu! le feu/Helas! ou sera pris confors/ Obediens usque ad mortem (Machaut, M10),
▶ Ex. 12.1, **231–44**, 653
    choice of tenor, 231–33
    relation to other motets, 241–44
    tenor disposition, 235–37
    tenor motives in upper voices, 237–40
    texts, 233*t*, 234–35

Hareu, hareu, je la [chace], 654

He compaignons (Du Fay), 283

He doux regars, 660

Hé! Mors com tu/Fine Amour/Quare non sum mortuus (Machaut, M3), 45–46

Helas j'ay lonetamps/Plains sui d'amere/Infelix, 656

Helas! pour quoy virent/Corde mesto cantando/ Libera me (Machaut, M12), 245

Herodis in pretorio/Herodis in atrio/Hey, hure lure, 458–59, 459n.21

Hic est precursor, 504*t*, 529

Hic est vere martir, 7, 570

Hodie puer nascitur/Homo mortalis, firmite/T/ Ct, 684

Honte paour (Machaut), 660

Hostis Herodes, 2

Humblement [chace], 657

Hunc diem festis celebremus hymnis /Precursoris verbi solennia/T/Ct, 666, 683

Ihesu salvator seculi/Quo vulneratus scelere (Hubertus de Salinis), 532*f*, 534*t*, 536, 537, 540*t*, 546–47, 548, **549*f***, 625–26

Impudenter circumivi/Virtutibus laudibilis (Vitry), 29, 34, 140, 141*t*, 162–63, 286, 532*f*, 533, 534*t*, 536, 537, 674

In dedicatione templi decantabat populus laudem, 358

In omnem terram, (tenor of *Apollinis* and *Sub Arturo*), 319, 329, 347, 349, 358, 375–76, 380, 381

In talem transfiguratur/Iubar lustrat radiosum/T/ Ct, 683

In virtute/Decens carmen/Clamor meus (Vitry), 653

Incessanter expectavi/Virtutis ineffabilis/Alleluya, 674–75, 683

Inclite flos orti Gebenensis (Matheus de Sancto Johanne), 460, 620, 639

Inter amenitatis/O livor/Reverrenti, 143–44, 656

Inter densas/Imbribus irriguis, 35–37, 53–55, 61–63, 415, 438, 472, 675

Iste confessor, 659

Isti sunt viri sancti, 394

Iubar solis universa/Fulgor solis non vilescit/T/Ct, 674–75, 682

J'ai . . . Imbertus/Hubertus de Salinis(?), 546*t*, 547

J'ai grant desespoir, 660

J'ai le chapelet, 654

Ja couars n'ara, 658

Je comence/Et se je serai li secons/Soulés viex, 657

Je languis, 296

Je voi douleur/Fauvel nous a fait/Autant, 79

Jour a jour la vie, 660

Jure quod in opere [recte opera]/Scariotis geniture/ Supreme matris, 66, 656

Karissimi, 657

Katerina pia virgo purissima, 528

Kyri sponse, 656

Kyrie Clemens pater, conditor syderum, 617–18, 638

Laissiez parler, 660

L'amoreuse flour/En l'estat d'amere/[Sicut fenum arui], 655

L'ardure qu'endure/Tresdouz espoir/Ego rogavi Deum, 647, 658

L'autre jour, 655

Las . . . (Hubertus de Salinis?), 546*t*

Lasse! comment/Se j'aim mon loyal/Pour quoy me bat (Machaut, M16), 653

Laudibus dignis merito (Jacopo da Bologna?), 504*t*, 509n.26, 570

Laurea martiri/Conlaudanda est/Proba me domine (Matteo da Perugia?), 502, 504*t*, 511, 512

Lay de Plour (Machaut), 269

Le ray au soleyl (Ciconia), 551, 625

Leonarde, pater inclite, 504*t*, 526, 533n.6

Letetur plebs fidelis/Pastor qui revelavit (Nicolaus Zacarie), 628

Letificans tristantes, 396

Li enseignement/De tous les biens/Ecce tu pulchra, 656, 672

Linor aula, 296

Los prijs honeur, 461n.29

Loyelon loielete, 658

Luce clarus, 298

Luceat laudis/Organizanter, 645, 654

Lucis eterne splendor/Veni, splendor mirabilis/T/Ct, 684

Lux purpurata/Diligite (Jacopo da Bologna), 504*t*, 509n.26, 511–14, 532–33, 532*f*, 534*t*, 536, 537

Ma dame m'a conge, 657

Magne Deus potencie/Genus regale esperie (Johannes Brassart), 35, 632–34, 639

Magni patris magna mira/Ovent Cyprus, Palestina/ T/Ct, 683

Marce Marcum, 504*t*, 511–14, 526, 533n.6

INDEX OF COMPOSITIONS   719

Maria, mare gratie/O Maria, celi porta/T/Ct, 683
Martine sancte pontifex, 296n.42, 631
Martyrum gemma/Diligenter/A Christo (Machaut, M19), 655
Mass (Machaut), **209–29**, 216*f*
   analysis of Gloria, 222–26
   contratenor, 223–24, 225–27
Mater alma clementie/Deitatis triclinium/T, 682
Mater digna Dei, 499n.8
Mater formosa/Gaude virgo, 140–41
Mater munda/Mater sancta Dei, 466, 471–72
Maugré mon cuer/De ma dolour/Quia amore (Machaut, M14), 653
Merci ou mort, 660
Miles Christi, 473–77
Mirar non posso (Hugo de Lantins), 628, 639
Missa Alma redemptoris (Leonel Power), 59
Missa Da gaudiorum premia (Dunstaple), 59
Missa Jesu Christe Fili Dei (Dunstaple) 59
Missa Rex seculorum (Dunstaple or Leonel Power) 59
Missa Sub tuum praesidium (Obrecht), 58–59
Misse Caput, 58–59
Mon chant en/Qui dolereux/Tristis est anima, 295n.39, 653, 674–75, 658
Mon mal en bien, en plaisir ma dolour/Toustens je la serviray/T/C, 674–75, 685
Monachant de morte wilhelmi (=Mon chant), 295
Mulierum, 658
Musicalis sciencia/Sciencie laudabili/[Alleluia Dies sanctificatus], ▶ Ex. 17.1, 50–51, 298, 306–8, 319–20, **325–41**, 349, 351–52, 353, 355–58, 363, 364, 372, 391–92, 397
   named musicians, 333–41
   taleae, 329
Musicorum collegio/In templo Dei posita/Avete, ▶ Ex. 18.1, 11–12, 26, 284–87, 306–8, 317, 329–31, 330*f*, **343–52**, 353, 355–58, 358, 372, 373, 377–78, 380, 381–82, 390, 391–92, 397
   calendrical aspects, 12–13
   relation to *Musicalis*, 329–30, 330*f*
Musicorum decus et species, 396
Musicorum inter collegia, 294–97, 396

Nate regnantis super astra/Maria, proles regina/T/Ct, 682
Natus in patris gremio/Apparuit sol hodie/T/Ct, 682
Nequicie peniteo, 296–97
Neuma, as tenor, 67, 94–95, 109, 131
Nicolai solemnia, 296n.42, 631n.98
Non eclipsis atra ferrugine, ▶ Fig. 21.1, 299, 392–95
Nova stella, 643, 658
Nove cantum melodie (Gilles Binchois), 283–84
Novum sidus orientis/Gaudeat et exultet, 4–5, 34, 499, 619–20, 638
Nulla pestis est gravior/Plange, nostra regia/Vergente, 68
Nuper rosarum flores (Du Fay), 636, 639
Nymphes des bois (Josquin), 284

O admirabile, 656
O Adonay, domus Israel /Pictor eterne syderum/Ct/T, 677*t*, 684
O amicus sponsi primus/Precursoris preconia (Johannes?), 26–28, **401–29**, **423***f*, 432, 448, 492
O Antoni expulsor demonum, ▶ Ex. 26.3, **527–28**
O beatum incendium (Ciconia), 553, 554*t*, 564, 571
O canenda/Rex quem metrorum (Vitry?), 37–38, 286–87, 338–39, 614, 652, 655
O clavis David aurea /Quis igitur aperiet/T/Ct, 684
O crux preciosa, 657
O dira nacio/Mens in nequicia/T, 20, 647, 654
O Emanuel, rex noster/Magne virtutum conditor/T/Ct, 684
O felix templum jubila (Ciconia), 504*t*, 512, 513n.43, 520, 547, 552–53, 554*t*, **556–68**, 557*f*, **590–94**, 591*f*, 592*f*, 595*f*, 628–29
O flos fragrans (Johannes Brassart), 633–34
O gloriosa domina, 356
O Maria virgo davitica/O Maria maris stella, 27–28, 27*f*, 295, 296–97, 504*t*, 510–11, 512, 558, 568
O Padua sidus preclarum (Ciconia), 504t, 513n.43, 554*t*, 563, 565, 587*f*, **595–601**
O Petre Christi discipule (Ciconia), 504*t*, 554*t*, 558, 564, **571–74**, 623–25, 638
O Philippe/O bone dux, 258, 655
O proles Hispanie/O sidus Hispanie (Du Fay), 564, 567, 570
O proles Yspanie/O proles nobile depositum (Ciconia?), 504*t*, 553–56, 554*t*, 564, 565, **567–71**
O que purificacio, 655
O Radix Yesse splendida /Cunti fundent precamina/T/Ct, 684
O Rex virtutum, gloria /Quis possit dign[e] exprimere/T/Ct, 684
O sacra virgo virginum/Tu, nati nata suscipe/T/Ct, 684
O Sapientia incarnata/Nos demoramur, benigne rector/T/Ct, 684
O virum omnimoda veneracione/O lux et decus tranensium/O beate Nicholae (Ciconia), 504*t*, 529, 552–53, 554*t*, 558–59, 559*f*, 561, 564, 566–67, 590
O vos omnes, 346
O/Nostris lumen tenebris, 140, 141*t*, 256–57, 610n.20
Omni habenti (probably not = Omnis terra/Habenti dabitur), 298
Omni tempore (Credo), ▶ Ex. 23.1, ▶ Fig. 23.1, **431–44**
Omnis terra/Habenti dabitur, 358n.7
Omnium bonorum plena (Loyset Compère), 284
On parole/A Paris/Frese nouvele, 44
Orbis orbatus/Vos pastores (Vitry?), 72, 142, **147–50**
Ore Pandulfum modulare dulci, 396
Oseletto selvaggio (Jacopo da Bologna?), 283, 509, 514

720 INDEX OF COMPOSITIONS

Padu[a]. . . ex panis . . . serenans/Tenor *Pastor bonus* (Ciconia?), 504*t*, 514, 553–56, 554*t*, 560–61, 563–65, **567–71**, 675

Pantheon abluitur/*Apollinis eclipsatur* (additional voice for *Apollinis*), 293–94, 308, **314–17** ▶ Ex. 16.3, 318–19, 321, 323, 351, 532*f*, 533, 534*t*, 536, 537

Par grant soif, clere fontainne/*Dame de tout pris*/T/Ct, 685

Par les bons Gedeons (Filippotto da Caserta), 621, 639

Par maintes foys, 295

Pastoribus, 658

Pater ave, 657

Patrem omnipotentem (Denis le Grant), 657

Patrem omnipotentem (Steve Sort), 658

Patrie pacis, 419n.34

Per grama protho paret/*Valde honorandus est beatus Johannes* (Vitry?), 131, 251–52, **608–14**, 638

Personet armonia dulcis cantus, melodia/*Consonet altisonis laudes notulis Katerine*/T, 675, 678–79, 683

Petre clemens/*Lugentium*/T (Vitry), **614–16**, 637, 638, 654, 672, 674

Petre petre, 655

Petrum Marcello/*O Petre antistes* (Ciconia), 35, 55, 504*t*, 510–11, 530, 552–53, 554*t*, 560–61, 563, 565, 567, 672n.42

Phi millies ad te/*O creator*/*Iacet granum*/*Quam sufflabit* (Vitry), 72, 102, 289, 312, 346, 616

Phiton le merveilleux (Machaut), 659

Pictagore per dogmata/*O terra sancta, suplica*/*Rosa vernans caritatis*, 393n.13, 618, 638

Pie pater (Antonius de Civitate; Antonio da Cividale), 561

Plasmatoris humani generis/*Verbigine mater ecclesia* (Nicolas Grenon), 562

Plaude decus mundi (Christoforus de Monte), 509n.30

Plausu querulo/*Plausu querulo*, ▶ Ex. 31.1, 20, 641, **651–52**, 651*f*, 655

Plures errores, 412

Porta celi fulgentibus/*Assit deus huic domui*/T/Ct, 682

Portio nature/*Ida capillorum*/*Ante thronum* (Henricus, or Egidius de Pusiex), 35, 338, 646–47, 653, 675

Post missarum solennia/*Post misse* (**Ivrea**), 37–38, 296–97, 421n.37, 448–52, 453*f*, 457–60, 654

Post missarum solennia/*Post misse* (Mayshuet?, **OH** and RC), 445, 449–52, 453*f*, 457–60, 458*f*

Pour ce que mes chans fais (Machaut), 332

Pour ce que point fui de la amere espine/*A toi, vierge, me represente*/T/Ct, 685

Povero zappator (Lorenzo da Firenze), 510, 560

Preco preheminencie/*Precursor premittitur*/ textless/ *Inter natos* (Dunstaple), 482–83, 490*t*

Presulum quo fantus, 499n.8

Principum nobilissime (Franciscus = Landini?), 288–89, 504*t*, 510, 533, 569

Prosapie, 656

Psallat chorus in novo carmine/*Eximine pater et regie* (Hubertus de Salinis), 532*f*, 534*t*, 536, 537, 540*t*, 543, 548, 550, 550*f*

Psallentes zinzugia (*additional voice to Apollinis*), ▶ Ex. 16.4, 287, **317–19**, 357, 380, 389, 536

Puisque pites, 654

Pura placens pulcra/*Parfundement plure Absolon*, 155–56, 458n.19, 658

Quant en moy/*Amour et biauté*/*Amara valde* (Machaut, M1), 248

Quant la pree, 656

Quant vraie amour/*O series summe rata*/*Super omnes speciosa* (Machaut, M17), 24–25, 24*f*

Quare fremuerunt, 77, 84, 83n.2, 610

Qui es promesses/*Ha! Fortune*/*Et non est qui adjuvat* (Machaut, M8), ▶ Ex.14.3, **272–79**, 276*f*, 278*f*, 646, 654

Qui patris atris honoris/*Paraclite spiritus*/T/Ct, 682

Quicunques vuet, 660

Quod jactatur (Ciconia), 405n.11, 625

Quorum doctrina fulget ecclesia (tenor of *Non eclipsis*), 392, 394

Reverenter veneremur/*Venerandum crucis lignum*/ T/Ct, 682

Revien espoir, 659

Rex Karole/*Leticie pacis* (Philippe Royllart), 4–5, 29, 35, 37–38, 97n.31, 286, 387, 397, **499**, 528, 532*f*, 533, 534*t*, 536, 537, 618–20, 646–47, 672

Rex rondellorum, 396

Rex sancte Edwarde, 482

Rite maiorem Jacobum canamus/*Artibus summis*/ *Ora pro nobis dominum* (Du Fay), 55

Romanorum rex (Johannes de Sarto), 283–84

Roses et lis (Magister Egidius Augustinus), 364

Rota versatilis, 678

S'il estoit nulz qui pleindre/*S'Amours tous amans joïr*/*Et gaudebit cor vestrum* (Machaut, M6), 53, 261

S'il m'est des d[. . .], 532*f*

Salvatoris mater pia/*O Georgi Deo care*/*Benedictus Marie Filius qui ve-* (Damett), 473, 475–78

Salve cleri speculum, 2

Salve mater Domini/*Salve templum gratie*/*-in nomine Domini* (Sturgeon), 473, 475, 477, 478–79

Salve regina 'Virgo mater ecclesie' (Hubertus de Salinis), 540*t*, 546n.47

Salve scema/*Salve salus*/textless/*Cantant celi* (Dunstaple), 490*t*

Sanctus (Pycard), 405n.10

Sanctus ('papale') (Du Fay), 639

Sanctus in eternis regnans, pater inque supernis/ *Sanctus et ingenitus pater atque carens genitura*/ T/Ct, 675, 683

INDEX OF COMPOSITIONS 721

Sanctus itaque patriarcha Leuntius (Antonio da Cividale), 528
Scariotis geniture/Jure quod/Superne matris (Vitry?), 68, 143, 144, 656
Schag melodie, 296
Se cuers ioans/Rex beatus/Ave (Vitry?), 68, 79–81, 140–44, 141*t*, 658
Se Galaas (Jo. Cunelier/Cuvelier), 544–46
Se grace n'est/Cum venerint (*Ite missa est* of Mass of Tournai), 20, 286–87, 452, 511, **579–80, 580***f*, 655
Se j'ai par la vostre, 655
Se j'onques a mon vivant, 141–42
Se je chant mains [chace] (Denis le Grant), 332, 336, 650, 654
Se je di qu'en elle tire/Tres fort m'abrasa/T/Ct, 685
Se Lancelot, 660
Se päour d'umble astinance/Diex tan desir estre amés de m'amour/Concupisco, 447–48n.5, 654; *see also Domine quis habitabit*
Servant regem/O Philippe (Ludowice)/Rex regum, 68, 79, 139–40, 142, 144, 610, 656
Sì dolce non sonò (Landini), 510
Si nichil actuleris/In precio precium (Hubertus de Salinis), 532*f*, 534*t*, 540*t*, 543, 548, 550
Solaris ardor Romani/Gregorius sol seculi/Petre tua navicula/Mariounette douche, 458n.19
Specialis virgo/Salve parens inclita (Dunstaple), 488, 490*t*
Stella celi (Cooke), 471
Ducalis sedes/Stirps mocinigo (Antonius Romanus), 636
Sub Arturo plebs/Fons citharizancium/In omnem terram (Alanus), ⊙ Ex. 20.1, 26, 284–85, 287, 288, 297–99, 304–8, 328–29, 347–349, 355–59, 362–63, **369–88**, 390–92, 393–95, 402, 411–13, 419–22, 436, 442, 462–64, 469–71, 487, 647
Suffragiose virginis, 419n.35
Summe summy (Gilet Velut), 673
Summus secretarius (Johannes Brassart), 633–34
Super cathedram/Presidentes, 142–44
Supremum est mortalibus (Du Fay), 635–36, 639
Sus une fontayne (Ciconia), 551, 566–67, 577, 625

Tant doucement (Machaut), 660
Te dignitas presularis (Johannes Brassart), 633–34, 639
Thalamus puerpere, thronus salomonis/Quomodo cantabimus sub iniqua lege/T, 101n.38
Thoma tibi obsequia, 411–12, 652, 655
Tous corps/De souspirant cuer/Suspiro (Machaut, M2), **260–62**
Toustans que mon esprit mire/Qui porroit amer/T/ Ct, 685
Tout autresi con l'ente fet venir/Le arrousers de l'eve qui chiet jus (Thibaut de Champagne), 269

Tra quante regione (Hugo de Lantins), 628
Trahunt in precipitia/An diex/Displicebat, 140–42
Tribum que non abhorruit/Quoniam secta latronum/ Merito hec patimur (Vitry), 20, 40, 67–81, 83–97, ⊙ Ex. 4.1, 141–45, 147–48, 497
    dating and relationship to *Aman* and *Garrit*, 67–81
    interplay with *Garrit gallus/In nova*, 104–9, 108*f*
    tenor, 91–96, 179
    texts, 88–91
Trinitatem, 504*t*, 513–14, 516–17
Triumphat hodie/Trop est fol – Si que la nuit, 458n.19
Trop ay dure/Par sauvage, 672
Trop plus est.belle/Biauté paree/Je ne sui mie (Machaut, M20), 56, 654
Tu qui gregem/Plange, regni respublica!/Apprehende arma et scutum et exurge (Machaut, M22), 29
Tu venerandus presul Amandus, 499n.8
Tuba sacre fidei proprie/In arboris empiro prospere/ Virgo sum (Vitry), 29, 123, 256, 286, 296n.42, 411–12, 657

Una panthera (Ciconia), 551
unidentified ballade (Hubertus de Salinis), 546*t*
unidentified virelai (Hubertus de Salinis?), 546*t*
Ut te per omnes/Ingens alumnus Padue (Ciconia), 55, 504*t*, 512, 554*t*, 564–66, 567n.42

Vasilissa ergo gaude (Du Fay), 628
Ve constat, 656
Venecie mundi splendor/Michael qui Stena domus/T (Ciconia), 504*t*, 509–10, 554*t*, 563, 565, 586, 587*f*
Veni sancte spiritus et emitte/Sancti spiritus assit (a3, Dunstaple), 488–89, 489*t*, 490*t*
Veni sancte spiritus et emitte/Veni sancte spiritus et infunde/Veni creator/Mentes tuorum (a4, Dunstaple), 35, 148, 469–71, 482–83, 489, 489*t*, 490*t*
Venite adoremus/Salve sancta (Carmen), 638
Vera pudicitia, 296
Veri almi pastoris musicale collegium (Conradus de Pistoria), 396, 639
Victima laudum pascalis/Victimis in pascalibus/ Victime paschali/Ct, 668, 677, 682
Virginalis concio, 346
    see also *En Katerine* (motetus)
Virginem mire pulcritudinis, 295, 631
Vos leonis, 654
Vos quid admiramini/Gratissima virginis species/ Gaude gloriosa (Vitry), ⊙ Ex. 8.2, 25–26, 51–52, **151–67**, 420, 655

Zodiacum signis (motetus of Apollinis eclipsatur) Zolomina zelus/Nazarea que decora/Ave Maria, 655

Index of Manuscripts

For these sigla see the List of Manuscripts on pp. xxvii–xxxiv. Archival sources are mostly not indexed here. For the benefit of digital users, indexed terms that span two pages (e.g., 52–53) may appear on only one of those pages. Where an item appears in a table, only the first page of that table is indexed (*t*).

Aachen, 151, 157–59, 160–61, 163, 448–49, 450n.8, 452–57, 615, 616, 638, 654–55
Ao, 502, 504*t*, 627
Apt, 653, 658–59
Arras983, 653, 659
Autun152, 659

Bamberg, 543n.32, 655
BarC853, 285, 293, 294, 309–10, **313–14**, 536, 653, 655, 638
BarC971, 293, 305, 309–10, 312, 319, 638, 653, 656, 658
Basel71, 499, 619, 638
Basel72, 34, 499, 619–20, 638
Belfast, 499n.8
Ber49, 653
Ber190, 659
Berlin, Staatsbibliothek, Ms. Mus.theor. 1325, 290n.22
Bergamo589, 659
Bern, 34n.38, 534*t*
Boverio, 624–25, 639
BOZ1, 296
BOZ2, 296–97
BOZ3, 631n.98
Br19606, 131, 139–50, 256–57, 653–59
Brescia5, 659
Brive, Bibliothèque municipale, MS 1, 527–28
Brno, 293, 309–10, 312–13, 319, 653
Brussels758, 655–56
Brussels5170, 151, 160, 165–66, 534*t*, 655
Br19606, 34, 84, 131, 139–143, 256, 333, 534, 658
BU2216, 554*t*, 558–59, 566, 636, 639
Bud298, 659

Ca29, 659
Ca165, 143–44
Ca1328, 131, 141–43, 151, 160, 166, 258, 650, 653–59
Canberra, ▶ Table 25.1
Cant128/6, 474n.20, 483

Ce70, 484
Ce300, 486
Chantilly, 3, 35, 287, 297, 353, 360, 361*f*, 362–63, 372, 376–77, 379, 381, 393n.13, 460, 463, 499, 542, 544–46, 546*t*, 620, 626, 628, 638–39, 641, 646–47, 649–50, 653–60
Civ57, 659
Civ98, 625, 658–60
Columbia, ▶ Table 25.1
Cop17a, 639
Cortona1, 651, 653, 655, 659
Cortona2, 295n.40
Cu710, 476n.24
Cu4435, 299, 395, 486 ▶ Table 25.1
Cu5963, ▶ Table 25.1
Cyprus, 661–82

Darmstadt521, 143, 534*t*, 657
Darmstadt3471, 543n.32
Darmstadt, Hessische Landes- und Hochschulbibliothek MS 705, 290n.22
Dor, 438
Douai74, 5, 5n.17, 104n.45, 289n.20, 387n.45, 412
Durham20, 29, 151, 155–59, 163–66, 287, 297, 343, 346, 458–59, 459n.21, 459*f*, 467n.5, 655, 658

Egerton, ▶ Table 25.1
Egidi, 504*t*, 521*f*, 526–27, 533n.6, 536
Esc10, 151–52, 157–59, 655

Faenza, 17, 659
Ferrell(Vg), 173, 261, 267, 274, 653–60
Fleischer, 658
Florence29, 543n.34
Fountains, 379, 421, 432, 438, 621–23, 638
Fp26, 550, 659–660
Franus, 294
Fribourg2, 358n.8
Fribourg260, 289n.21, 655–56

Gdańsk2315, 499n.8

724 INDEX OF MANUSCRIPTS

Ghent3360, 659
GR219, 659
GR224, 504*t*, 533n.6, 638
GRss, 638

Houghton122, 504*t*, 516, 540*t*, 546, 638

Ivrea, 29, 34, 151, 156–58, 160, 163, 164–66,
258, 274, 293, 309–12, 319, 379, 438n.15,
448–60, 614–18, 638, 646–47, 649–50, 653–
60, 672–75

Jena105, 653

Karlsruhe82, 20, 650, 656
Kassel1, 659
Koblenz701, 20, 141–43, 147–48, 650, 656
Kremsmünster149, 653

Lausanne8076, 527–28
Leiden342A, 653
Leiden2515, 293, 299, 309–10, 312, 392, 394–
95, 653–59
Leiden2720, 678
Leipzig223, 293, 309–10, 319, 653, 658
Leipzig431, 653
Lo4, 481n.29
Lo6, 17n.1
Lo12, 474n.17
Lo13, 481n.29
Lo24, 431n.2 ▶ Table 25.1
Lo36, 660
Lo53, 474n.18
Lo565, 474n.17
Lo763, 468
Lo861, 481n.29
Lo978, 3n.9
Lo1776, 481n.29
Lo4909, 17n.2, 19–20
Lo24198, 458n.19
Lo29987, 502, 504*t*, 538
Lo36579, 431n.2 ▶ Table 25.1
Lo40725, 431n.2
Lo54324, 486
Lo62132A, 101n.38
LoTNA, 285, 287, 293–94, 299, 313, 317–19, 389,
536, 653
Lwa12185, 101n.38, 161n.22, 421n.39
Lwa33327, 543n.32
Lucca184, 563

MachautA, 3, 28, 172–73, 259, 261, 267, 641, 653–60
MachautB, 653–60
MachautC, 173, 254–55, 259, 261, 268,
272, 653–60
MachautE, 226, 277, 646, 653–60
MachautG, 653–60

Maidstone, 486
Mainz, Stadtbibliothek, MS II 375, 290n.22
McV, 608, 612, 638, 657–59
Melk391, 660
Melk950, 296
Michaelbeuren10, 657
Mo, 33, 4n.16, 46n.17, 56n.43, 96n.28, 143–44, 283–
84, 331–32, 362, 543n.32, 655n.53
ModA, 396, 460n.26, 460n.27, 462n.36, 463, 499–
500, 502, 504*t*, 620, 625, 639, 659
ModB, 3–4, 483, 484, 639
Montefortino, 499n.8
Morgan396, 659–60
Morgan978, 115
Mu716, 657
Mu3223, 499n.8
Mu3224, 527
Mu15611, 659
Mu29775, 84–85, 142
MuEm, 27–28, 504*t*, 512, 543n.32, 639, 660

Newberry, 362–63
Norwich6, 486n.50
Nuremberg9, 499n.8, 631, 656
Nuremberg9a, 659

OH, 379, 384–86, 387, 405n.10, 415, 421, 431–32,
437–38, 443, **445–64**, **465–93**
dating, 465–66
Ox7, 155, 358, 447n.5, 458n.19, 482, 654, 658
Ox16, 504*t*, 517–20, 552, 554*t*, 563
Ox27, 431n.2
O31, ▶ Table 25.1
Ox32, 445–48, 450–51, 458, ▶ Table 25.1
Ox42, 497n.1
Ox81, 2, 148
Ox112, 504*t*, 508
Ox213, 35, 396, 437, 503, 504*t*, 534*t*, 536, 540*t*, 542,
545–48, 554*t*, 556, 563, 626, 628–29, 633–34,
638–39, 659, 662–64, 673
Ox271*, 141–43
Ox308, 332
OxAS56, 293, 650, 653, 656
OxC118, 484n.41
OxM267, ▶ Table 25.1
OxNC362, 458n.19
OxS26, 482n.33
OxU192, ▶ Table 25.1

Pad14, 658
Pad658, 293, 309, 312–13, 653
Pad675, 638
Pad1106, 27, 34, 289, 502, 504*t*, 510, 512,
514, 520, 533, 543n.32, 553–58, 554*t*, 561,
567–71, 574
Pad1115, 554*t*
Pad1475, 504*t*, 534*t*, 621, 638

Paris146, 2, 67–81, 83–109, 111–29, 135, 139–50, 257, 607–9, 655–58
Paris196, 659
Paris279, 68n.6, 376n.13
Paris568, 364, 659
Paris571, 68n.5, 77n.29, 84, 139–44, 255, 259, 655
Paris837, 115n.9
Paris844, 654
Paris934, 84, 155, 256, 412, 652, 655
Paris2195, 75n.27
Paris2444, 534t, 651, 655, 657
Paris3343, 615, 638, 654
Paris11411, 543n.32
Paris12044, 91–92
Paris14741, 272
Paris22069, 534t, 536, 651, 655, 657
Pepys1594, 659–60
Perugia2, 528
Perugia3065, 563
Philadelphia15, 659
Philadelphia614, 659
Philadelphia658, 487
Pic, 287, 297, 325, 327f, 330–32, 333, 650, 654, 656
Pra9, 659–60
Pra103, 296, 396n.17
Princeton103, 432, 437n.13

Q1, 540t
Q15, 3–4, 26–28, 34–35, 297, 372, 375–79, 388, 487–88, 499, 501–3, 504t, 512, 516, 528–30, 536, 542–43, 540t, 545–48, 550, 553–63, 554t, 557f, 562f, 567, 571, 616, 625–26, 632, 633–36, 638–39, 642, 662–64, 673

Redi71, 298n.46
Reina, 544, 639, 659–60
Robertsbridge, 346, 650, 656
Rostock, 84n.5, 142

SanGiorgio, 504t, 509
Seville25, 17n.1, 366, 500–1, 509
Siena30, 17n.1, 363n.17
Siena36, 528–29, 554t, 558
SienaRavi 3, 528
SL2211, 286, 293–94, 305, 314–17, 499–500, 504t, 513, 521f, 526, 529, 531–50, 552, 626, 638, 653, 655, 659–60
Solsona109, 658
Speciálnik, 294
Sq, 364, 538

Stras, 285, 293, 294, 297, 309–10, 312–17, 319, 338, 396, 396n.16, 536, 540t, 626, 638, 646, 653–60

Tallinn, 487, ⏵ Table 25.1
Tarragona1, 534t, 653
Tarragona2, 286, 293, 309–10, 653
Todi, 660
Toul94, 658
Tourn27, 655
Tr87, 143–44, 632–35, 639, 656, 659
Tr90, 639
Tr92, 639
Tr93, 639
Trém, 2–3, 144, 274, 286–87, 293, 331–32, 336, 448–49, 638, 641–60
Troyes1397, 534t
Troyes1949, 257n.40
Turin10, 660

Utrecht37, 536n.11, 540t, 548, 626, 660

V&A, ⏵ Table 25.1
Vat307, 148
Vat1260, 657
Vat5321, 18
Venice24, 286–87
Venice97, 515n.44
Venice145, 540t, 626, 638
Vienna123a, 657–58
Vienna2856, 657
Vienna3244, 653
Vienna4195, 615–16, 638, 654
Vienna5094, 294, 310, 312, 653, 657
Vienna661, 527–28
Vienna922, 294, 309, 653

W1, 7n.20
Warsaw378, 638
Warsaw8054, 553
Washington1400, 397
WashingtonJ6, 17n.1, 363n.17
WolkA, 660
WolkB, 660
Worcester160, 482
Wrocław16, 295, 296, 396n.16, 631, 638
Wrocław411, 653, 655, 658
Würz, 534t, 653, 657

YorkN3, 143–44, 656
Yox, 287, 297, 372–73, 377, 378, 379, 401–29, 431–44, 656

General Index

Incidental and ubiquitous mentions, and most footnote mentions, are not indexed. Principal entries are in boldface. For the benefit of digital users, indexed terms that span two pages (e.g., 52–53) may appear on only one of those pages. Where an item appears in a table, only the first page of that table is indexed (*t*). Where a figure or example extends over more than one page, only the first page is indexed (*f*).

accidentals, 228, 323, 348, 443

acrostics, 5, 115, 206, 252, 288–89, 338–39, 364, 508–10, 544, 570, 608, 612–14, 621, 666–67, 675, 682–84

Adam the Deacon, 369–72

Agincourt motets, 472–77

Alain, *see* Index of Compositions: *Fuiez de moi*

Alanus, J., 288, 297, 304, **369–87**, 463

see also Index of Compositions: *Sub Arturo plebs*

Alanus (Aleyn), Johannes (Chapel Royal member, canon of Windsor, d. 1373), 288, 383–84, 386–87, 463–64

Alebram, brother of Gwillelmus 'Malcharte', 464

Aleyn, W., 288

Alexander V, Antipope, *see* Filargo, Pietro

Alís Raurich, Cristina, 20, 135, 650

alliteration, 135, 173, 188–92, 277, 347, 418, 492–93, 675, 678–79

Allsen, Jon Michael, 35, 50

alteration, 36, 53–54, 101, 147, 155, 160, 259–62, 266–67, 310–13, 316–19, 359–62, 374, 378–79, 421, 432, 434, 436, 467, 479, 492, 520, 561–63

before or by a dot, 101–2, 147, 261–62

irregular, 157–58, 260–62

minim, 312–13, 316, 319, 331–32, 362, 379, 382, 402, 421

Amadeus VIII of Savoy (Antipope Felix V), 661–62

Amatori, Petrus, 355, 363, 366

analysis, relation to contemporary sources, 210–15

Andreas de Florentia, 500

Anne of Lusignan, Duchess of Savoy, 661–62, 681

and the Cyprus manuscript, 664–65

Antonio da Cividale (Antonius de Civitate or Civitato), 503; *see also* Index of Compositions: *Aurea flammigeri, Carminibus festos, Ducalis sedes*

Antonio da Tempo, *Summa artis rithmici vulgaris dictaminis*, 514–15

Antonio Zacara da Teramo, *see* Zacara

Antonius Romanus, 503; *see also* Index of Compositions: Gloria **Q15** no. 76 Apel, Willi, 49–50

Apollo, 301–2, 303–4, 380–81

Arnulf of St Ghislain, 579–80, 583

ars nova:

innovations, 143–44, 254, 311–12

treatises, 272

audience for motets, 13–14

Augustinian friars, 355–56 ·

Augustinus de Florencia, 353, 355, 362–63

Avogadro, Pietro, 680–81

B. de Cluni (Cluny), 288, 302–4, 307–8, 328, 357, 373, 394–95

signature in motet, 288

see also Index of Compositions: *Apollinis*

Bagarotti family, 680

Bartolomeus de Bononia, 396; *see also* Index of Compositions: *Arte psalentes*

Bate, Henry, 336

Beck, Eleonora M., 503–8

Becker, Ph. Aug., 115, 145

Becket, Thomas, 468, 652

Beggiamo family, 681

Benedict XII, Pope, 340–41, 614

Benedict XIII, Pope (Pedro de Luna), 364–66, 572

Bertrand, Pierre, Cardinal, 365

Besseler, Heinrich, 145, 147, 512, 558, 585, 635, 661–62, 665, 674, 680

on isorhythm, 13–14, 39–42, **46–52**, 55–57, 62

theory of *Harmonieträger*, 585

Bichomus, Nicholaus (Nicholas Beauchamp? Beecham?), 355, 362

Binchois, Gilles, *see* Index of Compositions: *Nove cantum melodie*

Bixolus, Belinus, 508

Blachly, Alexander, 118–23

Blavot, Petrus, 325–27, 335, 336, 340

Blithe, Richard, 369–72, 385–86

Boen, Johannes:

Ars [musice], 97n.31, 197n.3, 286

Musica, 136n.10, 328, 579–80, 580*f*

Boethius, 301–4, 308, 309, 357, 369–72, 373, 389, 390, 391–92

Boniface IX, Pope, 539, 545, 566, 624–26

Bonne of Luxembourg, 272

Boogaart, Jacques, 24–25, 187, 231, 233, 241–42, 250, 253, 260–61, 269, 276–77

728 GENERAL INDEX

Bowers, Roger, 383–87, 463–66, 468, 484–86, 621–23

Brassart, Johannes, 631–34; *see also* Index of Compositions: *Ave Maria gracia plena, Gratulemur Christicole, Magne Deus potencie, O flos fragrans, Summus secretarius, Te dignitas presularis*

Brownlee, Kevin, 5–6, 128, 170, 197, 202, 204*t*, 206, 208, 231, 233*t*, 263–65, 270, 275

Buff, Carolann, 387, 533n.8, 646

Bukofzer, Manfred, 58, 467, 488

Bus, Gervais du, 139–40

Butterfield, Ardis, 140–42

Byttering, *see* Index of Compositions: *En Katerine solennia*

caccias, 500–1, 503, 514–16, 531–32

cadence (*cadentia*), 12–13, **21–33**, 227–29, 232, 278, 330, 377, 415–17, 502, 585–88, 595–601

Caldwell, John, 403–4

calendrical allusions, 12–13, 191*t*, 305n.8, 347, 348, 349

Canel, Jean (Jean Hanelle?), *see* Hanelle, Jean

canon (instruction), 361*f*, 376–77, 415, 477, 489, 560–61, 562–63, 668–69, 670

within motet text, 374, 406–10

canons:

at the fifth, 404–6, 415

mensuration, 403–5, 415

on a chant, 405

rhythmic, 549, 549*f*

Caput masses, 58–59

Carmen, Jean, 645; *see also* Index of Compositions: *Venite adoremus*

Carrara, Andrea, Abbot, 504*t*, 554*t*, 565, 567

Carrara, Stefano, Bishop, 504*t*, 554*t*, 565

Cato, citations from, 125–26

Cattin, Giulio, 665

cauda hirundinis (swallowtail), 379, 388, 402, 421, 432

Cavalerius, Guillermus, 353, 355

Charles IV, Emperor, 365

Charles V, King of France, 286, 336, 499, 620, 643–44, 646–47

Charles de Valois, 133–35

Charlotte of Bourbon, Queen of Cyprus, 661–62

musicians of, 662–64

Chaucer, Geoffrey, and Machaut, 272

Christoforus de Monte, 503; *see also* Index of Compositions: *Plaude decus mundi*

Ciconia, Johannes, **497–530, 551–74, 575–602,** 606, 623–26

biography, 528–29, 551

cadences, 585–88, 595–601, 596*f*–99*f*

contratenors, 556–62

De proportionibus, 577

isorhythm in motets, 55, 563–64

Nova musica, 577

signature in motets, 288–89

texts, 564

see also Index of Compositions: *Albane misse celitus, Aler m'en veus,* [*Cristina*], *Doctorum principem,* Gloria *Suscipe Trinitas, Le ray au soleyl, O beatum incendium, O felix templum jubila, O Padua sidus preclarum, O Petre Christi discipule, O proles Yspanie, O virum omnimoda veneracione, Padu[a]... ex panis... serenans, Petrum Marcello, Quod jactatur, Regina gloriosa, Sus une fontayne, Una panthera, Ut te per omnes, Venecie mundi splendor*

Ciprianus, 353, 355

cithara, 357, 373, 380

Clark, Alice, 17, 154, 274, 278

Clement VI, Pope, 340–41, 605, **612–18,** 637

Clement VII, Antipope, 337, 364, 460–61, 499, 526, 606, 619–22, 639

Clement, Simon, 369–72

Clement de Berria (Clement de Berry), 355, 363

Clercx, Suzanne, 330, 334–40, 362–67, 551, 565, 572

Colonna, Oddo, 633

Colonna, Victoria, 639

color and *talea*, 12, 43–44, 61, 154*f*, 158*f*, 178*f*, 266–68, 266*f*, 298

non-coincidence of, 63, 177–78, 181, 319, 609–10

upper-voice, 40

see also talea

coloration:

for imperfection, 53, 304, 331, 379–80, 421–22, 468, 478, 528

interlocking, 155, 232

red, 101, 379, 402, 411–13, 466–67, 467*f*, 478–79, 669

reverse, 411–14, 623

for sesquialtera, 53, 467–68, 479

for syncopation, 377–79, 477–78, 67

split, 471, 477–78

tenor, 379, 514, 561, 623

to change modus, 150, 331

void, 331, 379, 402, 623

Compère, Loyset, *see* Index of Compositions: *Omnium bonorum plena*

composer signatures, motets with, 288–89

Conradus (Coradus) de Pistorio, Frater, 396; *see also* Index of Compositions: *Veri almi pastoris*

Contarini, Andrea, 504*t*, 533

contrafacta, 259, 447, 553, 554*t*, 571, 619–20

contratenor:

added, 259, 287, 317–19, 501–2, 556–62

essential, 154–60, 232, 353, 359–61, 404–17, 432, 452–53, 460, 502: *see also* solus tenor

inessential, 221–28, 460, 667–68

in Italian motets, 512

relation to tenor, 154–60, 404–17, 320–21, 582–83

Cook, Karen, 366

Cooke, J., 356n.5, 472–73; *see also* Index of Compositions: *Alma proles regia, Stella celi*

Corner, Marco, Doge, 526

Cossa, Baldassare, *see* John XXIII, Antipope
Council of Constance, 628–31
counterpoint:
  florid, 581, 588
  and harmony, 210–15
  strict, 579–80, 582–83
  see also successive procedures
Courtenay, Baudouin, Emperor of
    Constantinople, 336
Crawford, David, 635
Crocker, Richard, 211–12
Cubellus, Jacobus, 566
Cumming, Julie, 634–35
cursiva, 418, 432, 437
Cuthbert, Michael Scott, 155–56, 499n.8, 500–1,
    568, 569, 570
Cuvelier, Jacquemart le, 544–45
Cuvelier/Cunelier, Jo., 544–45; *see also* Index of
    Compositions: *Se Galaas*
Cyprian, 362–63
Cyprus manuscript, **661–82**
  Italian features in motets, 671–73
  motets in, 665–71
  stanza to *talea* relationship, 676–77
  texts, 674–76

Damett, 472; *see also* Index of Compositions:
    Salvatoris mater pia
Dandolo, Francesco, Doge, 504*t*
Dante, 128–29
De modo componendi tenores motettorum, **17–20**,
    43–44, **319–21**
  authorship by Egidius de Morino rejected, **17–20**,
    337, 364, 498
De Van, Guillaume, 41
Denis le Grant (Denis Normannus?), *see* le
    Grant, Denis
Denys de Collors, 345–46
Deo gratias motets, 445–462, 667
Desiderii (de Latines), Johannes, 353–55, 362–
    63, 366
Desmond, Karen, 96–97, 158–60, 162–63, 255–56,
    258–59, 262, 334, 339
Di Bacco, Giuliano, 539, 543–44, 566–67, 572–73,
    623–25, 651–52
diminution, 24–26, 48–54, 63–64, 235–36, 241, 349,
    359–60, 407*t*, 411–12, 439–42, 668–70, 672
  in Machaut Motet 2, 260–62
  in Machaut Motet 18, 250, 255–56, 258–59
Dionisius Normannus (Denis le Normand), 325–
    27, 336
dissonance, 362, 579–80, 581–82
  in added voices, 319
  in contratenors, 558–59
  judgement of, 576–77
  text-related, 348
Dit de Fauvain, 139
Docta sanctorum patrum, 254
doges, motets for, 504*t*, 509–10

Dolce, Brianne, 340
dots, 101–4, 147, 157–59, 260–62, 309, 394–95, 411,
    421, 432, 520
  for addition, 411
  for alteration, 101–2, 147, 261–62
  for division, 83, 102–4, 118–23, 143–44, 260–61,
    360, 362, 394–95, 467, 503–8, 520
  for perfection, 159, 266–67, 359–60
  for syncopation, 157–350, 362, 432, 478–79
double meaning, 10, 12, 70–71, 76, 83, 116, 127,
    133–37, 139, 207, 250, 406, 420, 433
Du Fay, Guillaume, 628, 662–63; *see also* Index of
    Compositions: Agnus *Custos et pastor ovium*,
    Apostolo glorioso, *Balsamus et munda cera*,
    Ecclesie militantis, *Fulgens iubar ecclesie dei*, *He
    compaignons*, *Nuper rosarum flores*, *O proles
    Hispanie*, Sanctus ('papale'), *Supremum est
    mortalibus*, *Vasilissa ergo gaude*
du Guesclin, Bertrand, 544
du Guesclin, Olivier, 625–26
du Pont, Jehan (Johannes), 325–27, 329, 335, 340
Dudas, Richard, 154, 156, 393, 651
Duèse, Jacques, *see* John XXII, Pope
Dunstaple, John:
  and the duke of Bedford, 484–86
  and events of 1416, 480–83
  motets with isorhythm, 488–92, 490*t*
  new discoveries, 486–88
  see also Index of Compositions: *Albanus roseo
    rutilat*, *Ave regina*, *Christe sanctorum*, Credo
    Anglicanum, *Descendi in ortum meum*, *Dies
    dignus decorari*, *Gaude felix*, *Gaude flore
    virginali*, *Gaude virgo salutata*, *Missa Da
    gaudiorum premia*, *Missa Jesu Christe Fili Dei*,
    Missa Rex seculorum, *Preco preheminencie*,
    Salve scema, *Specialis virgo*, *Veni sancte Spiritus*
    (a3), *Veni sancte spiritus et emitte* (a4)

Earp, Lawrence, 39–40, 154–55, 250–51, 253–54,
    255, 256–57, 272, 352, 411–12, 652
Easton, Adam, Cardinal, 622–23
echo imitation, 552
echo openings, 537
Edmund de Bury (*alias* Bokenham), 369–72, 384
Edmund de Miresco, 369–72
Edward III, King of England, 139–40
Egardus, 396
Eger von Kalkar, Heinrich, **289–92**, 328
Egidius Augustinus, Magister, 339, 364; *see also*
    Index of Compositions: *Courtois et sages*,
    Franchois sunt nobles, *Roses et lis*
Egidius Belwardi de Bruges, 339
Egidius de Aurolia (Giles of Orleans), 353–57,
    364 signature in motet, 288; *see also* Index of
    Compositions: *Alma polis*
Egidius de Flagiaco, 337
Egidius de Morino (Gilles de Thérouanne), 231–
    32, 301–2, 308, 325–28, 330–31, 333–34,
    337, 339

730 GENERAL INDEX

Egidius de Morino, author of *Tractatus figurarum*?, 319–20
   authorship of *De modo componendi tenores motettorum* rejected, 17–20, 319–21, 337, 364, 498
Egidius de Pusiex, 338; *see also* Index of Compositions: *Portio nature*
Egidius des Burces (Giles de Bruges), 325–27, 335, 339
Egidius of Orleans, Magister, *see* Egidius de Auriola
Egidius, Magister Frater, 339, 364
Elmham, *Liber metricus*, 481–83
Emiliani, Pietro, Bishop, 504t, 554t, 572–73, 574, 623–25, 636
Engelbert of Admont, 579
Eugene IV, Pope, 631–32, 634–39

Fallows, David, 56–57, 553, 566–67
Fauvain, 139
Fauvel, 69, 76–77, 134t
   marriage to Vain Glory, 133–35
Fauvel notation and dating, 251–52
Feragut, Bertrand, 635; *see also* Index of Compositions: *Excelsa civitas Vincencia*
Filargo, Pietro (Antipope Alexander V), 504t, 539–42, 545, 547–48, 554t, 572–74, **623–26**, 637
Filippotto da Caserta, *see* Index of Compositions: *Par les bons Gedeons*
Fontaine, Michael de, 643, 645
Foreastarius, Johannes (John Forester), 353–55, 362–63, 366
Fortuna, 85–86, 96, 115, 272–73, 274–79
   wheels of, 69, 74–76, 276–77
Foscari, Francesco, Doge, 509n.30
Franciscus, Magister, *see* Landini
Franciscus, *see* Index of Compositions: *De narcisus*
Franco of Cologne, 290–91, 369–72, 373, 379–80
Fuller, Sarah, 30, 585
Furnerii, Theobaldus, 366

G. d'Orbendas, 325–27, 329, 335, 340
G. de Horarum Fonte, *see* Tideswell, William of
Gace de la Buigne, 331–32, 336
Gallo, F. Alberto, 296, 503–8, 509–10
Galterius de Gardino (Walter de Gardino), 353, 355, 363
Garinus de Arceys, 337
Garinus de Soissons, 301–2, 325–27, 333–34, 335, 337
Gaston Febus, 544–45
Gaufridus de Barilio (Gaudefridus de Baralis), 335, 338
Geoffroy de Paris, 69
   Chronique metrique, 117–18
Gesta Henrici Quinti, 481–83
Gilles de Bruges, *see* Egidius des Burces
Gilles de la Thérouanne, *see* Egidius de Morino
Giovanni Gasparo da Castelgomberto, 573, 577

Girardus de Colonia, 353–55, 362–63
Godefridus (Gaudefridus) de Barilio (Godefroy de Baralle), 301–2, 325–27, 338
golden section, 207–8, 270, 391
Gómez, María Carmen, 313–14, 330
Gratiosus de Padua, signature in motet (?), 288–89 *see also* Index of Compositions: *Gratiosus fervidus*
Gratrus, 354–55, 363
Gregory the Great, Pope, 369–72, 373
Gregory XI, Pope, 618, 637
Grenon, Nicolas, *see* Index of Compositions: *Plasmatoris humani generis*
Grocheio, Johannes de, definition of motet, 1–2
Großtalea, *see* period
Guarin or Guerrinet de Soissons, *see* Garinus de Soissons
Guido d'Arezzo, 369–72, 379–80
Guilielmus de Francia, 339, 364
Guillaume de Trie, 252–54, 255–56, 259
Guillermus Cavalerii, 362–63
Guinigi, Lazzaro, 551
Guisardus de Cameraco (Guisard de Cambrai), 325–27, 335, 340
Günther, Ursula, 46, 49–50, 284–85, 304–5, 355–56, 358, 364, 366–67, 375–76, 460, 499–500, 544–45, 618, 645–47, 649
Gushee, Lawrence, 334
Gwillelmus 'Malcharte', see Malcharte

Haberl, Franz Xavier, 634–35
Hamm, Charles, 635
Hanelle, Jean, 662–65, 679–80
Hanelle, Mathieu, 662–63
Harrison, Frank Ll., 2, 284–85, 305, 316–17, 343, 345–46, 355–56, 366, 383–85
Hartt, Jared, 32–33, 149–50, 272
Hauboys, John (J. de Alto Bosco), 369–72, 385–86
Helene, Henricus, 301–2, 334, 338
Henricus, *see* Index of Compositions: *Portio nature*
Henry IV, King of England, 465–66
Henry V, Emperor, 67–68
Henry V, King of England, 465–66, 467, 473–77, 480, 481
Herlinger, Jan, 578
Hilarion, St, 661–62, 664–65, 666, 682
hockets, 179–81, 250–51, 258–59, 330, 514–15, 561
   criticised, 254, 328–29
   not breaking words, 245, 248–52, 249f, 250t, 254, 374–75
   at *talea* joins, 185, 233, 331, 350
Holford-Strevens, Leofranc, 125, 148, 155, 392, 564, 571, 572–74, 632, 651
Hoppin, Richard, 330, 334–40, 362–67, 661–64, 665, 666–67, 670, 671, 673–75, 676
Howlett, David, 163, 285, 301, 303, 314, 317–18, 325, 328, 343, 353, 369, 389, 390, 406, 428–29, 448, 485
Hubertus (Humbertus, Imbertus) de Salinis, 536, **539–50**, 625–26; *see also* Index of

GENERAL INDEX 731

Compositions: *Adieu plaisir, Bonté de corps, Con plus,* Credo *a3, En la saison,* Gloria *Jubilacio uni Deo,* Gloria *a3, Ihesu salvator seculi, J'ai . . ., Las . . ., Psallat chorus in novo carmine, Salve regina 'Virgo mater ecclesie', Si nichil actuleris,* unidentified ballade, unidentified virelai
Hughes, Andrew, 226
Hugo, named in *Musicorum collegio,* 343–45
Hugo de Lantins, 628; *see also* Index of Compositions: Credo **Q15** no. 68
Humfrey Duke of Gloucester, 485
Hydrolanos, 362–63

imperfection, 374, 378–79, 391, 394–95
   remote, 255–56, 262
indexes, 2–4, 8, 18–19, 437, 486, 500–1, 641–50, 653–59
instructions, 359, 562–63, 668–69, 670
   description within motet text, 303–4, 374, 406
   missing, 391, 406, 415–20, 433
   see also canon
introductions, 29
introitus, 28–29, 177–78, 184–85, 672
inversion, 275–76
Isabella, Queen of England, 139–40
isomelism, 52
isorhythm, **39–64,** 177, 240, 350, 458, 459–60, 468, 488–92, 490*t,* 670
   alternative terms for, 60–62
   15th-c. decline, 56–60
   in Italian motets, 510, 554*t,* 563–64
   notated in alignment, 330–31
   and tenor masses, 57–60

J. Anglicus (J. Langlois), named in *Musicorum collegio,* 343–46
J. de Alto Bosco, *see* Hauboys, John
J. de Corbe (J. de Corby), 369–72
'Ja', Magister, 501
Jacobus, *Speculum musice,* 304
   date of, 254–56
   on *cadentia,* 31–32
Jacobus (Jacques) d'Arras, 325–27, 329, 335, 336, 340
Jacopo da Bologna, *see* Index of Compositions: *Laudibus dignis merito, Lux purpurata, Oseletto selvaggio*
Janke, Andreas, 531–32, 538
Janus, King of Cyprus, 661–62, 664–66
Jean, duc de Berry, 364
Jean le Bon, 336
Jeanne de Boulogne, 364
Jeffroi de Barale, *see* Godefridus de Barilio
Jerome de Paris, 353–55, 362–63
Joanna I, Queen of Naples, 622
Johannes, named in *Musicorum collegio,* 343–45
Johannes de Sarto: *see* Index of Compositions: *Romanorum Rex*

John XXII, Pope, 252, 254, 339, 340–41, 362–63, 502, 607–14, 637
John XXIII, Antipope, 355–56n.1, 502, 504*t,* 624–25, 626, 627, 661–62
John II, King of Cyprus, 663–64
John II, King of France, 343, 345–46, 349
John, Duke (later king) of Aragon, 461
John Duke of Bedford, 480, 482–83, 484–86, 487
John of Bohemia, King, 327, 333–34, 339
John of Corby, 386
John of Exeter, 369–72, 384–86
John of Gaunt, 622–23
John of Ipswich (J. Episwich), 369–72
John of Tewkesbury, 151
John the Fearless, 642–43
Joseph of Exeter, 100, 149
Josquin des Prez, *see* Index of Compositions: *Nymphes des bois*
Jubal, 380–81
Julian of Speyer, 570

Katherine, Queen of England, 467
Katherine, St, 666, 678, 682
Kügle, Karl, 20, 37, 140, 147, 252, 332, 336, 457, 650, 662–67, 674–75, 679–81

Landini, Francesco, 500
   signature in motet, 288–89
   see also Index of Compositions: *De dimmi tu, Principum nobilissime, Sì dolce non sonò*
le Grant, Denis, 151–52, 291, 301–2, 331–32, 333–34, 335, **336,** 338, 340–41, 650; *see also* Index of Compositions: *Patrem omnipotentem, Se je chant mains [chace]*
Leech-Wilkinson, Daniel, 17–18, 39, 73, **209–29,** 251–52, 609
Leonel Power, 390, 465–66, 468, 485–86, 488; *see also* Index of Compositions: Credo *Opem nobis,* Missa *Alma redemptoris*
Leouns, 288, 389, 390
   signature in motet, 288
Lescurel, Jehannot de, 135, 140–42; *see also* Index of Compositions: *Gracieus temps est*
Levita, Adam, *see* Adam the Deacon
Loqueville, *see* Index of Compositions: Gloria
Lorenzo da Firenze, *see* Index of Compositions: *Povero zappator*
Louchart, Audefrois, 340
Louchart, Ingelbert or Engelbert, 325–27, 335, 339–40
Louis IX, King of France, 139–40
Louis X, King of France, 67–68, 79–81, 139
Louis I, duke of Anjou, 460–61
Louis, Duke of Anjou, 345–46
Louis, Count of Geneva, 661, 664
Louis of Bavaria, 613–14
Louis of Bourbon, 613
Louis of Toulouse, 611
Lucan, citations from, 125

732 GENERAL INDEX

Ludwig, Friedrich, 23
  on isorhythm, 39, 44–50

Machaut, Guillaume de, 301–2, 308, 309, 325–27,
  330, 335, 337, 340–41
  authorship, 288–89
  dissonances, 215–20, 222–26, 227–28
  epitaph, 209
  and isorhythm, 47–48
  manuscripts, 172–73, 288–89
  motets, 184t, 652
  non-coincident endings, 21–26
  tenors, 231–33
  see also Index of Compositions: *Amours qui a le
    pouoir, Biaute qui toutes, Bone pastor Guillerme,
    Christe, qui lux es et dies, Dame de qui, De
    bon espoir, De fortune, De petit peu, De toutes
    flours, En amer, Felix virgo, Fons tocius superbie,
    Hareu! hareu! le feu, Helas! pour quoy virent,
    Honte paour, Lasse! comment, Lay de Plour,
    Martyrum gemma, Maugré mon cuer, Phiton le
    merveilleux, Pour ce que mes chans fais, Quant
    vraie amour, Qui es promesses, S'il estoit nulz,
    Tant doucement, Tous corps, Trop plus est belle*
Mâcon, Jean, 643
madrigals, canonic, 514
Makhairas, Leontios, 662
Malatesta, Carlo, 628
Malatesta, Cleophe, 628
Malatesta, Pandolfo, 628
'Malcharte', Alebram, 397
'Malcharte', Gwillelmus, 397, 464
Malipiero, Francesco, Bishop, 635
manuscripts, related, 139–44
Manzari, Francesca, 544–45
Marcello, Pietro, Bishop, 504t, 554t, 565,
  572–73
Marchetto da Padova, 283, 288, 363, 501, 508–11
  Pomerium, 338–39, 362–63
  signature in motet, 288
  use of cross sign for natural, 578
  see also Index of Compositions: *Ave regina*
Marconi, T. (Thomas Marcon), 369–72, 385–86
Marcus of Viterbo, 504t, 527, 532–33
Marigny, Enguerrand de, **67–81**, 115–17, 124–
  25, 126–27
Marigny motets, **67–81, 83–109, 111–29**, 131, 133–
  35, 144–47
Martin V, Pope, 626, 628–31, 633, 639, 663
Martin, Arnaldus, 301–2, 335, 338
Matheus de Luceu (Mathieu de Luxeuil), 325–27,
  329, 340
Matheus de Sancto Johanne, 460–64, 620
  identification with Mayshuet rejected, 460, 463–64
  see also Index of Compositions: *Inclite flos orti
    Gebenensis*
Matteo da Perugia, 502, 624–26; *see also* Index
  of Compositions: *Ave sancta mundi, Laurea
  martiri*

maximodus, 349
Mayshuet, **445–64**, 471–72; *see also* Index of
  Compositions: *Are post libamina, Post missarum*
mensural transformation, 52–54, 58–59, 61, 62, 236,
  260–61, 359, 378, 391–92, 432, 438, 471–72,
  492, 563–64
mensurations, simultaneous, 255–56
Michael de Padua, 501
Michiel, Albano, Bishop, 504t, 554t, 565
minim rests, *see* rests
minim stems, 83–84, 118–23
Mocenigo, Tommaso, Doge, 509n.30
Molins, *see* Index of Compositions: *De ce que fol*
Morino, Egidius de, *see* Egidius de Flagiaco
motets:
  classification of, 48–51
  with composer signatures, 288–89
  dating of, 4–5, 126–27, 131, 133–37, 139–50
  five-part, 285, 313–14, 321, 389, 459–60, 471
  indexing by triplum or motetus, 2–3, 18–19, 259,
    272, 533, 645–46
  isoperiodic, 39–40, 46
  notational updating, 254–59
  origins and definitions of, 1–4
  for popes, **605–39**
Mugge, William (G. Muche or Mughe), 369–72, 384
Muris, Johannes de, 10, 151–52, 256-58, 301–4,
  308–9, 311, 325–27, 334–36, 614
  book loan to Vitry, 151–52
  Libellus, 311
  Notitia, 252, 255–56, 257, 258–59, 311, 362–63
musica ficta, 583–85, 601–2
Musserey (Mucherye), Jacob, 463–64; *see also*
  Mayshuet
Mutuilos, 353–55, 363

Nádas, John, 461–62, 531–32, 538, 539, 543–44,
  566–67, 572–73, 623–25, 651–52
Nevelon d'Amiens, 140–42
Nichasius, named in *Musicorum collegio*, 343–45
Nicholas V, Antipope, 613–14
Nicolaus/Guillermus, *see* Index of Compositions:
  Argi vices Poliphemus
Nicholas de Hermondivilla, 340–41
Nicholas of Hungerford (Nicholaus de Uado
  Famelico), 369–72
Nicholas of Trani, St, 566
Nicolaus Frangens de Leodio, 355–56n.1, 627
Nicolaus Zacarie, *see* Index of Compositions: *Già
  per gran nobeltà, Letetur plebs fidelis*
non-coincident endings, **21–28**, 267–68, 377,
  388, 415–17
Nosow, Robert, 482–83, 543–44, 629–31, 634
notation:
  conflicting, 310
  indicating English origin, 352
  Italian, 513, 672
  red, 101–4, 331–32
  void, 546–47, 623

Notitia del valore delle note del canto misurato, 297–98
number symbolism, 303–4, 306–7, 309, 328–29, 393–94

'O' antiphons, 667, 676, 677t, 682
Obrecht, Jacob, *see* Index of Compositions: *Missa Sub tuum praesidium*
onomatopoeia, 10, 188–90, 260
Orpheus, 357, 380–81
Ovid, quotations from, 76–77, 85–91, 96, 99–101, 104–7, 124, 125, 127–29, 149, 303–4
Oxwick, William (G. Oxwick), 369–72, 385–86

P. de Sancto Dionisio, *see* Pierre de St Denis
Padua fragments, 530, 536, 550, 553–56, 554t, 563, 567–68, 571, 621
    for individual items see Index of Manuscripts
Palacio, Robertus de, 301–2, 308, 325–27, 329, 335, 337
palindromes, 12, 75–76, 77–78, 89, 91–92, 94–95, 101–2, 107, 176, 192–93, 235, 265–66, 307, 432, 434f, 441–42, 443, 670
Pallart, J., named in *Musicorum collegio*, 343–45
Pandolfo III Malatesta, 396
panisorhythm, 49–51 parts, added, **313–21**: *see also* contratenor, added
Pennard, *see* Index of Compositions: Credo
period, supertalea or *Großtalea*, 163–64, 202, 239–40, 274–75
pes, 374
Peter of Dacia, 338–39
Petrarch, 3–4, 90n.13, 99–100, 365–66, 614
Petrus, Magister, 500–1
Petrus Amatori, 353, 355, 362–63
Petrus de Brugis (Pierre de Bruges), 301–2, 335, 338–39
Petrus de Sancto Dionisio, 362–63
    Tractatus, 257
Petrus dictus palma ociosa, 311, 581
Philip V, King of France, 67–68, 79, 99–100, 139–40, 253–54, 340–41
Philip IV, King of France, 67–68, 70, 76–77, 78, 79, 336
Philip the Bold, 642–43
Philipoctus or Egidius, *Tractatus figurarum*, 498
Philippe III, King of Navarre, 333–34, 336
Philippe d'Alençon, 551, 566–67, 621
Phoebus, 301–4, 392–94
Picquegny, Ferri de, 67–68
Picquigny, 67–68
Pierre de St Denis, 353–55, 362–63
Pierre Roger, *see* Clement VI, Pope
Pierre Roger de Beaufort, *see* Gregory XI, Pope
Pipudi, Magister Johannes, 357
Planchart, Alejandro, 570, 605, 628, 635, 674–75
Plumley, Yolanda, 545–46
Porta, J. de, 288, 353–56, **364–66**

signature in motet, 288
Porta, Johannes de Annoniaco (Annonay), 365–66
Power, *see* Leonel Power
Prosdocimus de Beldomandis, *Contrapunctus*, 577–85
Prosdocimus de Citadella, 508
puns, 11–12, 43–44, 90, 149, 207–8, 244, 250, 254, 270–71, 306–7, 347–48, 375–76, 391–92
    solmisation, 348, 375
Pycard, 464; *see also* Index of Compositions: Sanctus
Pythagoras, 301–3, 328, 370–72, 373, 382

Quatuor principalia, 346, 411
Queldryk, *see* Index of Compositions: Gloria

Racine, Guillaume, 345–46
Rainalducci, Pietro, *see* Nicholas V, Antipope
Raurich, *see* Alís Raurich
Reaney, Gilbert, 151, 211, 220, 460, 544, 626
refrains, 140–42
Regaudus de Tiramonte (Regaud de Tirlemont), 301–2, 325–27, **336**
Reginaldus de Bailleul, 325–27, **340**
Règles de la seconde rhétorique, 544
Renard tradition, 76–77
repeat signs, 177, 256, 261, 359, 668
rests, 95, 118–23, 143–44, 157–59, 160, 162–65, 260, 275, 328–29, 568
    as boundaries, 36, 39–40, 94–96, 104, 156, 160, 206, 235–36, 239n.28, 305–6, 331–32, 440
    coloured, 102f, 331–32, 406, 467f, 479f
    for displacement or syncopation, 53, 156, 157–59, 260–61, 359–60, 478–79
    with dots of addition, 411, 421
    at endings, 21, 23, 24–27, 35, 91
    in hockets 10, 163, 179–80, 185
    minim, 250–52, 256–57, 311–14, 331–32, 352, 374–75, 378–79, 610–11
    not breaking words, 160, 171, 185, 245, 248, 328–29, 374–75, 419, 468–69, 470f
    semibreve, 346, 352
        minor, or paired minim, 250–51, 256–57
        major, 331–32, 379, 421
    syllable placement in relation to, 10, 118–23
    text during rests, 11, 162–63, 166–67, 513
    undifferentiated, 251, 256–57, 257f, 331–32
retrograde, 50, 53, 84, 92, 176, 190, 192–24, 203, 276, 434, 442, 488–89, 510
rhythm:
    palindromic, 237
    restricted rhythmic vocabulary, 13, 165, 190, 191t, 440
    upper-voice, 240
Rizzuti, Alberto, 681
Robert d'Anjou, King of Naples, 338–39, 363, 613–14
Robert of Geneva, Cardinal, 461
Robertson, Anne Walters, 209
Robertus de Hoÿo (Robert de Huy), named in *Musicorum collegio*, 343–45

734 GENERAL INDEX

Roesner, Edward, 71–73, 76
Roger, Kévin, 358, 396
Rolandus de Casale, of Santa Giustina, 553–56, 570
Roman de Fauvel, 67–81, 83–109, 111–29
  chronological paradoxes, 69–81, 111, 126–27, 140–42, 145–47
Rosen, Charles, 42
Rossi da Giffoni, Leonardo, 504*t*, 526
'Roy Henry', 465–66
Royal Choirbook (RC), ⊙ Table 25.1, ⊙ Ex. 25.3, 445, 486–87
Royllart, Philippe, *see* Index of Compositions: *Rex Karole*

Sanders, Ernest, 57, 70, 71, 118–23, 131, 133–35, 140, 145, 150, 306, 497
Saucier, Catherine, 633–34
Schrade, Leo, 71, 83, 93, 131, 133, 145, 147
Sedulius, 356
self-recommendations, authorial, 347–48
semibreves:
  stemless, 250–51, 254, 331–32, 610, 651–52
  updated with stemmed minims, 140, 254–55, 311
  see also under rests
sharps, 123–24, 146, 471
Sigismund, Emperor, 480, 482, 632
similis ante similem, 157, 310
singers criticised, 447–48
solus tenor, 26–27, 29, 34–38, 232, 404–6, 413–16, 432, 437, 457, 512, 568, 615–16, 619, 649, 668
stems, 311–13, 394–95
  minim, 251, 254–55
Steno, Michele, Doge, 504*t*, 509, 554*t*, 565
Stephanus, named in *Musicorum collegio*, 343–45
Steve Sort, *see* Index of Compositions: *Patrem omnipotentem*
Stoessel, Jason, 573–74, 623
Stone, Anne, 545, 625
Strohm, Reinhard, 623, 625, 626, 643, 646, 667
Strutevilla or Struteville, J., 353, 355, 362
Sturgeon, Nicholas, 472; *see also* Index of Compositions: *Salve mater Domini*
successive procedures, 210–12, 220–25
supertalea, *see* period
syllables, placement of, 10
syncopation:
  of tenor and/or contratenor, 34, 156–60, 236–37, 266–67, 305, 359–62, 391, 467, 478–79
  of upper parts, 260, 275, 277–78, 319, 352, 362, 377–80, 421, 432, 440–42, 462–63, 671

talea, 182*t*, 202
  curtailed, 21–28, 163–64, 167, 377
  displaced, syncopated, 157–60, 180, 236, 266–67, 360–62, 467
  joins, 176, 180–81, 185, 232, 236, 238, 240
  non-coincidence with upper parts, 236–37, 305–6, 377–78, 437–38
  patterned by composer, 177–78

relation to text, 185–88, 186*t*, 202, 203–8, 233*t*, 241, 250*t*, 268–72, 328–29, 357
  stanza–*talea* correspondence, 241, 247–48, 374–75, 419, 452
  see also color and *talea*; period, supertalea or *Großtalea*
Tapissier, *see* Index of Compositions: *Eya dulcis*
Taxinus de Parisius, 353–55, 363
Templars, motets connected with, 68
tenors, 12–13
  ad longum, 35–37
  coloration, 652
  and contratenors, 37–38
  homographic, 21, 24–26, 35, 43–44, 49, 52–53, 55, 61–64, 94, 155, 261, 268, 374, 405, 414, 416, 459, 562
  in Italian motets, 511
  middle-voice, 20, 305, 310, 320–21, 508
  motives in upper voices, 13, 84, 91–96, 147, 238–39, 268, 275–76, 278, 308
  texts, 12, 84–85, 116–17, 175, 203–8, 271–72, 304–5, 394, 433
Terencinus de Verona Heremitarum, 501
texts, 9–13
text distribution, 241
Theobaldus, 353–55, 363
Thibaut de Champagne, 269; *see also* Index of Compositions: *Tout autresi con l'ente fet venir*
Thomas of Canterbury, St, 652
Thomas de Diciaco, 339
Thomas de Duacho (Thomas de Douai), 325–27, 339
Thomas Duke of Clarence, 465–66, 468, 471–72, 485–88
Thomson, Rodney M., 484
Tideswell, William of (G. de Horarum Fonte), 369–72
Tractatulus de cantu mensurali seu figurativo musice artis (Melk), 296
Tractatus de musica mensurabili (Wrocław), 295
Tractatus figurarum (Philippus de Caserta or Egidius), 17–18, 97n.30, 287, 319–20, 498
triplets, minim, 563
triplum–motetus, order of listing, 645–46
Trowell, Brian, 284, 382–86
Tubal (/Jubal), 369–72, 373, 381

Ugolino of Orvieto, 538; *see also* Index of Compositions: *Ce est la bele flour*
upper parts, in Italian motets, 511–12
Urban V, Pope, 527
Urban VI, Pope, 499, 526, 619, 621–23, 637

Vain Glory, 133–35, 134*t*
Valquerus de Valenciennis (Volquier de Valenciennes), 325–27, 335, 340
van den Borren, Charles, 542–43
Van, Guillaume de, 635
Vavassoris, Johannes, 5, 412; *see also* Index of Compositions: *Ferre solet*

Veliout, Gillet (Gilet Velut?), 662
Velut, Gilet, 662–64; *see also* Index of
    Compositions: *Benedicta viscera,*
    Summe summy
Vinderhout, Petrus, 339
Visconti, Anglesia, 662
Visconti, Bernabò, 662
Visconti, Giangaleazzo, 551, 625
Visconti, Luchino, 504*t*
Vitale-Brovarone, Alessandro, 661, 681
Vitry, Jean de, 340–41
Vitry, Philippe de, 301–2, 304, 308, 309, 325–27,
    329, 334, 335, 338–39, 612–13, 652
    attributions to, 9, 29, 71–73, 83, 102–3, 118–23,
        127, **139–50**, 151–67, 286–87, 288–89, 311–
        12, 346
    books borrowed from Muris, 151–52
    creator of isorhythmic motet, 47–48, 51–
        52, 59–60
    identity as Gallus, 99–100
    signature in motets, 288–89
    see also Index of Compositions: *Almifonis, Aman*
        novi, Amer amours, Apta caro, Beatius, Colla
        iugo, Cum statua, De terre en grec Gaulle
        . *appelle, Douce playsence, Firmissime fidem*
        teneamus, Floret cum Vana Gloria, Flos ortus,
        Garrit gallus, Impudenter circumivi, In virtute,
        O canenda, Per grama, Petre clemens, Orbis
        orbatus, Phi millies ad te, Scariotis geniture, Se

cuers ioans, Tribum que non abhorruit, Tuba
    sacre fidei, Vos quid admiramini
voice-crossing, 11, 124, 148, 171, 190–92, 195, 239,
    268, 275
voice exchange, 148, 406, 437–38
vowel rhyme, 10–11, 88–90, 161, 347–48, 356

Wathey, Andrew, 126, 139–40, 317, 333–34, 384,
    461–64, 611, 615–16, 643, 650
William of Exeter, 384–85
Wolf, Johannes, 45
word-painting, 11, 23, 123–24, 156–57, 164, 197,
    205–6, 244, 260, 275, 350
Wright, Craig, 643, 645, 647
Wright, Peter, 486–87

Ydrolanus, 353

Zabarella, Francesco, 504*t*, 510, 516, 554*t*, 565–66,
    569, 573, 623–25
Zacara (Zacar), Antonio, da Teramo, 472n.14, 514,
    539–42, 548, 551–52n.5, 572, 606, 623–26; *see*
    also Index of Compositions: [*Cacciando per*
    gustar], *Dime, Fortuna*
Zanobi da Strada, Giovanni, 365
Zayaruznaya, Anna, 29, 34, 39–41, 44, 252, 258, 274,
    448–49, 452–57, 612, 615–16, 650
Ziino, Agostino, 651
zodiac, 350–52, 357, 396